Forest Ecology

Forest Ecology

J. P. Kimmins *The University of British Columbia*

Macmillan Publishing Company
New York

Collier Macmillan Publishers
London

Macmillan Publishing Company
866 Third Avenue, New York, New York 10022

Collier Macmillan Canada, Inc.

Library of Congress Cataloging in Publication Data

Kimmins, J. P.
    Forest ecology.

    Bibliography: p.
    Includes index.
    1. Forest ecology. I. Title.
QH541.5.F6K55   574.5′2642   81-8190
ISBN 0-02-364050-2   AACR2

Printing: 1 2 3 4 5 6 7 8   Year: 7 8 9 0 1 2 3 4 5 6

ISBN 0-02-364050-2

The Importance of Forest Ecology in the Education of Forest Resource Managers

Over the past few decades there has been a gradual but steady change in public and professional attitudes towards our natural resources. Once the hallmark of environmentalists, concern over human population growth and resource depletion is now an accepted part of the dialogue between governments and financial institutions, corporations and industry, scientists and the general public. Whether this concern is truly altruistic or merely an expression of self-interest is of little consequence. The important fact is that there is a widespread and growing acceptance of limits to growth, and recognition that ultimately the limit will be determined by the supply and distribution of resources.

The growing perception of our dependency on finite and often rapidly diminishing resources requires significant changes in the education and training of resource managers, especially managers of those resources that are capable of being renewed. The need for a more complete understanding of the ecosystems in which these resources are found grows more urgent each year, as the strides of population growth outpace the often faltering steps of resource development and renewal. Nowhere is this more true than in the management of forested lands.

Until quite recently, the education and training of forest resource managers stressed the exploitation of existing timber resources. This focus is steadily being replaced by an explicit treatment of all aspects of the renewal and management of the total resource. Courses in the management of soil, water, fish habitat, wildlife, range and recreation have joined the more traditional subjects of timber management and forest protection in the core curriculum of most forestry schools. However, the simple inclusion of such courses in the curriculum is not in itself enough. They must be closely integrated to provide a well-rounded professional education in the field of *total landscape management*. In short, the management of the forest must be based on the view of the forest as an integrated ecological system or *ecosystem*. Such an integrated view is difficult to develop unless the education of forest resource managers is soundly based on a course in the ecology of the forest ecosystem. This book was designed primarily for use in such a course.

Why Write *Another* Ecology Textbook?

The past decade has witnessed a proliferation of ecology textbooks, representing a variety of approaches to the teaching of ecology. Many of these books are excellent for the

Preface

purposes for which they were written. They satisfy the requirements of courses specializing in a variety of ecological subdisciplines, but in my experience none of them satisfies the particular needs of an undergraduate course in forest ecology in a professional forest resource management program. These needs are:

1. A clear demonstration at the outset of the role of ecological knowledge in the management of forest resources. In many texts, the ecological role and current predicament of humans is either omitted or is relegated to the final and often unread chapter. Very few texts deal with the evolution and historical relationship between our species and the forest. The importance of these topics suggests that they should be discussed in some detail at the outset.

2. Use of the ecosystem concept as the central theme of the course. Foresters manage (or mismanage) ecosystems (entire landscapes), rather than individual trees, tree populations, or even tree-dominated biotic communities. In order to instill the importance of the integrated approach to management, the ecosystem concept should be introduced early rather than late in the course, and the ecosystem, rather than the individual, population, or community, should be the focus of the learning process.

3. A broad and balanced treatment of all aspects of forest ecology (the ecosystem concept; functional ecology; genetic aspects; components of the physical environment; components of the biotic environment, populations and communities; and temporal changes in ecosystems) is needed rather than an emphasis on any particular aspect. Rather than a course in autecology, or population ecology, or community ecology, foresters need a course in ecosystem ecology which includes all three of these subdisciplines. They manage ecosystems, not subsets thereof. Foresters must be exposed to all aspects of ecology.

4. A treatment of applied as well as basic forest ecology. It is not enough to teach forest resource managers the fundamentals of forest ecology. They must also learn about the day-to-day application of this knowledge in their work. Their training in ecology, and therefore the text that they use, should include a discussion of how to apply ecological information in the form of ecological classification of forested lands.

5. An introduction to the use of models and computer simulation in ecology and resource management. Because the power of computers is needed as much in basic and applied forest ecology as in any other branch of forestry, the topic of models and modelling and how these can be used to evaluate the environmental impacts of forest management should be introduced even in a first course in forest ecology.

How to Use This Book

The design of this text is based on seventeen years of experience teaching a second-year introductory course in forest ecology to future foresters at The University of British Columbia. Not all of these students have been budding ecologists and many might not have taken the course if they had not been required to do so. This posed a challenge to stimulate their interest and convince them that the considerable amount of work involved was worthwhile. The course has also been taken by many students of soil, landscape architecture, geography, botany, and zoology who have apparently found the approach to be useful. The book was not designed solely for this introductory course, however. It can also be used in fourth year courses in ecosystem classification and forest ecosystem function, and in graduate courses in forest ecosystem ecology, including simulation modelling of nutrient cycling and forest growth using FORCYTE (see Chapter 17).

The book is divided into three major parts.

Part I

The book opens with a review of human population growth and the current human predicament. This leads into a discussion of the role that interactions with the forest have played in recent human evolution, in the political history of the past few millenia, and in the development of ecology, forest ecology, and forestry. Chapters 1 and 2 provide a background to and rationale for Part II, the ecology of forest ecosystems.

Part II

Part II is divided into five sections: ecosystem function, genetic and evolutionary aspects, physical factors, biotic factors, and change.

Section A. After introducing the ecosystem concept, there is a detailed discussion of ecosystem function—ecological energetics and nutrient cycling. In many ecology texts these topics appear after the discussion of the components of the ecosystem. I believe that it is important to introduce students to ecosystem function at the outset. Virtually all resource management is involved with manipulating ecosystem function (the production aspects of function are the prime concern of most resource managers), and I view all other aspects of ecology as modifiers of ecosystem processes. The whole of life as we know it is a consequence of ecosystem function, and therefore it seems logical that this subject should be discussed early rather than late in an ecology course.

Section B. Reflecting the importance of the topic, the second section of the book reviews the genetic aspects of forest ecosystems. This provides the genetic background for Section C (which deals with the major components of the physical environment to which organisms must adapt if they are to survive and function) and for Section D (which deals with biotic interactions).

Section C. Once the forest has been described as a functional system, one may examine its components. Chapters 7 to 12 cover the physical environment: solar radiation, temperature, wind, soil, water, and fire: factors which act as major physical determinants of ecosystem function.

Section D. The book then discusses the biotic components of an organism's environment. First there is a rather conventional and necessarily brief treatment of population ecology. Second, there is a discussion of the structure and spatial variability of communities, and the variety of interspecific interactions that play such an important role in contributing to the diversity of living organisms and to the structure, composition and functioning of biotic communities.

Section E. Part II of the book concludes with an examination of how ecosystems change over time. Ecological succession is one of the most important topics of the book for foresters because much of a forester's professional life is involved in the manipulation of succession. A detailed discussion of succession is also useful in any course on the ecology of ecosystems, because understanding succession involves knowledge of all the subcomponents of ecosystems. Knowledge of ecological succession acts as a framework within which functional ecology, autecology, population ecology, and community ecology can be synthesized.

Part III

The final part of the book deals with the application of the information contained in Part II to the management of forested landscapes. The most fundamental application is in ecological classification, which is reviewed in detail.

A second application is in modelling the functioning of forest ecosystems, or parts thereof, and how they respond to management. The topic is treated at a conceptual level which should be comprehensible to any student, whatever his or her preparation in mathematics and computer programming. Examples are given of the use of models in some aspects of forest ecology and forest management.

Final chapters of books frequently remain unread. It is my hope, however, that Chapter 18 will not suffer this fate, because in closing the book I offer a philosophical view of resource management which I believe is helpful in thinking about resources and how they should be managed.

My hope in writing this textbook was that it would contribute to an improvement in how our forest environment, and our environment in general, are managed. If it does so, then the effort will have been worthwhile.

ACKNOWLEDGMENTS

I would like to gratefully acknowledge the contributions of John Worrall and Kim Scoullar to Chapters 6 and 17, respectively, and the assistance of various reviewers in improving the manuscript: Douglas M. Knudson, Purdue University; Carl Jordan, University of Georgia; Robert N. Muller, University of Kentucky; Larry Forcier, University of Vermont; Mohan K. Wali, State University of New York; and Brian McLeod for his editorial suggestions. The responsibility for any shortcomings must rest with me, however.

I owe my first interests in ecology to Paul Richards, Grieg-Smith, Bud Messenger and Paul Huffaker, but my greatest professional gratitude is reserved for Buzz Holling and Evelyn Hutchinson who first made me realize that within me there had always been an ecologist struggling to get out.

The launching of the book was made possible by a sabbatical leave financially supported by the Canada Council, to whom I offer my thanks.

My gratitude goes to Susan Phelps and Mary Saunders, who typed the early drafts of the manuscript, and especially to Patsy Quay, who was responsible for most of the final typing and for the numerous secretarial tasks involved in getting the book published. The patience of my production supervisor, Dora Rizzuto, is greatly appreciated.

My final and most deeply felt appreciation goes to my family: Ann, for so much help during the early stages of writing; Ann, Mark, and Shaun for all the time I did not spend with them while working on the book; and to all of them for encouragement and support during the long genesis of this book. It is dedicated to them.

J. P. K.

Contents

Section B   Genetic and Evolutionary Aspects of Ecosystems

6. Adaptation and Evolution: Genetic Aspects of Ecosystems

Section C   The Physical Environment

7. Ecological Role of Solar Radiation

8. Temperature as an Ecological Factor

9. Wind: Ecological Effects of Atmospheric Movements

10. Soil: The Least Renewable Component of the Ecosystem

PART I Man*and the Forest or Why the Science of Forest Ecology Developed

Forests were the evolutionary vessel in which was distilled the origins of that most remarkable of all animals: *Homo sapiens.* Forests were the habitat of our earliest evolutionary ancestors and have remained an important part of the environment of most branches of the human family tree. The rise and fall of empires, the conquest of nations, and the political, economic, and military power of human societies have been intimately related to the accessibility of forests and/or forest products for most of our recent history. While modern Man is no longer truly a forest animal, humans still are, and probably always will remain, dependent on forests for a wide variety of the necessities of life.

Part I examines the current human predicament and reviews the evolution and population growth that led to the present circumstances. It examines the history of our relationship to the forest, and the role that this relationship played in the development of forestry and forest ecology.

* While it is recognized that use of the word *man* as a collective term referring to the human race (i.e., the world population of *Homo sapiens*) may offend some readers, the author respectfully requests their tolerance of its occasional usage. In most cases, alternative words have been found, but in some places this traditional usage is retained because it seems to convey the intended meaning most easily.

1.1 Introduction

Correct decisions concerning how we should establish and manage our forests inevitably involve a consideration of the socioeconomic conditions that will exist when the tree crop is ready for harvest. In many parts of the world, the time involved in producing tree crops is so long that it is very difficult to predict these conditions, but it is clear that they will be closely related to the future growth of the human population. There is probably no other single factor that is a more important determinant of our future impact on the forests of the world than the future size of the human race.

Human impacts on the biosphere do not only depend on human numbers. They also depend on human attitudes towards the environment. Our future relationship to resources such as forests will therefore depend to a considerable degree upon our philosophical view of how we fit into the world ecosystem.

It is a common observation that an understanding of present day political and economic conditions and events is greatly assisted by knowledge of the past, and that such knowledge is indispensible in predicting the political and economic future. An understanding of our current impacts on the world's forests is likewise best achieved through knowledge of our evolution, population growth and historical relationship to forests, as is prediction of our future impacts.

This opening chapter will briefly examine the historical attitudes of Man towards the environment, the evolution of the human species, the growth in human numbers and the significance of this growth for forestry.

1.2 Evolutionary Origins

Man is a primate, a member of an order of terrestrial mammals, including lemurs, marmosets, monkeys, and apes, which had its origins in a line of ground-dwelling, insect-eating mammals that lived in tropical forests about 60 million years ago (Simmons, 1972). The environment of that time favored the evolution of this ground dwelling animal into several varieties of primitive tree-dwelling primates.

The change from ground to treetop habitat was accompanied by several important evolutionary changes. The problems posed by life in the new environment created selective pressures that favored a variety of new traits, some of which are believed to have created the evolutionary trends that produced *Homo sapiens*. Precision of movement and bal-

1 The Human Predicament: Evolution and Growth of Population

ance, dexterity of limbs with opposable thumbs, binocular and improved vision, and an increased mental capacity to accommodate these physical improvements were all highly advantageous attributes in the precarious treetop environment, and they became well developed. The difficulties of arboreal life also led to a reduction in the number of offspring in a litter and a lengthening of the gestation period; the young were large and well developed at birth, both mentally and physically.

There is disagreement as to which of these new developments was most important for the evolution of primitive man. It is probable that a unique combination of new traits was responsible rather than any single one, but there can be little doubt that the combination of grasping forefeet and upright stance was of major significance. It led to the evolution of the dependence on tools, which eventually resulted in the development of modern technology. The semiupright stance and powerful grasping forelimbs are attributes that were particularly well developed in primitive apes, who moved through the treetops by swinging from branch to branch (brachiating). It is from this line of primates that man eventually evolved.

Primate evolution occurred very slowly. It is thought to have taken about 30 million years for the three major lines of primates [monkeys, apes, and prosimians (lemurs)] to emerge from their ancestral ground-dwelling origins of 60 million years ago. The tropical forest environment of Africa where this evolution occurred extended far beyond its present limits, reaching northward to meet the Mediterranean Sea, which was then much larger. The range of the forest was not invariable, however. Its geographical limits ebbed and flowed across North Africa as ice ages came and went, resulting in alternate droughts and wetter periods (Moreau, 1966).

Periodic contraction of the tropical forest environment and its replacement by grassland gave a selective advantage to those primates with physical traits that allowed them to return from the treetop habitat back to the ground. These animals were able to augment their traditional treetop diet with food items from the ground, and eventually some of them were able to obtain all of their food supplies from the open grasslands. This would have reduced and eventually averted increasingly fierce competition for food experienced by those primates that remained in the diminishing treetop environment, and would have improved the survival and success of these pioneers. Both monkey and ape lines of primate responded to this type of selective pressure, leading ultimately to modern-day baboons and modern-day man, respectively.

Exploitation of this new and very different environment posed several problems for the early hominids. Lacking the claws, teeth, speed, and strength of the contemporary ground-dwelling carnivores (meat eaters), there was strong selective pressure for the evolution of tools (including fire), for cooperation in groups, and for the use of mental as well as purely physical solutions to problems. All of these attributes acted to greatly increase the physical capabilities of primitive humans and turned them into formidable hunters, thus guaranteeing success as a new evolutionary form. The extent of this success is thought to be reflected in the dramatic increase in the rate of extinction of species of large mammals that occurred during this period: the so-called Pleistocene overkill. For example, 71% of the genera of large mammals in North America became extinct shortly after the arrival of technologically advanced human predators (Martin, 1966, 1967). The success also led to a fundamental change. With the decreasing availability of game, humans changed from predominantly hunting to predominantly food gathering, and then from gathering to farming.

The evolution of tools, the harnessing of various forms of energy, and the securing of a reliable supply of food through domestication and farming led primitive humans from a purely biological evolutionary pathway into what has been called *cultural evolution*. The development of spoken

and written communication, the accumulation of knowledge and experience, and the development of a highly organized technical and industrial society have in the very recent stages of evolution changed humans into a being that appears superficially to be very different from other animals. However, beneath the disturbingly frail and ephemeral facade of our cultural evolution lies a basic similarity to our close evolutionary "relatives." All too easily, as in war or following an earthquake, humans lose the modest degree of independence from the environment that has been conferred on us by our cultural evolution, and our common heritage with other living organisms is revealed. We are ultimately as dependent on, and subject to, the exigencies of our physical and biotic environment as is any other animal. Humans are as natural a product of biological evolution as is a dinosaur or a bacterium.

1.3 Recent Evolutionary History and Past Growth in Numbers

As early humans evolved into successful group hunters using both stone weapons and fire, there was a gradual increase in numbers. From what is thought to have been an initial population of about 125,000 hominids 1 or 2 million years ago, numbers increased slowly to reach an estimated 1 million about 250,000 years ago, when *Homo sapiens* evolved as an identifiable species.[1] By the time of the Cro-Magnon and Neanderthal types of primitive man (30,000–40,000 years ago), the population had increased substantially to about 3 million; by 10,000 years ago, it is thought to have reached about 5 million.

The increase in hunting success and the concomitant improvement in diet that accompanied the development of weapons are thought to have stimulated the first of the three major changes that have occurred in the growth rate of the human population. In the first of these, there was probably only a marginal increase in the rate of population growth, which previously had been very close to zero. However, this small increase combined with the improvement in hunting ability appears to have resulted in the virtual decimation of much of the world's large game populations between 30,000 and 10,000 B.C.: the Pleistocene overkill mentioned earlier. Although there is some dispute as to whether all the Pleistocene extinction of larger mammals can be explained by human predation alone, the evidence of rapid declines in

---

[1] All population estimates prior to about A.D. 1800 are approximate guesses made by demographers and archaeologists. After 1800 the estimates become increasingly reliable, but even today we do not know exactly how many people there are on earth.

abundance of large mammals in several localities following the first invasion of hunting man is compelling.

Early human success at hunting provided the protein-rich diet necessary to support population growth, but it was not without its price. It created severe food shortages that initiated an important new evolutionary development. By 15,000–10,000 years ago, many populations of primitive humans had been forced back to the earlier ground-ape habit of food gathering rather than hunting. Grains of wild grasses became a staple food and it was not long (on an evolutionary time scale) before domestication and cultivation of both wheat and rice occurred. The nomadic hunters became territorial farmers, and the next two millenia saw the development of the great "hydraulic societies" based on irrigation agriculture in the Tigris-Euphrates, the Indus, and the Nile river valleys. This proved to be a highly successful development, which resulted in a large excess of food production over immediate needs and stimulated the second major increase in man's rate of population growth. From an estimated 5 million in 8000 B.C. (when agriculture was in its infancy), the human population grew to about 250 million by A.D. 1 and to 400 million by the late thirteenth century.

Although the agriculture of the eastern hydraulic societies was very successful, early European agriculture was much less productive. Because of the lack of methods for working the heavier, more fertile valley bottom soils, food production was largely restricted to areas with lighter, less fertile soils in valley-slope and ridge-top forests. These lower-productivity soils lacked the fertility to sustain continued cropping, and it was necessary to leave large areas in fallow each year. The invention in about A.D. 1000 of a new agricultural implement that was capable of tilling heavy soils rich in clay and silt (the moldboard plow) led to utilization of the richer and more productive valley-bottom soils, and significant increases in agricultural production. However, truly sustained-yield agriculture in Europe awaited the introduction of wheat–turnip–barley–clover rotation cropping in 1650. This system resulted in a dramatic increase in agricultural productivity and marked the beginning of the third and most spectacular increase in the rate of human population growth.

The explosive increase in agricultural production that followed the introduction of rotation cropping freed both labor and capital for the pursuit of scientific, industrial, and medical activities that were to transform Europe's population from 22 to 35% of the world's population in the short period from 1800 to 1930 (Russell, 1969). From a world population of about 545 million in 1650, there was an increase to 728 million in 1750, to 1171 million in 1850, to 2515 million in 1950 (Hauser, 1971), and to about 4000 million in 1975–1976. The growth of the human population over the past 2–5 million years is shown in Figure 1.1A.

The enormity of the recent increase in numbers of human beings is demonstrated in Table 1.1 in terms of both the change in the time required to double the population and the change in the time taken to produce successive billions of people. It is possible to arrive at some extraordinary conclu-

Table 1.1   Growth of the Human Population[a]

Date	Estimated Population, Millions	Estimated Time Required to Double the Population, yr	Estimated Time Required to Attain Successive Billions and Date Attained[b]
1,000,000 B.C.	0.125	35,000	
35,000 B.C.	3	35,000	1st billion—2–5 million years: 1800
8000 B.C.	8	5,500	
B.C. : A.D.	300	1,700	
A.D. 1400	400	1,700	
A.D. 1650	545	230	
A.D. 1750	800	139	2nd billion—130 years: 1930
A.D. 1850	1,300	116	
A.D. 1950	2,500	41	3rd billion—30 years: 1960
A.D. 1977	4,200	35	
A.D. 1984[b]	4,750	39	4th billion—15 years: 1975
Projections			
A.D. 2000[b]	6,130		5th billion—12 years: 1987(?)
A.D. 2025	8,297		6th billion—11 years: 1998(?)

[a]Except as noted, all data are from Deevey, 1960; Dorn, 1962; Hauser, 1971; and Coale, 1974.
[b]The Population Reference Bureau, 1983.

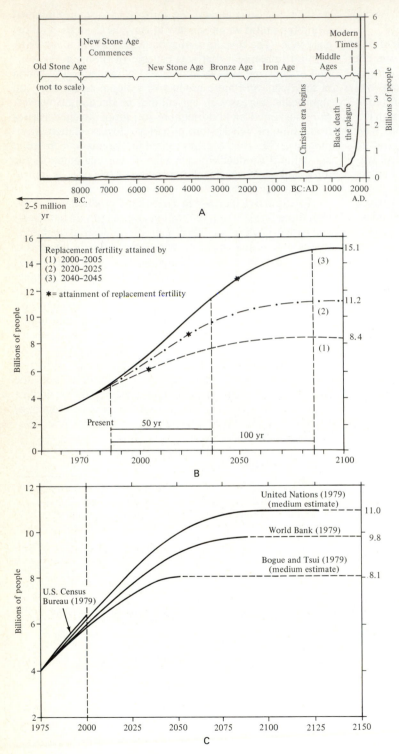

Figure 1.1

Growth of the human population. (A) The historical pattern of population increase over the past 2–5 million years. The majority of the growth in numbers occurred in the past 100 years. (B) Theoretical population projections which demonstrate the momentum of population growth. The population continues to increase after replacement fertility (see Chapter 13) is achieved because a high proportion of the population is in the reproductive and prereproductive age classes. The three projections differ in the year in which replacement fertility is attained. (C) Estimates of future population growth made in 1979 by four different authorities. The curves represent median estimates, each of which is accompanied in the original publications by upper and lower estimates. The wide divergence of these estimates emphasizes the high degree of uncertainty in population growth predictions. (After van der Tak et al., 1979. Courtesy Population Reference Bureau, Inc.)

sions from the available statistics on human populations and the projections as to the probable growth in numbers over the next few decades. For example, if current rates of population growth continue, between now and the end of this century we will be adding on the average about as many new people every decade as existed in the whole world in 1800 (1 billion). It is not yet clear whether this will be the case. There does appear to be a trend toward reduced family size and delayed family formation, but even if average family size undergoes a drastic reduction, populations will continue to grow for some time. The population increase has built-in momentum because such a large proportion of the population has yet to reproduce. Even if families are smaller, there will be so many more families than in the past that population growth will continue to increase after *replacement fertility* (when average family size equals the number of children needed to replace the parents) has been attained. This would be an average of slightly more than two children per couple, to allow for child mortality. Figure 1.1B illustrates this reproductive momentum. It presents theoretical population growth curves based upon three assumptions about when replacement fertility is obtained. In every case the population continues to grow for many years after replacement mortality was achieved.

The main impression that one gets from Figure 1.1A is that, compared to today's population, the number of human beings has been extremely small for almost the entire period of our evolutionary history. The explosive rise in numbers at the very end of the period (i.e., the past 200 years, especially the past 40 years) is unprecedented and at first glance appears to be quite out of character with the rest of human history. In fact, this is not the case. The pattern of low numbers sustained for most of the period followed by rapid increase toward the end of the period is characteristic of a process that has continued throughout human evolution: the process of *exponential growth*. The consequences of this are discussed in Section 1.5.

1.4 Predicted Future Growth in Human Numbers

The data in Figure 1.1 and Table 1.1 show that the world's population is increasing exceedingly rapidly. It is widely agreed among demographers (scientists who study population growth) that it is very difficult to predict future population growth for more than a few decades, but with an annual addition to the world's population (i.e., after deaths) in 1983 of about 84 million people per year (i.e., about 231,000 a day, or 9600 per hour, or 160 per minute—a rate approximately twice as fast as the human pulse), only the uninformed could fail to be concerned. At this rate the world's population will have increased by about 3200 while you have been reading this chapter.

Two sets of recent predictions about future population growth are given in Figure 1.1. All the predictions agree that we happen to be living at that point in human history at which the long sustained exponential population increase is starting to level off. However, as mentioned above, there is a momentum to population growth, and it will take many decades for the growth rate to drop to zero and population to stabilize. The only disagreement in the predictions is when and at what population size stability will be reached.

The most optimistic of the first set of predictions (Figure 1.1B) assumes that replacement fertility will be achieved by the period 2000–2005, and it suggests that the present population will approximately double to a final stable size of 8.4 billion. If replacement fertility is not achieved until the period 2020–2025, the population is expected to grow to 11.2 billion (a very plausible scenario), and if replacement fertility is not attained until the period 2040–2045, the population will increase to about 15 billion. These predictions suggest that forest crops established now for harvest at the end of a 50-year rotation must serve a human population that could vary from about 7.7 to 11.5 billion, 3.1–6.9 billion *more* than in 1983. Crops established now for harvest in 100 years may have to serve the needs of 3.8–10.4 billion *more* people than were alive when this book was written.

The second prediction set (Figure 1.1C) shows projections of human population growth made by four authorities. These are median projections; for two of them, the authorities have also provided a low and a high projection based on more optimistic and more pessimistic assumptions, respectively. As with Figure 1.1B, the variation in these projections shows how difficult it is to reach agreement about the probable course of human population growth. Even the low and high ranges about some of these median projections do not overlap!

1.5 Implications of Population Growth for Global Resources

An animal population is limited ultimately by aggression, disease, or lack of vital resources (food, water, shelter, space, or other material needs). These ultimate limits to growth are generally not reached because other, less violent control mechanisms maintain the population at much lower levels. Unfortunately, the majority of the human population does not appear to be exercising such restraints, and if current trends continue, it appears very likely that war, pestilence, starvation or shortage of some essential resource will be the means by which the population levels off and possibly declines to lower levels. As to when this will occur, opinions vary greatly. Most authorities judge food to be the most important, ultimate limiting factor, but there is a wide range of opinion as to how many people the world can feed. Optimistic estimates suggest that by applying state-of-the-art agriculture to all suitable land, we could feed 38–48 billion people (Revelle, 1974). However, such estimates of technological possibilities tend to ignore the large capital investment required for their attainment.

One of the conclusions of a study by the Club of Rome (Meadows et al., 1972) was that if present trends of population growth and resource depletion continue, the limits to population growth will be reached in less than 100 years. They concluded that although it is technologically possible to solve individual problems (such as food, minerals, pollution, and water supplies) by application of existing and new technology, competition for economic resources will prevent this from happening. The solution of the food problem would require the preemption of capital required to solve pollution or energy problems, which would then limit population growth. Solution of the pollution problem would limit the capital for agricultural expansion. Use of land to solve the food production problem would require the removal of large areas of forest and result in "timber famine." Political and social problems also limit the application of technology and capital: many countries spend far more on defense budgets than on trying to solve population and resource problems. More recently, it has been pointed out that even if vast increases in food production were achieved, many of the world's people would have no fuel with which to cook the food. Forest clearing to grow the food would have eliminated the supply of domestic fuel wood.

The Club of Rome study concluded that the human predicament is not hopeless—that we have much of the knowledge required, and still have the time in which to alter these growth trends and to establish a condition of ecological and economic stability that is sustainable far into the future. The sooner a start is made, the greater the chance that planned rather than cataclysmic controls will limit the world's population. However, unless major steps are taken in the next few decades, the chance of an innocuous solution to the population predicament (i.e., control by reducing the birthrate) will become very small, and solutions involving an increased death rate will inevitably prevail.

What is the meaning of all this for forestry? The seemingly inevitable doubling (to 8 billion), possible tripling (to 12 billion), and foreseeable quadrupling (to 16 billion) of the human population will place tremendously increased demands on the world's forest resources, demands that cannot easily be met because of the long time scale of forest crops in comparison with the rate of population growth. Some of the tree crops that we regenerate now will serve a world population twice as large and possibly as much as three to four times greater than at present. At the same time, the growing competition for land between forestry and agriculture will mean that in many parts of the world forest areas will be greatly reduced. The total world area of closed forest in 1978 was estimated to be 2.6 billion ha. It is believed that this will be reduced by 400 million ha by the year 2000, and that it will continue to decline until it reaches a long term stable area of 1.8 billion ha in about 2020: a reduction from 1978 of about 31% or 36 ha per minute (Council on Environmental Quality, 1980).

Recent estimates of deforestation in tropical areas, where forest clearance for food production has been most active, place the rate at between 11 and 30 million ha per year (or 21 to 57 ha per minute!) (Table 1.2). This is equivalent to a reduction of between 1.2 and 3% per year. Olsen (1982) challenges this figure. He estimates that the annual rate of loss is slightly less than 1%. Steinlin (1982) suggests 0.8%. However, many believe that except for parks and game reserves, the tropical rain forest as we now know it may be largely gone by the latter half of the next century unless present trends are changed (Spears, 1979).

In addition to forest clearance for agriculture, there are significant losses of commercial forestland to hydroelectric developments, power line rights-of-way, parks and environmental protection areas. Forestland is also being lost because of erosion accompanying poor-quality forest management. Much of the developing world is currently facing a serious timber famine which is likely to get substantially worse. The effects of this will have serious implications for human welfare.

Faced with such enormous human numbers, there is little that can be done. For example, the Club of Rome found that doubling the area of arable land available for agriculture (i.e., using *all* the world's potential arable land, involving very large development costs) would only delay the development of a critical shortage of such land by about 30 years. Similarly, if current population growth continues, doubling the area of the world's forests would merely postpone a global timber famine; it would not prevent it. Doubling the area of either agricultural or forest land would inevitably result in a major and unacceptable reduction of the other.

The relentless growth in human numbers will demand successful forest management. Successful forest manage-

Table 1.2 Estimates of the Area of Tropical Forests at Various Times Over the Past 30 Years and of Rates of Deforestation

Date	Area (km² × 10⁶)	Rate of Deforestation (10⁶ ha. yr⁻¹)	%	Reference
Original	15.9	Negligible	—	Woodwell et al., 1978
1950	17.0	—	—	Whittaker & Likens, 1973
1975	9.5	11	1.2	Woodwell et al., 1978
1977	10.0	30	3.0	Brunig, 1977
1979	11.0	20	1.8	Council on Environ. Qual., 1980
—	—	11.3	—	Development Forum, 1982

ment must, of necessity, be based on a thorough knowledge of ecology, the science dealing with the relationships between living organisms and their total environment. The present momentum of human population growth therefore requires that all resource managers have a good working knowledge of ecology. Anything less is unacceptable.

1.6 Philosophical View of Man's Place in the Biosphere

As noted above, population growth is not the only major determinant of future impacts on the environment and the world's forests. Our philosophical attitude towards the biosphere is also very important. There are two possible views of the relationship of humans to the living and nonliving environment: either that we are "different" and not a natural part of the environment, or that we are an integral and completely natural part of it.

Many "primitive" cultures had, or still have, a great reverence for the environment and the resources on which they depended. Offerings were made to the spirits of animals that were hunted and trees that were cut, and only as many resources were used as were needed to satisfy the essential needs of the community. However, as cultural evolution has proceeded, this attitude has often given way to a different view of things: the idea that we are "unnatural," that we are radically different from other animals, and that we are separate from and superior to "nature" and the "natural environment." This attitude is thought to have arisen as a result of more modern religious teachings and technological developments (White 1967; Moncrief 1970). The resultant philosophical view of our relationship to other organisms and the environment can lead, and it often has, to the attitude that since we are not a part of "the environment" we can modify it as we please, with little or no serious consequence to ourselves. The recent history of large-scale environmental alteration and the growing evidence of the undesirable consequences of many of these alterations demonstrate that this is clearly not a suitable philosophy on which to base the future conduct and development of the human race.

The environmental degradation resulting from these "traditional" attitudes led to a different philosophy. This also assumes that we are "unnatural" and an alien agent in the "natural environment," but it differs in that it concludes from this assumption that the only natural environment is one from which humans and their impacts are totally excluded. The environment is seen as something sacrosanct and holy, and it is felt that it is morally wrong for humans to modify the environment for their own use. This philosophy is just as unsuitable as a guideline for future evolution as the traditional view. It ignores the reality of the present abundance of the human species, its heavy demands on the environment, and the fact that human beings have for a long time been the major biotic force influencing the world. Exclusion of human influence on the environment is simply not a possible option.

Perhaps a more practical philosophical view of our place in the biosphere is one which considers us to be as natural and as much an integral part of our environment as any other living organism. Such a philosophy shows us that because we are inevitably a part of our environment, it is in our own self-interest to conserve it and manage it wisely. Similarly, the most rational basis for forest resource management is surely to consider the forester to be as natural a part of the forest as any other forest animal. The utility of this view lies in the inevitable conclusion that because we are still so heavily dependent on the forest, we misuse it at our peril.

1.7 Summary

Human beings are a product of biological evolution, and they share with other living organisms the fate of being dependent on the environment. Cultural evolution has certainly made humans appear to be different from other animals and has conferred on them a certain degree of independence from their environment. However, this independence is very fragile and there is no justifiable basis for claiming that human beings and their impact on the environment are any less natural than other species and their effects on the environment. The most useful view of our place in the world is to regard people as an integral and dependent part of the total environment.

Recent human evolutionary success has resulted in the attainment of a population level that is beginning to tax the ability of the earth to support it. Local populations have experienced shortages throughout much of human history, but there has nearly always been somewhere else people could turn to where resources were still in abundance. This situation has changed and the world's population has reached such a large size and is growing so rapidly that the number of unexploited areas and resources to which we can turn are rapidly diminishing. However, the problem is not always one of current shortages. Although these are common, for many resources we may have exploited only a modest proportion of what the world has to offer. The problem lies in exponential growth, because of which the sub-

stantial remaining resource reserve will be utilized in less time than it took to use the first few percent of the reserves. Thus, although we may appear to have so much reserve capacity of food, forest, mineral, and energy resources that we can defer serious consideration of resource depletion, the beginning of the twenty-first century will see serious shortages of several basic necessities for life because of exponential growth. There can be little doubt that technology can go a long way toward alleviating these shortages, but the evidence that acceptable technological solutions will be developed as rapidly as the population increases is not very reassuring. Neither is the thought of the accompanying environmental problems a pleasant one.

Managers of renewable natural resources face a tremendous challenge: that of greatly increasing production to satisfy the needs of the growing human population while reducing undesirable effects on other resources. In many cases, the increased production must come from a smaller area. Faced with this challenge, it should be obvious that only the highest-quality management will be acceptable. Such management can only occur if it is based on a sound understanding of the ecological relationships of the resource.

2.1 Introduction

The recent history of international conflict and economic disorder, and the consistent failure of many countries to achieve control of population growth and per capita resource consumption raises serious questions as to whether we are sufficiently rational to pull ourselves back from the exponential brink on which we are poised. However, not all the signs are negative. The world population growth rate of 2.1% in the 1960s declined to 1.9% by the mid-1970s and was around 1.7% by 1984. Ironically, it does rather appear that widespread recognition of the problems of exponential growth may well have developed at the precise point in human history at which the rate of population growth may have begun to decline (Kahn and Brown, 1975). Nevertheless, only time will tell whether this recent slight moderation in the rate of population growth will be sustained and followed by continuing declines.

In the developed countries of the world, the 1960s was a decade of concern over pesticides, pollution, environment, and, finally, population. The 1970s then became a decade of concern over resource depletion (especially energy), population, and economic instability. Now, in the 1980s, the danger of imminent resource depletion is widely recognized, and the economic constraints on solving the problem are paramount. The need for conservation and wise management of resources is gaining rather wide acceptance, at least in the developed countries, and an appreciation of the importance of renewable or ''inexhaustible'' resources is growing rapidly. Actual or incipient shortages of energy, raw materials, food, and water are influencing both the lives of individuals and the politics and policies of nations—as they always have done.

Resource depletion and resource scarcity are as real in forestry as in any other resource endeavor, and awareness of the need for improved resource management is probably as well developed in forestry as in any other resource field. A shrinking resource base due to poor management practices, competition from alternative land uses, and increasing economic inaccessibility of many forests almost certainly requires that increasing demands for forest products in the future will have to be satisfied from a smaller land area. Our dependence and impact on the forests of the world from our early evolutionary history until the present, and the historical pattern of development of forestry, show that the past 6000 years of cultural evolution has been molded to a considerable extent by the availability of wood, and that self-induced shortages of forest resources have been our frequent companion. Such shortages have often played a critical role in the unfolding of world history and were

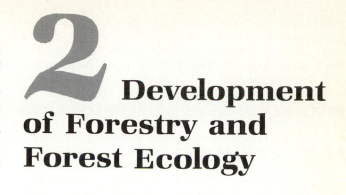

2 Development of Forestry and Forest Ecology

instrumental in the development of the science and art of forestry. The possibility that our dependence on the forest is about to increase again makes it necessary to review the history of this dependence and its effects on human cultural and political evolution. Much of the following discussion is based on that of Winters (1974); for an excellent review of human impacts on Mediterranean forests, the reader should consult Thirgood (1981).

2.2 Human Evolutionary Dependence on Forests

Humans almost always have been, and probably always will be to some extent dependent on forests. Having evolved from a primitive animal that lived in and depended on ancient tropical forests, human ancestors became totally tree-dependent, arboreal primates. Trees were their habitat, their environment, their source of food, and their protection from enemies. It was the reduction in area of ancestral tropical forests that generated the evolutionary pressures to leave the safety of the tree, to enter the more dangerous environment of the grassland, and to develop the physical and mental attributes that ultimately led to our current dominance over the plants and animals of the world. As our ancestors evolved from tree-dwelling primates into ground apes, they still depended on trees for escape cover, and the forest–grassland interface was probably a good hunting area.

Development of stone tools gave primitive humans a period of relative independence from the forest, increased their hunting ability, and stimulated the first of three major increases in population growth rate; this occurred between 1 million and 100,000 years ago. With the onset of the last ice age, this growth would probably have been reduced had the use of fire, using wood as fuel, not developed. Together with the use of furs and shelters, fire permitted the existence in cold areas of an animal that was thermally designed for a warm grassland environment. The development of wooden stockades and shelters gave increasing independence from cave dwellings and increasing protection from wild animals, and the construction of dry food storage facilities improved humans' ability to survive long, cold winters. As fire and wooden shelters became important, the earlier dependence on the forest began to return.

The second major increase in the rate of human population growth was associated with the development of agriculture about 8000 years ago. This development also marked the start of one of the major processes of deforestation: forest clearing for food production. Because the lighter soils used for early arable agriculture were frequently rather infertile, patterns of shifting agriculture developed that depended on the reinvasion of the forest to restore the fertility of the land. This method of food production has little long-term effect on forests. Major improvements in agriculture, and the concomitant deforestation, awaited the discovery of how to produce copper and iron by smelting, which was dependent on the use of wood charcoal as a fuel. The development of metal and wooden plows and the harnessing of domestic livestock power permitted the utilization of heavier, more fertile soils, and the development of metal saws and axes permitted the clearing of the much larger trees associated with these more productive sites.

The major agricultural advances accompanying these developments resulted in an excess of food production over current needs. This stimulated trade, which in turn gave rise to transportation needs involving wooden boats and animal-drawn wooden carts. The development of a merchant marine led to the need for a military marine to protect trading routes. As the growth of trade and commerce led to the growth of wealth and power, the earlier skirmishes and looting raids between rival tribes evolved into organized wars between nations competing for control over lands, resources, and trade routes. These wars were based for a pe-

riod of about 5000 years on a largely wooden technology, and preparations for war placed heavy demands on local forest resources. The great periods of naval warfare saw the supremacy of those nations that were able to secure ample supplies of shipbuilding timber, and they resulted in the denudation of substantial areas of forest and subsequent timber famines. Sometimes it was the quest for alternative supplies of timber to compensate for timber shortages that led to a subsequent war.

The importance of forests as commercial and strategic assets was recognized very early in the development of human culture. The ownership of forests played a major role in the history of human exploration, colonization, and international conflict. Several major events in human history of the last millenium have turned on the supply of timber for trade and warfare, and earlier history has many similar examples of the important role of forests. For example, it has been suggested that a significant factor in the British defeat in the American War of Independence was her inability to build and maintain a sufficient number of ships to attend to both her European and North American military commitments. Indeed, the reservation of extensive areas of New England forests for British naval use was probably a contributory factor leading to the war. The development of British colonial interests such as India in the eighteenth and nineteenth centuries were to a considerable extent related to shortages of home-grown ships' timbers to support British naval supremacy. The critically important supply of mining timbers (pit props) to Britain's coal industry was greatly reduced during World War I by the German naval blockade of the north Atlantic and other strategic supply routes, and pit prop reserves were at one point reduced to a 6-week supply. Without coal, Britain's war machine could not have continued, and European history over the past half century might have been substantially different.

The Industrial Revolution, now over two centuries old, could not have occurred without ample supplies of wood for buildings, machinery, and power. Although coal increasingly supplanted wood and charcoal during this period (largely because of a shortage of the latter), the coal could not have been obtained without adequate supplies of mining timbers, wooden carts, and other wooden paraphernalia that accompanied early coal-mining activities. Without the development of inexpensive paper derived from wood fiber, it is unlikely that the rapid accumulation and spread of knowledge and information that accompanied this period of technological revolution would have occurred. Although paper made from animal or grass fiber had been available from much earlier times, its use would have been too expensive or the supply too limited to support the knowledge and education explosion of the past century.

In addition to a direct dependence on trees, humans have also enjoyed and depended on many of the indirect benefits of trees. Regulation of stream discharge, maintainance of water quality, stabilization of steep hillsides, protection from high winds and avalanches, protection from marauding armies, provision of wildlife habitat for food and sport hunting, and provision of food for domestic livestock (beech and oak mast) have long been recognized as valuable forest-related assets. Deforestation eliminates these benefits and has resulted in reductions in the ability of the environment to sustain human beings in the regions where it has occurred.

It should be apparent from this brief review that almost all human evolution from primeval, primate stock to ground ape, and then through agricultural, technical, and cultural revolutions to the present time, has been intimately associated with, and conditioned by, forests. Whereas the enormous technical advances of the past 50 years appeared to offer alternatives or replacements for most forest products, many of these proved to require too much energy, to create too many problems of pollution, or to be inferior to wood products. Claims made during the past two decades that we were about to escape from our historic dependence on the forest have proved to be premature. Because of their renewability, forest products are likely to become more, rather than less, important in the future, and the indirect benefits of forests are receiving increasing recognition. There is good reason to believe that most human societies will continue to depend on forests for many basic resources, for energy, and for the maintenance of what is commonly referred to as a "high-quality environment."

2.3   History of Human Impacts on Forests

Although human populations have developed at different times in different parts of the world, it is possible to make a general statement about the characteristic pattern of growth of their impact on the forest. Of course, as was the case for population growth, it must be realized that this basic pattern has varied somewhat in different areas. Following this general statement, the development of human impacts on the forest in some specific areas is examined.

The effects of primitive humans on forests prior to 11,000 B.C. were very minor. Being hunters and gatherers, there was little reason to clear the forest, and with only crude stone tools, there was not the technology to do it. Undoubtedly, fire was used on some occasions to drive animals during hunting, and possibly to improve grazing. This

may have affected significant areas of forest locally, but human numbers were too few for this to have been a major force influencing the forests of the time. Their modest needs for fuel, tools, and shelter would easily have been met by the current growth of the forest, as is the case in some of the surviving examples of hunter–gatherer societies in the Pacific region and in South America. Humans at this stage of development had little more impact on the forest environment than did other inhabitants of the forest.

The first major change in the world's forests attributable to humans accompanied the development of agriculture. Clearings were made in the forest, and reinvasion by trees was sometimes prevented manually, by fire or by grazing. For a long time this patch-clearing agriculture was on a temporary, shifting basis, but as metal tools were evolved and heavier, richer soils were utilized, agricultural clearing accelerated and became permanent. The production of metal tools and weapons created a demand for fuel, and the combined effects of improved agriculture and metal technology produced further population increases and concomitant demands for more fuel and timber.

As humans evolved, both their numbers and per capita use of forest products increased. As a result, the rate of deforestation outstripped the simple growth in human numbers, larger areas were cleared, and forest regeneration was increasingly prevented by agriculture. The two processes of population growth and forest exploitation became linked in a positive feedback system: a process in which the size of A depends upon the size of B, which in turn depends upon the size of A. Any increase in A increases B, which in turn increases A, and so on, which results in an avalanche effect. Forest clearing for agriculture led to increased agricultural production, which led to an increase in population. This resulted in an increased demand for food, which led to further forest clearing for agriculture. This positive feedback process has continued with only temporary interruptions throughout most of the past 10,000 years, with increases in agricultural and other forest clearing surpassing the increase in human numbers. Only very recently has the rate of forest clearance for agriculture slowed down. With great increases in agricultural productivity, increased food production in many countries is being achieved from a constant or even shrinking land base, and recent forest conservation and replanting has led to a reduction in the rate of deforestation. However, the continuing population growth in some underdeveloped countries threatens to increase deforestation greatly over the next 50 years.

In spite of the tremendous inroads that agriculture has made, the greatest human impact on the world's forests has undoubtedly been associated with warfare. Although our current military adventures may appear to have little dependence on forests, this is a very recent development. Over the past 6000 years a very substantial part of the world's forests has been denuded in support of aggressive human activities. As early as 3500 B.C., the Egyptians were building large boats, and if Homer's mythological accounts of Agememnon's 1100 ships at the siege of Troy in 1100 B.C. are to be believed, the Greeks and the Romans had vast fleets of wooden boats. Considering that these boats are thought to have lasted only 10–15 years, the demands of timber for the construction and maintainance of such fleets must have been very substantial.

Naval warfare based on wooden ships was paralleled by "wood and metal" military activity on land involving wooden seige equipment, wooden defense works, and wooden and metal weapons and transport vehicles. The tradition of wooden warfare was continued until as recently as a century ago, and the vast European navies of the sixteenth to nineteenth centuries account for the denudation of large areas of the world's forests. Logging on its own did not eliminate the forest, but logging was often followed by grazing and fire, so that many areas were slowly denuded of tree vegetation following the initial selective harvesting of ships' timbers. Of course, this process of deforestation has not continued uninterrupted throughout recent human history. The decline of civilizations and periodic reductions of populations by disease and war permitted some of the cleared areas to revert to forest. However, many areas were so devastated by loss of soil that prompt return of the former forest vegetation was impossible, and early records indicate that large areas of present-day desert and semidesert were once forested. In some regions the conversion from forest to desert has probably resulted from climatic change, but this cannot account for all such conversions. It is apparent that human deforestation has also played an important part.

In addition to the direct military uses of wood, the use of wood in the production of metal for the manufacture of weapons and tools has been a major factor contributing to deforestation. Starting as early as 3200 B.C., the development of copper smelting, together with the discovery of iron, placed considerable demands on the forest in addition to those associated with the housing, feeding, and warming of the growing population.

2.4　Development of Forestry

Forestry is defined as "generally, a profession embracing the science, business and art of creating, conserving and managing forests and forest lands for the continuous use of their resources, material or other" (Ford-Robertson, 1971). It is a branch of human endeavor that has always developed because of need. It has arisen at different times and in different areas of the world, but its first appearance has always coincided with approximately the same stage in the evolution of the relationship between humans and the forest.

In the early stages of development of a human society, the forest is simply a part of the environment: the habitat of prey and enemies, and the occasional provider of certain necessities for life. As human utilization or removal of the forest increases, the forest is considered to be either a limitless resource or a limitless impediment: in either case, profligate use or energetic destruction is considered as an acceptable or even laudable activity. Initially, the resulting deforestation occurs only in isolated localities, but as the population grows, the geographical extent of forestless areas expands. Eventually, incipient shortages of forest products for certain uses are perceived, although frequently too late to prevent serious shortages. These generally lead to one of two alternative actions. In the first of these, sources of wood supply may be sought elsewhere and national policy is oriented toward development of trade with, or political control over, geographic areas that offer suitable supplies of forest products. This only postpones the second alternative, since the basic pattern of forest exploitation is repeated in any forested area that is colonized. The second alternative is the initiation of some form of forest regulation and management in order to conserve forest resources and avoid shortages.

Forestry has generally developed only after a period of exploitation that has created actual or potential future timber shortages. The earliest stages of forestry usually involve the institution of regulations designed to meet certain objectives. Characteristically, these regulations are based on administrative, short-term economic or strategic dictates and reflect little or no knowledge of the ecological nature and variability of the forest. As a consequence, such early attempts at forestry rarely succeed in solving the problems that were their genesis. Initial failures are almost invariably followed sooner or later by a continuing evolution toward an ever more ecologically rational set of management objectives and methods.

This predictable sequence in the evolution of forestry can be summarized into six major stages.

1. Unregulated exploitation of forests with no thought for depletion or conservation.
2. Perception of real or threatened future shortages of forest resources.

3. Exploitation of undepleted forests at more remote locations (stages 1 and 2 repeated), and/or,
4. Institution of simple, nonecological regulations concerning future forest cutting and management.
5. Realization that simple administrative dictates cannot ensure adequate future supplies of forest resources.
6. Initiation of a continuing development of ecologically based forest-resource conservation and management practices, usually accompanied by increasing success in the conservation and production of forest crops.

Precisely this sequence or parts thereof can be seen throughout human cultural evolution. The Egyptians got as far as creating local wood shortages, which were solved by either trade or invasion of forested areas such as Cyprus and Phoenicia. When these sources of timber were cut off by rival military powers, Egypt failed to proceed to the subsequent phase of establishing its own forest ordinances, possibly because by that time the population had grown to the point at which almost all suitable tree-growing land was being used for agriculture.

The Greeks and Romans progressed through similar stages, but both got as far as creating reservations overseas to ensure continued supplies. Reliance on overseas supplies relieved the need for the development of forestry in the home country, although planting of trees along rivers and canals was encouraged. Extensive deforestation of Greece led to severe soil erosion and land degradation, which in turn led to a switch from horses and cows to sheep and goats, animals which are able to survive on the nutritionally more marginal vegetation that grows on the severely eroded Greek landscape. This has had lasting consequences for the national diet. The soil erosion and land degradation was so serious that it led to large-scale emigrations from Greece between 750 and 550 B.C., and aroused interest in the biological nature and role of the forest. In 400 B.C., Plato wrote about the denudation of previously forested mountains, the drying up of springs, and the loss of soil. In the same period, Theophrastus (who is looked upon as the father of botany) developed an interest in plants and forests. He named and classified 500 plants and wrote about the ecology, technological characteristics, and utilization potential of different tree species and how the latter varied according to the type of site in which the trees were growing. Had the greatness of the Greek empire survived for another millenium, history might have recorded the development of modern forestry in Greece.

Knowledge of botany, of soil, and of methods of forest regeneration and culture was developed in Europe by monks in the eleventh century A.D. Control of substantial areas of forest by monasteries prevented wholesale deforestation and ensured a supply of charcoal and small wood, but it did nothing to prevent the shortage of large ships' timbers when the modern period of wooden navies started in the seventeenth century. Ordinances were introduced that stipulated cutting rotations, the retention of large trees, and the extent of large cuts. However, these early attempts at forest management were not entirely successful because they were excessively rigid and did not allow for natural biological variations or disasters. The subsequent four centuries have witnessed the successive modification of these early regulations and methods in the light of experience and new biological knowledge, culminating in a strong ecological basis for the present-day European practice of forestry.

The development of national forest ordinances in France predated the similar event in Germany. For political reasons, Germany did not develop national ordinances until near the end of the nineteenth century, although there were local and regional ordinances well before this, including a ban on clearcutting in the Salzburg area as early as 1237. Lack of national coordination permitted extensive deforestation in spite of these regulations, and with the exception of the less accessible mountain forests, much of the country had been deforested by the time a national organization was developed.

The history of forestry in North America follows the same general pattern, although the knowledge and experience gained in the development of European forestry had a restraining influence. The conservative attitude of the first settlers toward the forest reflected the more advanced stage in the evolution of forestry in their home countries. However, profligate use of the forest soon developed, returning the country to near the beginning of the development sequence. The denudation of North American forests by fire and logging appalled travelers returning from timber-short and frugal Europe, and they helped to stimulate public interest in conservation. The late nineteenth century saw the beginnings of modern forestry with the establishment of state forestry commissions, forest reserves, and a national forest service in the U.S. In the past half century, U.S. forestry has continued to evolve, with a steadily increasing emphasis on ecological principles.

In spite of, or perhaps because of, the extent and importance of its forest resources, the development of forestry in Canada postdates even that in the U.S. In some areas, forest management in Canada has started only very recently.

It is encouraging to note that in many countries around the world forestry is either in or has recently arrived at the sixth stage in its development from unregulated exploitation. Day-to-day practical application of forest ecology in forest management is no longer considered to be merely a central European idiosyncrasy. Unfortunately, this optimistic statement must be balanced by the fact that large-scale deforestation is not merely of historical interest. It is a present-day fact and probably an inevitable component of the human future. Every year, 5 million hectares of Asian forests are lost and millions more degraded by improper use (Ranjitsinh, 1979). The total area of forest in Thailand was reduced from 58.3% of the country in 1952 to 39% by 1973, and 33% by 1978. Afghanistan is being deforested so rapidly that the country could become essentially barren by 1990–95. For all practical purposes, Malaysia's forests could be gone by 1990. Nepal is likely to be denuded by the end of the century. The attention of politicians has been focused on this serious state of affairs and large programs of afforestation have been initiated. However, there are many ecological and institutional impediments to these programs, and it remains to be seen which of the two forces, afforestation/reforestation or deforestation, will win.

2.5   Forest Ecology: A Practical Means of Dealing with the Problems of Complexity

Forestry has always developed as the result of the need to ensure an adequate supply of certain desired goods and services from the forest. The development of forest ecology has been for similar reasons. Although it has also evolved into a branch of basic ecological science, the growth of forest ecology as an applied science can, in part, be related to the failure of early forestry to achieve its objectives. The development and acceptance of forest ecology by foresters occurred because it provided a means of recognizing, understanding, classifying and mapping the natural variation of forests: forest ecology provides the essential ecological basis for successful forest management.

It has been a consistent experience throughout the history of forestry that only by understanding the ecological characteristics of forests can they be managed successfully. The empirical approach of "try it and see" has made an important contribution to the development of forestry and will probably continue to do so. However, as the pressures of population growth and resource demands continue to increase, this approach will become less and less useful. The time required to produce an answer is too long and there is a decreasing acceptance of "mistakes." Today it is necessary to be able to make accurate predictions about the forest and its management without waiting decades or centuries for evidence on the success of our management methods.

Such predictions cannot be made without an understanding of forest ecology and the allied scientific disciplines.

Forests are difficult to manage because they are very complex and they vary greatly from one place to another. Forest ecology strives to reduce the complications posed by this complexity and variability by recognizing and understanding it. Perhaps the best way to explain this is by discussing the nature of biological causality and the principle of determinism.

It is a tenet of science that all things are determined. There is an explanation for all events or conditions (hereinafter referred to simply as events) in the form of a set of *antecedent*[1] conditions, factors, or *determinants* that collectively determine or "cause" the event. For example, the sun does not rise every morning in the east and set every evening in the west merely by chance. If this were so, it might periodically set in the north or the south. It sets in the west *because* (implying determinism or causation) of the way in which the earth moves in relation to the sun. The antecedent determinants of sunrise and sunset are thus all the factors of celestial mechanics that determine how the earth moves around its own axis and that of the sun. Similarly, if a tree dies, there will be a number of environmental and physiological factors that can be identified as antecedent determinants (hereinafter referred to simply as antecedents) of this pathological event. This scientific principle is called the *principle of determinism*.[2] It covers all categories of determinism from the simplest, in which there is a single antecedent (the *cause*) for each event, to the most complex, where there is an infinite number of antecedents for each event. This is represented diagrammatically in Figure 2.1.

The simplest case of determinism, the cause/event relationship, is referred to as *causal determinism*. A cause is defined as an antecedent that is both *necessary* and *sufficient* to determine a particular event. In other words, the event occurs *only* when the cause is present, and *every time* the cause is present the event will occur. This is a very rigid definition and such a relationship is largely theoretical. It probably never occurs in biological systems. Any biological event involves at the very least two, and most often several major antecedents. Events such as the setting of the sun and the death of a tree are thus examples of what is referred to as *multiple determinism*. Where the number of significant determinants is exceedingly large (more than 30, a condition rarely if ever observed in biological systems), one approaches the other extreme of determinism: *statistical determinism*.

[1] Antecedent: happening before the event.
[2] The terminology and concepts in this discussion are based on Bunge (1959).

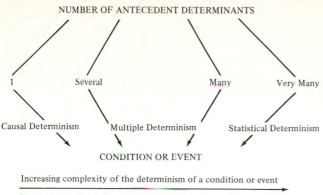

NUMBER OF ANTECEDENT DETERMINANTS

1   Several   Many   Very Many

Causal Determinism   Multiple Determinism   Statistical Determinism

CONDITION OR EVENT

Increasing complexity of the determinism of a condition or event

Decreasing predictability of the occurrence of a condition or event

Figure 2.1

Diagrammatic representation of the principle of determinism which states that all conditions and/or events are associated with a set of antecedent determinants. There is a large variation in the number of antecedent determinants that can be associated with a condition or event, from a single antecedent determinant (the *cause*) to some very large number. This results in three types of events/conditions: those that are causally determined, those that are multiply determined, and those that are statistically determined. The importance of this principle for resource management lies in the inverse relationship between the complexity of the determinism and the predictability of the condition or event.

The importance of the principle of determinism to science and forestry lies in the relationship between the predictability of an event and the complexity of the determination of that event. The fewer the antecedents, the more predictable the event. In causal determinism, one has perfect prediction because of the one-to-one relationship between antecedent and effect. In statistical determinism one has very low predictive ability since the very large number of antecedents combine to produce an apparently random, unpredictable occurrence of the event. In multiple determinism one has events that vary in their predictability from high (at the left side of Figure 2.1) to low (at the right side of Figure 2.1). The following examples illustrate the relationship between complexity and predictability.

First, consider a very simple case of determinism: a glass rod being broken by dropping it onto a stone floor. This is a reasonable approximation of causal determinism. Although there are several antecedents to the event of the rod being broken (e.g., the action of gravity, the fragility of the rod, the hardness of the floor, the weight of the rod, the elevation, and subsequent release of the rod at a height that will result in breakage), they are all considered to be known and invariable. One could say that the rod is broken *because* it is released and allowed to fall (the antecedent). The causal

nature of the event results in its predictability being 100%, and 100 repetitions of the antecedent (the action of dropping the rod on the floor) will always produce 100 broken rods.

Consider now the success of a blindfolded observer in predicting the fate of 100 glass rods dropped at random onto a stone floor, half of which is covered with small squares of rubber matting distributed at random. On average, 50 rods will land on stone and break, whereas the other 50 will land on rubber and remain intact. The blindfolded observer would be only 50% successful on average in predicting the breakage of the rods. Thus, by introducing one unknown antecedent, we have halved the predictability of that event. If, unknown to our blindfolded observer, we were to add a second unknown antecedent by replacing half of the breakable glass rods by unbreakable plastic rods, the observer's predictive success would be reduced to 25%. If we were to add a third unknown antecedent by dropping the rods alternately from 2 cm (generally, too small a drop for glass rods falling onto stone to break) and 2 m, the observer's average success in predictin the breaking of the rods would be further halved, to 12.5%. This sequence of declining predictability is shown in Figure 2.2. It should be obvious that there is little hope of success in accurately predicting events that have more than three or four unknown antecedents.

For a second example, let us consider a hypothetical relationship between clearcut logging and the occurrence of landslides. *If* there was a causal relationship between clearcutting steep hillsides and landslides, we could state categorically and unequivocally that a landslide will occur every time we clearcut a steep slope. If we were planning a series of clearcuts in a region that had 50% flat land and 50% steep land but we had no information as to the location of the cuts relative to the topography, our success in predicting landslides would, on average, be halved. However, we know that the determination of landslides is more complex than this. For example, we know that soils derived from volcanic rocks are more prone to landslides than are soils derived from granitic rocks. Thus, if we were planning clearcuts in a region containing an unmapped patchwork of steep and flat land with both volcanic and granitic soils (50:50), our ability to predict a clearcut/landslide event would be only 25% on average. Soil parent material is not the only soil factor determining landslides, however. The wetness of the soil and the rooting patterns of the trees and minor vegetation are two of several other factors that contribute significantly to the determination of a landslide event. As we add additional unknown antecedents to the determination of landslides following clearcutting, our success at predicting these events drops rapidly, as shown in Figure 2.2. Land-

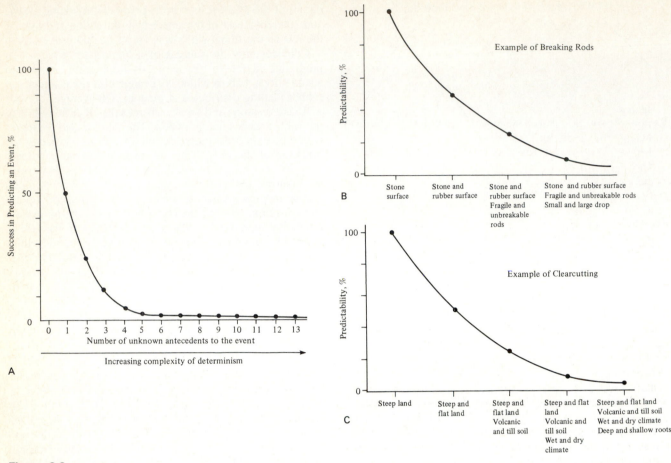

Figure 2.2
Some hypothetical examples of the relationship between the predictability of a condition/event and the complexity of its determinism. (A) General case. (B) Example of breaking rods. (C) Hypothetical example of clearcutting and landslides. See the text for explanation.

slides are very unpredictable events in those areas about which we have no information on topography, soils, rooting patterns, climate, and so on.

A forest is not merely a stand of trees. It is the total assemblage of

1. Trees.
2. The substrate on which they depend for support, nutrition, and moisture.
3. The other plants with which they interact in terms of mutual shelter, competition, benefit, or antagonism.
4. The animals that feed on, shelter under, or benefit the plants.
5. The microorganisms that exert direct or indirect benefi-

cial or antagonistic effects on the trees and other living organisms.
6. The soil and atmospheric climate, including fire and moisture, that influence the distribution and abundance of all the organisms in the forest.

The forest is a complex biological and physical system in which there is an enormous variety of interaction and interdependency among the different parts. Because of this great complexity, interaction, and interdependency, most events or conditions in a forest are determined by many antecedents: it is multiply determined. This has been expressed as follows (Major, 1951):[3]

[3]f: a function of.

vegetation = f(soil, climate, parent material,
             topography, biota, time)

and

soil = f(vegetation, climate, parent material,
        topography, biota, time)

Because of this complexity, attempts to predict vegetation or soil conditions in a region about which we have no knowledge of the factors on the right side of the equations will have a low probability of success.

Knowledge of the contribution of individual antecedents to the causation of a particular event effectively simplifies that causation. For example, in the case of the glass rod, the observer's predictive success improves if he or she knows the fragility of each rod and the height from which it is dropped. It is improved still further if a map of the location of the rubber pads is available and the observer knows where on this map each rod is to be dropped. Each time an antecedent is recognized and its role understood, we move one place to the left in Figure 2.1. By understanding all the antecedents in a complex, multiply determined event, we can effectively reduce it to a case of causal determinism as far as prediction is concerned. When we understand the contribution of soil parent material, soil moisture, vegetation rooting patterns, and all the other significant antecedents to the event, we can predict landslides very accurately if we have mapped spatial variations in these factors and if we know how they vary seasonally and annually.

Herein lies both the justification and the necessity for all foresters to have a working knowledge of both basic forest ecology and the ecological aspects of forestry. A forester's job is to contribute to the establishment of a set of management objectives and then find ways of achieving them. In helping to set objectives the forester must be able to predict the biological capabilities and tolerances of the ecological system under management. In deciding on the methods to be used to achieve these objectives the forester must be able to select from among a number of alternatives the one best suited to the situation at hand. This requires that the forester be able to predict the consequences of the various alternatives. Only in this way will he or she have a reasonable expectation of choosing the best alternative. However, to be able to make these predictions successfully in a highly complex system such as a forest, he or she must first have a good knowledge of the structure, function, and spatial variability of the forest. By understanding how soil, climate, microorganisms, plants, and animals influence each other, a forester can predict the growth and productivity of crop trees, since this knowledge effectively establishes causal

growth relationships. By understanding how such practices as clearcutting or slashburning affect the structure and function of forests, and by knowing the local conditions of soil, climate, and biota, foresters can predict the consequences of these treatments on a particular site. Through knowledge and understanding of forest ecology and of the local forest conditions comes predictability of those forests. Through predictability comes the selection of ecologically and economically rational objectives and the best methods of attaining them.

2.6   Summary

Throughout most of their evolution, humans have had a close relationship with forests. Wood and other forest products have played an important role in molding cultural evolution, and humans have radically changed the extent and composition of the world's forests. Unlike most other biological relationships, the interaction between humans and forest developed a positive feedback. As numbers grew, more timber was used and more forest was cleared for agriculture, and this led to further increases in the population. The process culminated at various times in various different countries in wood shortages that were of great political and economic significance and which led ultimately to the development of forestry. Early attempts to conserve and sustain wood supplies were largely unsuccessful. Regulations and ordinances based on military or short-term economic and/or political rather than on biological principles are not an adequate basis on which to develop successful sustained-yield forest management. The result of these failures was an effort to learn more about the ecological nature of the resource in order to develop more successful management objectives and methods. The failure of early forest management was the practical impetus behind the development of forest ecology.

Successful forest management requires the correct choice from among alternative methods of attaining management objectives. Such a choice requires the ability to predict the outcomes of the various alternatives so that the best can be selected. Accurate prediction is difficult in a forest because of the complexity of factors responsible for determining events and conditions. Accurate prediction in complex systems is possible, however, if the components and functional processes of the system are understood. The major role of forest ecology is to provide forest managers with a basic understanding of the way in which the forest ecosystem works: to familiarize them with the major determinants in the system.

PART II Forest Ecology: The Biological Basis for Management of Forest Resources

Having presented the case for forest ecology as an essential ingredient in the management of the world's forests, we turn now to the subject itself. This part of the book starts with an examination of the forest as a complex ecological system, an *ecosystem.* It then examines the major functional processes of such systems. This is followed by a chapter on the genetic and evolutionary aspects of ecology: the adaptation of the individual biological components of the ecosystem to the physical and biotic aspects of their environment. The major physical components of the environment are then described, followed by chapters on the biotic components of the environment: populations and communities. With all its major components examined, the ecosystem is then reassembled for a discussion of how it changes with time.

The structure of this part of the book is analogous to looking at an intact jigsaw puzzle of an ecosystem in order to gain an appreciation of the overall picture, then taking it apart to examine the component pieces and see how they fit together, and finally reassembling the picture in order to study and interpret it. Because Part II is so complex, it is subdivided into several sections.

A. Ecosystem ecology: the forest as a functional system.
B. Genetic and evolutionary aspects of ecosystems.
C. The physical environment.
D. The biotic environment.
E. Temporal changes in ecosystem structure and function.

Section A Ecosystem Ecology: The Forest as a Functional System

Many people think of a forest as a stand of trees, but it is far more than that. A forest is a complex, functional system of interacting and often interdependent biological, physical, and chemical components, the biological part of which has evolved to perpetuate itself through the production of new organic matter. From earliest evolution, humans have been interested in their environment as much for its functional characteristics as for any other attributes. Continuing this tradition, contemporary renewable-resource management is largely concerned with organic production and its manipulation through ecosystem modification.

Because of the importance of viewing any renewable resource as a system, and because of the preoccupation of renewable-resource management with ecosystem function, we consider first the nature of ecosystems, and then examine the two major aspects of ecosystem function: (1) energy capture, storage, and dynamics and (2) the input into, circulation within, and loss of nutrient chemicals from ecosystems.

3.1 The Science of Ecology and Its Historical Development

Ecology is the branch of biological science concerned with the distribution, abundance, and productivity of living organisms, and their interactions with each other and with their physical environment. As a scientific discipline, it is relatively young and lacks the large body of generally accepted principles and theories that characterize older disciplines such as physics and chemistry. It has been given various definitions, including *scientific natural history* (Elton, 1927), *the study of the structure and function of nature* (Odum, 1971), and *the scientific study of the interactions that determine the distribution and abundance of organisms* (Krebs, 1978). The choice of definition is not critical as long as it is remembered that the focus of ecology is on the interrelationships between living organisms and both their biotic (living) *and* abiotic (nonliving) environment.

The history of ecology dates from about the turn of this century, but the historical roots of the subject are much older. All animals, if they are to survive, must have an operational "knowledge" of those ecological relationships that affect them. The hunting success of early humans suggests that they must have known a lot about the behavior, food requirements, and habitat of both their prey and animals that preyed on them. Following the Pleistocene extinction, knowledge of plant ecology would have increased considerably as they changed from hunters to gatherers. Further improvements in knowledge of life histories and of environmental tolerances and requirements would have followed the development of farming and the domestication of plants and animals. This knowledge was purely empirical, of course. The development of scientific observation and the recording of relationships between animals, plants, and the physical environment awaited the development of Egyptian and Greek cultures.

The Egyptians left evidence in their sculpture and wall paintings of a well-developed appreciation of animals and plants, and the Greeks gave us the first formal record of botany and plant ecology. In the fourth century B.C., Aristotle wrote about plagues of field mice and locusts, echoing earlier concerns of Egyptian and Babylonian societies about outbreaks of animal pests. There is evidence in these early writings of a recognition of a "balance of nature" and a harmony among plants, animals, and humans. In about 300 B.C., Theophrastus, a pupil of Aristotle, demonstrated a clear understanding of habitat selection by different plants, the effects that different habitats have on the growth and

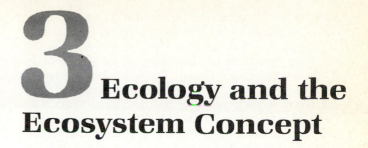

3. Ecology and the Ecosystem Concept

morphology of plants, and the implications of these effects for the utilization of trees by people (Kormondy, 1965).

> The differences between trees of the same kind have already been considered. Now all grow fairer and are more vigorous in their proper positions; for wild, no less than cultivated trees, have each their own positions: some love wet and marshy ground, as black poplar, abele, willow and in general those that grow by rivers; some love exposed and sunny positions; some prefer a shady place. The fir is fairest and tallest in a sunny position, and does not grow at all in a shady one; the silver-fir on the contrary is fairest in a shady place, and not so vigorous in a sunny one.
>
> Thus, there is in Arcadia, near the place called Krane, a low-lying district sheltered from wind, into which they say that the sun never strikes; and in this district the silver-firs excel greatly in height and stoutness, though they have not such close grain nor such comely wood, but quite the reverse,—like the fir when it grows in a shady place. Wherefore men do not use these for expensive work, such as doors or other choice articles, but rather for ship-building and house-building. For excellent rafters, beams and yard-arms are made from these, and also masts of great length which are not however equally strong; while masts made of trees grown in a sunny place are necessarily short but of closer grain and stronger than the others.

These early expressions of ecological awareness remained largely undeveloped for many centuries until the growing sophistication of agriculture led to an increase in practical knowledge of the relationships between plants and animals and between living organisms and their physical environment. European monastic settlements in the Middle Ages contributed to the growth of biological knowledge of forests, and this period saw the development of an interest in human populations (the beginnings of the science of *demography*) and natural history. The eighteenth century witnessed a general rejection of the view that the human situation could be perfected by social institutions alone. This view was replaced by a recognition that humans, animals, and plants are all held in check by the same general processes. Thomas Malthus in his famous *Essay on Population* (1798) told the world explicitly that humans, like any other organism, are ultimately resource limited. From this essay one can trace the development of Darwin's theories of evolution and natural selection, and much of the resulting conceptual base of biology.

Malthus' essay, which has been referred to as "certainly one of the most influential in the history of western thought" (McNaughton and Wolf, 1973), stimulated interest in the mathematical aspects of biology. It also led to the replacement of the ideas of *providential ecology* (a concept in which nature is thought to be designed to benefit and preserve each species) and *the balance of nature* by the ideas of *natural selection* and the *struggle for existence* (Egerton, 1968). The development of ecological thought was further stimulated by problems of agricultural pests and disease vectors, and by the end of the nineteenth century the recognition and description of plant and animal communities had gained considerable momentum.

A growing realization of the interrelatedness of living organisms and their physical environment led to a general recognition of the need for a new branch of science. The development of this recognition occurred earlier among soil scientists and silviculturists (foresters) than among other natural scientists (Sukachev and Dylis, 1964), but by about 1900 it had become widespread and led to the inception of the science of ecology. The name for the new science was coined originally as *oecology* by two German zoologists, Reither and Haekle, in 1869 (Kormondy, 1965). However, the word did not appear again until 1895, when a report on ecological plant geography was published by Warming, a Danish botanist. The word is derived from the Greek words *oikos,* meaning "house," and *logos,* meaning "the study of." Development of ecology gathered momentum in the first two decades of this century, but most of the major advances have been achieved in the past 60 years. Only in the past 30 years has it been recognized as a major branch of biological science.

Use of the word *ecology* was rare outside scientific circles as recently as 20 years ago. Today it is a household word. This semantic revolution has unfortunately been ac-companied by frequent misuse and misinterpretation of the word. It is commonly and wrongly used as a synonym for *conservation* and *preservation* and as a banner for the "environmental movement." As a science, ecology is amoral. It makes no moral or value judgments about the desirability or lack of desirability of any ecological condition or event. It merely describes the ecological characteristics or consequences of things. Judgments as to whether the characteristics of a particular ecosystem or ecosystem condition are any better or worse than those of any other ecosystem or condition must be made by society. Similarly, judgments as to whether the ecological consequences of particular events are good or bad, desirable or undesirable, can only be made using the prevailing measures of socioeconomic value. Ecological information is or should be used as an aid to the formulation of such value judgments, but most often they are made on the basis of social rather than ecological criteria.

3.2 Subdivisions of Ecology and the Levels-of-Biological-Organization Concept

There is frequently some confusion over just what ecology covers that is not already covered by other, more traditional disciplines such as botany, zoology, soil science, meteorology, and microbiology. In order to understand the unique contribution of ecology, it is necessary to understand the concept of *levels of biological organization* and the related concept of *levels of biological integration* (Rowe, 1961) that is discussed in section 3.4.

If all the knowledge of biology and closely related sciences is considered, we find that it can be arranged in a hierarchy of increasing biological complexity. In this hierarchy, each level incorporates knowledge of the level below. The lowest level is that of molecules in biological systems, which is successively based on the nonbiological levels of atoms and molecules (chemistry), energy and matter (physics), and space and numbers (mathematics). Various writers have identified successively more complex biological levels of organization: subcellular components, cells, tissues, organs, organ systems, and individual organisms. These are shown, together with the traditional scientific discipline that is most commonly associated with them, in Figure 3.1. Similar hierarchies could presumably be drawn up for the atmospheric and earth sciences, which emanate, together with the biological hierarchies, from the level of atoms and molecules.

It is apparent from Figure 3.1 that almost all of the traditional subdivisions of biology are concerned with levels of

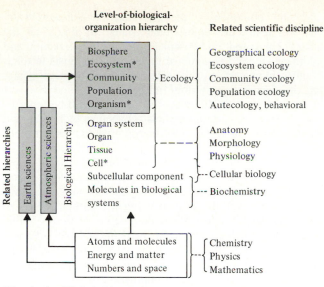

Level-of-biological-organization hierarchy   **Related scientific discipline**

*True levels of biological integration

Figure 3.1

Levels of biological organization and the related biological disciplines. The diagram shows three hierarchies of knowledge which lead from the fundamental subjects of mathematics, physics, and chemistry. These three hierarchies coalesce at the ecosystem level. Details are given only for the biological hierarchy. True levels of biological integration (according to Rowe, 1961) are marked with an asterisk.

organization at or below the individual organism. Ecology, on the other hand, is concerned with:

1. individual organisms in relation to other organisms and the nonliving environment,
2. groups of organisms of the same species (populations),
3. natural assemblages of populations of different species (communities), and
4. entire natural systems composed of communities and their physical environment (ecosystems).

In other words, ecology is concerned with levels of organization from the organism upward. In common with other biological disciplines, ecology knows no taxonomic boundaries. Just as the sciences of physiology, anatomy, and genetics can be applied to ferns and trees, insects and mammals, so one can study the ecology of mosses and shrubs, bacteria and birds. Ecology is a functional and organizational division rather than a taxonomic division of scientific knowledge.

The science of ecology has several subdivisions, each of which is associated with a different level of biological organization.

1. Study of the life history and the response to its environment of a single individual or species is frequently referred to as *autecology:* for example, the life history of an eagle, the food requirements of a deer, or the temperature tolerance of Douglas-fir seedlings.

2. Study of the abundance, distribution, productivity, and/or dynamics of a group of organisms of the same type (a single-species population) would be classified as *population ecology:* for example, an investigation of competition for light and nutrients in a pine plantation, the role of disease in controlling the numbers of insects on a tree, or the rate of growth and mortality of the individuals in a salmon population.

3. Studies involving the description and quantification of some aspect of a natural assemblage of different species of organisms are classified as *community ecology:* for example, the study, classification, and mapping of forest plant associations or forest types, the description of the animal community in a small lake, or a study of the change in plant and animal communities in an area over time. Population ecology and community ecology are sometimes referred to collectively as *synecology.*

4. Studies involving both the biotic community and its abiotic environment are classed as *ecosystem ecology.* Such studies may be primarily *descriptive,* as in the classification and mapping of different types of ecosystems. They can also be *functional,* such as a study of the interrelationships between the plant community and the soil, or the way in which energy and nutrients are distributed in and move through an ecosystem.

3.3   The Ecosystem Concept[1]

The word ecosystem has been used several times already, but its importance in forest ecology warrants further discussion. It is the central concept of this book, of ecology, and of the biologically rational management of forest resources. Our long-term survival on this planet will depend in no small part on our acceptance of the concept of ecosystem as a guide to our future conduct.

The term ecosystem was suggested by an English ecologist, Tansley. He defined it as including ''not only the organism-complex, but the whole complex of physical factors forming what we call the environment'' (Tansley, 1935).

---

[1] One of the important earlier collections of papers concerned with the application of the ecosystem concept in natural resource management can be found in van Dyne (1969). The reader is recommended to chapters by Major, Bormann and Likens, Schultz, and Bakuzis and Cooper.

There are several alternative definitions, all proposed by American ecologists. Lindeman (1942) proposed that ''an ecosystem is any system composed of physical, chemical and biological processes active within any space-time unit.'' Whittaker (1962) suggested that ''an ecosystem is a functional system that includes an assemblage of interacting organisms (plants, animals and saprobes) and their environment, which acts on them and on which they act.'' More recently, Odum (1971) proposed a longer but more explicit definition.

Any unit that includes all of the organisms (i.e., the community) in a given area interacting with the physical environment so that a flow of energy leads to a clearly defined trophic structure, biotic diversity, and material cycles (i.e., exchange of materials between living and non-living parts within the system) is an ecological system or ecosystem.

It is clear from these definitions that the term ecosystem is more of a concept than a real physical entity—a concept with six major attributes.

1. The attribute of *structure*. Ecosystems are made up of biotic and abiotic subcomponents. At the very least, a terrestrial ecosystem must have green plants, a substrate, and an atmosphere, and in most ecosystems there must be an appropriate mixture of plants, animals, and microbes if the ecosystem is to function. Terrestrial ecosystems normally consist of a complex biotic community, together with soil and atmosphere, a source of energy (generally the sun), and a supply of water.

2. The attribute of *function,* the constant exchange of matter and energy between the physical environment and the living community. Because living and nonliving things are both composed of energy and matter, and because it is often difficult to define when organic material is alive and when it is dead, there are considerable advantages in looking at an ecosystem in terms of a physical–chemical entity. Within this entity there is a constant exchange of matter and energy between different components, some of which have the characteristics of life and some of which do not. This way of looking at ecosystems in no way denies the importance of the more traditional genetic view of life; it is complementary to it.

3. The attribute of *complexity*, which results from the high level of biological integration that is inherent in an ecosystem. All events and conditions in ecosystems are multiply determined. They are therefore difficult to predict without a considerable knowledge of the structure and functional processes of the system.

4. The attribute of *interaction* and *interdependency*. So complete is the interconnectedness of the various living and nonliving components of the ecosystem that a change in any one will result in a subsequent change in almost all the others. The extent and completeness of this interaction and interdependency led some of the earlier ecologists to think of physical examples of the ecosystem concept (e.g., a hectare of forest, an agricultural field, or a small pond) as a sort of *superorganism*. This view has been rejected because although there are certain parallels between an individual and an ecosystem, the differences are too great to make the concept useful.

5. The attribute of *no inherent definition of spatial dimensions*. An individual organism is a tangible entity. It has a clearly defined physical size. Populations and communities are also spatially defined entities, although their size may sometimes be rather difficult to define. A flock of birds or a school of fish constitute easily identifiable populations, but their spatial boundaries may be difficult to establish because the space they occupy may change periodically. Similarly, identification of a population of spruce trees in the northern boreal spruce forest or of a biotic community in the open ocean may require a somewhat arbitrary definition of spatial boundaries. However, in spite of these problems, the focus of attention in the terms *population* and *community* is clearly on a real physical entity that often can be defined quite easily. The biotic community of a clearcut or of a wet valley bottom can be readily observed and its spatial limits described. The term *ecosystem,* on the other hand, focuses on the structure, the complexity of organization, the interaction and interdependency, and the functioning of the system, and not on the geographical boundaries of the system.

6. The attribute of *temporal change*. Ecosystems are not static, unchanging systems. In addition to the continuous exchanges of matter and energy, the entire structure and function of an ecosystem undergoes change over time.

The importance of the ecosystem concept lies in its explicit recognition of complexity, interaction, and functional processes. Its weakness lies in the difficulty of using the concept for the identification, mapping, description, and study of specific ecosystems because of its failure to define their physical boundaries. An alternative to the term *ecosystem* is the Russian term *biogeocoenose* (*bio,* the biotic community; *geo,* the abiotic environment; and *coenose,* the whole or system).

A biogeocoenose is defined as ''a combination, on a specific area of the earth's surface, of homogeneous natural phenomena (atmosphere; mineral strata; vegetation, animals, and microbic life; soil and water conditions). This combination is characterized by a specific type of interchange of matter and energy between its components and

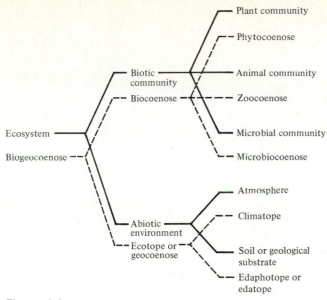

Figure 3.2

Comparison of the terms *biogeocoenose* and *ecosystem* and their subdivisions. The term ecosystem refers to an entity that has structural, functional, and dynamic attributes but which lacks a definition of its spatial boundaries. The term biogeocoenose refers to a specific ecosystem that has spatial boundaries and whose major components are relatively homogeneous.

with other natural phenomena, and . . . is in constant movement and development" (Sukachev and Dylis, 1964). This definition contains all the essential elements of Odum's definition of ecosystem: biotic and abiotic components, interaction between components, and exchanges of matter and energy. However, it has one important difference. It defines a specific area of the earth's surface by requiring that the biotic and abiotic components of the biogeocoenose are homogeneous (uniform or lacking in variation). Figure 3.2 shows the relationship between the terminology of the ecosystem and the biogeocoenose. Some people find the biogeocoenotic terminology difficult, and the term *ecosystem type* is often used as a synonym for biogeocoenose.

3.4 The Levels-of-Biological-Integration Concept

Before leaving the ecosystem concept, we refer back briefly to Figure 3.1, the levels of biological organization. Hierarchies that include such terms as tissues, organs, populations, and communities have been criticized (Rowe,

1961) on the grounds that although such levels of biological organization have merit as objects of study and focus for the associated biological subdiscipline, they do not represent true *levels of biological integration*. The only true levels in biology are cells, individuals, and ecosystems.

Rowe (1961) defined a true level of biological integration as one that is the total environment of all the levels of biological organization below *and* a structural and functional component of the next level above. He then noted that accurate prediction of events or conditions of any one level of biological organization can be made only on the basis of knowledge of the next true level of biological integration above. For example, the future development of a cell cannot be predicted merely from knowledge of the tissue that it is found in, nor of the organ in which the tissue is located. Only by knowing the physiological condition of the entire organism can a reliable prediction be made concerning all aspects of any one cell in that organism. An organism is therefore the next true level of integration above a cell. The fate of an individual organism cannot be predicted on the basis of a knowledge of the population to which it belongs, nor from an understanding of the biotic components of the community to which that population belongs. Only on the basis of knowledge of the ecosystem will all the relevant antecedents affecting that individual be identified and considered and a reliable prediction concerning that individual be obtained. Ecosystem is the only true level of biological integration above the individual.

The importance of this conclusion for ecology and forest management is that it points out the danger of trying to predict population or community events and conditions on the basis of knowledge about these levels of organization alone. This in no way denies the values of population and community ecology. It is vital that processes occurring at the population and community levels be understood. However, multiply determined events in ecosystems cannot be accurately predicted on the basis of causal mechanisms hypothesized from studies conducted exclusively at the population or community level. For example, predictions as to the future growth of a Douglas-fir plantation will not be very reliable if they are based only on a knowledge of the inherent growth abilities of this species, how the trees compete with each other, and their susceptibility to natural diseases and enemies. A knowledge of the other plants, animals, and microbes that enhance or impede the growth of the plantation will improve the prediction somewhat, but only a recognition of the entire variety of biotic, climatic, hydrologic, and edaphic (soil) factors affecting that population of Douglas-fir trees is sufficient to give completely reliable predictions as to their future. This does not imply

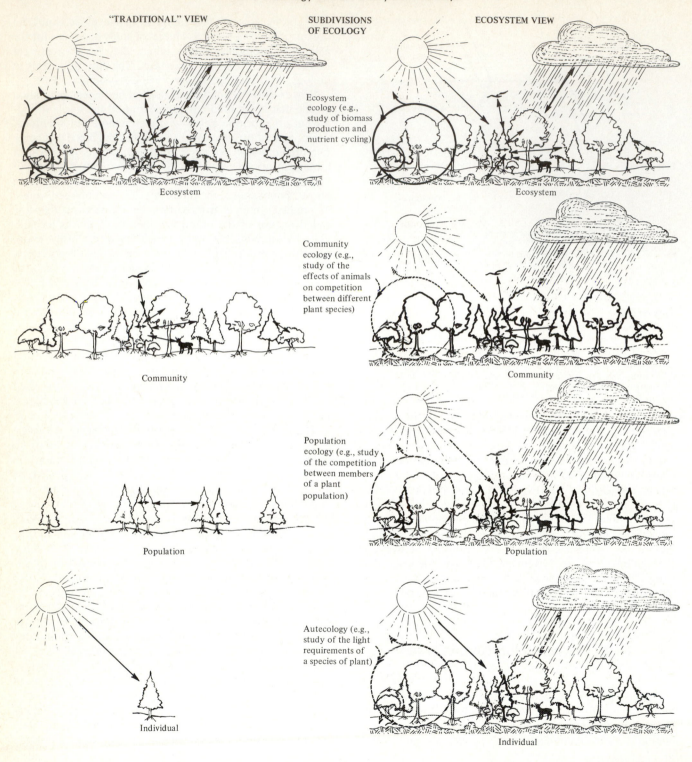

"TRADITIONAL" VIEW   SUBDIVISIONS OF ECOLOGY   ECOSYSTEM VIEW

Ecosystem ecology (e.g., study of biomass production and nutrient cycling)

Ecosystem

Ecosystem

Community ecology (e.g., study of the effects of animals on competition between different plant species)

Community

Community

Population ecology (e.g., study of the competition between members of a plant population)

Population

Population

Autecology (e.g., study of the light requirements of a species of plant)

Individual

Individual

Figure 3.3

''Traditional'' and ecosystem views of the subdivisions of ecology. In the traditional view, the focus is on the entity(ies) identified at the particular subdivision (e.g., the population at the population level). In the ecosystem view, the major focus is the same, but at every level the relationship between the object of study and the other components of the ecosystem is given explicit consideration. You will note that the two views are identical at the ecosystem level but differ at the other levels. Organisms, physical factors, and interactions in black ink are explicitly studied. Those in gray ink are explicitly recognized as potentially important determinants but are not necessarily studied. Their role in modifying the relationship being studied is frequently investigated.

that the silviculturist has to switch the focus of attention from the population of trees to every other factor of the biogeocoenose. It merely suggests that the population be examined with an explicit recognition of the effects of the other factors of the ecosystem on the population.

It has been suggested (Evans, 1956) that the basic unit of ecology should be the ecosystem (or biogeocoenose) rather than the individual, the population, or the community. If this is accepted, autecology becomes the study of the interactions of a single individual with its biotic and abiotic environment: an ecosystem with the organism being studied at its center. Synecology becomes the study of a group or groups of organisms reacting with their biotic and abiotic environment: an ecosystem with the population or community at its center. Ecosystem ecology is then left with the important jobs of studying the interactions, interdependencies, and exchanges of matter and energy between the components of the ecosystem, and of describing the temporal and spatial variations in ecosystems: a focus on the structure, functioning, and variability of the system.

By applying the ecosystem concept at all levels of ecology, Rowe's objections to the population and community levels are entirely overcome and population and community ecology attain their full potential. By considering individuals, populations or communities within an ecosystem context, we identify the total set of factors that determine the abundance, distribution and productivity of the biological object or system of interest. Natural phenomena exist and/or occur in natural landscapes: three-dimensional systems that have climatic, geological and biological components, and which vary in a fourth dimension—time. Consequently, we are unlikely to be able to understand and predict these phenomena unless we consider them as components of landscapes and of ecosystems.

Climate sets the overall framework for the biotic potential of an area: for example, tropical rain forest, desert, boreal forest or tundra. Within a climatic area, the landform (the shape of the landscape such as ridge top, midslope, lower slope or valley bottom), the origin of the surface materials (such as glacial deposits, water-sorted materials, wind-transported soils or organic materials), and the mineralogy of the inorganic soil matrix (for example, slowly weathering, nutrient-poor geological materials, or rapidly weathering, nutrient-rich materials) modify the climatically-set potential by determining the suitability of the substrate and the availability of moisture and nutrients to plants and animals.

The attainment of the physically-determined biotic potential depends on the types of organisms available to colonize and occupy the area: their genetic constitution (which defines their adaptations to, requirements for, and tolerances of the physical features of the environments) and how they interact with the other organisms of the area. The occurrence, distribution, abundance and productivity of any one organism are thus determined by the past and present climatic, geomorphological (landform), mineralogical, edaphic (type of soil), and biotic characteristics of the area in question.

The ecosystem concept is probably the single most important concept in ecology. It is the essential basis for successful intensive forest management. It is a prerequisite for the long-term survival of the human race on this planet. Mankind must learn that we are but one species in the world ecosystem; that our activities alter the world ecosystem which is our ''life-support system.'' Large-scale alterations of atmospheric chemistry (e.g., acid rain, atmospheric CO_2) will not only affect plants and other animals; they also affect us because we are a part of the ecosystem. Foresters must recognize that forest management affects the forest ecosystem, not just the tree crops which are merely a component of the ecosystem. And ecologists concerned with subsets of ecosystems must always remember the landscape setting of the phenomenon they are interested in.

These ideas are illustrated in Figure 3.3, which shows both the object of interest and the degree to which other factors are considered in ''traditional'' approaches and the ecosystem approach to the subdisciplines of ecology.

3.5 Summary

Ecology is one of the more recent major developments in the biological sciences, although its subject matter has been of vital interest to humans throughout their evolution. There has been a remarkable increase in scientific, political, and public interest in ecology over the past two decades. This has been accompanied by some confusion over the role of ecology in socioeconomic decision making. Quite incorrectly, ecology has been advanced by some as *the* basis on which socioeconomic decisions should be made. This is incorrect because the science of ecology itself provides no basis for value judgments and it is only one, albeit of preeminent importance, of several sources of information contributing to socioeconomic decisions.

Within a hierarchy of systems of increasing biological complexity, ecology begins where the more traditional branches of biology end: at the individual organism. Subdivisions of the science deal with individuals, populations, communities, and ecosystems, but the full potential of ecology is attained only when the ecosystem concept is employed, irrespective of the complexity of the ecological system in question. The term ecosystem provides the conceptual basis for ecology, but its shortcomings have led to the use of the term biogeocoenose (or ecosystem type) when identifying and mapping individual ecosystems in the field.

Forest ecology is merely the application of general ecology to a specific type of ecosystem: the forest. Forest ecology involves studies at the individual, population, community, and ecosystem levels, but such studies should always involve the ecosystem concept. Although forest ecology has traditionally been thought of as being concerned largely with the community level of organization, its full contribution can be realized only if all levels of biological organization within the forest ecosystem are studied.

4.1 Introduction

Energy is what life is all about, and everything about life is associated with energy. Organisms are accumulations of energy. Without a continuing supply of energy they die, and the energy accumulation is dispersed as their remains decompose. All organisms require a source of energy. To reproduce they require growth, to grow they require new energy, to acquire new energy they must do work, and to do work they must expend energy. Merely to stay alive requires energy. The study of the energy relationships (inputs, storage, transfer, and outputs) of ecosystems is called *ecological energetics*.

Both evolution and ecology can be viewed from an energy perspective. The evolutionary "struggle for existence" between organisms is basically a struggle to obtain sufficient energy in usable form to sustain and reproduce life. The abundance, productivity, and distribution of organisms (three central themes in population and community ecology) are all ultimately determined by the availability of energy. However, a large number of other factors are involved in determining this availability, and in many ecosystems factors other than energy play the primary role in determining the distribution and abundance of organisms. Thus, energy availability is often not the proximate factor, and the science of ecology involves far more than merely a consideration of energy. These points notwithstanding, energy remains the ultimate determinant of ecosystems and the central thread of ecology.

The origins of life on earth are thought to have resulted from the action of solar energy on the simple inorganic chemicals that were present on the sterile surface of the young planet. Organic molecules were produced that grew and replicated themselves by coalescing with and using some of the chemical bond energy contained in other such molecules. Different combinations of molecules resulted, and eventually pigments evolved that had the characteristic of absorbing solar radiation. This was stored as chemical bond energy by synthesizing additional complex organic molecules from simple inorganic substances in the environment. The following 2 billion years of evolution has elaborated a myriad of variations on this basic theme, but fundamentally the nature of life has not changed. Living organisms such as black spruce, bears, or bacteria are nothing more than highly organized associations between energy (largely solar energy) and inorganic chemicals from the soil and atmosphere. This viewpoint is substantiated by the example of a forest fire, in which the solar energy absorbed and stored by the plants is released as the heat and light of the flames, and the chemicals involved in capturing and

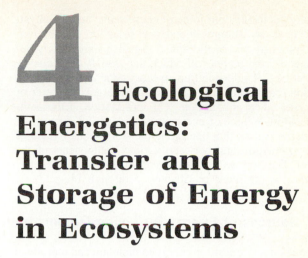

4 Ecological Energetics: Transfer and Storage of Energy in Ecosystems

storing the energy are released, often in their original form, as atmospheric gases or chemicals in the ash.

Life in general, and the forest in particular, is merely a complex physical–chemical organization that has evolved to become self-perpetuating. Although such a fundamental, functional view of life lacks the richness and appeal of the more traditional taxonomic approach (which considers life as a diverse assemblage of different organisms), it is essential if we are to gain a complete understanding of ecosystems. The manager of an electrical power station would be foolish to try to run the factory without a knowledge of electricity. Similarly, ecologists and ecosystem managers (e.g., foresters, agriculturalists, wildlife and fisheries managers) are unlikely to achieve their desired management objectives unless they are familiar with the distribution and movements of energy that are responsible for the character and productivity of the ecosystems under their management. Maximization of forest growth requires the maximization of energy capture and the minimization of energy losses from trees. High production of fish requires knowledge of where they get their energy from, what affects the supply and its utilization, and what limits the storage of this energy in fish biomass. Wildlife management requires a detailed understanding of energy flow in wildlife populations. All three of these crops are the result of the processes of ecological energetics. Their management inevitably involves the manipulation of these processes.

Energy is the driving force of ecosystems, and the physiology, anatomy, stature, abundance, behavior, distribution, and ecological role of individual organisms are largely determined by the manner in which they satisfy their energy requirements. Understanding an ecosystem requires (1) recognition that functional organization is largely a matter of energy transfers and storage, (2) appreciation of the pathways and magnitude of energy transfers, and (3) identification of the factors that determine the storage and dynamics of energy within and between various components of the system. The first two of these are discussed in this chapter. The third is the focus of Chapters 5 through 14.

4.2 Sources of Energy for Living Organisms

The relentless quest for energy to maintain and reproduce life has continued for billions of years. It has resulted in the evolution of a remarkable diversity of species of plants, animals, and microbes (approximately 2 million different species) that differ, among other things, in the source of their energy supply. This difference is the basis of a broad functional classification of organisms into a variety of *trophic* categories. The major division of this classification is between organisms that utilize abiotic energy sources *(autotrophs)* and organisms that depend on biotic energy sources *(heterotrophs)*.

Autotrophic (= self-feeding) organisms utilize energy sources that are independent of the activities of other organisms, energy that is available in completely abiotic environments. Autotrophs are referred to as *producers* (and sometimes as *primary producers*) because they produce the high-energy organic molecules that provide the energy source for nonautotrophic organisms. There are two subtypes, photo- and chemoautotrophic organisms.

Photoautotrophs utilize a portion of the electromagnetic energy from the sun (sunlight) in the process of photosynthesis. This process depends on chlorophyll pigments, which are capable of absorbing certain wavelengths of solar radiation and converting them into the chemical bond energy of glucose using carbon dioxide and water. All green plants are photoautotrophs.

Chemoautotrophs obtain their energy from simple inorganic chemicals: e.g., by oxidizing sulfide ions to free sulfur, sulfur to sulfate ions, ammonium ions to free nitrogen gas (N_2) or nitrite ions, and nitrite ions to nitrate ions, each oxidation being accompanied by a release of energy. The contribution of chemoautotrophs to total forest ecosystem energy flow is generally minor. However, their ecological role goes beyond their energy relationships because some of the oxidation products have important environmental effects. For example, sulfur-oxidizing bacteria can lead to the production of sulfuric acid and hence acidity in the water draining from piles of mining waste that contain sulfur, with subsequent leaching of highly toxic heavy metals into aquatic ecosystems. Conversion of ammonium ions to nitrate ions can increase the leaching of nitrogen from the soil into water bodies.

Heterotrophic (= other-feeding, i.e., feeding on others) organisms are unable to utilize either sunlight or inorganic chemical bond energy. They are dependent on energy obtained by oxidizing high-energy organic molecules such as carbohydrates, fats, and proteins synthesized by autotrophs. Heterotrophs are referred to as *consumers*, reflecting their dependence on the producers. The four subtypes are identified by their energy source.

Herbivores (primary consumers) utilize the energy contained in the organic matter of plants; that is, they are consumers of green plants.

Carnivores (secondary, tertiary, or higher-order consumers) utilize the energy contained in the organic matter of animals. Primary carnivores (secondary consumers) solve their energy needs by eating herbivores, secondary carnivores (tertiary consumers) by eating primary carnivores, and so on.

Omnivores utilize the energy contained in both plants and animals. Their diet will vary according to circumstance, and at any one time an omnivore may behave as either a herbivore or a carnivore. However, omnivores generally do best on a mixed diet of plant and animal material. Humans are omnivores.

Saprotrophs (decomposers, detrivores, or detritus-feeders) utilize the energy contained in dead organic matter of either plant or animal origin. Those that depend on dead plant materials or the feces of herbivores (including organisms living in the alimentary canal of herbivores) are analogous to herbivores, while those that depend on dead animals or the feces of carnivores (including organisms living in the alimentary canal of carnivores) are analogous to carnivores.

The assignment of a particular organism to a single trophic category is not always easy, since trophic dependencies may vary during a life history or with circumstances. Carnivores may be forced temporarily onto a plant diet at times of shortage of prey, and animals normally thought of as herbivores may become carnivorous if starving. Tadpoles are mainly herbivorous, whereas frogs are mainly carnivorous. Most green plants are entirely autotrophic, but there are certain species of algae that require certain complex substances which they cannot synthesize themselves and must get from the activities of other organisms; this makes them partly heterotrophic. Some plants trap and digest insects and other small animals and are therefore also partly heterotrophic. It has been reported that some phytoplankton (microscopic aquatic plants) in far northern lakes are autotrophic during the summer but heterotrophic during the long arctic night when they utilize organic substances dissolved in the water as a supplementary energy source (Rodhe, 1955).

4.3 Trophic Chains and Webs, Ecological Pyramids, and Energy Flow Diagrams

A. Trophic Chains

On first inspection by an untrained observer, an ecosystem might appear to be a relatively random assemblage of organisms. First appearances are often deceptive, however. There are, in fact, highly ordered sequences of energy or trophic (e.g., food) dependencies within an ecosystem. Each organism obtains the energy it requires for survival, growth, and reproduction in a manner characteristic of that species. The supply will be from a particular physical source or from a particular type of organism, and each organism is in turn the energy supply for some other organism. These characteristic sequences of energy transfers are referred to as *food chains* or *trophic chains*. Sequences that involve autotroph → herbivore → carnivore energy transfers are referred to as *grazing trophic chains*. Trophic chains commencing with dead organic matter and involving saprotrophs are referred to as *decomposer* or *detritus trophic chains*. The successive stages along a trophic chain are called *trophic levels*.

B. Trophic Webs

Ecosystems are complex (the importance of the fact justifies the repetition of this phrase almost *ad nauseum*), and although it is frequently both convenient and useful to examine the movement of energy along a single trophic chain, such knowledge generally does not provide an adequate understanding of the energy relationships of the whole ecosystem. Most plants are fed on by a variety of herbivores, and most herbivores feed on a variety of plants (except in those cases where coevolution has resulted in very high herbivore-plant specificity). Most herbivores are also prey to a variety of carnivores. Thus, trophic chains are but components of an intricate network or *web* of trophic dependencies. Figure 4.1 presents a greatly simplified *trophic web* for one portion of an oak woodland ecosystem in England. The major pathways of energy flow involved with insect defoliators in the tree crowns are indicated, as are the division of this flow into grazing and detritus food webs, and the major trophic levels within the webs. The distinction between the grazing and detritus trophic webs and the different trophic levels tends to become less and less clear the further one proceeds through the web.

C. Ecological Pyramids

The full complexity of most of the trophic webs that have been described has escaped complete identification, and diagrams such as Figure 4.1 are generally simplifications of reality. However, even such simplified representations can be rather confusing unless they are studied carefully. They often contain too much taxonomic information to permit easy comparisons between the trophic webs of different ecosystems, and yet not enough functional information to permit an accurate comparison of functional processes. This problem can be overcome by eliminating the taxonomic information and representing the trophic web as a series of stages or trophic levels in the transfer of energy through the system.

Much of the detail in Figure 4.1 can be summarized in a diagram referred to as an *ecological pyramid*. Three types of ecological pyramids can be used.

1. *Pyramid of numbers*. The simplest type of ecological pyramid is a pile of rectangles representing successive trophic levels in the trophic web, with the area of each rectangle proportional to the number of organisms in the corresponding trophic level. For some ecosystems the result is a pyramid-shaped figure, with fewer and fewer organisms as one proceeds through the trophic web. However, this is true only where the size of the organisms either remains constant or increases up the pyramid. In a forest ecosystem where the producers (trees) are very large relative to the consumers (e.g., defoliating insects), or in the situation in which primary and secondary consumers are successively smaller (e.g., a plant–parasite–hyperparasite trophic web), the numbers pyramid may take on a different shape (Figure 4.2).

Although the numbers pyramid is useful in describing the relative abundance of different types of organisms, it tells us little about overall ecosystem function and is therefore of little help in comparing the functions of different ecosystems. The shape of the numbers pyramid will change progressively from the early years of a forest plantation through to the mature tree crop and thus can provide some useful information to the forester. However, this type of pyramid gives no indication as to the total biomass and its rate of accumulation, and therefore gives no guidance as to the expected crop yield.

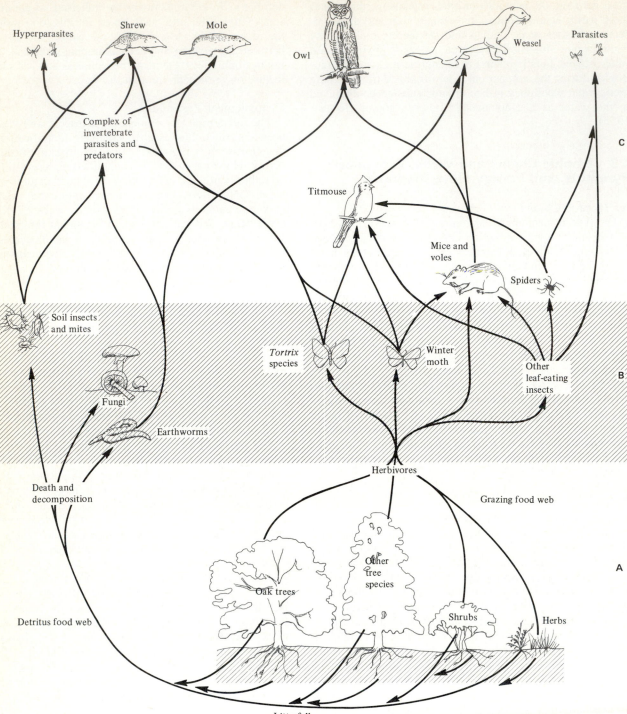

Hyperparasites

Shrew

Mole

Owl

Weasel

Parasites

Complex of invertebrate parasites and predators

C

Titmouse

Mice and voles

Spiders

Soil insects and mites

Tortrix species

Winter moth

Other leaf-eating insects

B

Fungi

Earthworms

Death and decomposition

Herbivores

Grazing food web

Detritus food web

Oak trees

Other tree species

Shrubs

Herbs

A

Litterfall

Figure 4.1

Energy flow through the trophic web of an English oak woodland (after Varley, 1970). The energy flow can be traced through two major pathways: the detritus food web and the grazing food web, each of which can be divided into trophic levels—stages of energy transfer through the web. (A) Primary trophic level: producers (plants). (B) Secondary trophic level: primary consumers (herbivores, saprotrophs). (C) Tertiary trophic level: secondary consumers (primary carnivores, omnivores). A fourth or quaternary trophic level may exist: tertiary consumers (secondary carnivores). In this example the weasel and the owl may act as secondary carnivores. (Courtesy Blackwell Scientific Publications, Ltd., Oxford, England.)

2. *Pyramid of biomass.* This type of pyramid differs from the pyramid of numbers in that the area of the rectangles is proportional to the biomass or weight of organisms occupying each trophic level. By accounting for size, the biomass pyramid gives a more accurate picture of the distribution of energy through the ecosystem. This facilitates comparison of the biomass present in different trophic levels and in different types of ecosystem (Figure 4.3). However, the biomass pyramid is not much better than the pyramid of numbers as a representation of ecosystem function and the dynamics of energy in the system, because no allowance is made for the longevity (life span) of organisms. One hectare of fast-growing but short-lived grass will have a very much smaller biomass of producers than 1 ha of slow-growing but long-lived trees, yet the grassland ecosystem can support a larger biomass of consumers than the forest.

The biomass pyramid of a forest will change through the life of the tree crop and will provide useful information on the size of the crop that can be harvested at any particular time. It tells us nothing, however, about how rapidly biomass is accumulating in each trophic level, and therefore provides no guidance as to the long-term yield that could be harvested. Although the biomass pyramid tells us a lot about the *inventory* of an ecosystem, it tells us little about

its *productivity.* It provides information that is of more value for short-term ecosystem exploitation than for long-term ecosystem management. Finally, although the biomass pyramid retains its upright form better than does the numbers pyramid, it can still be inverted in certain types of ecosystem; for example, there is a greater weight of herbivorous plankton than of phytoplankton in oceanic ecosystems (Figure 4.3).

3. *Energy flow pyramid.* The problems with the numbers and biomass pyramids can be overcome if we make the area of each rectangle proportional to the flow of energy through that trophic level. This type of pyramid should always be upright because of the second law of thermodynamics.[1] The loss of energy as it is transferred from one trophic level to the next means that there can never be more energy flow at any trophic level than at the next lower level (except on a temporary basis), with the one exception of energy imports, discussed below.

Figure 4.4 gives some examples of energy flow pyramids. Such pyramids provide information from which rates

---

[1] All transformations of energy (other than to heat) are incomplete because some of the energy is converted from nonrandom to random form (i.e., heat).

Trophic level

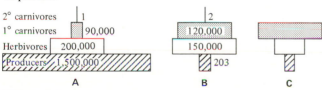

2° carnivores	1	
1° carnivores	90,000	
Herbivores	200,000	
Producers	1,500,000	

A   B   C

Figure 4.2

Examples of the pyramid of numbers (after Odum, 1971). The shape of the pyramid varies according to the type of ecosystem and can change with time, both seasonally and annually. (A) Temperate grassland in summer (numbers per 0.1 ha); producers are small. (B) Temperate forest in summer (numbers per 0.1 ha); producers are large. (C) Plant/parasite trophic web (hypothetical). (From *Fundamentals of Ecology,* Third Edition, by Eugene P. Odum. Copyright © 1971 by W. B. Saunders Company. Reprinted by permission of CBS College Publications.)

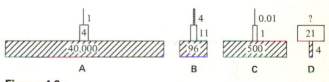

A   B   C   D

Figure 4.3

Examples of the pyramid of biomass. The numbers refer to grams (dry weight) of organisms per square meter (after Odum, 1971). These pyramids are much less variable in shape than the numbers pyramids. For most ecosystems they are upright, although they can be inverted in aquatic ecosystems. (A) Tropical rain forest. (B) Wisconsin Lake. (C) Abandoned agricultural field. (D) English Channel. (From *Fundamentals of Ecology,* Third Edition, by Eugene P. Odum. Copyright © 1971 by W. B. Saunders Company. Reprinted by permission of CBS College Publishing.)

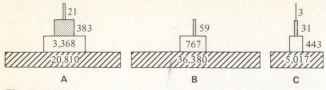

Figure 4.4

Examples of the pyramid of energy flow (kcal m^{-2} year^{-1}) (after Odum, 1971; Kozlovsky, 1968). These pyramids always retain their upright shape as long as there is no net import or export of organic matter into or out of the ecosystem. (A) Silver Springs (fresh water spring in Florida). (B) Salt marsh in Georgia. (C) Lake Mendota, Wisconsin. (From *Fundamentals of Ecology,* Third Edition, by Eugene P. Odum. Copyright © 1971 by W. B. Saunders Company. Reprinted by permission of CBS College Publishing.)

of biomass accumulation in different trophic levels can be deduced, but even the energy flow pyramid fails to give a complete description of ecological energetics, as we shall see shortly. The combination of energy and biomass pyramids is obviously essential for an understanding of ecosystem energetics, and the combination of all three types of pyramids gives an even more complete representation of the ecosystem. Unfortunately, there have been few studies in which all three types of information have been obtained.

D. Variations in Ecological Pyramids

1. Grazing vs. Detritus Trophic Webs. The first essential modification of simple ecological pyramids is the explicit identification of the energy flow to saprotrophs: the separation of energy flow into grazing and detritus trophic webs. In many ecosystems there is a greater flow of energy from producers to the detritus trophic web than from producers to the grazing trophic web. For example, in a densely stocked, intensively managed spruce plantation there will be very little herbivore biomass and grazing trophic web energy flow, but there will be a large flow to the detritus trophic web in the form of litterfall. Figure 4.5 provides a comparison between the biomass and energy flow in detritus and grazing trophic webs for two different types of ecosystem. It shows that the relative importance of the two webs varies greatly and that the energy flow in each web cannot be predicted from the biomass of that web. It also shows the variation in the biomass of detritus and grazing food webs when the detritus web accounts for either 99% or only 10% of post-producer energy flow.

2. Effect of Organism Size. As already noted, the functional importance of specific organisms within the ecosystem cannot be judged on the basis of biomass alone. The small biomass of producers in a marine bay ecosystem can have the same order of magnitude of energy flow as a forest

with a biomass several orders of magnitude greater. A very small biomass of detritus organisms in a freshwater spring in Florida (5 kcal m^{-2}) was found to account for five times as much energy flow (5060 kcal m^{-2} yr^{-1}) as a detritus biomass 22 times larger in a marine bay ecosystem (Figure 4.5A).

The unreliability of a biomass pyramid as an indicator of ecosystem function is related to the size of the organisms (Odum, 1956). It is known that there is a broad general tendency for the metabolism per unit weight of heterotrophic organisms (i.e., consumers) to be inversely proportional to body size (see Kleiber, 1961, or Gordon et al., 1968).

$$\text{Metabolism per gram} \propto \frac{1}{\text{body size}^{2/3}}$$

or

$$y = ax^b$$

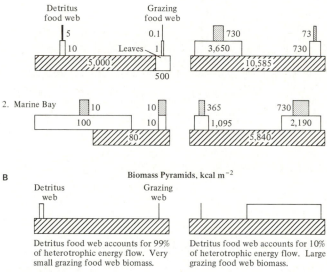

Figure 4.5

(A) Comparison of biomass and energy-flow pyramids for two different types of ecosystem. Grazing and detritus food (trophic) webs are shown separately (after Odum, 1957, 1962). The relative contribution of the detritus food web to heterotrophic energy flow varies between the two ecosystems and cannot be judged by the biomass of detrivores. (B) Effect on the biomass pyramid of variation in the proportion of heterotrophic energy flow accounted for by the detritus food web. (Reprinted by permission of Eugene P. Odum and *Japanese Journal of Ecology.*)

where y is the respiration rate, x the animal's weight in grams, and a and b are empirically determined constants (b is generally about 0.7).

Consider the time taken for about 600 kg of herbivores to convert approximately 900 kg of hay into herbivore tissue. A cow weighing about 600 kg will take 120 days with a daily heat loss of 20,000 kcal, whereas 300 rabbits, each weighing about 2 kg, will consume the hay in only 30 days with a daily heat loss of 80,000 kcal. Both cow and rabbits will gain a total of about 110 kg in weight and release 2.4×10^6 kcal of heat. The rabbits, each being approximately 1/300 the size of the cow, will complete the job in a quarter of the time because of their higher metabolic rate (Phillipson, 1966). An apparently similar relationship appears to hold for plants. Although very large plants require more energy per individual plant for maintenance metabolism than do very small plants, the maintenance metabolism per gram of tissue is much less in the large plant (Odum, 1956). This is partly because large trees contain a lot of dead supporting tissue that is not respiring.

Table 4.1 illustrates the relationship between the size of an organism and its contribution to energy flow. There is a general trend toward increasing energy flow per unit of biomass as size decreases. Inclusion of vertebrates, invertebrates, and microbes in the comparison results in there being no linear relationships, but within each group the trend can be seen. Figure 4.6 examines the effects that variation in organism size has on the shape of the biomass pyramid. Assuming that 50% of the total energy flow is in detritus food webs, the shape of the pyramid varies from inverted (for increasing organism size through the web) to a very flat right-side-up pyramid (where size decreases sharply through the web).

A consequence of the relationship between size and metabolic rate is that for a given biomass, a community of smaller organisms will have a higher rate of energy flow than will a community of larger organisms, and for a given

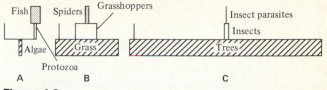

Figure 4.6

Influence of the size of organisms on the shape of biomass pyramids (after Odum, 1956). The diagrams assume no imports or exports of organic matter into or out of the ecosystem (photosynthesis = total ecosystem respiration) and 50 percent of the heterotrophic energy flow in the grazing food web. (A) Size increases up the pyramid. (B) Little change in size up the pyramid. (C) Size decreases up the pyramid. (Used by permission of H. T. Odum and the Ecological Society of America.)

energy flow a community of smaller organisms will have a smaller biomass than will a community of larger organisms. This consequence has very important implications for ecosystem management. Since the flow of energy through an ecosystem is ultimately limited by the availability of solar energy and by photosynthetic efficiency (see below), and since neither of these two parameters varies greatly in any particular climatic area, communities of large plants, such as trees, will support a larger biomass than will small plants, even though the smaller plants may actually produce new biomass at a faster rate.

Where it is impractical or uneconomical to harvest plants very frequently, large plants will be the most efficient way of harvesting sunlight energy because of the large biomass they sustain. On the other hand, if the production of plants can be harvested frequently and energy efficiently (such as by domestic herbivores or herbivorous fish), the use of small plants such as grasses, which have high metabolic and biomass production rates but small biomass accumulation, may be the most useful way for us to harvest sunlight energy. Which size of producer is best obviously depends upon whether one wants the energy in the form of timber or beef. However, the important point to note is that it takes energy to harvest a plant crop, and the more frequent the harvest, the less favorable the energy benefit/cost ratio is likely to be. By using animals to perform the harvest of rapidly growing but short-lived plants, we can largely avoid the direct energy costs of harvesting such plants.

3. Effects of Energy Imports or Exports. A third factor than can complicate the interpretation of the basic ecological pyramid is imports or exports of energy into or out of the ecosystem. In apparent contradiction of the second law of thermodynamics, the biomass and energy flow in heterotrophic trophic levels is sometimes larger than that of producer biomass and producer energy flow. In fact, the law is

Table 4.1 Energy Flow, per Unit of Biomass, in Six Primary Consumer Populations Differing in the Size of Individuals (Data from Odum, 1968)

Organism	Energy Flow, kcal day^{-1} g (biomass)$^{-1}$
Soil bacteria	1000
Marine copepods	1.25
Saltmarsh grasshoppers	0.4
Intertidal snails	0.1
Meadow mice	1.16
Deer	0.49

not violated: such anomalies result from imports of organic matter from another ecosystem. Similarly, heterotrophic energy flow and biomass may be smaller than prediced because of exports out of the ecosystem. For example, inputs of dead insects and leaves into stream ecosystems from streambank vegetation can support a level of biomass and productivity in populations of aquatic heterotrophs far in excess of that possible on the basis of aquatic primary production. Conversely, downstream drift of animals in well-illuminated but fast-flowing streams may result in heterotrophic biomass and energy flow pyramids that are much smaller than would be expected from the energy flow in the aquatic producer trophic level.

In a closed ecosystem the only input of energy is sunlight and the output is heat energy. The energy of photosynthesis equals the total loss of energy through respiration (heat loss through radiation from warm objects is ignored here but is discussed in Chapters 7 and 8). On the other hand, ecosystems receiving imports of energy in organic matter will have a total community respiration that is greater than photosynthetic production, and ecosystems experiencing exports of organic energy (out of the ecosystem or into long-term storage) will have a total community respiration that is less than their photosynthetic production.

E. Energy Flow Diagrams

The ecological pyramids discussed so far are useful as an overall summary of ecosystem function, but they omit a great deal of very important information. They give no information on significant flows of energy *between* grazing and detritus trophic webs (cf. Figure 4.1), and they fail to draw adequate attention to the consequence of the second law of thermodynamics: the loss of heat energy via the process of respiration each time there is an energy transformation. They also give no information on the relative magnitude of the several pathways of energy transfer that determine the biomass at any one trophic level. These deficiencies can be overcome by using *energy flow diagrams* that depict the biomass of trophic levels by boxes which are joined by pipes that represent energy transfers between trophic levels and between trophic webs. Figure 4.7 presents an energy flow diagram for the pine-forest pyramids presented in Figure 4.5. Only the major energy transfers are shown, but it is clear that there is a considerable amount of energy interchange between grazing and detritus trophic webs, and that their distinction becomes increasingly arbitrary as one proceeds through the trophic web. Individual organisms may change their trophic relationships according to the availability of food, so that they may alternately feed primarily in the detritus trophic web and primarily in the grazing trophic web.

Although energy flow diagrams present a static picture of what is in reality a dynamic and ever-changing network, they do provide a very useful summary of the functional character of an ecosystem and are more than merely an academic form of "doodling." Successful management of eco-

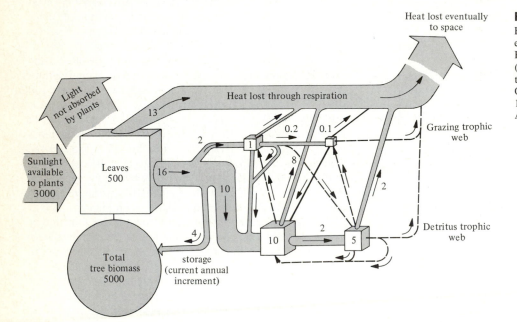

Figure 4.7
Energy-flow diagram for the pine forest ecosystem shown in Figure 4.5. Boxes represent the energy in biomass (kcal m^{-2}); pipes represent energy transfers (kcal m^{-2} day^{-1}). (After Odum, 1957, 1962. Copyright 1957, 1962 by the Ecological Society of America. Used by permission.)

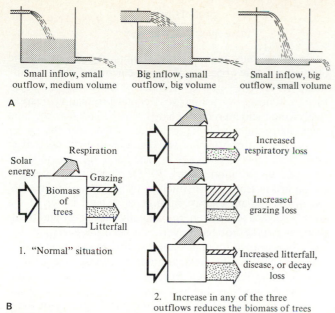

Figure 4.8
The relationship between inputs, outputs, and the size of a biomass compartment. (A) The volume of water in a tank depends on the rate of inflow and the rate of outflow. (B) Biomass in a trophic level depends on energy inflows and outflows (e.g., tree biomass in a 100-year-old stand).

systems for material products requires an understanding of the balance of energy inputs and outputs that determine the size of the crop. The relationship between energy inputs and outputs and the size of biomass compartments can be likened to that between the amount of water in a tank and the flows into and out of that tank. For a given rate of outflow, the volume of water will increase as the rate of inflow increases. For a given rate of inflow, the volume of water will decrease as outflow increases (Figure 4.8). For a given photosynthetic input of energy to trees, biomass in the trees will depend on the outflows of energy to respiration, grazing losses, or to litterfall. These are discussed below.

4.4 Energy Dynamics and Storage in Ecosystems

The productivity of ecosystems (i.e., the sum of the productivities of the component trophic levels) is determined by the efficiency with which energy enters and is passed through the trophic web. Forestry, wildlife, fisheries, and agricultural management are all concerned with production,

productivity, and the harvestable quantity of energy, and interest in ecosystem productivity has increased greatly in recent years (N.A.S., 1975). Successful management of organic production involves the correct choice of species, and this in turn involves a knowledge of the relative efficiencies with which different species acquire and store energy under particular environmental conditions. On dry and infertile soils, pines will harvest sunlight energy more efficiently than will spruces, and sheep are more efficient than cows at harvesting producer energy under marginal grazing conditions.

In this section of the chapter, we examine the biomass and productivity of different trophic levels and the efficiency with which energy passes between them. For each level we shall examine the input and output of energy and the resulting productivity and biomass. First, however, we must review the terminology used in discussions of this topic.

1. The *crop* is the total volume or weight of material that can be removed from a given area over a given period: for example, the weight or volume of Douglas-fir wood harvested from a hectare during a 60-year rotation. The magnitude of a given crop refers only to the material removed from the ecosystem, and therefore depends greatly on the proportion of the individual organism that is harvested. The crop from a hectare of pine forest might vary by as much as 300%, according to whether utilization is limited to logs larger than 10 cm in diameter or whether the complete tree, including branches, foliage, entire stems, stumps, and roots, is harvested.

2. The *standing crop* is the weight or volume of material that can be sampled or harvested by a particular method from a given area at a particular time. Crop and standing crop are the same at the time of harvest. As with a crop, the size of a standing crop depends greatly on the method of harvesting.

3. *Yield* is the average rate of accumulation of harvestable material: crop divided by the period of crop production. Because the time required to produce crops of different species varies, it is sometimes difficult to make comparisons between crop data. This problem is overcome by calculating yield over a year, although agriculturalists sometimes use yield per month during the growing season to overcome the problems of variable growing-season length. In terms of forest management, yield is the factor of greatest long-term interest because it determines the return on investment—essential information for production forestry.

The terms crop, standing crop, and yield are widely used in resource management. They are of less value to ecology, however, since they are not based on stable definitions and are subject to change according to technological and economic changes. Ecologists use the following three rather similar terms to overcome this problem.

1. *Production* (analogous to crop) describes the increase in total weight (biomass) or quantity of organic material on a given area over a defined period. It is usually used to refer to a specific population or trophic level, but it can refer to the whole ecosystem. It includes not only the increased quantity of material remaining on the area at the end of the time period, but also material that was produced and subsequently lost before the end of the period. Thus, production is equal to the crop plus the nonharvested and nonharvestable organic material produced over the period, plus losses to other populations, trophic levels or ecosystems, as appropriate.

Production can be subdivided into *gross production* (increase in organic material plus losses to respiration over the period) and *net production* (increases in organic material after losses to respiration). Production by plants is referred to as *primary production,* while production at higher trophic levels is referred to as *secondary production. Real photosynthesis* and *apparent photosynthesis* are terms used as alternatives to gross and net primary production, respectively, since autotrophic production is the result of photosynthesis.

2. *Biomass* (analogous to standing crop) refers to the total weight of organic material in a population, a trophic level, or an ecosystem in a given area at any point in time. It is equal to the standing crop plus all the unharvested and unharvestable organic material, and is the term used by ecologists to describe the quantity of biotic components of ecosystems: hence its use in biomass pyramids.

3. *Productivity* is the production per unit area per unit time, and is therefore analogous to yield. As with yield, the period over which production is calculated must be carefully defined. Productivity often varies considerably over the season, and if it is expressed over a short time period (e.g., a day) the value usually represents the average daily rate over the season. As with production, one can refer to gross, net, primary, or secondary productivity.

A. Producer Trophic Level

1. Inputs: Photosynthesis. We have already noted that with the relatively minor exception of chemoautotrophs, systems are organized and driven by inputs of solar energy to photoautotrophs, the green plants or *producers* of the ecosystem. The rate of primary production is therefore of great interest to both ecologists and ecosystem managers. The efficiency with which solar energy enters ecosystems is referred to as the *photosynthetic efficiency* (expressed as a %). It is defined as:

$$\frac{production}{incident\ radiant\ energy} \times 100$$

Great care must be taken when comparing photosynthetic efficiency figures because they are calculated in many different ways. One arrives at either gross or net photosynthetic efficiency by using gross or net production, respectively, and incident radiant energy may be based on the total solar energy falling on the area, the visible solar energy, or the energy of those visible wavelengths that are utilized in photosynthesis (see Chapter 7). The latter amounts to about 25% of total radiation (Gates, 1971). An additional complication arises from the distinction by some researchers between the radiant energy falling per square meter of the earth's surface and the energy actually falling on photosynthetic organs. Some have even estimated the energy that is actually absorbed by plants and use this to calculate photosynthetic ability. The most commonly used measure of photosynthetic efficiency is net production divided by the radiant energy reaching the surface of the vegetation in the wavelength range 0.4–0.7 micron (visible light). However, even this efficiency will vary according to whether it is based on radiation for the whole year, the leafy season or the growing season.

Photosynthetic efficiencies have been calculated for a wide variety of ecosystems. Values are generally small (1–5%) and surprisingly invariable in ecosystems that have a continuous plant community (Phillipson, 1966). In a large number of studies conducted since the 1940s, efficiencies (based on total incident radiation) of more than 3% have seldom been found, and 1% is typical, although when recalculated on the basis of energy in the visible range, these figures must be adjusted to 6 and 2%, respectively (Kormondy, 1969). Much higher efficiencies are attained over short periods when optimum conditions prevail, and efficiency increases as light intensity drops, approaching 20% at very low intensities under laboratory conditions (Collier et al., 1973). Efficiency also varies with leaf morphology and orientation; leaves that have developed in the shade are generally more efficient at lower light intensities than leaves that have developed in full sunlight.

Photosynthetic efficiencies calculated in the field over long periods are lower than those obtained in short-term studies. This is because for at least part of the growing season much of the light falls on nonphotosynthetic organs or on bare ground, and because conditions for optimum photosynthesis are present only part of the time. It has been calculated that if optimum conditions existed in the field throughout the growing season, net photosynthetic efficiency should be about 5% of the total incident solar radiation and 12% of the total visible solar radiation (Gates, 1971). The modest photosynthetic efficiencies achieved by many agricultural crops reflect incomplete coverage of the ground by leaves for much of the growing season. Figure 4.9 shows the development of leaf area of wheat and maize during a growing season in relation to photosynthetically active solar radiation. Maximum net use of sunlight is achieved at a *leaf area index*[2] of about 4, and it is apparent from Figure 4.9 that a significant proportion of available solar radiation during the growing season is not used by these two annual crops.

2. Losses:

a. RESPIRATION. According to the second law of thermodynamics, some of the energy of photosynthesis is used up during growth and maintenance, a process of energy loss referred to as *respiration*. Respiratory losses in plant communities vary from as little as 15% to more than 90% (Table 4.2), but the results of a wide range of studies suggest that, in general, autotrophic respiration accounts for about 30–40% of autotrophic gross production.

The temperature of the environment (especially nighttime temperature) and the size, rate of growth, and physiological condition of plants (i.e., metabolic rates) influence plant respiratory losses. The relative size of this loss is important in determining the productivity of the ecosystem (Figure 4.8B). The rate of growth and biomass accumulation of individual plants are in turn dependent on respiration losses, which will affect the competitive status of the plant in the community.

Respiration losses at the primary producer level appear to increase as one moves from polar toward tropical latitudes, presumably because of increasing temperatures (especially during the warmer nights). As a result, net primary production (NPP) in the tropics may not be very much greater than

[2]Leaf area index: the projected leaf surface area per unit of ground surface area. For a more complete discussion of leaf area in forests, see Section 4.6.

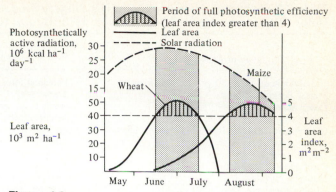

Figure 4.9

Development of leaf area in relation to the availability of solar energy for photosynthesis during the growing season for wheat and maize (after Niciporovic, 1968). Wheat is better able to exploit available solar radiation than maize because its maximum development of leaf area coincides with maximum solar radiation. Leaf area index is the ratio of horizontal leaf surface area to horizontal ground surface area. (Courtesy UNESCO.)

in temperate areas in spite of the higher gross production in the tropics. Lower gross production in higher elevations or more northerly areas is partly offset by reduced respiration losses, particularly during the cool nights that are characteristic of these areas (Tranquillini and Schutz, 1971). High nighttime respiration because of high nocturnal temperatures plays an important role in limiting the southerly or lower altitudinal extension of the range of some plants.

b. CONSUMPTION BY HERBIVORES. The extent to which plants are consumed by herbivores varies greatly between different types of ecosystem (Table 4.3). In grasslands, for example, a very high percentage of the aboveground plant biomass and the NPP is palatable, digestible, and within the reach of herbivores. In forests, on the other hand, the foliage is a much smaller proportion of NPP, the rest being woody tissues that are little used by herbivores (with the exception of fine roots and young twigs). Forest foliage

Table 4.2 Loss of Gross Primary Production to Respiration in Various Different Terrestrial Ecosystems

Ecosystem	Loss of Gross Primary Production to Respiration, %	Net Production Efficiency $\left(\dfrac{\text{net production}}{\text{gross production}} \times 100\right)$, %	Reference
Abandoned field, Mich.	15	85	Golley, 1960
Cornfield, Ohio	23	77	Transeau, 1926
Alfalfa field, U.S.	38	62	Odum, 1971
Scotch pine plantation, England	39	61	Odum, 1971
Oak–pine forest near New York City	55	45	Woodwell, 1970b
Tropical rain forest, Puerto Rico	71	29	Odum and Pigeon, 1970
450-year-old Douglas-fir forest, Ore.	93	7	Grier and Logan, 1977

Table 4.3 Extent of Consumption of Net Primary Production by Herbivores in Various Types of Ecosystem (After Wiegert and Owen, 1971; Ricklefs, 1973; Odum, 1962; Kozlovsky, 1968)

Type of Ecosystem	Type of Primary Producer	Consumption of NPP by Herbivores, %
Old agricultural field, 30 yr after abandonment	Perennial forbs and grasses	1.1
Mature deciduous forest	Trees	1.5–2.5
Desert scrub	Annual and perennial herbs and shrubs	5.5
Salt marsh	Perennial herbs	8.0
Old agricultural field, 1–7 yr after abandonment	Annual herbs	12.0
Conifer plantation	Pine trees	12.5
Lake Mendota, Wis.	Phytoplankton (algae) and macrophytes	14.7
Cedar Bog Lake, Minn.	Phytoplankton (algae) and macrophytes	21.8
Managed rangeland	Perennial grasses	30 –45
African grasslands	Perennial grasses	28 –60
Marine bay	Phytoplankton	75
Ocean	Phytoplankton	60 –99

		Consumption of Leaf Production, %	
		By Insects	By Birds and Frogs
Pine forest	Trees	9.2	1.5
Pine–oak forest	Trees	3.4	2.7
Pine–oak–alder forest edge	Trees	4.0	3.1

tends to be less palatable and digestible than grassland foliage because of its physical and chemical characteristics, and much of it is physically out of reach of many herbivores. Grassland plants experience between 28 and 60% loss of NPP to herbivores, while in forests only about 5–10% (an average of 8% is given by Bray, 1961, 1964) of the foliage is consumed. This average level represents only 1.5–2.5% of NPP except during periods of high insect herbivore abundance. Phytoplankton communities in aquatic ecosystems experience even heavier exploitation by herbivores (60–99% of NPP) than grassland communities because of the accessibility of phytoplankton and their low proportion of nondigestible supporting structures.

The importance of herbivores in the dynamics of energy is illustrated by some recent estimates of the consumption of NPP by termites and its conversion to CH_4 (methane), CO_2, and hydrogen gas (Zimmerman et al., 1982). Termites are exceedingly abundant in the tropical and subtropical areas of the world where they consume an estimated 37% of the NPP (this is equal to 28% of the world's terrestrial NPP). The final product of this consumption is thought to be about 152 million tons of methane, 50 billion tons of CO_2, and 200 million tons of hydrogen per year.

The figures given in Table 4.3 for forest ecosystems are examples of the exploitation of forest plants by herbivores under conditions of normal, stable herbivore populations. Anyone who has been in a forest during an outbreak of

defoliating insects will know that although these figures may be an accurate, or even an overestimate of the utilization of trees by herbivores under "normal" circumstances (periods of herbivore scarcity), they probably underestimate the long-term utilization. Forest insects periodically increase to epidemic proportions (e.g., the spruce budworm, the hemlock looper, the Douglas-fir tussock moth, the gypsy moth, or species of sawfly or tent caterpillar), at which time they can consume all of a deciduous tree's foliage or several years of evergreen foliage production in a single summer. Such massive transfers of energy to grazing and detritus food webs via insect frass (feces), dead insects, and dead trees result in reductions in NPP for several years and can drastically reduce the biomass of primary producers in the ecosystem (e.g., Morris, 1963; Rafes, 1970, 1971; Varley et al., 1973). Such pulses of energy flow from producer to primary consumer level may be reflected by temporary expansions in the magnitude of energy flow and biomass all the way up the trophic web.

It has generally been assumed that heavy defoliation kills or at least drastically reduces the growth of trees. This is undoubtedly true in many species, but some trees are apparently able to tolerate such defoliation remarkably well. Oak trees are often defoliated with only modest effects on growth because they quickly refoliate. Under some circumstances, Douglas-fir can recover from heavy defoliation by the Douglas-fir tussock moth (*Orgyia pseudotsugata*) with little growth reduction the following year (Majawa, 1977). This may be partly because tussock moth outbreaks often occur during a drought-induced period of slow tree growth. If the tree is partially defoliated during the period of moisture stress, the photosynthetic efficiency of the remaining foliage may be temporarily increased, largely compensating for the reduced foliar biomass.

Foresters and farmers are concerned with harvesting net primary production, either directly or via some desired species of herbivore. The growth of the vast pesticide industry over the past 30 years reflects our desire to prevent the energy of primary production from flowing to members of the secondary trophic levels other than ourselves or domestic herbivores. However, while transfer of energy from plants to herbivores may be considered undesirable in some ecosystems, in others it may be the objective of management. Pasture and stock farmers spend their working lives trying to promote such energy flow, by growing plants in a manner that optimizes energy flow into, and accumulation of energy in, herbivore populations (e.g., cows, sheep, or goats).

Herbivory in forests managed for timber production might appear to be unequivocally bad from the standpoint of timber management. But considered in terms of overall, long-term ecosystem energetics, a stable, low level of herbivory might in fact promote ecosystem productivity by stimulating litter decomposition and the circulation of nutrients. Also, it has been suggested that over a long period of time, defoliating insects may actually increase the productivity of unmanaged, unharvested (by foresters) ecosystems. It has been noted that insect outbreaks that result in extensive tree mortality are frequently associated with mature or overmature stands in which primary production has begun to decline. The insects remove these older, less productive stands which are then replaced by younger, more productive stands, thus increasing energy flow through the ecosystem (Mattson and Addy, 1975). Further studies of the overall effect of herbivores on ecosystem productivity are needed (e.g., Zlotin and Khodashova, 1980) to elucidate the overall role of herbivory in ecosystem function.

c. Litterfall. With the exception of heavy exploitation by herbivores during periods of high population, the greatest loss of forest NPP is by litterfall: the regular annual transfer of living plant material to the nonliving organic matter of the forest floor and mineral soil. Plant litterfall is obviously of less significance in ecosystems such as oceans and grasslands, in which much of the NPP is consumed by herbivores, but in many terrestrial ecosystems it is the major pathway of energy flow beyond the producer level. Leaves are the major component of aboveground litterfall in most ecosystems, although other components, such as bark, can be important in some areas (e.g., eucalyptus forests).

Table 4.4 summarizes the magnitude of aboveground litterfall in a variety of ecosystems (mostly forests) in comparison with aboveground plant biomass and NPP. Both total aboveground litterfall and leaf litterfall of forests increase

Table 4.4 Average Aboveground Litterfall in Relation to Phytomass (Plant Biomass) and Net Primary Production (Data from Ajtay et al., 1979)

Ecosystem Type	Total[a] Phytomass 10^3 g m^{-2}	Total NPP g m^{-2} yr^{-1}	Aboveground Litterfall g m^{-2} yr^{-1}	Aboveground[b] Litterfall as a % of Total NPP %	Litter Accumulation g m^{-2}
Arctic shrub tundra	2.3	350	200	58	5000
Boreal coniferous (open)	17	650	550	85	
Boreal coniferous (closed)	25	850	600	71	3500
Temperate evergreen coniferous	30	1500		57	
Temperate deciduous (mixed)	28	1300	850	65	3000
Temperate woodland	18	1500	1220	81	2500
Low tree/shrub savanna	7.5	2100	800	38	350
Mangrove	30	1000	600	60	10000
Tropical seasonal	25	1600	1300	81	850
Tropical humid	42	2300	1850	80	650

[a]To convert g m^{-2} to t ha^{-1}, divide by 100. e.g., 1000 g m^{-2} = 10t ha^{-1}. To convert 10^3 g m^{-2} to t ha^{-1}, multiply by 10.
[b]The data do not include root litterfall; total litterfall as a % of NPP would probably exhibit a different pattern.

from polar regions toward the equator. This parallels a similar variation in biomass and NPP since aboveground litterfall generally reflects aboveground forest productivity. The proportion of the total forest biomass invested in photosynthetic organs decreases as one moves from boreal to temperate regions, but increases again somewhat in tropical forests. This pattern reflects the evergreen character of northern forests, the deciduous character of temperate forests, and the evergreen character of tropical rain forests.

The annual quantity of aboveground litterfall obviously depends heavily on the proportion of the foliage biomass that dies each year; the longer the foliage retention, the less the quantity of leaf litterfall. For example, in coastal British Columbia, Pacific silver fir *(Abies amabilis)* retains about 6–9 years of foliage at the lower end of its altitudinal range (about 300 m near Vancouver, B.C.), about 13–19 years at midrange (about 1000 m), and about 22–26 years of foliage (oldest green needles on one branch were 31 years old) at the upper altitudinal limit of continuous forest (about 1700 m) (Kimmins, unpublished data). With relatively little variation in stand foliage biomass over this range, leaf litterfall will vary by a factor of about three. Foliage retention can vary latitudinally as well as with elevation, and this may help to explain the leaf litterfall pattern in Table 4.4. The ecological significance of evergreenness is discussed in greater detail in Chapter 5. A detailed review of this topic can be found in Chabot and Hicks (1982).

Aboveground litterfall varies with a variety of factors, including climate, soil moisture and soil fertility (greatest on moist and fertile sites), and altitude (often greatest at intermediate altitudes). Stand density, on the other hand, appears to make little difference. For example, little variation in either total or nonwoody aboveground litterfall was observed in four stands in Alaska ranging from a 12–30-year-old hardwood–conifer stand of 10,000 stems per hectare to a 132–163-year-old spruce–hemlock stand of 660 stems per hectare (Hurd, 1971). Several other studies have reached the same conclusion, including one that showed constant litterfall in eucalyptus forests varying in age from 55 to 200 years old and varying in density by more than fourfold. Understory vegetation contributed 25% of the aboveground litterfall in the oldest stand but only about 2.5% in the 55-year-old stand (Bray and Gorham, 1964).

Litterfall occurs either seasonally or continuously. Almost all aboveground litterfall in temperate deciduous forests occurs in the autumn, and several species of temperate conifers also shed most of their old foliage in the fall. In some climatic regions, deciduous leaf-fall may occur just before a dry season. Aboveground litterfall in tropical ever-green hardwood forests is distributed throughout the year, but minor peaks do occur in slightly drier months and in association with storms. In some species of pine, most needlefall occurs in the summer either before or during hot, dry periods. In species such as spruce, leaf-fall is continuous and rather random, occurring in response to random variations in such factors as weather and insect attack.

Until recently, most of the data on litterfall was for aboveground litter, which was assumed to be the major contribution of organic matter to the soil. This assumption is now known to be wrong. In many types of forest, shrub and herbaceous communities there is a greater annual turnover of organic matter below ground than above ground. A large proportion of a plant's net photosynthate is invested each year in relatively short-lived fine roots and mycorrhizal fungi (see Chapter 5), an apparently necessary strategy in the quest for the soil moisture and nutrients required to sustain photosynthesis. In some types of forest, such as in high-elevation subalpine areas, the majority of the annual input of organic matter to the forest floor comes from belowground "litterfall"—the annual, monthly, or weekly death of fine roots and associated microorganisms. In a recent study of Douglas-fir growing on poor (dry, low fertility) and good (moist, fertile) sites, Keyes and Grier (1981) reported a difference in total NPP of only 13%, compared with a net aboveground production difference of 188% (13.7 t ha^{-1} on the good site versus 7.3 t ha^{-1} on the poor site). This was explained by the difference in investment in the production of fine roots (<2 mm); 1.4 t ha^{-1} on the good site and 5.6 t ha^{-1} on the poor site. On the good site 8% of total stand dry matter production was in fine roots, compared to 36% on the poor site.

Litterfall is a very important parameter of energy flow. Its magnitude influences the proportion of the net primary productivity that is stored as permanent biomass. It is also the supply of energy to the detritus food web. In Chapter 5 we shall see that the quantity and qualitative characteristics of litterfall are very important in the overall functioning of the ecosystem.

3. Net Productivity and Biomass. Although energy gains by photosynthesis and energy losses by respiration, herbivory, and litterfall are individually of considerable interest, it is the combined outcome of these processes that is of greatest concern to ecosystem managers and ecologists: biomass and net primary productivity. Traditionally, foresters have been interested in the standing crop rather than biomass, but with the development of more complete utilization of trees, biomass is becoming their major focus. Productivity is generally reported in terms of the weight, volume, or energy content of the NPP per hectare per year.

Net primary productivity of a given type of vegetation generally increases as one moves from temperate to tropical areas, and within a given major climatic region, productivity increases as one moves from drier habitats to wetter habitats. Maximum productivity may be attained in semiterrestrial ecosystems (shallow water, swamps, marshes, or terrestrial sites associated with abundant supplies of water), although in many forest ecosystems productivity declines if the soil becomes excessively wet. Productivity also declines as one moves into larger bodies of water away from the land/water interface, such as the middle of large lakes or oceans. Forests generally exhibit productivities comparable to, if slightly lower than, agriculture. This is a rather surprising fact considering that forests tend to be located on less fertile sites in more severe climates than agricultural crops, and receive far fewer aids to production (fertilizers, insecticides, etc.).

Table 4.5 presents some aboveground productivity estimates for forests. There is a considerable variation between the estimates of different authors, but this is hardly surprising considering the difficulty of obtaining such data and the considerable natural variation in productivity within relatively small areas. In spite of this variability, the values shown in Table 4.5 are surprisingly consistent. Many of the estimates represent averages of stands of varying ages, which may account for some of the variability in the data. Gross productivity increases to a peak at intermediate ages and then declines slightly to a stable value that is sustained

Table 4.5 Average Net Aboveground Productivity of Various Forest Types Listed in Order of Increasing Productivity[a]

Forest Type	Climate	Net Aboveground Productivity[a] t ha^{-1} yr^{-1}	Reference[b]
Pine bog forest, U.S.S.R.	Boreal	3.4	Rodin and Bazilevich, 1967
Spruce, U.S.S.R.	Northern boreal	4.5	Rodin and Bazilevich, 1967
Pine, U.S.S.R.	Southern boreal	6.1	Rodin and Bazilevich, 1967
Spruce, U.S.S.R.	Mid-boreal	7.0	Rodin and Bazilevich, 1967
Spruce, U.S.S.R.	Southern boreal	8.5	Rodin and Bazilevich, 1967
Oak, U.S.S.R.	Temperate	9.0	Rodin and Bazilevich, 1967
Mangrove, U.S.	Subtropical	9.3	Rodin and Bazilevich, 1967
Birch, U.S.S.R.	Temperate	12.0	Rodin and Bazilevich, 1967
Beech, Europe	Temperate	13.0	Rodin and Bazilevich, 1967
Pine, England	Temperate	14.2	Rodin and Bazilevich, 1967
Deciduous forest	Subtropical	24.5	Rodin and Bazilevich, 1967
Rain forest	Tropical	32.5	Rodin and Bazilevich, 1967
Dry forest		3.1 (50%)	Odum, 1971
Coniferous forest	Boreal	4.5 (40%)	Odum, 1971
Moist forest	Temperate	10.0 (50%)	Odum, 1971
Wet forest	Tropical and subtropical	17.5 (70%)	Whittaker and Woodwell, 1971
Boreal forest		8.0	Whittaker and Woodwell, 1971
Temperate forest		13.0	Whittaker and Woodwell, 1971
Tropical forest		20.0	Whittaker and Woodwell, 1971
Woodland and shrubland		6.0	Whittaker and Woodwell, 1971
Pine	Temperate	8.0–9.5	Whittaker, 1966
Pine heath	Temperate	2.0–4.0	Whittaker, 1966
Hemlock forest	Temperate	8.5–11.5	Whittaker, 1966
Spruce–fir forest	Temperate	9.2–14.0	Whittaker, 1966
Fir forest	Temperate	4.7–6.5	Whittaker, 1966
Various hardwood forests	Temperate	5.0–14.0	Whittaker, 1966
Tulip tree forest	Temperate	24.0	Whittaker, 1966
Douglas-fir–hemlock	Temperate	12.7	Fujimori et al., 1976
Noble fir–Douglas-fir	Temperate	13.0	Grier and Logan, 1977
Hemlock–spruce	Temperate	10.3	Waring and Franklin, 1979
Douglas-fir	Temperate	10.9	Waring and Franklin, 1979
Coast redwood (stems only)	Temperate	14.3	Waring and Franklin, 1979

[a] A fuller list of biomass and net productivity of the world's forests is given by Art and Marks, 1971, and Cannell, 1982.

[b] Date of Rodin and Bazilevich, Odum, and Whittaker and Woodwell are average values for the type. Odum's data derived from gross productivity data based on the estimated percentage of respiratory losses shown in parentheses.

to an advanced age. However, respiration losses continue to increase as biomass accumulates, with the result that net productivity reaches a peak at an intermediate age and then declines (Figure 4.10). Other summaries of world forest biomass data can be found in Art and Marks (1971), and Cannell (1982).

Most published estimates of forest productivity are based on aboveground data, or if they include roots, they refer only to the large roots. Recent studies have shown that quite a different picture may emerge if one includes the production of fine roots. Keyes and Grier (1981) studied productivity in two stands of Douglas-fir that varied widely in stemwood production [site indices of 24 and 40 (m at 50 yr) for the poor and good stands, respectively]. They reported that aboveground and coarse root biomass increment on the poor site (8.4 t ha^{-1}) was about half that of the good site (15.3 t ha^{-1}). In contrast, the estimated *total* biomass increment for the poor site (15.4 t ha^{-1}) was about 87% of that for the good site (17.8 t ha^{-1}). This is because 36% of the NPP on the poor site was allocated to fine root production (5.6 t ha^{-1}) in comparison to 8% on the good site (1.4 t ha^{-1}).

A similar study in subalpine stands of Pacific silver-fir revealed a marked variation in allocation of NPP to fine roots as a stand ages: 36% in a 23-year-old stand, in comparison to 66.4% in a mature, 180-year-old stand (Grier et

al., 1981). Such age-related variation in the allocation of NPP between perennial and ephemeral tissues makes it difficult to compare the productivity of stands in which fine roots have not been studied. This study also examined the biomass of *mycorrhizae*.[3] These accounted for a mere 0.7 and 0.3% of the ecosystem biomass, but for 13.9 and 15% of the NPP in the 23- and the 180-year-old stands, respectively. Fine roots and mycorrhizae together accounted for 45 and 75%, respectively, of NPP (Vogt et al., 1982). This is an excellent example of the importance of mycorrhizae in ecosystem function, and of how a very small component of an ecosystem can play a pivotal role.

There are relatively few really detailed studies of the energetics of a forest ecosystem. Gathering the necessary data is expensive and laborious. One such study that demonstrates how stem mortality and respiration can exceed gross primary production in a very old forest and result in a decline in tree biomass is that of Grier and Logan (1977). They studied the biomass and energetics of five different forest plant communities in a 450-year-old Douglas-fir forest at the H. J. Andrews Experimental Forest in the western Cascade Range, Oregon. The results of their study are presented in Table 4.6.

The average total biomass of trees was 870 t ha^{-1}, a figure that is higher than most published values for forests except in the Pacific Northwest where exceptionally large quantities of forest biomass are accumulated. One community had a tree biomass of 1187 t ha^{-1}. The living trees represented 70% of the ecosystem biomass, and dead snags and fallen logs accounted for another 17%. The ecosystems had an appreciable average gross primary production of 161 t ha^{-1} yr^{-1}, but a high value for autotrophic respiration (93% of GPP) reduced net production to a value of 10.9 t ha^{-1} yr^{-1}. Annual losses of biomass from the live vegetation of 15.4 t ha^{-1} yr^{-1} resulted in a net loss of living biomass of 4.5 t ha^{-1} yr^{-1}. Although this is only a small proportion of the total biomass (0.5%) and could represent merely a short-term fluctuation around a long-term stable mean, it may also reflect the slow but prolonged decline of live tree biomass that occurs as an old forest changes from a healthy mature stand to a decadent, overmature stand. With total ecosystem respiration estimated to be about 158 t ha^{-1} yr^{-1}, or about 98% of gross primary production, it would certainly seem that this is a fully mature ecosystem that is close to its maximum biomass. Whether or not the organic matter content of such an ecosystem actually reaches steady state or whether it peaks and then

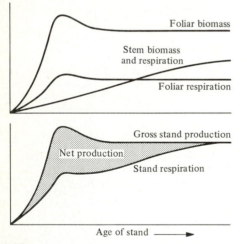

Figure 4.10

Variation in net production in forests during the life of a stand (after Kira and Shidei, 1967). As the living biomass increases, an increasing proportion of gross production is used in maintenance metabolism. In an overmature old-growth forest, respiration may equal photosynthesis and there may be no net production and no net biomass increase. (By permission of Dr. Tatuo Kira.)

---

[3] Symbiotic relationship between the fine roots of plants and soil fungi. The mycorrhizal relationship is discussed in Chapters 5 and 14.

Table 4.6 Summary of the Biomass (t ha^{-1}) and Ecological Energetics (t ha^{-1} yr^{-1}) of a 450-year-old Douglas-Fir Forest on Watershed 10, H. J. Andrews Experimental Forest, Ore. (Data from Grier and Logan, 1977)[a]

Parameter	Average	Range	Parameter	Average	Range
Biomass			*Energetics*		
Trees			Biomass increment (B)		
Foliage	12.4	8.6– 14.5	Trees	−4.3	−2.9– −6.2
Branches	52.6	35.9– 69.7	Lesser vegetation	0.6	.2– 1.2
Stem wood	576	399 – 794	Roots	−0.8	−0.5– −1.1
Stem bark	70.4	48.3– 96.9	Total	−4.5	−3.0– −6.1
Roots	153	106 – 204	Biomass loss, Litterfall		
Total	870	605 –1187	Aboveground ephemeral	4.3	3.8– 5.0
Lesser vegetation	6.4	5.6– 10.3	Fine root mortality	2.3	1.6– 2.6
Forest floor	51.2	27.5– 57.2	Stem and coarse root mortality	8.4	5.8– 11.5
Dead snags	24.6	3.8– 70.0	Other losses	0.4	0.4
Fallen logs	190	55.2– 581	Total loss of biomass	15.4	11.6– 19.2
Total detritus	266	108 – 696	Gross primary production (GPP)		
Soil organic matter	113	90 – 130	Above ground	124.1	86.2– 168.2
Ecosystem total	1249	1008 –1514	Below ground	36.8	25.0– 48.6
			Total	160.9	111.2– 216.8
			Autotrophic respiration		
			Above ground	116.1	79.9– 158.1
			Below ground	33.9	23.0– 45.6
			Total	150.0	102.9– 203.7
			Net primary production (NPP)		
			Above ground	8.0	6.3– 10.0
			Below ground	2.9	2.0– 3.3
			Total	10.9	8.3– 13.1
			Heterotrophic respiration		
			Forest floor	4.3	3.8– 5.0
			Decaying snags and logs	1.4	0.4– 4.3
			Below ground	1.8	1.3– 2.1
			Total	7.6	6.8– 10.2
			Net ecosystem production (NEP)		
			Above ground	2.3	−0.9– 4.7
			Below ground	1.0	0.7– 1.2
			Total	3.0	0.1– 5.6
			Ratio, %		
			NPP/GPP	6.8	6.0– 7.9
			ΔB/GPP	−2.8	−2.1– −3.1
			ΔB/NPP	−41.6	−29.0– −50.3

[a]Data for five different plant communities were gathered. Only the average and range of values are shown here. Note the variation in values that can be observed in a 10-ha watershed. Because of the use of averages, the sums of components do not necessarily equal the totals.

declines is difficult to ascertain because of the high probability that a forest will suffer some natural disaster before the very long-term pattern of organic accumulation becomes clear.

There was a great increase in concern about global ecology during the 1970s. Problems of air and water pollution, world food supply, overfishing of the world's oceans, and overcutting of the world's forests have stimulated increased efforts to quantify and understand world patterns of biomass and productivity. Global estimates are generally obtained by multiplying estimates of average biomass and productivity for different ecosystem types by estimates of the area of the earth occupied by the appropriate ecosystem type (Table 4.7). It is apparent from such estimates that the forest plays a major role in world ecosystems. The average productivity per hectare of the world's forests is more than four times as great as the average productivity for the whole world, more than twice the agricultural land average, and almost twice the terrestrial average. Although forests account for only 11 and 38% of the entire surface of the earth and the land surface, respectively, they account for 47 and 71% of the world and terrestrial net primary production, respectively, and about 93% of both the world and the terrestrial producer biomass (Whittaker and Woodwell, 1971). These data em-

Table 4.7 Estimates of Net Primary Productivity and Plant Biomass (Phytomass) for the Major Terrestrial Ecosystems of the World

Ecosystem Type	Surface Area $\times 10^{12}$ m^2	NPP g m^{-2} yr^{-1}	Total World Production (billion tons)	Living Phytomass kg m^{-2}	Total World Living Phytomass (billion tons)
1. Forests	31.3		48.68		950.5
Tropical humid	10	2300	23	42	420
Tropical seasonal	4.5	1600	7.2	25	112.5
Mangrove	0.3	1000	0.3	30	9
Temperate evergreen/conif.	3	1500	4.5	30	90
Temperate deciduous/mixed	3	1300	3.9	28	84
Boreal coniferous (closed)	6.5	850	5.53	25	162.5
Boreal coniferous (open)	2.5	650	1.63	17	42.5
Forest plantations	1.5	1750	2.62	20	30
2. Temperate woodlands (various)	2	1500	3	18	36
3. Chaparral, maquis, brushland	2.5	800	2	7	17.5
4. Savanna	22.5		39.35		145.7
Low tree/shrub savanna	6	2100	12.6	7.5	45
Grass dominated savanna	6	2300	13.8	2.2	13.2
Dry savanna thorn forest	3.5	1300	4.55	15	52.5
Dry thorny shrubs	7	1200	8.4	5	35
5. Temperated grassland	12.5		9.75		20.25
Temperated moist grassland	5	1200	6	2.1	10.5
Temperated dry grassland	7.5	500	3.75	1.3	9.75
6. Tundra arctic/alpine	9.5		2.12		13.05
Polar desert	1.5	25	0.04	0.15	0.23
High arctic/alpine	3.6	150	0.54	0.75	2.7
Low arctic/alpine	4.4	350	1.54	2.3	10.12
7. Desert and semidesert scrub	21		3		16.5
Scrub dominated	9	200	1.8	1.1	9.9
Irreversible degraded	12	100	1.2	0.55	6.6
8. Extreme deserts	9		0.13		0.78
Sandy hot and dry	8	10	0.08	0.06	0.48
Sandy cold and dry	1	50	0.05	0.3	0.3
9. Perpetual ice	15.5	0	0	0	0
10. Lakes and streams	2	400	0.8	0.02	0.04
11. Swamps and marshes	2		7.25		26.25
Temperate	0.5	2500	1.25	7.5	3.75
Tropical	1.5	4000	6	15	22.5
12. Bogs, unexploited peatlands	1.5	1000	1.5	5	7.5
13. Cultivated land	16		15.05		6.64
Temperate annuals	6	1200	7.2	0.1*	0.6
Temperate perennials	0.5	1500	0.75	5	2.5
Tropical annuals	9	700	6.3	0.06*	0.54
Tropical perennials	0.5	1600	0.8	6	3
14. Human area	2†	500	0.4	4	3.2
TOTAL	149.3	895	133.0	3.75	1243.9

Source: Ajtay et al., 1979. Copyright 1979 SCOPE. Used with permission.
Conversion Factors: To convert g m^{-2} yr to t ha^{-1} yr^{-1}, divide by 100; to convert kg m^{-2} to t ha^{-1}, multiply by 10.
*Annual average values.
†Of which only 40% (or 0.8 $\times$ 10^{12} m^2) is productive.

phasize the very important role that the world's forests play in global ecology, and stress the need for concern over global deforestation, which is estimated to be occurring at a net rate of about 25–35 ha min^{-1} (Spears, 1979; Council on Environmental Quality, 1980).

For a recent detailed analysis of biomass and of productivity in different types of forest ecosystem, the reader should consult O'Neill and De Angelis (1981), Gardner and Mankin (1981), De Angelis et al. (1981), Edwards et al. (1981), and Satoo and Madgwick (1982).

4. Distribution of Biomass Between Different Parts of Plants. The relative distribution of biomass between belowground and aboveground organs and between stem and reproductive organs is of great concern to farmers growing such crops as potatoes and corn. Similarly, the relative distribution of tree biomass between roots, stems, branches, and foliage is of more than academic interest to foresters. High productivity has little economic value if it is allocated to a nonmarketable part of the plant. Where forest harvesting is changing from the conventional utilization of only the larger parts of the stem to the utilization of the "whole tree" (all aboveground biomass) or even the "complete tree" (all biomass, including roots), the distribution between crowns, stems, and roots may be less important. Nevertheless, because of different end uses for, and value of, bark, wood, branches, foliage, and roots, it is still important to know the distribution of biomass between these components in a completely harvested crop. Such knowledge is also needed for the design of efficient harvesting equipment and processing techniques, and the advanced planning for post-harvest slash disposal.

The increase in total biomass along the transect from polar to equatorial environments is accompanied by a reduction in the relative magnitude of the root systems and a concomitant increase in the relative magnitude of aboveground biomass. This results in a general increase in the shoot/root ratio as one moves toward the equator. The investment in foliage varies according to whether the vegetation is deciduous or evergreen, but as we saw in Table 4.4, the amount of net primary production invested in foliage (and hence litterfall) does vary along the latitudinal gradient, generally being greatest near each end and least near the center of the gradient.

A study of the relative distribution of biomass components in both forest and agricultural crops on good- and medium-quality sites revealed that the proportion of stemwood in the total biomass of a spruce crop dropped from 42% on a good site to 27% on a medium site. Similarly, the proportion of a *Solanum* (potato) crop that was a harvestable product dropped from 75% on a good agricultural site to

68% on a medium site. For beech there was less change, the proportion of stemwood dropping from 41 to 39%; for pine there was a slight increase from 34 to 35% (Duvigneaud, 1971). Thus, there appears to be a change in the allocation of primary production to different components of biomass as the quality of the environment changes. The investment in stems is reduced while root biomass is increased on nutrient-poor sites because a larger root system is required to satisfy the moisture and nutrient demands of the aboveground parts (Keyes and Grier, 1981). Nutrient-demanding species show this change more sensitively than do non-nutrient-demanding species. Knowledge of this type of variation will become increasingly important in forest management in the future.

5. Concentration of Energy in Plant Parts. Plants do not store energy at the same concentration in all tissues, and different plant species vary in the concentration of energy in comparable biomass components. Table 4.8 presents data on the energy content of a variety of biomass categories: different biomass components within a community, different communities, the seeds of different species, and different types of animal. Within a community, the concentration of energy is lowest in woody and leaf material and highest in plant seeds, with animal tissues generally being intermediate.

Table 4.8 Energy Content of Various Biomass Categories

Material	Cal g^{-1} Dry Weight		Reference
	Boles	*Foliage*	
White ash	4674	4799	Musselman and Hocker, 1981
Red oak	4843	4967	Musselman and Hocker, 1981
Trembling aspen	4913	5360	Musselman and Hocker, 1981
White pine	5022	5226	Musselman and Hocker, 1981
Tropical rain forest	3897		Golley, 1961
Mangrove forest	3764[a]		Golley, 1961
Pine forest	4787[a]		Golley, 1961
Marshland	4072[a]		Golley, 1961
Grassy meadow	3905		Golley, 1961
Alpine meadow	4711		Golley, 1961
Oak seeds	4070		Turcek, 1967
Beech seeds	6700		Turcek, 1967
Spruce seeds	6100		Turcek, 1967
Invertebrates (excluding insects)	3000		Odum, 1971
Insects	5400		Odum, 1971
Vertebrates	5600		Odum, 1971

[a]Average for plant community.

Tropical plant communities have lower values than plants from more northerly communities, and there is a steady increase in energy concentration in plant tissue from the tropics to alpine communities along a gradient of decreasing available growing season solar energy (Jordan, 1971). The same pattern is seen in both woody and nonwoody plants, although the former generally have higher concentrations of energy.

B. Primary Consumer (Herbivore) Trophic Level

Energy flow above the primary producer level is influenced by several factors. The efficiency with which food resources are exploited, the efficiency of digestion, and the loss of energy in respiration all influence the rate at which energy is transferred from plants to herbivores. We shall discuss each of these parameters of energy flow in turn, referring to Figure 4.11 for clarification.

We have already seen that the proportion of primary producer energy that is exploited by the primary consumer trophic level (the *utilization efficiency*) is highly variable, but generally low for forest ecosystems. The utilization of vegetation by herbivores is determined by the palatability, nutritional quality, and physical availability of the plants to the herbivores, and by the abundance of the herbivores.

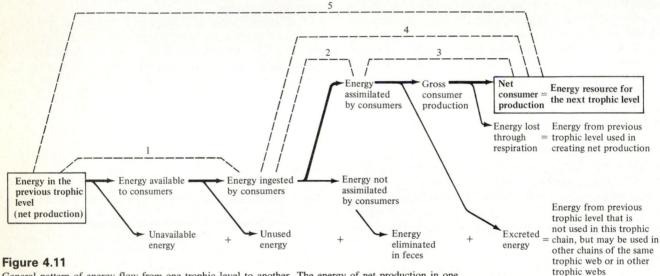

Figure 4.11

General pattern of energy flow from one trophic level to another. The energy of net production in one trophic level proceeds through various stages to become incorporated in the net production of the next trophic level of that trophic chain, to be transferred to another chain or web, or to be lost as heat during respiration. Various ratios that have been used to describe the efficiency of energy transfer at the various stages between two trophic levels are as follows:

1. Utilization (consumption or exploitation) efficiency

$$= \frac{\text{ingestion}}{\text{net production of previous trophic level}}$$

2. Assimilation (digestion) efficiency $= \dfrac{\text{assimilation}}{\text{ingestion}}$

3. Tissue growth (net production) efficiency $= \dfrac{\text{net production}}{\text{assimilation}}$

4. Ecological growth (gross production) efficiency $= \dfrac{\text{net production}}{\text{ingestion}}$

5. Trophic (ecological) efficiency $= \dfrac{\text{net production}}{\text{net production of previous trophic level}}$

For a comparison of different terms used to describe the efficiency of energy transfer, see Kozlovsky, 1968. (Used by permission of the Ecological Society of America.)

Levels of utilization that are sufficiently high to significantly reduce subsequent primary productivity are unusual.
They are normally associated with herbivore populations
that are in temporary outbreak condition.

The ratio of plant net production to plant biomass is often
used as a measure of the availability of plant production to
herbivores, since it reflects the relative allocation of production between woody and nonwoody tissues. Table 4.9
shows production/biomass ratios for a number of ecosystems, and a comparison with Table 4.3 reveals that there is
a close parallel between P/B ratios and consumption of net
primary production by herbivores. Agricultural ecosystems
have the highest P/B value for terrestrial ecosystems, a trib-
ute to the success of agricultural management in promoting
energy flow from plants to consumers (human beings or
domestic animals).

Ingestion of plants by herbivores does not necessarily
constitute a transfer of energy from producers to primary
consumers. Not all ingested plant biomass can be digested
and assimilated by herbivores. Much of it passes through
and out of the alimentary canal undigested, although digestion is aided in many herbivores by detritus organisms (bacteria) that live in the alimentary tract. The proportion of
ingested energy that is digested and assimilated into the
consumer's body is called the *assimilation efficiency*. It varies between different species and different ecosystems
(Table 4.10). High values are associated with foods such as
seeds (consumed by birds and small mammals) and aquatic
algae (consumed by aquatic herbivores) as these materials
have a high proportion of digestible material. Low values

are associated with browsers and grazers such as elephants
and grasshoppers, which eat woody or mature leaf materials
that are much less digestible.

High assimilation efficiency does not necessarily imply
high net production. *Tissue growth efficiency* (or net production efficiency) expresses the efficiency with which assimilated energy is converted into net production. It takes
into account losses of assimilated energy to respiration and
excretion. Tissue growth efficiencies are generally low
(Table 4.10), with a marked difference between the efficiency of invertebrates and vertebrates. Terrestial mammals
have very low efficiencies; values for terrestrial invertebrates are much higher, and aquatic invertebrates have the
highest values. A rather similar term, *ecological growth
efficiency*, expresses the efficiency with which ingested
energy is converted into net production; it accounts for both
assimilation efficiency and losses to respiration and excretion.

The difference between assimilation efficiency and ecological growth efficiency is accounted for by losses to respiration and excretion. Animals with a very high assimilation
efficiency, such as the sparrow or field mouse (Table 4.10),
often have lower ecological growth efficiencies because of
their high respiratory losses. More than 98% of the gross
production of these two species is lost through respiration.
Animals such as grasshoppers and leafhoppers, on the other
hand, have significantly higher ecological growth efficiencies, in spite of lower assimilation efficiencies, because
they are losing less than 70% of gross production to respiration.

An overall figure for energy transfer through consumer
trophic levels or populations can be obtained by calculating
the *trophic efficiency:* the ratio of net production in one
trophic level to net production in the previous trophic level.
This efficiency can be calculated by multiplying the net
production of the previous trophic level or prey population
by the percent efficiencies of utilization, assimilation, and
tissue growth of the level being studied to arrive at its net
production. Trophic efficiency represents the overall efficiency with which energy is passed from one trophic level
to the next, and is similar to the expression of energy flow
used in the construction of energy flow pyramids.

It is apparent from Table 4.10 that the efficiency of transfer of plant net biomass production into herbivore biomass
in terrestrial ecosystems is very low; less than 1% in most
cases. The explanation for these low trophic efficiencies
varies from one species to another. For some, it is primarily
the result of a low utilization efficiency, whereas in others it
is more a function of high metabolic rates and respiratory
losses. The efficiency in aquatic ecosystems is much higher

Table 4.9 Net Production/Biomass Ratios for Several
Types of Ecosystem (Whittaker and Woodwell, 1971;
Grier and Logan, 1977)

Ecosystem	Net Production/Biomass
Ocean	42
Coastal waters	35
Lakes and streams	25
Attached algae and estuaries	2
Agricultural land	0.65
Temperate grassland	0.33
Tundra and alpine	0.23
Savanna	0.18
Swamps and marshes	0.17
Woodland and shrubland	0.10
Temperate forest	0.04
Tropical forest	0.04
Boreal forest	0.04
Overmature old growth temperate conifer forest, northwestern U.S.	0.01

Table 4.10 Some Parameters of Energy Flow Through the Primary Consumer (Herbivore) Trophic Level[a]

	Utilization Efficiency, %	Assimilation Efficiency, %	Tissue Growth Efficiency, %	Ecological Growth Efficiency, %	Trophic Efficiency, %	Average Biomass g ha^{-1}	Average Biomass kcal m^{-2}	Gross Production Lost to Respiration and Excretion, %
Individual Species								
African elephant	9.6	32	1.5	0.5	0.48	12.7[b]	7.1	98.5
White-tailed deermouse	—	75	23	17.5	—	2.3	1.3	76.6
Sparrow	10–50	90	1.1	1.0	0.10–0.50	—	—	98.9
Field mouse	10–50	91	1.8	1.6	0.16–0.81	0.04	0.02	98.2
Vole	1.6	70	3.0	2.1	0.03	0.04–0.98	0.02–0.55	97.0
Rabbit	2.5	52	5.5	2.9	0.73	0.23	0.13	94.0
Cattle	—	38	11.0	4.2	—	—	—	89.0
Spittlebug	—	58	9.1	5.3	—	—	—	61.0
Grasshopper	2–7	16–37	37	10–14	0.27–0.94	0.5–1.8	0.28–1.0	63.0
Leafhopper	4.6	67	25.4	17.0	0.78	—	—	—
Pig	—	76	13.0	9.0	—	—	—	87.0
Tent caterpillar	—	29	57.0	17.0	—	5.5	3.1	43.0
Uganda cob	—	86	1.3	1.1	—	—	—	99.0
Ecosystem								
Old field (mouse trophic chain)	0.5	—	—	—	0.36–0.25	—	—	97.0
Forest	13	—	—	—	1.3	17.8	10	Approx. 80[c]
Salt marsh	—	—	—	—	—	—	—	78.0
Marine bay	75	—	—	—	25	1.8	1.0	67.0
Silver Springs, Fla.	38	—	44	—	17	65.9	37	56.0
Cedar Bog Lake, Minn.	22	86	62	—	12	—	—	38.0
Lake Mendota, Wis.	15	80	62	—	7	111	62.4	58.0

[a]Data from Odum, 1962; Odum, 1957; Kozlovsky, 1968; Golley, 1960; Cowan, 1962; Ricklefs, 1973; Wiegert and Evans, 1967.
[b]Calculated on the basis: 1 g dry herbivore = 5600 cal.
[c]Recalculated from Odum (1962) assuming a 40% assimilation efficiency.

because of the lower investment of energy in supporting tissues, which results in greater utilization and assimilation efficiencies. Because energy is passed through aquatic trophic webs more efficiently than through terrestrial webs, the former often have more trophic levels than the latter.

The data in Table 4.10 could give the reader the impression that there are abundant data on ecological efficiencies. There are, in fact, very few such data for anything other than simplified laboratory populations. Field studies of ecological efficiencies are very complex and very few researchers have attempted to characterize the energy flow through an entire natural ecosystem. Most of the examples where this has been done involved aquatic ecosystems, and these have already been referred to earlier in the chapter.

The biomass of herbivores varies greatly in different types of ecosystem, from high values in areas such as the east African grasslands to low values in hot, dry deserts. For example, the biomass of ungulates in the national parks of the U.S.S.R. varies from 22 to 52 kg ha^{-1} (Bannikov, 1967). Data on the total biomass of herbivores in ecosys-

tems are scarce, but estimates of secondary production and biomass in different types of ecosystems around the world are presented in Table 4.11.

C. Secondary Consumer (Carnivore) Trophic Level

The amount of energy diminishes rapidly as one proceeds along a trophic chain; so does our knowledge of that energy flow. We know a lot about energy at the primary producer level and quite a lot about the herbivore level, but relatively little is known about energy flow at the secondary consumer level and above. This is partly because agriculture and forestry have not considered carnivores to be commercial species. It is also because there are fewer carnivores than herbivores and they are frequently difficult to study.

Table 4.12 presents data on energy flow at the carnivore level. It is apparent that loss of gross production to respiration is high, although for terrestrial carnivores it is not substantially greater than for herbivores of comparable size and physiology. For aquatic carnivores, there does appear to be a higher respiratory loss than for aquatic herbivores.

Table 4.11　Secondary Production and Biomass in Different Ecosystems

Ecosystem Type	Primary Production Consumed by Herbivores, %	Herbivore Consumption,[a] 10^6 t yr^{-1}	Total Animal Production, 10^6 t yr^{-1}	Animal Biomass, kg ha^{-1}	Total Animal Biomass, 10^6 t
Terrestrial					
Tropical rain forest	7	2444	244	200	333
Tropical seasonal forest	6	667	67	120	89
Temperate evergreen forest	4	267	27	100	48
Temperate deciduous forest	5	422	42	156	111
Boreal forest	4	378	38	49	58
Woodland and shrubland	5	244	24	49	40
Savanna	15	1555	233	151	222
Temperate grassland	10	444	67	69	62
Tundra and alpine meadow	3	33	3	4.4	3.6
Desert scrub	3	40	6	4.4	8
Cultivated land	1	89	9	4.4	6
Aquatic					
Swamp and marsh	8	389	40	100	20
Lake and stream	20	267	27	49	12
Open ocean	40	16887	2533	24	800
Upwelling ocean	35	79	11	100	4
Continental shelf	30	2889	433	60	160
Algal bed and reef	15	167	24	200	12
Estuaries	15	367	56	151	21
Total marine	37	20387	3056	28	998
Total continental	7	7239	825	69	1016
Grand total	17	27626	3881	40	2013

Source: After Whittaker and Likens, 1973. Used with permission of the authors.

[a]Consumption, production, and biomass data obtained from original by multiplying carbon data by 2.22.

Table 4.12 Some Parameters of Energy Flow Through the Secondary Consumer (Carnivore) Trophic Level

	Utilization Efficiency, %	Assimilation Efficiency, %	Tissue Growth Efficiency, %	Ecological Growth Efficiency, %	Trophic Efficiency, %	Average Biomass, kcal m^{-2}	Gross Production Lost to Respiration and Excretion, %	Reference
Least weasel	—	97	2.3	2.2	—	0.0067	98	Golley, 1960
Marsh wren	—	70	0.5	0.4	—	0.17	99	Kale, 1965
Grasshopper mouse	—	78	5.7	4.2	—	0.033	95	Chew and Chew, 1970
Ecosystem								
Cedar Bog Lake, Minn.	44	91	42	38	19	—	58	Lindeman, 1942
Lake Mendota, Wis.	10	89	44	39	4	—	43	Juday, 1940
Silver Springs, Fla.	—	—	17	—	9	—	83	Odum, 1957

Intuitively, one might expect greater respiration losses at the secondary consumer level. After all, predators that must search for, pursue, overpower, and kill the cautious, swift, and strong herbivores that are their prey will have a large metabolic bill to pay for all that work. Herbivores, on the other hand, are generally moving through continuous communities of food plants which neither run away nor put up any physical resistance to being eaten. The situation requires more detailed consideration, however. Once a mammalian predator has captured an ungulate herbivore, it may not need to catch another for many days. Large carnivores often feed on the young, the old, the sick, or the maimed, and thus avoid the high energy cost of chasing and attacking fully grown, healthy adults. In contrast, the ungulate herbivore must spend almost all daylight hours searching for enough plant material of acceptable nutritional quality and palatability to satisfy its energy needs; a large proportion of the plants in a particular community will not satisfy these requirements. The metabolic costs to herbivores of processing large quantities of low-quality plant food is also higher than the cost to carnivores of processing smaller quantities of nutritious herbivore flesh. Some predators simply wait for their prey to come to them (spiders and ambush predators), whereas herbivores may cover long distances searching for food. With all these complications and with the relative scarcity of reliable data, one should be cautious in drawing firm conclusions about the relative magnitude of respiratory costs at the primary and secondary consumer trophic levels.

The assimilation efficiency of carnivores is generally higher than that of herbivores. Much of the plant material ingested by the latter is lignin and cellulose, which are often inefficiently used. On the other hand, only a relatively small proportion of herbivore biomass is indigestible to carnivores. The degree of chemical rearrangement between trophic levels is far greater between plants and herbivores

than between herbivores and carnivores, and the change is correspondingly less complete and more expensive in terms of metabolic energy.

D. Detritus Trophic Chains

We have already seen that in many terrestrial ecosystems, especially forests, herbivores normally utilize only a modest proportion of the NPP. Since much of this unused net production is invested in short-lived tissues such as leaves and reproductive structures, forests are characterized by substantial quantities of litterfall. This provides the major energy source for the saprotrophic organisms of the detritus trophic web, which also receive inputs from higher up the grazing trophic web. Because of low assimilation efficiencies, much of the plant material ingested by herbivores is promptly redirected to the detritus web in the form of feces, and additional transfers from the grazing to detritus webs result from the death of herbivores and carnivores, and carnivore defecation. The result is that for many ecosystems the detritus trophic web accounts for most of the postproducer energy flow.

Saprotrophic organisms such as seagulls, crabs, hyenas, and vultures are large and well known, but most of the decomposition of dead organic matter is accomplished by very small organisms: fungi and bacteria. The biomass of these decomposer organisms is often very small relative to the large quantity of energy passing through this trophic level—the result of the small size and short life span of many saprotrophic organisms. However, in some ecosystems the biomass of saprotrophs may be substantial.

Soil fauna (e.g., worms, millipedes, or springtails) are very important in the process of decomposition. The soft tissues of entire leaves are protected from decomposition by the surface cuticle, and even if this is removed, the rate of decomposition is often slow because the surface area of leaf fragments may be relatively small. Soil mesofauna break

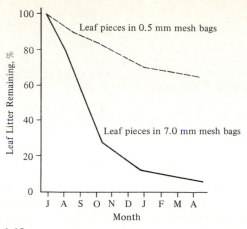

Figure 4.12
Decomposition of pieces of oak leaves contained in mesh bags that either exclude or permit entry of medium and large soil animals into the bags, where they can influence the rate of decomposition. (After Edwards and Heath, 1963. Used by permission of Dr. C. A. Edwards and North-Holland Publishing Company, Amsterdam.)

leaves up into large numbers of tiny pieces, which greatly increases the surface area available to microorganisms, exposes the more easily decomposed tissues, and may chemically alter the material in a way that improves it as a substrate for bacteria and fungi. Without this pretreatment, the fungi and bacteria that actually do most of the decomposition are must less efficient. This can easily be demonstrated by enclosing leaves in mesh bags of different mesh size and burying them in the forest floor. Leaves in bags that exclude the mesofauna decompose much more slowly than do leaves in bags that permit their entry (Figure 4.12).

Decomposition of litterfall varies in rate, in the chemical and physical products of decomposition, and in the organisms responsible. For example, bacteria tend to be dominant in the decomposition of deciduous angiosperm leaves,

whereas fungi normally dominate in the decomposition of the acidic litterfall of evergreen gymnosperms. Decomposition tends to be rapid when it is primarily bacterial, and slow when it is primarily fungal (Table 4.13).

Litter decomposition is influenced by several factors, including moisture, temperature, pH, the availability of O_2, the abundance of soil animals, the chemical and physical character of the litter, and the relative abundance of fungi and bacteria (see Section 4.9B and Chapter 5). These factors vary predictably between different geographical areas and it is possible to characterize different regions in terms of their rates of litter decomposition. A convenient way of expressing this rate is the ratio of the biomass of litterfall to the biomass of organic forest floor (Olson, 1963). The quantity of litterfall increases from the poles toward the equator, while the weight of forest floor shows the reverse trend. This pattern results because conditions of temperature and moisture and the chemical composition of the litter become less and less favorable for the organisms responsible for decomposition as one travels poleward from the equator. As a result, litterfall and net primary production both show an inverse relationship to the biomass of the forest floor, while the ratio of forest floor to litterfall (which is an index of resistance of litterfall to decomposition) increases as the weight of forest floor increases (see Figure 5.7).

The ratio of weight of forest floor to weight of annual litterfall has been called the organic matter *residence time* (Gosz, 1976). Generally, residence times have been based on aboveground litterfall. This can result in overestimates of residence time (underestimates of decomposition rates) in ecosystems where there is a large contribution of fine root litterfall. In Pacific silver fir stands in Washington, Grier et al. (1981) reported annual aboveground and belowground litterfall in a 23-year-old stand at 6.5 and 11.8 t ha^{-1}, with values of 4.6 and 12.2 in a 180-year-old stand. Organic

Table 4.13 Relationship Between Rate of Leaf Litter Decomposition and the Balance Between Bacteria and Fungi in Tennessee (Data from Witkamp, 1966)

Plant Species	Weight Loss in 12 Months, %	Carbon/Nitrogen Ratio	Number of Bacterial Colonies, millions g^{-1} dry weight of litter	Number of Fungal Colonies, thousands g^{-1} dry weight of litter	Bacteria/Fungi
Red mulberry	90	25	698	2650	264
Redbud	70	26	286	1870	148
White oak	55	34	32	1880	17
Loblolly pine	40	43	15	360	42

matter residence times in the forest floor based on aboveground litterfall only were estimated as 30 and 70 years in the young and old stands, respectively. Residence times based on *total* litterfall were reduced to 10 and 20 years, respectively (Vogt et al., 1983). Obviously, we will have to reexamine our understanding of forest ecosystem function as more data on fine root production and turnover become available.

There is a series of trophic levels beyond the saprotrophs analogous to secondary and tertiary consumers (primary and secondary carnivores) of the grazing food web. These levels involve larger organisms and therefore support a larger biomass than do the saprotrophs. The latter are generally analogous to herbivores because they depend primarily on energy in plant products, although some saprotrophs obtain their energy from the waste products and remains of consumers and are therefore analogous to carnivores. Secondary consumers in detritus food webs may feed exclusively in this web or they may feed in both detritus and grazing food webs. Microinvertebrates and earthworms are restricted to feeding on the bacteria and fungi decomposing soil organic matter, while a herbivore may consume the fruiting bodies of fungi as well as the green parts of plants. Generally, the farther up food webs one proceeds, the harder it is to categorize a particular organism as a member of either a grazing or a detritus food web.

4.5 Photosynthetic Efficiency of Forests

It was previously noted that the photosynthetic efficiency and productivity of forests often compares very favorably with that of agricultural ecosystems in the same region. This is rather interesting since many of the world's forests grow in inhospitable climates and/or on infertile soils in steep terrain. Most of the flat or gently sloping, adequately watered, well drained, and fertile land in areas with equitable climates was cleared for agricultural use centuries ago.

The apparent high efficiency and productivity of forests suggests that forests may be one of the more efficient forms of vegetation for converting light energy into plant material. We do not yet fully understand all the reasons for this, but it has been suggested that the following three factors may be important (Hellmers, 1964): (1) the degree of canopy closure, (2) the effect of light intensity, and (3) the retention of nighttime respiratory CO_2.

A. Degree of Canopy Closure

We have already seen in the discussion of photosynthetic efficiency that peak NPP is not reached until the horizontal upper surface area of leaves is about four times as great as the surface of land on which the plants are growing (i.e., a leaf area index of 4). We also saw that annual agricultural crops do not attain a leaf area index of 4 for several weeks after germination (Figure 4.9). Much of the growing season solar radiation falls on bare ground or on a photosynthetic surface with a leaf area index of less than 4. Agricultural yields have been shown to increase as leaf area index increases from 1 to 5, and it has been suggested that a value of 5 is required in grass communities in order to intercept 95% of the sunlight. Mature agricultural crops can have a leaf area index of 5 or more, but photosynthetic efficiency declines as the crops reach maturity, so we do not really know the relationship between production and leaf area index in annual crops at the higher index values (Wassink, 1959).

Most well-stocked forests have a leaf area index of 5 or more throughout most (deciduous trees) or all (evergreen trees) of the growing season. In some western U.S. conifer forests, total leaf areas of as high as 52 m^2 per square meter of ground have been observed (Waring et al., 1978). The high leaf area of forests is probably a partial explanation for their apparently superior photosynthetic performance. However, a word of caution is required concerning estimates of photosynthetic efficiency. Most estimates for forests have been obtained in medium-aged, well-stocked stands. It has been found that photosynthetic efficiency is lower in young and old beech stands than in medium-aged beech stands (Moller et al., 1954), a pattern similar to that of an agricultural crop. Because of this, it is possible that our view of the photosynthetic efficiency of forests is overly optimistic. If considered over the whole life of the crop (i.e., the rotation), the photosynthetic efficiency might be found to be somewhat lower than the published figures, although it would probably still be as high or higher than comparable figures for agricultural crops, and values for some young tree crops are known to be very high. Red alder growing in Vancouver, B.C., has been found to have a mean photosynthetic efficiency (based on growing season visible radiation) in the first 10 years of growth of 2.9%, with a range of 1.8–4.2% in stands of varying density (Smith, 1977).

B. Effect of Light Intensity

Photosynthetic efficiency increases as light intensity decreases (see Chapter 7). Values as high as 19% have been reported at intensities of one-tenth of full sunlight or less. It has been suggested that the average growing season light intensity is lower in areas in which the photosynthetic efficiency of forests has been measured than in areas for which we have agricultural efficiency data (e.g., Japan and Java for agricultural efficiencies, England and Denmark for forest efficiencies). This may contribute to the apparently higher efficiency of forests (Hellmers, 1964). However, it has not been definitely established that average light intensities were in fact different in the areas involved. Average light intensity was estimated by dividing total growing-season solar energy by the number of days in leaf, but unless one knows the number of daylight hours and how the light intensity varies over the growing season, this method does not give a reliable measure of actual light intensities. Although light intensity–efficiency relationships may well be involved, it is not yet possible to be certain just how important this relationship is in determining the apparent differences between forest and agricultural crops, and any real effect might be more a function of respiration than pho-

tosynthesis. Temperature differences accompanying differences in light intensity would affect the proportion of gross primary production that is lost in respiration, and vegetation in areas with cool nights would have a lower respiration loss and higher net photosynthetic efficiency. The tendency for many of the world's forests to grow in cooler areas with colder growing-season night temperatures than experienced by agricultural crops may contribute as much or more than light-intensity differences to the reported higher efficiency of forests.

C. Retention of Nocturnal CO_2

As we shall see in subsequent chapters, the availability of nutrients plays a very important role in determining the rate

Figure 4.13

Variation in atmospheric CO_2 concentrations at various heights within an oak-pine forest near New York. The data are for a 24-hour period during a temperature inversion (3:00 A.M. temperatures are shown). This climatic condition acts to restrict atmospheric stirring and to trap respiratory CO_2 in the layer of air near the ground. As a result, the daily depletion of CO_2 by photosynthesis and nocturnal enrichment by respiration can be seen. (After Woodwell and Botkin, 1970, Figure 3. Used by permission of Dr. G. M. Woodwell and Springer Verlag New York, Inc.)

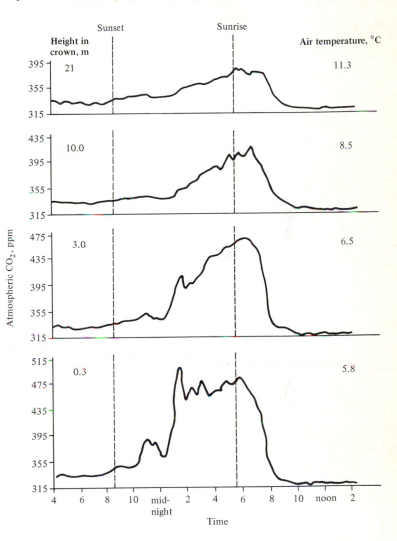

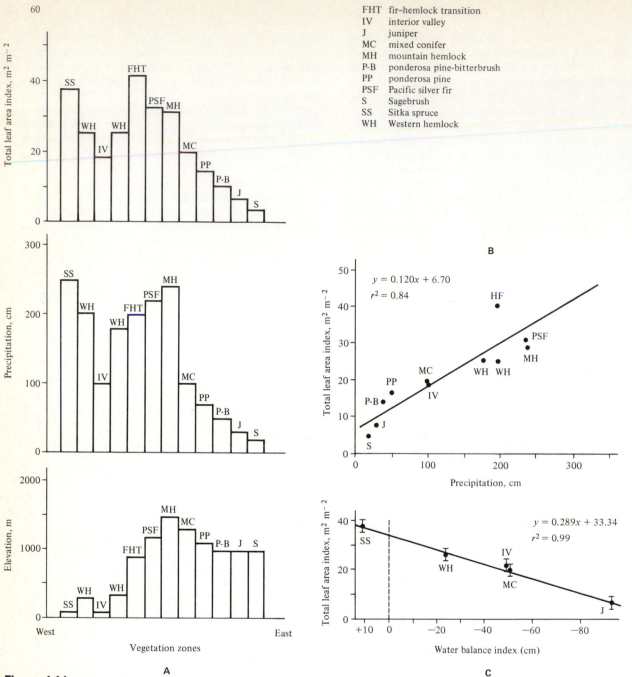

Figure 4.14
Total leaf area index (leaf surface area per m² of ground) and its relationship to elevation and precipitation in 12 major vegetation zones in Oregon (after Grier and Running, 1977). The vegetation zones lie along a W–E transect from the coast, over two mountain ranges, to a dry interior plateau. (A) Leaf area of major vegetation zones. (B) Relationship between leaf area and precipitation. (C) Relationship between leaf area and a water balance index for 5 forest zones. The water balance index is computed by adding soil water storage to measured growing season precipitation and then subtracting open-pan evaporation. (Used by permission of the Ecological Society of America.)

of plant growth. Carbon is one of the major constituents of organic matter, and it is taken up by the plant in the form of carbon dioxide (CO_2) gas from the air. CO_2 is present in the air at such low concentrations (about 0.03% by volume) that it is a limiting nutrient for photosynthesis and plant growth. Photosynthesis increases significantly with increasing concentrations of CO_2 and decreases at lower concentrations (Chapter 7). An actively photosynthesizing plant community depletes the CO_2 in the air around the leaves, whereas nocturnal plant respiration enriches it (Woodwell and Botkin, 1970) (Figure 4.13). This enrichment is augmented by the release of CO_2 from soil organic matter by saprotrophs in the detritus trophic web.

In an agricultural plant community there is an active exchange of air between the above- and within-crop air layers due to atmospheric turbulence. Only a fairly shallow layer of air near the ground is sheltered and calm. In contrast, forests have a deep layer of calm air below and within the lower canopy. Much of the CO_2 released at night in an agricultural crop is removed by air currents, only a small quantity being retained in the shallow calm layer. In forests, on the other hand, much of the nocturnal emission of CO_2 is retained within the air mass in contact with the tree crown until daylight, and morning photosynthesis in forests is supported by a greater supply of CO_2 than morning photosynthesis in an agricultural crop. It has been calculated that the extra CO_2 storage accounts for as much as 13% of the net production and photosynthetic efficiency in a forest stand (i.e., it could account for an increase in photosynthetic efficiency from 2.2 to 2.5%). In a 2-m-high agricultural crop it adds only 1% to production and photosynthetic efficiency (Hellmers, 1964).

Until our knowledge of photosynthetic efficiency under many different field situations is improved, we cannot be certain that forests are necessarily more efficient than agricultural crops. The available data suggest that they are, and there can be no doubt that even if their efficiencies have been overestimated, forests constitute a very efficient type of vegetation with which to harvest sunlight energy.

4.6   Leaf Area and Growth of Forests

Recent research in the Pacific Northwest has revealed some interesting relationships between the leaf area of forests and their growth (Gholz et al., 1976; Waring et al., 1978; Grier and Running, 1977; Waring et al., 1980). Total leaf area is reported to vary from 5 to 52 m^2 per square meter of ground surface, the highest values being found at

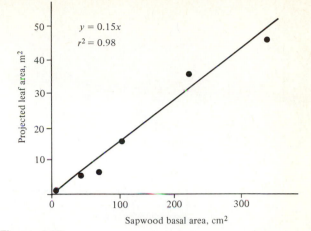

Figure 4.15
Leaf area of lodgepole pine *(Pinus contorta)* in relation to sapwood basal area. Projected leaf area is the horizontally-projected area of foliage, as opposed to the total leaf surface area. The data are for individual trees. (After Waring, 1980. Used by permission of Dr. R. H. Waring.)

middle elevations where winter snowpack accumulates and growing season temperatures are cool. Shrub and herb leaf area varies from 3 to 14% of the total. This variation in leaf area has been shown to be closely correlated with the water balance of the site (Figure 4.14); the drier the site, the lower the leaf area.

Leaf area is closely related to the basal area of sapwood (Grier and Waring, 1974), and, once the relationship for a species has been established (Figure 4.15), foliage surface area per tree can easily be estimated simply by boring the tree to obtain an increment core. Each tree species

Table 4.14 Ratios of Projected Leaf Area to Sapwood Basal Area for Selected Conifer Species Found Along a West–East Transect from the Humid Coast over Two Mountain Ranges to an Arid Interior Plateau in Oregon

Species	Environment	Ratio of Projected Leaf Area to Sapwood Basal Area, m^2 cm^{-2}
Sitka spruce	Humid	0.44
Douglas-fir	Moderate	0.32
Noble fir	Humid subalpine	0.27
Lodgepole pine	Continental	0.15
Mountain hemlock	Continental	0.16
Ponderosa pine	Semiarid	0.17
Western juniper	Arid	0.07

Source: Waring, 1980b. Used with permission of the NZ Forest Service and author.

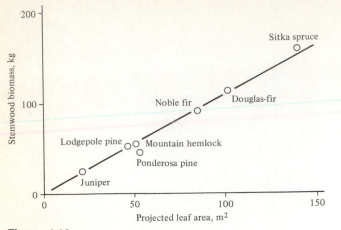

Figure 4.16
Relationship between biomass of stemwood and projected leaf area for individual specimens of seven tree species referred to in Table 4.14. All the trees had a dbh of 20 cm and 314 cm^2 of sapwood basal area. (After Waring, 1980. Used by permission of the NZ Forest Service and author.)

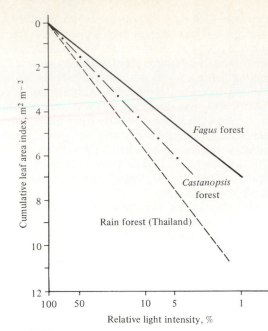

Figure 4.17
The intensity of light penetrating through a forest decreases exponentially as the leaf area increases. Each additional unit of leaf area index receives a rapidly diminishing quantity of solar energy and consequently contributes less and less to net growth. Note that the horizontal scale is logarithmic. (After Kira et al., 1969. Used by permission of Dr. Tatuo Kira.)

has a specific leaf area–sapwood basal area relationship, which reflects the type of climate in which it grows (Table 4.14).

Leaf area exhibits some interesting relationships to stemwood biomass on both an individual tree and a stand basis. Stemwood biomass shows a linear relationship to the projected leaf area of the tree, many species exhibiting a similar relationship (Figure 4.16). The potential maximum stemwood biomass accumulation in a stand also appears to be proportional to the development of stand leaf area (Waring, 1979).

Although high values for accumulated biomass are associated with high leaf areas, the efficiency with which the biomass is produced does not show a linear relationship to leaf area. As leaf area increases, an increasing proportion of the phytomass is operating in successively deeper shade (Figure 4.17) and therefore contributes less and less to the net production of photosynthate. This lowers the overall efficiency of growth per unit of leaf area as leaf area increases The result is that, in environments in which very high leaf areas can accumulate (humid forests), basal area growth for the stand may peak at less than maximum stand leaf area.

These relationships have not yet been studied under a wide range of conditions, but because they have very important implications for the management of commercial tree crops, they will undoubtedly receive more attention in the future.

4.7 Energy Cost/Benefit Relationships of Forest Production

Intensive forest management, especially forest harvesting, requires considerable amounts of energy. Road building, tree falling and bucking, log extraction, and transportation to the mill are all energy-intensive activities. As forestry becomes increasingly mechanized, the energy requirements of harvesting can, in some cases, increase by as much as 200%, although generally the switch from manual to fully mechanized harvesting would result in an increased use of petroleum products of only 15–30% (Bent et al., 1978). Increased use of fertilization, herbicides, insecticides, the introduction of mechanized thinning, mechanized site preparation, and mechanized planting are trends that are likely to continue, all of which will increase the energy demands of forest practice.

The processing of wood requires large amounts of energy, and in a forest-rich country such as Canada, wood

Table 4.15 Energy Benefit/Cost Analysis of Forest Production

A. Average Fuel Energy Costs of Silviculture

	kcal
Tree propagation (per kg seed)	
Seed collection	
Wild	126,413
Seed orchard	137,083
Seed processing	388,770
Regeneration	
Site preparation	
Southern U.S. (mechanical)	
Piling	823,696
Crushing	564,159
Western U.S. (burning)	323,923
Nursery production (per 1000 seedlings)	78,624
Greenhouse production (per 1000 seedlings)	41,198
Planting (per ha)	
Hand	388,560
Machine	306,987
Stand treatment (per ha)	
Brush control	498,752
Spacing	210,470
Fertilization	9,461,182

B. Energy Use by Silvicultural Activity

Activity	kcal	Per
Seed production	567,328	kg
Nursery seedlings	78,624	1000
Site preparation		
Slashburn: manual ignition	84,686	ha
Slashburn: helicopter ignition	323,799	ha
Mechanical piling	823,821	ha
Roll and chop	564,159	ha
Tree crush	564,159	ha
Ripping	564,159	ha
Bedding	270,248	ha
Planting		
Hand	388,560	ha
Machine	306,987	ha
Herbicide (aerial spray)	435,884	ha
Spacing	210,470	ha
Fertilizer (urea-N)	9,461,182	ha

C. Plantation Benefit/Cost Analysis

Species	Age	Management Intensity	Costs, kcal ha^{-1} × 10^3							Biomass Wood, m^3 ha^{-1}	Energy in Biomass, kcal ha^{-1}	Benefit/Cost Ratios	
			Site Preparation	Planting	Brush Contribution	Spacing	Fertilization	Fire Protection	Total Cost			1[a]	2[b]
Douglas-fir	30[c]	Average	324	388	—	—	—	74	786	301	4.35 × 10^8	554	22
	25[c]	High	324	558	529	210	9,462	62	11,147	308	4.45 × 10^8	40	15
	50[d]	High	324	558	—	210	56,766	121	58,513	1,239	17.8 × 10^8	31	12
Loblolly pine	25[c]	Average	887	388	—	—	—	62	1,337	244	3.4 × 10^8	264	21
	25[c]	High	887	561	529	29,683[e]	112,633	62	37,903	339	4.9 × 10^8	13	8

Source: Courtesy Weyerhaeuser Co., Tacoma, Wash.
[a]Energy content of wood produced/silvicultural energy costs.
[b]Energy content of wood produced/silvicultural + harvest + transportation-to-mill energy costs.
[c]Age at first commercial thinning.
[d]Age at final harvest.
[e]Spacing and a commercial thinning.

61

Table 4.16 Comparison of Energy Benefit/Cost of Harvesting in Scandinavia and Canada (Data from Ash et al., 1980)

| Location and Forest Type | Management Intensity | Energy Costs of Log Production, MJ m^{-3} | | | Benefit/Cost Ratio[a] |
		Harvest	Transport	Total	
Sweden	High	144	218	362	19
pine–spruce	Medium	37	41	78	90
Eastern Canada	High	243	264	507	14
spruce–fir	Medium	90	287	377	19
Western Canada	High	262	142	404	17
Douglas-fir–	Medium	90	90	180	39
Western hemlock					

[a]Energy equivalent of 1 m^3 of softwood = 6994 MJ. 1 MJ = 239 kcal.

processing is the largest single industrial user of power. Until the past decade, disposal of wood waste was a major problem for this industry, but the energy crisis has changed this. Use of mill wood waste to generate electricity is increasing, and many sawmills are now both energy self-sufficient and sellers of electrical power to the local grid.

The energy crises of the 1970's stimulated an examination of the concept of "the energy forest": a forest grown specifically to provide the fuel for a power station. At the present price of oil, the energy forest is not an economically viable prospect for most developed countries except in remote situations. However, fossil fuel may become more expensive and will eventually run out, and it is probable that energy forests will become a reality in some developed countries in the future. In countries like Brazil, this has already happened. Large areas of fast-growing *Eucalyptus* have been established there for the production of charcoal to be used to replace imported coal in the steel industry.

Forests can also contribute to the solution of the energy problem in other ways. Use of wood in buildings requires less energy than other materials, such as bricks, cement, or metal and plastic. The use of wood products for insulation reduces the use of fossil fuels for heating. The use of foliage and branches as cattle feed, or wood as a source of chemicals, can reduce the energy cost of cattle rearing and chemical production. Wood can also be converted to combustible gases or liquids that can themselves be used as fuel. Obviously, forests have an important role to play in the human energy budget, although this is not without potentially serious problems, some of which will be discussed in later chapters.

Until recently, energy benefit/cost analyses for contemporary forestry were harder to obtain than comparable figures for agriculture. There is increasing interest in such information, and in the next few years we should see many such analyses. Table 4.15 presents some data used by Weyerhaeuser Company to evaluate the energy benefit/cost ratio for forestry. Douglas-fir stands managed to first commercial thinning age yielded a benefit/cost ratio of 554 for average management intensity and 40 for intensive management, excluding the energy costs of harvest and transportation. Taken to a full rotation (50 years) with intensive management (five fertilizations with urea nitrogen fertilizer during the 20 years after commercial thinning), the ratio drops to 31. By comparison, average management to age 25 of a loblolly pine site would yield a ratio of 264, compared with 13 for intensive management. These ratios decline significantly when the energy costs of harvesting and delivery of logs to the mill, both energy-intensive activities, are included. However, final delivered-to-the-mill benefit/cost ratios varying from 22 to 8 still compare very favorably with agricultural values. Forestry is undoubtedly a relatively energy-efficient means of converting solar energy into biomass, harvesting the biomass, and converting it to a usable product. Table 4.16 presents some energy benefit/cost data for forest harvesting in Canada and Scandinavia. Figure 4.18 shows how the energy efficiency of forestry compares with that of other crop production activities.

4.8 Effects of Forest Management on Energy in the Forest Ecosystem

Forest management generally involves the production of a crop, and is therefore concerned with energy flow and storage. Many management practices influence energy in the forest, but this discussion will be limited to a consideration of the effects of clearcutting.

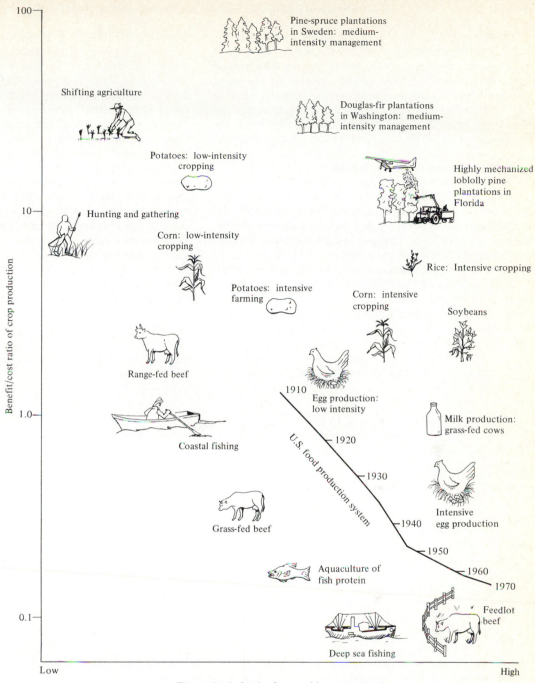

Figure 4.18

Energy benefit/cost ratios of various food and fiber crops produced with various levels of technological assistance. Primitive crop production (hunting-gathering and shifting agriculture) was much more energy efficient than modern feedlot production and deep-sea fishing. Low and medium intensity forestry are more energy efficient than high intensity forestry. Forestry is generally more energy efficient than agriculture. (After Steinhart and Steinhart, 1974. Copyright 1974 by the American Association for the Advancement of Science. Data on forestry from Ash et al., 1980, and J. E. Burks, personal communication.)

Clearcutting is a method of forest harvesting that has been used throughout the world, particularly in the harvest of previously unmanaged old-growth forests. The method has been variously defined as the removal of the entire standing crop; complete cutting; a silvicultural system in which the old crop is cleared over a considerable area at one time (Ford-Robertson, 1971). Basically, clearcutting is the removal of all of the trees on the logged area at one harvest.

A. Redistribution of Forest Biomass

The uncut mature forest represents an enormous accumulation of energy. Maximum aboveground biomass of 422, 575, and 415 t ha^{-1} has been reported for temperate deciduous, temperate evergreen hardwood, and tropical forests, respectively, while the biomass of cool temperate coniferous forests in Japan and the northeastern U.S. can exceed 600 t ha^{-1} (Art and Marks, 1971). An old-growth subalpine forest in southwestern British Columbia was reported to have an aboveground biomass of 731 t ha^{-1} (Krumlik, 1979), while aboveground biomass in Douglas-fir, western hemlock, and noble fir forests in the Oregon Cascade Mountains is reported to vary from 734 to 1773 t ha^{-1} (Zobel et al., 1976). Even higher values are reported for coast redwood forests in northern California where a stand

that exceeded 1000 years in age had a stem biomass alone of 3461 t ha^{-1} (Waring and Franklin, 1979). Converted to energy at 4000 cal g^{-1}, this would amount to 1.38 × 10^{10} kcal ha^{-1}, or the equivalent of about 2000 tons of coal. In addition to this, there is the energy contained in the forest floor. Forest floor biomass prior to logging in the Oregon coast range has been reported to vary from 22 to 85 t ha^{-1} (Youngberg, 1966). Table 4.17 shows forest floor biomass values for some other areas.

When a forest is clearcut, there are several important changes in the distribution of energy and the pathways of energy flow. First, by removing the overstory canopy, the entry of energy into the ecosystem by photosynthesis is more or less eliminated. Second, there is the potential for a large increase in the energy flow through the detritus food web. Depending on the type of harvesting, variable quantities of tree biomass *(slash)* are deposited on the ground. In *whole-tree harvesting* (removal of all aboveground biomass), very little slash is added to the forest floor (apart from the stumps and roots of the cut trees), whereas following clearcutting in some old-growth forests in the Douglas-fir region of western Oregon and Washington, the slash is reported to weigh between 67 and 516 t ha^{-1} (Dell and Ward, 1971).

Table 4.17 Forest Floor Weights[a] for Various Forest Types[b]

Location	Dominant Vegetation	Age, yr	Forest Floor Weight t ha^{-1}	Reference
Oregon, U.S.	*Abies, Tsuga* (46 sites)	Old growth	61	Williams and Dyrness, 1967
Alaska, U.S.	*Betula* (7 sites)	25–120	41	van Cleve and Noonan, 1971
Washington, U.S.	Conifers	Old growth	103	Gessel and Balci, 1965
Ontario, Canada	*Pinus contorta*	55	26	Foster and Morrison, 1976
Arizona, U.S.	*Pinus ponderosa*	49	47	Klemmedson, 1975
California, U.S.	*Pinus radiata*	30	60	Kittredge, 1940
New York, U.S.	*Pinus resinosa*	37	37	Stutzbach et al., 1972
Massachusetts, U.S.	*Pinus strobus*	34–96	43	Mader and Lull, 1968
Alaska, U.S.	*Populus* (7 stands)	20–120	42	van Cleve and Noonan, 1971
New Hampshire, U.S.	*Acer, Fagus*	200	89	Covington, 1976
New Mexico, U.S.	*Abies*	—	80	Wollom, 1973
Colorado, U.S.	*Abies lasiocarpa*	—	103	Snell et al., 1979
Germany	*Fagus*	80	39	Ulrich in Cole and Rapp, 1981
Alaska, U.S.	*Picea mariana*	55	133	van Cleve in Cole and Rapp, 1981
New Brunswick, Canada	*Pinus banksiana*	49	129	MacLean, 1978[c]

[a]Forest floor weight data are complicated by the failure to establish a common definition as to which root sizes are included in the estimate and which are excluded as being plant rather than forest floor materials.

[b]The examples were chosen to represent upper limits. Many studies have reported lower values.

[c]Datum from a fire-killed stand. The fallen dead trees, most of which were not yet incorporated into the forest floor, were included in the estimate. This provides a second illustration of the difficulties in comparing data from different studies.

B. Changes in Detritus Food Web Energy Flow

Following clearcutting there is characteristically a period of relatively rapid reduction in the thickness and biomass of the forest floor. For example, removal of tree cover in an eastern deciduous hardwood forest resulted in a loss of 23% of the biomass and 3 cm of the depth of the forest floor over the first three post-devegetation years (Dominski, 1971). This loss is partly due to the termination of litterfall inputs and partly to the accelerated decomposition that results from an increase in the flow of energy through the detritus food web.

Although there are reports of a marked decrease in the forest floor following logging in both hardwoods (e.g., Drobikov, 1969) and conifers (Cole and Gessel, 1963; Shibota et al., 1951), there are also a few reports of either no loss (Carmean, 1959; Suchting and Christmann, 1935) or of only very small reductions even after 10–20 years (e.g., Diebold, 1942).

Increased detritus energy flow following clearcutting is the combined result of both increases in the quantity of decomposable organic matter and changes in the condition of the forest floor. Summer daytime temperatures in the forest floor are warmer than before logging because of the removal of tree shade, and there is no longer any phenolic-compound-rich throughfall from the overstory that can inhibit decomposer organisms (Kowal, 1969; King and Heath, 1967). Cutting of trees results in the breakdown of mycorrhizal relationships, a reduction in the mycorrhizal fungi, and an increase in the activity of free-living saprotrophs. A study in New Zealand suggested that the fungal symbionts of *Pinus radiata* roots actually suppress the decomposition of the pine needle litter. By cutting a trench around small plots in a pine stand and thereby eliminating living mycorrhizal roots and their fungal symbionts, needle decomposition and loss of forest floor biomass were accelerated. A laboratory study showed that this was probably due to the suppression of free-living, litter-decomposing microbes by mycorrhizal symbionts (Gadgil and Gadgil, 1971, 1975).

The extent to which energy flow increases in detritus food webs following clearcutting depends upon the effects of the clearcutting on several factors (Bollen, 1974).

1. *Water*. Optimum conditions for microbial activity occur at 50% soil water-holding capacity. Excess moisture limits activity because of poor aeration, while decomposer organisms become inactive at low moisture levels. Clearcutting can reduce the rate of decomposition in hot, dry climates or where the clearcutting leads to soil waterlogging. Minimum and maximum water contents for active decomposition are 5 and 80%, respectively. When logs and forest floors become dry, decomposition becomes very slow.

2. *Temperature*. Extreme temperatures limit decomposer activity, and in areas with cold soils clearcutting will increase detritus energy flow by raising soil temperatures. Conversely, in areas with hot summers clearcutting can decrease decomposition by raising surface and/or slash temperatures to lethal levels. Minimum and maximum temperatures for decomposition are usually 2 and 40°C, respectively. However, in some environments (e.g., below the snow in subalpine forests) decomposition may be quite active at about 0°C.

3. *Aeration*. Maximum decomposer activity requires good aeration to supply O_2 and prevent toxic accumulations of CO_2. Where the activity of N-fixing bacteria plays a role in decomposition, exchange of N_2 may also be important. Where harvesting causes soil compaction and/or waterlogging, anaerobic conditions may be created which reduce decomposition.

4. *pH*. Low pH encourages fungal activity whereas bacteria are important in decomposition under less acidic conditions. Extreme pH values limit all decomposer activity; minimum and maximum values of pH for biological decomposition are about 4 and 10, respectively. Forest floor pH usually increases after clearcutting as the result of the release of divalent cations by the process of mineralization.

5. *Food supply*. Utilization of the energy in the forest floor requires that the microbes have access to an adequate supply of nutrients. If the C/N ratio is too high, the energy cannot be passed along the food web. Optimum rates of decomposition occur at a ratio of readily available carbon to nitrogen of about 25:1. Douglas-fir sapwood, heartwood, bark, and needles have ratios of 548:1, 429:1, 491:1, and 58:1, respectively. These components decompose slowly until the ratio approaches the optimum by loss of C or gain of N. In comparison, rapidly decomposing alfalfa hay has a value of 18:1 (Bollen, 1974). C/N ratio is not always a reliable predictor of decomposition rates, however. The presence or absence of various organic chemicals such as lignin and tannin can alter the relationship between C/N ratio and decomposition rate.

The acceleration in forest floor decomposition that characteristically follows clearcutting has been known for a long time (references in Lutz and Chandler, 1946), but has not been quantified for many forest types. Generally there is a period following harvesting when forest floor biomass declines, after which it rebuilds toward some eventual steady-state value. Whether or not this steady state is achieved depends upon whether or not another disturbance intervenes and again decreases forest floor biomass. Studies in the

Adirondack Mountains of New York suggest that a reasonably steady-state forest floor biomass is reached under yellow birch–red spruce stands at about 300 years of age with a value of about 265 t ha^{-1} (McFee and Stone, 1965). Attainment of steady state is believed to take longer in some western North American forests, if indeed it ever occurs. Fire, insects, disease, wind, or humans generally intercede before steady state is reached. A value of 158 t ha^{-1} has been reported for old-growth Douglas-fir (Gessel and Balci, 1965), while old-growth subalpine forests in southwestern B.C. have accumulations of up to 162 t ha^{-1} (Kimmins, unpublished data). In some cool, humid old-growth forests in coastal British Columbia that have been free of fire for many centuries, the depth of the forest floor on some sites can exceed 1 m, which would weigh in excess of 1200 t ha^{-1} if this depth is achieved over significant areas (based on a bulk density value of 0.12 g cm^{-3}).

Loss of forest floor biomass and depth following clearcutting can have several effects on the ecosystem. The water and nutrient storage capacity of the forest floor may be reduced, which can be undesirable in hot, dry climates and for infertile sites, but desirable for cold mineral soils. On sites where the forest floor has adverse chemical properties or where deep layers of low bulk density material pose problems for regeneration (because it dries rapidly in the summer), the reduction in depth may favor the reestablishment of a tree crop.

As the pioneer plant community reestablishes a foliage canopy, the entry of energy into the ecosystem is restored. This reestablishes litterfall inputs to the forest floor, much of which decomposes rapidly. The development of summer shading increases the moisture levels in the slash and forest floor, which promotes decomposition, especially in hot, dry environments. However, as a tree canopy develops and succession proceeds, the type of litterfall changes, mycorrhizal fungi begin to dominate the soil microflora, and decomposition rates slowly return to prelogging values. Replanting the area obviously influences both the speed with which these changes occur and the type of litter inputs to the forest floor.

C. Changes in Grazing Food Web Energy Flow

Accompanying the increase in detritus food web energy flow, there is a reduction in grazing food web energy flow. The degree of reduction is proportional to the reduction in usable and accessible living plant biomass. Where all living plants are eliminated, so is the grazing food web. However, clearcuts often leave advanced regeneration intact, and the shrubs and herbs in the understory often respond rapidly to the increased availability of light, moisture, and nutrients.

Coupled with the invasion of pioneer herbs and shrubs of early succession[4], this rapidly reestablishes the grazing food web, often at a higher level of energy flow than prelogging. The greater physical accessibility, palatability, and nutritive value of the early seral vegetation can result in more diverse, abundant, and productive animal communities in clearcuts than in the original uncut forest, as long as the animals' requirements for shelter and winter range are satisfied.

4.9   Summary

Energy is the single most essential ingredient of life, and all organisms are energy dependent. The quest for energy pervades the lives of all living things, and as a result ecosystems are organized into sequences of energy dependencies that give an internal structure to the system. This structure is in the form of a trophic web, which can be divided into a number of major stages (trophic levels) of energy transfer.

The efficiency of energy transfer from one trophic level to the next is generally low, but it tends to be greater in aquatic than in terrestrial ecosystems. As a consequence, aquatic trophic chains tend to have more stages (levels) than terrestrial trophic chains. The efficiency of energy transfer at specific points along a trophic chain depends more upon the size, metabolism, physiology, diet, and habitat of the organism involved than on the particular trophic level at which the transfer is taking place.

The biomass of any particular trophic level or population depends upon the balance of inputs and outputs of energy. The size and longevity of organisms are important determinants of biomass, but the contribution of a particular group of organisms to energy flow is not proportional to their biomass. Generally, the smaller the organisms, the greater their utilization of energy per unit of biomass.

Detritus trophic chains (which generally involve smaller organisms than grazing trophic chains) account for most of the post-producer energy flow in terrestrial ecosystems, whereas grazing trophic chains tend to dominate in aquatic ecosystems.

Forests constitute one of the most efficient types of terrestrial vegetation for harvesting solar energy, especially in inhospitable environments. They contribute to world net primary production disproportionately to their area and make up the majority of the world's living plant biomass. Forest productivity is closely related to leaf area, optimum

---

[4]The terms succession and seral are discussed in Chapter 15.

productivity in humid environments being attained at intermediate leaf areas.

By the beginning of the 1980s, it became apparent that after a brief absence (of about 100 years) from the energy scene, biomass is about to make a comeback as a significant contributor to national energy budgets in developed countries. Developing nations never escaped from this dependency, and with the real possibility of a world wood famine in the next few decades, wood appears to be about to regain some of its historic importance as a major factor in human cultural evolution.

Forestry practices have become increasingly energy intensive over the past three decades. Energy limitations will probably spur the development of "small technology," energy self-sufficiency, and biological solutions to problems in forestry.

Forest management has a significant impact on the quantity and distribution of energy in, and the subsequent energy flows through, the forest ecosystem. Production forestry is largely concerned with manipulating energy flows, and the forester should therefore understand the energy effects of management.

5 Biogeochemistry: Cycling of Nutrients in Ecosystems

5.1 Introduction

Chapter 4 examined the entry of energy into, its distribution and transfer within, and the ultimate loss of energy from ecosystems. This way of looking at ecosystems may be strange to some people. Our senses of sight, hearing, touch, smell, and taste recognize trees, shrubs, mosses, animals, fish, and birds rather than accumulations of solar energy at different trophic levels, yet this is what they are. We are aware of animals eating plants and other animals, and of fungi decomposing dead plant and animal material rather than energy flowing through grazing or detritus trophic webs, yet this is what is happening. Living organisms are fundamentally nothing more than accumulations of solar energy in association with certain chemical elements that have been sequestered from the soil and atmosphere. When we express concern about the productivity of a forest or a farm, we are really concerned about the flow of energy and the dynamics of the associated nutrient chemicals.

The beginnings of life are thought to have been the synthesis of organic molecules through the combination of solar energy (or chemical energy from the inorganic envi-

ronment) with appropriate assemblages of atoms (e.g., Dickerson, 1978). Without energy these atoms could not have been assembled into complex, high-energy molecules of living matter. Conversely, without the appropriate atoms, the energy necessary for life could not have been captured and stored. Movement and storage of energy in ecosystems are inseparable from the accumulation, storage, transfer, and recycling of the chemical elements associated with this energy. Understanding one requires knowledge of the other. The study of the distribution and dynamics of these chemical elements is the focus of the ecological subdiscipline known as *biogeochemistry*.

Almost all of the energy moving through ecosystems comes from a single source: the sun. In comparison, the source of the chemicals that make this energy flow possible is more complex. It includes the atmosphere, soil and rocks (the lithosphere), and water bodies (the hydrosphere). Although the sun is constantly losing energy and will eventually "burn" itself out, this event is occurring on an astronomical time scale. On a geological time scale, the supply of solar energy to a particular biogeocoenose can conveniently be considered to be inexhaustible. In contrast, the supply of chemicals for energy capture in that biogeocoenose is finite, as is the total quantity of chemicals on the earth (disregarding the small but continuous addition of meteorites from space). Of all the chemicals contained in the earth, only some of those in a thin layer at the interface of the atmosphere with the lithosphere and hydrosphere are available for participation in the energy fixation process.

Energy enters ecosystems almost entirely by the process of photosynthesis. It is stored temporarily in the energy bonds of various organic molecules such as adenosine triphosphate (ATP), a molecule that has been referred to as the "universal fuel of life" (Deevey, 1970). These organic molecules are passed along one or many trophic chains until the molecule is broken down into simple inorganic components, at which point the energy is released. This energy may be converted to heat and lost from the system in the performance of work. Alternatively, it may be reinvested in new chemical bonds during the synthesis of new organic molecules (with appropriate losses according to the second law of thermodynamics). In this way a quantum (a small "package" or quantity) of energy may be used as the bond energy of several different organic molecules before it is eventually converted into heat during the accomplishment of work and lost from the ecosystem.

Energy enters, flows through, and is ultimately lost from an ecosystem. It does not cycle because it is not reused once it has been converted to heat. The chemical elements involved in this energy flow behave differently. Once they are released from their association with energy in an organic molecule, they are returned to the nonliving part of the ecosystem, where they may again become available for uptake by plants. Once in plants, they are reunited with solar energy in the form of a new organic molecule. Alternatively, they may be moved to another ecosystem or may go into long-term storage. Chemicals associated with energy flow (hereinafter referred to as *nutrients*) are therefore cycled: they are reused within the ecosystem indefinitely, unless they are transferred to the cycle of another ecosystem or are converted to a long-term immobile form.

The nutrients necessary for organic production at either producer or consumer trophic levels are generally present in the abiotic environment at concentrations well below those required for active growth. In spite of this, organisms in mature ecosystems such as forests contain large quantities and appreciable concentrations of nutrients. That this can be so is evidence of the very well developed ability of plants and, to a lesser extent of animals, to concentrate nutrients from very low concentration sources in their environment. In fact, the processes of nutrient accumulation and conservation are so efficient that plant communities that have not been disturbed for a long time may become relatively independent of the mineral soil for the supply of many of their nutrient requirements. Their needs can be largely satisfied from the atmosphere and from the nutrients accumulated within the living or dead biomass in the system.

The cycling of nutrients in ecosystems is complex. Some elements cycle predominantly between the living organism and the atmosphere, whereas others generally cycle between organisms and the soil. Some elements follow both pathways. There is also an internal cycle within plants and animals that acts to conserve nutrients within individual organisms. Based on these differences, the cyclic movements of elements in ecosystems can be assigned to one or more of three major types of cycles: the geochemical cycle, the biogeochemical cycle, and the biochemical cycle (Figure 5.1).

1. *Geochemical cycles: exchanges of chemicals between ecosystems.* Wind transports nutrients in dust and rain from one biogeocoenose to another over distances that vary from as little as a hundred meters to as much as thousands of kilometers. Streamwater transports nutrients from forests to oceans, and water moving through the soil can carry nutrients from upslope to downslope ecosystems. Carbon dioxide (CO_2) released from a respiring tree in one valley may be blown over a mountain range to be reabsorbed by a photosynthesizing tree in the valley on the other side. The spatial scale of geological cycles is generally large (greater than hundreds of meters) and the cycle generally does not follow the same spatial pathway repeatedly. Once a nutrient has left a particular ecosystem, it will probably never return. The time scale is generally long (millions of years in the case of nutrients deposited in oceanic sediments), although it can be quite short, as in the case of CO_2, which may enter a forest ecosystem and leave again in a matter of hours. Alternatively, the CO_2 may be combined in organic matter that remains undecomposed in the same ecosystem for thousands of years.

2. *Biogeochemical cycles: exchanges of chemicals within an ecosystem.* Nitrogen absorbed by tree roots from decomposing litter on the forest floor may be translocated to the young developing leaves and returned to the forest floor when these leaves become leaf litterfall. Potassium in the foliage of shrubs may enter a grazing food chain when the shrubs are browsed by a deer, and may then be returned to the forest floor in the urine of a mountain lion that catches and eats the deer in the same biogeocoenose. Once in the forest floor, the potassium is generally recovered efficiently by the shrubs or other vegetation. The spatial scale of biogeochemical cycles is generally small, involving uptake from the soil beneath an individual plant and return to the same area. Animals, wind, or water may redistribute nutrients over longer distances within the biogeocoenose, and can also transfer nutrients from biogeochemical to geochemical cycles by transporting the nutrients out of the biogeocoenose. The time scale of biogeochemical cycles is generally shorter than geochemical cycles. It can be as short as a few hours, as in the case of potassium uptake and loss by foliar leaching, or as long as thousands of years as in the case of calcium stored in the woody tissues of long lived trees. Perhaps the major characteristic of biogeochemical cycles, especially in forest ecosystems, is that most of the nutrients in the cycle normally remain within a particular ecosystem (biogeocoenose). They are efficiently retained and accumulated with only modest losses to geochemical cycles.

3. *Biochemical cycles: redistribution of chemicals within individual organisms.* The term *biochemical cycle* has generally been used in reference to plants, although animals exhibit similar physiological functions. Nutrients are conserved within plants by removing them from short-lived tissues such as leaves before they are shed. The nutrients are translocated to younger, actively growing tissues or to storage sites. Animals regulate the chemical composition of excreta in a similar manner by removing required nutrients from, and adding unwanted or excess chemicals to waste material before it is eliminated from the body. Both the time and size scales of biochemical cycles are very much smaller

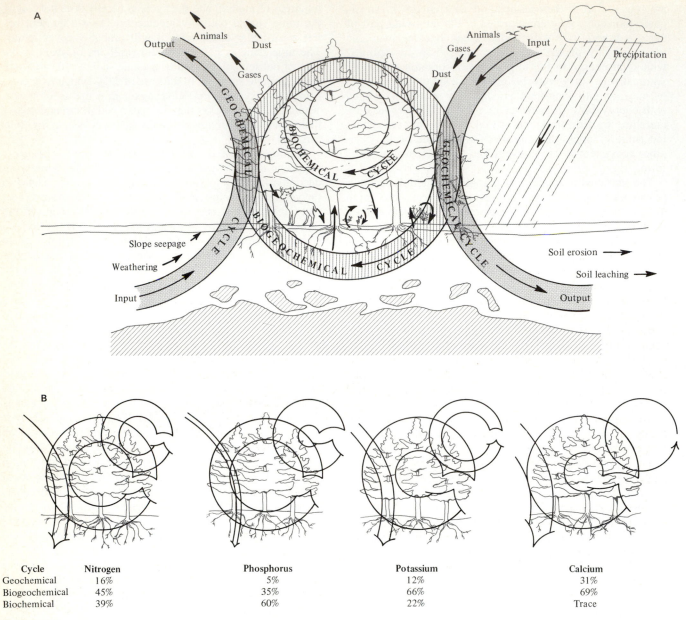

Figure 5.1

(A) The three major types of nutrient cycle: geochemical (between ecosystems), biogeochemical (within an ecosystem), and biochemical (within an organism; also referred to as internal cycling). (B) Percent of the nutrient dynamics in a forest ecosystem accounted for by the three cycles. The relative importance of the three cycles varies for different nutrients. Data for a 20-year-old loblolly pine plantation.

Cycle	Nitrogen	Phosphorus	Potassium	Calcium
Geochemical	16%	5%	12%	31%
Biogeochemical	45%	35%	66%	69%
Biochemical	39%	60%	22%	Trace

than the other two types of cycles because they occur within individual organisms as a part of active metabolic processes.

In this chapter we examine these three cycles in some detail. We then examine the biogeochemistry of some human activities, and how biogeochemical information can be useful in the classification and management of the world's forests. Before embarking on the discussion of cycles, it is necessary to consider the biological mechanisms by which the nutrients in these cycles help determine productivity and energy flow in ecosystems. These mechanisms are referred to as plant and animal nutrition.

5.2 Plant Nutrition: Energy and Nutrients at the Primary Producer Trophic Level

Life may have had its beginnings in shallow bodies of water as the chance combination of certain atoms in certain ratios. It is thought that under the influence of energy from ultraviolet solar radiation or lightning, this could have led to the formation of organic molecules. Such chance combinations would have occurred rarely, but it is thought that over millions of years, shallow lakes and coastal waters probably became dilute solutions of these organic molecules. Life itself is thought to have begun when certain of these complex molecules began to replicate themselves by acquiring the energy and atoms stored in other organic molecules. The earliest forms of life were probably similar to the anaerobic bacteria that we know today: saprophytic heterotrophs utilizing fermentation as the means of liberating energy from organic molecules in their environment.

Evolution has elaborated magnificently on this original theme, but the basic mechanisms of energy acquisition and storage are still present in all living organisms. Before either life, biosynthesis, or energy storage and transfer can occur, certain critical combinations of atoms at the approriate concentrations must be present. Life and energy flow are totally dependent on the adequate nutrition of individual organisms.

A. Inorganic Chemistry of Plants

Careful analysis will reveal that a very large number of chemical elements can be found in plants. Many or even most of these elements are present at very low concentrations: as low as one part by weight of the element to one billion parts by weight of the plant (one part per billion, or 10^{-9}, or ppb), or even one part per trillion (10^{-12}, or ppt). Only a few are found at concentrations greater than one part per million (10^{-6}, or ppm), and very few are found at con-

centrations that can be expressed as percentages by weight of plant substance (parts per hundred, or %). Many of the elements found in plants have no known role in plant metabolism. Others *must* be present before the plant can grow and function normally and are therefore referred to as *essential nutrients*. Whether or not a particular element is an essential nutrient cannot be guessed from its concentration. Some elements that are present at concentrations of only a few ppm (*micronutrients*) are as essential to the nutrition of the plant as elements that are present at concentrations of several percent (*macronutrients*).

Characteristic concentrations of the 16 elements that are considered essential for the growth of most plants are presented in Table 5.1. These figures represent average values for a wide variety of plants and will therefore be inaccurate for many individual species. For example, there are some plant species for which calcium is a micronutrient rather than a macronutrient. Some species require sodium or silicon as macronutrients. Most plants have no known physiological requirement for these elements even though they are found at some level in all plants. Selenium is toxic to most plants, but species that have evolved to tolerate selenium-rich soils may require it. The relative concentrations of different elements vary between different parts of the same plant, at different times of the year, and with variation in the age and physiological condition of the plant.

B. Acquisition of Nutrients

Approximately 95% of the dry weight of plants is accounted for by atoms of hydrogen, oxygen, carbon, and nitrogen, the major chemical constituents of biomass. The remaining 5% is divided unequally among the other 12 essential nutrients and numerous nonessential elements. Plants must obtain their nutrients in the required proportions from sources in their environment that have a very different composition, and selective uptake from the lithosphere, the atmosphere, and the hydrosphere is an essential part of plant physiology. The source of different nutrients for uptake varies according to their availability to plants rather than according to their absolute abundance. For example, although hydrogen and oxygen are abundant in the lithosphere, they are largely in an unavailable form, so plants must depend on the atmosphere and the hydrosphere for these two nutrients.

The earliest forms of plant life were aquatic. They were bathed in dilute solutions of nutrients, and since they were small, none of the cells were far from the nutrient solution. Consequently, these plants did not require any special morphological adaptations for nutrient acquisition. The situation on land is different, and the development of land plants could not occur until the problem of nutrient acquisition on

Table 5.1 Average Concentrations of Essential Nutrient Elements in Adequately Nourished Plants (After Epstein, 1972; Mason, 1966)

Element	Chemical Symbol	Atomic Weight	Concentration In Dry Matter ppm	Concentration In Dry Matter %	Relative Abundance of Atoms in Dry Matter	Average Concentration in the Earth's Crust, ppm
Macronutrients						
Hydrogen	H	1.01	—	6	60,000,000	1,400
Carbon	C	12.01	—	45	40,000,000	200
Oxygen	O	16.00	—	45	30,000,000	466,000
Nitrogen	N	14.01	—	1.5	1,000,000	20
Potassium	K	39.10	—	1.0	250,000	25,900
Calcium	Ca	40.08	—	0.5	125,000	36,300
Magnesium	Mg	24.32	—	0.3	80,000	20,900
Phosphorus	P	30.98	—	0.2	60,000	1,050
Sulfur	S	32.07	—	0.1	30,000	260
Micronutrients						
Chlorine	Cl	35.46	100	—	3,000	130
Boron	B	10.82	20	—	2,000	10
Iron	Fe	55.85	100	—	2,000	50,000
Manganese	Mn	54.94	50	—	1,000	950
Zinc	Zn	65.38	20	—	300	70
Copper	Cu	63.54	6	—	100	55
Molybdenum	Mo	95.95	0.1	—	1	1.5

"dry" land had been solved. The evolutionary answer to this problem was not to develop different biochemical mechanisms of nutrient uptake, but to make morphological adaptations that permitted uptake from solutions in the terrestrial environment. Roots exploited the soil solution, while modified leaves permitted the entry of gases into intracellular spaces where they were dissolved in thin films of water bathing the cells, and then absorbed.

The acquisition of an adequate, balanced supply of nutrients from the soil requires a major effort by terrestrial plants: the investment of a large proportion of their annual net production in the growth and maintenance of roots. Nutrient uptake from the thin layers of moisture surrounding soil particles requires very intimate contact between roots and the soil volume, and to achieve this, plants produce an extraordinarily large length and surface area of roots. A single rye plant grown for 4 months in approximately 0.05 m^3 (2 ft^3) of soil was found to have a root system with a total surface area of 639 m^2 (6875 ft^2) and a total length of 623 km (387 mi) (Dittmer, 1937). In a study of small and fine roots (<5 mm diameter) in subalpine forests of coastal British Columbia, Nuszdorfer (1982) found that the overstory had a root surface area of 7.3–11.9 m^2 m^{-2} and a root length of 3.8–6.5 km m^{-2}; understory values were 0.5–3.2 and 0.7–4.7, for ecosystem totals of 9.7–15.1 and 5.8–11.3 for area and length, respectively. This length is equal to between 1.5 and nearly 3 times the circumference

of the earth! It is not surprising that plants have been described as "solar-powered, chemical machines that mine the soils for minerals."

C. Nutritional Deficiencies

The definition of an adequate supply of a particular nutrient is difficult. It depends on the relative abundance and availability of other elements, the nutritional demands of the plant species, and the environmental conditions under which they are growing. Nutritional adequacy or deficiency has usually been defined empirically by observing the growth response of a plant to additions of the nutrient in question (Figure 5.2). Deficiency is defined as a condition in which an increase in the availability of a nutrient results in an increase in growth or reproductive performance of the plant. As the availability of a nutrient to a deficient plant increases, growth will increase rapidly, but the concentration of the nutrient in the plant will show little change because of dilution of the newly absorbed nutrient by the newly captured carbon, which is present in increased abundance because the improved nutrition has increased the rate of photosynthesis. As the condition of adequate nutrition is reached, or if some other nutrient or environmental factor becomes limiting to growth, uptake may continue and tissue concentrations will start to rise without any increase in the rate of plant growth or in biomass. If the rate of uptake increases further without any increases in growth or repro-

Figure 5.2

Relationship between the growth of a plant and the concentration of a nutrient in its tissue. (Modified after Ulrich and Hill, 1967.) If an addition of the nutrient increases plant growth but has little effect on the concentration of the nutrient in the plant, the plant is nutrient deficient. If such an addition results in little change in growth but an increase in concentration, the plant is adequately nourished. For an alternative method of assessing plant nutrition, see Figure 10.13. (Reproduced by permission of Soil Science Society of America and A. Ulrich.)

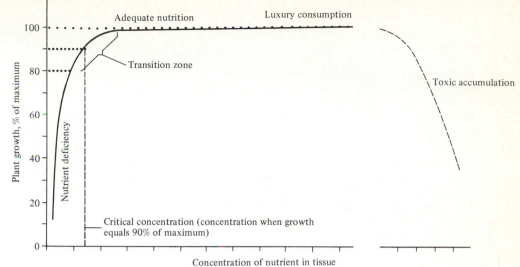

duction, the plant is said to be experiencing "luxury consumption." If high rates of luxury consumption continue, the element can accumulate to concentrations that are inimical to the plant, and growth may decline.

The concentration of nutrients in tree foliage is used by both foresters and agriculturalists to gauge the nutritional status of their crops. However, the concentration of a particular nutrient in a particular tissue cannot be used as a direct indicator of plant nutrient status.

The absolute level at which a nutrient is deficient often depends upon the level of other nutrients. For example, plants can be grown at very low levels of calcium when other divalent cations (ions with two positive charges) are absent. As the availability of these other cations increases, the calcium requirement increases greatly, and unless the calcium supply improves, growth ceases. Apparently, calcium acts not only as a nutrient, but also in the reduction of toxic effects of other cations. High levels of calcium in soil can induce phosphorus deficiencies, because at the high pH associated with calcium-rich soils, much of the phosphorus is tied up as insoluble calcium phosphate. As another example, the requirement for cobalt by plants with nitrogen-fixing root nodules is highest when neither nitrate nor ammonium ions are available to the plants. In the presence of abundant inorganic nitrogen, the cobalt requirement disappears. Sodium and strontium are not normally used in plant metabolism, but can be used to a limited extent as a substitute for potassium and calcium, respectively, when these elements are in short supply. Manganese can be toxic in the

absence of silicon, so that although silicon may not be an essential "nutrient," its presence may be necessary to permit plant growth under conditions of high manganese availability.

It should be obvious from these examples that the relative abundance of different elements is often as important as their absolute abundance. A Swedish tree physiologist, Ingestad, has shown the importance of nutrient ratios in the growth of tree seedlings. The use of *Ingestad ratios* is discussed in Chapter 10, as is the use of foliar analysis in the diagnosis of the nutritional status of trees.

Deficiencies of essential nutrients can induce a variety of biochemical responses that result in abnormal growth and metabolic performance. Deficiency of *nitrogen*, which is vitally involved in protein synthesis, affects the production of enzymes, amino acids, and nonenzymatic proteins, thus affecting all aspects of plant metabolism. The synthesis of chlorophyll (the plant pigment responsible for photosynthesis) is inhibited, and one of the first symptoms of nitrogen deficiency is yellowing of the leaves. Shortage of *phosphorus* restricts the synthesis of ATP, which is involved in all metabolic energy transformations. This immediately disrupts plant metabolism. Deficiencies of *iron* and *magnesium* interfere with chlorophyll synthesis and cause yellowing of foliage (as do a variety of other nutritional deficiencies). *Calcium* deficiency may induce toxicity from other nutrients, and it results in weaker cell walls because calcium is present in the middle lamellae of cell walls in the form of calcium pectate. Lack of calcium pectate reduces plant resistance to moisture stress, and the soil acidity that is often associated with low soil calcium renders soluble several metals that may be toxic to plants at high concentration (e.g., iron and aluminum).

D. Forest Nutrition

Plants are found growing in a very wide variety of environments, which vary from those having abundant supplies of nutrients to those having major deficits. Many forests fall into the latter category, and the supply of nutrients for uptake by trees during the active period of spring growth may be particularly inadequate. Plants are able to solve this problem to some extent by internal redistribution of nutrients from storage sites or from older tissues to the sites of active growth and synthesis. This can be important for elements such as potassium, nitrogen, and phosphorus, which are relatively mobile within the plant, but not for elements such as boron and calcium, which are rather immobile. Deficiencies of the latter two nutrients are particularly marked in the actively growing parts of the plant because of the low mobility of these elements. Plants with low nutrient uptake in the spring will not necessarily suffer deficiencies if they are successful in absorbing sufficient nutrients during the rest of the year to provide, by means of retranslocation, for the nutritional requirements of new growth the following spring.

Many of the world's forests are growing on soils derived from rock materials that weather very slowly and/or release very few nutrients. Where the relative abundance of the essential nutrients is favorable, this need not be a major determinant of low forest productivity. Forests have an impressive ability to accumulate and recycle nutrients, and if left undisturbed they appear to be well adapted to solving their nutrient needs. A more serious problem is imbalance of nutrients, caused by excesses or deficiencies of individual elements. Growth in many northern and high-elevation forests is limited by the low availability of nitrogen. Phosphorus deficiencies in some Australian, Brazilian, and British forest soils can severely limit growth both because of the lack of phosphorus and because this lack inhibits the utilization of nitrogen (Beadle, 1966; Loveless, 1961). If the phosphorus deficiency is alleviated, some of these forests subsequently exhibit symptoms of nitrogen deficiency.

The nutrient requirements of different tree species vary greatly. Pines, for example, can photosynthesize and grow efficiently on soils with very low levels of available nutrients. On the other hand, many hardwood trees will grow well only under conditions of moderate to good nutrition. This variation in the nutritional tolerances and requirements of plants plays an important role in determining their spatial distribution. Pines are frequently located on infertile, ridge-top soils, whereas hardwoods occupy richer valley soils. This does not necessarily mean that pines reach their greatest growth on poor soils, or that hardwoods could not grow on infertile soils. The actual distribution of plants is frequently determined by plant competition, with nutrition acting indirectly by influencing the relative competitive abilities of the various species on the different sites. However, there are cases where plants do exhibit very specific relationships to soil chemistry. Perhaps some of the best examples of the ecological importance of nutrition is seen in the difference in plant communities that grow on calcium-rich and calcium-poor soils, and on magnesium-rich (serpentine) and magnesium-poor soils (see references in Epstein, 1972, Chap. 10.)

Forest fertilization, a development of agricultural fertilization, has proven to be highly successful in many parts of the world, particularly in the case of micronutrient deficiencies in trees. Shortages of micronutrients such as zinc, boron, or molybdenum have seriously limited forest growth in areas such as New Zealand and Australia, and growth has increased dramatically following additions of the deficient element(s). Spectacular increases in tree growth have followed the addition of phosphorus to areas such as the phosphorus-deficient Brazilian savannah. Nutrient deficiencies may be harder to correct where the deficiency is the result of low availability rather than low total quantity, as is the case with nitrogen. However, nitrogen is the most widely used macronutrient fertilizer in forestry, and although recent increases in the cost and decreases in the availability of nitrogen fertilizers raise questions about the future of large-scale forest fertilization, the use of fertilizers in forestry will probably grow as the value of forest products increases.

Much of our present understanding of plant nutrition comes from studies of herbaceous agricultural plants which were bred for high productivity and growth under conditions of high nutrient availability. Much less is known about nutritional strategies of wild plants growing under conditions of nutritional stress. Such knowledge is essential, however, for forest management. A useful review of the nutrition of wild plants is given by Chapin (1980).

5.3 Animal Nutrition: Energy and Nutrients at Consumer Trophic Levels

Nutrition is just as important as a factor regulating the production of consumers as it is for producers. Being heterotrophs, animals require more than a handful of mineral elements in certain critical proportions. They also require a wide variety of organic substances, including amino acids, proteins, vitamins, fats, and carbohydrates. Some animals are more tolerant of varying nutrition than others because they have populations of saprophytic microorganisms in their digestive tracts. These microorganisms are able to synthesize some of the essential organic nutrients which are then available to the host animal. However, the symbiotic (mutually beneficial) saprotrophs also have nutritional tolerances and can synthesize these essential organic nutrients only if the host animal eats plant materials with an acceptable chemical composition.

A. Herbivores

The nutritional quality of food material varies considerably between herbivores and carnivores. Herbivores eat plant materials that vary widely in their organic and inorganic chemical composition, depending on the species, the part of the plant, the age of the plant, the time of year, and the physiological condition and nutritional status of the plant. For example, amino acid composition of conifer foliage varies between species, with the age of the tree and of the foliage, with the flowering condition of the plant, and with the fertility of the site (Gagnon, 1966; Kimmins, 1971). The amino acid composition of several tree species has been shown to vary according to whether the trees obtain their nitrogen as nitrate or ammonium ions, and mineral nutrition is known to affect the total amount and relative proportions of different soluble nitrogen compounds in trees (Durzan and Steward, 1967; Ebell and McMullen, 1970; Steinberg, 1951). The inorganic nutrient composition of plants also varies greatly. For example, it has been found that the concentrations of mineral elements in vegetables grown in different states in the U.S. can vary by a factor of 8 (Hopkins and Eisen, 1959).

The mineral content of tree foliage is known to reflect the nutrient status of the soil, and the chemical analysis of foliage has been widely used as a means of assessing soil fertility and the levels of plant nutrition. Wells and Metz (1963) found a twofold difference in foliar calcium and a threefold difference in magnesium concentrations in the foliage of loblolly pine growing on different soils; there was also a threefold difference in foliar phosphorus levels in young foliage. The mineral content of plants growing on Scottish heather moors was found to reflect the nutrient content of the underlying soil parent materials. Heather growing on soils derived from dioritic rocks contained higher levels of protein, phosphorus, and other minerals than did heather growing nearby on soils derived from granite (Jenkins et al., 1964; Robertson and Davis, 1965). Because of this dependency of plant chemistry on soil chemistry, herbivores living on areas underlain by different soil types or geological materials may experience widely different levels of nutritional value in their food supply.

In spite of the considerable variation in the organic and inorganic chemistry of the diets of herbivores, it is much less than the variation in the chemistry of the plants in a community. This difference is the result of selective feeding by animals. Insect herbivores have been shown to select the parts of the plants best suited to their nutritional needs and to vary their diet during the year to maintain the best available diet in the face of changing plant chemistry (Beck, 1956; Blais, 1958). Insects have also been shown to select from a number of different artificial diets the one that best satisfies their nutritional needs (House, 1967). Sheep, cattle, and deer exhibit great discrimination in the selection of their food, and nutrition is apparently a major factor in this behavior (Albrecht, 1958). Experiments have demonstrated that sheep can select plants with an average of 17% crude protein from a plant community with an average of 7% crude protein, and deer feeding in a nutritionally marginal salal (*Gaultheria shallon*) plant community are able to locate and select the 2% of the shrubs that are nutritionally adequate (Laukhart, 1962).

The nitrogen content of plants is only one of many nutritional attributes that are important to herbivores. However, because of its critical role in animal metabolism, and because the nitrogen content of plants is often low, herbivores often respond particularly to the nitrogen content of their food. A review of herbivory in relation to plant nitrogen content can be found in Mattson (1980).

Herbivores do not choose food plants solely on the basis of their inorganic and organic nutrient content. They also make their feeding selection on the basis of secondary plant chemicals. Plants growing in nutritionally deficient (e.g. the subarctic and parts of the tropics) and other environments in which it is difficult to replace losses to herbivory have evolved chemical defenses against herbivores, which avoid plants with high concentrations of these secondary chemicals (Chapin, 1980; Bryant and Kuropat, 1980; and Bryant et al., 1983). Physical defenses such as leaf toughness and hairyness may also be important (Coley, 1983).

B. Carnivores

The chemical composition of the food of carnivores is much less variable than that of herbivores. In spite of the considerable variation in dietary items consumed by herbivores and the large variations in the chemistry of those items, the average chemical composition of different species of large mammal differs surprisingly little (Davis, 1968). In elephants, sheep, human beings, hippopotamuses, and horses, mineral elements account for about 5% of the total biomass. Of this 5%, more than two-thirds is made up of calcium and phosphorus, the two mineral nutrients of prime concern in the nutrition of domestic livestock and wild mammalian herbivores.

The chemical composition of herbivores can vary, however. Phosphorus and calcium levels differ according to the content of these elements in the plant food. Herbivores fed entirely on old grass can become deficient in phosphorus, especially in areas with low soil phosphorus levels. Female mammals can become depleted in calcium while nursing their young because of the high calcium demand of milk production, and the calcium requirements of antler production places extra calcium demands on the males of antler-producing species. The ratio of fat to protein will also vary according to the nutrient status of the animal. Parameters such as age and health, time of year, and reproductive condition of the animal all influence body chemistry somewhat.

C. Micronutrients

Micronutrient deficiencies are as important in animals as they are in plants. Iodine, copper, selenium, and cobalt are important micronutrients known to produce deficiency diseases when in low supply. Animals have a fairly general requirement for sodium, but it is frequently lacking in the plant diets of herbivores. Since sodium is not an essential nutrient for plants, it is not conserved or accumulated by them, and sodium deficiency is common in herbivores (Orians and Pitelka, 1960). Farmers and wildlife managers solve this problem by providing mineral salt "licks" (lumps of salt-rich mineral material), and wildlife frequently use soil or rocks rich in sodium as natural salt licks. Wild animals are well known to have an appetite for salt, and animals living in sodium-deficient environments have been known to chew the wooden handles of tools or the canvas straps of backpacks that have been soaked with salty human sweat (Baestrup, 1940; Blair-West et al., 1968). Potassium is also important in animal nutrition, and potassium deficiencies can occur in areas of high rainfall because this element is readily lost from plants by leaching.

D. Importance of Nutrition in Animal Ecology

Animal nutrition has long been recognized by agricultural zoologists as a critical determinant of animal productivity. In contrast, some animal ecologists have been slow to recognize the fundamental role of nutrition in animal ecology in unmanaged or nonagricultural ecosystems. For example, Hairston et al. (1960) stated that since herbivore populations are nearly always limited in size in spite of the presence of an abundant, intact, green plant community, herbivores could not be food limited. However, from the

discussion above it should be clear that the productivity of herbivore populations can be limited in the presence of abundant *quantities* of plant biomass if the chemical quality is inadequate; both the utilization efficiency and the assimilation efficiency of herbivores are influenced by plant chemistry. It has been shown in experiments with an insect herbivore that a 50% dilution of an optimum diet with indigestible materials can result in a 20% increase in food intake but a lower total assimilation of protein, and a similar response has been demonstrated for mice (Dalton, 1963; House, 1965). Sheep are able to digest and assimilate 20–30% of the protein in their ingested food when it contains 3–5% protein. When the protein content of ingested food rises to 20–25%, the assimilation efficiency increases to 70–80% (Orians and Pitelka, 1960). There have been many reports of animals and birds dying with stomachs and crops full of indigestible (nutritionally inadequate) plant materials, and the ravages of malnutrition in people fed exclusively on white rice or white flour are known all too well. The chemical form in which energy is presented to a consumer ultimately dictates whether or not that energy is metabolically available to that consumer.

There is growing recognition of the importance of plant chemistry, nutritional and otherwise, as a regulator of the distribution and abundance of animals (Price et al., 1980; Mattson, 1980; Bryant and Kuropat, 1980), and it is likely that future theories about the regulation of animal numbers will reflect this recognition (Kimmins, 1970; White, 1969, 1974, 1976), Bryant et al. (1983) and Haukioja (1980).

5.4 The Geochemical Cycle: Nutrient Cycling Between Ecosystems

The geochemical cycle (or geological cycle as it is sometimes called) involves exchanges of chemicals between different ecosystems. These may be as close together as a mountain slope above a valley floor, or as far apart as an ocean and the center of a continent. The term *cycle* implies a repeated movement through a cyclic pathway; the removal of nutrients from one ecosystem to another and the subsequent return to the original ecosystem. Although this can occur for some of the elements that participate in the geochemical cycle, for most it does not. Geochemical cycling generally involves the removal of chemicals from one ecosystem and their deposition in another in which they may remain indefinitely, or from which they may be transferred to yet other ecosystems. These cycles constitute the inputs to and losses from biogeochemical cycles, and they play an important role in determining the quantity of nutrients cycling within an ecosystem, and therefore in ecosystem energy flow. For purposes of discussion it is convenient to categorize geochemical cycles as either *gaseous* or *sedimentary*.

A. Gaseous Cycles

Carbon, hydrogen, oxygen, nitrogen, and sulfur can all enter or leave ecosystems as gases or vapors, as solids or in solution. However, for nitrogen, carbon, and oxygen, the gaseous state is the predominant form of entry. Most types of rock contain little or no nitrogen (some sedimentary deposits may contain some), the oxygen in rocks is chemically bound, and carbon is either present at low levels or is released too slowly to satisfy the carbon requirements of plants (release of carbon from limestone deposits may be an exception). For sulfur, on the other hand, there is a substantial input from rock weathering. Sulfur does enter ecosystems as a gas, but in many ecosystems this is much less important than its entry as sulfates in solution. Plants in urban or industrial areas where there is abundant SO_2 in the atmosphere may take up a lot of this gas through their leaves. Much of the sulfur leaving ecosystems is in the form of ions dissolved in stream water, but there may also be a significant proportion in the form of gas.

The uptake of CO_2 from the air by plants is well known. Somewhat less well known is the uptake of atmospheric sulfur dioxide (SO_2), and direct uptake of gaseous nitrogen in the form of ammonia (NH_3) has been demonstrated. Most nitrogen enters ecosystems by the microbial fixation of nitrogen gas (N_2), but uptake of atmospheric NH_3 may provide up to 10% of the plant community's nitrogen requirements and amount to as much as 20 kg ha^{-1} yr^{-1} (Hutchinson et al., 1972). CO_2 and SO_2 are emitted by plants, while animals emit CO_2 and the reduced gases hydrogen sulfide (H_2S) and methane (CH_4). The contribution of animals to the carbon cycle has sometimes been underestimated by the failure to recognize the considerable production of methane. For example, it has been estimated (without the trace of a smile) that large herbivorous mammals release between 45 and 73 million tons a year of methane as flatulence (Ehhalt, 1973)! This figure appears small, however, compared to the estimate that termites in the tropical and subtropical regions annually convert 37% of net primary production into 50 billion metric tons of CO_2 and 152 million tons of CH_4 (Zimmerman, 1982). This release of CO_2 exceeds the annual release from the combustion of fossil fuels.

Gaseous cycles have attracted a great deal of attention over the past 20 years. Not only do they account for some of the major inputs and losses of macronutrients to and from ecosystems; they are the recipients of man's gaseous pollutants. Very large quantities of carbon monoxide, carbon dioxide, and the oxides of sulfur and nitrogen enter the atmosphere daily as the result of human activities, and a wide variety of organic chemicals and pesticides spend some time moving through these gaseous cycles. As we shall see later, the consequences of such large-scale additions to gaseous cycles and the fate of the added chemicals are of urgent concern. In particular, the addition of large quantities of the oxides of N and S to the atmosphere has resulted in the phenomenon of *acid rain*, which developed during the 1970s into one of the most widespread and insidious forms of global pollution. Acid rain is discussed in more detail in Section 5.11B.

B. Sedimentary Cycles

Although only a few chemicals are involved in gaseous cycles, all chemicals participate in the sedimentary type of geochemical cycle. For those elements that do have a gaseous phase, the relative importance of the two geochemical pathways depends upon the physical and chemical character of the element, its biological role, and the nature of the environment. For example, in a dry area much of the carbon and sulfur leaving an ecosystem will be in the form of gases. In a wet area a lot of the gaseous oxides of carbon and sulfur will be taken into solution and removed in streamwater.

Sedimentary cycles involve several different mechanisms of movement: meteorological, biological, and geological/hydrological.

1. Meteorological Mechanisms. These include inputs in dust and precipitation (rain and snow), and outputs as the result of wind erosion and transportation. Dust and pollen from land and salt spray from oceans are carried by wind to be deposited in some distant ecosystem during periods of precipitation or calm weather. Extreme examples of the potential of the meteorological pathway are dust and sandstorms and the deep layers of *loess* soil or the sand dunes that are produced. Ash from the 1980 eruption of Mt. St. Helens in Washington state was carried right around the globe, and the dirty color of old snow and of some glaciers demonstrates the considerable deposition of dust from the atmosphere even in periods when there is little volcanic activity. On a rather less dramatic scale, the dust from logging roads can result in an appreciable deposition of chemicals on nearby forests. In a single year, 1000 kg ha^{-1} of windborne material was deposited 80 m from the edge of a wood in Denmark (Holstener-Jorgensen, 1960). A total of 0.7 kg ha^{-1} of calcium and 0.1 kg ha^{-1} of potassium was deposited 20 m from a forest road in Sweden over a 2-week period in the spring (Tamm and Troedsson, 1955). The annual deposition of nutrients in dust from North American logging roads has not been measured but it must constitute an appreciable input to roadside ecosystems in some areas.

The combination of dry fallout (dust and aerosols settling out of the atmosphere during calm, dry weather) and wet fallout (dust, aerosols, and dissolved chemicals in rainfall, mist, or snow) results in a continuous input of nutrients into ecosystems that is small in some ecosystems and quite large in others. The quantity of nutrient elements in fallout varies at different times of the year, in different years, and in different places. It is greatly affected by the climate, the type of weather (which determines the source of air masses), and location relative to the sources of the fallout chemicals such as the ocean, areas of active wind erosion of soil, and areas of industrial air pollution.

The input of various chemicals in fallout has been measured in many parts of the world. Table 5.2[1] gives some example values for terrestrial ecosystems. Although this is not an exhaustive list and higher and lower values undoubtedly occur, it gives some idea of the variability of this part of the geochemical cycle. There is great variability even within small countries such as Scotland, reflecting the variable distance of sampling sites downwind (prevailing wind

direction) from the ocean, industrial centers, and areas of arable farming: three major sources of fallout chemicals. Nitrogen inputs range from less than 1 kg ha^{-1} yr^{-1} in areas immediately downwind of large oceans, to more than 21 kg ha^{-1} yr^{-1} in areas downwind of large industrial complexes. Phosphorus inputs are generally much smaller and less variable than for the other macronutrients, varying between 0.1 and 0.9 kg ha^{-1} yr^{-1}. Potassium inputs vary between 0.1 and 7.7 kg ha^{-1} yr^{-1}. Calcium inputs tend to be larger at between 2.3 and 52 kg ha^{-1} yr^{-1}, whereas magnesium inputs tend to be much lower (0.6–5.4 kg ha^{-1} yr^{-1}). Values for sulfur input lie between 3.5 and 18.3 kg ha^{-1} yr^{-1}. Chloride and sodium inputs reach extremely high values close to coastlines but are much lower inland.

Many of these values will actually be underestimates of atmospheric nutrient inputs to forests. They are based on precipitation collected in rain gauges, which do not collect fine rain, windblown rain, or dust as effectively as does a tree crown. For example, a study of a very windy exposed site in the White Mountains of northeastern U.S. revealed that positioning a plastic artificial foliage structure above the precipitation collector increased the catch of water, calcium, magnesium, sodium, and potassium by factors of 4.5, 8.3, 6.0, 4.9, and 5.7, respectively (Schlesinger and Reiners, 1974). A similar study in a much less windy location at low elevation in coastal British Columbia showed

[1]A much more complete set of data on many aspects of forest biogeochemistry can be found in Kimmins et al., 1985.

Table 5.2 Fallout of Chemicals in Various Parts of the World (Listed in Order of Nitrogen Inputs),[a,b] kg ha^{-1} yr^{-1}

| Location | N | | P | K | Ca | Na | Mg | S | Cl |
	NH$_4^+$	NO$_3^-$							
Europe	0.9–14.3	0.3–7.3							
England	8.2–14.0		0.3–0.9	3.1–4.8	9.0–13.1	25.5–35.1	3.2–5.4	12	
Mississippi	11.2		0.3	4.0	5.0		1.0	3.5	
Germany	4.8–5.7	2.9–4.1	0.1	1.7–2.1	52.1				
Denmark	4.6	2.3		3.1	6.5	16.1		12.9	26
New Hampshire	2.2	5.4		0.7	2.6	1.5	0.6	14.8	
Scotland	0.9–4.7	0.4–2.0		1.4–2.5	5.9–6.7	11.5–47.2	1.2–4.6	7.5–18.3	20–82
Belgium	1.8	4.2		2.9	9.1		2.3		
U.S.S.R.	5.6		0.5	7.7	15.4		2.5		
Sweden	0.9–3.7	0.5–1.5		0.6–3.7	2.6–13.9				
New Zealand	5.0		0.4	7.0	9.0	68	12	10	134
Haney, B.C., Canada	1.3	2.4		1.3	4.6	5.4	1.1	6.6	12.2
Vancouver, B.C., Canada	0.6	1.1	0.4	0.9	7.3	13.2	2.2	6.7	23.1
Washington	1.1			0.8	2.8				
Oregon	0.9–1.0		0.3	0.1–0.2	2.3–5.0	1.8	1.0		
Coweta, U.S.				3.2	6.0	5.4	1.3		
Fire Island, N.Y.				7.3	9.8	141.5	19.1		

[a]Data from Miller, 1979; Jensen, 1962; Grier et al., 1974; Switzer and Nelson, 1972; Weetman and Webber, 1972; Holden, 1966; Zeman, 1973; Feller, 1974; Likens et al., 1970; Crisp, 1966; Gore, 1968; Frederiksen, 1972; and Art et al., 1974.
[b]Values are probably underestimates because of failure to measure impact of aerosols on vegetation (see the text).

that artificial foliage positioned above a precipitation collector increased the collection of water by 8% and nutrient quantities by 25–150% (DeCatanzaro and Binkley, 1981). Although one cannot use these factors to estimate the true atmospheric inputs to a forested area, the results of these and similar studies indicate that the data in Table 5.2 are minimum estimates only of atmospheric inputs to forested ecosystems. The values in Table 5.2 are for areas with ample precipitation. Lower inputs can be expected in lower-rainfall areas, although dry fallout (i.e., dust) may compensate to a variable extent.

The data in Table 5.2 are for annual chemical inputs. If these rates of input are sustained, forest ecosystems will receive substantial quantities of chemicals over the life of a tree crop (a rotation, which is normally about 50–100 years). Where the nutrients are efficiently retained, these inputs may be sufficient to supply much of the annual requirements of the forest biota for certain nutrients. Where this is the case, it is possible for plant and animal communities to develop in relative nutritional independence of the soil. The soil is still vitally important, of course, since it determines in part the extent to which the nutrients added in rainfall and dust are retained and made available to plants. It is also important in water relationships and in providing anchorage for plants. However, the phenomenon of chemical fallout is one of the factors making possible the growth of productive old-growth forest on mineral soils with a very low nutrient status.

2. Biological Mechanisms. Redistribution of nutrients between ecosystems can occur as the result of animal migrations. Many of the animals that regularly participate in biogeochemical cycles also become involved in geochemical cycles because they feed in one ecosystem and defecate in another. Many species of flocking birds feed in agricultural areas during the day but return to woodlands to roost at night. In one woodland in England this resulted in an importation of about 6.1, 9.5, and 89.2 kg ha^{-1} of Na, K, and Ca by rooks over an 8-week period, compared to an annual input in rain of about 11, 4, and 24 kg ha^{-1}, respectively (Weir, 1969). The nighttime droppings of starling flocks in such woodlands can sometimes accumulate to a depth of several centimeters and kill the minor vegetation. However, in most terrestrial ecosystems, biological exports from one ecosystem will be balanced (or nearly so) by biological imports from another. Migratory birds feeding temporarily in an area will remove some nutrients but may defecate similar amounts that they imported from elsewhere. A study in a northern temperate hardwood forest ecosystem in the U.S. found that feeding by migratory birds resulted in an annual net removal of only about 3 g ha^{-1} of calcium and

nitrogen and less than 2 g ha^{-1} of sulfur and phosphorus (Sturges et al., 1974).

Snowy owls feeding on lemmings in the arctic cause a marked nutrient enrichment of the area around their nest because of the importation of lemming carcasses (and the nutrients contained therein) from the surrounding tundra. Salmon that have fed and grown in the ocean migrate back up rivers to the stream from which they originated, carrying with them nutrients from the ocean. Much of this nutrient input enters local terrestrial biogeochemical cycles when bears and eagles feed on the spawned-out salmon. Alternatively, the nutrients may temporarily enter stream biogeochemical cycles before being carried slowly back to the ocean.

Perhaps the best example of the biotic contribution to a geochemical cycle is the formation of phosphate deposits on the so-called *guano islands* off the west coast of South America. Phosphate arrives in the vicinity of these islands in nutrient-rich seawater upwelling from deep in the Pacific Ocean. The phosphorus enters a productive grazing trophic web that leads eventually to carnivorous seabirds. These catch fish at sea, but roost and nest on the islands. Fish carcasses, bird droppings, and dead birds accumulate on the islands in the almost rainless climate at a rate that has been estimated to be about 190,000 metric tons per year, containing 8800 metric tons of phosphorus (Hutchinson, 1950). Thus, seabirds are the critical link in building up a vast deposit of phosphorus, a process analogous to the biological events that have been involved in many of the world's sedimentary deposits of phosphate, carbon, and calcium.

Man's agricultural and forest management activities provide another example of biotic contributions to geochemical cycles. Fertilizers are dug up or manufactured in one ecosystem and distributed in another. Much of the accumulated capital of nutrients in a forest or agricultural crop may be removed at the time of harvest. Eventually, these nutrients find their way via combustion or waste disposal into the soil of some remote ecosystem or via sewers into remote water bodies.

Human beings differ from other animals in that we not only redistribute nutrients, but also concentrate, redistribute, and disperse a lot of nonnutrient elements and chemical compounds. Geological cycles form an intricate and amazingly well-balanced system which provides both terrestrial and aquatic ecosystems with sufficient nutrient inputs and outflows to keep their biogeochemical cycles running smoothly. However, we are altering the geochemical inputs to, and losses from, many ecosystems in a way that alters the energy flow patterns in those ecosystems, and in many cases these alterations are not desirable.

3. Geological/Hydrological Mechanisms. These involve inputs of nutrients to an ecosystem by chemical weathering of rock and soil minerals, or as nutrients dissolved in soil water or streamwater that is moving into the ecosystem. These mechanisms also involve outputs from an ecosystem of nutrients dissolved in soil water or surface water, or carried as particles in the form of eroded soil and organic matter.

In spite of the sometimes very considerable contributions of meteorological and biological inputs, the major supply of many nutrients for the biogeochemical cycle of many ecosystems is the geological process of weathering, erosion, and solution. Soil is formed by the physical and chemical breakdown of rock materials under the combined influence of climatic and biological processes. Nutrients that are released into solution during this process either enter a biogeochemical cycle or are removed by erosion (wind or water) or solution. The natural rate of weathering of rock or soil minerals and the subsequent release of nutrients is very difficult to measure, and there are few reliable direct estimates (Table 5.3).

The magnitude of this input to the geochemical cycle has usually been estimated indirectly as the difference between the quantity of chemicals entering the ecosystem by meteorological and biological processes and the quantity of chemicals leaving in water, assuming no change in the quantity of chemicals stored in the system. By basing the estimate on a small watershed with a watertight bedrock, the difference is equal to the net export of chemicals from the area in streamwater. Estimates derived in this way can underestimate the rate of weathering because the assumption of a watertight bedrock is often incorrect, although the error is partially offset by underestimates of atmospheric inputs (discussed

above). The estimate also assumes that the biomass (and its nutrient content) of the watershed is neither increasing nor decreasing. Over the short time period during which the estimate is made (a few years), this may well be in error. Losses of water to deep seepage, and short-term gains or losses of nutrients, appear to occur in most ecosystems (Curry, 1972). A final shortcoming of this method of estimating weathering rates results from biological and chemical processes within streams which take some of the nutrients leached from terrestrial into aquatic ecosystems out of solution (Perrin, 1981, Cummins, 1980, Triska and Cromak, 1980). These problems can cumulatively result in a significant error in estimates of geochemical weathering obtained by studying the balance between atmospheric inputs and outputs in streamwater.

Table 5.4 presents some examples of net losses of several chemcials from undisturbed, humid, temperate, forested watersheds. Losses of nitrogen dissolved in streamwater are always less than precipitation inputs, resulting in negative net output values. This reflects the much greater importance of gaseous cycles for nitrogen. Very little loss of phosphorus or potassium occurs, and in several ecosystems there is net accumulation of these elements (negative net output). Calcium and magnesium are lost in considerable quantities from most temperate ecosystems, which are normally well supplied with these elements, but they are efficiently retained in calcium-deficient tropical forests (see the discussion in Section 5.9). Losses of silicate and sodium, which tend to reflect chemical weathering of rock and soil more accurately than do macronutrients such as calcium and phosphorus (Johnson, 1971), are variable. This is the result of differences in both bedrock chemistry and rates of weathering.

Table 5.3 Estimates of the Rate of Release of Nutrients from Primary Minerals by Weathering, kg ha^{-1} yr^{-1}

Forest type	Bedrock type	Location	P	K	Ca	Mg	Reference
Northern hardwoods	Moraine/gneiss	Hubbard Brook, N.H.	—	7.1	21.1	3.5	Likens et al., 1977
Mixed hardwoods	Outwash sands	Long Island, N.Y.	—	11.1	24.2	8.4	Woodwell and Whittaker, 1967
Mixed hardwoods	Schists	Maryland	—	2.3	1.3	1.1	Cleaves et al., 1970
	Serpentine	Maryland	—	trace	trace	34.1	Cleaves et al., 1974
Coastal hardwoods	Quartz sand	Fire Island, N.Y.	—	0.01	0.04	0.01	Art et al., 1974
Aspen-mixed hardwoods	Glacial till	Wisconsin	0.9	3.6	7.1	—	Boyle et al., 1973
West coast conifers	Plutonic rocks	Southwestern British Columbia	0.33	1.7	34.4	6.6	Zeman, 1973
Cascade conifers	Dolomite	White Mountains, Calif.	—	4	86	52	Marchand, 1971
	Adamellite		—	8	17	2	
Cascade conifers	Tuffs/brecias	Oregon	—	1.6	47	11.6	Fredriksen, 1972
Tropical rain forest	Holocene alluvial deposits	Venezuela Soil age: 1000 yr	—	5.3–6.7	0.6–1.4	1.3–1.7	Hase and Foelster, 1983
		Soil age: 5000 yr	—	1.1–1.3	0.1–0.3	0.3	

Table 5.4 Net Losses of Several Chemicals from Undisturbed Forest Watersheds in Streamwater (Total Stream Chemical Content Minus Precipitation and Dry Fallout Chemical Content) in Various Parts of the Humid Temperate Regions of the World (Listed in Order of Calcium Loss)[a,b]

Location of Study Area	Hydrological Balance, mm		N		P	K	Ca	Mg	Na	S	Cl	Si
	Precipitation	Discharge	NH_4^+	NO_3^-								
Oak Ridge, Tenn.	1280	529	—	—	—	−1.6	58.6	46.7	−1.1	—	—	—
Oregon	2330	1525	−0.5		0.3	1.6	47.0	11.6	27.9	—	—	99.3
Oregon	—	—	−0.5		0.3	2.1	48.0	—	—	—	—	—
Great Britain[c]	2130	1731	−5.3		−0.1 to 0.3	5.9	44.8	—	19.7	—	—	—
Coastal B.C., Canada	4541	3668	−0.03	−0.3	0.1	1.7	34.4	6.6	12.4	0.8	15.0	91.3
Coastal B.C., Canada	2288	1080	−1.2	−1.9	0.0	0.6	14.8	2.9	8.2	1.5	0.3	—
Finland[d]	—	—		−4.0	−0.2	2.1	10.0	3.0		3.3	0.2	—
New Hampshire	1372	850	−2.0	−2.9	—	1.4	8.8	2.5	6.3	3.0	−1.0	17.0
Japan	—	—		−4.9	−0.4	−0.4	3.8	1.0	—	—	—	—
Coweta, U.S.	2035	1072	—	—	—	2.7	0.8	1.8	4.3	—	—	—

[a]Data from Swank and Elwood, 1971; Johnson and Swank, 1973; Fredrickson, 1972; Zeman, 1973; Likens et al., 1977; Viro, 1953; Miller and Williams, 1968; Cleaves et al., 1970; Iwatsubo and Tsutsumi, 1968; Crisp, 1966; and Grier et al., 1974.

[b]Values may be underestimates if there is appreciable undetected loss to deep seepage. They may be overestimates if precipitation inputs are significantly underestimated (see the text). Negative values indicate less output in streams than input in precipitation and dry fallout, indicating net accumulation in the ecosystem.

[c]Nonforested ecosystem.

[d]Estimate for the entire country.

5.5 The Biogeochemical Cycle: Nutrient Cycling Within an Ecosystem

Biogeochemical cycling involves a continuing cyclical exchange of chemicals between the biota and the physical environment within a biogeocoenose (Figure 5.1). It is the sequence of transfers of chemicals that occurs between the time an element enters a particular biogeocoenose and the time it leaves. Since nutrients in this cycle follow a continuous pathway, we could start the discussion at any point, but we shall begin with the uptake of nutrients by plants from the soil.

A. Nutrient Uptake by Plants

In common with all other life forms, plants satisfy much of their nutrient requirements by direct absorption of nutrients from solution in water. However, uptake of nutrients by roots from soil solution is not the only mechanism of plant nutrition nor is it necessarily the most important. In many soils, water contains low concentrations of macronutrients, and there may be relatively little direct uptake from solution. Direct uptake can occur from soil minerals that are in intimate contact with roots, and in some ecosystems, roots in contact with weathering rock surfaces are able to obtain much of their mineral nutrients directly from the rock (*lithoponics*[2]; see Chapter 10). Uptake can also occur through leaves if they are in contact with a nutrient-rich

solution, and this ability is used to advantage in some types of agricultural and horticultural fertilization practice in which nutrient solutions are sprayed onto the foliage. Uptake of carbon is almost entirely through the leaves, and foliar absorption of gaseous sulfur and nitrogen also occurs. Atmospheric CO_2, SO_2, and NH_3 dissolve in the film of moisture that covers the mesophyll cells inside the leaf and then move into the cells in solution.

1. From Soil Solution. A wide variety of physical and chemical characteristics of the soil will influence the concentration of nutrients in, and their uptake from, soil water, but there are three major factors that determine nutrient uptake by roots from soil solution.

1. The rate at which nutrients diffuse from the surrounding soil to the root (*diffusion transfer*).
2. The rate at which water containing nutrients moves from the surrounding soil to the root (*mass transfer*).
3. The rate at which new roots grow into unoccupied soil that contains unutilized pools of nutrients.

The relative importance of diffusion, mass transfer, and dispersion (diffusion enhanced by the mixing that is associated with massflow) varies for different nutrients. Different ions vary considerably in the rate at which they diffuse through soil. For those nutrients that diffuse slowly, such as phosphorus and potassium, the supply to the root will be more dependent upon the rooting pattern of the plant (which in turn controls the volume of soil in close contact with the root) than on the total amount of the nutrient in the entire

[2]This term was suggested to me by Dr. Harold Young, University of Maine, Orono, Me.

soil volume. On the other hand, the supply of nutrients that diffuse rapidly, such as nitrate, depends on the total quantity of nitrate available in the soil (Baldwin, 1975). The mass flow of nutrients to the root will depend on the amount of water in the soil and the rate at which it is moving toward the root. This in turn will be influenced by the rate at which the plant is transpiring water. In a study of Douglas-fir growing on a coarse, infertile soil it was estimated that somewhat less than 22, 37, and 80% of the N, K, and Ca taken up by the trees was provided by mass flow. Diffusion and dispersion, although limited by the low soil water content, were apparently very important in the transport of N to roots in this soil (Ballard and Cole, 1974).

Plants vary greatly in the quantity and spatial distribution of their small absorbing roots. Plants such as grasses and many species of deciduous tree (angiosperms) have finely divided root systems with an enormous total surface area and length. These grow through a substantial proportion of the soil volume, and such root systems are very efficient at exploiting the soil solution. In contrast, many conifers (gymnosperms) have root systems in which the root tips and find absorbing rootlets are restricted almost entirely to the surface layers of the soil, especially when growing an infertile soil (Figure 5.3). The roots are coarser and less branched and consequently less efficient on their own at filtering nutrients out of soil solution than are the root systems of most angiosperm plants. It has been suggested that this difference in root systems may relate to differences in the availability of nutrients in soil solution during the evolutionary periods when gymnosperms and angiosperm plants evolved (Voigt, 1968).

2. Via Mycotrophy. The characteristically low concentrations of dissolved ions in forest soil water, together with the form and distribution of their root systems, renders direct uptake of nutrients from soil solution by roots a rather inadequate mode of nutrition for many forest plants. It is generally recognized that total, direct nutritional dependence on the soil solution is abnormal. Most forest plants depend either completely or to a considerable extent on a mutually advantageous relationship between their roots and soil microorganisms, the most common of which is a root–fungus relationship called a *mycorrhiza*.

A mycorrhiza is an intimate association between a root tip of a higher plant and one of several species of fungus. The form of the relationship varies somewhat (see Chapters 10 and 14 for a more detailed treatment), but in one important type (*ectotrophic mycorrhiza*) the fungus forms a mantle of strands (hyphae) around the root tip and penetrates into the outer layers of the rootlet. Here the hyphae grow between the cells to form a network (the Hartig net).

The hyphae within the root are in continuous contact with the fungal mantle, which in turn is in continuous contact with a dense network of hyphae growing throughout much of the surrounding soil. The mycorrhizal association apparently confers many advantages on the plant. It improves nutrition under infertile soil conditions and confers greater resistance against disease organisms, drought, high temperatures, toxic substances in the soil, and extremes of soil acidity. The mycorrhizal relationship is probably one of the more important ecological relationships in forest ecosystems and the interested reader is recommended to reviews by Harley (1969), Hacskaylo (1971), and Marks and Kozlowski (1973).

The nutritional significance of the mycorrhizal relationship lies in the frequent observation that trees having mycorrhizal roots generally grow larger and absorb greater quantities of nutrients than trees without mycorrhizal roots. Uptake of N, P, and K is particularly enhanced. This is thought to be due to increased uptake of soil water (Duddridge et al., 1980), to an enlargement in the volume of the soil occupied by the root system and to its greatly increased effective absorbing surface. The fungi throughout the soil are essentially an extension of the roots with which they are associated, and it has been shown that this fungal mycelium (network of hyphae) is very efficient at absorbing nutrients from solution and holding them against leaching (Stark, 1972). The hyphae also increase the solubility of nutrients in the soil. Organic acids secreted by the hyphae and carbonic acid that results from the respiration of the fungi,

$$CO_2 + H_2O \longrightarrow H_2CO_3 \xrightarrow{\text{pH dependent}} H^+ + HCO_3$$

attack undecomposed soil minerals and organic matter, releasing previously unavailable nutrients which are then absorbed by the hyphae. Some of the nutrients entering

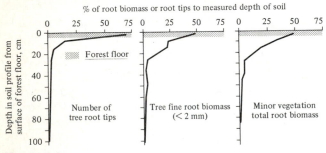

% of root biomass or root tips to measured depth of soil

Figure 5.3

Vertical distribution of tree root tips, tree fine root biomass, and minor vegetation root biomass in a 100–150 year old white spruce-subalpine fir stand growing on deep, infertile, moderately drained sand. (After Kimmins and Hawkes, 1978.)

hyphae in the soil subsequently become available to roots in mycorrhizal association with the fungus.

Mycotrophy, as plant nutrition with the aid of mycorrhizal associations is called, appears to be the normal mode of nutrition for most forest plants. For some plants the relationship is obligatory; they will die if grown in soils devoid of the fungal partner. For other plants it is apparently obligatory for survival on very infertile soils, but unnecessary on a fertile soil. The mycorrhizal association has been described as the keystone of the forest biogeochemical cycle; in many forest environments, active biogeochemical cycling and the existing vegetation could not occur without it.

The quantity of nutrients taken up annually by plants varies greatly. It is influenced by the availability of nutrients to the plants (i.e., site fertility) and their nutritional requirements, which in turn depend upon the species and their physiological maturity. The uptake varies during the development of a stand. It is very high during the early stages when there is a rapid accumulation of biomass of foliage and live woody tissues, and when the availability of nutrients in the soil is still high following the removal of the previous stand. Uptake then declines somewhat as the stand becomes more dependent on internal retranslocation of nutrients from old to younger tissues, thereby reducing the dependence of primary production on uptake. It may also decline because of (1) a decline in soil nutrient availability that results from a reduction in litter decomposition rates, and (2) the immobilization of an increasing proportion of the site nutrient capital in heartwood and/or slowly decomposing litter (see Heal et al., 1982 and references therein).

An accurate determination of the annual uptake of nutrients by a forest is a difficult task, and although many estimates have been made, most of these must be taken as very approximate. Uptake can only be measured indirectly, by measuring the net change in plant nutrient content and all losses of nutrients from the plants for the time period being considered. Uptake of nutrients = Net change in plant nutrient content + Replacement of nutrient losses from the plant. Alternatively, it can be approximated by measuring the nutrient content of all the new biomass and the internal redistribution of nutrients within the plant (see below). Uptake = Nutrient content of new biomass—contribution of internal cycling.

Although the work is laborious, it is reasonably easy to do this for the aboveground parts of forest plants. The nutrient exchanges of the root system, which may equal or exceed the aboveground exchanges for some nutrients, are much harder to measure. The work is much more laborious, many of the measurements cannot be made directly, and there are few studies that have quantified the nutrient dynamics of root systems. Consequently, most of the available estimates of uptake must be considered as just that—estimates.

Figure 5.4 shows the nutrient uptake (ignoring the root dynamics) by several different forests in comparison with three agricultural crops. Both the magnitude of the uptake and the relative importance of the different nutrients vary considerably. Hardwoods have the greatest overall uptake, with calcium being the dominant element. Nitrogen dominates the annual uptake of most conifers, although some genera of conifers (e.g., *Chamaecyparis, Thuja*) have an uptake pattern more like hardwoods. The uptake patterns in Figure 5.4 reflect site as well as species differences. The higher uptake by the mixed-oak forest compared to the oak–ash forest reflects higher levels of soil calcium on the former site. The differences also reflect variation in age; both the magnitude and the relative importance of the different nutrients vary with the age of the stand, making simple comparisons among the various estimates problematical. The magnitude of the annual uptake by agricultural crops is generally higher than that of most conifer crops. Conifer and agricultural crops differ in the generally lower requirement for calcium and the higher requirement for potassium in the latter.

Most nutrient uptake estimates were made before the magnitude of the annual production and turnover of tree fine roots was appreciated (c.f. Keyes and Grier, 1981). The nutrient uptake requirements of fine root production have not yet been quantified for many forests, and the reader is advised to interpret most nutrient uptake data with appropriate caution. For an example of the importance of the error, see Vogt et al. (1983).

Nutrient uptake estimates are not reliable as estimates of the minimum nutrient requirements for the primary production. Plants may absorb abundantly available nutrients in excess of requirements (luxury consumption) and may also absorb nonessential elements (e.g., sodium), and, conversely, much of the requirement for net production may be met by internal redistribution from older tissues (see below). Nor can requirements be gauged accurately from the levels of nutrients in the plant, just as energy dynamics cannot be gauged from the biomass pyramid. For example, a plant may have a low total content of an element that is readily lost (like potassium), but a high uptake requirement to replace the losses. An accurate assessment of the nutrient requirements of a forest must ultimately come from a comparison of uptake and productivity. Only recently has sufficient quantitative information been available to permit comparisons of uptake and requirement for net production in different forest types (e.g., Cole and Rapp (1981)).

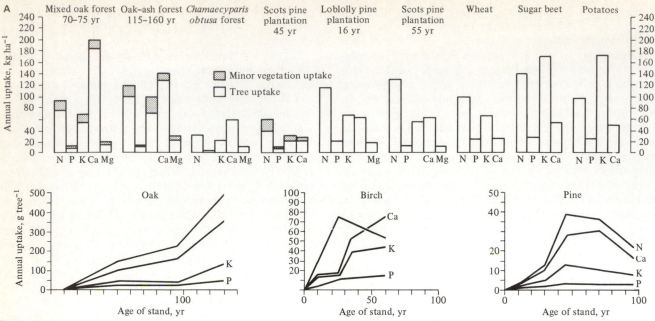

Figure 5.4

Nutrient uptake by forest crops. (A) Variation in the annual uptake of the major macronutrients by several different forest and agricultural plant crops. (B) Variation in uptake with age for three tree species. Some of these uptake estimates are based on studies of the aboveground organs alone (uptake = net increment of nutrients in aboveground parts + replacement of losses from aboveground parts). Inclusion of belowground biomass production and turnover (c.f. Keyes and Grier, 1981) could result in a considerable increase in the estimates. (Data from Duvigneaud and Denaeyer-De Smet, 1970; Mälkonen, 1974; Wells and Jorgensen, 1975; Tsutsumi, 1971; Remezov and Pogrebnyak, 1969.)

Comparisons are sometimes made between nutrient uptake and the total capital of nutrients in the soil. Such comparisons may be useful, especially for very mobile nutrient ions, but for many elements the comparison should be made with a knowledge of the distribution of the roots. This will strongly influence how much of the soil nutrient capital is readily available to the trees. In some soils, roots of trees can penetrate deeply, but most of the deeper roots are coarser, anchoring roots. As a general rule, the majority of the fine feeding roots of trees are restricted to the forest floor and the surface layers of the mineral soil. Results from one study showed that 82% of the fine roots of a 140-year-old Scots pine forest in the U.S.S.R. were in the top 20 cm of soil and 76% were in the top 10 cm. 93% of the roots of minor forest vegetation in a forest glade were in the top 20 cm of soil; 76% were in the top 10 cm (Vasil'eva, 1968). In a study in western Canada it was found that 71% of the conifer root tips in a white spruce/subalpine fir forest were in the forest floor, while 91% were in the forest floor and upper 10 cm of mineral soil (Figure 5.3). All these stands were on infertile sandy soils. On richer soils, a greater proportion of the fine root biomass and root tips are found at greater depths. However, many of the world's forests are growing on infertile soils, and for these forests the forest floor and superficial layers of mineral soil provide the majority of the nongaseous nutrients. The question as to the volume of soil that is being tapped by root systems is considered again in Chapter 10.

B. Nutrient Distribution in Plants

Once nutrients have been absorbed, they are transported to various parts of the plant for use in metabolic processes or storage. Just as uptake varies between species and sites, the relative distribution of nutrients between the various parts of forest plants varies considerably (Figure 5.5). This variation is a result of differences in both the distribution of biomass and the concentration of chemicals in the various tissues. Different plant species absorb and accumulate elements at very different rates. For example, dogwood trees have long been recognized as selective absorbers of calcium

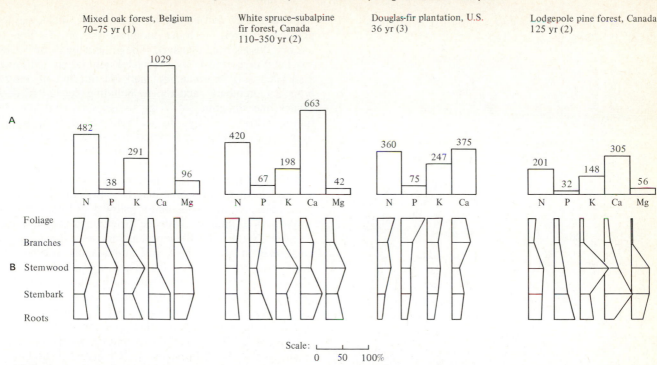

Figure 5.5

The tree nutrient content and its distribution in four different forest types. (A) The total content of five macronutrients in tree biomass (kg ha^{-1}). (B) Percentage distribution of this content between the five major biomass components. (Data from Duvigneaud and Denaeyer-De Smet, 1970; Kimmins, unpublished; Cole et al., 1967.)

(Thomas, 1969), which accounts for 2–4% of the leaf weight. The manganese content of plants in a Wisconsin forest was found to vary from as low as 20 ppm for a species of *Pyrus* to as high as 2999 ppm for a species of *Gaultheria* (Gerloff et al., 1966).

The relative distribution of nutrients varies according to the age of the plants. For example, the distribution of nitrogen among foliage, branches, and stems in a loblolly pine stand was found to vary as the stand aged. Most of the nitrogen in the very young stand was accumulated in the foliage, but by the time the plantation reached 60 years, the stems contained more than four times as much nitrogen as the foliage. This reflected the continued accumulation of stem and branch biomass throughout the 60 years, while foliage biomass peaked at about 25 years and then declined slowly over the rest of the period (Figure 5.6).

Within the crown, the chemical content of foliage varies according to the age of the foliage and its position in the crown. Nitrogen, phosphorus, and potassium concentrations of a given annual cohort of needles often decline with

age,[3] whereas calcium and magnesium concentrations tend to increase. The declines in concentration may either be because the needles continue to get heavier or because of an absolute loss of the chemicals. Since the chemistry of foliage is used as a diagnostic tool in assessing the nutritional status and fertilizer needs of forest trees, a knowledge of how foliage chemistry varies within tree crowns is of considerable practical concern. If foliage is sampled carefully, it can be a very useful index of the fertility of the site. This is discussed further in Chapter 10.

C. Nutrient Losses from Plants

All plants and animals are faced with continual losses of nutrients, and the majority of the annual uptake by plants simply replaces losses. A much smaller percentage is retained as the nutrient content of permanent new plant bio-

[3] This pattern is not *necessarily* found in the various age classes of needles on a single branch. Because of year-to-year variations in nutrient availability and growth conditions, the chemistry of new foliage may vary considerably from year to year, and this variation may persist until the needles are shed.

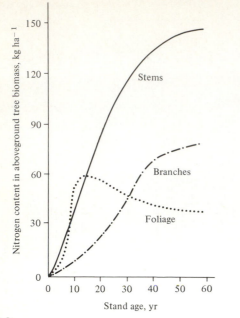

Figure 5.6
Variation with stand age in the relative contribution of stems, foliage, and branches to the aboveground nitrogen content of a loblolly pine stand. (After Switzer et al., 1968. Redrawn by permission of TVA and G. L. Switzer.)

mass. A certain amount of loss is undoubtedly necessary for both plants and animals to prevent toxic accumulations of chemicals, and either active secretion or passive loss enables the organism to regulate its internal chemistry within acceptable limits. House or greenhouse plants protected from rain may experience leaf damage because of toxic accumulations of chemicals that would have been lost by leaching in a natural environment. Similarly, agricultural crops in areas deficient in precipitation may experience disorders because of these accumulations. Natural populations in dry areas frequently have specialized morphological adaptations for the disposal of excess chemicals.

Under certain circumstances, losses of nutrients may be so great relative to uptake that the metabolism of the organisms may be adversely affected. This can occur in both plants (e.g., in areas of heavy rainfall or at times of heavy defoliation by herbivores) and animals (e.g., excessive sodium loss in humans through sweating). Thus, average rates of nutrient loss are the normal condition, while extremely high or very low rates of loss may interfere with normal metabolism.

Losses of nutrients from plants can occur in many ways: (1) leaching of above- or belowground organs by rainfall or

soil water; (2) defoliation by herbivores, including the physical removal of foliar biomass, the acceleration of leaching losses from damaged foliage, and the death of fine roots and mycorrhizae as a result of defoliation; (3) losses associated with reproduction; and (4) litterfall of leaves, branches, stembark, and roots, including the fall of dead tissues, the sloughing of living tissues (seasonal leaf and fine-root drop), and the physical removal of living tissues by mechanical force (e.g., wind and snow break).

Each of these will be discussed in turn.

1. Leaching by Rainwater. All plants experience losses of a wide variety of chemicals from leaves, bark, and roots by the leaching action of water. In some climates and for some nutrients, this is the major pathway of loss; it may be so great as to interfere with the growth and physiology of the plant (Stenlid, 1958). Inorganic micro- and macronutrients, other inorganic chemicals, amino acids, sugars, vitamins, growth-regulating substances (hormones), phenols, and many other plant chemicals are regularly washed off and out of plants when it rains. Of the inorganic nutrients, K, Ca, Mg, and Mn are usually leached in the greatest quantities, the amount depending upon the species of plant and the nature of the rainfall event (for a discussion of different types of rainfall events, see Chapter 11). Sodium, a nonessential chemical, is also very readily leached. Table 5.5 gives some examples of the variation in the inorganic chemistry of the water that has leached the aboveground biomass of forests. The nutrient quantities in this table include both materials leached out of vegetation and materials, such as dust, washed off the surface of the vegetation.

Although considerable quantities of inorganic nutrients are leached, it is organic substances that account for most of the chemicals in water reaching the forest floor (Tukey, 1970). Losses of up to 30% have occurred in agricultural crops as the result of heavy leaching of sugars from flowers and developing seeds. Palatability of soft fruits is reduced by heavy rains just before maturity and harvest because of the reduction in sugar content. The vitamin and nutritive value of forage crops is reduced by rain just before harvest, and the flowering of plants is affected by the leaching of plant growth hormones. Up to 800 kg ha^{-1} yr^{-1} of carbohydrate can be leached from apple trees compared with 20–30 kg of K, 10 kg of Ca, and 9 kg of Na. Leaching of inorganic nutrients is nevertheless considerable; up to 50% of the Ca and more than 80% of the K content of apple leaves can be leached in 24 hours (Tukey, 1970).

Deciduous hardwood trees generally lose more nutrients by leaching than conifers during the summer leafy period, but conifers may lose a greater total over the year because of leaching during a wet winter period. The greatest leaching

Table 5.5 Comparison of Some Macronutrients in Stemflow and Throughfall in Various Forests,[a] kg ha^{-1} yr^{-1}

Forest Type	N Thfl	N Stf	P Thfl	P Stf	K Thfl	K Stf	Ca Thfl	Ca Stf	Mg Thfl	Mg Stf	References
Douglas-fir, U.S., 36 yr old	1.5	0.3	0.3	0.1	10.7	1.6	3.5	1.1	—	—	Cole et al., 1967
Oakwood, Great Britain	3.7	0.1	0.3	0.1	8.6	1.6	6.4	2.0	3.5	0.7	Carlisle et al., 1967
Oakwood, Belgium	0.9	0.0	0.6	0.0	16.0	0.8	6.2	0.9	5.6	0.6	Duvigneaud and Denaeyer-De Smet, 1970
Hardwoods, U.S.	—	—	—	—	6.7	7.2	3.3	6.2	0.7	4.8	Torrenneva, 1975
Loblolly pine, U.S.	—	—	—	—	4.1	1.0	2.0	3.1	0.4	1.7	Torrenneva, 1975
Scots pine, Finland	4.8	0.1	0.1	0.0	5.8	0.2	7.4	0.4	—	—	Malkonen, 1974
Douglas-fir, U.S., 450 yr old	3.4	—	2.7	—	21.7	—	4.4	—	2.1	—	Abee and Lavender, 1972
Tropical forest, Ghana	11.0	—	3.3	—	196	—	26	—	16	—	Nye, 1961
Hardwoods, U.S.[b]	10.6	1.1	0.6	0.1	26.9	3.5	7.0	0.6	2.0	0.2	Eaton et al., 1973

[a]Much of the throughfall and stemflow nutrient content originates as "aerosols" intercepted by vegetation rather than materials leached out of vegetation. Thfl, throughfall: water falling through and dripping from tree crowns and minor vegetation foliage. Stf, stemflow: water reaching the soil by flowing down plant stems.
[b]Summer period only.

occurs in the tropics, where hardwoods hold their foliage all year round in a climate with abundant rainfall throughout the year. Leaching losses are influenced by the age of the foliage, and less leaching may occur from younger than from older foliage. However, leaching of nutrients such as N and P is greatest when these nutrients are in their most mobile state, which occurs in very young foliage during rapid early growth, and in senescent foliage prior to leaf fall. Consequently, there is no simple linear relationship between foliage age and leaching. Leaching is greater from damaged than from intact foliage, the undamaged cuticle acting as an efficient barrier to leaching. The extent of leaching during any particular rainstorm is greatly influenced by the duration and intensity of the rainfall and the time since the last rainfall (Attiwill, 1966; Miller, 1966). Annual leaching losses are determined by the quantity, timing, and character of precipitation. These vary from year to year, and therefore so does the total leaching loss.

Published values for the removal of nutrients from tree crowns by rain vary enormously: 0–12 kg ha^{-1} yr^{-1} for N, a trace to 8 kg ha^{-1} yr^{-1} for P, 1–320 kg ha^{-1} yr^{-1} for K, 0.2–194 kg ha^{-1} yr^{-1} for Ca, and 0.9–16 kg ha^{-1} yr^{-1} for Mg (Ovington, 1962; Attiwill, 1966; Madgwick and Ovington, 1959). The accuracy of these data as estimates of annual leaching totals is rather suspect. In many cases they are probably overestimates of vegetation leaching. They are calculated as the difference between the nutrient content of precipitation collected in the open and under the canopy, and the latter includes chemicals washed off the surface, as well as leached out of, vegetation. Also, vegetation (especially trees) is very efficient at intercepting fine rain, mist, and dust ("aerosols"), which are not sampled efficiently by traditional precipitation collectors. In a study of nutrient

cycling in Corsican pine in Scotland it was calculated that of the K, Ca, and Mg in throughfall[4] and stemflow, 53, 70, and 41% originated from intercepted aerosols rather than true foliar leaching (Miller et al., 1976). Estimates of N leaching, on the other hand, may be too low. Most studies measured only increased inorganic N in leachate, whereas the majority of the N may be in organic form.

The relative contributions of throughfall and stemflow also vary. They are largely determined by the morphology of the crown, which in turn is determined by the species, the age, and the structure of the stand. For example, the contribution of stemflow to the leaching of cations over a 6-month period in a 17-year-old Douglas-fir plantation varied according to the spacing of the trees, which in turn varied the morphology of the crown. At 3 × 3 ft spacing, the stemflow contributions were 44, 41, and 48% for K, Ca, and Mg, respectively, while at 12 × 12 ft spacing, they were 9, 9, and 3% (Kimmins, unpublished data; cf. Figure 11.2).

The leaching of foliage and other tissues is an important ecological process. By constantly returning a supply of nutrients to the rooting zone in a highly available condition, foliar leaching contributes to the nutrition of plants growing on infertile sites. For example, plants growing on calcium-deficient soils may experience calcium deficiency at the growing tips because, unlike nitrogen, phosphorus, and potassium, calcium cannot be easily retranslocated from old tissues to growing tissues. However, this lack of mobility can be partially compensated for by calcium leached out of the older foliage, absorbed by roots in the forest floor, and translocated directly to the growing tissues. The leaching of plant hormones, phenols, and other organic molecules af-

[4]Defined in Table 5.5.

fects rates of litter decomposition, the germination and survival of the seeds of other species, and the chemistry of the soil beneath a plant (Mahendrappa, 1974; Gersper and Holowaychuck, 1970). The supply of soluble carbohydrates to the forest floor in throughfall provides a readily available energy source for free-living microbes, and this may be important for the activity of free-living nitrogen-fixing microflora. We consider the ecological significance of some of these effects in Chapter 14.

2. Defoliation by Herbivores. The loss of chemicals from forest plants as the result of feeding by herbivores has received relatively little attention. This probably reflects the normally low levels of utilization of forest plants by herbivores (Table 4.3), but defoliation can be an important pathway of loss at times of herbivore epidemics.

Table 5.6 shows the amount of nutrients removed from an oak stand in litterfall during total defoliation by the gypsy moth. Substantial quantities of nutrients were removed in the insect feces (frass) and pieces of uneaten leaf, and the defoliation resulted in considerable increases in the loss of phosphorus, potassium, calcium, and magnesium. Heavy defoliation of a conifer stand will result in even larger losses since the accumulation of several years of foliage growth may be removed. A single complete defoliation of the 36-year-old Douglas-fir stand in Figure 5.5 would remove about 70 kg ha^{-1} of K, 82 kg ha^{-1} of Ca, 115 kg ha^{-1} of N, and 32 kg ha^{-1} of P, representing 28, 22, 32, and 43% of the total stand capital of these nutrients, respectively. By comparison, the combined litterfall and foliar leaching in this stand was 15 kg ha^{-1} of K, 16 kg ha^{-1} of Ca, 15 kg ha^{-1} of N, and 0.6 kg ha^{-1} of P (Cole et al., 1967). Frass from *Tortrix viridiana* larvae defoliating an oak stand in England made up only 15% of the carbon and energy (i.e., the biomass) of the annual litterfall but contained 24% of the N and 42% of the P in the litterfall (Carlisle et al.,

1966). This reflected the much higher concentrations of N and P in young oak leaves than in autumnal oak leaf litterfall.

The effects of defoliation on nutrient cycling are not limited to the increase in the litterfall pathway. If there is a lot of rainfall during the period of defoliation, leaching losses will be increased because the herbivore feeding impairs the ability of the foliage to resist leaching (Tukey and Morgan, 1963; Kimmins, 1972). Defoliation-induced increases in leaching will be greater in the spring, when nutrients are being actively transported to the foliage, than in the summer when this transport is greatly reduced.

In addition to its aboveground effects, defoliation is known to induce substantial root mortality. As much as 75% of the fine roots of balsam fir trees were found to be killed following the removal of 100% of the new foliage by spruce budworm (Redmond, 1959). This represents both a substantial loss of nutrients from the root biomass and a substantial temporary reduction in uptake to replace the losses. Similarly, severe or frequent grazing has been found to reduce the size and growth of roots in agricultural pasture plants. The loss of fine roots, together with the accompanying reduction in soluble carbohydrates, reduces the plant's ability to absorb nutrients (Alcock, 1964) either directly or with the assistance of mycorrhizae, an association that is very sensitive to the supply of carbohydrates to the roots. Reduced supplies of carbohydrates to the roots also result in the loss of nutrients from living roots back to the soil. Furthermore, the reduction in water uptake that accompanies heavy defoliation will reduce the rate of mass transfer of nutrients from the soil to the roots.

The effect of defoliation on the plant obviously goes beyond the mere removal of leaf material, and defoliation has biogeochemical impacts other than the removal of nutrients from plants. It can result in large transfers of frass and nutrients to streams and lakes, leading to an increase in aquatic

Table 5.6 Contribution of Defoliation by the Gypsy Moth to the Loss of Nutrients from 59-Year-Old Oak Trees, kg ha^{-1} yr^{-1} (Data from Rafes, 1971)

Litter type	Biomass	N	P	K	Ca	Mg
Frass (insect droppings)	750	24.4	1.5	24.1	14.0	5.7
Dead insects	35	3.4	0.5	1.1	0.1	0.1
Remains of eaten leaves	2176	37.4	3.6	32.1	44.0	7.3
Second flush of leaves	490	7.8	0.6	6.9	8.8	1.7
Total litter from defoliated area	3451	73.0	6.2	64.2	66.9	14.8
Total litter from undefoliated area	3480	68.7	3.6	47.4	55.6	9.4
Percent of increase in litterfall losses attributable to defoliation	—	6	72	35	20	57

productivity (Turner, 1963). Defoliation of overstory species is frequently accompanied by rapid growth of understory plants in response to the increased light, soil temperature, and nutrient availability. Because frass contains higher concentrations of nutrients and lower concentrations of various decomposition-inhibiting organic chemicals (such as tannins) than does leaf litter (e.g., Feeny, 1968, 1970; Feeny and Bostock, 1968), heavy inputs of frass to the forest floor will stimulate decomposition and mineralization of the litter.

3. Losses Associated with Reproduction. Horticulturalists and foresters have recognized for many years that the production of abundant crops of fruit and seeds tends to deplete the carbohydrate and nutrient reserves of plants (Kramer and Kozlowski, 1979; Gessel, 1962; Stenlid, 1958). This temporarily reduces their growth and the uptake of nutrients (Kozlowski, 1962). The initiation and development of flowers and seeds requires higher levels of nutrients than vegetative growth (Mustanoja and Leaf, 1965; Matthews, 1963), and plants in many areas are unable to produce a subsequent seed crop until they have rebuilt their reserves. It has been suggested that this is one of the determinants of the infrequent production of good seed years in northern forests and tundra regions (Kalela, 1962). The stimulation of flower and seed crops in trees by fertilization reflects the heavy nutrient demands of reproduction (Ebell, 1972).

As was the case with defoliation, there have been relatively few studies of the nutrient losses associated with reproduction. In one study, the male flowers of sessile oak were found to make up 4% of the litter biomass, but to contain about 11% of the N, 14% of the P, 12% of the K,

and 6% of the Mg in the total litterfall (Carlisle et al., 1966). The nutrient content of heavy crops of pollen and seeds has not been adequately quantified, but it is probably considerable.

4. Losses in Litterfall. Losses of nutrients by defoliation and reproduction can be substantial but they are characterized by great year-to-year variability. In a year with low herbivore populations, or a year without a heavy flower and seed crop, these losses will be very small. Conversely, in a year with an outbreak of insect defoliators or with a bumper seed crop, these losses will be high. Nutrient losses in leaf litterfall, on the other hand, tend to be somewhat more regular, since they are largely tied to the more predictable event of leaf shedding. Of all the pathways of nutrient loss from plants, aboveground litterfall has received the greatest attention. On the other hand, below-ground litterfall (the annual death of large quantities of fine roots) is one of the least studied pathways of nutrient removal from plants, in spite of the fact that in some forests it exceeds aboveground litterfall by several times.

Table 5.7 presents a summary of the quantities of certain macronutrients transferred from trees to soil by aboveground litterfall. The quantity is a function of the biomass, the type (leaves, branches, bark, etc.), and the nutrient concentrations in the litterfall, all of which vary from site to site. Litterfall losses are generally greatest on moist, warm, fertile, and other high-productivity sites and least on dry, cold, infertile, and other low-productivity sites. Table 5.8 shows how the biomass and litter chemical content varies in a Japanese hardwood forest along a topographic gradient from a moist valley bottom to a dry ridge top.

Table 5.7 Quantities of Certain Macronutrients in Aboveground Litterfall in Various Forests, Arranged in Order of Increasing N Content, kg ha^{-1} yr^{-1}

Location	N	P	K	Ca	Mg	Reference
Scots pine, Finland	11	1.0	2.5	7.8	—	Malkonen, 1974
Douglas-fir, Washington	13.6	0.2	2.7	11.1	—	Cole et al., 1967
Jack pine, Ontario, Canada	16.6	—	4.8	10.4	—	Foster and Gessel, 1972
Douglas-fir, Oregon	32.7	5.6	9.8	63.1	1.1	Abee and Lavender, 1972
Nothofagus forest, New Zealand	37	2.6	30	74	11	Ovington, 1962
Oak forest, England	41.0	2.2	10.5	23.8	3.4	Carlisle et al., 1966
Oak forest, Belgium	50	2.4	21.0	110	5.6	Duvigneaud and Denaeyer-De Smet, 1970
Spruce, U.S.S.R.	52	2.6	12.	48	7	Ovington, 1962
Hardwood forest, N.H.	54.2	4.0	18.3	40.7	5.9	Gosz et al., 1972
Loblolly pine, N.C.	58.2	7.8	16.0	29.2	6.9	Ovington, 1962
Oak forest, U.S.S.R.	59	3.0	62	86	13	Ovington, 1962
Birch forest, U.S.S.R.	66	5.0	13	54	19	Ovington, 1962
Beech, Sweden	69	5.0	14.4	31.7	4.3	Nihlgard, 1972
Red alder, B.C. Canada	137	5.4	16	51	10	Binkley, 1982
Tropical forest, Ghana	199.5	7.3	68.4	206	44.8	Nye, 1961

Table 5.8 Variation in the Macronutrient Content of Aboveground Litterfall Along a Topographic Gradient from a Valley Bottom to a Ridge Top in a Japanese Hardwood Forest, kg ha^{-1} yr^{-1} (Data from Katagiri and Tsutsumi, 1973)

Nutrient	Bottom of Slope (moist site)		Midslope		Ridge Top (dry site)
N	56.8	64.5	32.7	35.1	35.4
P	4.2	4.3	2.3	2.5	2.6
K	14.6	14.7	7.1	7.8	9.9
Ca	41.0	43.8	19.9	25.9	35.7
Mg	10.0	9.4	4.4	5.7	11.1
Biomass	4300	4728	2293	2640	3114

As was noted in Chapter 4, most of the existing litterfall data refer to aboveground litterfall only, which in many kinds of ecosystems may involve a much smaller turnover of biomass than belowground "litterfall" (it does not actually fall anywhere) which results from the annual production and mortality of fine roots. Although this aspect of litterfall has received little study, recent investigations have suggested that it is a major pathway of nutrient loss from plants. Measurements in an oak–hickory hardwood forest in Tennessee revealed that the death of fine roots accounted for a loss of 67.5 kg ha^{-1} yr^{-1} of N from the trees in comparison with 34 kg ha^{-1} yr^{-1} of N in leaf litterfall and 4.4 kg ha^{-1} yr^{-1} of N in aboveground leachates (Henderson and Harris, 1975). Death of fine roots in a 16-year-old loblolly pine stand in North Carolina accounted for a loss of 48.7 kg ha^{-1} yr^{-1} of N in comparison to 58.2 kg ha^{-1} yr^{-1} of N in aboveground litterfall and 9.6 kg ha^{-1} yr^{-1} in leachates (Wells and Jorgensen, 1975).

The importance of fine root litterfall varies according to stand age and site. Vogt et al. (1983) found that belowground litterfall was about double aboveground litterfall in a 23-year-old Pacific silver fir stand but more than four times as great in a 180-year-old stand. The difference in turnover of macronutrients between above and belowground litter varied from zero to about four times according to nutrient and stand age. Fine roots cycled 60, 10, 20, 30 and 10 kg ha^{-1} of N, P, K, Ca and Mg in the 23-year-old stand, and 110, 20, 20, 30, and 10 kg ha^{-1} in the 180-year-old stand (Vogt et al., 1982). Keyes and Grier (1981) reported that fine root litterfall in a dry ridge-top Douglas-fir stand was four times that of a stand on a moist lower slope site (5.6 vs 1.4 t ha^{-1} yr^{-1}).

It is probable that the annual death of fine roots constitutes a major proportion of the total litterfall of all forests. If this proves to be the case, total nutrient uptake by most forests has been very significantly underestimated, and

many of the values in Figure 5.4 may be much too small.

Litterfall generally accounts for the majority of the nitrogen, calcium, and magnesium loss from vegetation, and leaching generally accounts for the majority of the potassium loss. The major pathway of phosphorus loss is sometimes litterfall and sometimes leaching.

D. Litter Decomposition

Decomposition of litter and the release of nutrients is often the critical link in the forest biogeochemical cycle. If decomposition is too slow, most of the nutrients returned to the forest floor are removed from active circulation for long periods of time, and both nutrient cycling and forest productivity are reduced. Excessive accumulation of undecomposed litterfall can also lead to the development of forest floors that have undesirable physical effects on the soil. Deep forest floors can be excessively wet, excessively acid, and remain cold throughout most of the growing season. This results in poor root development, poor tree nutrition, and slow tree growth. Excessively rapid litter decomposition, on the other hand, can release nutrients faster than the plants and soil are able to retain them, and they may be leached out of the rooting zone. The loss of soil organic matter that will accompany excessively rapid rates of decomposition can also lead to the development of undesirable physical and chemical soil conditions, with serious consequences for site fertility, soil moisture status, and resistance to erosion and other forms of soil damage. Many of the major problems of forest tree nutrition and soil fertility are related to the amount and nature of the organic debris reaching the forest floor and its rate of decomposition (Waksman, 1932).

The rate of litter decomposition[5] varies enormously. It is often very rapid in humid tropical forests [between 6 and 10 times faster than in temperate forests (Madge, 1965)], where a leaf may decompose completely within weeks of falling to the forest floor. However, tropical decomposition rates can also be very slow (such as on highly weathered tropical white sands in Amazonia), variable (where there are seasonal dry periods), or moderate (in drier tropical forest). Litter decomposition is generally rapid (leaves decomposing in 1–3 years) in temperate hardwood forests, and slow to very slow in temperate and boreal conifer forests (4–30 years for needle decomposition). Arctic, alpine, and dryland forests have the slowest rates, needle decomposition requiring 40 years or more. The rate of litter decompo-

[5]Rate of litter decomposition can be calculated using the equation (Olson, 1963) $x_t = x_o e^{-kt}$, where x_t = amount of substrate at time t; x_o = initial amount of substrate; k = fractional loss rate per unit time; k is called the decay or decomposition constant.

sition generally increases as the quantity of litterfall increases, with the result that there is an inverse relationship between litterfall biomass and nutrient content, and the biomass and nutrient content of the forest floor (Figure 5.7). The very high aboveground litterfall of moist tropical forests on fertile soils is associated with little or no forest floor, while the small aboveground litterfall of cold forests is generally associated with very deep forest floors.

Most estimates of litter decomposition are based on short-term studies (1 or 2 years) of litter confined in litterbags or on a comparison of the forest floor biomass and the annual litterfall.[6] The latter may underestimate decomposition rates because of the general failure to include root death in the litter input rate. Vogt et al. (1983) reported that inclusion of root litter input data reduced estimated litter residence time estimates from 30 to 10 years in a 23-year-old stand and from 70 to 20 in a 180-year-old Pacific silver fir stand in Washington.

Litter decomposition is accomplished by the combined action of soil animals of various sizes (soil mesofauna and soil microfauna) and soil microorganisms (bacteria and fungi). The soil animals (worms, mites, springtails, beetles,

insect larvae, etc.) break down the litter into small pieces. This increases the surface area and ruptures the outer surface of the litter (the waxy cuticle), which otherwise restricts the access of the microflora to the more decomposable tissues inside the leaf. The soil animals bury the fresh litter, which places it in a moisture–temperature environment that is generally more conducive to decomposition, and by churning the soil they are constantly bringing nonmobile microflora (bacteria) into contact with decomposable materials. Some changes in the chemical composition of the litter material occur after it has passed through the gut of a soil animal, and this may result in faster microbial decomposition. However, it is generally agreed that the major contribution of soil animals to litter decomposition is the physical comminution of the material. These factors all combine to result in a very much more rapid rate of mineralization of fresh litter when there is an active community of soil animals.

The importance of these animals in decomposition has been demonstrated by comparing the rate of litter decomposition in the presence and absence of soil fauna. In one study it was found that the elimination of soil fauna by applying naphthalene to the forest floor reduced the normal loss of oak leaf material after 145 days by 50%, and in another it was reduced by 25% after 1 year (cf. Figure 4.12).

[6]The average residence time for litterfall organic matter in the forest floor is given by $T = H/L$ where T = organic matter residence time; H = forest floor weight minus the biomass of live roots; L = annual litterfall (Gosz et al., 1976).

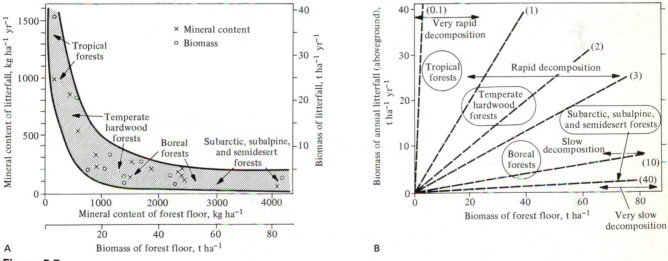

A

B

Figure 5.7

(A) Relationship between litterfall biomass and mineral content, and forest floor biomass and mineral content in different forest regions of the world. (B) Litter decomposition rates (numbers in brackets) expressed as the ratio of litterfall biomass to forest floor biomass. A ratio of 2 indicates that on average it take two years for the complete decomposition of one year's litterfall. (Data from Rodin and Bazilevich, 1967.) The litterfall data are for aboveground litter only, whereas forest floor biomass is derived from both above- and belowground litterfall. Consequently, decomposition rates shown in the diagram are underestimates.

After it has passed through a soil animal, litter is eliminated as fecal pellets which are rapidly invaded by fungi and bacteria. Intense activity by soil animals is normally a prerequisite for the high populations of soil microflora that are responsible for most of the actual decomposition. The relationship between rate of decomposition and abundance of soil microflora in various types of litterfall in Tennessee is shown in Table 4.13. Obviously, any explanation of the variation in rate of litter decomposition must be based on an understanding of the factors that control the abundance, species composition, and activity of the soil microflora. These include:

1. *The activity of the soil fauna,* including earthworms, enchytraeid worms, diplopods, isopods, dipteran larvae, collembolans, and orobatid mites (Edwards et al., 1970).

2. *The species of tree producing the litter.* Species vary in the physical and chemical properties of their litter, and in the soil microclimate and soil chemistry that they induce.

3. *The chemical composition of the litter.* This influences the acidity (pH) of the forest floor and the nutritional value of the litter to the decomposer organisms. The great variation in litter inorganic chemistry is illustrated in Table 5.9, and there is also an important variation in organic constituents of litter, such as sugars, amino acids, and phenols. These may affect the microflora directly, or indirectly by regulating the nutritional availability of other litter chemicals. The relative abundance of the different chemicals is also important. The carbon/nitrogen ratio has traditionally been considered a good indicator of decomposability; litter with a very high C/N ratio generally decomposes very slowly. This is partly because microbes need nitrogen in

order to be able to utilize carbon, partly because of the high acidity that generally accompanies high C/N ratios, and partly because the nitrogen in high C/N material is often complexed with decomposition-inhibiting chemicals such as tannins. However, a high C/N ratio does not necessarily correlate with slow decomposition. Low-C/N ratio material may decompose very slowly because all the easily decomposed carbon compounds have been used up, and high-C/N-ratio material with little tannin and lignin (e.g., straw) may decompose quite rapidly because the carbon it contains is accessible to decomposer organisms. Decomposition can sometimes be more limited by lack of available carbon than by lack of available nitrogen.

Decomposition rates determine the quantity of carbon stored in the soil and play a significant role in the global carbon cycle. Accelerated conversion of forest to agriculture has increased the loss of soil carbon and contributed to increases in atmospheric CO_2 levels (Clark, 1982, Bolin et al., 1979, Schlesinger, 1977). This topic is discussed again later in this chapter and in Chapter 8.

4. *The acidity (pH) of the litter and of the forest floor that it produces.* Many soil organisms are intolerant of very acidic forest floor conditions. Fungi are less adversely affected and dominate the soil flora in the decomposition of acid forest floors. Mites and springtails, which dominate the soil fauna under acidic conditions, decompose litter more slowly than bacteria and earthworms that dominate the soil flora and fauna, respectively, in less acid soils. Acid substrates are normally characterized by slow litter decomposition, although this is not always the case. Red alder (*Alnus rubra*) litter decomposes quite rapidly in spite of the low pH

Table 5.9 Variation in the Chemical Composition of Freshly Fallen Leaf Litter

Species	Composition, %					
	N	P	K	Ca	Mg	Ash
Sweet birch (*Betula lenta*)	0.72	0.17	0.75	1.65	0.28	—
Yellow-poplar (*Liriodendron tulipifera*)	0.51	0.11	0.95	2.56	0.45	10.67
Balsam fir (*Abies balsamea*)	1.25	0.09	0.12	1.12	0.16	3.08
Shagbark hickory (*Carya ovata*)	0.91	0.16	1.18	2.09	—	9.59
American basswood (*Tilia americanum*)	1.01	0.12	0.52	3.84	0.77	15.16
Cucumber tree (*Magnolia accuminata*)	0.58	0.28	0.76	1.71	0.29	—
Sugar maple (*Acer saccharum*)	0.67	0.11	0.75	1.81	0.24	—
Norway spruce (*Picea abies*)	1.02	0.09	0.39	1.96	0.23	—
Jack pine (*Pinus banksiana*)	0.58	0.04	0.16	0.61	—	4.15
Northern white cedar (*Thuja occidentalis*)	0.60	0.04	0.25	2.16	0.15	—
Eastern hemlock (*Tsuga canadensis*)	1.05	0.07	0.27	0.68	0.14	—

Source: Lutz and Chandler, 1946. Copyright John Wiley and Sons. Used with permission.

found in the forest floor beneath many red alder stands.

5. *The soil microclimate*. In common with other organisms, soil fauna and flora have certain climatic tolerances and are not active in soils that are either too hot, too cold, too wet, or too dry. The fastest decomposition occurs in the tropics, where the temperature and moisture conditions are almost constantly favorable for soil organisms. The slowest decomposition occurs where the soil is either very hot, very cold, very wet, or very dry for much of the year.

6. *The fertility status of the soil*. A plant growing on a fertile soil tends to have higher concentrations of nutrients in both foliage and litter than does the same plant growing on an infertile soil. Fertile soil generally supports plant species that have higher concentrations of nutrients and more decomposable litter than species that generally grow on infertile sites. Thus, by controlling plant species and litterfall chemistry, soil fertility exerts a major influence on the activity of decomposer organisms.

The discussion so far has referred primarily to leaf litter decomposition. Decomposition of large roots, branches, and stems involves different organisms, but the same principles hold true. Decomposition is relatively rapid where the material is initially comminuted (broken into small pieces) by the action of wood-boring animals (largely insects operating in conjunction with fungi), whose fecal pellets become the substrate for fungal and bacterial activity. Fungal activity alone will decompose woody material, but the process is very much slower than when fungi are preceded by soil fauna.

The end products of litter decomposition are CO_2, water, inorganic ions, and a variety of organic substances. The nature and abundance of these organic materials plays an important role in the development of the forest floor and the soil.

E. Role of Understory Vegetation

Discussions of nutrient cycling in forest ecosystems generally refer exclusively or mainly to the overstory tree vegetation. To understand how forests cycle nutrients, it is necessary to consider the contribution of *all* the vegetation, not only that of the dominant trees. This requires that our discussion be broadened to include understory trees, shrubs, herbs, ferns, mosses, and epiphytes (plants growing nonparasitically on other plants).

The biomass of understory and epiphytic vegetation can vary from nothing to as much as 15 t ha^{-1}, according to the tree species, the stand structure, the site type, and the climate (Rodin and Bazilevich, 1967). Particularly high values occur in "moss forests" (forests typified by a continuous

blanket of moss on the forest floor but little other minor vegetation). Dense shrub and herb growth often looks more impressive but generally amounts to far less weight per hectare than does a thick carpet of moss.

Minor vegetation biomass rarely constitutes more than a small fraction of the total forest biomass, but its contribution to nutrient cycling and total stand production can be very significant. It generally has higher concentrations of chemicals and higher rates of biomass turnover (i.e., less storage of net production) than does the overstory. As a result, the role of minor vegetation in total forest productivity and biogeochemistry is much greater than would be expected on the basis of biomass. For example, the understory of a 120-year-old pine forest in the U.S.S.R. was found to produce 16 times more biomass annually than the trees (P'Yavchenko, 1960). A study in three subalpine forest ecosystem types in coastal British Columbia (Figure 5.8) revealed that while minor vegetation litterfall accounted for only 3–11% of the aboveground litterfall biomass, minor vegetation contributed 16–38% of the N, 14–35% of the P, 5–31% of the Ca, 19–55% of the Mg, and an amazing 32–90% of the K in the total annual aboveground litterfall (Yarie, 1980). The understory also had a significant effect on nutrients in throughfall. This study demonstrates the importance of even a diminutive understory, and the fact that the quantity of nutrients circulating in the minor vegetation is sometimes greater than that circulating in the tree crop.

Table 5.10 presents some comparisons between the contributions of overstory and minor forest vegetation to leaching, litterfall, and nutrient uptake, and Figure 5.9 compares the importance of understory vegetation in K cycling in two different forest types. It is apparent from these data that estimates of nutrient turnover based on studies of the overstory alone will significantly underestimate the magnitude of the forest biogeochemical cycle in most types of forest.

A particularly interesting example of the significance of understory vegetation in nutrient cycling is the relationship between black spruce and the carpet of mosses on the forest floor in northern Quebec (Weetman, 1967; Weetman and Timmer, 1967). In these stands, the moss was found to contribute 33–50% of the total aboveground biomass production, while annual uptake of N, P, K, Ca, and Mg by the moss was estimated to be between 23 and 53% of the annual uptake by the trees. Studies of precipitation chemistry, moss decomposition, the rooting pattern of the black spruce, and the availability of nutrients in the forest floor led to the conclusion that the moss layer was the major source of nitrogen for the trees. Nitrogen from precipitation

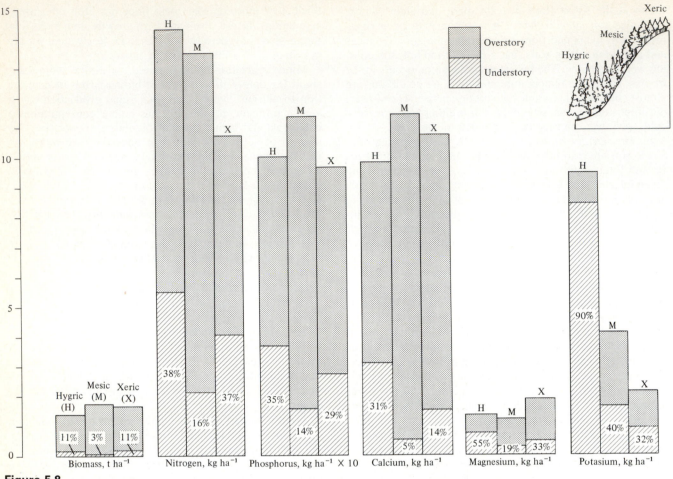

Figure 5.8
Contribution of understory and overstory to annual aboveground litterfall in three subalpine forest ecosystems along a minor topographic sequence of site types from dry (xeric) to moist (hygric) sites. The forest, which consisted of Pacific silver fir, mountain hemlock, and Alaska yellow cedar in various proportions, was up to 450 years old. (After Yarie, 1980. Used with the author's permission.)

and throughfall is absorbed by the moss layer, which holds it for 1–3 years before the moss starts to decompose. Nitrogen that is released is absorbed by mycorrhizal roots which grow in the layer of decomposing moss above the forest floor. Most of the nitrogen in the litterfall is thought to remain as unavailable organic nitrogen, the nitrogen cycle being driven by the 9 kg ha^{-1} that the tree canopy and moss layer filter out of the precipitation. The moss thus acts as an efficient biological filter that absorbs nutrients from solution in precipitation and throughfall and subsequently makes them available to the trees. Without the moss, much of the circulating nutrients would become immobilized in

the forest floor. There may also be some nitrogen fixation by the mosses or associated external microflora. Many species, especially *Sphagnum* and *Drepanocladus,* have both epiphytic and intracellular nitrogen-fixing algae and bacteria (Granhall and Selander, 1973; Granhall and Lindberg, 1977; Rosen and Lindberg, 1980).

The relatively high concentration of nutrients in the litterfall of understory vegetation (Table 5.10) has a generally beneficial effect on litter decomposition in the forest floor, and thus on site fertility. The beneficial effects on stand productivity of maintaining a light understory has long been recognized by European silviculturists.

Table 5.10 Comparisons of Some Biogeochemical Roles of Understory and Overstory Vegetation

A. Chemical Composition and Total Chemical Content of Understory (U) and Overstory (O) Vegetation Litterfall in Two Forest Types in Eastern U.S. (Scott, 1955)

	White Pine Plantation				Hardwood Stand			
	Concentration, %		kg ha^{-1}		Concentration, %		kg ha^{-1}	
Element	U	O	U	O	U	O	U	O
N	1.46	0.66	3.0	7.1	1.34	0.76	3.4	10.6
P	0.17	0.13	0.3	1.4	0.17	0.14	0.4	2.1
K	1.07	0.43	2.6	4.7	1.13	0.48	2.6	6.9
Ca	0.90	0.70	2.0	7.5	0.74	0.81	2.0	11.5
Mg	0.46	0.34	1.1	3.8	0.39	0.40	1.1	5.7
Biomass	—	—	206	1114	—	—	241	1402

B. Contributions to Leachate (Lch) and Litterfall (Ltfl) of Overstory and a Fern Understory in an Oak Wood in England (Carlisle et al., 1967)

	N, kg ha^{-1} yr^{-1}		P, kg ha^{-1} yr^{-1}		K, kg ha^{-1} yr^{-1}		Ca, kg ha^{-1} yr^{-1}		Mg, kg ha^{-1} yr^{-1}		
	Lch	Ltfl	Lch	Ltfl	Lch	Ltfl	Lch	Ltfl	Lch	Ltfl	Biomass, kg ha^{-1} yr^{-1}
Oak overstory	0.9	48.7	0.6	2.8	16.0	15.3	12.3	32.1	5.6	4.7	5196
Fern understory	0.3	12.9	0.1	0.9	9.4	6.9	0.1	4.0	1.0	1.3	1470

C. Contributions of Overstory and Understory Vegetation to Annual Nutrient Uptake in a Pine Stand in Finland (Malkonen, 1974).

	Percent of Total Uptake				Percent of Biomass	Percent of Annual Biomass Production
	N	P	K	Ca		
Pine overstory	54.6	53.6	54.1	58.4	84	71
Understory	45.4	46.4	45.9	41.6	16	29

F. Direct Nutrient Cycling

In many forests, recovery of nutrients by plants from decomposing litter involves the combination of uptake from soil solution by both mycorrhizal and nonmycorrhizal roots, and direct uptake by mycorrhizal fungi from decomposing organic matter. In some forests, nutrients are recovered almost exclusively by the latter method: the *direct nutrient cycling* pathway (Stark, 1972).

Direct nutrient cycling involves the invasion of fresh litter by the mycelium of a mycorrhizal fungus. The hyphae penetrate into the litter and decompose it, absorbing the nutrients as they are mineralized. Some of these nutrients become available to the mycorrhizal plant root. This decomposition pathway avoids the soil solution phase, which in turn prevents the nutrients from being leached away, and also prevents them from being immobilized by nonmycorrhizal microbes.

This is the most conservative of the biogeochemical pathways. Direct nutrient cycling ensures a very high efficiency of recovery of nutrients lost from plants in litter and thereby contributes to an almost closed biogeochemical cycle. It is particularly well developed on nutrient-poor soils where there has been strong selective pressure in favor of nutrient conservation. The pathway was first described for tropical forests growing on very nutrient deficient soils in the Amazon Basin, but it is probably also the dominant pathway of nutrient recovery on nutrient-poor sites in temperate and boreal forests.

For a recent review of nutrient cycling in various different types of forest ecosystem, see Cole and Rapp (1981).

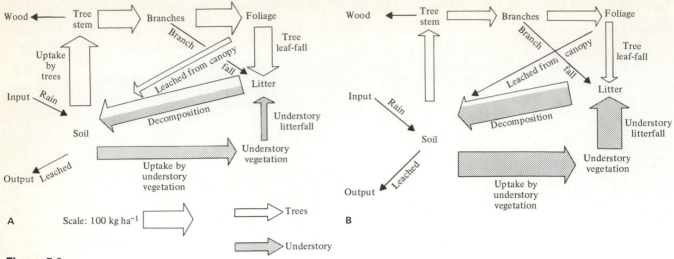

Figure 5.9
Comparison of the role of understory vegetation (shaded) in the potassium cycle in stands of two different species growing adjacent to each other on similar sites in England. (A) Pedunculate oak, 47 years old. (B) Scots pine, 47 years old. The magnitude of both the overstory and the understory cycle varies between the two stands. (After Ovington, 1965. Reproduced by permission of Hodder & Stoughton Limited and J. D. Ovington.)

5.6   The Biochemical Cycle: Nutrient Cycling Within Plants

Plants do not rely solely on root and foliar uptake to satisfy the current nutrient demands of height, diameter, and root growth. They are able to provide at least some of their needs by internal redistribution of nutrients that are already inside the plant. Animals behave similarly. There is a constant exchange of calcium between blood and bones, but in lactating female mammals there is a net withdrawal of calcium from bones to blood if the dietary intake of calcium is inadequate to meet the calcium demands of milk production. The internal redistribution of nutrients in plants, the *biochemical cycle,* constitutes an important mechanism by which plants conserve nutrients.

Plants would lose a much greater quantity of N, P, and K in litterfall if they were not able to remove a substantial proportion of these nutrients from old leaves before shedding them. In a study in Finland it was shown that 4-year-old needles of Scots pine lost 17% of their weight, 69% of their N, 81% of their P, and 80% of their K before they became litterfall. The nutrients were translocated out of the needles and stored initially in the bark and new wood of branches adjacent to the old needles (Malkonen, 1974). A study in the southern U.S. reported that loblolly pine needles lost 44, 38, and 58% of their N, P, and K, respectively,

and 14% of their weight just prior to abscission (Wells and Metz, 1963). Table 5.11 summarizes the efficiency of N and P retranslocation in a variety of tree species.

Trees are able to satisfy an appreciable proportion of their annual nutrient requirements by this mechanism. In one study, 20-year-old loblolly pines were found to satisfy 45% of their annual N requirement by translocation from yellowing needles (Switzer et al., 1968). The translocation out of old Scots pine needles in Finland was found to equal 23 and 33% of the N and K required for the production of new needles (Malkonen, 1974). Table 5.12 examines the importance of internal transfer in comparison with other sources of nutrients in satisfying the annual nutrient requirements of loblolly pine. Internal cycling is obviously very important for some elements in some species.

Redistribution of nutrients is important to plants in many ways. By conserving nutrients within their tissues, plants can sustain growth on sites on which the availability of nutrients for uptake from the soil is very low. They can also sustain growth at a time of year when nutrient availability in the soil is very low (e.g., in the spring on soils that are very cold and wet). Nutrients continue to be absorbed and stored by plants as they become available in the soil later in the season, even though they may not be needed right away for active growth. Redistribution also has some practical significance. The conservation of nitrogen within the tree crown

Table 5.11 Percentage of the Pre-senescence N and P Translocated out of Foliage Prior to Litterfall

	Nitrogen (%)	Phosphorus (%)	Reference
Douglas-fir: hygric	61	73	Parkinson, 1984
mesic	69	35	
xeric	61	1	
Douglas-fir: 42 yr	42	46	Turner, 1975
49 yr	36	63	
Loblolly pine	45	66	Switzer & Nelson, 1972
Scots pine	69	81	Malkönen, 1975
Evergreens-bog	45–71	45–75	Small, 1972
Evergreens-nonbog	51–73	66–98	
Deciduous-bog	23–68	46–80	
Deciduous-nonbog	1–52	4–71	
Scots pine: poor site	77	—	Stachurski & Zimka, 1975
Hornbeam: poor site	64	—	
good site	37	—	
Oak: poor site	63	—	
good site	45	—	
Alder good site	5	—	
Beech	72	70	Staaf, 1982
Chestnut Oak: better	80	65	Ostman & Weaver, 1982
poorer	76	61	
Eucalyptus	—	60	Attiwill, 1980
Eastern cottonwood	74	66	Baker & Blackmon, 1977
Mixed hardwoods	51	61	Ryan & Borman, 1982
Pin cherry	57	59	
Loblolly pine	52	47	Wells & Metz, 1963
upper crown	55	52	
mid crown	52	46	
lower crown	47	45	
Pine	43	—	Rapp et al., 1979
Subalpine conifers	54	59	Turner & Singer, 1976

may be one reason why the stimulation of tree growth by a single addition of nitrogen fertilizer persists for several years after treatment. If this is so, fertilization may have better results in forests where internal redistribution is well developed than in those in which it is providing only a minor contribution to tree nutrition.

The efficiency of nutrient recovery and redistribution at the time of leaf abscission can vary according to the availability of nutrients in the soil. It has been shown that the rate of nutrient withdrawal from aging radiata pine needles was much greater on nutrient-poor soils than on more fertile soils (Florence and Chuong, 1974). A confirmation of the relationship between internal cycling and external nutrient availability was provided by Turner (1977), who altered the availability of nitrogen in the forest floor of a Douglas-fir stand in coastal Washington by applying sucrose and sawdust to the ground beneath the trees. The provision of a readily available energy source greatly increased microbial activity, which in turn resulted in short-term immobilization of much of the available nitrogen in the forest floor. The trees responded to this sudden reduction in nitrogen availability by increasing the redistribution of nitrogen from old foliage to younger foliage and by shedding the oldest foliage, presumably because it no longer had sufficient N to operate efficiently; the old foliage was sacrificed in the face of serious N shortages in order to maintain the photosynthetic activity of young foliage. Table 5.13 summarizes the effects of the induced N deficiency (sucrose and sawdust) and also of induced N enrichment (fertilization) on internal cycling and foliage biomass. It can be seen that uptake of N provided only 15% of the N needed for new foliage production in the carbohydrate treatment, compared with 55% in the untreated control. The fertilized trees took up 26% more than was needed for the new foliage (luxury consumption).

Table 5.12 Relative Contributions of Different Nutrient Sources to the Annual Nutrient Requirements of a 20-Year-Old Loblolly Pine Plantation (Data from Switzer and Nelson, 1972)

Cycle	Nutrient Source	Percent Contribution to the Requirement of:				
		N	P	K	Ca[a]	Mg
Geochemical	Precipitation	16	6	12	31	16
	Mineral soil	0	2	0	0	6
Biogeochemical	Forest floor (litter decomposition)	40	23	16	47	38
	Canopy washing and leaching	5	9	50	22	16
Biochemical	Internal transfer	39	60	20	0	24

[a]Original data adjusted.

The efficiency of internal cycling is determined not only by the fertility of the soil. It is also affected by any factor that influences plant growth and plant uptake demand. Moisture thus has a major effect on internal cycling. Parkinson (1984) found that internal cycling of N did not vary much along a gradient of N availability in the soil because an accompanying increase in soil moisture enabled the tree to utilize all the available soil N even at the richest site. The confounding of moisture and nutrients may explain some of the inconsistencies in the literature on internal cycling.

It has been suggested that the physiological character of evergreenness (as opposed to deciduousness) may be related to the storage and conservation of nutrients (Muller-Stoll, 1947; Loveless, 1961; Beadle, 1966; Monk, 1966; Richards, 1968), and the observation that the degree of evergreenness of a given species varies in different habitats may in some cases be related to biogeochemical cycling. As noted in Chapter 4, Pacific silver fir in southwestern B.C. retains 6–8 years of needles at low elevation (300 m), 13–19 years of needles at medium elevation (1000 m), and up to 25 years (a maximum of 31 years) at elevations above 1500 m. Retention of a large biomass of old foliage provides a large volume from which nutrients may be withdrawn to support new growth when the air is warm but the soil is still cold or waterlogged—conditions that limit nutrient uptake. Having a large number of small annual foliage increments also means that only a very small fraction of the foliage is dropped each year. This reduces the need for a large recovery of nutrients at the time of litterfall, and it has been suggested (D. W. Cole, personal communication) that the degree of internal cycling is inversely proportional to the number of years of foliage retention. Deciduous conifers such as larch, and deciduous angiosperms that grow on infertile soils recycle a very high proportion of foliar N, P,

Table 5.13 Effect of Induced Increases and Decreases in Soil Nitrogen Availability on the Biomass, Nitrogen Content, and Internal Cycling of Douglas-fir Foliage

	N[a] Fertilization		Untreated Control		Carbohydrate Treatment	
	B[b]	N	B	N	B	N
Total foliage	10,340	137	9,400	94	8,480	80
Current foliage	2,550	37	2,200	22	1,790	19
Foliage litterfall	1,290	11.2	1,880	14.1	2,390	14.3
Uptake of N from soil	63		17		4	
Recycling from old foliage	−19		10		16.4	
Ratio: Uptake/ current tissue content (%)	126		55		15	

Source: Turner, 1977. Copyright American Society of Foresters. Used with permission.

[a]N, nitrogen, kg ha^{-1}; 880 kg ha^{-1} of urea.

[b]B, biomass, kg ha^{-1}.

and K. Pines that retain only 2–4 years of needles are somewhat less efficient, but still recover a large proportion of these nutrients prior to leaf fall. Species such as spruces and true firs, which carry many years of foliage, have a much lower need to develop highly efficient internal cycling.

Although the biochemical cycle has received less attention than the biogeochemical cycle, it obviously plays a vital role in plant nutrition and in determining the efficiency with which plants can utilize the solar energy available in a particular ecosystem.

Until relatively recently, biogeochemical studies have tended to focus on one of the three major cycles: geochemical, biogeochemical, or biochemical. This was very reasonable because the scarcity of data on all aspects of nutrient cycling required that a lot of detailed data gathering be undertaken. However, there now exists an extensive literature on forest biogeochemistry, and increasing attention is being paid to synthesis: to a consideration of the overall biogeochemical character of forest ecosystems, and how this varies between different ecosystems and between different developmental stages of a given ecosystem. A good example of such a comparison and synthesis can be found in Cole and Rapp (1981). For an excellent review of many aspects of global biogeochemistry, see Bolin and Cook (1983).

5.7 Cycling of Three Major Nutrients: Carbon, Nitrogen, and Sulfur

So far we have discussed the three major types of cycle in very general terms without reference to the variations that are associated with different chemical elements. In order to understand the complexity and interrelationships of geochemical and biogeochemical cycles more fully, we shall examine the cycles of carbon, nitrogen, and sulfur in some detail. The biogeochemistry of these three elements is rather similar in that all three require chemical reduction by biological processes before incorporation into living matter $(C \rightarrow CH, N \rightarrow NH, S \rightarrow SH)$.

On a global basis, the fixation and reduction of carbon, nitrogen, and sulfur are accomplished in the ratio $10:1:1$ by organisms that contain these elements, on average, in the ratio $554:7:1$ from an environment in which they are available in the ratio $1:103:34$ (Deevey, 1973). The exact details of these global cycles are still not well known. The following descriptions are based to a considerable extent on educated estimates.

A. The Carbon Cycle

Living organisms as a group contain the six major nutrients in the proportions: hydrogen 2960, oxygen 1480, carbon 1480, nitrogen 16, phosphorus 1.8, and sulfur 1.0 (Deevey, 1970). Carbon is therefore one of the major constituents of organic matter. It enters the biogeochemical cycle of terrestrial ecosystems primarily as gaseous CO_2, absorbed from the atmosphere by photosynthesizing plants. A small amount is also added as bicarbonate ions in rainwater and from the weathering of carbonaceous rocks. Carbon is lost from plants as respiratory CO_2, or it may enter grazing and detritus trophic webs. It is released from these primarily as the respiratory CO_2 of saprophytic organisms in the detritus trophic web, but a substantial additional amount passes back to the atmosphere as methane gas (CH_4). Some of the carbon released as CO_2 is promptly reabsorbed by photosynthetic organs or is dissolved in soil water and taken up by roots as bicarbonate ions, but most of it returns to the atmosphere or is carried off in drainage waters as bicarbonate ions. A smaller amount is returned to the soil in the form of organic molecules, such as amino acids, which can be absorbed by plant roots, but this pathway is relatively unimportant.

Most carbon atoms spend only a small proportion of their time in biogeochemical cycles, the majority of global carbon dynamics occurring in geochemical cycles. The residence time of carbon in the biosphere varies, of course, and we have already seen that the trapping and daytime reabsorption of nighttime respiratory CO_2 is more efficient in forests than in more diminutive plant communities in which most respiratory CO_2 is lost back to the atmosphere. Also, carbon fixed in permanent plant structures will remain for a longer time in an ecosystem with long-lived organisms than in one with short-lived organisms, and longer in ecosystems with low plant utilization by herbivores than in heavily grazed ecosystems. Carbon will therefore tend to remain longer in the biogeochemical cycles of forests than of ecosystems such as grasslands. The major pathways of the carbon cycle, and estimates of the quantities and rates of transfer within the cycle, are shown in Figure 5.10. The uncertainties in arriving at these estimates are considerable and the numbers should be used with appropriate caution, although the great public and scientific concern over the continuing rise in atmospheric CO_2 levels has led to a great improvement in our knowledge of the carbon cycle over the past decade.

Carbon dioxide is present in the atmosphere at a concentration approaching 340 ppm (about 0.03%) (Watts, 1982). This represents only a minute portion of the total carbon on the earth since about 99.9% of the world's carbon is locked up in deposits of coal, oil, limestone, and chalk. Atmospheric concentrations have not always been 340 ppm. At the beginning of the Industrial Revolution the level is

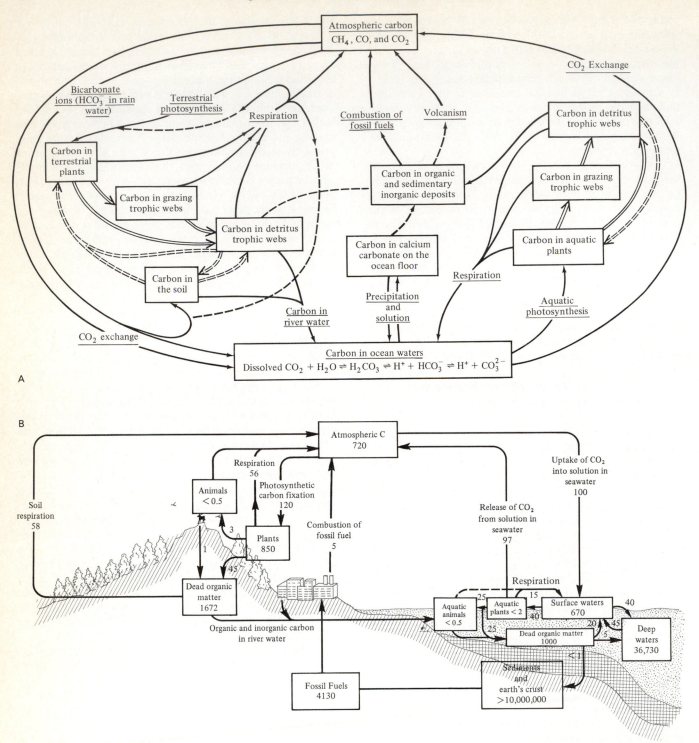

A

B

Figure 5.10

The carbon cycle. (A) Distribution and transfers of carbon in the biosphere. Double lines indicate the biogeochemical cycle, single lines the geochemical cycle. Solid lines indicate major transfers, dashed lines transfers of secondary importance. (B) Estimates of quantities and rates of transfer of carbon in the biosphere. Units are billions (10^9) of metric tons of carbon. Transfer rates are expressed on an annual basis. (Part B redrawn after Bolin et al., 1979; Clark et al., 1982. Reproduced by permission of Oxford University Press, *Scientific American*, B. Bolin, and W. C. Clark.)

thought to have been about 290 ppm. It has risen steadily since then, largely though not solely because of the release of CO_2 by the combustion of fossil fuels (Figure 5.11). By the year 2030 it may have doubled the level of 1900 A.D. to reach a concentration of about 600 ppm (Houghton et al., 1983), although others feel that this will not happen until about 2070 (Clark et al., 1982).

The estimated increase in atmospheric CO_2 concentrations since the middle of the nineteenth century cannot account for all the CO_2 that has been released by the combustion of fossil fuel during this period. In fact, the difference between the CO_2 content of the atmosphere in 1970 and in the mid-1800s is equal to only 65% of the calculated release of CO_2 by fossil fuel combustion (Machta, 1973). It is apparent that atmospheric CO_2 concentrations are under some type of regulatory control, an important part of which is provided by primary biomass production. Because photosynthesis is rather generally limited by the availability of CO_2, the world's vegetation acts as a negative feedback regulator which helps to moderate changes in atmospheric CO_2 concentrations. There is an estimated 5% increase in net primary production for each 10% increase in CO_2 concentrations when water, temperature, and other nutrients are

not limiting. Also, elevated CO_2 levels increase the water use efficiency of plants, thereby increasing net primary production in dry climates (Wong, 1980).

It is thought that prior to 1860, CO_2 uptake in net primary production balanced CO_2 release from the biosphere. Since 1860, there has been a net release from the biosphere due to clearance of forests for agriculture, burning of the wood, and decomposition of forest floors and soil organic matter. The magnitude of this net release back to the atmosphere is estimated to be 135–228 billion metric tons of C. Up until 1960, this net input exceeded that from fossil fuel combustion, and in 1980 alone it was estimated to be 1.8 to 4.7 billion metric tons. Since 1960, fossil fuels have taken over as the most important net contributor (Houghton et al., 1983).

The second major regulator of atmospheric CO_2 levels is the world's oceans. CO_2 dissolves in water to a degree that is controlled by temperature, pH, the atmospheric pressure exerted by CO_2, and the concentration of other nutrients in the water. Atmospheric CO_2 in contact with water forms the following series of chemical equilibria, which serve to maintain the air above the ocean at fairly constant CO_2 levels.

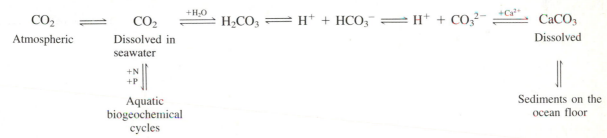

As the CO_2 concentration in the air increases, more gas goes into solution in the sea. This results in increased sedimentation of calcium carbonate and also in greater aquatic production if there are adequate supplies of dissolved nitrogen and phosphorus. Reductions in atmospheric CO_2, on the other hand, lead to a release of CO_2 from solution in seawater, the loss being made up by a chain of chemical adjustments leading ultimately to the uptake into solution of calcium carbonate deposits on the ocean floor. This mechanism is quite efficient at regulating atmospheric CO_2; it has removed 35% of what human beings have

added over the past century. The only snag is that the rate at which the mechanism operates is dependent on the rate of atmospheric and oceanic stirring and on the rate of response of the oceanic chemical equilibria (Broecker, 1973). Because these are all rather slow processes, the CO_2 control mechanism has not been able to keep up with the very rapid rate of CO_2 release from fossil fuels. Because of the lag in response of the oceanic control mechanisms, and because of the reduction in the terrestrial biospheric control mechanism, atmospheric CO_2 concentrations have risen.

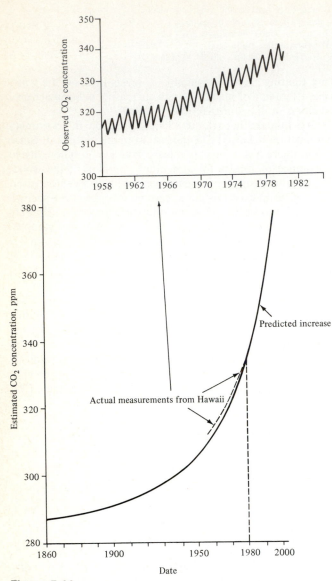

Figure 5.11

Estimated concentrations of CO_2 in the atmosphere from 1860 to the mid-1970s and predictions of increases to the year 2000 (after Machta, 1973). Actual data to 1980 from Mauna Loa, Hawaii are shown in the inset graph (after Watts, 1982) which shows both the annual variation and the overall upward trend. The variation in the data around the trend reflects the seasonal change in atmospheric CO_2 levels between summer and winter in the northern hemisphere: a result of the seasonal change in uptake by plants.

The regulation of atmospheric CO_2 is a good example of the complex processes that have operated for millenia to maintain the chemical conditions of this planet between the narrow limits within which life as we know it can exist. It has far-reaching significance for human beings and for other living organisms since the concentration of atmospheric carbon dioxide contributes to the regulation of the world's temperature in addition to its critical role in plant nutrition. Short-wavelength solar radiation (sunlight) can pass relatively freely through our atmosphere, but the long-wavelength energy (infrared radiation) that is reradiated from the surface of the earth cannot. It is absorbed by CO_2 and water vapor, and our atmosphere acts much like the glass in a greenhouse, maintaining a warm layer of air in contact with the earth (the atmospheric "greenhouse effect"). As atmospheric concentrations of CO_2 increase, more of the reradiated energy is absorbed by the atmosphere and its temperature increases. This, in turn, raises the temperature of the ocean, which causes more dissolved CO_2 to be released (the chemical equilibrium moves to the left), further enhancing the heating effect. This positive feedback mechanism cannot go on indefinitely, however, because a major increase in air temperature would accelerate evaporation of water from land and sea, leading to increased cloudiness. This would reflect more of the sun's short-wavelength radiation, leading to a cooling of the atmosphere. (This is discussed further in Chapter 8).

With such a mechanism regulating atmospheric CO_2 and temperature levels, it might be concluded that the continuing increase in atmospheric CO_2 poses no significant biological problems. Unfortunately, it is not certain that these mechanisms would act in time to prevent major changes in the earth's climate should our present rate of addition of CO_2 to the atmosphere be continued or increased. The failure of these mechanisms would have important consequences for all forms of life (Schneider, 1974, 1975). Major increases in atmospheric CO_2 concentrations have occurred before, perhaps as the result of periods of massive volcanic eruptions. There have also been major changes in the world's climate that have periodically redirected evolution and led to the extinction of many previously dominant life forms. The relationship between these two events is not known, but it makes interesting speculation. It is hoped that we will either run out of fossil fuel or voluntarily curb the production of CO_2 before we so change the atmosphere that we initiate a major alteration in the earth's climate. Improved knowledge of the biosphere would give us a better idea of how close we are to overloading the negative feedback mechanisms on which our life depends. For a recent review of the climatic impacts of increased CO_2 and other gaseous and aerosol emissions, and of the difficulties of quantifying biospheric and oceanic control of atmospheric CO_2 levels, see Bach et al. (1980), and Clark (1982).

B. The Nitrogen Cycle

The nitrogen cycle is somewhat different from the carbon cycle. Although both nutrients enter ecosystems from a reservoir in the atmosphere, the nitrogen reservoir is vast relative to the biological withdrawals from it, and it lacks the complex regulating mechanism that operates in the carbon cycle.

As a gas, nitrogen is as abundant in the atmosphere as carbon is scarce; it makes up about 79% of the world's atmosphere (i.e., 790,000 ppm). Unlike carbon, this vast atmospheric reservoir of nitrogen is unavailable to most organisms, and net production in much of the world's vegetation is limited by lack of nitrogen. This is a situation not unlike a person dying of thirst in the middle of the ocean— "water, water everywhere nor any drop to drink." [7] The nitrogen molecule, N_2, is an inert, unreactive gas that requires a high input of energy to break the N—N bond be-

[7] From the poem "The Rime of the Ancient Mariner" by S. T. Coleridge.

fore it will combine chemically with other atoms. Industrial fixation of nitrogen in the manufacture of fertilizers requires a temperature of 450°C and pressure of between 250 and 1000 atm. It is remarkable, therefore, to find that certain organisms have evolved the ability to reduce atmospheric nitrogen and combine it into organic molecules at 30–35°C under normal atmospheric pressure. This biological attribute is likely to be heavily exploited in the future as the cost of energy, and thus the cost of making nitrogen fertilizer, continues to rise.

The main pathways of nitrogen movement in geochemical and biogeochemical cycles are shown in Figure 5.12, together with estimates of the quantities involved. As with the carbon cycle, quantitative estimates of the world nitrogen cycle incorporate many uncertainties and must be accepted with appropriate caution. Nitrogen exists in the atmosphere as dinitrogen gas (N_2), ammonia gas (NH_3), and nitrate (NO_3^-), or ammonium (NH_4^+) ions, and can enter biogeochemical cycles in any of these four chemical forms. Ammonia gas is absorbed directly by plant foliage and such direct uptake from the atmosphere may account for up to 10% of the plants' nitrogen needs (Hutchinson et al., 1972). Nitrate and ammonium ions enter ecosystems as dry fallout or in precipitation, and this can add appreciable quantities

Table 5.14 Biological Nitrogen-Fixing Systems (After Epstein 1972; Bond, 1970; Youngberg and Wollum, 1970)

A. Symbiotic associations
   1. Root nodules
      a. Legumes with root-nodule bacteria (*Rhizobium*): peas, beans, clover, lupin, soybean, etc.
      b. Nonlegumes with root-nodule organisms (bacteria and actinomycetes): *Alnus, Arctostaphylos, Artemesia, Casuarina, Ceanothus, Cercocarpus, Coriaria, Discaria, Dryas, Elaeagnus, Hippophae, Opuntia, Myrica, Arafucaria, Ginko, Purshia,* and *Sheperdia*
      c. Nonlegumes with root-nodule blue-green algae; tropical trees of the order *Cycadales*
   2. Leaf nodules
      a. Nonlegume angiosperms with leaf-nodule bacteria; tropical trees; *Psychotrica, Ardisia,* etc.
      b. Nonlegume angiosperms with leaf-gland blue-green algae; herbaceous species in moist tropical habitats: *Gunnera* sp.

B. Less intimate associations
   1. Bacteria on the leaf surfaces of tropical rain forest trees
   2. Bacteria on the leaf surfaces of temperate zone trees
   3. Blue-green algae associated with ferns, liverworts, and fungi

C. Free-living organisms
   1. Blue-green algae (*Cyanophyta*): e.g., *Nostoc, Anabaena, Gleotrichia, Trichodesmium*
   2. Fungi, yeasts, actinomycetes
   3. Bacteria
      a. Aerobic: e.g., *Azotobacter, Beijerinckia*
      b. Facultative: e.g., *Aerobacter*
      c. Anaerobic
         i. Nonphotosynthetic: e.g., *Clostridium*
         ii. Photosynthetic: e.g., *Rhodospirillium*

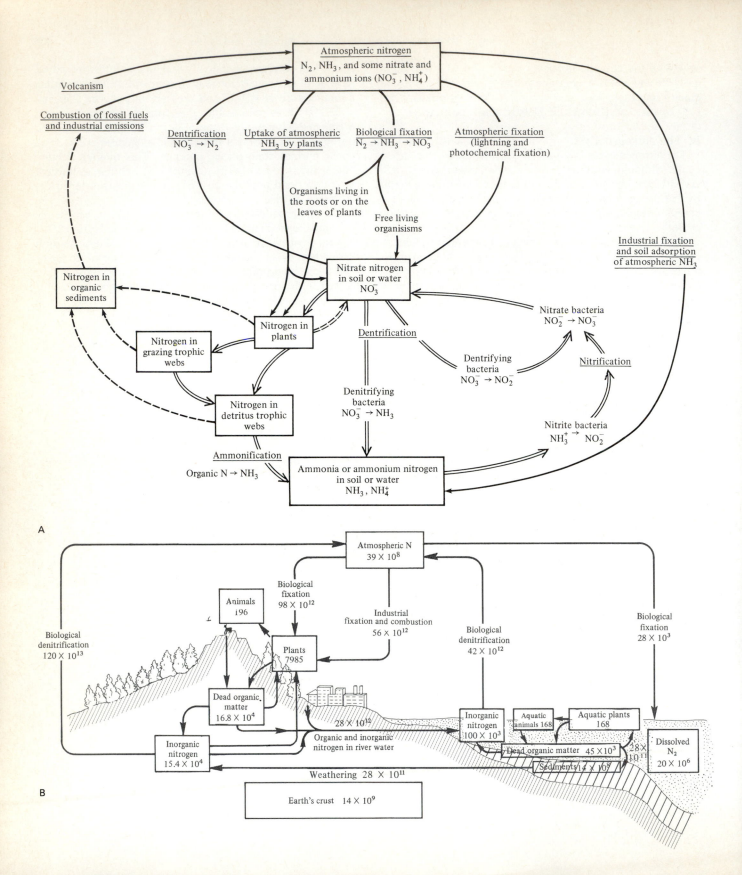

A

Atmospheric nitrogen
N_2, NH_3, and some nitrate and
ammonium ions (NO_3^-, NH_4^+)

Volcanism

Combustion of fossil fuels
and industrial emissions

Dentrification
$NO_3^- \rightarrow N_2$

Uptake of atmospheric
NH_3 by plants

Biological fixation
$N_2 \rightarrow NH_3 \rightarrow NO_3$

Atmospheric fixation
(lightning and
photochemical fixation)

Organisms living in
the roots or on the
leaves of plants

Free living
organisisms

Industrial fixation
and soil adsorption
of atmospheric NH_3

Nitrogen in
organic
sediments

Nitrate nitrogen
in soil or water
NO_3^-

Nitrate bacteria
$NO_2^- \rightarrow NO_3^-$

Nitrogen in
plants

Dentrification

Nitrogen in
grazing trophic
webs

Dentrifying
bacteria
$NO_3^- \rightarrow NO_2^-$

Nitrification

Nitrogen in
detritus trophic
webs

Denitrifying
bacteria
$NO_3^- \rightarrow NH_3$

Nitrite bacteria
$NH_3^+ \rightarrow NO_2^-$

Ammonification

Organic N $\rightarrow NH_3$

Ammonia or ammonium nitrogen
in soil or water
NH_3, NH_4^+

B

Atmospheric N
39×10^8

Biological
fixation
98×10^{12}

Animals
196

Industrial
fixation and combustion
56×10^{12}

Biological
denitrification
42×10^{12}

Biological
fixation
28×10^3

Biological
denitrification
120×10^{13}

Plants
7985

Dead organic
matter
16.8×10^4

28×10^{12}

Inorganic
nitrogen
100×10^3

Aquatic
animals 168

Aquatic plants
168

Organic and inorganic
nitrogen in river water

Dissolved
N_2
20×10^6

Inorganic
nitrogen
15.4×10^4

Dead organic matter 45×10^3

28×10^{11}

Sediments 14×10^9

Weathering 28×10^{11}

Earth's crust 14×10^9

Figure 5.12

The nitrogen cycle. (A) Distribution and transfers of nitrogen in the biosphere. Double lines indicate the biogeochemical cycle, single lines the geochemical cycle. Solid lines indicate major transfers, dashed lines secondary transfers. Nitrogen cycles in aquatic and terrestrial ecosystems are not shown separately. (B) Estimates of quantities and rates of transfer of nitrogen in the biosphere. Units for inventories (numbers in the boxes) are 10^{12} g (millions of metric tons). Transfer rates are expressed as g yr^{-1}. (Redrawn after Delwiche, 1981. Copyright John Wiley & Sons, Inc., N.Y. Redrawn by permission.)

of nitrogen annually to some ecosystems (Table 5.2). However, it is biological fixation of N_2 that accounts for the greatest nitrogen input in most ecosystems (Wollum and Davey, 1975), and estimates of up to 200 kg ha^{-1} yr^{-1} have been made for leguminous crops (Stewart, 1966), and 320 kg ha^{-1} yr^{-1} for stands of red alder (Newton et al., 1968). Terrestrial biological fixation has been estimated at about 98 million metric tons per year on land with an additional 28,000 tons in the oceans, (Delwiche, 1981).

Very few types of organism have evolved the ability to convert biologically unavailable N_2 into biologically available reduced or oxidized nitrogen; of those that can, all are microorganisms (Table 5.14). Many species of bacteria and algae are known to fix nitrogen. Some of these are free living, such as soil bacteria, the purple bacteria, several other photosynthetic bacteria, and several species of blue-green algae. Others operate symbiotically (a relationship between two different types of organisms which is favorable to both of them) with higher plants. The bacteria invade the living tissues of the plant and stimulate cell division and growth. This results in the formation of a nodule in which the bacteria live and fix atmospheric nitrogen. Bacteria of the genus *Rhizobium* stimulate root nodules on leguminous plants, and similar nitrogen-fixing root nodules are formed on the roots of alder (containing species of *Frankia*) and several other tree species. Nitrogen-fixing nodules also form on the leaves of some tropical trees, and nonnodule nitrogen-fixing bacteria are known to live on (or in?) the leaves of other trees, including conifers (Jones, 1970, 1976; Jones et al., 1974). With the help of the enzyme nitrogenase, these organisms are able to reduce N_2 to ammonia, which is converted to ammonium ions and incorporated into the metabolic activities of the plant. Nitrogenase contains iron and molybdenum, which, together with cobalt, are essential micronutrients for nitrogen fixation (Epstein, 1972). Excellent reviews of the role of nitrogen fixation in the production of forest biomass can be found in Fortin et al. (1980) and Chatarpaul and Carlisle (1983). The use of plants capable of N fixation will undoubtedly increase on N-deficient sites (e.g., Binkley, 1983).

The second most important source of nitrogen for terrestrial ecosystems is industrially-fixed fertilizer nitrogen. This

was estimated to be about 40 million metric tons in the mid 1970s and 50 to 60 million metric tons in 1980 (Delwiche, 1981; UN, 1981). The rate of fertilizer use has increased greatly in the past 25 years, and industrial nitrogen fixation could exceed natural biological fixation in the next few decades. Nitrogen fertilizer consumption in the continental U.S. rose from 870,000 metric tons in 1950 to 7,300,000 metric tons in 1972, and was expected to reach 10,900,000 metric tons by 1980 (Wollum and Davey, 1975). However, continued increase in industrial fixation may be limited by the future supply and cost of energy, so extrapolations of current trends should be treated with caution.

Once nitrogen has entered ecosystems, it undergoes a complex series of alterations. It is taken up by plants as NO_3^- or NH_4^+ and converted to organic nitrogen before proceeding along either grazing or detritus trophic chains to end up as soil nitrogen. Organic nitrogen may be stored in soils for many centuries or even millenia, but sooner or later much of it is converted to NH_3 or NH_4^+ by a variety of heterotrophic microorganisms (fungi, bacteria, and actinomycetes) in the process of *ammonification*. Nitrogen in this form may be taken up by plants, held by the soil, or converted to NO_3^- by a variety of either chemoautotrophic or heterotrophic bacteria in a two-stage process called *nitrification*. Nitrite bacteria (e.g., of the genus *Nitrosomonas*) convert NH_3 or NH_4^+ to nitrite ions (NO_2^-) which are the substrate for nitrate bacteria (e.g., of the genus *Nitrobacter*) which convert it to NO_3^-. The energy released during this oxidation is used to reduce and incorporate CO_2 into organic molecules that the microorganisms require for growth. Nitrification only occurs slowly under conditions of high acidity and low temperature, and may be inhibited by the presence of certain types of vegetation (Rice and Pancholy, 1972). It is therefore generally a less important pathway for nitrogen in coniferous than in hardwood forests, in northern than in southern forests, and in high-elevation than in lower-elevation forests. NO_3^- released by nitrification is either taken up by plants, chemically altered by other soil microbes, or held by the soil on the anion exchange capacity (AEC). Since the AEC of many forest soils is low, much of the nitrate that is not altered or absorbed by living organisms enters the geochemical cycle; it moves with soil water into other terrestrial or aquatic ecosystems.

A

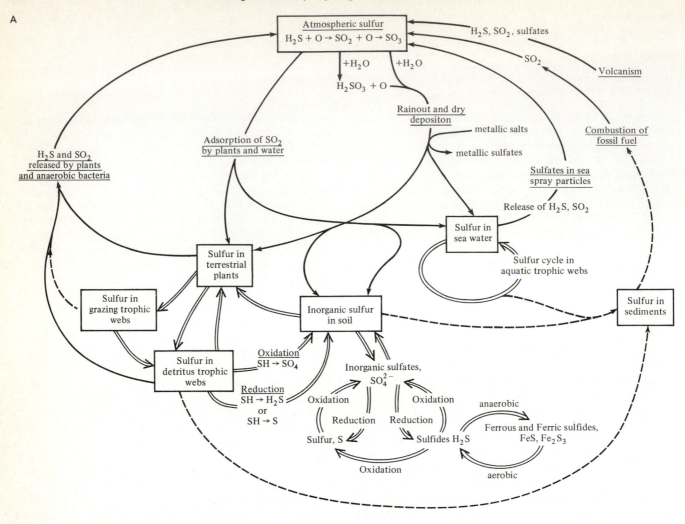

Inorganic nitrogen in soil or water may be subject to the process of *denitrification,* in which NO_3^- is reduced to NO_2^-, nitric oxide (NO), nitrous oxide (N_2O), N_2, or NH_3. Denitrification to N_2 can occur either abiotically or by the action of bacteria which use oxidized nitrogen as a source of oxygen; the latter is by far the more important mechanism. Some fungi and autotrophs are also capable of denitrification. The most complete denitrification occurs under anaerobic conditions, which are found in waterlogged soils, poorly aerated soils, or soils rich in decomposing organic matter. Under more aerobic conditions the reduction is less complete and may proceed only from NO_3^- to NO_2^-, which is then reoxidized by nitrate bacteria. Nitrogen that is reduced as far as N_2O, N_2 or NH_3 can be lost from the biogeochemical cycle. Under appropriate conditions, deni-

trification can result in losses of up to 50% of nitrogen that has been added to a soil in the form of fertilizer in a period as short as 2–4 days; it is therefore of considerable significance in the nitrogen balance of the ecosystem.

The circulation of nitrogen is thus seen to be under a greater degree of biological control than is the circulation of carbon. The atmospheric pool of nitrogen is so large [estimated to be 3.9×10^{21} g or 3,900,000 billion metric tons (Delwiche, 1981)] relative to the estimated annual withdrawals (about 210,000,000 metric tons) that its size can be considered to be independent of ecosystem processes. For this reason, interest in the nitrogen cycle focuses on biological processes within the biogeochemical cycle that control the circulation and retention of nitrogen, and the biologically controlled acquisition from and loss to the geochemi-

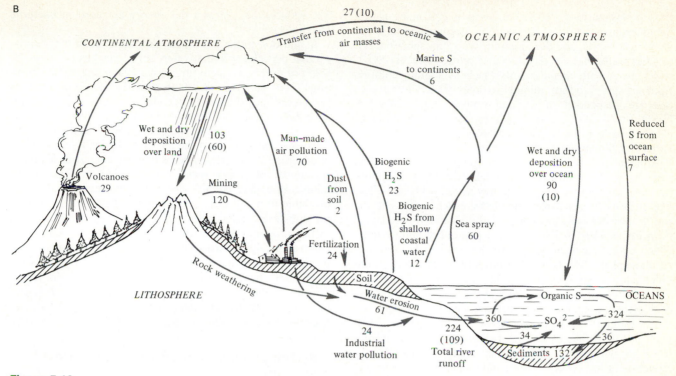

Figure 5.13

The sulfur cycle. (A) Distribution and transfers of sulfur in the biosphere. Double lines indicate the biogeochemical cycle, single lines the geochemical cycle. Solid lines indicate major transfers, dashed lines secondary transfers. (B) Estimates of quantities and rates of transfer of sulfur in the biosphere. Units are millions (10^6) of metric tons of sulfur. Numbers in brackets are estimates of anthropogenic contributions. Note the importance of air pollution from human activities in this cycle. (Part B redrawn after Ivanov, 1981, by permission of Scope and M. V. Ivanov.)

cal cycle. Abiotic inputs from the geochemical cycle are often of secondary importance, although with the increase in air pollution and the phenomenon of "acid rain," atmospheric inputs of nitrogen have become very important in some areas (see the discussion in Section 5.11B). Also, nitrogen dissolved in slope seepage waters can be a very important input into productive lower-slope ecosystems.

Useful reviews of terrestrial nitrogen cycles can be found in Söderlund and Svensson (1976), Clark and Rosswall (1981), Delwiche (1981), and Bolin and Cook (1983). An example of how this type of information can be applied in forest management is given in Heal et al. (1982).

C. The Sulfur Cycle

The geochemical cycle of sulfur bears similarities to both the nitrogen and the carbon cycles (Figure 5.13). Like carbon, the quantity of sulfur in the atmosphere is very much less than for nitrogen, and there is considerable exchange of gaseous sulfur dioxide (SO_2) between the ocean and the atmosphere. The details of this air/water SO_2 exchange are not as well known as the mechanisms of CO_2 exchange, but presumably there is a rather similar series of equilibrium conditions that tend to regulate the concentrations of SO_2 in both air and water.

Much of the sulfur taken up by plants is in the form of inorganic sulfates (SO_4^{2-}) absorbed from the soil, although there is some direct uptake of SO_2 from the air by leaves. The availability of sulfate in the soil is controlled by the activities of a complex assemblage of chemoautotrophic and heterotrophic microbes. These determine the chemical form of the sulfur in much the same manner as soil nitrogen.

Sulfur occurs in the atmosphere in the form of SO_2 and hydrogen sulfide gas (H_2S—"bad egg" gas). SO_2 combines with atomic or molecular oxygen (O or O_2) and ozone (O_3) to produce SO_3 (sulfur trioxide gas), while H_2S is oxidized to SO_2. Atmospheric SO_2 arises from emissions of SO_2 by plants, from seawater and volcanoes, and from the combustion of fossil fuels and organic matter (e.g., forest fires or slashburning). H_2S is released by volcanoes and by microorganisms during the anaerobic decomposition of organic matter. SO_2 and SO_3 combine with atmospheric water to yield sulfurous acid (H_2SO_3) and sulfuric acid (H_2SO_4), which react with metallic salts (such as sodium chloride from sea spray) to form minute particles of metallic sulfates that are suspended in the atmosphere (e.g., $2NaCl + H_2SO_4 \rightarrow Na_2SO_4 + 2HCl$). Atmospheric sulfate particles also originate from volcanic emissions, sea spray, and a variety of human terrestrial activities.

Atmospheric sulfate enters the biogeochemical sulfur cycle by several pathways. Plants absorb SO_2 directly into their leaves from the air just as they absorb CO_2 and NH_3. SO_2 is also absorbed from the air by water bodies and the soil. Rainwater and snow contain dilute sulfurous and sulfuric acids as well as dissolved and particulate sulfate ions, which contribute significantly to the acidity of rainwater. As atmospheric SO_2 concentrations have risen downwind of urban and industrial centers, so has the acidity of rainwater (the now well-known "acid rain problem") with important ecological consequences for recipient ecosystems (Brosset, 1973; Hill, 1973; Beamish, 1974, 1975; Almer, 1974; Dickson, 1975). Acidification of lakes has occurred in areas receiving acid rainfall, and this has been accompanied by a reduction or total loss of fish populations. In the 1960s and early 1970s the problem was best known in Norway and Sweden, but in the late 1970s and early 1980s it was recognized that acid rain had become one of the most serious environmental problems in eastern Canada and north central and eastern U.S. It is also found in other areas that are affected by industrial SO_2 emissions, and is one of the major environmental problems in central Europe. This topic is discussed in more detail in Section 5.11B.

Most of the sulfur that reaches the soil from the atmosphere is in the form of sulfates. It is taken up by plants and incorporated into organic molecules such as sulfur-containing amino acids. These eventually find their way into detritus food chains and thence to the soil, from which they may be decomposed or reabsorbed by plants. Under aerobic conditions, decomposition by fungi and bacteria (e.g., species of *Aspergillus* and *Neurospora*) produces inorganic sulfates. Under anaerobic conditions, bacteria such as *Beggiatoa* oxidize H_2S to S, whereas species of *Thiobacillus* oxidize it to SO_4^{2-}. Some bacteria require the presence of free oxygen before they can exploit this energy source, but others, such as the green and purple photosynthetic bacteria, can utilize chemically combined oxygen.

Reduced sulfur + $CO_2 \longrightarrow$

oxidized sulfur + reduced carbon + energy

The reduced carbon and the energy are used in bacterial metabolism.

In addition to the biological alterations in sulfur chemistry that occur in soil and water, some changes occur as the result of purely physical processes. Under anaerobic conditions, H_2S will combine with iron (Fe) to form ferric or ferrous sulfides (FeS or FeS_2) with important biogeochemical consequences. Under neutral or alkaline conditions, ferrous sulfide is insoluble and precipitates out of solution. This can render much of the sulfur biologically unavailable in anaerobic, iron-rich systems that are neutral or alkaline. A number of heavy metal micronutrients (copper, cadmium, zinc, and cobalt) associate themselves with these insoluble iron sulfides and can in turn become unavailable for uptake by plants. Similarly, the formation of ferrous sulfide promotes the conversion of phosphorus from a soluble to an insoluble form. This process is of great importance to phosphorus dynamics and organic productivity in lake ecosystems, but is beyond the scope of this book. For recent reviews of the global sulfur cycle, see Ivanov (1981) and Grant et al. (1976). The interactions between the N, C, and S cycles are discussed in Likens (1981).

5.8 Biogeochemical Efficiency of Forest Ecosystems

The combined action of the biogeochemical and biochemical cycles in undisturbed forest ecosystems results in active accumulation and retention of nutrients from the geochemical cycle. Many of the nutrients lost from forest ecosystems in streamwater come from soil below the main rooting zone or enter the stream directly as throughfall and litterfall from overhanging streamside vegetation. The organic forest floor that develops from decomposing litter promotes the chemical retention of nutrients, and the combined action of mycorrhizal roots and fungi provides an efficient biological mechanism for nutrient uptake and retention. Characteristically, at or near the surface of the soil there is a concentration of fine roots that are very efficient at absorbing nutrients in throughfall and nutrients released from decomposing litter. It is not surprising, therefore, that forest streamwater typically has very low levels of dissolved chemicals, a condition referred to as *oligotrophic* (as opposed to a *eutrophic* or nutrient-rich condition). Plants growing under conditions of low nutrient availability have evolved mechanisms for nutrient conservation, such as long foliage retention, leaching-resistant cuticles, chemical defenses against losses to herbivores, infrequent reproduction, and efficient internal recycling. A summary of these strategies can be found in Chapin (1980).

The biogeochemical efficiency of forests is one of the main reasons why forests are able to grow on soils of extremely low fertility, or on soils that are simply a thin layer of forest floor over unweathered bedrock. It is frequently observed that mature forests of remarkably similar composition and productivity can develop on areas varying in the inherent fertility of the soil. Part of this *apparent* independence of a mature forest from the nutritional status of the underlying mineral substrate arises from the tendency for forests to build up a forest floor, accumulate a capital of nutrients, and then operate largely from the nutrients within the biogeochemical cycle. In managing apparently productive mature forests on inherently infertile sites, it is vital to recognize the underlying biogeochemical character of the ecosystem so that the biological mechanisms that sustain the site productivity are not unwittingly impaired.

The efficiency of the forest in retaining nutrients can be demonstrated by examining the chemistry of water as it enters, at various stages as it passes through, and as it leaves a forest ecosystem. The result is a *water chemistry profile* (Figure 5.14). Commencing with low levels of chemicals dissolved in rain and snow, water becomes enriched as it leaches the tree crowns. Further increases occur as the water leaches the fresh litter on the forest floor. Chemical concentrations are then reduced as the water percolates down through the forest floor and mineral soil. The water that leaves the ecosystem as streamwater or groundwater may be in much the same chemical condition as when it entered as precipitation, with the exception of elements such as silicon, which are scarce in precipitation but can be abundant in streamwater as the result of rock weathering. The chemical composition of streamwater is certainly affected by the chemistry of the soil parent material and the rocks over which it passes in reaching the stream. In areas rich in calcium, magnesium, or other elements, the streamwater will be enriched in the corresponding chemical. Stream chemistry will also reflect regional precipitation, dry areas generally having higher concentrations of dissolved chemicals in streamwater than do wet areas. However, in many of the world's forests, forest streamwater is characterized by very low levels of dissolved nutrients because of both the efficiency with which forests retain nutrients, and within-stream nutrient cycling processes.

The biogeochemical efficiency of forests poses a potential solution to one of today's chronic environmental problems—what to do with polluted water and, in particular, what to do with human sewage. The water pollution that occurs when urban and industrial sewage is put into rivers or lakes can be avoided by applying the enriched water to the forest floor. Although this has not yet been done on a scale suitable for a large city, experimental schemes with smaller urban communities have been successful and have demonstrated the potential of this approach (Sopper, 1975). The forest ecosystem extracts most of the chemicals from the effluent, neutralizes pathogenic organisms, and delivers

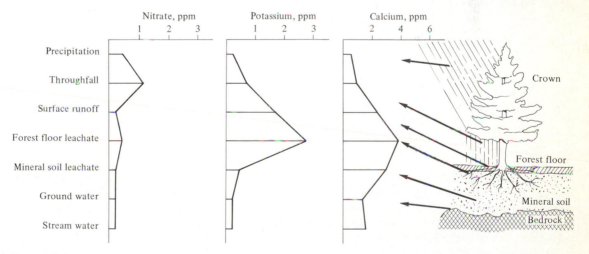

Figure 5.14

Water chemistry profiles for a mixed conifer forest. Concentrations of nitrate, potassium, and calcium ions in water are shown at seven stages of its passage through a 90-year-old west coast conifer stand in British Columbia. The shape of the profiles reflects the relative efficiency of the ecosystem at retaining these three ions within the biogeochemical cycle (high for NO_3^- and K^+, moderate for Ca^{2+}). (Data from Kimmins and Feller, 1976.)

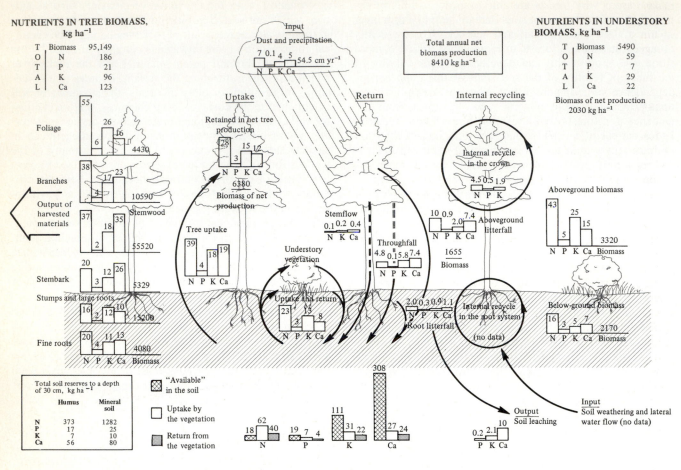

Figure 5.15
Summary of the biogeochemistry of a pine stand in Finland (data from Mälkonen, 1974) showing the distribution of four macronutrients in the biomass and soil and the dynamics of nutrients in the biochemical, biogeochemical, and geochemical cycles. The dynamics of nutrients within the understory plants is not shown. (Data used by permission of E. Mälkonen.)

relatively pure water to the streams, while the trees benefit by the improved water and nutrient availability. This method of cleaning up polluted water is not without its biogeochemical problems. For instance, litter decomposition can be accelerated to the point of eliminating the forest floor if the sewage solution is applied in too large a quantity. However, application of sewage to forests offers the possibility of solving a serious environmental problem while improving forest growth (Cole and Schiess, 1978; Sopper and Kerr, 1979; Cole et al., 1983). Urban solid waste can

also be applied to forest areas with positive effects on forest growth (Smith et al., 1979).

In order to make management decisions that are biogeochemically rational, the forester must have a good working knowledge of the biogeochemistry of a forest. He or she must understand geochemical inputs and outputs to and from the forest, the quantities, distribution, and cycling of nutrients within the forest, and the internal economy of nutrients inside plants and animals. The forester must know the nutritional requirements of a crop and the mechanisms by which they are satisfied. Examples of the types of information required are shown in Figure 5.15 for a conifer stand in Finland. We shall return to this topic later in the book to explain how this information can be used as an aid to forest management (see FORCYTE in Chapter 17).

5.9   Nutrient Cycling in Tropical Forest Ecosystems

Most of the early research on forest biogeochemistry was conducted in temperate and northern latitude forests, and until recently there has been a general scarcity of information on nutrient cycling at tropical latitudes. This situation is changing, and the 1970s witnessed a growing interest in this aspect of tropical ecology. Some of the earliest work on tropical forest biogeochemistry was done in west Africa (Greenland and Kowal, 1960; Nye, 1961). More recently, extensive studies have been undertaken in the tropical rain forest at El Verde, Puerto Rico (Odum and Pigeon, 1970), and a substantial literature is beginning to accumulate on studies in eastern Panama (Golley et al., 1975), in Costa Rica (Johnson et al., 1977, 1979; Gessel et al., 1978), in Brazil (Herrera et al., 1978), and in other Central and South American countries (see the references in Herrera et al., 1978). A general review of tropical ecology can be found in Farnworth and Golley (1973), Golley and Medina (1975), and UNESCO (1978). Nutrient cycling in the tropics is reviewed by Cole and Johnson (1980), and Jordan (1985). Nitrogen cycling in Southeast Asian wet tropical ecosystems is discussed in Wetselaar et al. (1981).

Great concern has been expressed by many scientists about the exploitation of tropical rain forests for timber and the clearing of forest for shifting cultivation or permanent agriculture. The tropical rain forest has been pictured as a highly diverse and very productive ecosystem characterized as having a large tree biomass, nutrient-poor soils, with the majority of the nutrients on the site contained in the vegetation, and a very large and rapid circulation of nutrients. Based on this concept of tropical forests, it has been suggested that removal of most of the vegetation may remove most of the site's nutrient capital. Like most ecological generalizations, this concept is only valid for certain types of tropical forest.

The native agricultural traditions in the tropics involve cutting down a small patch of forest, burning the slash after it has dried, and planting crops in the ashes that enrich the soil with nutrients and raise the pH of the very acid forest soil. This produces one or two good food crops, but the yield declines rapidly, supposedly because the ash nutrients are soon leached away or are removed in the harvested food plants, and the pH of the soil declines toward its original value. The area is then abandoned. Inputs of litterfall from adjacent forest, and reinvasion of herbs and trees (some of which are nitrogen fixers) gradually returns the area to its original fertility, and if the interval between successive cut-and-burns is not too short, this type of land use can continue indefinitely without degrading the productivity of the site (see further discussion in Section 5.12B). However, because of population growth, the interval between successive cut–burn–harvest events has been rapidly decreasing since World War II, and in some areas the soil has become so impoverished that the original forest species can no longer grow (Richards, 1973, 1977). There has been disagreement as to whether the yield decline is more closely related to nutrient depletion or to the buildup of pests and pathogens of the crop plant (Janzen, 1973), and the idea that nutrient leaching is always severe in the tropics has been challenged (Harcomb, 1977a, 1977b). Regardless of the outcome of the present debate, there is still widespread concern about the effects of short-rotation shifting agriculture on the soil, and about the intensive harvesting of tropical forests for timber. The long-term consequences of conversion from forests of indigenous trees to short-rotation exotic species are not well known, but many ecologists have expressed urgent concern about this trend (e.g., Richards, 1973; Cornforth, 1970) and investigations have been initiated (e.g., Russell, 1983).

Much of the argument about the effects of manipulating tropical forest has lacked a firm basis in scientific fact. Broad generalizations have frequently been made, such as that all tropical soils are lateritic, subject to irreversible hardening on exposure to sunlight, and/or they are inherently nutrient poor. It is now recognized that the diversity of soils, vegetation, and biogeochemical characteristics is as great in the tropics as at other latitudes, and that much more sophistication is required in our approach to evaluating the biogeochemical characteristics of tropical forests and the human impact thereon.

Studies in the Amazon Basin in South America have provided some very good insights into the adaptation of tropical vegetation to very nutrient poor soils. Forests growing on white sand soils (that are virtually devoid of nutrients) have evolved a number of adaptations that cause them to act like "a giant ion-exchange column that extracts nutrients from water passing through the ecosystem" (Herrera et al., 1978).

1. The forest develops a dense root mat on the soil surface. The rootlets do not have a well-developed geotropic response, and they soon grow over and cover any litter that

falls onto the root mat. Up to 60% of the tree biomass in some Amazonian forests is roots. This root mat has a very high nutrient retention capacity.

2. Direct nutrient cycling occurs from the litter to the roots via mycorrhizae. The fungal hyphae rapidly invade freshly fallen litter, absorbing inorganic nutrients before they can be leached into the soil and conducting them directly to the roots (Went and Stark, 1968). Radioisotopes have been used to demonstrate the very high efficiency with which the mycorrhizal hyphae that cover the surface of the soil and root mat are able to retain nutrients should they get into solution (Stark and Jordan, 1978). Almost none of the nutrients applied as an aqueous solution to the upper surface of this root mat were still in solution in water collected below the root mat.

3. Nutrients are conserved within the trees by efficient internal cycling before leaf shedding (Small, 1972; Montes and Medina, 1977), and by the reduction of herbivory through the accumulation of toxic secondary metabolic chemicals in leaves and roots. Annual loss of leaf area to herbivore consumption is only 1–2%, and the small size and low abundance of arthropods in such forests reflects the high levels of toxic alkaloids and polyphenols that are found in the plants (Janzen, 1974; Golley, 1977).

4. Adaptation of the plants to very acid soils, which are very low in Ca and P, high in H^+ and Al^{3+} ions, and frequently waterlogged. Adaptations to these harsh, oligotrophic conditions include sclerophyllous leaves (thick, leathery, and evergreen); tolerance of very low nutrient levels; efficient internal recycling of N, P, and K; and an evergreen habit. Calcium, which is one of the most limiting nutrients in the Amazon region, is not retranslocated but is efficiently recovered from decomposing litter.

5. The morphology of the leaves results in their arrangement on the forest floor after leaf fall so as to minimize their time of contact with throughfall, which could leach nutrients. The mineral soil tends to have many large pores, which promote rapid drainage and minimize leaching (Nortcliff and Thornes, 1977). It has been suggested that drip tips on leaves promote the shedding of water, thereby reducing nutrient leaching.

6. The multilayered structure of the rain forest canopy, together with the presence of many epiphyllous organisms (living nonparasitically on the leaves) such as mosses, algae, lichens, and bacteria, promote uptake of nutrients from precipitation and throughfall. The canopy scavenges nutrients from solution and combines them into organic forms that become available to the tree directly or via the litterfall pathway. As a result, concentrations of nutrients are lower in throughfall than in precipitation. Many of the epiphyllous organisms are capable of nitrogen fixation.

7. The high concentrations of secondary plant chemicals in litterfall of plants growing on tropical white sands impede decomposition, other than by mycorrhizal fungi. The secondary chemicals and the high acidity of the litter restrict the activity of bacteria. This ensures that virtually all the nutrients released through decomposition return to the plants via mycorrhizal fungi by the direct nutrient cycling pathway. It can also result in the buildup of a considerable forest floor, a situation that is not normally associated with tropical forests. The decomposition pathways that occur in such forests produce dark-colored organic acids as an end product. Under the prevailing acidic conditions, these organic acids are mobile and leach into streams, staining the water brown. This gives rise to the name *black water rivers* (e.g., the Rio Negro which combines with the clearwater Solimoes River at Manaus to form the Amazon). Such rivers have very low concentrations of dissolved nutrients, reflecting both the shortage of nutrients in the adjacent terrestrial ecosystems and the efficient retention of nutrients in the terrestrial nutrient cycle.

Removal or destruction of the vegetation in such nutrient-deficient ecosystems will result in rapid loss of the nutrient capital, and can convert tropical forest to wet deserts—areas of white sand virtually devoid of nutrients and vegetation. Occasional groups of plants may survive on "islands" of nutrient-containing organic matter. The efficiency of nutrient conservation and accumulation in such forests depends upon the living plants. Once these are gone, so are the mechanisms of nutrient conservation.

The scenario just described does not occur throughout the humid tropics. It occurs where the soils are very old and are the result of several cycles of erosion and deposition which have left little more than silica sand and silt. Much of the oligotrophic moist tropical forest in parts of the Amazon basin is growing on white sands derived from the weathering of nutrient-poor sandstone, and consequently many of the Amazonian forests are oligotrophic and exhibit the adaptations described above. Where the soils are younger, fine textured, and/or receive additions of nutrients from other geochemical pathways, the ecosystem nutrient capital is much higher and there is far less risk of nutrient exhaustion and ecosystem degradation. In areas with soils derived from recent volcanic materials, in areas where nutritionally exhausted surface soils are removed by erosion to expose nutritionally richer lower layers, and/or where fertile alluvial materials are deposited periodically, tropical soils can be as rich and fertile as temperate soils. However, because of the almost constant humid and warm conditions, the potential for rapid decomposition and nutrient loss following devegetation is generally greater than at higher latitudes, and most native humid tropical vegetation exhibits adaptations for nutrient conservation. This should warn us to be careful in our manipulation of the vegetation of these areas, and not to replace native vegetation with exotic species until we have demonstrated the ability of our managed ecosystems to conserve the soil nutrient capital.

Not all the tropics are uniformly humid. As one moves away from the equator, one first encounters seasonally dry forests (much of the Amazon basin experiences a pronounced dry season) and then increasingly arid woodlands. These have different soils and vegetation and markedly different biogeochemical characteristics. Consequently, experience of nutrient cycling in the humid tropics cannot be transferred to higher tropical latitudes without considerable modification, just as ecological wisdom gained at temperate latitudes is often an inadequate background for the wise management and conservation of the humid tropics.

A very useful comparison was made recently between oligotrophic and eutrophic forests in both the tropics and at temperate latitudes (Jordan and Herrera, 1981). This showed that the productivity and biomass of mature, undisturbed oligotrophic forests can be very similar to that of mature, undisturbed eutrophic forests, because adaptations for nutrient conservation in oligotrophic forests greatly reduce the problems of nutrient scarcity in the substrate. This is equally true in tropical and in temperate forests. The problems come when forests are removed. In oligotrophic ecosystems the nutrient capital is rapidly dissipated, the soil having little capacity to retain the nutrients. The rate of nutrient loss will be greatest in the tropics because of the more rapid decomposition and the greater risk of soil leaching losses. In eutrophic ecosystems, plant-related nutrient conservation mechanisms are relatively much less important, because the fertile soil is capable of retaining most of the nutrients released following deforestation, and has substantial nutrient reserves. This is true for both tropical and temperate forests, so the difference between temperate and tropical latitudes will be greatest on the oligotrophic sites.

Herein lies the explanation for much of the disagreement concerning the importance of nutrients in forest growth. Both tropical and temperate forests can grow on both nutrient-rich and nutrient-poor soils. Growth on the former depends mainly on the inherent fertility of the soil, and this is not usually reduced catastrophically by harvesting. Growth on the latter, on the other hand, depends on the plants themselves, and once plants and their biogeochemi-

cal effects are removed, the physical environment may not be capable of sustaining plant production.

In a review of nutrient cycling in tropical forests, Cole and Johnson (1980) concluded that because of our limited data base and the high diversity of tropical forests, few generalizations can be made. However, it does appear that, in general, leaf turnover (litterfall) in lowland tropical forests is more rapid than in other types of forest, decomposition is generally rapid, and mineral weathering and soil leaching rates are often high. They concluded that for many tropical soils, nutrient loss in harvested boles does not pose a serious threat to soil fertility, but that burning could cause significant losses of N. The presence of abundant HCO_3^- ions in tropical soil solutions creates a high leaching potential, but leaching is often only moderate in undisturbed forest because of a relatively low flux of water through the soil (Johnson et al., 1977) and the presence of a high anion exchange capacity, which limits the movement of P and S (Mekaru and Uehara, 1972; Bornemisza and Llanos, 1967). NO_3^- ions may be more important than HCO_3^- ions in the leaching of some tropical soils (Nye and Greenland, 1960).

Harvesting tropical forests causes a short-term increase in available nutrients, but this is followed within 3 years by a decline, presumably because of leaching and erosion (Nye and Greenland, 1964; Cunningham, 1963; Cornforth, 1970). Erosion losses can be very severe on steep slopes, accounting for a 74% decrease in the original site nutrient reserves. The extent of the postharvest nutrient loss will depend upon the speed with which the forest reinvades the site. Because reinvasion is normally rapid and because many of the invading species are nitrogen fixers, forestry in the tropics is potentially a much less damaging land use than agriculture. For a discussion of the biogeochemical effects of shifting cultivation in Central America, see Ewel et al. (1981).

5.10 Biogeochemical Classification of the World's Forests

The character of the nutrient cycle varies greatly from place to place as the result of variations in plants, animals, soil, and climate. This variability has been used as the basis of a functional classification of the world's vegetation. Rodin and Bazilevich (1967) identified 12 major types of vegetation on the basis of the magnitude of their biomass, their litterfall, the chemical composition of the litterfall, and the rate of litter decomposition (Table 5.14). This very broad classification is insufficiently detailed to have very much value for practical forest management, but there is

Table 5.14 Summary of Biogeochemical Classification of World's Vegetation (Rodin and Bazilevich, 1967)

Vegetation Type	Ecosystem Parameters[a]	Dominant Elements	Description[b]
Tundra (Boreal-nitric)	Biomass, Litterfall, Decomposition, Litter Chemistry (Index value scale to 10, 5)	N (K, Mn) Nitric	P: very low L: very light D: negligible LC: low concentrations
Boreal conifer (boreal-nitric)	(scale 9, 5)	N > Ca Calcic-nitric	P: low to medium L: light to medium D: very slow to rapid LC: very low concentrations
Boreal deciduous (boreal-nitric)	(scale 8, 5)	N > Ca (Si, Mg) Calcic-nitric	P: medium L: medium D: slow to medium LC: medium concentrations
Semishrub desert (desert-nitric)	(scale 10, 5)	N > Ca (Na, Cl) Calcic-nitric	P: very low L: very light D: very rapid LC: medium concentrations
Subtropical deciduous forest (subtropical-nitric)	(scale 10, 5)	N > Ca (Si, Al, Fe) Calcic-nitric	P: high L: heavy D: rapid LC: medium concentrations
Subboreal deciduous forest (subboreal-calcic)	(scale 10, 5)	Ca > N Nitric-calcic	P: medium L: medium D: slow to medium LC: medium concentrations
Subtropical desert (subtropical-calcic)	(scale 10, 5)	Ca > Si (Al, Fe) Silicic-calcic	P: very low to low L: light D: very rapid LC: high concentrations
Steppe (steppe-silicic)	(scale 8, 5)	Si > N Nitric-silicic	P: low to medium L: medium to heavy D: rapid LC: low to medium concentrations
Semishrub desert (desert-silicic)	(scale 10, 5)	Si > N (Cl, Ma) Nitric-silicic	P: medium L: medium D: very rapid LC: medium concentrations
Savanna (tropical-silicic)	(scale 9, 5)	Si > Na (Fe, Al) Nitric-silicic	P: medium L: medium D: very rapid LC: medium concentrations
Tropical rain forest (tropical-silicic)	(scale 10, 5)	Si > N (Al, Fe, Mn, S) Nitric-silicic	P: very high L: very heavy D: very rapid LC: medium concentrations
Desert (chloric)	(scale 10, 5)	Cl > Na Sodic-chloric	P: very low L: very light D: very rapid LC: very high concentrations

[a]The bars show the range of index values for four ecosystem characteristics in each of 12 different major vegetation types. Each type of plant community has a unique combination of parameter values.

[b]P = productivity; L = litterfall; D = decomposition; LC = litter chemistry.

Table 5.15 Application of Rodin and Bazilevich's (1967) Method of Regional Biogeochemical Classification of Ecosystems to a Local Topographic Sequence of Ecosystem Types in the Subalpine Coastal Mountain Hemlock Forests of British Columbia[a]

						Mineral elements			
Aboveground tree biomass, B, t ha^{-1}	NPP, P, t ha^{-1}	Litterfall,[b] L, t ha^{-1} yr^{-1}	True increment, I, t ha^{-1} yr^{-1}	Forest floor, F, t ha^{-1}	Litter turnover time,[c] D, yr	Accumulation in plant biomass, b, kg ha^{-1}	Uptake by NPP, U, kg ha^{-1} yr^{-1}	Returned with litterfall,[b] r, kg ha^{-1} yr^{-1}	Retained by true increment, $<I$, kg ha^{-1} yr^{-1}	Mean ash content of litterfall, A, %

Source: Krumlik, 1979. Used with permission of the author.

[a] The sequence of xeric (X)–mesic (M_1)–hygric (H) sites is a moisture-nutrient gradient (see Chapter 15). These sites were occupied by old-growth climax forest >350 years old. Mesic site 2 (M_2) was on poorer soil parent material than mesic site 1 (M_1). Values are the means of three plots.

[b] Total aboveground litterfall; includes epiphytes.

[c] Based on aboveground litter/forest floor ratio. This has been shown to overestimate litter turnover time (see Vogt et al., 1983).

some evidence that smaller units of forest vegetation can also be characterized by combinations of biogeochemical parameters. Since the biogeochemical character of a site influences how the site will respond to management, biogeochemical site classification may have some potential as a management tool.

Few attempts have been made to apply Rodin and Bazilevich's approach to the classification of biogeocoenoses, so it is too early to draw any firm conclusions about the potential value of their method for forest management. One example of such a local biogeochemical classification was a study of nutrient cycling in the overstory of a subalpine mountain hemlock forest in coastal British Columbia (Krumlik, 1979). It was found that the scales used by Rodin and Bazilevich covered too broad a range to permit the differentiation of individual ecosystem types, but by expanding the scales a reasonably good separation of the three sites was obtained (Table 5.15). A companion study of

production and nutrient cycling in the understory of these sites (Yarie, 1980) supported the idea of the biogeochemical identity of the three site types (see Figure 5.8).

5.11 Effects of Humans on Biogeochemistry and the Cycling of Toxic Substances

In our discussion of geochemical and biogeochemical cycles, we saw that animals play a critical role in forest biogeochemistry. Herbivores accelerate the transfer of chemicals from plants to the soil, the atmosphere, or the hydrological cycle, and by killing vegetation they can short-circuit important nutrient retention mechanisms. Animal migration can import or export nutrients to or from an ecosystem, and the activity of soil animals has a very important effect on litter decomposition. Human beings play a similar biogeochemical role, redistributing nutrients by the harvesting (or mining), transportation, consumption and waste of agricultural, forest, fish, and mineral products.

Any alteration of biogeochemical pathways involves work. Our biogeochemical role is far greater than that of other animals primarily because of the enormous energy resources at our command. Some of our biogeochemical alterations of the environment are deliberate and generally beneficial (''good'' being defined in terms of what society thinks it wants or needs): for example, the increased geological inputs and outputs involved in agricultural and forest fertilization and harvesting. Some are deliberate but harmful, such as the use of herbicides and insecticides in ill-conceived eradication programs. There are also many undesirable biochemical changes that are unplanned or unexpected consequences of deliberate biogeochemical activity; acid drainage often results from opencut mining, lakes downwind of industrial complexes are acidified, and lakes are overenriched by excessive use of agricultural fertilizers. Alterations of the biogeochemistry of an ecosystem that result in a lowering of the value of that system, or some part of it, to society are frequently referred to as *pollution*. For a discussion of the socioeconomic impacts of some aspects of

human changes to global chemical cycles, see papers in Likens (1981). We shall examine two examples.

A. Alteration of the Role of Vegetation: A Devegetated Watershed at Hubbard Brook, New Hampshire

We have seen that vegetation plays a very important role in ecosystem biogeochemistry. Nutrients are accumulated and conserved by the vegetation, and the capacity of mature vegetation and soil to recover nutrients generally appears to match approximately the rate at which they are released by decomposition. This results in characteristically low levels of nutrients leaving the ecosystem biogeochemical cycle dissolved in streamwater. However, if either the rate of nutrient uptake by vegetation or the rate of nutrient release by decomposition, or both, is altered, a change in the biogeochemical balance may occur. A good example of this is a study that examined the changes in the biogeochemical balance of a mature northern hardwood forest when nutrient uptake by the vegetation was eliminated through the use of clearcutting and herbicides. Nutrient retention in the undisturbed forest resulted in low levels of dissolved chemicals in

Table 5.16 Nutrient Capital and Turnover, kg ha^{-1}, in an Undisturbed 55-Year-Old Forested Watershed at Hubbard Brook, N.H.[a]

Component	Nutrient					
	N	P	K	Ca	Mg	S
Nutrient capital						
Aboveground plant biomass	351	35	155	383	36	42
Belowground plant biomass	181	53	63	101	13	17
Forest floor	1256	78	66	372	38	124
Annual inputs						
Precipitation	6.5	Trace	0.9	2.2	0.6	12.7
Aerosol/gaseous	14.2	—	—	—	—	6.1
Weathering	0	?	7.1	21	3.5	0.8
Annual outputs, streamwater						
Dissolved	3.9	Trace	1.9	13.7	3.1	17.6
Particulate	0.1	Trace	0.5	0.2	0.2	<0.1
Annual turnover						
Vegetation uptake	79.6	8.9	64.3	62.2	9.3	24.5
Aboveground litterfall	54.2	4.0	18.3	40.7	5.9	5.8
Root litterfall	6.2	1.7	2.1	3.2	0.5	0.6
Throughfall and stemflow	9.3	0.7	30.1	6.7	2.0	21.0
Root exudates	0.9	0.2	8.0	3.5	0.2	1.9
Net litter mineralization	69.6	?	20.1	42.4	6.1	5.7
Annual accretion						
Aboveground plant biomass	4.8	0.9	4.3	5.4	0.4	0.8
Below-ground plant biomass	4.2	1.4	1.5	2.7	0.3	0.4
Forest floor	7.7	0.5	0.3	1.4	0.2	0.8

Source: Likens et al., 1977. Copyright Springer-Verlag New York, Inc. Used with permission.

[a] A comparison of outputs with the nutrient capital and annual circulation shows that the ecosystem is efficient at retaining nutrients. However, when the watershed was deforested, this ability was drastically reduced.

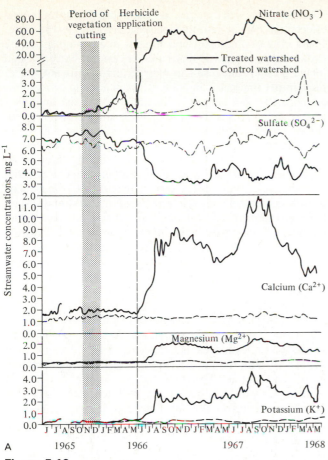

B

Figure 5.16

(A) Effect of the devegetation of a northern hardwood watershed in the mountains of Vermont, northeastern United States, on the chemistry of streamwater. All vegetation was cut and left in place at the end of 1965, and a herbicide was applied the following spring to prevent regrowth (after Likens et al., 1970). (B) Winter aerial photograph of two experimentally-logged watersheds; the furthest one is where the above data were obtained. (Part A reproduced by permission of the Ecological Society of America and G. E. Likens; Part B courtesy of J. W. Hornbeck.)

the stream draining the area in spite of the cycling of substantial quantities of nutrients in the forest (Table 5.16).

In the late autumn/early winter of 1965, all the vegetation on a small forested watershed was cut down, and all minor vegetation and regrowth of the hardwood stumps were eliminated the following spring and in subsequent summers by herbicide treatment. The result was dramatic (Figure 5.16). Previously rather constant low concentrations of cations dissolved in streamwater were increased in magnitude and variability, and the concentrations of anions were either in-

creased or decreased. Levels of nitrate increased from less than 0.5 ppm to as much as 80 ppm (eight times greater than the permissible U.S. federal water pollution standards) and averaged 38 and 53 ppm, respectively, during the 2 years following cutting. The increase in dissolved nutrients, together with the increased light and summer water temperatures that accompanied the removal of the forest canopy, led to the prolific growth of algae in the stream.

The rather dramatic outcome of the Hubbard Brook experiment is thought to have been the result of alterations in the pathway of nitrogen transformations in the litter decomposition phase of the biogeochemical cycle (Likens et al., 1969). Mature forest vegetation apparently inhibits the nitrification pathway, most soluble nitrogen in the forest floor being in the form of ammonium ions or amino acids. These are efficiently retained by soil chemical mechanisms or plant uptake, while any nitrate that is produced is absorbed by the vegetation. Removal of all plants resulted in several major changes. The inhibition of nitrification was terminated, nutrient uptake by plants was terminated, and the rate of litter decomposition was increased because of increased temperatures. These changes led to the production of large quantities of nitrate ions, which, in the absence of plant uptake, were leached out of the soil into the stream. For reasons to be discussed in Chapter 10, the presence of large quantities of soluble anions in soil solution results in the leaching of cations that would otherwise remain in the soil. The great increase in levels of cations in streamwater that resulted from devegetation in the Hubbard Brook study can therefore be explained in terms of the massive production of NO_3^-.

The findings of the initial Hubbard Brook study cannot be applied uncritically to other watersheds, because the treatment that was applied was not representative of conventional forest management. However, subsequent investigations of commercial harvesting of yellow birch in the Hubbard Brook region have yielded slightly less dramatic but essentially similar results (Hornbeck et al., 1975). More recent studies have shown that each of several different patterns of harvesting a watershed can result in different effects on water chemistry (Martin and Pierce, 1979). It therefore appears that under some conditions forest management practices do alter biogeochemical mechanisms in a way that leads to significant changes in the biogeochemical balance of a forest. This is considered further in Section 5.12. Readers interested in the mobility of nitrate ions in disturbed forest ecosystems, and in the regulation of the chemical composition of streams in northeastern U.S. should consult Vitousek (1977, 1981), Vitousek and Melillo (1979), and Vitousek et al (1979, 1982).

B. Acid Rain and Its Effects on Forests and Lakes

The phenomenon of acid rain has been alluded to several times. Described as Canada's premier pollution problem of the late 1970s and the 1980s, acid rain is no newcomer to many industrialized areas of Europe, and the problem is rapidly gaining attention in parts of the U.S. The early evidence of the acidification of the atmosphere included the absence of lichens on trees and gravestones in industrial England and Europe, and the crumbling of stone statues and cornices of buildings that had remained almost unchanged for centuries prior to atmospheric acidification. More recently, we have learned of a more insidious aspect of acid rain: its effects on rivers, lakes and forests.

The origins of acid rain lie in the accelerated release of sulfur dioxide and oxides of nitrogen to the air by the combustion of fossil fuels and other industrial materials. This greatly increases the atmospheric loadings of these gases, which in due course combine with water and are converted to sulfuric and nitric acid. These strong acids are highly ionized, and consequently the concentration of hydrogen ions in the atmosphere is greatly increased. Acidity is a measure of the concentration of hydrogen ions, so these processes lead to an increase in atmospheric acidity. This acidity is deposited in ecosystems by rain, snow, fog, or by dry fallout (dust); the latter may contribute up to 50% of the deposition of acidity. Acid rain can also result from releases of chlorine and hydrocarbons into the atmosphere.

Many ecosystems (especially forests) are chemically *buffered:* their chemical systems are able to resist change in the concentrations of various ions in solution, and consequently input of hydrogen ions may not lead to much change in their pH (the measure of acidity). Acid rain may have relatively little effect on such systems, at least in the short run, but the effects on poorly buffered ecosystems can be dramatic. Many oligotrophic lakes and streams in areas underlain by carbonate-poor granitic rocks are very poorly buffered, and inputs of acid rain result in biologically significant reductions in pH (increases in acidity). Such aquatic ecosystems are normally near neutral in reaction, and the fish and other aquatic organisms native to such lakes and streams are sensitive to acidity, especially in their reproductive stages. On average, oligotrophic lakes in areas with acid precipitation have experienced a pH drop of 2 units during the past 40 years. Because the pH scale is logarithmic, this means that the acidity in these lakes has increased 100 times. The growth in concern over acid precipitation was stimulated by the realization that fish have been eliminated from many oligotrophic mountain lakes in Scandinavia, and it is now recognized that the ''death'' of lakes in eastern Canada and northeastern U.S. from the effects of acid rain is occurring on a large scale. Thousands of lakes are now listed as ''dead.''

Paralleling the concern over the effects of acid rain on aquatic ecosystems is concern over its effects on forests. A considerable amount of research into these effects has been conducted in Scandinavia (Braekke, 1976; Jonsson and Sunberg, 1972), but the early results were contradictory and by the end of the 1970s there was no strong evidence of regional reductions in tree diameter growth in Norway that could be unequivocally attributed to acid rain (Strand, 1980). There is no doubt that acidic precipitation has a direct adverse effect on vegetation, including damage to the cuticle, interference with guard cells, disturbance of metabolism and poisoning of cells, interference with reproduction, accelerated foliar leaching, alteration of mycorrhizal and nitrogen-fixing associations, alteration of host–parasite relations, and increases in susceptibility to other stresses (Tamm and Cowling, 1976). However, much of the acidity in the rain is associated with N and S, both of which can be in limiting supplies in forect ecosystems. Adverse effects of the acid rain may therefore be balanced by beneficial, nutritional effects, at least initially.

The organic forest floor is a very well buffered chemical system, which is already quite acidic, and it appears that it may take many decades of acid rain to induce a major reduction in soil pH. However, there is evidence that acid rain may be accelerating the leaching of calcium and other cations out of forest floors, and decreasing the base saturation (see Chapter 10). Acid rain has also been shown to affect some soil animals by reducing their food supply (bacteria) and shelter (mosses) (Stachurska-Hagen, 1980). In the long run this could have an adverse effect on soil processes, soil fertility, and forest growth. In particular, the accumulated effects of acid precipitation may exacerbate leaching losses at the time of forest harvest (Tamm, 1976a).

The effects of acid rain on forest soils may in some cases be masked by the normal changes in soil pH that accompany changes in vegetation over time. Krug and Frink (1983) caution against ascribing declining soil pH values to the effects of acid rain unless the effects of past land use practices, secondary succession (Chapter 15) and stand development on soil pH have been accounted for. A very useful review of the effects of acid rain on forest soils and the types of soils on which serious effects might be expected is given by Johnson et al. (1982).

Recent investigations of dieback of spruce in the northeastern U.S. and eastern Canada (see Tomlinson, 1981), as well as studies in Germany (Ulrich et al., 1980), have suggested that on soils having a low capital of calcium, the deposition of acid lowers pH and results in the mobilization of aluminum, which then becomes toxic to fine roots. The loss of fine roots renders the trees more susceptible to drought and reduces their ability to absorb nutrients, which can lead to reductions in growth or even dieback. These effects will occur most strongly on soils derived from calcium-poor parent materials (granitic rocks) and will not be so prevalent on base-rich soils. In addition to soil effects, there are thought to be important direct adverse effects of SO_2 and other air pollutants on plant foliage (Knabe, 1976; Materna, 1979). These may involve direct effects on leaf physiology and photosynthesis (with accompanying fine root death), or may involve accelerated leaching of nutrients from foliage. We obviously do not yet know the full extent of the effects of acid precipitation on forests or the exact mechanisms of damage, and it would be premature to draw firm conclusions at this time. However, as in most ecological phenomena, it is probably safe to assume that a variety of mechanisms are involved.

The literature on acid rain is extensive. Interested readers are referred to Dochinger and Seliga (1976), Tollan (1978), Drablos and Tollan (1980), and an extensive series of articles about the effects of acid rain on forests and fish published by the SNSF project in Norway (SNSF Project, Box 61, 1432 Aas-NLH, Norway). Because of the rapidly increasing seriousness of acid rain in the U.S., a large-scale research program has been set up by the U.S. Environmental Protection Agency. Information on this program can be obtained from the Office of Exploratory Research, EPA, 401 MST, SW, Washington, D.C. 20460. Other useful references are Swedish Ministry of Agriculture (1982), Livingston (1982), Bangay and Riordin (1983), Morrison, (1984) and Smith et al. (1985).

5.12 Effects of Forest Management on Forest Biogeochemistry

Of all the environmental factors that determine energy flow and storage in forest ecosystems, the supply and circulation of nutrient elements is one of the most easily manipulated by the forest manager. Because of this, and because of the relationship between nutrition and productivity, it is important for the forester to understand how forest management can affect forest biogeochemistry. The effects may be either undesirable (nutrient loss or immobilization) or desirable (nutrient additions by fertilization, or improvements in rates of cycling and availability). The discussion will focus on two aspects of forest management: clearcut harvesting and postharvest slashburning.

A. Effects of Clearcutting

1. Losses in Harvested Materials. Trees contain nutrients, and consequently the removal of tree parts during a harvest results in a loss of nutrients from the site. The extent of the loss depends on the utilization intensity. The so-called "wasteful" harvesting that characterized the early days of logging in western North America utilized only large, sound logs, leaving much or even most of the forest biomass on the site. This resulted in only small withdrawals of nutrients because it harvested mainly heartwood, which generally contains low concentrations of nutrients. These "bad old days" have largely been replaced by a "less wasteful" type of harvesting that takes a much higher proportion of the tree stems. This is accompanied by an inevitable increase in nutrient withdrawals.

It is most unlikely that the continued growth in the human population (projected doubling of the world population to about 8 billion by the year 2020) will be matched by a similar growth in forest area. On the contrary, many countries will see a reduction in their area of productive forests over the next rotation. The impending famine of forest products that some believe will occur in the not-too-distant future can be delayed for a few years by increasing the intensity of production and harvest on existing land. A trend away from conventional stem harvesting with long rotations and toward shorter rotations and *whole-tree harvesting* (removal of all aboveground tree biomass from the site) is already developing. Some countries (e.g., Sweden) have gone the final step and are also harvesting tree stumps and root systems in what has been called *complete-tree harvesting* (Young, 1968). Stumps and large roots are also being harvested in the southern pine region of the U.S., together with all aboveground biomass of both thinnings and the

Table 5.17 Percentage Increase in Removal of Certain Plant Nutrients in Harvested Materials Accompanying the Switch from Conventional to Whole-Tree Harvesting[a]

Forest Type	Aboveground Biomass	Increase, %				Reference
		N	P	K	Ca	
Hemlock–cedar, <500 years old	43	165	117	77	95	Kimmins and Krumlik, 1976
Lodgepole pine, 125 years old	15	53	54	14	15	Kimmins and Krumlik, 1976
Spruce–fir, <350 years old	25	116	163	32	50	Kimmins and Krumlik, 1976
Hemlock–fir, <550 years old	20	86	67	48	48	Kimmins and Krumlik, 1976
Black spruce, 65 years old	99	288	367	236	179	Weetman and Webber, 1972
Cottonwood						
7 years old	25	127	—	—	—	Carter and White, 1971
9 years old	—	116	100	74	68	White, 1974
Jack pine, 65 years old						
Whole-tree harvest	26	120	250	80	46	Morrison and Foster, 1979
Complete-tree harvest	52	149	325	110	78	Morrison and Foster, 1979
Cryptomeria japonica, 25 years old	50	360	315	270	196	Tsutsumi, 1971
Loblolly pine						
4 years old	—	289	483	231	267	Haines and Sanderford, 1976
16 years old	25	35	107	85	—	Jorgensen et al., 1976
Douglas-fir, 15–20 years old	51	290	298	265	299	Webber, 1977
Mixed hardwoods, 45–50 years	39	72	77	78	83	Boyle and Ek, 1972
Boreal forest average	65	115	—	—	180	Marion, 1979
Temperate coniferous average	28	100	—	—	150	Marion, 1979
Temperate broadleaf average	60	215	—	—	110	Marion, 1979

[a]Further data of this type can be easily calculated from Kimmins et al. (1985) and Freedman (1980).

final crop (Koch, 1978, 1980). Even the foliage is harvested for processing into cattle feed or adhesives. Although one can applaud the apparent thrift of such a development, it is necessary to consider the full ecological effects of this type of forest harvesting, in particular the effects on nutrient withdrawals.

The current concern about harvest-induced site nutrient depletion was initiated in 1955 by Rennie (1955, 1957), who questioned whether or not it was reasonable to expect sustained production to continue indefinitely in conifer stands established on infertile soils. The development of concern over the nutritional aspects of intensive plantation management in the 1950s was reflected in the work of Ovington (1957, 1959), who documented the biomass and nutrient content of an age sequence of pine stands developing on sandy soils in eastern England and undertook nutrient-cycling studies in a wide variety of forest types in Great Britain (Ovington, 1961, 1962). However, it was not until the 1970s that the question of nutrient withdrawals in harvested materials received widespread attention by forest scientists.

During the past decade the effect of switching from conventional to whole-tree harvesting on the extent of nutrient withdrawals has been documented for a wide variety of forest types (Table 5.17). However, the consequences of these withdrawals for future tree growth are not easy to predict with confidence. They vary for different nutrients, with different species, with stand density, and with stand age because these parameters determine the relative proportions of stem biomass to crown biomass and therefore the difference in nutrient withdrawals between conventional and whole-tree harvesting. The effect of stand age is demonstrated in Table 5.18. In younger stands the ratio of sapwood to heartwood is higher than in older stands, as is the ratio of crown biomass to stem biomass. Sapwood generally has higher nutrient concentrations than heartwood; crown materials higher than stems. Shortening rotations reduces the age at harvest and therefore compounds the effects of increasing utilization standards by increasing the proportion of stems that is sapwood, and the proportion of crown material in the harvested biomass. For example, Boyle (1975) estimated that the change from a single 30-year rotation to three 10-year rotations in aspen stands (all with whole-tree harvesting) would increase the nutrient removal of N, P, K, and Ca by 345, 239, 234, and 173%, respectively. Obviously, *fiber farming* (full utilization with short rotations; Young, 1972) will have a much greater effect on site nutrient capital than did the "wasteful" logging of the past, which left most of

Table 5.18 Effect of Age of Stand on Percentage Increase in Loss of Nutrients After Conversion from Conventional to Whole-Tree Harvesting

Species	Age yr	Percent Increase in loss of				Reference
		N	P	K	Ca	
Norway spruce	18	195	233	161	206	Tamm, 1969
	50[a]	114	115	26	40	Tamm, 1969
	85[a]	91	104	42	29	Tamm, 1969
Scots pine	18	188	212	171	129	Wright and Will, 1958
	28	130	149	97	83	Wright and Will, 1958
	33	172	150	102	69	Ovington and Madgwick, 1959
	39	164	200	140	88	Tamm, 1969
	44	124	133	108	84	Tamm, 1969
	64	103	114	94	41	Wright and Will, 1958
	75	77	67	56	59	Tamm, 1969
Corsican pine	18	194	229	239	183	Wright and Will, 1958
	28	122	155	133	150	Wright and Will, 1958
	48	89	107	95	97	Wright and Will, 1958
Averages						
Pines	50	—	156	104	100	Rennie, 1955
	100	—	87	59	52	Rennie, 1955
Other conifers	50	—	170	127	138	Rennie, 1955
	100	—	87	56	59	Rennie, 1955
Hardwoods	50	—	122	92	67	Rennie, 1955
	100	—	69	47	37	Rennie, 1955

[a] Average of two stands.

the nutrients on the site where they could eventually be used by the next crop. Readers interested in this topic are referred to Leaf (1979).

It is much easier to evaluate the degree to which harvest-induced nutrient depletion occurs as the intensity of utilization increases than to determine how important such increased losses are in terms of reduced future wood production (Kimmins, 1977). The latter involves a variety of questions, many of which may be difficult to answer.

1. What proportion of the site nutrient capital is removed in harvested material?
2. What is the magnitude of other harvest-induced losses, such as soil leaching?
3. How frequently will harvest-induced losses occur; what is the rotation length?
4. How rapidly does the remaining site nutrient capital cycle? That is, how "available" are the remaining nutrients to the next crop?
5. How rapidly are the losses replaced by natural processes, and what are the processes? How are they affected by harvesting and stand treatments?
6. What are the nutrient requirements of the next crop? How do these requirements vary during the life of the crop?

7. How important is availability of nutrients in regulating production of the crop species?
8. How easily (economically and ecologically) are the harvest-induced losses replaced by fertilization or some other means?

In most cases we do not know the answers to these and other questions, but even if we did, the diversity of information involved makes it difficult to arrive at a conclusion concerning the long-term effects of intensive biomass harvesting. A simple graphical analysis (Figure 5.17) can show in general terms what may occur, but it is too simplistic to give much confidence in the predictions. The solution is to develop a computer simulation model that can handle all we know about the biogeochemistry of intensive harvesting (see Chapter 17).

Before we leave this topic, it should be emphasized that most investigations have concluded that medium to long (80–120 years) rotating harvesting of temperate forests in which only stems are removed poses little threat of site nutrient depletion. It is short rotations combined with intensive biomass utilization that may create problems of reduced soil fertility. This topic has received increasing attention recently, as exemplified by several symposia devoted to the question of long-term sustained forest produc-

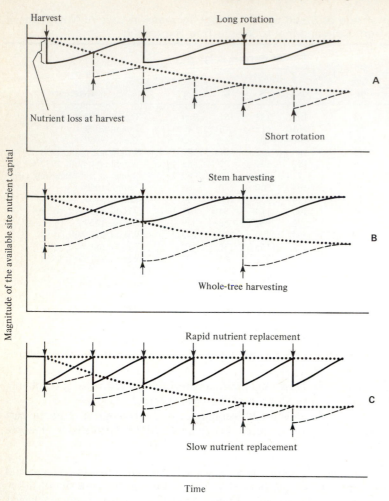

Figure 5.17
Simple graphical analysis of the relationship between the
available nutrient capital of a site and the (A) rotation
length, (B) intensity of utilization, and (C) rates of nutrient
replacement (i.e., inputs). The graphs are hypothetical because no long-term data of this type are available. The dotted lines indicate the expected long-term trends. Predictions
of this type are produced by some of the computer simulation models discussed in Chapter 17.

tivity under intensive forest management (Ballard et al.,
1983, Australian Forestry Council, 1981, SUNY, 1979).

*2. Increased Availability of Nutrients: The Assart Ef-
fect.* Clearcutting accelerates the mineralization of forest
floor materials present at the time of harvesting and adds a
variable quantity of logging slash to the forest floor. The
green foliage, fine twigs, and dead fine roots added as slash
contain substantial quantities of readily decomposable tissues that are relatively rich in nutrients, and there is commonly a "flush" of available nutrients that starts within a
year or two of logging. The flush continues until the readily
decomposed organic matter has been processed into more
stable microbial biomass, or mineralized, or converted into
relatively stable humus.

This fertilizing or *assart*[8] effect of clearcutting, which
continues until the nutrients have been taken up by plants,
immobilized by microbes or by soil chemical reactions, or
leached away, has been known for centuries. For millenia,
peasant farmers around the world have cleared forest and
planted crops that thrived on the accompanying flush of
nutrients. As the availability of nutrients and the productivity of the crops declined, the land was abandoned and
the forest allowed to reinvade and restore the diminished
fertility.

[8] An old English word meaning to grub up the trees and shrubs of a forest
or woodland to make the land arable, this term has been used recently to
refer to the post-clearcutting flush of nutrients.

A good example of the assart effect was provided by Weetman (1967). He cut a small area of a 90-year-old black spruce stand in Quebec and established on half of it a plantation of black spruce seedlings collected from the vicinity. On the other half he allowed natural regeneration to stock the area, a process that took about 8 years. Eighteen years later, the spruce planted immediately after cutting, which had the advantage of the assart effect, were about 5 m tall. The trees in the other area, which were more than half the age, were only about 50 cm or one tenth as tall. Forestry practice often calls for artificial regeneration only after a period in which natural regeneration is given an opportunity to restock the area. In many cases such a delay will mean that the next crop does not get the benefit of the flush of nutrients.

The assart effect can be responsible for fooling foresters about the quality of a site after clearcutting. Because nutrient availability is unusually high for a few years after clearcutting, nutrient-demanding species may initially grow well even on rather poor sites. However, once the assart effect is over, tree growth on such sites may decline drastically. In fact, once the flush of nutrients is over, nutrient availability and growth may actually decline to below the prelogging levels. While the increased microbial population is mineralizing the easily decomposable needles, twigs, and fine roots, it is also invading the larger woody materials, a process that is greatly aided if wood-boring insects are present because they introduce fungi into the logs. Before the fungi can utilize the energy contained in the high-C/N-ratio woody material, nitrogen and other nutrients are needed. These are believed to be withdrawn from the surrounding area by fungi, and translocated into and immobilized in the large woody material, resulting in a deficiency of available nutrients elsewhere in the soil. Tree growth under such immobilization conditions contrasts strongly with tree growth during the assart period. There is thought to be some fixation of N_2 by microbes decomposing logs, but the relative importance of fixation and translocation in increasing the N content of decomposing logs has yet to be established.

3. Leaching Losses Accompanying Clearcutting. The assart effect results from increases in the availability of nutrients. In the presence of nutrient-demanding plants, most of the nutrient release is taken up and retained. However, if the logging has left the area free of vegetation and if for some reason reinvasion is delayed and the soil is unable to retain them, the soluble nutrients released by mineralization of organic matter may be leached away. A high cation-exchange capacity will generally ensure the retention of cations, except where there is surface runoff or channeling of soil water through soil macropores or channels. However,

anions such as nitrate are poorly retained by many soils and are readily leached.

The most widely published example of the effect of vegetation removal on nutrient leaching is the experiment conducted in a climax eastern deciduous hardwood forest in New Hampshire, northeastern U.S. (Hubbard Brook). As we have already seen (section 5.11), the result was a dramatic and substantial alteration in water chemistry and in the nutrient budget for the watershed (Table 5.16). Figure 5.16 shows the changes in the concentrations of various chemicals, and Table 5.19 presents annual stream net nutrient budget data. During a 3-year period of deforestation, the total net loss of dissolved substances was increased about eightfold over the predeforestation value. Increases for individual elements were as follows: K, 20-fold; Ca, 8.6-fold; N, 160-fold (Bormann and Likens, 1979). Since many ecosystems are nitrogen limited, the last figure is particularly interesting. Subsequent studies comparing commercial clearcutting with the devegetation revealed less dramatic effects on stream nitrogen chemistry but similar effects on watershed nitrogen budget (Table 5.20).

The major difference between the Hubbard Brook devegetation experiment and commercial clearcutting is that concentrations of nutrients in streamwater in clearcut areas rapidly decline to levels that approach or even fall below those of the precutting period. The explanation for this decline is to be found in the rapid reestablishment of the plant community following clearcutting. Logged areas in the northern hardwood forest are rapidly invaded by various

Table 5.19 Net Gains and Losses, kg ha^{-1}, of Dissolved Substances for the Devegetated Watershed and a Control Watershed at Hubbard Brook, N.H., for the Water Years 1966–1969

Element	Net Gain or Loss[a]	
	Deforested Watershed[b]	Control Watershed
Nitrate N	−114.1	+1.6
Ca	−77.7	−9.0
Silicate Si	−30.6	−15.9
K	−30.3	−1.5
Al	−21.1	−3.0
Mg	−15.6	−2.6
Sulfate S	−2.8	−30.6
Cl	−1.7	+1.2
NH_4^+	+1.6	+2.2

Source: Bormann and Likens, 1979. Copyright Springer Verlag New York, Inc. Used with permission.
[a] Meteorological input minus streamwater output.
[b] Deforested November–December 1965.

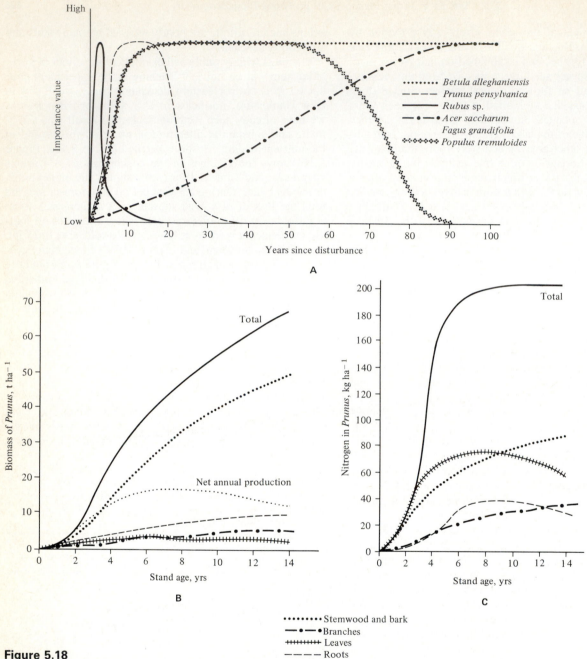

Figure 5.18

Role of pioneer plant communities in retention of nutrients following clearcutting. (A) Typical sequence of dominant plant species in a secondary succession in a northern deciduous hardwood forest in New Hampshire. Note the very rapid development of the pioneer vegetation. (B) Accumulation of biomass in components of the pin cherry *(Prunus pensylvanica)* community. (C) Nitrogen content of the pin cherry reaches nearly maximum values after only 6 years. Peak potassium values were observed after only 4 years. In this case, the pioneer vegetation played an important role in conserving the site nutrient capital. In other situations, the pioneer vegetation only develops a small biomass after clearcutting and may be proportionately less important in nutrient conservation. (After Marks, 1974. Reproduced by permission of the Ecological Society of America and P. L. Marks.)

pioneer shrubs (e.g., *Rubus* sp.) and deciduous hardwoods [e.g., pin cherry (*Prunus pensylvanica*) and birch (*Betula* sp.)]. These species accumulate biomass very rapidly, but even biomass accumulation is exceeded by the accumulation of nutrients. Maximum nitrogen content is achieved within 6 years of clearcutting, while peak potassium levels are reached within 4 years (Figure 5.18). Many logged areas in western North America are promptly invaded by fireweed (*Epilobium angustifolium*). This is a nutrient-demanding species whose presence is indicative of the postlogging nutrient flush. Fireweed accumulates biomass and nutrient capital rapidly, conserving some of the nutrients that otherwise might be leached away and holding them on the site until trees shade out the herb community and utilize the nutrients contained therein. Prompt reinvasion of any logged area will act to reduce nutrient losses and conserve the site nutrient capital, although it should be noted that in many cases the nutrient content of the pioneer vegetation may be much less than the quantity of nutrients released after logging because the biomass of this vegetation is often small.

The results of the Hubbard Brook studies have been interpreted by some as evidence that clearcutting causes serious disruption of ecosystem function. This stimulated studies in many other forest areas to ascertain if the same thing is true in other forest regions. For example, in a series of watershed studies in Oregon (Fredriksen et al., 1975), it was found that small increases in nitrate concentrations in streamwater do occur after clearcutting, typically with a delay of about a year. This delay occurs because with the low summer rainfall that characterizes much of the West Coast, products of decomposition are not flushed out of the soil until midwinter and because it usually takes at least one summer before appreciable mineralization can occur. The

extent of the increase varied in differnt parts of Oregon, but peak levels were generally only a few percent of the peak levels observed in New England. The increases declined rapidly as the watersheds revegetated, the duration of the increase being related to the speed of the revegetation.

The lower peak levels of stream nitrate observed in Oregon have been attributed to a greater quantity of high-C/N-ratio, slowly mineralizing material in the forest floor in Oregon than in New England, and to a delay in nitrification following disturbance because nitrifying organisms are less active in the lower quality forest floor materials of Oregon (Vitousek et al., 1982). There may also be a difference in the within-stream nutrient immobilization between Oregon streams and New England streams. Primary production in many West Coast streams is limited by lack of nutrients (Haydu and Thut, 1971), and streams are known to be active sinks for nitrate (Perrin 1981, Cummins 1980, Triska and Cromak, 1980). The difference could also be related to a greater importance of denitrification in the Oregon forests (cf. Martin, 1985).

A study of clearcutting effects in British Columbia revealed a somewhat greater response of stream chemistry than in Oregon, but much less than in New England (Feller and Kimmins, 1984). Losses of dissolved nitrogen in streamwater for 2 years after clearcutting were increased about 4 times the first year and 14 times the second year compared to the losses before clearcutting.

Evidently, it is necessary to investigate the biogeochemical effects of clearcutting on a site- and region-specific basis. Also, the considerable difference in stream chemistry that sometimes occurs in adjacent and apparently similar streams means that conclusions concerning the effect of clearcutting on ecosystem function based on streamwater chemistry can only be valid if, among other things, they include a pretreatment comparison of the streams. Broad generalizations that do not explicitly account for spatial and temporal variations in ecological conditions are unwarranted in the light of our present knowledge.

B. Effects of Slashburning

Clearcutting inevitably removes some nutrients from the site in harvested materials, virtually eliminates the biochemical cycle and much of the biogeochemical cycle, and can make a major modification in the geochemical cycle. The extent and duration of these effects are highly variable. Whole-tree harvesting can remove a significant proportion of site nutrients, and a delay in revegetation may permit leaching losses to occur on a significant scale. On the other hand, nutrient withdrawals in logs can be modest, and with prompt revegetation all three cycles return rather rapidly to

Table 5.20 Loss of Calcium and Nitrogen, kg ha^{-1}, from a Devegetated Watershed Compared to Losses from a Comparable Commercially Clearcut Watershed in New Hampshire (Likens et al., 1970; Pierce et al., 1972)

	Losses from Devegetated Watershed		Losses from Clearcut Watershed	
	N	Ca	N	Ca
Export in streamwater				
1st year	95	75	38	41
2nd year	140	90	57	48
Export in harvested products	0	0	144	221
Total 2-year export	236	165	239	310

something approaching the prelogging condition. Most of the site nitrogen is often retained by immobilization, lack of nitrate production, or plant uptake. Slashburning has a different effect. Although the question of wildfire effects is discussed in Chapter 12, a discussion of biogeochemical impacts of the prescribed use of fire in forest management is presented here.

Combustion of organic matter converts most of the chemicals therein to oxides. Many of these remain as solids because of high melting and gasification temperatures. They remain after the fire as ash, although a certain proportion of this is carried aloft by fire-induced convection currents and distributed to downwind areas. Where these air currents are strong, as in a hot fire covering many tens of hectares, a large proportion of the ash may be removed. For example, it is estimated that approximately 0.5–8 kg of fly ash is produced for every metric ton of fuel burned. Where there is a reduction of 50 t ha^{-1}, this would amount to between 25.0 and 400 kg ha^{-1} of mineral material (data in Cramer, 1974a). Estimates of particulate emissions as high as 29 kg of fly ash per metric ton of fuel have been reported at the head of a wildfire (Cooper, 1973), and presumably such high values may pertain under certain conditions in a slashfire. This fly ash may have the following composition: 0.0089% N, 11.7% Ca, 1.61% Mg, and 10.01% K (Grier, 1972).

Oxides that are gaseous at normal temperatures or the temperatures in the fire are lost as gases in the smoke plume, and most of the nitrogen and sulfur in the burned material will suffer this fate. Losses of the somewhat more refactory materials may also occur. It is customary to use temperatures lower than 480°C in preparing plant samples for analysis of cations because above this temperature potassium can be lost in significant amounts. Some phosphorus may also be lost at higher temperatures.

Calculation of the quantity of nutrients lost during a prescribed burn is difficult, and there are few published data. When heather (*Calluna vulgaris*) was burned in the laboratory by Allen (1964) at 800–825°C, the percentage losses of nutrient content were N, 76.2; P, 3.5; K, 4.9; Ca, 2.4; Mg, 2.1; and S, 56.3. At 550–650°C, the losses were 68 and 50% for N and P, respectively, and less than 1.4% for the others. Losses at higher temperatures were not reported. Knight (1966) burned forest floor material from a Douglas-fir stand and reported nitrogen losses of 410 kg ha^{-1} at 700°C and 167 kg ha^{-1} at 300°C. Much of this was probably as molecular nitrogen and is unlikely to be returned to the ecosystem by rain. Grier (1972) burned Douglas-fir slash on areas with average and four times average slash loadings and calculated the percentage loss of nutrients to

Table 5.21 Percent Loss of Biomass and Nutrients During Slashburning of Experimental Plots with Two Different Levels of Slash Loading (Grier, 1972)

	Loss with Standard Slash Loading,[a] %	Loss with Heavy Slash Loading,[b] %
Biomass	93	96
N	91	92
P	32	56
K	5	16
Ca	7	2
Mg	21	19
Na	0	25

[a] The standard loading was 75 t ha^{-1}
[b] The heavy loading was 320 t ha^{-1}.

gasses and fly ash. The results are shown in Table 5.21. In his study, fuel loadings (and therefore energy release) had an effect on the loss of P, K, and Na, but little effect on N, Ca, and Mg.

Feller and Kimmins (1984) reported on the loss of nutrients from the slash and forest floor during a slashburn in western British Columbia. Based on both field and laboratory studies, the quantities (kg ha^{-1}) of nutrients lost during the burn were calculated to be N, 982; P, 16; K, 37; Ca, 154; and Mg, 29. These amounts represented 41, 8, 24, 25, and 15%, respectively, of the total amounts of these nutrients in the forest floor and slash (Table 5.22). This compares with similar estimates (kg ha^{-1}) made for slashburns in Australia by Harwood and Jackson (1976): P, 10; K, 51; Ca, 100; and Mg, 37; and by Flinn et al. (1979): N, 220; P, 8; K, 21; Ca, 123; and Mg, 13.

Following the slashfire, the area is left covered with a layer of ash and charred material of varying depth. The fate of the nutrients contained within this layer is highly variable. If the soils have become hydrophobic[9] or the surface soil pores are plugged with ash, much of the ash may be washed directly into streams. At the other extreme, the ash may be washed into the upper layers of the soil, where all the cations are held by the soil cation-exchange capacity. Where water flow through the soil is predominantly in macrochannels, much of the nutrient material leached out of the ash may bypass soil exchange sites and rapidly reach groundwater and streams. Alternatively, if the burn results in the production of anions such as bicarbonate or nitrate, significant quantities of cations can be leached right through the soil (see the discussion of soil-leaching mechanisms in Chapter 10). Any of these situations can occur, and it is

[9] See Chapter 12.

Table 5.22 Nutrient Loss, kg ha^{-1}, from Two Treated Areas and a Control Watershed[a] at the Haney Research Forest, southwestern British Columbia, During the First Two Years After Treatment (1973–74, 1974–75) Compared to Nutrient Reserves in the Mineral Soil and Forest Floor in the Areas and Nutrient Inputs in Precipitation

	N			P			K			Ca			Mg		
	A	B	C	A	B	C	A	B	C	A	B	C	A	B	C
Exports															
Streamwater	11	3	1	0	0	0	11	9	3	44	55	55	9	10	9
Log	234	308	—	34	50	—	168	237	—	260	467	—	27	38	—
Atmospheric[b]	—	982	—	—	16	—	—	37	—	—	154	—	—	29	—
Total	245	1293	1	34	66	0	179	283	3	304	676	55	36	77	9
Reserves															
Forest floor[c]	1632	2180	1490	122	174	155	71	110	95	724	742	526	102	95	129
Mineral soil[d]	4566	4647	3924	18	16	7	87	148	85	489	332	149	38	25	16
Total	6198	6827	5414	140	190	162	158	258	180	1213	1074	675	140	120	145
Average annual precipitation input[e]	4	4	4	0	0	0	1	1	1	7	7	7	1	1	1

Source: Feller and Kimmins, 1984. Copyright American Geophysical Union. Used with permission.

[a] A = watershed A, a clearcut area; B = watershed B, clearcut and slashburned; C = control watershed C.
[b] Atmospheric exports following slashburning were obtained from Feller et al. (1983).
[c] Total quantities of nutrients present prior to clearcutting and burning.
[d] Quantities of total N, extractable P, and exchangeable K, Mg, and Ca present in the soil to rooting depth (70 cm in watersheds A and C, 65 cm in watershed B);
[e] Average for the seven water years 1971–72 to 1977–78.

difficult to predict the postfire movement of nutrients on slashburned areas without a careful preburn site assessment.

Studies of nutrient leaching in a burned area of pine forest in South Carolina revealed that the fire increased the solubility of cations as follows: Ca^{2+}, 20-fold; Mg^{2+}, 10-fold; Na^+, 2.3-fold; and K^+, 2.3-fold. Natural leaching reduced the yield of ions from the burned litter over a 1-month period by 80–83% for divalent cations and 45–63% for monovalent cations. The burn did not affect the level of nitrate and phosphate ions, but the solubility of N and P increased some time after the burn, probably due to microbial activity (Lewis, 1974).

Grier (1972) reported that over a 2-year period, 0.86 g m^{-2} of Ca, 4.24 g m^{-2} of Mg, and 49.1 g m^{-2} of K were leached from an ash layer after burning Douglas-fir slash in western Washington. These losses compared with the following release from unburned decomposing slash: 0.26 g m^{-2} of Ca, 1.4 g m^{-2} of Mg, and 3.67 g m^{-2} of K. In a study of a ponderosa pine site burned in a wildfire in central Washington, losses of 16.3 g m^{-2} Ca, 6.3 g m^{-2} Mg, and 7.9 g m^{-2} K were recorded (Grier, 1975). The differences between the two sites were explained in terms of differences in ash composition. Of the cations leached from the Douglas-fir ash, the following percentages were retained in the upper 30 cm of the soil: 62% Ca, 41% Mg, and 81% K.

In a study of the biogeochemical effects of shifting cultivation in the tropics, Ewel et al. (1981) cut and burned an area of second-growth tropical forest in Costa Rica. Harvest of the larger trees removed 18% of the S and, with the exception of N, more than 10% of the total initial inventory of other nutrients in the initial biomass and upper 3 cm of soil. Less than 5% of the initial N was removed in logs. Burning the slash volatilized 31% of the biomass, 22% of the N remaining and 49% of the remaining S. Postburn losses of N were equal to 16% of the initial inventory (probably leaching of NO_3^-). Loss of P, K, Ca and Mg were 51, 33, 45 and 40%, respectively; these occurred after the onset of rains. The impact of the postburn decomposition of soil organic matter was found to be as important as the loss during the burn. Decomposition released as much carbon in 154 days as was lost in the fire. Obviously, shifting cultivation involving fire can have a very significant effect on site biogeochemistry, especially if reinvasion of vegetation is inhibited, thereby facilitating the loss of ash minerals and soil organic matter.

Following a burn, the availability of many nutrients is initially increased, even if the total site capital of nutrients has been reduced. As a result, the vegetation that reinvades a slashburned site is initially well nourished, and the new flora will often contain species typical of much more fertile sites. Fireweed is a species that is favored by high nutrient availability. It is a fire follower largely because of the increased nutrient availability. The postfire flush of nutrients is not sustained, however; as the available nutrients are leached away, immobilized by microbes, or taken up by plants, indicators of high nutrient availability such as fire-weed generally decline.

On a fertile site, slashburning will generally have little adverse effect on the site nutrient capital and on postfire nutrient cycling. The soil is well endowed with nutrients, there is often a good rate of natural replacement, and most of the soil organic matter is mixed down into the mineral soil by animals where it is protected against consumption by fire. On nutrient-poor sites, on the other hand, loss of nutri-ents due to slashburning can result in a significant reduction in biogeochemical cycling and a concomitant reduction in subsequent NPP. The initial site nutrient capital is smaller, rates of natural replacement tend to be low, and much of the site's available nutrient capital is in the surface organic ac-cumulation, which may be burned off during the fire.

5.13   Summary

Because of the biochemical nature of ecological energet-ics, organic production can occur in ecosystems only if the appropriate chemical elements are available at appropriate concentrations, in the appropriate relative quantities, and in the appropriate total amounts.

The dynamics of nutrient chemicals in terrestrial ecosys-tems can be identified with one or more of three cycles: the geochemical cycle, which involves inputs into and losses of nutrients out of a particular ecosystem; the biogeochemical cycle, which involves the uptake by, storage in, and loss of nutrients from plants within an ecosystem, including move-ment of nutrients through grazing and detritus trophic webs; and the biochemical cycle, which involves an internal redis-tribution of nutrients within organisms that permits the or-ganism to satisfy some of its nutritional requirements for new growth from within its own nutrient capital. For each cycle, there is a variety of pathways which vary in relative importance among different species and different environ-ments.

Mechanisms have evolved to conserve and store nutrients within an ecosystem. Plants establishing on uncolonized mineral substrate will gradually remove available nutrients from the mineral layers and transfer them to living plant biomass and a surface accumulation of decomposing or-ganic matter. Atmospheric inputs are also accumulated within the ecosystem. Trees are particularly well adapted to accumulate nutrients from the geochemical cycle into a tight biogeochemical cycle, and after a period of time a forest may be able to live in virtual nutritional independence of the underlying mineral layers. This important phenomenon per-mits reasonably productive forest growth on some exceed-ingly nutrient-poor mineral substrates and is a major reason why forests are such a successful form of vegetation.

In managing ecosystems, the biogeochemical mecha-nisms responsible for production must be identified and conserved. Over the past two thousand years, and especially in the past 50 years, humans have been dislocating nutrient cycles on an ever-increasing scale. In many areas the accu-mulated nutrient reserves that have taken centuries, or even millenia, to build up have been dissipated. Natural proc-esses are fully capable of rebuilding these reserves in time, but generally too slowly for human purposes. The energy required to rebuild these concentrations of nutrients rapidly once they are dissipated would be enormous. Continued life as we know it will require that we conserve available nutri-ents by maintaining biogeochemical cycles intact, and nu-trient management will become as important in forestry as it is in agriculture.

Section B Genetic and Evolutionary Aspects of Ecosystems

The functional, production-oriented view of ecosystems is both useful and important, but it must never be forgotten that ecosystem function depends entirely on living organisms. These have evolved to be able to capture and store energy in particular environments, and the management of renewable resources will rarely be successful unless the adaptations of organisms to physical, chemical, and biotic conditions are given due consideration.

Ultimately, the success of a particular organism is determined by the nature of its environment, but the distribution, abundance, and productivity of living things are as much the result of their adaptations as of the actual nature of their surroundings. This section, consisting of a single chapter, is intended to remind the reader that biological conditions and events are largely determined by the genetic characteristics of the individual organisms involved, that all populations of organisms exhibit a variation in characteristics, and that organisms can acclimate and/or adapt to changing conditions. However, for any particular organism there is a maximum rate at which these two processes can occur and a maximum degree to which an organism can acclimate. This must be borne in mind when manipulating either the biotic or the abiotic components of ecosystems.

6 Adaptation and Evolution: Genetic Aspects of Ecosystems[1]

6.1 Introduction

In the discussion of ecosystems and their functional processes, the biota were considered in terms of functional levels (plants, herbivores, carnivores, and detrivores) rather than in terms of individual organisms. The processes of energy flow and nutrient cycling were also discussed as general ecological phenomena rather than as events in a specific ecosystem. This approach was used because the principles considered apply equally to all ecosystems. However, we must understand not only the functional processes of ecosystems, but also the ecological character of the individual organisms of which they consist. Knowledge of the behavioral, physiological, and morphological adaptations that permit a particular organism to survive in a particular environment is just as important as knowledge of the ecosystem processes in which that organism is involved.

All living organisms share the need for energy and for an appropriate supply of chemical elements with which to obtain, store, and utilize that energy. That they are able to do

this in almost all of the enormously varied environments present on earth is a reflection of the tremendous diversity of living organisms. This diversity is not merely a response to variation in the physical environment, for if this was so we might expect that the biota of any particular biogeocoenose would consist of only one, or at most a very few species at each trophic level (high beta diversity but low alpha diversity[2]). Although flora and fauna of very low diversity are found in some physically extreme environments, it is far more common to find a large number of different species participating in ecosystem processes. So great is the variety of species in most ecosystems that one is prompted to ask, as did Hutchinson (1959), why there are so many kinds of plants and animals. The answer to this question is to be found in one of the most important processes of ecology and of biology in general: *genetic adaptation* and *evolution*.

Biological evolution is the change in the genetic makeup of a species or population over time. It occurs because the individuals of any population differ from each other in their genotype (genetic constitution) and consequently, in many cases, also in their phenotype (behavioral, physiological, and morphological characteristics). Differences in survival and reproduction within the population are associated with variations in the genotype, and those genotypes producing individuals with phenotypes that are better adapted to their physical and biotic environment will contribute more offspring to the next generation than will less well adapted genotypes. Ricklefs (1973, p. 209) illustrates this principle well for the general case. Such successful genotypes have greater *fitness*. If the environment changes with time, different genotypes will prove to be best adapted to, or fittest in, these new environments. The genetic makeup of the population will change (i.e., evolution will occur) and better adapted phenotype(s) will be produced. The process by which this genetic change occurs is called *natural selection*.

In this chapter the genetic variability of populations and the importance of this variation for adaptation are examined, as are the importance of genetic variability to forest management and the opportunities and problems that it presents. The questions of adaptation and of acclimation are considered here only briefly, but additional examples are given at various points in the following chapters. Adaptation and acclimation enter into every aspect of an organisms's existence, and it is difficult to discuss any topic in ecology without reference to genetic variation and adaptation. A

---

[1] Much of this chapter was contributed by Dr. J. G. Worrall, Dendrologist, Faculty of Forestry, University of British Columbia, Vancouver.

[2] Alpha diversity—the diversity of species within a sampling unit (e.g., a biogeocoenose). Beta diversity—the variation in species composition between two different sampling units.

comprehensive account of this topic is given by Stern and Roche (1974). Earlier reviews can be found in Heslop-Harrison (1964) and Hiesey and Milner (1965).

6.2 Genetic Variation in Natural Populations: The Basis of Diversity in Living Organisms and the Raw Material for Natural Selection

The character of individual organisms in a population is varied. In a plantation of Douglas-fir (*Pseudotsuga menziesii* (Mirb.) Franco) some trees grow faster in height and diameter than others, and there may be similar variation in resistance to attack by insects and disease, the number and size of branches, bark thickness, wood specific gravity, the frequency and size of seed crops, and so on. The pattern of variation that is often observed is illustrated by the variation in height growth of black spruce (*Picea mariana* BSP) after two growing seasons in a forest nursery. Figure 6.1 shows the frequency of occurrence of seedlings in various height classes in this seeding population.

Many variables show this sort of (normal) distribution, where most values are clustered symmetrically about the mean. The distribution is completely defined by the mean and the standard deviation, which is a measure of the spread of the data. About 68% of values lie within one standard deviation of the mean, about 95% within two standard deviations, and 99% within three standard deviations. A population with a standard deviation of 5 and a mean of 100 is obviously less variable than one where the standard deviation is 5 and the mean 10, so that often the amount of variability is expressed as a ratio of the two (i.e., $^5/_{100} \times 100 = 5\%$ in the first case, $^5/_{10} \times 100 = 50\%$ in the second). This ratio is called the *coefficient of variation*.

The data in Figure 6.1 are from Morgernstern (1969), who investigated the height growth of black spruce seedlings of many different geographic origins. His results are shown in the first two columns of Table 6.1, while the third column presents values from the theoretical normal frequency distribution derived from the raw data. The mean is 11.31 cm and the standard deviation is 2.82 cm. The

Figure 6.1

Actual and expected distribution of heights of black spruce seedlings based on the data from columns 1–3 in Table 6.1.

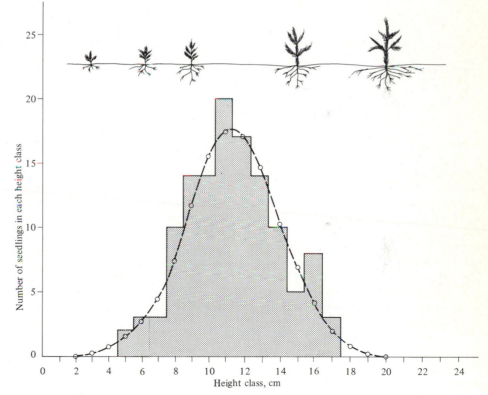

Table 6.1 Observed and Expected Frequencies of Black Spruce Seedling Phenotypes and Genotypes (data from Morgenstern, 1969)

Phenotype Height cm	Observed Frequency in Height Class	Expected Frequency in Height Class (normal distribution)	Assumed Genotype T	Assumed Genotype t	Binomial Expectations Parent Population	1st Generation of Selection Down	1st Generation of Selection Up	2nd Generation of Selection Up
1			0	24		.2		
2		.1	1	23		1.4		
3		.3	2	22		5.2		
4		.6	3	21	.2	11.7		
5	2	1.5	4	20	.6	18.7		
6	3	2.9	5	19	1.8	23.0		
7	3	5.5	6	18	4.3	22.2	.1	
8	10	8.6	7	17	8.3	17.5	.2	
9	14	12.6	8	16	13.2	10.8	.7	
10	14	15.5	9	15	17.7	6.1	1.8	
11	20	17.3	10	14	19.9	2.7	4.1	
12	17	16.7	11	13	19.1	1.0	7.8	
13	14	14.7	12	12	15.5	.4	12.4	.2
14	10	10.9	13	11	10.8	.1	17.2	.6
15	5	7.5	14	10	6.4		19.9	1.6
16	8	4.3	15	9	3.2		19.8	4.0
17	3	2.4	16	8	1.4		16.4	8.3
18		1.0	17	7	.5		11.4	14.5
19		.5	18	6	.1		6.6	20.9
20		.1	19	5			3.1	24.1
21			20	4			1.1	22.4
22			21	3			.3	15.7
23			22	2			.1	7.8
24			23	1				2.5
25			24	0				.4

chi-square value[3] is 9.14, indicating a fairly good fit between the observed and the normal distribution, since χ^2 .05 with 12 degrees of freedom is 21.0.

Morgernstern gives values for means and standard deviations of other morphological and physiological characters for these seedlings. In the case of morphological characteristics, the standard deviations are better expressed as a percentage of the mean (i.e., the coefficient of variation). For height growth this was 24.9%; for number of cotyledons, 7.1%; and for the amount of lammas growth[4], 44%. Coefficients of variation for other parameters generally fell between such limits, and averaged about 25%. For phenological variables, such as date of bud burst, the standard deviation was only 3.6 days, whereas for data on growth cessation it was 18.7 days. It might be inferred that the date of bud burst is more critical to successful survival (fitness) than the date of growth cessation and so is more strongly controlled (i.e., there is less variation).

All such phenotypic characteristics are ultimately controlled by the genetic makeup of the individual seedlings, modified to a greater or lesser extent by the environmental conditions. Where does this genetic variation come from? Before answering this question, a brief review of some basic genetic concepts is given for those readers unfamiliar with them.

A. Sources of Natural Variation

Most living cells contain nuclei the contents of which are clearly separated during cell division into rodlike structures. Having an affinity for particular dyes, these are called *chromosomes*. They consist of deoxyribonucleic acids (DNA), ribonucleic acids (RNA), and proteins. In the vegetative cells of higher plants, the chromosomes occur in (homolo-

[3]Chi-square (χ^2) is a distribution of ratios of variances (standard deviations squared), often used to test the goodness of fit of data to an assumed distribution (a normal distribution in this case). Large χ^2 values indicate poor fit.

[4]Height growth in many temperate zone species is completed quickly and quite early. A second flush of growth in late summer is called *lammas growth*, the bread-baking festival "Lammas Day" falling on August 1.

gous) pairs: for example, 13 pairs in Douglas-fir, 12 in beech (*Fagus* L.), and a higher and quite variable number in birch (*Betula* L.), for example, 14 or 28. In mitotic (vegetative) cell division, the chromosomes are duplicated so that each of the new cells contains the same number of chromosomes as the original cell: that is, the *diploid number*. But in reproductive cell division *via* meiosis, only one member of each pair of homologous chromosomes is represented in each resulting cell (gametes). These cells are *haploid*. Each parent contributes a haploid set of chromosomes to the zygote (the fertilized egg), which is the first cell of the next sporophyte or diploid generation.

Recognition of genetically controlled variation among individuals and the relationship between this variation and the evolution of different races and species is of recent origin, dating from the work of the great biologists Darwin, Wallace, and Mendel in the 1850s and 1860s. Much of the knowledge of how this variation arises has come from much more recent work, and the modern theory of genetics dates from only the 1930s. Around 1900 it was realized that the inheritance patterns for various traits described by Mendel could be explained by chromosome behavior during sexual reproduction if it could be assumed that discrete parts of chromosomes controlled specific phenotypic characters. DNA molecules in the chromosomes consist of two spiral strands, each consisting of multiples of the organic bases adenine, cytosine, guanine, and thymine bonded to pentose sugars, which are connected by phosphate radicals. Each spiral is held to the other by hydrogen bonds between ade-

nine and thymine and between guanine and cytosine to the inside. The base plus the sugar is called a *nucleotide*.

The four bases along a strand can be arranged into triplets in $4^3 = 64$ ways. One or more of these 64 triplets can be arranged in $64N$ ways to form a gene or unit of inheritance. Hall (1974) has estimated that there is enough DNA in the nucleus of jack pine cells (*Pinus banksiana* Lamb.) to provide more than 10^7 genes or genetic messages! In the simplest case, two genes govern a phenotypic trait, each at a similar position in the homologous chromosomes. These genes may be in several alternative forms (alleles), but often there are just two alleles of each gene. It is the enormously large number of possible combinations of the subcomponents of DNA and the existence of different (allelic) forms of these combinations that is the basis of the natural variation in populations.

B. Qualitative Variation

As an example of qualitative variation, consider *Fagus sylvatica* L., European beech, and one of its common ornamental forms, var. *larciniata*, the cut-leaf beech. Instead of having the normal ovate leaf, this form has deeply lobed, almost cleft leaves, as shown in Figure 6.2. If the normal and the cut-leaf types are cross-bred, the offspring (F_1) may be either all normal or half normal and half cut-leaf. Further breeding produces the following results. If the normal trees are self-fertilized, they yield offspring (F_2) that are 50:50 normal:cut-leaf. If two of the F_1 normal offspring are crossed with each other, their F_2 progeny are in the

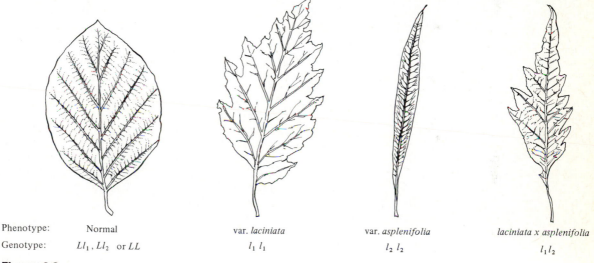

Phenotype:	Normal	var. *laciniata*	var. *asplenifolia*	*laciniata* x *asplenifolia*
Genotype:	Ll_1, Ll_2 or LL	$l_1 l_1$	$l_2 l_2$	$l_1 l_2$

Figure 6.2
Four leaf phenotypes of beech. The probable genotypes of each phenotype are indicated. (Based on Lamprecht, 1966; drawings from J. G. Worrall.)

ratio 3:1 normal:cut-leaf progeny. Further crosses between progeny have to wait for sexual maturity (about 40 years in beech, which illustrates why progress in tree genetics and tree breeding is relatively slow and why Mendel's choice of peas for his studies was a wise one). However, we may assume that the inheritance patterns would be exactly the same as those found by Mendel, which are shown in Figure 6.3, where L is the gene for normal leaves, which is dominant to the recessive allele (l) for cut-leaves. This type of diagram is called a *Punnett square*.

There are many other traits in trees that presumably are of this type, where a single dominant allelic form of a gene masks the recessive allelic form of that gene and there are only two phenotypes: the dominant and the recessive. The latter phenotype is seen only when the recessive allele is present on both chromosomes. There are numerous examples of this. Leaves vary in color, such as in the very dark leaved forms of European beech. In this "copper" beech, the gene (C) for anthocyanin production is dominant over (c), no anthocyanin, so that both CC and Cc genotypes have copper-colored foliage, whereas cc genotypes have normal green foliage (Blinkenberg et al., 1958). Most people are familiar with albinos (gg) in animals; the pigment gene (G) is dominant over no pigment (g). Such a condition is seen less often in plants because (gg) for no chlorophyll is lethal, and white seedlings live only a few weeks until food stored in the seed is exhausted. Heterozygous individuals, of normal phenotype, give a 3:1 ratio of normal:white progeny. The fastigiate[5] crown form, as seen in lombardy poplar (*Populus nigra* var. *Italica Muench.*) and in cultivars of such species as black locust (*Robinia pseudoacacia fastigiata* Dieck.) seems to be recessive to the normal oval crown forms. In the former case, the fastigiate form has erroneously been assigned varietal status, whereas actually it is merely a clone (or clones).

There is variation in the resin color in slash pine (Kraus and Squillace, 1964). Individuals occur rarely that have yellow resin and when these are bred with each other, they produce progeny with yellow resin. When crossed with normal trees which have colorless resin, the progeny usually have normal resin. Yellow resin is the result of the homozygous recessive condition.

Segaard (1969) studied disease resistance in *Thuja* L. (arbor-vitae) species. Western redcedar (or giant arborvitae) (*Thuja plicata* D. Don.) from western North America

[5]Fastigiate: an upright crown form, where laterals grow almost vertically, and are almost as long as the leading shoot.

Parental phenotypes:

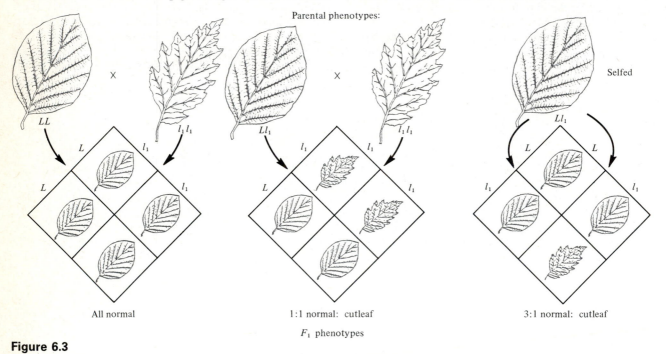

F_1 phenotypes

Figure 6.3
Inheritance patterns of the two beech leaf phenotypes, normal and cut-leaf (variety laciniata).

is susceptible to the rather serious cedar leaf blight (*Didymascella [Kiethia] thujina* (Dur.) Maire), whereas the closely related *Thuja standishii* (Gord.) Carr. (Japanese arbor-vitae) is not. Despite the fact that these species are separated by the Pacific Ocean and have been distinct for some time, they hybridize and these hybrids are fertile. The hybrid is resistant to the disease. The selfed hybrid yields progeny with a 3:1 ratio of resistant:susceptible. The backcross[6] to *T. standishii* is resistant; the backcross to *T. plicata* has a 1:1 ratio of resistant to susceptible plants. Evidently, this trait is governed by a single pair of genes, with the homozygous recessive being disease susceptible.

The European beech also serves to illustrate another point. There is a variety that has straplike leaves— var. *asplenifolia* (Figure 6.2). This is also due to a double-recessive condition, but the gene responsible is a third allelic form of the leaf-shape gene. Some genes exist in a whole array of allelic forms, three in this case.

C. Quantitative Variation

In the examples given above, phenotypes governed by a pair of genes were of only two kinds, because the homozygous dominant and the heterozygous genotypes produced indistinguishable phenotypes. With this type of inheritance, the phenotype is a direct reflection of the genotype in all but the most unusual environments and does not reveal variations in the intensity of action of a gene. For example, the (*G*) gene controls the production of a catalyst (an enzyme) that is involved in the synthesis of chlorophyll. Variations in the abundance of the catalyst make no difference to the rate of production of chlorophyll: it is all or nothing. Under special conditions, phenotypes may not reflect the genotype. If one were to grow seeds with genetic makeup *GG*, *Gg*, and *gg* (no catalyst) in the dark, all would produce white seedlings that would be phenotypically indistinguishable. This situation is, of course, a little artificial.

In natural populations, examples of all-or-nothing action of genes are relatively uncommon, but they have been widely studied because of their simplicity and have helped to elucidate the basic mechanisms of genetic inheritance. The more common situation is one in which phenotypic traits show a whole range of values. Many traits are quantitative.

Copper beech is not the only tree to have abnormally pigmented foliage. Many ornamental varieties of other tree species have unusual and attractive colors. Yellow foliage may result from a less than normal level of chlorophyll, so

[6]Backcross: a hybrid crossed with a parent.

that the carotene pigments are not so masked as they usually are. Such individuals are not normally very fit in natural environments, and they generally survive and reproduce only by the intervention of horticulturalists. However, occasionally trees with yellow foliage are found in the wild, for example, the ''golden'' sitka spruces (*Picea sitchensis* (Bong.) Carr.) of Queen Charlotte Island off the north coast of British Columbia. There is also an *aurea* variety of Norway spruce, *Picea abies* (L.) (Karst) (Langner, 1954). In both these cases, as before, only two genes are involved, but the three genotypes give rise to three instead of two phenotypes. The *G* gene for chlorophyll is not dominant over *g*, albino, so that the heterozygote (*Gg*) does have some chlorophyll, but not as much as the homozygote (*GG*). In this case the effects of each *G* gene are additive, the amount of chlorophyll depending on the number of *G* genes present. *GG* is normal, *Gg* is *aurea,* and *gg,* as before, is albino. Selfing of the *aurea* phenotype yields all three phenotypes, in the ratio 1:2:1 green:*aurea*:albino, as can be checked by drawing a Punnett square of the type in Figure 6.3. This particular genetic system is well known, since Langner was able to trace the distance and amounts of pollen flight from isolated *aurea* trees, because the progeny with adjacent normal trees will be in the 1:1 ratio of green to *aurea*. This is the simplest case of a quantitative trait. Another is the heterozygote $l_1 l_2$ of beech, which has leaves intermediate to $l_1 l_1$ cut-leaf and $l_2 l_2$ *asplenifolia* (the fourth leaf in Figure 6.3).

This simple case can be taken a step further. For instance, in domestic fowl, there is a phenotype ''frizzle'' that has curly feathers. This is homozygous (*FF*). When crossed with a normal fowl (*ff*), all the progeny are mildly frizzled (*Ff*), so that there are the three phenotypes, each produced by a different genotype. The *F* gene adds a certain amount of frizzle to the *Ff* heterozygote. However, there are other deviant feather types, from very mild frizzle all the way up to absurdly frizzled. Two pairs of genes govern this trait, so that there can be five genotypes and five phenotypes: *ffff*, normal; *Ffff*, mild frizzle; *FFff*, frizzle; *FFFf*, very frizzled; and *FFFF*, grotesque (Hutt, 1949).

The examples of qualitative and quantitative inheritance described above show that there is plenty of variation of both phenotype and genotype. Where does the variation in genetic structure come from? It is the result of mutation, caused perhaps by radiation, or by miscopying during chromosome duplication during cell division. This involves a change in the actual coding of a particular allele. For example, the *G* gene for chlorophyll production constantly mutates to *g* for albino, and vice versa, but the *g* gene is continuously removed from the population because of its zero fitness in the homozygous state. On a larger scale, chromosomes may break and rejoin in different order. They may be lost or gained in whole or in part. Whole sets of chromosomes may be gained when, during duplication, cell walls fail to form. This yields polyploid cells, as has been mentioned for birch, where the chromosome number may be $2n = 28$, or $2n = 56$ (i.e., tetraploid) or even hexaploid or octoploid. Such genetic variation is constantly arising, and many of modern technology's chemicals seem to accelerate it in a rather disastrous way (i.e., they are powerful mutagens).

The genetic variation present in a population or an individual may be expressed immediately as phenotypic variation. Trees containing a segment with different leaf color or form, or different phenology or branching pattern are seen quite commonly, this being the result of a somatic mutation in a meristem. More often, however, the variation is not expressed until the next generation(s), when independent segregation and assortment of genes produces new genotypes which express themselves phenotypically (e.g., Figure 6.3, or the *aurea* spruce mentioned above, which when selfed yields three phenotypes). Thus, constantly accumulating genetic variation is expressed via sexual reproduction, and on this resulting phenotypic variation, natural (and artificial) selection can act. It has been estimated that without sexual reproduction, evolution would proceed at less than 1% of its present rate.

There is plenty of scope for selection, since neither the seed nor seedlings resulting from sexual reproduction in plants, nor the offspring of animals, all survive. At equilibrium, each mature organism is replaced by only one of its progeny. In slash pine stands, each tree produces about 1500 seeds per year, and about half a million might be produced altogether during the life of a tree (Florence and McWilliam, 1956). In small fruited species such as red alder (*Alnus rubra* Bong.) there are close to 10 million potential progeny throughout the life of the parent. Few seed will germinate, since most will fall on unsuitable sites or succumb to rodents or fungi and insects. Those that do germinate are not likely to survive a full season; very few will grow to reproductive age; still fewer will reach maturity. At every stage of their life, organisms have many physical and biotic factors working against their survival, and only those individuals that have the phenotypic characteristics that make them well adapted to their environment (and some good luck) will survive and reproduce.

In summary, there is variation, some of which is genetic and is inherited. Not all progeny survive, so it would seem

that the stage is set for selection, adaptation, and evolution. Have they happened?

6.3 Examples of Selection, Adaptation, and Evolution

A. Man-Made Selection Pressures

1. The Theoretical Case. If selection pressures based on tree height were applied to the black spruce seedlings of Table 6.1 and Figure 6.1, some trees would be eliminated because they proved to be unfit under these particular pressures. As a result, the proportion of T genes in the remaining population would change. For example, if all seedlings greater than 9 cm tall were destroyed, the proportion of T genes, $p(T)$, in the remaining population of 18 seedlings would become $< .2338$, and their mean height would be 6.37 cm. The selection differential (the original population mean minus the mean of the selected individuals) is $11.31 - 6.37$ or 4.94 cm. If they were of reproductive age (actually about 15 years in spruce) these selected seedlings would produce a population of offspring that had a height distribution (at the same age) as shown in column 7 of Table 6.1; they would retain the same mean as the parent population (6.37 cm). This distribution was calculated using the binomial[7], as was the theoretical distribution for the original population. Similarly, we could select against small size and promote tallness in the population by selecting the tallest: the top 16 individuals in the original population. These have a $p(T)$ value of .5972, and a mean height 14.3 cm. The theoretical distribution of their progeny is shown in column 8 of Table 6.1. If selection for tallness were to be continued by selecting only those individuals in the second generation that were taller than 18 cm [theoretically, there would be 11.2 individuals with a $p(T)$ value of .786] the resulting progeny would have a distribution of height growth as shown in column 9.

These distributions are shown in Figure 6.4. The means are diverging from that of the original population. Selection that produces diverging means is called *directional selection*. Interestingly, new types are appearing, types that did not exist in the original population. For example, there were no plants as tall as 24 cm in the original population, but these are present after selecting for tallness for two generations. In theory, at least, it appears that a variable popula-

---

[7] In the binomial distribution, an event has the probability p of success, $q(= 1 - p)$ of failure. If repeated n times, the number of successes $r = \binom{n}{r} p^r q^{n-r}$.

tion can, as a result of selection, yield forms that could not have been predicted.

The selection gain just described is theoretical only. In practice, the selection gain expected from the selection differential is rarely if ever obtained. This if for many reasons, perhaps the most important of which is that the individual effects of genes are not strictly additive. For instance, in the *aurea* spruce varieties, the phenotypes corresponding to the genotypes that have two genes for chlorophyll *(GG)*, 1 gene for chlorophyll *(Gg)*, or no genes for chlorophyll *(gg)*, do not contain chlorophyll in amounts $2:1:0$. Instead, the ratio is closer to $7:1:0$. The realized gain expressed as a propor-

tion of the selection differential is called the *heritability,* and for many traits in trees it is about 25%.

2. Actual Examples of Selection Pressures:

a. INTENTIONAL. One has only to look at the products of many generations of selection by agriculturalists to see that the theoretical prediction made above (i.e., that selection in a variable population can yield unexpected phenotypes) is also true in practice. Domestic animals and plants can hardly be recognized as being the same species as their wild ancestors. Compare, for example, the huge red, shiny, juicy (and almost totally tasteless) fruit of McIntosh apples, with those of *Malus pumila* Mill., the common crabapple of Eu-

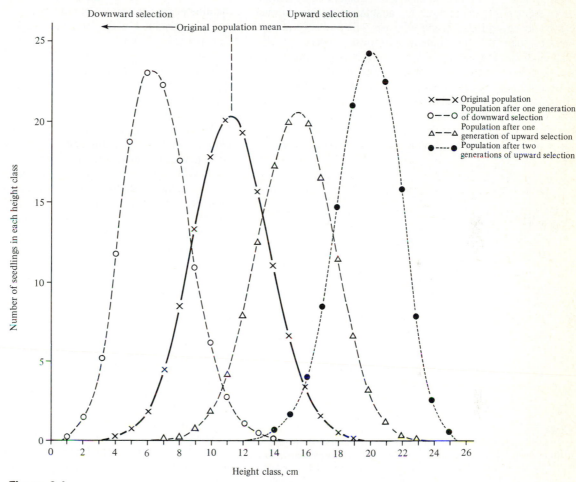

Figure 6.4

Theoretical distributions of seedling height after one generation of downward selection and one and two generations of upward selection. The data are from columns 6–9 of Table 6.1.

rope. Darwin was fascinated by the variability of pigeons and bred them to investigate the heritability of the variation in these birds. The modern "fancy" breeds that have resulted from over a century of selective breeding bear little resemblance to the ancestral rock dove (*Columbia livia* Gmelin) and in fact make one hope that we do not ever initiate selective breeding programs in human beings. Who knows what the results might be? Such spectacular results of selection are also the aim of tree breeders.

Figure 6.5 shows the results of selection, both for and against, DDT resistance in the fruit fly (*Drosophila melanogaster* Meigen). Within 15 generations approximately 25-fold changes were produced in this characteristic, both up and down. This indicates the tremendous potential that insect populations have for adaptation against human efforts to control them, and why we will probably always have to share the environment with pest insects.

It is disturbing to consider the same sort of "progress" that has been made in disease-causing bacteria, many of which are now resistant to antibiotics. Such resistance can be induced rapidly merely by exposing the parent bacteria to low doses of such antibiotics in the process of screening out the susceptible ones (see the coevolution example below for an explanation of the possible mechanism involved).

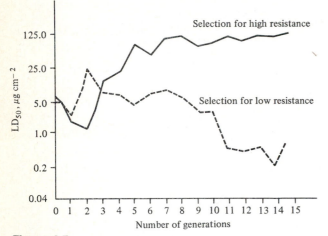

Figure 6.5

Variation in resistance to DDT in populations of the fruit fly, *Drosophila melanogaster,* subject to selection over 15 successive generations either for or against resistance to DDT. Resistance was increased by a factor of about 40 in in the former and reduced by a factor of about 6 in the latter. The technique involved selection of genetic variation that was already present in the original population (sib-selection). (After Bennett, 1960. Reproduced from *Heredity* by permission of Genetical Society of Great Britain and J. Bennett.)

b. ACCIDENTAL. In natural environments, populations undergoing selection are not artificially kept separate from one another as is the case in experimental selection. In accidental as opposed to deliberate human-induced selection there is a free exchange between the selected and original populations.

The classic case of human activities causing differentials between populations is that of industrial melanism in the peppered moth (*Biston betularia* Guenee), which lives in the woodlands in England. There is a good record of the phenotypic appearance of this moth over the past 150 years because specimens of this species are to be found in moth and butterfly collections made periodically throughout the period. Most of the specimens dating from the beginning of the nineteenth century are of the "typical" variety, which is whitish, speckled with gray and black—hence the name "peppered." A dark-colored or "melanic" variant occurred in the early collections, but apparently it was rare. Selection pressure from predators would have favored the typical form because of its better concealment as it rested on the lichen-covered bark of tree species such as birch (Figure 6.6). The melanic form did not remain rare, however. Its frequency has increased steadily over the past century until in many parts of England today it represents the more common form. Only in the less industrialized parts of Britain has the typical form retained its earlier frequency.

The change in the relative frequencies of the typical and melanic form parallels the increase in air pollution that occurred in Great Britain over the last century. Increasing air pollution led to two important changes in the environment of the peppered moth: the killing of the pale-colored lichens that covered dark tree trunks, lichens being extremely sensitive to SO_2, and darkening of the pale tree trunks by the deposition of soot (carbon particles). These changes in the moth's habitat improved the concealment of the melanic form from avian predators as the moths rest on the tree trunks, but virtually eliminated concealment for the typical form. The resulting changes in selection pressure altered the relative fitness of the two forms and led to a change in their frequency in the population. This change has not been permanent, however. Pollution control programs have significantly reduced air pollution in some areas of Great Britain, with parallel increases in the frequency of the typical form (Cook et al., 1970).

Similar accidental selection has resulted in mosquito populations that are resistant to DDT, which is no longer effective in the control of malaria in areas in which DDT has been used extensively. The production of the resistant strain followed much the same path as depicted in Figure 6.5 for the fruit fly. A similar phenomenon, which is of considerable interest to foresters and wood users, is the evolution, after 50 or so years of selection, of forms of shipworm *(Teredo nervalis)* that are not affected by creosote. This means that wooden marine installations must now be protected by some other method, such as pentachlorophenol.

There are comparable examples in plants of evolution induced by our efforts to control pests and by the widespread pollution of the environment. It has been shown (Marriage and Warwick, 1980) that in response to herbicide application, pigweed *(Chenopodium album)* types have evolved that are resistant to the chemicals involved. Bradshaw (1952) showed that races of grasses such as *Agnostis tenuis* have evolved that are so tolerant of high concentrations of heavy metal they can grow on mine tailings rich in such elements as zinc and lead.

B. Natural Selection Pressures

A species is a genetic grouping of organisms (a *gene pool*) whose genetic constitution *(genome)* is sufficiently homogeneous to allow sexual reproduction *(gene flow)* between individuals of the group (species), but different enough from that of any other species to preclude or severely limit gene exchange between the groups. In fact, this definition often does not work very well, since individuals from opposite ends of the range of a widely distributed species will not breed with each other, and so could be called separate species. However, gene exchange between these remotely located individuals can occur by breeding them with individuals from the middle parts of the range.

Since most species have a geographical range that includes considerable variation in the character of the environment, different local populations of a species will experience either slight or significant differences in selection pressure. The continuing operation of this natural selection will result in the survival of those individuals and their offspring whose genetic makeup best suits them for life and reproduction in their particular environment (i.e., gives them a high fitness). As Darwin put it, life involves a "struggle for existence," leading to "survival of the fittest," and this results in the development of locally adapted genotypes or *ecotypes,* a genetic subdivision of a species in response to local environmental conditions.

The classic example of the presence of genetic variation within a species between different parts of its range is found in the studies of yarrow (*Achillea* spp.) by Clausen, Keck, and Hiesey (1948) [see also the review of the physiology of races and species by Hiesey and Milner (1965)]. This and other examples are discussed by Jones and Luchsinger (1979). Yarrow is a herbaceous plant which grows widely across California from sea level to elevations over 3000 m

in the Sierra Nevada. The tallness of the plant varies greatly over its range (Figure 6.7), with a general decrease in size from the San Joaquin Valley toward the Pacific Ocean, and with increasing elevation eastward. This phenotypic variation does not prove the existence of ecotypes (i.e., local genotypic variation) since many species have the capacity to *acclimate* (i.e., produce different phenotypes from a single genotype) when grown in different environments. Acceptance of the existence of yarrow ecotypes requires demonstration of the fact that these differences (or others) are heritable, and that they will appear when plants from across the range are grown together in a single environment (i.e., in a provenance test).

In order to test for ecotypes, Clausen et al. collected seed from several locations *(provenances*[8]*)* along the altitudinal range of yarrow, and planted them in prepared seedbeds at sea level (Stanford), and at medium- (Mather) and high-elevation (Timberline) sites. These experiments showed that height growth is indeed inherited (that in this case the different provenances are different ecotypes), but that the genetically controlled variation in height growth is greatly modified by the environment. The ecotypes performed best (if tallness is considered "best") on sites closest to the elevation of their origin (in many species this is not the case). Moving ecotypes from low to high elevation was generally more deleterious than the reverse, indicating that it is easier for an ecotype adapted to a severe environment to exploit a moderate one than vice versa. The survival of the yarrow ecotypes in environments that were markedly different from their location of origin indicates that this species has a considerable ability to acclimate. However, this was a controlled experiment under ideal conditions (gardens, where competing vegetation was eliminated). In natural conditions, the "foreign" ecotypes would quite likely be eliminated by competition from other species (see the discussion of ecological niches in Chapter 14, section 14.6).

A similar example for trees occurs in those species such as Douglas-fir and black cottonwood (*Populus trichocarpa* Torr. and Gray), which grow in areas differing widely in the length of the growing season (the number of frost-free days). Provenances of these species (in this case ecotypes) from the continental climate east of the coast range in British Columbia survive when grown on the coast but perform poorly. Conversely, coastal provenances fail completely when grown in the interior of the province because of frost injury. The explanation is the same in both cases. Coastal

---

[8]The term provenance differs from the term ectotype; the former refers to the geographical location in which a genotype has evolved; the latter is the genotype that is adapted to the conditions of that location.

Unpolluted Area

Moths on a tree trunk in
an area without air pollution

Variants of Moth

○ typica form
● carbonaria form
⊙ insularia form

Polluted Area

Moths on a tree trunk in
an area with heavy air pollution

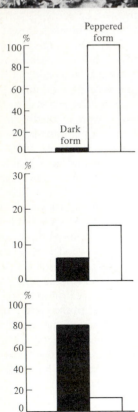

% frequency of dark and peppered forms
in local populations

% recapture of marked dark and peppered
forms released in woods

% of dark and peppered forms in observed
cases of predation by birds

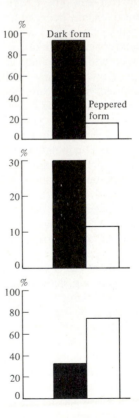

Figure 6.6 *(on facing page)*

The effect of changing selection pressure on the frequency of dark (melanic or carbonaria) and peppered (typica) forms of the peppered moth. The photo on the left shows adults of this species at rest on the lichen-covered bark of a tree trunk in an unpolluted area. The photo on the right shows two individuals on a tree trunk from which lichens have been eliminated by air pollution and which has been darkened by the deposition of air-borne soot. The change in the frequency of the two forms is probably related to predation by birds that use visual clues in searching. (Data from Kettlewell, 1956, 1958; photos from the experiments of Dr. H. B. D. Kettlewell, Oxford University. Reproduced with permission from *Heredity*.)

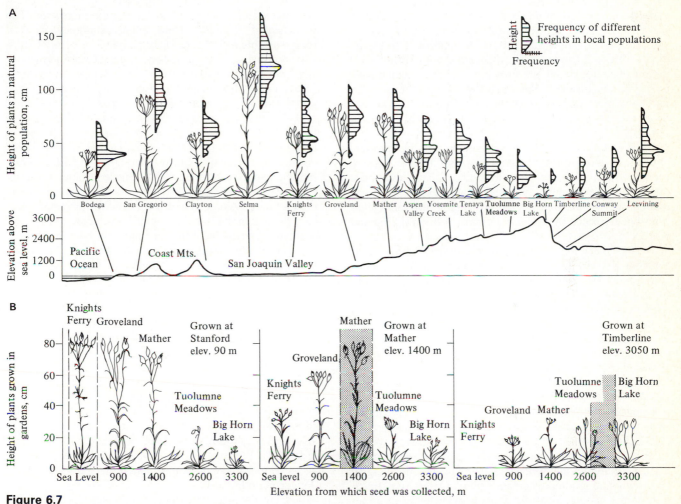

Figure 6.7

Evidence for the existence of ecotypes: the classical study of variation in height growth of yarrow *(Achillea millefolium)* (after Clausen et al., 1948). (A) Variation in the average height growth of ecotypes of yarrow along a W-E transect across California. The variation in height growth around the average for these local populations is also shown. (B) Height growth of five ecotypes from across the elevational range when they were grown together in gardens at three elevations. A stylized representation of the plants is used. (Reproduced by permission of Carnegie Institute of Washington.)

provenances cease growth and acclimate to the coming winter when the length of the shortening daylight period is about an hour longer than it will be when the first killing frost will occur. They still do this when grown in the interior, but unfortunately the first frost in this region occurs about a week *before* the critical coastal day length occurs. Because of their adaptation to local conditions, interior provenances cease growth and become frost hardy earlier than the coast provenances, when the day length is still relatively long, and so are not damaged. When grown on the coast, these provenances cease growth unnecessarily early, and so do not grow as well as the coastal provenances. *After* growth cessation, the coastal and interior provenances show little difference in absolute frost hardiness. Their differences are associated with fitting their period of activity into the growing season to which they have become adapted. Similar differences occur between north and south provenances. Such photoperiodic[9] ecotypes were originally shown in grasses and trees by Vaartaja (1959).

Other examples of ecotypic variation in trees include variation in height growth of ponderosa pine (*Pinus ponderosa* Laws) from different elevations, and differences in photosynthesis, respiration, and leaf characteristics of sugar maple (*Acer saccharum* Marsh) growing at different elevations but separated by a distance of only 0.8 km (Ledig and Korbobo, 1983).

We have seen that local differences in the physical environment give rise to locally adapted genetic subpopulations called ecotypes. Where there is a sudden change in environmental conditions, such as in steep mountain country, or where there is a sudden change in the chemical and physical properties of soil, local ecotypes may be clearly differentiated. An example of the latter is the local ecotypes of various plants growing on serpentine soils (rich in magnesium) (Kruckeberg, 1954). Similarly, if there is a sudden change in the biological significance of a physical factor along a gradient of gradual change in that factor (e.g., 0°C along a gradient of temperature), clearly differentiated ecotypes will occur. However, where the spatial variation in the physical environment is very gradual, there will be a similar gradual change in the genetic constitution of the population. Such a continuous and gradual change in genotype along an environmental gradient is called a *cline*. Objective delineation of the geographical distribution of different ecotypes along a cline is difficult or even impossible.

Unlike different species which are normally genetically isolated from each other, different ectoypes are capable of interbreeding. Sometimes the offspring that result are larger and more vigorous than either parent. This phenomenon is known as *hybrid vigor* and is widely used in the breeding of improved strains of agricultural and horticultural crops and also in tree breeding. More frequently, the hybrid offspring have characteristics that are intermediate between those of the two parents. Hybrid populations generally contain more variation than the parent populations. This increased variability increases the possibilities for selecting new and fitter combinations of alleles. Hybridization thus increases the potential for evolution and adaptation.

Do species and ecotypes both evolve the same way? The circumstantial evidence from plant geography is very strong, since there is a remarkable number of pairs of similar species that seem to have a common ancestor and whose range was split into two parts by a geographic feature or climatic event. In North America we have eastern white pine–western white pine (*Pinus strobus* L.–*Pinus monticola* Dougl.), eastern hemlock–western hemlock (*Tsuga canadensis* (L.) Carr–*Tsuga heterophylla* (Rafn.) Sarg.), Canada yew–Pacific yew (*Taxus canadensis* Marsh.–*Taxus brevifolia* Nutt.), and so on. It is thought that each pair had a common species as an ancestor, whose original transcontinental range was split by the formation of the prairies. This split prevented gene exchange, and the different selection pressures in the two subpopulations, acting on varying phenotypes caused by different randomly occurring mutations, eventually produced separate species. Fraser fir (*Abies fraseri* Poir.) is very similar to balsam fir (*Abies balsamea* Mill.) and perhaps originated when populations adapted to low temperature migrated north or up the mountains of eastern central U.S. after glacial periods in order to stay within the temperature range to which they were best adapted. The mountain populations eventually became separated from the main population by low-altitude warm areas and hence developed into a separate species. The same sort of origin for jack (*Pinus banksiana* Lamb.) and lodgepole (*Pinus contorta* Dougl.) pines seems likely, but in this case the jack pine spread west on the north side of the prairies and is now sympatric with lodgepole in two locations. In these areas it hybridizes with lodgepole pine, producing fertile hybrids. Presumably, evolution to true species would have occurred if the populations had remained separated for a longer period.

There are also striking pairs of similar species on the west coast of North America and the east coast of Asia, such as Japanese (*Acer japonicum* Thunb.) and vine (*Acer circinatum* Pursh.) maples. Did these originate from a species that inhabited the Bering area before the continents became separated by the Straits? Similarly suggestive are the North

---

[9]Photoperiodicity is discussed in Chapter 7.

Pacific distribution of the *Pseudotsuga* genus, and the existence of only two *Liriodendron* species, yellow poplar (*Liriodendron tulipifera* L.) in North America and *L. chinense* Sarg. in China.

The average conditions of the physical environment are reasonably stable. Changes in regional precipitation or temperature regimes and changes in soil conditions generally occur so slowly that even long-lived organisms have ample opportunity to adapt to them. Year-to-year variations in weather pose greater evolutionary difficulties. A period of 10 years of rather mild, moist weather will favor genotypes that may be poorly adapted to the two years of drought and late spring frosts that follow. Such unpredictable periodic fluctuations in weather tend to maintain a high degree of genetic variability in populations with an annual life history, which populations are entirely replaced every year, and to promote phenotypic adaptations such as acclimation in long-lived organisms such as trees, which are generally less variable genetically.

6.4 Coevolution and the Biotic Environment

Factors of the physical environment cannot on their own explain evolution. Natural selection is also guided by environmental differences that are caused by living organisms. Consider, for example, the evolution of species of land plant that do not require much light. Before there were large land plants, there were virtually no shady environments for our present shade-tolerant plants to exploit. They evolved when shady environments were created by other plants. But creation of new physical environments is not the only way in which the biota have influenced evolution. Interactions between individuals of the same species and between individuals of different species have also been extremely important. Species evolve in a manner that promotes beneficial interactions and/or favors a particular species in some antagonistic interaction such as competition or predation. This currently controversial topic is explored more fully in Chapter 14. (For a recent treatment see Thompson, 1982, and Futuyama and Slatkin, 1983.)

Consider, for example, the relationship between a population of herbivores and the population of plants that they are eating. Because of natural variation in plant populations, some of the plants will be either less attractive, less palatable, or less nutritious to the herbivores, and will be less utilized by the herbivores than will the other members of the population. These plants will tend to survive better and produce more seed than will the more heavily utilized

individuals. Over many generations of herbivore pressure, the frequency of these fitter individuals in the plant population will increase. This will lead to a general decrease in the suitability of the vegetation for the herbivores whose abundance will gradually decline. However, this will generate selection pressure on the herbivores, leading to above-average survival and increased fitness of those herbivore genotypes that can successfully utilize the less desirable plant form. After many generations the frequency of these tolerant herbivore genotypes will increase, leading to a gradual recovery in their abundance and a renewal of herbivore-induced selection pressure on the plant population, and so on.

This sort of evolution is very important in forest pathology (diseases); for instance, the evolution of white pines and the fungal disease white pine blister rust (*Cronartium ribicola* Fisher). This Asian disease has historically applied pressure to its white pine hosts, which resulted in more resistant Asian white pines. These resistant hosts obviously applied pressure to the blister rust, which resulted in a more virulent disease. After many generations a very virulent form of the disease developed, but did not do a great deal of damage to its now highly resistant host. However, in North America white pines have not been selected for resistance to blister rust, which is not native, and it is now apparent that very few, if any, of the North American white pines have any resistance to the disease. Large-scale destruction of white pine populations occurred when the disease was introduced into this continent. There are numerous other examples of disastrous effects of introduction of nonnative organisms of all kinds. The examples of chestnut blight and Dutch elm disease in the eastern U.S. are well known, as is the recent case of the reintroduction of a more virulent form of the latter disease back into England. It appears likely that few of the present English elms will survive the current scourge (this example is discussed further in Chapter 14).

The alternating evolution of two species of organisms in response to mutual selection pressures is called *coevolution*. Sometimes coevolution results from attempts by one species to reduce the impacts of another species, as in the example just given. Sometimes it involves attempts to strengthen relationships between two species. For example, the development of a plant characteristic (such as nectar production) that is beneficial to a species of animal (such as a nectar-feeding insect) may lead to improved pollination of that plant. This will generate selection pressures in the plant population favoring the genotypes producing the most nectar, and in the insect population for those genotypes that select this genotype in preference to others. Such a sequence of mutually beneficial developments can lead to a high degree of specificity between certain species of plants and animals. The importance of this type of evolutionary process is seen in the many amazing adaptations of plants and insects to each other, some of which will be examined in Chapter 14.

Coevolution is an important concept. Since most of the species in a particular biogeocoenose have coexisted for thousands or even millions of years, it is most likely that some degree of coevolution will have occurred, whether this has been to favor or impair relationships between species. The addition or removal of species to or from the ecosystem can therefore be expected to influence both the performance and evolutionary development of the remaining biota. Good survival and high productivity in its native habitat is no guarantee that an organism will perform similarly if transferred to a completely different biotic environment. Similarly, the rarity or unimportance of an organism in its native environment is no guarantee that it will not become a pest species or have great economic potential when introduced into a new environment. A change in the biotic environment of an individual can have as great or even greater effect on a population than can a change in the physical environment. The character of an organism in a particular physical environment is largely a function of its adaptation to the other biotic components of that physical environment.

Coevolution has undoubtedly played a major role in the evolution of many different kinds of organisms. The continuing pressure of competition for energy and material resources and of exploitation by other organisms has selected from among the natural variation within populations those genotypes with the greatest fitness. Divergence in morphological, physiological, and behavioral characteristics has resulted, leading ultimately to the formation of genetically isolated species. The combination of adaptations to the enormously variable physical environment and adaptation to other organisms struggling to survive in that environment is responsible for the enormous diversity of life that exists today.

6.5 Evolutionary Time Scales

The rate at which evolution can occur is highly variable. It depends upon several factors, and has been discussed by Pollard (1979). Ultimately, new variation in a population is the result of mutation, and major evolutionary change is limited by the rate at which new mutations enter the population. However, smaller evolutionary adjustments to the genetic makeup and the fitness of a population are the result

of the variation that results from the rearrangement of existing genetic information during sexual reproduction. The potential rate of evolution and adaptation is therefore closely related to the frequency and abundance of sexual reproduction. An insect species with 10 generations a year will tend to be capable of faster genetic change than will a tree with one generation per century, but it will exhibit slower genetic change than will a species of bacterium or virus that may have hundreds of generations a year. A plant species that produces many thousands of seeds per year will generally be capable of faster genetic change than will a plant species with an annual production of a dozen seeds.

The potential rate of evolution of an organism has important consequences for ecosystem management, since human beings act as a potent force of natural selection and our activities may deliberately or accidentally accelerate rates of evolution. Action by farmers or foresters to reduce the losses of their crops to pest species places selection pressure on the pest populations. This has frequently resulted in the evolution of a new pest genotype that is not affected by the control measure. Perhaps the best examples of management-induced counterevolution is the evolution of resistance to chemical poisons in populations of insect pests. When the insecticide DDT was first introduced, extremely small doses resulted in almost total mortality of the target insects. However, after several years of application, the doses required to produce the same level of mortality increased, and after many years of exposure to DDT, some insect populations became so resistant to it that other insecticides had to be used. However, resistance to these also developed and during the past 15 years the situation in some agricultural areas of the U.S. developed into a race between the evolution of new insecticides by human beings and the counterevolution of resistance by the target pests. It is clear that chemical control measures that must be applied frequently to a pest that has a rapid potential rate of evolution constitute at most a very temporary solution to the problem. Figure 6.5 showed how DDT resistance in a population of fruit flies can be raised or lowered by artificial selection.

Rates of evolution of crop species can be speeded up artificially. By selecting seed from trees with desirable properties such as wood strength, growth rate, or resistance to frost, disease, or insects, the forest geneticist can alter the genetic makeup and thus the phenotype of the population to a condition that has improved economic value. In terms of improved technical characteristics, and in terms of improved adaptation to climatic factors (which have a long time scale of directional change), such accelerated evolution is likely to have a beneficial outcome. In terms of adaptations to factors of the biotic environment which are themselves evolving, the outcome of artificial manipulation of evolution is less predictable. Breeding resistance in trees to diseases and insects (accelerated counterevolution) undoubtedly offers a potential solution to some insect and disease problems, but it may merely lead to counterevolution by the pest and only temporary relief from the problem. In agricultural crops where the generation time of the crop is not greatly different from that of the pest, the problems of coevolution may be manageable. In forest crops, which have generation times on the order of decades or centuries, the possibility of counterevolution by pests with annual generations poses potential difficulties to long-term genetic solutions for pest problems.

6.6 Implications of Genetic Variability, Evolution, and Adaptation for Forestry

Recognition of genetic variability and adaptation has proven to be as important for forestry as it has for biology in general. All too often, poor survival, low productivity, and undesirable growth form have been the dominant characteristics of tree plantations grown from seed collected in areas that differed from the plantation in elevation, latitude, climate, and/or soil. These expensive demonstrations of the limitations imposed by the genetic constitution of a plant on where and under what conditions it may be successfully grown have led to planting restrictions in many countries. For example, the British Columbia Forest Service in Canada has a requirement that the seedlings to be planted on a particular site must be grown from seed originating within 150 m elevation and 2 degrees of latitude and longitude of the location of planting. All seedlings must be grown from seed collected in the same seed collection zone as the area in which they are to be planted. It is hoped that these restrictions will ensure that the thousands of years of selection that have resulted in our present-day heritage of locally adapted ecotypes are not squandered by thoughtless clearcutting and subsequent regeneration with nonadapted genotypes.

Where natural selection has not produced commercially desirable attributes of growth and tree morphology, programs of artificial selection and breeding offer the possibility of augmenting the natural process of selection. Care is required in the conduct of such programs, however. We have already seen that the genome of natural ecotypes generally represents a compromise between several opposing forces of selection. Competition from other trees will promote *stabilizing selection,* which reduces the variety of genotypes by favouring the most competitive type. On the other hand, the spatial variability of the physical environment

within any locality will tend to promote *disruptive selection,* which increases the variety of genotypes within the local population.

A population of very similar, well-adapted genotypes has the advantage of all the individuals growing, competing, and reproducing successfully under "normal" conditions (the conditions to which they are adapted). It will have the disadvantage of being susceptible to unfavorable conditions. If random fluctuations of weather produce climatic conditions to which these genotypes are not adapted, or if an insect or disease organism arrives that finds these genotypes to be a desirable food supply, a high percentage of the prey may be killed or adversely affected. A population with a wide variation in genotypes may be less successful in terms of overall growth and survival under stable environmental conditions. Only a small proportion of the population may be really well adapted to the environment at any one time. But such a population is generally able to survive under fluctuating environmental conditions or in the face of an insect or disease attack because at least some of the population will be resistant to the unfavorable conditions.

Genetic tree-improvement programs are generally a form of stabilizing selection in which an attempt is made to regenerate the forest with genotypes that are superior in some respect. Seed is collected from a restricted range of parent genotypes, and nursery culling of excessively large or small individuals may further reduce variability. This is fine as long as the resulting population retains sufficient variability or has sufficient powers of acclimation to resist unpredicted variation in the environment. However, if the genetic improvement selects an ecotype with relatively little variability in adaptation and with little ability to acclimate to varying conditions, the benefits of improved growth and form could be outweighed by lack of resistance to unpredictable variations in environmental factors, both physical and biotic.

The native organisms inhabiting a particular biogeocoenose may be well adapted to the problems of energy acquisition in their environment, but do not necessarily represent the best possible, or the best living, adaptation to that environment. Mountain and ocean barriers to the dispersal of organisms may have excluded species or ecotypes that are better adapted than the native biota. Time lags in evolution, time lags in the invasion of new genotypes into a rapidly changing environment, and the constraints that develop through coevolution may mean that imported species can perform better than native species, at least initially. This has been demonstrated both by the successful planting of "exotic" (i.e., from a different region) tree species in afforestation and reforestation programs, and by epidemics of accidentally introduced insect pests and diseases.

Having made this point, one can say that, in general, a locally adapted ecotype will be better able to survive and produce biomass in a given environment than will an imported ecotype. Its genotype has been molded by long experience to give the balance of phenotypic characteristics that allow it to survive the variety of stresses that it will experience in that particular environment. Consequently, it is in the best interest of forestry to create and conserve reserves (gene pools) of local ecotypes, even if they do not offer immediate commercial values. Adaptive phenotypes are not always highly productive or of desirable morphology, but should the more commercially desirable genotypes prove to be poorly adapted, the forester can go back to using the original genotype or introduce some of the original genes into the crop gene pool. Perhaps the best strategy for the forester is to marry the local ecotype to a genotype of desirable physical characteristics, thus gaining the best of both worlds. As forests become more intensively managed, and as genetically improved planting stock is used more widely, it will become increasingly important to create *ecological reserves:* examples of the unmanaged condition containing the local ecotypes. These must be conserved as gene banks from which the forester can make withdrawals should his or her initial investments in genetic improvement prove to be unwise.

6.7 Evolution of Ecosystems

The beginnings of life are thought to have involved the chance combinations of chemical elements and energy into various organic molecules that were sufficiently stable to accumulate in sheltered environments. Life itself probably began when, through some chance event, combinations of molecules occurred in which some of the molecules were able to chemically degrade some of the other molecules and to use the liberated energy and atoms to synthesize duplicates of themselves. Arrival at this stage would have taken a great deal of time, because of the low probability of the appropriate molecular combination. This probability has been likened to the probability of assembling letters of the alphabet at random and producing a book on forest ecology. For example, the probability of combining groups of four letters of the alphabet at random into the word TREE is one in 456,976 (i.e., 26^4). The probability of assembling molecules at random into self-replicating aggregations was perhaps about the same as assembling letters at random and producing an intelligible sentence, and the probability of the evolution of complex single-celled organisms might have been equivalent to the probability of producing a good short story (Ricklefs, 1973). There were probably innumerable chemical developments during the first 3 billion years of the earth's existence of which only one basic pattern survived and evolved to the point of leaving fossil evidence of its existence.

Evolution during the subsequent 500–1000 million years has been a steady process of adaptation of a few surviving early life forms to exploit new opportunities for the acquisition and storage of energy. As all the opportunities to obtain energy by one method were used up in a particular type of environment, the resulting selection pressure generated by competition produced organisms with new methods of energy acquisition. As photosynthesizing organisms (photoautotrophs) completely exploited the light energy in an environment, some of these organisms adapted to become herbivores, and selection subsequently led some of these to become carnivores. When all the trophic possibilities of one environment were exhausted, selection pressure led to the adaptation of some of the organisms to the utilization of energy sources in a new environment. In this way, land areas were colonized by the life forms that had evolved in the water. The organisms we observe today represent the outcome of billions of years of adaptation to solve the most basic need of life: the need for energy. May (1978) discusses the evolution of ecological systems.

6.8 Summary

Ecosystems are biogeochemical systems that have evolved to trap, concentrate, and accumulate energy. The biological components of this system all utilize the same basic mechanism for energy accumulation and transfer, but evolution has produced a remarkable number of variations on the basic theme of life. Thousands of millions of years of natural selection induced by unfavorable physical conditions, competition for energy and other resources, and exploitation by other organisms has diversified life into a myriad of different types of organism. Each type has become specialized in competing, surviving, and reproducing itself in particular types of physical and biotic environment, but is also capable of adaptation to changing conditions. This ability arises from the natural variation in morphology, physiology, and behavior that is present in all natural populations of organisms. As conditions change, different genotypes within the population become the best adapted and are favored by natural selection. In this way species evolve.

Organisms have adapted to the physical environment: their needs and tolerances are attuned by natural selection to the physical conditions and resource availabilities experienced by their recent predecessors. They have also coevolved with other organisms. This has resulted in the development of mutual dependencies between many organisms as well as the development of chemical, physical, and behavioral mechanisms of defense and offense. The interdependencies that have evolved between the plant and animal members of biotic communities give an internal structure and character to many communities.

Adaptation and natural variation pose both problems and possibilities to the ecosystem manager. Adaptation places constraints on which organisms can be grown in a particular environment, and coevolution may determine the mixture of organisms that are necessary for the production of one of them. Adaptation also limits some of the possible methods of dealing with animal and plant pests. Natural variation provides the possibilities for the artificial production of desired genotypes: the genetic composition of the plant and animal community can be changed. In managing a forest ecosystem, the forester must recognize local adaptation in the form of ecotypes or provenances. In attempting to improve the production of the forest, care must be taken to conserve the natural gene bank and wherever possible to incorporate natural adaptations in any improved genotypes used in regeneration programs.

The individual organisms in the ecosystem have evolved with the physical environment and with each other. The phenomenon of coevolution has resulted in many of the organisms in the ecosystem becoming so dependent, directly or indirectly, on each other that they are only able to accumulate energy efficiently in each other's presence. Consider, for example, the fungal and tree partners in the mycorrhizal association, or the relationship between moss and spruce trees described in Chapter 5. The marked degree of interaction and interrelationship that characterizes the biota of many ecosystems led to the idea of the ecosystems as a "supraorganism" in which the various species are compared with the various organs of an individual organism. This idea contributed to the development of the ecosystem concept by Tansley, but there are so many differences between an individual organism and a biogeocoenose that the idea has fallen into disrepute. It would be unwise to reject the analogy completely, however. An ecosystem is a highly interdependent biotic/physical system, the components of which have evolved together to the point at which some of the relationships are essential to the normal functioning of the other parts. The forester is wise to remember this before making major changes in the ecosystem. He or she must remember that forest management can act as a powerful force of genetic selection, and must ensure that the results of all such selection pressures direct evolution in ways that are in the long-term interests of society.

Section C The Physical Environment

The physical environment provides the basic necessities for autotrophic life: energy, and the nutrients needed to capture and store it. But in order to be able to utilize available energy and survive, organisms must be adapted to the physical conditions they encounter. Much of the diversity of life reflects the evolution of adaptations to factors of the physical environment; adaptations that permit life forms to exist in virtually all the physical environments that can be found on earth.

This section examines solar radiation, temperature, wind, soil, water, and fire, their effects on organisms, and some of the adaptations that have evolved in response to these effects. It is important that renewable-resource managers understand the adaptations of both desirable and undesirable species to these physical factors in order that desired species can be matched with the appropriate environment, and to ensure that any management-induced change in the physical environment favors the desired structure and function of the biota. Knowledge of such adaptations in undesirable species can be invaluable in controlling their distribution and abundance.

7.1 Introduction

Solar radiation is the major source of energy for life, and consequently photoautotrophs are the dominant producers in the trophic web of most ecosystems. The ecological role of solar radiation is broader than merely the provision of energy, however. Its fate as it passes through the atmosphere and at the earth's surface plays a major role in determining world temperatures, climates, and weather patterns. Variation in the wavelength of radiation in the visible part of the solar spectrum *(light)* gives rise to the visual sense of color in animals, and this has led to a wide variety of adaptations in both plants and animals. These organisms have evolved the use of color to provide protection against sunburn, for display purposes (to repel enemies or attract mates and beneficial organisms), and to provide camouflage for security against predators. The continuing alternation of day and night provides an environmental clock that determines patterns of physiology and behavior, while the seasonal variation in the relative length of day and night provides an environmental calendar that schedules the life histories of most of the organisms on earth. The intensity of light regulates rates of activity and behavior patterns in some animals, influences the pigmentation of both plants and animals, and can affect the morphology of plants. Light also acts as one means by which both animals and plants orient themselves in space.

Solar radiation is thus the source of most life, and a major determinant of the physiology, morphology, behavior, and life history of most organisms. The term ''light'' will be used as a synonym for solar radiation in this chapter because many of the ecological effects of solar radiation are the result of wavelengths in the visible part of the spectrum.

7.2 Physical Nature of Solar Radiation and Its Variations in Time and Space

Before examining the ecological role of, and the adaptations of organisms to solar radiation, we will review briefly its physical nature, how it varies geographically, daily and seasonally, and how it determines the energy balance and temperature of the world.

Because of its high temperature, the sun is continuously emitting vast quantities of energy in the form of electromagnetic waves of various wavelengths. These form a continuous spectrum of wavelengths from very short wavelength gamma rays (3×10^{-6} micron, a micron being one-thousandth of a millimeter) to medium-wavelength infrared rays (up to 5 microns). *Light* is those wavelengths between about

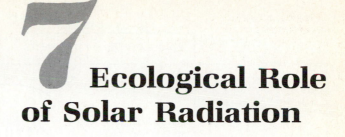

7 Ecological Role of Solar Radiation

0.39 and 0.76 micron (i.e. 390–760 nm). Most solar radiant energy is emitted at wavelengths between 0.4 and 2.0 microns (visible light and infrared). Nearly 50% is in the visible part of the spectrum; infrared accounts for most of the rest (Figure 7.1).

As solar radiation passes down through the atmosphere, it experiences changes in both quantity and spectral composition. Clouds and water vapor reflect, scatter, or absorb radiation of all visible wavelengths more or less equally, with the result that clouds, overcast skies, and very humid skies look white. Atmospheric dust also absorbs, reflects, and scatters solar radiation, but the longer visible wavelengths are scattered more than the other visible wavelengths, so that very dusty atmospheres (heavily polluted air over urban and industrial regions, and very smoky air following forest fires or slashburns) have a brownish or reddish tint. Molecules of atmospheric gases, on the other hand, scatter the shorter wavelengths more than the other visible wavelengths, with the result that clear, clean skies look blue. Under these atmospheric conditions the sun becomes red when it is close to the horizon because of the scattering of the shorter wavelengths, while the sky on each side of the sun remains blue. On the other hand, if the atmosphere

149

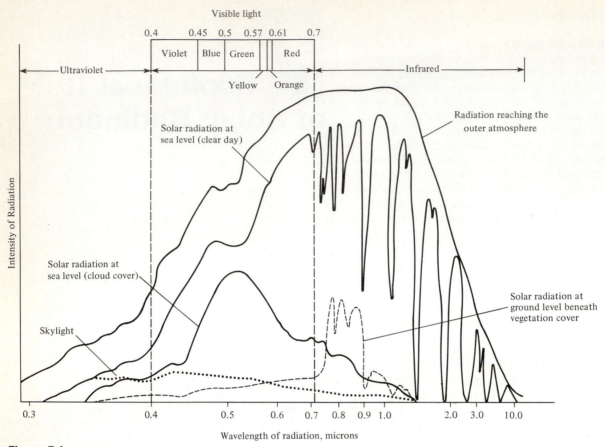

Figure 7.1

Change in the quantity (shown on the graph as Intensity of Radiation, also called Spectral Irradience) and quality of solar radiation as it passes through the atmosphere on either clear or cloudy days and penetrates through a canopy of vegetation. The spectral composition of skylight (radiation from a clear blue sky) is also shown. This graph expresses radiation intensity as the energy per micron of wavelength x (wavelength^2), which causes the line to increase from UV to IR wavelengths. In fact, the greatest energy levels are found in the visible wavelengths (about 0.5 micron). If the values in this graph are divided by (wavelength^2), the true energy distribution can be seen—strongly peaked in the visible, with low values in UV and IR. (Modified after Gates, 1965. Reproduced by permission of the Ecological Society of America and D. M. Gates.)

contains a lot of dust, the sky on each side of the sun near the horizon will also look red because of the preferential scattering of the longer wavelengths.

Ultraviolet and infrared wavelengths are largely lost from solar radiation as it passes down through the atmosphere because of a number of absorption processes. Ultraviolet is largely absorbed by the layer of ozone (O_3) that is present in the upper atmosphere, while infrared is absorbed by carbon dioxide gas and water molecules. Because of this filtering action by the atmosphere, the solar spectrum is significantly depleted in most wavelengths other than the visible ones by

the time it reaches the earth's surface. It is therefore not surprising that so much of the ecological role of solar radiation (energy source, sight, color, etc.) is related to these visible wavelengths. The other wavelengths are also very important, of course, and we should not overlook the important ecological role of ultraviolet and infrared radiation.

When solar radiation reaches the earth's outer atmosphere, it has a total energy of about 2 cal cm^{-2} min^{-1} at a surface at right angles to the sun's rays. This quantity, which is called the *solar constant*, varies slightly with the seasons (about 3%) since the earth has an elliptical orbit around the sun. As the radiation passes through the atmosphere, it is reduced in intensity by reflection, absorption, and scattering, and by the time "sunlight" reaches sea level at midday in summer at latitude 40°, it is normally reduced in intensity by between 12 and 50%. During periods of heavy cloud cover it is reduced much more.

Reduction in the intensity of radiation is greatest in areas where the air is very humid, where there is frequent cloud cover, where and when the sun is low in the sky, and where the air is very turbid from dust or air pollution. Cities tend to have 10–25 times as much dust and air pollution, 15–20% less total solar radiation, and 5–10% more clouds than do comparable rural areas (Landsburg, 1958). The importance of atmospheric turbidity is demonstrated by the observation that during one winter, the city of Chicago received only 55% as much radiant solar energy as the less industrialized city of Madison, Wis., to the west (Trewartha, 1954). Smoke from wildfires and slashburns in western Canada in the summer and fall of 1950 was implicated in a 54% reduction in normal levels of solar radiation in the city of Washington, D.C., over 3000 miles to the east, and a noticeable effect on solar radiation was recorded in Europe (Lull, 1951).

The total amount of radiation reaching the earth's surface does not depend only on the attenuation of radiation by the atmosphere. It also depends upon the number of hours of daylight. For example, maximum solar radiation in the summer in Alaska is only about 0.5 cal cm^{-2} min^{-1}, but since the day is 24 hours long, daily totals of 300–500 cal cm^{-2} day^{-1} are accumulated. This is sometimes greater than the daily accumulations in the tropics, where maximum solar radiation may be 1.6 cal cm^{-2} min^{-1}, but the day is only 12 hours long. The greatest amount of solar radiation is experienced in summer in the middle latitudes, where clear, clean, low humidity skies are combined with moderately long days. It comes as a surprise to some that the total growing season solar radiation energy at high latitudes can compare very favorably with lower latitudes because of the long days and clear skies, conditions that result in the highly productive summer agriculture that can be conducted at high latitudes.

The discussion of radiation energies so far has assumed a flat surface at right angles to the sunlight. However, both slope and aspect can either increase or decrease the radiation reaching the ground, depending on the location and the time of year. Aspect and slope also have an important effect in determining the distribution of solar intensities through the day. Easterly aspects will receive maximum intensities in the morning, while westerly aspects experience peak illumination in the afternoon. Midday is the time of highest light intensity for northerly and southerly aspects. The effects of easterly and westerly aspects is amplified by increasing slopes.

The effect of aspect on radiation intensities is modified somewhat by atmospheric conditions. On a clear, sunny day about 5% of the radiation reaching the ground is *skylight* (scattered sunlight), while under average conditions the value is commonly about 17% (Collier et al., 1973). On completely overcast days it is 100%. In clear, sunny weather a northerly aspect in the northern hemisphere may receive much less solar radiation than a southerly aspect, whereas on a completely overcast day both aspects will receive virtually the same quantity. Thus, the effect of aspect is most apparent in clear weather and cloudless regions, and least apparent under overcast conditions and in cloudy regions.

Some of the solar radiation that does not reach the earth's surface is reflected back to space and plays no further role in the earth's ecology. However, much of it is absorbed by the atmosphere, and the resulting atmospheric warming contributes to the determination of world climates. Uneven heating of different parts of the atmosphere results in convection currents and atmospheric stirring that produce cumulus clouds, help regulate atmospheric CO_2 levels (see Chapter 5), disperse air pollution, and contribute to the determination of regional weather patterns.

Once solar radiation has reached the surface of the earth, it is either absorbed or reflected. The percentage of the incident radiation that is reflected is called the *albedo,* and it can vary from as much as 95% (deep, fresh snow) to as little as 3% (deep oceans and forests) (Table 7.1). Albedo measures the overall reflectance of a surface, but the various wavelengths of sunlight are not normally reflected equally, which gives rise to the variable color of surfaces. Snow reflects visible wavelengths uniformly, giving a white

Table 7.1 Albedo Values for Various Surfaces (Geiger, 1965*)

Surface	Albedo, % Reflectance
Fresh snow cover	75–95
Old snow cover	40–70
Sand dunes, ocean surf	30–60
Sandy soil	15–40
Meadows and fields	12–30
Fresh grass	26
Dry grass	15–25
Dark cultivated soil	7–10
Woodland	5–20
Forest	3–10

* Copyright Harvard University Press. Used with permission.

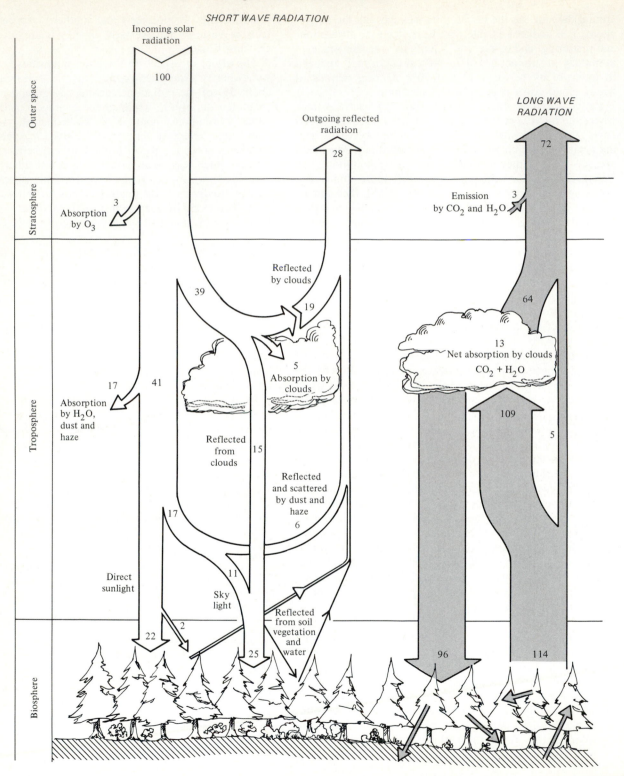

SHORT WAVE RADIATION

Incoming solar
radiation

100

Outer space

Outgoing reflected
radiation

28

LONG WAVE
RADIATION

72

Stratosphere

Absorption
by O₃

3

Emission
by CO₂ and H₂O

3

Reflected
by clouds

39

19

64

5
Absorption by
clouds

13
Net absorption by clouds
CO₂ + H₂O

Troposphere

Absorption
by H₂O,
dust and
haze

17   41

Reflected
from
clouds

15

109

5

Reflected
and scattered
by dust and
haze

6

17

11

Direct
sunlight

Sky
light

Reflected
from soil
vegetation
and
water

Biosphere

22   2

25

96

114

Figure 7.2
Radiation balance at the earth's surface. The importance of long-wave radiation is apparent. The numbers show the relative magnitude of different radiant transfers, with incoming short-wave radiation equal to 100. (After Schneider and Dennett, 1975. Redrawn by permission of the Royal Swedish Academy of Sciences and S. H. Schneider.)

color, and the green color of forests results from their preferential reflectance of green wavelengths. Invisible wavelengths are also reflected differentially. The variation in ultraviolet reflection by flowers is "visible" to, and important for, pollinating insects, while both the reflection and emission of infrared wavelengths by plants varies with their physiological condition. This is the basis of methods for detecting the effects of diseases and insects on forest and agricultural crops by aerial photography (remote sensing) (e.g. Puritch, 1981, Sabins, 1978). The very low albedo values of forests show that they are among the most efficient radiation-absorbing surfaces on earth.

Of the solar radiation that is reflected at the earth's surface, some is lost to space while the rest is either reflected or is absorbed and then reradiated back to earth by the atmosphere. This explains why in winter, cloudy days can be warmer than clear days. The clouds prevent much of the reflected radiation from escaping from the atmosphere by returning it back to the surface.

The solar radiation that is not reflected from the surface of the earth is absorbed by soil, rock, water, or living organisms. The absorbed energy may raise the temperature of the absorbing material, evaporate water from it, or, in the case of green plants, be incorporated into high-energy chemical molecules in the process of photosynthesis. If the absorption of energy results in an increase in the temperature of an object, some of this energy will be reradiated. In fact, most of the visible portion of the solar spectrum that passes through the atmosphere is absorbed by terrestrial or aquatic surfaces, raises their temperature, and is subsequently reradiated. However, this reradiated energy is at much longer wavelengths than the incoming radiation. Peak terrestrial radiation is at 1.0 μm (infrared) compared with peak solar radiation at 0.5 μm (blue-green); the atmosphere is almost opaque to these longer wavelengths (cf. Figure 7.1), which are consequently absorbed. This warms the air, which then reradiates some of the energy back to earth.

As a result of these processes, the atmosphere acts in much the same manner as the glass of a greenhouse, which is transparent to visible solar energy but opaque to reradiated infrared energy, which is consequently trapped. A greenhouse acts as a solar energy accumulator, maintaining itself at a much higher temperature than its surroundings. By creating a "greenhouse effect," the atmosphere (mainly

atmospheric H_2O and CO_2) accumulates solar energy and thereby plays a critical role in maintaining the temperature of our ecosystems within a range that is suitable for existing forms of life: a range that maintains that critical medium for life, water, in a liquid rather than a solid or vapor form. The growing recognition of the importance of atmospheric ozone and carbon dioxide concentrations for the maintenance of life on earth has led to increasing concern over the possible long-term effects of the changes that we are causing in atmospheric chemistry (discussed in Chapter 5). Figure 7.2 summarizes the energy balance of the earth's surface.

Solar radiation varies not only geographically but also with time. The rotation of the earth on its axis gives rise to alternating light and dark periods, and the intensity of radiation varies during the day as the distance that the radiation travels through the atmosphere changes. The long atmospheric path length early and late in the day results in lower radiation intensities than at midday, when the path length through the atmosphere is shortest. The duration of the daily light period (photoperiod) also varies because the plane of rotation of the earth around the sun is different from the plane of rotation of the earth around its axis. When the earth faces the sun squarely with the equator closer to the sun than any other point on earth (as it does at the spring and autumnal equinoxes: March 21 and September 23, respectively, for the northern hemisphere's spring and fall), the day length and night length are equal at 12 hours all over the earth. Three months after the March equinox, when the earth has progressed one-fourth of its way around the sun, it reaches the point at which the Tropic of Cancer is the closest point of the earth to the sun (June 21: the northern hemisphere's summer solstice). Day length in the arctic becomes 24 hours, while in the antarctic there is perpetual night. Equatorial areas continue to receive about 12 hours of daylight, while in the temperate regions the nights become short or long depending on the hemisphere. As the earth progresses farther around its solar orbit, it reaches the September equinox, when day length returns to 12 hours over the whole earth; 3 months later, on December 22, the northern hemisphere's winter solstice is reached. Arctic nights become 24 hours long while perpetual day occurs in the antarctic; the northern temperate areas experience winter day lengths while southern temperate regions have long summer days.

7.3 Ecological Effects of Variations in the Spectral Quality of Solar Radiation

Some of the evolutionary adaptations to solar radiation reflect the alteration of the solar spectrum by the earth's atmosphere (Figure 7.1). The wavelengths least affected are those between 0.4 and 0.7 micron (visible light). These are the wavelengths that are absorbed by the pigments of plants and that are perceived by the eyes of most animals. Some plant functions can be completed satisfactorily in light depleted in some of these wavelengths, but most plants grow best when exposed to the full visible spectrum (Daubenmire, 1974). Some animals have the ability to detect and may even be able to "see" (i.e., form an image on a retina) wavelengths other than visible light. Pit vipers are known to have infrared (IR) sensors that enable this type of snake to detect and strike at living enemies or prey in the dark, and IR sensors are thought to be important for some insects. Certain wood-boring beetles that use freshly fire-killed timber as a substrate for their larvae are thought to be able to detect forest fires many miles away using these sensors, and other phytophagous insects may possibly use IR sensitivity to detect physiologically weak plants (cf. human use of IR imagery in remote sensing). Insect parasites and predators may use IR detectors to locate concealed living prey. Ultraviolet (UV) wavelengths are also detected by some animals. Many insects use the variation in UV reflectance for plant recognition, and nectar-gathering insects use patterns of UV reflected from flowers as a guide in their search for nectar.

Much of UV radiation from the sun is absorbed by the ozone layer in the upper atmosphere, and consequently UV comprises only about 2% of the solar radiant energy at the earth's surface. The cuticle of plants is largely opaque to these wavelengths and they are absorbed by the cell sap, so it is not surprising that UV plays no known essential role in plant physiology. Cells not protected by a cuticle, by layers of other cells, or by UV-absorbing pigments can suffer injury from the high photochemical energy levels of these wavelengths. Algae, fungi, and bacteria are all sensitive to UV, a phenomenon that is given practical application in the use of UV radiation to sterilize surfaces and to kill microorganisms.

UV radiation induces a reversible inhibition of growth in plants, either by destroying the auxins (growth-regulating hormones) that control cell division and enlargement, or by affecting the ability of a plant to respond normally to auxins. The very short growth form and stunting that are characteristic of many alpine plants have sometimes been ascribed to higher exposure to UV at high elevation, but such a relationship has not been definitely established. Whereas the quantity of UV in direct sunlight increases with increasing altitude, the amount of UV in skylight decreases with altitude. High-elevation areas are sometimes cloudier than low-elevation areas, which results in greater atmospheric UV absorption, and consequently the increase in total UV radiation with increasing elevation is not always very great. Also, alpine plants have become adapted to the somewhat higher levels of UV. They have thicker cuticles and more UV-absorbing purple *anthocyanin* pigment, and therefore the living cells may not actually experience more UV than do the cells of a lower-elevation plant (Caldwell, 1968).

The production of protective pigments by plants is a common phenomenon. Just as human beings develop a suntan to protect skin cells from damage (sunburn) by photochemically active short-wavelength solar radiation, so plants protect their cells by the production of anthocyanin pigments. It is a common observation that the fleshy, pale green stems and leaves of many plants grown indoors over the winter rapidly develop purple, red, or brown pigmentation if placed in direct sunshine in the spring.

UV radiation produces a very important effect when it falls on fatty substances such as sterols. It changes some of them into vitamin D, a very important substance for animal nutrition, but one that most vertebrate animals cannot synthesize for themselves and that occurs at very low levels in plants. UV radiation falling on the skin of animals (including humans) converts sterols into vitamin D and acts as the major source of this vitamin for many organisms. Children living on inadequate diets in urban areas with heavy air pollution (which virtually eliminates UV wavelengths from sunlight), or in other environments in which they are not exposed to sunlight, tend to develop vitamin D deficiency symptoms (e.g., rickets, the malformation of bones). These can be alleviated by exposure to sunlight containing UV, or simply by artificial irradiation using UV lamps. The importance of UV synthesis of vitamin D to animal populations is not known, but variations in the abundance of certain animals in north-central U.S. have been shown to parallel variations in the intensity of solar UV radiation (Shelford, 1951a, 1951b). Migratory birds prevented from traveling south from northern regions have been reported to develop vitamin D deficiency during the sunlight-deficient winter (Clarke, 1967).

Light passing through a canopy of vegetation experiences changes in spectral composition, as well as in intensity, because of differences in the reflectance, absorbance, and transmittance of the different wavelengths (Figure 7.1). The pigments responsible for photosynthesis absorb radiation most efficiently in the violet-blue and orange-red wavelengths, permitting both reflectance and transmittance of green to exceed those of other visible wavelengths. The spectral alteration of solar radiation by vegetation varies somewhat between species. It is greater for hardwood forests with their translucent leaves than for conifer forests with their opaque needles which act more like neutral density filters, reducing all wavelengths equally. Most of the light reaching the forest floor in a conifer forest is in *sunflecks:* small patches of direct sunlight or skylight shining through gaps in the canopy (Vezina and Boulter, 1966).

One of the best known and most easily perceived ecological aspects of the spectral quality of light is the adaptation of animal species to the selective pressures of predation by the development of protective coloration. The case of the peppered moth discussed in Chapter 6 exemplifies the almost universal phenomenon of camouflage. In some cases, such as the peppered moth, the coloration does not change during the life of the adult. In others it may change as the spectral character of the organism's environment changes. The varying hare ("snowshoe rabbit") and arctic ptarmigan have white fur and feathers, respectively, in winter to blend with the snow and brown fur and feathers in the summer to blend with their snow-free surroundings. Species of flat fish will change color and pattern within hours or even minutes of being placed on a different-colored ocean floor, and animals such as the chameleon lizard or the squid are able to change color in minutes or less to blend with their background. Not all coloration is for concealment. Many species of fish, insects, and birds are brilliantly colored, although often this is only true for the male. Female birds generally have coloration that conceals them when they are sitting on their nest. Brilliant coloration may serve the various functions of sexual displays, aggressive displays, distraction of predators from a concealed mate on a nest, warnings of chemical defense mechanisms, and mimicry.

7.4 Ecological Effects of Variations in the Intensity of Solar Radiation

Nowhere on earth is the intensity of solar radiation so great that it has prevented the evolution or maintenance of life. High temperatures and the resulting moisture stress that accompany high intensities of sunlight do have a marked effect on life processes and may greatly restrict or even prevent the sustained existence of life. However, where these indirect effects are not overpowering, ecological adaptation has been able to solve most of the problems of high levels of light.

Lack of light has a more potent effect, and environments completely lacking visible radiation are devoid of most

or all forms of permanently resident organisms. Chemoautotrophs and the organisms dependent thereon can survive in dark places, as can detrivores if organic debris finds its way into such environments. This accounts for life in the soil, in the depths of lakes and oceans, and in underground caves and rivers. Alternatively, organisms can exist in dark environments if they make periodic forays into the light world. This is an adaptation found in bats, which are equipped with guidance systems (hearing or smell) that are independent of light so that they can navigate in their dark environments, as well as on nocturnal hunting trips. Plants are organisms that are able to live half in a dark environment (the soil) and half in a light environment. This is made possible by differences in morphology and function in the root and the aerial systems. Another adaptation to life in dark environments is the production of light by the organisms themselves. This phenomenon, known as *bioluminescence,* is perhaps best known in oceanic plankton and deep-sea organisms, and in glowworms and fireflies.

A. Effects on Plants

1. Photosynthesis. Photosynthesis is a light-dependent process in which the rate of photosynthetic fixation of both CO_2 and solar energy is largely dependent upon light intensity.[1] However, this relationship is not a simple linear one. It does not hold true at all light intensities, and it can be modified by a wide variety of other factors.

Consider the rate of net photosynthesis in a plant as the intensity of light increases from zero (Figure 7.3). Photosynthesis increases rapidly, but initially there is no net CO_2 fixation (and therefore no increase in biomass) because the rate of CO_2 loss in respiration is greater than the rate of CO_2 fixation. As light intensity continues to increase, a point is reached at which respiratory losses are exactly balanced by photosynthetic gains. This light intensity is called the *compensation point* (CP). Above the CP, the rate of photosynthesis continues to increase rapidly with increasing light intensity, but this relationship is not sustained. With continued increases in light, the rate of increase in photosynthesis diminishes until the *saturation point* (SP) is reached, beyond which further increases in light intensity result in little or no further increases in net CO_2 fixation. At very high light intensities, net fixation may drop because of damage to the photosynthetic apparatus or for other reasons.

---

[1] For simplicity, the term *light intensity* is used throughout the following discussion to refer to the intensity of *photosynthetically-active radiation* (PAR). The correct term for this intensity is *photosynthetic photon flux density* (PPFD).

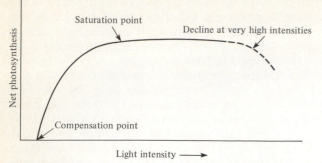

Figure 7.3
Generalized relationship between net photosynthesis and increasing light intensity. The compensation point is the light intensity at which photosynthesis equals respiration. The saturation point is the light intensity above which no further increase in net photosynthesis occurs.

Compensation points and saturation points vary considerably among different species, among different individuals of the same species, among different parts of a single individual, and under different environmental conditions (Figure 7.4). Leaves with very thin cuticles and algae that have no cuticle to reflect and absorb light have net photosynthesis under very low light intensities (i.e., very low CPs). Plants with a high ratio of photosynthetic biomass to living supporting biomass (e.g., algae, mosses) will have lower CPs than plants with a low ratio (e.g., trees) because they (the algae) have less respiratory loss of CO_2 to compensate for. Plants with low CPs often have lower SPs than plants with high CPs. It takes less light to provide all the solar energy that the photochemical system can use in an algal cell than in a tree leaf cell. Within a tree crown, leaves growing in full sunlight (sun leaves) have higher CPs and SPs than do leaves growing in deep shade (shade leaves) because of differences in leaf morphology (Figure 7.4A). A single, fully illuminated leaf will exhibit lower CP and SP values than the leaves in a crowded group of plants, where there is a lot of mutual shading. Many of the leaves in such a group of plants will be below their CP or SP until quite high light intensities are reached (Figure 7.4B). Species that are adapted to growing at reduced light intensities (which are referred to as *shade tolerant,* e.g., dogwood, hemlock, maple, or redwood) generally have lower CPs and SPs than do species adapted to high-light-intensity environments (e.g., pines and *Eucalyptus*), which may not reach SP even at full sunlight because of the morphology and arrangement of their foliage (Figure 7.4C).

The intensities of light at which compensation and saturation points occur depends upon several other factors. Photosynthesis is a highly complex chemical process that is de-

pendent on a variety of chemical raw materials, including CO_2 and H_2O. SP values can be greatly increased by raising the concentration of CO_2 in the air surrounding plants, a fact well known to horticulturalists who raise CO_2 levels in greenhouses to increase growth rates of various plants (Figure 7.4D). The increased growth and yield following fertilization reflects the improved ability of plants to utilize sunlight energy as the supply of nutrients is increased (Figure 7.4F). CPs are higher under conditions of moisture stress. Photosynthesis is impaired by water stress, and it drops off rapidly as the plant approaches its wilting point (see Chapter 11), so that much higher light intensities are required for survival in dry environments or where there is severe competition for water. Water stress may kill a plant by literally starving it to death by preventing net photosynthesis (Figure 7.4E).

The relationship between light intensity and net photosynthesis is very complex and under the control of many factors. It is not surprising, therefore, that net photosynthesis in natural stands of plants does not always follow the daily variation in light intensity. In clear weather there may be a morning peak in net photosynthesis followed by a midday dip and a second peak in the afternoon (Figure 7.4I). It has been suggested that this midday dip may result from one or more of the following factors:

1. Overheating of leaves.
2. Excessive respiration.
3. Water deficits.
4. Accumulation of products of photosynthesis in the leaves.
5. Photooxidation of enzymes and pigments.
6. Closure of stomata.
7. The depletion of CO_2 in the air surrounding the crown that accompanies high intensities of solar radiation in the middle of the day.

Conifers may or may not show this bimodal pattern of photosynthesis. Scots pine, noble fir, and grand fir were reported to have a bimodal pattern on a clear day with a high vapor pressure deficit (VPD), but a unimodal pattern on an overcast day with a low VPD (Hodges, 1967).

The effects of temperature on photosynthesis and respiration are shown in Figure 7.5. Gross photosynthesis responds rapidly to initial increases in temperature, but the rate levels off as lethal temperatures are approached. Respiration exhibits the opposite pattern, increasing slowly in the lower part of the temperature range and rapidly at the upper part of the range. The sum of these two relationships results in maximum net photosynthesis at relatively low to intermediate temperatures.

The relationship of photosynthesis to light intensity is thus seen to be very complex, and recent research in this field has employed computer modeling as a means of handling this complexity (see Chapter 17). The interested reader is referred to Kramer and Kozlowski (1979) and Cannel and Last (1976).

As mentioned above, the CP is reached at very different light intensities by different species (Table 7.2). Quite often, the average light intensity found beneath a well-stocked forest stand is lower than the CPs of most plant species (compare Tables 7.2 and 7.3); under such conditions, net photosynthesis can occur only when a *sunfleck* falls on the plant. The existence of sunflecks may permit a significant understory to develop in stands in which the *average* light intensity is below the CP of the understory plants. Consequently, data on the average light intensity beneath a canopy is often not particularly useful. Whereas much of the forest floor may receive intensities of less than 1% full sunlight, the sunflecks that move over the forest floor as the day progresses temporarily provide seedlings and understory plants with light that may be as much as 50% as intense as full sunlight. In a study of a tropical rain forest, it was found that 20–25% of the forest floor at noon was illuminated by sunflecks that accounted for 70–80% of the total solar energy reaching the ground (Evans, 1956). The comparison of Tables 7.2 and 7.3 should be made with this in mind.

Although the CPs shown in Table 7.2 were obtained under experimental conditions and will be subject to some modification for field conditions, they give a reasonably good indication of the relative minimum light requirements and shade tolerances of the various species. The highest CP values are for those species such as pines that are adapted to

Table 7.2 Compensation Points of Seedlings of Several Tree Species Expressed as a Percentage of Full Sunlight (Burns, 1923; Bates and Roeser, 1928)

Species	Compensation Point, %
Ponderosa pine	30.6
Scots pine	28.7
Northern white cedar	18.6
Tamarack	17.6
Douglas-fir	13.6
Lodgepole pine	13.6
Oak	13.6
Engelmann spruce	10.6
Eastern white pine	10.4
Norway spruce	8.7
Eastern hemlock	8.4
American beech	7.5
Sugar maple	3.4

Table 7.3 Light Intensities Beneath Various Types of Forest Expressed as a Percentage of Full Sunlight (from Reifsnyder and Lull, 1965; Geiger, 1965)

	Percent of Full Sunlight	
Forest Type	Winter Leafless Period	With Foliage
Red beech	26–66	2–40
Oak	43–69	3–35
Ash	39–80	8–60
Birch	—	20–30
Tropical rain forest	—	0.2–2.0
Jack and red pine		7–15
Eastern white pine		27
Western white pine		6–15
Scots pine		11–13
Norway spruce		2–3
Silver fir		2–20

high light intensities; the lowest CPs are for those species (such as hemlock, beech, and maple) whose seedlings normally grow in deep shade.

The presence of seedlings on the forest floor is not necessarily evidence that the light intensity is above their CP. Seedlings of species with large seeds can exist for several years below their compensation points by using energy stored in the seed. Also, the light requirements and CP of a species may change as it ages, so that intensities that are adequate for a young seedling become inadequate as it grows older. Norway spruce seedlings were found to survive for 1–2 years at light intensities of less than 5% full sunlight, whereas intensities of 15–24% were necessary if the plants were to grow satisfactorily at 10–15 years of age. Optimal seedling survival and growth occurred at 35–50% of full sunlight (Rousell, 1948). Seedlings of the European ash (*Fraxinus excelsior*) will grow in heavily shaded hedgerows and limestone crevices, but the species becomes light demanding as it gets older. It has been found that in general at least 20% of full sunlight is required for tree survival over a period of many years (Spurr and Barnes, 1973) and almost all species make their maximum biomass growth under conditions of full sunlight. As the ratio of photosynthetic biomass to nonphotosynthetic biomass decreases, the respiratory load on the photosynthetic apparatus increases, with possible increases in CP values.

Rate of height growth of seedlings generally increases as light intensity increases from low values. The light intensity at which maximum height growth is reached varies considerably, but the seedlings of most species attain maximum height growth under partial shade. Light-demanding species, such as pines, do attain maximum height growth in full sunlight, but light intensity can be reduced by as much as

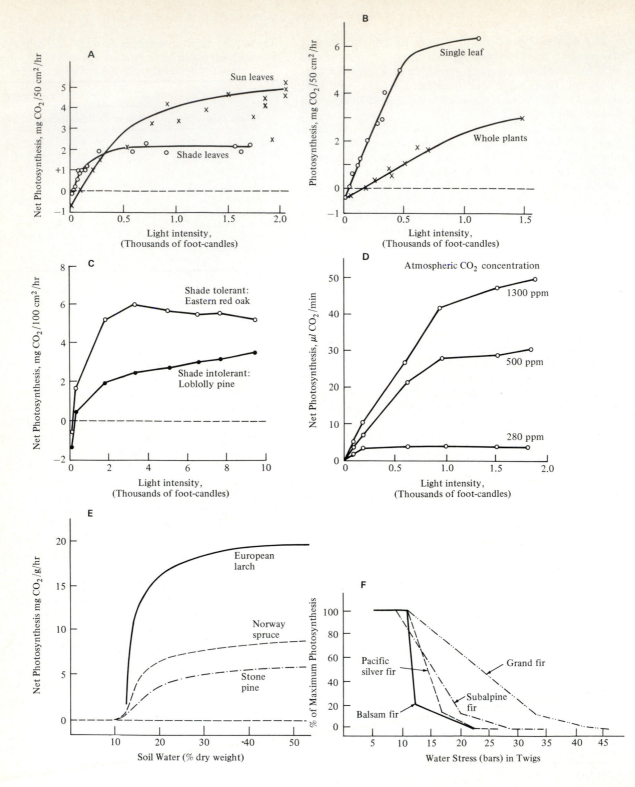

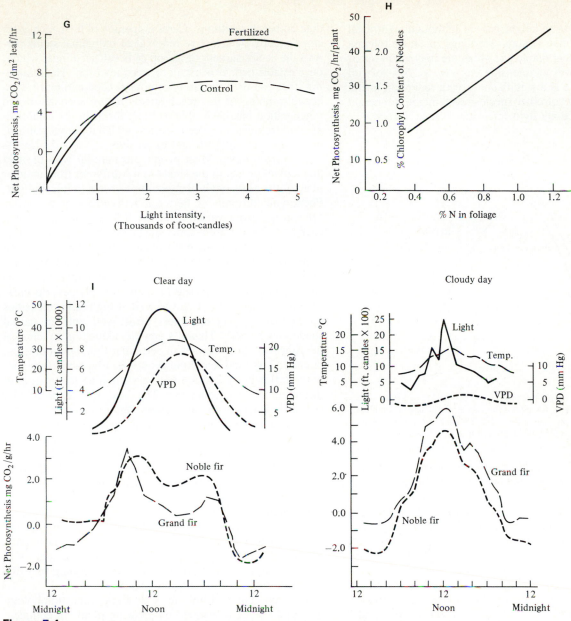

Figure 7.4

Variations in the rate of photosynthesis with a variety of variables. (A) With foliage type (sun and shade leaves) in European beech (after Boysen-Jensen, 1932). (B) With degree of mutual shading in white mustard *(Sinapis alba)* (after Boysen-Jensen, 1932). (C) With difference in shade tolerance (after Kramer and Decker, 1944). (D) With concentration of CO_2 in the atmosphere surrounding the foliage of wheat seedlings (after Hoover et al., 1933). (E) With soil moisture status in three species of conifer (after Havranek and Benecke, 1978). (F) With variation in internal plant moisture stress for four species of *Abies* (after Puritch, 1973). (G) With nitrogen fertilization of Douglas-fir (after Brix, 1971). (H) With foliar nitrogen concentrations in Norway spruce (after Keller, 1971). (I) With time of day in two tree species (after Hodges, 1967). (Reproduced with permission.)

50% with little loss in height growth (although significant loss in diameter may occur). Seedlings of shade-tolerant species such as sugar maple and sycamore may attain maximum height growth at intensities as low as 20% of full sunlight, and there is a significant growth reduction in full sunlight. Seedlings of other species reach maximum height growth at intermediate light intensities (Table 7.4).

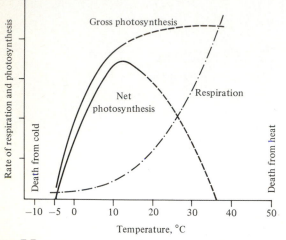

Figure 7.5
Effect of temperature on photosynthesis and respiration of *Pinus cembra*. The broken lines for photosynthesis at the higher temperatures are estimates. (Based on Tranquillini, 1954; after Kramer, 1957. Reproduced with permission of W. Tranquillini and P. J. Kramer.)

The light intensity reaching the forest floor varies greatly according to the tree species, the density of the canopy, and the local solar radiation levels. The light conditions experienced by a forest plant will vary according to average light conditions in the stand and the position of the plant in relation to the rest of the canopy. A crown dominant will receive full sunlight, while codominant, subdominant, suppressed, and understory plants will generally receive progressively less light. Table 7.3 gives some average light intensities beneath various forest types. The wide variation is the result of differences in age and density of stands. Figure 7.6 shows how the radiation reaching the forest floor varies with crown density, spacing (number of stems per hectare), height above the ground (note the variation according to cloudiness), and time of day.

Silviculturalists use a knowledge of the relative CPs of crop and weed plant species and of the relationship between crown density and forest floor light intensities to influence the composition of vegetation on the forest floor. Many of the weed species in French beech forests have higher CPs

than do beech seedlings. Careful opening of the beech overstory canopy by selective removal of individual stems permits the establishment of a crop of beech seedlings, which, once established, is resistant to weed invasion. The remaining trees can then be safely removed. Clearcutting or even heavy thinning of the beech stands before adequate beech regeneration has been obtained can result in the establishment of troublesome weed species, which make reestablishment of beech difficult and expensive.

2. Morphology. Most people are familiar with the fact that a plant grown in the shade looks different from another plant of the same or similar genotype grown in full sunlight. Phenotypic differences between individuals of a species often result from variation in the light conditions experienced by the different individuals. Such differences may also be partly due to such factors as temperature, wind, and moisture, which tend to vary as light intensity varies. Individual factors never act alone in ecosystems, and, as stressed earlier, causal determinism probably never occurs.

Some plants will only grow well at high light intensities *(heliophytes)*, whereas others grow well only in partial shade *(sciophytes)*. This is a genetic adaptation to increase the fitness of these species in particular light environments, but heliophyte and sciophyte genotypes frequently lack phenotypic flexibility and are not very good at acclimating to different light environments. The lack of a thick cuticle, supporting and conducting tissues, and roots makes mosses efficient at photosynthesis in deep shade, where they are protected from excessive moisture loss, but makes them poorly adapted for survival in full sunlight. The thick cuticles and mutual shading of pine needles enable them to operate under conditions of very high light intensity and the temperature and moisture stress that often accompany high light intensities, but prevent them from acclimating to a shaded environment. Other plants, such as many of the hardwood tree species and understory plants, have great powers of acclimation, and a single genotype can grow in widely differing light environments by developing very different morphological characteristics.

The importance of light in controlling plant morphology can easily be demonstrated by growing plants in complete darkness. The distribution of new biomass between roots and stems, and within stems between height growth and diameter growth is regulated by growth hormones that are produced at the growing tips. These hormones, which are sensitive to light and which are partially or completely destroyed under high light intensity, stimulate rapid cell division and cell elongation. In bright light, most of the hormone produced is destroyed, so that growth in length is moderate and the remaining growth materials contribute to

Table 7.4 Effect of Light Intensity on Height Growth, Biomass Accumulation, and Shoot/Root Ratio in Seedlings of Several Tree Species (Kozlowski, 1962; McDermott, 1954; Logan, 1966a)

Species	Light Conditions	Height Growth, cm	Biomass, g Shoot	Root	Shoot/Root Ratio
Jack pine (4 yr old)	Full sun	112	52.7	30.0	1.8
	Partial shade	99	32.1	17.2	1.9
	Full shade	40	2.7	1.0	2.7
Eastern larch (4 yr old)	Full sun	158	31.8	29.8	1.1
	Partial shade	170	27.9	20.5	1.9
	Full shade	64	4.0	2.5	1.6
Loblolly pine (2 yr old)	Full sun	42	25.2	20.1	0.8
	Full shade	35	6.1	7.2	1.2
Overcup oak (2 yr old)	Full sun	59	21.1	44.1	0.48
	Full shade	66	20.1	38.7	0.52
River birch (10 wk old)	Full sun	41	—	—	3.6
	Partial shade	52	—	—	8.3
	Full shade	26	—	—	13.4

root and stem diameter growth. In the dark, the hormones are not destroyed, cell division and elongation are promoted, and development of leaves, supporting tissues, chlorophyll, and root systems is suppressed. The result is rapid growth of a long, thin, weak, fleshy stem lacking chlorophyll and normally developed leaves as the plant attempts to grow into an area with higher light intensities. Plants exhibiting such morphological changes in response to inadequate light intensity are said to be *etiolated,* a phenomenon familiar to anyone who has kept potatoes or dahlia tubers in the dark for too long. Etiolation is seen best in herbaceous light-demanding species. It generally does not develop in shade-tolerant plants. Evolution has "taught" them that sacrificing everything in favor of rapid stem elongation is not the best strategy, and many shade-tolerant plants have adapted to restrain rapid elongation under shaded conditions (Grime, 1966).

Dramatic cases of etiolation are not normally observed in forest trees, but light-controlled variation does occur in the allocation of new biomass to various parts of the plant. Under high light intensities, seedling root biomass may increase as fast or even faster than stem biomass, but under reduced light intensities most of the net biomass production is invested in stem height growth, thus increasing the *shoot/ root ratio*. The response of trees and tree seedlings to reduced light intensity is generally not so much one of increasing height growth, although this may occur (Table 7.4). It is rather one of reducing root and stem diameter growth to sustain height growth. Trees growing in overcrowded plantations or densely stocked natural stands de-

velop tall, thin, and weak stems with very small crowns and very small root systems, and tree seedlings growing in densely stocked or excessively shaded nursery beds will also have high shoot/root ratios.

If a seedling is to survive light competition from its neighbors, it must expose its foliage to adequate light intensities. Producing a strong, thick stem and a large root system will do little to help the long-term survival of a plant if this strategy maintains the plant in the shade of its competitors. Competition for light was probably one of the most powerful selection factors during the development of the first land plants, and the development of erect stems to hold the photosynthetic apparatus up to the light was one of the earliest terrestrial plant adaptations (Wilson, 1970). Although the plant must be careful not to overcommit its limited resources to aboveground growth, the evolution of a significant environmental control over the genetically determined shoot/root ratio in order to optimize fitness in the struggle to survive was probably a very early development. Table 7.4 shows how the stem height, stem biomass, root biomass, and shoot/root ratio of seedlings of several species vary with light conditions. A considerable variation in response is apparent. Light-demanding species such as jack pine show a much greater reduction in height and biomass growth and a greater increase in shoot/root ratio as light intensity decreases than do shade-tolerant species.

Leaves show a great range of morphological variation in response to varying light intensities. Leaves grown in deep shade *(shade leaves)* are normally larger, thinner, less lobed, and have fewer layers of *palisade cells* than leaves grown in full sunlight *(sun leaves)* (Figure 7.7). Palisade

Figure 7.6

Effect of forest cover on the intensity of solar radiation reaching the forest floor. (A) Variation with crown closure, conifer forest, Sierra Nevada mountains, California (after U.S. Corps of Engineers, 1956). (B) Variation with tree spacing; the jack pine plantation at 6 × 6 and 8 × 8 ft had not yet closed canopy (data from Reifsnyder and Lull, 1965). (C) Variation with height above-ground in a beech stand in sunny and overcast conditions (after Reifsnyder and Lull, 1965). (D) Effect of time of day (angle of sun in the sky) on light intensity reaching the top of the canopy and the ground in a tropical forest as percent of midday full sunlight (after Longman and Jenik, 1974). (Reproduced with permission.)

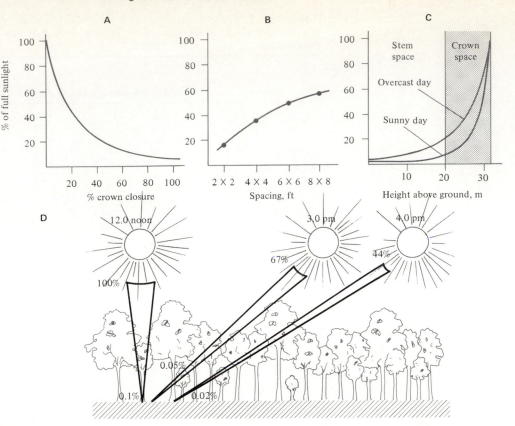

cells are the closely packed mesophyll cells that occur in one or more layers beneath the leaf epidermis. In most leaves they are found only on the adaxial (upper) side of the leaf, but they can also occur on the abaxial (lower) side. Palisade cells usually contain the majority of the chloroplasts which are responsible for photosynthesis. In a study of a variety of herbaceous plant species, it was found that the distribution of chloroplasts between the palisade parenchyma cells and the spongy parenchama cells was 69–86% in the palisade and 14–31% in the spongy mesophyll (Schurhoff, 1924).

As light passes through the palisade layer(s) some of it is absorbed, and at low intensities insufficient light penetrates through the upper palisade layer to produce net photosynthesis in lower palisade layers or the spongy mesophyll. Under very high light intensities, the quantity of light penetrating through the first two layers of palisade cells may be greater than the compensation point of the individual cells, and there may be a third palisade layer.

The importance of the palisade layer is reflected in the fact that the palisade tissue exposes 1.6–3.5 times as much surface within the leaf for gaseous exchange as the spongy mesophyll. Where there are many palisade layers, the internal surface of the leaf may be very high. For example, the internal leaf surface of a 21-year-old *Catalpa* tree was reported to be 5100 m^2, whereas the outer leaf surface was only 390 m^2 (Turrell, 1934). The ratio of internal to external leaf surface is greater in xeromorphic sun leaves (17.2–31.3) than in intermediate leaves (11.6–19.2) and shade leaves (6.8–9.9) (Turrell, 1936). Thus, the area of internal leaf surface available for gas exchange varies according to the ecological conditions. The larger internal surface area in xeromorphic leaves presumably compensates for the smaller overall size of sun leaves. For further details of leaf anatomy, see Esau (1963) or another standard work on plant anatomy.

Shade leaves have a thinner cuticle and fewer cuticular hairs, thus reducing reflection and absorption and increasing the transmission of light to the palisade cells. The epidermis of shade leaves may transmit as much as 98% of the light energy, whereas the value for sun leaves may be as low as 15% (Daubenmire, 1974). Shade leaves also have

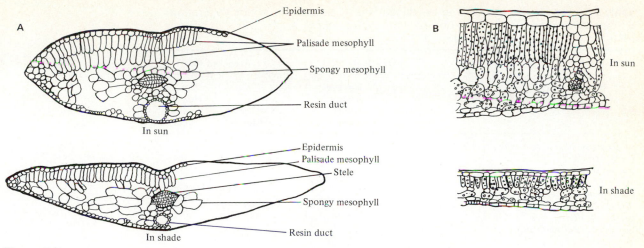

Figure 7.7

Variation in leaf morphology in response to light intensity. (A) Cross sections of leaves of western hemlock developed in full sunlight and in the shade of a dense Douglas-fir canopy (after Tucker and Emmingham, 1977). (B) Cross sections of leaves of sugar maple from the southern edge (full sunlight) and the center of the crown (shade) of an isolated tree (after Weaver and Clements, 1938). (Copyrights Society of American Foresters (A) and McGraw-Hill Book Co. (B). Reproduced with permission of Soc. Amer. For., McGraw-Hill, and W. H. Emmingham.)

better developed mesophyll layers through which CO_2 is absorbed and H_2O evaporated. As a result of these morphological characteristics, shade leaves have a much higher photosynthetic efficiency than do sun leaves (as high as 20%; Daubenmire, 1974). This does not mean that trees in deep shade will grow faster than trees in full sunlight. The total amount of CO_2 fixation is normally lower in shade leaves than in sun leaves in spite of this high efficiency because of the much lower levels of light to which shade leaves are exposed.

3. Shade Tolerance. For many centuries, foresters have classified plants as *shade tolerant* or *light demanding* (shade intolerant). The emphasis of this classification has always been on light conditions, but we now know that the reaction of plants to shade conditions in natural situations is only partly a matter of photosynthesis/light intensity relationships. Just as plant height growth is controlled by a large number of genes and environmental variables, so tolerance of shade is a multiply determined characteristic.

Much of the early work on compensation points showed that under experimental conditions individual seedlings can exist at lower light intensities than those occurring in woodlands and forests that lack any understory vegetation. This observation threw doubt on the theory that shade tolerance was directly related to the compensation point. Several investigations in the first half of this century showed that if root competition for moisture and nutrients was eliminated

by digging a trench around an area of shaded forest floor lacking any vegetation, the area was rapidly invaded by overstory and understory seedlings. Studies showed that trenching increased soil moisture, leading to improvements in the germination, growth, and survival of tree seedlings (Korstian and Coile, 1938). More recent trenching experiments have demonstrated increases in mineralization of organic matter and a great improvement in nutrient availability (Gadgil and Gadgil, 1971, 1975; Vitousek et al., 1979). Table 7.5 presents a comparison between trenched and untrenched plots 8 years after trenching, and Figure 7.8 shows how rapidly these vegetation changes occur once root competition is removed. From these trenching experiments we can conclude that shade tolerance is as much a matter of availability of and competition for moisture and nutrients as competition for light.

The high shoot/root ratios and small root systems of shade-intolerant plants grown at low light intensities puts them at a disadvantage in the competition for moisture and nutrients with overstory plants whose canopies are fully illuminated. These morphological effects of light may reduce the fitness of the plants in shaded environments from which they are therefore excluded. Successful plants in such environments are those which have been molded by evolution to have adaptations that ensure adequate supplies of light, moisture, and nutrients under the very low light conditions. The rootless mosses that dominate the ground vegetation in

Table 7.5 Height Growth of Tree Seedlings and Abundance of Minor Vegetation 8 Years After Removal of Root Competition by Trenching (data from Toumey and Kienholz, 1931)

	Control Plot		Trenched Plot	
	Number of Seedlings	Average Height of Seedlings, cm	Number of Seedlings	Average Height of Seedlings, cm
A. Response of tree seedlings				
Eastern hemlock	3	7	11	96
Eastern white pine	6	7	26	36
B. Response of herbaceous plants				
White violet (*Viola* sp.)	39		764	
Blackberry (*Rubus* sp.)	18		357	
Five finger (*Potentilla* sp.)	12		279	
C. Percent total vegetative cover	8.1		80	

very shaded conditions obtain most of their nutrients from throughfall, minimize moisture loss by their prostrate growth form, tolerate drying out, and have very low compensation points because almost all of their biomass is photosynthetic; there is almost no respiration "tax" imposed by nonphotosynthetic organs such as roots and stems.

Plants growing in low light intensities produce shade leaves that are designed to optimize photosynthesis: large leaves with thin cuticles and few lobes, held horizontally in a pattern that minimizes mutual shading. The leaves (and the plants in general) have a higher ratio of photosynthetic biomass to nonphotosynthetic biomass than do plants in high light intensities, and there is a lower respiration rate. These adaptations combine to reduce compensation points, improving the chances of survival of adapted plants in low light environments (Table 7.6).

Survival of seedlings in the shade is related to seed size. A common adaptation of shade-tolerant plants is to produce relatively few seeds of large size with abundant energy reserves. Large, heavy seeds have less chance of being widely dispersed than small, light seeds, and tend to remain close to the parent plant where there is often significant light competition. The large store of energy enables them to survive with an inefficient dispersal system. Some large seeds are able to reach higher light environments by having wings or relationships with animals to aid dispersal.

Some tree species which can grow in deep shade have evolved to sacrifice height growth in favor of maintaining branch elongation and root growth. It is not uncommon in dense old-growth subalpine forests in coastal Pacific North-

west U.S. and B.C. to see 1 m tall Pacific silver fir saplings of up to 100 years in age with a branch spread of as much as 4 m in diameter, and a height increment of less than 1 cm. There is a greater chance of finding light by going outwards rather than upwards, a strategy that maintains an understory of stunted saplings, many of which can resume normal rates of height growth if a gap is created in the overstory.

Shade tolerance may also be affected by disease organisms. The higher humidity that occurs in shaded environments favors the growth of various fungal pathogens of tree seedlings (Vaartaja, 1952), and shade tolerance may be related to resistance to these pathogens.

It should be apparent from this discussion that whether or not a seedling can establish and grow in a particular shaded environment is not simply a question of light intensity and compensation points. As with most ecological phenomena, several factors are involved, and shade tolerance is a good example of multiple determinism.

B. Effects on Animals

Variations in the intensity of solar radiation are generally of less direct consequence to animals than to plants, but light intensity nevertheless plays an important role in the lives of animals. Most animals depend to a considerable extent on their eyesight for finding food, for detection of enemies and for navigation, although in many cases the senses of hearing, smell, and taste may be as important or even more important. The intensity of light plays an important role in the level of activity of many animals which enter a resting period during darkness (called "sleep" in some ani-

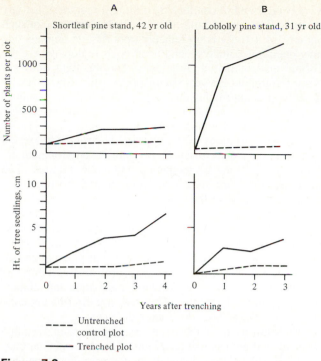

Figure 7.8

Effect of removal of root competition by trenching on the height growth of tree seedlings and the total number of plants on the trenched plots in two different pine stands. (After Korstian and Coile, 1938. Copyright Duke University, School of Forestry and Environmental Studies. Reproduced with permission.)

Table 7.6 Relative Growth and Respiration Rates in Seedlings of Shade-Tolerant and Light-Demanding Tree Species (data from Grime, 1966)

Species	Growth rate,[a] mg g^{-1} hr^{-1}	Respiration rate,[b] mg g^{-1} hr^{-1}
Shade tolerant		
Eastern hemlock	2.9	2.2
Pacific yew	—	1.2
American beech	—	2.6
Red maple	5.5	2.1
Sugar maple	0.6	1.8
Chinese chestnut	1.8	1.2
Northern red oak	0.6	1.8
Shade intolerant		
Tulip tree	—	3.9
Black walnut	—	2.7
Black cherry	—	4.8
Aspen	—	4.2
Sweet birch	4.5	3.6
Sumac	2.8	6.6
American elm	3.9	—

[a]Growth rate of 1-week-old seedlings in full sunlight: mg weight gain per gram of dry seedling per hour.
[b]Respiration rate of leaf discs over 12 hours: mg weight loss per gram of dry leaf per hour at 25°C.

mals) and become active in the light. The speed of movement and general activity of many animals, such as insects and crabs, increases as light intensity increases, a phenomenon known as *photokinesis*.

Some heterotrophic organisms have evolved to become active mainly at times of low light intensity because of the concealment conferred by darkness, and some species are entirely nocturnal in their activities. The nocturnal habit undoubtedly developed first in herbivores as an adaptation to avoid predation. Respite from their enemies was probably short-lived, however, as the eyesight of their predators evolved to enable them to hunt their prey using visual clues at very low light intensities. The eyes of vertebrate animals are generally able to detect the movement of small objects at light intensities as low as one ten-billionth of full sunlight (Clarke, 1967). Natural selection obviously had the genetic material ready at hand with which to produce nighttime vision.

Light plays an important role in the orientation of both plants and animals. In plants the response is called *photo-tropism;* the orientation and movement of an animal in relation to a light stimulus is termed *phototaxis*. The orientation may be either toward (positive) or away from (negative) the light source or at some angle to it, and the direction of the response may vary under different conditions. Spruce budworm larvae have a positive phototaxis which leads them out to the end of branches during bright sunshine, and negative phototaxis under overcast conditions when the source of light is diffuse. Many animals have a complex orientation behavior in which the angle of the sun in the sky is used for orientation, allowance being made for the change in the angle of the sun as the day progresses.

Information about its discovery of a new source of pollen or nectar is relayed by a bee to other bees in the hive by means of a waggle dance, in which the distance of the new resource is indicated by the duration of the dance, the magnitude of the resource by the enthusiasm and persistence of the dancing bee, and the direction relative to the angle of the sun in the sky by the orientation of the dance on the honeycomb (von Frisch, 1967). Both bees and birds have been shown to have eyes that are sensitive to the angle of polarization of sky light, an adaptation that permits unerring navigation over featureless expanses of forest, ocean, or desert even on a cloudy day.

7.5 Ecological Effects of Temporal Variations in Solar Radiation

The survival of an organism is determined by both the factors of the physical environment and the other organisms with which it interacts. Success at exploiting favorable opportunities and at avoiding unfavorable circumstances in an environment that varies both daily and seasonally depends to a great extent on the ability of an organism to do things at the correct time. Predators must be in the right place at the right time if they are to eat. Insect pollinated flowers must flower when the adults of their insect pollinators are around, and the food needs of nectar-feeding insects must coincide with the flowering period of their host flowers. Long-distance migrations of animals away from environments that are about to become unfavorable must often start at a time when food and temperature conditions are still favorable if the animals are to reach the security of more equitable environments before bad weather arrives. Plants living in areas with low winter temperatures must initiate physiological changes (which may take several weeks for completion) in time to become resistant to unfavorably low temperatures when they occur. In short, organisms need to have a sense of time.

The environment exhibits two major types of predictable variation that require some means of timekeeping by the organism: the day–night variation and the seasonal variation. There is also a monthly periodicity in the activity of some animals in response to the phases of the moon (Clarke, 1967); most of the examples are marine organisms, for which monthly tidal variations are important.

The alternation of day and night and the annual "march of the seasons" give rise to variations in the availability of food (or nutrients) and shelter, in the activity of natural enemies, in temperature, and in the availability of water. An organism that is unable to organize its daily and annual activities to take advantage of good conditions, and to complete all of its essential activities and functions in time to prepare for a period of unfavorable conditions is very unlikely to survive. Consequently, most organisms are adapted to a *diurnal* (day/night) periodicity, while those that live in a seasonal environment also have an annual periodicity. Those organisms that live in a relatively nonseasonal (equatorial areas) or unpredictable (desert) environment may lack a strongly seasonal periodicity.

In some organisms, the variation in day/night activity is largely a matter of photokinesis; the organisms are simply more active in the light. In others, the rhythm is more deeply engrained. Certain species of small mammals brought into the laboratory and kept in complete darkness have been found to continue their diurnal rhythm of activity for up to 7 months (Clarke, 1967). The maintenance of such patterns of activity is presumably important to animals that may overwinter underground or in polar regions where the normal environmental stimulus of varying light does not occur throughout the year. Many plants only grow normally if exposed to alternating day and night conditions, and their metabolism becomes abnormal if they are exposed to continuous day for prolonged periods.

Seasonal variations in the physical environment and the consequent seasonal variations in the biotic environment are largely phenomena of temperate and polar regions. The small seasonal variations in temperature and moisture conditions that occur at the equator are thought to be of relatively minor consequence. But as one moves away from the equator toward either of the poles one soon encounters areas in which ecologically important seasonal dry periods occur. In the middle latitudes, marked seasonal fluctuations of both moisture and temperature are characteristic, while farther poleward, the season of favorable moisture and temperature conditions is greatly shortened; a period of unfavorably low temperatures dominates the year.

Organisms living in these seasonal regions need a reliable "calendar of environmental events." Such a calendar cannot be based on light intensity or temperature alone, because although these vary with the season they are subject to the unpredictable effects of unseasonal weather. Snow in midsummer and sunbathing temperatures in midwinter are not unknown at temperate latitudes, at least for a day or two. The calendar must therefore be based on a reliably predictable environmental factor that varies in phase with the average onset and termination of unfavorable environmental conditions. The annual variation in the relative lengths of day and night provides just such an environmental timekeeper, although organisms normally use other environmental clues such as temperature in conjunction with day/night length.

The sensitivity of organisms to the length of daylight is called *photoperiodism*. Actually, for plants it is the length of the uninterrupted dark period that is important, as can be demonstrated by interrupting the middle of a long dark period (short day) with a brief period of light (Figure 7.9). This produces the same result as a short "night" (i.e., long day) treatment, because plant response to light is based on a light-absorbing pigment known as *phytochrome*. This pigment can exist in two different forms: a biologically active form, which absorbs radiation in the far-red part of the spectrum (PFR), and a less active form that absorbs in the red wavelengths (PR). During the day, the red portion of the visible spectrum converts most of the phytochrome into the biologically active form, thereby promoting activity. During the dark period, there is slow conversion to the inactive form; the longer the dark period, the greater the proportion of the phytochrome in the inactive form and the smaller the response of the plants to the light. This can be summarized as follows:

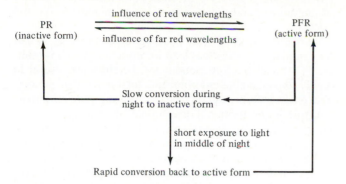

PR (inactive form) ⇄ PFR (active form)

influence of red wavelengths

influence of far red wavelengths

Slow conversion during night to inactive form

short exposure to light in middle of night

Rapid conversion back to active form

When most of the phytochrome is in the inactive form, active growth ceases and the plants enter dormancy (Downs, 1962). With long-day and short-night conditions, most of the phytochrome is in the active form and the plant responds actively to light. Interruption of a long dark period by a brief period of light converts much of the inactive phytochrome back to active form and therefore simulates a short-night condition.

Photoperiodism can be found in all types of organisms and, perhaps surprisingly, at all latitudes. It is best developed in areas with highly variable but seasonally predictable climates (e.g., alpine or polar regions). Its occurrence in some tropical organisms may reflect the phenomenon of continental drift. Present-day land masses were not always in their present positions. They have moved slowly over the surface of the earth as the result of horizontal and vertical movements of the earth's crust (tectonic movements), and present-day equatorial areas have occupied positions at higher latitudes in the past. Equatorial photoperiodism may also reflect our failure to detect some current seasonality of ecological importance in equatorial regions (e.g., there is a much greater seasonality in precipitation and humidity in many tropical forests than is generally recognized), or it may simply be the result of an incomplete understanding of photoperiodism.

An enormous variety of biological phenomena has been shown to exhibit some degree of photoperiodism (Vince-Prue, 1975). Its major role is in regulating the onset of reproduction in plants and animals and in preparation for dormancy prior to the onset of a climatically unfavorable season. Photoperiodic responses are classified into one of the following three categories according to the reproductive or other response of the individual.

1. *Short-day organisms.* Animals that reproduce, plants that flower, or flower most rapidly, and organisms that enter dormancy or complete some other aspect of their life history with fewer than some critical number of hours of daylight. The term "long-night organisms" would actually be more appropriate because the length of the uninterrupted dark period is the critical stimulus.
2. *Long-day organisms.* Organisms that respond as in 1, but to more than some critical number of hours of daylight.

12 hours

12 hours + 1 hour of light in the middle of the dark period

20 hours

Figure 7.9

Photoperiodism in trees. The effect of interrupting the dark period on the photoperiodic response in plants. Douglas-fir grown with a 12 hour photoperiod enters dormancy, but if the 12 hour dark period is interrupted in the middle by a 1 hour light period, growth continues and achieves almost as much total growth as plants under a 20 hour photoperiod. (After Downs, 1962. Copyright Ronald Press. Redrawn by permission of John Wiley & Sons, Inc. and R. J. Downs.)

3. *Day-length indifferent (day-neutral) organisms.* Organisms that complete their life history events irrespective of the day length.

For short-day organisms, there are two occasions each year when the day-length stimulus and the temperature conditions satisfy the requirements for reproduction: the spring and the fall. Some organisms will breed at both times (Allee et al., 1967), but most short-day organisms require a dual stimulus and reproduce only once a year. Long–short-day organisms respond to short-day conditions only following a period of long days (i.e., in the fall), and short–long-day organisms respond only to a period of short days when the days are getting longer. Triggering of the photoperiodic stimulus may involve temperature and other environmental factors. The critical photoperiod for short-day organisms is usually fairly broad, from 2 to 15 hours of light, while the critical photoperiod for long-day organisms is from 16 up to 24 hours. There may also be some intermediate-day-length organisms responding to periods of 12–16 hours of light (Figure 7.10).

Short-day photoperiods occur much of the year near the equator, and in the spring and fall at intermediate latitudes. At high latitudes, there are too few days that have both 2–15-hour photoperiods and favorable temperatures to permit the completion of short-day-induced life stages. Short-day organisms are therefore most common at the middle and lower latitudes. Conversely, long-day photoperiods never occur near the equator and last for only a very short time (the middle of summer) at middle latitudes. They are most common at high latitudes (northern forest and polar regions), and this is where long-day organisms are found.

A few organisms (day-neutral) appear to ignore the seasons and to grow and flower (plants) or reproduce (animals) whenever environmental conditions are favorable, irrespective of the length of the photoperiod. Such organisms are found only in the less extreme seasonal environments. In the more severe climates, most organisms are obliged to "tow the seasonal line."

A. Role of Photoperiodism in Animals

The phenomenon of photoperiodism was first demonstrated experimentally in plants (Garner and Allard, 1920), but it has subsequently been shown to be the factor responsible for the timing of many of the critical events in the lives of animals in seasonally variable environments. It plays a critical role in regulating the onset of reproduction, the start of migrations, and the seasonal change in color of fur and feathers.

A characteristic of most photoperiodic responses is that they initiate activities that lead to future events whose timing is critical. Such responses are therefore less useful in highly unpredictable environments than in regular, predictable environments, although they may still play an important role in the former. For example, the timing of spring rains in temperate deserts and the brief flush of plant and animal activity that follows cannot be accurately predicted, and therefore a rigid photoperiodic control of spring reproduction in desert areas would not always synchronize reproduction with the period of abundant food. It has been found in certain species of desert birds that spring photoperiods initiate the development of the sexual organs but do not actually stimulate reproduction. A state of sexual readiness is prepared and maintained during the period when rains are most likely to occur, but reproduction itself occurs in response to some stimulus associated with the rains themselves (Marshall and Disney, 1957).

Most animals in seasonal environments bear their young in the spring so that they have time to grow to a size and maturity that will permit them to survive the following winter. Synchronization of births with favorable spring food and temperature conditions requires that mating takes place sufficiently long before the birth event to allow for the gestation (pregnancy) period. Animals such as deer, sheep, and goats which have a fairly long gestation period must mate in the fall or early winter, and sexual activity is stimulated by short days following long days. On the other hand, animals with a very short gestation period can safely wait until late

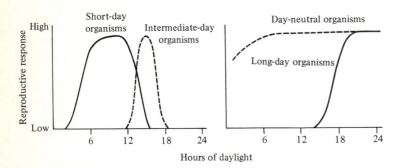

Figure 7.10

Photoperiodism. Variation in the reproductive response of the three major photoperiodic types of organism as day length varies. Other photoperiodic responses show a similar range of types. (After Vince-Prue, 1975. Amended and redrawn by permission of McGraw-Hill Book Company (UK) Limited and D. Vince-Prue.)

winter or early spring to mate, and they may have a short-day-following-a-period-of-low-temperature photoperiodic response, or even a long-day response. Initiation of preparations for reproduction must start in advance of sexual activity, so that courtship, selection and establishment of nesting sites or territories, and preparation of a shelter or nest must be initiated by photoperiodic stimuli that permit sufficient time for these activities to be completed before the onset of breeding. An illustration of this is the fact that birds feeding on early spring insects have a shorter day stimulus for nest building than do summer migrant visitors or midsummer insect feeders such as swallows.

The migration of birds and other animals between polar and lower latitudes to avoid periods of winter cold has been known for a long time, but only in the past half century was it realized that photoperiod was the environmental trigger that initiated migrations. The really long migrations from polar areas require that animals leave before temperature and food conditions become unfavorable, and migrations are initiated at about the same time each year in good or bad weather. Only the evolutionary experience that to delay can sometimes be fatal, coupled with the dependable environmental calendar set by day length, can ensure a consistent departure date irrespective of the current conditions. The rigidity of this adaptation will sometimes result in birds arriving at northern locations before winter has given way to spring. As with most adaptations, photoperiodicity represents a compromise between the conflicting pressures of selection induced by biotic factors and selection induced by physical environmental factors that results in maximum fitness of the species.

Seasonal variation in the color of the fur and feathers of terrestrial animals is a common adaptation to seasonal changes in the color of the physical environment. Animals that are well camouflaged in the summer would be very obvious against a background of winter snow, and evolution has produced a genetically controlled color change in many of the animals that spend the winter above the snow in seasonally snowy environments. Animals of the tundra that overwinter beneath the snow (such as the lemming) do not change color. The timing of color changes is controlled by photoperiod, as in the case of the varying hare (or snowshoe rabbit, *Lepus americanus*) which begins to change from producing brown fur to producing white fur when the day length drops below 18 hours. The reverse change occurs as day length increases beyond 18 hours. White fur can be induced in the middle of summer by exposing the animals to light periods of less than 18 hours, and brown fur is produced in midwinter by animals given an artificially extended photoperiod (Allee et al., 1967).

Many animals solve the problems presented by winter low temperatures by going into a dormant condition (see Chapter 8) and photoperiod is generally involved in initiating the physiological changes required for dormancy.

B. Role of Photoperiodism in Plants

Photoperiodism in plants plays a major role in the control of the cessation of growth and the onset of dormancy in the late summer or fall, and in many plants it regulates flowering and fruiting in the spring and summer. It also plays a role in the breaking of dormancy and resumption of growth in the spring in some perennial plants. It is thought that control of flowering and fruiting in woody plants is generally not under direct photoperiodic control, but our understanding of many aspects of photoperiodism in trees is still incomplete as most of the research on this topic has been conducted on herbaceous plants. Much of the work carried out on woody plants has used seedlings or cuttings, and

Table 7.7 The Length of the Effect of Photoperiod on Growth in Height and Gain in Weight of Various Conifers. Expressed as Percentages of Maxima Achieved with Optimum Photoperiods (based on data from Downs, 1962)

Species	Percent of Maximum Growth in Height at Various Photo-Periods, hr						Percent of Maximum Growth in Weight at Various Photo-Periods, hr						Duration of Experiment (months)
	8	12	14	16	20	24	8	12	14	16	20	24	
Coastal redwood	—	77	94	100	90	77	—	68	87	100	93	79	12
Montery pine	55	59	64	64	—	100	55	67	68	60	—	100	7
Japanese larch	—	8	44	62	69	100	—	17	71	66	80	100	4
Sitka spruce	—	13	17	75	—	100	—	14	20	71	—	100	17
Douglas-fir	—	4	11	51	100	88	—	4	23	83	77	100	—
Jack pine	12	20	40	56	—	100	4	11	39	88	—	100	8.5
Eastern white pine	3	13	13	23	—	100	1	3	14	23	—	100	15
White spruce	—	13	16	28	50	100	—	11	17	28	50	100	4
Norway spruce	1	1	1	8	—	100	1	1	1	9	—	100	11

photoperiodic responses of mature trees, particularly the control of reproduction, are not yet well known. Flowering in many tree species appears to be day-neutral, and the trees will break spring dormancy equally in total darkness or continuous light, indicating that termination of dormancy is not a light-mediated phenomenon (Pauley, 1958). Temperature frequently acts as an important complementary factor in photoperiodic responses.

Short-day plants are those that flower naturally only under short days and long nights, and are found only at middle or low latitudes. Short days do occur at higher latitudes, but they are more frequently accompanied by frost or snow than at lower latitudes. Spring short-day plants include certain annuals and perennials. The seed of the annuals must germinate early in the spring if the plants are to grow, mature, and reproduce before they are killed by fall frosts. Spring short-day perennials are those that are likely to experience strong competition for light, moisture, or nutrients from other species later in the season. Many understory species in deciduous woodlands initiate growth and flower before the overstory species come into leaf and light conditions become unfavorable. Flower buds are normally set the previous summer or fall to avoid any delays in the spring. Other short-day perennials flower in the fall.

Long-day plants are those that flower only when the days are long and the nights are short, a condition that is met only in the higher latitudes. Such plants break dormancy and return to dormancy at much longer day lengths than short-day plants, reflecting the environmental hazards of being an "early bird" or a "hanger-on." Many economically important conifers are long-day plants, becoming dormant if grown at photoperiods of 16 days or less, and many achieve their full growth potential only under 24-hour photoperiods. Some species, such as the coastal redwood and Monterey pine from California, are relatively day-neutral (Table 7.7), reflecting the lack of any selective advantage of having a photoperiodic response in the equitable environments in which they have evolved. Figure 7.11 shows the variation in growth response to varying photoperiods between the relatively short-day Japanese larch, which enters dormancy at photoperiods of less than 14 hours, and white spruce, which enters dormancy at photoperiods of less than 16–20 hours.

Because of the importance of photoperiodism to the survival and fitness of organisms, it is not surprising that there is considerable variation in photoperiodic response in a species across its geographical range, and photoperiodic ecotypes have been recognized in many species. The date of occurrence of unfavorable temperature and moisture conditions will vary between the coast and inland, between a frosty valley bottom and valley slopes, between high and

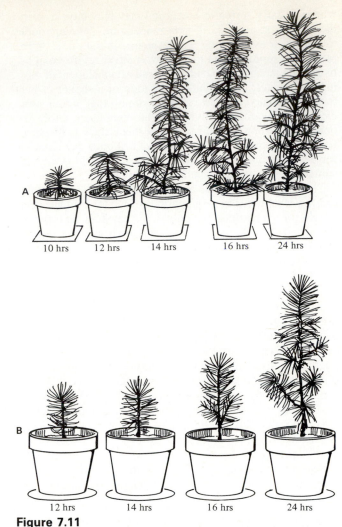

Figure 7.11
Growth of conifer seedlings over a four month period at various photoperiods. (A) Japanese larch. (B) White spruce. (After Downs, 1962. Copyright Ronald Press. Redrawn by permission of John Wiley & Sons, Inc. and R. J. Downs.)

low elevations, between north and south portions of the species range, and between north and south aspects. Consequently, the photoperiodic "calendar" selected for by organisms living in these different environments will vary. An example of this is spring bud burst in Douglas-fir, which appears to have a long-day photoperiodic response in high-elevation ecotypes, whereas low-elevation ecotypes at the same latitude have no such adaptation (Ingrens-Moller, 1957).

In a study of ecotypic variation in photoperiodic responses, seed was collected from black cottonwood *(Populus trichocarpa)* growing over a wide geographical area and grown near Boston, Massachusetts at about 42° north latitude. The date at which the seedlings entered dormancy was recorded and compared with the latitude of origin (Figure 7.12). A clear relationship between latitude of origin and date of cessation in height growth was observed, with some southern ecotypes (which had been moved north) continuing growth until late October. In fact, some did not stop growing until their shoots were killed by the first fall frosts. The date of cessation of growth also showed a good

relationship with the length of the growing season in the region of origin, indicating that the length of the growing season is a genetic characteristic of a species that is related to, and modified by, variations in the photoperiod. Both relationships depicted in Figure 7.12 exhibited considerable variation. Seed from latitudes 44–46°N varied in date of cessation of height growth from mid-July to late October, and ecotypes that stopped growing in mid-September were from regions with growing seasons of between 140 and about 220 days. This variation reflects variations in local conditions due to aspect, elevation, and so on, and the interaction of photoperiodic responses with factors such

Figure 7.12

Experimental demonstration of photoperiodic ecotypes in black cottonwood. Variation in the date when height growth stopped in black cottonwood ecotypes collected from a wide latitudinal range and grown together at Boston, Massachusetts (approx. latitude 42°). The variation of the data about the mean reflects differences in elevation and climate in different localities at any one latitude. The date of cessation in height growth, a genetically controlled photoperiodic response, reflects the average length of the growing season in the location of origin. (Pauley, 1958. Copyright Ronald Press. Redrawn by permission of John Wiley & Sons, Inc. and S. S. Pauley.)

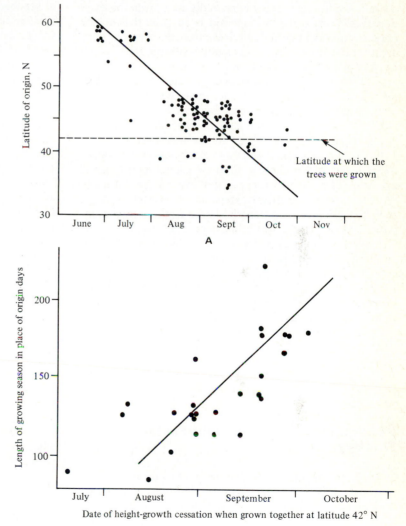

as temperature. It is also an expression of the natural variation in characteristics that can be found in most populations.

When short-day plants are moved northward, they often grow larger than they would in their native locality because of the greater number of hours of light per day and because the short photoperiod required to stimulate dormancy does not occur until very late in the summer or fall. However, because the onset of dormancy is delayed, the plants may not become dormant before the first killing frosts, and plants moved north typically suffer a higher incidence of frost damage. Flowering may also be inhibited because of the long photoperiods. On the other hand, long-day plants moved south often experience reduced growth or even dwarfing because the photoperiod is so short that it may only permit a short period of release from dormancy or none at all. In the black cottonwood study just mentioned, movement of northern ecotypes southward reduced annual height growth from 130 cm to between 15 and 20 cm, height growth being terminated in late June, whereas ecotypes from southern localities grew as much as 200 cms (Pauley, 1958). Flowering was inhibited because the photoperiod never became long enough to initiate reproduction.

It should be apparent from these examples that photoperiodic adaptations will help to limit the natural migration and extension of a species' range. They can also pose a major limitation on the artificial extension of a species' range, such as the planting of "exotic" trees (species from a different country or region) by foresters. The success in using North American species at more northerly latitudes in Britain, maritime Europe, and Scandinavia reflects the increased growth of ecotypes when moved north; the relatively moderate climate of these areas (because of the Gulf Stream) removes the normal impediment on south-to-north movements of plants. The reverse process of moving high-latitude ecotypes native of Europe into more southerly areas in the U.S. has not met with notable success (Pauley, 1958).

For a more detailed treatment of photoperiodism in plants, see Salisbury and Ross (1969).

7.6 Importance of the Light Factor in Forestry

There can be little doubt that the light factor plays a very important role in the management of forest ecosystems. Failure to recognize the role that light intensity plays in determining the morphology of plants can result in planting failures, loss of productivity in established stands, and the production of timber of reduced economic value. Failure to recognize the adaptation (genetic or phenotypic) of local tree ecotypes (provenances) to both the intensity and periodicity of light can result in planting shock or seedling death, poor growth or temporary growth reduction of advance regeneration, and death or severe reduction in growth of suppressed saplings if the overstory is removed too suddenly or at the wrong time of the year. The following are a few examples of the practical importance of the topics discussed in this chapter.

The forest nurseryman should be aware of the influence of light on plant morphology. Maximum seedling height growth for some species may be obtained by partial shading of seedbeds or by dense stocking of seedbeds, but shading must be applied with caution because the resulting seedlings will generally have thinner and weaker stems than seedlings grown in full sunlight, and they will have higher shoot/root ratios. For plantation establishment in a moist, sheltered site, these characteristics may be desirable, but they are unlikely to aid the seedling in its struggle for survival if planted on an open, exposed site. Seedlings grown in the nursery or the forest at low light intensities will have shade leaves. If suddenly exposed to full sunlight and the accompanying altered temperature and moisture conditions by planting on an exposed site, or by the sudden removal of the overstory canopy, these plants will experience some degree of light shock. This may either kill them or result in a reduction or cessation of growth for one or more years until appropriately adapted sun leaves or needles are produced. The poorly adapted foliage is frequently shed by the plant. Nursery light conditions should be manipulated to produce seedlings with root/shoot ratios, leaf morphology, leaf pigmentation, height, and diameter characteristics that will give them maximum fitness in their struggle for survival against the moisture stress, high- or low-light-intensity stress, wind abrasion stress, and plant competition stress that they will experience when planted out. By manipulating light intensity with shades or by varying seedbed density, different phenotypes can be produced that are adapted to a variety of different planting sites. There is of course an interaction between light, moisture, and nutrient conditions; nursery managers can vary all three of these factors to produce seedlings of the desired morphology.

Damage to plants as a result of a sudden increase in light intensity often involves the foliage (e.g., damage to conifers when released from competing vegetation), but light can also affect stems because of the heating effects of solar radiation. *Sun scald*, the killing of bark by lethally high temperature following sudden exposure to sunlight, commonly occurs when thin-barked species growing in dense stands are suddenly exposed to direct sunlight by the removal of adjacent trees. Sun scald is mainly a winter phenomenon because it is associated with rapidly fluctuating temperatures rather than with high temperature alone. Another effect of sudden stem exposure is the stimulation of new or *epicormic* branching. This is very common in previously shaded hardwood stems that experience a great increase in light intensity, but it is also seen in some conifers. Epicormic branching can have important implications for timber quality, and European foresters have developed silvicultural techniques to reduce it to a minimum.

Failure to recognize light intensity–plant morphology relationships in the forest stand can result in poor resistance to wind, snow, and drought damage, poor growth form with heavy branching, and long crowns due to poor natural pruning. Thin-barked species can suffer sun scald damage and hardwood trees may form epicormic branches. The light intensity in a stand will influence the stem taper, the stem straightness (especially in hardwood stands), the frequency of knots and the proportion of knot-free wood in the stem, the diameter growth, and the proportion of the net photosynthetic production that is put into usable stem growth. Rapid removal of an overstory of weed species in the middle of summer may result in a reduction in the growth of the released crop tree for several years, rather than the expected increase in growth, thereby negating the benefits of weed control.

Failure to recognize the role of photoperiodism in synchronizing the activities of most forest plants and animals can result in planting failures, susceptibility to frost, and poor growth. Planted seedlings must have received the correct light and temperature conditions in the nursery and in storage if their physiology is to be correctly synchronized with their new environment. The generally poor adaptation to the physical environment of ecotypes from very different elevations at the same latitude, or from different latitudes at the same elevation, renders them increasingly susceptible to competition and pathogens. Having said this, it must be noted that establishment of plantations with seedlings of the wrong photoperiodic ecotypes will not always have undesirable results. As with the agricultural examples of maize and tobacco plants, a change in photoperiod may suppress reproduction so that all of the available nutrients and energy are put into vegetative growth. However, there have been so many cases of plantation failures resulting from the use of nonnative ecotypes that the forester must give careful consideration to the photoperiodic adaptation of the plants that are to replace the harvested crop.

7.7 Summary

The fundamental role of solar radiation is as the major source of energy for life, but this is not its only ecological effect.

The interaction of solar radiation with water and the atmosphere maintains global temperatures within a range that has proved to be suitable for the evolution of life. Without the temperature-regulating aspects of solar radiation, life as we know it could not have evolved and, given our present technology, could not continue.

Although the energy aspects of solar radiation are extremely important, they are preeminent only for the photoautotrophs. For most heterotrophic organisms, other aspects of the sun's energy emissions are more important. Vision, the ability to see one's surroundings, is of critical importance to most animals, some of which have become adapted to "see" wavelengths other than the visible, or to see at light intensities that are so low that for most other organisms it is dark. Color, the visual response to different wavelengths, adds an ecologically important dimension to vision, which has led to adaptations for concealment, mimicry, and a variety of visual signals that assist organisms in organizing their behavior in a way that increases their genetic fitness.

Variations in light intensity as the result of either location or competition have resulted in a wide variety of adaptations, especially in green plants. For such organisms, light is potentially both beneficial and harmful, and adaptations include protective mechanisms as well as mechanisms to enhance the exposure to and interception of light. These involve both morphological and physiological modifications that enable organisms to survive and compete successfully in various different light environments. Adaptations to variations in the quantity of solar radiation are not restricted to plants; animals also exhibit a variety of adaptations to light intensity.

Most organisms require a sense of time; an environmental clock and/or calendar by which their activities can be scheduled to take advantage of favorable conditions and to avoid adverse conditions. The daily and seasonal variation in light intensity and the seasonal variation in photoperiod apparently provide the best available environmental timepiece; in most terrestrial organisms light seems to have been selected by evolution as the most important timekeeper. However, few organisms exhibit a slavish adherence to photoperiod. It is more common for light to be one of several factors that, in combination, schedule the biological events in the lives of living things.

Because organisms have adapted to particular solar-radiation conditions, care must be taken when moving organisms from one geographical location to another. Raising a plant in a light environment that is different from that of its native location can sometimes induce growth patterns that are desirable for human uses of the plant, but optimum growth and survival are generally obtained when a plant genotype is kept in its native light environment.

Of the three major aspects of solar radiation that can be varied on any particular site, the forest manager can control only the intensity factor. This involves the choice of harvest method (clearcutting vs. selective or small patch cutting) and the manipulation of light competition between crop trees and other vegetation early in the life of the crop, and between individual crop trees later on in the life of the stand. Consideration of the light intensity requirements of the crop is important and will play a major role in how a particular site is managed. Radiation quality and periodicity can be varied significantly only by moving plants to different geographic locations.

8.1 Introduction

Temperature is probably the environmental factor most familiar to the average person, a fact that suggests its ecological importance. Our cultural evolution has made us very dependent on an artificially regulated temperature environment, and many of the cultural variations between different races, such as style of clothing, type of housing, and daily and seasonal activity patterns, reflect the overriding influence of the temperature factor. A significant portion of the human economy is expended in overcoming the constraints that the temperature factor places on human activity and population development. Similarly, much of the energy budget of most terrestrial and some aquatic animals is allotted to maintaining within acceptable limits the temperatures that they experience.

Temperature is a measure of the intensity or concentration of heat energy in an object. It is determined by both the amount of heat energy in, and the heat capacity of the object. Thus, a piece of dry wood (low thermal capacity) will have a much higher temperature than a piece of iron (high thermal capacity) of the same size when both objects contain the same amount of heat energy, and when both the iron and the wood have the same temperature, the iron will contain much more heat energy than the wood. A small addition of heat energy to the piece of wood will raise its temperature significantly, whereas the same amount of heat energy added to the iron will alter its temperature very little.

The temperature of a body generally goes up as heat energy is added and drops as it is lost, but this is not always the case. Water gives out a great deal of heat energy without changing its temperature as it freezes, and ice absorbs a lot of heat energy as it melts, again with no change in temperature. This exception to the general rule is due to the *latent* (or hidden) *heat of crystallization*. The *latent heat of vaporization* results in a similar phenomenon as water changes from the liquid to vapor state. Because of the large amount of latent heat associated with freezing and vaporization, and because of its high thermal capacity, water retains its liquid properties under widely varying levels of heat energy. It has been estimated that the melting of the winter ice on Lake Mendota in Wisconsin involves the absorption of heat energy equivalent to 195,000 tons of anthracite coal, with no change in temperature (Allee et al., 1967). A similar quantity of heat must be given off before the water can refreeze, resulting in a substantial delay in transformation of the liquid back to the solid form. The remarkable temperature properties of water make it a very suitable medium for life

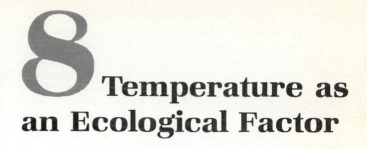

8 Temperature as an Ecological Factor

processes, and provide a partial explanation as to why all living organisms conduct their chemical processes in solution in water.

In this chapter we consider how the temperature of the environment varies from place to place and from time to time, and the significance of these variations for plants and animals. We then discuss the role of temperature in limiting the geographical distribution of species, and the importance of the temperature factor in forestry.

8.2 Geographical and Temporal Variations in Temperature

Temperature exhibits a number of well-defined cycles of variation that are directly attributable to the rotation of the earth around its axis and around the sun. These rotations lead to a daily and seasonal variation in the amount of radiant energy reaching a particular part of the earth, and consequently in its temperature. In the tropics, the diurnal variation in temperature may be only a few degrees, whereas in continental regions it can be as much as 50°C in either winter (e.g., −49 to 6.5°C in Montana) or summer (e.g., 2–50°C just above the ground in some deserts). These large ranges sometimes involve extremely rapid changes in temperature, such as a 27°C change in 2 minutes recorded in South Dakota. Islands in the Pacific Ocean may have an annual variation in daily mean temperatures of as little as 11.8°C (19.6–31.4°C), while the comparable figure for parts of Siberia is 107°C (−70° to 37°C). The lowest recorded temperature is −88°C in Antarctica, while temperatures as high as 60°C for air and 84°C for surface soil have been recorded in desert areas (Clarke, 1967; Spurr and Barnes, 1973; McWhirter and McWhirter, 1975).

Temperature exhibits long-term as well as short-term and geographical variations. On a geological time scale of hundreds of thousands of years, temperatures have varied as ice ages have come and gone, accompanied by shifts in the location of the major climatic zones. Variations in mean annual temperature of as much as 10°C have occurred since the last glacial period (the Wisconsin glaciation), and although this may not result in great changes in a hot climate, it is of great significance in a cold climate. A 1°C reduction in the mean annual temperature (1°C drop in every monthly average) of Akureyri, Iceland, would reduce the growing season from 158 to 144 days, and a 2.4°C drop would reduce it to 118 days (Bryson, 1974). A "little ice age" occurred from the sixteenth to the nineteenth centuries, followed by a general warming period of nearly 100 years. There was a rise of up to 1.7°C in the mean annual temperature of the eastern U.S., a change in climate equivalent to a 300-m change in elevation or about 170-km change in latitude (Spurr and Barnes, 1973). This warming trend was reflected in the retreat of glaciers, but it appears to have ended and the climate may now be reverting to a condition similar to that which prevailed in the nineteenth century (Wahl, 1968; Wahl and Lawson, 1970).

The three most important variables determining the geographical variation of temperature are latitude, altitude, and the proximity of large bodies of water such as oceans or large lakes. Both latitude and altitude influence the radiation budget, while convection and conduction processes move heat from large water bodies to the air in winter, and from land to the air in summer. Temperature extremes are greatly modified in the vicinity (especially downwind) of large bodies of water. Aspect and topographic position are also important determinants of local temperature conditions.

A. The Radiation Budget

The temperature of a terrestrial object is often largely determined by its radiation budget; the balance between the quantity of radiant energy impinging on the body from solar or terrestrial sources, and the quantity of energy leaving the body due to reflection or reradiation. Heat exchange by conduction and convection also contributes to the determination of temperature, but radiant-energy exchanges are frequently more important in terrestrial situations. In contrast, the temperature of objects in aquatic situations is mainly controlled by conduction.

Because of the close relationship between the radiation budget and temperature, geographical and temporal variation in temperature is very similar to geographical and temporal variation in net radiation budgets. Days are warmer than nights. Cloudy areas are cooler in the day and warmer at night than clear areas (Figure 8.1). Northern aspects are cooler than southern aspects (in the northern hemisphere).

The radiation budget of an organism consists of energy gains through the absorption of short (solar)- and long (atmospheric and terrestrial)-wavelength radiation, and energy losses from the emission of long-wavelength radiation. At temperatures above absolute zero (−273°C) all objects emit radiant energy, the wavelength of which varies with the temperature of the object: the higher the temperature, the shorter the wavelength. Table 8.1 presents a radiation budget for a meadow community in central Europe in summer and winter, showing the importance of long-wavelength radiation in comparison with the more readily perceived short-wavelength radiation. This is in agreement with Figure 7.2, which shows the importance of long-wave radiation in the global radiation budget.

The radiation budget of an object is greatly influenced by its "view factor": the proportion of its radiating environment that is accounted for by the sky. A rabbit in the middle of a flat area of desert has a "view" of all of the sky and therefore has a high view factor; a seedling growing beneath a small opening in the forest canopy has a very small view factor. Almost all of its radiating environment is occupied by overstory trees. On a clear day, a location with a large view factor will have a strongly positive net radiation budget because of the high intensity of short-wavelength radiation and high temperatures may occur. On a clear night, such a site will have a strongly negative net budget and low temperatures may occur. The "cold," clear sky will emit or reflect very little long-wavelength radiation to balance the outgoing radiation. A situation with a small view factor, on the other hand, will have only weakly positive and negative day and night net budgets, the latter because inputs of long-wavelength radiation from the surrounding vegetation at night partially compensate for radiation losses (Figure 8.1). The view factor is less important in cloudy than in clear weather because of the reduced

Figure 8.1

Effect of cloudiness on daytime
(A) and nighttime (B) radiation
budgets.

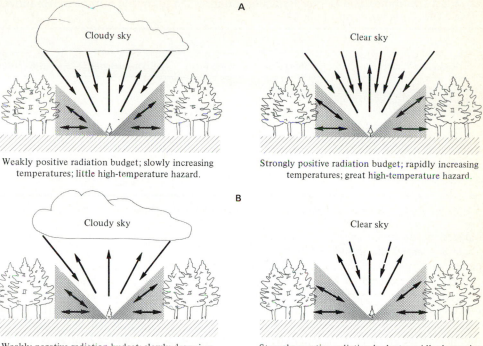

A

Weakly positive radiation budget; slowly increasing
temperatures; little high-temperature hazard.

Strongly positive radiation budget; rapidly increasing
temperatures; great high-temperature hazard.

B

Weakly negative radiation budget; slowly dropping
temperatures; little ground frost hazard.

Strongly negative radiation budget; rapidly decreasing
temperature; great ground frost hazard.

intensity of daytime short-wavelength radiation and because of long wavelength reradiation from the cloud at night. In a forest situation, the view factor of a seedling is determined by microrelief (stumps, logs), aspect, and the size of canopy opening relative to the height of the surrounding trees. The importance of tree height, clearing size, and view factor in determining radiation balances is reduced in areas with predominantly cloudy climates.

Radiation budgets are greatly modified by albedo. Energy that is reflected rather than absorbed does not increase the heat content of an object, and therefore does not affect its temperature. Forest canopies, which have a low albedo, warm up rapidly, whereas a white sandy beach or snow surface reflects most of the solar energy that is received, and such surfaces warm up slowly. Snow covered with dust melts faster than clean snow because of the lowered albedo and increased absorption. Dark-colored soil absorbs much more radiant energy than light-colored soil and therefore reaches much higher temperatures. However, the air temperature above the lighter-colored soil may be greater than above dark-colored soil because of the greater reflection from the former (Figure 8.2). A layer of snow increases the daytime temperature of the air just above it (because of light

reflection), and plant parts just above the snow may be damaged by the resulting wide diurnal temperature fluctuations and high light intensity.

Radiation budgets at ground level are greatly affected by vegetation. We saw in Chapter 7 that there is a great reduction in short-wave solar radiation as light passes down from the upper surface of the vegetation to the forest floor and that this results in lower summer air and soil temperatures below the forest canopy than in adjacent clearings. The forest vegetation also acts as a blanket, eliminating the view factor and covering the area with a radiation absorbing and emitting layer. Net nighttime radiation losses from the soil, understory vegetation, and ground-dwelling fauna are much less than in open areas, and there is a reduced risk of *ground frost* (radiant cooling of the soil and adjacent air layers to below 0°C). Winter nocturnal soil and air temperatures are often higher inside the forest than in adjacent clearings, but daytime temperatures are generally reduced because of the weaker daytime net radiation budget. Shrubs, herbs, and even a moss layer can exert a similar insulating effect on the ground.

Forest cover reduces the range of temperatures (annual, monthly, or diurnal), and the mean monthly range may be

Table 8.1 Summer and Winter Radiation Budgets[a] in a Central European Meadow, Langleys/day (data from Reifsnyder and Lull, 1965)

Radiation Source	June			December		
	Short-wave	Long-wave	All Wavelengths	Short-wave	Long-wave	All Wavelengths
Downward from space: direct solar radiation	+248	—	+248	+12	—	+12
Downward from atmosphere: skylight and atmosphere reradiation	+218	+728	+946	+39	+582	+621
Upward from earth's surface: reradiation and reflection	−93	−807	−900	−18	−621	−639
Net budget	+373	−79	+294	+33	−39	−6

[a] A positive net radiation budget indicates increasing temperatures, while a negative budget indicates falling temperatures.

reduced by as much as 7°C in July and 3°C in January. Table 8.2 shows the influences of forest cover on air temperatures in various U.S. forests. Maximum temperatures are generally reduced by forest cover, whereas minimum temperatures are generally increased. The reduction in monthly maxima is more pronounced in July (up to 4.6°C) than in January (up to 1.7°C), while the increase in monthly minima can be as much as 3–4°C in both summer and winter. These data apply mainly to closed forest stands. Shrub and open forest communities can produce the opposite effect, with increased monthly temperature ranges (Kittredge, 1948).

The temperature effects of a net radiation budget are greatly influenced by the thermal capacity of the objects receiving the radiation. Water has a very high thermal capacity and therefore the moisture content of an object affects its temperature response. A wet soil warms up and cools down more slowly than dry soil, and the high water content of living organisms helps to regulate their temperature fluctuations. Water bodies such as large lakes and oceans have an enormous thermal capacity, and they experience only minor and very gradual temperature changes.

B. Conduction and Convection of Heat

The radiation budget is not the sole determinant of the heat energy content of an object; other processes are also involved. Plants, animals, and soil lose or gain heat from the atmosphere by conduction and/or convection. This can maintain low temperatures even when there is a positive net radiation budget, and vice versa. The importance of conduction and convection to the temperature of an organism depends to some extent on the thermal properties of its surface. Where conductivity is low, such as tree bark, seal blubber, or the fur of mammals at high latitudes, conduction

and convection are of reduced importance. In warmer climates where efficient loss of excess body heat is necessary, these processes are more important.

In addition to their contribution to the thermal balance of individual organisms, conduction and convection play a major role in world ecology by transferring energy between land and water surfaces. Air in contact with water exchanges heat by conduction, and the resulting atmospheric temperature gradients lead to convection currents that distribute the effects of the heat exchange over large areas. The enormous store of summer heat in a large lake or an ocean warms the air passing over it during the winter, raising temperatures in downwind land areas. In the spring and summer the relatively low temperature of large water bodies results in the opposite effect. The Japanese Current in the north Pacific and the Gulf Stream in the north Atlantic are good examples. They deliver warm water from tropical to higher latitudes on the west coasts of North America and Europe (Scandinavia), which warms the air moving from the ocean to the land in these areas. This produces a remarkably equitable climate in these coastal areas, permitting the northward extension along the coast of many lower-latitude species. The Alaskan coast and northern coastal Norway are warmer in January than areas in the middle of large continents several thousand miles to the south. In contrast, the east coast of Canada experiences currents from cold northern waters, and these make the climate of Labrador and Newfoundland much colder in the summer than comparable latitudes elsewhere.

Conduction plays a very important role in determining the distribution of temperature with depth in the soil. Dry organic soils have an extremely low thermal conductivity (heat energy moves through them slowly), whereas the conductivity of mineral soils is low to moderate. Wet soils con-

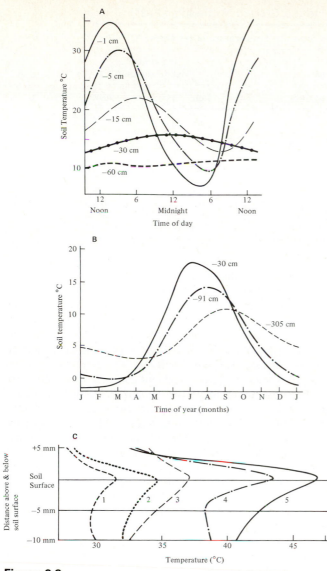

Figure 8.2

Soil temperature profiles; their diurnal and annual variations, and variations according to color, moisture content, and exposure to light. (A) Diurnal variation in temperature at various depths in a subalpine soil in British Columbia. (After Ballard, 1972. Reproduced with permission of the Regents of the University of Colorado.) (B) Variation in mean monthly temperature at various depths in the soil at Bozeman, Montana. (After Fitton and Brooks, 1931. Reproduced with permission of the American Meteorological Society.) (C) Variation in vertical gradients of soil temperature with color, shading, and moisture content. (After Daubenmire, 1974. Reproduced with permission of John Wiley & Sons, Inc.) Key: 1 = grey, dry, shaded soil; 2 = grey, wet, exposed soil; 3 = white, dry, exposed soil; 4 = grey, dry, exposed soil; 5 = black, dry, exposed soil.

duct heat better than do dry soils, but even in wet mineral soils heat conduction is not fast enough to give a uniform distribution of temperature through the soil. Peak soil surface temperatures may be reached at noon or early in the afternoon, but peak temperatures at successively deeper points in the soil occur at successively later times. Similarly, minimum diurnal temperatures in the soil lag behind minimum surface temperatures (Figure 8.2A). There is also a lag in the annual variation in soil temperatures, with maxima and minima at depth in the soil occurring several months after those at the soil surface (Figure 8.2B). This may permit the activity of roots and soil organisms to continue throughout the autumn and into winter, long after the aboveground parts of plants have become dormant.

Many northern and high-elevation soils freeze in the winter. In very severe climates this occurs irrespective of snow cover, and the soil may be perpetually frozen throughout most of its depth (*permafrost*). In somewhat less frigid climates, soils may remain more or less unfrozen for most or all of the winter if a deep layer of snow accumulates before low temperatures occur. The snow acts as an efficient insulation against low winter temperatures, and animals such as lemmings can continue their activities uninterrupted beneath the arctic snow. Snow also reduces radiation losses from the soil. Where there is permafrost, plant roots are confined to the superficial "active layer" of soil, which melts in the summer. This restricts root growth and the availability of nutrients, and is an important determinant of the low productivity of northern forests. Deeper thawing of permafrost soils due to warmer summers, removal of vegetation, or disturbances of surface organic layers improves the availability of nutrients and is associated with improved plant and animal productivity (Lutz, 1956; Schultz, 1969).

Where frozen mineral soil is exposed to sunlight in the spring and early summer, its temperature rises rapidly. Where it is covered by a layer of organic material, mineral soil warms up very slowly and may remain frozen for much or even all of the growing season. Much of the northern permafrost regions owes its ecological condition to the layer of insulating organic matter laid down by the vegetation, and massive soil thawing, slumping, and erosion frequently follows the removal of the organic surface layer and exposure of frozen soil. The concern over use of tracked vehicles in oil exploration and construction of oil pipelines in the arctic is related to the thermal fragility of these northern ecosystems.

C. The Role of Topography

High-elevation areas have lower average temperatures than do low-elevation areas, because air temperatures nor-

Table 8.2   Effects of Forest Cover on Air Temperatures near to the Ground (Kittredge, 1948*)

| | Departures from Air Temperature in the Open, °C | | | |
| | Monthly Mean Maximum | | Monthly Mean Minimum | |
Forest Type in the U.S.	Jan.	July	Jan.	July
Beech, N.Y.	—	−4.6	—	+2.5
White pine, Idaho	—	−3.3	—	+3.9
Hemlock, N.Y.	—	−2.7	—	+2.2
White pine, N.H.	—	−2.7	—	+1.8
Douglas-fir, 9000 ft, Colo.	−1.7	−1.2	+1.2	+1.4
Jeffrey pine, 6000 ft, Cal.	+0.4	−0.8	+2.0	+3.7
Jack pine, Neb.	−0.1	−0.7	+0.6	−1.6
Aspen–Engelmann spruce, 9000 ft, Colo.	−1.0	−0.6	−0.1	−0.6
Ponderosa pine, 7250 ft, Ariz.	−0.6	0	+3.3	+2.8
Chaparral, 6000 ft, Calif.	+0.8	+2.8	−0.9	−1.2

*Copyright D. D. Kittredge. Used with permission.

mally decrease at a rate of about 0.4°C per 100 m of elevation (the *lapse rate*) as one proceeds up a mountain. The air at low elevation is denser and therefore absorbs more radiant energy than the air at higher elevations; it also receives heat by conduction and convection from the ground. Under conditions of low atmospheric humidity, the lower, warmer air expands and becomes lighter than the colder air above. Convection currents develop in which plumes of warm air rise high into the atmosphere, forming cumulus clouds. If the lower air is very humid, the atmosphere is more stable, the convection columns do not develop as readily, and there is little atmospheric stirring. Should rapid nocturnal radiant cooling occur under these stable conditions, the air close to the ground may become colder than the air above it and a condition of atmospheric stability called a *temperature inversion* may develop. During an inversion, air temperature increases with increasing distance above the ground up to a certain height and then resumes the normal lapse rate.

Temperature inversions can occur as the result of nocturnal radiant cooling and certain other meteorological processes. Nocturnal inversions generally break up as soon as the ground is warmed by sunlight the following day, but in other circumstances they can be much more persistent. Inversions can also occur as the result of topography. Radiant cooling of high ground flanking a valley gives rise to a layer of cold, dense air in contact with the surface. This air flows slowly down the valley slopes, displacing warmer air in the lower part of the valley and creating an inversion (Figure 8.3). When the cold air draining into the valley is below 0°C, frost occurs on the valley floor, while much warmer temperatures will be experienced in the "thermal belt" higher up the slopes. This is of great importance to fruit

growers, and orchards are often located in the thermal belt. Forest insect problems are sometimes associated with this belt because the milder winters experienced in the thermal belt may increase the winter survival of insect defoliators [e.g., the lodgepole pine needle miner in the Canadian Rocky Mountains (Stark, 1959)]. The warmer winter air temperature of the thermal belt may also give rise to winter moisture stress in plants (*red belt* damage: see Chapter 9).

The cold air drainage that produces valley temperature inversions can also have important small-scale effects. Small topographic depressions tend to fill up with cold air, creating *frost pockets,* and small openings in the forest may fill with cold air and be frostier than a large opening in which the cold air can drain away or be swept away by winds. Frost pockets sometimes create local variations in plant and animal life in environments that lack apparent variation in any physical attribute other than their topographic position.

D. Soil Temperatures

The temperature of soils has already been mentioned several times, but its importance deserves some additional comment. Because of the high thermal capacity of water, wet soils require more heat to raise their temperature than do dry soils; a volume of water requires five times as much heat as the same volume of dry mineral soil to produce the same temperature change. Poorly drained organic and clay soils thaw and warm up much more slowly than do loamy soils (moderately well drained), which are in turn slower than freely drained sandy soils. Frost damage to roots in the fall is most common on light, freely drained soils which

Figure 8.3

Vertical temperature profiles in a valley on a cool, clear day (A) and a cold, clear night (B). The day-time profile near the valley floor is inverted during the cold night.

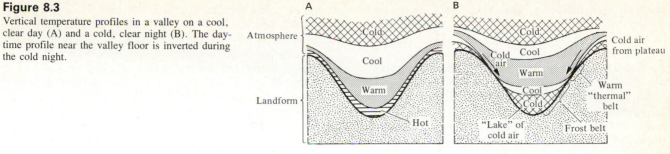

rapidly lose their warmth. The heavier, wetter soils are kept warm far into the fall by the large quantity of summer heat that they contain.

The color of soil has an important effect on its temperature, as demonstrated in Figure 8.2C. Light-colored soils absorb radiant energy less efficiently than do dark-colored soils, and therefore stay cooler. Soil blackened by charcoal is an excellent absorber of radiation, with an albedo approaching zero. Dry, charred organic matter has a very low thermal conductivity, and this, together with its high absorptivity, can give rise to very high temperatures in a thin layer at the surface. In a study of soil temperatures, charred organic matter, grey mineral soil, and yellow mineral soil exposed to full sunlight on a day with an air temperature of 38°C were found to have surface temperatures of 73, 64, and 62°C, respectively (Isaac, 1938).

The importance of thermal conductivity in determining surface temperatures was shown in a study of white pine forest floors in the northeastern U.S. Pine needle litter reached a temperature of 68°C on a day when the air temperature was 24°C, while bare mineral soil reached 36°C and a moss carpet reached 39°C. Soil color also affects soil temperature by influencing reradiation. Light-colored soils are less efficient at radiant heat loss than dark soils, and the surface of an organic soil can drop to below freezing (because of efficient reradiation and poor conduction to replace the lost heat from deeper layers) under conditions in which a light-colored mineral soil would remain above freezing. The resulting damage to superficial feeding roots in organic soils can be lessened by covering the surface of the soil with light-colored sand, which reduces reradiation and increases conduction (Haines, 1922). This technique is sometimes used in forest nurseries to prevent frost problems.

E. Climate and Microclimate

In Chapter 7 we saw that the light conditions experienced by two seedlings growing 10 cm apart on the forest floor can vary greatly. Similarly, the temperature conditions experienced by an insect feeding on the uppermost branches of an overstory tree are quite different from those experienced by an insect feeding on minor vegetation. In discussing any climatic factor, it is necessary to distinguish regional or macroclimate from microclimate; the climatic conditions actually experienced by an individual organism. The microclimate of a person dressed in a sweater and overcoat is very different from the winter macroclimate of the person's hometown; the temperature experience of a diminutive spring-flowering herb is very different from that of a nearby tree 20 m in height. Surface soil and adjacent air temperatures in late winter or early spring in a spot sheltered from the wind may be high enough to promote plant growth when the air 2 m above the ground is still too low to break dormancy. A herb in a shallow frost pocket may experience frost damage while a taller shrub next to it does not: the frost-sensitive organs of the shrub are located above the frost layer. In one study it was found that a small frost pocket had a frost-free period of only 77–104 days, compared with 161 days for a nearby location with good cold-air drainage (Spurr, 1957). On the other hand, a plant in a small, steep-sided depression will have a smaller view factor than one in a flat, open location, and it will be less susceptible to radiation ground frosts. Clearly, the regional macroclimate merely sets the overall climatic framework within which microclimate is determined by many modifying factors.

In discussing the ecological effects of temperature, a further cautionary note is necessary. Temperatures are frequently quoted as annual or monthly means. By itself, the former is an almost worthless piece of information, since a mild coastal climate can have the same mean annual temperature as a continental climate with bitterly cold winters and very hot summers. Mean monthly temperatures give a more realistic picture, but the combined graphs of mean monthly maximum and mean monthly minimum temperatures with an indication of extreme daily values gives a much better basis for comparing the temperature regimes of two environments.

F. Human Effects on the World Radiation Budget and Global Temperatures

We cannot close this section of the chapter without speculating briefly on the effects of human activities on the global radiation budget, on global temperatures, and on world climate. In Chapter 5, the effect of human activities on atmospheric CO_2 levels was explored. The possible effects of elevated CO_2 concentrations and other consequences of human activity on world temperature will be considered briefly here.

Figure 8.4 presents a model of the regulation of the world's climate. Many of the determinants in the model are altered by human activities, and great concern was expressed in the late 1970s and early 1980s about human-induced alteration of climates, especially the CO_2 issue. Carbon dioxide in the atmosphere acts much like the glass in a greenhouse: it permits light to enter but traps long wavelength (thermal infrared) radiation. This leads to atmospheric warming. Human activities have increased the

atmospheric CO_2 concentrations by about 7% over the past two decades and about 15–20% over the last century. It is projected that if the present rates of increase in fossil fuel consumption were to continue, the concentration might be approximately doubled in the next 100 years (to a level of about 600 ppm (Clark et al., 1982; Dickson, 1982). There is, of course, great uncertainty about future trends in fuel consumption, and this leads to a great variation in predictions concerning future increases in CO_2 and consequent effects on world temperatures (Figure 8.5).

Recent (post 1970) estimates of the average surface air temperature changes accompanying a doubling of CO_2 levels range from 0.1 to 3.9°C (Clark et al., 1982). However, CO_2 is only one of several absorbers of CO_2 in the atmosphere (Dickson, 1982) and an inadequate understanding of future changes in the concentrations of other gasses such as methane (CH_4), ozone (O_3) and nitrous oxide (N_2O) that may contribute to climatic change complicate the issue. Hydrates of methane exist in ice and below permafrost in the arctic. Warming of the atmosphere would melt ice and some permafrost, releasing methane which could in turn increase atmospheric heating (Bell, 1982). Because of all these difficulties, it will probably not be possible to measure

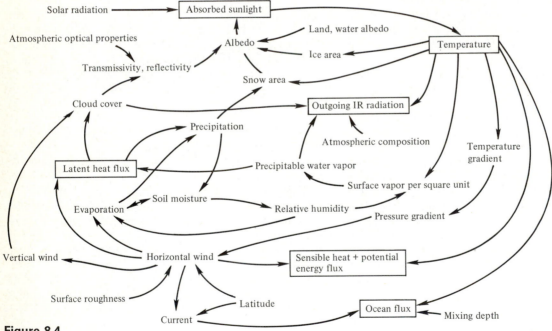

Figure 8.4

Model of world climate. The large number of determinants and the resulting complexity makes it difficult to predict with confidence the effects of human activities on the world's climate. (After Schneider, 1974. Redrawn with permission of Royal Swedish Academy of Sciences and S. H. Schneider.)

with certainty the contributions of elevated CO_2 levels to atmospheric warming until early in the next century (Hansen et al., 1981). The climate is also sensitive to the reflection of short wave radiation by clouds and aerosols (from volcanic eruptions and air pollution).

What is the contribution of forestry–deforestation to changes in atmospheric CO_2 levels? Estimates made between 1970 and 1982 of the annual net contribution of changing land use to atmospheric carbon varied from none to 8 Gt (a gigaton = 10^9 t or 10^{15} g) (data in Clark et al., 1982). Estimates for 1980 range from 0.5 to 2.0 (average of 0.8) Gt (Olson, 1982) and 1.8 to 4.7 (average of 2.6) Gt (Woodwell, 1982). Of these totals, 1.5 to 1.6 Gt are contributed from forest clearing and fuelwood consumption, 0.9 to 3.1 Gt from loss of soil organic matter, while net regrowth of forest removes 1.7 to 1.9 Gt. Fossil fuel emissions in the early 1980s of about 5.3 Gt thus compare with an estimated contribution from changing land use of about 1 to 2.5 Gt. Deforestation, reduction of forest biomass and

loss of soil organic matter may therefore be making a significant long-term contribution to CO_2-induced changes in atmospheric temperatures. The question as to whether or not the remaining terrestrial biosphere is presently acting as a net sink or a net source of atmospheric CO_2 cannot yet be answered unequivocally because of the formidable difficulties in measuring accurately the global dynamics of CO_2 (Brown et al., 1981). For a recent discussion of the potential ecological effects of CO_2-induced climatic change, see McBeath et al. (1984) and Seidel and Keyes (1983).

8.3 Some General Ecological Concepts Concerning Temperature

There is a great temptation to describe climates as *severe, extreme, favorable,* or *unfavorable*. These adjectives reflect our own response to climatic conditions and are not necessarily accurate as descriptions of the response of native organisms. The fact that we find −30°C very cold does not mean that this is an extreme or unfavorable temperature for a tree in midwinter in northern Canada or the U.S.S.R. The response of an organism to a particular temperature is conditioned by the adaptation of the organism to that temperature. A species that has survived in a particular environment is adapted to the conditions of that environment, and those genotypes that cannot tolerate the conditions are eliminated. The unfavorableness of a temperature therefore depends on whether or not it is "unusual" in terms of the organism's recent evolutionary history. Very low or very high temperatures that have been a regular feature of the species' experience over many generations are not necessarily unfavorable. Medium temperatures that have not been such a regular feature may be highly unfavorable and can accurately be described as "severe." Fish from arctic seas will die if transferred to tropical waters, and the same fate would befall tropical fish put into the sea off the north coast of Greenland. Mild frost at the time of flowering may be disastrous for a plant population that can tolerate extremely low winter temperatures.

Other adjectives that are commonly used to describe temperature are *optimum, maximum,* and *minimum* (referred to as *cardinal* temperatures[1]). These terms can be used correctly only if adequately qualified. Optimum for what? A temperature that is optimum for survival may not be optimum for reproduction. Growth is not causally determined

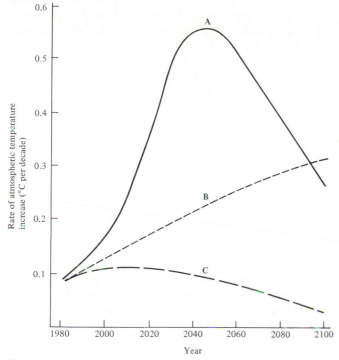

Figure 8.5

Predicted rates of CO_2-induced atmospheric temperature change with (A) a rapid increase in the use of fossil and synthetic fuels, (B) a slow increase, and (C) no increase in fossil fuel use and their gradual replacement by nonfossil fuels. (After Clark et al., 1982. Redrawn with permission of Oxford University Press and W. C. Clarke.)

[1]Cardinal temperatures are the set of temperature that define the temperature adaptations of an organism, including the temperature requirements and tolerances for different life stages, life processes and parts of the organism.

by temperature, and the optimum temperature for growth will probably depend upon conditions of moisture, nutrition, light, competition, and so on.

In defining maximum and minimum temperatures, the length of exposure, time of year, and stage in the organism's life history must be defined. The eggs and larvae of a species of fruit fly are killed by 7 weeks of exposure to 7°C, but death occurs after 3 weeks at 1°C. Flower farmers sometimes immerse their bulbs briefly in nearly boiling water to kill surface fungi and pests without harming the bulb; prolonged immersion at this temperature would "cook" them. Maximum and minimum temperature information is obviously of limited value unless accompanied by information on exposure (Figure 8.6).

A further complication arises because different parts of the same organism may have different cardinal temperatures. Roots have lower minimum temperatures than shoots, so that the relative temperatures of soil and air may have a pronounced effect on the welfare of some plants. The extremities of polar animals have temperatures in winter that would be lethal to the main body of the animal. Cardinal temperatures vary at different times of year and at different stages of an organism's life history.

To clarify the situation and render comparisons meaningful, the following terms should be employed (Table 8.3). The *effective temperature range* is that range of temperatures over which the existing population of genotypes can

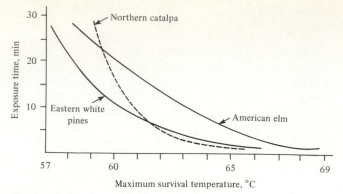

Figure 8.6

Variation in the maximum survival temperature of three tree species with different lengths of exposure. The graph shows the exposure time at different temperatures that is required to kill cortical parenchyma cells. (After Lorenz, 1939. Reproduced with permission of University of Minnesota.)

conduct all their normal life functions and persist indefinitely. It is limited by the maximum and minimum effective temperatures. The *survival temperature range* is the maximum temperature range over which the population can survive. It is limited by the maximum and minimum survival temperatures, which will vary with time of year, stage of life cycle, duration of exposure, and rate of temperature change at the extreme temperatures. The rate of temperature change is sometimes more important than the actual temperature. A plant that is gradually cooled to below freezing and then gradually thawed may suffer no harm, whereas it would be killed if frozen and thawed rapidly. Acclimatization enables organisms to change their cardinal temperatures, but it will occur only if the rate of temperature change is not too great.

Organisms can be classified into two major groups: those that regulate their internal temperature within narrow limits, so that for much of the time it is different from that of the environment (*homeotherms, endotherms,* or warm-blooded animals), and those that allow their internal temperature to equilibrate more or less with that of their environment (*poikilotherms* or *ecotherms*—plants and cold-blooded animals). Some animals (notably hibernating birds and mammals) are homeotherms most of the time, but sometimes allow substantial changes in their body temperatures. Such animals have been referred to as *heterotherms*.

A. Excessively High Temperatures

Temperatures may be too high for a variety of reasons. Metabolic and respiratory rates increase with temperature, and for every organism there is a temperature at which the

Table 8.3 Temperature Relationships of Living Organisms (After Clarke, 1967)

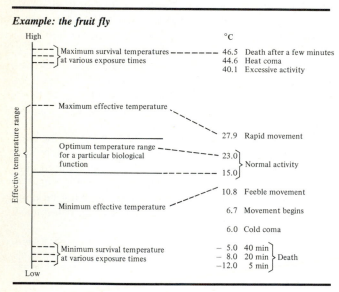

Example: the fruit fly

	°C	
High		
Maximum survival temperatures at various exposure times	46.5	Death after a few minutes
	44.6	Heat coma
	40.1	Excessive activity
Maximum effective temperature		
	27.9	Rapid movement
Optimum temperature range for a particular biological function	23.0	Normal activity
	15.0	
	10.8	Feeble movement
Minimum effective temperature	6.7	Movement begins
	6.0	Cold coma
Minimum survival temperature at various exposure times	−5.0 40 min	
	−8.0 20 min	Death
	−12.0 5 min	
Low		

loss of energy in respiration is greater than the rate at which it is replaced by photosynthesis or ingestion/assimilation (leading to starvation) or by mobilization from reserves (leading to heat exhaustion). In plants and cold-blooded animals, metabolic rates commonly double or triple for every 10°C increase in body temperature. Such organisms are said to have a $Q10$ value of 2 or 3, respectively. Different metabolic functions have different $Q10$ values, and the effective temperature range may be that range over which all functions are synchronized. As this range is exceeded, the different $Q10$ values put different aspects of the metabolism out of synchrony and the organism eventually dies. This condition occurs in homeotherms with a much smaller change of internal temperatures than in poikilotherms.

Temperatures above 50°C induce changes in the molecular structure of most proteins. Boiling an egg at 100°C causes the proteins to coagulate, but sustained temperatures of only 30–50°C will cause sufficient alterations in most proteins to interfere with their normal function (Spurr and Barnes, 1973; Daubenmire, 1974). A few organisms can survive at temperatures of about 90°C, such as algae in hot springs and certain desert animals, but there are few records of poikilothermous animals living permanently at temperatures above 45°C (Clarke, 1967). Poikilotherms can tolerate much greater increases in body temperatures than homeotherms, for which the margin of safety between normal and lethal body temperature may be only a few degrees (2°C for some birds; 3–5°C for human beings). However, for most poikilotherms, optimum temperatures for many functions are only just below maximum survival temperatures (Figure 8.7), so temperature regulation at the optimum range is just as important as for homeotherms. Maximum survival temperature (with long exposure) for plants is commonly about

55°C, but respiration generally exceeds photosynthesis at about 50°C (Spurr and Barnes, 1973), although some desert plants have been shown to grow when their tissues are at 56.5°C with an air temperature of 58°C (MacDougal and Working, 1921).

Perhaps one of the most important effects of high temperature is the associated loss of moisture. Water is lost either as a cooling adaptation or simply because of increased evaporation at higher temperatures, and a significant proportion of deaths of nonaquatic organisms from high temperatures are probably cases of dehydration. Changes in behavior and metabolic derangement due to loss of water, and attempts to locate water and cooler environments can all have important effects on the survival of animals.

High temperatures may increase the susceptibility of aquatic organisms to diseases, and reduce the concentration of dissolved oxygen to critical levels. Excessive fluctuation of water temperature can affect the solubility of nitrogen in the blood of aquatic animals, leading to death from the "bends": bubbles of nitrogen forming in and blocking the bloodstream.

B. Excessively Low Temperatures

There is also a variety of reasons why temperatures can be too low. Variations in $Q10$ values can be responsible for metabolic derangement at low temperatures, or metabolism may simply be slowed down to the point at which other factors become lethal. If unusually low winter temperatures delay the development of salmon eggs and alevins (young fish) in the gravel beds of a temporary stream (one that dries up in the summer), the young fish may not be sufficiently well developed to emerge from the gravel and migrate to a permanent water body before the stream dries up and they are killed. The rate of movement of poikilotherms is greatly reduced at low temperatures, rendering them more susceptible to predation. Low temperatures can cause the precipitation of proteins or lead to the formation of intracellular ice crystals. These may rupture the cells, destroy their internal organization, or dehydrate them by withdrawing liquid water; frozen tissues often exhibit symptoms of dehydration (Weiser, 1970).

Although freezing damage occurs in many species, freezing is not always harmful. Ice crystals are known to form in the tissues of Norway spruce without damaging them, and a species of algae has been unharmed after being frozen at −182°C for an hour (Clarke, 1967). Alternate ice crystal formation and melting can occur many times in a single day in pine needles without apparent harm (Christersson and Sandstedt, 1978). Certain species of algae that inhabit snow or marine environments may complete their life cycle en-

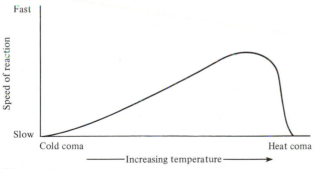

Figure 8.7
Generalized relationship between animal activity and temperature. The range in body temperature between cold coma and heat coma is much greater for poikilotherms than for homeotherms. (After Allee et al., 1967. Copyright W. B. Saunders Company. Reproduced by permission.)

tirely at temperatures below 0°C. Freezing of animal tissues frequently ruptures blood vessels and leads to the degeneration of cells, but the Alaska black fish can recover normal activity after 40 minutes at −40°C. Obviously, generalities about the biological consequences of temperature are meaningless unless adequately qualified.

8.4 Effects of Temperature on Plants

A. Growth Response

Both temperature and physiological response to it vary considerably in different parts of a plant. Roots normally assume the temperature of the soil around them, which in areas away from the equator is lower than shoot temperature in the summer and may be higher in the winter. Shaded stems approximate the air temperature below the crowns, although the insulating properties of bark cause the temperature of the stem to lag behind that of the air. A stem illuminated by full sunlight may experience appreciable increases in temperature, particularly if it has a dark color, although movement of cool water up the stem from the roots may keep stems cooler than the air and prevent excessive temperatures in exposed stems. This can be particularly important at the root collar of a seedling, which may find itself in contact with a midsummer soil surface temperature of over 60°C. Leaves may have temperatures higher, lower, or the same as the air. Thin leaves with high rates of transpiration may be as much as 15°C cooler than the air in summer, even in full sunlight, because of evaporative cooling. Thick leaves may be as much as 30°C warmer than the surrounding air in winter. In some cases, the respiratory activity of the plant may increase tissue temperatures slightly, but this is normally unimportant (Daubenmire, 1974).

The cardinal temperatures for different plant functions vary enormously. Gross photosynthesis reaches a peak at a much lower temperature than respiration, which increases almost up to the maximum survival temperature (see Figure 7.5). Net photosynthesis reaches a maximum at intermediate temperatures. This may help to explain why plants transferred to cooler climates than those to which they are accustomed (higher latitude or altitude) frequently grow faster, and plants moved to warmer climates (lower latitude or altitude) are frequently less productive than in their native environment. The midday decline in net photosynthesis and the rapid carbohydrate accumulation in some crop plants as temperatures decline at the end of the growing season may also reflect differences in respiratory and photosynthetic cardinal temperatures.

Cardinal temperatures vary between different plant organs. As noted above, roots have lower minimum effective temperatures than shoots, and can continue to grow in the fall when the shoot has become dormant. Spring root growth can begin when the soil is still cold but increasing air temperatures have stimulated shoot growth. Predictably, plants exhibit cardinal temperatures commensurate with their environment. High-altitude, high-latitude plants have lower values than low-altitude, low-latitude plants (Figure 8.8). The variation in cardinal temperatures as a plant ages has already been mentioned.

Plant metabolic activity and growth depend upon the availability of water in liquid form, and they cannot continue when the tissues are frozen. Plants can continue to photosynthesize at leaf temperatures a few degrees below freezing because cells do not freeze at these temperatures, and photosynthesis has been measured in some conifers at even lower air temperatures (Parker, 1953). However, the needle temperature in these studies was probably substantially higher than the air temperature. Leaves can act as miniature greenhouses, maintaining temperatures many degrees above that of the surrounding air (see Figure 9.5). Low-temperature photosynthesis permits alpine and arctic plants to start growth in the spring beneath the snow, and winter photosynthesis by evergreen plants in sunny weather. The extent of this winter activity is limited, however, because of the reduced ability of plants to absorb nutrients and moisture, and to translocate them from the roots to the shoots at low temperatures.

All plants experience variations in temperature associated with diurnal variations in the net radiation budget. Plants living away from the equator also experience seasonal temperature variations. Plants are generally sensitive to these variations and will grow normally only when exposed to the particular diurnal and seasonal temperature changes to which they are adapted, a phenomenon called *thermoperiodism*.

Diurnal thermoperiodic responses generally involve a difference in temperature between day and night. Low night and moderate day temperatures are important to flowering and fruiting, and affect the quality of crop plants and fruit (Treshow, 1970). Maximum height growth in loblolly pine and Douglas-fir seedlings occurred when day temperatures were 12 and 10°C warmer, respectively, than night temperatures (Kramer, 1957; Hellmers and Sundahl, 1959). For some species, such as Engelmann spruce and ponderosa pine, the night temperatures are more critical to seedling growth than day temperatures. Conversely, variation in day temperatures produced a greater variation in redwood seedling height growth than did variation in night temperatures

Figure 8.8

Variation in the temperature optimum for photosynthesis in trees. (A) An elevational sequence of tree species from central Europe. (Data from Pisek et al., 1969. Reproduced by permission of VEB Gustav Fischer Verlag.) (B) An elevational sequence of balsam fir ecotypes from New England, U.S. (After Freyer et al., 1972. Reproduced by permission of the *Canadian Journal of Botany*.)

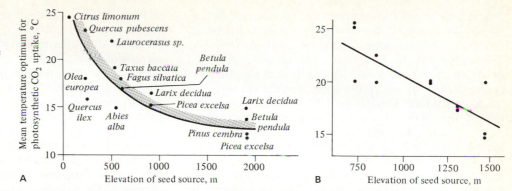

(Figure 8.9). Maximum height growth of red fir seedlings was achieved at both 17 and 23°C daytime temperatures, but only when the former was accompanied by a 4°C, and the latter by a 10°C night temperature (Hellmers, 1966a). Cool days required cold nights, and warm days required cool nights. The diurnal thermoperiodic responses of ponderosa pine have been found to vary somewhat over its range, with maximum height growth occurring with cool days and warm nights (17°C/22°C) in an Arizona ecotype, warm days and warm nights (23°C/23°C) in Washington and Colorado ecotypes, and in both warm day/cool night (23°C/14°C) and cool day/warm night (17°C/22°C) combinations in a Californian ecotype (Callaham, 1962). The height-growth response of red maple seedlings in the U.S. to day and night temperatures also varied in different parts of its range, optimum growth occurring at temperature combinations that resembled those normally prevailing in the area from which seed was collected (Perry, 1962).

Seasonal thermoperiodic responses play an important complementary role to a plant's photoperiodic responses. Whereas photoperiod plays the major role in the initiation of winter dormancy, temperature conditions predominate in the termination of dormancy in the spring and in control of the timing of flowering. Release from dormancy in many plants requires chilling at temperatures of 0–10°C or below for periods of 260–1000 hours, depending on the species. Peach trees require 400 hours, blackberry bushes need 800 hours, and apple trees require even longer. In some cli-

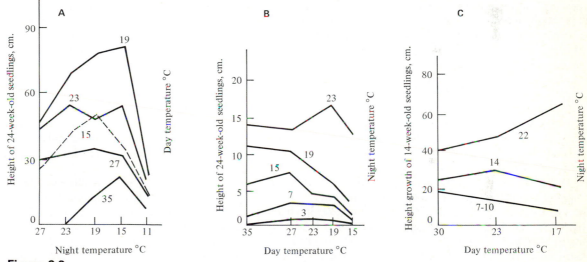

Figure 8.9

Height growth in California redwood (A), Colorado Engelmann spruce (B), and Arizona ponderosa pine (C) seedlings exposed to various combinations of day and night temperatures (after Hellmers, 1966; Hellmers et al., 1970; and Callaham, 1962). The difference between day and night temperatures clearly has an important influence on height growth of these species. (Reproduced with permission.)

mates, this chilling requirement may have been satisfied by January or February, but new growth does not normally commence until temperatures become favorable (Wareing, 1969). However, if plants from lower latitudes are moved poleward, their modest chilling requirements will be met before the risk of late spring frosts is over, and they may suffer frost injury. Conversely, high-latitude plants moved toward the equator may not get sufficient winter chilling, and bud break, leaf and flower development may all be inhibited. Plants from winter-cold environments may exhibit a similar response if kept in a warm greenhouse over winter. Not all species require chilling. Growth of birch and European beech seedlings can be stimulated simply by transferring from short to long photoperiods.

Seeds of many species require chilling before they will germinate. Temperatures of 0–5°C are most effective, and adequate aeration and moisture are required. Germination of some hardwood tree seeds is greatly enhanced by *stratifying* them in damp sand at cool temperatures for a period before they are sown. The chilling requirements of seed of some species can be eliminated by removing the seed coat, but in many species the embryo itself has a chilling requirement.

Initiation of flower buds and flowering in many species requires an exposure to low temperatures, a fact that limits the spread of certain species to warmer climates. The stimulating effect of low temperature on flowering is used to advantage by farmers in the process of *vernalization:* the induction of flowering by cold treatment. The short growing season of northern areas poses problems for the production of grain crops such as rye, which is day-neutral but will not flower until it has produced 22 leaves. This requires most of the growing season, but if the seed is moistened and held at 1°C for several weeks before planting, the plant becomes sensitive to the long days that occur at high latitudes, and flowering may be initiated when as few as eight leaves have been produced. Vernalization is more complex than merely a temperature treatment, and the desired results cannot be obtained without the correct oxygen and light conditions (Hillman, 1969).

The response of a plant to temperature is not fixed. It depends on the temperature experiences in the plant's recent past because of the ability of plants to acclimatize. If a plant is exposed to slowly diminishing temperatures, it will eventually be able to survive at very much lower temperatures than if it is suddenly exposed to a low temperature. This ability of metabolic processes to acclimatize is exemplified by the cardinal temperatures of photosynthesis, which change in response to changes in environmental temperatures. For example, a Californian shrub was found to attain its peak photosynthetic rate at 12–15°C after being exposed for 12 days to a 15°C day/2°C night temperature regime (Figure 8.10). After being switched to a 30°C environment for 23 hours with continuous light, the photosynthetic rate increased and the optimum temperature range occurred at about 21–28°C. Photosynthetic temperature acclimitization in a Californian perennial herb showed the same pattern, although the shift in optimum temperature range was much smaller for an alpine ecotype than for a coastal ecotype. The phenomenon of acclimatization poses yet another problem for the definition of cardinal temperatures, which are valid only for the temperature conditions under which they are measured. The degree to which plants can alter their cardinal temperatures in response to slow changes in environmental temperatures will vary greatly between species.

Because the rate of metabolic processes increases with temperature, there is a reasonably good correlation between the growth of experimental plants and the *heat sum* expressed as daily degree hours [the daily sum of: temperature (in degrees Celsius) × number of daylight hours at that temperature]. The heat sum is a measure of the amount of heat to which the plants are exposed, and different species exhibit optimum growth at different daily heat sums (Figure 8.11).

Rate of growth is strongly influenced by temperature, and because plants must complete a certain minimum amount of growth before they can flower, the poleward and upper altitudinal distribution of plants corresponds to some extent to the geographical distribution of annual heat sums. Many attempts have been made to correlate these two parameters, with variable success. Heat sums have been calculated in many ways (Wang, 1960), but the commonly used measure of annual heat sums is *degree days:* the annual or growing season sum of the daily difference between mean daily air temperature and some threshold temperature. For example, the heat sum required for flowering of grain crops in Ohio is 600–1050 degree days, using 6°C as a threshold (Clarke, 1967). This heat sum is accumulated earlier in a hot summer than in a cold summer, contributing to variation in date of flowering.

The use of heat sums to predict plant distribution has been criticized because it ignores the complications of thermoperiodism, the variation in cardinal temperatures as the plant matures, differences between species and between ecotypes, the variation in the day length during which high temperatures occur, and because growth and distribution are also influenced by other environmental factors. Generally, the heat relationships of plants are too complex to permit simple correlations with geographical distribution, but in spite of these criticisms, northern tree lines do show a good

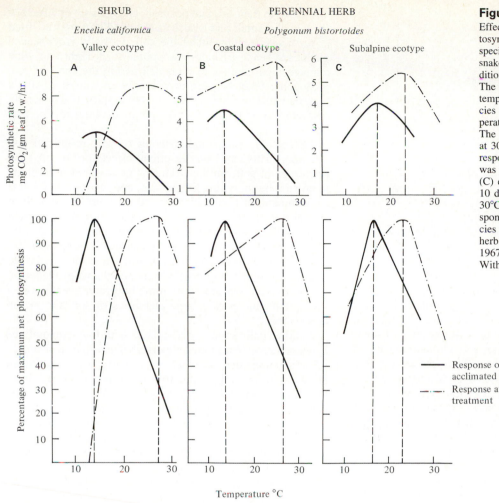

SHRUB

Encelia californica

Valley ecotype

PERENNIAL HERB

Polygonum bistortoides

Coastal ecotype   Subalpine ecotype

Figure 8.10

Effect of varying temperature on the photosynthetic rate of two California plant species, Encelia *(Encelia californica)* and snake weed *(Polygonum bistortoides)*, conditioned to low and high temperatures. (A) The photosynthetic response to various temperatures was tested on the shrub species after exposure to 12 days of low temperatures (15°C daytime, 2°C nighttime). The plants were then exposed to 23 hours at 30°C and the photosynthetic-temperature response redetermined. The experiment was repeated for coastal (B) and subalpine (C) ecotypes of the perennial herb, with 10 days cold treatment and 25 hours at 30°C. Differences in photosynthetic response are apparent between the two species and between the two ecotypes of the herb. (After Mooney and Shropshire, 1967. Reproduced from *Oecol. Plant.* With permission.)

— Response of cold-acclimated plants

—·—·— Response after heat treatment

Temperature °C

correlation with temperature. North of the line, the warmest summer month generally has a mean temperature of less than 10°C, while south of the tree line the value is higher (Mikola, 1962). Vegetative growth usually requires lower temperatures than reproductive growth, and the tree line may reflect a failure to reproduce rather than a failure to grow.

B. Temperature-Related Injuries

Two aspects of temperature are responsible for most of the temperature-related injuries to plants: rapid change in temperature and the occurrence of unseasonal temperatures. Unusually hot summers and unusually cold winters can certainly produce pathological symptoms in plants, but low growing-season and high winter temperatures are generally much more damaging, particularly if accompanied by rapid temperature changes. If dormant woody plants are cooled slowly, they can survive temperatures far below those attained even in polar regions (Weiser, 1970), reflecting the ability of plants to change their cardinal temperatures to some extent by acclimatization. In addition to the general effects of temperature extremes discussed in the preceding section, plants exhibit the following responses.

1. Low-Temperature Injury. Frost damage to plant tissues as the result of seasonally low temperatures is uncommon. The delicate leaves, flowers, and stems of deciduous and annual plants are generally shed before low temperatures occur, and the leaves of dormant evergreens are very resistant to low-temperature damage. In contrast, unseasonably low temperatures can be very damaging, even if they

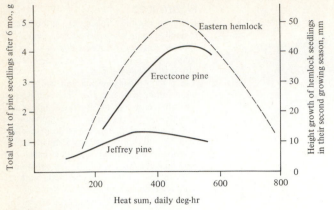

Figure 8.11
Seedling growth of three tree species at various different daily heat sums. (After Hellmers, 1962. Copyright Ronald Press. Redrawn with permission of John Wiley & Sons, Inc. and H. Hellmers.)

are not actually very low. Unseasonal frost can kill flowers, which are the most frost-sensitive parts of a plant. Freezing of leaves during the growing season can lead to disorganization, wilting, water loss, and death, while freezing of stems can result in the death of patches of the cambium which develop into lesions and permit the entry of pathogens. Efficient emission of radiation and low conductivity lead to rapid surface cooling of woody stems on clear nights with low air temperatures. The outer layers of the stem contract more rapidly than the inner layers, which creates tensions that can cause the stem to crack. These *frost cracks* are particularly common in regions subject to sudden drops in air temperature, such as the west coast of north America. The normally mild winter air masses on the coast are periodically replaced by polar air masses spilling over the coast mountains, producing dramatic drops in temperature (Figure 8.12). As the temperature in the stem again becomes uniform, the cracks close and heal over, but they remain permanent points of weakness. The differential stem shrinkage that causes frost cracks can also cause bark to separate from the stem.

An indirect form of low-temperature damage that is of both ecological and practical interest results from rapid alternate freezing and thawing of the soil. Rapid radiation cooling results in the freezing of soils from the surface downward. Water is drawn up to the frozen layer, where it freezes and forms a gradually thickening layer of vertically oriented ice crystals (*needle ice*). The frozen surface soil together with small plants can be lifted as much as a decimeter by this needle ice, and then lowered again as the ice melts. Roots pulled up from lower unfrozen soil layers can-

not return to their original position, and over several freeze–thaw cycles small plants such as tree seedlings may be lifted (*frost-heaved*) right out of the soil. Partially frost-heaved plants are rendered more susceptible to drought and wind damage, and damage to roots can permit the entry of root pathogens. Frost heaving occurs only on soils that have a high moisture content and which cool rapidly: it is generally restricted to exposed mineral soils of medium to fine texture.

Alternate freezing and thawing of soil results in *soil churning*. This can have beneficial effects on the physical properties of soil, but may render fine-textured soils prone to erosion by loosening the surface, and in arctic and alpine environments it may inhibit growth of most or even all of the vegetation. In severe cases, rocks and stones are brought to the surface and arranged in various patterns (stripes or polygons). On steep slopes it can cause soil creep (*solifluction*), in which wavelike lines of soil are gradually moved downslope by the alternate freezing and thawing. Plants are tipped over, roots are torn from the ground, and over a geological time period large quantities of soil are moved downslope.

Another indirect injury associated with low temperatures is water stress. Warm air temperatures in winter (especially when accompanied by wind) or an early, warm spring in areas where the soil is still frozen can remove water from plants at a time when it cannot be replaced. Even if the water is not frozen, winter water stress can occur because of the doubling of the viscosity of water between 25 and 0°C. Plants growing on soils that are cold or frozen in winter often exhibit the same morphological adaptations as plants growing on summer-dry sites. The water imbalance caused by high air temperatures and low soil temperatures is referred to as *physiological drought*. When severe, it can

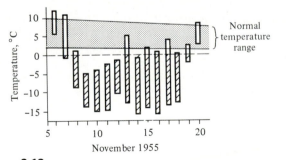

Figure 8.12
Effect of the invasion of a polar air mass into a coastal region on the diurnal temperature range. Data are for Centralia, Washington. Plain bar indicates above-freezing, striped bar below-freezing, temperatures. (After Daubenmire, 1974. Redrawn with permission of John Wiley & Sons, Inc. and R. F. Daubenmire.)

cause browning of the foliage (e.g., the redbelt damage in the mountains of western North America) and even the death of the entire plant.

By killing buds or new terminal twigs, early frost in the autumn can alter the shape of a plant. Stems become crooked or have multiple leaders, and may become bushy. In extreme cases the plant may be killed back to ground level each year and never gain the size and shape that it would have in a less frosty environment. Plants damaged by frost or subjected to a prolonged period below their optimum temperature range are frequently more susceptible to damage by insects and diseases.

2. High-Temperature Injury. The most common deleterious effects of high temperatures are the excessive loss of moisture and the stimulation of excessive respiration rates. *Sun scald,* mentioned in Chapter 7, results from the rapid heating and cooling of stems during the winter dormant period, but this is more a function of rate of temperature change than of high temperatures per se. High temperatures are responsible for *stem girdle* in seedlings. Because of the low albedo and low conductivity of many soils, surface temperatures frequently become very high, and young plant stems not yet protected by thick layers of bark may be damaged where they contact the soil surface. A band of cambium a few millimeters wide is killed around the stem, and this results in the death of the plant either because of the interruption of internal translocation or because of the entry of pathogens.

C. Adaptations of Plants to Unfavorable Temperatures

In common with other organisms, plants have adapted to the temperature factor both morphologically and physiologically.

1. Morphological Adaptations. Morphological adaptations to high temperatures include leaf shape, size, and orientation. Long, thin leaves are oriented to maximize mutual shading (e.g., pines) or minimize sunlight interception during midday heat (e.g., *Eucalyptus*). Cuticles are thick, scaly, or hairy, to increase albedo and reduce transmittance, and protective pigments further reduce the heat balance of foliage. Rapid evaporation of water from leaves cools them, but this is a luxury that many plants in hot environments cannot rely on. In fact, an important adaptation to high-temperature environments is a leaf morphology that reduces evaporation. Adaptation to physiological drought associated with low temperatures also involves leaf morphologies that regulate water loss.

Many trees have morphological adaptations to enable them or their progeny to survive brief exposure to high temperatures in forest fires. The thick bark of redwoods and many species of pine confers a high degree of resistance to surface fires. Some trees have the power to resprout if crowns are burned off, such as the epicormic sprouting of redwoods and the production of new foliage by seedlings of long leaf pine *(Pinus palustris)* following a fire. Many species of pine have *serotinous* cones in which the scales are held closed by resin and will only open to release the seed after exposure to high temperatures. Such temperatures occur during a forest fire or when the cones are lying on hot ground in midsummer following removal of the tree cover by wind, insects, disease, or logging. The occurrence of serotiny appears to be related to the incidence of forest fires (Ledig and Fryer, 1971).

Adaptation to low temperature includes the formation of a morphologically (and physiologically) different stage, such as a seed or spore, that either resists low temperature or finds its way to a more sheltered location (e.g., the soil), or the development of different overwintering forms *(life forms)* of the permanent plant. Morphological adaptation to low temperature is so common that it is the basis for a plant classification scheme developed by the Danish botanist Raunkiaer (1934). The classification is based on the vertical location, and hence the degree of protection, of the dormant buds during the period of dormancy. Some of the major categories of the classification are shown in Figure 8.13.

The relative abundance of the different life forms (the *life form spectrum*) varies in environments that differ in their temperature characteristics (Table 8.4). *Phanerophytes* dominate tropical environments where there is little or no need to protect the dormant bud from extreme temperatures. Temperate, moist climates are dominated by *hemicryptophytes,* whereas tundra environments are dominated by *chamaephytes* and *hemicryptophytes*. *Cryptophytes* are most common in temperate climates, and *therophytes* dominate the floras of desert regions, reflecting the severe temperature stress of this type of environment (Raunkiaer, 1934). The survival of chamaephytes in very cold environments may reflect the presence of insulating layers of snow and the increase in air temperature close to the ground. Although these life forms are adaptations to temperature, they are almost certainly adaptations to other factors as well, such as wind and water stress.

2. Physiological Adaptations. Physiological adaptations are largely related to the water aspect of the temperature factor. Winter freezing damage is avoided in seeds and spores by the elimination of virtually all free water, and dry seeds have been successfully germinated after 3 weeks of exposure to a temperature of $-190°C$ (Clarke, 1967). Alternatively, where water is retained in a plant, freezing can be

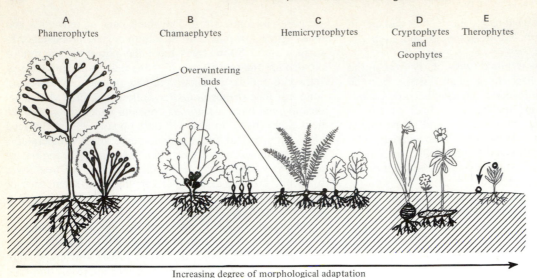

| A | B | C | D | E |
| Phanerophytes | Chamaephytes | Hemicryptophytes | Cryptophytes and Geophytes | Therophytes |

Increasing degree of morphological adaptation

Figure 8.13
The major life forms of plants according to Raunkiaer (1934). Lighter-colored parts are ephemeral; darker parts are perennial. (A) Trees and tall shrubs with dormant buds and shoot tips that project high into the air with little or no protection other than bud scales and sticky substances. (B) Low shrubs with dormant buds and shoot tips borne above but close to the ground. (C) Herbaceous plants with dormant buds and shoot tips at the soil surface or beneath an organic layer. (D) Tuberous and bulbous herbs with dormant buds buried at various depths in the soil. (E) Annuals with the embryonic bud protected by a seed coat; located on or in the soil surface during the dormant period.

avoided at moderately low temperatures by increasing the concentration of dissolved and colloidal substances. This enables metabolic processes to continue at reduced temperatures, but at very low temperatures freezing becomes inevitable and plants become *dormant* (a physiological condition in which plants become very resistant to damage by low temperatures). The damaging effect of both high and low temperatures rarely occurs in the absence of physiological activity, suggesting that such damage is associated with a derangement of active metabolic processes.

Physiological preparations for dormancy are primarily under the control of shortening photoperiods, and city plants maintained artificially on a long photoperiod because of illumination by street lights may have a long delay in the onset of dormancy. However, photoperiod does not have exclusive control of dormancy. Low temperatures, nutrient supply, soil moisture, and other factors can modify or even substitute for the photoperiod stimulus in some plants.

Dormancy can occur in several degrees of intensity. Before the onset of *true dormancy* there is a *predormancy*, which is marked by a cessation in growth and an increased resistance to low temperature (first stage of acclimation, Figure 8.14). This condition can be broken and growth resumed if there is a return to warmer temperatures and longer photoperiods prior to the development of *full dormancy* (second stage of acclimation), which occurs as photoperiods continue to shorten and temperatures drop. Full dormancy, which may be triggered by exposure to the first

Table 8.4 Variation in the Frequency of Five Life Forms in the Plant Communities of Various Environments (After Dansereau, 1957; Richards, 1952)

| Environment | Approximate Percent Occurrence of Each Life Form[a] | | | | |
	Phanerophyte	Chamaephyte	Hemicryptophyte	Cryptophyte	Therophyte
Wet tropical	92	7	0	1	0
Subtropical	62	13	9	3	12
Temperate	17	5	46	23	9
Hot desert	19	14	19	6	42
Arctic	0.5	22	60	15	2

[a]Mean of 2 or 3 locations.

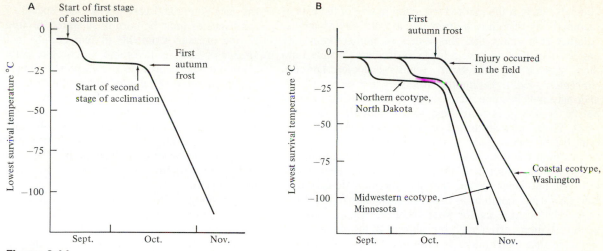

Figure 8.14

The development of cold resistance in the living bark of a hardy shrub, red-osier dogwood *(Cornus stolonifera),* in Minnesota. (A) Typical pattern. (B) Variation in the pattern among ecotypes from three different climates when grown together in Minnesota. Only the coastal ecotype suffered frost damage because the other two ecotypes had already passed through their first stage of acclimation by mid-October. (After Weiser, 1970. Copyright AAAS 1970. Redrawn with permission of AAAS and C. J. Weiser.)

frost, is marked by deciduous leaf-fall and a dramatic increase in cold resistance. A period of chilling is required before full dormancy can be broken and growth resumed. A temperature of 5°C is optimum and freezing is not required. In fact, temperatures below 0°C and above 10°C will not satisfy the requirement. The chilling must continue for a specific period, the length of which depends upon the species, but for most northern hemisphere plants the requirement is satisfied by the end of December. Trees transferred to the greenhouse at this time will break dormancy and resume growth, although expansion of new leaves and active growth normally requires a period of exposure to some critical higher temperature. Elm trees near Chicago require 310 hours at about 25°C prior to leaf break; temperatures above 30°C and below 10°C are ineffective. There are many minor deviations from this general pattern, but they are beyond the scope of this book (see Perry, 1971; Weiser, 1970). For an earlier review of cold resistance in plants, see Parker (1963).

The date of onset and termination of dormancy and the degree of acclimatization varies from species to species and between different ecotypes of a single species, as was the case for photoperiodicity.

The seeds and resting stages of some plants will only emerge from dormancy and resume activity after exposure to a high temperature. This may be an adaptation to keep them dormant in a deeply shaded location in which they would die for lack of light. When light conditions become favorable for survival, the accompanying high temperatures stimulate growth. It may also be an adaptation to fire (see Chapter 12).

8.5 Animal Adaptations to Temperature

A. Some General Relationships

At temperatures below their effective range, animals enter a cold coma and if not aroused within a certain period of time will eventually die. As body temperatures increase, activity rates increase up to a maximum, above which activity declines and the body enters a heat coma. The temperature of optimum activity and efficiency is closer to the maximum than to the minimum survival temperature (Figure 8.7). As with plants, the cardinal temperatures of animals vary between species, with age and physiological condition, with the duration of exposure, and according to the recent temperature experiences of the animal. Most poikilotherms are active between 6 and 35°C, but there are examples of activity well outside this range.

The relationship between animal morphology and environmental temperatures has attracted attention for a long time, and various general relationships or "rules" have been proposed. The *Allen rule* states that, in general, the extremities of homeotherms are smaller in cold than in hot climates, such as the marked reduction in size of the ears of mammals as one moves from hot to cold environments. Another rule states that the bodies of homeotherms are larger, stockier, and have a lower surface area/weight ratio than species of the same genus at lower latitudes (*Bergman's rule*). Yet another rule says that races of birds and mammals become increasingly darker in skin, fur, and pelage as one goes from high to low latitudes (*Golger's rule*). These rules are based on observed patterns of variation, but they have been criticized because of the existence of exceptions and because of the implication that temperature acts as a causal determinant in producing these variations. It has been argued that the variation described in Bergman's rule could be as much an adaptation to predator–prey relationships as for heat balance, which could be achieved more efficiently by improved insulation. It is probable that temperature is only one of several determinants involved in the variation.

B. Poikilotherms and Homeotherms

It has already been mentioned that animals exhibit two major responses to temperature: poikilothermy and homeothermy. The more limited case of heterothermy has also been mentioned.

Poikilotherms in aquatic environments generally show little deviation from the temperature of the water because of the efficiency of conduction in exchanging heat between the organism and water. Their temperatures are stable because there is little diurnal temperature variation in most aquatic environments. Marine tidal rock pools are an exception, becoming warm or even hot during day-time low tides, and dropping as much as 25°C with the first large wave of the incoming tide. Terrestrial poikilotherms behave differently; they normally experience a wide diurnal temperature fluctuation, and their body temperature can differ substantially from air temperature. An animal with a low skin albedo on a clear but cold day may attain a body temperature well above that of the air, just as a conifer needle may attain temperatures that permit active photosynthesis when the air temperature is far below freezing. The inefficiency of thermal energy loss by the processes of conduction and convection in dry air permits the existence of steep gradients of temperature between a terrestrial poikilotherm and its medium. This enables terrestrial poikilotherms to control their temperature somewhat. By regulating their radiation budget, they can control their heat load and consequently their temperature between unexpectedly narrow limits.

Homeotherms are able to maintain remarkably constant temperatures over wide limits of environmental temperature. This ability varies with age and is poorly developed in the very young and very old of many species. The young of such species must be born in sheltered environments and at a time of year when the air temperature in their burrow, shelter or nest, is favorable. Arctic homeotherms such as seals and whales provide an exception to this rule since their young are born well equipped to regulate their internal temperatures. The degree of homeothermy may vary through the life of an animal; birds are essentially poikilothermous until they develop feathers, when they become homeothermous (Allee et al., 1967). Homeotherms have to pay a high energy bill to maintain a steep gradient between their bodies and their environment, and some animals permit their internal temperatures to drop at certain times to improve their energy budget. Winter-hibernating mammals permit their internal temperatures to vary seasonally as an adaptation to low temperatures and low availability of food, and hummingbirds permit their temperature to drop at night as an adaptation to conserve energy in the face of their high metabolic rate. Sometimes the distinction between homeotherms and poikilotherms becomes a little fuzzy, as in the case of honeybees which are able to regulate the temperature of their hive between fairly narrow limits by varying their behavior pattern.

C. Adaptations of Animals to Temperature Conditions

Adaptations by animals to temperature extremes may involve attempts to regulate their heat balance, and therefore their temperature, by varying conduction, convection, radiation, and evaporative cooling. Alternatively, the tolerance of the animals may be changed by alteration of their cardinal temperatures.

Methods of regulating heat balance vary depending on the relative importance of the different pathways of heat loss. In insects such as cockroaches, 80% of the total heat energy loss is by convection and 20% is by radiation. Almost none is lost by evaporation of water because, in common with many other organisms, cockroaches have evolved very efficient methods of water conservation. The python and the tortoise, which inhabit hot, dry environments, only lose 0.1–0.3% of their body weight per day in evaporated water: cockroaches lose about 4%. In contrast, woodlice, which live in humid microenvironments and will die if left for several days in a dry environment, lose 14%. Salamanders lose 95% of their body weight of water per day if placed in a dry environment and are completely intolerant of dry microclimates. Evaporative cooling could potentially be important to woodlice and salamanders, but since they confine themselves to humid microenvironments, water loss is not a significant mechanism of heat loss (Gates, 1962).

Birds lose most of their excess heat by radiation because their feathers greatly reduce conductive and convective losses. Birds that have access to ample water supplies may use evaporative cooling by panting and what is called *gullar flutter* (rapid flapping of the floor of the mouth). This is absent in birds from hot, dry regions. In general, birds tend to conserve water.

Sheep lose 48% of their heat by radiation, 38% by convection, and 14% by conduction. By comparison, a naked human loses 47% of his or her energy by radiation and 53% by convection: in a fully clothed human the figures are 55 and 45%, respectively (Gates, 1962).

Adaptation to low temperatures is necessary because most animals are injured or killed if their tissues freeze or if their internal temperature drops below their lower effective or survival temperature for a critical period. Mortality may be a consequence of physiological or morphological damage, or may result from increased susceptibility to disease or natural enemies. Adaptation to high temperatures is necessary to avoid death following heat coma, derangement of physiological processes, excessive loss of moisture, or physiological exhaustion due to hyperactivity. Many animal adaptations parallel those of plants since the biochemical systems of plants and animals have many similarities, reflecting their common biogeochemical origin.

Animal adaptations can be classified as physiological, morphological, or behavioral, although many adaptations fall into more than one of these categories.

1. Physiological Adaptations. The adverse effects of temperature extremes on physiological processes and on the availability of food and water are avoided in many animals by undergoing a period of reduced physiological activity. This results in an alteration in their cardinal temperatures. Many poikilotherms undergo a period of winter rest that involves a variety of physiological as well as behavioral and morphological changes. Such a rest period in insects is called a *diapause*.

As with dormancy in plants, diapause is initiated by decreasing photoperiods and temperature, and termination of diapause has a chilling requirement. Diapause can be affected by photoperiod, moisture, the level of nutrition prior to diapause, and other factors. The requirements for termination of diapause may sometimes be satisfied by midwinter, but activity is not resumed until temperatures increase in the spring. Insects may also have a period of physiological rest in response to stressfully high temperatures. This is known as summer *(aestival)* diapause, and is also initiated by temperature and/or photoperiodic stimuli. Many aestivating animals do not require any specific stimulus (as they do in winter diapause) for the resumption of normal activity, which occurs as soon as the temperature returns to a favorable level. Dormancy in insects can be found in the egg, larval, pupal, and adult life stages.

While in diapause, insects are highly resistant to cold, and they can safely overwinter in environments subject to very low temperatures. Many other poikilotherms are not resistant to freezing and seek out sheltered habitats for their winter dormancy. Many amphibians and aquatic animals bury themselves in the mud on a lake bottom or seek the deeper waters that do not freeze. Snakes retreat into deep rock crevices or caves, frequently with large numbers occupying the same shelter. Some poikilotherms bury themselves deep in the soil. All these environments are characterized by rather stable temperatures above freezing.

Many homeotherms that live in environments with low winter temperatures are able to continue normal physiological activities by means of behavioral and morphological adaptations. They may confine their activities to below the snow, as do the lemmings of the arctic, or develop better insulation as polar bears or arctic foxes do. However, where these adaptations are inadequate, increased metabolism may be employed as a means of creating metabolic heat to compensate for increased losses to the environment. Figure 8.15 shows how the metabolic rate increases with decreasing temperature in homeotherms from three different temperature environments. This physiological adaptation is most pronounced in the tropical homeotherm that has no morphological adaptation to deal with low temperatures. The eskimo dog is so well insulated that it employs this physiological adaptation only at very low temperatures.

There is a high metabolic price to be paid for sustained activity during a period when food and water may be scarce, and some animals that are normally homeothermic during the active season avoid this metabolic cost by permitting their body temperature to drop during a period of winter dormancy, or at other times. These animals are the *heterotherms* and their winter dormancy is called *hibernation*. It is a highly variable phenomenon which may be initiated by shortening photoperiods, decreasing temperatures, or shortage of food and water. It may be *permissive,* in which case hibernation is an optional, but not obligatory response to unexpected stress. It may be *seasonal,* in which body temperatures drop in a regular seasonal rhythm under internal control even in a constant temperature environment. No stress is required and the adaptation is initiated before the period of stress. Alternatively, hibernation may be *obligate,* as when it is triggered by stress such as low temperature or reduced food supply. Some carnivores, such as bears, badgers, and raccoons, do not go into a true hibernation. They merely experience a period of winter lethargy when their

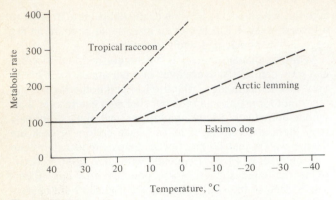

Figure 8.15
Increase in the metabolic rate of homeotherms from warm, cold, and very cold environments in response to decreasing environmental temperatures. Metabolic control of internal temperatures is least important for the well-insulated dog and most important for the tropical raccoon, which is not morphologically adapted to maintain internal temperatures in a cold environment. (After Irving, 1964. Copyright American Physiological Society, Washington D.C. Reproduced with permission.)

body temperature drops 4–5°C, and their metabolic rate falls by 40–50%. The hearts of these animals cease to function at a body temperature of 17–21°C, whereas the hearts of some true hibernators continue to beat at tempeatures of 0°C or even slightly below.

Heterotherms seek out sheltered habitats for their hibernation, and hibernation is less common in environments in which animals cannot find shelter from very low temperatures. Some of them allow their body temperature to drop to within a few degrees of the surrounding air temperature, but most are aroused as their bodies approach 0°C, so they can only hibernate in microenvironments that remain above or close to freezing. Hedgehogs can hibernate in air as cold as −5°C, maintaining a body temperature 2–5°C, but the optimum air temperature for their hibernation is 4°C. In contrast, arctic marmots can hibernate at air temperatures as low as −48°C with peripheral body temperatures as low as −5°C. Termination of hibernation normally occurs as temperatures increase. Hedgehogs wake up after 4–5 hours of exposure to 12°C, arctic marmots at temperatures above 14°C, while the Mohave ground squirrel can remain dormant even at 27°C (Folk, 1974), this high value corresponding to the higher-temperature regime of its environment.

Insect diapause and heterotherm hibernation are accompanied by reduced metabolism and energy utilization. They are not only adaptive characteristics in terms of surviving low temperatures; they also effect a considerable savings in an animal's energy budget. Small homeotherms, such as mice, bats, and hummingbirds, which have very high metabolic rates during the day (or night for nocturnal animals) would suffer substantial losses of energy if they sustained this rate during their period of rest. This is avoided by becoming heterothermic, permitting the body temperature to drop and entering a condition of torpor during the nonactive hours. Some birds undergo a similar torpor during the coldest parts of the year.

A second major type of physiological adaptation involves avoidance of freezing by lowering the freezing point of cellular fluids. Very few animals can survive actual freezing, but by lowering the freezing point of the body, many poikilotherms can survive very low temperatures. Reducing the water content and increasing the fat content of the body, increasing the concentrations of organic and inorganic materials dissolved in cellular fluids, and the formation of colloids can lower the freezing point of insects by as much as 50°C (Allee et al., 1967). An alternative to this antifreeze strategy is the elimination of all free water, such as in the eggs, spores, or resting stages of some poikilotherms. Once in a waterless condition, temperatures approaching absolute zero (−237°C) can be tolerated.

A third type of physiological adaptation involves different cardinal temperatures for different parts of an animal. With an air temperature of −16°C, the foot of a seagull may approach 0°C, while the upper leg is at 38°C. An eskimo dog may have a central body temperature of over 37°C while the air temperature is −30°C, its snout is at 5°C, and its foot pad is at 0°C (Figure 8.16). Heat loss from the body is greatly reduced by tolerating reduced temperatures in those parts of the body from which heat could be lost most easily.

2. Morphological Adaptations. These are largely concerned with regulating radiation, convection, and conduction. The development of fur, feathers, or thick layers of fat (blubber) beneath the skin acts to lower heat loss from the surface by reducing surface temperatures, while the layer of low conductivity air trapped beneath fur and feathers greatly reduces conduction of body heat to the surface. Variation in the thickness of fur and in total insulation reflects the winter temperature environment of the animal and the degree of reliance on subcutaneous fat deposits and metabolic heat to regulate internal temperatures. The reduction in the size and projection of extremities beyond the body and fur in high-latitude animals (Allen's rule) lowers the surface area over which heat loss can occur, and in addition to insulation many animals living in cold (or rapid heat loss) environments have a heat-exchange mechanism that reduces the flow of heat from the center of the body to the skin or cold extremities. Arteries carrying warm blood from the central body area are in close contact with, or are surrounded by an

Figure 8.16

Temperature variation between the body and the extremities in two homeotherms living in cold environments. The temperatures at various points from the body to the extremities are shown. (After Irving, 1964. Copyright American Physiological Society, Washington, D.C. Reproduced with permission.)

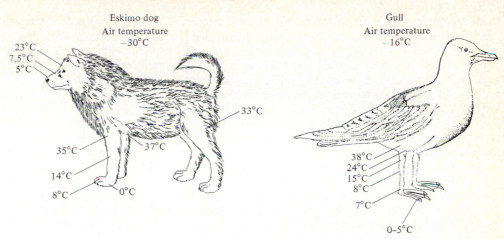

Eskimo dog
Air temperature
−30°C

23°C
7.5°C
5°C
33°C
35°C
37°C
14°C
8°C
0°C

Gull
Air temperature
−16°C

38°C
24°C
15°C
8°C
7°C
0–5°C

intertwining network of veins carrying cold blood back from the extremities. Much of the heat in the arterial blood is transferred by conduction and convection to the cold venous blood, which is thus warmed and carries heat back to the heart. Many animals also have the ability to constrict the flow of blood to the skin or extremities. Vascular constrictor muscles divert much of the warm arterial blood directly into veins, thus reducing heat loss. Heat loss from extremities in contact with cold surfaces is also reduced by having a horny, scaly, or fatty pad with low thermal conductivity, very low freezing point, and little or no blood or living cells. This is a common adaptation in animals, although other adaptations can be found. Wolverines have pads on their feet which have high thermal conductivity and which aid in the dissipation of excess heat in summer. Hair grows to cover these pads in the winter and the feet can be in contact with snow at −55°C with little temperature loss.

Morphological adaptations to promote heat loss in the summer are numerous. Shedding of heavy winter fur and reduction of fat layers under the skin promote summer heat loss. Male deer and other male cervid ungulates develop antlers in the summer that serve as heat-exchange organs. The developing antler is covered by a furry skin (velvet) that is rich in arteries and veins, promoting convection and radiant losses of heat. As temperatures drop in the late summer, the blood supply to the velvet is cut off, the velvet dries up, and it is removed when the animal rubs its antlers against vegetation. After the mating season in the fall, the antlers are knocked off, only to regrow the following spring. The antlers are used in sexually oriented aggressive activities in the fall, but it is thought that heat regulation is one of their primary functions. The fact that the females do not grow antlers may explain their preference for the shade.

Animals in hot environments tend to have longer extremities and thinner fur than those in cold environments. Many desert animals have long legs to raise their bodies off the hot surface and above the surface few millimeters of hot air. The ears of elephants provide this bulky animal with a large surface area for heat exchange. The ears are continually flapped like fans to keep the air in contact with the body in motion, thus promoting convection heat loss. This source of heat loss is of vital importance; if an elephant is immobilized in the hot tropical environment and unable to maintain the flow of air over its body, it will soon enter heat coma and will eventually die.

Some animals have morphological skin adaptations that promote heat loss by evaporative cooling. Man has specialized skin glands that emit water (sweat) when increased heat loss is required. The high latent heat of vaporization provides an effective cooling mechanism as this surface water evaporates.

3. Behavioral Adaptations. Most organisms augment their morphological and physiological adaptations with behavioral adaptations that promote either heat conservation or heat loss. It has been noted that poikilotherms do not regulate their temperatures internally and will tend to equilibrate with the temperature of their environment. However, studies have revealed that many poikilotherms are able to maintain their body temperatures within fairly close limits in spite of fluctuating environmental temperatures. Lizards, insects, and snakes shelter overnight in environments that remain warmer than in the open. In the morning they move to the warmest location, if possible in full sunlight. Once they have reached "operational" temperature they go about their daily activities, distributing their time between sunny and shaded locations, and orienting their bodies to the sun in order to maintain almost constant optimum body temperature (Bogert, 1959). If they get too hot, they move to aquatic, deeply shaded or windy locations where they can reestablish an optimum body temperature. Such short distance or local movements undertaken to regulate body temperature are referred to as *thermal migrations* (hibernation involves thermal migration to local environments that have a favorable temperature regime for this physiological adaptation). Where vegetation is used to help regulate the internal thermal regime of animals, it is referred to as *thermal cover*. Maintenance of appropriate thermal cover, both for shelter from winter cold and from summer heat, is an important component of wildlife habitat management. Where thermal migrations are inadequate to regulate daytime body temperatures in very hot environments, organisms may become nocturnal or restrict their activity to dawn and dusk.

Many organisms that live in environments subject to temperature extremes avoid the associated problems by undertaking long-distance migration to more equitable climates. Most birds that breed in the Arctic fly south for the winter to avoid low temperatures and the accompanying lack of food and water. In large, well-insulated birds such as geese, the migration away from the poles may not involve long distances, but smaller birds such as swallows and hummingbirds, which are dependent on airborne insects and flowers for food, may follow the summer from one hemisphere to the other. Annual migrations of as much as 25,000 miles are made by shorebirds utilizing the arctic and South America, while the arctic tern holds the long-distance commuter record with a yearly round trip of 35,000 miles (Wetty, 1963).

Most of the long migrations are made by birds, but it is not an exclusively avian adaptation. The monarch butterfly makes an annual migration from its winter location at Pacific Grove, California, to Alaska and back. The barren ground caribou of northern Canada migrate south from their summer range in the arctic tundra to their winter range in the northern spruce forests, where they find some shelter from the arctic weather, and food in the form of lichens and mosses (Kelsall, 1968). Many animals also make altitudinal migrations, moving down the mountains into valleys in the winter to avoid deep snow, low temperatures, and lack of food. All these migrations are regular seasonal events in response to temperature or temprature-related variations in the availability of food energy. Other long-distance migrations occur that are not directly related to a temperature factor. Many species of *anadromous* fish migrate from their spawning and rearing grounds in freshwater lakes and rivers to distance oceans, where they feed and mature, returning to the same stream to spawn several years later. Such migra-

tions are probably the result of a complex of factors, many of which are not yet completely understood.

A combined behavioral–physiological adaptation to high temperature that is found in many animals is panting combined with salivation. This induces evaporation of water from the mouth and lungs resulting in cooling. In some animals, these air movements are restricted to the mouth and throat (e.g., gullar fluttering in desert birds) to reduce water loss or to avoid undesirable changes in blood chemistry that can result from excessive ventilation of the lungs (Ricklefs, 1973).

8.6   Role of Temperature in Limiting the Distribution of Organisms

If a population of animals is placed in an experimental environment varying in temperature, they will tend to gather in that part of the environment which most closely matches their temperature adaptations. Similarly, if plant seed is sown throughout the experimental environment, the resulting plants will grow best in the temperature regime that matches that of their native environment most closely. Temperature exerts a powerful influence in determining the geographical distribution of organisms. Although natural selection and acclimatization can change the temperature relations of a population, there is a limit to the genetic and phenotypic adaptability of any population. Competition from species that are adapted to different temperature regimes also acts as a powerful deterrent to major changes in the temperature adaptations of a species which is therefore largely restricted, under undisturbed conditions, to those areas that provide optimum temperature conditions for that species. Temperature conditions can limit the distribution of populations in several ways.

A. Polar and Upper Altitudinal Limits

1. Low Winter Temperatures. These can derange metabolism, freeze tissues, reduce the availability of food and water, or cause mechanical injury. The direct effects of low winter temperatures on organisms can determine the upper altitudinal and poleward extension of species, but they are frequently less important than indirect effects such as soil churning, frost heaving, and solifluction, which are the result of fluctuating temperatures. Unseasonable low temperatures in early fall or late spring frosts may also be more important than low winter temperatures, because they can determine the limit of species by restricting flowering and/or by killing seedlings.

Low-temperature limitation results in an approximately east–west poleward limit to a species distribution, which bends north along the coast (effect of the ocean) and south in the interior (cold, continental winter). The poleward distribution of migratory animals varies during the year, moving poleward in the summer and toward the equator in the winter.

2. Insufficient Summer Warmth for Growth and Reproduction. Where summers are short and/or cool, insufficient gross photosynthesis may occur to balance the respiration and litterfall of plants, eliminating net growth. Long-term occupation of an area is obviously impossible under these conditions. Even greater quantities of summer warmth (greater heat sum) are necessary to produce viable seeds. The upper altitudinal and poleward limits of a species range are often set more by the temperature requirement for reproduction than for growth alone. Animals similarly require a minimum period above some critical initial temperature if young are to develop successfully, with poikilotherms being more sensitive than homeotherms. However, the warmer microclimate near the ground, the sheltered microclimate of a nest or den, and homeothermy make animals generally less sensitive to low heat sums than are plants.

If lack of summer warmth were the factor controlling distributions, it would also produce an overall east–west poleward limit, but unlike the distribution determined by low winter temperature, it would bend south on the coast and north in the interior. The reduced vigor and slower development of organisms near these limits render the organisms increasingly susceptible to diseases and exploitation by natural enemies.

B. Lower Latitudinal or Altitudinal Limits

1. High Summer Temperatures. These result in the derangement of metabolic processes, heat mortality, excessive loss of water, high respiration rate, and a reduction in the availability of food and water. Plants that have a favorable photosynthesis/respiration balance may be restricted from moving to lower elevations or latitudes because the increase in nocturnal respiration is greater than the increase in daytime photosynthesis. These factors result in an east–west lower altitudinal boundary to species' distributions which bends south on the coast and north in the interior of continents.

2. The Lack of a Winter Chilling Period. Inadequate duration or intensity of winter chilling will limit the lower latitudinal or altitudinal range of species that require chilling to break dormancy or stimulate flowering. Insects and plants of the temperate region will not spread into subtropical regions because of the lack of chilling. It is well known

that apples cannot be grown in fruit-growing areas at lower latitudes for this reason.

Different species of plants and animals vary as to which temperature factor limits distribution. Some are limited poleward by low winter temperatures. Others are limited by inadequate summer heat. This variation results in a complex overlapping pattern of the ranges of different species. It also results in spatial variations in the overall character of the vegetation that are repeated all over the world wherever similar temperature conditions occur. Traveling from the equator to the poles over the continents, one passes along a temperature gradient which results in bands of major vegetation types running roughly east–west across the continents. A similar temperature gradient and pattern of vegetation can also be found with increased elevation near the equator. The evergreen tropical rain forest found at the equator at sea level is replaced by semideciduous and deciduous hardwood forest toward the poles or at higher elevation (Figure 8.17). This in turn gives way to dry forest, grassland, and, in some areas, desert. Further poleward or higher up this is replaced by deciduous forest, which gives way eventually to evergreen conifer forest. At very high latitudes and tropical altitudes, conifer forest is displaced by tundra vegetation, which continues until bare rock or permanent ice is reached. In South America, the alpine tundra is called *paramo*. The dry desert or grassland vegetation may be absent from this sequence if the interaction of temperature, moisture, fire, and herbivory permit continuous tree growth.

The characteristic bands of vegetation and associated animal and microbial communities that occur along altitudinal and latitudinal temperature gradients are called *biomes,* and the regions that they occupy are called *life zones:* areas in which mature or climax vegetation (see Chapter 15) is dominated by plants of a given life form. Tropical evergreen hardwood forest, grassland, or conifer forest are three examples of biomes. The overall east–west alignment of biomes is greatly modified by mountains, lakes, oceans, and regional atmospheric circulation patterns, all of which modify temperature gradients. The distribution of biomes is further modified by local variations in moisture, fire, soils, and animals, and by human effects on the distribution of plants and animals. Biomes are shifted toward the equator as one goes up in elevation, and reach higher elevations on southern aspects than on northern aspects.

The consistent patterns of biomes around the world gave rise to Hopkins' *bioclimatic rule,* which says that biological events in the spring are delayed 3–4 days for each higher degree of latitude, and for each 100–130 m increase in alti-

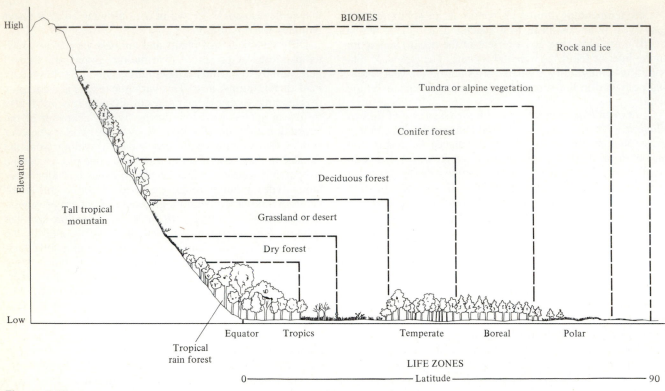

Figure 8.17
Latitudinal and altitudinal patterns of vegetation that reflect gradients of temperature and moisture. The exact vegetation patterns shown in the diagram rarely occur along a straight line from the equator to the poles, nor do they always occur as shown from sea level to mountaintop, but the general sequence can be observed in many parts of the world.

tude. The situation is reversed at the end of the summer. Hopkins (1920) also claimed that there was a seasonal retardation of 4 days for each 5° longitude from west to east in the U.S. It is generally felt that although some species may conform to the bioclimatic rule, the complex determination of most ecological events means that the rule will not apply to all circumstances.

Because of variations in temperature adaptations, species vary in their geographical ranges. Species appear and disappear rather irregularly along the gradient from the equator to the poles, or from low to high elevation, and this often results in very indistinct boundaries between different biomes or community types within a biome. This is not always the case, and groups of species sometimes replace each other rather completely over relatively short distances (see Chapter 14). Where this occurs there will be a rather sharp boundary between life zones, and many species may have the same limit to their distribution. Sometimes this

may coincide with a physical discontinuity in the environment, such as a change in soil, but it is frequently related to a biologically critical point in a continuous temperature gradient. The plant community of a frosty valley floor is often markedly different from that of the thermal zone on the valley slope, and as one travels poleward from the equator the point at which winter frost first occurs is marked by the sudden loss of many frost-sensitive species. Perhaps the best defined interface between life zones is that between conifer forest and either alpine or arctic tree lines. The environmental determination of tree lines is extremely complex, as we shall see in Chapter 14, but temperature plays an important role through its influence on snow depth, soil churning, solifluction, permafrost, flowering and seed production, seed germination, and seedling survival.

The role of temperature in the distribution of plants and animals has attracted a lot of attention and deserves a fuller treatment than is possible here. The interested reader is recommended to the extensive treatment of temperature and life in Precht et al. (1973). We will encounter the temperature factor again in subsequent chapters because of its important interaction with several other parameters of the physical environment.

8.7 Importance of the Temperature Factor in Forestry

Approximately 10% of the world's surface and 33% of the land surface is covered with forest, woodland, and shrubland (Whittaker, 1975a).Closed forest accounts for about 20% of the land surface (Council on Environmental Quality, 1981). Of the forest area, approximately half is tropical forest growing in environments where temperatures are relatively unvarying and generally not extreme. The other half is characterized by temperatures that limit biological activity and may pose problems for the forest manager at some time of the year. Much of the world's timber is grown and harvested in environments where either macroclimatic or microclimatic temperatures can influence forest land management in some manner.

Extreme temperatures and rapid changes in temperature can damage trees in many ways. Bud killing can result in multiple leaders. Stem girdling or patch killing of the cambium can either kill trees or create lesions that lead to infection by decay organisms. Rapid drops in temperature or very low temperatures can result in frost cracking of stems, which reduces timber values and can lead to invasion by decay organisms. This is frequently more severe on the most productive sites, where very fast-grown trees appear to be more susceptible than their slow-grown counterparts on drier, less productive sites.

Periods of warm weather during winter when soils are either dry or frozen can lead to damage to tree crowns because of moisture stress. Hot weather in the spring at the time of tree planting can result in heavy mortality of planted seedlings even if the soil is moist because the seedlings have not had time to produce enough new roots to compensate for the damage done to their roots during transfer from the nursery and planting. Fall (autumn) planting may avoid this problem. Soils remain warm in the fall much longer than the atmosphere, which permits continued root growth so that the trees are equipped to deal with spring moisture stress when it occurs. However, soils are often drier in the fall than in the spring, and ''Indian summer'' weather in the fall can induce lethal moisture stress in planted seedlings. Except for the surface few centimeters, soil temperatures in northern areas may remain low far into the growing season.

This limits root growth and makes regeneration after clearcutting very difficult. The seedlings develop shallow root systems, which makes them susceptible to spring and fall frost heaving if the forest floor is removed, and summer drying of the surface of the soil if the forest floor is left undisturbed.

Another temperature-related problem results from the variation in the temperature adaptations of different ecotypes. Winter hardening of seedlings is regulated by the combination of exposure to lower temperatures and decreasing photoperiod. Ecotypes from different regions have a different ''environmental calendar,'' and if moved to a new climatic region they may suffer frost damage because of inadequate hardening. Seedlings grown in nurseries at lower latitudes or altitudes may suffer frost damage when planted out at higher latitudes and altitudes if their temperature experiences in the nursery have not prepared them for the temperature conditions at the planting site.

Species vary greatly in their temperature adaptations. The planting of a single species over a wide range of sites, aspects, altitudes, and latitudes that vary greatly in temperature has naturally resulted in very variable regeneration success. A species that may regenerate satisfactorily in the cool microclimate of an open forest on a southerly slope may fail entirely in the hot microclimate of a large clearcut on the same site. A species that regenerates and grows well in a midslope position may fail or grow poorly on a frosty valley bottom or at higher elevations. The problem is not always directly related to a temperature effect. Douglas-fir in coastal British Columbia suffers serious leader damage in areas of heavy snowfall and freezing rain, whereas the same ecotype may grow well 200 m lower in elevation, where temperatures are only a few degrees warmer, but where most of the precipitation falls as rain.

Microclimate, especially the thermal regime of microenvironments, is often very important for forestry. Microsites that are only a few meters apart may differ greatly in temperature regimes according to aspect, slope, view factor, shading, soil moisture, and soil color. Frost pockets may preclude reforestation of microsites that are adjacent to areas only a couple of degrees warmer but in which regeneration is successful.

The factors responsible for the natural distribution of many tree species are still not completely understood, but temperature plays an important role. Adequate summer warmth for growth and reproduction, winter temperatures that satisfy chilling requirements, freedom from damage caused by temperature extremes or rapid rates of temperature change, soil temperatures, and the interaction between temperature and moisture are all important. In addition, temperature plays a major role in determining nutrient availability. Decomposition is much slower in cold than in warm environments, and fertilization experiments have demonstrated that the temperature related climatic limitation of tree growth in the north is as much the result of temperature-regulation of nutrient cycling as of more direct effects of temperature on plant physiology. Some of these temperature limitations on where trees can be grown can be modified by forest managers, but some cannot, and this places constraints on how forest ecosystems are managed.

Of all forest management activities, it is clearcutting that has the greatest effect on temperatue because of its alteration of the radiation-energy balance (Figure 8.18). Forests have a much lower albedo than clearcuts, so less total energy is absorbed by clearcut than by forested areas (R_n is lower). However, most of the absorbed radiation reaches the ground, and much more heat is conducted down into the soil in a clearcut (G is higher) than in the uncut forest. Because of the active transpiration by an uncut forest, much of the net radiation is lost as latent heat of evaporation (LE). LE has a low value in a clearcut, at least initially, and consequently more of the absorbed energy is available to raise the temperature of objects (M), which in turn warms the air, which then carries the heat away (sensible heat flow, H). Approximately 30% of the net radiation in a forest with adequate water supplies is dissipated as sensible heat. In contrast, the sensible heat flow from a dry, bare soil may be as much as 70% of the net radiation. Table 8.5 compares the

Table 8.5 Energy Balance Comparison Between an 18-Year-Old Douglas-fir Plantation and a Clearcut at Solar Noon on a Clear Day at the UBC Research Forest, Haney, B.C. (After McNaughton and Black, 1973; Black, 1977)

	Parameter	Energy Flux, W m^{-2}	
		Douglas-fir Stand	Clearcut (no vegetation regrowth)
R_n	Net radiation flux density	520	550
G	Soil heat flux density	32	40
LE	Latent heat flux density	301	70
H	Sensible heat flux density	183	440
M	Rate of heat storage in vegetation (on an area basis)	4	0

parameters of the energy-balance equation for a clearcut and an 18-year-old Douglas-fir plantation in coastal B.C.

Alteration of the radiation balance following clearcutting influences rates of snow melt in the spring, which can have a profound effect on the hydrological cycle, the availability of moisture in the summer, and the stream environment. Radiation frosts and cold air drainage can create frost pockets following clearcutting, which may lead to the total failure of plantations or significant damage to the trees.

The reduction in forest cover increases the view factor of seedlings in a clearcut. The further from the stand edge, the greater the exposure of the seedling to the sky (Figure

Figure 8.18

The radiant-energy balance of a forest. R_n = net radiation absorbed by the ecosystem; G = conduction of heat away through the soil; H = convective removal of heat by the atmosphere; LE = heat lost through evaporation of water in transpiration; M = increase in the heat contained in the ecosystem (i.e., its temperature).

$$R_n = G + H + LE + M$$

Incident radiation

Reflection and reradiation

Atmosphere

LE H

R_n

Forest/soil surface

M

Soil/ground

G

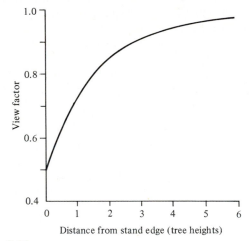

Figure 8.19

View factor (proportion of sky that is visible) at ground level in a large rectangular opening in a lodgepole pine forest as a function of distance from the stand edge. (After Cochran, 1969a. Reproduced with permission of P. H. Cochran.)

8.19). This in turn results in higher summer daytime temperatures and lower summer nighttime temperatures than in the adjacent forest (Figure 8.20), the degree of difference depending upon the size of the clearcut. Table 8.6 summarizes the effect of clearcut size on a number of meteorological parameters.

Slope, aspect, altitude, and latitude all affect the change in temperature conditions that accompany clearcutting. Similarly, the radiative and thermal properties of the soil surface are important. Surfaces such as a dark-colored organic forest floor, which has low thermal capacity, low thermal conductivity, and low albedo, develop very high daytime surface temperatures. Light-colored mineral surfaces that have high albedo, high thermal capacity, and high thermal conductivity do not develop high surface temperatures. The former type of surface can reach such high temperatures that seedling mortality occurs as a result of the death of stem tissues. The importance of this is seen in the variation in mortality of seedlings that, because of the angle at which they are planted, either shade their own stems at ground level or do not. A study 60 years ago reported that seedlings inclined to the south on southerly aspects (in the northern hemisphere) had a higher survival rate than seedlings inclined to the north (Table 8.7).

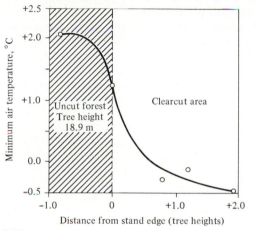

Figure 8.20
Average minimum air temperature 6.4 cm above the soil surface for 18 days in summer in a clearcut and an adjacent lodgepole pine stand. Radiation frost occurred in the clearcut but not in the uncut stand. (After Cochran, 1969a. Reproduced with permission of P. H. Cochran.)

Table 8.7 Summer Mortality of Engelmann and Norway Spruce Transplants in Their First Year in the Field due to Stem Girdling, as Affected by Aspect and Direction of Inclination of the Trees (data from Korstian and Fetherolf, 1921)

Species	Aspect	Inclination[a]	Mortality, %
Engelmann spruce	Level	South	3.7
	Level	Vertical	11.4
	Level	North	30.6
Norway spruce	Level	South	8.5
	Level	North	33.5
Engelmann spruce	South	Vertical	7.0
	Level	Vertical	11.4
	North	Vertical	2.4

[a]Where the trees were inclined so that they shaded their own stems (south), mortality was much lower.

Table 8.6 Effect of Forest Clearing Size (Expressed in Terms of Diameter and Diameter/Tree Height Ratio) on Some Microclimatic Parameters (Geiger, 1965*)

Microclimatic Parameter	Size of Forest Clearing[a]					
	Diameter, m: 0	12	22	38	47	87
	Diam/tree ht: 0	0.46	0.85	1.47	1.82	3.36
Mean angle of shielding (h), degrees	90	72	59	48	40	26
Outgoing radiation as percent of open land value	0	11	31	52	66	87
Precipitation as percent of open land value	—	87	—	105	—	102
Midday July temp: excess of clearcut over forest, °C	0	0.7	2.0	5.2	5.4	4.1

*Copyright Harvard University Press. Used with permission.
[a]Only the largest clearing would be considered to be a clearcut.

8.8 Summary

Temperature is one of the more important environmental variables. It plays a critical role in the availability and ecological effectiveness of that vital component of all life systems: water. It influences the availability of food to heterotrophs, and the availability of nutrients to autotrophs. Slower decomposition and a reduction in nutrient uptake by plants when temperatures drop results in a significant difference in the biogeochemistry of forests growing in warm and cold environments, and between summer and winter in the latter. Temperature influences the geographical distribution of different organisms and plays a major role in determining the life form and species composition of plant communities.

The temperatures experienced by animals are modified by physiological, morphological, and behavioral adaptations. Both homeotherms and poikilotherms are generally able to restrict their temperature experiences to a narrower range of temperatures than that occurring in their environment. Plants have somewhat fewer options, owing to their lack of mobility and fewer possible physiological and morphological adaptations, and they generally cope with problems by becoming inactive during periods of unfavorable temperatures. Their physiological adaptations involve sensitivity to a variety of "clues" which increase the chances of being prepared to meet unfavorable conditions. These clues include photoperiod and temperature experiences. Plants also exhibit a considerable ability to alter their cardinal temperature by acclimatization in response to changed environmental temperatures. This ability permits them to continue growth under fluctuating environmental conditions and in a variety of environments. However, every individual has a range of tolerances beyond which its biological functions will be impaired.

Recognition of the temperature factor is important in forest management, whether the main concern is with timber, wildlife, fisheries, range, or recreation. The forester can modify the microclimate significantly within any macroclimatic region by appropriate manipulation of the forest, but must recognize the overall limitations on the options imposed by the macroclimate.

9.1 Introduction

The quantity of incident solar energy and the proportion that is absorbed by either the atmosphere or the surface of the earth varies from place to place. This results in regional variations in atmospheric and surface temperatures, which in turn result in differences in atmospheric pressure. Such differences lead to the movement of air (i.e., wind) from areas of high to areas of low pressure. Wind is thus the result of the conversion of solar radiation to thermal energy, and thermal energy to the kinetic energy of wind systems.

Winds have a wide variety of ecological effects. They transport water vapor from lakes and oceans to the land, and thus ensure the supply of rainfall. The friction of one turbulent air mass on another generates static electricity, which results in lightning, which in turn may start wildfires and contribute nitrogen to ecosystems by producing oxides of nitrogen in the atmosphere. Wind removes dust and organic particles from one ecosystem and deposits them in another, sometimes to the extent that a deep layer of *loess* soil develops. The removal of fine soil particles by wind can convert medium-textured soils to sand or rocky substrates, with accompanying changes in soil fertility and moisture. This is an important mechanism in the process of *desertification*. Wind influences evaporation and transpiration, and can produce desiccation damage and even the death of plants. Wind transports heat energy. By carrying warm air to cold regions and hot air to cold regions, it serves to moderate temperatures. By transporting pollen grains, spores, and seeds of plants, wind plays an essential role in the reproduction and dissemination of vegetation. Animals are also transported by wind currents. Seagulls will follow a ship for miles without wing beats by riding on the air turbulence in the wake of a ship. Insects, spiders, and other small animals are dispersed by wind, and it is believed that surprisingly large animals are occasionally transported long distances by unusually high and turbulent winds. This is believed to be important in the development of both flora and fauna on new islands formed by volcanism.

Wind is important to humans in many ways. It is an important means of dispersing atmospheric pollutants, and many cities would have far more serious air pollution problems if it were not for the cleansing action of wind. In contrast, high winds can destroy property, uproot trees, sink ships, erode soil, and destroy farm and forest crops.

This chapter examines the spatial and temporal variations of wind and the relationship of wind to topography. Effects of wind on plants, animals, and entire ecosystems are dis-

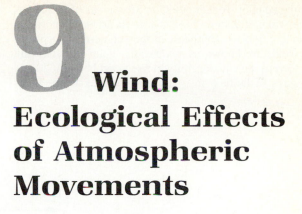

9 Wind: Ecological Effects of Atmospheric Movements

cussed, as well as the important reciprocal effect of plants on wind. The chapter concludes with a discussion of the importance of wind for forestry.

9.2 Temporal and Spatial Variations in Wind

Wind results from the differential heating of the atmosphere, which in turn results largely from differential heating of the earth's surface. As the earth rotates, areas are sequentially warmed and cooled, giving rise to global variations in air pressure which drive the global air circulation systems, and thereby determine to a large extent the world's variation in climate.

Low-latitude regions between the tropics and the equator are constantly warm, while the polar regions are always cold. In between lies a broad zone in which there is an exchange between equatorial and polar air. This exchange serves to prevent equatorial areas from getting ever hotter and polar areas ever colder. The transfer of excesses and deficits of heat is accomplished by a systematic global circulation of air masses. In simple terms, air rises in equatorial regions and travels poleward, sinking as it goes, returning to the equator from about 25 to 30 degrees of latitude as surface winds that blow from the northeast in the northern hemisphere and the southeast in the southern hemisphere; these winds are known as *tradewinds*. Polar air sinks and flows toward the equator, only to rise again between 60 and 50 degrees of latitude in a counterflow back to the pole.

Between these two circulation systems is a midlatitudinal circulation that gives rise to the westerly winds of midlatitudes. Actually, this is a highly simplified representation of world air circulation. In reality, the pattern shows much more diversity as the result of the continental land masses and the change of the seasons.

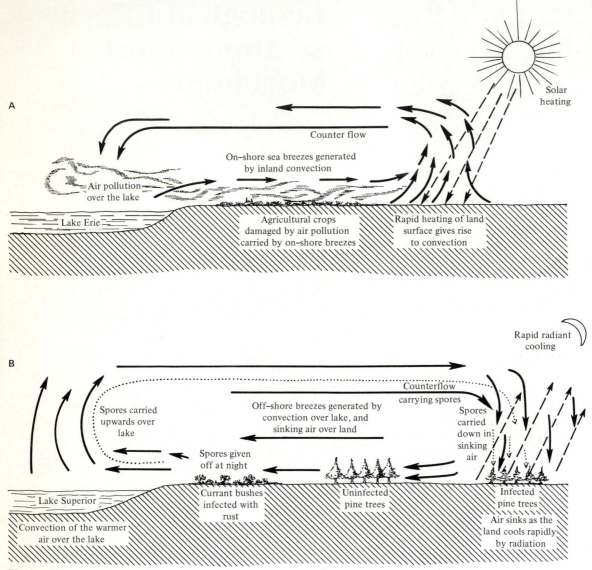

Figure 9.1
Air circulation systems between land and water bodies are found along ocean or lake coastlines during anticyclonic weather. (A) The daytime water-to-land system for Lake Erie showing the transport of ozone, as described in the text. (B) Nighttime land-to-water system for Lake Superior, showing the transport of blister rust spores, as described in the text.

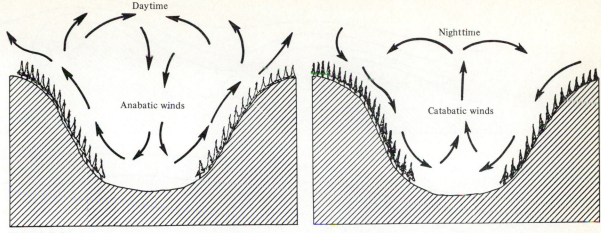

Figure 9.2
Anabatic and katabatic winds shown in a cross-section of a mountain valley. (Modified after USDA, 1964.)

Land surfaces warm up faster during the day than do water surfaces. The air in contact with land is heated, causing it to expand and rise, while cooler air moves landward from over the water. This creates local onshore breezes that are independent of regional air circulation systems. The reverse occurs at night. The land cools faster than the water surface and the direction of local breezes become offshore (Figure 9.1). Such land–water air circulation systems develop only during anticyclonic weather when the atmosphere is relatively stable. They are prevented by cyclonic winds, and also by cloudy weather, which prevents the development of thermal differences between the land and the water. The onshore winds can extend inland as far as 30 km and affect airflow up to a height of 1–2 km (Oke, 1978).

The ecological significance of such winds is exemplified by two interesting situations which occurred around Lakes

Erie and Superior. In the first case, ozone damage to tobacco plants growing near the shores of Lake Erie was shown to result from air pollutants originating from industrial areas around the lake. Ozone was formed from these pollutants by phytochemical action at some height above the lake, and brought down to low levels by the daytime circulation (Figure 9.1A). The ozone was then carried with the onshore breezes to the land, where it damaged the crops (Mukammal, 1965). In the second case, blister rust disease was found to be infecting pine trees in an area about 15–20 km inland from Lake Superior. To the surprise of investigators, the disease was not found in pine stands between the infected area and an area 8 km closer to the lake in which currant bushes (the alternate host for the disease and the source of the spores infecting the pine trees) were growing. The explanation for this unexpected distribution of the

Figure 9.3
Valley and mountain winds during the day (A) and night (B) in a mountain valley. (Modified after USDA, 1964.)

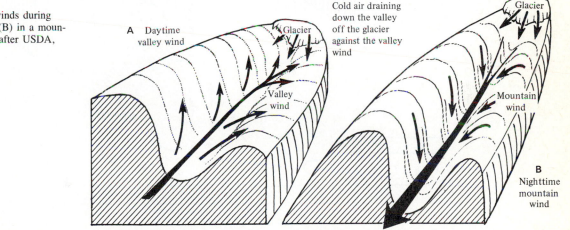

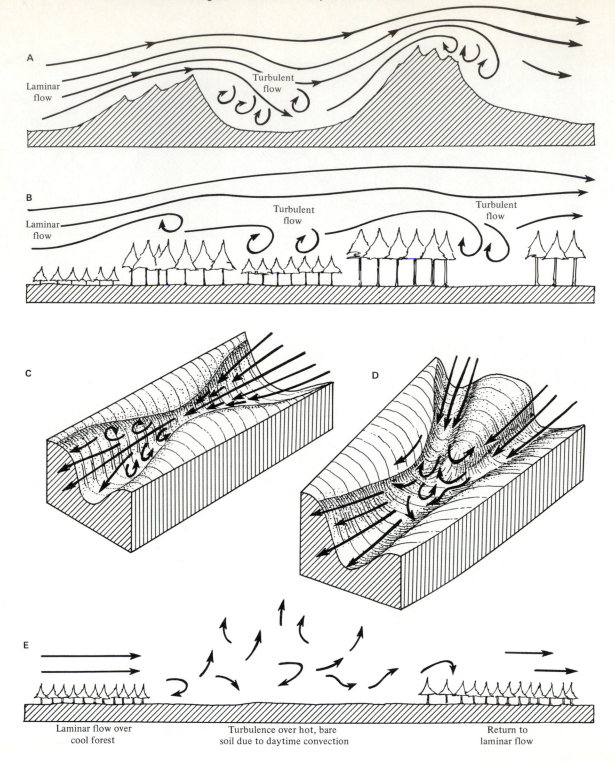

A

Laminar flow

Turbulent flow

B

Laminar flow

Turbulent flow

Turbulent flow

C

D

E

Laminar flow over cool forest

Turbulence over hot, bare soil due to daytime convection

Return to laminar flow

Figure 9.4

The change from laminar to turbulent air flow occurs as winds cross topographic barriers and move over vegetation of varying height, or over land surfaces of varying temperature. (A) Topographic barriers produce turbulence with strong updrafts and downdrafts on the lee slopes. (B) Vegetation of varying height produces turbulence above the vegetation. (C) Acceleration through a narrow valley produces lateral turbulence. (D) Turbulence occurs when laminar flows from two valleys meet at a valley junction. (E) Turbulence occurs when air moves over surfaces of varying temperature. (Modified after USDA, 1964.)

rust lies in the fact that the spores of the rust growing on the currant bushes were released only at night, when they were carried out over the lake by the nocturnal offshore breeze. The nocturnal counterflow (Figure 9.1B) then carried the spores to higher altitudes and back over the land, where the subsequent downflow deposited them on the trees in the infected area. This explanation of the unusual pattern of infection was supported by tracing the air movements with smoke and balloons (van Arsdel, 1965).

Valleys, especially those in mountainous regions, produce their own wind systems as a result of differential heating of different aspects or parts of the valley. As with the water–land circulation system, such winds are best developed during anticyclonic summer weather. There are two types of valley wind. One type results from the daytime warming and nighttime cooling of the valley, which results in daytime upslope winds (anabatic) and nighttime downslope winds (catabatic) (Figure 9.2). The second type involves a plain-to-mountain flow of air in the daytime because air in valleys becomes heated and rises more than air over plains; this results in up-valley air movements (valley winds). At night, the mountain ridges cool by radiation loss faster than the plain. The lower layers of the air over these ridges cool and slide down into the valley, where they combine to form a down-valley air movement (mountain winds) (Figure 9.3). Glaciers and snowfields can result in catabatic air movements even in the daytime, although such winds are often overcome by the daytime valley winds.

Air may move either as *laminar flow* or as *turbulent flow*. In the former, the different air layers ride over each other with little mixing. Such flow is rare in natural situations. More commonly, airflow is turbulent, with large-scale mixing of air from different layers, and repeated changes in the direction of the movement of the body of air. Turbulence results from friction between the air and the surface or because of obstructions to laminar flow. It can also occur as a result of the convectional currents that arise from differential heating of the earth's surface.

Mountain topography produces large eddies in the lee of ridges, especially during high winds. Airflows tend to be more laminar upwind and downwind of such features; the slower the wind, the more laminar the flow in the lee area. The narrowing of valleys accelerates winds and can

lead to eddying. Rough vegetation surfaces and the heating of the land surface can also give rise to turbulence (Figure 9.4).

Chinook or *foehn* winds are a particular type of wind experienced on the lee side of mountain ranges (also the *Santa Anna* winds of California). Moist ocean winds moving inland over mountains lose more and more moisture as they are forced up and over successive mountain ranges. On descending the lee side of the last few ridges the winds warm up as they are compressed by increasing atmospheric pressure (approximately 1°C increase for every 100 m dropped) and attain a great drying power, which can result in rapid evaporative loss of snowpacks in winter and in moisture removal from the vegetation and soil in summer or winter.

9.3 Effects of Wind on Vegetation

Wind affects plants in a variety of ways: by disseminating pollen, spores, or seeds, by influencing plant physiology (Whitehead, 1968), and by influencing plant morphology.

A. Dissemination of Reproductive Propagules

Most plants depend upon wind at least in part for the dissemination of reproductive structures. Dissemination of pollen by wind (*anemophily*) is common among the more primitive taxonomic groups (e.g., the conifers), and most plants of cool and cold climates are wind-pollinated. Such plants require the production of much larger quantities of pollen than plants which are animal-pollinated. The extent of pollen production is reflected in the frequently observed coverage of soil and water by a yellow film of pollen in the spring in areas of coniferous forest. Evidently, the advantages of widespread distribution of pollen by wind justify the apparently profligate expenditure of energy and nutrients on pollen production.

Wind dissemination of reproductive propagules (*anemochory*) is even more widespread than anemophily. It usually involves seeds and spores, but can also be involved in asexual reproduction, as in the case of the distribution of living twigs of poplar, which are physiologically abscissed (*cladoptosis*), complete with functional green leaves, (Galloway and Worrall, 1979) and will take root if disseminated by wind and/or water to a suitable rooting medium.

Some plants produce seeds which are so small that they can be carried considerable distances by wind. Members of the orchid and heather families produce seeds which often weigh no more than 0.002 mg. Such seeds, together with spores of algae and fungi, can be carried to great heights in the atmosphere and transported over long distances by even moderate winds. Larger disseminules are often provided with long hairs, which increase the frictional surface (i.e., act as a "parachute") and enable the wind to transport them over considerable distances. Seeds of plants such as dandelions (Compositae), willow (Salicaceae), clematis, and fireweed (*Epilobium* sp.) can be carried for hundreds of kilometers.

Even larger seeds or one-seed fruits (e.g., elm, maple, ash, birch, and members of the Pinaceae family) are provided with wings to ensure dispersal away from the parent plant. Distance carried depends upon the height of the tree, the strength of the wind, and the size and shape of the disseminule and its wing. Douglas-fir seed in Oregon is regularly carried 300 m from the parent tree (Isaac, 1930) and much further during periods of strong winds.

B. Effects on Physiological Processes

Wind has a marked effect on the exchange of gases between plants and the atmosphere. If leaves are bent as they flap in the wind, air is pumped in and out of the leaf air spaces through the stomata, and this accelerates the exchange of CO_2 and O_2. Wind prevents or reduces nocturnal accumulation of respiratory CO_2 within and below the vegetation canopy, thereby reducing the rate of early morning photosynthesis.

Loss of water from plant surfaces is markedly affected by wind. Removal or reduction in the thickness of the boundary layer of humid air around leaves by wind accelerates the diffusion of water vapor out through the stomata. This can increase evaporation even when the vapor pressure deficit is zero because of the important effect of convection on evaporation (Daubenmire, 1974). However, water loss does not increase linearly with increasing wind speed; it increases with the square root of wind velocity. Initially, there is a large increase in loss of water as wind speed increases from zero, but there is little difference in the rate of loss between medium and strong winds. Above wind speeds of 6 km h^{-1}, evaporation is mainly determined by the vapor pressure deficit of the air. Wind also accelerates water loss by the pumping action, as already mentioned.

The effect of wind on the moisture balance of plants is demonstrated by red belt damage to conifers during the winter in the mountainous areas of western North America (MacHattie, 1963) and other topographically similar areas in the world. The chinook or foehn winds that occur in such areas have a remarkable drying power. As they flow down over the mountain forests, they accelerate transpiration loss, which desiccates the foliage if the soils are frozen or dry. The desiccation damage (browning of foliage) occurs only in a horizontal midelevation belt because cold air in the valley bottoms prevents the warm, dry air from affecting valley bottom stands, while at high elevations the winds do not have as much drying power. Winds during dry, cold, sunny anticyclonic winter weather can produce similar desiccation damage in other areas. Tree seedlings growing in forest nurseries can suffer extensive damage during such weather unless precautions such as spraying (to encase the seedlings in ice) or windbreaks are employed.

Wind-induced desiccation damage is not restricted to cold winter weather, and even plants growing on moist soil can be exposed to moisture stress if exposed to drying winds. Lethal leaf water deficits can develop in many species at winds of $50-70 \text{ km h}^{-1}$ when soil moisture is not limiting (Whitehead, 1968). The result can be the killing of needles and even the death of buds.

Bending of plants by wind influences the physiology of growth. The distribution of available growth substances between root growth, stem diameter growth, and stem height growth is influenced by stem movements. Experiments in which trees were prevented from swaying by guy lines resulted in the development of smaller root systems and thinner, weaker stems in comparison with trees that swayed naturally in the wind. Trees guyed halfway up developed normal stems above the point of guying, but the stationary stem below the point of guying failed to increase in strength and became progressively weaker relative to the unguyed stem. A significant difference was observed after only 2 years of guying. Trees that have grown in a dense stand where they are protected from wind have slim and cylindrical stems that are easily broken if the stand is thinned or suddenly exposed to wind. Trees in such dense stands usually have poorly developed root systems, so they are also very subject to windblow (Larsen, 1963). However, the reader should remember that wind does not act as a causal determinant in this matter. The influence of light competition on root-shoot ratios and other factors that influence the distribution of photosynthate between growth in height and growth in diameter are also important.

By increasing the evaporation of water from leaves and by removing a layer of warm air from around the plant, wind acts to lower plant temperatures. This is beneficial to plants in hot environments because it can prevent high-temperature damage, but in cold environments the cooling effect can be detrimental. Metabolic rates, which are already low because of suboptimal temperatures, may be reduced to the point at which plants are unable to complete necessary physiological processes. It has been reported that wind in arctic and alpine environments can reduce leaf temperatures by 7°C (Wilson, 1959), and a study of Scots pine needle temperatures in central Sweden showed that even a gentle wind can have an important cooling effect. On an April day with variable cloudiness, very light wind and an air temperature of −1 to 0°C, leaf temperature was equal to air temperature in cloudy periods but rose to 7 to 8°C above air temperature during sunny periods. On a sunny day with an air temperature of 1 to 2°C and gentle wind, needle temperature varied from 3 to 7°C, but rose to 12 to 15°C above air temperature when the needle was sheltered from the wind (Figure 9.5).

C. Effects on Morphology

Wind plays an important role in determining the phenotypic appearance of plants. We have already seen that wind affects stem and root morphology by affecting the distribution of growth. When exposed to frequent drying winds, many plant species fail to obtain the size that is characteristic of the species in a sheltered location. Such plants become dwarfed because their cells have insufficient water to expand to full size and because the moisture stress may inhibit cell division. Leaves exposed to wind become thicker and smaller and have a lower rate of water loss per unit area than do leaves growing in nonwindy situations. The cooling effect of wind also contributes to dwarfing by reducing growth rates, and the death of buds and foliage by desiccation also acts to prevent an increase in stature of the plants. For many plants, a 27–36 km h^{-1} continuous wind results in some reduction in leaf size and internode length. Continuous wind over 70 km h^{-1} results in great growth reduction and ultimately in death (Whitehead, 1968). Plant

dwarfing by wind is a common phenomenon in alpine environments, but once again it must be stressed that wind is not a casual determinant of alpine plant morphology. Later in the book we shall examine the multiplicity of factors that determine plant growth at alpine tree lines.

The effect of wind on plant morphology sometimes results from materials carried by the wind rather than from the wind itself. In windy areas near the ocean, where the wind carries salt or sand, all the foliage and buds exposed to the full effects of the wind can be killed. This can be the result of desiccation, the toxic effects of salt spray, or the physical abrasion caused by wind-driven particles: the foliage and buds are literally sandblasted.

Windblown sand can remove all the bark from trees planted in sand dune areas, and windblown ice crystals can kill all the foliage and buds of trees in a narrow zone just above the maximum depth of winter snow. Buds and foliage growing in the lee of the stem are less affected, with the result that crowns become flag-shaped (Figure 9.6).

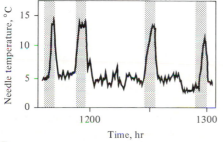

Figure 9.5

Temperature variation in a Scots pine needle in April, with and without shelter from the wind. The shading indicates the presence of a windshield around the needle. The air temperature was 1 to 2°C, and the needle was illuminated by full sunlight. (After Christersson and Sandstedt, 1978. Used by permission of *Canadian Journal of Forest Research* and the authors.)

Figure 9.6

Flag-shaped crown of Douglas-fir at tree-line caused by prevailing winds killing the buds on the windward side of the tree.

Such wind training of vegetation is responsible for the typical wedge shape of tree crown development along windswept coastlines, and for the development of *krummholz* tree growth. This term refers to the shrublike growth form of trees at altitudinal tree lines, where dwarfing and wind training result in dense, low, multistemmed growth of trees in the shelter of rocks or slight depressions. In very extreme cases where the terminal bud is repeatedly killed, only leeward branches survive, with the result that the plants develop a horizontal stem growing in the downwind direction of the prevailing wind. Any plant part growing upward out of the sheltered area is killed (Figure 9.7).

Wind training can also occur simply as the result of prolonged unidirectional wind pressure on developing branches. Twigs that start growing in an upwind direction are bent around to a downwind direction and eventually become permanently oriented in that position (Lawrence, 1939).

The input of sea salts along the coastal fringe is often responsible for a narrow coastal strip of vegetation that differs in both form and species composition from that inland where the spray input is less intense. Cordes (1972) found that the narrow strip of Sitka spruce that grows along the sandy beaches of western Vancouver Island, British Columbia, was correlated with a high input of salt spray from the nearby ocean. Western hemlock and western redcedar, which are less tolerant of the salt spray, are largely excluded from this strip.

Modification of stem shape is a common response of trees to wind. The bending forces in coniferous tree stems during prolonged periods of unidirectional wind result in the

Figure 9.7
Wind training of *Pinus albicaulis* on Mt. Lassen, California. Only buds in the lee of a rock and the plant stem survive. This results in the tree developing a procumbent stem that is, in fact, a branch, all leaders having been killed.

development of enlarged annual rings of *compression wood* on the leeward side, and the reduction or even elimination of some annual rings on the windward side of the tree. The stem develops an elliptical cross section with the long axis in the direction of the prevailing wind. Angiosperm tree species have a somewhat different response to such wind pressure. They develop *tension wood* on the windward side, which serves in the same manner as compression wood to resist the bending pressure of the wind and maintain the stem in an upright position. An extreme example of wind modification of stem shape is a case of a Monterey cypress stem growing on the coast near Carmel, Calif. At a height of 7 m from the ground, the stem was 188 cm in diameter in the direction of the prevailing wind, but only 23 cm in diameter at right angles to the wind. The central growth ring was situated only 8 cm from the windward side, there being 180 cm on the leeward side. Three hundred and four annual rings were counted to the leeward of the central growth ring, whereas only 50 growth rings were counted on the windward side (Oosting, 1956).

Stem tensions that result from the swaying of trees produce another form of morphological adaptation: buttress formation. Ring growth is accelerated in the angles between the lower stem and the larger roots, and this results in the formation of large stem buttresses, especially at positions on the trunk that give the tree most support against the prevailing winds. Such buttresses are particularly well developed on very large trees in tropical forests subject to high winds, but they can also be seen to a lesser extent on large trees in windy locations at temperate latitudes. Stem buttresses result in a serious loss of timber since buttressed stems are difficult to process in a sawmill.

The effects of wind on plant morphology discussed above are generally the result of moderate wind speeds sustained over long periods. More dramatic effects can occur when the vegetation is subject to high winds or very turbulent winds over shorter periods. The whipping of branches in the wind can result in *wind tatter*. Just as the free end of a flag tatters in high winds, so the foliage at the end of a branch becomes tattered during periods of high and turbulent air movement. This phenomenon has been put to practical use in afforestation of windswept areas in Great Britain. Small nylon flags are sometimes placed along a gradient of increasing wind (e.g., with increasing elevation on exposed coastal mountains), and the rate at which the free edge tatters over one year is measured. This rate is then compared with the survival and growth of trees planted along the same transect, and a threshold tatter rate beyond which tree growth is unsatisfactory is established. "Tatter flags" are then put out wherever plantations are contemplated in very

windy areas to ascertain the likelihood of success of reforestation efforts and the elevation beyond which planting
would be unsuccessful (Lines and Howell, 1963) (Figure 9.8).

Crown tattering also occurs when the branches of adjacent trees batter each other during a windstorm. Large
quantities of small branches bearing green foliage may be
broken off. Sometimes this results in the forest floor of
coniferous forests being covered by an almost continuous
carpet of green foliage following a winter wind storm, with
significant consequences for decomposition and nutrient
cycling.

Exceedingly violent winds can result in *windbreak*. The
stem is snapped off at some height above the ground, while
the lower part of the stem remains upright, still anchored by
its roots. Except in trees with fungal decay in the stem, such
breakage in undisturbed stands is not common except during periods of very high wind velocity (typhoons, tornadoes, or hurricanes) or excessively turbulent windstorms. It
is most common where trees previously sheltered in dense
stands are exposed to even moderate winds by clearcut harvesting of the adjacent stand or by roadbuilding activities
through a previously undisturbed stand. Stem breakage
tends to be more common in dense stands, where the stems
are tall and slender, than in open-grown stands, where the
stems are thicker and more tapered. It also occurs more

Figure 9.8

The use of "tatter flags" to gauge the
effect of wind on planted tree seedlings. (A) Relationship between the
rate of tatter of the free edge of a cloth
flag and the mean annual height
growth of planted lodgepole pine trees
in Scotland and northern England (after
Lines and Howell, 1963). (B) Rate of
tatter of standard flags at various elevations in the western Cairngorm
Mountains of Scotland (after Pears,
1972). Areas above 400 m elevation
are questionable sites for initial plantation establishment. The dotted line indicates suggested critical level of tatter
for adequate seedling growth. (Lines
and Howell, 1963. Used by permission
of the Forestry Commission, U.K.,
and the authors.)

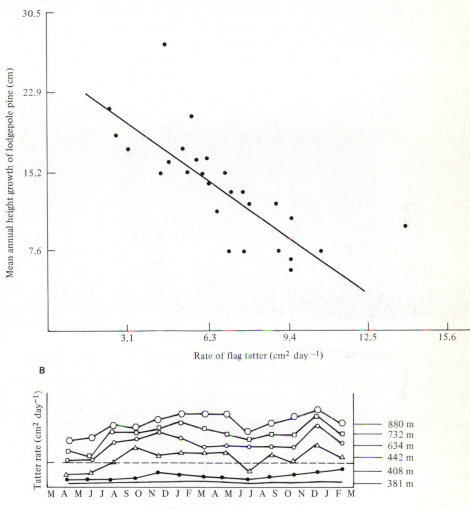

frequently where the trees have well-developed root systems and are well anchored. In most other situations, such damaging winds result in *windthrow* rather than windbreak: the roots are pulled out of the ground and the intact trees are toppled over (Figure 9.9). (*Windblow* and *blowdown* are other terms used for wind damage to trees.)

Windthrow is more common in shallow- than in deep-rooted species, more common in shallow and/or wet soils than in deep and/or dry soils, and more common where soil, stand, or pathological conditions have resulted in small, irregular, shallow, or asymmetrical root systems. Thus, trees growing on thin soil over bedrock, saturated soil, compacted soil, or soil with shallow pans, and trees in which deformation to roots has occurred during nursery growth and/or planting, tend to have a higher than normal susceptibility to windthrow. Windthrow is also a common result of damage to root systems by pathogenic organisms or some mechanical agency. Turbulent wind tends to produce windthrow more than laminar flow because the rocking motion produced by turbulence reduces the friction between the roots and the soil more effectively than does unidirectional wind pressure from laminar wind flow. A study of wind damage in mixed white fir–red fir stands adjacent to clearcuts in California implicated bole rot (30%), fire scars (19%), and root rot (18%) as the main causes of wind damage to mature trees, the remaining 33% of damaged trees being associated with shallow soil, logging damage, dwarf mistletoe, and stem deformities. Wind damage accounted for 60% of all tree damage and death, compared with 30% for insects and 6% for snow (Gordon, 1973).

Windthrow played a very important role in the development of the classical methods of European and tropical silviculture (Godwin, 1968). Bad experiences with clearcutting in windy regions led to the development of a wide variety of silvicultural systems and patterns of forest harvesting, each one tailored to a particular combination of topography, soils, tree species, and wind.

Figure 9.9
Wind damage to an Engelmann spruce-lodgepole pine-Douglas-fir stand in central British Columbia. The majority of the trees were blown over, but trees with particularly strong roots and/or weak stems experienced stembreak. (Photo courtesy of Ministry of Forests, British Columbia.)

D. Influence Through the Distribution of Precipitation and Snow

Wind affects the availability of moisture to plants by transporting moist air to a locality and by removing it again. Atmospheric circulation systems determine the precipitation of a region, and wind greatly affects the loss of that moisture by evapotranspiration. Wind redistributes winter snow, and this can have important consequences for vegetation. Soil beneath snowdrifts in grasslands receives substantially more water in the spring than soil in areas where the snow is thinner, and the resulting increase in spring soil moisture levels may enable trees to invade the area. Adjacent areas not associated with winter snowdrifts become too dry for tree establishment and survival during the spring and summer.

9.4 Effects of Wind on Animals

Wind affects animals in a variety of ways. Although wind effects have generally not received as much attention from animal ecologists as have the effects of other physical factors, such as temperature and moisture, the effects of wind are nevertheless of considerable importance.

Wind influences the behavior of animals. Many species of birds and insects are restricted to sheltered microenvironments during high winds, and prolonged periods of wind may seriously interfere with feeding activities with potentially adverse consequences for the animals' energy balance. Because of this, small animals generally live in microhabitats that experience very much lower winds than occur in the general environment. Many leaf-eating insects will drop to the ground when the vegetation on which they are feeding is violently shaken by wind, and will remain there until the wind drops. Butterflies and moths flatten themselves against the ground to avoid being swept away. There are even birds in the windy desert of high Tibet which are reported to build a rampart of pebbles on the windward side of their nests (Allee et al., 1967).

Homeotherms are affected by the "chill factor" of wind, which increases both the convective loss of heat and cooling by evaporation of water. Greater insulation or restriction of activities to sheltered locations is necessary during periods of high winds and low temperatures. Poikilotherms are also affected by wind chill. Their internal body temperatures are largely determined by behavior, and therefore wind-induced changes in their thermal load may require a change in behavior in order to maintain body temperatures within a particular range.

Rapidly moving air has a substantial kinetic energy and can transport surprisingly large objects. Even gentle winds play an important role in transporting smaller animals, but windstorms of great violence can transport quite sizable organisms. The fauna of the Greater Antilles Islands in the West Indies is evolutionarily related to the fauna of Central America, yet no convincing evidence exists that there was ever a land bridge connecting the island to the mainland. It has been suggested that the similarity of animals as large as rodents and snakes between the two areas is the result of wind transport of the species between the two areas (Darlington, 1938) (This does not discount the important contribution of water transport). The exceptional lifting and carrying power of wind is illustrated by the "rain of fishes" which occurred in Marksville, Louisiana, in 1947 (Bajkov, 1949). On the morning of October 23, fish ranging between 5 and 23 cm in length fell from the sky in a density of up to one per m^2. The species involved were the same as those in nearby ponds, and several small tornadoes had been noticed in the area that day. The incident was explained in terms of local high-velocity winds which had sucked up the surface of the water of the lakes together with the aquatic organisms contained therein. Fish transport by local violent air currents may sometimes have been involved in the introduction of fish into landlocked ponds or lake systems not connected with other freshwater areas in which the species occur.

There are many instances of insects being transported over long distances by wind. Species such as the spruce budworm (*Choristoneura fumiferana*) are dispersed over many hundreds of kilometers by convective windstorms as a result of the behavior of the adult moths. A sudden decrease in light intensity caused by a heavy cloud, or a sudden drop in air pressure ahead of a convective storm stimulates the moths to rise above the trees for a brief period of flight. If a cold front with its associated convective updrafts passes over the area at this time, the moths are carried aloft and transported for long distances, and then deposited as the storm disperses. Wind dispersal can initiate outbreaks of destructive pests in areas far removed from infestation centers and can hasten the decline of the infestation in the source area by removing large numbers of the female moths (Henson, 1962).

The location of areas plagued by locusts in East Africa has been shown to be influenced by winds, which tend to concentrate the swarms into fairly well defined areas. Locust problems are particularly severe in the intertropical convergence zone (Figure 9.10), where winds appear to keep the swarms within a fairly well defined east-to-west band. Movement of the swarms to the north or south of this band is correlated with north or south shifts in the intertropi-

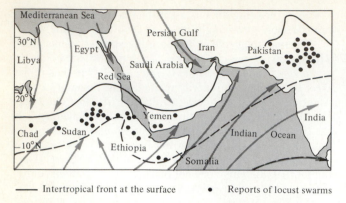

— Intertropical front at the surface   • Reports of locust swarms

— — Limit of upper northerlies   ➤ Major air movements

Figure 9.10
The Intertropical Convergence Zone and the reported distribution of locust swarms during the period July 12–31, 1950, in eastern Africa, the Middle East, and India. The convergence of major air circulation patterns serves to concentrate locust swarms within a well defined east-west band. (After Rainey, 1973. Used by permission of the Royal Meteorological Society and the author.)

cal front. Similarly, infestations of the African army worm (*Spodoptera exempta* Walk), which attacks cereals and grasses in eastern and southern Africa, can be predicted using synoptic meteorological data (Rainey, 1973).

9.5   Effects of Wind on Ecosystems

Wind can alter ecosystems in a variety of ways. Wind transport of pathogens and insects can lead to the destruction of all or some of the vegetation. The loss of vegetative cover alters the habitat for other animals in terms of both shelter and food. If the loss is extensive, it may expose the soil to sunlight, wind, and rain, with a variety of consequent effects.

Wind erosion of soil can significantly alter an ecosystem. The surface layers of the soil are generally the most important in terms of plant production, and their loss through wind erosion can lower soil fertility. This is particularly serious in dryland arable farming where soil cultivation techniques render the surface soil particularly prone to removal by wind. The dust storms that are an unfortunate characteristic of hot, dry agricultural areas represent both a nuisance to human comfort and a degradation of ecosystem productivity in the eroded areas.

Deposition of wind-transported soils can have a variety of effects. Small annual additions of fine mineral and organic particles act as a fertilizer and generally improve the productivity of a site, but where the deposition rate is too great,

the vegetation may be killed. Most plants cannot tolerate the sudden addition of many decimeters of soil parent material to the soil surface. Small plants are totally buried, and larger plants may die because their deeply buried roots are unable to obtain the necessary oxygen.

Certain plant species have become adapted to, and can survive burial by, wind deposits. Marram grass (*Amophila arenaria*), which grows on coastal sand dunes, is able to survive burial to a depth of about 1 m. It responds by sending up a rhizome to within a few centimeters of the new surface, and growing new aerial shoots from the elevated rhizome. The buried portions of the plant then die. If a sand dune is excavated, the remains of marram grass can be found at many depths within the dune, tracing the history of growth of the dune by deposition during storms. Another example of adaptation to burial is exhibited by the ohia tree (*Metrosideros collina*), which grows in areas of recent volcanic activity on the islands of Hawaii. Such trees may be subject periodically to the deposition of as much as several meters of fine-textured volcanic ash. Close to the eruption, where the ash is hot, the trees are killed, but further away, where the ash is cool, the trees are able to survive the deposition of more than a meter of ash by the development of aerial roots.

Wind swaying of very large trees in steep mountain topography is sometimes responsible for landslides. The soil is loosened by the heaving of the root systems as the trees sway, and the slope hydrology may be altered by the pumping action of the roots. The net effect is to increase the soil shear stress and reduce its shear strength to the point at which slope failure occurs and a landslide is triggered. This effect of wind is thought to contribute to the occurrence of serious landslides in old growth forests in the coastal mountains of British Columbia during wet and windy winter weather.

Air transportation of pollution can have a dramatic effect on ecosystem structure and function. Figure 9.11 shows an area downwind of a smelter at Sudbury, Ontario, where all the vegetation has been eliminated by sulfur fumes. Ponderosa pines in the mountains to the east of the city of Los Angeles are being adversely affected by smog, and this species may be eliminated in some areas unless the pollution is reduced.

9.6   Effects of Vegetation on Wind

Vegetation exerts a marked effect on winds close to the ground. The roughness of the vegetation provides a friction surface which significantly reduces the overall wind velocity but increases wind turbulence. Forests are particularly

Figure 9.11
Landscape denuded of vegetation by sulfur fumes in Sudbury, Ontario. (Photo courtesy of Dr. T. Hutchinson.)

effective at modifying winds because although they are porous, allowing some wind movement through them, the very large surface area of leaves, branches and bark provides a very large frictional surface, which effectively reduces wind speeds. Table 9.1 lists values for Z_0, the roughness length (an index of the frictional resistance of surfaces to air movement), for a variety of surfaces.

The profile of wind in a forest depends upon the tree species, the density of the stand, and the stand structure. Even-aged stands without any understory may have low wind speeds in the crown but appreciable winds between the crown and the ground, whereas multilayered forest communities have reduced wind speeds at all heights below the upper crown. The reduction of wind speed is much greater for high winds than for low winds. A 6-km h^{-1} wind in the open may be reduced by only 2 km h^{-1} at the same height in the forest; a 50-km h^{-1} wind in the open can be reduced to as little as 7 km h^{-1} in the forest (Anonymous, 1964). Table 9.2 lists examples of the reduction of wind by various types of forest stand.

The effects of vegetation on wind have been recognized and employed to advantage for centuries. Shelterbelts of trees are planted by farmers to reduce wind velocity over fields and to provide livestock with shelter from the wind

Table 9.1 Roughness Length (Z_0) Values for Various Surfaces (Data from Oke, 1978)

Type of Surface	Roughness Length, m
Water (calm, open sea)	$0.1–10.0 \times 10^{-5}$
Snow	$0.5–10.0 \times 10^{-4}$
Sand desert	0.3×10^{-3}
Soils	$0.1–1.0 \times 10^{-2}$
Grass (0.02–1.0 m high)	$0.03–1.0 \times 10^{-1}$
Agricultural crops	0.04–0.20
Orchards	0.05–1.0
Forests	1.0–6.0

Table 9.2 Effect of Forests on Wind Velocities (Data from Kittredge, 1948)

Forest	Wind Speed in Open, km h^{-1}	Reduction in Forest, %
Western white pine, Idaho	2.4	82
Jack pine, Neb.	13.1	72
Aspen, Col.	5.3	68
Douglas-fir, Col.	3.9	67
Ponderosa pine, Ariz.	9.0	49

(e.g., Read, 1964). In many parts of the world, agriculture would be much less productive without such shelter, and shelterbelts would probably be of great benefit in many areas that currently do not have them. Trees are also planted to reduce heat loss from buildings and to reduce wind erosion of soil. They are used to capture blowing sand and have been used extensively to stabilize areas of shifting sand dunes. They are also important in causing the deposition and accumulation of blowing snow. The latter is of great importance to agriculture in areas where the soil moisture required for spring and summer crops comes more from melting snowpack than from growing season precipitation.

The effect of shelterbelts on wind depends very much on the permeability of the belt. Impermeable belts result in maximum downwind reduction of velocity, but speeds increase rapidly further downwind and there is a lot of turbulence. Permeable belts are associated with less reduction in velocity but also with less turbulence and a more persistent downwind effect (Figure 9.12). The choice of windbreak will depend upon the local wind conditions, the type of crop, and the type and degree of wind modification desired by the land manager. Deciduous hardwood belts are not used to provide livestock with shelter from winter winds because of inadequate reduction of wind speed in the lee of the belt, and impermeable conifer belts will not be used to shelter grain crops from summer winds because of the problems of downwind turbulence and the short distance over which wind-speed reduction is achieved.

The flow of wind over unbroken forest in level terrain is approximately laminar (except where small-scale turbulence occurs within the tree canopy), but it may become turbulent as the wind passes into harvested areas (Figure 9.13A). Turbulence often develops along the windward edge of a clearcut and this can result in windblow or other damage. However, turbulence is not usually the major cause of tree damage in clearcuts. That place is reserved for the acceleration of wind as it leaves the clearcut.

As wind passes over the leading edge of a logged area, the wind drops from canopy height to move over the ground. In order to leave the clearcut again, the wind must regain its original height by rising up over the uncut stand at the downwind end of the opening. This involves some acceleration of the wind. The degree of acceleration depends upon the shape of the clearcut. Where the cut is wedge-shaped with the narrow end pointing upwind, there may be little or no acceleration; the wind enters the clearcut along a narrow front and leaves on a broad front. Where the broad end points upwind, a large volume of wind enters the area along the broad front, but has only a narrow area through

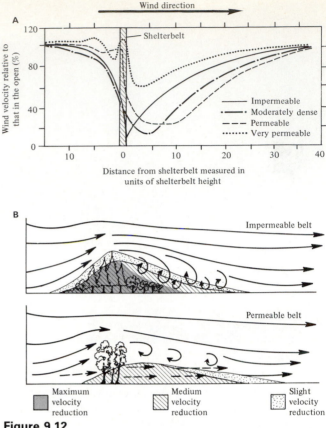

Figure 9.12
Effects of shelter belts on wind velocities. (A) Extent of wind reduction by shelter belts of different permeability. (B) Turbulence and generalized wind velocity profiles over permeable and impermeable shelter belts (hypothetical). (After Nägeli, 1945. Used by permission of L'Institut Féderal de Recherches Forestiers, Zurich.)

which it must pass on its exit. This results in an acceleration of the air mass in the same way that a broad, slow-moving river speeds up as it passes through a narrow gorge. The increased velocity increases the kinetic energy of the wind and some of this energy is transferred to the trees as the wind leaves the area. This can result in windblow (Figure 9.13B).

Windblow is far more common in stands adjacent to clearcut areas than in stands well away from clearcuts. Trees in a fully stocked stand provide each other with mutual shelter, and only the uppermost part of the crowns of the largest trees experience the full force of the wind. Additional stability is provided by the intertwining and grafting of root systems; each tree gains some stability from the root systems of the adjacent trees. Trees at the edge of a clearcut are exposed to the full strength of the wind, and as the roots of the adjacent cut stumps decay and lose strength, these edge trees lose some of their rooting stability. Windblow is most common where newly exposed trees experience wind acceleration and turbulence, although sometimes they can be blown over even in moderate wind speeds without turbulence. For a discussion of windblow and forestry, see Palmer (1968).

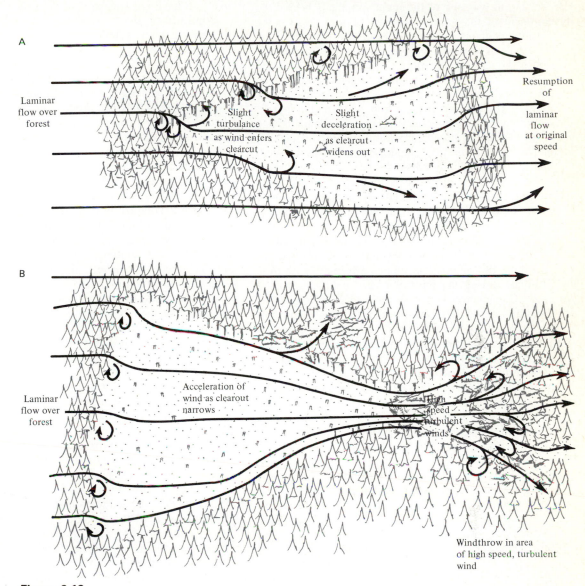

Figure 9.13
The influence of clearcut shape and orientation on the incidence of windthrow. (A) Cone-shaped opening with narrow end toward prevailing high winds. This minimizes the risk of wind damage. (B) Cone-shaped opening with broad end toward prevailing high winds. This produces the greatest risk of wind damage. The wind damage continues downwind until speed and turbulence decrease, or until wind-firm trees are encountered.

9.7   Significance of Wind for Forestry

Wind has played an important role in the development of forestry. Windblow was one of the factors that wrecked early attempts to provide secure future supplies of timber in Europe, and it was one of the main stimulants behind the development of the various patterns of forest harvesting used in mountainous European forests.

The effect of wind on the water balance of plants can determine the success or failure of planting. The moisture stress caused by wind can be fatal to a young seedling even on a moist site because of the resistance to water uptake that is caused by the lack of fine roots, root hairs, and/or mycorrhizal associations. Reducing the size of clearcuts and planting in the lee of stumps, microtopographic features, or logging debris, all of which reduce the exposure of seedlings to wind, can help to reduce desiccation-induced seedling mortality. Wind also affects natural regeneration by determining the distribution of seeds and can damage young plantation trees by loosening their root systems in the soil by frequent violent rocking (Edwards et al., 1963).

Windblow continues to be a problem in many parts of the world. Planted trees frequently develop root forms that differ from those of "natural" seedlings. This may result from root damage during the nursery phase or at the time of planting. The abnormal root systems tend to reduce the wind stability of the trees, even though the tops of the trees may grow normally. Consequently, the problem is not noticed until the trees blow over. Site preparation by ploughing can result in an abnormal orientation of the root system, with concomitant reductions in stability. Several of the "container" methods of planting young trees result in root deformation and/or abnormal development of the root system, and it remains to be seen whether the move from bare root stock[1] to container stock[2] in artificial forest regeneration will be accompanied by an increase in wind-related problems.

The problems of windblow should play an overriding role in determining the shape, size, and layout of clearcuts in areas where wind is an important factor. Small patches of trees left to protect streams and lakes or to provide wildlife habitat often blow down, and foresters frequently resist leaving such patches because of windblow.

[1] Bare root stock: seedlings that are grown in open soil beds in the nursery, dug up when large enough, and planted in the forest with bare roots.
[2] Container stock: seedlings grown in the nursery in soil that is held in some type of container, and planted out when large enough either in the container or removed from the container with the "plug" of soil around which the roots have grown.

9.8   Summary

The atmosphere is the medium that surrounds terrestrial animals and the aboveground parts of terrestrial plants. Movements in that medium, known as wind, are therefore likely to have significant effects on these organisms.

Wind affects the growth and morphology of plants by influencing their water balance, their gaseous exchanges, the distribution of net growth between different parts of the plant, and the survival of buds and leaves. Although a certain amount of wind can have a beneficial effect, moderate wind speeds generally exert an adverse influence on tree growth. High winds can produce mechanical damage, and sustained, directional winds can reduce the quality of stemwood for human uses thereof by causing the formation of tension or compression wood, stem buttresses and marked stem taper. Mechanical damage can become particularly severe if the wind carries ice or mineral particles.

Many animals are affected by wind. Small animals may be unable to conduct their normal activities when winds are strong because of the risk of damage or displacement. High winds may aggravate the loss of water and heat, which may lower body temperatures below the effective or even the survival range. Conversely, the cooling effect of wind may permit an animal to survive in a very hot environment.

Transportation of materials and objects by wind is undoubtedly one of its most significant ecological roles. It removes human atmospheric pollution from its source area, transferring any resulting problems downwind (e.g., acid rain). It transports small animals, some of which are totally dependent on air currents for their dispersal to new areas. It carries seeds and spores over long distances, and therefore constitutes a major force in determining the patterns of vegetation development in an area. The wind transportation of pollen is essential in the life history of many plant species. Without wind, many ecosystems would be much less productive because wind provides a continuing input of nutrient-containing dust particles and precipitation.

Wind has always been a major factor in the management of forests. Periodic destruction of forests by wind, the effect of wind on seed distribution (and therefore on natural regeneration), the effect of wind on the survival of planted seedlings, and wind damage to stands adjacent to clearcuts were important factors in the development of a variety of silvicultural systems and forest management strategies in Europe over the past three centuries. The ecological effects of wind remain an important consideration in the management of both plant and animal populations, and it will always be an unwise forester who fails to give the wind factor due consideration.

10.1 Introduction: The Nature of Soil

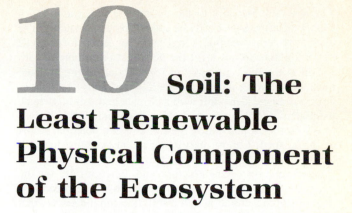

10
Soil: The Least Renewable Physical Component of the Ecosystem

The terms *plant* and *animal* are widely understood by both the lay and scientific communities. The term *soil*, on the other hand, has many connotations. Soil scientists have traditionally considered soil to be the "unconsolidated mineral material on the surface of the earth that serves as a natural medium for the growth of land plants." More recently they have added to this definition the requirement that soil can be either mineral or organic material, that it must be at least 10 cm thick, and that it must be "naturally occurring" material. This results in the following definition for soil:

. . . the naturally occurring, unconsolidated, mineral or organic material at the earth's surface that is capable of supporting plant growth. Its properties usually vary with depth and are determined by climatic factors and organisms, as conditioned by relief and hence water regimes, acting through time on geological materials to produce genetic horizons that differ from the parent material. In the landscape, soil merges into nonsoil entities, such as exposed, consolidated rock or permanent bodies of water at arbitrarily defined boundaries.[1]

The disturbed surface of a logged site or a farmer's field is soil, but displaced materials such as a gravel dump or a mine spoil tip are not.

Geologists use the term in a broader sense to refer to all materials produced by weathering of the surface of the earth. To an engineer, soil is ground material that can be excavated by earth-moving equipment without blasting. To the layman, soil is simply "dirt"—the substance that sticks to the shoes, dirties the gardener's hands, or has to be moved while digging a hole. Ecological definitions include "any part of the earth's crust in which plants are anchored" (Daubenmire, 1974) and "the net result of the action of climate and organisms, especially vegetation, on the parent material of the earth's surface" (Odum, 1971).

To a forester, soil is those upper layers of the unconsolidated surface of the landscape that provide forest plants with the following major necessities of life: water, nutrients, and a firm anchorage. It may be mineral or organic, deep or shallow, extensively weathered or only slightly weathered. This is a somewhat broader definition than that used by the Soil Science Society of America (1973):

The unconsolidated mineral matter on the surface of the earth that has been subjected to and influenced by genetic and environmental factors such as *parent material, climate* (including moisture and temperature effects), *macro-* and *microorganisms*, and *topography,* all acting over *time* and producing a product—soil—that dif-

fers from the material from which it was derived by many physical, chemical, biological, and morphological properties and characteristics.

The SSSA definition is useful because it reveals the complex nature of the phenomenon that we call soil. It is sometimes expressed in the simpler form (Jenny, 1961):

Soil = f(parent material, climate, biota, topography, time)

where f means "a function of" or "is determined by."

Soil is thus not merely the unconsolidated mineral material at the interface between the solid geological surface of the earth and the atmosphere. It is not primarily a physical, geological phenomenon. It is the combined result of atmospheric and biological processes acting on geological materials over a period of time.

The term *solum* is used to refer to that part of the unconsolidated surface material that is soil. Between the solum and the bedrock is relatively unaltered material that has traditionally been referred to as *parent material* (the unconsolidated and more or less chemically weathered mineral or organic matter from which the solum or soil is developed by pedogenic processes). The solum, however, may have developed in transported materials that are unrelated geologic-

---

[1]L. M. Lavkulich, personal communication.

ally and pedologically to the underlying materials, which cannot therefore legitimately be called "parent" material. The alternative term *"nonsoil,"* has been suggested for surficial materials that do not meet the accepted definition of soil.

Soil is the basic resource of foresters and agriculturists; trees, cows, and cabbages are merely the crops. A forest or a farm is a landscape unit with a climate and soil that create the potential for organic production that can take the form of an economic crop. Destroy the soil and that potential is lost or diminished. Careful harvesting of these crops does not "destroy" the forest or farm; it merely creates temporary changes in ecosystem structure and function. If, on the other hand, the harvest is accompanied by widespread loss or catastrophic alteration of the soil, one can indeed say that the forest or the farm, at least the present form thereof, has been "destroyed" for the period of time that it will take for natural or human-accelerated processes to return the ecosystem to a productive condition (see Chapter 15).

Soil is one of the three major components of the ecosystem. To understand it requires every bit as much effort as that required to understand the other two thirds. It is a highly complex assemblage of geological materials, dead organic matter, living roots, animals and microbes, soil water, and soil atmosphere. Together, these components form a dynamic system in which the line between living and dead frequently becomes academic. Together, they provide the physical and chemical conditions necessary for plant life, and consequently for most forms of animal and microbial life.

Both ecologists and natural resource managers should learn as much as they can about soil; this critically important but somewhat neglected ecosystem component. The acquisition of a complete understanding of soil is a lifetime activity, and the present chapter can serve only as an introduction to one of the most important aspects of both ecology and resource management. Readers interested in soils are referred to such books as Remezov and Pogrebnyac (1969), Hunt (1972), Armson (1977), Pritchett (1979), Jenny (1980), Ulrich et al. (1981), or any standard soil science text (e.g., Brady, 1984).

10.2 Physical Properties of Soil

A. Texture

Soils are made up of various combinations of organic matter and mineral particles of various sizes organized in characteristic patterns. Variation in the relative abundance of different sized particles in the <2 mm diameter mineral material results in differences in the *texture* of soils. Three major size classes in the <2 mm material are recognized: sand, silt and clay, the size limits of which are shown in Table 10.1. These particle sizes are combined in various proportions to produce the various textural classes: sand, sandy loam, silt loam, clay loam, and clay (note that sand, silt, and clay can refer both to a particular size class and to a textural class). Figure 10.1 shows how these and other textural classes are defined in North America, and Table 10.2 gives a guide to the field recognition of the six basic classes.

Particles larger than 2.0 mm in diameter [pebbles (2–20 mm), cobbles (20–200 mm), and boulders (200–2000 mm)] have traditionally been excluded from textural classifications. This reflects the preoccupation of soil science with agricultural soils, in which parameters such as aeration, soil moisture, root penetration, soil structure, and fertility are generally most closely related to the relative frequencies of particles smaller than 2 mm. It also reflects the historical fact that farmers recognized the importance of understanding soils long before most foresters did. In contrast to agricultural soils, particles larger than 2 mm occupy a considerable portion or even the majority of the soil volume in many forest soils, and it is not uncommon to find trees growing directly on fractured bedrock or on organic layers lacking a substantial mineral particle component. Consequently, the use of texture to indicate soil fertility is not always as useful in forestry as it is in agriculture.

B. Structure

In most soils, groups of individual mineral particles are bound together (cementation) into aggregates or *peds:* units of soil structure formed by natural processes. The binding agents may be colloidal clay or organic matter, but other

Table 10.1 American and International Classifications of Soil Particle Size

	Particle Size, mm
American system	
Clay	<0.002
Silt	0.002–0.05
Very fine sand	0.05 –0.1
Fine sand	0.1 –0.25
Medium sand	0.25 –0.5
Coarse sand	0.5 –1.0
Very coarse sand	1.0 –2.0
International system	
Clay	<0.002
Silt	0.002–0.02
Fine sand	0.02 –0.2
Coarse sand	0.2 –2.0

Figure 10.1

Triangular summary of the sand, silt, and clay content of the major textural classes recognized in North America. The relative frequencies of these three particle-size classes can be read from the diagram by projecting scale lines from each of the scales. The example shown, which has a clay texture, contains 60% by weight of clay, 20% by weight of silt, and 20% by weight of sand. (After Armson, 1977. Used by permission of the University of Toronto Press and the author.)

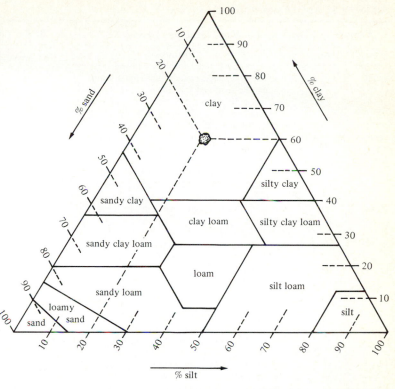

chemicals can also be involved. The size and shape of the aggregates vary greatly, from spheroidal aggregates as large as 10 mm in diameter (called *crumbs* if they are porous and *granules* if not) up to blocks or prismlike units as large as 50 mm in diameter. Where there is no such aggregation, the soil is described as being *structureless* or *massive*. Structure may be a fairly permanent feature, but in some types of soil (e.g., certain clays) it can change according to the prevailing soil moisture condition.

Structure develops as a result of physical and chemical processes in the soil, often in association with biological activity. Wetting and drying cycles in soils containing clays that shrink on drying can develop a *blocky* or *prismatic* structure. Alternate freezing and thawing can break such large aggregates into smaller ones or initiate development of structure in massive materials. The presence of colloidal clay or organic matter binds larger particles (silt and sand) together to give a crumby or granular structure, although the binding efficiency of the cementing material may depend upon chemical factors. Where there is an abundance of monovalent sodium (Na^+) in the soil, clay particles tend to disperse and peds will break down or not form. Where divalent cations such as calcium (Ca^{2+}) dominate in the soil,

formation of stable aggregates is promoted by the process of *flocculation*. These doubly positively charged ions effectively neutralize the negative charges on clay particles that create mutual repulsion between the particles and resist aggregation. Flocculation is a less permanent condition than aggregation by cementation, but seems to be a prerequisite for it and is important in fine-textured soils. In very acid or very alkaline soils, where there is little free calcium or magnesium or where there are high levels of sodium and to a lesser extent potassium, flocculation is inhibited; such soils tend to be rather structureless or massive. Colloidal materials (clay and organic matter) tend to be washed down to deeper layers of the soil under such circumstances. Coarse-textured soils (sands and gravels) also have little structure and are sometimes termed *single-grained soils*.

Organic matter, the presence of roots, and the activities of soil animals are important in the development of soil structure. Many types of organic compound can act as a binding agent, especially those that have colloidal properties. Roots exude organic substances, which, either alone or in association with microorganisms, bind particles into aggregates. The formation of root channels opens up the soil, and the churning action of roots helps to break up massive

Table 10.2 Field Determination of Soil Texture

A. Features That Are Useful in Hand Texturing (Armson, 1977)

Soil Texture	Features
Sand	Loose and single-grained. Individual grains can be seen and felt. Squeezed in the hand when dry, it will fall apart when pressure is released. Squeezed when moist, it will form a cast that will crumble when touched.
Sandy loam	Contains enough silt and clay to make it somewhat coherent. Sand grains are readily seen and felt. Squeezed when dry, the cast will readily fall apart. Squeezed when moist, the cast will bear careful handling without breaking.
Loam	Mellow, with a somewhat gritty feel, yet fairly smooth and plastic when moist. Squeezed when dry, the cast will not break if handled carefully. Squeezed when moist, the cast can be handled freely without breaking.
Silt loam	When dry it may appear cloddy, but the lumps are easily broken. When pulverized it feels soft and floury. When wet the soil puddles. Casts formed of either dry or moist soil can be readily handled without breaking. When moistened soil is squeezed between thumb and finger it will not ''ribbon,'' but will form flat ''pastry flakes.''
Clay loam	When dry it forms hard lumps or clods. When moist it can be squeezed to form a thin ribbon, which will break readily, barely sustaining its own weight. When moist the soil is plastic and will form a cast that will take much handling.
Clay	Forms very hard aggregates when dry. When wet it is plastic and sticky. Moist clay can be pinched out between thumb and finger to form a long flexible ribbon. Note that some clays are friable and lack plasticity in all moisture conditions.

B. Key for Field Assessment of Soil Texture (Belisle, 1980)

Moist cast test	Moist soil (dampened if necessary) is compressed in the clenched hand. Some soils bind together in a cast, which is then tossed from hand to hand to assess its strength.
Ribbon test	Moist soil is kneaded with the fingers, rolled into a cigarette shape and then squeezed out between the thumb and forefinger to form the longest and thinnest ribbon possible.
Feel test	The soil is rubbed between the thumb and forefinger to gain a feel for its coarseness or fineness. The soil is then rubbed in the palm of the hand to dry it and to separate and estimate the size of the individual sand particles. The sand particles are then allowed to fall off the hand, and the amount of finer material remaining (silt and clay) is noted. Sand has a grainy feel; silt feels floury; clay feels very smooth.
Taste test	A small amount of soil is worked between the front teeth. Sand is distinguished as individual grains that grit sharply against the teeth. Silt particles are identified as a general fine grittiness, but individual grains cannot be identified. Clay particles have no grittiness.
Shine test	A small amount of moderately dry soil is rolled into a ball and rubbed once or twice against a hard, smooth object such as a knife blade or thumb nail. A shine on the ball indicates clay in the soil.

materials. Animals mix soil, which promotes the incorporation of organic matter deep into the mineral soil. Their burrowing opens and loosens the soil, and the feces of many soil animals become small peds.

C. Porosity

Porosity is a measure of the amount of pore space in a soil, or the volume of the soil not occupied by solids. It is a critically important parameter of soil because it influences the movement of water and gases, which in turn determine the activity of roots and soil organisms. The porosity of structureless (massive) soils is much lower than that of well-aggregated soils because the latter have abundant larger pores between the peds. However, total porosity may be less important than the distribution of the pore space. If all the space occurs as large pores, as it does in gravel or coarse sandy soil, water will drain very freely and the soil will be subject to drought. Conversely, if all the pores occur as minute spaces between clay particles, the movement of gases and water will be extremely slow, and plants growing in the soil will experience waterlogging and oxygen deficiency. The ideal pore distribution is that which retains sufficient water and yet permits adequate diffusion of oxygen and carbon dioxide to satisfy the requirements of desired

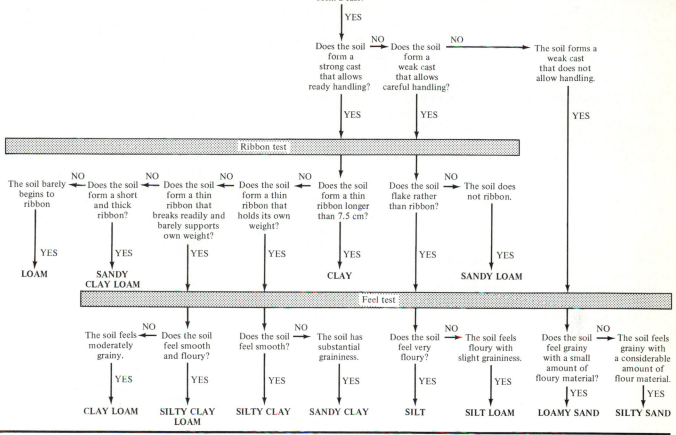

species of plants, soil animals, and soil microbes. Generally, this is found in a well-structured soil with most of the small pores within, and the larger pores between the aggregates. Total pore space in a poorly structured soil may be as little as 35%, whereas a well-structured soil with the same texture may have as much as 65% pore space.

D. Consistence

Soils vary in the degree to which the particles or peds stick together. Soil *consistence* refers to the stickiness of soils and their ability to resist deformation under stress. A soil that can be rolled into a cylindrical shape when moist is said to be plastic. This is a feature of clay-rich soils which is used to assess the textural class of a soil in the technique of *hand texturing* (cf. Table 10.1). If the clay becomes too wet it looses its plasticity and becomes sticky. When dry, it is hard. The consistence of soil is important because it helps determine soil stability, erodibility, and trafficability under various moisture conditions.

E. Bulk Density

The structure, texture, and porosity of soils, together with their organic matter content, combine to determine the *bulk density* of a soil: the kilograms of soil material per cubic meter of soil volume. Measurement of bulk density is widely used to estimate porosity.

Expressed in the older units of g cm^{-3}, the bulk density of clay, clay loam, and silt loam surface soils normally ranges from 1.00 to as high as 1.60, depending upon their condition. Sands and sandy loams have values of 1.20–1.80. Very compact nonsoils may have bulk densities of 2.0 or even higher (Brady, 1984). Forest floor bulk densities also vary. For example, values of 0.12–0.16 g cm^{-3} have been reported for yellow birch–red spruce stands in the Adirondack Mountains of New York (McPhee and Stone, 1965). A 500-year-old subalpine forest in coastal British Columbia was found to have mean values of 0.14–0.18 (Kimmins, unpublished data). Much higher values (0.27 for a forest in New Hampshire; Hoyle, 1973) and much lower values (0.056 for undecomposed moss peat; Boelter, 1964) can also be found. One reason for this variation is the variation in biomass of live small and fine roots (<5 mm diameter) in forest floors and in the extent to which they were removed prior to calculating bulk density. Forest floors in areas of heavy winter snowpack tend to have higher bulk density than those in snow-free areas.

F. Aeration

Organisms living belowground exchange gases just as their aboveground counterparts do. Most soil organisms require an external supply of oxygen and release carbon dioxide, which must diffuse out of the soil, be carried away dissolved in water or otherwise be absorbed if toxic accu-

mulations are not to occur. Inadequate gaseous or dissolved oxygen results in the reduction of oxidized soil chemicals such as iron and sulfur by anaerobic soil microbes. This leads to the production of materials such as ferrous iron and hydrogen sulfide which are toxic to the roots of many plants. Figure 10.2 illustrates the effect of reduced oxygen concentrations on height and root growth in seedlings of a number of tree species. The root surface area of black spruce seedlings (2 years old) was found to be more sensitive to soil oxygen levels than was height growth.

Soil aeration is determined by total soil porosity, the distribution of the pore space, and the proportion of the space that is filled with water. Soils with high porosity can be poorly aerated if constantly wet, whereas soils with medium to low porosity can be reasonably well aerated if not too wet and if the pores are of medium size. Even soils with good drainage, high porosity, and good pore distribution can become poorly aerated if the structure of the upper few millimeters of the soil is damaged by such things as heavy rain or mechanical compaction. A thin layer of soil in which the structure and porosity has been lost can effectively block gaseous exchange between the soil and the atmosphere. A soil whose surface structure has been lost due to mechanical impacts is said to have been *puddled*.

G. Temperature

Chapter 8 presented a brief summary of soil temperature relationships and the reader may wish to refer back to the appropriate section of that chapter before proceeding.

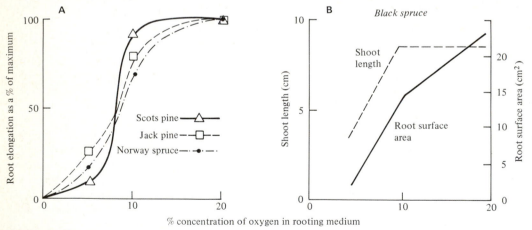

Figure 10.2
Effect of reduced oxygen levels on the growth of shoots and roots of several conifers. (A) Variation in the rate of root elongation in seedlings of three species growing in solutions containing various concentrations of oxygen. (After Leyton and Rousseau, 1958. Redrawn by permission of John Wiley & Sons, Inc.) (B) Variation in shoot length and root-surface area of black spruce seedlings under simulated out-planting conditions and varying oxygen tensions. (After Armson, 1977. Redrawn by permission of the University of Toronto Press.)

Temperature is an important parameter of soil since it influences the activity of roots and soil organisms, rates of decomposition, and nutrient uptake. Organic materials have a lower thermal conductivity and volumetric heat capacity[2] than do inorganic materials, and consequently the forest floor serves to modify greatly the temperature of the underlying mineral soil. The presence of a forest floor reduces daily temperature variations and retards the spring warming and autumn cooling of the mineral soil.

Soil temperature regimes are influenced by soil porosity and texture. Thermal conductivities generally increase with increasing particle size, so that sands have higher conductivities, warm up faster in the spring, and cool down more rapidly in the fall than do clays. Denser materials have higher conductivities than those that have a lower bulk density.

Water content has a very important effect on soil temperature. Wet soils have a higher thermal conductivity than dry soils, but they generally warm up and cool down more slowly because of the high volumetric heat capacity of water and because much of the incoming solar energy may be utilized in evaporating water at the surface.

Soil temperature is largely determined by the balance of incoming and outgoing radiation. By shading the soil, vegetation exerts a dominant influence on the radiation balance at the soil surface. Vegetative cover results in a reduction in maximum and an increase in minimum soil temperatures, although the latter may be due more to the formation of a surface litter layer than to shading. The influence of soil color was mentioned briefly in Chapter 8.

10.3 Soil Water

Although water relationships are, strictly speaking, a physical characteristic of soils, they are sufficiently important that the subject is treated in a separate section. Some aspects of soil water are discussed in Chapter 11.

Water can exist in soil as a liquid, a vapor, or a solid. Water vapor can be significant in dry soils with fluctuating temperatures because vapor movement and condensation can appreciably effect the availability of liquid water. Water vapor diffuses upward from lower layers of the soil and condenses in surface layers which have undergone nocturnal radiative cooling. Ice or frost can have an important effect on soil water content and water movement in soils in cold areas. Frost churning can affect soil structure and development, while frozen soil restricts the infiltration of

water, thus reducing the total amount of water in the soil later in the season. These points notwithstanding, the most important form of soil water is liquid.

Aspects of soil water that have attracted most attention are its movement and storage in the soil. Both of these are in turn determined by the energy relationships that exist between water and soil particles. Water moves from areas of higher energy to areas of lower energy and is held within the soil when the energy of the water is less than the energy of the soil holding it.

Water in the soil has three types of energy (generally called *water potential*).

1. *Osmotic potential,* which is a measure of the concentration of dissolved chemicals (solutes). These lower the vapor pressure of water, reducing evaporation. There will be a net movement of water vapor from water with low solute concentrations (high osmotic potential) to water with high solute concentrations (low osmotic potential). This type of water potential contributes relatively little to the movement of soil water except in saline and desert soils, but it is of considerable importance in plant–water relations.

2. *Gravitational potential,* which is the potential energy that the water has by virtue of its position or elevation within the soil. Water at the surface of the soil has a higher gravitational potential than does water 1 m beneath it. The

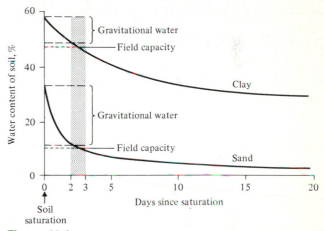

Figure 10.3

Loss of water from two different soils following saturation. Water content at field capacity (defined as water content after 2–3 days of drainage following saturation) is shown. Water in excess of field capacity is gravitational water. It is, obviously, easier to distinguish gravitational from capillary movement in the coarse- than in the fine-textured soil because of the marked change in slope of the graph in the former, before and after the 2–3-day time period. (Hewlett and Nutter, 1969. Redrawn by permission of the University of Georgia Press and the authors.)

---

[2] Volumetric heat capacity: the quantity of heat required to raise the temperature of 1 cm^3 of the material by 1°C.

potential is zero when the water reaches the surface of the water table. Gravitational potential is the energy that is generally (but not always) responsible for the drainage of water down through the soil.

3. *Matric potential,* which is the energy of water associated with the forces of *capillarity* and *adsorption*. It is a negative potential (and is therefore sometimes called *matric suction*) since it opposes the action of gravitational and osmotic potentials; water moves from areas of low matric potential to areas of high matric potential. *Capillary* forces occur in the smaller pore spaces; they act to lower the energy level of the water and thus hold it in the pores. *Adhesive* forces that result from the molecular structure of water bind water molecules to the soil particles with which they are in contact. In coarse-textured soils the surface area of pore walls available for adsorption and the capillarity of these pores are negligible compared with those of fine-textured soils, and the importance of matric potential in determining water movement is negligible or sizable, respectively. The importance of matric potential changes as the soil dries out, because as it does so the remaining water is restricted to smaller and smaller pores, in which matric potential is increasingly significant.

The amount of water stored in soil is determined by the relative magnitudes of gravitational and matric potentials. Consider a saturated soil in which all pore spaces are filled with water (e.g., at the end of a prolonged heavy rain). As soon as the rain stops, water in the larger pores will drain downwards toward the water table because the positive gravitation potential (GP) exceeds the negative matric potential (MP) in these pores. The water that is lost is called *gravitational water.* Water will remain in those pores for which the MP is greater than the GP. The soil is then said to be at *field capacity:* the condition that occurs in non-vegetated soil 2–3 days after a rainfall that saturated it. It is an imprecise term because water drainage continues for much longer than 2–3 days. This is especially true in a fine-textured soil (Figure 10.3) because, as the soil becomes drier, capillary forces begin to predominate and water drains more slowly. The term is most useful for coarse-textured soils, in which matric potential is less significant.

The majority of the water in a saturated, coarse-textured soil is gravitational water, and it is lost by the time field capacity is reached (Figure 10.4A). In fine-textured soil there may be little gravitational water, so at field capacity this type of soil retains a much higher percentage of its saturated water content than does a coarse-textured soil. However, most of this water is held in such small capillaries that the matric potential is greater than the *plant potential* (the ability of plants to withdraw water from the soil) and the water is unavailable to plants. The matric potential at which soil water becomes unavailable (referred to as the *permanent wilting point*) is considered to be about 1500 kPa (a soil water tension of about −15 atm). A fine sand will

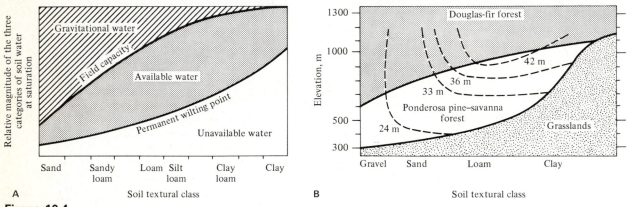

Figure 10.4
Relationship between the availability of water to plants and soil texture. (A) The distribution of soil water between the three main categories of soil water varies in soils of different texture. Very fine- and very coarse-textured soils have less available water than does medium-textured soil. (After Hewlett and Nutter, 1969. Used by permission of the University of Georgia Press and the authors.) (B) Relationship between major climatic climax vegetation types, soil texture, and elevation in south-central British Columbia. The mean tree heights of dominant trees at age 100 years are also shown. The vegetation type and the tree height growth vary as soil texture changes, which reflects texture-controlled soil moisture conditions. The interaction between elevation and soil texture results from elevation-dependent precipitation changes and the effects of texture on the availability of precipitation to plants. (After Brayshaw, 1970. Used by permission of the British Columbia Provincial Museum and the author.)

have approximately the same quantity of available water at field capacity as a clay, even though it contains only about half as much water. Loamy soils can contain nearly twice as much available water as clays, although they contain significantly less total water. These generalizations will obviously be modified by variations in soil structure.

The movement of water in saturated soil approximates Darcy's law:

$$Q = kA \times H/L$$

where Q is the volume of flow per unit time, k the hydraulic conductivity, A the cross-sectional area through which water is flowing, and H/L the hydraulic gradient (hydraulic head per unit of column length).

Water flow in unsaturated soils behaves differently. As soil dries out, hydraulic conductivity decreases because the water is flowing in smaller and smaller capillaries (rate of flow varies as the fourth power of the radius of the capillary, so a reduction of radius by 50% reduces flow rate 16-fold). Also, as water leaves the larger pores they fill with air, which provides a barrier to the flow of water remaining in the isolated small pores that connect the larger ones. As a result, water movement is rapid in coarse soils when they are saturated, but it declines dramatically and becomes very slow as the soil dries. Water movement at saturation is slower in fine-textured than in coarse-textured soils, but as the soil dries the rate decreases more slowly and remains appreciable even when the soil becomes fairly dry. This means that although a coarse soil initially loses water rapidly by gravity and evaporation after the termination of a rainstorm, losses decline rapidly and the remaining water may be held for a long time, maintaining a moist soil condition. In contrast, although a fine-textured soil does not lose water as rapidly at first, losses may continue until the soil becomes very dry. It also means that movement of water to the zone of depletion around a root is much slower in a coarse-textured soil than in a fine-textured soil, rendering such coarse soils "drier" to plants than they really are.

10.4 Chemical Properties of Soil

Soils have characteristic chemical properties that are the result of weathering of their mineral components, decomposition of organic material, and the activity of plants and animals. After a discussion of weathering, we will examine the following soil properties: cation and anion exchange capacity, pH, and the forms and availability of macronutrients.

A. Weathering

Weathering of mineral materials involves both physical and chemical processes. Physical weathering is the breakdown of rocks into increasingly smaller particles by mechanical action during transportation by water, wind, or ice, or as the result of temperature fluctuations, particularly freeze–thaw cycles. It is more important in the preparation of mineral particles for soil-forming processes than in the actual development of soil, a process that is dominated by chemical weathering. Chemical weathering results in the release of elements from soil minerals and the alteration of the chemical form of the residual materials.

Chemical weathering involves a variety of processes. Simple exposure to water may result in *solution* or *hydrolysis*, a reaction in which a compound reacts with water to form two different molecules. For example, water combines with some primary minerals such as feldspars to yield salts and complex compounds containing aluminum and silicon. These compounds can recrystallize into clay minerals (aluminosilicates).

$$KAlSi_3O_8 + H_2O \rightleftharpoons HAlSi_3O_8 + KOH$$

$$\downarrow \text{decomposes}$$

$$H_4SiO_4 + Al_2O_3 \cdot 3H_2O$$

Silicic   Gibbsite
acid

(Armson, 1977)

The intensity of hydrolysis increases with increasing temperature as long as moisture is adequate. It is therefore a more active process in the tropics than in temperate regions, and tropical soils tend to be more deeply and completely weathered than do their temperate counterparts. Water can also combine with minerals in the process of *hydration*. This results in the formation of secondary minerals which are softer and more easily weathered physically than the original primary mineral.

When there is abundant carbon dioxide present in the soil solution, hydration together with *carbonation* can alter feldspars to clay minerals.

$$CaAl_2Si_2O_8 \cdot 2NaAlSi_3O_8 + 4H_2CO_3 + 2(nH_2O) \longrightarrow$$

Sodium-calcium feldspar   Carbonic   Water
acid

$$2Al_2(OH)_2Si_4O_{10} \, nH_2O + Ca(HCO_3)_2 + 2NaHCO_3$$

Clay   Calcium   Sodium
bicarbonate   bicarbonate

(Hunt, 1972)

Oxidation and *reduction* are both important types of chemical weathering. Oxidation is the loss of electrons from a molecule; reduction is the gain of electrons. These processes not only alter the chemical form of the material, but render the material more susceptible to other weathering reactions such as hydrolysis. Reduction of some insoluble substances (such as ferric iron to ferrous iron: $Fe^{3+} \rightarrow Fe^{2+}$) makes them more soluble; oxidation reverses the process. Oxidation–reduction weathering is particularly important in soils where there is a seasonal fluctuation between saturated and nonsaturated conditions. Such soils, which have a mottled, gray-brown coloration as a result of the alternating oxidation and reduction, are called *gleysols;* the process by which they are formed is called *gleyzation.*

Loss of silica from primary minerals is an important type of chemical weathering under certain climatic conditions (hot and moist). This type of weathering *(laterization)* is important in the formation of *laterites,* a type of soil found in some parts of the tropics and in some wet and warm temperate areas. Laterization results in the formation of *plinthite,* a nonindurated (the soil scientists' term for not physically hardened) mixture of iron and aluminum oxides, clay, quartz, and other diluents that commonly occurs as red soil mottles. Plinthite is usually arranged in platy, polygonal, or reticulate patterns through the soil matrix. It changes irreversibly to ironstone hardpans or irregular aggregates on exposure to repeated wetting and drying. Removal of vegetation from lateritic soils (oxisols) in the tropics exposes plinthite to heating and drying, and this has frequently resulted in the development of serious land management problems. An example of laterization is the conversion of the dark-colored mineral biotite to iron oxide, clay, salts, and silica.

$$2KMg_2Fe(OH)_2AlSi_3O_{10} + O + nH_2O \longrightarrow$$
    Biotite

$$Fe_2O_3 \cdot H_2O + Al_2(OH)_2Si_4O_{10} \cdot nH_2O + 2KHCO_3 +$$
Iron oxide   Clay   Potassium
                                             bicarbonate

$$4Mg(HCO_3)_2 + 2SiO_2 + 5H_2O \qquad \text{(Hunt, 1972)}$$
Magnesium   Silica   Water
bicarbonate

Another category of weathering that is thought to be particularly important in forest soils is *chelation* or the formation of organic matter–element complexes: the reaction between metallic ions and certain organic compounds which can act as electron donors. Metallic elements such as iron, aluminum, and copper are frequently held and moved in the soil as organic chelates or complexes. It is believed that chelation can lead to the decomposition of silicate minerals. Chelation reduces the toxicity of substances such as iron and copper, increases their mobility in the soil, and may facilitate their uptake by plants.

Weathering is important for a variety of reasons. By physical comminution, smaller particles with increased surface area are produced; a prerequisite for the formation of mineral soils. Chemical weathering releases nutrient elements required by plants and microbes and results in the formation of clay minerals. The most abundant primary minerals are the silicates, the most common of which are the feldspars. As these weather they produce one of several different types of clay, including montmorillonite, a type that shrinks and swells as its drys and wets; illite, a nonexpanding clay; and vermiculite and chlorite, clays that expand but less so than montmorillonite, kaolinite, and halloysite. In all clays except kaolinite and halloysite there is considerable replacement of aluminum by iron or magnesium. In some of the clays, elements such as potassium can fit between the layers of the crystal lattice and become firmly bound. Clay exerts a dominant influence over the chemical properties of mineral soils, and also on their physical properties (porosity, structure, texture, drainage, etc.). Perhaps its major contribution to soil chemical properties is the phenomenon of cation exchange.

B. Cation and Anion Exchange Capacities

Both clay and colloidal organic matter are negatively charged and therefore can act as anions. As a result, these two materials, either individually or combined as a *clay–humus complex,* have the ability to absorb and hold positively charged ions (cations). This gives soil containing clay or organic matter a *cation exchange capacity* (CEC).

The CEC of soil clay minerals and organic matter varies widely. Measured in units of milliequivalents[3] per hundred grams of dry material (meq per 100 g), CEC values vary from as low as 3–10 for kaolinite, 15–40 for illite, and 30 for vermiculite to 80–120 for montmorillonite (Brady, 1984). Values for organic matter vary from 50 to 250, but since the bulk density of organic matter is much lower than that of clay, organic matter may have a smaller total CEC than would the same volume of clay. The CEC generally declines as the soil becomes more acid, but the relationship depends on the material. The CEC of humus is more affected than that of clays.

[3] Milliequivalent: the amount of an element or compound that will combine with or replace 1 mg of hydrogen. It equals the atomic weight in milligrams divided by the valence.

All cations can be held on the CEC, but they vary in how firmly they are held. Generally, the greater the number of electrical charges, the firmer the absorption, so Ca^{2+} ions are held more firmly than K^+ ions. This does not apply to ions such as Al^{3+} and Mg^{2+} if they are hydrated, in which condition they are held less firmly than K^+ and NH_4^+. Also, the density of negative charges on the clay or organic matter affects which ion is held. The composition of the ionic population associated with the CEC is also influenced by the chemical composition of the soil solution. Where this has high concentrations of any particular ion, that ion will tend to displace other ions on the exchange sites, irrespective of their relative absorption or replacing powers. For example, soil solution containing large numbers of hydrogen ions will result in the displacement of much of the population of other types of ions from the CEC. The degree to which basic ions occupy the CEC is called the *percent base saturation:* the sum of the "exchangeable" cations, other than hydrogen and aluminum, on the CEC expressed as a percentage of the total CEC.

Surfaces of roots have negative charges which attract and promote the absorption of cations, and organic substances secreted by the roots create a CEC in the *rhizosphere* (soil zone immediately around roots). Living roots can therefore provide a CEC in a soil in addition to that provided by clay and humus.

Soils also have an anion exchange capacity (AEC), but this is generally much less than CEC. Some clay and organic colloids are amphoteric (they can carry either negative or positive charges) and any iron or aluminum oxide present provides additional positive charges to which anions can be attracted. The AEC is pH dependent; generally, it is greater in acidic than in neutral or basic soils.

C. Soil Reaction or pH: Acidity and Alkalinity

Soil reaction refers to the activity of hydrogen ions in the soil. It is measured in units of *pH,* which is the logarithm of the reciprocal of the hydrogen ion activity. The scale goes from 1 to 14, there being a tenfold difference in concentration between successive units (i.e., pH 3 is 10 times more acid than pH 4 and 100 times more acid than pH 5). At 22°C, pure water will contain 1 g of hydrogen ions per 10 million liters, giving a concentration of 0.0000001; the logarithm of the reciprocal of this concentration is 7. Consequently, the pH of pure (or neutral) water is 7: solutions having a pH of less than 7 are acid, and of more than 7 are alkaline. Hydroxyl and hydrogen ions are present at equivalent concentrations at pH 7. Hydroxyl ions are less abundant than hydrogen ions below pH 7 and more abundant above pH 7.

"Soil pH" may refer to either the pH of the soil solution or the total quantity of hydrogen ions held on the exchange sites in the soil. Some of the hydrogen ions on the cation exchange sites are held so tightly that they are not measured under most experimental conditions: this is called *exchange or reserve acidity*. These "reserve" H^+ ions are released as the acidity of the solution is reduced and this tends to *buffer* the pH of the soil; it serves to resist changes in soil pH. Both of these types of acidity vary with the type of soil, depth in the soil, type of vegetation, season, and weather. Consequently, generalized statements about soil reaction should be treated with appropriate caution.

Soil acidity can develop in several ways. Acid precipitation is a significant source in some regions, but generally it is relatively unimportant. Weathering of light-colored igneous rocks which are rich in silica can result in the production of acidic materials. Soil organisms produce acids in several ways. Organic acids may be created as a by-product of their metabolism, the organisms may cause alterations in their chemical environment that lead to the release of H^+ ions (e.g., organic nitrogen → nitrate ions → nitric acid), and acidity is formed when respiratory CO_2 combines with water to produce carbonic acid. Acids may also be produced during the decomposition of soil organic matter; litter of most conifers and of mosses such as *Sphagnum* becomes very acidic as it decomposes.

Soil alkalinity originates largely from salts, such as calcium carbonate, that hydrolyze to form strong bases. These salts originate from the weathering of rocks such as limestone or dark-colored igneous rocks which yield basic compounds as they decay. Alkalinity can also originate from the importation of basic salts in drainage water which subsequently evaporates. Highly alkaline (solonchak) or saline (solonetz) soils are frequently formed by this process in arid regions.

D. Availability of Nutrients

The nutrients required for plant growth are present in the soil in a variety of forms. They may be dissolved in the soil solution, from which they can be utilized directly. They may be absorbed onto exchange sites, from which they may enter soil solution or be directly exploited by tree roots or microorganisms that contact the exchange sites. Alternatively, they may be firmly fixed in clay lattices, immobilized in decomposition-resistant organic matter, or present in insoluble inorganic compounds. pH is important in determining the availability of many elements, because of its relationship to solubility and rates of decomposition. Figure 10.5 shows approximately how the availability of various nutrients varies with pH. Most of the macronutrients exhibit

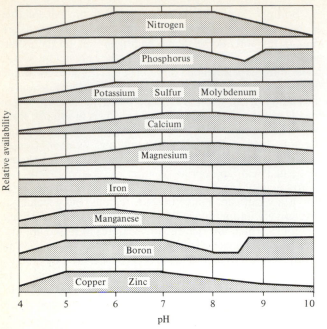

Figure 10.5
Effect of soil pH on the relative availability of twelve different nutrients. (After Truog. Reproduced from *Soil Society of America Proceedings,* vol. 11, 1946, pp. 305–8, by permission of the Soil Science Society of America.)

maximum availability at pH values between 6.5 and 7.5 (slightly acid to slightly alkaline), although metallic ions are generally less available above pH 7. Optimum availability of nutrients for most plants appears to be between pH 6 and 7 (slightly acid to neutral). Of course, pH is not the sole determinant of availability, and Figure 10.5 is only a broad generalization to which there are many exceptions.

Nitrogen occurs in both organic and inorganic forms in the soil. Except in carbon-rich sedimentary rocks, sources of soil nitrogen are exclusively from the atmosphere (pollution and fertilization being notable exceptions in certain localities). The most frequent inorganic forms of nitrogen are nitrate (NO_3^-) and ammonium (NH_4^+) ions, but in poorly aerated soils, nitrite (NO_2^-) may be formed and accumulate to toxic concentrations. Nitrate occurs almost entirely in solution and is therefore readily available to plants. Most ammonium ions are held in a readily exchangeable form on cation exchange sites. Others are fixed between the lattices of clay minerals from which they are released only slowly. Plants use both forms of inorganic nitrogen. Some species appear to favor nitrate, some flourish on ammonium nitrogen, and still others appear to grow best with a balance of

the two. Some plants actually accumulate nitrate ions in their foliage. Plants also exploit nitrogen in organic compounds. Simple amino acids can be absorbed by roots, and mycorrhizal fungi can exploit several forms of organic nitrogen. Nitrogen is available over a wide pH range, but decreasingly so below pH 6 and above pH 8, an important reason being the adverse affect of pH extremes on soil microbes. Details of the nitrogen cycle are given in Chapter 5. For a review of nitrogen in forest soils, see Wollum and Davie (1975) and Knowles (1975).

The main source of soil *phosphorus* is weathering of soil minerals, there being very little phosphorus in the atmosphere. It is available over a narrower range of pH than nitrogen, availability declining above pH 7.5 and below pH 6.5. In acid soils (pH less than 5), phosphorus in the $H_2PO_4^-$ form reacts with iron and aluminum to form insoluble compounds. Above pH 6, phosphorus reacts with calcium to form insoluble calcium phosphate, although there is generally not a great amount of free calcium in the soil until the pH rises to pH 7 or above. Maximum availability occurs at about pH 6.5. As a result of these processes, phosphorus is found only at very low levels in the soil solution (and is therefore not very subject to leaching) and many forest plants must depend upon mycorrhizal fungi to obtain the phosphorus they need. Phosphorus can exist in a number of organic forms, including chelates of iron and aluminum phosphate, and these may increase its availability to plants. It is also held on anion exchange sites.

Potassium occurs in a wide range of soil minerals and is readily available where there is active weathering of such materials. In the soil it exists almost entirely in inorganic forms, being rapidly released from organic matter following death. It is found in solution, on cation exchange sites, or ''fixed'' in the lattices of expanding clays. There is an equilibrium between these different pools of potassium, which serves to maintain fairly constant levels of availability to plants in spite of additions to or losses from the soil solution or CEC. Levels of available potassium are generally higher in organic than in mineral horizons because ''fixing'' in clay lattices in the mineral soil removes it from solution, but organic soils can be short of potassium because of the lack of inputs from mineral weathering.

As with potassium, *calcium* and *magnesium* in soils originate largely from the weathering of primary minerals. In alkaline soils they may accumulate as free carbonates (detected by the effervescence of CO_2 upon treatment with dilute hydrochloric acid), whereas in acid soils in humid climates much of the calcium and magnesium released by weathering may be leached out of the soil. Calcium is found on cation exchange sites and also in soil solution. It is present in organic matter and released on decomposition, but more slowly than potassium because it is a structural component of plant tissues, whereas potassium is a component of the easily decomposed cellular protoplasm.

Sulfur is present in soil minerals as sulfides which are weathered to sulfate (SO_4^{2-}) ions. It also reaches soil from the atmosphere as the result of direct uptake of gaseous SO_2 by plants and in precipitation. As with nitrogen, the dynamics of sulfur in soil are largely under the control of microbes.

There are small quantities of micronutrient and nonnutrient trace elements in most minerals (ore deposits excepted, of course). Their availability is low in alkaline soils. It increases as the pH drops, but in highly weathered and acidic soils availability may again be low because of leaching losses and the lack of a reservoir in unweathered materials.

E. Leaching

The chemical composition of soil is strongly affected by its water relationships. The chemical products of mineral weathering accumulate in the upper layers of soils in regions in which evaporation exceeds precipitation, resulting in alkaline (solonchak) or even saline (solonetz) soils. In humid areas, where there is an excess of precipitation over evapotranspiration, at least seasonally, chemicals released by weathering may be leached out of the upper layers of the soil. However, leaching of chemicals from soils is not dependent solely on water movement through the soil. Whether or not it occurs also depends upon the cation and anion exchange capacities of the soil, the uptake of chemicals by plants, and the balance of ions in solution.

There are two requirements for the leaching of chemicals out of soils. First, the chemicals must be in ionic form, and second, there must be hydrogen ion—mobile anion couples in the soil solution. These requirements are necessary because water draining out of soil is electrically neutral; soil water contains as many cations as anions. Ions on the exchange sites will not be leached out of the soil in spite of large water flows unless there is an adequate supply of ions in the solution: hydrogen ions to displace the other cations and anions with which the displaced cations can associate.

The process of leaching is illustrated in Figure 10.6. Soil water entering the forest floor may pick up a variety of anions, such as bicarbonate anions formed from the dissociation of carbonic acid (which is first formed by the combination of water and respiratory CO_2), nitrate ions produced by nitrifying bacteria, sulfate ions derived either from atmospheric inputs, from decomposition, or from the activities of sulfur oxidizing bacteria, and chloride ions released

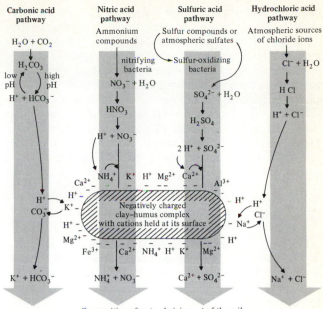

Composition of water draining out of the soil

Figure 10.6

Schematic representation of mechanisms of soil leaching. The anions involved may be predominantly bicarbonate (HCO_3^-), nitrate (NO_3^-), sulfate (SO_4^{2-}), chloride (Cl^-), or anions of organic acids (such as fulvic acid) produced during decomposition of organic matter. (After Likens et al., 1970; Cole et al., 1975; Kimmins and Feller, 1976. Based on a figure in Cole et al., 1975. Redrawn with permission of Les Presses de L'Universite Laval and D. W. Cole.)

by decomposition or from direct inputs from the atmosphere. The relative importance of these different ions varies according to the climate and soil type. In some soils bicarbonate will be the most important anion, in some nitrate will dominate, whereas in others there may be a mixture of the various different inorganic anions. The soil solution in some forest soils is dominated by organic substances such as fulvic acid or oxalic acid, which provide the majority of the anions that are involved in the leaching of cations. As this hydrogen- and anion-rich water enters the mineral soil, cations held on the negatively charged clay humus complex will be displaced. The water will pass down through and out of the soil, carrying with it salts of these anions unless they are taken out of solution by plant and microbial uptake, or unless changes in solution pH (because of the loss of H^+ ions) cause them to precipitate out of solution.

In soils characterized by high rates of CO_2 production and a pH value that permits both the formation of carbonic acid and its dissociation into bicarbonate ions (HCO_3^-) and hydrogen (H^+) ions, leaching is largely controlled by the pH-dependent abundance of bicarbonate. This has been shown to be of importance in the tropics and some temperate forests (Cole et al., 1976; Cole, 1976). In soils where there is a great abundance of nitrate ions (NO_3^-) released by chemoautotrophic nitrifying bacteria, the leaching pathway may be dominated by this ion (Likens et al., 1970). In situations such as polluted environments or near coastlines with prevailing onshore winds, chloride (Cl^-) or sulfate (SO_4^{2-}) may be important (Kimmins and Feller, 1976). The addition of nitrate or sulfate ions with fertilizers may result in the leaching of cations from the surface layers of soils.

10.5   Soil Organic Matter

Because of its intimate association with soil chemistry, the discussion of soil organic matter could have been included in the preceding section. It is accorded a section of its own to stress its preeminent importance in most forest soils.

The input and decomposition of organic matter in the form of litterfall was discussed in Chapters 4 and 5. The reader is remined that recent studies have suggested that in many forests the largely unmeasured below-ground litterfall (annual mortality of small roots and their mycorrhizal symbionts) may equal or exceed aboveground litterfall, so that most existing estimates of total annual additions of organic matter to the soil are probably low.

Litterfall is important as the source of the majority of the nutrients taken up annually by plants. It forms a superficial organic layer that plays an important role in the protection of soil against erosion and in regulating soil moisture status. Organic matter favors the activity of soil animals, and colloidal organic matter promotes soil aggregation and a favorable structure and porosity. Once decomposed into humus, the organic matter contributes significantly to CEC, while organic acids released during decomposition promote the weathering of soil minerals and the leaching of mineral nutrients. The presence of organic matter is one of the parameters that differentiates soil from "parent material" or "nonsoil."

When litter reaches the surface of the soil it undergoes physical and chemical degradation in the process of *decomposition* (see Chapter 4). In warm humid environments this is rapid and virtually complete to inorganic constituents, so that no permanent organic accumulation develops. In most forests decomposition is slower than additions, with the result that a layer of organic matter called the *forest floor* builds up. In very dry environments decomposition may be exceedingly slow, with relatively little change in the litter

other than oxidation and minor fungal decomposition. In such environments, frequent ground fire may have been the major natural agent of mineralization in the past. In more humid environments, microbial decomposition is the major agent.

Mature forests floors (those that have developed for a sufficient period of time to exhibit the features that are characteristic for the vegetation, soils, and climate of the area) can be subdivided into three distinct horizontal layers: the litter layer (L), the intermediate layer (F) (sometimes called the fermentation layer, but since decomposition in this layer is generally aerobic and fermentation is anaerobic, the term is a misnomer), and the humus layer (H):

The L layer consists of recently fallen aboveground litter that has not markedly changed in shape, form, or color from when it fell: its origin is still obvious.

The F layer is where most of the decomposition occurs, and it is frequently rich in fungal mycelia and fine tree roots which together bind the disintegrating litter into a loose mat. Physical comminution and decomposition reduces the litter to small pieces in this layer, but much of it is still recognizable as to its origin. The material is moister and darker in color than that in the L layer.

The H layer is normally more compact, darker, moister, and made up of well-decomposed material that is generally unrecognizable as to its origin (the remains of cones, rotting logs, or large bark slabs may be an exception). It may or may not be mixed with the underlying mineral soil.

Not all of these layers are always present or recognizable, and their depth and detailed characteristics vary considerably according to the type of forest floor. Often, the designation of layer boundaries is difficult, as they tend to grade into each other. In cool, moist environments the mortality of fine roots may be the major addition of organic matter to the F and H layers. Where this is the case, litterfall may be added annually throughout the forest floor and differentiation of F and H horizons may be difficult. In very humid, acid environments much of the colloidal humus of the H layer is leached down to the mineral B horizon so that a typical H layer may be absent and the forst floor may be predominantly a deep F layer. On some sites this layer may have such profuse fungal mycelium that the material is light gray rather than the normal dark brown.

In spite of these local variations in the general pattern, forest floors can generally be divided into three major categories, which represent the two extremes and the median condition of what is in reality a continuum: mor, moder, and mull.

Mor (also called *raw humus*) forest floors are generally acid and occur in cool, moist climates under temperate or boreal vegetation. Decomposition of litter is generally slow and incomplete, leaving a residue of humus, and there is an abrupt transition from the forest floor to the underlying mineral soil. The L layer varies in depth from a few millimeters to many centimeters and overlies an F layer rich in fine roots and fungal mycelia. This layer, which is of variable thickness, grades into a well-decomposed H layer, also of highly variable thickness depending upon time of development, soil, and climate. The humus can vary in texture from granular to fibrous to greasy-amorphous. It may contain large quantities of fungal mycelium and fine roots, or relatively little. In cool, humid climates, humus may be leached down into the mineral horizons, endowing them with a dark color and leaving relatively little H layer in the forest floor. In mor forest floors there is generally little activity by soil animals that are large enough to produce significant mixing of mineral particles into the humus layer. Consequently, mor humus layers usually contain very small amounts of mineral particles. The scarcity of large soil animals is beneficial for the development of fungi which dominate the microflora. Mor forest floors are characteristic of climates that inhibit decomposition, of plant species that produce slowly decomposing litter, and of very infertile soils, irrespective of climate (mor forest floors can be found from the tropics to the arctic).

Moder (also called *duff mull*) forest floors are characterized by a higher pH, more rapid and complete decomposition of litter and a more gradual transition from the forest floor to the mineral soil than in the mor type. The L layer, of variable thickness, overlies an F layer that has less abundant fungal activity than in mor forest floors (because of the increased activity of soil animals), but generally an abundance of fine roots. It grades into an H layer, which is generally quite thin (only a few centimeters) and which frequently is partially mixed with and grades into the underlying mineral soil. This reflects greater soil animal activity than in mor types. Moder forest floors are more acid than mull forest floors and there is correspondingly less faunal mixing. The humus generally has a loose, crumbly texture.

Mull forest floors are characterized by little or no L layer for most of the year in spite of considerable litter inputs, although considerable autumnal accumulations may occur in deciduous hardwood forests. The F layer is virtually absent because decomposition is so rapid, so that for much of the year the soil surface is the H layer. This is frequently an A_h[4] layer, where there is intimate mixing of the organic and underlying mineral soils, which grades almost impercepti-

---

[4]A_h: surface mineral horizon enriched with organic matter; contains less than 17% organic C by weight.

bly into underlying inorganic horizons. In some mull forest floors, the upper layer of the soil is composed entirely of earthworm casts. The active mixing of the organic material inhibits the development of fungal mycelium, and consequently bacteria dominate the microflora. Mull forest floors are characteristic of mild, moist climates and fertile soils, conditions that promote rapid decomposition and vegetation that produces readily decomposable litterfall. In less favorable climates, they can be found only on very fertile sites. In more favorable climates, they can be found on most sites.

10.6 Soil Biology

Irrespective of the physical characteristics of the land surface and the degree of physical and chemical weathering, the abiotic surface only constitutes a soil-forming potential and not a soil. Only when the lifeless geological substrate is occupied and modified by living organisms does the dynamic physical–chemical–biotic system that we call soil develop. Without biotic modification the physical components of many soils would be completely unproductive. The biota literally create their own soil environment.

The term *soil biota* refers to the organisms that spend all or part of their life cycle in the soil. They can be divided into soil flora and soil fauna. The flora will be considered first because it provides energy needed by the fauna.

A useful review of soil biology can be found in Burges and Raw (1967).

A. Soil Flora

The term *soil flora* refers to a diverse group of nonanimal soil organisms that include bacteria, actinomycetes, fungi, and algae (all members of the microflora) and those parts (the roots) of higher plants (macroflora) that occupy the soil. The macroflora will only be given partial treatment here since they are discussed in a subsequent section.

1. Microflora. The soil microflora can be classified either functionally or taxonomically. The group includes autotrophs and heterotrophs. The former consists of both photoautotrophs and chemoautotrophs; the latter includes symbiotic, parasitic, and saprophytic species.

a. BACTERIA. Soil bacteria can be classified by their shape or by how they take up stains. For our purposes, a classification based on their ecological function is more useful.

i. Autotrophic bacteria. These are all chemoautotrophs which satisfy their energy needs by utilizing energy released during transformations of inorganic compounds. The genera

Nitrosocystis, Nitrosogloea, and especially *Nitrosomonas* can convert ammonium nitrogen (NH_4^+) to nitrite nitrogen (NO_2^-), and *Nitrobacter* oxidizes it further to nitrate nitrogen (NO_3^-). This process of *nitrification* is particularly active in soils at pH values close to neutral, with mild temperatures, moist soils, and a supply of readily decomposable ammonium substrate. Relatively little nitrification occurs in forest soils with low pH, but there may be a great increase in the activity of nitrifying bacteria when such soils are limed (Figure 10.7), or following clearcutting (Martin, 1985) or devegetation (Figure 5.16). Other bacteria use nitrate nitrogen as a source of oxygen, reducing it to gaseous N_2 or N_2O, a process called *denitrification*. Certain species of *Bacillus, Pseudomonas,* and *Achromobacter* are involved in this process.

Both sulfur and iron are also utilized by chemo-autotrophs. Some species of bacteria can oxidize sulfur or sulfides to sulfate ions (and hence to sulfuric acid): *Thiobacillus, Beggiotoa,* and *Thiothrix.* This ability is put to practical use in forest nurseries where "flowers of sulfur" mixed with organic matter is added to forest nursery soils to reduce an undesirably high pH. Sulfur may also be added with insoluble fertilizers such as rock phosphate. The sulfuric acid that results from the bacterial activity converts the insoluble material to soluble monocalcium phosphate, which is readily available to plants. Oxidized sulfur compounds may also experience reduction by anaerobic bacteria. For example, *Sporovibrio desulphuricans* is important in reducing sulfates to hydrogen sulfide in poorly drained organic soils. The resulting toxic accumulations of this gas are partly responsible for the poor growth of trees in stagnant swamps. Apparently, these sulfur-reducing bacteria are not very active at pH values below 5.5.

Iron bacteria such as *Crenothrix, Leptothrix,* and *Gallionella* derive their energy from the oxidation of soluble ferrous iron to almost insoluble ferric iron, while under anaerobic conditions other bacteria reconvert ferric forms back to the ferrous state. The red staining of rocks by water draining from puddled or gleyed soils is largely the result of the activities of these iron bacteria. Manganese experiences similar transformations and toxic levels of the soluble reduced forms of these two elements are partly responsible for poor root development in such anaerobic soils. Water flowing out of such soils often has what appears to be a film of oil on the surface. Closer inspection reveals that the water is coated with a thin film of microscopic crystals, which form as the ferrous iron–rich deoxygenated water contacts atmospheric oxygen. These crystals act as a defraction grating which produces the colors of the spectrum.

ii. Heterotrophic bacteria. The abundance of hetero-

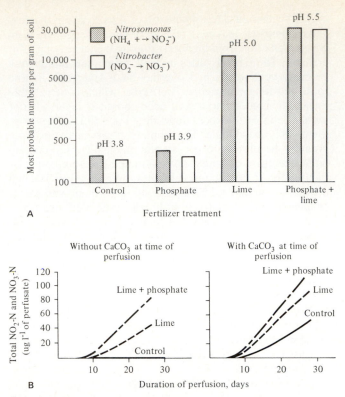

Figure 10.7

Effect of liming on the abundance and activity of nitrifying bacteria in an acidic forest soil under a beech-maple stand in Ontario. The study was conducted 8 years after the lime (in the form of ground dolomitic limestone) and phosphorus were applied. (A) Effect of lime, with or without phosphorus fertilizer, on the abundance (expressed as most probable numbers) of nitrifying bacteria and the pH of the humus layer of the forest floor. The limiting pH for the bacteria was apparently between 3.9 and 5.0. (B) Effect of lime, with or without phosphorus, on rate of nitrifaction of added ammonium sulfate; and with or without additions of $CaCo_3$ at the time of the study to further increase the pH (Perfusion is a laboratory technique used in studies of nitrification). The delay in the nitrification response is time needed for bacterial numbers to increase in response to the addition of ammonium nitrogen. (After Corke, 1958. Used by permission of Michigan State University and the author.)

trophic bacteria in soils appears to be related to two major factors: the availability of a suitable energy substrate and a tolerable pH. Temperature and moisture are also important regulators of these saprotrophs, as is the inhibitory effect that other soil flora have on them. Heterotrophic bacteria utilize simple sugars and starches, but can also utilize cellulose, hemicellulose, and proteinaceous substances (especially species of *Bacillus*) by means of enzymes that they secrete.

An important role of heterotrophic bacteria is the breakdown of complex nitrogen-containing molecules to ammonium nitrogen, which then becomes the substrate for the chemoautotrophic nitrogen bacteria. A lot of the nitrogen in readily available forms (NO_3^- and NH_4^+) is rapidly taken up and retained in bacterial biomass (in a process known as *microbial immobilization*), so much of the nitrogen released by microbial decomposition is not available to plants. Bacteria require nitrogen and other nutrients in order to exploit the energy in the cellulose and other organic molecules of undecomposed organic matter. Large quantities of such matter in soils can result in nitrogen-deficiency symptoms in plants, as most of the available nitrogen is immobilized by the microbes. Similarly, nitrogen fertilizer is often less effective on soils that have a high carbon-to-nitrogen (C/N) ratio and a lot of undecomposed woody material. As the C/N ratio is lowered and wood materials are decomposed, much of this microbial nitrogen is released and plant nitrogen nutrition is improved.

The overall role of heterotrophic bacteria in the decomposition of complex organic matter is hard to assess. They are known to prepare such material for faunal consumption and are important in fertile soils of near-neutral reaction. They also play an important role in organic decomposition as the gut flora of soil animals. They are much less important than fungi in acid forest soils and their activity is probably inhibited by soil fungi in much the same way that pathogenic bacteria are inhibited by secretions from fungi of the genus *Penicillum*. It has been shown that elimination of mycorrhizal fungi from the forest floor of a radiata pine plantation in New Zealand results in a greatly accelerated activity of nonmycorrhizal saprophitic organisms and more rapid litter decomposition; the *Gadgil effect* (Gadgil and Gadgil, 1975).

One group of heterotrophic bacteria have the ability to fix atmospheric nitrogen (N_2, sometimes called dinitrogen). Both aerobic *(Azotobacter, Achromobacter, and Biejerinckia)* and anaerobic *(Clostridium)* nitrogen fixers have been identified. Bacteria of the genus *Clostridium* are also noteworthy because of their ability to decompose cellulose and because they are more tolerant of acid soils than are *Azotobacter*. For example, the most probable numbers[5] of *Clostridium* in a fertilized maple–beech stand in Ontario 8 years after fertilization were 19,000 (lime treatment; pH 5.0) to 92,500 (lime + phosphate treatment; pH 5.5) per gram of humus, while *Azotobacter* were undetected. In the untreated control plot (pH 3.8) a value of 80,000 was found. *Clostridium* was thought to be the major organism

responsible for the fixation of 44 kg ha^{-1} yr^{-1} of nitrogen in a mull humus forest floor beneath a stand of sugar maple (this was increased to 60 kg ha^{-1} yr^{-1} by the addition of glucose as an energy substrate), while less than 1 kg ha^{-1} yr^{-1} was fixed in a mor humus forest floor beneath American beech (Knowles, 1965). Fixation of about 33 kg ha^{-1} yr^{-1} under aspen (Brouzes et al., 1969) and 15–18 kg ha^{-1} yr^{-1} under Douglas-fir (Fortin et al., 1979) has been reported.

iii. Symbiotic bacteria. The symbiotic (mutually beneficial) relationship between various nitrogen-fixing bacteria and higher plants was discussed in Chapter 5 (see Table 5.4). The relationship between *Rhizobium* and many species of legume is well known, but many nonlegumous perennial plants also have root nodules containing nitrogen-fixing bacteria. These associations give higher plants the ability to colonize and grow in nitrogen-deficient environments and are an important aspect of plant succession (Chapter 15). Such nodulated plants have a stimulatory effect on nonnodulated plants growing with them.

b. ACTINOMYCETES. This is a group of organisms sometimes (but wrongly) grouped with the fungi. They exhibit characteristics of both fungi and bacteria, consisting of nonseptate branching hyphae which are often brightly colored. These hyphae are easily broken into short rods resembling bacteria. In contrast to fungi, they are sensitive to acidity and are absent at pH 4.7 or lower. An outstanding characteristic is their ability to produce antibiotics of high toxicity to other microbes. They are most abundant in grassland or agricultural soils but are also found in forest soils. As heterotrophs, they can decompose cellulose, hemicellulose, and simple carbohydrates, and some species can decompose chitin (found in insect exoskeletons and cell walls of fungi).

Of major ecological significance is the involvement of soil actinomycetes of the genus *Frankia* in symbiotic nitrogen fixation. The actinomycetes invade the root hairs of nonlegumes and form distinctive nodules which can equal or exceed the nitrogen-fixation rate of *Rhizobium*–legume nodules. About 160 species from 13 genera of nonlegumes are known to develop nodules (Bond, 1977), of which the most significant for forestry is the *Alnus–Frankia* relationship. Conifers such as Douglas-fir attain much better growth on nitrogen-deficient soils when there is a subordinate layer of red alder. As much as 320 kg ha^{-1} yr^{-1} peak additions of nitrogen have been estimated for temperate red alder stands (see Chapter 5), and mean values under five species of alder range from 12 to 300 kg ha^{-1} yr^{-1} (Tarrant and Trappe, 1971). An understory of another actinomycete-nodulated species, snow brush *(Ceanothus),* in Oregon forests has been shown to contribute up to 20 kg ha^{-1} yr^{-1}

[5] A commonly used unit of estimated bacterial numbers.

(Figure 10.8). For further reading on N-fixation, see Fortin et al., 1979 and Chatarpaul and Carlisle, 1983.

c. FUNGI. The fungi make up the majority of the saprotrophic heterotrophs (decomposer organisms) in many forest soils, especially in acidic soils with mor humus. They are most abundant and obvious in the F layer, where they form an interconnecting web of white, yellow, or dark-colored strands which frequently form small fan-shaped mycellial networks clearly visible to the naked eye. Microscopic examination reveals their presence in both the L and the H layers of the forest floor and also in the underlying mineral horizons, but their abundance drops off rapidly with depth. A study in a pine stand in Scotland revealed concentrations of fungal hyphae (expressed as meters of hyphae per cubic centimeter of soil) of 5.6 m cm^{-3} in the organic H horizon and only 0.4 m cm^{-3} in the mineral B horizon (Burgess, 1963).

Fungi vary in their ability to utilize organic matter. Some species utilize cellulose but not lignin, darkening the material they decompose and making it weak and crumbly (brown rot). Others attack lignin but leave the cellulose, which results in a fibrous residue with a lighter color (white rot). There is often a characteristic sequence of fungi participating in the decomposition of decaying wood. Such tissue is first invaded by fungi utilizing sugars and other simple carbon compounds. They are followed by cellulose decomposers, and finally lignin decomposers take over. This sequence of decomposition may vary in different soils.

Perhaps the most significant group of fungi are those that form symbiotic mycorrhizal associations with tree roots. The mycorrhizal phenomenon is not yet completely understood, but good reviews can be found in Bjorkman (1970),

Hacskaylo (1971), and Harley (1969). The nutritional significance of mycorrhizae was mentioned in Chapter 5. It has been shown that they increase the efficiency of uptake of nutrients which are at very low concentrations in soil solution, and it is believed that they accelerate mineral weathering and absorb the nutrients that are released thereby. They facilitate the uptake of phosphorus and organic forms of nitrogen and promote the fixation of nitrogen by other organisms (see references in Voigt, 1971).

Mycorrhizae may prolong the life of roots, increase their diameter and branchiness, and even inhibit the attack of pathogenic fungi. It has been estimated that mycorrhizae increase the surface area of pine roots by hundreds or even thousands of times in comparison to unaffected roots. In fact, pine trees do not exist in nature without mycorrhizae. It has also been observed that pines have a stimulatory effect on other trees growing with them in nitrogen-limited environments that resembles the effects of nitrogen fertilizer. The process involved is not known, but it may be either that the pine mycorrhizae are mobilizing previously unavailable nitrogen resources or that they stimulate nitrogen fixation. Mycorrhizae increase the tolerance of roots to extremes of pH caused by high levels of soil sulfur and aluminum. They increase the resistance of roots to other toxins, to high temperatures, and to drought (Marx and Brian, 1976). Mycorrhizae also improve the ability of trees to exploit soil water (Read, 1980).

With this long list of advantages, it is not surprising that the mycorrhizal habit is the most common root condition for a great many plants, and it appears that mycorrhizae have been selected in evolution rather than uninfected root systems (Harley, 1969).

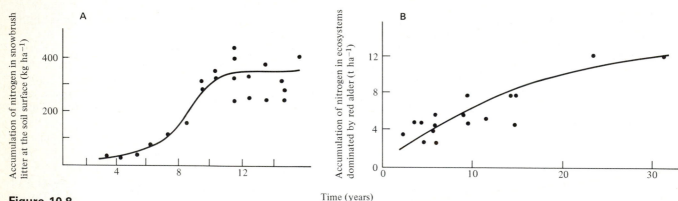

Time (years)

Figure 10.8

Accumulation of nitrogen by communities of (A) snowbrush, *Ceanothus velutinus* and (B) red alder in Oregon. (A, after Zavitovski and Newton, 1968a. Redrawn by permission of the Ecological Society of America and the authors; B, data from Newton et al., 1968.)

There are two major forms of mycorrhizae: *ectotrophic* and *endotrophic*. Ectotrophic mycorrhizae, or simply ectomycorrhizae, consist of a short, thickened side branch of a fine root around which fungal mycellium has grown as a sheath. This sheath is connected to hyphae throughout the surrounding soil, and hyphae from the sheath penetrate the outer layers of the root and form a network (the *Hartig net*) around the cortical cells. Endotrophic forms (endomycorrhizae) do not have the outer fungal sheath and the hyphae of the Hartig net penetrate the cells of the cortex (Figure 10.9). An intermediate form, the *ectendomycorrhizae*, has a sheath but also penetrates into the cells, where they form swellings called *vesicles* or *arbuscules*. Ectomycorrhizae in particular are thought to be an adaption to nutrient-deficient soils and most of the work on the value of mycorrhizae to trees has been done on this form. Relatively little work has been done on endomycorrhizae, but it is thought that they confer the same general benefits with the exception of the increased resistance to root disease.

Mycorrhizal associations are not permanent. Initial formation occurs in the first growing season after the primary leaves of the seedling have been produced. The association lasts for about one year, after which the infected root tip may die or may grow rapidly in length, thereby throwing off the fungal sheath and becoming a normal nonmycorrhizal root. New mycorrhizal associations are formed each year. Formation of mycorrhizal associations is promoted by moderate nutrient deficiency, and seedlings grown in pots with repeated fertilization have fewer mycorrhizae than do unfertilized control trees. If the nutrient deficiency is extreme, the development of mycorrhizae is inhibited because the trees are unable to provide the roots with the supply of carbohydrates that is apparently necessary for the maintenance of the association.

Inoculation of nursery stock with mycorrhizal-forming fungi offers great potential for improvement of artificial forest regeneration. Many cases of poor growth of seedlings on infertile nursery soils, of failures of introduced species (especially pines) in Australia, New Zealand, and Great Britain, and of failures in reforestation of prairies and heaths have been corrected by inoculating the problem area with appropriate fungi. Failure of trees to invade grasslands may in part reflect the antibiotic effect of grass roots on the fungi that form mycorrhizae with trees. Several studies have demonstrated satisfactory tree growth when such areas are planted with tree seedlings grown in nursery soils inoculated with specific ectomycorrhizal fungi (Moser, 1959; Theodorou and Bowen, 1970; Lamb and Richards, 1971).

There has recently been great interest in the fungus *Pisolithus tinctorius* as a mycorrhizal symbiont. It stimulates much greater development of dichotomous roots compared with natural symbionts, and greatly increases the rate of biomass accumulation in nursery seedlings. Table 10.3 shows the effects of this fungus on the growth of lodgepole pine, Douglas-fir, and loblolly pine seedlings in the nursery. The efficacy of this species of mycorrhizal symbiont when the seedlings are planted out in the forest has yet to be assessed.

d. ALGAE. Free-living algae occur at the interface of the soil and the atmosphere. Of the several groups that occur, the blue-green algae are capable of nitrogen fixation, and this is thought to be of considerable importance during the colonization of exposed mineral soils by plant communities.

2. Macroflora (Plant Roots). Roots play an important role in soil development and function. They penetrate mineral soil, sometimes to considerable depths. Organic matter is contributed to the lower soil horizons when roots die, increasing CEC and promoting the formation of soil structure. The channels left in the soil after the dead roots have decayed improve soil aeration and facilitate the movement of gravitational water—important changes in fine-textured soils. Roots increase the rate of weathering of primary soil minerals and rock, either because of organic compounds they secrete, or because of the activities of the microorganisms that live in association with roots. These include most mycorrhizal fungi and a variety of microorganisms that live in the *rhizosphere*. Where there is a lack of mineral soil, trees may be able to obtain their mineral nutrients directly from rock surfaces by this means (lithoponics).

The rhizosphere is that portion of the soil in which the abundance and composition of the microbial population is influenced by the presence of the roots. The roots release carbohydrates, vitamins, and amino acids into the surrounding layer of soil, which results in increases in bacterial numbers by as much as 20 times (Katznelson, 1965). This increase in microbial metabolic activity accelerates mineral weathering, and the rhizosphere microbial community is frequently enriched in species that either fix atmospheric nitrogen or hydrolyze organic nitrogen to ammonium forms (ammonifiers). Formation of soil structure is also facilitated by the increased microbial activity. Some of the organisms in the rhizosphere produce growth-regulating compounds (auxins) that modify the form of root growth. These would include root nodule–forming bacteria and mycorrhizal-forming fungi (Slankis, 1958).

One of the important effects of roots on the soil results from the high turnover of fine roots. Root mortality in grasses results in a great enrichment of organic matter in mineral layers in prairie soils, and the accumulation of forest floors can be as much or more the result of the produc-

ECTOMYCORRHIZAE

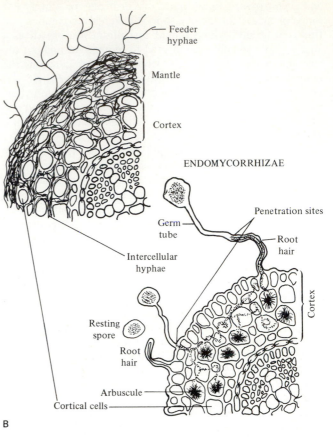

Figure 10.9

Mycorrhizae. (A) Ectomycorrhizal shortroots
formed by *Pisolithus tinctorius* Myl. on lodgepole
pine. (B) Diagrammatic cross-section of ecto- and
endo-mycorrhizae on tree roots. (C) Photo of
Douglas-fir seedlings in an Oregon forest nursery
recently converted from a grass field. Only the
larger seedlings in the center were infected with
mycorrhizal fungi. (D) The growth and survival of
mycorrhizal seedlings shown in C was substantially
better than the non-mycorrhizal seedlings (A, courtesy of V. G. Marshall, Canadian Forest Service.
B, C, and D adapted from DeYoe and Cromak,
1983. Used by permission of Oregon State University Extension Service and authors.)

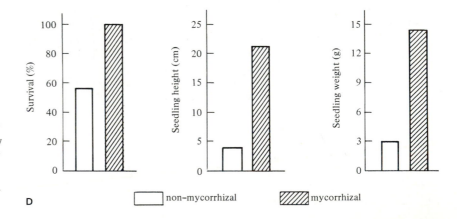

Table 10.3 Growth of Seedlings of Three Species With and Without Incorporation of *Pisolithus tinctorius* Inoculum into the Nursery Soil Mix in Which the Seedlings Were Grown

Species and Treatment	Weight at 16 Weeks after Seeding, mg			Shoot/root Ratio
	Shoot	Root	Total	
Douglas-fir[a]				
Inoculated	354(51)[b]	151(35)	505(40)	2.36
Control	235	112	347	2.11
Lodgepole pine[a]				
Inoculated	129(55)	120(48)	249(52)	1.08
Control	83	81	164	1.03

	Wt. in g. of 7 Month Seedling					
	Shoot	Root	Total	Shoot/root Ratio	Ht. (cm)	Stem diam. (mm)
Loblolly pine[c]						
Inoculated	8.9(112)	2.6(86)	11.5(105)	3.42	36(38)	8.2(37)
Control	4.2	1.4	5.6	3.00	26	6.0

[a]Data from J. A. Dangerfield (unpublished).
[b]Percent increase attributable to inoculation.
[c]Data from Marx and Bryan (1976).

tion and death of fine roots and mycorrhizal fungi as it is of aboveground litterfall. As already mentioned, this poses problems in the classification of forest floors into L, F, and H layers since fine-root mortality may add fresh "litter" to each of these three layers annually.

Roots provide plants with a number of important requisites for life: stability, water, and most of the necessary nutrients. Their importance is reflected in the considerable investment by plants in root biomass: as much as 20–45% of tree biomass in polar areas and as little as 10–20% in tropical areas. More than 50% of annual biomass production may be invested in root production, and one reason for the small aboveground production on infertile sites is believed to be the high production of fine roots necessary to obtain the required nutrients.

Root systems can take a variety of forms [taproot, heart root, and flat root (Figure 10.10)] as a result of the influence of a variety of factors (see reviews in Sutton, 1969; Bilan, 1971; and Herman, 1977). These forms are more under environmental than genetic control. For instance, spruce trees, long thought to be shallow-rooted, can have heart roots and even taproots extending to a considerable depth when grown on suitable soils. Pines, which have traditionally been thought of as having deeply penetrating taproots, can have flat roots on soils that restrict rooting. The evolutionary relationship between certain tree species and certain types of sites certainly does result in trees having inherent root growth forms, but these are broadly modified by the rooting environment. Some species have highly plastic root forms: environmental factors can easily modify them. Other species have nonplastic root forms: the genetically controlled form is apparent irrespective of soil types (e.g., black spruce).

The stability that roots confer is particularly important for tall plants such as trees. The resistance to windthrow depends partly on rooting depth and volume and partly on the tolerance of the tree species to soil conditions. Spruces, which tolerate severe restriction of root penetration when they grow on swampy soils, are often more resistant to windthrow on such sites than are pines. Species of the latter genus are adapted to drier sites and are less tolerant of the extreme root modification that occurs on the wet sites.

Nutrients and moisture are absorbed from the soil with an efficiency that depends to a considerable extent upon root distribution relative to the resources of moisture and nutrients. Most nutrient uptake occurs in fine roots (less than 2 mm in diameter) which tend to be concentrated in the surface soil horizons (cf. Figure 5.3), especially in acidic, nutrient-poor soils. Conversely, moisture is taken up throughout the profile wherever the moisture is available to the roots. The following factors are important in determining the vertical distribution of roots in forest soils.

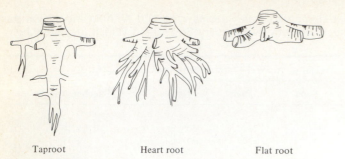

Taproot   Heart root   Flat root

Figure 10.10
The three major types of root system commonly found in trees. In some tree species the form of the root is under strong genetic control, whereas in others the root form is more a reflection of the soil conditions under which the tree is growing. Intermediates between these three main types are common. (After Armson, 1977. Used by permission of the University of Toronto press and the author.)

1. *Physical soil properties*. Roots cannot penetrate into excessively hard material such as solid bedrock or hardpan (a compacted or cemented horizontal layer in the soil) and will be shallow where such obstructions are close to the surface.
2. *Soil moisture and aeration*. Roots cannot grow indefinitely in dry or oxygen-deficient soils. Fine roots may grow into such zones but will die sooner or later, so that larger roots can never develop. In humid forests there is abundant rooting in the F and even in the L layer of the forest floor: in dry climates fine roots are absent from the L and much of the F layer of forest floors and may even be absent from the H layer. In such forests they are restricted entirely to the moister mineral soil. Lack of oxygen and/or toxic accumulations of carbon dioxide may exclude fine roots from lower layers of soil with poor aeration, and from structureless soils.
3. *Soil temperature*. Although roots have lower cardinal temperatures than shoots do, reduced temperatures do limit root growth. Surface soils warm up much earlier in spring than deeper soils do, so new root growth tends to be concentrated on the surface layers. Permanently frozen soils completely restrict root growth.
4. *Nutrition*. Roots that grow into more fertile soil tend to grow faster than those that grow into less fertile soil. Consequently, root growth tends to be more prolific in the surface organic horizon or the most fertile mineral horizons. The poorer the soil, the more superficial the fine roots: the richer the soil, the more uniform the distribution of fine roots with depth. This is only true, however, where moisture is not severely limiting.
5. *Competition or interaction with roots of other species*. Roots of established lesser vegetation (e.g., grasses or

shrubs) compete effectively for moisture and nutrients in the surface soil and may effectively exclude or restrict the roots of planted trees or invading woody plants. Some plants exude chemicals from their roots that inhibit the root growth of other species (alellopathy; see Chapter 14). Root competition can result in the failure of regeneration on grassy and shrubby sites.
6. *Soil chemistry*. Toxic accumulations of chemicals such as iron or aluminum, or a chemical in a toxic reduced form may inhibit fine-root growth. This may prevent roots from penetrating down into the soil B horizon. The damaging effects on trees of acid rain is thought to be related to the mobilization of iron and aluminum which inhibits fine root development, impairing tree nutrition and resistance to summer drought.

B. Soil Fauna

The soil fauna include all animals that spend at least part of their life in the soil. They are a diverse group, ranging from moderately large mammals that excavate underground burrows, to microscopic mites, nematodes, and even protozoans that live in films of water coating soil particles (Figure 10.11). Reviews of soil animals can be found in Wallwork (1970) and Jackson and Rowe (1966). Soil fauna can be classified in a number of ways.

1. By size:
   a. Macrofauna. Animals whose body size is greater than 1 cm: vertebrates, mollusks, earthworms, and larger arthropods.
   b. Mesofauna. Body size from 0.2 mm (the smallest size visible with a hand lens) to 1 cm: mites, springtails *(Collembola)*, potworms *(Enchytraeids)*, and larger nematodes.
   c. Microfauna. Microscopic organisms less than 0.2 mm: smaller mites and nemotodes, and protozoans.
2. By habitat:
   a. Animals that inhabit the surface litter (e.g., snails) because they are too large to penetrate the soil.
   b. Animals that live in the pore spaces of structured soil.
   c. Burrowing animals such as worms or ants (burrowing vertebrates are generally of local rather than general importance).
3. By trophic relationships:
   a. Bacteria and some protozoans are preyed upon by other protozoans, and mites graze on the fungi that are decomposing the organic matter.

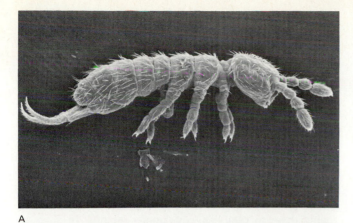

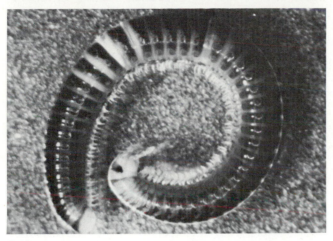

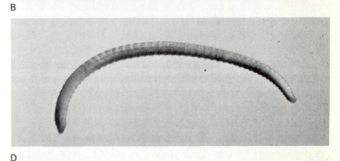

Figure 10.11
Some of the more common types of soil animal found in forest floors:
(A) A springtail (Colembola; Arthropoda); (B) A pseudoscorpion (Pseudoscorpionida; Arthropoda); (C) A millipede (Diplopoda; Arthropoda); (D) Enchytraeid worm (Annelida); (E) Orabatid mite (Acari; Arthropoda). (Photos courtesy of Dr. V. G. Marshall, Canadian Forestry Service.)

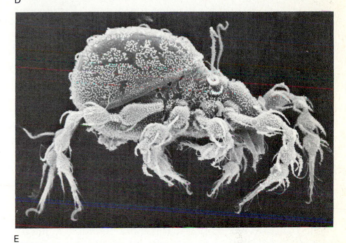

b. Mites are consumed by other arthropods, which together with earthworms are preyed upon by burrowing mammals.

c. The feces of soil animals are rapidly invaded by fungi and bacteria, which are then grazed by various animals, including earthworms. There is a marked succession of fungi and fauna during the various stages of breakdown of organic matter.

1. Macrofauna: a. SOIL VERTEBRATES. Soil vertebrates influence soil and vegetation in several ways. Their burrowing activities influence soil aeration and structure, soil drainage, and soil development. By active churning of the soil, the development of typical soil horizons may be prevented. Many soil vertebrates feed on insects and plant seeds at the surface of the soil and thus have a significant effect on the overall composition of the soil fauna and on vegetation development. Tree invasion of prairies and sub-alpine meadows may be inhibited by animal consumption of tree seed and damage to roots or girdling of the stems of seedlings. Plant community species composition and rates of succession in general are affected. Predation of Douglas-fir seed by the white-footed deer mouse *(Peromyscus maniculatus)* in British Columbia frequently precludes natural regeneration of this tree except in years of very heavy seed crops. This mouse, which can reach densities of 30 per hectare, can consume up to 300 seeds per night (Sullivan, 1968b). It has been suggested that the marked periodicity of Douglas-fir seed crops could be in part an evolutionary response to this very heavy seed predation.

b. MOLLUSKS. Mollusks are particularly abundant on richer soils, where the calcium needed for their metabolism is abundant. Some feed on living plants, some are sapro-phytic and utilize litter, and some are predatory and feed on earthworms. In some forest types, large slugs are the major herbivore feeding on minor vegetation (e.g., on the coast of British Columbia); they can also be major herbivore pests in agricultural ecosystems (Rollo, 1978).

c. EARTHWORMS. Earthworms have received more attention than any other group of soil animals. There are many different genera and species with widely varying habitat requirements, which occur from low-elevation agricultural soils to high-elevation subalpine forest soils. Earthworms are responsible for large-scale soil mixing. This takes surface organic matter deep into the mineral soil, promoting good soil structure, and bringing mineral material from lower horizons to the soil surface. By their burrowing activities, earthworms can, over a period of centuries, bury large rocks and even the ruins of old stone buildings. Their burrows aerate the soil and provide channels for water movement. Their feces are invaded by bacteria and form fairly stable soil aggregates, so that soils with abundant earthworm activity are generally well aerated, well structured, and fertile.

Forest floors influenced by earthworms are mulls, and may consist almost entirely of worm casts and aggregates formed by microbial activity. The worms convert the organic matter to a condition that is more favorable to microbial decomposition, and this may be the most significant overall effect of earthworms (Satchell, 1967). Mulls can develop within a few years of the introduction of earthworms to wormless soils with mor forest floors (Langmaid, 1964) (Figure 10.12). Earthworms do not tolerate flooding, and will come to the surface during heavy rain. Neither do they tolerate drought. During hot, dry weather, worms will move to deeper, moister layers in the soil.

d. MILLIPEDES. Millipedes play an important role in the initial comminution and decomposition of organic matter in forest soils. They tend to be most abundant on moist sites with moder or mull humus types.

e. TERMITES. Termites play a major role in many tropical soils. Soil mixing and incorporation of organic matter occurs as with earthworms. The construction of termite mounds from the finest soil particles apparently results over long periods of time in a fine-textured, gravel-free upper soil layer which is more susceptible to some forms of soil erosion than the original soil (Nye, 1954).

2. *Mesofauna:* a. ANTS. Ants alter the bulk density of soils in the vicinity of their burrows, and this change can extend to some depth in the soil. Their social organization enable them to establish populations rapidly. In areas of prolific ant activity, considerable quantities of material are brought to the surface from lower horizons. This material accumulates at the surface and after a prolonged period it forms the surface mineral layer in much the same way that termites affect surface texture in the tropics. As predators, ants affect the composition of the soil fauna. Their overall effects on soil have not been studied in detail.

b. MITES (Acari). Mites are one of the most numerous groups of animals in most forest soils; their numbers can go as high as 10,000 per cubic meter. They are located mainly in the organic surface layers, where they are important in decomposition. In addition to feeding directly on organic matter, they graze on bacteria and fungi.

c. SPRINGTAILS (Collembola). Springtails are another very prolific group of soil animals, especially in the surface organic layers. They have been reported to reach densities approaching 50,000 per square meter in a Douglas-fir plantation (Poole, 1961). They are more abundant in moder and mor forest floors than in mulls, possibly because of their habit of feeding on fungi, which are much less abundant in mull than in mor or moder humus. They also feed on living and dead plant material, feces, bacteria, and algae (Armson, 1977).

d. POTWORMS (Enchytraeids). Potworms are small white worms that can attain amazing numbers [250,000 per square meter (O'Connor, 1957)]. Potworms are thought to feed primarily on dead organic matter, but also on small feces. They ingest small mineral particles and are probably important in mixing organic matter into the mineral soil.

e. NEMATODES. These are small round worms that are best known for their parasitism of plants. Some nematodes are predaceous on other soil organisms. They are not thought to be involved in the decomposition of organic matter.

Figure 10.12

Conversion of a podzolic mor-forest floor to a mull-forest floor following the invasion of the site by earthworms in a New Brunswick coniferous-deciduous forest ecosystem with a silt-loam soil. Over a 3-year period virtually all of the forest floor was incorporated into the upper mineral soil. Similar effects were observed in sandy, silty, and slaty soils. In all cases there was a general increase in the pH of the surface mineral layers, in some cases by as much as 0.6 pH unit. (After Langmaid, 1964. Used by permission of the Agricultural Institute of Canada.)

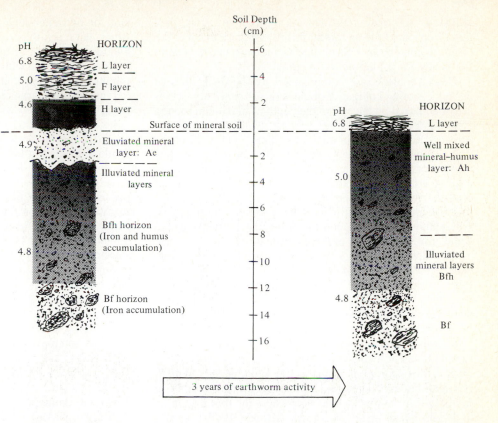

3. *Microfauna.* a. SMALLER MITES AND NEMATODES. Essentially similar to larger mites and nematodes of the mesofauna. Owing to their great numbers, mites play a major role in producing the friable crumb structure of some humus forms.

10.7 Soil Fertility

Soil fertility is "the status of the soil with respect to its ability to supply the nutrients essential to plant growth" (S.S.S.A., 1973). Soil fertility can be considered either in terms of the availability of nutrients to plants or in terms of plant nutrition. Nutrient availability is determined by the sum total of the physical, chemical, and biological characteristics of the soil, and consequently assessment of soil fertility is no easy matter. Tree nutrition is an equally complex subject because of the interactions between different nutrients, the variation in nutrient demand with species, age and physiological condition, and because of a general lack of knowledge as to the nutrient requirements of trees.

Soil fertility is so complex that only a rather brief summary is possible here. A more detailed treatment of the topic can be found in Tisdale and Nelson (1966), Morrison (1974), and Armson (1977). However, in spite of the difficulties in defining soil fertility, it continues to be of great interest to growers of plants because the nutrient regime is one of the principal environmental factors over which some degree of control can be exercised. Various approaches have been made to the assessment of site fertility.

A. Measurement of Levels of Nutrients

The total quantity and the "availability" of nutrients in the soil can be measured analytically. Interpretation of such measures is usually based on the results of agricultural studies, but often there is little correlation between conventional analytical measures of nutrient availability and the growth of forest trees. Different analytical methods yield widely varying estimates of availability and it is frequently unclear which estimate is the most reliable. Analytical measurement of the total nutrient levels in the soil are more reliable, but although such totals represent a long-term reservoir, they may contribute little to current fertility because much of the reservoir may be in a form that will remain unavailable to the plants for a long period of time.

These problems are compounded by the difficulties of defining rooting volume. Estimates of soil nutrient reserves are often based on the soil to the depth of maximum rooting (*root system sorption zone:* rooting depth × area of root spread). In Chapter 5 it was noted that virtually all of the fine feeding roots may be concentrated in the upper few centimeters of the soil, even though the depth of maximum rooting may be as great as 2 m. The nutrient reserve in the root system sorption zone may therefore be a gross overestimate of the pool of nutrients being exploited by the trees. Alternatively, one can consider only the nutrients within some arbitrary distance of the individual roots (e.g., 1 cm), a zone defined as the *root surface sorption zone* (Voigt et al., 1964). Table 10.4 compares the available amounts of three nutrients in these two zones. From this discussion it should be obvious that conclusions concerning fertility depend very much on the analytical procedures used and on the volume of soil that is being considered.

A further problem is that conventional analysis of a soil sample taken at a single point in time ignores mass movement or diffusion of elements to tree roots in soil solution. Nutrients contained in downslope seepage are a major factor in the fertility of lower slope sites where the rooting zone is underlain by an impervious layer (Klinka, 1976), but this important type of nutrient input is ignored by conventional soil analysis. Shorter-distance movements are also impor-tant for nutrients such as potassium and nitrate nitrogen, which can reach the roots from variable distances in the soil by either diffusion or mass flow (Ballard and Cole, 1974).

Other problems with the soil analysis method of deter-mining fertility are that it gives a static picture of what is a dynamic soil parameter, and a small capital of nutrients being rapidly cycled will result in a more fertile soil than a large capital of nutrients cycling slowly. Fertility is also related to the demands of the plant crop. A site may be quite fertile in terms of the low demands of a pine crop, whereas the soil might be infertile in terms of the requirements of a more nutrient-demanding crop such as spruce or fir. A soil that is quite fertile in terms of the modest requirements of many species of conifer may be very infertile in terms of the demands of many species of deciduous hardwood.

Once the relationships between plant growth and some selected soil analysis parameters have been established, the method is relatively quick and inexpensive. Unfortun-ately, establishing these relationships can involve consid-erable effort and expense and the method is compounded by the problems of soil heterogeneity. The high cost of soil analysis often restricts the number of samples so much that this method cannot give an accurate picture of site fertility.

B. Foliar Analysis

An alternative and commonly used approach is to mea-sure the concentration or content of nutrient elements in plants, although the relationship between foliar chemistry and soil fertility is not a simple one. If the plant is growing particularly well it may have lower concentrations of certain elements (because of the dilution by all the carbon, oxygen and hydrogen that is being incorporated in the biomass) than if the plant were growing only moderately well. Very low concentrations of essential nutrients are normally associated with slow growth, but the relationship is not necessarily causal. Factors such as adverse climate, root pathogens and soil moisture conditions can result in low foliar con-centrations on fertile soils or quite high foliar concentra-tions of some nutrients in trees that are growing slowly on dry sites.

Foliar analysis is quick and relatively inexpensive once reliable relationships between foliar chemistry and growth performance have been established, but there are some drawbacks. Considerable effort and expense are involved in establishing such relationships, especially since ratios of elements may be more important than absolute levels, and the technique is hard to apply once trees get larger because

Table 10.4 Comparison of Exchangeable Nutrient Reserves in the Root System Sorption Zone and Root Surface Sorption Zone for 5 to 9-Year-Old Pitch Pine Trees (Data from Voigt et al., 1964)

	Nutrient Availability, mg		
	P[a]	Ca	K
Amount in the root surface sorption zone	2[b] 35[c]	198	35
Amount in the root system sorption zone	148 2430	16,400	3530
Total in tree	154	415	247
Annual uptake	19	53	28

[a]For phosphorus, two different estimates are given which were derived from two different analytical methods. Obviously, estimates of soil nutrient reserves vary enor-mously depending on the method of chemical analysis and the method of calculating reserves from the data.

[b]H_2O-soluble.

[c]NH_4F–HCl-soluble.

of the difficulties of sampling crowns in tall trees. Despite these problems, it is generally a more successful means of assessing fertility than soil analysis.[6] For reviews of this approach see Morrison (1974), van den Driessche (1974), and van den Burg (1976).

A recent development of foliar analysis as a means of predicting the nutritional status and potential response of trees to fertilization is the use of short-term foliar response to fertilizer additions (Figure 10.13). The technique involves plotting foliar concentration (%) against the nutrient content (weight × concentration) of foliage (expressed as mg/100 leaves or some similar unit), and superimposing on this graph lines of weight per 100 leaves (or some similar unit). Data on nutrient concentration and content obtained before, and one growing season after, a spring addition of fertilizer are plotted, and interpretations of nutritional status and fertilizer response potential are made according to the change in the position of the foliage data on the graph. For further details of this useful technique, see Timmer and Stone (1978), Morrow (1978), and Weetman and Fournier (1982).

The question of nutrient ratios has been extensively investigated by Ingestad (e.g., 1967a,b, 1971, 1979, 1981), who reported that optimum growth of seedlings occurs only when the ratios of macronutrients lie within a fairly narrow range. For birch, pine, and spruce seedlings, optimum nutrition occurred at the following relative levels: N = 100, P = 13, K = 65, Ca = 6, Mg = 8.5. Alternatively, one can express each element as a percent of total concentration; for pine, N/P/K = 67:7:26 (Lavrichenko, in Morrison, 1974).

C. Assessment of Fertility by Plant Production

The fertility of the soil is ultimately expressed in the growth of plants. Plant productivity is a good empirical measure of soil fertility as long as climate, pathogens, herbivores, plant competition, and rooting patterns permit the plants to exploit and reflect the availability of nutrients in the soil. Where nutrients are not the major limiting factor, this method will not yield a good assessment of the fertility of the soil. A fertile soil in a climate that restricts plant growth will not yield high plant production. Nevertheless, the method will give a good estimate of the total productive potential of the site, and ultimately this is the objective of

[6]Recent developments in this field include computer programs that will compare foliar nutrient analysis data with data banks on foliar chemistry and growth of the species involved and produce a nutritional diagnosis and fertilizer recommendations (e.g., the work of Dr. T. M. Ballard, Faculty of Forestry, UBC, Vancouver, B.C.)

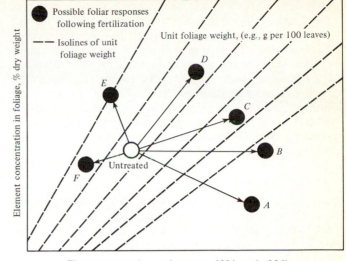

Interpretation of the Change

Direction of Shift	Response in			Interpretation	
	Needle Weight	Nutrient Conc.	Nutrient Content	Nutrient Status	Possible Diagnosis
A	+	−	+	Dilution	Nonlimiting
B	+		+	Unchanged	Nonlimiting
C	+	+	+	Deficiency	Limiting
D		+	+	Luxury consumption	Nontoxic
E	−	++	±	Excess	Toxic
F	−	−	−	Excess	Antagonistic

Figure 10.13

Graphical analysis of the nutritional status of trees. The change in the relationship between nutrient concentration, nutrient content, and dry weight of foliage following fertilization. (After Timmer and Stone, 1978. Adapted from *Soil Science Society of America Journal,* Vol. 42, pp. 125–30 by permission of Soil Science Society of America.)

soil fertility assessment. A major drawback of the method is that it takes a long time to assess fertility in this way.

D. Plant–Site Relationships

Another way of assessing soil fertility is to examine site–plant relationships. Plant production is examined as moisture and nutrient conditions change, and mathematical relationships between biomass parameters and various soil parameters (depth, texture, moisture, etc.) are developed. This method requires a lot of initial work and it is unclear how general such relationships may be; interaction and compensation of environmental factors may restrict the use of relationships to the region in which they were developed. An example of this type of approach is that of Steinbrenner (1976). In this study, site index [average height of dominant trees at some index age (formerly 100 years; recently 50 years)] of western hemlock *(Tsuga heterophylla)* was related to total and effective soil depths, gravel content, depth of A horizon, percent clay in the A horizon, silt and clay in the A horizon, elevation, precipitation, slope position, and several other soil parameters. Separate equations were formulated for residual and glacial soils. The best equation for residual soils was found to be

Site index (in m) at 50 years = 32.75 + 0.265 (depth of A horizon) − 0.12414 (depth of A horizon)^2 − 0.24409 log (depth of A horizon) + 101.42 (silt and clay content of A horizon) − 0.00111 (elevation)^2 − 0.04795 (slope position).

In a somewhat more comprehensive approach, Baker and Broadfoot (1977) related the site index of eight species of hardwood trees in the southeastern U.S. to a complex of 23 nonvegetation parameters. The contribution of each factor to site index was determined for each species and charts were prepared that enable the user to estimate site index for each species even when the site is devoid of vegetation. By way of example, the charts for cottonwood *(Populus deltoides)* and a sample of the use of the system are shown in Figure 10.14. The method was tested for approximately 20 sites for each species and resulted in a correlation coefficient between observed and predicted values of 0.99 for cottonwood (best) and 0.93 for sweetgum (worst).

Eis (1962) correlated eight topographic features and eight soil and water regime features with the site index of various west coast tree species at the University of British Columbia Research Forest near Vancouver. The soil and moisture regime accounted for 55% of the variability of site index, while landform accounted for 40%. Soil and moisture variables were able to account for 81% of the variability in site index observed within individual plant associations (defined by the composition of the minor vegetation).

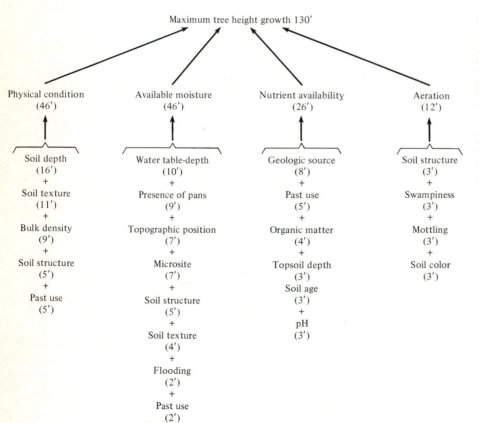

Figure 10.14

Site evaluation based on four major soil properties: physical condition, available moisture, nutrient availability, and aeration. Contribution of various soil-site properties to the four major soil factors, and the estimated contribution of each property to the height growth of eastern cottonwood (130 ft at age 30 years) on an ideal site. Addition of all estimated contributions produces a total of 130. A key is provided giving ranges for each property, from best to poor. Using this key, the site index (see Chapter 16) of any site can be determined. (After Baker and Broadfoot, 1979. Used by permission of the authors.)

E. Field Fertilizer Trials and Assessment by Visual Symptoms

Perhaps the most reliable and widely used method of assessing soil fertility is the empirical approach of field fertilizer trials to establish nutrient deficiencies: the "try it and see" approach. Such trials are time consuming and can be expensive but are generally favored for predicting response to fertilizers. Although less costly and time consuming, pot trials in the greenhouse have proven to be less satifactory since it is often difficult to establish relationships between pot and field responses. Field trials have often made use of visual symptoms such as foliar discoloration, needle twisting and fusing, premature leaf fall, resin exudation, and/or deformation of young shoots to indicate deficiencies. The predictive efficacy of such symptoms depends upon the degree of correlation between the symptoms and field response to fertilizers. The increasing use of color charts that provide objective descriptions of color should help to improve the technique. Some of the major problems with the method are that many symptoms are nonspecific and are usually evident only when deficiencies are severe, and even then only at certain times of the year. Also, it has recently been suggested (Ingestad and Lund, 1979) that visual deficiency symptoms may be a better indicator of changing nutrient conditions than of a permanent deficiency. If plants are given sufficient time to adapt to low nutrient availability, deficiency symptoms may disappear. Table 10.5 presents the principal visual symptoms that typically accompany severe deficiencies of various elements.

Table 10.5 Principal Visual Symptoms Accompanying Severe Instances of Deficiency as Observed in Both Culture- and Field-Grown Trees (Morrison, 1974)

Element	General Appearance
Nitrogen	General chlorosis and stunting of needles, which increases with severity of deficiency; in the severest cases needles are short, stiff, yellow-green to yellow; in some cases purple tipping followed by necrosis of needles occurs at end of growing season.
Phosphorus	Youngest needles green or yellow-green, older needles distinctly purple-tinged; purple deepens with severity of deficiency; in very severe cases in seedlings, all needles purple.
Potassium	Symptoms vary: usually needles short, chlorotic, with some green near base and, in some severe cases, purpling and necrosis with top dieback; sometimes little or no chlorosis, but purpling, browning, or necrosis of needles evident.
Calcium	General chlorosis followed by necrosis of needles, especially at branch tips; in severe cases, death of terminal bud and top dieback; resin exudation.

Table 10.5, continued

Element	General Appearance
Magnesium	Yellow tipping of current needles followed in severe cases by tip necrosis.
Sulfur	General chlorosis of foliage followed in severe cases by necrosis.
Iron	More or less diffuse chlorosis; in milder cases, confined to new needles; in more severe cases, bright yellow discoloration with no bud development.
Manganese	Needles slightly chlorotic; in severe cases, some necrosis of needles.
Boron	Tip dieback late in growing season with associated chlorotic-to-necrotic foliage, intergrading to dieback of leading shoot with characteristic crooking.
Zinc	Extreme stunting of trees with shortening of branches; needles yellow, short, crowded together on twig, sometimes bronze-tipped; older needles shed early, with resultant tuffing of foliage; in severe cases, trees rosetted with top dieback.
Copper	Needles twisted spirally, yellowed or bronzed; "tipburn" or necrosis of needle tips evident; in severe cases, young shoots twisted or bent.
Molybdenum	Chlorosis of leaves followed by necrosis of tissue, beginning at tip and eventually covering whole leaf.

10.8 Soil Development

A. Major Factors that Determine Soil Development

The nature of a soil depends on several factors: the character of the materials from which it develops, its topographic position in the landscape, the climate, the biota (mainly the vegetation), and how long soil development has been occurring.

1. Materials from Which Soils Develop. The character of the soil is markedly influenced by the geology and mode of origin of the parent material from which it develops.

The geological origin determines the mineral content, the resistance to weathering, and the release of nutrients during weathering of parent material. Soils derived from light-colored, quartz-rich, decay-resistant plutonic rocks are generally coarser textured and less fertile than soils derived from dark-colored geological materials such as volcanic rocks that are rich in easily-weathered minerals. Sandstone rocks derived largely from quartz particles will yield less fertile soils than siltstones and shales. Limestones will give rise to richer soils than granite.

The mode of origin of the parent material influences the texture and coarse fragment content of soil:

a. *Residual soils* are developed by *in situ* weathering of bedrock, are usually finer textured at the surface, and become less weathered and have a higher coarse fragment content with depth.

b. *Transported soils* tend to be more uniform in textural composition with depth but can vary greatly in texture. Soils derived from wind-transported materials (*aeolian* or *loess* soils) and from materials deposited by water in lakes (*lacustrine*) tend to be uniformly fine textured (clays, silts and fine sands). Materials deposited in flood plains by rivers (*alluvial*) are fine to coarse textured (silts, sands and gravels). Materials deposited by glacial meltwaters (*glacio-fluvial*) are normally very coarse (gravels and stones). The coarse fragments in these water-transported materials are generally well rounded. Materials transported and deposited by glaciers (*glacial till*) are characterized by an unsorted mixture of a wide range of particle sizes from large stones to clay, the particular mixture depending on the geological nature of the material. The coarse fragments vary from well rounded to sharp edged. The texture of *colluvial* materials that have been transported downslope under the influence of gravity will depend on the nature of the material prior to downslope movement (e.g. glacio-fluvial or till). *Talus* parent materials are composed of rock fragments that have been dislodged from cliffs or steep rocky slopes and accumulated downslope. They are extremely coarse textured and generally unstable, although they may overlie more finely textured colluvial materials. Colluvial materials can move downslope either slowly or rapidly: the former is referred to as *soil creep*, the latter as *mass wasting*.

2. Topography. Topography—slope, aspect, elevation, and position in the landscape (ridge top, midslope, or valley bottom)—exerts a strong influence on soil development. Steeper slopes and ridge tops undergo more rapid erosion and consequently often have thinner soils with a coarser texture than do more gentle slopes. Water drains rapidly from such sites and therefore the soils are drier. Colluvial action on steep slopes stirs the soil, restricting the development of characteristic horizons. Valley bottom and lower slope soils are moister, finer textured, and deeper because they receive additions of fine-textured materials eroded from upslope, and are more fertile either because they receive additional nutrients in downslope seepage water and/or because the improved moisture status increases the availability of nutrients by favoring soil weathering and litter decomposition. Equatorward aspects (i.e., southern aspects in the northern hemisphere) produce hotter, drier soils than poleward aspects. High-elevation soils are generally cooler than low-elevation soils and may be wetter in the growing season because of snowmelt water.

3. Climate. Given sufficient time, climate may ultimately become the dominant factor controlling soil development. This is referred to as the *zonal concept* of soil development: a zonal soil is one whose characteristics are determined predominantly by the regional macroclimate.

In areas where there is substantially more precipitation than evaporation, at least for a major part of the year, there is net drainage down through the soil. This results in the leaching of certain chemicals from the surface to lower layers and the development of *soil horizons,* horizontal layers that differ in physical and/or chemical properties. The abundant moisture facilitates the development of forest vegetation and a characteristic accumulation of organic matter at the surface of the mineral soil, the *forest floor* (called the LFH or O horizon). Decomposition of the organic matter in the forest floor produces organic acids, which are leached down to the surface of the mineral soil (the A horizon) where they accelerate the weathering of primary minerals. Salts produced by this weathering are then leached (a process called *eluviation*) further down into the mineral soil, either in solution or chelated by soluble organic matter. This removes colored substances such as iron, leaving a pale or bleached surface horizon (the A_e or A_2, also called the *eluvial* horizon). Much of the eluviated material is deposited in the next lower layer, where it produces a strongly colored horizon; the B or *illuvial* horizon. The coloring can also result from the release of iron by weathering of minerals in the B horizon.

Such soils have been broadly referred to as *pedalfers* (leached soils; e.g., podzols, some brunisols, luvisols) (Figure 10.15). Because there is a net leaching of mineral cations from these soils they tend to be acidic (lost cations are replaced by hydrogen ions), at least in the surface horizons, and they are sometimes less fertile than the other major group of soils: the *pedocals* (incompletely leached soils; e.g., chernozems, some brunisols).

Pedocal soils develop where the combined evaporation and transpiration exceed precipitation for most of the year. The soil is rarely wet enough to permit appreciable drainage to the groundwater table. Products of weathering are leached downward from the surface to deeper horizons during a rainfall but are returned to the surface either via uptake by plants or by upward capillary movement as the surface soil layers dry. The drier, hotter climate of the areas where such soils develop usually produces savanna forest, grassland or desert types of vegetation. There is little or no surface accumulation of organic matter in these types because of one or more of the following: rapid and complete decomposition, low productivity, (and hence low aboveground litterfall), heavy browsing by herbivores, and a high

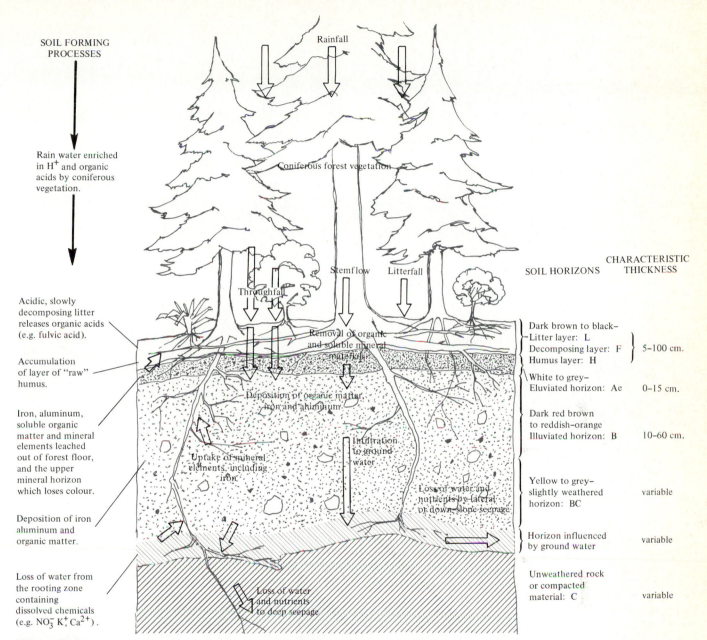

Figure 10.15

Characteristic major horizons and soil-forming processes of a typical coniferous forest podzol, a pedalfer type of soil.
(After Clarke, 1967. Copyright 1967 by John Wiley & Sons, Inc., New York. Used by permission.)

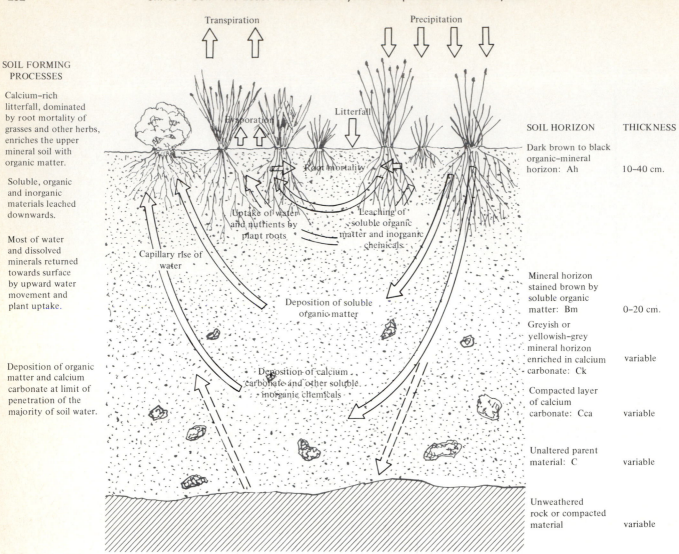

SOIL FORMING PROCESSES

Calcium–rich litterfall, dominated by root mortality of grasses and other herbs, enriches the upper mineral soil with organic matter.

Soluble, organic and inorganic materials leached downwards.

Most of water and dissolved minerals returned towards surface by upward water movement and plant uptake.

Deposition of organic matter and calcium carbonate at limit of penetration of the majority of soil water.

SOIL HORIZON	THICKNESS
Dark brown to black organic–mineral horizon: Ah	10–40 cm.
Mineral horizon stained brown by soluble organic matter: Bm	0–20 cm.
Greyish or yellowish–grey mineral horizon enriched in calcium carbonate: Ck	variable
Compacted layer of calcium carbonate: Cca	variable
Unaltered parent material: C	variable
Unweathered rock or compacted material	variable

Figure 10.16
Characteristic major horizons and soil-forming processes of a typical grassland chernozem, a pedocal type of soil. (After Clarke, 1967. Copyright 1967 by John Wiley and Sons Inc., New York. Used by permission.)

frequency of fire. Most of the soil organic matter that accumulates in these soils is in the upper mineral horizons as the result of production and turnover of roots. The annual addition of large quantities of dead roots to the surface layers of grassland soils results in the formation of a characteristic dark colored, organic-rich surface horizon. Such soils are called *chernozems* (Figure 10.16).

4. Biota. Although climate has an important direct influ-

ence on soil development, it has an equally important indirect influence because of its effect on the fauna and flora. Two areas of the same parent material and the same climate will produce two different types of soil if one is maintained under a conifer forest and the other under herbaceous vegetation. Differences in the patterns and extent of rooting, in nutrient uptake, in the chemistry and decomposition of the litter, and in the associated soil fauna and microflora lead to

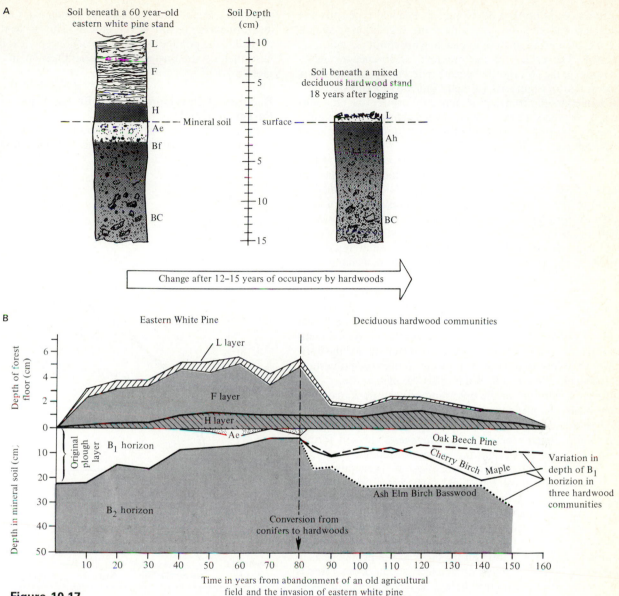

Figure 10.17

Effect of vegetation change at Harvard forest on characteristics of the soil profile. (A) Logging of a 60-year-old eastern white pine stand, growing in New England on an acid podzol with a thick (10 cm) mor-forest floor, was followed by invasion of mixed deciduous hardwoods (birch, oak, maple, ash, and cherry). 18 years later, after 12–15 years of occupancy by hardwoods, the forest floor was mull with <1 cm surface organic accumulation, and the upper mineral soil enriched with humus as a result of abundant earthworm activity. (After Fisher, 1928. Used by permission of the Ecological Society of America and Harvard Forest.) (B) Changing characteristics of the soil profile in an age sequence of white pine stands that developed on abandoned fields, and in an age sequence of mixed hardwood stands that developed after the pine stands were logged. Organic matter is transferred from mineral soil to forest floor in the pine sequence, while the reverse occurs under hardwoods. The depth of the B_1 ("dark brown" horizon) varied in proportion to the rate of decomposition of leaf litter. In ash-elm-birch-basswood stands, litter decomposed rapidly. In oak-beech-pine stands, it decomposed more slowly. (After Griffith et al., 1930. Used by permission of Harvard Forest.)

differences in horizon development. Pedocal-type soils can develop into pedalfer-type soils if the vegetation is altered (e.g., afforestation of grasslands with conifers, and vice versa). The effects of the presence or absence of earthworms on the soil profile beneath a given vegetation type is illustrated in Figure 10.12, and Figure 10.17 shows the effect of changing from a predominantly conifer to a predominantly deciduous forest cover. Such a change may require a long period of time to occur or it may be relatively rapid, as was the case in Figure 10.17A.

Over the past few millenia, man has become an important factor in soil development. Ploughing and fertilization of agricultural soils gives them a character that is quite distinct from that of unploughed soils. Erosion resulting from agriculture, forestry, fire, and other aspects of human stewardship of the earth has altered or removed soils in many parts of the world. Human effects certainly constitute one of the major biotic factors influencing the present-day character of the world's soils.

An important aspect of forest soil development is the mixing of horizons that accompanies the uprooting of trees. In windy areas, this may happen sufficiently frequently that the normal development of soil horizons is prevented completely. In many forest areas it is characteristic for the horizons to be discontinuous or to occur in unexpected vertical sequences as the result of the upheaval of tree roots. Even though windthrow or the uprooting of dead trees may happen relatively infrequently in terms of the human time scale, the resultant churning action is often rapid relative to the rate of pedogenic processes (*pedogenesis,* or soil formation) that are responsible for horizon differentiation.

5. *Time.* Soil-forming processes are generally slow compared with most biological time scales, although the time required for the development of characteristic soil properties is highly variable. In extreme environments (e.g., very hot, cold, arid, or saturated) or where one is dealing with structureless or consolidated materials, many millenia may be required for the processes of pedogenesis to result in the development of characteristic horizons. This is especially true when considering the development of residual soils from solid rock. In less extreme environments and/or on materials in which pedogenesis is rapid, characteristic horizons may develop much faster. Perceptible podzolization can appear in sand dune soils in 100–200 years, especially under forest, although 1000–1500 years is considered necessary for the development of typical podzols (Lutz and Chandler, 1946). In many situations zonal soils may never develop because processes of soil additions, soil erosion, and soil mixing occur more rapidly than climatically determined soil horizon development or because factors of to-

pography, parent material, fire, and biota exert an overriding influence on soil development. This is leading to a decline in the popularity of the zonal concept of soils, which nevertheless remains a useful generalization in some regions.

B. Rates of Development in Different Types of Parent Material

Residual soils generally develop slowly (although the rate is greatly influenced by the climate and vegetation), and in

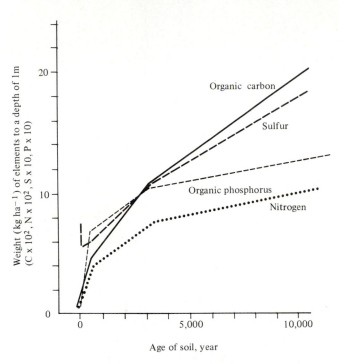

Percent Change in Soil Chemical Content Per Year

Soil Age (yr)	Organic Carbon	Nitrogen	Sulfur	Organic Phosphorus
0–50	+4.64	+2.76	−0.48	+0.66
50–500	+0.36	+0.27	+0.02	+0.52
500–3000	+0.06	+0.04	+0.03	+0.03
3000–10,000	+0.01	+0.01	+0.01	+<0.01

Figure 10.18
Weights of organic carbon, nitrogen, sulfur, and organic phosphorus in mineral soil of different ages, derived from windblown sand in New Zealand. The maximum rate of change occurred during the first 50 years, very slow changes occurring after 500 years. (After Syers et al., 1970. Used by permission of Blackwell Scientific Publications, Ltd., Oxford, England, and the authors.)

the absence of major disturbance they remain approximately the same over prolonged periods (e.g., many centuries). Ice-transported materials also change slowly once the ice has retreated, little change occurring over several centuries after an initial period of more rapid change (discussed in Chapter 15). In contrast, types of parent material that are the result of continuing deposition are subject to continuing change, as in the case of alluvial deposits. Strang (1973) estimated that silt deposits in a northern Canadian valley were being added at a rate of between 0.3 and 1.3 cm yr^{-1}. Aeolian materials such as loess or sand dunes are frequently subject to additions, losses, or movement, while colluvial soils are frequently subject to movement and mixing.

Figure 10.18 shows the changes in organic carbon, nitrogen, sulfur, and organic phosphorus in sandy soils of aeolian origin in New Zealand varying in age from 0 to 10,000 years since deposition. After a rapid gain of C, N, and organic P during the first 500–1000 years, the rate of accumulation slowed down, especially for P and N. Initially, the increases were restricted to the surface horizons, but with time the lower horizons also became enriched in these nutrients, which are still accumulating in the soil even after 10,000 years. Cumulose (organic) soils can develop over rock surfaces quite rapidly (several centuries) in humid environments, or more slowly (several millenia) as the result of the natural succession from a shallow pond or lake to a fen or bog. Several more examples of temporal changes in soils are given in Chapter 15.

10.9 Ecological Significance of Soil

Soils provide a variety of essential prerequisites for plants, and hence for animal life. These requisites include anchorage, moisture supply, and nutrient supply for plants, a refuge and a place to live for soil animals, and a substrate for aboveground terrestrial animals.

A. Importance for Plants

1. Anchorage. A rough surface such as that provided by soil is necessary for colonization by most vascular plants. Seeds falling on bare rock are usually washed or blown away before they can become established. Once established, the plants must be able to hold their photosynthetic organs in the appropriate position and arrangement relative to the sun's rays. This generally requires a firm anchorage for the roots. Where there is little or no soil, adequate anchorage may be provided by the penetration of roots into cracks and crevices, and trees growing on rocky ridges can be very wind-firm if the rock is fractured. Such roots may penetrate more than 20 m down into fractured or eroded rock. Where there is no mineral soil and the bedrock is unfractured, a surface accumulation of organic material may suffice for anchorage, although trees are generally susceptible to windthrow on such sites. As a result, areas of thin soil over unfractured bedrock often remain unforested for a long time following a disturbance.

The relationship between soil characteristics and the stability of plants is complicated by the fact that plants provide each other with mutual shelter and support. Trees in dense forests have interwoven root systems and crowns, which may provide stability in situations where the root systems are quite inadequate to support the aboveground parts. The stability provided by root anchorage often proves to be inadequate in the face of strong wind once the continuity of such a stand is broken. This can happen when trees are removed during road construction and when previously sheltered trees are exposed at the edge of a clearcut.

Utilization of soil by roots is strongly conditioned by both physical and chemical conditions. Poor aeration, physical compaction, chemical cementation (iron or calcium pans), high water tables, toxic chemical conditions, and low soil temperatures can restrict root activity to a shallow surface layer of soil. Consequently, deep mineral soils do not necessarily provide better anchorage and wind stability for trees than do shallower soils. Forests on deep but saturated (either permanently or temporarily) soils are often more susceptible to windthrow than are trees on thin rocky soils.

2. Supply of Moisture. One of the major ecological roles of soil is to act as a sponge: to absorb and store water. A major reason for the lack of vegetation in areas lacking soil of any kind is the lack of moisture storage. Life is thought to have evolved in water, and only when adaptations such as roots and lungs evolved did terrestrial life evolve. These adaptations maintain at least a part of the organism in a humid environment where the vital process of chemical exchange can occur.

Soils that have extremely low moisture storage capacity (e.g., coarse gravels, pumice soils) may remain unvegetated or carry only a sparse growth of drought-resistant plants. Soils that have an excess of water are also unsuitable for most forms of plant growth because they lack the oxygen necessary for root growth and frequently have soil chemical conditions that are toxic to plant roots. On the other hand, soils that are well drained but which remain moist throughout the growing season are generally highly productive and support lush vegetation. These are useful generalizations, but it must be remembered that one cannot predict the composition and productivity of the vegetation of a site merely on the basis of soil moisture conditions. Soil structure, porosity, aeration, and the local climate are all important in determining the relationship between plant growth and soil moisture conditions, and optimum plant growth occurs only in soils with the appropriate balance between air-filled and water-filled pores.

Soil organic layers are often particularly favorable to good moisture status because they can hold a lot of water but also contain a lot of larger air spaces. In cool, humid regions where forest floors can accumulate to depths approaching 1 m and where they commonly exceed 20 cm, potentially xeric sites may in fact have quite a favorable moisture status. For example, there are many productive forests in western Canada that are growing on variable accumulations of organic matter over solid rock. These stands frequently achieve levels of organic production rivaling that of adjacent stands growing on glacial till soils several meters deep. In a dry climate this is less common because of the much thinner forest floors and the general lack of moisture. Under dry conditions organic layers are generally inferior to mineral soils in providing moisture for plants. Organic layers can dry rapidly because of the large air spaces, and the lost moisture is not replaced efficiently from the underlying mineral soil because of the hydraulic discontinuity between the mineral and organic layers, because dry organic matter has a low hydraulic conductivity and because it may become *hydrophobic* (water repellent). Organic soils can also pose problems of excess moisture. Soils derived from sphagnum moss may retain so much water that the surface organic layer is almost permanently saturated, which makes it unsuitable for most plants.

Soil texture becomes critical at the dry end as well as at the wet end (saturation) of the soil moisture spectrum. We have already seen that although fine-textured soils generally hold more water than coarse-textured soils do, they may sometimes be drier in terms of moisture availability to plants. Brayshaw (1970) found that Douglas-fir (only moderately drought tolerant) was restricted to coarser soils than ponderosa pine (very drought tolerant) in the hot, dry, southern interior of British Columbia because the coarser-textured soil had a higher soil moisture availability than the finer-textured soil (Figure 10.4).

3. Supply of Nutrients. We have already seen that plants obtain the nutrients required for new growth in a number of ways: by absorption from the atmosphere and soil solution, from weathering of soil minerals, from decomposing organic matter, and by internal redistribution of their existing capital of nutrients. It has also been noted that mycotrophy is almost universally important.

Trees obtain most of their annual uptake of most nutrients from the biogeochemical cycle, and the major contribution of the soil to this cycle is usually the forest floor (especially for N and P). The geochemical cycle adds to and sustains the biogeochemical cycle, the relative contributions of the different geochemical inputs varying from site to site. The contribution of the mineral soil depends upon its mineralogy, its physical and chemical characteristics, its water relationships, and the distribution of the roots; in some cases, the contribution may be very minor. For example, forests with a well-developed forest floor, an active biogeochemical cycle, and a humid climate may grow quite productively on rocky landscapes that have little or no mineral soil; inputs from the geochemical cycle via *lithoponics* are the major source of mineral nutrients on such sites. Such examples notwithstanding, the mineral soil is normally a major source of nutrients for plants. Also, the presence and the physical and chemical condition of the mineral soil have an important influence on the soil fauna, which in turn affect nutrient cycling and soil fertility.

From this brief discussion it should be clear that it is difficult to generalize about the ecological significance of soil. The answer to the question "do plants require soil?" requires a consideration of what plants require and how they are able to satisfy these requirements. Under certain climatic and geological conditions, plants are able to satisfy their minimum requirements for anchorage, moisture, and nutrients in the virtual absence of soil. However, before this can occur, a considerable organic accumulation is usually necessary, and the highest levels of plant production are normally attained on a well-structured, medium-textured, well-aerated mineral soil with a rapidly decomposing surface accumulation of organic matter.

The organic and mineral soil horizons contribute differently to the needs of plants in different situations, but rarely can plant production be improved by the large-scale removal of any of the soil horizons. There are some exceptions, of course. Where the soil in the rooting zone is completely weathered and largely depleted in nutrients (this occurs in some very old residual soils in the tropics), erosion of such soils can expose the less weathered deeper soil layers which have greater reserves of unweathered minerals. This may result in increased plant production. Similarly, excessive accumulations of certain types of organic matter can render a site swampy, cold and/or depauperate in available nutrients. Removal of some or all of such organic layers can improve moisture, temperature and nutrient conditions.

The complexity of soil–plant relationships has led some ecologists to focus their attention on the plant components of the ecosystem rather than on the plant–soil complex. The often overriding influence of climate and the ability of plants to modify the moisture and nutrient conditions of the soil sometimes create the impression that plants can behave relatively independently of the soil, and this may have reduced the concern about the soil resource. However, although it is true that plants can create their own soil environment (see Chapter 15), there can be little question that soil conditions exert an extremely important influence on the biotic composition and productivity of ecosystems. In Chapter 14 we examine the distribution of plants along environmental gradients that are largely gradients of soil conditions, and we will see that soil–plant relationships, although complex, are a dominant feature of most ecosystems. The ecology of an area cannot be understood adequately unless there is an appropriate understanding of the soil.

B. Importance for Animals

Animals are affected by soils both directly and indirectly. Burrowing animals cannot live in very stony or rocky areas unless there are natural caves, and animals do not hibernate in areas of frozen soils because of the difficulty of excavating suitable shelters. Animal appendages are adapted for the type of substrate they contact; animals that walk on moist, low-bearing-capacity soils have larger feet than those accustomed to dry, firm ground. Animal nutrition is influenced by soils because plant chemistry reflects soil chemistry. In humid climates or areas with low soil-sodium levels, plants may be short of sodium and other minerals. In some areas micronutrients are in short supply in the soil, and this is also reflected in plant chemistry. Animals that feed on plants from such areas may develop deficiency symptoms unless they can make up the deficiencies by eating soil or licking mineral deposits. The availability of such *salt licks* may be a major factor in determining animal abundance, and animals will travel considerable distances to get to a lick. Soils in alpine environments are typically short of sodium, and it is not uncommon to have the straps of a packsack or a wooden spade handle gnawed by salt-hungry animals. We shall return to this topic later.

10.10   Importance of Soils for Forest Management

Soils are the productive potential of forests. They are a nonrenewable [7] component of our renewable resource. Certainly, there are other important nonrenewable components, such as the genetic constitution of the biota. Once an entire gene pool is lost, it may never be recreated. But of all the

[7]For a discussion of the renewability of resources, see Chapter 18.

nonrenewable aspects of the forest, soil is probably the hardest to replace once lost. Biota can normally be reintroduced from other areas. Except on a limited basis, this is not usually possible for soil.

Much of the really fertile soil on moderate topography in areas with climates that are suitable for high-production forestry have already been sequestered by agriculture. Our desire for food has traditionally overriden our desire for forest products. The forester is frequently left with the less productive soils, soils that for reasons of topography, texture, depth, minerology, moisture status, chemistry, temperature, fertility, and/or economics are not required for food production. Because of these limitations, the forester generally has fewer options for manipulation of soil physical and chemical parameters than does the farmer. Certainly, the forester can fertilize some types of sites, and the use of fire or mechanical treatment may improve the fertility of some areas following harvesting. But compared with most farmers, foresters must generally produce their crops with the soil resource that they have inherited.

Forest harvesting is an engineering activity that is rife with possibilities for adverse effects on the soil. There is a variety of effects.

1. *Soil disturbance.* Forest harvesting generally produces disturbance to the soil surface. This can vary from a slight disturbance of the forest floor to the complete loss of the upper soil horizons. The most important factor determining the degree of ground disturbance is the type of harvesting equipment used, followed by the time of year. Table 10.6 shows a comparison of the degree of soil disturbance associated with various different extraction methods (yarding) in the western U.S.

The least soil disturbance occurs with skyline yarding, in which the logs are moved from the stump to the landing (point of loading onto trucks) suspended in the air by a taut

Table 10.6   Degree of Soil Disturbance Associated with Various Methods of Harvesting Trees in Western North America[a]

Method of Logging	Total Soil Disturbance, % of Area	Mineral Soil Exposed, % of Area
Horse	12	12
Tractor	21–87	21–69
Jammer	15	15
High lead	11–90	5–56
Skyline	6	6
Helicopter	36	5

[a]Data from Bockheim et al., 1975; Garrison and Rummell, 1951; Wooldridge, 1960; Dyrness, 1965; Ruth, 1967.

cable. There are few data available on horse yarding, but the extent of soil disturbance would appear to be relatively small. High lead yarding, perhaps the most common method on the west coast of North America, produces significantly more soil disturbance than does either of the previous two methods. In high lead yarding the logs are dragged to a central landing by a slack cable, and there is considerable soil disturbance on the ''yarding roads'' along which the logs are moved. According to the topography, the front end of the log may be raised off the ground, but often the log is in contact with the ground along most of its length for much of the trip from stump to landing. The highest degree of soil disturbance is associated with tractor or skidder yarding, in which a wheeled or tracked vehicle travels to the log and then drags it to the landing by cable.

Table 10.7 presents some results of a detailed study of soil disturbance, vegetation cover, and regeneration on clearcuts in the mountains of southeastern B.C. Both yarding method and season of logging were important in determining the degree of soil disturbance. Roads (main haul roads and skid trails) constituted by far the most important source of soil disturbance. Skyline yarding, which does not require the clearcut to be roaded, produced the smallest degree of soil disturbance. Ground skidding produced the highest degree of disturbance. However, there is a wide variation in the extent of disturbance associated with this method in different regions.

2. *Effects on soil stability.* Unfortunately, damage to soils by clearcutting is not limited to surface disturbance. On steep slopes, the stability of the soil may be reduced to the point at which *mass wasting* occurs (slumps, slides, and debris avalanches). A study of soil mass movements in the H. J. Andrews forest in the Cascade Mountains of Oregon revealed that 83% of all soil mass movements were associated with slopes of more than 45% (24°) and that 72% of all

events and about 50% of all soil material moved were associated with roads; 17% of the observed events were in logged areas between roads, and 11% occurred in areas not disturbed by humans (Dyrness, 1967).

A study of the impact of clearcutting and road construction on soil erosion by landslides in the western Cascade Range in Oregon demonstrated the importance of the nature of the underlying geological materials (Swanston and Dyrness, 1975). At elevations above 900–1000 m in the H. J. Andrews experimental forest, the soil is underlain by lava-flow bedrock. This type of material produces a stable soil mantle that has a low susceptibility to landsliding following clearcutting, and in the 1950–1972 period only two small road-related slides occurred in clearcut areas. At lower elevations, altered volcanic-clastic rocks have a very unstable soil mantle. Clearcutting in this area has increased slide erosion by 2.8 times from prelogging levels. Along road rights-of-way the increase has been 30 times. With roads covering about 8% and clearcuts 92% of the harvested area, roads contribute about half of the management-related slides. Roads and clearcuts combined have increased slide activity by about five times over a 20-year period.

A study of landslides in the Maybeso Creek Valley in southeastern Alaska revealed a dramatic effect of clearcutting on the incidence of soil mass movements. Most of the increase occurred on the slopes of steep, V-shaped side drainages, but there was also some increase on smooth uniform slopes of the main valley (Table 10.8).

The increase in slides is due partly to the disruption of slope hydrology and slope stability by roads and partly to the loss of root strength as stumps and large roots decay. Roots are believed to play a major role in holding soil mantles in place on steep slopes in areas such as western North America. Following clearcutting there is a delay of 3–10 years in the onset of slides, which corresponds to the timing

Table 10.7   Soil Disturbance Associated with Forest Harvesting and Postharvest Site Treatment in Southeastern British Columbia (Data from Smith and Wass, 1976)

Logging Method	Area Disturbed by Roads, %		Area Disturbed Between Roads, %	
	Slashburned	Not Slashburned	Slashburned	Not Slashburned
Summer ground skidding	36	42	8	4
Winter ground skidding	19	25	8	5
Summer high lead	15	9	14	8
Winter high lead	—	16	—	0.5
Summer grapple yarding	—	27	—	2
Winter grapple yarding	—	22	—	0
Summer jammer yarding	—	8	—	5
Summer skyline	—	0	—	8

Table 10.8   History of Landslides[a] in the Maybeso Creek Valley near Hollis, Southeastern Alaska, Illustrating the Effect of Clearcutting on Soil Stability

Time Period	Length of Period, yr	Number of Slides	Number of Slides Per Year	Total Area of Slides, ha	Area Per Year ha yr^{-1}
1848–1948 (approx.)	100	12	0.12	11.1	0.11
1948–1952	4	1	0.25	1.6	0.40
Clearcutting started 1953					
1952–1959	7	20	2.9	2.5	0.36
1959–1961	2	28	14.0	7.7	3.85
1961–1962	1	68	68.0	36.8	36.8

Source: Bishop and Stevens, 1964. Used with permission.

[a] The number and area of slides were monitored by aerial photography.

of loss of root strength (Swanston, 1974; Bishop and Stevens, 1964; Fujiwara, 1970; Rice and Foggin, 1971; Swanston, 1969; Turmanina, 1965). This is followed by a period of several decades of soil instability until new root systems are formed which restabilize the soil mantle (Figure 10.19). Loss of root strength was reported to contribute to soil mass movements following high elevation clearcutting in southwestern B.C. (Utzig and Herring, 1975).

3. *Loss of soil organic matter and nutrient content and changes in soil chemistry.* These topics have already been covered in the discussions of effects on biomass and energy (Chapter 4) and on biogeochemistry (Chapter 5).

4. *Alteration in soil temperature.* Important changes in soil temperature occur as the result of clearcutting. The extent of these changes depends to a considerable extent on the degree of mineral soil exposure and the reduction in the depth of the surface accumulation of organic matter. In winter-cold environments, the productivity of the plant community may be influenced markedly by the late thawing and slow warming of the mineral soil. Roots are largely confined to the surface organic layers, which warm up somewhat more rapidly than the deeper layers because of their lower thermal capacity and greater exposure to sunlight. Where these organic layers contain nutrient-poor and slowly decomposing material, the plants will experience inadequate nutrition and grow slowly. Also, the restriction of roots to the surface of the forest floor, which may dry out in the summer, can render seedlings very susceptible to drought injury or death. Soil disturbance that exposes mineral soil and the reduction in the depth of forest floor that generally occurs following logging can have very beneficial effects on soil temperature and plant productivity in such environments. Exposure of mineral soil also reduces diurnal temperature extremes at the soil surface with beneficial con-

sequences for seedlings. In summer-hot environments, soil temperatures may increase to levels that are lethal for many plants (see Chapter 8).

5. *Alteration of soil physical properties.* Use of heavy machinery can alter soil structure, porosity and density, pore size distribution, aeration, water retention, infiltration capacity, and hydraulic conductivity. The degree of alteration depends upon the weight of equipment and logs being yarded, the number of times heavy objects pass over the soil, and the soil water content. In one study, soil density increased exponentially with increasing number of passages of a tractor (Foil, 1965); one trip of the tractor on wet soil resulted in as much compaction as four trips on a dry soil (Steinbrenner, 1955). Compaction during tree-length-log skidding by tractor in Minnesota was reported to be only about half (5%) that with full-tree skidding (stem plus crown) (11%) (Mace, 1970). Loss of the forest floor exposes the mineral soil to compaction and to the impaction of rain, both of which can lead to loss of surface soil structure and "puddling." A structureless surface layer only a few millimeters in thickness can be enough to alter the infiltration rate radically and result in surface runoff and erosion.

Unless an ecological approach is taken to harvesting and site treatment, forest management is unlikely to attain its objectives, and to a considerable extent this is the result of adverse effects on the soil. One of the essential educational requirements for foresters and other renewable resource managers must surely be a sound working knowledge of soils.

Above all it must be remembered that in most cases the productive potential of the site is vested in a relatively thin surface layer of soil, and erosion of only the surface few centimeters may be accompanied by significant reductions

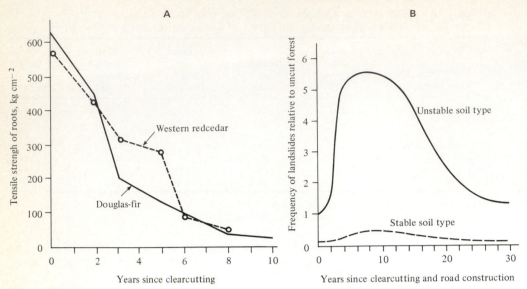

Figure 10.19

(A) Loss of root strength in a clearcut in coastal British Columbia. (After O'Loughlin, 1974. Used by permission of the National Research Council of Canada, and the author. See also Ziemer, 1981; O'Loughlin and Ziemer, 1982.) (B) The consequent period of soil instability on steep slopes. The graph shows relative frequency of landslides on stable and unstable soil types in the western Cascade Range of Oregon. The curve for unstable soil is based on data; that for stable soil is hypothetical. (After Swanson and Dyrness, 1975).

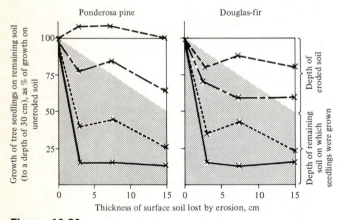

Figure 10.20

The importance of upper layers of soil for site fertility and tree growth is shown by the loss of seedling growth when grown in pots of soil from profiles whose progressively thicker surface layers have been removed to simulate progressively more serious erosion. The four lines are for soil samples taken from four different areas in Washington. The significance of soil erosion for the growth of seedlings of these two tree species varies, obviously, from one site to another, and there is a difference in the response of the two species. (After Klock, 1982. Used by permission of the American Society of Agronomy, and the author.)

in plant growth. Figure 10.20 shows the reduction in seedling growth when seedlings are grown on soil from different depths in the profile. This is a measure of the growth of seedlings following progressively more serious soil erosion. A loss of the upper 2 cm of mineral soil from a site on the east side of the Cascade Mountains in Washington was associated with an 80% reduction in seedling growth.

Knowledge of soils is important in all phases of forestry. The choice of harvesting method and type of equipment will be influenced by soil fertility, soil stability, soil compactability, and soil erodability. Postharvesting site treatments, choice of species, and method of regeneration will similarly be strongly influenced by the soil properties of the site. The behavior of herbicides in the environment is largely determined by soils, as are the effects and fate of fertilizers. In short, soil considerations should influence every aspect of forestry.

10.11   Soil and Man

There is increasing concern over the effects of humans on soils. Pimentel et al. (1976) compiled a sobering assessment of the effects of urbanization, highway construction, and agriculture on the soil resource in the U.S. Each year more than 1 million hectares of arable land is lost to highways, urbanization, and so on. This is partly offset by the addition of about 0.5 million hectares through irrigation and drainage. The total loss since 1945 is an area equivalent in size to the state of Nebraska (18.2 million hectares). For many years the significance of this loss was downplayed by many because of an agricultural land reserve of 23.5 million hectares. However, 16.5 million hectares of this land have had to be put back into production, greatly diminishing the reserve. Also, the reserve consists of marginal lands which require high inputs of fossil energy to render them productive, whereas most of the continuing withdrawals are from the most productive land area. History shows that cropland is twice as likely to be urbanized as non-cropland. Up until 1976, about 8 million hectares of former cropland had been converted to urban uses, while about 13 million hectares have been covered by highways and roads. In the past 200 years, nearly 1000 million hectares in the U.S. have been lost from crop production, more than half as much as what is now being cultivated.

It has been estimated that during the last 200 years at least a third of the topsoil in U.S. croplands has been lost. By 1935, erosion had already ruined 40.5 million hectares for practical cultivation, and up to 50% of the topsoil had been lost from a further 40.5 million hectares. Soil formation processes have replaced some of this loss, although the extent of the replacement is highly variable and difficult to measure. Under ideal conditions soil can form at about 1 cm in about 12 years, but under average natural conditions the rate is closer to 1 cm in 120–400 years. Under average agricultural conditions it is about 1 cm in about 40 years.

Water erosion is clearly the dominant form of soil loss in the U.S., delivering approximately 4 billion tons yr^{-1} of sediment to waterways in the 48 contiguous states, 75% of which comes from agricultural lands. About 75% of the eroded soil ends up in reservoirs, lakes, and rivers, the rest in the ocean. The annual cost of dredging this lost agricultural wealth from waterways was about $250 million in 1976. Reduction in the life of reservoirs costs an additional $75 million annually. This and other sediment damage was estimated to cost the U.S. $500 million in 1976.

Wind erosion is thought to be less severe than water erosion (about 75% of the total erosion loss), but can be severe locally. It has been estimated that 850 million tons of soil is removed by wind per year in the western U.S. alone. In one semiarid portion of the Great Plains, an average of 23 cm (3336 tons ha^{-1}) of topsoil was removed by wind from cultivated fields over about 20 years; in Ohio, 321 tons ha^{-1}

were removed from experimental corn land in one season. In total, it is estimated that wind removes about 1 billion tons of topsoil per year. Added to soil erosion, this makes a grand total of about 5 billion tons of topsoil that is transferred to streams or elsewhere (some may fall on other eroded land): equivalent to 18 cm of soil lost over 2 million hectares.

By comparison, annual soil loss is only about 0.07 ton ha^{-1} from permanent grassland, and less than this for undisturbed forests.

Soil erosion from agricultural lands in the U.S. removes more than 50 million tons of plant nutrients annually. The cost of replacing the N, P, and 25% of the K lost from agricultural soils was about $7 billion in the early 1970s.

To feed the world population that is predicted for the year 2000, food production would have to be doubled. This would require a threefold increase in the use of energy, which is unlikely to happen, since developing countries are already using 60% of their energy for their food production systems. On a worldwide basis, nearly 25% of all energy, including wood, goes into food production.

The consequences of all this for forestry are as follows. First, the most fertile and productive forestland will probably be converted to agricultural uses, reducing the land base for wood production. This will happen in the face of a growing world timber famine. Second, forests will be used increasingly as an energy source as more and more conventional energy is committed to the production of food. Use of forestland for energy production will then exacerbate the fiber famine. The obvious conclusion is that we simply cannot tolerate continuance of the present levels of soil erosion and loss of productive lands to other uses.

The land base on which to grow forests, and the productivity of the soil on that land base, must be preserved. This will happen only if the importance of soils becomes widely recognized and if this is accompanied by a greatly improved understanding of soils by resource managers. All field managers should be capable of describing and interpreting the soils under their management, and a pocket field manual for describing soils should be a standard part of their field equipment.

10.12 Summary

Cows and cabbages are merely crops; it is the soil that is the essence of a farm. Crops can be replaced. Once soil is lost, it may be economically and/or ecologically impossible to replace it or restore it to its original condition within our lifetime. The same holds true for forests. The trees are replaceable, as long as the gene pool is not lost, and displaced animals will rapidly reinvade a denuded area as soon as the redeveloping vegetation provides a suitable habitat. But if the soil is lost through fire or landslide, it may be many centuries or even millenia before new soil has developed to the extent of that which has been lost. Thus, for most forests, the soil is the resource; the trees, merely a crop. This requires that managers have *at least* as good a knowledge of the soil as of the crop, a situation that rarely pertains. A sound appreciation of the nature and ecological role of soils is equally important for those ecologists who wish to understand ecosystems.

Soil provides plants with a variety of basic necessities for life: anchorage and support, moisture, nutrients, and a supply of oxygen for the roots. The availability of these necessities depends upon the characteristics of the soil.

Soil texture, structure, porosity, and temperature exert a major influence over soil moisture conditions, aeration, the potential fertility of the soil, and the ability of root systems to occupy and exploit the soil. The physical properties of the soil also influence soil stability, erodability, and trafficability.

Soil water is one of the major factors controlling plant growth. The amount of water stored in the soil, its availability to plants, and the rate at which it is lost through drainage and evaporation are all determined by physical features of the soil, as well as the climate and topography.

Soil fertility, the ability of soil to provide plants with the nutrients they require, is a complex phenomenon. It is determined by soil chemistry, soil organic matter content, soil moisture, soil aeration, soil animal and microbial activity, and soil temperature. These are not independent factors.

They all interact with and influence each other and other soil parameters. Additional complication arises from the fact that soil fertility is more closely related to the balance of different nutrients and to their rate of circulation within the ecosystem than to absolute levels of nutrients in the soil. The fertility of forest soils is often more closely related to the input to, and rate of decomposition of organic matter in, the soil than to the chemistry of the mineral layers.

Soil is the product of biological processes acting in concert with physical and chemical processes to alter soil parent material. These biological processes involve the activity of soil fauna and flora, and plants require the presence and activity of at least some soil organisms. The mycorrhizal relationship between fungi and plant roots is particularly important, but the roles of other soil microbes in the nitrogen cycle and of soil animals and microbes in organic matter decomposition and the development of soil structure and porosity are equally significant. Soil is partly biological in nature, and due consideration must be given to this fact.

The luxuriance of undisturbed, mature plant communities has often fooled people into misinterpreting the ability of soil to sustain plant productivity in the face of intensive cropping. Experience has shown that many soils are only fertile if left under undisturbed vegetation for considerable periods. Frequent disturbance and intensive harvesting of biomass may degrade soil fertility because of the physical loss of soil through erosion, the loss of soil organic matter, changes in soil physical properties, the loss of nutrients, or any combination of these factors. Soil is not an inert, physical phenomenon. It is a dynamic physical-chemical-biological entity. This must be recognized if ecosystems are to be managed intensively for plant crop production.

11.1 Introduction

Second only to energy, liquid water is the most important prerequisite for life as we know it. It is commonly believed that organisms evolved following the synthesis and subsequent combination of simple organic molecules in shallow bodies of liquid water, and all life processes involve chemical reactions in aqueous solutions. Water vapor in the air protects organisms from the harmful effects of ultraviolet radiation, and by trapping long-wave radiation it contributes to the maintenance of atmospheric temperatures in the range over which water can exist in the liquid form. The oceans and large lakes regulate atmospheric concentrations of CO_2, which influences both atmospheric temperature and global organic production. Water is thus the very essence of life, and it is almost impossible to discuss the ecology of any organism without reference to its adaptations to the moisture conditions of its environment.

The remarkable fact of life is to a great extent a reflection of the remarkable properties of water. It is one of the few inorganic substances that is liquid at summer air temperatures, and without a liquid solvent the chemical processes of life could not occur. It has a higher *specific heat* (the amount of heat required to raise the temperature of 1 g of a substance 1°C) than any other common substance, which gives it the ability to absorb or give out large quantities of energy with relatively minor changes in temperature. The abundance of liquid water at the surface of the earth and water vapor in the atmosphere greatly reduces temperature fluctuations, a fact to which a comparison of coastal and continental climates will attest. A high heat of *vaporization* (heat absorbed during the change from liquid to vapor phase; 536 cal is required to convert 1 g of liquid water to water vapor) inhibits evaporation and acts to maintain water in the liquid form. It also means that water is an extremely effective coolant. Large quantities of heat are absorbed by the evaporation of modest quantities of water. Life in exposed or hot environments would be impossible for many plants and animals without the cooling that is provided by evaporation. Of equal ecological importance is the relatively high *heat of fusion* (heat given off during the change from liquid to solid phase; 80 cal must be removed from 1 g of liquid water in order to freeze it), which acts to resist the freezing of water and reduces the rate at which the temperature of aquatic ecosystems drops in the winter. Finally, water reaches maximum density at 4°C, not 0°C, a fact that prevents lakes and rivers from freezing solid. Ice has lower density than water and therefore floats; the heavier, 4°C water sinks to the bottom, where it is protected from further cooling.

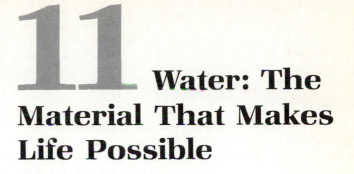

11 Water: The Material That Makes Life Possible

In addition to these temperature attributes, water is an excellent solvent for ionic substances and has a high density and viscosity. The high density provides support to aquatic organisms but it means that water is crushingly heavy at depth, and the high viscosity impedes movement. Water also has a poor ability to dissolve oxygen, a fact that may limit the activity of aquatic organisms to shallow areas or the surface of deep water bodies.

All these physical characteristics of water can be attributed to the nature of the water molecule. Although it is electrically neutral, with two H^+ atoms and one O^{2-} atom, the two hydrogens are arranged asymmetrically, so that one side of the molecule is somewhat positive and the other side is somewhat negative. This type of molecule is called a *dipole*. The negative side of one molecule attracts the positive side of another, resulting in hydrogen bonds that hold the molecules together. This hydrogen bonding accounts for the high values of such things as heat of vaporization and specific heat. Heat energy is absorbed in overcoming hydrogen bonds rather than raising the temperature. It also accounts for the solvent properties of water. The attraction of the different sides of the water molecule to oppositely charged ions of a solute is so great that it overcomes the attraction that holds the two ions of the solute together. The ions separate and become associated with the water molecule; the solute "goes into solution." For example, when soluble ammonium nitrate fertilizer is placed in water, the force holding the NH_4^+ and the NO_3^- ions together is less than the attraction of these ions to different sides of the water molecule. Consequently, the fertilizer molecule dissociates, and the two ions are held by hydrogen bonds to the water molecules.

Water is of enormous significance to all plants and animals and no less so to humans. It acts as the medium in which all life processes (i.e., chemical processes) occur. It acts as a transport system permitting nutrient uptake from the soil, moving metabolites around, supplying oxygen to oxygen-demanding tissues, removing waste products and regulating the temperature of organisms, and supporting and protecting aquatic organisms. For humans, water has the added significance of being a source of power (hydroelectricity) and a means of disposing of undesirable wastes, heat, and materials. Lack of water may well become more important than lack of energy as a major factor limiting our population growth: water to grow food, water to flush away our wastes, and clean water to drink.

In this chapter we examine the water cycle and the availability of water to plants and animals. An examination of adaptations to the water factor is followed by a consideration of how water affects the distribution of plants and animals. The chapter concludes with an introduction to the human effects on the water cycle and the significance of water to forestry. For a recent review of water relations and hydrological cycles of forest ecosystems, see Waring et al. (1981).

11.2 The Water Cycle

Like nutrient cycles in general, the water cycle is driven by inputs of solar energy. Vast quantities of radiant energy are absorbed in the process of evaporating water from the warm areas of the world's oceans. The energy is transferred to the atmosphere as the water vapor condenses, thereby driving our climate and creating our weather. The warm, moist air creates clouds as it rises, and the winds formed by the resulting processes of atmospheric stirring move the clouds over the land, where some of the moisture falls as precipitation. Some of this is reevaporated directly back to the atmosphere and some is subsequently transpired by plants. The rest enters water courses and returns to lakes and eventually to oceans, from which it is once again evaporated. We shall discuss each stage of the water cycle (Figure 11.1) in turn.

A. Precipitation and Other Inputs of Moisture into Ecosystems

Precipitation occurs when air becomes saturated with water vapor and condensation occurs to form clouds. Under certain conditions (which are not yet fully understood), the cloud droplets coalesce and grow in size until they are too large to remain suspended in the air, and they fall as rain. The quantity of water vapor that a volume of air can contain depends upon its temperature: the higher the temperature, the greater the quantity. As air temperature drops, the amount of vapor that it can hold also drops, until at a certain temperature (the dew point) it becomes saturated and condensation occurs. The conditions for precipitation are created when air masses containing water vapor cool to below their dew point. Such cooling can occur in several ways, and consequently there are several types of precipitation.

1. *Convectional Rainfall.* This results when differential solar heating of the earth's surface and lower air layers results in air masses rising by convection. As the air rises, it expands because of lower atmospheric pressure. As it expands it cools, and convectional clouds are formed. The resulting rain is usually local in distribution and of short duration, but it can be of high intensity. This type of precipitation is most common in the summer when there is moist warm air near the ground and sufficient solar energy to cause convectional stirring.

2. *Orographic Precipitation.* This occurs when warm moist air is forced upward over hills or mountain ranges by the general movement of the air mass. Mountains, particularly those that have mild climates and are immediately downwind of large bodies of water, typically have clouds around their tops for much of the year even when the sky elsewhere is cloud free. Some mountains are associated with "standing clouds," which never move in spite of strong winds. They represent the cooling of air as it passes over the mountain, and the subsequent rewarming as the air drops in elevation behind the mountain.

3. *Frontal or Cyclonic Precipitation.* This precipitation occurs when warm moist air is forced to move upward over a layer of cold air. This generally produces prolonged rain over large areas, frequently of only moderate or low intensity. Local high-intensity frontal precipitation may occur at the interface when large masses of warm, moist air meet large masses of cold air.

Moisture may be transferred from air to land in a variety of ways. The most obvious of these are rain and snow, the ecological effects of which are determined not only by the total quantity per year but also by their seasonal distribution and their intensity: the rate of precipitation per unit time (usually per hour or per day). Precipitation with a droplet

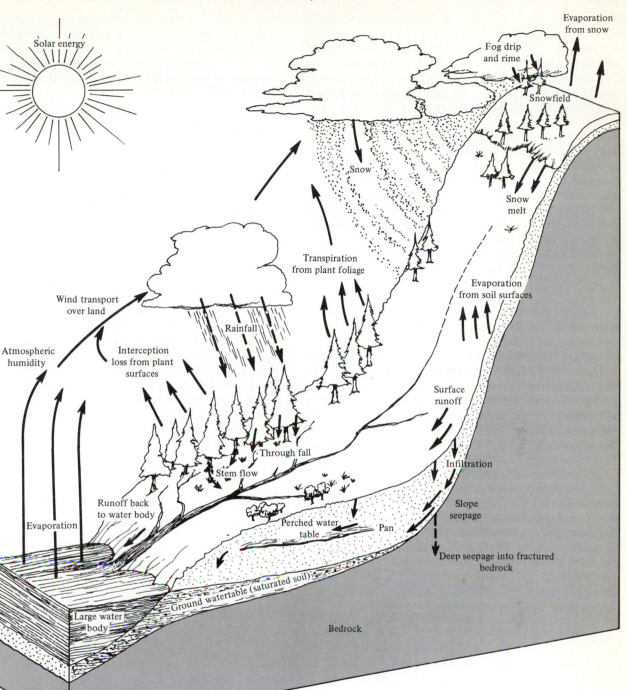

Figure 11.1
Diagrammatic summary of the major components of the water cycle. This cycle is driven by inputs of solar energy that generate evaporation and atmospheric stirring.

size of less than 0.5 mm and an intensity of about 0.25 mm hr^{-1} is called drizzle; heavy rain has droplets 2.5–6.4 mm in diameter, intensities of 15–100 mm hr^{-1}, and a velocity of about 20 mm sec^{-1}, nearly twice that of drizzle (Hewlett and Nutter, 1969). Rainfall intensity has important ecological implications. Heavy rain can strip foliage from plants, beat down herbaceous vegetation, alter the structure of the surface layers of the soil, erode soil and silt up streams, and kill, displace, or interfere with the feeding activities of small animals. Drizzle makes a given amount of rain more available to plants, as it is delivered over a longer period. It is also more effective in leaching chemicals from plant foliage than is a brief period of heavy rain delivering the same quantity of water. On the other hand, heavy rain is more effective than light rain at leaching chemicals through soils.

The distribution, intensity, and characteristics of snow are also important. A heavy fall of wet snow can trap and strand wildlife or inhibit their migration. It can strip branches from trees; break off their leaders (growing tips), resulting in forked stems; break the stems; or result in the uprooting of the whole tree. Sometimes this is highly destructive. At other times it merely results in the death of diseased or suppressed trees, leaving more growing space for those remaining. Other ecological aspects of snow will be discussed later.

Under certain low-temperature conditions, rain forms ice particles *(hail)* rather than snow. Hail can reach several centimeters in diameter and can damage vegetation by stripping foliage and branches. Animals caught in such heavy hail can be killed or wounded.

Dew is the condensation of water vapor on snow, cold soil, or cold plant surfaces, and it can be an ecologically important addition of water in some types of ecosystems. It usually occurs on clear nights when such surfaces cool by radiation loss. By forming a film of moisture on foliage, overnight transpiration is reduced, conserving soil moisture for use the following day. When the dew is heavy, water may run down stems or drip to the ground, where it becomes available for daytime use. This can be an important source of soil moisture for dryland species such as bunch grasses, and small, shallow-rooted desert annuals may depend as much on dew as on rain. The maximum amount of dew that can be deposited per night is about 1 mm, although it is usually much less than this (Slatyer, 1967b). It is generally thought that dew is not of great significance to the overall water balance of mature plants in nondesert areas, but dew may be important at the time of germination and in the survival of young trees planted on dry sites. Dew has

been shown to increase the survival of pine seedlings rooted in dry soil, and this may be important in determining tree regeneration in dry areas (Stone and Fowels, 1955; Stone, 1957, 1958). Dew is a significant input of moisture to alpine snowfields. In 1957, condensation in an alpine snowfield in the Colorado Rockies exceeded evaporation by an average of 14,600 L ha^{-1} day^{-1} during the month of August. The maximum observed gain due to condensation was equivalent to 0.086 mm hr^{-1} or about 1000 L ha^{-1} hr^{-1} (Anonymous, 1958).

Another less well recognized input of moisture is the result of the formation of *rime*. This is a layer of ice that develops on surfaces by one of two processes: the impaction of fog particles on freezing surfaces or the growth of ice crystals on freezing surfaces that are in contact with warmer, moist air. When the ice melts, the water can be absorbed by plants either directly or after the water has dripped down to the soil. The accumulation of rime can be an important moisture input in some environments. For example, the amount of water reaching the ground beneath stunted trees at high elevations in the New England mountains was found to be about four times that in the open as the result of the formation of rime on the vegetation (Schlesinger and Reiners, 1974). Rime contributed 7–10 cm additional precipitation over the winter in a lodgepole pine forest in Washington (Berndt and Fowler, 1969). Rime can accumulate to a thickness of several centimeters on minor vegetation in clearcuts in clear, cold, fall or spring weather.

Fog drip is an input of water that results from fog and mist particles (0.01–0.1 mm in diameter) coming in contact

Table 11.1 Fog Drip Under Vegetation at 1783 m Elevation on Mt. Wilson, California (Data from Kittredge, 1948)

Vegetation Type	Precipitation Beneath the Vegetation, cm	Fog Drip, cm
Open (no vegetation)	58	0
Shrubs:		
Ceanothus sp., 2.4 m tall	58	0
Trees		
Canyon live oaks, 13.7 m tall	121	63
Pseudotsuga macrocarpa, 12.2 m tall	122	64
Pinus ponderosa, 24.4 m tall	154	96

with vegetation surfaces. Fog drip is particularly important in forests at high elevations or in humid coastal or foggy areas. For example, fog drip contributed water equivalent to 150 cm of precipitation during a 40-day summer rainless period at a location near San Francisco (Oberlander, 1956). Twenty-five percent of the water reaching the soil beneath a ridge-top conifer forest about 4 km inland from the Oregon coast was found to be from fog drip (Isaac, 1946). An 18-week study in a Sitka spruce/western hemlock stand in Oregon recorded 29 cm of fog drip while precipitation was recorded as 64 cm. It has been suggested that water input below forest cover in foggy weather generally exceeds that in the open by 30–50%: peak values are generally found in ridge-top locations. Table 11.1 shows some fog drip data obtained under different vegetation types on Mount Wilson, California. Fog drip increased with increasing height of the vegetation: the taller the vegetation, the greater the volume of air from which fog particles could be scavenged.

The efficiency of trees at removing fog particles from the air has been utilized in Japan, where belts of trees have been planted around fog-plagued cities. Studies revealed that these tree belts can remove about 3370 L ha^{-1} hr^{-1} under certain conditions of wind and fog; this is equivalent to about 0.34 mm hr^{-1} precipitation or the equivalent of a moderate rainfall intensity. Adjacent grassland captured only 10–17% as much (Hori, 1953). The effect of fog drip on soil moisture can be very significant. For example, the surface 30 cm of soil beneath a plantation of Monterey pine and eucalyptus at about 500 m elevation in the Berkeley hills of California contained a higher midsummer moisture content than that under adjacent grassland. The difference, which was equivalent to 5–8 cm of precipitation, was attributed to fog drip (Means, 1927). Forests have sometimes been planted in foggy areas to increase the yield of water. *Araucaria* forests were planted on ridge tops on the Hawaiian island of Lanai when it was discovered that such plantations could yield up to 75 cm of fog drip (Ekern, 1964). Many estimates of water inputs into forests have ignored fog drip. It is apparent that in certain types of forest this may be a significant oversight (see the review in Kerfoot, 1968).

The atmosphere is not the only source of water for an ecosystem. In fine-textured soils, water can reach vegetation by capillary rise from water tables well below the depth of rooting. Lower-slope ecosystems receive seepage water flowing downslope through the soil over an impermeable layer. Springs can augment the water supply of lower-slope areas even where slope seepage does not occur.

From this brief review it should be clear that although rain and snow are the major sources of water input for many ecosystems, there are several other ecologically important sources.

B. Do Forests Influence Water Inputs into Ecosystems?

In the earlier part of this century there was a great deal of controversy about the relationship between forest cover and precipitation. It was claimed by some that in comparison with other forms of vegetation, forests increase precipitation and also recharge the air with moisture which promotes precipitation in downwind areas. Forest removal was thought to reduce precipitation and hence stream flow.

Analysis of this question for temperate forests (e.g., Kittredge, 1948) has revealed that while the removal of forest can reduce total stream flow in some situations, this is mainly through reductions in fog drip; direct effects of forests on precipitation are probably minor. It has been suggested that the maximum effect that a forest could have on precipitation in temperate regions is a 5% increase, but that this maximum is attained only in particular circumstances (Golding, 1970). However, there is growing concern that deforestation in the Amazon basin could significantly affect atmospheric humidity and precipitation over large areas downwind, and this topic will doubtless become a focus of future research as the deforestation of the humid tropics accelerates. Much of the almost daily rainfall in the Amazon basin is promptly reevaporated and transpired back to the atmosphere, maintaining high atmospheric humidity and generating the clouds that provide the next day's rain. Without forest vegetation, most of the water would enter rivers, resulting in the progressive drying of the air. Even with the forest, many trees die each year during the dry season, and there is concern that large-scale conversion of forest to agricultural land could so reduce atmospheric humidity and precipitation that many of the tree species in the remaining forest would die.

C. Interception of Precipitation by Vegetation

Not all the precipitation reaching the surface of the vegetation arrives at the soil surface, as anyone who has taken shelter beneath a tree during a rainstorm can tell you. Similarly, much of the dew or rime accumulated overnight is evaporated the following morning and never reaches the soil. The loss back to the atmosphere of precipitation that has been intercepted by vegetation is called *interception loss*.

The magnitude of interception loss depends upon the *interception storage capacity* of the vegetation, on the total energy available to evaporate water held by the vegetation, and on the movement and humidity of the air. Water is held as a film on plant surfaces, in bark cracks, needle angles, and so on, the water capacity of which varies on different types of vegetation. Much of this water will be released if the vegetation is shaken by wind, which serves to reduce interception. Heavy rain also serves to shake much of the stored water from the crown. Evaporation of the stored water requires energy and is promoted by air that has a high *vapor pressure deficit* (VPD), which is the difference between the actual vapor pressure of the air and the saturation vapor pressure at that temperature. It is a measure of the drying power of the air. Evaporation loss is thus high during summer when there is a high VPD, abundant energy for evaporation, and a long time between storms. Winters in winter-wet climates have little interception loss because of little energy for evaporation, low or zero VPDs, and short periods of time between storms, which gives little chance for evaporative loss to occur. However, some evaporation does occur even in winter and there can be surprisingly rapid evaporation between winter showers (Rutter, 1963).

The absolute amount of interception loss is relatively independent of storm size since it is determined by interception storage capacity, which is more or less constant. By the same argument, it becomes a decreasing percentage of total precipitation as storm size increases. Interception storage for tree and shrub cover has been reported to range between 0.25 and 7.6 cm of rain and up to 2.5 cm (water equivalent) of snow (references in Satterlund, 1972). Interception loss of rain by trees can be 100% for light summer showers in dry climates and 0% for heavy or continuous rain in winter in humid climates. It is much reduced in deciduous trees in the nonleafy period.

Table 11.2 presents some figures for interception loss in various forest types in the U.S. The loss of water through interception is very dependent on crown structure, which in turn varies with the tree age and the density of stems in the stand (Table 11.3). Interception can also occur for snow that builds up on tree branches. In humid climates there is little evaporative loss for such snow, but in continental climates there may be an appreciable loss to evaporation; the snow loses water vapor directly to the air without melting. This is discussed in more detail later.

Interception losses make it difficult to arrive at accurate figures for fog interception, and vice versa. Most fog drip estimates are the net contribution of fog drip after interception loss has occurred. Interception loss also reduces the quantities of dew and rime water that reach the ground.

D. Redistribution of Water by Vegetation

Precipitation in nonvegetative areas reaches the ground fairly uniformly over distances measured in tens of meters (heavily localized convectional storms excepted). Beneath all but the most diminutive vegetation, the situation is different. Water intercepted by tree crowns is redistributed into two major subtypes and reaches the floor very nonuniformly: (1) *throughfall*—that portion of the incident precipitation which drips from or falls through the vegetation canopy (sometimes divided into canopy drip and throughfall that does not touch any vegetation), and (2) *stemflow*—that portion which reaches the soil by flowing down the stem.

The importance of stemflow varies greatly. It is generally insignificant in climax humid West Coast forests, where the pendulous branches serve to divert almost all precipitation to throughfall (Figure 11.2A). Immature forests, forests of

Table 11.2 Annual Percent Interception Loss in Various Different Mature Forest Types in the U.S. (Data from Kittredge, 1948)

Forest Type	Location	Interception, %
Mature hardwoods	S. Appalachian Mts.	12
Oak–pine	New Jersey	13
Quaking aspen	Colorado	16
Ponderosa pine	Idaho	22
Lodgepole pine	Colorado	32
Douglas-fir	Washington	34
Ponderosa pine	Arizona	40
Maple–beech	New York	43
Eastern hemlock	Connecticut	48

Table 11.3 Effects of Stand Age and Tree Spacing on Interception Loss

	Age, yr	Interception Loss, cm	Interception, %
Eastern white pine, S. Appalachian Mts.[a]	10	30.5	15
	35	38.1	19
	60	53.3	26
Spacing Stems/ha			
Douglas-fir, 18 yr old, Coastal British Columbia[b]	10,000	12.7	15
	3,000	19.5	23
	1,370	20.4	24
	730	22.0	26

[a] The data for white pine are for annual interception losses (Kittredge, 1948).
[b] The data for Douglas-fir apply to an 8-month period, May–December (Kimmins, unpublished data).

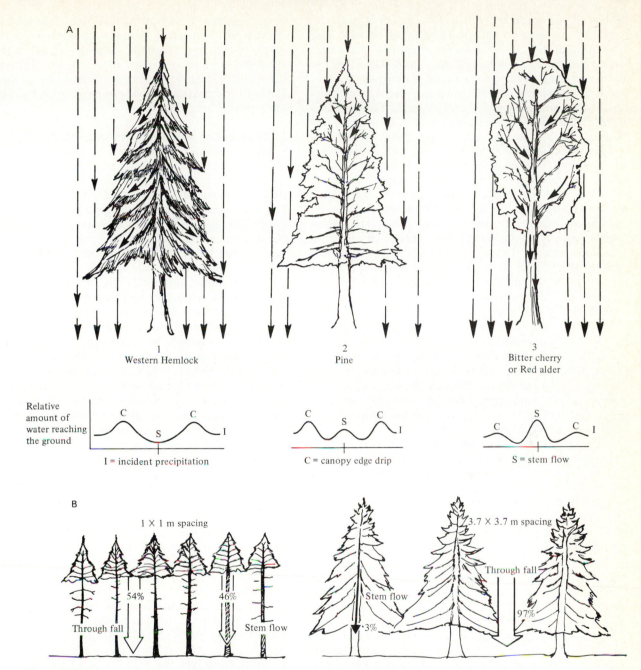

Figure 11.2
Effect of variation in crown morphology and stand density on the relative importance of stemflow and throughfall.
(A) Tree species with pendulous branches tend to have little stem flow and redistribute much of the precipitation into canopy-edge drip. Species with erect or acute-angled branches have much more stemflow and less canopy drip.
(B) The closer the spacing in a stand, the higher the proportion of acute-angled branches and the greater the importance of stemflow: data from an 18-year-old Douglas-fir plantation.

hardwoods such as cherry (*Prunus* sp.) or alder *(Alnus),* and forests of pine tend to have more stemflow because their upturned branches act as a funnel. Stemflow also varies with stand density. A 6-month study (May–December) in an 18-year-old Douglas-fir spacing plantation near Vancouver, B.C. (Kimmins, unpublished data), revealed that interception loss varied from 15 to 26% of incident precipitation as the number of trees per hectare went from about 10,000 to about 730, and that the relative proportions of stemflow to throughfall declined from 44% (i.e., 44% of the water reaching the ground beneath the trees was stemflow) in the most dense stand to 3% in the least dense stand. This difference was attributed to differences in crown morphology (Figure 11.3B). The increase in interception loss with decreasing stand density resulted from the greater interception storage capacity of the large, long crowns of the more widely spaced trees. The small crown storage, and upturned branches of the trees in the dense stand delivered a higher proportion of the incident precipitation to the soil via stemflow than did the less dense stand.

Stemflow is also affected by bark roughness. Smooth-bark species have little stem water storage capacity, and stemflow will commence on smooth-barked species such as beech after only a little more than 1 mm of rain has fallen (Voigt, 1960; Leonard, 1961). Rough-barked species such as spruce, cedar, or mature Douglas-fir have a large stem storage capacity, and appreciable stemflow may not reach the ground until more than 2 cm of rain has fallen (Helvey and Patric, 1965).

Where stemflow is appreciable, it serves to concentrate a lot of the incident precipitation close to the base of the trees. In a study of the distribution of radioactive fallout in the soil beneath beech trees in Ohio, it was found that soil at the base of a tree where there was abundant stemflow contained five times as much radioactivity as soil where there was no stemflow. The amount of water arriving per unit area over a small area close to the tree bases was found to be seven times that of the incident precipitation (Gersper and Holowaychuk, 1970). The water delivered to the base of trees as stemflow penetrates the soil rapidly by following large roots. Therefore, forests with a high proportion of stemflow may have a different hydrological character from those with a low proportion of stemflow. The rapid entry and deep penetration of stemflow into the soil reduces losses by evaporation and therefore increases the availability of water to plants. This can be very important to vegetation in dry areas, and many species in such areas have a morphology that promotes stemflow.

It has been suggested (Horn, 1971) that the geometry of below-ground biomass reflects the effect of aboveground biomass geometry on water distribution. Tree species with crowns and stems that promote stemflow tend to have deeply penetrating taproots, whereas those with little stemflow and a lot of canopy-edge drip tend to have more superficially located root systems: heart roots and flat roots. This will optimize the recovery of moisture and nutrients by the plants.

E. Interception and Redistribution of Snow

Snow is also intercepted and stored on the crowns of plants, sometimes to a greater extent than rain. Except in windy weather, it remains on trees longer than rain and is therefore potentially susceptible to greater evaporation losses. Snow was observed to remain on tree crowns for up to 50% of the snow season at a study site in the Sierra Nevada mountains in California, and more than 60% in some upstate New York locations; there may be continuous retention of snow on tree canopies in northern Canada (references in Satterlund, 1972). In contrast, snow does not remain on tree crowns for very long in snowy environments subject to periodic above-freezing temperatures, such as subalpine coastal forests in western North America.

When snow falls from tree crowns, much of it is redistributed into canopy-edge snowfall. This contributes to the characteristic pattern of peak snow accumulation under canopy edges and minimum accumulation close to the stem, but redistribution by crowns is not the sole cause of this pattern of accumulation. Redistribution by wind, water dripping from snow melting in the crowns, and melting of snow by radiation from tree trunks also help to determine the observed patterns of snow depth in forests. Snow tends to accumulate in small openings in the forest more than in closed forest or large openings because wind eddies in small openings favor the deposition of snow. In a study in the eastern foothills of the Rocky Mountains in Alberta, greatest snow accumulations in a lodgepole pine forest were found in openings equivalent to two to three times the tree height, but the longest duration of snowpack was found in openings equivalent to the height of the surrounding stand. In smaller openings than this, the long-wave radiation from the trees accelerated snowmelt, while in larger openings the greater exposure to sunlight accounted for a faster rate of melt (Golding and Swanson, 1978).

F. Infiltration into the Soil

Water reaching the ground can either flow laterally over the surface or penetrate the soil in a process called *infiltration*. Once within the soil, the movement of water is known as *percolation*. The term infiltration can apply either to the organic forest floor or to the underlying mineral soil, but since the rate of water movement into the forest floor almost always exceeds rates of precipitation, and since the condition of the forest floor is subject to modification and is therefore less permanent than the mineral soil as a site feature, the term is applied most frequently to the mineral soil.

Entry of water into the forest floor is normally rapid because of the many large pores and the organic nature of the forest floor, which gives it a high moisture-holding capacity. However, forest floors that have become very hot and dry during the summer may exhibit *hydrophobicity* (literally, water hating), which makes them very difficult to rewet. As a result, the rate of entry and movement of water during the first fall rains may be reduced. Hydrophobicity can also be induced by fire (see Chapter 12). It is not a permanent condition and once the forest floor has been rewetted, hydrophobicity does not re-form upon mild drying.

Once wet, forest floors can hold between one and five times their own weight of water (Kittredge, 1948); the more decomposed the organic matter and the more rotting wood in the forest floor, the more water it can hold. Only the water in excess of the field capacity of the forest floor will infiltrate into the mineral soil, and it may take many weeks and many centimeters of rain before the mineral soil beneath the forest floor becomes wet in the fall following a dry summer.

Infiltration into moist forest floors is normally rapid, and it has been widely thought that little or no surface flow or runoff occurs. This is not always true, because short-distance runoff can occur on sloping forest floors as the result of the arrangement of leaf litter (leaves or needles arranged like the tiles of a roof) or because of a compact surface growth of liverworts or mosses that makes surface flow easier than infiltration. Considerable runoff has been measured on sloping sites in wet western hemlock forests in British Columbia (Feller, 1974). Such flows only occur over short distances (a few centimeters to a few meters), because before moving very far, the water forms into pools behind logs or collects in microdepressions and then infiltrates the forest floor. Alternatively, the water may encounter a vertical plant stem, down which it flows rapidly.

Infiltration into mineral soils is determined by both soil texture and soil structure, parameters that define the size and arrangement of pores in the soil. Infiltration involves movement under the action of gravity into larger pores or old root channels (tubular spaces ramifying through the soil, formed by roots that have died and decayed). Where large pores are frequent (sands, gravels, or well-structured silts or clays), infiltration rate will be high. Where they are few, much of the water must infiltrate the smaller pores by the process of capillary action [you will recall that this is the

process that causes water to rise up inside a narrow (e.g., 1-mm diameter) glass tube when its surface is touched to the water surface]. The smaller the pores, the more rapid the initial entry of water into the surface pores but the slower the movement through the soil once the surface pores are filled.

Movement of water into and through the soil is affected by the amount of organic matter and swelling clays in the soil. These swell on wetting and act to clog the pores, reducing rates of water movement and thus the infiltration rate. If the infiltrating water is dirty (e.g., a suspension of clay particles or organic matter), the surface pores may become clogged and infiltration reduced.

In all but very coarse types of soil, the crumb structure of the surface mineral soil is critically important. If this is destroyed, infiltration is greatly reduced. Compaction by grazing animals or harvesting equipment, loss of structure by plowing, or damage to the surface structure of exposed mineral soils by the impact of rain can all reduce infiltration. Heavy raindrops falling from branches can rapidly damage exposed mineral soils. The kinetic energy of these drops is transferred to soil crumbs upon impact and this process may separate the crumbs into their component particles. It is important to maintain a forest floor in which the kinetic energy of the falling rain can be dissipated without effecting the soil structure.

G. Water in the Soil

This topic was introduced in Chapter 10 but some additional concepts will be discussed here. In Section 10.3, we saw that water in the soil is classified as gravitational, available, and unavailable. The relative proportions of these three types of water varies according to the relative abundance of different pore sizes, which in turn depends upon soil structure and texture. Coarse soils (sands and gravels) have many large pores, and most of the water in the soil at field capacity is available. Fine soils (clays and silts) have many capillary-sized pores, and much of the water at field capacity (a very imprecise term for such soils) is unavailable. The movement of water through soils under saturated conditions follows D'Arcy's law, which says that water flow is proportional to the product of hydraulic conductivity (a function of pore size and distribution), the hydraulic gradient, and the cross-sectional area of soil through which the water is flowing.

Water moves through the soil in response to hydraulic gradients, capillary forces, and gravity. This combination generally results in downward movement during wet periods when there is a high input of water to the soil surface, but in summer when there is a net loss by evaporation from the surface, upward movements may occur. Water moving down through the soil may encounter less pervious or even impervious layers. These may be lenses (strata) of finer-textured materials in stratified transported soils, or layers in which pedogenic processes have deposited materials. Iron, calcium, organic matter, clay, and other materials are often deposited or accumulated in lower horizons, and this tends to obstruct percolation. Where such layers are impervious, downward movement is prevented and a *perched water table* is formed. Such perched water tables may be extensive and result in swampy conditions overlying dry, freely drained geological deposits. More frequently, they are intermittent, and result in a mozaic of wetter and drier soil conditions.

In the absence of pans, water drainage will continue until the *groundwater table* is encountered. This is a layer of saturated soil in contact with an underlying impermeable layer of bedrock or compacted material. Water will remain at this level, percolate slowly down into cracks in the underlying material, move laterally under the influence of gravity (seepage water), or move back up through the soil as it dries from above (a process known as *capillary rise*). The layer of soil above the water table that remains moist because of capillary rise is called the *capillary fringe*. Seepage water moves downhill until it joins either a water surface or a subterranean body of water.

H. Loss of Water to Evaporation and Transpiration

Water is lost from soil by three major pathways: drainage to groundwater, evaporation back to the atmosphere, and uptake by plants. The equivalent of 760 mm of precipitation is delivered to the 48 coterminous U.S. states each year, and of this about 370 mm is lost back to the atmosphere by evaporation from forests and wildlands (Hewlett and Nutter, 1969). By comparison, Australia receives 420 mm of precipitation and loses 370 mm by evapotranspiration. Canada receives the equivalent of 600 mm precipitation, of which 230 mm is lost to evapotranspiration (den Hartog and Ferguson, 1978).

1. Evaporation. Evaporation from the soil surface requires two preconditions: energy in the form of solar radiation (580 cal is required to evaporate 1 g of water), and an upward flow of water from lower in the soil to maintain water in the surface layer, where the energy is available for evaporation. Evaporation from bare soil in the summer is initially rapid, but water evaporates first from the larger pores, and when the rate slows down as these are emptied, water is withdrawn from smaller pores. Upward capillary movement is slow, and under conditions of rapid evaporation all water may be removed from the surface soil. When

this happens, the continuity of the water columns from the surface to the lower soil layers is broken, continued upward capillary movement essentially ceases, and evaporation is reduced to upward movement of water vapor. This sequence of events occurs more in coarse-textured than in fine-textured soils. Thus, summer evaporation from bare coarse and medium textured soil is initially rapid, but once the surface layer dries out it drops to very low levels, and soil a few centimeters down may remain near field capacity. In fine textured soil, capillary columns remain intact for much longer and the lower soil layers may therefore become much drier. In the winter there is usually insufficient energy for much evaporation and the soil surface of most soils remains moist.

Under a continuous cover of vegetation, insufficient energy reaches the soil to produce much evaporation, even in the summer. Where there is an organic accumulation, evaporation from the mineral soil is further reduced because of the lack of continuous pores from the mineral soil to the surface of the forest floor; water rising in the mineral soil is blocked by the hydrological discontinuity of the mineral–organic interface. A well-decomposed forest floor resists drying out because much of the water is held by colloids, but even if it does dry, it constitutes an efficient vapor barrier which reduces loss of water from the mineral soil.

Evaporation of snow occurs in continental climates where there are many clear sunny days with dry air in the winter. The rate is lower than the evaporation of water from soil, since snow has a higher albedo (most of the energy is reflected and therefore not available for evaporation), much of the energy is used to raise the temperature to 0°C, and 84 cal g^{-1} is required to melt the snow. A total of about 664 cal is required to evaporate 1 g of snow at 0°C. In coastal climates, evaporative losses will be less because of the lower levels of solar energy available during the cloudy winter.

Measurements at an elevation of about 2100 m in Utah revealed evaporation of about 7 cm of snow over a 180-day period, which represented about 14% of the snowfall (Kittredge, 1948). Studies in an open meadow, an open pine forest, and a closed fir stand near Lake Tahoe, Nevada, revealed a November to March loss of snow equivalent to 22, 12, and 6 cm of water, respectively. The difference was related to differences in the quantity of solar energy available for evaporation at the surface of the snow, which resulted from shading by the vegetation.

Evaporative loss is particularly rapid during periods of warm winds in the winter (e.g., the chinook winds in the Canadian Rocky Mountains). Based on an energy calculation, it was estimated that there was an evaporative loss of

Table 11.4 Variation in Transpiration Losses of Water from Forest Trees

Species	Biomass of Foliage, kg ha^{-1}	Daily Transpiration of Leaves, g H$_2$O (g green leaves)$^{-1}$	Annual Transpiration of 40–50-yr-old Stands cm H$_2$O[a]
Birch	4,940	9.5	17
Beech	7,900	4.8	14
Larch	13,950	3.2	17
Pine	12,550	1.9	8.6
Spruce	31,000	1.4	16
Douglas-fir	40,000	1.3	19

Source: Data from Rutter, 1968. Copyright Academic Press. Used with permission.
[a] Water loss expressed in terms of cm H$_2$O per unit area.

snowpack of 1.2 and 2.0 mm day^{-1} during chinooks in 1975 and 1976, respectively, on the east slope of the Rockies west of Calgary, Alberta. The higher value in 1976 was attributed to higher wind speeds that year. The highest daily evaporative loss calculated during these two years was estimated to be 10.4 mm (Golding, 1978).

2. Transpiration. Loss of water from within the living cells of plant tissues to the atmosphere by vaporization is called *transpiration*. Water absorbed by roots from soil is translocated upward to the foliage in the xylem of the roots and stem. This uptake and translocation is driven by solar energy falling on the leaves and stems, which causes water to evaporate from the moist outside surfaces of mesophyll cells into air spaces within the leaf. The water vapor either diffuses out to the atmosphere through stomata or evaporates directly through the cuticle of leaves. This vaporiza-

Table 11.5 Utilization of Water by Forests in Various Parts of the World (After Rutter, 1968)

Forest Type	Annual Precipitation, cm	Annual Evapotranspiration Loss		Growing Season Soil Water Deficit
		cm	%	
Northern taiga conifer forest, USSR	52.5	28.6	54	Negligible
Southern taiga conifer forest, USSR	60.0	32.9	55	Negligible
Spruce stand, Great Britain	135.0	80.0	59	Negligible
Mixed conifer and deciduous stand, Switzerland	165.0	86.1	52	Negligible
Mixed conifer and deciduous stand, N. Japan	261.7	54.2	21	Negligible
Evergreen rain forest, Kenya	195.0	157.0	81	Small
Deciduous forest, European USSR	45.7	42.4	93	Moderate
Coulter pine, California	123.0	63.7	52	Severe
Ponderosa pine, California	126.0	58.0	46	Severe
Coulter pine, San Dimas, Calif.	52.5	63.7	75	Extreme

tion produces a water deficit within the foliage cells which is transmitted via the water columns in the branches, stems, and large roots to the fine roots, where uptake from the soil occurs. The resultant reduction in water in the rhizosphere sets up moisture gradients that result in movements of water from the surrounding soil to the roots.

The amount of water transpired by forests varies according to the species, the quantity of foliage, the availability of water in the soil, and the availability of solar energy to evaporate water from the leaves. The variation between species results from differences in stomatal resistance (the resistance to diffusion of water through the stomata, which will be higher where the stomata are sunk deeply in a thick cuticle and lower in leaves with a thin cuticle), internal resistance to water movement in the plant (a function of internal morphology of conducting elements), and resistance to uptake from the soil (a function of root morphology). Table 11.4 shows how transpiration varies according to species and foliage biomass. Birch has a very high transpiration rate per unit leaf weight, but because it has a modest leaf biomass its annual transpiration rate differs little from that of species with low transpiration rates per unit weight but high foliage biomass. Within one species or type of plant (e.g., conifer vs. deciduous hardwood), leaf biomass is related to leaf area, so the more fully stocked a stand or the greater the leaf area index, the greater the transpirational loss if there is sufficient solar energy available. Thus it can be seen that annual transpiration per unit area of fully stocked forest varies much less than the rate per unit of leaf biomass.

Table 11.5 shows how the annual evapotranspiration rate varies in different types of forests around the world. It can be seen that the percentage of the annual precipitation that is transpired varies considerably, but not necessarily in proportion to the growing-season soil-moisture deficit (annual growing season precipitation minus potential growing season evapotranspiration). Northern areas tend to have negligible deficits and lose only a modest percentage of annual precipitation by transpiration. Much higher transpiration losses might be expected in a hot, dry climate, yet two studies involving ponderosa and coulter pines at San Dimas, California, found only 46 and 52% transpiration loss associated with severe soil-moisture deficits. The lack of the expected correlation relates to the annual distribution of precipitation: winter precipitation experiences much smaller evaporation losses than does summer precipitation. At San Dimas, there is little or no water to transpire in the summer, when the potential for loss is high: the rains come in the winter, when potential transpiration is much lower.

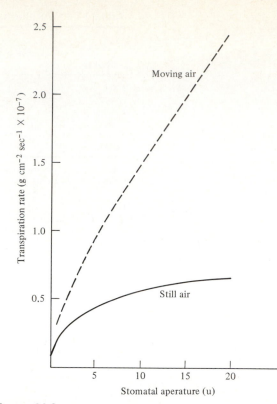

Figure 11.3

Effect of air movement on transpiration loss from *Zebrina* leaves. The graph shows transpiration rates at different stomatal apertures in still and moving air. In still air, water vapor accumulates in a thin layer of air around the leaf. This layer inhibits transpiration, so that water loss becomes relatively independent of stomatal aperture. In moving air this boundary layer is removed, and transpiration becomes very sensitive to stomatal aperture. (After Bange, 1953. Used by permission of the Koninklijke Nederlandse Botanische Vereeniging, The Netherlands, and North-Holland Physics Publishing.)

The importance of stomatal opening in the control of transpiration loss warrants a brief discussion of the topic. Stomatal opening and closure are thought to be largely determined by intercellular CO_2 concentration; when this is low, stomata open, and when it is high, they close (Slatyer, 1967). Both temperature and light have a direct effect on stomatal opening, but most of this effect is indirect, via the effect of temperature and light on internal CO_2 concentrations. These drop during the day because of photosynthesis (stomata open) and increase at night (stomata close) because of respiration. Stomatal opening is also influenced by water stress, because stomatal opening depends on the turgor of the guard cells; this can override the effects of light, temperature, and internal CO_2 levels. However, water deficits do not affect closure until some critical level of water stress has been reached. Sudden increases in stress can actually cause a temporary increase in stomatal aperture because more rapid water loss may occur from cells adjacent to the guard cells than from the guard cells themselves.

Transpiration rate is also affected by wind. As water vapor emerges from the stomata and the cuticle, it enters the thin layer of air that is in contact with the leaf (the *boundary layer*). This increases the partial pressure of water vapor in the boundary layer, which in turn depresses the diffusion of vapor out of the leaf and reduces the rate of transpiration loss. If this layer is continually removed by wind and replaced by drier air, transpiration continues unimpeded. Figure 11.3 shows the effect of air movement on transpiration loss from leaves. As stomatal aperture increases in still air, transpiration slows down because of a buildup of water vapor around the leaf. In moving air, transpiration continues to increase with increasing stomatal aperture. Wind speeds of 13 km hr^{-1} have been estimated to increase transpiration by 20%, with a 50% increase in 40-km hr^{-1} winds (Clarke, 1967).

11.3 Availability of Water to Plants and Animals

The hydrological cycle is a description of the distribution and movement of water between water bodies, the atmosphere, and terrestrial ecosystems. It does not define the consequences for living organisms of the distribution and movements of water.

The availability of water to organisms, its ecological effectiveness, is determined by several factors.

1. *Timing*. The moisture requirements of terrestrial organisms vary from season to season. Greatest demands are usually during the growing season or metabolically active period, and requirements may be very small during the rest of the year. Therefore, annual precipitation figures are often of limited use in ecology. Many parts of California, which have extreme soil moisture deficits during the growing season, have the same annual precipitation as some continental locations which have only a small growing-season soil moisture deficit. The difference results from the California sites receiving almost all of their rain in the winter, whereas in the interior of the continent there is a more even distribution throughout the year. Only precipitation that is available to an organism when it is needed is of significance to the water balance of that organism.

2. *Soil moisture storage*. Dry sites are very often dry because of rapid drainage and a small water storage capacity

in the soil, rather than because they receive less precipitation. A coarse gravel soil will be much drier in the summer than an adjacent loam soil. In the former, water tensions may approach the wilting point within few days of a rainstorm, whereas a subsequent rainstorm may well occur before the moisture stored in the soil pores of the loam soil has been depleted to the wilting point.

3. *Rapidity of drainage losses*. The longer moisture remains within the rooting zone, the more ecologically effective it will be to plants. Steeply sloping land sheds moisture more rapidly than flat land and consequently is drier, unless it receives seepage water from upslope drainage. In very deep soils, moisture may drain so far below the rooting zone that it is of no consequence to the vegetation. As a result, shallow coarse soils over an impermeable layer can be moister than very deep, finer-textured soils. In the former, rapid drainage is arrested at a point that is still accessible to the plant.

4. *Physical state of the water*. Frozen water is unavailable to most organisms and water vapor is of much less direct significance to organisms than liquid water. Although ice, snow, and water vapor all have important ecological effects in terrestrial ecosystems, as a usable source of water they are generally insignificant. The availability of water varies somewhat between the extremes of freezing point and boiling point. At the upper end of this scale water is generally unavailable because it is above the cardinal temperature of the organism. At lower temperatures, uptake by plants may be reduced because of an increase in the viscosity of water in both the soil and the plant.

5. *Chemical composition of the water*. Water is available to organisms only if it is in the appropriate chemical condition. Human beings will not drink heavily polluted water, and will die on a prolonged diet of seawater. Water with high concentrations of solutes cannot be absorbed by the roots of most plants. In fact, roots will tend to lose water and become desiccated if immersed in water with high concentrations of solutes. Plants growing in bogs frequently experience high moisture tensions because of the tendency for the solute-rich bog water both to resist uptake and to remove moisture from the plants. Only specially adapted plants can survive in such ecosystems. As a result of these adaptations, some tree species that grow on bogs can also be found growing on dry, gravely, or rock ridges. Both black spruce and lodgepole pine behave this way in western Canada, and western redcedar can be found growing on both wet lower-slope sites and dry ridge tops. Presumably, the adaptations that permit water uptake in the physiologically dry bog also equip the trees for survival on the dry ridges.

The effects of water chemistry on an organism's water balance are of particular significance to aquatic organisms.

These are divided into two groups according to their adaptations: *stenohaline* organisms are those that are adapted to only a narrow range of solute concentrations, and *euryhaline* organisms are tolerant of a wide range of solute concentrations. Plants or animals that live exclusively in the ocean or in fresh water are generally stenohaline, whereas those that live in the tidal portions of estuaries and are alternately exposed to salt and fresh water are euryhaline. The difference between euryhaline and stenohaline is not absolute. Anadramous fish (those that spend part of their life cycle in the ocean and part in fresh water) may have to spend a period in the brackish waters at the mouth of the river while the necessary physiological adjustments are made. They will be killed if transferred directly from salt to fresh water, or vice versa. Tolerance to a range of salinities may therefore be dependent on the rate of change in salinity.

6. *Intensity of Precipitation.* Water that falls on vegetation only to be lost through interception is not available to plants, apart from minor quantities that might be absorbed by the foliage. Similarly, small quantities of precipitation that reach the soil surface may be reevaporated rapidly and serve no useful function for plants. Precipitation distributed into many light showers may therefore be less available to plants than precipitation in fewer but moderate intensity showers. If all the rain falls in a single intense storm, its availability is again reduced because much of it is lost as surface runoff or subsurface storm flow. Maximum availability occurs when the rain comes in moderate intensity storms in which the rain penetrates more deeply into the soil, where it remains available to plants.

7. *Evaporative power of the air.* Except during a rainstorm, and sometimes even then, the atmosphere is almost always dry enough to permit evaporation and transpiration to occur. The drier the air (high VPD values) and the greater the energy available for evaporation, the shorter the period of time over which water is available to plants and the less effective a given amount of precipitation. As already discussed, wind influences evapotranspiration greatly, so moving air normally reduces the residence time of moisture in an ecosystem. Approximately 38% of the 600 mm of annual precipitation in Canada (a cool-to-cold high-latitude country) is lost to evapotranspiration (den Hartog and Ferguson, 1978). In the coterminous United States, a lower-latitude country with a hotter climate, approximately 70% is lost in this way, while the comparable figure for Australia, a country characterized by an arid climate, is estimated to be 88%. Obviously, evapotranspiration has a great effect on how long rainfall remains available in the soil.

11.4 Adaptations of Plants to Excess or Deficit of Water

Plants require water for almost every part of their life cycle. Seeds require moisture to germinate and will remain dormant if they fall on dry soil, even if chilling and/or heating requirements have been satisfied. This moisture requirement may result from the need to leach growth inhibitors from the seed coat (particularly important in desert plants, where inhibitors prevent germination after a light shower and delay it until the heavy winter rains), to soften hard seed coatings so that the root radicle can emerge, and/or to permit the seed to swell and burst its covering.

Moisture is required for growth because with inadequate moisture, gaseous exchange in the foliage is drastically reduced. Plants regulate water loss from leaves by developing a waxy surface layer, the cuticle, which is nearly impervious to water. Unfortunately, cutin is also rather impervious to carbon dioxide and oxygen, which must be exchanged if the plant is to grow. This problem was solved with the evolution of stomata, which connect the leaf atmosphere with the external atmosphere.

Active uptake of moisture is important to plants since they rely on the *transpiration stream* to transport nutrients from the roots to the leaves. Movement of water and nutrients from roots to leaves promotes uptake of both from the rhizosphere, which in turn causes water and its solutes to move from remote soil pores to the rhizosphere.

Plants withdraw water from the soil until there is no longer a gradient of moisture tension between the plant and the soil. Transpiration creates a water stress in the plant that results in moisture tension within the roots. When the soil is moist, water moves into the roots in response to this tension. As the soil dries, the gradient between the plant and the soil diminishes and less water is absorbed. When a soil has dried to the point at which soil moisture tension approaches the plant moisture tension, uptake suddenly declines sharply, the plant wilts, the stomata close, and transpiration virtually ceases. The soil-moisture potential at which this occurs is referred to as the *temporary wilting point* (temporary wilting can also occur because transpiration exceeds uptake and translocation even when the soil is wet). Plants will recover turgidity when soil moisture tension drops again or the transpiration rate drops. However, if the soil water potential decreases further, plants will wilt to the point at which they will not recover turgor. The soil water potential at which this occurs is called the *permanent wilting point*. The amount of water in the soil (percentage by weight) at the permanent wilting point is called the *per-*

manent wilting percentage (PW%). This varies greatly according to the texture of the soil because texture dictates the tension with which the remaining water is held in the capillaries as the soil dries. Table 11.6 shows the relationship between texture and two measures of soil moisture that are of significance to plants.

The variation in the PW% of different species of plants growing on the same soil is generally much less than the variation for a single species growing on different soils, and some ecologists have claimed that the PW% is essentially common for all plants—that it is a soil parameter rather than a plant parameter. Contrary to this point of view, it has been shown that there is a significant variation in permanent wilting percentage between different plants and that a variation in PW% as small as 0.5% or less (which is within the limits of experimental measurement of PW%) may be of great significance to a plant. This is because a small variation in PW% may be associated with a large variation in soil moisture potential (Table 11.7). In some soils such a small difference in PW% could supply a plant with enough moisture to keep it alive for 6 full days (Levitt, 1958), which

could make the difference between survival and death of the plant. Another argument against the theory that PW% is only a soil parameter is that early investigations of PW% rather ignored plants that do not conserve water: called the water spenders (discussed below). Although water absorption by these types of plants may be greatly reduced under conditions of low soil water availability, they are able to resist permanent wilting to a lower soil water content than other types of plants.

Plants can be classified according to their adaptations to water stress.

1. Those adapted to partial or complete submergence in free water are called *hydrophytes*. Such plants cannot grow at soil moisture tensions greater than 500–1000 kPa.[1]
2. Terrestrial plants adapted to moderate water supplies are called *mesophytes;* they can grow at soil moisture tensions of up to 2000 kPa. They lack the specialized adaptations to excess or deficits of moisture found in hydrophytes and xerophytes, respectively.
3. Plants adapted to arid zones are called *xerophytes*. They can grow under moisture tensions as great as 4000 kPa. They are characterized by a variety of xeromorphic and physiologic adaptations, but attempts to define xerophytes on the basis of morphology have been unsuccessful.

Table 11.6 Effect of Soil Texture on the Availability of Water to Plants (Data from Veihmeyer, 1956)

Soil Textural Class	Moisture Equivalent[a]	Permanent Wilting %[b]
Clay	28.4	13.4
Loam	21.7	10.3
Silt loam	16.1	7.5
Sandy loam	9.5	2.9
Fine sand	3.2	1.0

[a]Moisture equivalent is the percent of water in an initially saturated soil remaining after a centrifugal force equal to 1000 × gravity has been applied to it for 10–40 min.
[b]Permanent wilting percent equals the water in the soil at the permanent wilting point as a percent of the soil by weight.

Table 11.7 Variation Among Plants in the Permanent Wilting Percent, Soil Water Potential at the Permanent Wilting Point and the Final Soil Water Content after Permanent Wilting (Data from Slatyer, 1957)

Plant	Permanent Wilting %	Soil Water Potential, atm	Final Soil Water Content, %[a]
Tomato	11.8	−18	9.8
Cotton	10.2	−38	7.0
Privet	9.7	−47	6.9

[a]Water uptake by plants generally continues after the permanent wilting point is reached, so the final soil water content is lower than the permanent wilting percentage.

A. Excess Moisture

The term *hydrophyte* includes strictly aquatic plants, including those that grow in bogs, swamps, and marshes. Nonhydrophytic plants are generally excluded from these saturated semiterrestrial habitats because of the soil oxygen deficiency that accompanies saturation. The tolerance of hydrophytes to this condition can be explained partly by the characteristic presence of internal cavities and spongy tissues in many hydrophytes. These facilitate the movement of oxygen from leaves and stems to roots, thus permitting them to function in an oxygen-deficient environment. A good example of this is the rice plant *(Oryza sativa)*, in which the submerged roots may contain up to 18% O_2, whereas the muddy substrate contains none (Daubenmire, 1974). Restriction of roots to the better aerated surface soil, development of *pneumatophores* (special root branches that grow vertically upward until they emerge into the air and which are usually equipped with stomata and a well-developed intercellular system of air spaces), the ability to respire

[1]Pa = pascal, the metric unit of pressure. 1 Pa = N m^{-2}, where 1 N (Newton, unit of force) = kg m s^{-2}.

anaerobically for limited periods of time, and an overall low requirement for oxygen are other modifications that permit plants to grow in saturated terrestrial environments. Some species of mesophyte have the ability to develop these hydrophytic adaptations when growing in wet soil.

B. Moisture Deficits

Although hydrophytes are an important group of plants, there has been much more interest in xerophytes and the adaptations of plants to moisture deficits (e.g., Slatyer, 1967; Kozlowski, 1968; Levitt, 1972). Xerophytes can be classified according to the manner in which they respond to moisture stress (Levitt, 1972):

1. Drought escapers: ephemeral plants.
2. Drought Resisters.
   a. Avoidance of drought stress: water savers, water spenders.
   b. Tolerance of drought stress: avoidance of dehydration, tolerance of dehydration.

1. Drought Escapers: the Ephemerals.   These are plants that escape from the adverse effects of drought on internal water balance by eliminating most or all of their water and suspending metabolic functions that depend upon water. They can do this by entering the seed or spore stage. Arid regions usually support a wide diversity of small annual plant species that flower only during rainy seasons, which may occur annually or only every few years. These plants often lack the xeromorphic charcteristics of other xerophytes, and they cannot tolerate soil drought. Their main characteristics are small size, a high root/shoot ratio, and an ability to complete their life cycles very rapidly. Germination, growth, flowering, and seed set are all completed within the few weeks following the rainy period when the soil has sufficient moisture for the plant's needs. Because desert annuals cannot actually tolerate soil drought, they are not always considered to be true xerophytes. It is worth noting that the seeds of most plants are drought resistant, that not all annuals can survive in arid conditions, and that most desert ephemerals do not grow outside arid regions.

2. Drought Resisters.   a. AVOIDANCE OF DROUGHT STRESS.   This involves the maintenance of a high water potential when a plant is exposed to an external water stress. There are two major adaptations: water conservation *(water savers)* and water utilization *(water spenders)*. Early investigators noted the striking morphological characteristics of xerophytes and assumed that drought resistance resulted from water conservation. This assumption was challenged when it was discovered that some xerophytes lose water faster than some mesophytes when both plants are grown in

a moist habitat. It is now known that both adaptations exist. Water savers may lose as little as $1/4300$ of their weight of water per day, whereas water spenders may lose up to five times their weight of water per hour (Kilian and Lemee, 1956). Thus, water spenders may lose water as much as 500,000 times as rapidly as water savers.

i. Water savers. The best examples of water savers are the succulents (e.g., cacti) and some sclerophylls. Both are able to restrict transpiration long before wilting occurs. Succulents avoid drought by absorbing large quantities of water whenever it is available and storing it in swollen parenchymatous tissues and vacuoles. Their roots tend to be very superficial, so that they can exploit even light rainfall that only wets the surface soil. The roots are often drought-deciduous, dying shortly after a rain and regrowing when moisture is next available. Loss of water is avoided because the stomata open only at night and for a short time in the morning. They remain closed during the heat of the day. The CO_2 required during the day for photosynthesis is obtained from organic acids accumulated at night (Ting and Duggar, 1968). Water loss is also reduced by having a very small surface area-to-volume ratio. Leaves are reduced or even eliminated, the plant being merely a swollen stem. Water loss as a result of damage to the cuticle by herbivores is avoided by the development of sharp spines and chemical defenses.

Nonsucculent water savers include drought-resistant conifers and evergreen angiosperms. Their primary adaptation is having very impermeable cuticles. Cuticular transpiration in water savers is a much smaller fraction ($1/5$ to $1/50$ of stomatal transpiration) than in mesophytes ($1/2$ to $1/3$ of stomatal transpiration). As water is lost, cuticular transpiration decreases even more and may become negligible before wilting occurs. The deposition of additional lipids in the cuticle also helps to slow cuticular transpiration.

ii. Water spenders. Accelerated water absorption permits the maintenance of high internal water contents in spite of high transpiration rates by xerophytic water spenders. It enables them to keep their stomata open in the day, and water spenders are associated with higher rates of photosynthesis and growth than the water conservers. There are several adaptations that permit this apparently profligate use of water. Leaf veins are closer together and there is a higher density of veins than in mesophytes, which results in a more rapid delivery of water to the leaf surface and a higher transpiration rate. Smaller leaves have a smaller frictional resistance to the flow of water than large leaves and can transpire more rapidly.

Very high root/shoot ratios provide plants with a larger soil water capital to draw on which helps to sustain transpiration, and the larger root systems may penetrate down to water supplies deep in the soil. Artificial reduction of the root/shoot ratio reduces drought resistance in water spenders. For example, it was found that *Cryptomeria japonica* was more resistant than *Chamaecyparis obtusa* when the roots were allowed to penetrate freely in deep soil, but the resistance order was reversed when rooting was restricted by growing the trees in shallow containers (Satoo, 1956). *Pinus densiflora,* which had the highest root/shoot ratio, was the most drought resistant of several conifers tested. Plants that characteristically root down to a water table are called *phraeatophytes,* an extreme case of which is *Prosopis favata,* a desert plant of the near east, the roots of which extend 15 m down to the water table (Oppenheimer, 1951). The roots of Jarrah trees *(Eucalyptus marginata)* growing in southwestern Australia have also been measured to a depth of 15 m (Kimber, 1974). A final root adaptation is the ability to send out new roots into unexplored soils during a drought. The survival of many species in dry regions depends upon this adaptation. Water spenders also have the adaptation of a reduced permanent wilting point.

Water spenders may be able to partially alleviate drought stress by absorbing atmospheric moisture or nocturnal dew directly through the foliage. This may be of importance to plants in foggy localities or areas characterized by hot, dry days and cold nights. It is thought that dew absorption may play a significant role in the survival of planted tree seedlings in dry sites that are subject to dew in the evening. Water spenders also have the ability to become water savers when the water supply becomes extremely limiting.

b. TOLERANCE OF DROUGHT STRESS. Tolerance to drought conditions, which is exhibited by many plants and may involve either tolerance or avoidance of dehydration, can be achieved by a variety of mechanisms. High levels of solutes in cell sap give cells a low osmotic potential (high osmotic pressure) which keeps them turgid even under drought stress, thereby avoiding dehydration. Death from drought may result from the "starvation" that accompanies restricted exchange of CO_2. Tolerance to drought may therefore be achieved by maintaining stomata open in spite of reduced plant water content, thereby avoiding CO_2 starvation. Under these conditions, transpiration is reduced by low cell osmotic potential but CO_2 exchange continues. Alternatively, starvation can be avoided by having a lower metabolic rate. This reduces the demand for CO_2 uptake and makes the available photosynthate last longer. The low dry matter content of succulents is associated with low metabolic demands per volume of leaf and a tolerance of CO_2 starvation. Similarly, the drought-related death from starvation that accompanies a loss of protein may be either

avoided or tolerated. Finally, some plants simply are not damaged by being dried out. Mosses, lichens, and some ferns (sometimes known as "resurrection" plants) can remain in an air-dry condition for prolonged periods without injury. Growth resumes when the plants are able to reabsorb water. Epiphytic ferns are often particularly tolerant of being dried out. For example, a fern *Polypodium polypochoides* was found to survive uninjured after losing 97% of its normal water content (Stuart, 1968).

Drought tolerance, like tolerance to low temperatures, is influenced by preconditioning or "hardening": the exposure to a sublethal stress that results in resistance to an otherwise lethal stress. Table 11.8 shows how moderate levels of water stress result in an increase in drought tolerance of birch and aspen.

c. XEROPHILY: MORPHOLOGICAL AND PHYSIOLOGICAL ADAPTATIONS TO DROUGHT. The following are common xeromorphic characteristics (Levitt, 1972; Daubenmire, 1974). They may be under genetic control and therefore be rather invariable. In some species they vary according to the environmental moisture conditions to which the plant is exposed.

1. Morphological characteristics
   a. Reduced shoot size.
   b. Increases in the extent of the root system.
   c. Reduced size of leaves.
   d. Thicker leaves.
   e. Smaller leaf cells.
   f. Thicker cell walls.
   g. Smaller stomata, crowded together more densely.
   h. Presence of leaf hairs (pubescent).
   i. Thicker cuticle with more lipids.
   j. Better development of palisade mesophyll.
   k. Less pronounced development of spongy mesophyll.
   l. Smaller intercellular spaces.

Table 11.8 Effect of Moderate Drought Preconditioning on Drought Tolerance in Two Tree Species (Data from Jarvis and Jarvis, 1963)

Species	Preconditioning Water Stress, bars	Drought Tolerance, bars
Birch	0.1	34
	1.0	50
	2.0	60
Aspen	0.1	48
	0.5	56
	1.0	58
	4.0	75

    m. Smaller xylem cells.

    n. Higher proportion of heavily lignified tissues.

    o. More deeply sunken stomata.

2. Physiological characteristics

    a. Accumulation of sugars.

    b. Higher cell sap concentration.

    c. Lower osmotic potential.

    d. Lower cellular water content.

    e. Higher rate of transpiration per unit area of leaf.

    f. More rapid photosynthesis per unit area of leaf.

    g. Lower starch/sugar ratio.

    h. Lower protoplasmic viscosity.

    i. Increased protoplasmic permeability.

    j. Greater resistance to wilting.

    k. Earlier flowering and fruiting.

    l. Greater longevity.

    m. Increase in the percent of bound water absorbed by colloids per unit weight of dry tissue.

11.5   Adaptations of Animals to Excess or Deficit of Water

Water makes up a large proportion of the body weight of animals (70–90% of protoplasm), all of which must maintain an appropriate water balance in order to survive. Most of the adaptations to water found in terrestrial animals are related to restricting the loss of water while permitting exchange of respiratory gases and the elimination of wastes. Aquatic animals also have adaptations to maintain gaseous exchange (gills and/or gas-pervious outer layers), and they can experience an excess or deficit of water if their internal osmotic potential does not match that of the surrounding water. The necessary physiological changes required during the migration of anadromous fish have already been mentioned. Interesting though such aquatic adaptations are, the following section will focus on adaptations in terrestrial animals.

Many land animals employ the evaporation of water as a cooling mechanism. Sweating and panting are important means of maintaining internal temperatures in homeotherms, but this can result in excessive loss of moisture. Animals in dry environments have evolved a variety of mechanisms to ensure moisture conservation.

1. *Impervious integument.* Only animals with a relatively impermeable body covering (such as reptiles, birds, mammals, and insects) can remain permanently in dry terrestrial environments. Animals with moist skins, such as amphibians, are restricted to sites such as swamps or moist soils, and are frequently nocturnal in habit. Desert environments are normally inhabited by reptiles and insects, which have a dry and extremely impervious exterior, but certain nonsweating mammals and birds can also survive in such environments. The survival of these dry-skinned animals is totally dependent on the integrity of their impervious outer layers, and insects such as cockroaches can be killed almost as readily by carborundum powder as by insecticides. If the powder becomes trapped between the overlapping scales of the abdomen, it abrades the waterproof layer, permitting unregulated water loss and the subsequent death of the animal by desiccation.

2. *Internal lungs.* Exchange of oxygen and CO_2 between the blood and the atmosphere requires exposure of moist, blood-bearing tissues. In a dry atmosphere water is lost rapidly from such surfaces, which both impairs the efficiency of gaseous exchange and threatens the water balance of the animal. Organisms were unable to invade terrestrial environments until evolution had overcome this problem. The solution for insects is a series of sinuous branching pipes called *trachea* that leads from the exterior opening (the *spiracle*) to the site of gaseous exchange. Most of the exchange is by diffusion rather than by pumping, which reduces the forceable expulsion of moisture vapor. The spiracles close under excessively dry conditions, restricting moisture loss still further; the insects rely on oxygen within the trachea while the spiracles are closed. Moisture loss from animals with lungs is restricted by the location of the lungs deep within the body. The oxygen exchange sites (alveoli) are joined to the exterior by the system of finely divided pipes called the *bronchioles*.

3. *Dry excretion.* An important role of water in animals is to transport waste materials out of the body. In many environments use of water for this purpose would constitute profligate waste, and animals in such environments have evolved a more conservative approach to excretion. Urine is concentrated to a much lower osmotic potential than blood by active recovery of water, and in the most water-conserving animals such as insects, reptiles, and some birds, nitrogenous wastes are excreted as solid uric acid. Animals inhabiting moist environments may have rather liquid feces (e.g., cows). Animals of drier environments (e.g., rodents, sheep, or antelopes) have relatively dry feces. In human beings, the concentration of urine and the moisture content of feces tends to decrease as the body becomes progressively dehydrated.

4. *Suspended animation.* Animals can avoid drought by suspending the metabolic activities that require moisture or increase the loss of moisture. Such periods of suspended animation are called *aestivation*.

5. *Burrowing and nocturnal behavior*. Restriction of activity to the dark hours reduces the moisture stress experienced by organisms, by exposing them to lower temperatures and higher atmospheric humidity. During the day nocturnal animals generally remain underground, where humidity is much higher. During prolonged drought, they seek out areas of moist soil and remain there until the end of the drought.

6. *Drought-resistant stages*. Some animals die during drought periods, leaving drought-resistant eggs that hatch and resume activity when the availability of moisture increases again.

7. *Humidity control*. The construction of enclosed nests and covered runways, as exhibited by termites and some species of ant, permits animals that are susceptible to moisture loss to exist in dry environments, with only short forays into fully exposed habitats. Animals such as isopods restrict their activity to high-humidity environments such as beneath rocks or rotting logs.

8. *Migration and nomadism*. Many birds and animals migrate or become nomadic in response to drought. Migration of birds and animals from cold winter areas is in part a response to the reduced availability of water due to low temperature. Nomadism in desert areas is largely a response to variations in available water either directly from water sources or indirectly through the availability of water-containing food items.

9. *Water from food*. Some animals depend entirely on water contained in their food and rarely consume free water. The only moisture available to herbivores and carnivores for prolonged periods in dry grasslands may be the water contained in plants or in the blood and flesh of herbivores, respectively. For animals consuming high-moisture-content food, relatively modest water conservation adaptations may ensure an acceptable water balance. However, for animals such as the granary weevil, which feeds on dry materials such as stored wheat, there obviously have to be highly efficient water conservation adaptations. The moisture content of the granary weevil is about 48%, compared to 9% for its food, indicating very efficient water acquisition and conservation.

10. *Utilization of metabolic water*. Insects such as dry wood termites, death watch beetles, and powder post beetles survive in environments in which there is virtually no free molecular water. Such animals obtain the necessary water by oxidizing their food to create water metabolically. Some desert animals use a combination of metabolic water and other sources. The camel, for example, can provide some of its internal water requirement by oxidation of the fat stored in its hump.

Various combinations of these moisture adaptations permit animals of some type to survive in virtually any terrestrial environment. Only the very hottest and driest environments are unsuitable for permanent occupation by animals, and even these may be occupied for at least a part of the year. As a consequence, life in the desert is generally abundant and varied in spite of what appears to us to be a harsh environment.

11.6   Effect of Moisture on Plant Distribution and Production

Plant geographers of the nineteenth century noted a close relationship between major types of vegetation, such as deserts, grasslands, deciduous forests, and coniferous forests, and major differences in the climate. As one travels from sea level to mountaintops or from the equator to the poles, one experiences predictable changes in temperature and precipitation, and these are accompanied by fairly predictable changes in the life form (physiognomy) of the vegetation (Figure 8.17). Although the relationship between these patterns of vegetation and climate is complex, the correlation between the two is good enough that the early plant geographers used climate to classify and map vegetation, and early climatologists used vegetation to classify and map climates (see Chapter 16). These classifications involve various combinations of temperature (or net radiation) and moisture, and it is certainly not possible to separate out the effects of water alone.

Some of the more recent ideas about vegetation–climate relationships have stressed the energy balance approach, in which the climate is defined in terms of precipitation and the availability of solar energy to evaporate water. These ideas are centered on the availability of water to plants. It has been found that the ratio of precipitation (centimeters of rain per year) to potential evaporation (centimeters of evaporation per year from an open water surface), or P/E ratio, during the frost-free season correlates reasonably well in the coterminous U.S. with very broad patterns of vegetation (Figure 11.4). P/E ratios greater than 100 (found in the southeast, northeast, and northwest) indicate that the water supply is greater than the potential loss during the frost-free season. Values less than 100 indicate the reverse. P/E ratios of less than 20 correspond approximately with the occurrence of deserts, while the 60 line approximately separates the short grass and the tall grass prairies (Clark, 1954). Studies in Oregon forests have established relationships between the dominant tree species and gradients of moisture (expressed as predawn plant moisture stress measured dur-

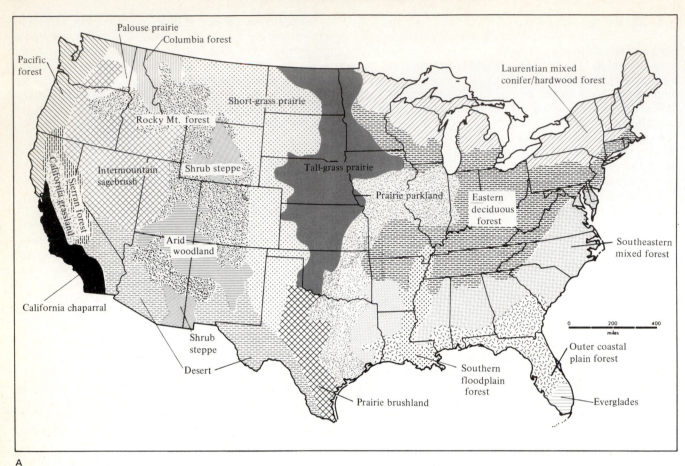

A

Figure 11.4
(A) Comparison of the geographic distribution of broad vegetation types (based on Ecoregions) in the U.S. (Only major divisions of the ecoregion map are shown) with (B) variation in the precipitation-evapo-transpiration ratio during the frost-free period. These maps are greatly simplified and are only intended to indicate broad relationships. (After Bailey, 1976 and Livingston and Shreve, 1921. (A) Carnegie Institution of Washington Publication 284. (B) Forest Service, USDA Miscellaneous Publication 1391.)

ing the driest part of the year) and temperature (a physiological assessment of daily soil and air temperatures throughout the growing season) (Figure 11.5). These relationships permit a reasonably accurate prediction of potential vegetation using temperature and moisture indices. The regeneration potential of different tree species can be predicted in a similar manner. Studies of a variety of other indices of plant water relationships have revealed predictable differences between a hot, dry environment and a cool, moist environment (Table 11.9), and it is possible to characterize plant communities in terms of these indices.

The relationship between moisture and plant productivity is extremely complex, and it is very difficult to separate the influence of moisture from the influence of other closely related factors. In particular, the availability of moisture is very closely related to plant nutrition. Soil water stress can result in reduced photosynthesis because the closure of stomata limits the uptake of gaseous nutrients from the atmosphere. In extreme drought, the plants may actually be CO_2 starved and lose biomass. Lack of an active transport stream limits internal movements in plants of inorganic nutrients, amino acids, and the products of photosynthesis, thus inter-

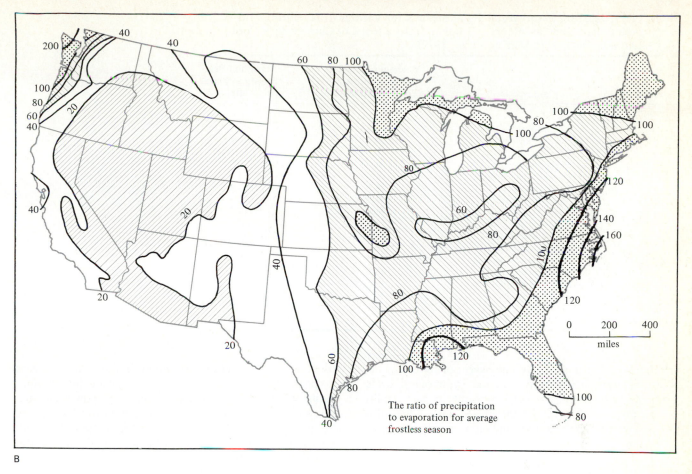

The ratio of precipitation to evaporation for average frostless season

B

fering with metabolism and growth. Lack of soil moisture restricts the mass movement of nutrients into the rhizosphere, the uptake of nutrients from the rhizosphere and the growth of fine roots into soil containing unexploited nutrients. The lack of uptake of nitrogen may lead to protein starvation and a consequent loss of production. Lack of soil moisture reduces litter decomposition and mineralization, reducing the levels of soil nutrients available to plants. Obviously, water stress is inextricably related to plant nutrition. The joint effect of moisture and nutrients is seen in characteristic patterns of variation in tree height (or site index) and volume growth along topographic sequences of plant communities from xeric ridge tops downslope to moist, fertile lower-slope situations. Figure 11.6 shows the variation between height growth class and soil moisture for

three tree species in coastal British Columbia, and Figure 11.7 shows estimates of the variation in growth class as a function of moisture and nutrients for two tree species.

11.7 Forestry and the Water Factor

Forests grow in the humid regions of the earth, and as a result of interception loss, redistribution by crowns, evapotranspiration, and control of snowmelt, they exert a major influence on the water cycle. There is considerable interest in what happens to the cycle when the forest is removed by harvest.

Earlier in the chapter, brief mention was made of the controversy as to the effects of deforestation on regional

Table 11.9 Selected Plant–Water Relationships for Various Tree, Shrub, and Herbaceous Plant Species Along a Gradient from a Hot-Dry Climate to a Cool-Moist Climate (Data from Waring et al., 1972)

Climate	Plant Species	Maximum Potential Transpiration, g cm^{-2} (April–Sept.)	Maximum Plant Moisture Stress, atm
	Trees		
Hot-dry	*Arbutus menziesii*	30.0	30.0
	Quercus kelloggii	30.0	30.0
	Pinus jeffreyi	25.0	25.0
	Pinus ponderosa	21.4	25.4
	Pseudotsuga menziesii	21.4	25.4
	Abies magnifica	12.5	19.1
	Picea engelmannii	11.0	12.8
Cool-moist	*Tsuga mertensiana*	11.0	19.1
	Minor vegetation		
Hot-dry	*Rhus diversiloba*	30.0	25.4
	Arctostaphylos viscida	30.0	25.4
	Xerophyllum tenax	19.5	19.1
	Rubus parviflorus	16.8	16.2
	Achlys triphylla	16.8	16.2
	Viola glabella	13.1	12.8
Cool-moist	*Valeriana sitchensis*	7.8	5.2

precipitation, but this is only one aspect of the interaction between forest management and the hydrological cycle.

Manipulation of forest vegetation results in many modifications of the water cycle in the treated area. Removal of tree cover reduces interception and eliminates canopy redis-

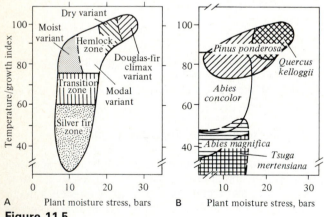

Figure 11.5
Relationship of moisture and temperature indices to the distribution of forest types (A) and natural regeneration of tree species (B) in Oregon. (After Zobel et al., 1974, and Waring et al., 1972. Used by permission of the authors.)

tribution. It eliminates transpiration, but may also increase evaporation. It influences water input by reducing or eliminating fog drip, and it alters the patterns of snow accumulation and the rate of snowmelt. Movement of water into and through the soil may be effected if the harvesting has affected infiltration rates and soil hydraulic conductivity. This will depend upon the degree to which harvesting has removed or modified the forest floor. Increased overland flow and accompanying erosion may occur. Total stream flow is increased by the reduction of interception and transpiration, and peak storm flow will be increased if surface runoff to streams is increased significantly.

Increased stream discharge produces a variety of changes in the stream environment, such as bank erosion, flooding, and disturbance to fish habitat. Removal of streambank vegetation reduces stream shading, which has implications for stream temperature, aquatic primary production, and the behavior of aquatic organisms. The change in the timing of snowmelt and the alteration of evapotranspiration affect the timing of spring runoff with significant consequences for summer stream flow and summer soil moisture.

Moisture stress (excess or deficit) plays a major role in determining the success of artificial regeneration programs. There has been a general lack of appreciation of the resistance to water uptake in newly planted trees, which suffer

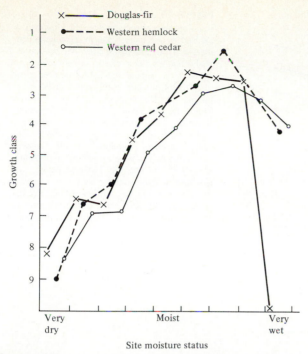

Figure 11.6

Relationship between growth class (based on height) and three species of tree growing in the Coastal Western Hemlock Zone of British Columbia. The moisture scale is relative, rather than absolute. It represents the range of edaphically and topographically-induced soil moisture conditions found within a particular climatic zone. All three species are adversely affected by excess soil moisture, but especially Douglas-fir. (Data from Klinka, 1976. Used by permission of the author.)

high mortality if exposed (as they often are) to moisture deficits before they are able to develop a new fine-root system. The alterations in the hydrological cycle following logging can play a major role in determining the success or failure of regeneration programs.

Tree productivity in the developing stand is closely related to soil moisture conditions, both because soil moisture dictates the biomass of foliage (Chapter 4) and because moisture stress affects the photosynthetic efficiency of that foliage. Any forest management activity that reduces the moisture status of either dry or moist sites will probably be accompanied by a loss of production. On an excessively wet site, a reduction in moisture will normally be highly beneficial for tree growth.

Water is critically important in forestry. It is needed to grow trees, but at the same time forests are responsible for

maintaining the quality and *regimen* of streamwater (the timing of delivery of streamwater: daily and seasonal) that make it a suitable environment for aquatic life and a useful commodity for agricultural, domestic, and industrial use. In many parts of the world, the socioeconomic value of stream flow regulation, streamwater quality control, and maintenance of fish habitat may exceed the socioeconomic value of timber in many watersheds. In such areas, timber management must take second place to watershed management. This may require radical modification of harvesting plans, or even a total restriction on harvesting.

11.8 Summary

The presence of liquid water on the earth is believed to have been the vital factor that permitted life as we know it to evolve. The unique physical and chemical properties of water make it an ideal medium for biological processes, and access to water or the ability to create it metabolically is indispensable for life. The character of ecosystems is closely related to the quality and quantity of water and how these vary through the year.

Understanding the water factor in ecosystems must be based on a knowledge of the water cycle: the inputs of water to, movement and storage of water within, and loss of water from ecosystems.

The moisture status of a site is not determined simply by precipitation inputs, and the availability of water to organisms is not determined simply by the moisture status of the site. The physical character and timing of water inputs to the site, the nature of the soil and topography, the physical and chemical state of the water, the nature of the climate, and the adaptations of the organisms all influence the availability and ecological efficiency of water.

Both plants and animals exhibit a broad range of adaptations to either excesses or deficits of water. These adaptations permit life to continue in almost any type of water environment that can be found on earth, but for each species there is a rather limited range of moisture conditions that can be tolerated, and the water factor is a major determinant of plant distribution. The effect is not necessarily direct, however; water interacts with a wide variety of other ecological factors, especially nutrients.

Although the total quantity of water in the world far exceeds human requirements, most of it is unavailable, and lack of water of suitable physical and chemical quality will be a significant barrier to human ambitions in the next few decades. Because forests grow in the humid parts of the

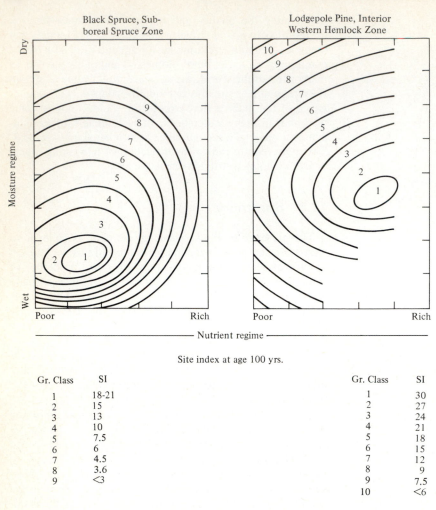

Figure 11.7
Relationship between tree-height growth (expressed as site index—the average height in meters of the 200 tallest trees per hectare at 100 years) and gradients of soil moisture and fertility for black spruce and lodgepole pine growing in different biogeoclimatic zones in British Columbia. (A) Black spruce, Sub-boreal Spruce Zone. (B) Lodgepole pine, Interior Western-Hemlock Zone. This type of graphical presentation is based on the edatopic grid matrix (or edaphic grid) of Pogrebniak (1930). Neither of the gradients has been quantified in absolute terms (see Chapter 16). The grids show isoclines of tree-growth class for all combinations of moisture and fertility. (After Krajina, 1969. Used by permission of the Department of Botany, University of British Columbia, and the author.)

Site index at age 100 yrs.

Gr. Class	SI
1	18-21
2	15
3	13
4	10
5	7.5
6	6
7	4.5
8	3.6
9	<3

Gr. Class	SI
1	30
2	27
3	24
4	21
5	18
6	15
7	12
8	9
9	7.5
10	<6

world, they have a major influence on the quantity and quality of streamwater and the timing of its delivery to streams. Management and harvesting of forests can have a major impact on all three of these attributes of the water cycle, and watershed management is an important component of forest management in most forests. Because of the importance of water in growing tree crops, the forester must understand the hydrological character of forests, the adaptations of the forest organisms to water, and how management influences this important ecological factor.

12.1 Introduction

Precipitation is a common event and one with which most of us are all too familiar. We are all aware of light, wind, and temperature as factors of our environment. We experience soil by growing plants in it, by having to move it, or simply by walking on it. Fire, on the other hand, is an environmental factor with which most people have had little firsthand experience. We have been conditioned by years of antifire propaganda to consider fire as inherently bad and largely the result of human activities. There has been a widespread failure to recognize fire for what it really is: a natural ecological factor that is as important as wind or precipitation in determining the structure and function of many of the world's ecosystems.

Except in the very wettest, very hottest, and very coldest environments (there is nothing to burn in the latter two!), fire has played a role virtually everywhere on terrestrial earth. Fire was ecologically important long before it was used by humans, as evidenced by the presence of charcoal buried deeply in ancient sedimentary deposits. Such fires were the result of volcanic activity, spontaneous combustion, or lightning, the latter being the most important. It has been estimated that there are about 40,000 thunder clouds active over the whole world every day (Schonland, 1950). For Canada alone, almost 10,000 lightning fires were recorded during a 10-year period (Bennett, 1960), and lightning is believed to account for 27% of all Canadian forest fires (McLean and Lockman, 1967). About 25% of forest fires in Alaska, accounting for 75% of the area burned, have been attributed to lightning (Hardy and Franks, 1963).

Fire was perhaps the first major force employed by humans to alter their surroundings (Stewart, 1956). In addition to using fire for heating and cooking, fire was employed to drive game, to improve grazing, to remove vegetation in order to facilitate travel, to clear land for agriculture, and in both aggressive and defensive encounters with other humans. Man's use of fire extended over most of the earth, and there is evidence that fire of anthropogenic origin has influenced even the humid tropical forest for many thousands of years in the form of cut-and-burn shifting agriculture.

Fire is generally an environmental factor of low frequency but of considerable potency. Because it produces such radical environmental changes so rapidly, a frequency of once in several centuries is quite sufficient to maintain an ecosystem condition quite different from that which would eventually develop in the absence of fire. This is seen in

12 Fire: A Pervasive and Powerful Environmental Factor

some of the eucalypt forests of Australia, which are maintained by a fire frequency as low as once in 350 years. In the prolonged absence of fire, the eucalypts would be replaced by forests of southern beech (*Nothofagus* sp.) and tree ferns (*Dicksonia*) (Gilbert, 1959; Gill, 1975). Fire frequency varies enormously from one region to another, and from one ecosystem type to another within a region. Dry ridge tops may be burned every few decades or centuries, whereas moist valley bottoms may only burn once every few millenia. Table 12.1 shows a range of fire frequencies for selected vegetation types in North America.

In this chapter we review briefly the types of fire that occur and their effects on soils, plants, animals, and ecosystem function. General reviews of the ecological role of fire in Canada and elsewhere can be found in Lutz (1956), Ahlgren and Ahlgren (1960), Cooper (1961), Kayll (1968), Slaughter et al. (1971), Washburn (1973), Kozlowski and Ahlgren (1974), Wells et al. (1979), and Wein and MacLean (1981).

Table 12.1   Fire Frequencies from Selected Vegetation Types in North America

Vegetation Type and Location	Record Type and Period	Fire Frequency (years)	Reference
Prairie, Missouri	—	1	Kucera and Ehrenreich (1962)
Long-leaf pine and blue stem ranges, southeast U.S.	—	3	Duvall and Whittaker (1964)
Mixed conifers, California	Fire scars on trees (1581–present)	7–9	Wagener (1961)
Ponderosa pine, Arizona	Fire scars on trees (1700–present)	5–12	Weaver (1951)
Mixed forest, Minnesota	Lake sediments (1000 years)	60–70	Swain (1973)
Boreal conifers, Northwest Territories	Fire report records (1966–1972)	110	Johnson and Rowe (1975)
Mixed forest, New Brunswick	Fire report records (1920–1975)	230–1000	Wein and Moore (1977)

Source: After Wein, 1978. Copyright Plenum Press. Used with permission.

12.2   Types and Occurrence of Fires

In the mind of the average layperson a fire is simply a fire. Unfortunately, things are not so simple. The ecological effects of fire vary enormously according to the time of year; the quantity, condition, and distribution of the fuel; the prevailing climatic conditions; the duration and intensity of the fire, the slope, aspect, and elevation; the type of vegetation and soil; and so on. Generalizations about fire and its effects on ecosystems are fraught with the danger of inaccurate representation of the real situation. Discussion of fire should always specify the type of fire and type of environment.

Fires can be divided into three major types: (1) *ground fires*—largely flameless fires which burn slowly through thick surface accumulations of organic matter; (2) *surface fires*—rapidly burning fires that sweep quickly over an area, consuming litter and the aboveground portions of herbs and shrubs; and (3) *crown fires*—fires that burn through the crowns of woody vegetation, frequently leaving most of the stem and the forest floor relatively untouched.

Various technical terms are applied to fire, including duration, intensity, and rate of spread. *Duration* refers to the time over which energy release occurs at any particular location. *Intensity* refers to the flux of energy (cal cm^{-1} sec^{-1}) released by the fire. *Rate of spread* refers to the speed with which the leading edge of the fire travels downwind.

The three types of fire can occur in any combination. Sometimes a crown fire will be accompanied by both surface and ground fires, resulting in the total consumption of all organic matter above the mineral soil. Even roots deep in the mineral soil may be burned. Alternatively, crown fires driven by strong winds may race through the tree crowns consuming foliage and twigs only, leaving stems and the forest floor virtually intact. Such fires leave most of the biomass and almost all of the minor vegetation intact. Some trees are killed by having their crowns burned, but others, such as redwoods (*Sequoia* sp.) and ponderosa pine *(Pinus ponderosa),* are able to regenerate branches and foliage.

Surface fires generally burn off just the litter layer and the aboveground parts of herbs and shrubs. These are often able to resprout from below-ground perenating organs, depending on the depth of heat penetration into the soil and the depth of the lowest perenating organ of the plant (Flinn and Wein, 1977). Trees may or may not be killed, depending on their bark thickness. Ground fires tend to be more destructive, since they kill and consume all the roots in the forest floor, which generally prevents resprouting from underground organs. Ground fires can kill large trees by this means while the stems and crowns remain untouched. Consumption of forest floor may eliminate most of the dormant seeds on the site, slowing revegetation of the area. However, viable seeds are sometimes found buried in the mineral soil, where they may escape destruction by ground fires and contribute to revegetation (Moore and Wein, 1977). The loss of forest floor exacerbates the ecological consequences of the loss of all living vegetation, but the subsequent fall of dead but unburned shrub and tree materials contributes to a rebuilding of this layer.

Fire occurs mainly in the dry season, which occurs at different times of year in different parts of the world. It can occur at the beginning, middle, or end of the dry season, with markedly different ecological effects. A dry spring may be associated with high fire hazard in areas without a snowpack, but in many regions middle to late summer has the highest risk of fire. A spring surface fire will have a very different effect than a late summer fire, which is often a combined crown–surface–ground fire. Following a spring fire, plants will resprout and there may be relatively little change in the vegetation for the following year. In contrast, a late summer or early winter fire will leave the ground bare of vegetation throughout the following winter.

Information on the causes of fire is of some interest because it permits a comparison of the importance of humans as a cause of ignition with that of other causes. However, such data are often of little value in determining the contribution of man-made fires to the overall ecological effect of fire because many man-made fires are promptly extinguished. They generally do not burn large areas, whereas many lightning fires do.

12.3 Effects of Fire on Soil

Soil properties are strongly influenced by living vegetation and accumulated dead organic matter, both of which are removed to a variable degree by fire. Consequently, fire has the potential to induce major changes in soils. Such changes are sometimes deleterious, but in those ecosystems in which fire is a frequent and natural component, the effects on soil may be benign or even desirable.

The degree to which soil properties are altered by fire depends upon the fire intensity and the amount of organic matter that is consumed. These in turn are influenced by the amount of organic fuel available, its distribution and moisture content, and the prevailing weather conditions. Because these parameters are so variable, it is very difficult to make reliable generalizations about the effects of fire. A low-intensity surface fire may have very little effect on soils, and a rapidly moving crown fire might also have little effect if the vegetation resprouts rapidly. Conversely, fire may have a great effect if all the vegetation is killed because of the resulting losses of shade, root strength, and transpiration that lead to significant changes in soil temperature, stability, and moisture. Ground fires generally have a marked effect by removing the surface accumulation of organic matter, while high-intensity ground–surface–crown fires during the heat of the summer can result in a massive alteration or the total loss of soil.

Because fire can create major changes to soil characteristics, because soil is so important to the forester, and because fire, both wild and managed, is such a common feature of the forest environment, it is very important that resource managers have a clear understanding of its effects. These can be divided into physical, chemical, and biological. For a detailed treatment of the effects of fire on soil, the reader is referred to U.S.D.A. (1971, 1979a), Kozlowski and Ahlgren (1974), Cramer (1974b), Bell et al. (1974a,b), and Wells et al. (1979).

A. Physical Changes

1. Organic Matter. Loss of organic matter is one of the most important effects of fire on soils. Fire speeds up the normal process of mineralization of organic matter, achieving in a few minutes what would have taken microbes several years for materials such as dead foliage or fine roots, and decades or even centuries for large fuels such as stumps and logs. Generally, fire is restricted to the surface of the organic accumulation because of the need for oxygen and because deeper layers are often too wet to burn. However, ground fires can smolder slowly into deep layers of even moist organic matter, the heat from the fire drying the material ahead of it. Organic matter incorporated into the mineral soil is normally unaffected by fire, but in extremely hot fires the penetration of heat down into the mineral soil can destroy colloidal organic matter. Fire can penetrate deeply into the soil by burning along dead roots.

The loss of surface organic accumulations depends upon fire duration, intensity, and fuel moisture. A fire in the spring when the forest floor is moist may burn off the fresh litter only, leaving the F and H layers intact, whereas a midsummer fire might remove the L, the F, and much of the H. Hot fall fires can remove up to 50 cm of organic matter over rock on dry sites (Figure 12.1). Armson (1977) reported that a light early spring (April) surface fire in mixed white pine and sugar maple forest in southern Ontario resulted in no significant reduction in surface organic matter. In contrast, natural fires in the boreal region of Ontario reduced the LFH layer by approximately 50%. Viro (1974) reported a 25% reduction in the F and H layers from 33 to 25 t ha^{-1} following burns in Finland, while organic matter in the mineral soil fell by 17% in the upper 10 cm and 7–10% lower in the profile. Consumption of F and H layers in pine stands in eastern Canada was found to be related to the percent moisture content before the fire (Figure 12.2). The effects of fire on total soil organic matter will depend on how much organic matter there is in the mineral soil. Where there is a lot, the loss of surface organic accumulations may not constitute as serious a loss as first appears.

2. Structure and Porosity. Fires that remove only the L horizon will have little effect on soil structure, whereas a fire that removes all the forest floor and exposes the mineral soil to the impact of raindrops can lead to a loss of structure in the surface layers. This can reduce infiltration rates and increase surface runoff, which can lead to erosion. In a hot ground fire, colloidal organic matter in the surface mineral layers may be destroyed, accompanied by a loss of structure and a reduction in porosity (Fuller et al., 1955). Opposing these changes is the increase in pH and divalent cations that accompanies fire, which can lead to an increase in flocculation and an improvement in the structure of surface layers of finer-textured soils.

3. Moisture. Fire reduces transpiration and interception losses in proportion to the reduction in foliage. Where all vegetation is killed, the soil may be correspondingly wetter, but this depends on the effects of the fire on soil organic matter and soil structure. It is true only where the fire leaves the forest floor more or less intact. In coarse-textured soils, much of the soil moisture storage capacity is provided by organic matter, and if this is burned off, the soils may become much drier. If there is a reduction in infiltration because of the fire, less water will enter the soil and less will be available for storage; again the soil becomes drier. Fire will also increase soil evaporation losses if all the forest floor is removed: losses that are restricted in the absence of fire by the hydraulic discontinuity at the mineral/organic interface. In a hot, dry climate with a medium-textured soil, such evaporation losses may be considerable.

Fire can reduce infiltration in several ways: by loss of mineral soil structure, by the plugging of macropores with ash, by the formation of a charred crust, and by the development of a water-repellent layer. In an extremely hot and adequately aerated fire, all carbon compounds are oxidized to CO or CO_2. However, in many fires, there is insufficient heat and/or oxygen for combustion and many organic compounds are simply vaporized. Much of the vapor leaves in the smoke column, but some of it is driven downward into the unburned soil, where it condenses on the cooler, unburned materials. Subsequent penetration of heat drives the most volatile constituents even deeper into the soil, broadening the band of soil affected by the condensate (Savage, 1974). This leads to the development of a well-defined layer of material, which, because of the coating of volatile substances, displays the phenomenon of *hydrophobicity* or water repellency. This hydrophobic layer reduces the rate of infiltration into the remaining forest floor and/or underlying mineral soil.

The occurrence of hydrophobicity is highly variable. It varies according to the type of fuel, the type of fire and the type of soil. Sand, with its relatively small surface area, is much more affected than silt or clay soils, which have a very large surface area (DeByle, 1973). Hot fires with tem-

A

B

Figure 12.1

Loss of forest floor following slashburning. (A) Rocky slope in southwestern British Columbia, which had a thick forest floor beneath a mature stand of western hemlock, Pacific silver fir, and western red cedar prior to clearcut harvesting and a hot fall slashburn. (B) Close-up of a stump on a bare rock, which had previously been covered with at least 15 cm of organic matter (based on the space between many of the large roots and the rock surface).

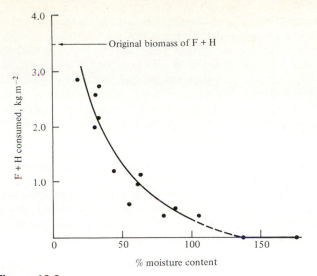

Figure 12.2
Effect of F and H layer moisture content on F and H layer consumption by fire in pine stands in Ontario. (After van Wagner, 1972. Reprinted by permission of the National Research Council of Canada and the author.)

peratures of about 500°C or greater do not induce hydrophobicity because the hydrophobic substances are destroyed. Temperatures of 425–500°C begin to destroy the hydrophobic property after 10 minutes, while 260–315°C for 10–15 minutes will produce a persistent and highly water-repellent layer (Debano et al., 1967).

The best known examples of hydrophobicity occur under chaparral brushlands in southern California. Wildfires in moister and cooler northern forests are less likely to cause a significant increase in hydrophobicity. This is because mor forest floors under these forests are normally hydrophobic when dry, a condition that is attributed to the abundance of fungal mycelium and spores in these F and H horizons (Debano and Rice, 1973). Intense fires can produce a short-term increase in mineral soil hydrophobicity (Table 12.2), but some fires may actually reduce it by eliminating the fungus (DeByle, 1973). Water repellency has been reported in burned Jeffrey pine stands in Nevada (Hussain et al., 1969) and lodgepole pine stands in Oregon (Table 12.3).

Because of the natural hydrophobicity of dry mor forest floors, exceptions can be found to the generalization that organic matter improves the moisture status of coarse soils. For example, organic matter contributes little to soil aggregation in a sandy soil, and by coating the mineral particles it may make the soil water-repellent and therefore drier. The LFH layers that accumulate on such soils in dry climates may be very hydrophobic during the growing season, preventing the infiltration of summer rain down to the rooting zone. Removal or diminution of this layer by fire can improve the moisture status of the site. In contrast, the large surface area of the particles in a clay soil diminishes water repellency, while the organic matter promotes aggregation, structure, and drainage. This improves the permeability and moisture status of clay soils. Removal of surface organic matter from clay soils can have adverse effects on soil moisture status.

It is generally thought that hydrophobicity lowers soil moisture levels by impeding infiltration, although this effect may be offset by a reduction in evaporation loss. This occurs because the hydrophobic layer impedes nonsaturated

Table 12.2 Percent of Soil Samples Found to Be Hydrophobic on Various Aspects in Clearcut and Slashburned Areas[a] in Montana and the Duration of the Condition (Data from DeByle, 1973)

Time of Sample	Soil Depth, cm	% of Samples that Were Hydrophobic, by Aspect			
		North	East	South[b]	West
Preburn	0–5	3.1	0	10.5	7.1
	5–10	0	0	0	0
Immediately postburn	0–5	14.3	21.4	56.2	27.3
	5–10	0	7.1	25.0	9.1
One year postburn	0–5	0	6.2	16.7	5.0
	5–10	0	0	5.6	0
Two years postburn[c]	0–5	0	0	25.0	0
	5–10	0	0	0	0

[a]The area had supported old growth stands of western larch, Douglas-fir, and Engelmann spruce.
[b]Hydrophobicity was greater on the southerly aspect both before and after burning.
[c]On most areas, pretreatment levels were approached after two years.

Table 12.3 Effect of Fire on Infiltration Rates (Water Drop Penetration Time) in Lodgepole Pine Forests in Oregon

Fire Treatment	Soil Depth, cm	Water Drop Penetration Time
Unburned	0 – 5.0	1346[a]
	5.0–91.4	0
Light burn	0 – 2.5	1
	2.5– 7.6	[b]
	7.6–15.2	170
	20.3–30.5	1
Severe burn	0 – 6.4	0
	6.4–15.2	[b]

Source: Debano and Rice, 1973. Copyright Soc. Amer. For. Used with permission.

[a]Note the hydrophobicity of the unburned surface layer, and the progressive increase in depth of the hydrophobic layer in the mineral soil with increasing fire intensity.

[b]Water drop evaporated without penetration.

water flow upward through the surface layers of the soil, which acts to conserve soil moisture (Figure 12.3).

4. Temperature. Low soil temperature is a major limiting factor in many poleward and high-elevation forest ecosystems. It is primarily the result of long cold winters and thick forest floors that prevent summer warmth from reaching the underlying mineral soil. In very cold climates this leads to the lower layers of the soil being permanently frozen.

Low soil temperature slows decomposition and limits rooting depth, both of which reduce plant production by limiting the supply of nutrients. The effect of temperature on decomposition is indicated by the amount of CO_2 given off from the forest floor materials incubated at various temperatures. Viro (1974) found that raising the temperature at which Finnish forest floor material was incubated from 6°C to 12.5°C doubled CO_2 evolution, while 20°C quadru-

pled it. Permafrost close to the surface also leads to poor soil drainage, which further limits forest growth.

Fire affects soil temperatures in both the long and the short term. The long-term effects generally involve an increase in soil temperatures. By darkening the soil surface, fire promotes absorption of solar energy, and by reducing the depth of the surface organic accumulation, transfer of heat to the mineral soil is promoted. Table 12.4 shows soil temperatures in forest, clearcut, and burned areas. Removal of tree shade increased soil temperature, but fire increased it by as much again. The effect can be seen down to a depth of 20 cm in the mineral soil.

In addition to the general increase in soil temperature, fire sometimes results in a reduction in surface temperature. In hot climates with open forests, very high temperatures can occur at the surface of the forest floor. This is a consequence of the high solar energy input to, and the low thermal conductivity and thermal capacity of, dry litter. Removal of the LFH exposes mineral soil, which has both a high thermal conductivity and a high thermal capacity. Because of these thermal properties, high mineral soil surface temperatures are uncommon. However, if the fire leaves a layer of black charcoal, it will have the opposite effect; it will result in increased surface temperature because of the lower water-holding capacity and greater absorbancy (lower albedo) of the burned surface.

Energy released during a burn creates short-term effects on soil temperature. Surface soil temperatures as high as 1000°C have been recorded (references in Ahlgren, 1974), but because of the remarkable insulating properties of forest floors, heat penetration is generally limited. For example, temperatures of 350–900°C were recorded at the soil surface under burning slash in Australia, while at 5–10 cm depth in the soil the temperature was only 100°C (Humphreys and Lambert, 1965). In a jack pine prescribed burn in Minnesota, surface temperatures exceeded 800°C for

Table 12.4 Effect of Burning and Shading on Summer Soil Temperatures

Sampling Depth	Temperature, °C		
	Uncut Forest[a]	Clearcut Area	Slashburned Clearcut
Air, 5 cm above forest floor	20.6	24.8	23.6
Forest floor surface	18.0	24.4	31.3
Mineral soil			
Surface	9.1	12.8	16.0
10 cm	8.7	10.6	12.5
20 cm	8.3	10.2	12.0

Source: Viro, 1974. Copyright Academic Press. Used with permission.

[a]The data are for 1400 hours in a 100-year-old spruce stand in south Finland.

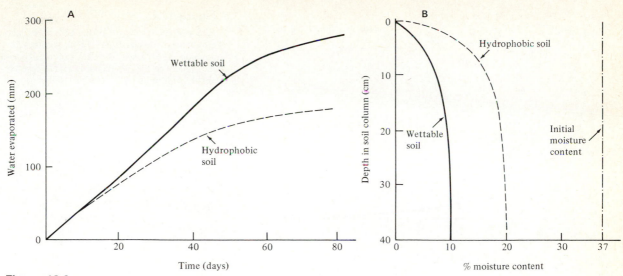

Figure 12.3
Effect of hydrophobicity on soil moisture conditions. (A) Cumulative evaporation from soil columns containing wettable and nonwettable soil. (B) Soil moisture distribution in the columns after 109 days of evaporation. Hydrophobicity reduced evaporation which resulted in the soil retaining a higher moisture content (After Debano et al., 1967. Used by permission of the USDA Forest Service, and the authors.)

1 minute, 500°C for 9 minutes, and 300°C for 17 minutes. The organic–mineral interface at depth of 5–8 cm from the surface reached 300°C for 14 minutes, and was above 50°C for 72 minutes (Ahlgren, 1970).

An experiment in Australia examined the soil heating in fires ranging from a surface fire of 45 minutes' duration to an 8-hour fire that consumed all the trees and shrubs on the test plot. The short-duration fire resulted in a maximum temperature of 50°C at a 2.5-cm depth. The 8-hour fire raised the temperature at a 7.5-cm depth to 223°C (Beadle, 1940). Fire of high intensity generally occurs on only a small proportion of an area, so that heating of the mineral soil beneath burning forest floors is not normally very intense. In a study of 44 fires in Florida, it was found that temperatures rarely exceeded 52°C for more than 15 minutes at depths 3–6 mm below the surface (Heyward, 1938).

The major temperature-dependent stages of ignition are (Ralston and Hatchell, 1971): (1) 100–200°C—nondestructive distillation of volatile organic compounds, (2) 200–300°C—destructive distillation of up to 85% of organic substances, and (3) >300°C—ignition of carbonaceous residues. A comparison of these numbers with those in the preceding paragraph explains why much forest floor remains unburned even under quite hot surface fires.

B. Chemical Changes

1. pH. When fire oxidizes organic compounds, elements that form anions (e.g., N, P, and Cl) are lost in much greater quantities than elements such as Ca, K, and Mg, which form cations. The ash left by the fire consists largely of soluble oxides of these alkali earths. These oxides are rapidly changed to carbonates, which have an alkaline reaction and tend to neutralize acidity in the soil. Consequently, soil pH generally increases following a fire. The extent and duration of the increase will depend on the intensity of the fire, the amount of organic matter consumed, and the buffering capacity of the soil. Viro (1974) reported an increase of 2–3 pH units in the forest floor following burning in Finland, returning to original levels after 50 years (Figure 12.4). The underlying mineral soil was less affected, but an increase of 0.4 pH unit persisted for 20 years, and even after 50 years was still a difference of 0.2 pH unit.

Smaller changes in pH have been reported in areas of the eastern and southeastern U.S., where burns of various frequencies produced pH changes of only about 0.5 pH unit. The degree of change is related to the cation exchange capacity of the soil, as is the speed with which the pH returns to its original levels. The growth of herbs and shrubs that frequently follows a fire helps to slow the return to the

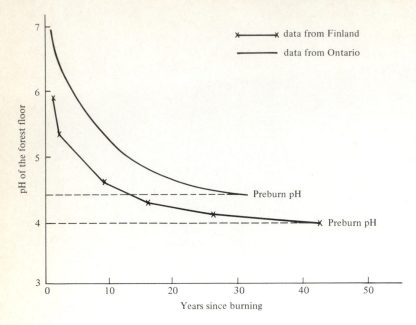

Figure 12.4

Effect of fire on the pH of the LFH layer, and rate of recovery of the original pH. (From data in Viro, 1974, and Armson, 1977. Used by permission of Academic Press Inc., and The Finnish Forest Research Institute; the University of Toronto Press; and the authors.)

original level of acidity by reducing the leaching of cations and by active circulation of nutrients. The pH change accompanying fire may be one of the main benefits of burning in tropical shifting agriculture. Highly leached tropical soils derived from poor parent materials often have such a low pH (in the 3 to 4 range) that food crops cannot be grown satisfactorily unless the pH is raised by ash from burning the vegetation.

2. Site Nutrient Capital and Nutrient Availability. Fire induces a variety of chemical changes in the soil. As organic matter is burned, carbon is released as gaseous oxides, and nitrogen is lost increasingly as temperatures rise above 300°C. Sulfur and phosphorus are also subject to gasification losses, and some potassium may be lost at temperatures greater than 500°C. Boron is also subject to loss during a fire (Moore and Norris, 1974). Many other nutrients are removed from the site in the form of fly ash that is carried up with the smoke. In very hot fires with high fire-induced winds and a strong convection column, most of the ash and the nutrients contained therein may be removed from the site. In cooler fires, most of the elemental content of the burned material remains on site. Because of this, the total quantity of chemicals such as Ca and Mg in the forest floor may be increased significantly by a low to moderate intensity fire through the addition of ash from incinerated minor vegetation and tree crowns. This increase generally does not persist indefinitely. Some of the chemicals in the ash are leached down into the mineral soil, and some are taken up by the vegetation.

A major effect of fire is to convert unavailable mineral nutrients in undecomposed organic matter to a soluble form that is available to plants. This means that even when fire causes a substantial decrease in the total soil mineral nutrient capital due to gasification, fly ash, and/or leaching losses, it may actually improve the availability of nutrients. The higher nutrient availability is seen first in the forest floor (with the exception of very soluble elements such as K), but forest floor levels decline with time because of leaching to lower horizons, uptake by plants, and microbial conversion back to unavailable forms. Increases in levels of available nutrients lower in the profile occur after a delay of several years.

Of all the macronutrients, nitrogen is the most susceptible to loss during a fire, and postfire NPP may be significantly reduced because of a reduction in soil nitrogen. However, if the fire merely burns off the L and upper F layers, postfire nitrogen availability may actually be increased because of a pH and temperature-induced increase in mineralization of the remaining F and H materials. Where the fire burns off all the forest floor, nitrogen availability will be greatly decreased unless this results in postfire invasion of the site by free-living or symbiotic nitrogen fixers. Fire-induced changes in site biogeochemistry are discussed further in Section 12.6B.

C. Biological Changes

Although soil temperature may not be high enough during a burn for ignition to occur, it may be high enough to affect soil animals. The meso- and microfauna of the L and F horizons have limited mobility and are normally killed during a fire, but survivors in the lower H horizon or in islands of unburned LFH provide a source for recolonization, and numbers recover within a few years. The effects are therefore related to fire frequency, as has been demonstrated in studies of prescribed burning of pine stands in South Carolina. Annual burning significantly reduced the abundance of mites and springtails, whereas burning every 5 years produced no long-term change in numbers (Metz and Farrier, 1971). Where intense fires eliminate all surface organic accumulations, virtually all meso- and microfauna can be eliminated for many years, although such fires are generally limited to the summer, when surface dryness and heat would have already driven these animals down into the moister, cooler, mineral soil, where they would survive the fire.

The literature on fire reveals that effects on microflora are highly variable because of the great variability in the effects of fire on soil temperature, moisture, and pH (Ahlgren, 1974). Because of the mobility of their reproductive propagules, bacteria and fungi are usually able to reinvade and recolonize a burned area promptly, and therefore fire-induced microfaunal changes often tend to be less persistent than other fire-related environmental changes. Typically, fires produce an initial reduction in microflora populations, followed in many cases by an increase, which frequently occurs after the first postfire rainfall (Ahlgren and Ahlgren, 1965). The abundance of these postburn populations may exceed preburn levels because of increased pH, reduced microbial competition, and improved availability of nutrients. Sometimes fire can sterilize an area, permitting the replacement of the original microfauna by a different set of species. Loss of mycorrhizal fungi from a burned area due to such microfaunal replacement may be related to the regeneration failures and/or poor seedling growth that sometimes occur following a burn. The persistence of microfaunal changes will depend on the persistence of changes in critical soil conditions.

It has sometimes been suggested that the initially improved nitrogen nutrition of plants following a moderate burn may reflect atmospheric nitrogen fixation by free-living bacteria. Grass growing in burned areas is frequently reported to be more lush, to have a darker green color, and to have a higher protein content than grass in unburned areas, implying higher availability of nitrogen. Both wildlife and domestic livestock will seek out and browse the vegetation of burned areas. Direct evidence of such fire-induced fixation is lacking, but it may occur as the result of the increased pH (Armson, 1977). Burning has been reported to increase the abundance of the nitrogen-fixing *Azotobacter* and *Clostridium* species. Fire can increase nitrogen mineralization for up to 12 years (references in Ahlgren, 1974), although the opposite effect may occur in dry soils (e.g., Meiklejohn, 1953).

12.4 Effects of Fire on Plants

Because fire has been such a characteristic feature of most ecosystems, a wide variety of plant adaptations has evolved. Fire may affect any stage in a plant's development (vegetative, flowering, fruiting, or dormant) and there is a corresponding variety of adaptive traits.

A. Adaptations to Fire in the Vegetative Stage

Plants can be classified into several categories based on vegetative characteristics that affect their reaction to fire. Some plants achieve resistance by protecting themselves from damage, whereas others are able to tolerate the damage.

Fire-resistant bark is one of the more common adaptations to surface and ground fires. Trees such as western larch (*Larix occidentalis*), Douglas-fir (*Pseudotsuga menziesii*), and ponderosa pine (*Pinus ponderosa*) develop a very thick layer of dead bark as they mature, which enables them to survive quite hot ground and surface fires (Figure 12.5). Some angiosperms, such as some *Eucalyptus* sp., also have fire-resistant bark. There is disagreement over the nature of a bark's protective value. Some researchers claim that the bark of different species has a similar thermal diffusivity irrespective of a wide range of moisture content and structure: that bark thickness is the most important variable. Others claim to have demonstrated wide species differences in heat penetration of bark (see Gill, 1975). The protection conferred by bark will also depend on its flammability and how quickly the burned bark is replaced. Where replacement is slow, a severely burned bark may be susceptible to a subsequent fire of much lower intensity. Species that shed bark rapidly and accumulate bark and other aboveground litter around their base will be more susceptible to fire damage than will those without such an accumulation.

Reduced flammability of tissues will reduce the spread and intensity of a fire, reducing the risk of fire damage. Species with high foliar moisture content and low resin or oil content will generally be much more fire resistant than the resin- and oil-rich conifers. Mixed angiosperm–

Figure 12.5
Douglas-fir stump in south-central British Columbia, showing the great thickness of bark that confers on this species a high resistance to surface fires.

coniferous stands will be more resistant than pure coniferous stands partly because of the break in continuity of flammable crown fuels.

Protected buds confer on plants the ability to continue to grow and to recover from the loss to branches, foliage, or even the entire aerial shoot. Some conifers, such as pitch pine *(Pinus rigida),* redwoods *(Sequoia* sp.), and ponderosa pine, are able to replace the foliage and branches lost in a crown fire by means of adventitious or latent auxiliary buds. Similarly, leaf scorch of eucalypts stimulates the development of epicormic shoots, although the ability to recover from crown damage in this manner varies considerably between different species. Younger trees of any species have a greater ability in this respect than do older trees.

Many species are able to replace entire aerial shoots by developing new shoots from underground buds that survive the fire. Many angiosperm trees, shrubs, herbs, and even some conifers have this ability. When the aerial shoot of aspen *(Populus tremuloides)* is killed by fire, sucker shoots develop from adventitious buds on lateral roots growing in the surface layers of the soil. When the crown and stem of a coast redwood *(Sequoia sempervirens)* are consumed by fire, sprouts form around the base of the stem which results in the clumping of stems in the subsequent stand around the old stumps.

Plants that have *lignotubers* are able to produce new shoots more rapidly than those lacking this adaptation because of the food reserves provided by the tuber. A lignotuber is a conspicuous swelling of the main axis, mostly or entirely below the ground surface. The tuber forms at the root/stem junction by the process of bud multiplication, and it is consequently a rich source of sprouts if the aerial shoot is killed. This adaptation enables some eucalypts to reoccupy and dominate a site very rapidly after a fire (Mount, 1969). It is most obvious at the environmental extremes of the genus, and the adaptation is absent in the most productive forest sites of southern Australia. It is therefore thought that lignotubers probably represent a generalized adaptive trait for recovery from stress-induced damage rather than a specifically fire-induced adaptation (Gill, 1975).

Plants that have *rhizomes* (horizontal, underground stems) are also able to sprout rapidly following fire and are highly resistant to damage by fire. The success of the rhizomatous fireweed *(Epilobium angustifolium)* and bracken fern *(Pteridium aquilinum)* in fire environments exemplifies the success of this adaptation.

B. Adaptations to Fire in the Reproductive Phase

Evolution has selected a variety of reproductive traits that increase the fitness of plants exposed to frequent fires.

Precocious flowering reduces the time from germination to seed production in perennial plants, and species such as lodgepole pine *(Pinus contorta)* can produce seed in as little as five years (Fowells, 1965), which is normally before the next fire occurs. Frequent fire eliminates species that flower infrequently or only after a long juvenile period, unless there are other adaptations.

Fire has been shown to cause a *stimulation of flowering* in some plants. For example, the reproductive success of some members of the genus *Xanthorrhoea,* a fire-adapted Australian shrub, is greatly enhanced by fire, although some interfire flowering does occur (Specht et al., 1958). This may be a temperature response or may merely reflect a reduction in competition for light, moisture, and nutrients. It could also be an effect of smoke. It is known that ethylene, a component of wood smoke, stimulates flowering, a fact that was once put to good use by pineapple farmers in Puerto Rico, who flooded their fields with wood smoke to initiate flowering. Ethylene gas is sometimes used by itself to stimulate flowering (Komarek, 1971).

Seed dispersal is influenced by fire in some species. Lodgepole pine, jack pine *(Pinus banksiana),* and black spruce *(Picea marina)* are three North American conifers that have *serotinous* cones, the scales of which are prevented from opening by a resinous bond (Figure 12.6). The resin of jack pine cones melts at temperatures greater than 60°C, and the seeds can remain viable within cones exposed to a temperature of 370°C for 60 seconds (Beaufait, 1960). Certain species of several Australian genera [e.g., *Banksia, Casuarina, Calothamnus, Hakea,* and *Xylomelum* (refer-

Figure 12.6
Serotinous cones of lodgepole pine. The cone scales will only open after being heated to a critical temperature, such as in a fire, or when lying on a forest floor exposed to full sunlight (e.g., after clearcutting).

ences in Gill, 1975)] also depend on heating for seed dispersal. For example, the shrub genus *Banksia* produces flowers in dense, spikelike inflorescences. The resulting hard woody fruits (or *follicles* since they are developed from a single carpel) open freely without fire in some species, whereas in others only about 1% of the fruits open unless the plant is exposed to fire. In all these species, seed release involves the breaking of a zone of abscission cells. Desiccation increases the tension across this abscission zone, and in many species this is sufficient to open the fruit; in others, the additional heat treatment provided by fire is necessary. In species such as *Eucalyptus* and *Casuarina*, the protective woody fruits only open upon desiccation. This occurs following death by fire, but does not actually require heat treatment (Gardner, 1957).

C. Effects of Fire on Germination

The seeds of many species lie dormant in the soil until the area is burned. Shrubs of dry areas such as *Acacia, Arctostaphylos, Ceanothus,* and *Rhus* produce large quantities of hard-coated seeds that germinate only when they have been heated. This may be achieved by exposure to full sun as well as to fire, but fire is generally the agent that removes the shade and is therefore either directly or indirectly responsible for the heating.

Many plants germinate better on mineral soil than on a loose surface organic accumulation. This can be explained in terms of better moisture and temperature conditions on the mineral soils, and/or the removal of chemicals that may serve to inhibit germination (*allelopathy;* see Chapter 14).

A feature of chamise communities (*Adenostoma fasciculatum,* a shrub found in Californian "hard chaparral") is the virtual absence of herbs until after a fire that removes the aerial shoots of the shrub. Experiments showed that although some of the increase in herbaceous growth could be attributed to the fertilizer effect of the ash and to some reduction in small-mammal seed predation, fire appeared to be the most important factor (McPherson and Muller, 1969; Muller et al., 1968). Other chaparral species are known to release a variety of terpenes, phenols, alkaloids, and other organic chemicals that inhibit the germination and growth of competing species. These *allelochemicals* accumulate in the surface soil, from which they can be removed by fire, permitting the invasion of previously excluded species. The rapid and prolific invasion of burned-over forest in northern areas by fireweed and its superior growth in such areas may well involve a similar release from inhibition, although the improved nutrient availability in burned areas is probably the major factor.

D. Evolution of Increased Inflammability

Some fire-adapted species have apparently evolved along a totally different line. Rather than evolving resistance to fire, they have evolved an increased susceptibility of the vegetative stage to fire, coupled with seed adaptations. It is intriguing that, rather than being fire-resistant, many plant species in fire environments actually burn more readily and destructively than plants of environments in which fire is uncommon. It has been suggested (Mutch, 1970) that this represents a successful adaptation which increases the fitness of the species. For example, jack pine (a species with precocious flowering and protected seeds) forms stands that under natural conditions burn with monotonous regularity. Fire eliminates the light-demanding pine, but it also kills the competing tree species that would replace it in the absence of fire. Continued occupancy of the area by jack pine is thus ensured because the precociously produced seeds protected in their serotinous cones promptly regenerate the burned area. A similar example is provided by fireweed and bracken fern, which produce highly inflammable litter that accumulates because of slow decomposition. This increases the chance of fire, which benefits these rhizomotous species while eliminating the woody species that would shade them out.

E. Other Adaptations

Another adaptation to fire that is found in some fire-adapted species is very rapid early growth. This undoubtedly benefits the plants in other ways as well, but rapid elevation of the terminal bud and foliage out of reach of surface fires, and rapid development of thick bark are un-doubtedly of advantage in a fire-dominated ecosystem. An interesting and well-known example of this type of adaptation is provided by longleaf pine *(Pinus palustris)*. The terminal bud remains close to the ground for about 5 years after germination, while the seedling develops a large root system. During this period the bud is protected from the frequent ground fires that characterize the region where this species grows by long fire-resistant needles that form a dense circle around the bud (the so-called grass stage of the tree). Many 1- and 2-year-old seedlings are killed by fire, but for those that survive the first 2 years, the fires merely scorch the ends of the needles. The grass stage ends when the well-rooted seedling begins a period of rapid height growth which carries the fire-sensitive bud well above the reach of surface fires.

Longleaf pine is not only extremely resistant to fire damage: it also depends upon fire. This species is very susceptible to a foliage fungus (brown spot disease, *Septaria acicola*) which is eliminated or reduced by fire, and longleaf pine stands are deliberately burned in the grass stage to control the disease. The species is also unable to compete with the understory hardwood species that would invade the site in the absence of fire.

Because of the variable degree of fire adaptation in different plant species, fire plays a major role in determining the structure and composition of many of the world's plant communities. It has been called the dominant fact of forest history by Spurr and Barnes (1973), who review the role of fire in determining the composition of forests in the U.S. Fire has been implicated in the maintenance of grassland around the world (although some grasslands are climatically determined), and extensive heath lands in Europe were created by deforestation followed by frequent fires. Much of the vast area of pine, Douglas-fir, and eucalypts in the world are of fire origin, and extensive areas of oak in Europe and the eastern U.S. owe their existence to a history of forest fires (Brown, 1960). Without it, these species would be partially or completely replaced by other species. In many cases, a relatively low frequency of fire is all that is necessary.

12.5 Effects of Fire on Animals

Antifire educational programs have engendered the popular conception that forest and grassland fires are always accompanied by a mass evacuation of the local fur and feather populace in a general state of panic. The image of the singed bear cub or fawn left to a fiery fate by the general exodus of animals has convinced many that fire is the enemy of both human and beast, and that at the first smell of smoke animals evacuate. However, the scientific literature does not give unequivocal support for this view, and the fact that animals can be more abundant in fire-dominated than in fire-free environments does not lend much credibility to this popular view. Much of the unreferenced discussion below is based on the excellent review of the extensive literature on the effects of fire on birds and mammals given by Bendell (1974).

Fire affects animals in two major ways: the direct effects during the burn, and the indirect effects that result from changes in the animal's environment.

Evidence for the direct effects of fire on animals is mixed. These effects depend upon the mobility of the animals, the completeness and size of the burn, the rate of spread, and the intensity of the fire. There are reports of many mammals, large and small, swimming across large rivers to escape a 1915 fire that covered 1,600,000 km² in western Siberia. The smoke from this fire is reported to have covered an area the size of Europe. In contrast, neither birds nor animals undertook more than local movements during fires covering about 35,000 ha on the Kenai peninsula in Alaska in 1969. Small mammals were affected more than large mammals and birds. The literature suggests that most animals are able to avoid adverse effects of fire by moving into burrows (e.g., small mammals), to islands of vegetation that are not affected by the fire, or into lakes or rivers. Obviously, fire will have adverse effects on animals with low mobility such as the young, the egg and fledgling stage of birds, and the old, the maimed, and the sick. These are animals that are normally subject to above-average mortality rates, and in many cases fire-induced mortality may only hasten the inevitable. In very large and intense fires, smoke and/or lack of oxygen may cause more harm to animals than the direct effects of heat.

The indirect effects of fire on animals are of much greater import than the direct effects. Most animals are highly habitat specific. For reasons of food, cover, microclimate, and competition from other species, each type of animal tends to be associated with specific vegetation types in a specific type of landscape. As fire changes the environment, there is normally a change in the abundance, distribution, productivity, and species of animal occupying an area. When a fire burns erratically through an area, it produces a mosaic of old and young vegetation types, each with its own characteristic fauna. Such fires serve to increase both the diversity and the abundance of fauna. In contrast, many species of birds and animals are absent in either continuous, dense old growth forest or an extensive, completely burned area.

Many animals use different types of vegetation for different stages of their life cycle and therefore require a mosaic of vegetation. For example, Figure 12.7 shows the use of hardwood forest of different ages by ruffed grouse. Mammals that depend on late stages of forest development and which may be eliminated or displaced by fire are: mountain, woodland and barren-ground caribou, marten, red squirrel, grizzly bear, wolverine, and fisher. Species of large mammal favored by fire include moose, white- and black-tailed deer, elk, cougar, coyote, black bear, beaver, and hare. Birds such as the wild turkey; ring-necked pheasant; bobwhite quail; short-tailed, ruffed, and blue grouse; willow ptarmigan; and some of the waterfowl are benefited by fire, whereas birds like the spruce grouse, which depend upon dense forests, are adversely affected. Table 12.5 summarizes some of the literature on species changes following fire.

Fire plays an important role in maintaining grasslands against invasion by trees. It has been suggested that herbivores contribute to this role of fire by feeding more on the fire-sensitive, less flammable species. By leaving the most flammable species, the animals contribute to the future reburning of the area and the maintenance of habitat suitable to them. Examples to the contrary can also be found.

There is a particularly important relationship between fire and large mammals in northern areas. Where vegetation develops in the continued absence of fire, postfire birch and aspen stands are replaced by dense spruce stands. These shade the soil and lead to the development of a thick moss layer and forest floor. This insulates the soil and leads to a rise in the level of permafrost in the soil, which in turn leads to a decline in the chemical quality of the vegetation (see Chapter 15). Fire leads to a warming of the soil, a drop in the level of permafrost, the replacement of conifers by hardwoods, and a general improvement in plant and animal nutrition. Wildfire from lightning is an important natural component of Alaskan ecosystems without which the wildlife ecology of the area would be radically altered (Lutz, 1956). In fact, it is felt that more ecological damage is done by fighting fire in northern areas than by the fire itself (references in Slaughter et al., 1971). Fire can increase the depth of the active layer (soil unfrozen above the permafrost in midsummer) from about 55 cm to 100 cm, with recovery to prefire values in about 50 years (Viereck, 1973). However, fire in the north is not always benign, and it can have an adverse effect on fine-textured, high-ice-content soils of arctic and subarctic regions. When fire removes the protecting vegetation and organic blanket, the ice melts, leading to soil subsidence and silt flows. Once this process is started, extensive areas of stable soil and vegetation can become an eroding morass of silt (Mackay, 1970; Heginbottom, 1971; Viereck, 1973).

Animals living in fire-affected environments have evolved various adaptations to this environment. These ad-

Figure 12.7

Variation in the utilization of aspen forest by ruffed grouse and other wildlife species during the first 90 years postfire. (After Gullion, 1972. Used by permission of the author.)

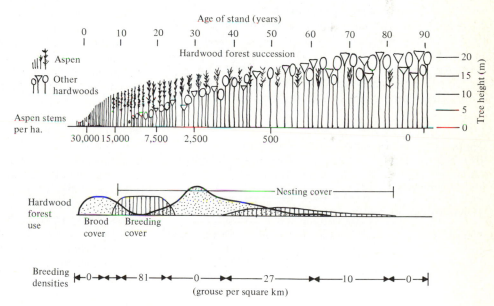

Table 12.5 Changes in Species of Breeding Birds and Mammals (Excluding Predators and Large Mammals) Following Burning

Foraging Zone	Number of Species					
	Before Burn	After Burn	No. of Sp. Gained	%	No. of Sp. Lost	%
A. Species of birds						
Grassland and shrub	48	62	18	38	4	8
Tree trunk	25	26	5	20	4	16
Tree	63	58	6	10	11	17
Totals	136	146	29	21	19	14
B. Species of mammals						
Grassland and shrub	42	45	7	17	4	10
Forest	16	14	2	13	4	25
Totals	58	59	9	16	8	14

Source: After Bendell, 1974. Copyright Academic Press. Used with permission.

aptations include high dispersal rates and the ability to respond to the newfound opportunities created by fire by having a high and variable birthrate. Species of such environments must be able to tolerate rapid changes in their environment. Animals of fire areas tend to be larger and of the browser and grazer types, whereas animals of relatively fire free forests generally tend to be smaller. An example of adaptation to fire habitats is provided by Geist (1971), who compared population characteristics of a fire follower, the moose, with those of the bighorn sheep, which lives in a stable, relatively fire-free environment. Moose are adapted to exploit new habitat by their ability to disperse and quickly increase numbers in a new, fire-created habitat. For sheep, new habitats appear rarely, so dispersal is not an advantage, and the birthrate is stable and low with a death rate that is determined mainly by food supply. Table 12.6 summarizes some characteristics of the two populations.

Table 12.6 Comparison of Some Population Characteristics of Fire-Adapted (Moose) and Nonfire-Adapted (Bighorn Sheep) Large Mammalian Herbivores (Geist, 1971)

Population Characteristic	Moose	Bighorn Sheep
Birthrate	High and variable	Low and constant
Dispersal rate	High	Low
Abundance	Fluctuating	Steady
Major population limitation	Food supply	Food supply

12.6 Effects of Fire on Ecosystems and Ecosystem Processes

By influencing plants, soil, and animals, fire induces several changes in ecosystem processes. We will discuss the effects on energy flow and forest biogeochemistry.

A. Energy Flow

Energy flow out of the system is greatly increased during a fire, and decomposition following fire may also be accelerated, although decomposition of charred logs may be slower than uncharred logs. Primary production is decreased by the reduction or elimination of plants, and where a fire has reduced the moisture and fertility status of the soil, primary production may be depressed for a long time. Alternatively, primary production may be increased by fire because of the change in species composition and more favorable soil conditions. After a fire, primary production is initially by ephemeral species with little biomass accumulation. These species are replaced by herbaceous and shrubby perennials, in which much of the initial biomass accumulation may be below ground. Only when trees recolonize the area does a significant aboveground biomass begin to reaccumulate.

Secondary productivity in grazing food chains is generally increased by fire except where severe soil damage has occurred. Immediately after a fire there may be no secondary production, but as herbaceous and shrub primary production increases, herbivore production generally increases, usually to above prefire values. This continues until plants that have lower value to herbivores invade and dominate the area.

Much of the effect of fire on energy flow is the result of change in the biogeochemistry of the ecosystem.

B. Forest Biogeochemistry

Forest biogeochemistry is considerably altered by fire. The output of nutrients in smoke and flyash has been mentioned. Reduced infiltration leads to overland flow, which may wash the ash directly into water courses. Even where such overland flow is relatively short distance, there may be a significant redistribution of nutrients within an area by this mechanism. We have already seen that there is a change in the availability of nutrients to plants, and in the vertical distribution of chemicals within the soil profile. The effects of fire on these parameters is obviously highly variable because of the variability of fire. The following gives some indication of the effects that can occur.

In August 1970, much of north-central Washington State, including the Entiat Experimental Forest, was swept by lightning fires that covered about 47,000 ha. Streamflow and streamwater chemistry had been measured on several watersheds (473–564 ha in area) in this experimental forest for nearly 10 years prior to the fire. The watersheds carried forests of ponderosa pine, Douglas-fir, and lodgepole pine with an understory including *Ceanothus* species, bitter brush *(Purshia tridentata),* pinegrass *(Calamagrostis rubescens),* and numerous forb species. The watersheds, which range in elevation from 550 to 2100 m, are on the east side of the Cascade Mountains. They receive an annual precipitation of about 58.4 cm.

The Entiat fire produced an average ash weight on the soil surface of 2900 kg ha^{-1}, containing the following amounts of nutrients (in kg ha^{-1}): N, 23; Ca, 314; Mg, 54; K, 70; and Na, 22 (Grier, 1975). Nutrient losses during the fire as the combined result of volatilization and ash convection were estimated to be (in kg ha^{-1}): N, 855; Ca, 75; Mg, 33; K, 282; and Na, 698. The nitrogen loss was considered to be directly proportional to loss of plant biomass and forest floor.

During the first year after the burn, leaching of ash resulted in the following measured transfers down into the mineral soil (in kg ha^{-1}): N, trace; Ca, 149; Mg, 50; K, 92; and Na, 33. Of these amounts, the following percentages were retained in the upper 19 cm of mineral soil: 90% of Ca, 96% of Mg, and 91% of K. A net loss of 29 kg ha^{-1} of Na was observed in this soil layer. Because the nutrient content of the vegetation prior to the fire was not estimated,

and because much of this would have been added to the soil as ash, it was not possible to measure accurately the percentage of the ecosystem nutrient capital that was lost due to the fire. However, by ignoring the problem of additions of plant ash to the forest floor, it was estimated that 39, 11, 15, 35, and 83% of the N, Ca, Mg, K, and Na capital of the ecosystem was lost. These are most probably conservative figures.

Losses of these chemicals in streamwater increased, partly because of increases in streamwater concentrations but also because of the increased stream flow (a 15% increase, equivalent to 8.9 cm of precipitation over the first postfire year (Helvey, 1972; Berndt, 1971). Concentrations of nitrate-nitrogen rose from 0.005 ppm to 0.042 ppm in the burned watershed, and to 0.310 ppm when a burned watershed was subsequently fertilized with urea. This is equivalent to an annual loss (in kg ha^{-1}) of 0.008 before the fire, 1.92 after the fire, and 3.28 after the fertilization, which was at a rate of 78 kg ha^{-1}. Thus, the losses in streamwater were insignificant compared to the losses in the fire itself.

The small contribution of stream export to nitrogen losses reflects both the loss of most of the nitrogen on the site to the atmosphere during the fire and the efficient retention of most of the leached nitrogen by the upper mineral soil. It may also be the result of the fact that energy-flow in the aquatic food webs of many streams and rivers is nutrient limited, especially by nitrogen and phosphorus. Much of the inorganic nitrogen entering a stream is rapidly taken up by microbes and deposited as organic sediments within the stream, immobilized by large woody debris, carried downstream as living organisms or suspended organic matter, or lost to the atmosphere by microbial denitrification. Any or all of these processes can act to reduce streamwater exports to a value well below the actual loss of nitrogen from land to the stream.

Loss of chemicals from an ecosystem following fire can lead to the creation of shrub-dominated heathlands, particularly on coarse-textured, low-fertility soils. These so called *fire barrens* can be seen in Scandinavia (Viro, 1974), Canada (Damman, 1971; Strang, 1972), the U.S. (Forman, 1979), and as extensive *heathlands* in Great Britain (Gimingham, 1972). The ericaceous shrubs that dominate these heaths are thought to impoverish the soil further by promoting podzolization, and inhibit invasion of trees by interfering with the formation of mycorrhizal associations.

Fire in chaparral has been shown to increase the availability of soil nitrogen (Christensen, 1973). Both nitrate and ammonia levels increase greatly following burning from typically low preburn levels. This may be because fire removes chemicals that are present in the unburned chaparral which inhibit nitrogen mineralization by bacteria. Peaks in the nitrate content of unburned soil normally occur following the first fall rains after a dry summer, but these are thought to be the result of foliar leaching of nitrate rather than a stimulation of nitrification. The ash from the burned chaparral contains appreciable quantities of ammonium nitrogen because of incomplete combustion (the ash contained 38% by weight of organic matter), and the high postfire nitrate level undoubtedly results from microbial nitrification of this ammonium nitrogen.

Of all the losses of nutrients during a fire, perhaps the most difficult to measure is the loss in smoke and fly ash. Several studies have reported large loses of volatile nitrogen during fires (Allen, 1964; Knight, 1966; Debell and Ralston, 1970; Feller et al., 1984), and large losses of phosphorus during the burning of herbaceous communities have been reported (Lloyd, 1971). Not all of these local losses are permanently removed from the ecosystem. A fire in a South Carolina pine forest resulted in a doubling of the cation content of rainfall and dry fallout downwind (Lewis, 1974), while 30% of the elements lost as fly ash during the burning of an old field in Ontario were deposited in the adjacent downwind area (Smith and Bowes, 1974).

An intense fire that occurred in a Douglas-fir–Ponderosa pine forest in Idaho produced a large pall of smoke through which rainfall fell over the following few days. This precipitation was found to have concentrations of N, K, Ca, Mg, and Na that were 21, 38, 19, 27, and 71 times higher, respectively, than rain falling before the fire. Although this appears to be a dramatic increase, the estimated addition of nutrients gained from the smoke through wet and dry impaction were calculated to provide only 1–4% of the average net annual increase in forest biomass nutrient content. Consequently, this return is probably of limited ecological significance, most of the fire losses being removed from the general area of the fire (Clayton, 1976).

The complexity of fire effects on nutrient cycling are so great, and our knowledge of these effects is so inadequate that quantitative predictions concerning the long-term effects of fire on forest biogeochemistry and productivity are not possible for most fire-affected ecosystems. Most studies have focused on the changes in the distribution of nutrients that are caused by fire. Few studies have quantified long-term effects on ecosystem function. Faced with this high complexity and frequent lack of long-term response data, forest scientists often resort to the development and use of computer simulation models. This topic is discussed in Chapter 17, but a good example of the application of modeling to the effects of wildfire on a forested ecosystem can be found in MacLean and Wein (1980). A useful review of the effects of fire on nutrient cycling is provided by MacLean et al. (1981).

12.7   Effects of Fire Exclusion

Because fire is a natural factor of the environment, fire-affected ecosystems have become adapted to a particular frequency and intensity of fire and will remain in their natural condition only if this frequency and intensity remains the same. Human activities have often altered both of these. Fire has been introduced to ecosystems in which it has historically been rare, and the occurrence of fire has been greatly reduced in some ecosystems in which it was almost an annual event. In the former case, fire-sensitive communities have been replaced by fire-resistant communities. In the latter case, conditions have been created in which the relatively benign natural fire has gained the potential to produce widespread destruction.

In fire-adapted forests with natural fire frequency, fuel accumulation is prevented and regeneration is limited, so that surface fires tend to be of low intensity and do not turn into crown fires. Such low-intensity surface fires generally have a net beneficial effect on ecosystem function. When fire is excluded from this type of forest, ground fuels accumulate, eventually resulting in intense ground and surface fires. Dense regeneration of trees provides a *fire ladder* by which a crown fire can be created from a surface fire (Cooper, 1961). In fact, the net result of 50 years of successful fire suppression in fire-adapted forests has been the creation of a greatly increased risk of fire of greatly increased destructiveness. This problem has attracted a lot of attention recently and attempts are being made to reintroduce fire to fire-adapted forests (see Biswell, 1960; Oberle, 1969; Dodge, 1972; Kilgore and Briggs, 1972; Habeck and Mutch, 1973; Agee, 1974; Wright, 1974).

An interesting example of the effect of fire on the interaction between organisms is the case of dieback of jarrah *(Eucalyptus marginata)* in Australia. This large tree is susceptible to an introduced root pathogen, *Phytophthora cinnamomi,* which can cause extensive tree mortality. Hot wildfires promote the growth of legumes, which increase site nitrogen status through symbiotic nitrogen fixation, thereby increasing the vigor of jarrah and its resistance to *Phytophthora.* Hot fires also remove *Banksia grandis,* another tree species that is highly susceptible to *Phytophthora.* Dieback of jarrah forest is particularly severe when there is an understory of banksia because the fungal infection builds up on the banksia and then spreads to the jarrah. Low-intensity prescribed fires, on the other hand, promote the growth of banksia and the subsequent dieback of jarrah. Control of wildfires and their replacement by prescribed burning has rendered the jarrah forest far more susceptible to this root pathogen (Christensen et al., 1981; Shea, 1979). Additional examples of the complex interactions between fire and the biota can be found in Gill et al. (1981).

Fire is thought to be the primary natural ecological factor governing the distribution and abundance of dwarf mistletoes in North American forests (Alexander and Hawksworth, 1976). Its effect is complex and fire may either encourage or discourage these parasites. Where the burn is complete over large areas, fire excludes dwarf mistletoe because this parasite recolonizes an area slowly. Conversely, partial burns that leave scattered groups of infected trees create ideal conditions for rapid spread of the parasite throughout the subsequent young stand. Wildfires also exacerbate this pathological problem by converting nonsusceptible climax (see Chapter 15) forests, such as spruce–fir in the Rocky Mountains, into susceptible seral forests such as lodgepole and jack pine forests. Frequent fires also prevent the natural selection of mistletoe-resistant genotypes.

12.8   Fire and Forest Management

Uncontrolled wildfire and intensive forest management have traditionally been considered incompatible. The forester wants to harvest much of the biomass that is consumed in a wildfire and does not want the undesirable changes to soil and the hydrological cycle that are the frequent aftermath of an intense summer wildfire. On the other hand, fire does have some uses in forestry. It can be used to manipulate the depth, chemistry, and decomposition of the forest floor and the temperature of the mineral soil. It can be used to sanitize an area of diseases, parasites, and insect pests. It can dispose of unwanted biomass (postharvest logging residue or *slash*), thus reducing the fuel accumulation problems, improving regeneration possibilities, and improving access for wildlife. Brush problems can be abated temporarily by fire, and established stands can be fireproofed by periodic prescribed burning.

There can be little doubt that managed or prescribed fire has an important role to play in forest management, especially during the conversion of overmature virgin forests into second-growth forests. There can also be little doubt that we will continue to suppress many wildfires. To be useful to the forester, prescribed fire must be applied at the time of year when there is a reasonable chance of achieving given objectives, and the forester may deliberately burn an area in the spring or fall in which money and time were invested putting out a fire the previous summer. The important difference between managed fires and wildfires must be made clear to the public so that they will accept what may to a layperson appear to be an extraordinary policy.

12.9   Summary

Relatively few terrestrial ecosystems have not, at one time or another, been affected by fire. For most ecosystems, the frequency of fire is low, but fire is such a powerful ecological factor that even at a frequency as low as once every two or three centuries it may be a major determinant of ecosystem character.

Generalizations about the ecological effects of fire are very unreliable because of variations in the frequency, duration, intensity, and type of fire, in the character of the physical environment (climate and soil), and in the species and their adaptations to fire. The effects on vegetation can vary from beneficial to highly detrimental, while the major effects on animals will depend upon whether or not the species is favored by the changes in the environment wrought by the fire.

Fire does have direct adverse effects on plants and animals, but these are often relatively short-lived. In contrast, the indirect effects that result from fire-induced alterations in soils can be much more persistent. Soil structure, organic matter content, and nutrient status can all be adversely effected by hot, persistent fires, with consequent reductions in plant productivity. On some sites in some forest types, the long-term reductions in forest productivity may be more serious than the killing of the present forest cover.

For good reasons, foresters have traditionally considered wildfire as an enemy to be excluded at all costs. However, there is growing evidence that fire plays an important and either a beneficial or a benign role in some ecosystems. The organisms native to such areas have evolved with fire and may grow better with a natural fire frequency than with no fire. Overprotection from fire can result in undesirable changes in the plant community and render the community susceptible to serious damage should a fire occur. Much more needs to be known about the effects of fires of different types on particular ecosystems so that we can prevent destructive wildfire but retain benign and beneficial fire where it is a natural and desirable environmental factor.

Section D The Biotic Environment

If organisms existed apart from each other, evolution would have resulted in adaptations only to physical factors. That this is not the case can be attributed to the important role that other organisms play in the life of any particular plant, animal, or microbe: an importance that is reflected in a wide variety of adaptations to the biotic component of an organism's environment.

In very severe physical environments, organisms may not be abundant enough for interactions to play the dominant role in evolution, but in the more moderate environments that cover much of the earth's surface, the evolutionary development of organisms and the form and functioning of ecosystems have been very strongly influenced by inter- and intraspecific interactions. In such environments, coevolution has frequently been a major force in determining the character of the community. Managers of renewable resources must be mindful of the wide variety of interrelationships between organisms of the same and of different types. Such relationships can be important in determining the success of forest resource management.

13.1 Introduction

Living organisms rarely exist for long as isolated individuals. Certainly, individual trees can be found growing by themselves many kilometers from any other trees, and individual animals may be driven by the elements far from the other members of their population. However, such individuals do not remain alone for long. They may reproduce (if they are able to do so on their own) and create a new population, return to the population from which they came, be joined by other individuals of the same species, or die. Most organisms exist for most of their life history as members of a population, and other individuals of the same species are often as important a component of the environment of an individual as are the factors of the physical environment.

A. Spatial Arrangement of Organisms

The individual members of most plant, animal, and microbial populations are not distributed over the ground at random. They exhibit a definite pattern or *dispersion*. Many types of organism in most types of environment exhibit marked clumping of the individuals, with the clumps distributed either randomly or nonrandomly. Other types of organisms in some types of environment are rather regularly spaced apart; their dispersion approaches a uniform distribution. It is common to find coniferous trees in an even-aged, single-species stand fairly evenly spaced as the result of competition for light, while competition for moisture may lead to a rather even spacing of large species of cacti or pines in desert and dryland forest, respectively. The same thing can be seen in animal populations. Many bird species divide the environment up into rather uniformly sized territories, so that the birds may have a fairly uniform rather than a random distribution. However, completely uniform distributions are very rare in nature.

Clumping of individuals in a population (which is said to be *contagiously* distributed or to exhibit *contagion*) can be the result of several processes.

1. *Dispersal of seed or young.* Because of wind and water movements, many seeds and spores may come to rest in the same general area, and this can lead to clustering of the individuals in the next generation. Wind-dispersed insects may all land in the same locality and therefore have a very nonrandom distribution. Collection and storage of seed by animals can result in clumped growth of plants.

2. *Reproduction.* Lack of medium- and long-distance dispersal of reproductive propagules or offspring may result in the clumping of subsequent generations as a more or less pure population around the site of the parent organism(s). Longer-distance dispersal will tend to produce a mixture of species and less obvious clumping. Vegetative reproduction

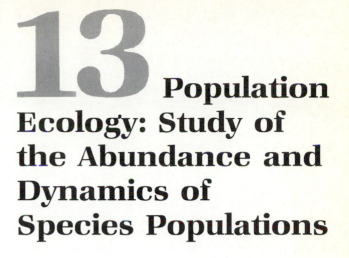

13 Population Ecology: Study of the Abundance and Dynamics of Species Populations

will lead to the establishment of new shoots in the vicinity of the reproducing plant and produce a spreading mat or clump of a single species.

3. *Variations in the physical environment.* Dispersal of reproductive propagules can result in either a random or a uniform distribution over a large area, but only those that land on a suitable substrate will become established. For moisture-requiring species, only those propagules that land on moist soil will survive, giving rise to a clumping of individuals and species on such sites. Seeds of light-demanding plants may germinate all over the forest floor, but only those located under gaps in the canopy will survive. Similarly, spatial variations in soil chemistry and microrelief can result in a markedly nonrandom distribution of plant individuals and species. Many animals also have rather narrow habitat requirements and will be found aggregated in areas where they experience appropriate food, shelter, and environmental conditions.

4. *Active locomotion in response to a common stimulus.* Members of a particular animal species will tend to have the same or a similar response to environmental stimuli, which can cause them to aggregate in the same general area.

5. *Modification of the physical environment by the organisms.* An interesting example of clumping is the character-

305

istic *tree islands* found in subalpine meadows near the tree line (Figure 13.1). The snow close to the stem of an isolated tree melts earlier than in the surrounding meadow, as a result of canopy drip and radiation of heat to the snow from the stem. This accelerated snowmelt exposes the ground close to the stem several weeks earlier than in the surrounding meadow, lengthening the snow-free growing season close to the tree. The earlier snowmelt facilitates the growth of shrubs and other trees in the "snow crater" and leads to the formation of a tree group (in closed forest) or island (in subalpine meadows). In the meadow away from the tree island, the prolonged snow duration precludes the growth of trees and large shrubs. In this example, the presence of one individual modifies the environment so that other individuals of the same or other species can survive. Similarly, the growth of mosses adapted to acid conditions on sites with nonacidic soils is made possible by the presence of trees with acidic litter, and the growth of calcium-demanding herbs on rather calcium-poor soils is facilitated by the presence of hardwood tree species that have significant levels of calcium in their throughfall and litterfall.

6. *Aggregation as the result of biotic factors.* Contagion in animal populations can occur because the presence of other individuals modifies the biotic hazards of the environment. Many species are restricted to, or clumped in, those environments or microenvironments in which they can resist diseases or escape the depredations of natural enemies. Heavy grazing pressure may eliminate forbs from grasslands, restricting them to clumps of shrubs that protect them from herbivores, and animals may be clumped in places where they can escape their predators and parasites. Alternatively, clumping of prey organisms may simply result from random searching by natural enemies.

B. Advantages and Disadvantages of Being a Member of a Population

Aggregation into populations confers both advantages and disadvantages on the member organisms (Allee, 1931, 1951). We will discuss the advantages first.

1. *Protection.* Plants gain mutual protection from the rigors of the physical environment, such as wind and temperature extremes. Many mature forests just below timber-

A

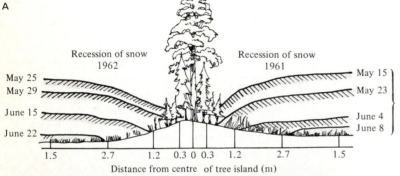

B

Figure 13.1

(A) Diagram of a small subalpine tree island in a subalpine meadow in coastal British Columbia, showing its associated snow crater and the springtime recession of the snow in 1961 and 1962. The area within 30 cm of the central tree had almost 4 weeks more snow-free period than the area 3 m away from the tree. (After Brooke et al., 1970. Used with permission of the Department of Botany of The University of British Columbia and the authors.) (B) Snow craters in closed forests can sometimes be 2 m deep with vertical walls at a distance of 50 cm from the tree trunk. The photo shows a snow crater in closed montane forest close to the forest limit in southwestern British Columbia. It is common to find two or three trees growing close together in these craters.

line are often very difficult to replace if the area is extensively deforested because the combined effects of wind, full insulation (high summer temperatures), and/or frost heaving can make reforestation by natural or artificial means very difficult. The present tree line in the Grampian Mountains of Scotland is thought to be about 200 m lower than the climatic potential for the area (Pears, 1968) because historic deforestation has allowed wind velocity to increase near the ground to the point at which seedling establishment and growth is prevented. Undoubtedly there are other determinants of the lowered tree line in the Grampians, but the loss of shelter by other trees is probably a major cause of regeneration failure.

Many animals also depend upon mutual shelter. Bees form tightly packed swarms inside hives in the winter to conserve heat, while in the summer, hive temperatures are kept down by some of the bees fanning their wings at the entrance to the hive (Uvarov, 1931). Larger animals will huddle together in winter for mutual warmth and shelter from wind, and even animals that are aggressive and solitary in the summer may become gregarious during cold winter weather [e.g., the winter wren (McLachlin, 1983)]. Aggregation of seabirds in densely populated breeding colonies, fish in schools and large ungulates in herds achieve protection from predators because the members of the group are individually less susceptible to predation than are individuals on their own.

2. *Reproduction*. Many species have a critical lower population size (numbers) and density (dispersion) that is necessary for successful reproduction and survival. Animals of the open ocean, such as whales and deep-sea fish, obviously have a serious reproduction problem if they become separated from other individuals of the same species; they cannot find a mate. Some animals require a certain minimum aggregation of individuals before breeding will begin. A population density of less than one pair of muskrats per 1.6 km of stream or per 35 ha of marshland is not commensurate with successful breeding (Errington, 1963). Crowding in aphid populations triggers a switch from the production of wingless to the production of winged females, which are then able to disperse to new host plants.

The stimulation of reproduction by crowding is also seen in birds that breed in colonies (Darling, 1938), and it has been suggested that a minimum of 10,000 birds at a mean density of three nests per square meter is necessary for the establishment of a successful breeding colony of the guano-producing cormorant on the islands off Peru (Hutchinson, 1950). Apparently, the stimulation provided by the noise and movement of other birds is necessary to prepare them for mating, nest building, incubation, and feeding the young. As a result of this requirement, large concentrations of birds promote synchrony of reproduction, which is thought to confer benefits to the individuals in the population by lowering the risk of predation. By synchronizing the production of seeds, eggs, or young, organisms can "swamp the market." Predators are often intimidated by or cannot cope with large numbers of their prey. Alternatively, the predators simply cannot "keep up" and therefore most of the offspring survive (see Section 13.5B).

3. *Genetic diversity*. The aggregation of organisms promotes genetic variation and polymorphism in a population. High genetic diversity improves the ability of a population to survive in a changing, unpredictable, and variable environment. It facilitates the development of a broad geographic range and helps the species to cope with interspecific competition. If a population is too small, inbreeding will lead to reduced genetic diversity and increased risk of population extinction.

The reduction of genetic diversity in small populations may have led to the extinction in the U.S. of the passenger pigeon and the heath hen. The latter was formerly abundant in Massachusetts and probably also from Maine to Delaware (Gross, 1928). By 1880, the species was restricted to Martha's Vineyard, an island off the east coast of Massachusetts, and a large reservation was established to preserve the species. Numbers increased to 2000 in 1916, but a fire, a gale, and a hard winter combined with an influx of avian predators (goshawks) decimated the population, leaving fewer than 50 breeding pairs. Numbers declined thereafter until in 1927 only 20 birds were left. The last bird seen was reported in 1932. Apparently, the natural disasters of 1916 reduced the population below some critical level, after which it was doomed.

4. *Intraspecific competition*. Although it can have adverse effects, intraspecific competition (between members of the same species) often acts to keep a population healthy and well adapted to its physical environment. Sick and poorly adapted individuals do not survive the competition. By selection for high fitness in the intraspecific sense, such competition may render the population more successful in interspecific interactions (between members of different species).

5. *Division of labor and cooperation*. Colonial and social behavior has proven to be a successful evolutionary development, as evidenced by ants, wasps, bees, and human beings. All these animals have gained advantages by the development of cooperation and of division of labor. Many individuals working together can achieve more than that number working alone, because cooperation facilitates the development of specialization, with its attendant in-

creased efficiency. Worker bees and ants, freed from the time and energy demands of reproduction, can invest all their efforts in food gathering, nest building, and maintenance. Specialized soldier ants and termites lessen the need for defensive adaptations in, and activities by, the workers, with consequent energy savings. Cooperation among predators greatly increases their power and efficiency. A single wolf could never bring down a healthy, mature moose, whereas a large pack of determined wolves might eventually prevail.

Against the advantages of aggregation must be set a number of disadvantages.

1. *Intraspecific competition.* Because natural selection operates to reduce competition between species, individual organisms often suffer more adverse effects from competition with individuals of the same species than with individuals of some other species. Although intraspecific competition can have the beneficial effect of weeding out those individuals that are sick or which have physiological, anatomical, or behavioral abnormalities that prevent them from competing successfully, generally the effects of intense competition within a population are adverse. As Darwin (1859) put it: ''The struggle will almost invariably be most severe between individuals of the same species, for they frequent the same districts, require the same food and are exposed to the same dangers.''

Overpopulation can produce a variety of types of competition. Trees in an overstocked forest compete for space to spread their branches, for light, soil moisture, and soil nutrients, and for the rooting volume needed to provide stability. Overstocking in dry environments can result in the stagnation of the entire population since none of the individuals obtain sufficient resources to be able to outcompete their neighbors and cause natural thinning. This is a common situation in Douglas-fir, lodgepole pine, and ponderosa pine stands in dry areas of western North America (Figure 13.2). The effects of reduction in competition following removal of large overstory dominants or following the thinning of overstocked stands can be seen clearly in Figure 13.3.

Overpopulation in animals can lead to severe competition for food. If a few individuals exert dominance over the others, this competition may simply reduce numbers to the point at which all remaining animals receive sufficient food. In the absence of such dominance, all of the population will suffer deficiencies and all may die of starvation.

2. *Increase in levels of stress.* The physical proximity of other members of the population may increase the stress to which an individual is exposed. Stress produces physiological changes (e.g., changes in the production of hormones such as adrenalin by the endocrine system) that may alter

Figure 13.2
Chronically overstocked lodgepole pine in central British Columbia. Large numbers of seeds were released from serotinous cones by a fire, and the failure of the stand to undergo natural thinning has resulted in stagnation of growth. Numbers of trees as high as 500,000 per hectare are not uncommon.

behavior and susceptibility to pathogenic factors such as disease or environmental extremes. For example, it is generally felt that human beings are much more likely to become sick following a period of stress than when they are unstressed. Stress-induced changes in hormone levels can induce marked behavioral changes, which may have adverse consequences for the individual and the population.

3. *Alteration of the environment.* The population density of arctic lemmings periodically increases to a level at which they browse the vegetation so heavily that they virtually eliminate the cover needed for escape from predators. Some animals foul their environment with their wastes or metabolic by-products if the population density gets too high (e.g., human populations in overcrowded cities). This can so degrade the environment for that species that its numbers are drastically reduced.

4. *Disease transmission.* Parasites, predators, and disease organisms are generally benefited by high densities of their host organisms. More prey and more frequent encounters between prey facilitate the spread and growth of disease and parasitic organisms. The spread of insect pests and diseases through mixed-species forests is often much slower than through single-species stands.

5. *Physical interference.* If animal populations become too dense, encounters with other individuals become so frequent that normal patterns of behavior are interfered with. This can interrupt feeding and breeding activities.

Figure 13.3

Cross-section of a Douglas-fir tree showing the effects of moisture competition and release therefrom. The first 80 or more years of growth was as a suppressed sapling, competing for moisture with a scattered overstory of large mature trees. When these were removed, thereby reducing competition for moisture, the trees grew rapidly. The stem disc was about 7 cm diameter at age 80, and 14 cm diameter eight years after release. (Courtesy A. Vyse, British Columbia Ministry of Forests.)

These adverse aspects of intraspecific interactions all serve as a negative feedback on population growth. We will examine some of them in more detail later in the chapter.

13.2   Population Growth and Demographic Characteristics of Populations

Most of the research on population growth has been done by zoologists working with animals and using the number of individuals as an index of population. However, the first significant paper in population biology was not written by a zoologist but by a botanist in 1874, and Malthus had earlier (1798) made it clear that the fundamental characteristics of populations are found equally in both plants and animals (Harper, 1977). The focus on animals probably occurred because most animal species lend themselves to population census better than most plant species. It is easy to monitor the change in number of adult animals in a population as it increases over time, whereas for plants it is not clear exactly what should be measured. Does one count seeds, seedlings, or mature plants? For annual plants a census may in fact be a reasonably easy and realistic measure of the population. For perennials, and particularly for long-lived woody tree species, numbers may not be a very good measure of the population. Biomass or basal area may be better.

Simple, free-living algae or free-floating aquatic plants are analogous to individual insects or mammals. They can be investigated experimentally in much the same manner as the simple animals that were used by researchers such as Gause (discussed later in this chapter) to develop the basic concepts of population ecology. Unfortunately, the analogy does not hold for large plants such as trees, which are more analogous to a termite colony or a bee's nest. Functionally, a tree is a population of leaves or of buds connected by woody structures, with a high degree of central organization and integration. Each leaf on the plant is in some ways like an individual organism, in that it has a life history, it competes with other leaves, and it is a member of a population. A study of the change in number of complex plants in an area over time is therefore more analogous to a study of the number of bees' nests or ant colonies in an area than to a study of the number of individual bees or ants. We have already seen that the leaf area index of a particular ecosystem is a characteristic of that system and that maximum leaf area is attained rapidly and is more or less sustained for long periods. The numbers of leaves or the leaf area index grows in much the same way that a population of animals increases toward and fluctuates around its carrying capacity. Because of these considerations it is not always possible to apply population theories developed for animal populations to plant populations. Recently, plant population dynamics has developed as a branch of ecology in its own right (Harper, 1977). We return later to a discussion of the characteristics of plant populations. For now, we focus primarily on animal populations.

Before we can discuss the central question of population ecology (what regulates the abundance and distribution of a species), we must consider how populations develop over time from a single reproductive unit (a male–female pair for sexual reproduction, or a single individual for asexual or self-fertilizing reproduction).

A. Geometric Growth

If a reproductive unit of a species with a short generation time is placed in an environment that provides all requisites for life in excess of needs, the numbers of the organism will increase over time as indicated in Figure 13.4. This pattern of population change is called *geometric growth*. The abundance of the population shows a curvilinear increase with time as does the rate of change in abundance from generation to generation.

If the organism in question has discrete, nonoverlapping generations (e.g., annual plants or an insect with a single generation per year in a seasonal environment), the curve in Figure 13.4 can be described by

$$N_{t+1} = R_0 N_t$$

where N_t is the population size at generation t, N_{t+1} the population size in the subsequent generation, and R_0 the net reproductive rate, or the number of female offspring produced per female per generation (assuming sexual reproduction and a constant ratio of males to females). If R_0 remains constant at a value greater than one, the population increases. The higher the value of R_0, the more rapid the population growth.

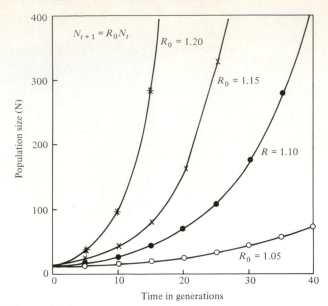

Figure 13.4

Geometric increase in numbers of organisms with discrete generations starting with 10 individuals and various net reproductive rates (R_0). (After Krebs, 1972. Copyright C. J. Krebs. Used with permission of author and Harper & Row, Publishers.)

If, on the other hand, the organism in question breeds continuously throughout the growing season of the year, and if the population is made up of overlapping generations (e.g., humans or a population of aphids on a rose bush with many generations during one growing season), population growth must be described using differential equations. Under these circumstances, the population curve in Figure 13.4 would be described (Lotka, 1922) as

$$\frac{dN}{dt} = rN$$

| Rate of change in number per unit time | = | natural rate of increase | × | number in the population |

The term r, the *natural rate of increase* (or *biotic potential*) of the species, is a parameter that incorporates both additions to the population (births) and losses from the population (deaths). It is the rate of population growth per capita and expresses the result as growth rate per individual. Birthrate on its own is not enough to describe population growth, since growth will vary with different death rates even if the birthrate remains constant (Figure 13.5).

Because additions to and losses from a population vary widely according to the size and condition of the population and the nature of the environment, r is very variable for any

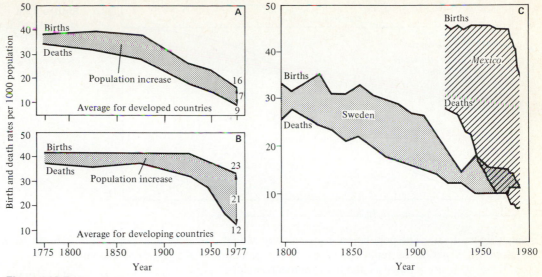

Figure 13.5
Effect of birth rates and death rates on population growth. Where there is no net immigration or emigration, rate of population increase equals birth rate minus death rate (shaded portion of graph). Average values of birth and death rates for human populations in developed (A) and developing (B) countries are shown with one example for each type of country (C). (After van der Tak et al., 1979. Used with permission of the Population Reference Bureau and the authors.)

species. In order to permit comparisons between r values for different populations, ecologists use the parameter r_m. This is called the *innate capacity for increase* of the species. It is defined as the maximum rate of increase attained by a species at a particular combination of temperature, humidity, and so on, when the quantity of food (and/or nutrients), space, and the numbers of other individuals of the same species are kept at optimum values and other species are excluded (Andrewartha and Birch, 1954). The term r_m is thus a parameter that is obtained under and refers to ideal laboratory conditions. Its value with reference to field populations is that it provides a standard with which to compare the performance of field populations and how close they are able to come to obtaining their maximum theoretical rate of increase.

B. Logistic Growth

Geometric population increase is characteristic of the early phases of population growth, or the growth of a population that has recently escaped from some traditional population control (e.g., the human population as described in Chapter 1). Most populations exhibit relatively little change in numbers from year to year. In 1944 it was estimated that there were about 125 million ducks in the U.S., which pro-

duce 10–16 eggs per pair. Had all the adults and offspring survived, there would have been about 900 million ducks the following year. In reality, the numbers remained approximately the same. Queen termites are said to be capable of laying tens of millions of eggs, and oysters reportedly can discharge 500 million ripe eggs in one spawning. Even these astronomical numbers are dwarfed by the reproductive excesses of fungi which can release billions of spores per night from a relatively small area of substrate (references in Clarke, 1967). Yet, in spite of these enormous reproductive potentials, populations of such organisms grow at a geometric rate only for a very brief period, and except following some major disturbance, they generally do not show sustained growth over many generations.

The reason for this lack of sustained growth is that as a population grows in numbers, so does the negative feedback caused by competition, diseases, stress, and so on. This negative feedback is referred to as the *environmental resistance* (Chapman, 1928). As a population starts to increase from a single breeding unit, this resistance is low and the population expands geometrically. So does the environmental resistance, which steadily reduces the rate of population growth until the resistance becomes so great that no further increase is possible. Such population growth has an S or sigmoidal shape and is called a *logistic growth*

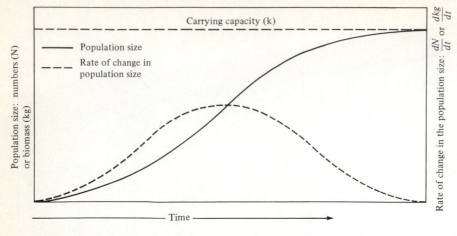

Figure 13.6
Idealized logistic growth curve. The graph shows the sigmoidal increase in numbers over time and the asymptotic approach to K, the carrying capacity. The rate of change in numbers (or biomass) is also shown.

curve (Figure 13.6). The population grows slowly at first, followed by a period of rapid increase. The population growth rate then slows down as numbers approach an upper limit (*K*, the *carrying capacity*) asymptotically. When the carrying capacity has been reached, the environment is "saturated" with that particular species.

The environmental resistance that prevents the biotic potential of the species from being realized can be described mathematically and incorporated in the geometric growth equation to convert it into a logistic equation. For the case of nonoverlapping generations, R_0 varies according to how

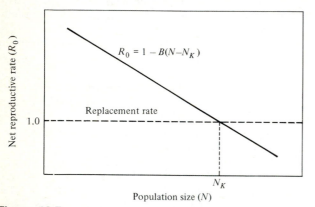

Figure 13.7
Relationship between net reproductive rate (R_0) and population size (*N*). R_0 is equal to 1.0 when the population is at its equilibrium density (i.e., at carrying capacity, $N = N_K$, and $-B(N - N_K) = 0$). The slope of the line is equal to $-B$, the coefficient relating change in reproductive rate to change in population size. (After Krebs, 1972. Copyright C. J. Krebs. Used with permission of author and Harper & Row, Publishers.)

close the population size is to K (Figure 13.7). Thus, $N_{t+1} = R_0 N_t$ becomes

$$N_{t+1} = [1 - B(N_t - N_K)]N_t$$

where $-B$ is the slope of the line relating net reproductive rate (R_0) to the number of individuals in the population (*N*) (Figure 13.7) and N_K is the maximum size of the population at carrying capacity.

For any population there will be a critical value of $-B$ at which the population increases smoothly up to the carrying capacity and levels off. If the slope is greater than this equilibrium value, the population will grow more rapidly, overshoot *K*, and establish a sustained oscillation around it. If the slope is too great, the oscillations may become larger and larger, with R_0 eventually becoming zero and the population becoming extinct (Figure 13.8).

For the case of overlapping generations and continuous breeding, the geometric differential equation

$$\frac{dN}{dt} = rN$$

becomes

$$\frac{dN}{dt} = \frac{rN(K - N)}{K} \qquad \text{or} \qquad rN\left(1 - \frac{N}{K}\right)$$

$$\begin{array}{c} \text{Rate of growth} \\ \text{of population} \end{array} = \begin{array}{c} \text{per capita population} \\ \text{growth rate} \end{array}$$

$$\times \begin{array}{c} \text{population} \\ \text{size} \end{array} \times \begin{array}{c} \text{proportion} \\ \text{of carrying} \\ \text{capacity that} \\ \text{remains unused} \end{array}$$

As *N* approaches *K*, both $(K - N)$ and $(1 - N/K)$ approach zero, and $rN(K - N)/K$ and $rN(1 - N/K)$ become very

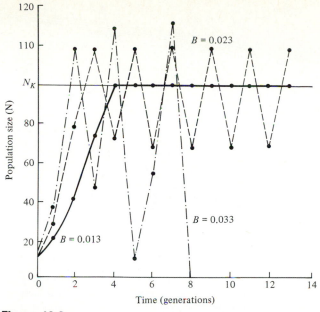

Figure 13.8
Population growth of a hypothetical organism with discrete generations and a linear relationship between population density and net reproductive rate. The population trend is shown for a starting population of 10, an equilibrium density (N_K) of 100 and for three different values of B. The larger B is, the greater the instability of the population. (After Krebs, 1972. Copyright C. J. Krebs. Used with permission of the author and Harper & Row, Publishers.)

small. The population essentially stops growing. If N is greater than K, population ''growth'' becomes negative and the population will decline. An area cannot sustain for more than a brief period a greater number of individuals than the carrying capacity. It cannot exist permanently in an ''oversaturated'' condition.

C. The Logistic Growth Equation and Actual Populations

The differential logistic equation of population growth was proposed for the human population as early as 1838 by Verhulst and again in 1920 by Pearl and Reed in a study of the U.S. population. A more recent analysis of the U.S. population growth incorporating more recent census data showed that these authors were overoptimistic about when the human population would start to exhibit a logistic pattern of growth. Until very recently, it has continued to grow geometrically. This raises a question as to the generality of the logistic growth model for natural populations with overlapping generations.

Numerous studies have compared actual population growth with the idealized logistic model. Growth of yeast and bacteria cultures or simple organisms such as protozoans raised under constant conditions with a continual supply of food does approximate the logistic curve. Laboratory populations of more complex organisms such as flour beetles initially conform to the logistic, increasing sigmoidally to an asymptote (Gause, 1934), but if the experiment is prolonged, the population is found to fluctuate widely around the asymptote and eventually decline (Park et al., 1964).

A search of the literature reveals that there are no documented cases in which the population of an organism with a complex life cycle has maintained a steady population at the upper asymptote of the logistic curve for more than a brief period, and that population growth often fails to conform to the shape of the logistic curve (Krebs, 1978). This is probably because the logistic growth curve is based on various assumptions that are frequently not met in either experimental or natural conditions. We will examine four aspects of populations that may interfere with the attainment of logistic growth: lack of response to K, time lags in response to K, changes in K induced by high populations or other factors, and the age class structure of the population.

1. Lack of Response to K. Some species do not exhibit a marked negative feedback between population density and growth rate. In a survey of 64 studies of population growth in which there was a significant directional trend in numbers with time, evidence for a negative feedback was found in 47 species, whereas no such evidence was found in 16 species (Tanner, 1966). In only one species was there any evidence for a positive feedback, where the rate of population growth was positively correlated with population size (density). The species was *Homo sapiens*. This analysis suggested that 73% of the populations studied exhibited the negative feedback necessary for population stability. However, there is some question concerning the statistical validity of this conclusion and several population ecologists feel that there are few cases where there is strong evidence of an effective negative feedback component in population growth.

2. Time Lags. If a population is so responsive to intraspecific interactions that there is an immediate negative feedback between an increase in population and the population growth rate, one might expect population growth to be sigmoid. If, on the other hand, there is a delay in such a feedback, one would expect populations to overshoot the carrying capacity: the greater the time lag, the greater the overshoot.

3. Reduction in K by High Population Density. For some species, the attainment of high populations is accompanied by a decrease in the carrying capacity and an accompanying decline in the population. This is not true for organisms such as trees, which respond to the attainment of K (in terms of volume or basal area) by reducing population density in favor of increased size of the surviving individuals. When the carrying capacity for volume or leaf area is attained, some individuals are able to continue growing by outcompeting and killing other individuals. Some species of animal are able to avoid overshooting and degrading their carrying capacity by dividing the resource up between the individuals in the population. Territories are established, the size of which depends upon the resource requirements of the individual, so that the population never exceeds K and never degrades the carrying capacity of the resource (see the discussion of territorial behavior in grouse later in the chapter).

For nonterritorial herbivores, K can easily be depressed if populations get too high. Reindeer have been introduced into many parts of Alaska during the past century to replace dwindling caribou herds. Two of the Pribilof Islands in the Bering Sea received such introductions in 1911. Four males with 21 females were released on St. Paul's Island (106 km²) and 3 males with 12 females were released on St. George's Island (91 km²), where the populations were unmolested by predators, including humans. The St. George's population grew to a peak of 222 animals early in the 1920s and then declined to a reasonably stable herd of 40–60 animals. The St. Paul population initially increased at a similar rate to the St. George population, but instead of declining it started growing geometrically in the mid-1920s, reaching a peak level of about 2000 animals in 1938. This high population overgrazed its food supply (slow-growing lichens) and then declined rapidly to a level of only 8 animals in 1950 (Figure 13.9). The experience on St. Paul's Island was reproduced when reindeer were introduced to St. Matthew's Island (332 km²) in 1944. An initial population of 5 males with 24 females had increased to 1350 by 1957 and reached a peak of 6000, after which it crashed to 42 in 1966 following overgrazing (Klein, 1968). Similar events have occurred in New Zealand following the introduction of the Himalayan thar (a hollow-horned ungulate animal resembling a goat), and in several other parts of the world (see references in Caughley, 1970). Such population *eruptions* appear to be initiated by an improvement in food supply (an increase in food-regulated carrying capacity), or introduction to an unexploited food supply, and terminated by overgrazing, which lowers the carrying capacity and prevents a sigmoid pattern of population growth.

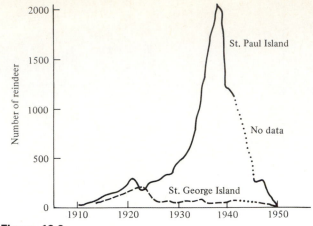

Figure 13.9

Reindeer introduced onto St. Paul Island in the Bering Sea without any natural enemies increased to levels of abundance at which they overgrazed their food supply (lichens), thereby lowering K and almost driving the population to extinction. A similar population introduced to St. George Island declined before it had much effect on K. (After Scheffer, 1951. Copyright American Association for the Advancement of Science. Used with permission of AAAS and the author.)

4. Age Structure of the Population. The logistic growth equation is based upon the assumption that a population will eventually attain a *stationary age distribution*. By this we mean that the ratios of reproductive propagules to immature individuals, and of immature individuals to reproductive adults, remain constant over time, and that natality equals mortality. It is the distribution of ages in a population that has ceased to grow and is at equilibrium with its total environment. If the population fails to achieve or sustain this type of age structure, the population will not follow the logistic growth curve.

The importance of age structure in the dynamics of populations requires that we examine it in some detail. Taking the human census data for Canada as an example, one finds tables (called *life tables*) which list the numbers of people in each 4-year age group from birth to an age of 85 years or older. These life-table data can be displayed graphically in the form of an *age-distribution diagram*. Figure 13.10 compares such diagrams for Canada, the U.S., and India for various dates, and one can see that there has been a considerable change in the shape of the distribution. Early in this century, while the Canadian and U.S. populations were expanding rapidly, most of the population was in the younger age classes, representing both a greater rate of reproduction and a greater rate of immigration of young people than occurred in the 1970s. Also shown is a graph of the

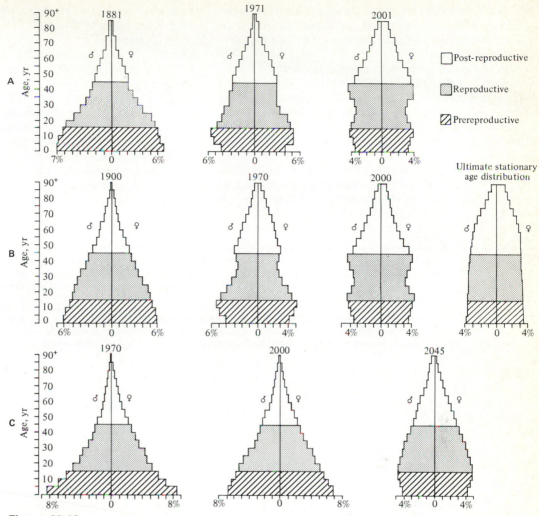

Figure 13.10

Historical and predicted patterns of change in the age distribution in the human populations of (A) Canada, (B) the US, and (C) India. The horizontal scale is the percent of the population in each 5 year age class by sex. It would appear that in the move toward a stationary age distribution, India was about 100 years behind the two North American countries in the 1970's, but that it will only be about 75 years behind in the eventual attainment of this demographic condition. (Data for (A) from Statistics Canada, 1976. Used by permission. Data for (B) from C. F. Westoff, The population of developed countries. Copyright © 1974 by Scientific American, Inc. All rights reserved. Data for (C) from T. Frejka, 1974. Used by permission.)

expected distribution of age classes when the population eventually stops growing (the predicted stationary age distribution) and the predicted trend for India. It can be seen that there are far fewer young people and far more older people in a population that has ceased to grow than is found in an expanding population. This obviously has very important implications for social organization. Fewer schools will be required, more geriatric hospitals will be needed, and there will be fewer people in the work force to support the enlarged nonproductive older age classes. Fewer people will be creating the capital necessary to provide the inflation adjustments for the pensions of large numbers of older people. The human age distribution obviously has very important implications for the human population. Similarly, the age distribution is an important determinant of the dynamics of other populations.

A life table is a somewhat morbid document! It provides a summary of the schedule of deaths in a population and may list the causes of mortality in each age group. A decline in numbers between two adjacent age classes generally means that deaths have occurred, although it can also indicate emigration. The life-table technique of summarizing the nature and occurrence of mortality and the survivorship (percent survival from one age class to the next) of a population was first developed by students of human populations (human *demographers*), with major contributions from life insurance companies, which are interested in knowing when people are likely to die.

An example of a life table's age-specific summary of mortality is given in Table 13.1. It shows the numbers of survivors at the start of each age interval (age class), the number dying in each age interval, the rate of mortality (numbers dying per 1000 individuals), and the mean expectation of further life for individuals alive at the start of each interval. The shorter the time interval, the greater the detail of information on when mortality occurs, which helps to identify the causes of mortality. Each of the columns of a life table can be calculated from any of the other columns. The various columns merely represent different methods of presenting the basic survivorship data.

Table 13.1 Life Tables

Age Class (x)	Number of Survivors at the Beginning of Age Class x (l_x)		Number of Deaths during Age Class x (d_x)		Mortality Rate Per 1000 Individuals $(1000q_x)$		Mean Expectation of Further Life at Beginning of Age Class (e_x)	

A. Life table for red deer stags on the Isle of Rhum, Scotland. The table was constructed on the basis of a census in 1957 (Lowe, 1969). Such a table is called a *time-specific* or *static life* table as opposed to a *dynamic* or *cohort* life table in which the survival of an initial group or cohort of young is monitored until all individuals are dead. Figures in brackets show cohort life table data for the first 9 years for the 1957 cohort.

Age Class	l_x		d_x		$1000q_x$		e_x	
1	1000	(1000)	282	(84)	282.2	(84.0)	5.81	(4.70)
2	718	(916)	7	(19)	9.8	(20.7)	6.89	(4.15)
3	711	(897)	7	(0)	9.8	(0.0)	5.95	(3.25)
4	704	(897)	7	(150)	9.9	(167.2)	5.01	(2.23)
5	697	(747)	7	(321)	10.0	(430.0)	4.05	(1.58)
6	690	(426)	7	(218)	10.1	(512.0)	3.09	(1.39)
7	684	(208)	182	(58)	266.0	(278.8)	2.11	(1.31)
8	502	(150)	253	(130)	504.0	(866.5)	1.70	(0.63)
9	249	(20)	157	(20)	630.6	(1000.0)	1.91	(0.50)
10	92	(0)	14	(0)	152.1	(0.0)	3.31	(0.0)
11	78		14		179.4		2.81	
12	64		14		218.7		2.31	
13	50		14		279.9		1.82	
14	36		14		388.9		1.33	
15	22		14		636.3		0.86	
16	8		8		1000.0		0.50	
17	0		0		0.0		0.0	

B. Life table for a hypothetical striped maple population (Hibbs, 1979)

Age Class	l_x	d_x	$1000q_x$	e_x	Cause of Death
1	10,000	8750	875	4.1	43% eaten 16% winter kill 41% other
2–15	1250	low	low	28.2	little mortality
16–40	1250	1205	38.4	14.2	$P:R < 1$
41–100	45	43	15.6	33.6	Crown closure, physical damage
+100	2	—	low	—	

Perhaps the most commonly used information in a life table is the number of survivors at the start of each age interval. This can be presented graphically in the form of a *survivorship curve,* of which there are two categories: the *cohort* or *dynamic* type and the *stationary age distribution* or *static* type, each of which represents a different type of life table. *Cohort life tables* are constructed by following the survival of a particular group of individuals (a cohort, e.g., all Douglas-fir seedlings on a 1-ha plot that germinated in 1980) until they are all dead. *Static or instantaneous life tables* are made by examining the age distribution of the population at the time of a census (e.g., the age distribution of trees in a 1-ha Douglas-fir forest at the time of measurement). Survivorship curves often present surviving numbers on a logarithmic scale because of heavy juvenile mortality.

There are four major types of survivorship curve (Figure 13.11). In Type I, the population suffers very little mortality until near the end of the physiological life span; most dying organisms are old. Mortality in Type II populations is distributed evenly across all age classes (there is a constant number of deaths per unit time), while in Type III, a constant percentage of the survivors die in each time interval. In Type IV, heavy juvenile mortality is followed by low and fairly constant mortality for the rest of the life span. These four curves are hypothetical and few populations conform to them exactly. *Homo sapiens* in developed countries conform fairly closely to Type I, except for a brief period of infant mortality in the first few days of life. Many bird species conform approximately to Type II, while Type III is characteristic of many fish and marine invertebrates. Plants may conform to any one of these types. Many species have heavy juvenile mortality followed by rather constant adult mortality intermediate between Types II and III. Others are intermediate between Types I and II.

The survivorship curve is not a fixed characteristic of a population. It changes if the action of the agents of mortality changes. Introduction of hunting or the removal of predators will significantly affect the curve for a deer population. The curve for light-demanding tree seedlings will change if defoliating insects cause heavy mortality in the overstory, thereby reducing seedling mortality. As mortality and natality vary from time to time, so does the shape of the age distribution. However, a population in which mortality and natality rates remain constant for a considerable period has a very regular and constant age distribution. In steadily increasing and in steadily declining populations, the age distribution is said to be stable. A *stable age distribution* is one in which the *shape* of the survivorship does not change but the total number of individuals in the population is changing. Where mortality exactly equals natality, the population will remain constant and will eventually achieve a stationary age distribution. The latter is equivalent to the survivorship curve for a population that is neither growing nor decreasing and which is at equilibrium with its environment.

Populations that have a stable age distribution but which have higher numbers in the younger age classes than the stationary age distribution will grow geometrically. If the age distribution changes with time toward the stationary form, a sigmoidal growth curve will result. Thus one cannot interpret the probable future growth of a population from the age distribution alone. One also needs to know the characteristic or stationary survivorship curve.

From this discussion it can be seen that in many cases the logistic growth equation is too simplistic to accurately represent what happens in nature. Nevertheless, some populations do conform to this type of growth, and the idea of environmental resistance constraining the biotic potential of a species is useful.

13.3 Major Determinants of Population Size

The number of organisms in a population results from the combined action of four major population parameters: natality, mortality, immigration, and emigration.

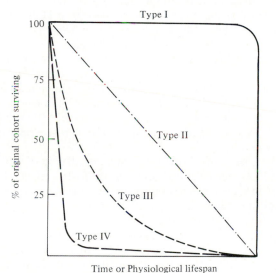

Figure 13.11
The four major types of survivorship curve. (After Slobodkin, 1961. Used with permission of L. B. Slobodkin.)

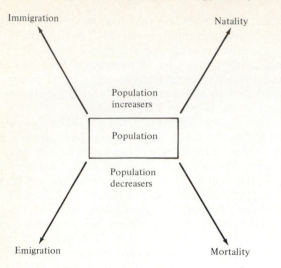

There are many factors that influence these four parameters, and much time and energy has been spent trying to decide on their relative importance in regulating population size. We will consider each in turn and then discuss the various theories concerning population regulation.

A. Natality

Natality refers to the process of producing new individuals, whether this is by sexual (birth, hatching, or germination) or by asexual reproduction. It is a rate that can refer to the actual number of new offspring produced per female per unit time (the *fertility* of the female) or the maximum potential rate of which the females of a particular species are capable (the *fecundity* of the species). The fecundity of *Homo sapiens* is one birth per 9–11 months per female during the reproductive years. The greatest reported fertility is 27 (a Russian living in the last century), although there is a claim (unsubstantiated) that a Brazilian couple in this century have produced 32 children (McWhirter and McWhirter, 1975). Fortunately, two offspring per female is becoming common in developed countries and some women choose to have no children, thereby offsetting families of more than 2 children. Gradually, human fertility is approaching *replacement fertility:* the level of fertility at which each breeding unit (a couple) on average produces only enough children to replace themselves.

Measurement of natality is complicated by the variety of breeding patterns found in organisms. Some breed once a year, some several times a year, and some continuously. Sometimes the fertility rate will be reported on an annual basis, sometimes on a generation basis, and sometimes on the basis of some arbitrary age class.

Natality varies during the life of an organism. There is always a prereproductive period and some organisms survive to a postreproductive stage. Trees from temperate latitudes vary in the age at which they first reproduce (Table 13.2), as do animals (Table 13.3). The longer reproduction is delayed, the slower the rate of population growth, and delaying marriage and family formation is often proposed as an alternative to reduced family size as a way of regulating the rate of growth of human populations. For example, compare the contribution of a couple that produces a family of six children in their late thirties and early forties with a couple that produces a family of three children when they are in their late teens and early twenties. If their offspring behaved the same way as their parents and had similar survivorship, both family groups would leave about the same number of offspring after 120 years.

The number of offspring per reproduction (*brood size* when referring to animals) varies greatly between different types of plants and animals. Brood size is under genetic control and is believed to represent the optimum allocation of resources for the particular species in its particular environment. For example, tropical birds tend to lay smaller clutches of eggs than do temperate and northern birds (Skutch, 1967; Cody, 1966). Apparently, it is better to lay fewer larger eggs in the tropics and a larger number of smaller eggs at the higher latitudes. At any one latitude, clutch size varies with species; gulls normally lay three eggs while the Canadian goose lays four to six eggs. Brood size is also influenced by the availability of food. It has been reported that the great tit *(Parus major)* in Holland has a smaller average clutch size and fewer pairs raise second broods in years when the birds are abundant than when they are scarce. This was tested experimentally by tripling the population by providing nesting boxes, thereby increasing competition for food. This reduced average clutch size by two eggs (from about 10) and the proportion of pairs raising second broods from 63% to 16% (Kluijver, 1951). Klomp (1970) has reviewed the question of clutch-size determination in detail.

Mammals also show a considerable degree of environmental control on brood size. Arctic foxes produce larger litters in years when lemmings are abundant than when lemmings are scarce. Lions in South Africa were reported to have litters of four to five cubs when game was plentiful compared with two to three cubs per litter when game was scarce (references in Lack, 1954). In a study of North American elk, 20–25% of the hinds bore twins in an area with ample food, whereas almost no twins were produced on a range that had been heavily overgrazed. The same thing has been reported for deer.

Table 13.2   Age at Which Forest Trees Begin to Reproduce Abundantly

		Early,[a] 10–20 yr	Intermediate, 20–40 yr	Late, 40–60 yr
Conifers	Pines	Jack, pitch, lodgepole, knobcone, Virginian, sand, Monterey, bishop, slash, loblolly	Red, eastern white, shortleaf	Sugar, western white, ponderosa, limber, whitebark
	Other	Tamarack, black spruce, northern white cedar, Port Orford cedar, southern white cedar, cypress	Red and white spruce, balsam, fir, Douglas-fir	Spruce, true firs
Hardwoods		Willow, cottonwood, aspen, alder, gray birch, paper birch, pin cherry, red maple, bigleaf maple, box elder, scrub oak, and other fast-growing short-lived trees that produce small seeds	Hickories, maple, basswood, ash, elm, sycamore, chestnut, buckeye	Beech, oak

Source: After Daniel et al. Copyright McGraw-Hill Book Co., NY. Used with permission of publisher and authors.
[a] Many of these species may produce appreciable quantities of seed after as few as 5 years.

Fecundity estimates are often included in life tables. Table 13.4 presents a fecundity schedule for the hinds in the red deer population on the Isle of Rhum, referred to in Table 13.1. For each age class it shows the sex ratio, the number of female offspring per female (m_x), and the fertility of the age class obtained by multiplying m_x by the number of hinds in the age class (l_x). The net production rate for the species is obtained by summing ($l_x m_x$) for all age classes.

The number of offspring produced by an organism is believed to represent a balance between the energy costs of producing more offspring and the benefit of the increased contribution of those offspring to the genetic composition of the next generation. If a 20% increase in offspring reared means that each offspring receives 20% less food, fewer offspring may survive and contribute their genes to the next generation. In this case there would be strong selection to reduce the number of offspring to the point at which each

Table 13.3   Age at Which Animals Start to Reproduce (Kendeigh, 1961)

Type of Animal	Age of First Reproduction
Planktonic organisms	Few days
European voles	Few weeks
Tropical sparrow	6–8 months
Nontropical songbirds	1–3 years
Beaver, wolf, lion, and whale	2 years
Deer, bison, bear	3 or more years
Elephant	8–16 years
Rhinoceros	20 years

receives adequate food. Conversely, if a 20% rise in the number of offspring increased the contribution of the genotype to the next generation, selection will favor more offspring.

From the discussion above it is obvious that a species has a "choice"[1] to make. It can allocate its available energy and nutrient resources to a large number of small offspring, as is done by many tree species and aquatic invertebrates, or it can produce fewer, larger offspring that are better equipped for survival. Where the environment is very patchy and unpredictable, where the risk of mortality to any one individual is high, or where there is very little competition from other organisms, the optimum evolutionary "strategy"[1] is to produce large numbers of small offspring. Such species are called *r-strategists* and have been produced by *r-selection*. Species in more predictable and uniform environments with high levels of inter- and intraspecific competition are selected to produce fewer but larger offspring with greater competitive abilities. Such species are called *K-strategists*. Some characteristic features of *r*- and *k*-strategists are listed in Table 13.5.

B. Mortality

The topic of mortality was introduced in the discussion of life tables and survivorship curves and it was noted that two populations with the same total abundance can have quite

[1] The use of these and other anthropomorphisms is justified by their utility in the learning process. The reader is reminded that there is no such thing as a strategy (implying advanced planning) in evolution, and other species do not make evolutionary choices in the sense that humans do.

Table 13.4 Schedule of Fecundity for Hinds in the Isle of Rhum Population (Lowe, 1969)

Age Class, yr (x)	Percent of Offspring That Are Female	Female Offspring Per Female (m_x)	Net Production Rate (R_0 or $l_x m_x$)
1	—	—	—
2	—	—	—
3	50	0.311	0.242
4	50	0.278	0.193
5	50	0.302	0.184
6	61.9	0.400	0.210
7	61.9	0.476	0.210
8	61.9	0.358	0.128
9	61.9	0.447	0.081
10	61.9	0.289	0.017
11	50.0	0.283	0.014
12	50.0	0.285	0.012
13	50.0	0.283	0.010
14	50.0	0.282	0.007
15	50.0	0.285	0.005
16	50.0	0.284	0.003

different growth patterns because of differences in age structure, and hence, mortality. One can be expanding, if most of the individuals are young. The other can be on the point of collapse because most of the individuals are old and it has no juveniles at all. Similarly, two populations, both with the same number of individuals, can have totally different temporal changes in abundance according to when the mortality occurs: before or after the reproductive period.

Mortality can occur as the result of many different processes, including disease, predation, parasitism, antibiosis, physical conflict, starvation, malnutrition, temperature effects, and dehydration.

C. Immigration and Emigration

For some species, the arrival of individuals from, or their departure to, remote areas constitutes the major factor regulating the actual number of organisms in a locality. One of the best known examples in which dispersal is the major determinant of animal numbers in an area is immigration of African locusts (Johnson, 1963). Locusts appear periodically in plague proportions through much of Africa, wrecking havoc on the vegetation wherever they settle (Albrecht, 1967). The desert locust was at plague levels for 37 of the 56 years from 1908 to 1964, and can cover areas as large as 17 million square miles (Waloff, 1966). Individual swarms can cover areas as large as 400 square miles, contain 1.6×10^{10} locusts and weigh about 50,000 tons (Gunn, 1960).

Prior to the work of a Russian entomologist (Uvarov, 1961), who developed the *phase theory* of locusts, the sudden, almost magical appearance of vast swarms of locusts and their equally rapid disappearance had baffled researchers. Uvarov showed that locusts have two phases, which differ in behavior, color, physiology, and morphology. In the *solitary phase,* locusts behave much like any other grasshopper; a local nuisance but never aggregating into swarms of plague proportions. Rainfall in areas inhabited by solitary locusts is followed by plant growth, improved locust nutrition, and an increase in population density; wind movements can increase the density of the locust populations even more by concentrating the insects in a particular locality. When a sufficient concentration has developed, the behavior of the insects change and they actively aggregate. The resulting increase in frequency of interactions between individuals leads to the formation of the *gregarious phase,* in which swarm formation and emigration occurs (Key, 1950). Although active flight is undertaken, the subsequent distribution of the swarms to new areas is largely by wind, the locust swarms often being blown in the opposite direction to the one in which the insects are flying (Rainey, 1963; Johnson, 1963).

In the case of the African locust, immigration is an important component of the initial rise in population density that is needed to trigger the switch from solitary to gregarious phase, and emigration is important in moving the swarms from area to area. The size of the locust population

Table 13.5 Some Characteristic Features[a] of *r* and *K* Strategists and Their Environments

Feature	*r*-Strategists	*K*-Strategists
Climate	Variable and/or unpredictable	Fairly constant and predictable
Mortality	Often catastrophic, undirected, density independent	Directed, density dependent
Survivorship curve	Often Type III[b] (Figure 13.11)	Usually Types I and II (Figure 13.11)
Population size	Variable, nonequilibrium: usually well below carrying capacity; unsaturated communities; recolonization often occurs annually	Fairly constant, equilibrium value: at or near carrying capacity of the environment; saturated communities; annual recolonization not usually necessary
Intensity of competition	Variable and often low	Usually high
Lifespan	Short, usually less than 1 year	Usually more than 1 year and often many years
Selection favors	Rapid growth	Slower growth
	High r_m	Greater competitive ability
	Early reproduction	Delayed reproduction
	Small body size	Larger body size, often very large
	Single reproduction/life cycle	Repeated reproductions/life cycle

Source: After Pianka, 1970. Copyright The University of Chicago Press. Used with permission.

[a] Obvious exceptions will be found. For example some trees are *r*-strategists and some are *K*-strategists, and yet they may be very similar in size and longevity.

[b] Deevey, 1967.

in any one area is therefore more affected by immigration and emigration than by any other population parameter.

Many animals produce offspring in excess of the carrying capacity of the environment. These excess individuals then disperse to new areas and thereby avoid populations in excess of the carrying capacity in the home area. Human history is replete with examples of Europeans and Scandinavians leaving overcrowded home countries to seek new territories, and in many other overcrowded countries around the world emigration has historically been an important mechanism to ease population pressures. The resulting immigration into recipient countries has often had a greater short-term effect on population increase than has natality in the existing population.

In a study of the regulation of field mice, Krebs and Myers (1974) established that dispersal was a critical component of population regulation in these small mammals. By fencing an area and preventing the dispersal that normally occurs during a period of population growth, mouse numbers increased to three times the density in an unfenced control area. This led to overgrazing and starvation, which reduced the population to about half that in the unfenced area; 56% of the males and 69% of the females produced during a population increase were lost from the control area by dispersal.

Dispersal is also important in territorial animals. Once all the choice territories are occupied, remaining animals disperse to marginal habitats, thus preventing the population from reaching deleteriously high densities. More will be said about this later.

13.4 Theories About the Natural Regulation of Population Size

The basic elements of population growth have been known for a long time. Greek philosophers such as Plato understood that population growth could be stimulated by compulsory and early marriage and by large family size, and that overpopulation could be avoided by infanticide, abortion, celibacy, and emigration. However, the first clear statement that populations do not grow indefinitely but reach some upper level awaited the writings of an Italian by the name of Botero in 1588. He noted that in spite of an undiminished power of increase, population growth is halted by such events as famine, disease, wars, earthquake, and floods, and that the most fundamental limitation was lack of food. Two centuries later, Malthus (1798) enunciated his famous principles of population growth: that a population has the potential to increase geometrically but is restrained by the finite carrying capacity of its environment. He noted that increased population density was accompanied by increased mortality from disease and increased violence. Many others both before and after Malthus have contributed to a growing knowledge of population regulation [for a full discussion, see Cole (1957)], but the foundations of the modern theories about populations were developed by applied ("economic") entomologists interested in the control of insect pests.

There are two major properties of populations that need to be explained: variation in mean abundance between different environments and temporal variation in the numbers of individuals about the mean in any one environment. Some of the theories described below refer mainly to mean abundance, whereas others refer mainly to temporal fluctuations.

The various theories about population regulation that have been developed over the past 70 years can be grouped into several schools of thought: the *biotic* or *density-dependent* school, the *abiotic* or *density-independent* school (these two schools can be combined as the *extrinsic* regulation school), the *self-regulation* (or *intrinsic* regulation) school, and the *comprehensive* school.

A. Biotic or Density-Dependent School

Howard and Fiske (1911) contributed the first major paper in the modern discussion of population regulation. Working on the biological control of the gypsy moth and the brown-tail moth in the eastern U.S., they presented the idea that populations exist at approximately constant levels because of a *balance of nature*. They classified natural mortality factors as *facultative* and *catastrophic*. Facultative mortality agents operate more intensely as the population increases and are said to be *density dependent*. Conversely, the action of catastrophic agents (such as the climatic factors of wind and temperature) is unaffected by population density; organisms are killed in numbers that bear no relationship to their abundance. Such catastrophic agents are said to be *density independent*. Howard and Fiske believed that parasitism is the only truly facultative mortality factor. They felt that predators could act in a similar manner, although some predators take a constant number of prey from year to year and therefore are not facultative.

The next important contribution to this branch of ecology [sometimes referred to as the most important single paper written on the topic of population regulation (Tamarin, 1978)] was made by another entomologist, Nicholson, in 1933. He supported Howard and Fiske's contention that the balance of nature could be produced only by the action of density-dependent factors, but he maintained that it is competition for resources rather than natural enemies that accounts for balance in population abundance. Although he conceded that parasites do act in a density-dependent manner, he pointed out that because of time lags, their populations may produce oscillations of increasing amplitude rather than balance. It is intraspecific competition, according to Nicholson, that determines the levels at which populations exist in balance with their environment. Nicholson's views were later supported by Milne (1957, 1962), also an entomologist, who claimed that intraspecific competition is the only factor affected solely by numbers. However, Milne noted that populations are often maintained below the density at which competition becomes significant, and he felt that at those times population density is held in check by density-independent or imperfectly density-dependent factors.

The concept of the balance of nature was further developed by Smith (1935), an entomologist working on biological control of pests in California, who actually coined the terms "density dependent" and "density independent" for the two main types of mortality factors. He noted that populations exhibit two major growth phenomena: a tendency to vary in numbers over time, and a tendency for this variation to vary about a mean abundance that is characteristic of a particular environment but which can vary in different environments. Smith claimed that average density can never be determined directly by density-independent mortality factors, but noted that such density-independent factors as climate can act in a density-dependent fashion under some circumstances. If a species requires a protective refuge to avoid climatically induced mortality, and if such refuges are in limited supply, the mortality would increase as population increased since the number of sheltered individuals remains constant. As an applied entomologist, Smith felt that parasites, predators, and diseases were of prime importance in determining mean population densities, but he concluded that weather plays an important role and that this is reflected in fluctuations about the mean.

Another advocate of the biotic concept of population regulation was Lack (1954), a British ornithologist. He noted that most birds vary in numbers between rather narrow limits and felt that this indicates the action of density-dependent factors. In his studies he found that the variation in fertility between high- and low-density populations was not sufficient to account for the observed changes in numbers, and concluded that mortality, especially juvenile mortality, must be the dominant mechanism of population regulation. He found that 82–92% of passerine birds die within a year of hatching. In considering the possible causes of this mortality, he felt that food, predation, and disease were the only candidate factors and that, for birds, competition for food was the most important. Extrapolating from his work with birds, Lack suggested that food was the major limiting factor for most vertebrates, but that plant-eating insects are rarely limited by food. He also stated that although climate often causes severe losses of birds, populations usually recover rapidly and therefore climate cannot regulate bird populations in the Nicholsonian sense.

B. Abiotic or Density-Independent School

Applied entomologists also led the field in the first major challenge to the biotic school. Bodenheimer in 1928 suggested that many immature insects that are parasitized would be killed by climatic factors anyway (*compensatory mortality* [2]) and that parasitism is therefore subordinate to climate in the regulation of population density. The importance of climate in determining the distribution and abundance of insects was reaffirmed in a major review by Uvarov (1931), who noted that up to that time most applied entomologists had been ''ecological historians,'' recording and trying to explain past events. What was required were some ''prophets'' who could predict future entomological events, and he felt that in doing this the relationship between climate and insects was the most useful predictive tool.

Perhaps the best known exponents of the abiotic school are two Australian entomologists, Andrewartha and Birch (1954), whose ideas were refined by Andrewartha and Browning (1961) and Browning (1962). They rejected the division of regulatory processes into density-dependent and density-independent categories and claimed that investigations of animal populations should focus on the individual rather than the population; it is the individual that suffers mortality, not the population. Explorations of the abundance and distribution of individual organisms should be based on an investigation of the influence of the following four factors of an individual's environment on its chances of survival and reproduction: weather, food, other organisms, and a place in which to live. They felt that of these, climate was the dominant factor since it affected food, other organisms, and ''the place in which to live.'' However, these authors did recognize the importance of biotic factors and their theory is, therefore, not totally abiotic.

[2] Because of compensatory mortality, it is difficult to judge the importance of any particular mortality factor in population regulation. If one factor does not kill an organism, it may die anyway because of the action of a second factor.

Other advocates of the abiotic school include ecologists who have attempted to explain cyclic population fluctuations in terms of variations in sunspot activity and ultraviolet radiation.

C. Self-Regulation or Intrinsic Regulation School

Implicit in all the theories discussed so far is the view that all individuals in the population are identical in their characteristics, needs, and responses. These theories all overlook the natural genetic and phenotypic variation in any population. Parasites, predators, food quality and quantity, competition from other species or from other individuals of the same population, and climatic factors such as cold, heat, rain, and wind, all act on the individuals in a population as forces external to the individual. Because of genetic variation, there is variation in the response of the individual members of the population to these factors, and if the genetic composition of a population changes over time, so will its response to these factors. The self-regulation school holds that variation over time in the quality of individuals within a population is an important and major component of population regulation: that population fluctuations are produced by changes that are intrinsic to the population individuals themselves. There are two types of intrinsic mechanisms that can be involved: phenotypic and genotypic.

One of the first suggestions that there could be a genetic cause of population fluctuations was given by the British geneticist Ford in 1931. He noted (Ford, 1975) that as the environmental conditions undergo their normal temporal variation and become favorable to a species, numbers increase and at the same time selection pressure is reduced. This favors the survival of genotypes that would not survive under harsher conditions. As environmental conditions return to ''normal'' or become harsher than usual, these genotypes are removed and the population declines.

The idea of genetic self-regulation was largely developed by Chitty (1960, 1971) working with population fluctuations in small mammals. He suggested that under favorable environmental conditions, indefinite increase in population density is prevented through a deterioration in the ''quality'' of the population. As populations grow there is selection for genotypes that are more aggressive, which leads to increased mortality and a reduction in the rate of population growth. Selection for appropriate behavior to deal with the more frequent intraspecific interactions is thought to be accompanied by reduced selection for ability to survive other natural hazards such as inclement weather. The combination of altered behavior and reduced resistance to physical extremes leads to a population decline. As this occurs, selection for aggressiveness is weakened and selection for survival in the face of other mortality factors is strengthened. This in turn leads to a change in behavior, an increase in survival, and regrowth of the population. In Chitty's conception, population regulation includes the action of abiotic factors, such as weather. These factors act in a density-dependent fashion since their effect becomes more intense as density rises and population "quality" falls.

Another form of self-regulation in animal populations is based on behavioral mechanisms. Wyne-Edwards (1962, 1964, 1965), a British ecologist who has worked mainly with birds, noted that although food is ultimately the most critical resource for animals, birds have evolved behavioral mechanisms to limit populations before they threaten the future supply of food. This can be done in any of several ways. Birds that nest in colonies may, as a group, limit the area of nesting sites. Adjacent, apparently suitable sites, are "taboo" to the birds and remain unused. Another mechanism that occurs in a wide variety of animals is social structure or *pecking order*. Because dominant animals have first access to food and other resources, there is little need for constant physical dispute over rights. The remaining food and resources are available to progressively lower order individuals. As resources become scarce, the higher-order animals continue to be well provided for and survive, whereas low-order individuals are excluded and die. This perpetuates the population in situations in which equal division of resources would spell disaster for the entire population.

A final social mechanism is that of *territoriality*. Breeding pairs set up territories, the size of which determines the size of the breeding population in that year. As the supply of resources varies, territory size may vary, producing a fluctuation in the population density. A particularly good example of the relationship between territoriality and population size is the study of red grouse populations in eastern Scotland. Historically, the grouse has been an aristocratic bird in Great Britain, being regularly hunted by monarchs, and even today the start of the shooting season still coincides with the start of the summer recess for the House of Commons. Concern over periodic bad years for grouse shooting led to an investigation of the so-called "grouse disease" (periodic declines in numbers) early this century. The preliminary conclusion of this study was that the periods of grouse scarcity were due to the action of a parasitic nematode (Lovat, 1911), but after further research it was suggested that food shortage was the primary determinant of the population fluctuation. More recent studies have implicated territorial behavior related to food quality and quantity as an important determinant of the temporal variation in numbers.

Cock grouse set up territories with hens in the autumn. These territories may be abandoned during snowy winters, but with the onset of milder weather in February the cocks return to their territories. Fixed pairing occurs and birds without territories disperse to suboptimum habitats, where many of them die. One brood is raised per year, with the eggs laid in late May or early June. On hatching, the young chicks join the juvenile population, feeding initially on insects and later on young heather shoots. Juveniles that survive their first winter may join the breeding population the following spring. There is a marked annual variation in the proportion of unmated cocks because of variation in territory size, and there is a variation in average clutch size and in the survival of the eggs and young. The size of individual territories is determined by male aggressiveness. When this is low, individual males tolerate much closer proximity of other males and hence territory size is small. When males are aggressive, tolerance of proximity is reduced and larger territories are defended.

Having established that the breeding population of red grouse on the Scottish moors is largely controlled by behavior, the determinants of behavioral variation were investigated. Although it has not been conclusively proven, it appears likely that periodic variations in the nutritive quality [e.g., N and P concentrations and organic constituents (possibly the result of plant defensive mechanisms)] and the quantity of succulent heather tips influence the aggressiveness of the males (Moss, 1967a,b, 1972; Jenkins et al., 1963; Miller et al., 1966). Another very interesting example of how nutrition can influence population fluctuations through the behavior of individuals is provided by Wellington (1957, 1960, 1964, 1965).

A final example of self-regulation theories is the theory that implicates a behavior–endocrine feedback system (Christian and Davis, 1964). Developing an earlier idea about the effect of prolonged stress on the endocrine system (Selye's 1946 general adaptation syndrome), it was suggested that as populations increase in density, the accompanying increase in interactions and interference between individuals stimulates the adrenopituitary system, which causes changes in behavior (e.g., heightened aggression in all animals and decreased maternal care of the young in overcrowded laboratory rodent populations), reduced reproduction (diminished production of sex hormones), and eventually a rise in mortality due to hypoglycemia and a variety of specific symptoms collectively referred to as "shock disease." This theory differs from that of Chitty, in that it involves a physiological rather than a genetic basis for the altered behavior at high densities.

One problem with the stress theory is that natural populations rarely become as dense as the laboratory populations in which the phenomena was identified. However, an undefined "shock disease" has been reported in wild populations of snowshoe hare declining from high numbers in Canada (Green and Larson, 1938). Changes in the adrenal system similar to those observed by Christian and Davis were reported in rabbits in subalpine regions of the Snowy Mountains in Australia (Myers, 1967), but this was thought to be associated with low sodium levels in the diet rather than with crowding per se (Blair-West et al., 1968).

D. Comprehensive or Compromise School

Although several researchers have proposed that populations are regulated by a single factor, a much larger number of population ecologists have subscribed to the idea that the abundance and distribution of most populations are determined by a combination of extrinsic and intrinsic, biotic and abiotic, and density-dependent and density-independent mechanisms. The particular combination of regulating factors will vary from case to case. Homeothermic animals may be regulated differently than poikilotherms. Organisms living in physically extreme, widely varying, or unpredictable environments may be regulated differently than organisms living in physically moderate, relatively constant, and highly predictable environments. The mechanisms of regulation may vary at different stages of the life cycle and from year to year. The regulation of populations is seen to be the result of a complex of mechanisms and factors.

Huffaker and Messenger (1964) proposed the use of the terms *conditioning mechanisms* and *governing mechanisms* as a replacement for the controversial terms "density-independent" and "density-dependent." Conditioning mechanisms are defined as "environmental factors or agents which, uninfluenced by density, contribute to the setting or fixing of a framework of potential environmental

carrying capacity or affect interim population regulation when capacity is not attained." Conditioning factors determine the general levels that a population may attain in an environment: whether the population is generally very low or very high. Governing mechanisms are defined as "the actions of repressive environmental factors, collectively or singly, which intensify as the population density increases and relax as the density falls."

Conditioning factors tend to be more important than governing factors in determining animal abundance in physically unfavorable or extreme environments, and the converse is true for favorable or moderate environments (Figure 13.12). This is because in environments in which the conditioning mechanisms set a low population potential, the population never attains densities at which density-dependent factors become effective. Governing mechanisms are therefore relatively unimportant contributors to the setting of population levels, and the population responds directly to variations in the low carrying capacity. In environments in which conditioning factors set a high population potential, populations increase to the point at which the density-dependent governing factors act strongly on the population, and these factors are preeminent in determining population numbers (Figure 13.12). Where the population potential set by conditioning factors is substantially above the level set by governing factors, the former will appear to play little or no role in population regulation. The relative importance of governing and conditioning factors for a given species will vary in different parts of its range and at different times as the species range expands and contracts. Near the center of the range, governing factors will dominate, whereas conditioning factors will play the major role at the periphery of the range (Figure 13.13).

The comprehensive approach to population regulation suffers from one major weakness as far as traditional scientists are concerned: it is very difficult to prove a comprehen-

Figure 13.12

Variation in the importance of density-dependent and density-independent mechanisms of population regulation in different types of environment. (A) Importance of conditioning (i.e., density-independent) and governing (i.e., density-dependent) mechanisms in different environments. By scanning across the graph at any point on the vertical scale, you can see the relative importance of the two mechanisms for that particular type of environment. (B) Correlation between population density change and conditioning and governing mechanisms. (Modified after Huffaker and Messenger, 1964. Copyright Chapman and Hall Ltd. London. Used with permission of the publisher and the authors.)

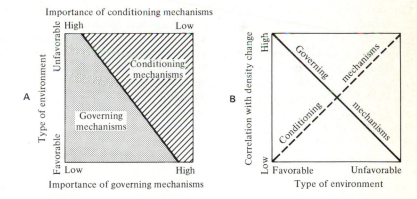

sive theory wrong. Science advances by a process of logical reasoning. A scientist examines the known facts about a phenomenon and by *inductive reasoning*[3] formulates an initial theory about it: a statement of what he or she thinks are the reasons for the known facts. This theory is then subject to experimental testing in an attempt to *prove it wrong*. This is done by making predictions *(hypotheses)* from the theory (by *deductive reasoning*[3]), which are then tested in carefully designed experiments. The experimental observations (results) are then used in conjunction with inductive reasoning to evaluate the initial theory. If proved wrong, the theory can be reformulated to account for the experimental evidence, or replaced by a more plausible theory, and then retested. If, after repeated attempts to disprove it, the theory still fits the facts, it may be accepted as a reasonable approximation of reality. If the theory remains after many years of testing, it may be elevated to the status of a *principle* or *law*. This process, *the scientific method,*[4] requires that a theory generate testable, refutable hypotheses. The problem with comprehensive theories of population regulation is that they rarely generate easily refutable hypotheses; because of their inherent complexity they tend to generate complex hypotheses that are not easily tested in simple experiments. This shortcoming has been used by some to reject the comprehensive approach (e.g., Chitty, 1967) in favor of theories based predominantly on the action of a single factor.

There can be little disagreement with the desire to advance our understanding of natural phenomena, or with the claim that science is advanced by rigorous testing of inductive-derived theories. However, to force our ideas about the regulation of a natural population into the scientific straightjacket of a simple, testable hypothesis for the convenience of science may overlook the fact that in reality some populations may be regulated by a complex set of factors. It may be necessary to have complex theories to account for multiply-determined phenomena. It must also be recognized that although the scientific method may work admirably in mature sciences such as physics and chemistry, it may be inappropriate for the juvenile stages of a young science like ecology. Many of the branches of ecology are still in the early descriptive stages in which the experimental scientific method may not always be very useful. It must also be realized that although the scientific method may be well suited to examining subcomponents of ecosystems, this does not necessarily qualify the method as the ideal or only tool for advancing knowledge about entire ecosystems, at least not with our present incomplete knowledge of these ecosystems. A better approach is to design methods for the scientific evaluation of ecosystem-level theories that *can* deal with greater complexity. Such methods are to be found in multivariate statistics and computer simulation (see Chapter 17).

Comprehensive theories vary greatly in the number and type of factors that are included. This variation reflects the experience of the theorist, the species involved, and the type of environment. Climatic effects may be invoked directly and/or indirectly by their action through the soil, plants, or other animals. For herbivores, the effects of parasites, predators, diseases, competition, and food availability and quality may be included. For parasites and predators, the role of climate, disease, and the availability and nutritional value of the host may be important. A good example of how population theories are increasing in complexity is provided by Price et al. (1980), who argue that realistic progress in understanding the population dynamics of insect herbivores will not be made unless we consider the interactions between three trophic levels: plant–herbivore interactions and herbivore–parasite interactions. They note that it may not be possible to understand herbivore–parasite relationships unless we first understand herbivore–plant interactions. This includes the important question of herbivore nutrition (e.g., Mattson, 1980).

An example of the need for a comprehensive approach to explaining animal population dynamics is the history of attempts to explain the fascinating phenomenon of *cyclic population fluctuations* that characterize some species of herbivores that live at high latitudes.

Population cycles are fluctuations of relatively constant period (significantly different from random) around a long-term mean population density. Cyclic population fluctuations are seen in various parts of the world in different kinds of animal populations, including mammals, birds, and insects. They have always fascinated humans because in a variable and unpredictable world, predictable, regular change in animal abundance is unexpected. Perhaps the best known example of cyclic population fluctuations is that seen in Canada, where many different species of wildlife, including snowshoe hare, lynx, muskrat, and various species of tetraonid birds (e.g., grouse), exhibit an approximate 10-year cycle of abundance with a marked degree of synchrony between species and between widely separated areas (Keith, 1963).

Among the bewildering array of explanations that have been advanced to explain population cycles, are the following theories.

---

[3] Inductive reasoning: from the specific to the general. Deductive reasoning: from the general to the specific.

[4] The scientific method is discussed again in Chapter 17.

1. Cosmic theories, based on such things as sunspots, lunar cycles, variation in ultraviolet radiation (Douglas, 1919; Elton, 1924; Delury, 1932; Huntington, 1945; Rowan, 1950; Shelford, 1951a,b; Grange, 1949; Siivonen and Koskimmies, 1955; Koskimmies, 1955; Errington, 1963).
2. Climatic theories (Anderson, 1952; Williams, 1954; Frank, 1957; Watt, 1968).
3. Predation theories (Pitelka, 1957, but see Gilpin, 1973; Marshall, 1954; Chitty, 1960; Murray, 1965).
4. Disease theories (Lovat, 1911; Clarke, 1936; MacLulich, 1937; Errington, 1963).
5. Physiological ''shock'' theories (Green and Larson, 1938; Green and Evans, 1940; Christian, 1950, 1961, 1971).
6. Food supply theories (Lack, 1954).
7. Food quality theories (Elton, 1924; Braestrup, 1940; Hutchinson and Deevey, 1949; Carpenter, 1940; Mackenzie, 1952; Moss, 1967a,b; Siivonen, 1957; Laukhart, 1957, 1962; Kalela, 1962; Schultz, 1964; Pitelka, 1964; White, 1969, 1974, 1976).
8. Genetic-behavioral theories (Chitty, 1960, 1971; Krebs et al., 1973; Krebs and Myers, 1974).
9. Ecosystem theories, which consider all the major determinants of population regulation within a single conceptual framework. As an example of this type of theory,

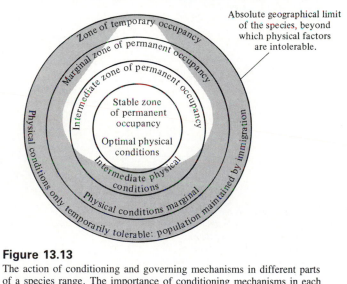

Figure 13.13

The action of conditioning and governing mechanisms in different parts of a species range. The importance of conditioning mechanisms in each zone is represented by the proportion of that zone which is shaded: of little or no importance in the central, stable zone, but preeminently important in the outer zone of temporary occupancy. (Modified after Huffaker and Messenger, 1964. Copyright Chapman and Hall Ltd. London. Used with permission of publisher and the authors.)

Figure 13.14 presents a conceptual ecosystem-level model of the 10-year cycle of wildlife in Canada's northern forests.

We still do not have a good explanation for cyclic population fluctuations, in spite of sixty years of work. Our failure to achieve an understanding of this phenomenon may well be the result of seeking *causal* explanations for a multiply determined phenomenon. Perhaps Elton's (1924) original ecosystem-level concept of these events (reflected in Kimmins, 1970: see Figure 13.14) may eventually prove to be fairly close to the truth.

13.5 Role of Predation in Population Regulation

Interest in predator–prey interactions was stimulated largely by Elton's (1924) descriptions of cyclic animal population fluctuations, and as with population growth in general, the topic soon became the subject of mathematical analysis. In the mid-1920s, simple equations were derived to describe, for populations with overlapping generations and continuous breeding, the effects of prey–population size on the dependent predator population, and vice versa (Lotka, 1925; Volterra, 1926). These involve a modification of the geometric growth curves for prey due to the presence of the predator.

$$\frac{dN}{dt} = r_1 N$$

becomes

$$\frac{dN}{dt} = (r_1 - k_1 P)N$$

where N is the numbers of prey, P the numbers of predators, r_1 the innate capacity for increase for the prey, and k_1 is a constant that measures the ability of the prey to escape predators.

The equation for the predator population in the absence of prey (assuming a geometric decline in the absence of food) is

$$\frac{dP}{dt} = -r_2 P$$

where r_2 is the death rate of predators in the absence of prey. This is modified as follows for the presence of prey:

$$\frac{dP}{dt} = (-r_2 + k_2 N)P$$

where k_2 is a measure of the ability of the predator to catch prey.

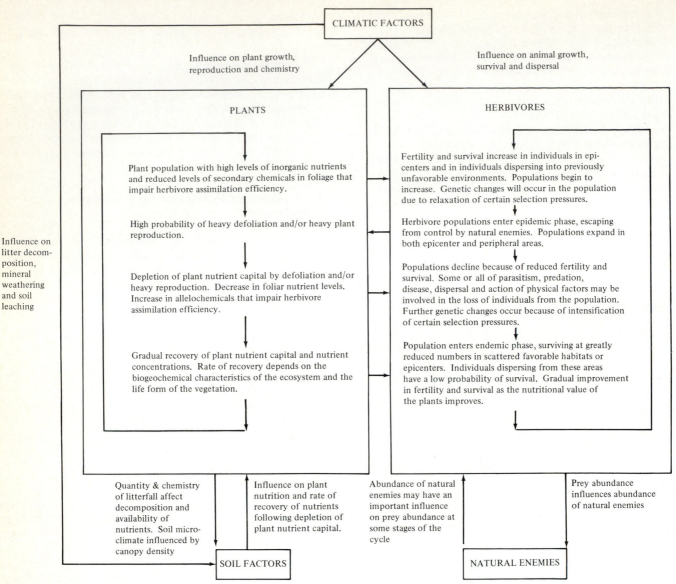

Figure 13.14

Summary of an ecosystem theory of the 10-year cycle of wildlife in Canada's northern forests (based on Kimmins, 1970). According to the theory (which is speculative and has not been tested), the period of the cycle is related to the biogeochemical characteristics of the northern forest type of ecosystem and the life form of the boreal vegetation. These give to these northern ecosystems a characteristic "resonance frequency" in response to large scale biogeochemical perturbations. Synchrony between populations in different regions is hypothesized to be under the control of infrequent large-scale weather patterns. These physical and chemical factors act as conditioning mechanisms which, in concert, produce a cyclic variation with a period of about 10 years in the potential for energy flow from plants to herbivores. The attainment of that potential is influenced by a variety of largely biotic factors, including several types of governing factors. The nutritional quality of the winter food supply is thought to be a critical factor in determining population size and in synchronizing the cycles of different cyclic species (see also Keith and Windberg, 1978).

Solving both these equations from some initial starting value produces oscillations of the two populations that are slightly out of phase with each other (Figure 13.15). The magnitude of the oscillation depends on the starting densities of the populations. Figure 13.15 can be summarized in a graph (a *phase diagram*) of predator density against prey density which eliminates the time dimension. Figure 13.16 presents phase diagrams for a variety of initial starting populations. From this type of graph one can predict those combinations of predator and prey densities that will permit the prey to increase in numbers, and those combinations that will lead to a decline in prey abundance.

Although this method of evaluating predator–prey interactions has its uses, mathematical and graphical analyses of interspecific competition and of population growth have rarely proven to be an accurate description of populations in their natural environments. There are too many aspects of population growth and of competition that are ignored in simple equations (too many antecedent determinants of population growth are left unaccounted for). The equations are helpful in that they give us a basic pattern of processes, but we must go to the field if we are to really understand what is happening. With this in mind, we can ask the question: How realistic are the predictions of these simple predator–prey equations?

A. Experimental Investigation of Predator–Prey Relationships

The first test of the predictions was made by Gause (1934) in a laboratory study in which he attempted to raise a population of protozoans *(Paramecium caudatum)* together with a predator *(Didinium nasutum)* in a liquid nutrient medium made by boiling oats in water and using the clear supernatant liquid with an inoculation of bacteria as food for the *Paramecium*. In a series of experiments in which he varied the starting population size and the size of the container, Gause experienced nothing but failure. An initial

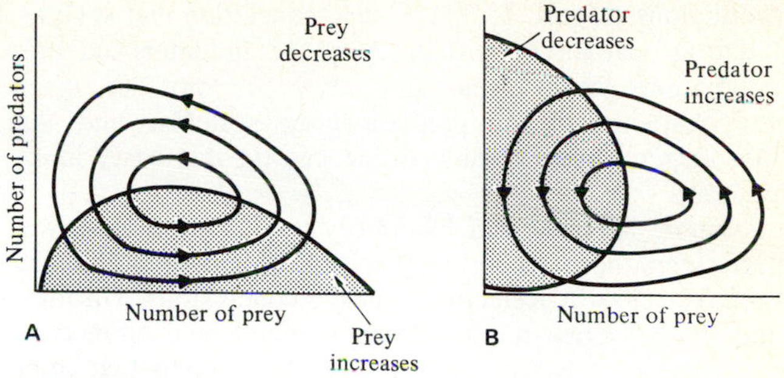

Figure 13.16

Classical Lotka-Volterra predator-prey oscillations expressed without the time dimension in the form of a phase diagram. The curves show the direction of change in numbers over time associated with various combinations of predators and prey. Following a curve around the circle defines the numbers of predators and prey over a time sequence. The shape of the curves depends on the values of r_1 and r_2, k_1 and k_2. The concentric lines represent different initial combinations of predators and prey. (A) Predator-prey combinations for which prey increase (shaded area) or decrease. (B) Predator-prey combinations for which predators increase (shaded area) or decrease. (Based on Rosenzweig and MacArthur 1963. Copyright The University of Chicago Press. Used with permission of the publisher.)

increase in *Paramecium* led to an increase in *Didinium*, which ate all the *Paramecium* and then starved to death. Only when he introduced a refuge where *Paramecium* could hide from *Didinium* could he change this pattern. When he replaced the clear liquid medium with the entire boiled oats medium (which resulted in a sediment of oat fragments in the bottom of the container), some of the *Paramecium* entered the sediment and thereby escaped predation. The *Didinium* eliminated the *Paramecium* from the liquid medium and starved to death as usual, but then the *Paramecium* emerged from the sediment and entered a period of geometric increase in the liquid. Gause then examined the effect of repeated additions of predator and prey to a simple nutrient medium. This stratagem finally resulted in something that approximated the Lotka–Volterra

Figure 13.15

Classical predator-prey population oscillations as predicted by the Lotka-Volterra equations described in the text, with $r_1 = 1.0$, $k_1 = 0.1$, $r_2 = 0.5$ and $k_2 = 0.02$. (After Krebs, 1972. Copyright C. J. Krebs. Used with permission of the author and Harper & Row, Publishers.)

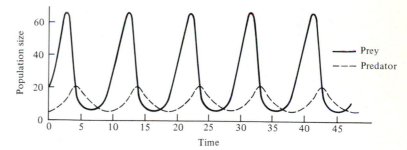

predictions (Figure 13.17). Gause concluded that such oscillations cannot be produced by the predator and prey populations themselves, that they are not an inherent characteristic of predator–prey systems, and that they depend upon outside influences (in this case, immigration).

A more sophisticated laboratory test of these ideas was performed more recently by a Californian entomologist, Huffaker (1958). Rejecting Gause's conclusions, Huffaker undertook a series of experiments in which he examined the relationship between two mites: the six-spotted mite *(Eotetranychus sexmaculatus), which feeds on oranges, and a predatory mite (Typhlodromus occidentalis),* which feeds on *Eotetranychus*. The main feature of the experiments was a progressive increase in the degree of complexity and spatial heterogeneity of the mites' environment as the series progressed.

To start with, the predator was placed on a single orange infested with six-spotted mites, which were rapidly eliminated, followed by the death by starvation of the predatory mite. The experiment was then repeated with 40 oranges, some of which were partly covered with paraffin or paper to act as refuges for the prey and barriers to the dispersal of the predator. In other 40-orange experiments Huffaker replaced some of the oranges by balls so that he could vary the dispersion of feeding sites. As with the single orange, the 40-orange experiments all led to a final elimination of both mites. However, as the complexity of the experiment was increased in succeeding experiments, something approximating a Lotka–Volterra oscillation was eventually obtained in an experiment involving 252 oranges separated by a complex system of barriers and vertical sticks that facilitated the distribution of the six-spotted mite. Whenever a predator discovered an orange with a prey population on it, the prey was eliminated, but sufficient numbers of the prey mite dispersed and founded new populations on uncolonized oranges that its overall population survived. When the predator reduced the prey populations markedly, the prey became very hard to find and the predator population declined.

The conclusion drawn from this experiment was that if the experimental environment is heterogeneous enough and large enough to permit the normal local movements of predator and prey, reasonably stable predator–prey oscillations can be sustained for considerable periods. There is evidence that if such experiments are successfully maintained for many generations, adaptations may occur that reduce the amplitude of the oscillations and thereby reduce the risk of the populations being eliminated (Pimentel et al., 1963).

Apparently, the classical predator–prey oscillation can occur in diverse laboratory habitats. Does this mean that predators play a major role in regulating populations in nature? The answer to this is "it depends upon the species." The conclusion from many studies is that in noncyclic, nonterritorial species, predation may be very important in regulating population levels. In territorial animals and in populations subject to cyclic population fluctuations, predators appear to act as a compensating mortality factor: the prey species would die anyway. This is not to say that predation of one sort or another cannot be very important. The biological control of prickly pear in Australia, *Lantana* in Hawaii, St. John's wort in United States, and many other successful cases of biological control of weeds by introduced phytophagous insects shows the power of herbivory. Many plant species in the world are maintained at low populations by herbivores that are scarcely ever even noticed, so low is their population. Biological control of insect pests has been equally successful. Perhaps the best known example of successful biological control is the case of the vedalia beetle *(Rodolia cardinalis),* which eliminated the cottony-cushion scale *(Icerya purchasi)* as a major pest problem after the vedalia was introduced to California fruit orchards in 1888. In 1887 the California citrus industry was threatened with destruction from massive infestation of the scale. The successful solution to this serious economic problem was the beginning of the increasingly popular practice of biological control of insect pests by the use of predators.

B. Functional and Numerical Predator Responses

We cannot leave the subject of predation without a brief review of one of the most significant attempts to understand how predators work and why they are sometimes able to control populations and sometimes not. Holling (1959, 1965), then an entomologist working on European pine sawfly populations in Canada, investigated the ability of a predator of this sawfly to respond to changes in the abundance of its food. The masked shrew (*Sorex* sp.) feeds on sawfly cocoons which are hidden in the forest floor of pine plantations. By examining the basic components of predation (searching time, capture time, handling time, appetite satiation, and recovery from satiation), Holling was able to describe the *functional* response of a predator to its prey population. This is defined as the change in number of prey eaten per predator per unit time as the population of its prey increases.

Investigations revealed three basic types of functional response:

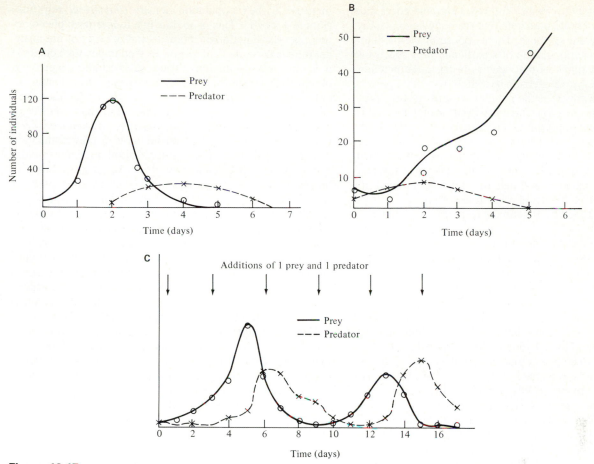

Figure 13.17
The interaction of two ciliated protozoans in a laboratory culture. (A) The prey *(Paramecium caudatum)* is eliminated by its predator *(Didinium nasutum),* which then starves. (B) The addition of a refuge for the prey in the bottom of the container resulted in the elimination of the predator and the subsequent increase in prey numbers. (C) A more permanent predator-prey oscillation in the absence of a prey refuge was attained by periodic additions (immigration) of one prey and one predator. (After Gause, 1934.)

In Type 1, the number of prey consumed per predator per unit time increases linearly with increase in prey density (as predicted by the Lotka–Volterra model) until some saturation value is reached, at which the number of prey taken per predator becomes independent of prey density; the rate of ingestion of prey equals the maximum digestion rate of the predator. In this type, the predator takes a constant proportion of the prey as the population grows until saturation density is reached, when the proportion starts to decline.

In Type 2, the increase in the number of prey taken for each increase in prey declines steadily until it levels off and the predator becomes insensitive to prey density. Type 2 is found in many invertebrate predators and is largely the result of handling time. It takes a finite amount of time to locate a prey, but this decreases as prey density increases. Handling time (the time to overpower and consume the prey) remains constant irrespective of density. Consequently, even if the predator can eat continuously, an upper level of prey consumption is set by how quickly the predator can consume each prey. In this type, the proportion of the population taken by the predator is initially high but declines steadily.

Type 3 functional response follows a sigmoid curve and is typical of vertebrate predators that are *polyphagous* (prey on several different species). The response of the predator to increases in the population of a particular prey species is small at low densities of that species because the predator would gain little by transferring its search from other prey to this species. However, as the population density of the prey species continues to grow, predators start switching to this improved feeding opportunity and form a *search image* for the species (Tinbergen, 1960). They learn to recognize the particular prey and where and when it may be found, which increases their rate of predation on this species. At higher prey densities, satiation and handling time act to level off the response curve as in the other two curves.

These three types of functional response are shown in Figure 13.18.

The slopes of the three response curves vary according to the efficiency of the predator at finding the prey. In Type 3 it also depends upon the degree of polyphagy in the predator. A predator that prefers a particular prey or is opportunistic (it recognizes a good opportunity when it sees it) will show a much more rapid functional response than will a species that also feeds on other prey, whose numbers may not be increasing. Holling found that the short-tailed shrew (*Blarina* sp.), which is a comparatively uncommon but opportunistic feeder, responded to the density of pine sawfly cocoons much more rapidly than did the deer mouse (*Peromyscus* sp.) or masked shrew (*Sorex* sp.) (Figure 13.19A). Because of the rapid nature of its numerical response, *Blarina* is an important component of the contribution of predators to population regulation as long as the prey population does not get close to the upper asymptote of the response curve.

Predators can also respond to greater prey numbers by an increase in their population density (*numerical response*) (Figure 13.19B). This is obviously a longer-term phenomenon than the functional response, and because of the inherent time lags, numerical responses tend to generate classical predator–prey oscillations. There can be three major types of numerical response: (1) predator populations may increase, (2) they may show no response, or (3) they may decrease as prey populations increase. For many species of predator, immigration, greater natality, and reduced juvenile mortality accompanies an increase in prey population density, and this leads to a growth in the predator population (type 1). The predator numbers do not grow linearly, however, since food is not the only determinant of predator carrying capacity. If the predator feeds on other species, it may respond to an increase in one prey species simply by switching its feeding to that species with relatively little change in either total predation or predator population density (type 2). As the prey species declines, the predator switches back to alternative foods. Increase in prey abundance may result in increased abundance of, and competition from, other species of predator, and this may lead to a decline in numbers of the first predator (type 3).

Numerical and functional response information is interesting, but it is the *total response* (functional × numerical) that is of real interest in assessing the importance of predation in population regulation. Figure 13.19C shows the total response of the three species of small mammals preying on European pine sawfly. Note that below a certain density of sawfly cocoons, each of these predators responded effectively to prey density. However, for each species, and for their combined activity, there was a prey density above which they became less and less effective as a population control factor. This critical prey density is called *escape density*.

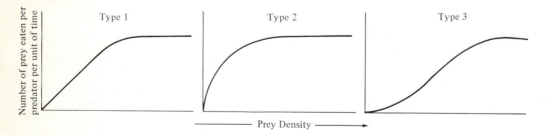

Figure 13.18

Three major patterns of functional response of predators to increasing prey populations as proposed by Holling (1959). In Type 1 there is a linear increase in number of prey consumed per predator per unit time, up to some upper limit. In Type 2 there is an asymptotic approach and in Type 3 a sigmoid approach to the upper limit. (Copyright Entomological Society of Canada. Used with permission of Ent. Soc. Canada and the author.)

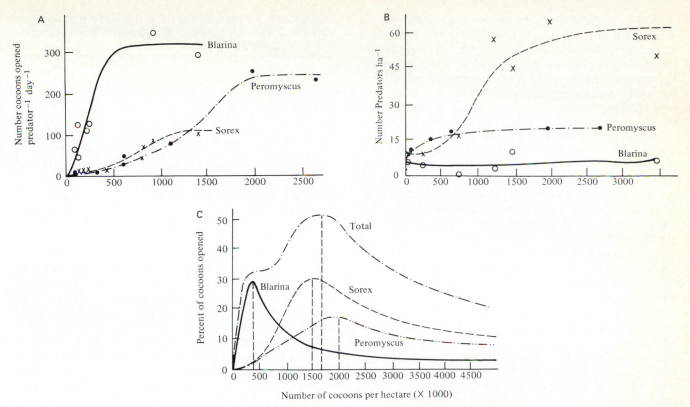

Figure 13.19

Functional (A), numerical (B), and total (C) response of three species of small mammalian predators to changes in the density of one of their foods: cocoons of the European pine sawfly (after Holling, 1959). *Blarina* had the greatest and most rapid functional response, but because of its negligible numerical response it is only an effective predator at lower population densities. *Sorex* was the most effective predator because although it had only a modest functional response, it had the highest numerical response. The vertical dotted lines in (C) show prey escape densities, above which the individual predators, or their combined activity, become progressively less effective in controlling the prey. (Copyright Entomological Society of Canada. Used with permission of Ent. Soc. Canada and the author.)

13.6   Plant Population Biology

In spite of the fact that the earliest writings in the modern period of population ecology related to plants, much of the work on populations has been done by animal ecologists. Notable exceptions can be found in the work of people like Harper (1977) and his students. In some ways plants are easier to study than animals because they are stationary, because they are easy to enumerate, and because behavior does not complicate matters. However, from the population dynamics standpoint, plants can present problems because in some respects a plant is more like a colony than an individual animal. Each leaf on the plant competes with other leaves for the basic necessities of life: water, nutrients,

light, and space. Each leaf has its own life history from birth (as a primordium on a meristem) through growth to maturity and eventual senescence, unless it succumbs to some mortality factor first. Populations of leaves have a survivorship curve and an age-class structure, and they undergo population growth from a small number of cotyledons on the germinating seedling to the large population on the fully mature plant. The leaf population may have discrete generations, as in deciduous perennial or annual plants, or overlapping generations, as in evergreen conifers that maintain their leaves for many years. In fact, a plant really is analogous to a population of buds or of leaves.

Plant population biology is classified by Harper into several different phases. The first phase, which he calls the *seed rain,* is analogous to the two population processes of natality and dispersal. Plants have a genetically determined fecundity (potential maximum number of reproductive propagules per plant per year or per generation) and an environmentally determined fertility (number of reproductive propagules actually produced per plant per year or per generation). The seed rain varies as a function of distance from the plant (Figure 13.20), wind, and any other factor that influences seed dispersal. The seed rain contributes to the *seed bank:* the population of living but ungerminated seeds contained in the soil (Figure 13.21). The seed bank of forests can be as large as 3000 seeds per m² (Table 13.6).

Each cohort of reproductive propagules has a characteristic survivorship curve in any particular environment. As in many animal populations, there is heavy juvenile mortality in most plant populations. Figure 13.22 shows the causes of mortality among seedlings of Douglas-fir on six different substrates under three light regimes in a clearcut area in Oregon. Interestingly, the total mortality did not vary greatly by substrate or light condition even though the type of mortality agent or the relative importance thereof varied. Compensatory mortality appears to have been important in this study.

Tree populations have survivorship curves and age-class distributions which vary greatly between species and the stage of development of the plant community. Light-demanding pioneer species tend to have a small number of age classes (i.e., are even-aged) that pass up and out of the age-class distribution as the species is eliminated in the

Table 13.6 Number of Seeds in the Seed Bank of Various Different Forests in Maine (Data from Olmsted and Curtis, 1947)

Vegetation	Seeds[a] m⁻²
White pine (70-yr stand)	1000 (173)
White pine (80-yr stand)	320 —
Spruce, fir (30-yr stand)	2850 (49)
Red pine plantation (24-yr stand)	532 (5)
Beech, yellow birch, sugar maple (110-yr stand)	1000 (91)
Beech, yellow birch, sugar maple (50-yr stand)	218 (42)
Sugar maple (150-yr stand)	122 (11)

[a] Values without parentheses are direct counts by microscopic examination. Values in parentheses are the result of germination tests.

course of successional development (see Chapter 15). Shade-tolerant climax species in old growth forests have a more stable age distribution (Figure 13.23). Figure 13.24 presents survivorship curves for various tree species on the eastern slope of the Rocky Mountains near Boulder, Colorado. The different shapes of the curves match the successional status of the trees. Lodgepole pine is a pioneer species which, in the absence of fire, is normally excluded in 100 years, Ponderosa pine is a midseral species, and the mature (climax) forest is dominated by Engelmann spruce (Knowles and Grant, 1983). Survivorship curves and life table analysis were used by Yarie (1981) to determine the historical frequency of forest fires in Alaska.

Figure 13.20

The seed rain from *Picea engelmannii* in three forest clearings in Utah as a function of distance from the stand edge. (Data from Roe, 1967.)

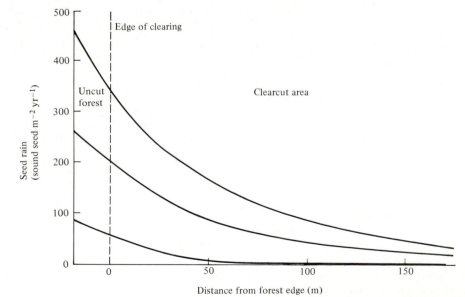

Plants compete for limited resources in their environment, and both their population development and the carrying capacity may be determined by density-independent factors. The carrying capacity for foliage (or leaf area index) has been shown to be strongly influenced by available soil moisture (Grier and Running, 1977), and the biomass of stems, foliage, and so on, is much greater on a fertile site than an infertile site. Since leaves can be considered to have some of the characteristics of individuals in socially structured populations, available moisture can be considered as a density-independent factor determining leaf populations (see Figure 4.14). Density-dependent factors also play a role and intraspecific competition can severely limit population development. For example, following wildfire, lodgepole pine *(Pinus contorta)* may regenerate at densities as high as 1,235,500 stems per hectare (Smithers, 1957), and densities of nearly 250,000 stems per hectare have been reported in a stand 70 years old (Mason, 1915). Under these conditions none of the individuals get enough light, moisture, and nutrients to develop properly and the population stagnates (Figure 13.2). Such stands may only reach a height of 1.2 m at an age of 50 years (Horton, 1956).

Interspecific competition is also a significant factor, shade-intolerant species being outcompeted by shade-tolerant species, while trees tolerant of low fertility will outcompete nutrient-demanding species under conditions of low

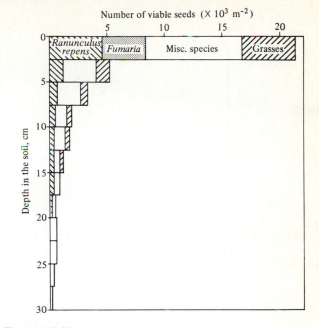

Figure 13.21

The seed bank in a rich hay meadow in Wales. The graph shows the number of viable seeds of various species at various depths in the soil. (Data from Chippindale and Milton, 1934; after Harper 1977. Used with permission of Academic Press and author.)

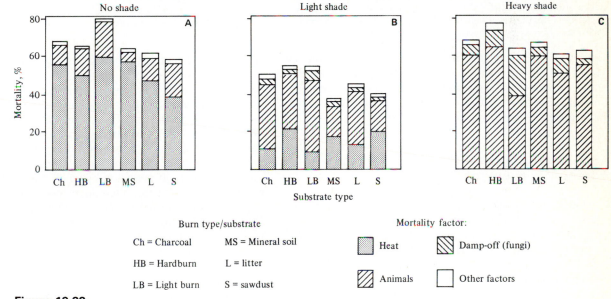

Figure 13.22

Causes of Douglas-fir seedling mortality on six different substrates under three degrees of shading in a clearcut in Oregon. (After Hermann and Chilcote, 1965. Used with permission of R. K. Hermann.)

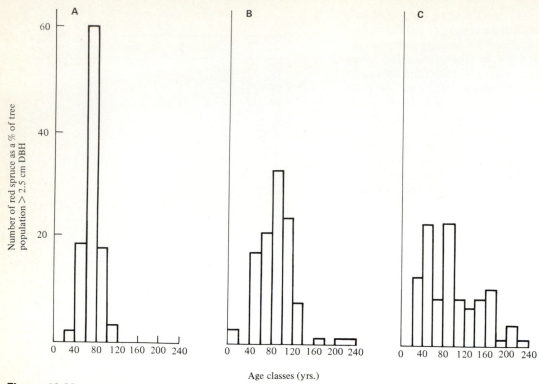

Figure 13.23

Age distributions among red spruce *(Picea rubens)* populations in early, mid, and late seral stages of the spruce-fir forests of the Maine coast. (A) Pioneer deciduous hardwood stage. (B) Seral red spruce stage. (C) Spruce-fir climax stage. (Data from Davis, 1966; after Harper, 1977. Used with permission of Academic Press, J. L. Harper, R. B. Davis, and The Ecological Society of America.)

fertility. Natural enemies also play an important role in plant population dynamics. We have already discussed examples in which diseases and/or herbivores have virtually eliminated certain species of plant over large areas, and more examples are given in Chapter 14.

13.7 Importance of Population Ecology in Forest Management

Timber management is, to a large degree, applied population ecology. Foresters attempt to establish a population of a particular genotype of a particular species with the objective of attaining a particular number of mature individuals of a particular size at a particular age. This involves manipulation of the age-class structure to achieve a predetermined age-class distribution, which in turn requires a knowledge of the survivorship curve of that genotype under the particular conditions. In the nursery, the forester must

account for percent viability and percent seedling mortality if he or she is to sow enough seeds to achieve production goals. The forester must know about intraspecific competition in the seedbed and its effects on seedling morphology if he or she is to get the right type of seedling for planting out. When direct seeding of clearcuts is used, the forester should have a life table for those seeds in the application area, to know how many seeds to apply to achieve a desired population of seedlings. If predation by small mammals is an important mortality factor, alternative foods can be provided (e.g., sunflower seeds) to cause predator switching (Sullivan, 1980). During stand management the forester should know the natural mortality rate of the trees so that he or she can plan the intensity and frquency of thinning (subject, of course, to economic and manpower constraints). This type of information is sometimes provided to foresters in the form of natural stocking curves, but unfortunately the population information needed for sophisticated population manipulation is frequently lacking.

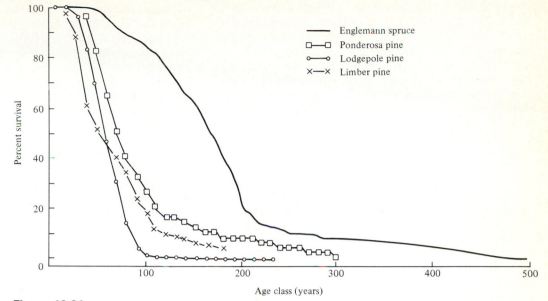

Figure 13.24
Survivorship curves for four species of conifer in the Rocky Mountains of Colorado. Engelmann spruce and ponderosa pine are climax dominants on the appropriate sites, whereas lodgepole pine is a pioneer species which colonizes burned areas. The limber pine is neither climax nor pioneer. It can play either role, but is often found in patches at a variety of seral stages. (After Knowles and Grant, 1983. Used with permission of the Ecological Society of American and P. Knowles.)

Wildlife management, range management, and fish management, which are all variously associated with forestry, are areas where there is a great need for improved knowledge of population ecology. Much more information is required concerning carrying capacity, natality, mortality, dispersal, survivorship curves, stationary age-class distributions, and the nature of population regulation (e.g., the importance of weather, territoriality and other self-regulating mechanisms, parasites, predators, disease, food availability and quality, etc.) if we are to be more successful in managing animal populations in forest ecosystems.

Control of insects and diseases is a vitally important area of forest management. Enormous quantities of potentially harvestable biomass are lost annually to these biotic mortality agents. Their control is expensive and not always biologically or economically warranted. They may merely kill trees that would otherwise be killed by some other mortality agent. Control is often not initiated until a point in the outbreak at which the population is declining naturally, and high pest population levels early in the pest's life history may not necessarily mean economic damage if some severe mortality agent operates on later stages of the pest population. In the absence of adequate population information, the forester may be committed to expensive, unnecessary, and ineffective control measures. If the forester is to be able to predict the course of pest population trends accurately enough to be able to apply control measures in an ecologically sound manner, the major determinants of their populations must be known.

13.8   Summary

For many ecologists, understanding what controls the distribution and abundance of organisms is the focus of their science. These population ecologists are concerned with the four major factors that determine population size and distribution: natality (the rate at which individuals enter the population through reproduction), mortality (the rate at which individuals die), and immigration and emigration (the rates at which individuals enter and/or leave the population through movement). These four processes are in turn regulated by a wide variety of physical and biological factors.

Populations have a set of attributes that are unique to this level of biological organization. They have a pattern of dispersion in their environment, there are characteristic patterns of change in abundance over time (either increasing or decreasing), there is a characteristic schedule of mortality over the life of a particular cohort, and there is an age-class structure to the population. Understanding populations involves understanding how these attributes are determined.

Development of theories about the regulation of the abundance of animal populations has engaged the minds of population ecologists for more than three-quarters of a century. The early theories were causal in nature; they sought to explain population dynamics in terms of a single factor or a limited set of factors. Great controversies raged for many decades about whether density-dependent biotic factors, especially competition, were preeminent, or whether density-independent factors, especially physical factors of the environment, were primarily responsible for controlling abundance and distribution. Most of these early theories were based on the action of factors external to the population, but over the past three decades additional theories have been developed, based on behavioral, physiological, and genetic mechanisms—factors internal to the population. A more recent school of thought has taken a position midway between these competing ideas. The comprehensive school suggests that many different types of factor are involved, but their relative importance varies for different types of organism and in different types of environment.

Predation is a mechanism of population control that was long felt to be important in regulating prey populations. Analytical investigations have shown that in some circumstances, especially at low to moderate prey population, predation can be a major factor preventing increase in prey abundance, but that above a certain density it becomes relatively unimportant. This threshold density is specific to each particular predator-prey system. Knowledge of the functional, numerical, and total response of predators to varying prey abundance is of critical importance to the design of programs of biological control of pests based on predation.

Population ecology has traditionally been the domain of animal ecologists, but in the past few decades a school of plant population ecology has been developed. There are strong parallels, but also significant differences, between plant and animal populations that require slightly different approaches for the two groups. Despite these differences, considerably improved insights into the best way of managing plant populations can be obtained by applying concepts and techniques developed for animal population ecology.

Forest resource managers are concerned with ecosystems, and the ecosystem approach must be the basis on which they conduct their activities. However, their immediate concern is often with populations and therefore their knowledge of ecosystem ecology must be complemented by a sound appreciation of population ecology. As noted in Chapter 3, a focus on populations is completely compatible with the ecosystem concept as long as there is explicit recognition of the ecosystem framework within which populations exist.

14.1 Introduction

The survival, abundance, and distribution of a species depend upon its adaptation to the physical environment and to the other living organisms with which it shares that environment. In Chapter 13 we examined the role of intraspecific interactions and of the physical environment in determining the abundance, distribution, and population dynamics of a species, as well as certain interactions between species in different trophic levels (predator–prey interactions). This chapter focuses on the structure and organization of the complex mixture of species populations that exist together in what we call the *biotic community*, and on relationships between different species occupying the same or different trophic levels.

Populations do not exist in isolation, except in artificial experimental environments. Nor do they exist in nature in association with only a population of a single species of host, competitor, or natural enemy. Even in a wheat field or a dense young plantation of Douglas-fir trees there will be other species of plants (agricultural weeds, or mosses, lichens, and other minor forest vegetation, respectively), the number and variety of which will tend to increase as the age of the stand increases.

Dense monocultures (communities dominated by one species of plant) do occur in unmanaged forests or native grasslands, but they are much less common than are mixed communities. The dominant plant is usually accompanied by a surprising variety of other organisms. Botanists and zoologists studying the relatively species-poor beech forests of Switzerland concluded that this type of community contains approximately 10,500 species of plants, animals, and microbes (Daubenmire, 1968). Even in dense man-made monocultures of conifers, one is still confronted by an amazing diversity of organisms coexisting and interacting in still incompletely understood ways. Decomposer organisms in the soil, fungal and insect pathogens, various species of lichens and mosses, a scattered ground flora of herbs and shrubs, and the bird and animal populations that are inevitably associated with any plant community together form an integrated, interacting system that is responsible for the observed patterns of energy flow, biomass accumulation, and nutrient cycling.

The biotic community has been defined as "an assemblage of plants, animals, bacteria and fungi that live in an environment and interact with one another, forming a distinctive living system with its own composition, structure, environmental relations, development and function" (Whittaker, 1975a). Each community is characterized by a particular species composition, vertical structure, patterns of

14 Community Ecology

change over time, biomass, energy flow, and nutrient cycling. It is the biotic component of the ecosystem: the biocoenose of the biogeocoenose. In common with the term ecosystem, *community* has no implicit definition of spatial extent or boundaries, although its geographical extent can be defined by the *plant association* or phytocoenose.

The community can be split into three subdivisions for purposes of study and description: the plant community, the animal community, and the microbial community. It is often convenient to make this subdivision, but it must be remembered that the intimate degree of association and interaction among these three components requires that they are never considered in isolation. We have already seen that although a clear understanding of intraspecific mechanisms of population increase and decline is essential to an overall understanding of ecosystem structure and function, only when such an understanding is placed within an ecosystem framework will it confer reliable powers of prediction about the ecosystem. Similarly, knowledge of the plant community alone is frequently insufficient on its own as the basis for reliable predictions about the biotic community or ecosystem as a whole (see also the discussion in Chapter 16).

Early interest in communities focused on the plant component. From the time of Theophrastus until the middle of the nineteenth century, little or no recognition was given to the important role of animals or microbes. Karl Mobius, a marine biologist who studied oyster communities in the late nineteenth century, has been credited with being the first to emphasize the importance of studying the entire biotic community. He recognized the intimate association among oysters (the object of his study), the algae on which they feed, the parasites that prey on them, and other organisms (e.g., sponges) that compete with the oysters for space. Recognition of the integration of the components of a biotic community into a functional system led to the idea of the community as a *supraorganism,* which in turn led the English ecologist Tansley to develop the ecosystem concept in 1935. More recent studies in the ecological subdisciplines of energetics and biogeochemistry have confirmed many of the early ideas concerning the holistic and integrated nature of the biotic community.

Development of the analogy between the community and the individual organism is largely attributed to the American ecologist Clements. He compared the developmental stages of a community, as it progresses from a group of pioneer organisms that invades an unoccupied area to a final, mature, self-replacing, or *climax* community (see Chapter 15), with the developmental stages of an individual from birth to maturity. He felt that a community, like an organism, is born, grows, matures, reproduces, and dies. The fact that the climax community on many sites can repeatedly redevelop through a fairly regular pattern of stages following successive disturbances was used to support the analogy.

The concept of the community as a supraorganism has never received widespread acceptance and is not popular today because of the numerous fundamental differences between a community and an individual organism. For instance, the death of an organism is not really comparable to the replacement of a climax community by the community of an earlier stage of ecosystem development. Similarly, the successive replacement of communities through successional development cannot be compared with the growth of an individual. Certain successional stages can sometimes be omitted from certain types of successional sequence, but it is impossible for any of the stages of ontogeny to be omitted from the development of an individual organism. Above all, communities lack the strict genetic definition that is inherent in the individual. In spite of these reservations, it is generally recognized that communities are organic entities in which there is a considerable degree of internal interconnectedness, and many ecologists still accept the concept of the community as a *quasiorganism*. This simply says that

there are certain similarities and parallels between these two different levels of biological organization.

The early focus on plant communities probably occurred because plants account for the majority of the organic biomass in most terrestrial ecosystems and because plants are frequently the physically dominant and visually most impressive members of the community. While the animal community often plays an important role in regulating the composition and structure of the plant community, the former is largely dependent on the latter for food and shelter. Consequently, animal communities are generally more determined by the plant community than vice versa, notable exceptions notwithstanding. Animal and microbial communities are also more difficult to study than is the more static plant community.

This chapter begins by examining the structure and pattern of plant communities. This is followed by a discussion of how these parameters vary along environmental gradients, both locally and continentally. A description of tree lines will be followed by a description of the major types of interaction between the different species in the community. The chapter concludes with a discourse on the diversity of communities.

14.2 Structure and Growth Forms of Plant Communities

Plant communities have several characteristics by which they can be described: structure, life form, spatial pattern, species composition, successional stage, biomass, and functional processes (energy flow and nutrient cycling). We start by examining structure, life form, and pattern.

The *structure* of a plant community refers to the vertical arrangement and spatial organization of the plants. It does not require many visits to a forested area to give one the impression that vegetation occurs in distinct *layers* (subdivisions of the vegetation based upon plant height) and that each layer is characterized by one or more distinct groups or *synusiae* of plants. In a tropical forest the tree layer consists of a tree synusia and a woody climber synusia. The herb layer of a temperate forest may include a perennial herbaceous grass synusia, an annual herb synusia and a bulbous perennial herb synusia. Visits to forests in different localities within a climatic region and to forests in various climatic regions will expand this impression to include the fact that the structure or layering of forests varies between different sites within a region as well as between different regions. In fact, community structure is a characteristic feature of different sites and regions. The structure of the plant community on a dry, rocky ridge is different from that in the valley below (see Figure 16.10). The structure of the boreal forest varies from that of temperate deciduous forests, and both differ from the structure of a tropical rain forest (Figure 14.1).

The vertical structure of plant communities is the consequence of variations in the *growth form* or gross morphology of the plants (cf. the life forms of Raunkiaer, Figure 8.13). The overall growth form of communities is referred to as their *physiognomy*. A forest is an ecosystem characterized by a plant community dominated by plants with a tree physiognomy. A prairie is an ecosystem dominated by plants with a herbaceous, graminoid physiognomy. The physiognomy of the plant community is defined by the dominant plant species, but most communities also include species representing several other growth forms organized into one or more subordinate layers. For example, forest plant communities are generally composed of five major layers (Figure 14.2): (1) *trees*—plants with large woody, perennial, aboveground stems, generally taller than 3 m; (2) *shrubs*—plants with medium to small, woody, perennial aboveground stems, mostly less than 3 m tall; (3) *herbs*—plants without a perennial aboveground stem; (4) *thallophytes*—nonvascular plants without perennial underground or aboveground stems; and (5) *epiphytes*—plants growing wholly aboveground on other plants. An additional layer found in tropical and some higher latitude forests is (6) *lianas*—woody climbers or vines.

Most of these layers can be subdivided on the basis of height. In the description of plant communities, ecologists may divide the tree layer into three sublayers and the shrubs into two sublayers. Some foresters divide the tree layer into several *crown classes* (e.g., dominant, codominant, intermediate, and suppressed) on the basis of the competitive status of the crown. These classes are used for both stand description and for prescribing thinning treatments for over-

Table 14.1 Kraft's Classification of Trees by Crown Class (Based on Baker, 1950)

Tree Class	Description
Dominant	Crowns are somewhat above the general canopy level and are therefore fully exposed to overhead light and partially exposed to lateral light. In multi-aged stands, dominants may develop very large, coarse branches and wide crowns. Such dominants are called *wolf* trees. Wolf trees, which can also develop in even-aged stands, may result for genetic as well as for environmental reasons.
Codominant	Together with dominants, codominant trees form the main canopy. They are not quite as tall as the dominants and receive light predominantly from overhead. They are normally almost as vigorous (thrifty) as the dominants.
Intermediate	Crowns are definitely subordinate to the main canopy trees, and because they experience strong lateral competition for light and space the crowns are often narrow. However, crowns of intermediate trees do form a component of the main canopy. Light is received from overhead through gaps between the codominants and/or dominants.
Suppressed	Crowns are below and do not penetrate up into the main canopy. They receive little direct overhead light. Most light comes from sunflecks or indirect light. Suppressed trees are commonly weak and slow-growing. However, some trees in this crown class may be growing up vigorously towards the overhead canopy in which an opening has recently been made.
Dead trees	

Table 14.2 Major Growth Forms of Terrestrial Plants (Beard, 1973)

Trees (larger woody plants, mostly well above 3 m tall)
  Needle-leaved (mainly conifers—pine, spruce, larch, redwood, and so on)
  Broad-leaved evergreen (many tropical and subtropical trees, mostly with medium-sized leaves)
  Evergreen-sclerophyll (with smaller, tough, evergreen leaves)
  Broad-leaved deciduous (leaves shed in the temperate zone winter or in the tropical dry season)
  Thorn-trees (armed with spines, in many cases with compound, deciduous leaves)
  Rosette trees (unbranched, with a crown of large leaves—palms and tree-ferns)
Lianas (woody climbers or vines)
Shrubs (smaller woody plants, mostly below 3 m in height)
  Needle-leaved
  Broad-leaved evergreen
  Broad-leaved deciduous
  Evergreen-sclerophyll
  Rosette shrubs (yucca, agave, aloe, palmetto, and so on)
  Stem succulents (cacti, certain euphorbias, and so on)
  Thorn-shrubs
  Semishrubs (suffrutescent, i.e., with the upper parts of the stems and branches dying back in unfavorable seasons)
  Subshrubs or dwarf shrubs (low shrubs spreading near the ground surface, less than 25 cm high)
Epiphytes (plants growing wholly above the ground surface, on other plants)
Herbs (plants without perennial aboveground woody stems)
  Ferns
  Graminoids (grasses, sedges, and other grass-like plants)
  Forbs (herbs other than ferns and graminoids)
Thallophytes
  Lichens
  Mosses
  Liverworts

A   B

Figure 14.1
Structure of forest communities. (A) Black spruce stand in Quebec exhibiting the characteristic structure of many boreal forests on mesic sites: dense, rather uniform stocking with trees of rather uniform size, low tree species diversity,
and an understory limited mainly to a thick carpet of mosses. (B) Temperate deciduous hardwood forest: a second-
growth stand on the Allegheny Plateau of northwestern Pennsylvania. Sugar and red maples, beech, black cherry, and
yellow poplar are the major species in an overstory of moderate diversity. Such stands are often multi-aged and
multi-storied, with a considerable understory. (Photo courtesy of D. A. Marquis; see Marquis, 1975, 1981.) (C) *Left,*
Tropical rain forest near Manaus, Amazonas, showing the vertical complexity of the vegetation (several canopy layers). *Right,* When the large emergent trees die or blow down, large gaps are created, which creates the characteristic
hetero-geneity of the structure and composition of tropical rain forests.

crowded plantations or natural stands (Table 14.1). For a
summary of dominance classifications, see Daniel et al.
(1979).

Most of the major growth forms have several subdivisions. *Herbs* can be split into *grasses, ferns,* and *forbs*
(herbs that are neither ferns nor grasses). Trees can be split
into needle-leaved trees, broad-leaved evergreen trees,
broad-leaved deciduous trees, rosette trees, and so on.

Thallophytes can be divided into those that grow on the
ground, those that grow on rock *(epiliths),* and those that
grow on rotting wood *(epixyles).* Epiphytes can be classified according to whether they grow on foliage, branches,
or stems. A list of the major terrestrial growth forms is
presented in Table 14-2.

Plants occupying a particular layer exhibit adaptations to
the conditions they experience in that layer. Trees that are

c

exposed to the physical stresses of wind, to high light intensities in the upper crown, and to rapid transpiration stress have strong woody stems and branches, large spreading or deep root systems, and bear foliage with xeromorphic characteristics. Forest forbs, on the other hand, have little need for the strength of woody stems, but they must be able to photosynthesize efficiently at low light intensities. They typically have higher levels of foliar nutrients and often have broad, thin leaves, features that improve photosynthetic efficiency and permit survival, growth, and reproduction at the low light intensities that exist below the tree canopy. The lack of woody tissues means that virtually all net photosynthates can be used for root, leaf, and reproduction, but it places greater importance on cellular turgidity for the maintenance of plant shape and orientation. Consequently, most forbs are restricted to moist soils, where they can maintain their turgidity. Good nutrition is necessary to permit net photosynthesis to occur at low light intensities, and this restricts most forbs to fertile sites.

The number of layers of vegetation in a plant community reflects the character of the physical environment. Dry environments such as grasslands or deserts often have only one or two layers: a layer of perennial herbs in the grassland, and a perennial shrub layer plus an ephemeral herb layer in the desert. As one moves into more humid environments a tree layer is added, and as moisture becomes increasingly abundant, perennial herb and epiphyte layers are added. Thallophytes may be present in almost any environment, although they tend to become increasingly abundant along a transect from hot and dry to cool and moist environments.

Structural change along environmental gradients results in characteristic combinations of growth forms (cf. life-form spectra, Chapter 8) at different points along the gradi-

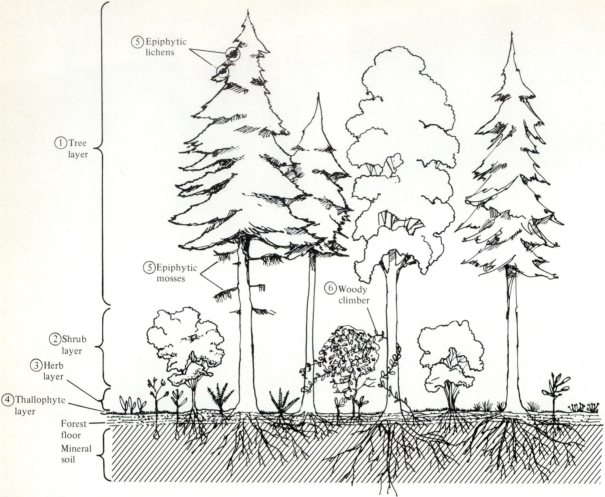

Figure 14.2
The five major layers of a forested plant community. Each layer can be subdivided into sublayers or synusiae. A sixth layer, woody climbers, may also be found.

ent. This occurs on all continents and results in broad divisions of a continental flora that are called *plant formations* and which are found on most of the large continents. Because major gradients such as temperature and moisture tend to run north–south on large continents, plant formations tend to occur as east–west bands across the continents. However, the east–west orientation is greatly modified by mountains and deserts and also by the variation in climate between coastal and interior locations on large continents. The temperate deciduous forest of Europe is a different formation from the temperate deciduous forest of North America, although both belong to the same *formation type* (all

similar formations around the world are grouped in one formation type).

A plant formation on a particular continent together with its associated animal and microbial community and physical environment is called a *biome,* a group of ecosystems in which the primary producers have similar growth forms and consumers have broadly similar feeding habits. Similar biomes (those with the same plant formation type) around the world form a *biome type,* such as the temperate deciduous forest biome type or the boreal forest biome type. The physical environment (climate, topography, geology, soils) of a biome is called a *life zone.*

14.3 Distribution of Species Along Environmental Gradients

Communities vary in their composition according to variations in the physical environment, and both local and regional gradients of physical factors are associated with characteristic patterns of ecosystem types and biome types, respectively. The variation in physiognomy along such gradients is accompanied by variations in species composition. The exact nature of the patterns of community variation along environmental gradients has emerged as one of the more controversial topics in plant synecology. The controversy is important since it involves the philosophical basis for conflicting views about the nature of plant communities.

The sequence of biotic communities along an environmental gradient is called a *coenocline* or simply a *community gradient*. The assemblage of physical environmental factors that change as one moves along a coenocline is called a *complex gradient*, while the combined community–environment gradient is called an *ecocline*. Thus, as one travels from sea level to the top of the mountain one can observe a sequence of biotic communities (the coenocline) and a sequence of physical environments (the complex gradient), which together form a sequence of ecosystem types (the ecocline).

A. Possible Patterns of Species Distribution

There are several possible ways in which plants could distribute themselves along environmental gradients (Figure 14.3).

1. If there is a strong association between the dominant and subordinate vegetation, and if the dominant species occupy sharply defined segments of the environmental gradient, plants form characteristic groupings of species from all layers and these groupings exclude each other along sharp boundaries in all layers (Figure 14.3A). In this situation, strong competition between dominant species produces strong mutual exclusion, so that each dominant species occupies a particular section of the complex gradient. Each dominant species creates, or is associated with, a particular habitat in which a characteristic group of subordinate species develops. The groupings represent adaptation of the subordinate vegetation to the presence of the dominant species, to each other, and to the physical environment. This pattern is characteristic of steep environmental gradients (i.e., a marked change in environmental conditions over relatively short distances).

2. Similar to pattern 1 but with broadly overlapping ranges because of less intense competition and less competitive exclusion among the dominant species. There are iden-

tifiable groupings involving all layers, but their ranges overlap broadly (Figure 14.3B). This pattern is characteristic of gentle environmental gradients.

3. If the species in any layer compete strongly with other species in that layer but exhibit only a weak response to species in other layers, there is very little overlap in the ranges of species within a particular layer but little or no grouping of species between layers. There is little association between species in different layers and therefore no clearly identifiable plant associations as one proceeds along the gradient. This occurs where the complex gradient and intralayer competition are the major determinants of species distributions (Figure 14.3C).

4. Similar to pattern 3 but with broadly overlapping ranges of species with any layer. There is some degree of mutual exclusion within a layer, but no obvious associations of species in different layers (Figure 14.3D).

5. If the dominant species do not exhibit mutual exclusion but the subordinate species do, the species in the upper layer (i.e., the tree canopy) have broadly overlapping distributions along the complex gradient, while species in the lower layers show marked grouping. This pattern occurs where there are relatively few species in the dominant layer, all of which are responding primarily to climatic factors (which vary gradually along a major complex gradient), and there are many species in the lower layers which are responding primarily to a complex of local site factors (such as soil characteristics), which vary considerably over short distances (Figure 14.3E).

6. If all the species distribute themselves along the environmental gradient solely in response to their environmental tolerances and independently of the presence of other species, species in all layers would appear and drop out again in an irregular fashion as one moves along the complex gradient. There would be neither identifiable grouping between layers nor sharp exclusion of species within a layer. Rather, there would be a *continuum* of vegetation change along the environmental gradient (Figure 14.3F).

7. The distribution of species along the gradient can exhibit various combinations of the foregoing patterns at different locations on the gradient, or can have a bimodal or multimodal distribution (Figure 14.3G).

B. Major Schools of Thought Concerning Species Distribution

European schools of plant synecology have traditionally maintained that species are associated in characteristic groups that are more or less mutually exclusive and limited by fairly distinct boundaries (Figure 14.3A). Such groups, which are characteristic of particular types of physical envi-

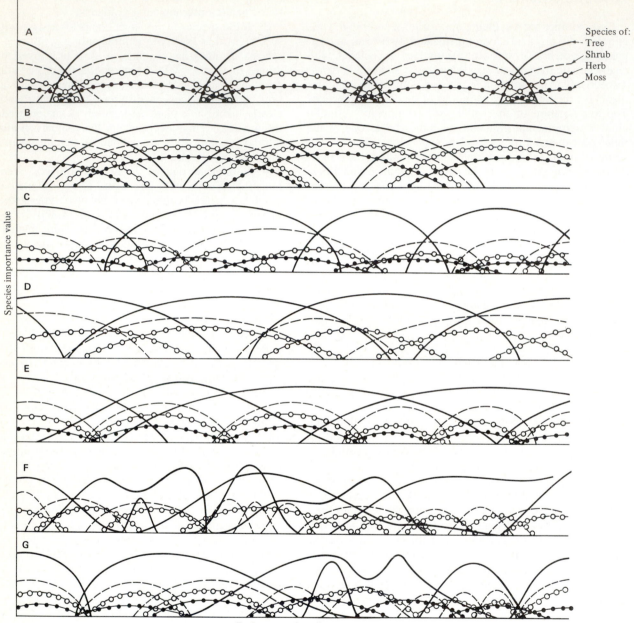

Species of:
- Tree
- Shrub
- Herb
- Moss

Species importance value

Environmental gradient

Figure 14.3

Seven hypothetical patterns of distribution of plant species along an environmental gradient such as moisture or elevation. (A) Mutually exclusive associations with little overlap. (B) Mutually exclusive associations with broad overlap. (C) Mutual exclusion within a layer, but no association between layers. (D) Similar to C, but with broad overlap of species distributions within a layer. (E) Tree layer shows broad overlap of species distributions, but lower layers exibit mutually exclusive associations. (F) The species in all layers enter and drop out of the community irregularly along the gradient without any identifiable groupings or patterns of exclusion. (G) Species distributions exhibit various combinations of the above, with different patterns of species replacement in different parts of the gradient. Each line can represent a single species or a group of species in a particular layer. (Reprinted with permission of Macmillan Publishing Company from *Communities and Ecosystems,* Second Edition by Robert H. Whittaker. Copyright © 1975 by Robert H. Whittaker.)

ronment, are termed *associations:* plant communities of definite species composition and characteristic physiognomy, growing in particular, homogeneous habitat conditions. Because an association is defined by its entire plant membership, it is comparable to the phytocoenose of a biocoenose. However, there is a difference. The term "association" refers to any abstract entity, as does the term *species*. The phytocoenose, on the other hand, refers to an actual assemblage of living organsims in the field and is thus comparable to an *individual* of a particular species.

The term "association" has not always been used in this context. American ecologists in particular have tended to apply it more broadly to include all communities dominated by a particular species. For example, a Douglas-fir "association" would include all plant communities in a region that are dominated by Douglas-fir.

The essence of the European association concept is that (1) the individual species in the association are, to some extent, adapted to each other; (2) the association is made up of species that have similar habitat requirements; and (3) the association has some degree of holistic integration.

The association concept involves the idea of *ecological groups*. Although no two species have identical ecological relationships, many species are so similar to certain other species in their tolerances and distribution that they can be considered to have essentially the same overall adaptations to their environment and belong to the same ecological group. The term can be applied to either the total set of species from all synusiae that share the same tolerances, or to groups of plants restricted to a single synusia. It can refer to the total set of ecological attributes of a species or to a restricted set, such as the moisture or the nutritional tolerances. The existence of ecological groups and the adaptation of the members of an association to each other results in some degree of mutually exclusive grouping of species along environmental gradients. A large number of ecologists have subscribed to this viewpoint, and it is a common experience to observe discrete associations while passing

through a forest. Figure 14.4 illustrates the idea of an ecological group.

A different concept of vegetation was developed independently by two plant ecologists in the 1920s: Ramensky (1924) in the U.S.S.R. and Gleason (1926) in the U.S. These ecologists considered that species are distributed along environmental gradients solely according to their individual adaptations and tolerances. The community of plants observed in a particular habitat consists of populations of those species which are able to successfully invade, survive, and reproduce in that environment. Each species is distributed independently of other species according to genetic, physiological, and life-cycle characteristics which determine how it relates to both its physical environment and to other species. Because of the multifactorial nature of species characteristics, no two species are alike in distribution. This lack of similarity results in a scattering of the centers of species distributions along the gradient, generally with broad overlap. Communities that consist of species whose distributions happen to overlap intergrade continuously except where marked environmental discontinuity or disturbance by fire, logging, and so on, occur (Whittaker, 1975a). This *individualistic* and *continuum hypothesis* of plant distributions views the vegetation of a region as a series of plant species populations distributed independently of each other along the physical gradients of the environment, as suggested in Figure 14.3F.

The evidence used by Whittaker in support of the individualistic hypothesis was obtained in studies of the distribution of tree and subordinate plant species along altitudinal gradients in various mountainous regions of the U.S. (Whittaker, 1956, 1960). Other evidence has come from studies of forests in Wisconsin (e.g., Curtis, 1959; Curtis and McIntosh, 1951). Using the approach to vegetation analysis known as *gradient analysis* and the technique known as *ordination*, it was concluded that there was so much overlap in the distribution of species along gradients that distinct groupings could not be identified (Figure 14.5).

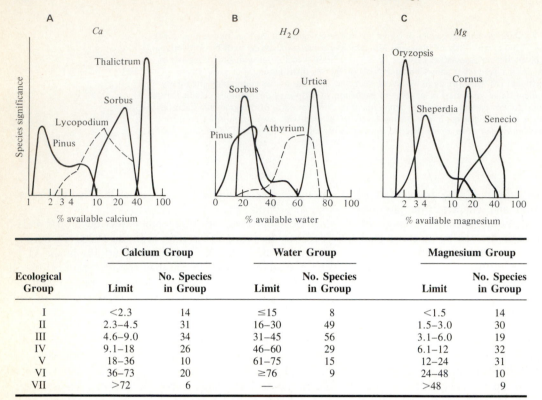

Ecological Group	Calcium Group		Water Group		Magnesium Group	
	Limit	No. Species in Group	Limit	No. Species in Group	Limit	No. Species in Group
I	<2.3	14	≤15	8	<1.5	14
II	2.3–4.5	31	16–30	49	1.5–3.0	30
III	4.6–9.0	34	31–45	56	3.1–6.0	19
IV	9.1–18	26	46–60	29	6.1–12	32
V	18–36	10	61–75	15	12–24	31
VI	36–73	20	≥76	9	24–48	10
VII	>72	6	—		>48	9

Figure 14.4
Distributions of selected plant species along gradients of available (A) soil calcium, (B) moisture, and (C) magnesium in north-central British Columbia. Ecological-group limits for these three parameters in this area and the number of species in each group are listed below. The horizontal axis and group limits are expressed in terms of percent of the maximum value recorded for the parameter. For example, 80 on the calcium scale means a value 80% as large as the highest calcium value recorded. Only the generic names of the species are shown. (Modified after Wali and Krajina, 1973. Used with permission of Dr. W. Junk Publishers and M. K. Wali.)

Although the entire community was studied by these ecologists, the focus of attention tended to be on the tree layer, and the resulting analyses lend support to the continuum theory. This may, however, be as much a result of the emphasis on overstory species as of a lack of associations. Identifiable groupings of plant species tend to be much more evident in subordinate or understory vegetation than in the overstory layer, because many tree species grow on a range of sites within a given climatic region, whereas many herbs and shrubs are only found grouped in restricted locations along an environmental gradient. Although all plants are affected by both climatic and soil factors, trees tend to be more influenced by the former (which tends to change slowly and continuously) and minor vegetation more by the latter (which tend to vary more abruptly and over shorter distances). Thus, analysis of tree data will often support the continuum hypothesis, whereas analysis of minor vegetation will often support the individual association concept. Analysis of community data from areas with a diverse tree flora and a poorly developed or poorly studied subordinate flora will tend to support the continuum theory more than data from areas with very few overstory species and a well-documented subordinate flora.

A major problem in considering the distribution of plants along environmental gradients arises from the confounding of gradients of soil moisture and fertility (associated with local topographic features) with climatic gradients (associated with major topographic features (Figure 14.6)). Species may have discontinuous local distributions and form local associations, and at the same time exhibit more of a continuum of change along regional climatic gradients.

Figure 14.5

Distribution of tree species along a topographic moisture gradient. The upper graph uses data from the Siskiyou Mountains in Oregon (760–1070 m). The lower graph uses data from the Santa Catalina Mountains in Arizona (1830–2140 m). The graphs show numbers of stems greater than 2 cm diameter per ha. (Reprinted with permission of Macmillan Publishing Company from *Communities and Ecosystems*, Second Edition by Robert H. Whittaker. Copyright ©1975 by Robert H. Whittaker.)

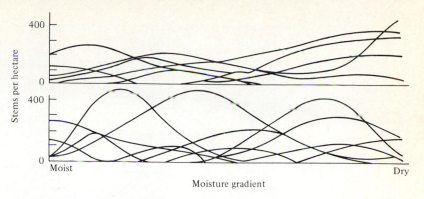

14.4 Major Forest Ecotones: The Interface Between Forests and Communities of Different Physiognomy

If it is agreed that a coenocline may sometimes be made up of a series of discrete communities, transitions between the communities can be identified. These transitional areas are zones of tension between the two adjacent biotic associations in which the member species of each community compete with those of the other community for resources and occupancy of the land. These transition zones, which are called *ecotones*, can be seen most clearly where the adjacent communities have a different physiognomy as well as a different species composition, as they do at the interface between grassland and forest, or between the community of a clearcut and the adjacent uncut forest.

Ecotones are interesting because the plants in them are often growing under conditions of considerable physical and biotic stress. By studying the reasons for natural ecotones, we can reveal much about the complexity of the way in which the structure and function of biotic communities are determined. Perhaps the best known examples of ecotones are tree lines: the interface of forest and grassland, of forest and alpine meadow, and of forest and arctic tundra.

A. Low-Elevation Tree Lines

Low-elevation tree lines occur where forest gives way to grassland. The ecotone may be very narrow, with a sharp transition from grassland to forest, such as the conifer forest–grassland transition common in the western mountains of North America. Alternatively, it may be more gradual, as in the transition from long-grass prairie to eastern deciduous hardwood forest in the Midwest.

The western low-elevation tree lines are often the result of sudden changes in soil texture that induce sudden changes in soil moisture availability. For example, valley bottom soils in many interior valleys in southern British Columbia are deep, fine-textured lacustrine deposits laid down in extensive postglacial lakes. With the present-day climate, such soils are too dry for tree growth and support native bunchgrass or semi-desert shrub communities. In contrast, the valley slopes have medium-textured till soils, often with slope seepage within the rooting zone. Such soils generally support Douglas-fir–ponderosa pine forests (Figure 14.7).

The broad prairie ecotone is under the primary control of climate (Curtis, 1959; Weaver, 1968). There is a gradual increase in precipitation and P/E ratio (see Chapter 11) as one moves east from the open grassland to the closed forest, and the location of the ecotone correlates reasonably well with a critical range of P/E values. However, insufficient precipitation alone is not an adequate explanation for the distribution of the prairie grasslands and the ecotone. Scattered patches of tree growth occur throughout most of the prairie (Wells, 1965), and the climate of much of the area is not too dry for trees (Eyre, 1968). Fire and grazing have also played important roles, both singly and in combination.

Fire has been an important natural component of grasslands, especially autumnal fires started by lightning or humans. The early colonization of the prairies was apparently affected by these grass fires, because settlers would not build their houses beyond the shelter of woodlands due to the danger posed by grass fires (Sauer, 1969). Fire kills tree seedlings that are invading grasslands, but it can actually increase the productivity of the grasses (Kucera and Ehrenreich, 1962). This may be because the removal of the mulch of dead grass permits the soil to warm up more rap-

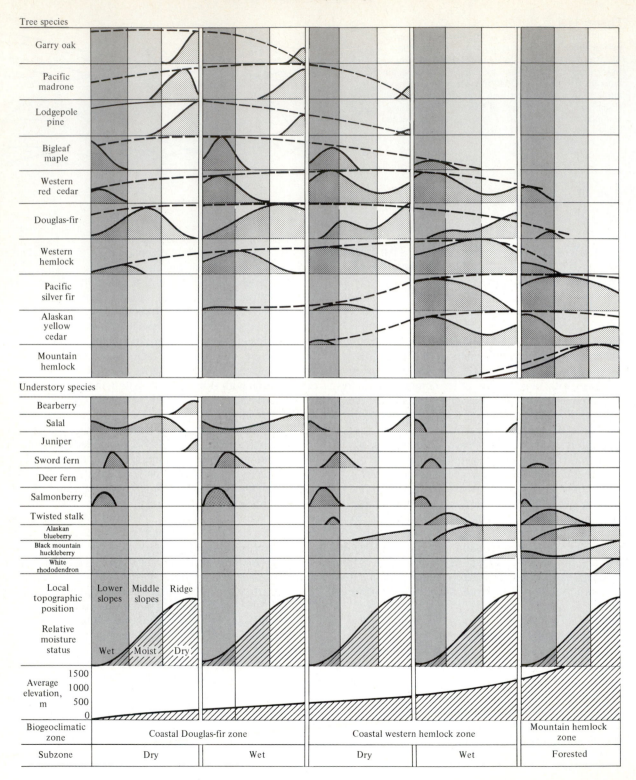

Figure 14.6

Distribution of major tree and selected herb and shrub species along local topographic sequences, and along the major elevational gradient from sea level to 1500 m near Vancouver, British Columbia. Species can have unimodal or bimodal distributions along local topographically-induced moisture/nutrient gradients with quite sharp boundaries to their discontinuous distributions, whereas their overall elevational distribution may be unimodal (shown for trees by dotted line). Note that the distribution of most of the understory species is much narrower than that of most of the overstory species. The trees are strongly influenced by the climate as well as the soil, whereas the understory vegetation is more strongly influenced by local soil conditions.

idly in the spring (promoting root growth) while burning releases nutrients and may destroy toxic organic compounds in the litter (Weaver and Roland, 1952). However, fire does not always have a beneficial effect on the growth of grasses, and it can increase tree invasion by reducing competition for soil moisture. Burning very dry grassland may adversely affect both grasses and trees because the accumulated grass litter serves as a vapor barrier which limits evaporation and thus conserves soil moisture (Dix, 1960). Also, by removing the shade provided by the grass, fire can raise surface soil temperatures to levels that are lethal to tree seeds and young seedlings.

Grazing affects the nature and location of the ecotone by killing small seedlings and modifying competition between trees and grass. Occasional heavy grazing, such as was produced by the original roaming herds of native ungulates, does not adversely affect the production of native grasses (Alcock, 1964), but sustained heavy grazing can lead to a change in the species composition of the grass community and/or a replacement of the grasses by shrubs or trees because of reduced competition for soil moisture (e.g., Buffington and Herbel, 1965).

The location of the low-elevation tree line shows a temporal variation because of alternate invasion of trees into the grassland and loss of trees from the ecotone. These events are erratic and depend to a considerable extent upon climatic cycles. Periods of wetter summers, greater snowpack, lower fire frequency, and reducing grazing pressure are generally accompanied by an invasion of the grassland by trees. Periodic intense droughts [(e.g., the 1934–1941 period in the Midwest, when it was estimated that 50–60% of the trees in Nebraska and Kansas died (Weaver, 1968)], higher frequency of fire, lower winter snowpack, and increased grazing tend to result in a slow expansion of the grassland. Patterns of tree seedling invasion of grassland that are often hard to explain on the basis of midsummer studies may be related to differential snow accumulation in the winter. Seedlings in low elevation forest–grassland ecotones have a higher survival rate in areas that carry large winter snow drifts than in areas of average or below-average snowpack because the prolonged snowmelt of the former

area keeps the surrounding soil charged with moisture far longer into the hot, dry summer.

In addition to the factors of precipitation, P/E ratio, soil texture, fire, and grazing, low-elevation tree lines can also be a product of cold-air drainage. Billings (1954) reported that the lower limits of a pine–juniper woodland on a mountain in Nevada seemed to coincide with a pronounced temperature inversion. Temperature inversions in valleys can result in grassland or meadow vegetation because of frost damage to trees or because cold air increases snow duration. Although snow accumulation generally promotes tree invasion into grasslands, if the snow-free period is too short, the trees will be adversely affected and a meadow will develop.

The low-elevation forest–grassland ecotone is of considerable interest to forest management. Should such areas be subjected to periodic prescribed burning to promote grass production for use by wildlife and/or domestic livestock, or should they be protected and tree production encouraged? World food shortages and increased hunting pressure favor the former option, whereas the increasing evidence of actual and impending timber famines leads some to conclude that the land base for tree production should be maintained against encroachment by other land uses.

B. High-Elevation Tree Lines

The ecotone between alpine and montane forest plant communities is perhaps the best known and most studied example of tree lines. The term *timberline* is sometimes used synonymously with *tree line,* but the two terms are in fact different. Timberline refers to the upper elevational limit of commercial timber, which is normally the upper elevational limit of closed forest. The timberline is thus synonymous with the *forest limit.* Trees in the ecotone area [correctly referred to as the *subalpine* zone (Love, 1970)] either do not reach commercial size or if they do, they are scattered in "tree islands" that have low commercial value and therefore cannot be considered as "timber" (Figure 14.8). Stunted individual trees (*krummholz* growth form) may be found growing many hundreds of meters above the forest limit, so that the *tree line* or *tree limit* is often very different from the forest limit or timberline (Figure 14.9). In

Figure 14.7
Low elevation tree line where forest gives way to grassland—the interface between valley bottom grasslands and ponderosa pine-Douglas-fir forest in south-central British Columbia.

some areas, such as the high-elevation *Nothofagus* forests of New Zealand, the tree limit and the forest limit coincide; there is a sudden transition from commercial forest to alpine vegetation.

Elevational timberlines may be formed by either conifers or angiosperms. The Pinaceae are the predominant timberline trees in the northern hemisphere (mainly species of *Pinus, Picea, Abies, Tsuga,* and *Larix,* although *Juniperus* and *Chamaecyparis* of the Cupressaceae are also represented). Species of *Betula* and *Alnus* form both northern and upper elevational tree lines over much of Scandinavia and in

parts of the Alps and British Columbia. *Fagus sylvatica* is an important timberline species in central and southern Europe and the Caucasus, and *Acer, Sorbus, Populus,* and *Quercus* species are also found at the timberline (Wardle, 1974). In the southern hemisphere, *Eucalyptus* and *Nothofagus* are the important timberline genera. Table 14.3 summarizes the elevation and species at timberline in various parts of the world.

The explanation of the location of either the tree line or the timberline is very complex. Numerous environmental factors act to inhibit the upward extension of closed forest

Figure 14.8
Tree islands of *Abies lasiocarpa* in the subalpine ecotone of the coastal mountains of British Columbia. Once established as a tree island, the trees grow relatively well. Establishment in the meadow is very difficult.

Figure 14.9

Variation in tree growth form in the subalpine zone as one proceeds from closed montane forest to open alpine communities. (A) Engelmann spruce, Rocky Mountains, Colorado. (B) Lodgepole pine (given as *Pinus murrayana* Balf.), Sierra Nevada, California. (After Wardle, 1968, and Clausen, 1965. Used by permission of the Ecological Society of America and Society for Study of Evolution and the authors.)

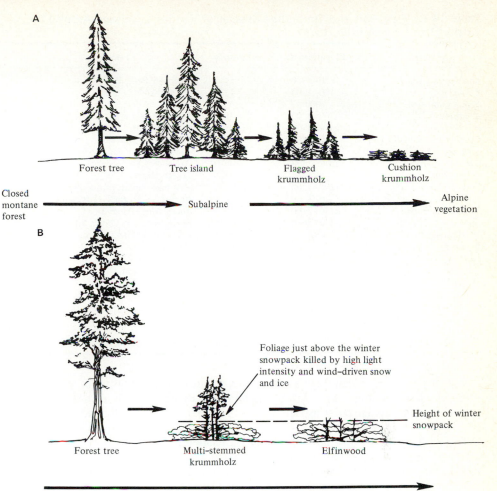

into the subalpine and alpine zones. The importance of any one factor varies from place to place, so that no single explanation will fit all circumstances. Each potential factor will be considered in turn.

1. Temperature. There are several facts which suggest that tree lines are largely determined by temperature. These are:

a. The elevation of timberline increases from polar regions toward the equator, leveling off at about 30°N and 25°S, with a possible dip near the equator. This change in elevation approximates that of isotherms (110-m change per degree of latitude) in North America.

b. The elevation of timberline is lower in coastal than in interior mountains, which mirrors summer temperature isotherms that dip farther south (in the northern hemi-

sphere) along the coast than in the interior of continents. The difference can also be due to the *Massenerhebung effect* if the coast mountains are less massive than the interior mountains: there is a lower temperature lapse rate and therefore higher climatic–biotic zones on larger and higher than on smaller and lower land masses (Wardle, 1974). The greater temperature range of continental interior areas also serves to raise timberlines since the lower winter temperatures have much less effect than do the greater summer temperatures. For a given average annual temperature, interior areas will be warmer in the summer than coastal areas.

c. High elevation tree lines are higher on south aspects than on north aspects in cold, humid climates in the northern hemisphere, where lack of summer warmth is critical. In

Table 14.3. Elevation and Timberline Species at Various Locations Around the World (Data from Wardle, 1974)

Species	Elevation, m	Latitude	Location
Abies lasiocarpa	1850–1900	50°N	Garibaldi Park, B.C.
A. mariessii	1400–1500	41°N	Mt. Hakkoda, Japan
Betula pubescens	1000	63°N	Harjedalen, Sweden
B. utilis	3500–4200	29–35°N	western Himalaya
B. verrucosa	up to 2500	41–44°N	Caucasus Mts., U.S.S.R.
Eucalyptus coccifera	1200–1300	43°S	Mt. Field, Tasmania
E. niphophila	1850–2000	36°S	Snowy Mountains, N.S.W., Australia
Larix decidua	up to 2300	46°N	Poschiavo, Switzerland
L. griffithii	3800	28°N	eastern Himalaya
Nothofagus menziesii	1200–1300	42°S	west coast South Island, N.Z.
N. pumilo	1650	40°S	Andina de Nenquen, Argentina
Picea engelmannii	2150–2300	50°N	Rocky Mts., Alberta
	3350–3600	39°N	Frong Range of Rocky Mts., Colo.
P. likiangensis	4500	38°N	southeast Sinkiang, China
P. sitchensis	900	60°N	Haines, Alaska
Pinus albicaulis	3300	38°N	Sierra Nevada Mts., Calif.
P. cembra	1900	47°N	Glarns, Switzerland
P. hartwegii	up to 4100	19°N	Iztaccihuatl, Mexico
P. sylvestris	500	57°N	Cairngorm Mts., Scotland
	(600–700 potential)		
Podocarpus compactus	3900–4100	6°S	Mt. Wilhelm, New Guinea
Polylepis tomentella	up to 4900	19°S	northern Chile
Rhododendron sp.	3600–3800	27°N	eastern Himalaya

hot, dry climates, where high summer temperatures are an important limiting factor, low elevation tree lines are lower on the cooler polar aspects.

These observations, together with the broad relationship between temperature and biological phenomena in general, support the idea that temperature plays a key role in determining tree line elevations. The concept of heat sums and its relationship to northern treelines was mentioned in Chapter 8. Nineteenth-century work on this topic suggested that the climatic limits of cold timberlines roughly parallel the isotherms for the mean temperature of the warmest summer month (Daubenmire, 1954). Above tree lines there is insufficient warmth to permit tree growth. Success of woody plants at high altitudes depends to a considerable extent on their ability to ripen and "harden off" new shoots in time for this new growth to survive low winter temperatures and winter desiccation, the latter being the most important. Where there is insufficient total summer warmth (heat sum) to permit the necessary physiological processes to be completed in time, trees cannot survive.

Other aspects of the temperature explanation of tree lines are lethal maximum summer temperatures and frost heaving. High-elevation plants may experience intolerably high temperatures for short periods of time (Gates and Janke,

1966). For example, surface temperatures of 84°C have been recorded in subalpine areas in Austria (Aulitzky, 1961), and the surface temperature in a subalpine meadow in British Columbia was reported to go as high as 49°C, approaching the range that is lethal for some young tree seedlings (Ballard, 1972). Frost heaving and its effects on tree seedlings were discussed in Chapter 8. Subalpine areas can experience radiation frosts almost throughout the year, and tree invasion of subalpine meadows is often restricted to drier mounds, where frost heaving is less intense. Frost heaving is often the factor that excludes all vegetation from alpine areas.

The temperature explanation of tree lines is supported by the observation that tree growth-form changes from upright to krummholz to a shrub or scrub form as one proceeds from closed forest up to the tree limit (Figure 14.9). Fully illuminated foliage of *Nothofagus solandri* 2 m above the ground in New Zealand was observed to be 0.5–2°C above air temperature during much of the day, with occasional increases to 6°C above air values. In contrast, fully illuminated shoots of the sprawling shrub *Podocarpus nivalis* within 3 cm of the ground usually exceeded air temperature by 5–11°C and occasionally more (Wardle, 1974). Thus, trees are able to satisfy their heat requirements as elevation increases by growing closer and closer to the ground.

2. Carbon Balance. Several authors have suggested that the tree limit represents the elevation at which trees can no longer achieve a positive carbon balance from year to year. The fact that most timberline species are evergreen has been cited in favor of this idea since deciduous species would require higher levels of summer energy fixation (more positive CO_2 balance) to compensate for the annual loss of all their foliage and the lack of any winter photosynthesis to offset winter respiration (Bliss, 1966). At a certain elevation there is insufficient summer photosynthesis because of low temperatures and short growing season to generate enough net photosynthesis to support winter respiration *and* growth, let alone reproduction. For example, bristlecone pine *(Pinus aristata)* at timberline in California requires 117 hours of photosynthesis at the peak summer rate (equal to half the growing season) to redress the total winter negative balance of 140 mg CO_2 g dry wt^{-1} (Schulz et al., 1967).

Studies of *Pinus cembra* at timberline in Austria have shown that this species only used 33% of the carbon assimilated annually for respiration and increase in dry matter, which suggests that carbon balance may not be limiting. It is thought that the remaining 67% of assimilated carbon may have been transferred to mycorrhizal fungi (Tranquillini, 1959), which are known to be capable of using a significant portion of the net photosynthate produced by the plant (e.g., Schweers and Meyer, 1970). This "loss" to mycorrhizae represents the energy cost to plants of obtaining the nutrients and moisture needed for survival in what is a dry and nutrient-poor environment.

Some authors question the importance of the carbon-balance theory. Nevertheless, there can be little doubt that alpine herbs are at an advantage over trees in that they produce less nonphotosynthetic aboveground biomass and do not have to support the respiration of overwintering aboveground biomass. They are able to use much more of their photosynthate for the production of photosynthetic and reproductive structures.

3. Wind. Timberline trees in most extratropical regions are so dwarfed and wind-trained (Figure 9.6) that for many years ecologists have attributed tree lines to wind. Projecting twigs frequently show the effects of fatal winter desiccation (often due to wind-induced transpiration loss), and at the upper tree limit the krummholz or scrub growth is typically confined to the lee of rocks, other vegetation, or sheltered depressions (Figure 9.7). Timberline can extend more than 500 m higher on leeward than on windward slopes of mountains (Schroter, 1926). Pears (1968) has shown that tree lines in the Grampian Mountains of Scotland have been considerably depressed by human activities over the past few millenia, and feels that wind is a major factor that has

prevented a return of the forest limit to its original elevation. Reestablishment of conifer plantations on windy moorland in Great Britain is similarly limited by wind (Lines and Howell, 1963). Wind velocities often rise rather sharply with elevation, in contrast to the more gradual increase in temperature (Daubenmire, 1954).

Typically, tree growth on windy ridges is luxuriant up to the height of winter snowpack. Any growth above the level of snowpack is killed during the winter by mechanical damage or desiccation (also by high light intensities just above the snowpack). Where this winter wind damage is serious, the height of krummholz may be limited by snow depth. Wind aggravates the problem of low temperature and desiccation, and wind-induced mechanical and physiological damage near the tree line is more significant than at lower elevations because of the very slow growth to replace these losses.

Against the wind theory must be set the observation that high winds are often more common in valleys than on the higher slopes above them and the fact that deformed but surviving trees are found in very windy locations. Obviously, wind alone cannot explain tree lines.

4. Snow Duration. The transition from closed forest to alpine conditions may represent a critical point on the snow duration curve at which the snow-free period is too short to permit the establishment and growth of trees. Long snow duration lowers the total warmth (heat sum) available to seedlings and small trees in climates that more than satisfy the requirements of trees above the snowpack. This affects the hardening off and net carbon balance of the seedlings and may prevent their establishment and/or survival. The snow craters that melt around the stems of trees in the closed forest near timberline permit the establishment and growth of shade-tolerant seedlings close to the parent tree, whereas the snowpack between trees may persist an additional month and preclude seedling establishment (Figure 13.1). This leads to the characteristic clumping of trees in the closed forest–subalpine interface. In southwestern British Columbia it is possible to predict the location of this ecotone by measuring the length of the snow-free period (or vice versa) (Brooke et al., 1970).

In northern latitudes, tree growth sometimes occurs well above the general timberline along the southfacing rim of exposed east–west ridges, in spite of the low temperatures and high winds to which such a location is exposed. This observation can be explained by the fact that these locations lose their snow cover many weeks earlier than either the north-facing rim, where cornices form if the prevailing winter wind is from the south (Figure 14.10), or the slope below, where the deep snowpack persists long into the summer.

Figure 14.10
Effect of snow duration on mountain vegetation in high snowfall areas, facing east along a ridge in coastal British Columbia. Trees grow on the south side of the ridge crest where wind prevents deep snow accumulation and there is early snowmelt. Deeper, more prolonged snowpack on the north side and lower on the south slope precludes the establishment of trees. In such environments the south crest may be sparsely forested while the north aspect has meadow vegetation.

Another line of evidence in favor of the snow duration hypothesis comes from observations of widespread invasion of subalpine meadows by conifers in the Cascade Mountains in Oregon, Washington, and British Columbia (Franklin et al., 1971; van Vetchen, 1960; Brink, 1959). Tree invasion of subalpine and alpine meadows is normally a slow process. One tree establishes and survives. Its presence reduces snow duration, leading to further seedling establishment around it and the formation of a tree clump. Vegetative reproduction (lower branches touching the ground develop roots and form new individuals) and/or sexual reproduction then enlarge the groups to *tree islands,* which may eventually coalesce into closed forest, thus raising the tree line. This is a slow process requiring many centuries and is quite different from the sudden appearance of seedlings over large portions of the subalpine such as occurred between 1923 and 1944. Studies of these invasions eliminated grazing and fire as causative agents. They revealed that at the time of the invasion the local glaciers were in decline, with a steady recession from 1910 to 1953. After this, the glaciers readvanced. The warmer, drier period that triggered the glacial recession would have been accompanied by lower snowpacks and earlier snowmelt, facilitating the invasion of snow-determined meadows by trees.

5. Fire. There can be little doubt that fire has depressed alpine tree lines in many areas. It is the most important catastrophic event affecting timberline, and its effects last longer than those of windthrow, avalanche, or insects since it usually kills seedlings and consumes forest floor and seeds as well as killing the overstory. Burned areas are usu-

ally invaded by luxuriant communities of flowering plants, and many subalpine meadows of high recreational value owe their existence to lightning fires. Reinvasion by trees is often slow because fire followers such as lodgepole pine and aspen are not normally timberline species (Wardle, 1974). In the Australian Alps, timberline *Eucalyptus* can survive destructive crown fires by regenerating from lignotubers.

6. Animals. Domestic grazing, excessive wild populations of introduced grazers (e.g., goats), and outbreaks of insects (defoliation or bark beetles) can all influence elevational tree lines by killing seedlings or mature trees. Grazing tends to be a more insidious factor than catastrophic insect outbreaks, because the latter occur only periodically and usually do not kill all the trees and their seedlings. Consequently, insect outbreaks do not usually lower the tree line, whereas grazing eliminates tree seedlings, so that the tree line is gradually lowered as the old trees die. The loss of forest cover changes the microclimate (mainly wind and temperature), and this may preclude reinvasion. The herbaceous vegetation above tree lines encourages burrowing animals such as marmots and pocket gophers. The soil-churning, the winter consumption of vegetation below the snow and damage to seedling root systems caused by these animals may serve to limit tree invasion of the meadows in which these herbivores live. Bark stripping of seedlings by small mammals can also be a potent force restricting tree invasion into meadows.

7. Other Plants. The area above tree lines is characterized by vigorous communities of shrubby or herbaceous growth forms that are well adapted to the alpine environment. Tree lines may sometimes represent the elevational point at which competition between trees and alpine–subalpine plant species is balanced.

8. Pathogens. Trees at timberline are under physiological stress and are therefore more subject to disease and parasite attack than when growing at lower elevations. Trees in alpine meadows are often adversely affected by snow fungus, which may kill part or all of the foliage, weakening or killing the tree.

No single explanation for elevational tree lines has emerged that is satisfactory for all situations. It is clear that these ecotones are almost always determined by a complex of environmental factors, the relative importance of which varies from place to place. Sometimes it is wind, sometimes it is snow duration, and sometimes it is summer warmth that is important, but never do these and other factors act alone. Sometimes, tree lines coincide with abrupt changes of physical factors along an elevation transect. More often they represent the point along a steady gradient of physical conditions at which the trees can no longer tolerate their environment or can no longer compete with other life forms. Readers interested in this topic are recommended to the detailed analysis of tree growth at high altitudes by Tranquillini (1979), and to Benecke and Davis (1980).

C. Polar Tree Lines

The most northerly forest type in the northern hemisphere is the boreal, which gives way on its northern boundary to the shrub–herb formation of the tundra. The species composition at the northern forest ecotone varies in different parts of the world. In most of North America, black and white spruce are dominant. In Scandinavia, pine, spruce, and birch combine at the forest margin, while larch dominates at the ecotone in Siberia (Hustich, 1953).

As with elevational tree lines, it is much easier to define the northern limit of continuous forest (± 25–30 km) than to define the northern tree limit, because the latter depends partly on how one defines "tree." The northern limit of a tree species is highly irregular, diffuse, and difficult to map.

It is generally felt that the position of the northern forest ecotone is predominantly determined by climate, especially temperature. There is a good correlation between potential evaporation (a direct function of temperature) and the major forest types in Canada (Table 14.4). Temperature is more important than moisture, and the isopleth of 10°C accumulated month-degrees above a 6°C threshold shows a close correlation with the northern forest limit in Canada. In Alaska there is a correspondence between the forest limit

and both day-degrees above 10°C and the mean temperature of the coldest month (references in Larsen, 1974).

The climate of the arctic ecotone is influenced by airmass climatology. It has been observed that the ecotone coincides with the path of summer cyclonic storms, and that the forest border coincides with the mean summer (July–October) position of the climatic boundary between arctic air to the north and pacific and continental air masses to the south. Similarly, the forest–tundra ecotone in Eurasia approximates the median location of the arctic front. Exactly how these air masses influence the vegetation is still a subject of speculation (Larsen, 1974).

Temperature regimes in arctic and alpine regions are significantly different from each other because areas with similar mean temperatures differ in the amplitude of temperature fluctuations. In alpine environments, the low mean daily summer temperature is the combination of warm daytime temperatures and low night temperatures. In the arctic, where the difference between summer day and night temperatures is much smaller due to the short nights, the same mean daily temperature is associated with much cooler days. This has implications for many life forms. For example, the number of insect species, their rate of development, and the rate of organic decomposition are all greater in alpine than in arctic areas of similar mean summer temperatures (Remmert and Wunderlung, 1970).

Temperature affects arctic vegetation in several ways. Low temperatures not only reduce metabolic rates but also produce soil churning and permafrost. Soil churning inhibits the establishment of tree seedlings and damages the roots of established trees, while permafrost limits root activity, tree stability, and tree nutrition. Soil under trees is often colder than under the diminutive tundra vegetation to the north, and trees at the forest limit are often associated with permanent ice lenses. As a tree grows, it shades the ground

Table 14.4 Relationship Between Potential Evaporation (cm) and Major Ecotones in Canada (Data from Larsen, 1974)

Ecotone	Typical PE Value, cm
Tundra–forest/tundra	30–32
Forest/tundra–open lichen woodland	36–37
Open lichen woodland–closed boreal forest	42–43
Closed boreal forest–mixed conifer/ hardwood forest	47–48
Mixed conifer/hardwood forest– Great Lakes/St. Lawrence mixed forest	50–51

beneath its crown, thereby preventing the summer melting of permafrost in the shaded area. This leads to the development of a lens of ice that grows in thickness each year to form a mound with the tree on top. Eventually, the moss layer over the mound becomes broken, exposing the ice lens, which then melts, collapsing the mound and killing the tree. The result is a *frost scar* (a gap in the organic layer that exposes the mineral soil) along the edge of which tree seedlings establish to repeat the cycle (Figure 14.11). For a discussion of permafrost, see Ives (1974).

As with elevational tree lines, both wind and fire influence the polar extension of trees. Wind, which helps to determine the potential location of the forest ecotone, acts more through its effects on temperature than its mechanical effects. Fire is an important factor in determining the actual location of the ecotone, which often differs from the potential location. Lightning fires burning through the ecotone eliminate trees, the reinvasion of which is very slow. The action of fire may be one reason why the northern forest ecotone is frequently broad, with islands of trees occurring far to the north of the main body of continuous forest.

As with the elevational forest ecotone, the polar ecotone varies in location with time. Griggs (1946) reported on a major northern advance of the forest border around Kodiak, Alaska, over the past two centuries. Presumably this reflects the changes in world temperatures that have occurred over this time period. The determination of the northern ecotone is complex, and the interested reader is referred to sources such as Hansen (1966) and Ives and Barry (1974).

14.5 Interactions Between Species in a Community

Certain types of relationships that exist between different species were dealt with in Chapter 13 because they have traditionally been thought of as major determinants of population dynamics. There are many other important types of interspecific relationships that have not yet been mentioned, and they will be examined in this section.

The biotic component of the environment of any individual organism is extremely important to it. In some environ-

Figure 14.11
Cycle of development and collapse of frost mounds associated with white spruce in Mt. McKinley National Park, Alaska. (After Viereck, 1965. Used by permission of the Arctic Institute of North America and the author.)

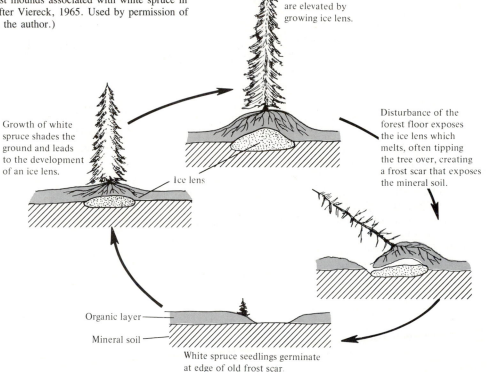

Tree and forest floor are elevated by growing ice lens.

Disturbance of the forest floor exposes the ice lens which melts, often tipping the tree over, creating a frost scar that exposes the mineral soil.

Growth of white spruce shades the ground and leads to the development of an ice lens.

Ice lens

Organic layer

Mineral soil

White spruce seedlings germinate at edge of old frost scar.

ments, physical factors are dominant in determining the characteristics of the biotic community, but in most ecosystems the organisms themselves and the way in which they interact are equally important. The presence of another species may be vital for food and/or shelter, or it may constitute a major threat in terms of disease, predation, parasitism, or competition.

Beneficial or harmful relationships may exist between organisms of similar size, as in the case of a Douglas-fir tree competing for light with a western hemlock tree. Such relationships also occur between organisms of vastly different size, as in the case of the mycorrhizal relationship between a giant tree and a microscopic fungus, or between a whale and the minute aquatic animal that it eats. Interspecific relationships which are not always readily apparent may be the major factor controlling the performance or even the presence of a species in a particular ecosystem.

Interspecific interactions can be classified according to whether they are harmful or beneficial, whether they involve a continuous or an intermittent interaction, and whether they are vital (obligate) or not (facultative or opportunistic). The major types of interactions are shown in Table 14.5. Frequently, a relationship may be intermediate between these classes, which merely represent a convenient division of what is in reality a continuum of relationships. Also, relationships can change from one class to another as time passes and conditions change. For example, mutualism can grade into parasitism, and commensalism can grade into physical exploitation or parasitism. For a recent review of species interactions and the consequent coevolution, see Thompson (1982) and Futuyama and Slatkin (1983).

A. Symbiotic Interactions

The term *symbiosis* was coined in 1879 by a German botanist, DeBarry, to describe the relationship between certain species of algae and fungi that live together to form lichens. He defined it as the living together of two dissimilar organisms in close association or union. Sometimes the term is applied to all interspecific interactions, as originally intended by DeBarry (Whittaker, 1975), but it is commonly restricted to those interactions that are predominantly beneficial or which lack a negative effect on either of the partners. The term is used in the latter sense in this book. Symbiosis defined in this manner can be subdivided into two subtypes: *mutualism* and *commensalism*.

1. Mutualism. This type includes all interactions in which both partners benefit. It includes a wide variety of interactions, from permanent intimate contact between partners, to situations in which there is no actual physical contact.

a. WITH CONTINUOUS CONTACT. There are numerous examples of this interaction that will be well known to most readers. One of the best known is the intimate association that develops when the cortex of the smallest order of secondary roots is invaded by specific fungi during periods of active root growth. Where the invasion of the cortex is *intercellular,* the association is called an *ectomycorrhiza;* where it is *intracellular,* the term *endomycorrhiza* is used. Where both inter- and intracellular infection occurs, the relationship is called an *ectendomycorrhiza*. These associations increase the solubility of minerals, improve uptake of nutrients by the host plant, transport water to the root over ecologically significant distances, protect the roots against pathogens, produce plant hormones, and move carbohydrates from one plant to another. As noted in Chapters 5 and 10, mycorrhizal roots are the norm in most plants. A mycorrhiza is not a permanent relationship, most mycorrhizae being re-formed each year.

The mycorrhizal relationship develops only when both partners benefit. In a nutrient-rich soil, many trees will develop normal long roots with root hairs rather than short roots with mycorrhizae: the tree does not "need" the association. Trees that are growing extremely poorly may also lack mycorrhizae; the fungus cannot obtain sufficient carbohydrate from the root to support the relationship and it may become parasitic on the root. Mycorrhizae have been called "the ultimate in reciprocal parasitism" (Hacskaylo, 1972). If one partner no longer needs the other, the relationship changes from symbiotic to antagonistic. Reduced light intensity and stem girdling, or heavy defoliation caused by insects or foliar diseases can also reduce the incidence of mycorrhizae, because these treatments reduce the supply of carbohydrates to the root.

The formation of mycorrhizae is a complex matter which depends on more than just the level of root carbohydrate: the internal balance of inorganic nutrients and organic me-

Table 14.5 Types of Interspecific Interactions

Category of Interactions	Type of Interaction	Effect on	
		Species A	Species B
Symbiosis	Mutualism	+	+
	Commensalism	+	0
Antagonism	Exploitation		
	physical	+	−
	parasitism	+	−
	predation	+	−
	Antibiosis, including allelopathy	+	−
	Competition	−	−

tabolites are also thought to be important (Slankis, 1971). For some tree species (all pines and some species of the genera *Quercus* and *Fagus)* the relationship is generally obligate, and many attempts to establish plantations of nonnative pines on nonforest soils in various parts of the world failed until the soil was inoculated with the appropriate mycorrhizal fungi. For example, slash pine introduced as seed into Puerto Rico grew 30 cm in 3 years, was chlorotic, and had few needles. Plants inoculated with mycorrhizal fungi were 244 cm tall and had a full complement of needles at the same age (Hacskaylo, 1972). It is now recommended that when new forest nurseries are established in areas lacking mycorrhizal fungi of the species being grown, the nursery soil be inoculated with the appropriate fungus (Mikola, 1970).

A mycorrhiza is a mutualistic relationship that exists only when there is continuous contact, although both partners can, under certain circumstances, exist alone. This is also true of the mutualistic relationship that we call a *lichen*. These life forms do not represent individual genetic packages as do life forms such as a ponderosa pine or a blacktailed deer. In spite of the fact that we classify lichens with generic and specific names as we do plants and animals, they are in fact nothing more than a mutualistic relationship between particular species of fungus and algae. When crustose lichens reproduce, they release two different types of propagule: fungal spores and algal spores. If the former land on a suitable substrate, the spores germinate and develop a small mat of mycelium. This mycelium will perish unless spores of an appropriate species of alga land on and become entrapped in the mycelium; the fungus is a heterotroph and is adapted to obtain its energy supply from the alga. The algae of some lichens are of the nitrogen-fixing blue-green variety, which provide the fungi with a supply of nitrogen in addition to carbohydrates. The algae may be able to exist independently, although this is unlikely since they are adapted to the lichen symbiosis. The fungus provides them with shelter and improved availability of moisture and nutrients. Some lichens are only known to reproduce sexually in this mannner. Others are only known to reproduce asexually; small fragments containing both fungus and algae break off and are distributed by wind. Some reproduce both ways. The lichen association permits these two organisms (fungus and algae) to exist in environments, such as bare rock or the tops of trees, which are unsuitable for most other life forms. The relationship enables them to avoid competition and makes them a very successful life form.

The difficulty of obtaining nitrogen has led to the development of many mutualistic relationships between heterotrophic microbial nitrogen fixers and autotrophic plants not capable of exploiting atmospheric N_2. The invasion of roots of leguminous plants by bacteria of the genus *Rhizobium* and the subsequent formation of root nodules has already been mentioned (Chapter 5). The bacteria gain a shelter and plant carbohydrates as a source of energy, and the host plant gains a secure source of nitrogen. This enables the plant to grow in nitrogen-deficient environments and gives it a competitive edge over plants without such symbiotic associations. The invasion of alder roots by nitrogen-fixing actinomycetes and the formation of leaf nodules were mentioned in earlier chapters.

Another important example from the microbial world is the relationship between intestinal bacteria and the host animal (Howard, 1967). Ruminant herbivores are able to exist on woody plant species because bacteria in their ruminant stomachs alter the cellulose to chemical forms that the host can digest. By converting a lot of the organic matter to CO_2 and methane [the flatulence for which such animals are renowned (see Chapter 5)], these bacteria increase the concentration of nitrogen in the nongaseous material passing through the animals' intestine, thereby facilitating its utilization. Insects also depend on gut flora to enable them to survive on nutritionally marginal material. This is especially important in wood-boring species. Their gut flora are able to synthesize amino acids and other essential organic nutrients, enabling the host insects to survive on a diet that is lacking a number of essential constituents.

b. WITHOUT CONTINUOUS CONTACT. Many examples of this type of relationship can be found in the animal kingdom, but it also occurs between other life forms.

The literature is replete with fascinating examples of mutualistic relationships between animals. For example, many large ungulate herbivores permit certain species of birds to land on them to feed on external parasites such as ticks. The cowbird of North America and the little white heron in Africa both feed on such external parasites to the mutual benefit of both bird and ungulate.

A wide variety of symbiotic relationships have been reported between ants and various other life forms. Most gardeners are familiar with the solicitous attention given to aphids by ants on rose bushes. The ants protect the aphids from parasites and predators and in turn obtain a supply of ''honeydew'' from the aphids. This is the liquid excreta of the aphids: essentially plant sap plus aphid excreta less the nutrients that have been removed from the sap by the aphids' digestive system. The degree of contact between the ants and aphids varies. In some species, the aphids are kept right in the ants' nest, feeding on plant roots. In others, the aphids may feed above ground but be carried to the nest and to other plants by the ants. Sometimes, the ants merely attend the aphid population where they find it on the plant. Aphid eggs may be carried to the nest for the winter, and the young aphids hatching in the spring are used to repopulate host plants.

The parallel between the human farmer/domestic livestock relationship and the ant/aphid relationship is remarkable. No less remarkable is the parallel between the methods used by farmers of arable land and the cultivation of fungi by certain beetles, ants, and termites (Batra and Batra, 1967). Tropical leaf-cutting ants (*Atta* sp.) cut up green leaves and carry the pieces to their nests. There they are chewed up and the resulting pulp is spread out in special underground chambers to form a substrate on which spores of a particular species of fungus are planted. The developing mycelium is carefully cultivated by the ants, which remove other species of fungi and prevent the fruiting of the desired fungus since they feed on the mycelium (Brues, 1946).

Many wood-boring beetles have a special morphological adaptation (called a *mycangium*) located at some part of their body in which wood-rotting fungal spores accumulate (Francke-Grosmann, 1967). When the beetles invade a new tree to breed, they excavate a tunnel in which to lay their eggs, infecting the area with fungal spores as they work. These germinate and spread through the wood, softening it, and enriching it with organic nitrogen. By the time the beetle larvae hatch, they are surrounded by a zone of wood containing fungal mycelia, which also lines the tunnels in which the larvae feed. This is an ideal environment and food supply in which to mature, and the presence of fungal spores in their food and their environment ensures that the mycangia of the developing larvae become suitably charged with spores so that the next generation will be equally well supplied.

Janzen (1966) has described a fascinating case of ant–plant mutualism between the ant *Pseudomyrex ferruginea* and the Bull's-horn acacia *(Acacia cornigera)* in Central America. The ants protect the acacia plants from insect pests and modify competition by other plants, and in exchange the ants obtain food and a nesting site from the plant. To start a colony, the queen ant bores a hole in one of the swollen acacia thorns and hollows out its soft interior to make space for eggs and larvae. When the first thorn is filled, the next thorn is utilized. Food is "provided" by the plant in the form of nectaries at the base of the leaves and nutritious nodules that form at the tips of the leaves.

In some ant–acacia associations, both partners can exist independently, although both benefit from the relationship. The *Pseudomyrex/Acacia* symbiosis, on the other hand, is obligate and borders on being a case of continuous contact mutualism. To sustain the intensity of the relationship, both partners have developed special adaptations. For their part, the ants are active 24 hours a day to provide continuous protection; this is unusual for ants, which normally have a diurnal behavior pattern. The acacia is evergreen, which ensures a continuous supply of food for the ants; most closely related species of acacia are deciduous in the dry season.

To demonstrate the degree of protection provided by the ants, Janzen prevented ant colonization of acacia shoots by means of ant poison, and then measured growth and survival of shoots with and without ants. Table 14.6 demonstrates that the symbiosis is highly beneficial to both growth and survival of the acacia shoots.

Insect pollination is another well-known example of mutualism without continuous contact. Flowering plants have evolved nectaries with showy flowers which are often equipped with ultraviolet reflecting lines to guide insects to them. These plants invest a considerable part of their energy budget in the production of flowers, pollen, and nectar to gain the advantage of between-plant transfer of pollen. The most highly developed plant-pollinator relationships are found between the orchid family and euglossine bees. So highly developed is this relationship that the flowers no longer have nectaries and they are visited only by male bees. The flowers have such specialized perfumes that in many cases only one species of bee is attracted (Dressler, 1968; Dodson et al., 1969). Similarly, the peculiarly enclosed flowers of the commercial fig are pollinated only by wasps of the genus *Blastophaga,* which lay their eggs in special floral structures. The complexities of the fig–wasp mutualism have recently been reviewed by Wiebes (1979) and Janzen (1979). Yet another obligate and specific symbiosis is found between the yucca plant and the yucca moth (Hartzell, 1967). The female moth visits the yucca flower in

Table 14.6 Effect of the Ant-Acacia Symbiosis on the Growth and Survival of Bull's-horn Acacia in Mexico (Data from Janzen, 1966)

Parameter	With Ants	Without Ants
Growth of shoots May 25–Aug. 3, cm	104	16
Survival of stumps over a 10–mo. period, %	72	44
Mean weight of shoots per stump after 10 mos. growth, g	579	44
Mean number of leaves per stump after 10 mos. growth	108	52
Mean number of swollen thorns per stump after 10 mos. growth	104	39

the evening and collects a ball of pollen from the anthers. Then, holding the pollen ball in specially adapted mouth parts, she flies to another plant, pierces the ovary of the flower with her ovipositor, lays her eggs, and then deposits the pollen ball into the stigma. As with so many mutualistic symbioses, the evolutionary development of such a relationship taxes the imagination.

2. Commensalism. When the relationship between two different species benefits one partner (guest) but neither benefits nor harms the other (host), it is termed a *commensal symbiosis* or *commensalism*. As with mutualism, the commensal relationship is not a fixed one. If the guest partner becomes too prolific, it may adversely affect the host partner and the relationship may become *antagonistic*. Alternatively, if some advantage to the host develops as the commensal relationship evolves over a long period, the affair will develop into mutualism.

A common example of commensalism is the nonparasitic growth of one type of plant on another. Some types of forest are characterized by tree crowns festooned with epiphytic mosses and/or lichens. By growing in the crowns, these life forms avoid competition from herbs and shrubs on the forest floor, benefit from the nutrients in the throughfall of the host, and are held up to the light. The host suffers virtually no loss where the growth of the epiphyte is modest, or where it occurs on the stem. If, on the other hand, the development of crown epiphytes becomes excessive, a tree may suffer some loss of light to its foliage, and one sometimes observes a tree in obviously poor health that is smothered in lichens. The conclusion that the epiphyte has become antagonistic may not be warranted, however. It is just as likely that the epiphyte is responding to an independently caused pathological condition in its host. Also, some epiphytes are nitrogen fixers, and as they die and become litterfall they contribute to the nitrogen economy of the trees. What appears to be a commensal relationship may thus in reality be mutualistic. It may well be that many examples of commensalism are merely examples of mutualism that we do not yet fully understand.

Examples of apparent commensalism are common among animals. Scavenging hyenas and vultures that follow the large African predators benefit from the leftovers of a kill but contribute little to the predators' economy. Similarly, remora fish, which attach themselves by a sucker to sharks and whales, benefit in terms of transportation and protection and may obtain scraps of food left over as the host feeds. They are small enough that their presence does not seem to hinder their powerful hosts.

Many animals seek shelter in the nests of others. Some species of birds inhabit the abandoned nests of others, and there are numerous examples of small animals sharing the abodes of larger animals. An example of a more intimate shelter relationship is seen in the case of the intestinal flora of human beings (including *Escherichia coli*), which serves no known beneficial function, but neither does it do much harm in healthy individuals. Such flora may be an evolutionary "leftover" from our recent evolutionary past when our diet contained large proportions of plant material of low nutritional value. Under conditions of disease, stress, or injury, in infants, or in older debilitated individuals, *E. coli* can produce intestinal diseases or enteritis. *E. coli* is thus usually nonpathogenic but opportunistic; it will produce disease if it gains access to susceptible tissues or organs, such as the bladder, where it causes cystitis. In many cases these shelter arrangements are probably truly commensal, but in some the host may benefit by the scavenging activities of the guest, which serves to "keep the house clean."

Vegetation in general participates in a very important commensal relationship with animals by providing shelter. Many animals require shelter to feel secure, and they obtain this from plants without affecting them in any other way. Documented examples of such a symbiosis are far too numerous to mention here. The interested reader is referred to Henry (1967), Cheng (1970), and Jennings and Lee (1975).

B. Antagonistic Interactions

All relationships in which at least one of the partners is adversely affected are included in the general category of *antagonism*. Such relationships play a major role in determining the abundance and distribution of species populations and the diversity of species in a community. They are also important in the evolution of species characteristics.

Antagonistic relationships can be subdivided into (1) nonconsumptive physical exploitation, (2) consumptive physical exploitation (including parasitism and predation), (3) antibiosis (including allelopathy), and (4) competition.

The first three types generally involve benefit to one partner and harm to the other. The fourth type involves mutually adverse effects.

1. Physical Exploitation: a. NONCONSUMPTIVE PHYSICAL EXPLOITATION. Many forest plants invest a considerable portion of their energy budget in building a strong stem with which to hold up their foliage to the light and to resist the damaging effects of wind. If it were not for this evolutionary strategy, we would have neither forests nor a forest industry, and the human species might never have evolved. Not all plants solve their problems this way, however. Shade-tolerant herbs get by with lower light intensities by having large shade leaves, by operating seasonally, and by saving energy by dispensing with woody perennial stems. Climbing plants also dispense with strong woody stems by using other plants for physical support. This adaptation is well developed in tropical forests, where the trees are draped with lianas and other climbing plants (Figure 14.1C), but it is also seen in temperate ecosystems, where plants such as ivy *(Hedera helix)* and *Clematis* sp. exploit trees and bushes (Figure 14.12). Initially, the climbers may act as commensals, but they often grow over and kill their host.

Physical exploitation is seen in several species of birds. The antarctic penguin will steal nest-building materials and may even steal unattended eggs. Piratical behavior is seen in birds such as eagles, skuas, and jaegers, which will attack lesser birds of prey that are carrying fish, forcing them to release their capture and then consuming it themselves. Hijacking of food is also seen in the insect world. Tropical flies of the genus *Bengalia* will lie in wait for ants returning from a hunting raid on a termite nest. They attack ants carrying dead termites, causing them to drop their booty, which the fly promptly consumes (Clarke, 1976).

That harbinger of springtime in the English woodland, the cuckoo bird *(Cuculus canorus),* exploits smaller birds in a particularly insidious way. After mating, the female cuckoo seeks out the nest of a smaller bird in which it lays an egg. This generally occurs after the nest owner has already laid a clutch, possibly because the large cuckoo must feed for longer in the spring to generate its comparatively large eggs (Lack, 1966). The host species may recognize the cuckoo's egg as an interloper and eject it from the nest, but frequently this does not happen and the cuckoo egg is incubated and hatched. The host bird dutifully feeds the resulting chick, which may ungratefully dispatch its nest mates by tipping them out of the nest or may contribute to their starvation because the smaller chicks of the host species cannot compete with the vociferous cuckoo chick for the attention of the parent bird at feeding time. The cuckoo chick quickly outgrows the hardworking but unwitting foster parents, which faithfully feed it until it is ready to fly.

This type of relationship is often called *brood parasitism* and could just as easily have been discussed below under

Figure 14.12

Physical exploitation. (A) Ivy *(Hedera helix)* climbing on and smothering ash trees *(Fraxinus excellsior)* in southern England. (B) Tropical climbers smothering trees in Hawaii.

A

B

parasitism (consumptive physical exploitation). The cuckoo certainly diverts energy from the host population, weakening and killing some of that population. However, brood parasitism is included here since parasites are normally thought of as organisms that actually consume part of the living body tissues of their host.

A similar type of relationship, but with an interesting twist to it, exists in the cowbird in Panama. In this region the giant cowbird is a brood parasite of another bird, the chestnut-headed oropendula, which builds a sacklike nest that hangs from the branches of large trees. Natural selection has acted on species that are subject to brood parasitism so that they are able to recognize the difference between their own eggs and those of a brood parasite. However, selection has also acted on the parasite to produce eggs that mimic those of the host so well that they avoid detection. In a study of the oropendula–cowbird relationship in the Panama Canal zone, a curious phenomenon was discovered (Smith, 1968). It was found that in some oropendula colonies, the cowbird eggs were mimics, whereas in others the eggs of the two species were distinctly different. The explanation for this enigma was found in two additional relationships: a parasitic one and a commensal one.

Oropendula chicks are subject to parasitism in the nest by bot flies, which lay their eggs on the naked skin of the newly hatched birds. The chicks are unable to groom themselves to remove these parasites because their eyes do not open for 6–9 days after hatching. The cowbird chicks hatch 5–7 days earlier, are born with a covering of down (which deters the bot flies from laying eggs on them), and open their eyes within 48 hours. The active cowbird nestlings snap at anything small that moves in the nest, including the adult bot flies, and they also remove larvae from the skin of the oropendulas (Table 14.7). The brood parasite in this case has both a mutualistic relationship and an exploitive relationship, which apparently compensate for each other in

natural selection. Consequently, there is no selective advantage to the oropendulas in discriminating against cowbird eggs where there are bot flies, and in such areas egg mimicry has not been selected for.

If this is the correct explanation, why has selection favored cowbird egg mimics in other oropendula colonies? Smith discovered that all oropendula colonies in which the birds discriminated between their own and other eggs and ejected nonconforming objects were close to nests of bees or wasps. Bot flies rarely approach close to the nests of these insects, the proximity of which confers on the oropendulas an immunity against bot fly parasitism (i.e., there is a commensal relationship between the bees/wasps and the oropendulas). This immunity in turn eliminates the selective advantage of having a cowbird in the nest and makes its presence exploitive rather than mutualistic.

The study of the cowbird–oropendula relationship is an elegant demonstration of the need to recognize variations in intraspecific relationships if we are to understand the form and function of ecosystems.

b. CONSUMPTIVE PHYSICAL EXPLOITATION. This category includes relationships in which, (1) one organism consumes part of the blood or tissues of a host organism, often weakening and sometimes killing it (parasitism), (2) one animal kills and consumes all or part of another animal (predation), and (3) a herbivore consumes all or part of a plant, possibly killing or weakening it.

Essentially, this category of antagonism accelerates the loss of energy and biomass from the individual organism.

i. Parasitism. As with many interspecific interactions, there is no clearcut distinction between parasites and predators. Parasites are normally very much smaller than their hosts and generally exist in more or less continuous contact with them. When a host–parasite relationship has existed for many thousands of generations of the host, the parasite is rarely lethal, although if its population becomes too high it may be so debilitating that its host succumbs to other mortality factors. The situation is quite different when a new host–parasite relationship is established. When a plant parasite has recently been introduced to an area previously outside its range, or a new, more virulent genotype of a pathogen has evolved, the relationship may well be fatal. This early stage of a parasite relationship, which is called the *epidemic phase,* is transient because natural selection develops host resistance and reduces parasite virulence to the point at which a stable relationship is established or restored (the *endemic phase*). An example of this evolution in parasitic relationships is the malarial parasite, which, in the absence of medication, can be fatal to people from non-

Table 14.7 Relationship Between the Incidence of Bot Fly Parasitism of Oropendula Nestlings and the Presence of Cowbird Chicks in the Nest (Data from Smith, 1968)

Cowbird Nestlings	Number (Percent) of Oropendula Nestlings	
	With Bot Fly Parasites	Without Bot Fly Parasites
Present	57 (8.4)	619 (91.6)
Absent	382 (90.1)	42 (9.9)

malarial areas. Human populations exposed to malaria for many generations have a high incidence of sickle cells in their blood, which are thought to confer some resistance to the parasite.

There are several interesting examples of this type of interaction from the world of forestry. Prior to 1900, the American chestnut was a major species in the eastern hardwood forest of the U.S. In the early 1900s, a fungus (*Endothica parasitica,* the chestnut blight) was accidentally introduced from Asia, where it existed as an endemic parasite. Within 20 years, most of the mature chestnut trees in New England were dead, and by the 1940s the same fate had befallen the chestnut all the way to the southern end of its distribution in the southern Appalachians. Chestnut still sprouts from the old root stocks but never survives long enough to become a canopy tree. It is likely that if the species can continue to survive as a shrub, a more stable endemic relationship will eventually evolve that will result in the return of this species as a major tree in the region.

A rather similar example is found in the history of the Dutch elm disease, caused by the fungus *Ceratocystis ulmi.* This fungus, which is endemic on elms in Europe where it causes only occasional branch mortality, is spread by a bark beetle with which it has a mutualistic relationship. Logs containing live bark beetles were shipped to the U.S. in about 1930. The beetles rapidly spread the disease to the native North American elms, which proved to be highly susceptible and which have been virtually eliminated from much of the eastern U.S. and Canada. During this period of epidemic conditions, the fungus apparently evolved a more virulent strain, which was then accidentally introduced back into England in the early 1970s. There, the U.S. experience was repeated. Spreading out in concentric rings from the points of introduction (ports into which beetle-infested logs were imported), the virulent disease has eliminated most of the 5 million hedgerow and ornamental elms in southern England (Figure 14.13).

ii. Predation. In contrast to typical parasites, typical predators are often larger than their prey (or at least not many orders of magnitude smaller), are free living, and generally have only a single successful encounter with their "host" (*prey* or *victim* would be a more appropriate epithet). The predator is sometimes said to live on "the capital" of its food resource, whereas a parasite utilizes "the interest." Although this metaphor has some reality in terms of the individual host, it loses its currency when applied to host–prey populations in general. Parasites can so weaken host individuals that the population goes into a decline, while predators may only take diseased and old individuals

or those that are in excess of the carrying capacity. By so doing, predators may actually sustain the health and abundance of the prey population.

As with a parasitic relationship, a recently developed predator–prey relationship can be unstable. When a predator population is introduced to a prey population that has been without predators for some time, its activities can virtually decimate its prey (this is generally the basis for biological control programs). If both populations survive through several predator–prey cycles, a stable relationship may be established.

Predation can occur between a wide variety of organisms. Herbivores are normally considered to be predators, and plants the prey, but the tables are turned in plants such as sundew (*Drosera* sp.) and the pitcher plant (*Sarracenia* sp.), which are insectivorous; the plants are the predator and insects the prey. Herbivores of various types are the prey for primary carnivores, which in turn become the prey for secondary carnivores. Soil fauna prey on soil fungi in much the same way that herbivores prey on plants, but here again the hunter can become the hunted because certain species of soil fungi are predaceous on soil fauna much larger than themselves. One species of fungus produces a chain of cells in the form of a loop. Should a nematode or other soil microorganism insert part of its body through the loop, the cells contract, tightening the loop sufficiently to kill the victim (Bessey, 1950).

The general public often views predators as "red in tooth and claw": as vicious, savage, and undesirable. In almost all cases this is a misconception. Predators generally act to remove the sick, the maimed, and the dying from the prey

Figure 14.13

Elm trees *(Ulmus sp.)* in southeastern UK, killed by Dutch elm disease following the introduction of a virulent strain from the US. The photograph was taken in midsummer.

population. They help to keep the population below its carrying capacity and thereby prevent the carrying capacity from being degraded. Certainly, there are examples of wanton killing by predators, but this usually represents situations where the normal adaptations between predator and prey have been upset by human action or some other environmental factor. Killing of domestic livestock by large predators or of deer by packs of semiwild domestic dogs represent unnatural situations that cannot be compared with natural predator–prey relationships.

2. Antibiosis. Many if not all organisms interact with each other chemically as well as physically. Such chemical interactions occur between microbial life forms, between plants and animals, between different species of animals, and between different species of plants. Such interactions are broadly referred to as *antibiosis*. There are many well-known examples of interaction between microbes. Perhaps one of the best examples is the production of penicillin by fungi (belonging to the genus *Penicillium*), which inhibits the growth of bacteria in the vicinity of these fungi. There is frequently intense chemical competition between different species of crustose lichens invading rock surfaces, and between the fungi and other microbes occupying the soil. These organisms employ antibiotic substances to influence the growth of competing species. For example, in a study of interactions between actinomycetes and fungi isolated from soil and tree seedlings, antagonistic effects were found in the majority of over 200 different combinations that were examined (Vaartaja and Salisbury, 1965). Many plant species produce antibiotics that inhibit the growth of microbes (Stoessl, 1970). Members of the family *Cupressaceace,* which are well known for their durability and decay resistance, produce a substance, β-thujaplicin, which inhibits the growth of a wide variety of bacterial species and is bactericidal to several species (Trust and Coombs, 1973).

Many plants contain chemicals that make them unpalatable to herbivores. Larvae of the winter moth can only eat young oak leaves because old oak leaves contain high levels of tannin which render the leaves unpalatable (Feeny, 1968, 1970). Trees injured by insect feeding may produce polyphenols which can inhibit the population growth of the insects. Altered polyphenol metabolism was noted in Scots pine attacked by the European sawfly (Thielges, 1968), and there is a growing body of evidence that this may be a rather general phenomenon (e.g., Haukioja, 1980). Recent studies have suggested that willows fed on by snowshoe hares in Alaska become unpalatable by producing secondary chemicals, and that this may be a part of the mechanism of the 10 year cycle (Bryant, 1986; Bryant et al., 1983; Bryant and Kuropat, 1980). Where activities of one herbivore stimulate

plant defense mechanisms, other herbivores feeding on the same plant may be adversely affected, leading to some degree of synchronization in their population fluctuations (Haukioja, 1980; Kimmins, 1970). Recently, it has been suggested that when some species of plant are attacked by herbivores, they may produce volatile chemicals that stimulate the chemical defenses of neighboring plants: a plant "early warning system" (Baldwin and Schultz, 1983).

Interaction and chemical coadaptation between plants and herbivores may have been a major factor in the evolution of high species diversity in terrestrial ecosystems (Erlich and Raven, 1967). Any explanation of the great diversity of species in tropical rain forests must include chemical adaptations of plants to herbivores, and evolution of plant diversity in response to the chemical effects of plants on each other is probably one of the major explanations for the evolution of species diversity higher in the food web. For a recent treatment of the interaction between herbivores and plant secondary chemicals, see Rosenthal and Janzen (1982).

3. Allelopathy (Antibiosis Between Plants). One of the best known cases of antibiosis is that which occurs between plants. The metabolism of plants is extremely complex, involving a very large number of organic molecules involved in a very large number of processes. With such chemical complexity it should not be surprising that evolution has failed to fine-tune plant biochemical systems to the point at which there are no waste products or metabolic "leftovers." Many of these *secondary plant chemicals* are of no value to the plant, but some are, because they modify the growth and behavior of other organisms to the benefit of the plant. Chemicals that inhibit the germination, growth, or occurrence of other plants are referred to as *allelochemicals* and the phenomenon as allelochemical antibiosis, or *allelopathy*.

Examples of allelopathy have been reported since the nineteenth century. Perhaps the best known is the example of walnut trees (*Juglans* sp.). It has long been observed that very few species of herbs and shrubs will grow beneath a canopy of walnut trees and that this is not the result of mere competition for light, moisture, and nutrients. The walnut tree produces an allelochemical called *juglone*, which occurs in a water-soluble, nontoxic form (hydroxyjuglone) in leaves, fruits, and other tissues. This is washed into the soil by rain, where it is oxidized to juglone, which inhibits the germination and growth of many other plant species.

A somewhat different case of allelopathy is found in the hot, dry climate of southern California. Grasslands in this area are invaded by a community of low shrubs known as soft chaparral. This community is dominated by a sage brush *(Artemesia californica)* and a mint *(Salvia leuco-phylla)*, both of which produce volatile allelochemicals that fill the air above the community with a characteristic fragrance. Experiments have shown that the characteristic absence of grasses and herbs from the areas occupied by, and in a belt 1–2 m surrounding the shrub clumps is not the result of competition, water-soluble allelochemicals, or the effects of animals, but that it is the result of the volatilization of terpenes (camphor and cineole) from the shrubs into the surrounding air. These terpenes have a marked inhibitory effect on germination and growth of seedlings, and also on soil bacteria. The terpenes are absorbed onto clay particles in the soil surface, rendering the soil unsuitable for the growth of other plants until the chemicals are either driven off by fire or washed away by rain. In wet years there is an increased abundance of other plants in the belts around the shrubs, while the wet season following a fire in chaparral is characterized by the conspicuous blooming of annual plants that were mostly absent before the fire (Muller, 1966, 1969; Muller et al., 1968).

Allelopathy is now thought to be the rule rather than the exception in the ecosystem. Evolution has favored plant forms that have allelopathic metabolic waste products and/or metabolites. The more this form of interspecific interaction is investigated, the more it appears that allelochemicals have played a major role in the evolution of biotic diversity and that they are a major factor determining the form and functioning of biotic communities. Allelopathy is found in both plants and microbes, and it has been observed in a wide range of climates and plant communities. The allelochemicals may be released as volatile gasses (mostly in species from dry areas, which tend to be more aromatic than species from wet areas), or as water-soluble substances that are exuded, excreted, or leached. They may be released from aboveground or belowground living plant parts, or they may be released only after death and decay. The chemicals involved in allelopathy include phenolic acids, coumarins and quinones, terpenes and essential oils, alkaloids, and organic acids.

Allelochemicals act in a wide variety of ways. They may inhibit the germination of seeds, the activity of nitrogen-fixing bacteria, or interfere with the formation of mycorrhizae. For example, heather *(Calluna vulgaris)*, which makes the Scottish moors famous, releases substances that can inhibit the formation of mycorrhizae on the roots of some trees. Early attempts to afforest these moors with Sitka spruce met with failure because the planted seedlings grew exceedingly slowly. Physical removal of the heather resulted in the appearance of mycorrhizal fungi and the development of increased vigor in the trees (Handley, 1963).

Ploughing, which turns over a sod and kills the underlying heather, had a similar beneficial effect. In contrast to the effect on the introduced spruce, heather has much less effect on the native Scots pine (Malcolm, 1975) and the presence of pines apparently improves the growth of planted spruce.

Bracken fern *(Pteridium aquilinum)* is also believed to have an allelopathic effect on young trees. Dense areas of this fern (referred to as "deer forest" in Scotland) are very resistant to invasion by trees. This is partly because of competition for light, nutrients, and moisture, partly because the dead fronds smother the young trees, and partly because of chemical effects. Figure 14.14 shows the effects of phenolic acids exuded by bracken fern on root growth in barley plants.

Interference with nitrogen-fixing bacteria by allelochemicals has been observed. The decay products of some grasses tolerant of low nitrogen availability inhibit nitrogen-fixing bacteria in the soil, which in turn retards the invasion of the area by nitrogen demanding species (Rice, 1964, 1965). Pioneer plants may also interfere with symbiotic nitrogen fixation (Rice 1967, 1968). This effectively reduces competition and prolongs the occupancy of the area by the pioneer species.

It is probable that allelopathy has been selected for in many, if not most, pioneer species. Crustose lichens colonizing bare rock compete with each other using secondary chemicals, and the persistence of some pioneer mosses may have some chemical basis. Climax species may also prevent the invasion of pioneer species by allelopathy. Root growth in yellow birch seedlings (pioneer species) has been shown to be inhibited by the presence of maple seedlings (climax species), the inhibition being caused by substances leached out of the maple root tips. The difficulty of regenerating yellow birch in areas occupied by sugar maple may well be the result of these allelopathic effects (Tubbs, 1973).

The allelopathic effects of a species are not fixed in time. Other species adapt and eventually the allelopathic effect may become less potent. For example, stands of a given species of *Eucalyptus* in the U.S. sometimes contain almost no other plants, whereas stands of the same species in its native Australia have a well-developed understory. The inference is that there has been sufficient evolutionary time in Australia for minor vegetation species to develop tolerance to the eucalypt allelochemicals, whereas U.S. plants have not had time to adapt to this recently introduced species. Similarly, a species of buttercup *(Ranunculus testiculatus)*, a native of southeastern Europe and central Asia, excluded all other species over large areas when it was introduced to dry areas of Utah and the interior of Oregon and Washington. Tests showed that allelochemicals from the buttercup

Figure 14.14
Effect of allelochemicals produced by bracken fern on
barley plants grown in a nutrient solution. The plants
on the left also received an aqueous extract of bracken
plants. Root growth was severely depressed by the
phenols contained in the extract. (Photo courtesy of
A. D. M. Glass; see Glass, 1976.)

strongly inhibited the germination of native forbs and
grasses. The effect was greatest on sandy soil and least on
fine-textured soils, in which the allelochemicals are presumably absorbed and rendered ineffective (Buchanan et
al., 1978).

Allelopathic effects of overstory dominants on understory
plants are thought to contribute to the patchy distribution of
minor vegetation that is characteristic of forests of mixed
species dominance. Understory species also experience allelochemicals produced by other understory species. It has
been reported that a composite, *Hyoseris scabra,* grows in
the presence of a wild onion *(Allium chamaemoly),* but only
if a third species, *Bellis annua,* is also present. The latter
mitigates for itself and the *Hyoseris* the allelopathic effects
of the onion (Whittaker, 1970).

Allelopathy is not a peculiarity of a few species, but a
widespread and normal, although generally inconspicuous
phenomenon of natural communities. Dramatic cases of allelopathy are easy to recognize (Muller, 1968). In a much
wider range of cases allelochemical effects are less obvious
but may, nevertheless, make significant contributions to
plant competition.

Allelopathic effects are probably far more important in
both forestry and agriculture (Tukey, 1969) than is generally realized. Most home gardeners will recognize the adverse effects of tomato plants on ornamental plants, of ivy if
it is allowed to climb over other plants, and of various species of conifers in the area beneath their crowns, effects that
cannot be explained in terms of simple competition for
space, light, water, nutrients, and so on. Similarly, under-

standing how forest ecosystems operate must involve a recognition of the chemical interactions of species. For a recent
review of allelopathy, see Rice (1984).

4. Competition. Interspecific competition occurs wherever two different species attempt to utilize the same resource when that resource is in limited supply. There is no
competition when they share a common resource that exceeds their combined demands on it. Competition can also
occur when the resource is not in short supply but the two
species interfere with each other's use of it.

We saw in Chapter 13 how growth equations have been
used to describe population growth, including *intraspecific*
competition. The Lotka–Volterra logistic equations that
were discussed can be extended to describe *interspecific*
competition, and used to predict the probable outcome of
such interactions.

When we recognize that environments have a carrying
capacity, and that individuals in the population compete for
the resources that determine that capacity, the simple
growth equation

$$\frac{dN}{dt} = rN$$

becomes

$$\frac{dN}{dt} = rN \left(\frac{K - N}{K} \right)$$

This equation must be further modified where we have populations of two species competing for the same resources.
For species 1, we can rewrite the equation to include $-N_2$,

the negative effect of individuals of species 2 on the carrying capacity of the environment for species 1, either because of competition for a common resource or because of interference in the use of a resource:

$$\frac{dN_1}{dt} = r_1 N_1 \left(\frac{K_1 - N_1 - N_2}{K_1} \right)$$

or

$$\frac{dN_1}{dt} = r_1 N_1 \left(1 - \frac{N_1}{K_1} - \frac{N_2}{K_1} \right)$$

where r_1 is the per capita rate of population increase of species 1, N_1 is the number of individuals of species 1, K_1 is the carrying capacity of the environment for species 1, N_2 is the number of individuals of species 2, N_1/K_1 is the portion of the carrying capacity for species 1 used up by N_1, and N_2/K_1 is the portion of the carrying capacity for species 1 used up by N_2. Thus, the greater the number of individuals of species 2 competing with species 1, the lower the value of $(K_1 - N_1 - N_2)/K_1$, and the lower the rate of population increase for species 1. Similarly, for species 2,

$$\frac{dN_2}{dt} = r_2 N_2 \left(\frac{K_2 - N_2 - N_1}{K_2} \right)$$

or

$$\frac{dN_2}{dt} = r_2 N_2 \left(1 - \frac{N_2}{K_2} - \frac{N_1}{K_2} \right)$$

The greater the number of N_1 individuals, the less the remaining unused carrying capacity for species 2 and the lower its population growth rate.

This formulation is reasonable as long as both species place the same demands on the resource and the ability to exploit the resource is the same for individuals of both species. If they differ, a further modification must be made. Rather than reducing the carrying capacity for species 1 by the *number* of species 2, we must reduce it by the number of species 2 expressed in terms of the equivalent number of species 1. For example, if species 2 eats twice as much as species 1 (i.e., $N_2 = 2N_1$), we would reduce K_1 by $-2N_1$ rather than by $-N_2$. To generalize, we can say that

$$N_1 = \alpha N_2 \qquad \text{and} \qquad N_2 = \beta N_1$$

where $\alpha = N_1/N_2$, or the ratio of resource use by species 1 to resource use by species 2, and $\beta = N_2/N_1$, or the ratio of resource use by species 2 to resource use by species 1. The terms α and β are called the *competition coefficients*. If two species are competing in an area, the number of species 1 that the area can carry is reduced by the number of species 2 present multiplied by species 2 competition coefficient, and vice versa. In other words, $K_1 - N_1 - N_2/\beta = 0$, and $K_2 - N_2 - N_1/\alpha = 0$. The relative numbers of the two species will depend on the value of α and β. This can be described graphically (Figure 14.15).

Figure 14.15

Graphical representation of the change in numbers of two species that are competing with each other. (A) Change in abundance of species 1 as the abundance of a competitor, species 2, varies. When the abundance of species 1 falls in the shaded area, species 1 increases until the stability line value is reached. When there are K_2/β or more individuals of species 1, species 2 is eliminated. When there are K_1/α or more individuals of species 2, species 1 is eliminated. If the abundance of species 1 falls in the unshaded area, numbers will decline until the stability line is reached. (B) Change in abundance of species 2 as the abundance of a competitor, species 1, varies. The same comments apply as for A. The small graphs show the position of the stability line for strong, weak, or no interspecific competition.

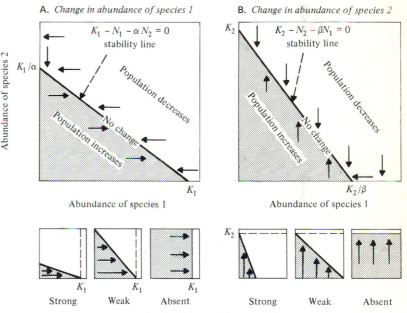

A. *Change in abundance of species 1*

$K_1 - N_1 - \alpha N_2 = 0$
stability line

Population decreases

Population increases   No change

Abundance of species 2 (vertical axis), K_1/α

Abundance of species 1, K_1

B. *Change in abundance of species 2*

$K_2 - N_2 - \beta N_1 = 0$
stability line

Population increases   No change   Population decreases

K_2, K_2/β

Abundance of species 1

Strong   Weak   Absent   Strong   Weak   Absent

K_1 K_1 K_1 K_2

Level of interspecific competition

Interspecific competition attracted the attention of several biologists in the early decades of this century, including a Russian biologist, Gause, who examined the outcome of competition under laboratory conditions between two closely related species of protozoa (*Paramecium* sp.) utilizing the same food resource. His experiments all ended the same way: one species became dominant and finally eliminated the other species (Gause, 1934, 1935). This type of experiment has been repeated many times, including the benchmark work of Park (1962) and his colleagues with the flour beetles *Tribolium castaneum* and *T. confusum*. When these two species were grown together in a bottle of flour, one species always eliminated the other. The successful species depended on the conditions of the experiment. *T. castaneum* prevailed in warm, moist conditions, while *T. confusum* succeeded under drier, cooler conditions, although when grown alone both species did best under warm, moist conditions. This type of experiment has also been performed with plants (e.g., Harper, 1961) with essentially the same results: where two species were forced to compete in a simplified laboratory environment, only one species was able to persist (Figure 14.16).

The results of these experiments led to the *competitive exclusion principle* (Hardin, 1960), which says that two species competing for the same resource cannot coexist indefinitely. One of the two species will eventually dominate. This principle, which is sometimes referred to as *Gause's hypothesis*, has attracted a lot of attention over the past half century. It led to the development of the concept of ecological *niche*.

14.6   The Competitive Exclusion Principle and the Ecological Niche Concept

The competitive exclusion principle works rather well in simple laboratory experiments with two competing species, but in natural ecosystems one can find numerous examples that initially appear to contradict the theory. Consider, for example, the numerous species of phytoplankton in the sur-

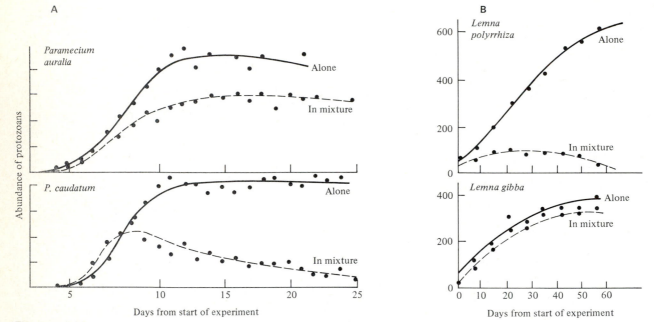

Figure 14.16

Classical studies of competition between closely related species under laboratory culture conditions. (A) The original experiments by Gause (1934, 1935) which led to the development of the competitive exclusion principle. Competition between *Paramecium aurelia* and *P. caudatum* leads to the elimination of *P. caudatum*, although *P. caudatum* can equal *P. aurelia* in population growth when grown alone. (B) Essentially the same results were obtained by Harper (1961) for two closely related species of duckweed *(Lemna),* a small floating plant of calm freshwater ecosystems. *Lemna gibba* excludes *L. polyrrhiza* even though the latter has a greater productivity than *L. gibba* when grown alone. (After Gause, 1934, and Harper. 1961. Used by permission of the Society of Experimental Biology and J. L. Harper.)

face few centimeters of ocean water, all of which are competing for limited nutrients. Why do so many species persist in the face of this competition? One could also ask why so many different species of insect herbivore feed on oak trees. Why are there so many species of birds that prey on a population of insects when it is in outbreak? These questions have fascinated ecologists for years and there have been numerous excellent studies that have helped us to arrive at some answers and to understand the important role that interspecific competition has played in evolution. We shall examine three examples of competitive exclusion in natural ecosystems and then discuss the theory in general terms.

Forests generally have a variety of bird species feeding on the canopy insects. For example, the boreal forests of New England are inhabited by five species of warbler (*Dendroica* sp.), all of which are about the same size and have a similar insect diet. How can these apparently competing species coexist? The answer was revealed in studies (MacArthur, 1958) which showed that coexistence was made possible by a physical and temporal division of the food resource that served to reduce interspecific competition to a lower value than intraspecific competition. The division was achieved by differences in feeding behavior and in the timing of breeding, which varies the time of peak food requirement (Figure 14.17). The Cape May warbler

feeds only on the outer branches in the upper crowns of trees and is abundant only during outbreaks of species such as the spruce budworm. The bay-breasted warbler feeds mainly on the middle parts of the crown, with limited additional feeding in the inner parts of the upper and lower crown. It is also most successful during periods of superabundance of food. The blackburnian warbler feeds mainly in the outer part of the upper two-thirds of the crown. The black-throated green warbler feeds in the middle and outer sections of the branches in the middle of the crown and also on the branch ends of the upper crown. The myrtle warbler is less abundant than the other species and less specialized in its feeding behavior, but it exhibits a tendency to feed in the lower crown. It depends on having a very large territory and is able to maintain a fairly constant population through periods of low insect abundance.

Three of the five species of warbler appear to be able to coexist by a combination of some degree of spatial and temporal separation of their feeding and by differences in feeding behavior. One species can coexist by being a more general feeder and by concentration on the lower crown area, which is underutilized by the other three species. The fifth species can coexist in anything more than very low numbers only when a superabundance of foods reduces the competitive pressure from the other species. This study of warbler coexistence revealed a complex of adaptations by which these closely related species are able to share the same environment.

A somewhat similar example of coexistence was observed in a study of six closely related species of leafhopper (*Erythroneura* sp.) on sycamore trees (*Pseudoplatanus* sp.) in Illinois (Ross, 1957). All six species appear to have very similar habits and life cycles, and it was concluded that this invalidated the competitive exclusion principle. However, it is not clear that severe interspecific competition did in fact occur between these species. The leafhoppers differed slightly in preferred feeding position, and this type of sap-sucking insect has modest food requirements; a large, vigorous tree is able to support very large numbers of them. Also, the action of other population regulators may well have limited the total numbers of leafhoppers to below the levels at which interspecific competition became significant. All six species were found together only on trees in moist, fertile locations, where the trees would probably be able to produce enough photosynthate to support their own minimum requirements and those of the hoppers. In contrast, only two species were found on trees in droughty areas, where the trees would produce less photosynthate. Large populations were found in the fertile locations and small populations in the droughty areas. It may well be that

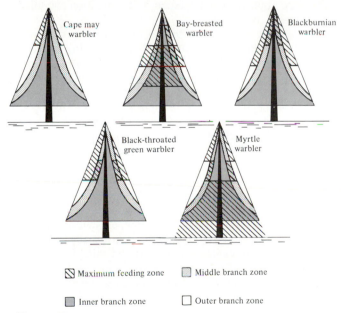

Maximum feeding zone   Middle branch zone

Inner branch zone   Outer branch zone

Figure 14.17
Distribution of feeding activity of five species of warbler in the crowns of conifers in northeastern US. (After MacArthur, 1958. Used with permission of the Ecological Society of America.

interspecific competition is unimportant on the fertile sites but that it prevents four of the six species from coinhabiting the trees on droughty sites. Competitive exclusion can take place only where competition is severe, which probably never occurred on the fertile site.

The enigma of high diversity in populations of oceanic plankton may be explained by the fact that competition between these microscopic autotrophs of the open ocean never continues long enough to permanently favor any one species. It was noted earlier in the discussion that the outcome of competition between two species in the laboratory depends upon the conditions of the experiment. If these conditions are continually changing, neither species will hold the competitive edge long enough to dominate the other. The surface of the ocean is being continually stirred, so that the conditions of light, temperature, and water density to which the plankton community are exposed are continually or at least frequently changed. Under these conditions of environmental diversity and instability, many competing species can coexist.

In contrast to these examples, one can find cases where competitive exclusion has been clearly demonstrated. Numerous examples occur where a species of plant or animal has been introduced from another country without its normal complement of parasites and predators. Uncontrolled, such species multiply rapidly and occupy areas previously occupied by native species which are competitively excluded. For example, when the prickly pear (*Opuntia* sp.) was introduced to Australia in the nineteenth century, it spread over large portions of the continent, excluding native vegetation. By 1900, six species had become established on more than 4 million hectares. By 1925 the cactus occupied an area of nearly 25 million hectares; on half of this area the cactus had become so dense that it was practically impenetrable by human beings or large animals. In a similar example, the Klamath weed *(Hypericum perforatum),* which was first reported in the U.S. in California in 1900, increased until by 1944 it dominated nearly 1 million hectares of rangeland in the western U.S.

A case of competitive exclusion reported from California resulted from attempts to control an important pest species on orange trees, the California red scale *(Aonidiella aurantii).* This pest became heavily parasitized by a parasitic wasp, *Aphytis chrysomphali,* which was accidentally introduced into southern California around 1900. In 1948, another species of *Aphytis (A. lingnanensis)* was introduced from China. Sharing the same food source, it spread rapidly and succeeded in displacing *A. chrysomphali* from an area of about 400 mi² in about 10 years (DeBach and Sundby, 1963). In the late 1950s a third species *(A. melinus)* was

introduced from India. Upon release it began to displace *A. lignanensis* from hotter interior areas but not from the cooler coastal areas. The mechanism of displacement is still not known, but it has been shown that none of the species can coexist in laboratory populations even in the presence of excess supplies of food.

A common means by which closely related species are able to coexist is the evolution of morphological differences that enable them to utilize different resources or slightly different types of environment. Two well-known examples of this are the cases of Darwin's finches *(Geospizinae)* from the Galapagos Islands (Lack, 1947), and the honeycreepers *(Drepanididae)* on the Hawaiian Islands (Amadon, 1947). Beak length varies significantly among each of these two groups of closely related bird species. The different beak size restricts feeding by the birds to different types of food, thereby avoiding competition.

An interesting example of competitive displacement was described among pocket gophers (Geomyidae) in Colorado (Miller, 1964). Four species occur: the Plains, the yellow-faced, the Botta's, and the northern pocket gopher. The four species always occupy different areas, although a study revealed that frequently more than one species could have lived in any one area in the absence of the other species. The most critical factors determining the observed distribution of the gophers were interspecific competition and tolerance of soil conditions.

The relative competitive abilities of the four species were observed to be in the order Plains > yellow-faced > Botta's > northern. That is, the Plains pocket gopher could outcompete the yellow-faced pocket gopher, and so on. The Plains gopher is found only over a narrow range of soil conditions: deep sandy loams. The yellow-faced gopher also prefers deep sandy loams, but cannot compete with the Plains gopher, which excludes it from these preferred habitats. The yellow-faced gopher can tolerate heavier, more compact soils and drier sites, which is where it is found when the two species are sympatric (their ranges overlap). The Botta's gopher will occupy a wide range of soils, being absent only from hard clays and very coarse textured materials, but because it is unable to compete with either the Plains or the yellow-faced gopher, it is usually excluded from the more favorable medium-textured soils. Finally, the northern gopher, which is adapted to a wider range of soils and topography than any of the other three species, prefers and is most abundant in deep, easily worked soils. However, because it can tolerate very shallow and coarse soils and very compacted soils that are beyond the tolerance of the other three species, and because of its low competitive abilities, it tends to be restricted to these marginal sites when the other three species are present. Figure 14.18 summarizes the fundamental and realized niches (see below for explanation) of these four species.

Species avoid competition by evolving different adaptations, tolerances, requirements, behavior, and so on. As Gause predicted, no two species that have the same set of characteristics can compete indefinitely. The fact that species do coexist means that they do not compete intolerably: that they differ in their set of requirements. This observation led to the development of the concept of ecological *niche:* a term that expresses the total role of an organism in the environment. The term was first used by an animal ecologist (Grinnel, 1917) to refer to the *habitat,* the *geographical range,* and the *adaptations* of the bird that he was studying, the California thrasher. The use of the term has changed since 1917. Its current usage encompasses three major concepts:

1. Niche refers to the *functional role* of a species in an ecosystem. It stresses the entire complex of characteristics exhibited by that species. Is it a plant, animal, or microbe? Is it large or small? Is it autotrophic or heterotrophic? What is its productivity and role in nutrient cycling? In other words, how does the species fit into the complex functional processes of the ecosystem? An analogy has been drawn between this aspect of niche and the *profession* or *occupa-*tion of a human being. How does the organism "make its living"? The English ecologist Elton (1927) had this in mind when he defined niche as the relationship of an animal to food and enemies. "The ecologist should cultivate the habit of looking at animals from this point of view as well as the ordinary standpoints of appearance, names, affinities and past history. When an ecologist says 'there goes a badger' he should include in his thoughts some definite idea of the animal's place in the community to which it belongs, just as if he had said 'there goes the vicar'." The "profession" of an animal defines how it "makes its living," when it makes its living, and how it interacts with other species. When we define a person as a forester, a wildlife manager, a fisherman, or a miner we have defined much of how that person makes a living and the role of that person in the local economy and community. We have defined the functional aspects of the person's niche in the community.

2. Niche refers also to the *habitat* of a species: the type or range of environments in which it lives. By defining the habitat, the range of physical conditions to which the species is exposed is also partially defined. Thus, definition of a species niche includes its adaptations to light, temperature, moisture, nutrients, soil, fire, and so on, and the amplitude of these factors to which it is exposed at various times.

Figure 14.18

Fundamental and realized niches of four species of pocket gopher in Colorado expressed in terms of soil texture. All four species achieve peak abundance on loose sandy-loam soils, but there is a progressive exclusion to increasingly marginal soil types as competitive ability declines. (Based on Miller, 1964.)

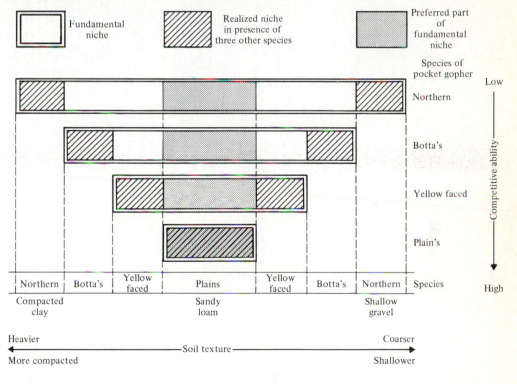

3. Definition of niche involves a statement of the *geographical area* in which a species is found (e.g., its territory or home range). Area is different from habitat. The latter is concerned with the factors that determine where a species is found, whereas the former is concerned with the geographical extent and location of its range.

Niche thus refers to the functional, adaptational, and distributional characteristics of a species. Definition of the niche of a species is obviously complex, involving a large number of parameters. Also, the definition cannot be fixed, in that species interactions, habitat adaptations, and area are all variable over time. The niche of an individual when it is young may differ from its niche when it is old.

The niche of a species has been likened to a volume within which the species is competitively supreme. For example, if we could define the niche of three species of trees in terms of light requirements, nutrient requirements, and moisture requirements, we could represent their niches graphically as in Figure 14.19. The American ecologist Evelyn Hutchinson (1957) introduced this idea when he described niche as an *n-dimensional hypervolume* (*n* = the

number of parameters being used to characterize the niche). He also noted that it is necessary to identify two hypervolumes: a *fundamental niche,* which contains a smaller *realized niche* (Figure 14.18). The fundamental niche represents the maximum niche that the species could occupy in the absence of competition from other species. The realized niche is that portion of the fundamental niche occupied by the species in the face of competition. In an ecosystem that has been relatively undisturbed for a long time, the geographical range of species will reflect its realized niche. Following disturbances such as fire, extensive logging, or removal of some component of the community by biotic processes, a species may spread to occupy much or all of its fundamental niche.

Douglas-fir has been planted in western North America over a much wider elevational and soil moisture range than is normal in old-growth forests, where it is restricted to a much narrower realized niche. Some of these plantings have failed because the species has been planted outside its fundamental niche (i.e., outside the range of physical environments to which the species is adapted). Others have failed

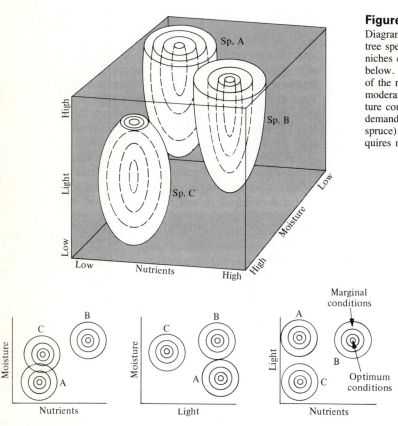

Figure 14.19

Diagrammatic representation of the realized niche volumes of three tree species, defined in terms of light, moisture, and nutrients. The niches defined in terms of two parameters at a time are shown below. The concentric volumes (circles) represent various portions of the realized niches, from optimum to marginal. Species A is moderately light demanding but tolerant of low nutrient and moisture conditions (e.g., a species of pine). Species B is also light demanding, but requires high moisture and nutrient levels (e.g., a spruce). Species C is tolerant of low light and nutrients, but requires moderate to high levels of moisture (e.g., a hemlock).

because although the plantings were done within the fundamental niche, competition from other species was too high: the species was planted outside its realized niche. Artificial manipulation of competition by manual, mechanical, or chemical weeding can permit a species to greatly expand its realized niche compared to that of an undisturbed system. Also, where a species is introduced to a new environment without the natural enemies and competitors with which it has evolved, its realized niche may become very extensive (e.g., prickly pear in Australia, radiata pine in New Zealand and Australia).

14.7 Community Diversity

Community diversity refers to the number of different species in the community. Some plant communities are characterized by low diversity: for example, a lodgepole pine forest on a rocky ridge in coastal British Columbia. Others, such as the herb and shrub-rich forest in the valley below, have a very high diversity. Diversity can refer to all organisms in the community, but it is more frequently used to refer to one type or group of organism. Thus we can talk about the diversity of vascular plants, of birds, of mammals, and of the soil fauna.

Diversity expressed as a species list does not give an adequate picture of a community because the *relative abundance* and *importance* of the different species can vary. Two forests, both with 20 species of plants, can differ greatly in their characteristics. One could be a conifer forest dominated by a single overstory species with occasional specimens of three other tree species and a very sparse understory of 16 species, most of them mosses, with two species accounting for the majority of the understory biomass. On the other hand, the overstory could be an intimate mixture of six species of conifer with a well-developed understory of 12 species of shrubs and herbs, all rather similar in abundance.

Any analysis of diversity should include measures of both species diversity and individual species importance. The *importance value* of a species in a community can be assessed in various ways. The number of individuals per unit area (density or abundance) is often used for animal species, but it is not very useful when comparing the importance of organisms such as moose and white-footed deer mice, or Douglas-fir and stepmoss *(Hylocomium splendens)*. The problem is somewhat reduced by the use of biomass per unit area. For plant populations, *percent cover* (percentage of the horizontal surface that is occupied by the *crowns* of each species) or a combined cover-abundance estimate is commonly used to indicate species importance. Productivity of the different species has also been used as a measure of importance.

Once an importance value has been assigned to each species, the allocation of the community's resources between the member species can be summarized graphically by plotting the *relative importance value* (this is calculated for each species by dividing the importance value of that species by the sum of the importance values for all the species in the community) of each species in descending order of species importance. Because communities typically have a few species with high importance values and a lot of species with low values, such graphical representations are typically plotted on a logarithmic scale.

Figure 14.20 shows the three major types of species importance curves that have been observed. Line **A** (a geometric series) is typical of the low-diversity communities of severe environments in which dominance by a few species is well developed. The plants of subalpine or boreal forest would approximate this type of importance curve. Line **B** (called the log-normal distribution) is typical of communities rich in species, such as the tropical rain forest and some semidesert areas. It involves a few species with high values, and a large number of species that are uncommon or rare. Samples from heterogeneous environments that include several different plant associations also exhibit this distribution of importance values. Line **C,** in which several species have high importance and there are few rare species, is characteristic of small samples of taxonomically related animals from a narrowly defined, homogeneous community (e.g., nesting birds in a woodland).

Attempts to produce meaningful generalizations about the observed variations in species diversity in different environments has absorbed much time and energy and has elicited extended argument between ecologists. Some of the earlier generalizations (e.g., that diversity increases during successional development from pioneer to climax, that the most diverse communities are the most productive and stable, or that diversity increases along moisture and nutrient gradients) have been shown to be inaccurate, and today a much more cautious approach is taken to the subject than previously. A detailed treatment of the topic is beyond the scope of this chapter; only a brief summary will be presented. The topic is discussed more fully in texts such as Ricklefs (1973), Krebs (1978), and Whittaker (1975).

Two categories of diversity can be identified. The number of species present in a sample for a particular community is referred to as *alpha diversity*. A lodgepole pine–*Cladonia* lichen forest will have a low alpha diversity, whereas a tropical rain forest will have a high alpha diversity. The variation in species composition between two adjacent communities on an environmental gradient is called *beta diversity*. The beta diversity of an area containing both grassland and closed forest will generally be greater than that of an area containing two different coniferous forest associations or two different grassland associations.

Alpha diversity can be measured in a variety of ways, including:

1. *Species diversity:*

$$d = S/\log A \quad \text{or} \quad S/\log N$$

where d is the species diversity, S the number of species in a sample of standard size, A the sample area, and N the total number of individuals in the sample.

2. *Simpson's index:*

$$C = \sum_{i=1}^{s} (n_i/N)^2$$

where C is Simpson's index, n_i the importance value of the ith species, and N the total importance value for all species.

There is also a wide choice of methods for measuring beta diversity, of which the following two are commonly used:

1. *Coefficient of community*

$$CC = \frac{2\,S_{ab}}{S_a + S_b}$$

Figure 14.20
Species importance curves for three different types of environment. (A) Vascular plant species in a subalpine fir forest in Tennessee. Species importance is measured by net production. (B) Vascular plant species in a deciduous "cove forest" in Tennessee (such forests are characterized by high species diversity). Species importance is measured by net production. (C) Importance of bird species in a deciduous forest in West Virginia, measured by densities of nesting pairs. (Reprinted with permission of Macmillan Publishing Company from *Communities and Ecosystems,* Second Edition by Robert H. Whittaker. Copyright © 1975 by Robert H. Whittaker.)

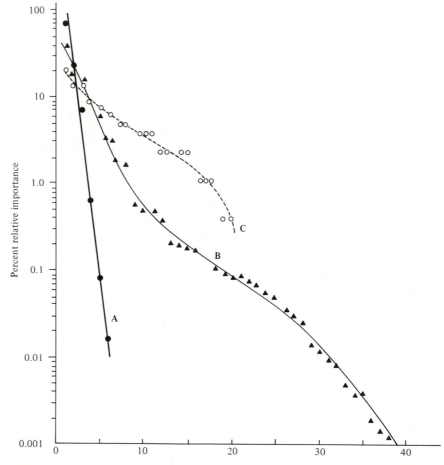

where CC is the coefficient of community, S_a the number of species in community a, S_b the number of species in community b, and S_{ab} the number of species that occur in both communities.

2. *Percent similarity and Euclidian distance*

$$PS = 1 - 0.5\Sigma(P_a - P_b)$$

or

$$ED = \sqrt{\Sigma(N_a - N_b)^2}$$

where PS in the percent similarity, ED the Euclidian distance, P_a and P_b are the decimal importance value for a given species in communities a and b; N_a and N_b are the importance values for a given species in communities a and b.

A detailed treatment of these measures of diversity is beyond the scope of this book. The interested reader should consult Kershaw (1973) or Mueller-Dombois and Ellenberg (1974).

Perhaps the only reliable generalization that can be made about biotic diversity in terrestrial ecosystems is that alpha diversity for most groups of organisms generally decreases from lowland tropical to high-latitude or high-altitude ecosystems. A tropical rain forest in Malaysia can contain up to 227 tree species on about 2 ha (Richards, 1969), whereas the central hardwood forests of eastern U.S. may have 10–40 overstory species (Clark, 1976) present in an area, and the boreal forest in Canada may have only one to four species. The number of ant species varies from 222 in Brazil to 63 in Iowa and 3 in arctic Alaska (Fischer, 1960). There are about 600 species of breeding land birds in Panama, 150 in Oregon, and 26 in the Alaskan north coast (MacArthur and Wilson, 1967). The number of land mammal species increases from 15 in northern Canada to more than 150 in Central America (Simpson, 1964). An example of how the diversity of tree species can vary latitudinally and longitudinally is given in Figure 14.21. This shows tree species diversity in British Columbia. The greatest diversity is found in mountainous regions in the southern part of the province at the interface between coastal and interior climatic conditions.

Many explanations have been advanced to explain the global pattern of latitudinal variation in diversity:

A. Time Hypothesis

One of the earliest suggestions was based on the greater age of tropical ecosystems, where evolution has supposedly continued with relatively little interruption for millions of years. Glaciation in the recent past makes many temperate areas very young by comparison, giving less time for high diversity to evolve. Certainly, the fossil record, although very incomplete, does suggest a latitudinal gradient in species diversity, and it has been pointed out that the diversity of insect species feeding on trees is related to the time over which the insect–host relationship has developed (Southwood, 1961). For example, sessile oak, which is native to Britain, is associated with 284 species of insect, whereas evergreen oak, introduced in 1580, has only two associated insects. A graph of the present-day number of associated insect species plotted against the length of the fossil record of the host tree species in Britain shows a reasonably linear trend (Figure 14.22). The validity of the time hypothesis is difficult to assess because of the incompleteness of the fossil record and because unequivocal proof would require actual observation, which is nearly impossible considering the time scale. Consequently, there has been more interest in the alternative hypotheses.

B. Rate of Speciation Hypothesis

It is widely held that the rate of speciation (evolution of new species) is faster in the tropics than in temperate or arctic environments. The longer growing season and relative lack of seasonal environmental extremes in the tropics permits many generations per year and maintenance of populations close to their K value (carrying capacity). This intensifies interspecific competition and creates a more favorable environment for speciation. Many animals and birds in the tropics are more sedentary than at higher latitudes and altitudes. This characteristic reduces the flow of genes between populations that are diverging genetically and thereby facilitates speciation. The high mountains of many tropical countries tend to be a greater barrier to bird and animal movement than do the mountains of temperate zones; high mountain passes are climatically much more different from lowland habitats in the tropics than in temperate zones (Janzen, 1967).

Natural selection in tropical environments is predominantly in response to biotic factors (interspecific interactions), whereas at higher latitudes and altitudes, physical factors play a major role (Dobzansky, 1950). The release of adapting systems from the physiological constraints imposed by the demands of the physical environment allows a more rapid evolutionary response to biotic factors in the tropics. This encourages the development of a positive feedback between the development of diversity in different components of the community; increased diversity of animals leads to a diversification of the vegetation which creates the potential for a greater diversity of animals.

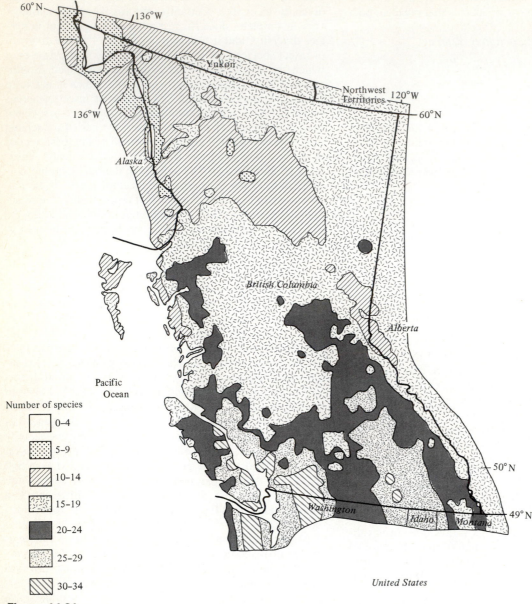

Figure 14.21
Tree species diversity in British Columbia. The highest diversity occurs in the area of climatic transition from coastal to interior climatic conditions. The area is mountainous and there is a high diversity of physical environments based on variation in elevation, aspect, and location within the transition area. (After Krajina, Klinka, and Worrall, 1982. Used by permission of J. G. Worrall.)

Figure 14.22

The relationship between the length of the fossil record of several British tree species and the number of insects known to be associated with them. The number of fossil records of tree remains for the Quaternary (=Pleistocene and recent geological periods, approximately the last million years) is a measure of how long the tree species has occurred in Britain and how long insect-tree coevolution has been occurring in this area. (After Southwood, 1961. Used with permission of Blackwell Scientific Publications.)

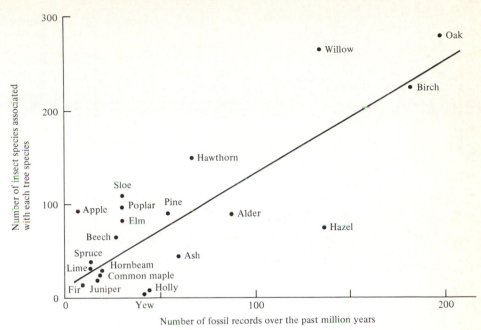

C. Predation Hypothesis

Another theory about tropical diversity suggests that there are more predators and parasites in the tropics than elsewhere and that these serve to hold down prey populations to such low levels that competition among prey species is reduced (Paine, 1966). This permits the addition of more prey species, which in turn supports new predators. The addition of more prey species tends to reestablish interspecific competition, which in turn promotes further speciation. There is some evidence in favor of this idea. It has been shown that in some communities the removal of predators lowers the diversity of prey species because it permits the development of dominance by a few species.

Janzen (1970) has suggested that seed predators contribute to the low density of adult trees of any one species in species-rich, lowland tropical forests, and to the regular spacing of such trees. Many tropical seed eaters are host specific and tend to be aggregated around the host tree. This produces a "seed shadow" around each tree and a steady increase in seedling establishment with increasing distance from the seed source, until one approaches maximum dispersal range (Figure 14.23). Survival of a tree's offspring is reduced within its own seed shadow, permitting other species to grow there and producing a high alpha diversity. Janzen's hypothesis requires that seed predation is less efficient in the less diverse temperate and high latitude/altitude environments. In support of the theory is the report by Harper (1969) that the herbaceous vegetation on an island off the coast of England was more diverse when heavily browsed by rabbits than after removal of the rabbits by myxamitosis (a virus disease).

The exact role of predation in population regulation is still unclear and so also is the role of predation in determining diversity. There is a lack of data to test this hypothesis critically, and it may be that predation is more important in explaining alpha diversity in the tropics than in explaining the global latitudinal gradient in species diversity.

D. Environmental Stability Hypothesis

An important difference between tropical and polar environments is the degree of environmental stability. Environments with low biotic diversity tend to be severe or unpredictable, or both, whereas those with high biotic diversity tend to be either stable or predictable, or both. The surprising fact that biotic diversity is greater in deep-sea communities than in very shallow water communities has been used to challenge the theory that diversity is related to temperature: that high temperatures encourage the development of high diversity and low temperatures induce low diversity (deep-sea temperatures are low). It has been proposed that diversity is not related to temperature per se but to the stability of that temperature and the predictability of its

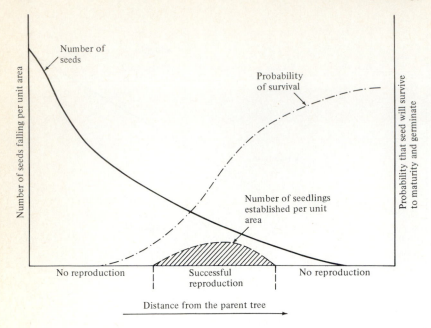

Figure 14.23

Graphical presentation of the suggested explanation for the lack of self-reproduction in the vicinity of tropical trees ("seed shadow"). This phenomenon is thought to contribute to the high diversity of tropical rain forests. (After Janzen, 1970. Copyright University of Chicago Press. Used with permission of the publisher and author.)

changes. Stable climates permit the development of more finely adapted species and therefore more potential niches than erratic climates in which there is a strong selective advantage to having broad adaptations. Against this argument is the fact that there are many hot desert and semidesert environments which are markedly unstable in terms of moisture and yet have high plant diversity. This would support the idea that temperature, rather than either moisture or the stability of environmental conditions, has a key influence on terrestrial vascular plant diversity (Whittaker, 1975).

E. Environmental Heterogeneity Hypothesis

There appears to be a relationship between diversity and environmental heterogeneity. The more heterogeneous and complex the physical environment, the more complex the plant and animal communities. Mountainous areas are associated with higher species diversity than areas of gentle topography. Mountainous Columbia has more species of birds than Brazil, which has a more uniform topography. The Pacific coast and Sierra Nevada mountains in the U.S. have a higher diversity of mammals than do the high plains or Mississippi Valley. In Canada, conifer forests of topographically and climatically diverse British Columbia have in total a much greater diversity than coniferous forests in the less variable physical environments of provinces such as Saskatchewan, Manitoba, and Ontario. The greatest diversity in British Columbia is found in the coastal mountains in the transition zone between interior and coastal climatic regions (Figure 14.21). This area has a particularly high diversity of physical environments. Mountainous relief is characterized by marked variations in elevation, aspect, slope, climate, and soils, and this heterogeneity is associated with a considerable diversity of plant and animals.

An interesting aspect of spatial heterogeneity is found among birds. A study of bird diversity in the deciduous forests of the eastern U.S. revealed that there was a stronger relationship between bird species diversity and foliage-height diversity than between bird diversity and plant species diversity. Foliage-height diversity is a measure of the stratification of the plant crowns. High foliage-height diversity occurs where foliage extends continuously from ground to upper canopy, whether this is because of a variety of species or a variety of age classes of a single species (MacArthur and MacArthur, 1961).

F. Size and Spatial Isolation of "Islands"

The diversity of species on islands, peninsulas, or isolated patches of vegetation (e.g., "islands" of forest in grasslands, or the vegetation on a tall, isolated peak) presents a special case. It has been observed that the number of species on islands depends upon the size of the island (Figure 14.24) and that the shape of the relationship is reasonably constant. The number depends on two factors: the rate at

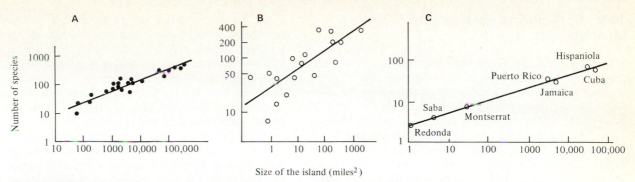

Figure 14.24
Species diversity and the area of islands in various parts of the world. The graphs show how the number of species increases as the size of an island increases. (A) Terrestrial and freshwater birds on the Sanda Islands, the Philippines, and New Guinea (after MacArthur and Wilson, 1967). (B) Terrestrial plant species on the Galapagos Islands (after Preston, 1962). (C) Amphibians and reptiles in the West Indies (after MacArthur and Wilson, 1967). (Figures A and C from Robert H. MacArthur and Edward O. Wilson, *The Theory of Island Biogeography.* Copyright © 1967 by Princeton University Press. Reprinted by permission of Princeton University Press. Figure B from Preston, 1962. Used with permission of the Ecological Society of America and F. W. Preston.)

which species become extinct and the rate at which extinction losses are replaced by immigration to the island. The explanation for reduced island diversity is that the small supply of resources on small islands cannot support large populations and/or many species, and therefore the extinction rate is higher than on a large island with many resources. It is thought (MacArthur and Wilson, 1967) that islands distant from the source of immigrants will have a lower rate of immigration and therefore will support a lower equilibrium diversity than islands near to a mainland source. The species-area curve should rise more rapidly on islands close to the mainland than on remote islands. Many recent studies support this theory, and the topic has received increasing attention in the past few years (e.g., Burgess and Sharpe, 1981).

The question as to how large an area must be in order to maintain a given diversity of species has important practical implications. As more and more of the world's mature, unmanaged forest is logged, the remaining areas of parks, nature reserves, and the like become "islands" in a "sea" of different vegetation and/or land uses. If these reserves are too small, the very species they were created to protect may not survive. Definition of the critical minimal area necessary for the preservation of a given species or community is thus essential in designing parks, reserves, and "leave blocks." For example, minimal area requirements may mean that it is better to have one large park than several smaller parks of the same total area. The issue is important

whenever large scale deforestation is occurring, especially in the tropics where patchwork clearance for agriculture may leave areas of forest that are too small to sustain the desired diversity of native vegetation and animal life (Lovejoy and Oren, 1981, and other references in Burgess and Sharpe, 1981).

From our present knowledge it appears that useful generalizations about patterns of diversity that are valid for all groups of organisms will continue to elude us. Variation in species diversity is complex and does not form a smooth, steady gradient from the equator to the poles. Different factors appear to be involved in determining the diversity of different species groups: vegetation structure for birds, environmental stability in oceanic-bottom organisms, temperature, moisture and nutrient conditions for terrestrial plants, and so on. Diversity can vary widely at different times in any particular environment. Diversity generally increases with time (at least initially) after a disturbance event has eliminated the fauna and flora, as the result of both reinvasion (short-term change) and evolution (long-term change). However, diversity changes produced by ecological succession can exhibit a variety of patterns (Chapter 15), and evolution can lead to temporary declines in diversity if a species evolves that exerts strong dominance in the community. There is no clear relationship between productivity and diversity, nor is there any clear and/or consistent relationship between diversity and various measures of ecosystem stability (Chapter 15).

14.8 Community Ecology and Forest Management

Foresters are concerned with the structure and functioning of forested ecosystems. Although this concern requires that due consideration be given to *both* the abiotic and biotic components, it is the latter part of the ecosystem that is often of greatest immediate interest. Chapter 3 stressed the need to consider the biotic community in an ecosystem and landscape context. However, there are several aspects of community ecology that have value for forest management, with or without a broader ecosystem framework.

In Chapter 16 we will see that knowledge of life forms, their relative frequencies (life form spectra), and the vertical layering and percent cover of the various layers in plant communities can be very useful in the description, classification, and identification of forest ecosystems. Strand structure is important in timber, wildlife, water, range, and recreation management, so most categories of forester should have a basic knowledge of community structure.

Classification of forest ecosystems involves division of the landscape into classes. This can be done in a number of ways, but it is often based solely or partially on the plant community. Development of a practical plant-community-based system of forest classification involves a recognition of how species are distributed along environmental gradients. A system that assumes discrete associations will not work well where there is a continuum of vegetation change, while the assumption of a continuum ignores the advantages that can be gained in those regions where there are mutually exclusive associations that reflect significant variations in the productive potential of the physical environment. Knowledge of species distributions along environmental gradients can help in predicting such things as the correct tree species for the site, the brush hazzard, and the appropriate silvicultural regime.

One of the most important aspects of community ecology is the diversity of interspecific interactions. Most foresters are well aware of antagonistic interactions between their tree crops and some of the other species in the community, but the full significance of interspecific interactions for the composition and productivity of the community is not always recognized. The geographical range of a species may be determined as much by its susceptibility to a herbivore or a pathogen as its ability to tolerate some climatic or edaphic factor (note that biotic and abiotic factors interact). The growth of a tree species may not be possible in the absence of some mutualistic interaction (e.g., mycorrhizae or N-fixing microbes), while the presence of a noncommercial but deeply rooted species with nutrient-rich, highly decomposable litterfall may significantly increase the production of a shallow-rooted crop species.

Recognition of the importance of interspecific interactions and how the forester can influence them creates the possibility of managing these interactions to our advantage. Improved mycorrhizal and symbiotic nitrogen associations offer the possibility of significant increases in tree growth. Understanding the nature of competition can facilitate wise investment of time and energy in alleviating competition or can lead to the use of competition as a biological method of weed control.

Community ecology considered in an ecosystem context leads to the concept of ecological niche. Knowledge of the fundamental niche of a tree species can indicate the potential geographical and habitat range over which the species might be grown; but successful extension of a species outside of its realized niche involves an understanding of the biotic interactions that act to exclude the species from those areas of its fundamental niche that it does not normally occupy. Only if the forester is able to modify these interactions appropriately will crop establishment outside of a species' realized niche be successful. Harvesting and postharvest site treatment can so alter the physical characteristics of a site that the area can become part of the realized niche of a species that is normally excluded. By this means, the forester may be able to expand the range of a desirable species, (and may also expand the range of a pest species). However, it must be recognized that unless the physical changes are maintained, antagonistic biotic interactions that normally exclude the species may intensify and result in the eventual failure of the crop. The complex interplay between biotic and abiotic factors that determines a species range is seen most dramatically in tree lines. A consideration of this type of ecotone is helpful in appreciating the complexity of ecosystems.

Much has been written about the relationship between species diversity and community productivity and stability. Few practically useful generalizations have emerged, but it does seem that diversity can be a useful parameter in defining ecosystems. More research is required before we are able to assess for most sites the relative desirability of low and high species diversity.

It should be apparent from this brief review that community ecology involves a variety of topics that are of value to foresters. Much of the value relates to an understanding of ecosystem change and the application of community ecology in ecological classification. These topics are covered in the next two chapters.

14.9 Summary

There are two major components in the environment of any organism: abiotic factors (physical and chemical) and biotic factors. The latter can be further subdivided into organisms of the same type (other members of the same species population) and organisms of some other type. These two subcomponents give rise to intraspecific and interspecific interactions, respectively, both of which are important in determining the abundance and distribution of organisms. This chapter has been concerned with the second of these two types of interaction.

Mixed-species communities have three dimensions to their structure, two of which were considered in this chapter: the vertical structure and the horizontal structure. The third dimension, change in structure over time, is discussed in the next chapter. Communities vary in the number of layers of vegetation they have, which depends on the variety of life forms represented in the community, which in turn reflects soil and climatic conditions and the actions of biotic factors. The floristic composition and structure change as these two physical features change, which gives rise to the spatial variation in communities.

The question of how species and/or communities are arranged along environmental gradients has been as controversial among community ecologists as the question of population regulation has been among population ecologists. For several decades there were energetic arguments between supporters of the continuum and association schools of thought, but as with the population question, time has mellowed the argument. It is now generally recognized that the pattern of species replacement along environmental gradients varies between different climatic, physiographic, and floristic areas, that it may vary in different layers of the community and at different times, and that one's view of the pattern of distribution may depend on how one looks at it.

Irrespective of exactly how species arrange themselves in space, there is little question that the distribution is related to the ecological niches, both fundamental and realized, of the species concerned. These niches are defined both in terms of the physical requirements and tolerances of the organisms and in terms of the rich diversity of interspecific interactions that exist in any community. As with population regulation, the relative importance of physical and biotic factors in determining community structure, composition, and variation along environmental gradients will differ between different climatic, physiographic, and biotic regions.

Community diversity has been the subject of much discussion. Earlier ideas that there was a positive relationship between the diversity and the stability of the community have had to be reevaluated, partly because no simple relationship seems to exist and partly because it is so difficult to decide just what we mean by stability. All that can be said at this point is that stability, however this term is used, is determined by far more than floristic diversity.

The diversity of climates and soils around the world has permitted the evolution of diverse forms of terrestrial life, which are arranged in broad biotic assemblages over the surface of the continents. These assemblages are characterized by the life form of their vegetation (i.e., the plant formation) but include all the animals and microbes with which the plants are associated. The term biome refers to these broad regional biotic assemblages and their associated abiotic environments.

Community ecology is important in forest resource management because in attempting to favor particular species, the manager must understand the species' niche, both fundamental and realized, and the variety of interspecific interactions that will determine, in large part, the success or failure of his or her activities. Interactions that are adverse for the desired species must be controlled, and those that are beneficial should be promoted.

Section **E** Temporal Changes in Ecosystem Structure and Function

Sections A–D have presented an introduction to the ecosystem, how it functions, the importance of the genetic constitution of the biota in determining this function, and the physical and biotic factors and processes that affect the biota. Having examined the system and its components, we now consider change in ecosystems over time and how such change influences ecosystem structure and function. Of the various types of temporal change, the single chapter in this section will focus on the relatively rapid changes that occur in the structure and composition of the biotic community in an area following some disturbance of the original community; a type of change called ecological succession. This type of change is produced, either intentionally or otherwise, by forest management, and much of a forest manager's life is spent manipulating succession. It is therefore extremely important that foresters have a sound grasp of this topic.

15.1 Introduction and Terminology

Change is one of the most fundamental characteristics of ecosystems. Just as individual organisms change through the various stages of their life history, so the characteristics of ecosystems alter as time passes. Three major categories of ecosystem change can be identified.

1. *Long-term changes in the physical environment.* Ice ages come and go, soils develop or they may be eroded, and lakes become shallower and may eventually disappear as they are filled in with sediments. This type of change normally occurs very slowly, and generally we cannot observe the consequences for biotic communities within our lifetime. The resulting changes in the physical environment tend to be directional over long periods; those in the vegetation can be seen in the composition of pollen found at various depths in the sediments or peat of lakes and bogs (cf. Figure 15.7). Sometimes, the change occurs more rapidly and we can observe the effects in decade-to-decade changes in plant and animal populations. For example, several decades of weather that is warmer and drier than average may result in alpine meadows being invaded by trees. Several decades of weather that is cooler and wetter than average may result in the invasion of dry grasslands by the forest. Such medium-term climatic changes, however, are rarely directional and generally do not produce consistent directional changes in the biota. Rather, they produce medium-term variations around the average condition; the position of the alpine meadow–forest or grassland–forest ecotone fluctuates about a long-term average.

2. *Changes in the genetic constitution of organisms as the result of natural selection.* This type of change is occurring continually and is called evolution (Chapter 6). It can occur rapidly in response to rapidly changing physical or biotic selection pressures, but it also occurs on a longer time scale in response to slow but directional changes in climate, soil conditions, and other organisms. Natural selection is constantly altering the genetic constitution of populations in a manner that increases their genetic fitness. With continual changes in the physical and biotic environment there is continual genetic adjustment to maintain fitness.

3. *Changes in the types, numbers, and groupings of organisms occupying an area and concomitant changes in certain features of the physical microenvironment.* This type of change occurs in both newly exposed, previously uncolonized physical environments, and in previously colonized areas following disturbance to the indigenous community. The changes in the biota are accompanied by changes in the microclimate and soil. Sometimes these

15 Ecological Succession: Processes of Change in Ecosystems

physical changes result from the changes in the biota; sometimes vice versa.

Of these three categories of change, we are most familiar with the last one: the temporal development of and change in ecosystem structure and function. If we give up the fight with weeds in our garden, or if an economically marginal farm is abandoned, the freshly exposed soil will soon be colonized by a variety of plants, most of which are annuals. Within a few years, these will have been joined by perennial weeds and, unless we are in a very arid climate, it will not be too long before woody plants make their appearance: either shrubs or trees. In many areas, the first trees to become established are hardwoods (angiosperms). These may be successively replaced by other species of hardwood trees, but in many parts of the nontropical world we would probably live to see the day when coniferous tree species make their appearance and initiate what may be either a slow or a rapid replacement. In several other parts of the world, conifers may be the pioneers and be replaced by hardwoods.

This type of change is of enormous importance to humans. It lies behind the need for farmers to plow fields and to employ selective herbicides. It is the ecological rationale for the practices of clearcutting and prescribed burning in the management of certain types of forest. It is why we spend so much of our summer weekends on our knees in our gardens. It is called *ecological succession* (or simply *succession*) and is the topic of this chapter.

The term *succession* can be used in two ways. It can refer to the sequence of plant, animal, and microbial communities that successively occupy an area over a period of time, such as the changes that can be observed over the hundred years following the abandonment of a plowed field (Figure 15.1). It can also refer to the *process of change* by which these biotic communities replace each other and by which the physical environment becomes altered over a period of time. When the term is used in this latter sense, the *product* of succession is called a *sere:* the characteristic sequence of biotic communities that successively occupy and replace each other in a particular environment over time following disturbance of the original community or the formation of a new, previously uncolonized environment. The various communities that together make up a sere are called *seral stages*. Throughout this chapter, *succession* will be used to refer to the process of change, and *sere* will be used to refer to the product of succession.

Ecological succession, the process of ecosystem development, occurs in virtually every type of environment found on earth, although the details vary according to the type of ecosystem. It is called *primary succession* when it begins in environments that lack organic matter and which have not yet been altered in any way by living organisms. A fresh rock surface exposed by a landslide, a layer of till deposited by a retreating glacier, a new lake formed by the construction of a dam, or a new island created by volcanic eruption would undergo primary succession. Where succession begins in an environment that has already been more or less modified by a period of occupancy by living organisms, it is called *secondary succession*. Forest clearcuts and abandoned agricultural fields both undergo secondary succession.

Succession in very dry (xeric) environments is called *xerarch succession;* that in moist (mesic) and very wet (hydric) environments is called *mesarch* and *hydrarch succession,* respectively. The resulting seres under these three different moisture conditions are called *xeroseres, mesoseres,* and *hydroseres. Psammoseres* result when succession occurs in sand dune environments, and the sequence of communities in salty environments such as salt marshes is called a *halosere*. Succession on rock surfaces produces a *lithosere.*

A further distinction is sometimes made on the basis of the fertility status of the environment. *Oligotrophic succession* occurs in nutrient-poor environments; comparable terms for moderately fertile and rich environments are *mesotrophic succession* and *eutrophic succession,* respectively. These adjectives have traditionally been used to describe different stages of a hydrosere, but there is no a priori reason why they should not also be used to describe variations in succession between any environments varying in nutrient status. The successional pattern of plant communities on an oligotrophic soil is generally very different from that on a eutrophic soil.

The driving force behind succession, the reason why change occurs, is not always the same. If classified according to the driving force, three main categories of succession can be identified. In many cases, the replacement of one community by the next results from changes in the physical environment that have been produced by the resident organisms. These changes often render the site less optimal for the organisms producing the change and more optimal for those organisms that replace them. Such a process is called *autogenic succession,* in contrast to *allogenic succession,* which occurs when geological processes cause changes in the physical environment, which in turn lead to changes in the biota. The filling in of a lake with sediment and the resulting changes in the biota are an example of allogenic succession, whereas the subsequent biotically controlled conversions from bog community to forest are an example of autogenic succession. A third and somewhat less common type, *biogenic succession,* occurs when there is sudden interference with an autogenic or allogenic succession by a living organism which becomes the major agent of successional change, at least temporarily. A sudden change in herbivore pressure on the plant community or the sudden removal of a segment of the plant community by a pathogen are two examples of biogenic succession. The maintenance of grasslands in some areas of the world has been attributed to the activity of browsing and grazing herbivores. Successional change toward a conifer forest can be hastened by insect or disease removal of an earlier hardwood seral stage.

Although change in the composition of the biota over time is a fundamental characteristic of all ecosystems, the rates of change vary widely in different seres and between the different stages of a single sere. In most areas, change does not continue indefinitely. Communities develop in which rates of change become exceedingly slow, or in which the composition of the biota remains approximately constant for a long period of time. Such relatively stable communities, which represent either the final or an indefinitely prolonged stage of a sere, are called *climax communities*—or simply *climax*. The climax can be considered both in terms of physiognomy and in terms of structure and

Figure 15.1

Typical sequence of plant communities that might be observed occupying a plowed field or scarified clearcut in coastal British Columbia over the subsequent 100-year period. The photographs show representative communities for three stages: (A) herb-shrub-young deciduous tree; (B) deciduous tree; and (C) maturing conifer. (D) A drawing showing the variations over the period in the importance values of the different vegetation forms. In similar "old-field" successions in other regions, a conifer forest stage (frequently consisting of pines) may follow the shrub stage, to be replaced in time by a final deciduous stage.

floristic composition. Thus, the term can be used to refer both to plant formations or biomes and to plant associations.

Most of the above successional terminology refers to a progressive, forward development of the ecosystem toward a climax condition. *Successional retrogression,* on the other hand, refers to the effects of disturbance in altering the seral condition of an ecosystem back to an earlier stage: for example, when fire destroys a climax community and leads to the development of a pioneer primary or secondary successional community, depending on the severity of the fire.

As we will see by the end of the chapter, the simple, progressive development of a sere from a bare, unvegetated area through a predictable series of stages to a stable climax is not an accurate description of what really happens in many kinds of ecosystem. Many ecologists whose experience is limited to anthropogenically disturbed environments do not find the concept of a linear development to a predictable climax community very useful, and it is now recognized that the pattern of seral stages is often variable. However, the linear concept of successional development will serve as a useful starting point for our discussion.

Ecological succession is one of the most important topics of both basic and applied ecology. Understanding the processes, rates, and patterns of ecosystem development, and how these vary in different types of ecosystems, is a key factor in successful management of ecosystems. Whether one's goal is the management of a wilderness or a city park, a valley-bottom farm or a mountain rangeland, a sea-level plantation or a subalpine forest, a herd of mountain caribou or of black-tailed deer, it is necessary to understand the vegetation potential and patterns of vegetation development over time that characterize the area. In this chapter we review the history of concepts about succession and consider why species and communities replace each other over a period of time. We consider the three major types of sere and how rates of succession vary in different environments. A discussion of the concept of climax leads to a consideration of changes in the structure and function of the ecosystem during succession, and the chapter concludes with a brief comment on the importance of succession to humans.

15.2 Brief Review of Concepts and the Classical Models of Succession

Few topics in ecology have been argued about more than succession and the related concepts of diversity and stability. Descriptions of succession to be found in many earlier ecology textbooks did not correspond very closely to succession as it can be observed in forested ecosystems, and

there continues to be discussion concerning the mechanisms of succession and exactly what constitutes a climax. However, significant advances in our understanding of succession have occurred over the past ten years. These advances, together with the shortcomings of earlier theories, are discussed in the following reviews which are recommended to the interested reader (Drury and Nisbet, 1973; Horn, 1974); Botkin, 1980, MacMahon, 1980, and numerous useful articles in West, Shugart and Botkin, 1981).

Many of the shortcomings of conventional theories about ecological succession have resulted from the uncritical extrapolation of the earliest studies to a variety of different types of ecosystem, and from a preoccupation among North American ecologists during the decades of the 1950s and 1960s with two particular cases of succession: abandoned farmland (''old-field'' succession) and prairie succession (MacMahon, 1980). There was a conspicuous failure to differentiate adequately the major types of succession, and the interpretations of many earlier authors were heavily influenced by their own field experience. Ecologists from the eastern deciduous hardwood forest region of the U.S. tended to present a view of succession based on studies of eastern forest ecosystems that was not always accurate or appropriate for northern or even western North American environments, and the opposite is also true. Similarly, the traditional North American view of succession has not always been very useful in other parts of the world.

The problem of parochialism has occurred in many branches of ecology, and many energetic arguments in the ecological literature can be related in part to the different field experiences of the participants. One of the easiest mistakes to make in ecology is to attempt to apply a general theory developed under a restricted range of ecological conditions to a very different type of ecosystem. Although it is one of the aims of ecology to develop broadly applicable theories about the patterns in nature, it must never be forgotten that the theory must fit the facts rather than the other way around. The reader must remember that the author of this book also has a limited experience of the vast range of ecosystem types in the world and that the view of succession presented here is undoubtedly influenced by that experience. However, a conscious attempt has been made to consider the variety of successional conditions that can be encountered, and hopefully the ensuing discussion will apply to most forested environments.

A. Early References to Succession

A recognition that vegetation undergoes change over time is recorded in the earliest of botanical writings. Theophrastus wrote about it in 300 B.C. and the pattern of development of vegetation in bogs in Ireland was described in print in 1685. A French botanist, Buffon, noted the succession of tree species in French forests and recognized the process of autogenic succession as early as 1747. Many descriptions of vegetation change were published in the nineteenth century; a period when many of the earlier empirical observations and experiences of foresters were formalized into published statements concerning vegetation change in managed forests.

In 1863, the American philosopher and naturalist, Thoreau, described the succession in which even-aged hardwood stands replace pine stands after logging in the northeastern U.S. He coined the term "forest succession" to describe the change. It was not until the turn of the century, however, that Thoreau's early statement was developed into a formal concept of plant succession by the work of two American plant ecologists: Cowles and Clements. Their ideas, which were developed while studying vegetation sequences in sand dune areas on the shores of Lake Michigan, developed the earlier work of European ecologists, including a Danish botanist, Warming, and led to the first theory of succession: the *monoclimax theory* (see reviews in Clements, 1916; Drury and Nisbet, 1973; and Whittaker, 1974).

B. The Monoclimax Theory

The monoclimax theory states that the species composition and structure of the terminal community of all seres is determined by the regional macroclimate. The climax consists of those plants that can reproduce successfully beneath their own shade and therefore maintain the community indefinitely under the prevailing climatic conditions. The theory does not require that all areas in a given region support the climatic climax at any given time, since many areas will be occupied by earlier seral stages which are actively developing toward the climax following a disturbance. In fact, the theory allows that none of the vegetation in a region may be in the climatic climax condition, and that development in some areas may be arrested and attainment of the climatic climax conditions greatly delayed or permanently prevented because of the action of soil, animal, fire, or other environmental factors that override the effect of climatic factors. All it requires is that there be a definite linear development *toward* the climatic climax. Proponents of the monoclimax theory have produced a series of terms with which to describe these "atypical" conditions.

Where succession is arrested early in the sere, such as a spring-fed bog on which the vegetation is unable to alter the moisture conditions, or a lichen community on a steep exposed rock face, a *serclimax* (pronounced sere-climax) results. Such seral communities may persist indefinitely.

Where development proceeds but is arrested permanently or for a very long period at the stage immediately preceding the climax, a *subclimax* results. For example, fire, wind, or logging can maintain in perpetuity a forest of pioneer tree species such as birch, pine, or Douglas-fir, rather than climatic climax species such as beech, hemlock, or cedar. A *disclimax,* (disturbance climax) occurs where communities are held in a stable early successional condition by the activities of humans or other animals. Farmland generally represents a disclimax, as do those subalpine meadows that are maintained in their recreationally valuable condition by the activities of burrowing animals. Removal of these animals would, in many cases, result in the reinvasion of these meadows by subalpine forest communities. A classic case of a disclimax is the calcarious downlands (low, rolling chalk hills) of southern England. It was once thought that soil conditions were responsible for the grassland community that had characterized the downs for centuries, which were therefore regarded as a serclimax. However, drastic reduction of rabbit populations by disease in the 1950s was followed by prompt succession toward climax hardwood forest, demonstrating that the grasslands were really a disclimax.

Early discussion of the monoclimax theory linked it with the idea that the climax was analogous to a "supraorganism." Following the removal of a mature climax community (analogous to the death of an old organism), a new succession is initiated (analogous to the birth of an organism) which leads through a fixed series of seral stages (analogous to stages in the life history of an organism) to culminate in the reestablishment of the climax (analogous to the attainment of maturity in an organism). A corollary of the supraorganism concept is that succession can no more fail to result in the ultimate reestablishment of the climax than germination can fail to lead to another mature individual of the same type. While the monoclimax theory recognizes the existence of *relatively* stable communities that do not yet reflect the regional climate, these are thought of as but temporary delays in the ultimate and inevitable progress toward the climatic climax: the principal, prevailing undisturbed plant community of a region which best expresses the regional climate.

Another corollary of the monoclimax theory is the principle of *ecological convergence*. This states that since succession is regulated primarily by climate, the biotic communities occupying all site types within a given climatic region will converge in structure and species composition to arrive eventually at a single climax community type: the *climatic climax*. Within any region there is always a variety of physical environments differing in moisture status, fertility, type of soil, and so on. Early seral communities in these diverse environments differ greatly in structure, floristic composition, and function. However, over a period of time, which may be very prolonged (centuries or even millennia), the combined activities of the plants, animals, microbes, and physical processes gradually modify the extremes of the physical environment. Dry sites become wetter and wet sites become drier. Very fertile (eutrophic) sites become less fertile and infertile sites (oligotrophic) become enriched. According to the theory, this convergence in the soil

and microclimatic conditions eventually permits the same biotic community to occupy all sites irrespective of the original condition of the physical environment. Figure 15.2 presents an idealized example of ecological convergence for low-elevation forests in coastal British Columbia. Ecological convergence may also be refered to as *successional convergence*.

Since the monoclimax theory was first advanced by Clements in 1916 it has generated both intense argument and strong support. The main point of contention initially

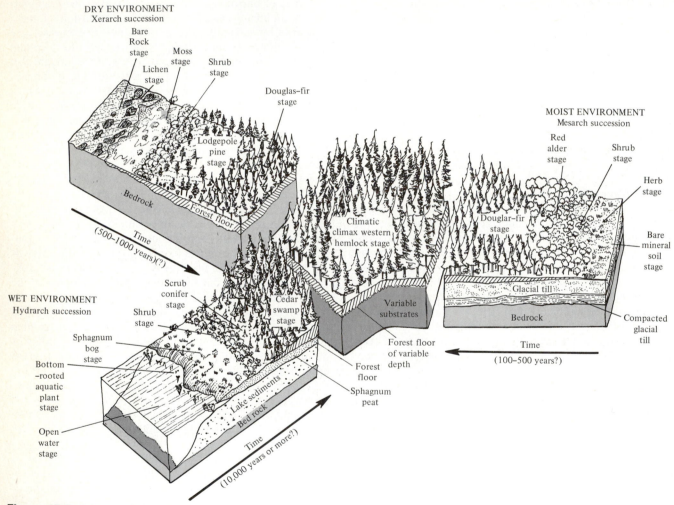

Figure 15.2
Idealized representation of ecological succession and convergence in the three major types of environment of the Coastal Western Hemlock Zone of British Columbia. The seral stages illustrated represent typical but not necessarily inevitable components of the convergence. The time scales are not linear, nor are they comparable for the three types of sere. Estimates of the probable ranges in time scales for the three seres are given.

was the concept of the climax as a "complex supra-organism," which implies an invariable sequence of stages within any type of sere, leading inevitably to a single climax type: the climatic type. Studies of secondary succession on power rights-of-way, abandoned farmland, and forest clear-cuts have revealed that expected seral stages may frequently be omitted, that early or midseral stages can sometimes be surprisingly stable, and that the floristic composition of seral communities can vary greatly from time to time and from place to place in similar physical environments. This obviously invalidates the comparison between a sere and the developmental stages of an individual organism. Another major point of contention is the idea that vegetation will continue to develop towards the same end point over periods of several centuries. This point is challenged by the evidence of major changes in climate and vegetation in North America over periods considerably shorter than that required for complete ecological convergence (Botkin, 1980).

C. The Polyclimax Theory

Although the concept of the climax as a supraorganism has not been without its supporters (e.g., Phillips, 1931, 1934, 1935a, 1935b), it has been criticized by proponents of the second major theory of succession: the *polyclimax theory* (Tansley, 1920, 1935, 1939, 1941). This theory notes that many factors can intervene to prevent an area from reaching the climatic climax condition. In many parts of the world, frequent natural fires serve to maintain grass-lands or forests of midseral tree species in areas in which the climatic conditions would indicate progression to an open forest or a forest of later-successional tree species, respectively. The presence of outcrops of serpentine soils rich in magnesium or of limestone soils rich in calcium in an area dominated by acid igneous rocks will result in local climaxes that are floristically different from the regional climax. The activities of grazing animals, already referred to, can maintain grassland communities in a climax condition, preventing the invasion of woody species. Areas of thin soil and steep topography will support stable communities that differ from those of flat, valley-bottom areas. Thus, according to the environmental factor acting to prevent convergence to the climatic climax, we can have a *pyral climax* (fire), *edaphic climax* (soil), or a *biotic climax* (animal influence) in addition to the climatic climax.

In the polyclimax theory, the vegetation of a region is viewed as a mosaic of communities at different stages of succession, some of which may reach climatic climax relatively rapidly (a few centuries or less). Some of the communities may be developing slowly toward a climatic climax,

but so slowly that the climate may have changed before the climax is reached. For these areas it becomes academic to talk about a climatic climax. Other areas may never approach the climatic climax condition for the region because factors other than climate are dominant in determining the structure and composition of the community. Thus, according to the theory, succession in a region does not lead toward a single climax but toward a mosaic of different climax communities determined by the mosaic of habitats.

In defense of the monoclimax theory it should be noted that the supraorganism analogy is not a necessary part of the theory, that in some types of sere the overall sequence of broad seral stages is remarkably invariable, and that in some climates ecological convergence does occur. As with so many ecological theories, the monoclimax theory is a reasonable approximation of reality in some parts of the world, whereas in others the polyclimax theory fits the facts better.

D. The Climax Pattern Hypothesis

A third and more recent model of succession is called the *climax pattern hypothesis* (Whittaker, 1953). Both the monoclimax and the polyclimax theory assume the existence of discrete, mutually exclusive plant communities, an assumption that is rejected by some plant ecologists on the grounds that vegetation forms a continuum in which species are distributed and replace each other independently along environmental gradients (see Chapter 14). Individual species are combined in many different ways into communities and a single species may be shared by many communities (Gleason, 1926, 1939). Vegetation is seen as a complex pattern of integrating communities rather than a mosaic of distinct communities. Succession within this complex pattern will result in a corresponding complex pattern of individualistic climax communities.

E. Some Thoughts on the Concept of the Climax Community

Some ecologists have concluded that the concept of climax, as well as the arguments over which of the three viewpoints is correct, has outlived its usefulness. Others maintain that the concept continues to have value. Its contributions include:

1. The expression of a real and important difference in stability (in the sense of persistence) between successional and self-maintaining communities; it provides an indication of the direction and degree of vegetation development in a region.
2. The provision of a basis for comparative studies of the composition, structure, function, and practical manage-

ment of successional communities. By selecting areas with a common climax, one can make more meaningful comparisons between seral stages.

3. The provision of a means of identifying particular types of physical environment and of defining local macro-climates and variations in soil conditions.

Undoubtedly, the concept of climax is more useful in some types of environments than in others, and for some branches of ecology than others. In physically extreme environments, seres may be telescoped into two or even a single stage in which pioneer and climax organisms are one and the same species. In such environments the concept is less useful than where succession involves a sequence of seral stages leading to a distinct climax.

A final question must be answered: How does one recognize that a particular community is or is not climax? The definition of climax is: a self-replacing seral stage that is relatively stable (in the sense that it persists for a long time relative to the other seral stages). As we shall see, there are problems with this definition since the early seral stages of some primary seres may outlast the climax, and seral communities may be self-replacing for many generations before they are in turn replaced. However, such early stages are subject to directional change (albeit slow), whereas in the absence of catastrophic disturbance the climax tends to exhibit only minor fluctuations around an average composi-

tion and structure over long periods of time (centuries). By examining a series of areas varying in age since disturbance it is possible to construct the probable seral sequence (or range of alternative sequences) for any region, and an examination of the population age-class and/or size-class structure of the dominant vegetation will confirm a climax or seral interpretation. If the dominant species exhibit a reverse J-shaped age or size frequency curve, one may perhaps conclude that the area is climax, whereas if the curve is bell-shaped the species is probably not replacing itself and may be seral (Figure 15.3).

Before leaving the discussion of climax it is worth reiterating that a climax community occurs for one or more of the following reasons:

First, there are no rapid allogenic changes in the environment and the living community is not capable of inducing any further autogenic change. Consequently, the community becomes self-replacing since it represents the group of organisms best adapted to compete for and utilize resources on that site under those particular conditions.

A second reason is that although the climax community may be capable of inducing further autogenic change in the environment that would eventually lead to the replacement of that community by another, the natural incidence of fire, wind, disease, or the action of herbivores prevents these changes from occurring. For example, the invasion of pine

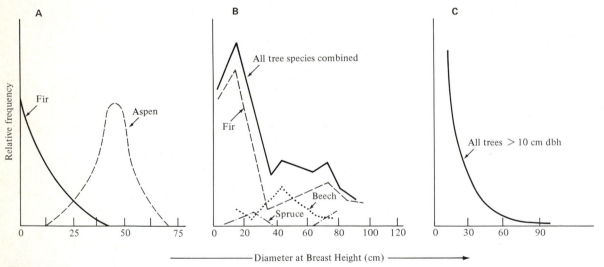

Figure 15.3

Size frequency curves for the dominant trees in three forests. (A) Temperate seral forest. A successional forest in Arizona in which aspen is failing to reproduce itself and is being replaced by white fir (*Abies concolor*). (B) Temperate climax forest. An apparently climax forest in the Carpathian Mountains. The trees do not exhibit a perfect reverse-J shape, probably because regeneration and mortality of larger trees occur sporadically rather than continuously. (C) A climax tropical rain forest. (After Whittaker, 1975, and Cousins, 1974.)

forests by later successional species may depend upon amelioration of microclimate and soil nutrient and moisture conditions by the pine trees. Frequent ground fires may prevent the accumulation of the forest floor material needed to produce amelioration of soil conditions, and thereby maintain an open stand structure. This in turn maintains the site in a condition that is unfavorable for the species of the subsequent seral stage.

Third, the invading species of a subsequent seral stage are constantly removed by fire, herbivores, disease, or climatic factors that operate to prevent colonization. This is somewhat similar to the preceding reason, but it differs in that the environment is capable of supporting the next seral stage but colonization is prevented. For example, many grasslands that could sustain a climatic climax forest remain as grasslands because of the action of fire or herbivores or both. Many of the *Eucalyptus* forests of Australia are prevented from being replaced by a climatic climax dominated by southern beech (*Nothofagus* sp.) by a frequency of fire approximately once in 350 years (Beadle, 1966).

A fourth reason is that allogenic or autogenic changes may continue, albeit at a reduced rate, but there are no organisms in the region that are better adapted to occupy the site or capable of competing with the climax organisms. In such a case the continuing allogenic changes may eventually become unfavorable to the climax community, which can become over-mature and senescent (decadent). Very old climatic climax forests sometimes attain this condition, which sets the stage for a natural disturbance event, such as fire, insects, or wind, that initiates a new secondary succession.

15.3   Mechanisms of Successional Change

If we are to understand the dynamics of vegetation, we must first answer the question: Why does change occur? If we wish to go further and make our understanding of succession useful in the management of natural resources, we have to ask the additional question: How rapidly does succession occur? In answering these questions we will discover that the driving force and rate of succession vary from site to site, from region to region, and between different seral stages on a given site.

Succession occurs as the result of either autogenic processes (associated with the living community) or allogenic processes (associated with the physical environment). Examples of allogenic succession can easily be observed along the banks of a meandering river in a valley floodplain, where succession starts on recently deposited sandbars and

is directed initially by subsequent alluvial deposits (e.g., Van Cleve and Viereck, 1981). Such examples are less common than the products of autogenic succession, which is the result of three major biotic mechanisms: colonization, alteration of the physical characteristics of the site, and displacement of species by competition or antibiosis.

A. Colonization

Colonization is a process with two components: invasion and survival. The rate at which a site is colonized depends on both the rate (numbers per unit time) at which individual organisms (seeds, spores, immature or mature individuals) arrive at the site, and on their success at becoming established and surviving. For a given rate of invasion, colonization of a moist, fertile site is likely to be much more rapid than that of a dry, infertile site because of poor survival on the latter. A fertile, plowed field is rapidly invaded by a large variety of weeds, whereas a neighboring construction site from which the soil has been removed to expose a coarse, infertile parent material may remain virtually free of vegetation for many months, in spite of receiving the same input of seeds as the plowed field.

Both the rate of invasion and the rate of extinction vary greatly among different plant species. *Pioneer* or *fugitive* species (those that only occur in the earliest seral stages) tend to have high rates of invasion because they produce very large numbers of reproductive propagules and because they have an efficient means of dispersal (normally, wind). For example, a study of succession in African grasslands revealed that the average number of seeds produced per plant was 20,700 for pioneer colonizing species, 6200 for the initial grass species, 272 for secondary grass species, and only 27 for the climax species (Jones, 1968). Production of reproductive rather than vegetative biomass also varies with time within a seral stage. Burning a tall grass prairie in Illinois was reported to increase the percentage of the annual biomass production invested in flower stalk production to 53% from the 7% value found on unburned plots. This reduction of flowering with time following burning is ascribed to the effects of the accumulation of undecomposed grass litter on unburned areas (Old, 1969).

If colonizers produce short-lived reproductive propagules, they must produce very large numbers unless they have an efficient means of dispersal to suitable new habitats. Many plants rely on wind and produce abundant quantities of small, relatively short-lived seeds to compensate for the fact that wind is not a reliable means of reaching the appropriate type of habitat. Alternative strategies have evolved in some plants, such as those that produce fewer but larger seeds which are dispersed to suitable sites by birds or small mammals, or those that produce long-lived seeds. Many forest plants apparently exhibit the latter adaptation, and viable seeds of pioneer species can be found in large numbers in some forest floors. For example, as many as 1125 viable seeds per square meter were found in a 100-year-old Douglas-fir–western hemlock forest in coastal B.C., 69% of which were from the pioneer tree, red alder, 30% of which were from species not present in the stand at the time of sampling, and 22% of which were from species not found in west coast forests. Nearly all the germinating seeds were from early successional species (Kellman, 1970). The extremely prompt colonization of such sites following disturbance by clearcutting is undoubtedly in part a reflection of the large seed bank in the forest floor.

Another adaptation exhibited by many early colonizers is a symbiotic association with nitrogen-fixing organisms. Lichens, typical colonizers of bare rock or dry, nutrient-poor soils, may be partially composed of nitrogen-fixing algae, while plant species such as red alder and lupine have symbiotic nitrogen-fixing microorganisms within nodules on their root systems. Lack of available nitrogen is a characteristic feature of early stages of primary seres and this results in very low survival of plants that are not equipped to overcome this problem.

A further adaptation that is well developed in colonizing species is a high degree of variation (polymorphism) in germination behavior. Seeds of a given species exhibit a wide range of germination dates (Cavers and Harper, 1966; Salisbury, 1970), increasing the probability that at least some of the seeds will germinate during a period of favorable environmental conditions. This is particularly important for species colonizing an abiotic environment where there is no existing vegetation to ameliorate microclimatic extremes and in which there may be great microclimatic heterogeneity. It is also important to note that there is a significant year-to-year or decade-to-decade variation in the amount and timing of precipitation. Polymorphism increases the population's ability to deal with such variation.

Variation in rates of invasion and growth is claimed by some authorities to be the major factor in succession, especially secondary succession. Early seral species are those that produce abundant seed which is successfully distributed to new sites. Such species generally grow very rapidly and fully occupy such sites, excluding other species with lower invasion and growth rates (Drury and Nisbet, 1973). The first community occupying a disturbed area may simply reflect species with the highest rate of invasion, while the community of the subsequent seral stage may consist of plants with similar survival rates but lower invasion rates. The observation that, at least on mesic sites, species from almost any seral stage can grow in almost any other seral stage if established before competition becomes severe is given as evidence of this view. However, growth under such circumstances is generally much less than that achieved under the seral conditions with which the species is normally associated, and environmental alteration by pioneer species is frequently a prerequisite for successful establishment of later successional species. It is probable that invasion rate is a more important determinant of successional patterns in mesic than in xeric and hydric seres (see below), and more important in secondary than in primary succession.

Before leaving the topic of colonization we must consider the relative importance of what has been termed the *relay floristics* and the *initial floristic composition* patterns of succession (Egler, 1954). The conventional view of colonization has envisaged waves of plants successively colonizing, occupying an area, and being replaced by the subsequent wave of new species. Each seral stage prepares the site for the next stage. However, in some types of sere it is apparent that seeds or plants of later successional stages are present from the outset. Different seral stages merely represent variable periods of occupancy before the species becomes dominant. The seeds or diminutive plants of shrub species may be present during the herb stage but remain ungerminated or unnoticed by the casual observer. Similarly, trees species may be present from the outset but take many years before they germinate and/or overcome the shrubs and become dominant (Figure 15.4). Undoubtedly, both relay floristics and initial floristic composition are important in succession, but their relative importance will vary. In mesarch succession (old-field succession, for example), initial floristic composition may often be the dominant pattern, whereas in hydrarch and xerarch succession, relay floristics will dominate. Similarly, initial floristic composition will generally be more important in secondary succession than in primary succession.

Knowledge of the relative contributions of these two patterns to secondary succession in clearcuts is important for the design of ecologically sound strategies for weed control. Control of vegetation that is competing with planted trees will differ if the weed problem arises from a seed and/or bud bank already on the site (initial vegetative composition) or from current colonization of the ecosystem (relay floristics).

B. Alteration of the Physical Characteristics of the Ecosystem

Survival of a species that has invaded a site is a measure of its adaptation to and tolerance of the physical and biotic conditions of the site. However, by occupying the site, a

Figure 15.4

Diagrammatic representation of (A) relay floristics and (B) initial floristic composition types of old-field succession as envisaged by Egler (1954). Most successions will exhibit some combination of these two patterns. (Reproduced by permission of the International Society for Vegetation Science and the author.)

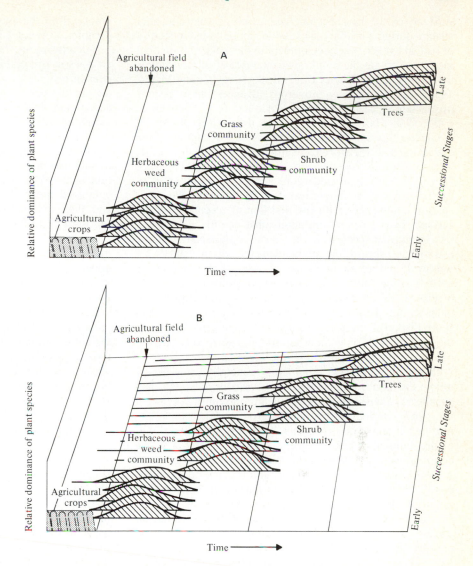

species inevitably changes the site conditions, and the changes are frequently not favorable to the continued occupancy of the site by that species. The changes may either reduce the competitive abilities of the resident species or increase those of the invading species, or both. The net result is the replacement of one group of species by another group. For example, shade-intolerant pioneer species create so much shade as their community develops that their own seedlings either cannot survive or they grow poorly, while shade-tolerant seedlings of invading species flourish. Failing to reproduce themselves, the pioneers are replaced by the subsequent seral community. Similarly, the change in

soil pH accompanying the accumulation of tree litter and the development of a forest floor generally favors the nutrition of climax tree species over early or midseral herb, shrub, and tree species. In some types of primary succession, such alteration of the physical environment is an absolute prerequisite for the establishment of later seral stages. In this type of situation, environmental modification is probably the major driving force of succession, and the relay floristics model of succession would apply. In other types of primary succession and in many secondary successions this mechanism contributes to the successional process but is not necessarily the major driving force.

Some of the best documented cases of environmental change during a primary succession can be found in studies of soil and vegetation development in the wake of retreating glaciers. Perhaps the best known example of such a study is that conducted at Glacier Bay, Alaska (Crocker and Major, 1955). There have been numerous advances and recessions of glaciers since the Pleistocene ice age (e.g., Lawrence, 1950, 1958; Harris and Farr, 1974), the most recent retreat at Glacier Bay starting in the mid-eighteenth century at the end of the post-Pleistocene "Little Ice Age." The area that was exposed during the current retreat of approximately 96 km (60 miles) has undergone succession resulting in an age sequence of communities of up to 180 years old. Succession commences with the invasion of recently exposed surfaces by a pioneer community that can include mosses (*Rhacomitrium* species), herbs (fireweed, horsetail, sedges, and rushes), shrubs [mountain avens (*Dryas* sp.) and dwarf willows], and trees (cottonwoods). Almost all of the major species of the entire succession are physiologically capable of colonizing the bare surfaces, the observed sequence of communities being due partly to differences in seed and spore dispersal and partly to differences in growth rates of the species with or without environmental modification—especially the addition of organic nitrogen.

Plants in the pioneer community generally grow poorly unless the shrubs mountain avens (*Dryas drummondii*) and soapberry (*Sheperdia canadensis*) are present (Lawrence et al., 1967). Both these species have root nodules containing nitrogen-fixing microorganisms. The nitrogen-fixing ability of the mountain avens (a creeping shrub) gives it a strong competitive advantage in the nitrogen-poor environment exposed by the retreating glacier, and it generally develops to form a continuous mat between the initial pioneer community and the subsequent seral stage of shrubby willows. The shrub (willow thicket) stage does not last very long, for it is invaded by red alder (also a nitrogen-fixing species) and occasional cottonwood trees, which form a dense thicket that resists invasion for many decades but which is eventually replaced by a pure sitka spruce forest. The spruce is not climax, however. In the absence of disturbance, spruce stands are invaded by mountain and western hemlocks to give a mixed spruce–hemlock climatic climax. The rate of succession is not uniform over the entire area and some bare ground remains uncolonized for a long time. However, the transition from the pioneer community to the willow–alder thicket stage generally begins about 15–20 years after the exposure of the surface and complete cover by alder thickets is achieved after another 35–40 years. The alder holds its own for about 50 years, but by about 120 years after initial colonization the succession to spruce stands is essentially complete (Figure 15.5A).

Accompanying the changes in vegetation are some major changes in soil conditions. These are studied by examining sites of progressively increasing age since the retreat of the ice. In the early stages the soils are merely disorganized accumulations of morainal debris and till exhibiting little regular change in properties with depth. Following invasion there is a progressive modification of many of the soil's properties, starting at the surface and gradually progressing down through the soil profile. Bulk density of the fine fraction of the soil, which averages about 1.4 g mL^{-1} in uncolonized areas, is reduced somewhat by frost heaving, and then exhibits a continuing decrease to about 0.7–0.8 g mL^{-1} in the spruce stage. These changes are largely confined to the upper 15 cm, the zone that contains most of the roots. The values shown in Figure 15.5B are for the upper 5 cm, with a progressive increase with depth to 15 cm. All sites had a value of about 1.4 below 15 cm, irrespective of time since glaciation.

Soil pH, which is initially high (8.0–8.4) because of the presence of calcium carbonate-rich rocks, decreases with the colonization of the surface at a rate that depends on the type of vegetation. Whereas uncolonized surfaces exhibit virtually no drop in pH over 30 years, 20 years of colonization by cottonwood, willow, or mountain avens is associated with a reduction in the pH to about 7.8. The alder thicket stage is associated with a more dramatic drop to values in the surface soil of about 5.0 after 35–40 years of occupancy. This reflects a litter pH of 5.6–6.1 in the early stages and 4.2–4.6 in the late stages of alder dominance (Figure 15.5C). The rapid decline in pH ceases after the alder thicket stage, the spruce litter being no more acidic than the alder litter. Changes in pH were largely restricted to the upper 25 cm, although some changes could be detected as deep as 41 cm. Similar drops in soil pH accompanying postglacial retreat succession have been recorded in many other studies: 2.3 pH units over 250 years in central Alaska, 2.8 units over 500 years in Switzerland, 4.5 units over 50 years in northern Sweden, and 3.0 units over 200 years in Australia. Primary succession on sand dunes is also accompanied by pH declines: 2.7 units over 280 years in western England and 0.9 unit over 235 years in eastern England (Major, 1974).

Accumulation of organic carbon in both the mineral and organic soil layers increased at a fairly constant rate during the alder stage but leveled off during the spruce stage, at about 130 years after the retreat of the ice. The rate of accumulation in the upper 46 cm of the mineral soil (most

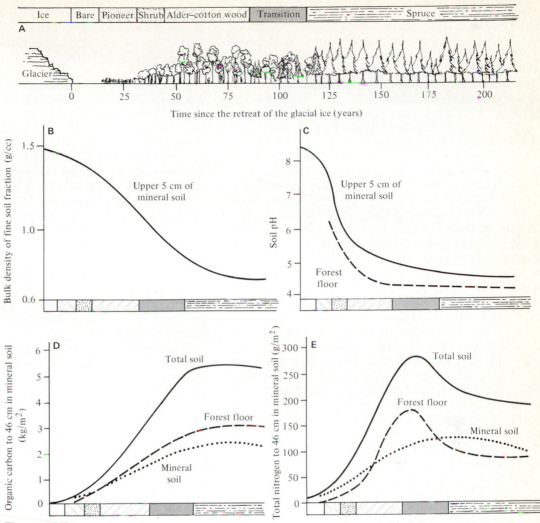

Figure 15.5

Changes in soil characteristics accompanying primary mesarch succession at Glacier Bay, Alaska (after Crocker and Major, 1955). (A) Vegetation sequence over 200 years following the retreat of the glacial ice. (B) Changes in mineral soil bulk density. (C) Changes in soil pH. (D) Changes in soil organic carbon. (E) Changes in soil nitrogen. Note the rapid accretion of nitrogen in the forest floor during the alder stage, followed by a decline during the spruce stage. Much of this apparent nitrogen loss may be incorporation into spruce biomass. (Copyright Blackwell Scientific Publications Ltd. Used with permission.)

of it in the upper 15 cm) was rather similar to that in the surface organic layers: about 15 g m^{-2} yr^{-1} (Figure 15.5D). The biomass of the forest floor increased most rapidly during the alder thicket stage, but accumulation continued throughout the 180-year age sequence of communities, to reach a maximum mean depth of 13 cm and a biomass of 90–100 t ha^{-1}. This is similar to the accumulation of

212 t ha^{-1} forest floor material with a mean depth of 16 cm under a spruce–hemlock stand developed over 300 years on a landslide area elsewhere in Alaska (Gregory, 1960).

The continued accumulation of organic carbon is believed to be related to the pattern of nitrogen accumulation. Initial nitrogen accumulation has been ascribed to fixation by the algal crust that develops on bare areas, and to the root nodules of the soapberry and mountain avens in the pioneer shrub community. Far greater accumulation occurs during the alder stage, which has an estimated net fixation rate of 62 kg ha^{-1} yr^{-1}. Nitrogen accumulation in the forest floor levels off in the alder–spruce transition stage and then declines substantially, probably due to reduced nitrogen fixation and to uptake and incorporation in spruce biomass. The decreasing nitrogen and constant carbon levels in the forest floor result in an increase in C/N ratio from about 13 in the alder stage to 33–36 for the spruce forest floor. Undoubtedly, this reduces rates of litter decomposition and results in the continued accumulation of forest floor biomass.

Other studies of changes in soil accompanying succession have reported similar results. Olson (1958) documented soil changes over a 10,000-year successional sequence on sand dunes on the shores of Lake Michigan. This psammosere develops from bare sand surfaces through grass and shrub stages to seral communities of pines or balsam fir. These communities give way to a climatic climax beech–maple community, but many areas are characterized by prolonged occupancy by a subclimax black oak–blueberry community. Surface soil pH changes during this succession from 7.7 to 4.0 over an estimated 10,000 years. A bleached Ae layer (the eluvial surface mineral horizon common to many podzol soils) with a pH of about 4.5 forms after 1000 years (a similar period to that reported for Ae development in southwest Alaska (Chandler, 1942), although Alaskan podzols have been reported to develop in as little as 150 years (Ugolini, 1966)), decreasing to 3.6 units after 10,000 years. Organic carbon in the surface soil increases from about 0.05% in a 5-year-old dune to about 1% at 80 years beneath a pine–bunchgrass community and to more than 2% beneath a black oak–blueberry community at 10,000 years. The persistence of the subclimax black oak is interpreted to be the result of the acidity of the accumulating organic layer, which inhibits invasion by maple and beech.

A third type of environment in which an age sequence of successional communities can be studied is river terraces. Fonda (1974) examined the communities of the successively older river terraces to be found with increasing distance each side of the Hoh River in western Washington. A pioneer community of willows and herbs colonizing gravel bars is replaced by alder as the bars develop into alluvial flats (80–100 years). The alder is replaced by a sitka spruce–bigleaf maple–cottonwood community on the first river terrace (400 years). This gives way to a sitka spruce–western hemlock community on the second terrace (750 years), while climax hemlock stands are found on the older third terrace, areas first exposed by the retreating Pleistocene alpine glaciers. Table 15.1 shows the variation in soil physical properties observed along this chronological sequence. Nitrogen concentrations decline over the first three stages; organic matter, phosphorus, and moisture-holding capacity all tend to increase; and pH shows a sustained decline.

Studies of succession on north-facing slopes in interior Alaska have revealed a progressive change in soil nitrogen and phosphorus and the development of sphagnum bogs on sites formerly occupied by productive forest (Heilman, 1966, 1968; also, Van Cleve and Viereck, 1981). The succession starts with a productive birch–alder community which is gradually invaded by white and black spruce. This leads to the formation of a black spruce–moss community characterized by *Hylocomium*, *Pleurozium*, *Polytrichum*, and *Dicranum* mosses. The buildup of the moss layer insulates the soil, lowers soil temperatures and raises the level of permafrost in the soil. Under these conditions, the above moss species are replaced by the peat-forming moss *Sphagnum*. The accumulation of *Sphagnum* peat further reduces soil temperatures and increases water-logging of the upper layers of the soil, which leads to a decrease in the density of the black spruce stand and the formation of an open *Sphagnum*–black spruce bog.

Temperature and moisture changes beneath the developing vegetation are undoubtedly driving mechanisms in the succession, but it has been suggested that the concomitant change in soil nitrogen and phosphorus is also very important (Figure 15.6). As succession proceeds, the concentrations of available nitrogen and phosphorus in the rooting zone (the upper soil layers) declines because of lower soil temperatures, increasing moisture content, and the formation of low-bulk-density moss peat that has very low concentrations of nutrients. The highest soil nutrient concentrations are found in progressively lower and colder layers of the soil, out of reach of the trees, which consequently expe-

Table 15.1 Variation in Soil Properties of the Upper 4 cm of the Mineral Soil in a Chronosequence of Communities on the Banks of the Hoh River, Washington (Data from Fonda, 1974)

Soil Property	Seral Stage			
	Alder	Spruce–Maple–Cottonwood	Spruce–Hemlock	Hemlock
% nitrogen	0.77	0.20	0.14	0.47
% phosphorus	0.58	0.70	0.47	1.08
% organic matter	4.5	7.2	5.5	18.6
pH	5	4.9	4.4	4.0
Moisture retention value	7.4	11.6	19.7	24.8

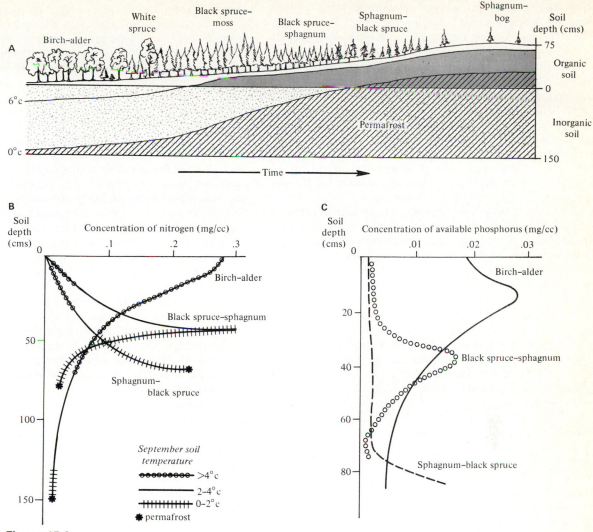

Figure 15.6
Variation in the distribution of nitrogen and phosphorus with depth in the soil during a successional sequence on a north-facing slope in interior Alaska (after Heilman, 1966, 1968). The process whereby soil nitrogen and phosphorus become located in deeper and colder layers of the soil as succession proceeds as the result of the accumulation of an increasingly deep layer of moss is readily apparent. (A) Vegetation sequence and changes in the depth of the organic layer and in September soil temperature (tree height and soil depth not drawn to the same scale). (B, C) Variation in the concentration of total nitrogen (B) and available phosphorus (C) with depth in the soil. (Copyright Ecological Society of America. Used with permission of ESA and the author.)

rience increasing nutrient deficiency. The more-nutrient-demanding birch and alder are replaced by the less-demanding black spruce, but even this species is adversely affected as the availability of nutrients continues to decrease. The productivity of the spruce decreases and eventually even this species is excluded, leaving a sphagnum bog.

A new theory concerning the succession that leads from forest to bog in coastal Alaska has recently been advanced by Ugolini and Mann (1979). They examined a sequence of communities from a recently established forest on coastal beach deposits, through a mature sitka spruce stand, into a spruce–sphagnum community and eventually a sphagnum bog. The spruce stand that develops on the freely drained mineral beach materials develops a thick, acidic forest floor. Under the cool, humid, high-precipitation climate of the region, this leads to podzolization of the mineral soil. Iron is leached from the upper mineral horizons to be deposited as a B_f horizon. After centuries of this process, the iron accumulation becomes so great that an *iron pan* is formed: a layer of mineral soil in which the mineral particles are cemented together by iron and aluminum oxides. The iron pan develops to the point at which it impedes drainage and the soil becomes boggy. This leads to the development of sphagnum moss and a layer of sphagnum peat, which, in conjunction with the impeded drainage, leads to the death of the trees. The result is a sphagnum bog.

Ugolini and Mann's theory seems very plausible until one realizes that few of these coastal sphagnum bogs are presently underlain by an iron pan. But there is an explanation. As the sphagnum bog builds up, organic acids are produced which form organic complexes with the iron. Over a long period of time, the result is the dissolution and disappearance of the pan. This does not lead to a reversion of the area back to forest, however. The thick layer of sphagnum peat that has developed by the time the pan disappears is more than capable of reproducing the hydrological effects of the pan. A similar change in vegetation and soil conditions is reflected in a pollen profile from a bog forest in central coastal British Columbia (Figure 15.7).

In addition to the very important effects of succession on soils, the successional development of vegetation produces significant alterations in microclimate. Since the effect of vegetation on microclimate was discussed in Chapters 7 to 10, the topic will not be elaborated here. It will suffice to remind the reader that light intensity and wind speed are reduced, temperature extremes are moderated, relative humidity is increased, and the evaporative power of the air beneath the vegetation canopy is reduced. For example, Cain and Friesner (1929) found that loss by evaporation from porous ceramic bulbs declined through successive seral stages from 14.6 mL day^{-1} in an old-field to 4.7 mL day^{-1} in a climax forest. Such changes in microclimate are of great significance for plants, animals, and microbes.

C. Displacement of Species by Antibiosis, Autotoxicity and Competition

Not only do plants alter the microclimate and the physical and inorganic chemical characteristics of the soil, they also alter their organic chemical environment. In the discussion of allelopathy (Chapter 14) it was seen that plants produce a wide variety of chemicals to inhibit germination and/or growth of other species. This adaptation plays a significant role in succession. In some cases allelopathy serves to accelerate succession, whereas in others it impedes it.

The order in which different species of plant invade abandoned fields in Oklahoma has been shown to be related to the plants' nitrogen requirements, and the low level of soil nitrogen that is characteristic of such fields appears to be a major factor in determining the successional sequence (Rice, 1964, 1967, 1968). Any factor influencing the availability of nitrogen would thus affect the rate of succession. Several of the pioneer plants in this old-field succession that are tolerant of low nitrogen availability have adapted to prolong their occupancy of the site by producing allelochemicals that inhibit nitrogen-fixing and nitrifying bacteria and thereby impair the growth of later seral plants. This may be a fairly common adaptation among early seral plants. For example, clover plants exhibiting extremely poor root nodulation and having very poor survival in the presence of certain species of grass in New Zealand failed to respond to even heavy fertilization, with or without trace elements. Killing of the grasses by herbicide, on the other hand, permitted normal growth of, and nitrogen fixation by, the clover by eliminating the nodule-inhibiting influence of the grasses (Beggs, 1964). However, the success of a formalin treatment of the soil in overcoming the inhibition of the clover, and of nodulation, suggests that soil microflora may also have been involved.

In contrast to the findings in Oklahoma, an early seral species in old-field succession in North Carolina has been shown to produce a substance that hastens its own demise and speeds the transition to the subsequent community. Horseweed *(Aster canadensis),* a winter annual, is the first species to colonize abandoned fields, but it rapidly disappears from the community because growth of additional horseweed seedlings is inhibited by chemicals released from the decaying roots of the parent plants (Keever, 1950). There are numerous other examples of such *autotoxicity* among pioneers in old-field and other successions (see Whittaker, 1970). For example, the allelochemical habit of chaparral can turn to autotoxicity and kill the center of old shrub patches if such heavy accumulations of terpenes (which reduce competition from grasses) occur that they become toxic to the producing plants (Muller, 1966, 1969).

Sometimes, the loss of vigor or the death of plants in the center of shrub patches is more the result of old age than autotoxicity, as is the case in heather *(Calluna vulgaris)* in Scotland (Watt, 1947, 1955; Barclay-Estrup and Gimingham, 1969). But heather does provide us with an interesting case of indirect allelopathy that impedes the progress of succession. It produces chemicals that inhibit mycorrhizal

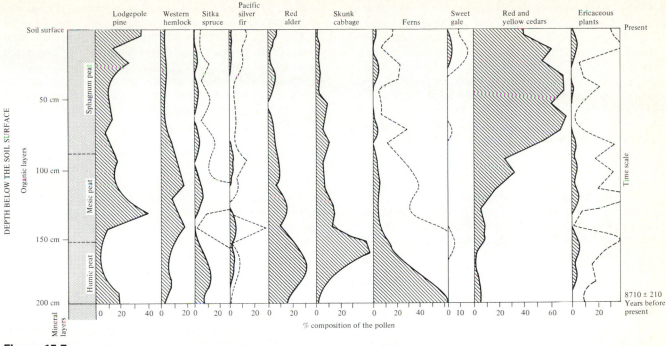

Figure 15.7

Vegetation change in central coastal British Columbia since the retreat of glaciers as reflected in the pollen profile from a bog-forest near Prince Rupert. The change in vegetation certainly reflects changes in climate over the past 9000 years, but it also reflects changes from a community growing on fertile mineral soil to a community growing on 2 m of slowly decomposing, nutrient-poor peat; a change that has resulted from the processes of succession (Banner et al., 1983). The area beneath the dotted line represents a 10X expansion of the striped area beneath the solid line. (Copyright National Research Council of Canada. Used with permission of NRC and the authors.)

fungi and thereby prevent the invasion of the site and the displacement of the heather by trees (Harley, 1952).

An interesting and important case of a shrub serclimax (a very stable and persistent shrub seral stage) which may possibly involve allelopathic mechanisms is that of the ericaceous shrub *Kalmia angustifolium* in eastern Canada. If this species becomes well established, such as after a fire, it can form a dense shrub community that resists tree invasion for extremely prolonged periods. Damman (1971) studied balsam fir, black spruce, and a *Kalmia* heath (heath refers to a plant community dominated by ericaceous shrubs) growing on very similar mineral substrates in western Newfoundland. He found that the *Kalmia* heath had a raw humus layer weighing 293 t ha^{-1}, in comparison with weights of 87 t ha^{-1} in the *Picea* forest and 65 t ha^{-1} in the *Abies* forest. These accumulations represented 78, 21, and 14 times the annual litterfall, respectively, implying very slow litter decomposition on the *Kalmia* heath. Mineralization of N and P showed similar trends and Ca mineralization

was much slower in the heath than in the forest. Interestingly, a net increase in nitrogen of 23 kg ha^{-1} yr^{-1} was calculated for the heath. Only half of this could be accounted for by precipitation, and, in the absence of known nitrogen-fixing plants, the difference was ascribed to dust, pollen, or the direct absorption of ammonia from the air by plants or the soil. This study shows that *Kalmia* heaths inhibit mineralization and accumulate nutrients in an unavailable form. Whether the resulting low availability of nutrients is sufficient to explain the lack of tree invasion, or whether the chemicals that inhibit decomposer organisms also inhibit tree mycorrhiae and/or tree root development, is unclear. It would be interesting to investigate whether or not *Kalmia* resists tree invasion by the same mechanisms as *Calluna*.

Allelochemicals serve to modify the competitive relationships of species, but competition itself, particularly for light, is also important. Early successional plants are generally shade intolerant and small in stature, whereas later successional species are generally shade tolerant and taller in stature. Shaded seedlings are more susceptible to attack by fungi (Vaartaja, 1962), and the ability to resist such attacks is important in determining the role of a species in succession. As noted in Chapter 7, ability to survive in the shade is related to seed weight and respiration rate. Seeds of shade-tolerant, late successional species are often larger and the seedlings often have lower growth and death rates in the shade than shade-intolerant, early successional species. However, early successional species have a much higher growth potential than shade-tolerant, late successional species when they are all fully illuminated (Grime, 1966; Grime and Jeffrey, 1965). It has been suggested that successional replacement is closely involved with competition for light and that light adaptation represents a compromise between ability to grow rapidly in full light and ability to survive fungal attack under shaded conditions.

These examples will suffice to demonstrate that plants do not occur in successional sequence merely as a result of the physical conditions of their microenvironment. Interactions between different plant species and between plants and microbes also contribute significantly to the order and rate with which species replace each other.

As noted at the beginning of this section, the explanation for the successional replacement of species varies from one situation to the next. Various combinations of invasion rate, shade tolerance, allelopathy and autotoxicity, environmental modification, nutrient and moisture competition, old age and senescence, seed longevity and availability of seed sources, and ability to sprout from subterranean organs are responsible for the general patterns of species replacement, which can show considerable variation from site to site and from one time to another. Understanding plant succession obviously requires a good knowledge of *physiological ecology:* the physiological adaptations of plants that determine their responses to the physical environment and the other plant and animal species (Bazzaz, 1979; Bazzaz and Pickett, 1980; Rice 1984).

15.4   Rates of Successional Change

The rate at which succession proceeds is highly variable. It depends upon

1. The degree of environmental change that must occur before one community can be replaced by another: the greater the change, the more prolonged the stage.
2. The productivity of the organisms and the efficiency with which they produce environmental change: the

more productive and efficient the organisms, the shorter the duration of the seral stages.
3. The longevity of the organism dominating each seral stage: the longer lived the organisms, the longer the stage may last.
4. The degree to which communities at any particular stage occupy and dominate the site and resist invasion by other species: the better developed the community, the more resistant to invasion and the longer lasting it will be.

A. Degree of Environmental Change During a Succession

If one considers the total set of ecological conditions at the beginning and end of a xerosere, a mesosere, and a hydrosere, it becomes obvious that a far greater change occurs during xerarch and hydrarch than during mesarch succession. In a typical primary lithic xerosere, one starts with a completely unmodified microclimate, and little soil or unconsolidated soil parent material. There is little or no soil moisture storage capacity, nutrient retention capacity, or available nutrient capital, and little in the way of a rooting medium to provide stability for higher plants. At the climax one finds a forest microclimate, a well-developed organic layer, the beginnings of a mineral soil, a relatively large site nutrient capital, an active nutrient cycle, a significant soil moisture storage capacity, and reasonably good physical support for the trees (Figure 15.2).

The typical primary hydrosere also involves extensive change in the physical and chemical environment. From a nutrient-poor aquatic environment one proceeds through a semiterrestrial condition to a forested condition that will eventually bear a close resemblance to the climatic climax of the xerosere and mesosere. The ecological conditions between the start and finish of the sere are enormously different.

The typical mesosere, on the other hand, involves much less environmental change. Soil moisture conditions generally do not change radically, and with the important exceptions of the accumulation of an organic layer, the development of soil horizons, and a change in site nutrient capital and availability, there may not be a very great change in the soil. The major changes are in microclimate and surface soil conditions. As a result of these differences, xerarch and hydrarch succession tends to be slow, while mesarch succession tends to be rapid.

B. Rate at Which the Biota Alter the Environment

The living community in early xerarch and hydrarch succession is composed of small organisms that either grow very slowly or are very short-lived and accumulate very little biomass. Lichens grow so slowly that there is even a science of *lichenometry*, which measures time since historical events in terms of lichen growth. Pioneer dryland mosses similarly lack the high biomass production that characterizes mosses in later stages of mesoseres in humid climates. Phytoplankton in early hydrarch succession may have quite high individual photosynthetic efficiencies (if not limited by low levels of nutrients), but they do not accumulate much biomass because they are so short lived and heavily grazed, and most of their remains decomposes fairly rapidly. In common with the roots of higher plants, lichens and mosses produce organic acids which accelerate the weathering of rock. This biochemical weathering is important, but in pioneer xeric stages it is limited by the lack of moisture and the low biotic productivity, and it is certainly much less significant than the more extensive chemical breakdown of rock that occurs under well-developed, moist organic layers later in xerarch succession. Thus, the extensive ecological changes that are necessary early in xerarch and hydrarch succession are associated with diminutive and frequently slow-growing life forms. Consequently, rates of autogenic succession are very slow in these seral stages. The allogenic processes of lake sedimentation and bedrock weathering are also extremely slow, so these early stages are generally very long—often as much as hundreds or even thousands of years.

The situation in mesarch succession is quite different, with very much less environmental alteration involved, and a productive, rapidly growing community of plants involved in causing it. Relatively little in the way of allogenic processes is involved and the autogenic changes generally proceed just as fast as the vegetation is able to develop. Most mesarch seral stages involve a single generation of plants, whereas most xerarch and hydrarch seral stages involve many generations. Consequently, the early stages of mesarch succession develop rapidly and are associated more with the next two factors than with the preceding two.

Succession generally proceeds faster in humid, mesothermal climates which favor the fast-growing plants that produce autogenic change quickly. The slow plant growth that is characteristic of very hot, cold, dry or excessively humid (e.g. some high elevation tropical cloud forests) climates is associated with correspondingly slower successional change.

C. Longevity of the Organisms Dominating the Site

In mesarch succession, the length of a seral stage is partly determined by the longevity of the organisms involved, especially in midseral and subclimax stages. The duration of the alder–thicket stage at Glacier Bay is largely determined by the physiological longevity of the alder, which resists invasion until it begins to senesce. The shrub stage on subhygric and hygric sites in coastal B.C. can last for several decades until the salmonberry thickets which frequently develop on such sites start to senesce. The subclimax Douglas-fir stage in the western hemlock zone of British Columbia can last for many centuries before it is replaced by the climax western hemlock–western red cedar, simply because of the great age reached by Douglas-fir. Similarly, the subclimax sitka spruce stage on the B.C. and Alaska coast may last for as long as half a millenium or more before being replaced by the climatic climax (western hemlock), simply because of its longevity. The short duration of early mesosere stages may simply relate to the high percentage of annuals or biennials in the early plant communities of this sere.

D. Degree to Which Communities Dominate the Site and Resist Invasion

The climax community persists because it fully occupies and dominates the site and resists the invasion of nonclimax species. It may do this by competing efficiently for light, by making nutrients unavailable to all but appropriately adapted climax species (cf. direct nutrient cycling), by competing for moisture, or by inhibiting germination of seeds of other species by allelochemical mechanisms. Similarly, earlier seral communities can become very long lasting if they ever become so well established that they are able to dominate the site and resist invasion. Shrub stages in particular, once well established, may become extremely resistant to invasion and colonization by the tree species of the subsequent seral stage. Ordinarily, seedlings of such trees become established beneath the shrub community soon after it gains control of the site, and after a relatively brief period of competition, the trees grow above the shrubs and shade them out (initial vegetative composition). However, if invasion by the trees is delayed until the shrubs have become large and completely occupy the site, it may be many decades before the trees can enter the community. This phenomenon has been applied on a limited scale in the establishment of virtually maintenance-free, low-stature vegetative cover below power lines as an alternative to continual mechanical or herbicidal control of tree growth (Bramble and Byrnes 1972; Egler, 1953; Niering and Egler, 1955).

Variable combinations of these four determinants of the rate of succession and duration of particular seral stages precludes any reliable general statement about rates and durations. The following points are probably as far as it is reasonable to go at present. The reader is reminded that as with all generalizations, they will not always hold true.

1. Overall rates of succession are generally much slower in primary than in secondary succession because of the greater degree of environmental alteration that is involved. For comparable seral stages in primary and secondary succession (i.e., middle stages of primary succession compared with early stages of secondary succession), the difference in rates is less than for the entire sere.

2. Rates of succession are much faster in mesarch than in xerarch and hydrarch succession.

3. Rates of succession in the earlier stages of xeroseres and hydroseres are slower than in later stages. The opposite is true for mesarch succession, in which earlier stages are succeeded more rapidly than later stages.

4. The duration of any particular stage will be greatly influenced by the timing and rate of invasion of the site by reproductive propagules of individuals of the subsequent seral stage. Where such invasion is slow or delayed, a seral plant community may become very well established, resist invasion, and consequently last very much longer than where such invasion is rapid and immediate (cf. relay floristics vs. initial vegetative composition). The relative duration of different stages is consequently quite variable.

5. Succession will be much faster in climates that promote high rates of NPP and biomass accummulation than in climates that limit plant growth.

15.5   The Three Major Types of Sere

Succession and the resulting seres occur on a wide variety of terrestrial substrates: fine-textured alluvial deposits, glacial tills and coarse, gravelly river terraces, sand dunes, and rock surfaces, all of which can vary in chemistry from limestone to silaceous sandstone. It also occurs in climates that vary from equatorial to polar, and alpine to marine. It is to be expected, therefore, that although succession generally follows one of a few broad patterns, the details vary greatly from place to place.

The major classification of seres is not based directly on soil texture type, depth, or chemistry but on variations in the availability and ecological effectiveness of water (see Chapter 11). The moisture status of a site is often closely related to other soil characteristics, and such a classification implicitly reflects many other soil physical and chemical properties.

Seres are classified as *xeric, mesic,* or *hydric.* These terms were introduced in Chapter 11, but the reader is reminded that they can be used in either an absolute or a relative sense and that this can easily result in confusion. The former refers to the absolute water content of the soil, whereas the latter refers to the availability of soil water to organisms relative to the regional climate (see Chapter 16). In successional terminology these terms are used to imply very dry, moist, and very wet environments.

Xeric, mesic, and hydric sites represent the two extremes and the modal conditions in what is in reality a continuous variation in moisture status. Most sites represent an intermediate situation. However, these three seral types serve as a useful framework for the discussion of succession, and the following descriptions of examples of these three seres serve as a model with which real examples of succession in other areas can be compared. The examples given below are from the western hemlock biogeoclimatic zone of coastal British Columbia (Krajina, 1965): a humid region with warm summers, mild winters, and annual precipitation of 110–439 cm. Different species will be involved in other climatic areas and quite different patterns of succession can be found. However, the overall pattern and processes of community changes described are common to the primary successions of many temperate forest regions.

A. Primary Xerarch Succession and the Xerosere

Typical primary xerarch succession (see Figure 15.2) can be observed on a rock surface exposed by a landslide, a road cut, or on a rocky ridge following a severe wildfire or escaped slashburn. Such succession results in a primary lithosere. The physical environment at the start of the sere is inhospitable for most life forms. There is little or no water storage capacity on the site, and water is limiting to plant growth, especially during the growing season. Daytime temperatures can be very high due to full illumination, and radiation cooling at night can result in a large diurnal temperature fluctuation. Unless the rock is well fractured or fissured, the lack of soil for physical support precludes the growth of plants with an upright growth form, and there is virtually no capital of nutrients available on the site for plant growth. Nitrogen in particular is limiting, and although mineral nutrients are released from the weathering surface of the rock, most of them are washed away because of the lack of cation exchange sites and plant roots. The major source of many nutrients may be precipitation and dust.

Seeds and spores of many plants are continually arriving at such sites. Most are either blown or washed away, fail to germinate, or the young plants die shortly after germination for lack of the basic prerequisites of plant life. Thus, the pioneer plant community is limited to crustose lichens and pioneer mosses (such as *Rhacomitrium* sp.) that are tolerant of drought, infertility, and lack of physical support. The former grow very slowly but gradually cover the surface of the rock with a thin layer of organic material containing nitrogen (often fixed by the algae in the lichens) and other nutrients, and providing a very limited but ecologically significant storage of water.

The organic layer produced by the lichens undoubtedly gives an advantage to invading mosses, although there may be allelopathic mechanisms affording protection to the lichens against their ultimate fate of being overgrown by a carpet of mosses. The mosses grow faster than lichens and accelerate the process of humus accumulation, but depending on the climate and the species involved, their growth in an early xerosere is generally slow compared to that of the higher plants that occupy the area in later seral stages. In the drier parts of coastal B.C., it may take many decades or even centuries before the mosses develop sufficient nutrient capital, moisture storage capacity, and physical support to permit permanent occupancy and growth of dryland shrubs such as salal *(Gaultheria shallon)* and certain species of *Vaccinium*. In high rainfall areas, the process may require only a few decades.

The rate of organic accumulation increases as the shrub seral stage develops. The aerial cover of the shrubs greatly modifies the microclimate at the soil surface, and the area is invaded by species of moss and lichen that are not found in the pioneer stage. After a variable period of the shrub stage, tree seeds that have been reaching the site all along will successfully germinate, and seedlings of species that are tolerant of the xeric and oligotrophic conditions of the site (such as lodgepole pine and Douglas-fir) will survive. Growth of trees at this stage is characteristically slow, and many trees die when they reach a certain size because the site can no longer satisfy their increasing moisture and nutrient requirements (especially if there is an unusually hot, dry summer), or they may be blown over. However, their litterfall contributes to the buildup of organic matter and eventually the site reaches a condition that can support a continuous cover of slowly growing closed forest.

The establishment of a closed forest is followed by a long period in which there is a slow but continuing buildup of the organic layer, which in the prolonged absence of fire can eventually reach depths of 1 m or more if the climate is humid. As the layer builds up, the moisture storage capacity and the nutrient capital of the site steadily increase, and may eventually permit invasion of the site by shade-tolerant tree species such as western red cedar and western hemlock. The process of conversion from a lodgepole and/or Douglas-fir forest to a climatic climax cedar–hemlock community is very slow, generally requiring many centuries for completion, but in the prolonged absence of disturbance by wind, fire, erosion, disease, insects, or logging, and of significant climatic change, it will eventually develop. In the drier parts of coastal B.C., these late seral species may invade the site and persist as small trees in the understory but never become a part of the main canopy. They die of heat and drought as they move from the sheltered microclimate of the understory into the harsher microclimate of the main canopy.

B. Primary Mesarch Succession and the Mesosere

Typical mesarch succession (see Figure 15.2) occurs on deep (usually >1 m), medium-textured soil (which is often of moderate fertility) or soil parent material. If the topography is sloping, there must be sufficient upslope drainage area to compensate for the downslope loss of water from the site, and this type of sere frequently occurs midslope. It also occurs on ridge tops if the soil is moderately thick and has good soil moisture retention characteristics, and in flat areas, where soil drainage is moderate but there is no upslope drainage area to provide additional moisture. Primary succession is much less common on mesic sites than on xeric sites because the probability of any disturbance removing all the products of the previous succession (organic matter, a well-developed soil, soil fauna and flora, and an accumulation of plant spores and seeds) is much lower for a mesic site than for a xeric site. Consequently, most successions on mesic sites are secondary. Primary succession occurs where logging or fire followed by extensive sheet erosion removes everything above the C soil horizon. Areas subject to mechanical land-clearing operations, landslides, or deposition of alluvial materials would also undergo primary mesarch succession.

The pioneer stage of this sere is frequently dominated by herbaceous plants unless the availability of nitrogen is low (as in primary succession, in which case plants associated with symbiotic nitrogen-fixing microbes or with very low nitrogen requirements may dominate). In coastal British Columbia, for example, the herbaceous pioneer stage is frequently missing or poorly developed on sites that are very poor in nitrogen; such sites are rapidly colonized by dense stands of red alder, which has nitrogen-fixing root nodules. If the site is somewhat more fertile, invasions by red alder may not occur until after a stage dominated by herbs such as bracken fern *(Pteridium aquilinum)* and shrubs such as salal, species of *Vaccinium*, elderberry *(Sambucus* sp.), and possibly salmonberry *(Rubus spectabilis),* although the latter species is more typical of wetter sites (hygric to subhydric).

Red alder, which is the fastest-growing tree on such sites in its early years, may occupy the site for 30–60 years, gradually giving way to either Douglas-fir or western hemlock and western red cedar, depending upon aspect, seed source, and local climate. If a well-stocked Douglas-fir seral stage does occur, it may be very prolonged since the tree is long lived. However, since Douglas-fir is shade intolerant on this site in the more humid low elevation areas of coastal B.C., regeneration beneath the Douglas-fir will be climatic climax hemlock and cedar. These will eventually replace and exclude the Douglas-fir unless the canopy is sufficiently opened by disturbance (windthrow) to increase light penetration to the point at which some Douglas-fir seedlings can survive. If such disturbance does occur, seral Douglas-fir can exist more or less permanently as scattered individuals or small groups in the shade-tolerant climax community.

C. Primary Hydrarch Succession and the Hydrosere

Primary hydrarch succession (Figure 15.2) starts in newly formed lakes such as those that develop in the wake of a retreating glacier, or when a river is dammed by a landslide or through deliberate human activity. Aquatic succession is a major topic in its own right but is beyond the scope of this book. Our interest in the hydrosere is confined largely to the later semiterrestrial and terrestrial stages.

All lakes undergo a progressive process of filling in. For large lakes, this is generally a process measured on a geological rather than a biological time scale, although even large lakes can fill with sediments fairly rapidly. For example, Lake Mead, formed by Boulder Dam on the Colorado River in the southwestern U.S., is estimated to have a life of only 150 years because of deposition of the enormous load of silt carried by the Colorado River (Sawyer, 1966). Inputs of sediments in drainage water, wind-carried dust, and the accumulation of organic material from autotrophic and heterotrophic production in such lakes all serve to reduce the depth of water. Initially, organic production in the lakes is limited to food chains based on phytoplankton. In oligotrophic (immature, nutrient-poor) lakes, such production is very slow, and lake fill-in is largely a geological process.

As the lake matures and becomes shallower, bottom-rooted aquatic plants and lakeshore vegetation contribute increasingly to the accumulation of organic sediments. Where the land shelves gently into the lake and where the lake is mesotrophic to eutrophic, marsh and swamp plants such as sedges, rushes, and shrubs form a distinct zone around the margin of the lake. In oligotrophic lakes (as shown in Figure 15.2), the lake-edge environment may be dominated by *Sphagnum* mosses and shrubs tolerant of acidic bog conditions, the dead remains of which decompose slowly and produce an ever-thickening, floating layer or shelf of peaty material that may extend out many meters over the surface of the lake. Eventually, the layer becomes so thick that its lower surface rests on the bottom of the lake, converting that portion of the area from an aquatic to a semiterrestrial ecosystem.

Once a continuous layer of sphagnum peat has been established or the lake sediment level has reached the water surface, further plant litter accumulation serves to raise the surface of the organic litter above the water table. This produces a drier layer which is invaded by a variety of shrubs, which, under acidic, oligotrophic conditions in coastal B.C., include Labrador tea *(Ledum groenlandicum),* sweet gale *(Myrica gale),* swamp laurel *(Kalmia polifolia),* and hardhack *(Spirea douglasii).* Continued litter production and evapotranspiration by this shrub stage raise and dry the surface layers of the soil to the point at which trees such as lodgepole pine, western white pine, western red cedar or western hemlock, and larger shrubs such as crabapple *(Malus diversifolia),* ninebark *(Physiocarpus capitatus)* and high-bush cranberry *(Viburnum edule),* can become established. Tree growth is slow initially, but after a prolonged period of accumulation of leaves, needles, branches, and logs, the surface of the organic soil becomes sufficiently elevated above the water table to permit moderately productive growth of all the conifers listed above, although the light-demanding pines are frequently ousted by the shade-tolerant hemlock and cedar. The result of hydrarch succession is concentric bands of vegetation radiating outward from the water body, eventually developing into climatic climax western hemlock stands.

In comparing the descriptions of these three particular seres, there is one point that should have become apparent. In environments characterized by moisture extremes, a certain sequence of seral communities is more or less mandatory. The shrub seral stage in the primary xerosere cannot occur before the moss stage. The tree stage generally cannot occur before the shrub stage, and the climatic climax stage *cannot* occur until the subclimax forest has wrought very considerable changes in the moisture status of the site. Similarly, the shrub seral stage in the hydrosere cannot occur until the combination of allogenic and autogenic processes has ameliorated the moisture status of the substrate sufficiently, and the closed forest seral stage cannot occur until after the shrub stage. In the mesosere, on the other hand, climax tree species can participate in the pioneer community, especially if the microclimate is cool and humid (higher elevations and northerly aspects). Almost any of the intermediate seral stages can be omitted or greatly truncated, although greatest productivity of later seral communities generally occurs following the environmental modification (largely the accumulation of organic matter and nitrogen) that accompanies the earlier seral stages. Arguments about whether or not succession must follow a fixed pattern have generally failed to recognize the different nature of these three types of succession. They have also frequently failed to recognize that the need for environmental modification before a particular seral community can colonize an area applies far more in primary succession than in the much more common but variable secondary succession.

15.6 Linear and Cyclical Succession: The Problem with the Concept of Climax

The pattern of succession that has been described so far has been based on the implicit assumption that there is a linear development from a postdisturbance condition to a final, self-perpetuating, and therefore "stable" climax that persists for a very long time. This view of linear or "directional" succession (Knapp, 1974) accepts that the climax community eventually may become senescent, leading to its removal in a catastrophic manner by fire, wind, insects, or disease. This initiates a secondary linear succession leading back to the climax. However, the view assumes that the more common pattern is where the climax is permanently self-perpetuating (i.e., over many generations), with seedlings of the same species replacing individuals as they die of old age. The linear concept of succession does not allow for the situation in which the sequence of seral stages may eventually lead back to the "initial" stage without some catastrophic event.

A number of vegetation studies have reported that in certain types of ecosystems one can observe a patchwork of communities that are successively replacing each other in a cyclical sequence. This cycle may involve only the final stages of the sere, or there may be a cyclic repetition of the entire seral sequence. The former case has been referred to as a *regeneration complex* or *stand cycle;* the latter is called *cyclic succession* (Watt, 1947, 1955).

In studies of the patchwork of microcommunities in a British heathland, Watt (1947, 1955) identified four phases (pioneer, building, mature, and degenerate, which leads to the reestablishment of the pioneer phase) and described these for a variety of plant communities. For example, vig-

orous young heather *(Calluna vulgaris)* growing on an English moorland ages, becomes senescent, and dies, leaving a patch of bare organic soil which is rapidly invaded by young heather (Figure 15.8A). The height and number of shoots per plant, and the depth of the mor humus beneath the heather, exhibit a cyclical variation. Left undisturbed (by fire) for many years, a heather moor becomes a mozaic of small areas (a few square meters) of the four phases. At any one time, the majority of the area is in the building phase.

In the second example (Figure 15.8B), a tussock-forming species of moorland grass, *Festuca ovina,* creates a sequence of microtopographic conditions which are associated with four vegetation phases: hollow, building, mature, and degenerate. Grass seedlings invade areas of exposed mineral soil or erosion pavement. The activity of ants and earthworms together with the deposition of soil by wind and splash erosion from adjacent degenerating or hollow phases builds up the mineral soil around these seedlings, whose roots stabilize the accumulating soil and thereby build a "tussock." As the grass ages, it becomes senescent and is replaced by various species of lichens and bryophytes. These fail to stabilize the soil, which is gradually eroded back down to the erosion pavement, at which time grass seedlings become reestablished and initiate a new tussock-building phase. As with the heather, the four phases of the tussock grass community form a mozaic of small patches.

A similar regeneration cycle (wave regeneration; Sprugel, 1975) has been documented in the Adirondack Mountains of the northeastern U.S. The climax dominant *Abies balsamea* becomes susceptible to a variety of environmental stresses, notably wind, as it approaches maturity at about 60 years of age. The death of individual trees exposes the crowns of lee trees, which are damaged and then killed, exposing the next group of trees downwind. Prolific and regular production of seed crops by the *Abies* ensures prompt regeneration of this species below the dead and dying trees, and the net result is a series of crescent-shaped bands of dead and dying trees moving slowly across the forest with a frequency of about one wave every 60 years (Figure 15.9).

Examination of the climax in many types of ecosystem has revealed that the regeneration complex—consisting of a patchwork of communities or community conditions, each patch depending upon its neighbors and developing under conditions partly imposed by them—is common in many types of environment. This observation suggests that the climax should be considered as a "steady state" of repeated short-term cyclic variations in the composition of small patches of vegetation around a mean community condition, rather than a stable, unvarying condition in which there is

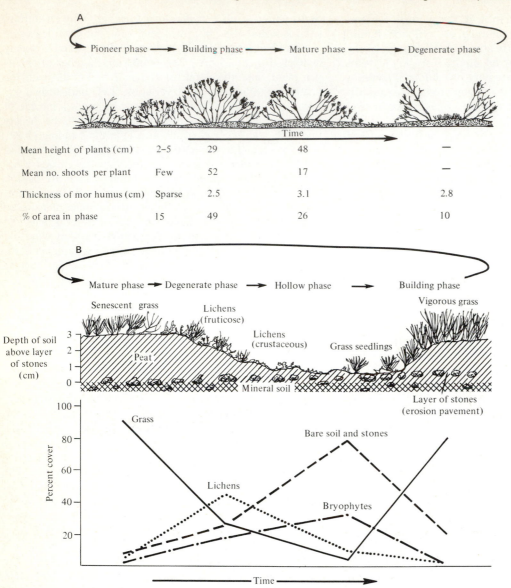

A				
Pioneer phase → Building phase → Mature phase → Degenerate phase				

		Time →		
Mean height of plants (cm)	2–5	29	48	—
Mean no. shoots per plant	Few	52	17	—
Thickness of mor humus (cm)	Sparse	2.5	3.1	2.8
% of area in phase	15	49	26	10

Figure 15.8
Two examples of the regeneration complex form of cyclical succession (after Watt, 1947, 1955). (A) Heather growing on an English moorland. Senescence of the vegetation is followed by a period of absence of the dominant plant and then by recolonization. (B) Regeneration complex in a sheep's fescue (*Festuca ovina*) grassland in England. (Copyright Blackwell Scientific Publications Ltd. Used with permission of the publisher.)

an individual-by-individual replacement. Although the latter does occur in some situations, either the frequency and intensity of natural disturbance (see the references in Vitousek and Reiners, 1975) or the normal pattern of senescence and death more commonly produces patch replacement: the regeneration complex. Recognition of the importance of such small-scale disturbance has resulted in a growing interest in *gap dynamics* in forest ecosystems (e.g., Doyle, 1981; Shugart et al., 1981; Shugart and West, 1980).

Cyclical succession involving the entire sere occurs over a much longer time scale than the regeneration complex or stand cycle. The best example is seen in the development of forests and bogs on northern slopes in Alaska (Heilman, 1966, 1968; Viereck, 1970; Neiland, 1971). This has already been described partially (Figure 15.6), but was portrayed as a linear succession. If the area is fairly flat and the succession is considered over a much longer period, however, it can develop into an example of cyclical succession. As the accumulation of sphagnum peat continues, it may

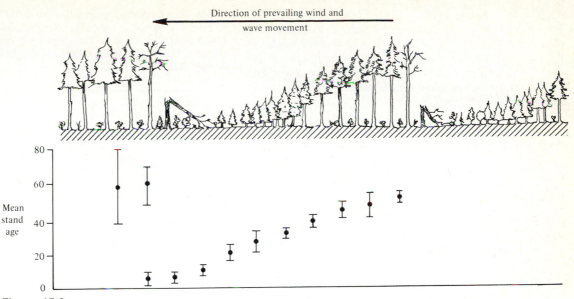

Figure 15.9

Wave regeneration in a climax balsam fir forest on Whiteface Mountain in the Adirondack Mountains, New York State (after Sprugel, 1976). Wavelength varied from 50 to 150 m, while tree age at the wave edge was as great as 79 years (based on the study of 11 waves). The diagram shows the variation in stand structure and tree age across one wave (±1 standard deviation). (Copyright Blackwell Scientific Publications Ltd. Used with permission of the publisher and author.)

produce a lens-shaped bog whose center is higher than its edges (called an *ombrotrophic* bog, in which the only source of water and nutrients for plants is precipitation). This may eventually lead to the formation of streams draining the bog. As these streams erode their way down into the peat, the area may become drier and warmer, the permafrost level recedes, the peat starts to decompose more rapidly, and the area may be invaded by birch and alder, reinitiating the sequence already described. The process of self-drainage is a very slow one, and fire usually intercedes before the drainage is complete, burning off the surface of the accumulated peat, lowering the permafrost, and reinitiating the succession.

15.7 Recent Models of Succession

The classical concepts of succession expounded by Cowles (1899), Clements (1916), Weaver and Clements (1938), and developed by Odum (1969) have received an increasing number of criticisms by field ecologists, particularly those working in ecosystems affected by fire. The view that following a disturbance a community gradually regains the structure and floristic composition of adjacent undisturbed communities on comparable sites by an orderly and predictable series of species replacement has been widely challenged. It has been claimed (Noble and Slatyer, 1977) that this traditional view implies altruism on the part of the species in each of the early successional stages; it requires that they alter their environment so that it becomes less suitable for their own persistence and more suitable for colonization of the subsequent seral community. Theories based on altruism are not widely accepted in ecology, and although these classical models of succession may have relevance for primary succession in severe environments (involving the relay floristics type of species replacement), they are not very useful for the analysis of the more common secondary succession.

One of the major difficulties with the classical models[1] of succession is that they are based on a community-by-community rather than a species-by-species replacement sequence. The idea of individualistic species-by-species replacement, suggested originally by Thoreau (1860) and developed by Gleason (1926), was given new life in a series of models of succession by Connell (1972), Drury and Nis-

[1] The nature of models and the process of modeling are discussed in Chapter 17.

bet (1973), and Horn (1974, 1976). These ecologists noted that studies in several forest regions had shown that succession rarely conforms to the classical Clementsian model—that later seral-stage replacement sequences are not consistently undirectional, and sere climaxes are common. Existing communities frequently impede rather than facilitate the development of a subsequent community. These observations led to the following hypothesis: that succession occurs as the result of differential survival and growth of individual species that are adapted to grow best at different stages in the successional sequence. This hypothesis led to the development of probabilistic Markov models.

A. Markov Models

This type of model is based on the idea that successional sequences are the direct result of *stochastic* (randomly occurring) processes of plant species replacement. Each plant in a community has a certain probability of being replaced by another individual of the same species in any time period, and for each other species that might replace it there is also a certain probability of replacement. The direction and pattern of succession is determined only by the original composition of the community and the matrix of replacement probabilities for the species in the region. The pattern is independent of how the system evolved to its present state, but for a given matrix of replacement probabilities, the community composition will always tend to converge toward a "climax" state, irrespective of the nature of disturbance. An example of this type of model was given by Horn (1976) for succession in a hardwood forest on abandoned farmland in the eastern U.S. (Table 15.2).

Markov models have been shown to predict some secondary successions very accurately, but they have a number of drawbacks. Replacement probabilities are assumed to be constant over time and the species replacements are assumed to take place at discrete intervals. The lack of any description of the functional processes involved in species replacement make this type of model rather inflexible.

The Markov type of model can be applied to community-by-community replacement as well as to species-by-species or tree-by-tree replacement.

B. Stand Models

In an attempt to overcome some of the deficiencies of Markov models, several people have developed stand models. These are far more detailed than the simple Markov type of model, and may include information on seed supply, the growth and death of individual trees, and how they compete with each other. This often involves a description of the spatial distribution of individual trees and the vertical structure of the community.

Table 15.2 Matrix of Species-by-Species Replacement Probabilities for a Model of Succession in a Deciduous Hardwood Forest on Abandoned Farmland in New Jersey, U.S., and Predictions of the Model Concerning Future Forest Composition After Starting with a Pure Gray Birch Stand

A. Probability that the species in vector A will be replaced by the species in vector B over a 50-year period.[a]

	Vector A			
Vector B	Gray Birch	Black Gum	Red Maple	Beech
Gray birch	.05	.01	.00	.00
Black gum	.36	.57	.14	.01
Red maple	.50	.25	.55	.03
Beech	.09	.17	.31	.96

B. Predicted future composition of a forest initially composed of pure gray birch, using the probability matrix in A.

Species composition of the forest at various times in the future (%)

	0 yr	50 yr	100 yr	150 yr	200 yr	Very Old Forest
Gray birch	100	5	1	0	0	0
Black gum	0	36	29	23	18	3
Red maple	0	50	39	30	24	4
Beech	0	9	31	47	58	93

Source: After Horn, 1976. Copyright Blackwell Scientific Publications Ltd. Used with permission.

[a] For example, the probability that a gray birch tree will be replaced by a red maple tree in this time period is $50/100$ or one in two.

Stand development simulators of this type have been applied to coniferous ecosystems in the Pacific Northwest (Reed and Clark, 1976). Figure 15.10 shows some of the details of how successional change is simulated in the Reed and Clark model. Starting with a particular ecosystem condition (the state of the ecosystem, which was established in the previous time period), a comparison is made between this condition and the niches of the available species. Recruits of the appropriate species are established where there is some unoccupied niche space, and all existing plants are grown by an amount appropriate for the simulated time interval and for the current environmental conditions. Optional perturbations can then be applied to the model and their consequences examined. These may cause a certain amount of plant mortality and environmental modification, which defines the state of the ecosystem at the start of the subsequent iteration, and creates some unoccupied niche space. Alternatively, the mortality may be caused by competition. One of the most elaborate forest dynamics models

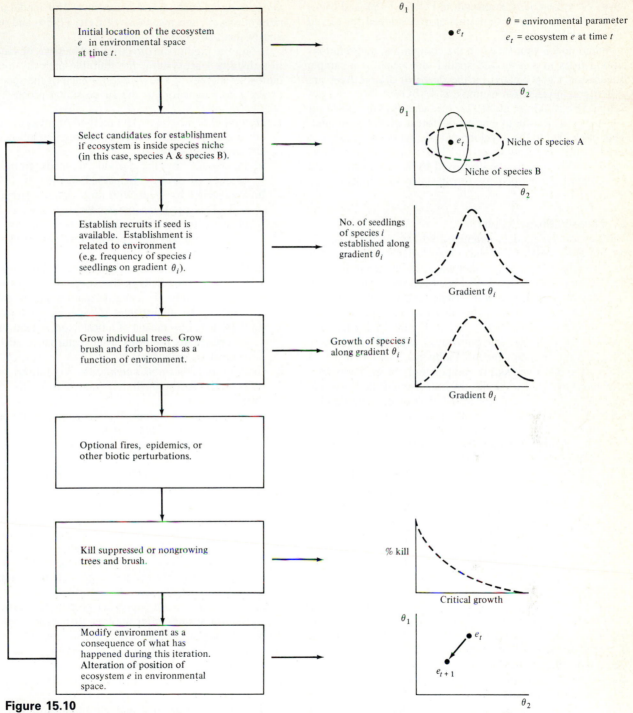

Figure 15.10
Flowchart of the annual update algorithm for the stand succession model developed by Reed and Clark, 1976. (Used with permission of the author.)

based on individual tree growth is FOREST (Ek and Mon-serud, 1974), a succession simulator developed for mixed forests in Wisconsin.

Stand models that focus on the competitive interrelations among trees in a restricted spatial unit, such as a sample quadrat or a gap created by the death of a large tree, are called *gap models*. An example is JABOWA, a model developed by Botkin et al. (1972) (see also Botkin, 1981) for the northern deciduous hardwood forest in New England. This model led to the development of a whole generation of similar models (Shugart et al., 1981; Shugart and West, 1980). Other models are discussed by Means (1982), and for a detailed treatment of forest succession models, see Shugart (1984).

C. Three-Pathway Model

Many of the models examined so far involve a single pattern of successional replacement. Egler's (1954) model, which includes two major pathways, is an exception. Recently, a more complex model has been proposed (Connell and Slatyer, 1977), which in essence is an amplification of Egler's model to include the idea of sere climaxes. The *three-pathway model,* illustrated in Figure 15.11, has one pathway (the *facilitation* pathway), which is essentially Egler's relay floristics model. Pathways 2 and 3 are based on Egler's initial vegetative composition model. Pathway 2 (the *tolerance* pathway) differs little from Egler's second pathway—the environment at the start of the sere permits invasion by any species. Early seral species are merely those that are adapted to rapidly colonize disturbed sites and which are shade intolerant and are therefore competitively excluded by the shade-tolerant later seral species. Pathway 3 (the *inhibition* pathway) invokes the idea of serclimaxes. The early occupants of the site act to inhibit establishment of seedlings of either early or late seral species. Species change can occur only when the death of individuals or a disturbance creates the possibility of new colonization.

D. Multiple-Pathway Model

Although the successional models discussed above all represent some degree of improvement over the original Clementsian model, they have been criticized (Noble and Slatyer, 1977; Cattelino et al., 1979) because of their inapplicability to fire-dominated ecosystems, their failure to quantify the effects of disturbances of different intensity and frequency, and because they do not explicitly incorporate the adaptations of species that determine the model's response to different types of disturbance. Because of the high diversity of species adaptations and the intensity, type, and frequency of disturbance, these authors have developed a

multiple-pathway model of succession. This model incorporates classical concepts, those of Egler (1954) and of Drury and Nisbet (1973).

In order to predict the direction and patterns of succession in a disturbed ecosystem, the multiple-pathway model requires three types of knowledge for each of the species that exerts a dominant role in the successional process:

1. *Method of persistence*. The method of invasion and colonization, or of persistence of propagules following disturbance (four classes).
   a. Persistence by the arrival of seeds from remote sources (D species: dispersed seed).
   b. Persistence by seeds with long viability stored in the soil. This pool can persist through several disturbances without replenishment, because not all the seeds germinate after the first disturbance (S species: stored seed).
   c. Persistence of seed surviving on the site in protective cones or fruits held in the vegetation canopy; seeds available only if sexually mature plants available prior to the disturbance (C species: canopy seed).
   d. Persistence by means of a protected vegetative organ that resprouts promptly after disturbance (V species: vegetative recovery).
2. *Conditions for establishment*. The conditions required (tolerated) for establishment and growth to maturity (three classes).
   a. Species able to establish at any time, in the presence of mature individuals of the same or different species; able to tolerate competition (T species: tolerant).
   b. Species able to establish only immediately after disturbance when competition is usually reduced; intolerant of competition (I species: intolerant).
   c. Species able to establish only after the environment has been modified by the presence of mature individuals of the same or other species (R species).
3. *Critical life history events*. The time taken to reach critical stages in the life history (e.g., age of reproduction, longevity) (four classes).
   a. Replenishment of supply of propagules sufficient to replace species after another disturbance (event p).
   b. Attainment of maturity; production of sufficient propagules to enable the species to persist through another disturbance (event m).
   c. Senescence and loss of the species from the community (event l).
   d. Loss of propagules and elimination of the species (event e).

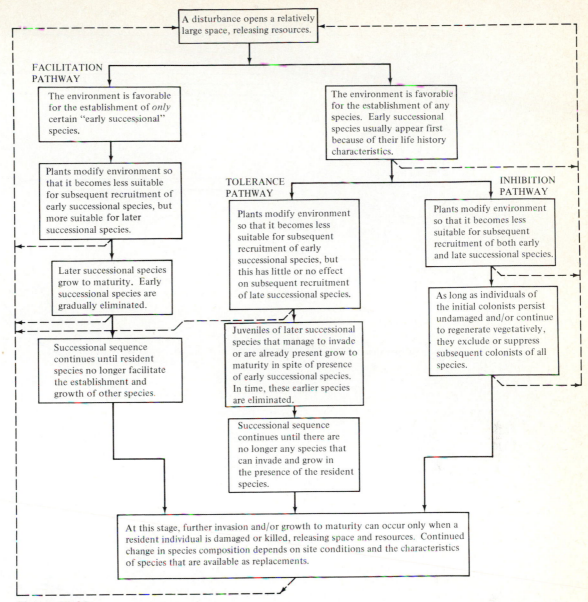

Figure 15.11
The three-pathway model of succession of Connell and Slatyer, 1977. (Copyright The University of Chicago Press. Used with permission of the publisher and authors.)

Using this information, diagrams can be prepared that predict and summarize secondary succession. For example, patterns of succession in two different forest types in northwestern Montana are shown in Figure 15.12, and a further discussion can be found in Noble and Slatyer (1980).

This approach has been extended recently in the form of a quantitative simulation model of succession, which deals with both overstory and understory species and accounts for the effects of fire intensity and the height to which flames scorch the foliage on the sequence of species replacements.

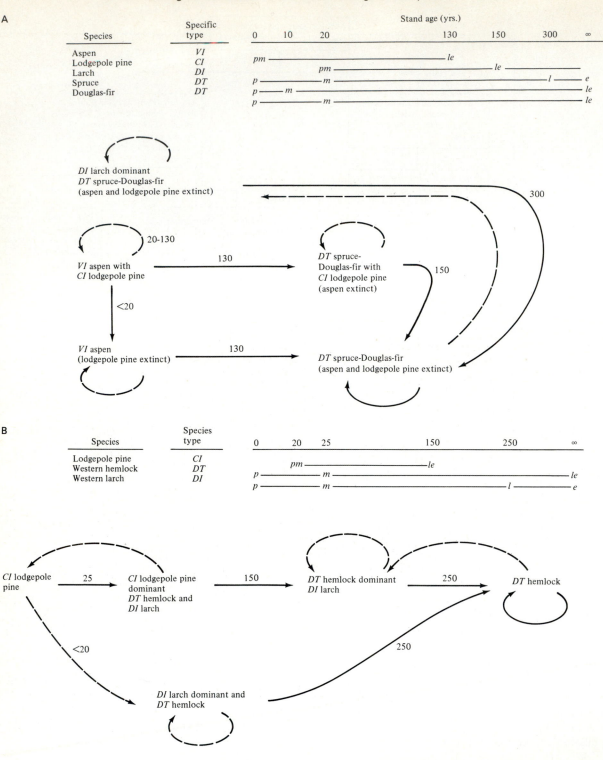

Figure 15.12

Life history characteristics and species replacement sequences in two community types in northwestern Montana. (A) Aspen community type. (B) Hemlock community type (after Cattelino et al., 1979). Numbers on solid lines indicate the time (years) for transition in the absence of disturbance. Numbers on dashed lines indicate frequency of disturbance by fire. (Copyright Springer-Verlag New York Inc. Used with permission of the publisher and authors.)

An example of the model is given in Figure 15.13 and Table 15.3. For details, consult Kessell and Potter (1980). This simulation model is an example of the type of predictive tool that ecologists and resource managers will probably make increasing use of in the future.

Succession is such an important but complex and variable aspect of ecology that there will undoubtedly be continued development of successional models. A useful review of the successional literature up to 1979 can be found in Mac-Mahon (1980). Other recent treatments are presented in van der Maarel (1980), West et al. (1981), Mooney and Godron (1983), and Shugart 1985. Reviews of succession models are given by Shugart and West (1980) and Loucks et al. (1981). Knapp (1974) also reviewed models of succession.

Table 15.3 Species Composition for each of 13 Successional States for the PSME/SYAL *(Pseudotsuga menziesii/Symphoricarpos albus)* Habitat Type in Western Montana

	Succession Model States												
	1	2	3	4	5	6	7	8	9	10	11	12	13

The values in the tables are species importance values.[a] The data are for the model shown in Figure 15.13.

	1	2	3	4	5	6	7	8	9	10	11	12	13
Trees (>1.4 m tall)					OVERSTORY SPECIES								
Pinus contorta (lodgepole pine)			3	2	1								
Pinus ponderosa (ponderosa pine)			2	2	2	2	1	1			3	3	2
Pseudotsuga menziesii (Douglas-fir)			4	4	5	5	5	6	6		4	4	5
Tree seedlings (<1.4 m tall)													
Pinus contorta (lodgepole pine)	1	1											
Pinus ponderosa (ponderosa pine)	1	1								1			
Pseudotsuga menziesii (Douglas-fir)	1	1	1	1							1	1	1
Total canopy cover			4	4	4	4	4	4	4		4	4	4
Shrubs and subshrubs					UNDERSTORY SPECIES								
Juniperus communis			2	1							2	1	
Potentilla fruticosa				1	1	1	1	1	1			1	1
Ribes spp.	2	2											
Rosa spp.			1	2	2	2	2	2	2		1	2	2
Shepherdia canadensis			2	1	1	1	1	1	1		2	1	1
Spiraea betulifolia			2	2	2	2	2	2	2		2	2	2
Symphoricarpos albus	1	1	2	2	2	2	2	2	2	1	2	2	2
Berberis repens			1	1	1	1	1	1	1		1	1	1
Total shrub cover	2	2	4	4	4	4	4	4	4	2	4	4	4
Forbs and grasses													
Calamagrostis rubescens	1	1	3	1	1	1	1	1	1	1	3	1	1
Carex geyeri	2	2	3								2	3	
Festuca scabrella	1	1	1		1						1	1	1
Gramineae	1	1		1	1						1		1
Arnica spp.			2		1	1	1	1	1		2		1
Astragalus spp.			1	1	1	1	1	1	1		1	1	1
Fragaria spp.	2	2	1		1	1	1	1	1	2	1		1
Total forb and grass cover	5	5	3	2	1	1	1	1	1		5	3	2

Source: After Kessell and Potter, 1980. Copyright Springer-Verlag New York, Inc.

[a]Importance values are expressed on a seven-point scale. Blank = <1%:; 1 = 1–5%; 2 = 6–25%, 3 = 26–50%; 4 = 51–75%; 5 = 76–95%; 6 = >95%. Importance values for trees at least 1.4 m tall are relative density; all other importance values are absolute cover.

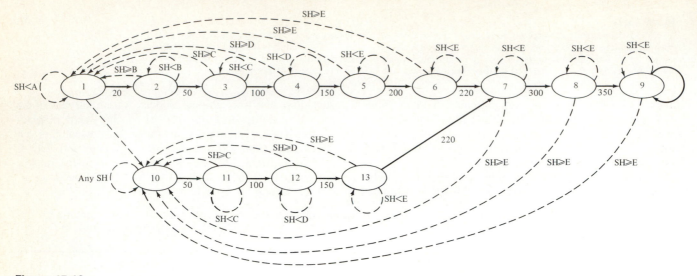

Figure 15.13

Pictoral representation of a computer simulation model developed to describe and predict overstory succession in nine Montana forest habitat types. Transition from one vegetation state (numbered circles) to the next depends upon stand age. Regression to an earlier state depends upon the scorch height of wildfires. Critical scorch height values are given in Kessell and Potter, 1980. Solid lines indicate vegetation transitions in the absence of disturbance. Dotted lines show transitions accompanying wildfires of indicated scorch height (SH). Numbers by solid lines are the cumulative years free from fire disturbance. (Copyright Springer-Verlag New York Inc. Used with permission of the publisher and authors.)

15.8   Changes in Ecosystem Function During Succession

As an area proceeds from early to late seral stages of a linear succession, or from one point to another of a cyclic succession, there is a marked change in several characteristics of the community. The life form and longevity of the dominant plants, the structure of the community, its productivity, and the ratio of green to woody biomass all undergo changes. In this section we examine under three headings the changes in ecosystem function that accompany changes in ecosystem structure: ecological energetics, nutrient cycling, and ecosystem stability.

A. Ecological Energetics

It is difficult to generalize about the variation in energy flow at different stages of succession since this will differ so much among xeric, mesic, and hydric environments, and between primary and secondary successions. No rigorous, comparative analysis of these patterns has ever been made (largely for lack of adequate data), and therefore the following model must be considered hypothetical. There is growing interest in such comparisons, and the next decade of research should provide a much improved understanding of this topic.

At the beginning of each seral stage, net productivity (excess of photosynthesis over respiration) will generally increase until perhaps the middle or later part of the stage, then level off, and finally decline somewhat as transition to the next stage occurs. Various combinations of incomplete occupancy of the site by the invading community, competition between the invading community and the remnants of the previous community, and occupancy of part of the site by senescent individuals of the previous community will all serve to prevent maximum primary productivity at the beginning of a seral stage or during the transition to a new seral stage. As the seral community fully occupies the site and develops toward maturity, net productivity will peak, only to decline as the ratio of photosynthesizing to respiring biomass decreases, as competition within the community increases, and as the individuals in the community become senescent.

Net productivity in a mesosere in a moderate climate will rise rapidly from the pioneer community and peak during one of the intermediate seral stages (Figure 15.14B). This may occur in the shrub stage if it is succeeded directly by

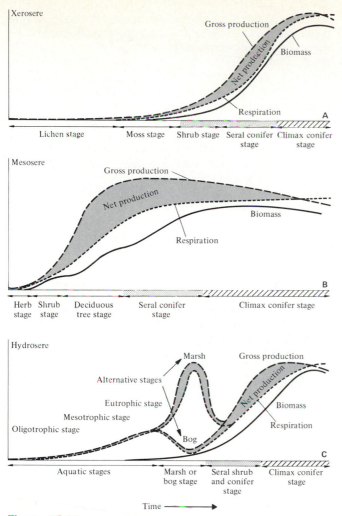

cause later successional species have been selected during their evolution more for survival than for rapid growth. However, it is more difficult to make generalizations about mesoseres than about hydroseres and xeroseres because, as we have seen, mesoseres tend to follow a less consistent pattern of succession. It may well be that in those cases in which an area reforests directly with climax species following disturbance, productivity in the young climax community would be just as high as that of earlier seral communities had they been occupying the site.

Living biomass may approach its maximum value in the middle stages of the mesosere, with only modest increases after either the deciduous or the pioneer conifer stage. On the other hand, total biomass accumulation may continue almost indefinitely since trees stems may be incorporated into the forest floor in a largely undecomposed condition as they die and are replaced.

The pattern of production for xeroseres and hydroseres is considerably different. In a xerosere, gross production, net production, and biomass are all very small during the pioneer lichen stage (Figure 15.14A). Production and biomass increase slightly during the moss stage and again in the shrub stage. Increases continue throughout the seral conifer stage, reaching a peak only when the area has converged to the climatic climax community. In the absence of complete convergence, biomass and production will peak in the terminal seral stage.

In a hydrosere, productivity increases from the oligotrophic to the eutrophic lake stage, but very little living biomass accumulates. Productivity may drop somewhat as one passes through the transition from aquatic to wet terrestrial stages (bogs), although marsh ecosystems are sometimes associated with very high productivity (Chapter 4). Productivity may then either drop or increase, according to the productivity of the semiterrestrial stage (depending largely on nutrient status), rising further as succession approaches the climatic climax (Figure 15.14C).

It has been suggested that the ratio of total ecosystem production to total ecosystem respiration (the P/R ratio) is a good index of the degree of successional maturity. Where the ratio approaches 1 (no net biomass accumulation), the ecosystem is said to be approaching a climax condition, whereas a high value indicates an early seral condition. Less than 1 should indicate a senescent climax condition (Whittaker and Woodwell, 1968). Although this may be a useful approach to an overall evaluation of ecosystem maturity in some types of ecosystem, it is to be expected that there will be variation in P/R ratio within any single stage as the seral community progresses from juvenility to maturity to senescence. Also, we do not have enough information from

Figure 15.14
Hypothetical model of the overall variation in autotrophic production and biomass accumulation during primary succession in three types of environment. Time scales for the three graphs differ, and none of the scales are linear. The mesosere is much shorter than the other two seres. No actual time scales are given since the duration of any stage can vary greatly. The curves are smoothed to show overall trends. In reality, each stage probably has an initial increase in biomass and production followed by a slight decline late in the stage. Respiration is shown to exceed gross production late in the climax stage resulting in a biomass decline. In some forest ecosystems biomass may continue to accumulate in the climax community for a very long time.

conifers, in an early hardwood tree stage (such as red alder in coastal British Columbia), or in an early conifer tree stage (such as pine or Douglas-fir). Net productivity may decline somewhat as the climax community develops, be-stands of varying successional conditions to be completely confident that the P/R ratio does vary as suggested. An additional problem lies in the implicit assumption that respiration equals gross production at climax. Experience in forestry suggests that biomass can continue to accumulate for very prolonged periods (hundreds, and perhaps even thousands of years) in climax communities. In the Pacific Northwest, ratios may exceed 1 in 1000 year-old stands, and yield is sustained in 300 year-old stands in Utah (Mac-Mahon, 1980). Only in overmature, senescent climax communities will net biomass accumulation approach zero or become negative (cf. Table 4.10).

B. Biogeochemistry

Not only does the magnitude of nutrient turnover vary during succession but so also does the relative importance of the three pathways of nutrient movement: the geochemical cycle, the biogeochemical cycle, and the biochemical cycle.

1. Geochemical cycle. At the start of the pioneer stage of primary succession, the addition of nutrients to the ecosystem in dust, precipitation, seepage water, biotic imports, biological fixation of gases, and the weathering of rock and soil minerals is most probably balanced by outputs in biotic exports, water and wind erosion, and soil leachates. The extent of the latter loss is determined by the cation and anion exchange capacities of, and the production of anions in, the mineral soil (Cole et al., 1975; cf. Figure 10.6).

As succession proceeds, the unconsolidated layers of surficial deposits (where they exist) are occupied by plant roots and their mycorrhizal associates, and a soil organic layer is formed which greatly increases the ability of the abiotic environment to conserve nutrients. Nutrient output from the system is also substantially reduced by the uptake of nutrients by plants and their incorporation in plant, animal, and microbial biomass. Weathering of primary minerals and rocks is accelerated by the organic acids produced by decomposing organic matter, by roots (Voigt, 1968), and by soil fungi (Silverman and Munoz, 1970), so that the rate of mineral nutrient input will be higher during succession than before it starts (cf. lithoponics). The rate of nitrogen input will also vary through succession as the activity of nitrogen-fixing organisms varies. This is still an incompletely understood topic, but nitrogen inputs will generally peak during seral stages dominated by plants such as alder, which have a symbiotic relationship with nitrogen-fixing microorganisms (Chatarpaul and Carlisle, 1983).

During periods of high biomass accumulation, output of essential nutrients from the ecosystem will be less than inputs because of their incorporation in the accumulating

biomass. Table 15.4 shows the average growing season concentrations of six ions in streams draining nine late-successional ecosystems and five mid-seral ecosystems that resulted from logging. The lower values for the latter reflect the rapid biomass accumulation in seral forests. As net biomass accumulation decreases, the rate of nutrient accumulation also slows down until outputs once again equal inputs at the climax stage, as shown in Figure 15.15 for a mesosere. The input/output balance for xeroseres and hydroseres will also reflect biomass accumulation, and one could say that balance in the geocycle is largely a function of patterns of biomass accumulation (Figure 15.14). Natural catastrophies such as fire or logging, which temporarily devegetate an area and speed decomposition, result in a sudden increase in output from the system as organic matter is lost. This net loss is temporary and is reversed to become a gain as soon as biomass accumulation begins.

Our knowledge of the variation in the balance between geochemical inputs and outputs during succession is far from complete, and there is need for a lot more research in this field (Gorham et al., 1979). This is an important topic. Human begins are influencing the geochemical balance of the earth in as yet incompletely understood ways (e.g., acid rain), which may have significant effects on ecosystem function.

2. Biogeochemical Cycle. This cycle varies according to biomass turnover (litterfall) and leaching losses from plants. The high turnover of relatively nutrient-rich biomass in pio-

Table 15.4 Average Growing Season (1 June–30 September 1973 and 1974) Concentrations of Five Ions[a] in Streamwater Draining Five Mid-Successional and Nine Late-Successional Ecosystems, New Hampshire

	Streamwater Concentrations,[b] μeq L^{-1}		
Ion	Late-Successional Watersheds	Mid-Successional Watersheds	Ratio of Concentrations
NO_3^-	53 (5)	8 (1.3)	6.6
K^+	13 (1)	7 (0.5)	1.8
Mg^{2+}	40 (4.9)	24 (1.6)	1.7
Ca^{2+}	56 (4.5)	36 (2.5)	1.6
Cl^-	15 (0.3)	13 (0.3)	1.2
Na^+	29 (2.6)	28 (0.9)	1.0

Source: Vitousek and Reiners, 1975. Copyright the American Institute of Biological Sciences. Used with permission.

[a]Note the relative absence of any effect of logging on sodium and chloride ions: nonnutrient elements.

[b]Standard error of the means is shown in parentheses.

Figure 15.15

Model of the response of an ecosystem to disturbance. (A) Variation in biomass accumulation. (B) Balance between nutrient inputs and outputs. In a mature forest prior to disturbance, nutrient outputs will generally equal or exceed inputs. As succession starts there will be a brief period of high nutrient loss, but as biomass accumulates, outputs will fall below inputs for essential nutrients; nonnutrient elements remain unaffected (after Vitousek and Reiners, 1975). This example is probably valid for mesoseres, but xeroseres and hydroseres may exhibit somewhat different patterns. (Copyright American Institute of Biological Science. Used with permission of the publisher and authors.)

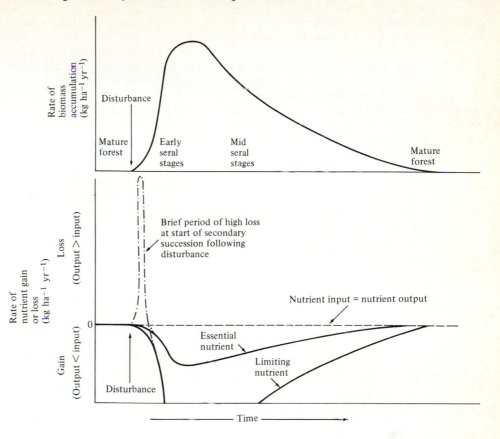

neer, shrub, and seral hardwood stages can exceed the turnover in late successional conifer stages, so that in mesoseres the biogeochemical cycle can peak in an early seral stage. In xeroseres and hydroseres, it is more likely that nutrient turnover will peak in the immature climax or later subclimax stages because the organic production of these stages is higher than that of earlier stages. Biogeochemical cycling in the mature climax stage is probably largely confined to direct nutrient cycling (tree → forest floor → tree), and since decomposition tends to slow down at the climax stage because of changes in the organic and inorganic chemistry of the litter, nutrient turnover is probably reduced. The apparent adaptation of "hoarding" nutrients by promoting direct nutrient cycling and inhibiting mineralization probably helps the climax community to perpetuate itself and to compete with other species even if it does reduce rates of nutrient turnover and productivity.

3. Biochemical or Internal Cycle. Internal nutrient cycling is an important conservation mechanism exhibited by many, if not all plants. Not enough is known yet about the variation in internal cycling during different stages of succession to present a clear picture, but accompanying the hypothesized trend toward "nutrient hoarding" within the ecosystem as succession proceeds, one might expect a trend toward a greater degree of internal cycling. By removing a greater proportion of the nutrients in its old foliage prior to abscission, a plant can "hoard" nutrients more efficiently, thereby rendering them less available to competitors. One might expect, therefore, that internal cycling will become more efficient as succession proceeds. Further studies are necessary to test the validity of this hypothesis, and it is certainly not universally true. *Eucalyptus* species, which are often subclimax, are outstandingly good at internal cycling of phosphorus (Attiwill, 1980; Ferreira, Kimmins and Barros, 1984), and the low nutrient availability in the soil early in some successions and the high growth rate potential of many pioneer plants may in some ecosystems result in greater internal cycling early than late in succession.

15.9 Relationship Between Ecosystem Stability and Successional Stage

Ecologists have spent a great deal of time over the past decade discussing the concept of *stability in ecosystems*. Lack of agreement over just what is meant by stability has contributed to the longevity of the debate. Many ecologists have claimed that the diversity of the biota increases during succession and that there is a concomitant increase in stability, but it is now recognized that there are probably no simple relationships between diversity and stability (see reviews by Orians, 1975; Margalef, 1975; May, 1975; Whittaker, 1975; and Botkin, 1980).

The concept of stability usually refers to the tendency of a system to remain in its present condition or return to that condition following a disturbance. The term has been used with a number of connotations (Orians, 1975) and therein lies part of the difficulty. The following meanings of the term ''stability'' have been used (Figure 15.16).

1. *Constancy*. The lack of change in some parameter(s) of the ecosystem such as the number of species, the life form of the community, or physical features of the environment.
2. *Persistence*. The length of time over which the ecosystem is constant or maintains a particular condition within specified bounds.
3. *Inertia*. The ability of the ecosystem to remain constant or to persist in the face of disturbing factors such as wind, fire, disease, herbivore outbreak, and so on.
4. *Resilience*. This term has been used as a synonym for elastic stability.
5. *Elasticity*. The speed with which the ecosystem returns to its original condition following disturbance.
6. *Amplitude*. The extent to which an ecosystem can be changed and still return rapidly to its original condition.
7. *Cyclic stability*. The property of an ecosystem to change through a sequence of conditions that bring it back to the original condition (i.e., the regeneration complex of a heather moor; even the Alaskan forest–bog cyclic succession could be said to have a form of stability).
8. *Trajectory stability*. The tendency of ecosystems to return to a single final condition after disturbance has altered the initial condition to a variety of new conditions. Ecological convergence following successional retrogression is an example of trajectory stability.

Of these terms, constancy and persistence can be used to refer to the stability of individual seral stages. Cyclic and trajectory stability can be used to refer to the overall stability of successional patterns, the former referring to cyclical succession and the latter to ecological convergence. Inertia, resilience, elasticity, and amplitude can be used to refer to the degree of successional retrogression following a disturbance and the subsequent rates of succession back to the initial condition.

The problem with the quest for a predictable relationship between diversity and stability arises from the fact that a given ecosystem may be stable according to one of the above definitions, and unstable according to another. For example, diverse (species-rich) tropical forests may have a high inertial stability, but low elastic and amplitude stability. Conversely, many of the less diverse temperate forests may have a lower inertial stability, but a higher elastic and amplitude stability.

Ecosystem stability will vary between different types of sere, between different seral stages, and between primary and secondary successions. The inertial stability of a mesosere will be greater than that of a xerosere or hydrosere (it takes a greater degree of disturbance to produce a major change), and mesoseres are more elastic (they return to the climax more rapidly). They also tend to have a greater amplitude stability (they can be pushed much further back in succession before the return to climax is significantly delayed) than xeroseres and hydroseres. Early stages of primary seres will have lower values for several of these stability indices than will early stages of secondary seres.

Early seral stages may or may not be more stable than late seral stages or climax according to these definitions. Whereas a low intensity surface fire may destroy an early seral stage, a climax forest may be relatively unaltered by it. The opposite may be equally true, depending on the species involved. On the other hand, whereas a windstorm may destroy a climax forest, it may have no effect on a shrub stage. It has been argued that early stages are more stable than climax stages, since it obviously takes longer to return to the climax following severe disturbance than to return to a much earlier stage (Horn, 1974). This idea may be justifiable in terms of elastic stability but overlooks the fact that such early stages have low constancy and persistence stability compared with the climax, have lower amplitude stability, and both stages may merely be parts of the same overall trajectory stability. The greater susceptibility of agricultural ecosystems to erosion by wind and flood compared with that of the regional climax ecosystems in all but the driest climates is an example of the instability of these early seral stages.

Much of the discussion about ecosystem stability has focused on ecosystem structure: the species composition and spatial arrangement, the depth and composition of the forest floor, etc. More recently, the evaluation of stability

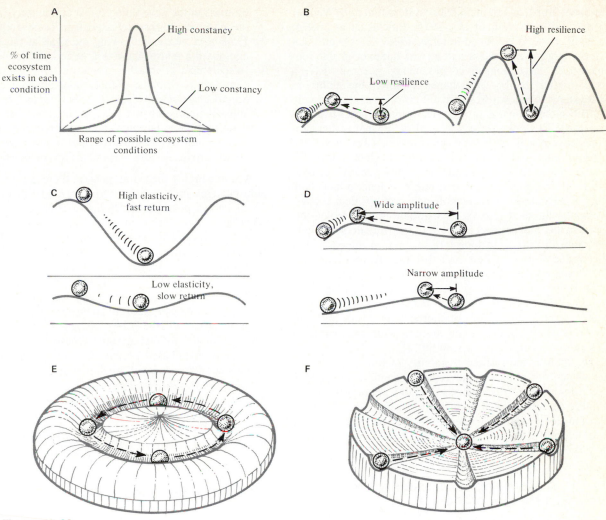

Figure 15.16

Diagrammatic representation of various concepts of ecosystem stability (modified after Orians, 1975). In B–F the condition of an undisturbed ecosystem is represented by the position of a ball in a hollow. Horizontal displacement of the ball from its resting position indicates a change in ecosystem condition. The shape of the hollow reflects the various aspects of ecosystem stability since the shape determines the ease and direction of the movement of the ball when displaced (i.e., how the condition of the ecosystem changes when disturbed). While it remains within the lip of the hollow (the limit of stability of the ecosystem), the ball always returns to its initial condition when released from disturbance. If pushed over the lip, the ball will continue to move until it reaches some new resting condition (i.e., another hollow). (The ball-hollow analogy was borrowed from Holling, 1973.) (A) *Constancy*—lack of change in ecosystem condition (defined by one or more parameters). (B) *Inertia* or *resilience*—degree of resistance of the ecosystem to change. Vertical rise to the lip is a measure of the ecosystem resilience. (C) *Elasticity*—speed with which a disturbed ecosystem returns to its initial condition. (D) *Amplitude*—degree to which ecosystem can be changed but still return to its initial condition following termination of the disturbance. (E) *Cyclic stability*—the condition of the ecosystem changes through a cyclic sequence of conditions. (F) *Trajectory stability*—ecosystem will alaways return to the same condition irrespective of condition when released from disturbance. (Copyright Dr. W. Junk Publisher, Netherlands. Used with permission of the publisher and author.)

has been broadened to include ecosystem function (Webster et al., 1975; O'Neill et al., 1975; Reichle et al., 1975; O'Neill, 1976; O'Neill and Reichle, 1980). Ecosystems that have a large live biomass and a slow turnover of that biomass (i.e., large, long-lived organisms) generally have a high inertial stability. Resilience stability, the ability of ecosystems to recover from change, is often associated with a small biomass that is turning over rapidly (short-lived organisms). However, a large capital of organic matter provides a reservoir of energy and nutrients that drives the heterotrophic and autotrophic activities which return the ecosystem to its initial condition. Consequently, ecosystems rich in organic matter and nutrients tend to have both higher inertial and higher resilience stability than ecosystems lacking such reserves. Disturbances that deplete organic matter and nutrient reserves (e.g., fire) are potentially far more disturbing to long-term ecosystem function than disturbances (e.g., windblow) that merely re-arrange organic matter and nutrient pools within the system.

Different components of terrestrial ecosystems may confer different types of stability on the ecosystem. Forests usually have an understory of shorter-lived plants that confer a degree of resilience to the system, while the long-lived overstory provides inertial stability.

The inertial and resilience stability of forest ecosystems are sometimes related to spatial and genetic heterogeneity (i.e., diversity) of the biomass, but this relationship is extremely complex, and it is difficult to generalize. The ability of an ecosystem to recover from perturbation is probably more closely related to its ability to process energy than to its diversity *per se*.

15.10   A Model of Succession for the Northern Hardwood Forest

Studies conducted in the Hubbard Brook Valley within the White Mountains of the northeastern U.S. have led to the development of a conceptual model of the changes in forest ecosystem characteristics during secondary succession (Figure 15.17A). The model identifies four phases in this succession.

1. *Reorganization phase*. This is a period of one or two decades following a disturbance (e.g., clearcut harvesting) that removed the previous forest. During this phase, there is a steady decline in total ecosystem biomass because decomposition and erosion losses exceed net biomass production by the early seral vegetation.
2. *Aggradation phase*. For more than a century following the reorganization phase, there is a net accumulation of

biomass in the developing forest community. The end of the phase is marked by a peak in ecosystem biomass.
3. *Transition phase*. Following the peak at the end of the aggradation phase, there is a period of biomass decline as the forest approaches a mature, climax condition in equilibrium with the climatic and edaphic conditions.
4. *Steady-state phase*. This is a period that lasts until a subsequent disturbance takes the area back to the reorganization phase. During the steady-state phase, the ecosystem biomass fluctuates about a mean value that is characteristic for the particular type of ecosystem.

Accompanying these four phases, there are fairly predictable changes in ecosystem structure and function. Figure 15.17 shows postulated patterns of change in habitat and plant species diversity, in net biomass storage, and in the export of dissolved substances in streamwater during the four phases (Bormann and Likens, 1979).

It is important to understand how ecosystem structure and function are affected by disturbance, and how the duration of the various phases is affected by the type of disturbance and the type of ecosystem. In some ecosystems, the reorganization phase will be brief, whereas in others it may be very prolonged following some types of disturbance. The duration of this phase has important consequences for forest biogeochemistry and soil organic matter, and consequently for the pathway followed in the subsequent secondary succession. A detailed treatment of the ecosystem conditions associated with each of these four phases in the northern hardwood forest of the United States has been given by Bormann and Likens (1979).

15.11   Succession in Animal Communities

So far we have talked about succession as though it involved only plants, but succession happens to ecosystems, not merely to plant communities. Animal and microbial communities each undergo a sequence of changes that parallel the seral stages of the plants. Most animals are habitat-specific, and most microbes are substrate or host specific. Consequently, both groups change in response to the allogenic or plant-induced autogenic changes in the ecosystem. Sometimes they are themselves the agents of successional progression, retrogression, or stagnation (e.g., animal-induced climax). Insect defoliation of seral hardwoods can speed their replacement by conifers by as much as half a century, and defoliator-induced mortality of climax conifers can initiate a secondary succession beginning with a hardwood stage. Heavy browsing by deer, rabbits, or sim-

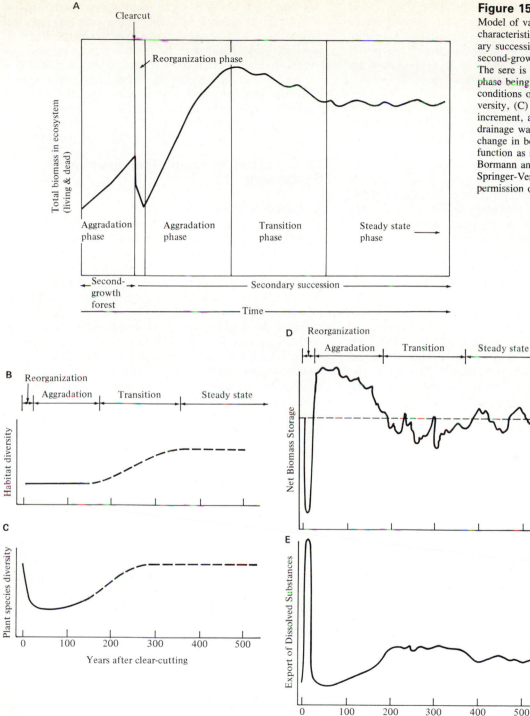

Figure 15.17
Model of variation in various ecosystem
characteristics during a prolonged secondary succession following clearcutting of a
second-growth northern hardwood forest.
The sere is divided into four phases, each
phase being characterized by particular
conditions of (A) biomass, (B) habitat diversity, (C) species diversity, (D) biomass
increment, and (E) export of chemicals in
drainage waters. There is a characteristic
change in both ecosystem structure *and*
function as succession proceeds. (After
Bormann and Likens, 1979. Copyright
Springer-Verlag New York Inc. Used with
permission of the publisher and authors.)

ilar animals can maintain grassland ''permanently'' in areas that would normally proceed through one or more additional seral stages. Figure 15.18 shows the effect of wildlife browsing on tree regeneration (plants less than 10 years old) in a German forest, and the composition of a grassland before and 10 years after protection from moderate wildlife browsing.

Each seral plant community is associated with a particular group of birds and other animals, a fact well known to the hunter. Early seral stages, in which most of the biomass is green, digestible, and within reach of ground-dwelling herbivores, tend to support a higher secondary productivity and biomass of herbivores and associated carnivores than do late seral and climax stages. The climax is far from devoid of animal life, however. The many species of insect that feed on climax tree seed and foliage provide food for a variety of insect-feeding birds. Many species of small mammals and birds also feed on climax tree seed. Specialized herbivores, such as mountain caribou, feed on the lichens that grow in climax conifer forests. Many species of large ungulate herbivores feed in early seral stages in the summer, but require late seral stages in the winter both for protection against deep snow and for food (arboreal lichens and green leaf litterfall). Recent research in coastal B.C. has revealed that the ungulate-carrying capacity of old-growth climax forests is far higher than previously thought and may even be substantially higher than that of managed second-growth forests.

Figure 15.19 shows a sequence of bird and animal species associated with old-field succession in Illinois. While this diagram is not representative of other regions because of species differences, it demonstrates that some animal species have narrow seral ranges, that others occur in almost all stages, and that the overall pattern of bird and animal species replacement with time is very similar to that of plant species succession. The explanation for this similarity lies in the dependency of many animal species on particular seral stages. As the plant communities change, so do the animal communities.

15.12 Effect of Forest Management on Succession

A. Effects of Clearcutting

As discussed above, a seral stage is defined in terms of microclimatic, soil, vegetation, animal, and microbial conditions. The living community that characterizes a particular stage of a particular sere consists of those organisms that are adapted to the physical and biotic conditions of that stage. Clearcutting alters all of these ecosystem parameters to a greater or lesser extent.

Where the objectives of management require that a mid-seral tree species form the next crop, it is obviously desirable to disturb the forest sufficiently to create physical and biotic conditions favoring the growth of that species. This requires the creation of an early seral–midseral microclimate, minimal competition, and a midseral forest floor-soil condition. Clearcutting may achieve the first two requirements, but may not satisfy the third. If there is a thick,

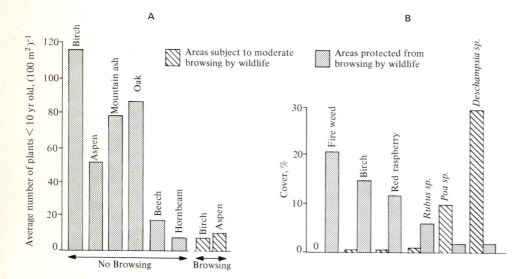

Figure 15.18

Effects of protection from browsing on the composition of the vegetation in two areas in Germany. (A) The number of tree seedlings in a forest with and without browsing. (B) The abundance of two species of grass (*Pao chaixii* and *Deschampsia flexuosa*) and other components of a grassland with and without browsing (after Knapp, 1974). Browsed and unbrowsed areas were on the same site type in both studies. The effects of such wildlife browsing on succession are obvious. (Copyright Dr. W. Junk Publisher, Netherlands. Used with permission of the publisher and author.)

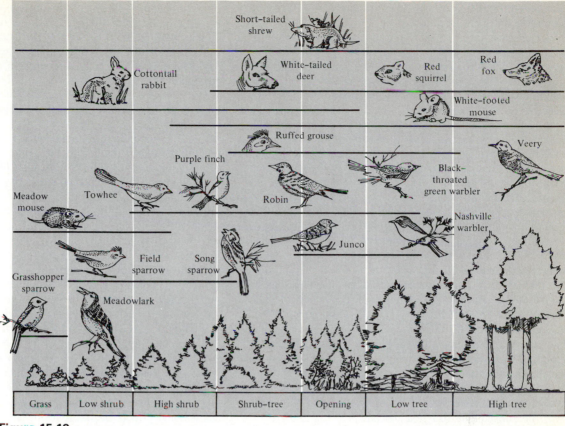

Figure 15.19

Sequence of animals associated with the stand cycle of pine plantations in central New York (after Smith, 1980). Species vary in the number of stages they are associated with. A succession of wildlife is found accompanying all plant successions. (Copyright R. L. Smith. Used with permission of the publisher and author.)

late-seral (climax) forest floor condition that remains largely undisturbed after clearcutting, seedlings of the early seral–midseral crop species may not grow well, especially if there are high surface temperatures and low surface soil moisture conditions. They have the appropriate microclimate, but an inappropriate soil condition. Late seral species will not do well either because the early seral microclimate is inappropriate and its effects on the otherwise suitable soil surface are intolerable. Essentially, the two major physical components of the seral stage have got "out of step" with each other (cf. the use of bark mulch on flowerbeds to inhibit the invasion of weeds). Few plants are able to cope with such a combination of conditions, and such sites tend to revegetate slowly after clearcutting. Either forest floor reduction through decomposition, fire, or disturbance must occur, or there must be some modification of the microcli-

mate by some hardy plant that can tolerate the "unusual" combination of conditions. Thus, although concern is often expressed over the degree of soil disturbance that accompanies tractor logging, in some cases the disturbance may be desirable. It may serve to "resynchronize" the microclimatic and forest floor components of the seral stage. In fact, where accidental disturbance is inadequate, the site may be deliberately disturbed by soil *scarification*.

Resynchronization by disturbance of the forest floor may be a reasonable thing to do in well-structured loamy soils on gentle topography. It is less reasonable on very wet or very dry sites, the extremes of which would be a hydrosere and a lithic xerosere, respectively. Disturbance in a hydrosere tends to raise the water table, which has already been raised by the reduction in transpiration loss. Disturbance in a lithic xerosere degrades the moisture, nutrient, and tree stability characteristics of the area. If clearcutting poses problems of parameter desynchronization on such sites, the answer lies in not creating the marked change in the microclimate. In fact, as pointed out earlier, maximum production is generally attained by the climax seral stage of such seres (Figure 15.14) and therefore major successional retrogression is usually undesirable anyway. Consequently, the size of clearcut openings should generally be restricted on such sites. Harvesting should be by small patch, strip or individual tree removal that maintains a permanent forest influence on the site. This conclusion will be modified by the climate of the area. Loss of forest influence is of much greater consequence in hot and dry climates than in mesothermal climates, and in winter-cold climates the soil warming caused by clearcutting may be beneficial to ecosystem function.

Another way of judging the desirability of harvesting disturbance is to consider the disturbance in relation to rate of ecosystem recovery from that disturbance. Figure 15.20 shows three hypothetical primary seres that are not unlike the typical seral development which can be observed in hydric, mesic, and lithic–xeric environments at low to middle elevations in southern coastal British Columbia (cf. Fig. 15.2). Beneath each sere there are two families of arrows. The upper family shows the degree of successional retrogression (hypothetical) that would accompany various intensities of harvest-induced disturbance in these three types of environment. The lower family of arrows indicates the hypothetical degree of successional development of the area over the subsequent 100-year period.

Although there are no quantitative data to substantiate this hypothetical model of retrogression and recovery, it is supported by qualitative field observations. The figure suggests that significant retrogression in xeroseres and hydroseres is followed by very slow rates of recovery and that such retrogression may be considered to be semipermanent in terms of forest management. On the other hand, retrogression to the very beginning of the sere in mesic environments will generally not prevent succession from replacing at least the midseral or even the late seral stage over the subsequent 100 years. Moderate retrogression may permit the redevelopment of near-climax conditions in this time period. The reader should be able to make an analysis of this type for the forests with which he or she is familiar.

In summary, clearcutting inevitably creates successional change; it pushes an area back to an earlier seral condition. In many cases this is desirable. In some it does not create enough disturbance; then it must be combined with soil scarification or slashburning in order to synchronize the soil surface and the microclimatic conditions or simply to create an earlier seral stage. Unfortunately, the effects of clearcut-

ting are not always so benign. In xeroseres and hydroseres it can produce combinations of soil and microclimatic conditions that are unsuitable for the most desirable species of plant, at least initially, and cannot be rectified by further disturbance. It may lead to soil erosion and mass wasting that, instead of merely initiating an earlier stage of secondary succession, may push the area back to the start of a primary succession and even cause a change from one type of sere to another (e.g., mesosere to xerosere). Thus, clearcutting is a powerful tool of successional manipulation, but it can be abused if the user is not aware of its full range of environmental consequences, and how they vary in different sites and in different climates.

B. Effects of Slashburning

The successional consequences of slashburning depend upon the aggregate of all the other environmental effects of slashburning, on the type of fire, and on the type of site. A hot burn on a late seral xerosere might eliminate all the surface organic accumulation and lead to the erosion of much of whatever mineral soil has developed. This would transform the area to the beginning of a primary xerosere. Alternatively, a slashburn on a moist fertile site might act to accelerate the development of a secondary sere. By suppressing shrub growth that might otherwise form a shrub community, and by promoting the reestablishment of a tree crop, slashburning might hasten the redevelopment of a climax stand. Obviously, reliable generalizations about the successional effects of slashburning are impossible.

Although clearcutting results in successional retrogression, it often has a greater effect on microclimate than on forest floors. As discussed above, this can render different parameters of successional condition out of phase with each other. Mechanical scarification can sometimes rectify the situation, but where topography and/or stumps and slash make this impossible, fire can be used. By reducing the depth of low bulk density L-F layers and by altering forest floor chemistry, prescribed fire can return climax forest floors to an earlier seral condition that matches the early seral microclimate. Where doing this has unacceptable results in terms of ecosystem function, one might conclude that radical changes in microclimate as a result of clearcutting should not be permitted. Small patch cutting or using the shelter-wood method would permit the maintenance of a forest microclimate, reducing the need for radical alteration of forest floor condition. In dry, hot environments, these harvesting methods will often be preferable to conventional large-scale clearcutting. In cooler and more humid environments, especially with very old and overmature forests, clearcutting, sometimes accompanied by slashburning, will

Figure 15.20

Diagrammatic representation of the successional consequences of different levels of disturbance during harvesting of the penultimate successional stage of three different types of sere in coastal British Columbia. Arrow 1
represents minimal disturbance which permits succession
to proceed to climax, over the subsequent 100 years.
Arrow 2 represents the degree of disturbance necessary
with a 100 year frequency to maintain the penultimate
successional stage in perpetuity. Arrows 3 and 4 represent increasing levels of disturbance. The variation in the
successional consequences of heavy disturbance between
the three seres can readily be seen. (A) In the xeric environment, successional changes accompanying disturbance include loss of nutrients and of nutrient and moisture storage capacity. Recovery from excessive
disturbance is slow and cannot readily be accelerated.
Patterns of recovery are predictable. (B) In the mesic-
hygric environment, overall successional changes accompanying disturbance are modest and recovery is generally
rapid. Recovery can fairly easily be accelerated when it
is undesirably slow. Note that both the degree and pathway of successional recovery are variable and difficult to
predict. (C) In the hydric environment, the major successional changes accompanying disturbance are increasing
wetness and loss of soluble nutrients. Recovery tends to
be slow but can be accelerated by such techniques as
drainage. As with the xeric environment, the pattern is
very predictable. (After Kimmins, 1972. Copyright Canadian Institute of Forestry. Used with permission.)

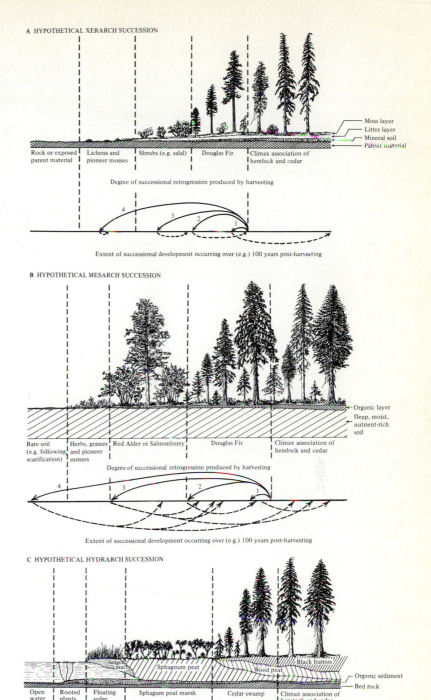

A HYPOTHETICAL XERARCH SUCCESSION

Moss layer
Litter layer
Mineral soil
Parent material

Rock or exposed parent material | Lichens and pioneer mosses | Shrubs (e.g. salal) | Douglas Fir | Climax association of hemlock and cedar

Degree of successional retrogression produced by harvesting

Extent of successional development occurring over (e.g.) 100 years post-harvesting

B HYPOTHETICAL MESARCH SUCCESSION

Organic layer
Deep, moist, nutrient-rich soil

Bare soil (e.g. following scarification) | Herbs, grasses and pioneer mosses | Red Alder or Salmonberry | Douglas Fir | Climax association of hemlock and cedar

Degree of successional retrogression produced by harvesting

Extent of successional development occurring over (e.g.) 100 years post-harvesting

C HYPOTHETICAL HYDRARCH SUCCESSION

Sedge peat | Sphagnum peat | Wood peat | Black humus
Organic sediment
Bed rock

Open water | Rooted plants | Floating sedge peat | Sphagum peat marsh | Cedar swamp | Climax association of hemlock and cedar

Degree of successional retrogression produced by harvesting

Extent of successional development occurring over (e.g.) 100 years post-harvesting frequently continue to be the best management strategy, at least in the first rotation.

Because slashburning has the potential, in some environments, for great and relatively permanent change in the seral condition, it can affect the classification status of a site. If the hygrotope and trophotope (see Chapter 16) are altered on more than a temporary basis, the floristic composition and productivity of the plant community will be changed. Such changes may be accompanied by alterations in soil characteristics. The combined changes in vegetation and soil may mean that the classification status of the area may change; it has become a different biogeocoenose or ecosystem type. This situation must be differentiated from short-term effects on microclimate, soils, and floristics, which can revert fairly rapidly to the original condition through the process of secondary succession.

15.13   Summary

One of the characteristics of ecosystems is change. Soils develop or are eroded. Weather varies seasonally and climates exhibit long-term variation. Individual organisms develop, mature, reproduce, and die.

Throughout these continual changes in the physical, chemical, and biological environment, the processes of energy capture, its storage in biomass, and the cycling of nutrients continue. The community of organisms responsible for these processes changes, the pattern of change reflecting the type of physical and chemical environment and the successive modification of that environment by both the biota itself and various combinations of geological and climatic processes. It is this process of change in ecosystems that we call *ecological succession,* while the pattern of ecosystem conditions observed over time in a particular location is called a *sere*.

Early attempts to describe general patterns of vegetation change following disturbance resulted in the theory (monoclimax) that there is a fixed sequence of communities that inevitably succeed each other in a region until a stable, self-replacing climax in equilibrium with the regional climate is produced. The attractive simplicity of this theory resulted in its survival for many decades until its preeminence was challenged by a second theory (polyclimax), which claimed that community composition and stability are under the influence of many factors, any one of which may be dominant at different times and places. Succession will not necessarily always follow the same pattern and stabilize with the same climax community. The result is a patchwork of different types of climax communities which are at equilibrium with a number of different factors. A third theory (climax pattern) considers that since communities integrate with one another, because of the individualistic distribution of individual organisms along environmental gradients, the climax community will similarly exhibit an integrating pattern. The climax community that occupies the largest proportion of habitats that are not special or extreme for the area is considered to be the prevailing climatic climax and to express the climate of the area.

Succession occurs for a variety of reasons that vary in their importance from place to place and from time to time. Biotically-induced change is probably the major driving force of most successions, but geological processes can also be important. The various processes of succession occur in a wide variety of environments with the result that there is an enormous variety of seres. This variety can be classified, one of the most useful ways of doing so being according to the moisture status of the site.

The variation in mechanisms and physical environments involved in succession produces great variation in rates of succession and the duration of different seral stages. Rates and durations tend to be characteristic for each major type of sere, but there is a considerable range within each type, and generalizations must be made with caution. There can also be a great variation in the pattern of seral stages in some types of sere.

Changes in the structure and species composition of the community are accompanied by changes in ecosystem function. Productivity, biomass, and the exchange of energy between different components of the ecosystem all vary between different seral stages and between different types of sere. Nutrient cycling similarly shows a pattern of change as succession proceeds.

Much of the theory and discussion of succession is concerned primarily with plant succession. However, succession refers to ecosystem events, and there are concomitant successions in the animal and microbial communities. Since these organisms are largely dependent on autotrophic production and the plant-controlled microenvironment, such successions tend to follow in the wake of plant succession. There are, however, numerous examples in which animals and microbes play a major role in determining the course, the speed, and the outcome of plant succession. Succession is thus an ecosystem phenomenon, and it is not the special domain of any particular branch of ecology.

As a component of ecosystems, human beings' day-to-day activities are intimately affected by succession. Both farming and forestry, two fundamental human activities, are constantly working to manipulate successions in order to optimize the availability of certain seral conditions.

Without an adequate theoretical and/or empirical knowledge of succession, successful land management is generally a matter of luck, and many of the common examples of unsuccessful management could have been avoided by applying a knowledge of succession. Our current environmental predicament and the fact that we still appear to be losing ground, literally and metaphorically, are in no small degree due to a failure to recognize and understand succession as it occurs in the wide variety of terrestrial and aquatic environments on earth.

PART III Application of Ecological Information in the Management of Forest Ecosystems

Human beings are thinking animals, and therefore knowledge has a value for human societies that is independent of its practical application. However, the value of knowledge is greater if it can be put to use in improving the human condition and our understanding of how to conduct our activities without degrading the environment.

Part III examines the ways in which principles of forest ecology (the information contained in Part II) can be used to increase the success of renewable-resource management. Ecological classification uses knowledge of ecosystem structure and function to identify and describe different types of ecosystem, each of which has a characteristic response to management. Identification of ecosystem types greatly improves our ability to predict the response of our forests to management. A second application of such knowledge is in the development of conceptual and computer models of forest ecosystems and the impacts of management thereon. Models provide a mechanism by which to organize our knowledge about a particular ecosystem type and use it to make predictions about the future condition of that ecosystem under alternative management regimes.

The book concludes with a philosophical view of the management of renewable resources.

16.1 Introduction

The desire to create order where there is disorder, to explain the unknown, and to predict events or conditions in the future is a characteristic of most, if not all human beings. We have an innate desire to explain, understand, and predict ourselves and our environment. Unfortunately, this is a very difficult goal to achieve, given the diversity and complexity of ecosystems. We have neither the time, the energy, nor the mental capacity to know everything about all things. Our response to this problem has typically been to arrange objects or facts about objects into groups of like individuals. This enables us to extrapolate our knowledge about one or two individuals to all the members of such a group. For example, by stipulating that a particular animal is a dog, it is in most cases unnecessary to say that it has four legs, a tail, and a fur-covered skin. One can also infer that the animal is most probably larger than a rat and smaller than a horse, that it generally does not eat human beings, and that it probably has a strong predilection for chasing cats. Similarly, by saying that an object in a forest is a coniferous tree, it is immediately apparent that it is an immobile organism requiring light, water, nutrients, and a secure anchorage, and that it is a very uncomfortable experience to have a mature specimen fall on you.

Classification, the act and the result of arranging facts or things into groups or classes of like individuals, permits confident statements to be made about all the members of a class based on the knowledge gained from the study of only a few members of that class. The degree of confidence one has in such statements varies depending on the breadth (i.e., homogeneity) of the class and the characteristics used to define the class. The experience of swimming safely in a lake containing trout or in the sea in the presence of mackerel is not a reliable basis on which to predict the safety of swimming in piranha- or shark-infested waters. The class of objects called *fish* is very broad, and the definition does not specify whether or not members of the class might be inimical to human health or whether human beings constitute part of the group's diet. To make such a prediction with confidence would require splitting fish into two subgroups: man-eating and non-man-eating. The usefulness of a particular classification and the criteria that should be used in defining classes will depend on the heterogeneity of the classes and the purposes for which the classification is to be used.

Classification is, as far as we know, a uniquely human attribute. It is undertaken with the objective of reducing the heterogeneity of a group of objects in order to increase our understanding and ability to predict the characteristics of any one of the objects. In its very essence, it is *purposive:* it

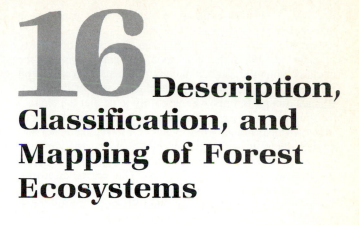

16 Description, Classification, and Mapping of Forest Ecosystems

is done for a reason, not as an end in itself. Purpose is implicit in all classifications and different purposes lead to different classifications. There can be no single "best" classification that will serve all purposes under all circumstances, although there will nearly always be a best method for a specific application.

The ideal forest classification for forest management would be one that satisfies the needs of the forest resource manager and other forest users with minimum cost, time, and commitment of resources. Such a classification should be formulated using those ecosystem characteristics that will give to the classification the predictive powers necessary to achieve the stated objectives of forest management. For example, in the development of a virgin forested valley we might wish to have a land classification that would predict the location of unstable soil and shallow, rocky soil to minimize the cost of road construction, to make road maintenance as easy as possible, and to reduce impacts of the road on resource values. On the other hand, if we wanted to be able to make reliable long-range plans concerning site-specific harvesting methods and postharvesting site treatment, or if we wanted to predict the recreational potential of the forest, a different classification would be required. It is unlikely that a single classification could be optimum for all possible applications, but some classifications can serve a broader range of purposes than others.

Forest classification is undertaken to improve our ability to make reliable statements about the characteristics, the resource potential, and/or the environmental constraints on the management of any particular forest stand or land area. It is an attempt to improve our ability to predict the characteristics of forest ecosystems by reducing the number of unknown determinants (cf. Figure 2.2). The large number of such determinants, together with the wide variety of uses of classification in forest management, suggest the need for a variety of different classifications. This has the disadvantage, however, that it can result in an undesirable duplication of effort and expense, and although useful forest classifications are not *necessarily* immensely complex, single-parameter classifications often have limited utility and may not satisfy the complex requirements of multiple-use forest management.

As an alternative, one might decide that the only ecological classification approach that will be really useful in forestry is one that provides *all* possible ecological information desired by forest resource users and managers: a classification explicitly incorporating all major parameters of the ecosystem. Although this may be true in some situations, it is not necessarily the best approach, for the following reasons:

1. Homogeneous classes defined by all major parameters of the ecosystem can result in dividing an area up into such small units that the classification is virtually unusable.
2. Such a classification can be very expensive to formulate and apply in mapping. Classification is purposive, and it is justified only when the resulting benefits exceed the costs. Consequently, expensive classifications are generally regarded with less favor than are inexpensive ones.
3. Many of the characteristics of ecosystems are closely correlated (i.e., when characteristic A increases, so does characteristic B), so that it is not always necessary to classify every characteristic. For example, on a given aspect at a given latitude and longitude, temperature varies in a more or less predictable manner with elevation, so it is not necessary to include both these parameters in a classification.

The "best" classification is generally a compromise between the need for simplicity and the need for sufficient detail to make the classification effective. In this chapter we review briefly the various approaches that have been made to forestland classification. The important topics of field data gathering, analysis of vegetation data by traditional and "numerical" techniques, and of vegetation/ecosystem mapping cannot be covered here for lack of space. Throughout the chapter we assume that the primary objective is classification and mapping of the forest resource, rather than ordination of the vegetation and gradient analysis. The issue as to whether vegetation organizes itself into discrete communities that are repeated in similar environments throughout the landscape, or whether vegetation is a continuum made up of species populations distributed independently along environmental gradients, was discussed in Chapter 14. Readers who are interested in fuller details of classification, field sampling, data analysis, and mapping are referred to Kuchler (1967), Shimwell (1971), Whittaker (1973a), and Mueller-Dombois and Ellenberg (1974). A useful review of site classification in the U.S. is provided by Carmean (1976).

There have been many different approaches to the classification of forests. Some have focused on those aspects of the physical environment that determine the characteristics of the vegetation. Others are based on the vegetation itself. Some approaches attempt to incorporate all the major ecosystem determinants in combined vegetation–environment or ecosystem schemes (called *ecosystematic* approaches). The reader is reminded that there is no single best or correct classification. "Best" is defined by application and needs that change with time, and a classification that was good 25 years ago under the prevailing circumstances is not necessarily adequate under current conditions.

Classification is not a static, once-and-for-all activity, and present-day classifications will undoubtedly evolve to meet the future needs of forestry. However, it should be noted that where the initial classification involves a comprehensive, ecosystematic approach, it should be possible to adapt the basic classification to changing needs, eliminating the need for costly reclassification. If the initial work involves the establishment of a basic taxonomy of ecosystems, the classification will be much more adaptable than where it is based on a small subset of ecosystem parameters. The classification approaches discussed here are *climatic, physiographic, vegetative,* and *ecosystematic.*

16.2   Climatic Classification

Climate is generally accepted as one of the major determinants of vegetation. Major plant formations are closely correlated with major climatic zones, and local variations in climate are reflected in changes in species composition within a biome. Climate is important in forestry because it influences the suitability and productivity of a tree species

Table 16.1 Köppen's System of Climatic Classification as Modified by Trewartha (Based on Money, 1972)

Major Climatic Types			Climatic Subtypes		
Symbol	Climate	Definition	Symbol[a]	Climate	Definition
A	Tropical rainy	Hot climate with no cool season. Temperature of the coldest month over 18°C	f	No dry season	Driest month has >60 mm precipitation.
			m	Short dry season	Rainfall sufficient to support rain forest.
			w	Dry winter, wet summer	Driest month has <60 mm precipitation.
B	Dry	Evaporation exceeds precipitation W = arid, desert S = semiarid, steppe	Wh	Hot desert	Mean annual temperature over 18°C.
			Sh	Tropical and subtropical semiarid	A short rainy season.
			Wk	Middle latitude interior desert	Large annual temperature range. Persistently dry.
			Sk	Middle latitude semiarid	Meager rainfall, mostly in summer.
C	Humid mesothermal (moist temperate)	Temperature of coldest month between 18 and 0°C	s	Subtropical, dry summers	Wettest winter month has 3× rain of driest summer month. Driest month has <30 mm.
			sa	Hot summers	Warmest month averages over 22°C.
			sb	Warm summers	Warmest month averages less than 22°C.
			a	Humid subtropical hot summers	Warmest month over 22°C.
			fa	No dry season	Driest month has >30 mm rain.
			wa	Dry winters	Wettest summer month has 10× rain of driest winter month.
			b	Marine climate, cool–warm summers	Rain at all seasons. Warmest month <22°C.
			fb	No dry season	Warmest month <22°C.
			c	Marine climate, short cool summers	Less than 4 months >10°C. Rain at all seasons.
D	Humid microthermal (rainy/snowy, cold)	Temperature of coldest month less than 0°C, warmest month over 10°C	a	Humid continental warm summers	Warmest month >22°C. Rain in all seasons with summer maximum. Winter snow cover. Variable weather; alternating polar and tropical air.
			b	Humid continental, cool summers	Warmest month <22°C, as for "a," but large snow cover.
			c	Subarctic	Warmest month <22°C. <4 months >10°C. Cold winter. Light precipitation.
			d	Subarctic, very cold winters	Coldest month <−38°C. Very light precipitation.
E	Polar	Temperature of the warmest month less than 10°C	T	Tundra	Mean temperature of the warmest month >0°C. Light precipitation, mostly in summer.
			F	Ice cap. Perpetual frost	No month with mean temperature >0°C.

[a] f = no dry season   S = steppe climate   b = mean temperature warmest month 22–10°C, 4 months have mean temp. >10°C.
w = winter dry season   h = mean annual temperature >18°C   c = mean temperature warmest month 22–10°C, <4 months have mean temperature >10°C.
s = summer dry season   k = mean annual temperature <18°C
W = desert climate   a = mean temperature warmest month >22°C   d = mean temperature coldest month <−38°C.

on a particular site, and because it affects every aspect of forest management from regeneration to harvesting (Thornthwaite and Hare, 1955). Many of the earliest attempts at broad vegetation classification by plant geographers were based on climate parameters, and present-day ecosystematic approaches incorporate climate as a major component of the classification. All climatic classifications involve various combinations of degree of aridity (dryness) and warmth. Aridity is not just a matter of precipitation; it is determined by the ecological effectiveness of precipitation, as discussed in Chapter 11.

Perhaps the most durable of the climatic classifications used in vegetation ecology is that proposed by Köppen (1923). Building on the ideas of an earlier bioclimatologist, de Candolle (1874), Köppen made careful observations of

the climatic conditions required for the growth of various groups of plants, and he related variations in vegetation to temperature and precipitation characteristics of the climate. He proposed a world classification consisting of five major climatic types: Tropical Rainy, Dry, Humid Mesothermal (warm temperate), Humid Microthermal (cold boreal forest), and Polar (tundra). These types were defined by rather arbitrary temperature limits. For example, the warmest month of the Humid Microthermal climate has an average temperature above 10°C, and the coldest month has an average temperature less than −3°C. The former is claimed to be correlated with the poleward limit of tree growth and the latter with the equatorward limit of permafrost. Neither of these correlations is very precise (Money, 1972). Each of Köppen's types is subdivided by the addition of subscript

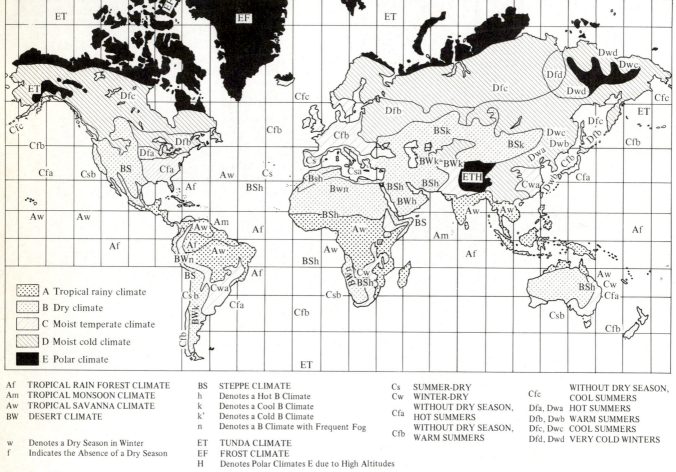

Af	TROPICAL RAIN FOREST CLIMATE	BS	STEPPE CLIMATE
Am	TROPICAL MONSOON CLIMATE	h	Denotes a Hot B Climate
Aw	TROPICAL SAVANNA CLIMATE	k	Denotes a Cool B Climate
BW	DESERT CLIMATE	k'	Denotes a Cold B Climate
		n	Denotes a B Climate with Frequent Fog
w	Denotes a Dry Season in Winter	ET	TUNDA CLIMATE
f	Indicates the Absence of a Dry Season	EF	FROST CLIMATE
		H	Denotes Polar Climates E due to High Altitudes

Cs	SUMMER-DRY	Cfc	WITHOUT DRY SEASON, COOL SUMMERS
Cw	WINTER-DRY		
Cfa	WITHOUT DRY SEASON, HOT SUMMERS	Dfa, Dwa	HOT SUMMERS
		Dfb, Dwb	WARM SUMMERS
Cfb	WITHOUT DRY SEASON, WARM SUMMERS	Dfc, Dwc	COOL SUMMERS
		Dfd, Dwd	VERY COLD WINTERS

Figure 16.1

Köppen's system of classification of world climates. Only the major classes of climate are shown.

letters resulting in more homogeneous climatic subunits (Table 16.1). The world distribution of Köppen's climatic types is shown in Figure 16.1.

An alternative system based on the effectiveness of precipitation was developed by Thornthwaite in 1931. This is now largely of historical interest, and it was replaced in 1948 by a second classification based on potential evapotranspiration (PE), defined by temperature and the water budget. Vegetation boundaries in the eastern U.S. coincide reasonably closely with PE values (Figure 11.4), but unlike his 1931 and Köppen's classifications, Thornthwaite's 1948 classification does not use vegetation boundaries to define climatic areas. Thornthwaite's system is not very satisfactory in tropical and subtropical areas (Barry and Chorley, 1968), and the climate/vegetation/soil relationships are useful only at a continental level. Further details may be found in Thornthwaite (1948) and Thornthwaite and Hare (1955).

More recent developments in climatic classification have stressed the energy-balance approach (Budyko, 1974). PE is defined more by available energy (net radiation) than by temperature per se. Net radiation available annually for evaporation from a wet surface (R_n) is compared with the heat required to evaporate the mean annual precipitation (L_r). The ratio R_n/L_r (the *radiative index of dryness*) has values less than 1.0 for humid areas and greater than 1.0 for dry areas; (e.g., desert, >3.0; semidesert, 2–3; steppe, 1–2; forest, 0.33–1.0; and tundra, <0.33). The relationships among net radiation, the radiation index of dryness, vegetation zones, and the hydrological balance are shown in Figure 16.2.

The climatic classes in the classifications described above are generally too broad to render them useful for site-specific management decisions. They do, however, indicate the general vegetation potential and are therefore useful in

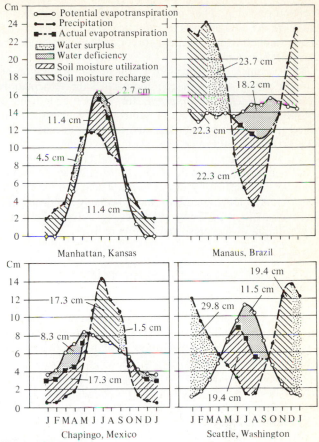

Figure 16.3

Climatic diagrams developed by Thornthwaite and Hare (1955) for locations in Kansas, Washington (U.S.), Mexico, and Brazil. (Used with permission of the Food and Agriculture Organization of the United Nations and the authors.)

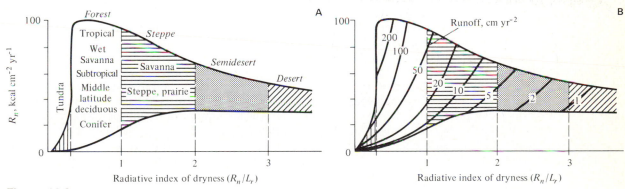

Figure 16.2

Relationships of net radiation (R_n) and the radiative index of dryness to vegetation (A) and river runoff (B). (After Budyko, 1974. Copyright Academic Press, Inc. Used with permission of the publisher and author.)

regional planning. They provide the logical framework for the more detailed ecosystem classifications to be described below, and climatic data are incorporated into most modern classification activities.

Most climatic classifications result in the preparation of climatic maps. An alternative approach is the presentation of individual *climatic diagrams* for various geographical locations. These permit the presentation of much more detailed information on moisture and temperature conditions and are more useful in detailed ecological or resource management work than are the more general climatic schemes described above. Climatic diagrams for the whole world have been published by Walter et al. (1975) and the resulting Climatic Diagram Maps have been synthesized into world climatic maps. Some examples of Thornthwaite's climatic diagrams are presented in Figure 16.3.

16.3   Landform or Physiographic Classification

The basic resource in forestry is the soil and its associated landforms. Soil and landform play a major role in determining forest structure, composition, and productivity, and they form the basis of *physiographic* classifications.

The main advantage of the physiographic approach is that it lends itself to remote sensing, which enables large areas to be mapped relatively rapidly and inexpensively. There are several other advantages. Since it is based on relatively permanent site features (macroclimate, landforms, and soil), it is a relatively permanent classification, resulting in relatively unchanging maps. Since the classes are defined by parameters that determine vegetation composition, structure, and productivity, the classification has a sound ecological basis. There are, however, a number of disadvantages. One of these is the fact that it is difficult to use the many continuously variable parameters of climate, landform, and soil to produce units of classification that are appropriate to vegetation classification without reference to the vegetation itself. Thus, physiographic approaches tend to evolve with time into biophysical or ecosystematic approaches by the explicit inclusion of vegetation parameters. For an example of a physiographic system, see Burger (1972) and Hills (1976). A brief comparison of physiographic approaches in Canada, Australia, and the U.S. is given in Wertz and Arnold (1975).

Many physiographic classifications have used both soils and landforms to define classes. Some have used just soils, such as those in Germany (Wittich, 1962) and in the U.S. (review in Jones, 1969). Where soils are classified accord-

ing to ecological rather than purely pedogenic (soil development) criteria, the correlation between soils, vegetation, and overall ecosystem characteristics may be fairly close. However, where soil classes are fairly broad and are basically pedogenic, correlations with vegetation may be rather poor and of relatively little use as the basis for forest classifications. Also, soils data alone cannot provide all the information needed by the resource manager because of the complex interactions among soil, climate, topography, water, vegetation, and fauna.

Soil classifications are extremely useful in all aspects of forest management even if they fall short of the ideal classification. They help identify areas of unstable or erodable soils, areas of high or low road-building suitability, areas that will be difficult to regenerate, and areas that are suitable for particular crop species. They are also valuable in recreation, wildlife, and watershed management (Crawford, 1975). They can give a good indication of productivity if appropriately classified (see Thomas and Burroughs, 1975). Knowledge of the soil, the forester's basic resource, is the first step toward understanding the overall functioning of ecosystems, and soil classification is an essential component of any ecosystematic or integrated classification.

One of the interesting approaches to soil classification for ecology and forest management is the *edaphic grid* (Remezov and Pogrebnyak, 1969), which depicts the occurrence and growth of plants under various combinations of soil moisture and nutrients. The edaphic grid and its application in forestry is described in a later section of this chapter.

16.4   Vegetation Classification

Climatic and physiographic classifications are an indirect approach to the classification of forest ecosystems. Their classes are defined by factors that determine vegetation. To the extent that an indirect approach can perceive, measure, interpret, and incorporate all significant physical factors, it should be similar to ecosystem classification in its ability to predict the ecosystem. However, rarely do such classifications incorporate all significant physical factors, and there is frequently a problem of knowing what parameters to measure and how to interpret the significance of the resulting data for vegetation. Consequently, the soil scientist often uses the vegetation to help in the mapping and interpretation of soils, and many people have felt that it is therefore more logical to classify and map the vegetation (or the basic biotic community) itself. The biota constitutes the best measurement and integration of the total physical and biotic environment (Daubenmire, 1976), and it generally reflects the overall ecological characteristics of a site more faithfully than is possible with other approaches, given the current level of ecological understanding and ability to measure the environment. The widespread use of vegetation in classification and mapping of soil and climate supports this point of view.

Vegetation classification attempts to identify discrete, repeatable classes of relatively homogeneous vegetation communities or associations about which reliable statements can be made. Once a classification has been established, field mapping of vegetation may be undertaken. Classification assumes either that natural vegetation groupings (communities) do occur, or that it is reasonable to separate a continuum of variation in vegetation composition and/or structure into a series of arbitrary classes.

Vegetation classification can be approached in many different ways: structure and life form, dominance, floristic composition, or plant productivity. Each of these approaches can involve different methods of investigation and different criteria for the definition of classes. The choice of criteria to be used depends upon three points (Whittaker, 1973b): (1) *accessibility*—criteria that are easily observed and measured in the field; (2) *significance*—ability of criteria to distinguish one community from another (i.e., the degree of correlation between the criteria and characteristics of the community and its environment); and (3) *effectiveness*—suitability for expressing environmental differences or producing units of classification at the required level of detail.

Different approaches to classification have been triumphed vigorously by ecologists working in different countries and biomes. These diverse views will probably persist, and it is unlikely that a single common method will ever be adopted because differences in environmental and biotic conditions and in classification needs will favor different approaches at different times and places. In the following section the various approaches are described briefly. Some of the more important methods are presented in more detail in a subsequent section. For a detailed treatment of this topic, see Whittaker (1973a) and Mueller-Dombois and Ellenberg (1974).

A. Classification of Structure and Life Form: Physiognomic Classification

The earliest attempts at vegetation classification were made by the plant geographers Humboldt and Grisebach during the first half of the nineteenth century. They characterized classes of vegetation by the *growth form* of the dominant plants and the type of environment in which they grow. These classes were called *formations:* major kinds of plant communities on a given continent characterized by their physiognomy and a range of environments to which that physiognomy is an adaptation. Definition of the type of environment is important. Tropical grassland (savanna), temperate grassland (steppe), alpine meadow, and salt-marsh are all dominated by plants of the same life form, but they are all regarded as different formations because of differences in the physical environment (Beard, 1973). As noted earlier, formations are analogous to biomes.

The physiognomic approach was developed by the Danish ecologists Warming (1909) and Raunkiaer (1934). Warming defined an association as a community of definite floristic composition within a formation, and noted that a formation is an expression of certain defined conditions of life. It does not define the floristic character of the vegetation. Raunkiaer introduced the *life-form* classification (discussed in Chapter 8) and the concept of *biological spectra* (percentages of the species in a community that belong to various life forms), but his approach has remained less influential in physiognomic classification than the central concept of the growth form of the vegetation dominants. A recent listing of the major growth forms of terrestrial plants was presented in Table 14.2; major formation types are given in Table 16.2, and their distribution in relation to mean annual temperature and precipitation is shown in Figure 16.4.

Table 16.2 Terrestrial Formation-types of the World (After Whittaker, 1975a)

1. Tropical rain forest
2. Tropical seasonal forest
3. Temperate rain forest
4. Temperate deciduous forest
5. Temperate evergreen forest
6. Taiga (subarctic–subalpine needle-leaved forest)
7. Elfinwoods (subalpine zone forest on tropical mountains)
8. Tropical broadleaved woodlands
9. Thornwoods
10. Temperate woodlands
11. Temperate shrublands
12. Savannas (tropical grasslands)
13. Temperate grasslands
14. Alpine shrublands
15. Alpine grasslands
16. Tundra (treeless arctic plains)
17. Warm semidesert scrubs
18. Cool semideserts
19. Arctic–alpine semideserts
20. True deserts (subtropical)
21. Arctic–alpine deserts

[a]The relationship of these formation types to world-scale gradients of temperature and moisture are shown in Figure 16.4

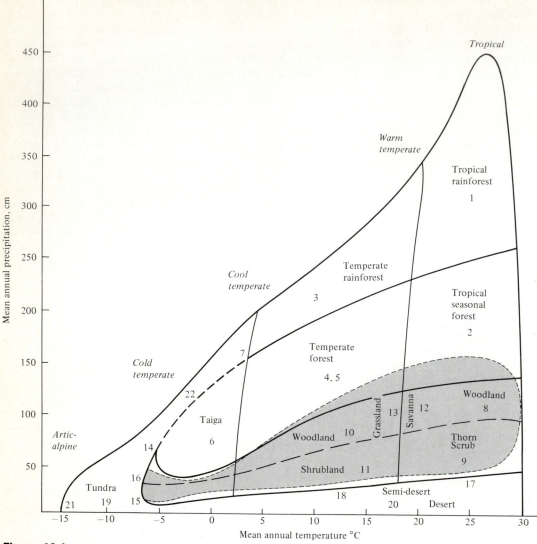

Figure 16.4
Relationship between world formation types and climate (temperature and humidity). The numbers refer to the formation types of Whittaker (1975) as given in Table 16.2. The shaded area enclosed by the dashed line is a range of environments in which either grassland or woody plants dominate. (After Beard, 1973; based on Holdridge, 1947. Copyright Dr. W. Junk Publishers, Netherlands. Used with permission of the publisher and author.)

Physiognomic classification can be based on a direct description of vegetation structure. This method was introduced by Kuchler (1947) and subsequently modified and improved by Dansereau (1951, 1957). They described vegetation using six parameters: growth form, size, "function" (coniferous, deciduous, etc.), leaf shape and size, leaf texture, and ground coverage. Each category is divided into three to six subcategories, which are associated with two sets of symbols, one alphabetic and the other pictorial. The former is used to produce a descriptive formula, and the latter to prepare stylized diagrams of the vegetation structure.

A somewhat analogous approach is that of *profile diagrams,* which were developed for use in the description and classification of tropical forests (Davis and Richards, 1933, 1934), where either floristic complexity or incomplete floristic information makes a floristic approach difficult. This method involves the preparation of a descriptive diagram of the vertical structure of the vegetation, in which the relative positions of the various layers of the vegetation are accurately depicted (Figure 16.5). Such diagrams can be used to portray the variation in formation types along major environmental gradients, and they are helpful in explaining the complexity of the vegetation mosaic that occurs in mountainous topography. They can also be used in the description and classification of individual plant communities.

As the earliest approach to vegetation description and classification, the physiognomic approach remains the principal basis for treating vegetation on a broad scale in relation to climate, and it is an important basis for vegetation research in certain parts of the world. It is one of the best ways of comparing communities on different continents and is particularly useful in the initial description and classification of diverse forest or other vegetation types about which there is little or no immediately available taxonomic information. However, the approach is less useful than some of the alternatives as a basis for site-specific forest management, especially in areas with relatively simple floras and readily available taxonomic information. Description of other physiognomic methods of classification can be found in Mueller-Dombois and Ellenberg (1974).

B. Classification Based on Dominance Type

Plant formations are often divided into subordinate vegetation units on the basis of their dominant species (dominant in terms of biomass, density, height, coverage, etc.). In both British and American plant ecology, classification of communities has often been based on the dominant plant species. Individual, easily noticed plant species provide the simplest floristic tool by which to create some order in the great variability of plant communities, and dominance has traditionally been used in describing types of forest: beech forest, pine forest, or spruce forest. The national system of forest classification in the U.S. (forest cover types) is based on the dominant tree species in the overstory (Society of American Foresters, 1980) (described in section G), and in the past this type of classification has been preferred by many applied ecologists, foresters, and range and wildlife managers in many countries.

Because some species attain dominance over a wide geographical area whereas others occupy a restricted range of habitats, vegetation classes defined by dominance vary greatly in their heterogeneity. In areas with a diverse flora, the selection of dominant species by which to define the class may be very arbitrary, and a dominance type cannot therefore be a particular, standardized type of community unit. Dominance types are poorly suited to the construction of a formal hierarchical classification of vegetation in such areas (Whittaker, 1973b). On the other hand, in areas with a simple flora, dominance types may adequately describe the major features of the vegetation, and may be detailed enough to define at least some of the smaller vegetation units. The information requirement for this type of classification is generally much lower than that of other floristic approaches, which may make the method attractive in spite of its several shortcomings.

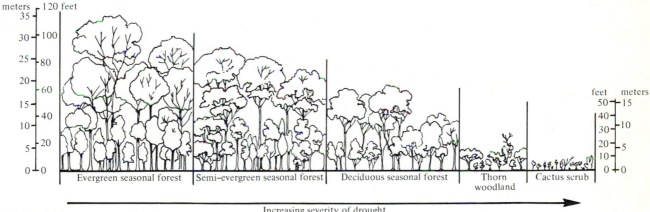

Figure 16.5

Profile diagram showing the sequence of formation types that has been described along a moisture gradient in Trinidad. (After Beard, 1973. Copyright Dr. W. Junk Publishers, Netherlands. Used with permission of the publisher and author.)

C. Classifications Based upon Floristic Composition

Floristic classifications constitute the best developed approach to vegetation classification. Most European and Soviet schools of plant ecology utilize this approach, and it has been widely applied in Canada and elsewhere. The approach can be broken down into three major subdivisions: emphasis on ground or subordinate vegetation, emphasis on overstory vegetation, and emphasis on the entire plant community.

1. Ground Vegetation. Emphasis on ground vegetation characterizes the classification scheme developed in the Scandinavian and Baltic region. The approach is especially associated with the work of Cajander (1926) in Finland: the *forest site–type* classification. The Baltic region is characterized by few tree species, each of which can occur over a wide range of sites with different undergrowth associates, the distribution of which is *relatively* independent of the overstory. The understory vegetation provides much more information about, and expresses more effectively, the habitat conditions than does the species-poor overstory. Successful application of the system requires a good knowledge of succession and of the undergrowth–environment species relationships, because the overstory composition and structure of stands representing a given habitat or site type can vary considerably. The site type is an abstraction based on the climatic climax condition, with a number of variations according to the seral stage.

The Finnish system is applied in three stages.

1. *Site-type classes.* Finnish forests are divided into five such classes on the basis of broad features of the site (moisture and fertility status): dry and poor (heathlands), fresh-mesic (mossy forests), fresh-and-rich (broad-leaved forests), wet-and-rich (inundated forests), and wet-and-poor (bog forests) site types. Site-type classes represent a broad division of the vegetation into plant formations, and of ecosystems into biomes. Each site-type class is divided into a number of site types.

2. *Site types.* These are generally identified on the basis of the entire understory vegetation, although where the flora is very simple the definition may be based largely on one or two dominant species which give the name to the site type. In the boreal conditions of Finland, Cajander stressed dominance and competition within the understory vegetation, but a full characterization of site type involves specification of dominant, constant characteristic and differential species (defined below) of stable climax stands. Since the characteristic climax ground vegetation establishes itself within decades following disturbance, this approach permits accurate assignment of seral stands to site-type classes with rela-

tive accuracy and ease. Using dominant ground vegetation, Cajanda separated the heathland site-type class into five site types: *Cladina* type, *Myrtillus–Cladina* type, *Calluna* type, *Empetrum–Myrtillus* type, and *Vaccinium* type. Other site-type classes are similarly subdivided. Most site types are further subdivided into forest types.

3. *Forest types.* Except at the extremes of moisture and nutrient conditions, a given site type can carry different tree species or have different proportions of a mixture of tree species. Medium and rich site types can thus be divided into a number of *forest types,* which are identified by both understory and overstory species composition. For example, the *Vaccinium myrtillus* site type is divided into several forest types on the basis of the association of this species with either pine or spruce in the climax condition, and either birch or aspen in the seral condition.

The Finnish system has been widely applied in Finnish forest management. Forest composition and species productivity have been studied and volume vs. age curves have been produced for the various site types (Figure 16.6). Site-type classifications have also been applied in Sweden, eastern Canada (Burger, 1972), parts of the U.S., and the U.S.S.R. (Frey, 1973), and the units of this classification have proven to be useful for making decisions about forest regeneration and forest management strategies. The method has been most successful under boreal conditions, where the diversity of the flora, the climate, and the edaphic conditions is low (e.g., Rowe, 1956; see the review in Burger, 1972). Similar applications of the Finnish system have been made elsewhere, as for example the height vs. age and volume vs. age curves that were prepared for Douglas-fir site types in Washington, Oregon, and southwestern British Columbia (Spilsbury and Smith, 1947). The method did not work very well in this region because of the higher diversity of the trees and minor vegetation and the greater diversity in the physical environment. The same conclusion was reached in Ontario and Quebec in eastern Canada: the Finnish system worked well in the central and northern areas of these provinces, where boreal conditions occur, but the system was rejected in favor of a total community classification in the floristically richer southern areas. The work on the Finnish system in the Pacific Northwest is now largely of historical interest.

2. Overstory Composition. The focus of attention in forestry has frequently been on the tree crop: its composition and productivity. Both Canada and the U.S. have national classifications/inventories of forest vegetation based on the species composition of the overstory, and these have been widely used by both the professional and scientific commu-

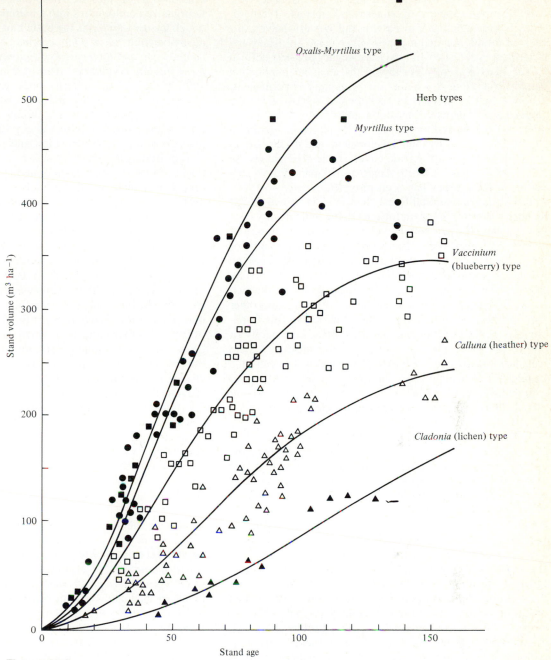

Figure 16.6
Volume-over-age curves for five forest site types in Finland, from a moist, fertile herb type *(Oxalis-Myrtillus)* to a poor, dry, lichen type *(Cladonia)*. The spread of the data about the lines varies between types. (After Frey, 1973; based on Cajander and Ilvessalo, 1921, and Cajander, 1949. Copyright Dr. W. Junk Publishers, Netherlands. Used with permission of the publisher and T. E. Frey.)

nities as a standardized description of forests. The U.S. classification[1] (Society of American Foresters, 1980) divides North America into eastern and western halves, for each of which the major *forest cover types* are listed and described. A forest cover type is a category of forest defined by the trees presently occupying the area, no implication being conveyed as to whether it is temporary or permanent. A *forest type* is defined as "a group of stands of similar character as regards composition and development due to given ecological factors. . . . " Emphasis is given to "composition" rather than development, and the classification is based on existing tree cover. Table 16.3 shows the forest cover types for North America. No map of the distribution of these types has been provided.

The Canadian national forest classification (Rowe, 1972) identifies *forest regions,* defined as stable, climatically controlled plant formations characterized by the presence of certain tree species: the climax dominants. The regions, of which there are eight (plus two nonforest regions: grassland and tundra), are subdivided into *forest sections,* defined by the consistent presence of certain "associations" and which show, in the mass, a character that is different from other parts of the region. The term "association" in this Canadian system is used to describe a recurring community of one or more tree species. Actually, the Canadian system was developed as an inventory of the nation's forests, the components of which were subsequently assigned to classes using criteria that were defined after the inventory was completed. Thus it differs somewhat from a classification in the pure sense.

3. Composition of the Entire Plant Community. Two classification systems which are based predominantly on the entire plant community will be described.

a. THE CENTRAL EUROPEAN OR BRAUN–BLANQUET APPROACH. Perhaps the most widely applied approach to floristic classification involves the study of entire plant communities. These are conceived as types of vegetation recognized by their structure and floristic composition, which are considered to be a better expression of between-community differences and community–environment relationships than any other community characteristic. Among the species in the community, some are more sensitive than others in expressing certain relationships, and this approach, which was developed in central Europe and which is generally referred to as the Braun–Blanquet method, seeks *diagnostic species* that are effective indicators of the

relationships of interest. These diagnostic species are used to organize communities into a hierarchical classification of which the *association* is the basic unit. Used in this context, an association is: *a plant community of definite floristic composition and uniform physiognomy which occurs in uniform habitat conditions*. This definition was adopted in 1910 at the Brussels International Botanical Congress and has become the generally accepted use of the term "association" throughout Europe. It should be noted that the uniform habitat criteria is not always met, emphasis being placed on floristic composition and physiognomy.

The Braun–Blanquet approach accepts a view of the plant community that is intermediate between the superorganism concept and the individualistic or continuum concept. It recognizes the reality of continuous species distributions but emphasizes interactions between species that lead to relative discontinuities between communities. A more or less discontinuous continuum of species distributions results from the combination of competition (and the resulting development of ecological niches), coevolution (development of obligate or facultative interspecific relationships), and the fact that the dominant species in the community often play a major role in determining the physical characteristics of the microenvironments in which the subdominant species grow. There is continuous variation in community composition along an environmental gradient, but the degree of change per unit length of the gradient is very low in some sections of the gradient (associations) and very high in others (transition zones between adjacent associations).

The Braun–Blanquet approach stresses the distinction between the abstract idea of the *association* (an idealized vegetation class of floristic classification; for a history of the various definitions of the term association, see Westhoff and van der Maarel, 1973) and the real *plant community* that is growing in a real physical environment and which is assigned to a particular abstract class or association. This is similar to the distinction between an individual eastern hemlock tree in a stand and the abstract idea of the eastern hemlock species to which this individual plant is assigned.

The hierarchical levels of the classification are defined by three types of *diagnostic species:* character species, differential species, and constant companion species. *Character species* are those that are largely restricted to the unit of vegetation under consideration, and each level in the hierarchy has a list of character species. To qualify as a character species for the association level, a species must have a narrow habitat distribution and be almost, if not entirely, restricted to that particular association (i.e., the range of the species should more or less coincide with the range of the association). Its degree of restriction to one association is

---

[1] This was also listed under dominance types of classification. Originally a dominance classification, it is now a hybrid between overstory dominance and overstory composition.

Table 16.3 Forest Cover Types of North America

Eastern Forest Cover Types   **Western Forest Cover Types**

Boreal forest region
Boreal conifers[a]
  Jack pine[b](1)[c]
  Balsam fir (5)
  Black spruce (12)
  Black spruce–tamarack (13)
  White spruce (107)
  Tamarack (38)
Boreal hardwoods
  Aspen (16)
  Pin cherry (17)
  Paper birch (18)

Northern forest region
Spruce-fir types
  Red spruce (32)
  Red spruce–balsam fir (33)
  Red spruce–Fraser fir (34)
  Red spruce–yellow birch (30)
  Red spruce–sugar maple–beech (31)
  Paper birch–red spruce–balsam fir (35)
  Northern white-cedar (37)
Pine and hemlock types
  Red pine (15)
  Eastern white pine (21)
  White pine–hemlock (22)
  Eastern hemlock (23)
  White pine–northern red oak–red maple (20)
  White pine–chestnut oak (51)
  Hemlock–yellow birch (24)
Northern hardwoods
  Sugar maple (27)
  Sugar maple–beech–yellow birch (25)
  Sugar maple–basswood (26)
  Black cherry–maple (28)
  Beech–sugar maple (60)
  Red maple (108)
Other northern types
  Northern pin oak (14)
  Gray birch–red maple (19)
  Black ash–American elm–red maple (39)
  Hawthorn (109)

Central forest region
Upland oaks
  Post oak–blackjack oak (40)
  Bur oak (42)
  Bear oak (43)
  Chestnut oak (44)
  White oak–black oak–northern red oak (52)
  White oak (53)
  Black oak (110)
  Northern red oak (55)
Other central types
  Black locust (50)
  Yellow-poplar (57)
  Yellow-poplar–eastern hemlock (58)
  Yellow-poplar–white oak–northern red oak (59)
  River birch–sycamore (61)
  Silver maple–American elm (62)
  Sassafras–persimmon (64)
  Pin oak–sweetgum (65)
  Pitch pine (45)
  Eastern redcedar (46)

Southern forest region
Southern yellow pines
  Sand pine (69)
  Longleaf pine (70)
  Longleaf pine–slash pine (83)
  Shortleaf pine (75)
  Virginia pine (79)
  Loblolly pine (81)
  Loblolly pine–shortleaf pine (80)
  Slash pine (84)
  South Florida slash pine (111)
  Pond pine (98)
Oak-pine types
  Longleaf pine–scrub oak (71)
  Shortleaf pine–oak (76)
  Virginia pine–oak (78)
  Loblolly pine–hardwood (82)
  Slash pine–hardwood (85)
Bottomland types
  Cottonwood (63)
  Willow oak–water oak–diamondleaf oak (88)
  Live oak (89)
  Swamp chestnut oak–cherrybark oak (91)
  Sweetgum–willow oak (92)
  Sugarberry—American elm–green ash (93)
  Sycamore–sweetgum–American elm (94)
  Black willow (95)
  Overcup oak–water hickory (96)
  Baldcypress (101)
  Baldcypress–tupelo (102)
  Water tupelo–swamp tupelo (103)
  Sweetbay–swamp tupelo–redbay (104)
Other southern types
  Ashe juniper–redberry (Pinchot) juniper (66)
  Mohrs ("shin") oak (67)
  Mesquite (68)
  Southern scrub oak (72)
  Southern redcedar (73)
  Cabbage palmetto (74)
  Sweetgum–yellow-poplar (87)
  Atlantic white-cedar (97)
  Pondcypress (100)

Tropical forest region
(Florida only)
Tropical hardwoods (105)
Mangrove (106)

Northern interior (boreal)
White spruce (201)
White spruce–aspen (251)
White spruce–paper birch (202)
Paper birch (252)
Balsam poplar (203)
Black spruce (204)
Black spruce–white spruce (253)
Black spruce–paper birch (254)

High elevations
Mountain hemlock (205)
Engelmann spruce–subalpine fir (206)
Red fir (207)
Whitebark pine (208)
Bristlecone pine (209)
California mixed subalpine (256)

Middle elevations, interior
Interior Douglas-fir (210)
White fir (211)
Western larch (212)
Grand fir (213)
Western white pine (215)
Blue spruce (216)
Aspen (217)
Lodgepole pine (218)
Limber pine (219)
Rocky Mountain juniper (220)

North Pacific
Red alder (221)
Black cottonwood–willow (222)
Sitka spruce (223)
Western hemlock (224)
Western hemlock–Sitka spruce (225)
Coastal true fir–hemlock (226)
Western redcedar–western hemlock (227)
Western redcedar (228)
Pacific Douglas-fir (229)
Douglas-fir–western hemlock (230)
Port Orford-cedar (231)
Redwood (232)
Oregon white oak (233)
Douglas-fir–tanoak–Pacific madrone (234)

Low elevations, interior
Cottonwood–willow (235)
Bur oak (236)
Interior ponderosa pine (237)
Western juniper (238)
Pinyon–juniper (239)
Arizona cypress (240)
Western live oak (241)
Mesquite (242)

South Pacific except
for high mountains
Sierra Nevada mixed conifer (243)
Pacific ponderosa pine–Douglas-fir (244)
Pacific ponderosa pine (245)
California black oak (246)
Jeffrey pine (247)
Knobcone pine (248)
Canyon live oak (249)
Blue oak–Digger pine (250)
California coast live oak (255)

Source: SAF, 1980. Copyright Society of American Foresters. Used with permission.
  [a]Type group   [b]Type name   [c]Type number

referred to as its *fidelity*. Table 16.4 gives definitions of both presence and fidelity classes, and defines the various classes of diagnostic species. Figure 16.7 illustrates the concept of fidelity class.

Character species are not necessarily dominants. In fact, they can be species with low abundance and cover. Fidelity to the association (not occurring elsewhere—fidelity classes III–V are required for a character species) and high presence value (present on a very high proportion of the plant communities representing the association in question—presence class V is often required, but class IV may be accepted if the fidelity is high) are the key attributes. Of the two attributes, fidelity is more important than presence, and the presence or absence of a particular character species is less important in the definition of the vegetation unit than the *characteristic combination of character species*. The

Table 16.4 Definition of Constancy and Fidelity and the Criteria for Differentiating Values of Species (Shimwell, 1971; Mueller-Dombois and Ellenberg, 1974)

A. Presence or Constancy Classes

Presence Class	Percent of Plots in Which Species Occurs
r	<1
I	1–20
II	21–40
III	41–60
IV	61–80
V	81–100

B. Fidelity Classes (see Figure 16.7)

Fidelity Class V: Exclusive species. Species exclusively or almost exclusively restricted to a particular vegetation unit.

Fidelity Class IV: Selective species. Species with a strong preference for a specific vegetation unit but also found infrequently in other units.

Fidelity Class III: Preferential species. Species often occurring in other vegetation units but with their optimum or maximum expression in one unit.

Fidelity Class II: Companion species. Species without a definite preference for certain vegetation units, but which are frequently present on a particular unit.

Fidelity Class I: Strangers or accidental species. Species which have a definite preference for other vegetation units but which are occasionally present; may be a relict from previous seral stage.

C. Differentiating Values

1. Character species: must have presence class ≥IV and fidelity class ≥III.
2. Constant dominant: presence class V; mean species significance ≥3.0.
3. Constant: presence class V; mean species significance <3.0.
4. Important companion: presence class ≥III: fidelity class II.

association is recognized by a characteristic association between a typical group of species of high fidelity.

Subassociations, the level of the hierarchy below the association, are defined by *differential species*. These are species that do not have high enough fidelity or constancy to be character species for the association, but which permit subdivision of the association into two or more subunits.

A problem with the definition of fidelity classes arises from variations in the adaptations of different ecotypes. A species that may have a fidelity class V in one part of its range may have a much lower fidelity in other parts.

A full treatment of this and other aspects of the Braun–Blanquet approach is beyond the scope of this book, so the interested reader is recommended to fuller treatments in Shimwell (1971), Whittaker (1973a), and Mueller-Dombois and Ellenberg (1974).

b. THE HABITAT-TYPE APPROACH OF DAUBENMIRE. A somewhat different approach to vegetation classification employing the entire plant community is used in the northwestern U.S. (Daubenmire, 1952; Daubenmire and Daubenmire, 1968). The vegetation is classified primarily by differences in the overstory, the resulting units or *unions* being subdivided according to the dominant shrub or herb species. The combination of overstory and understory unions defines ''associations,'' which are named after the dominant overstory species and the dominant or characteristic understory species (shrub or herb). Only climax associations are considered in the nomenclature, but seral variants of these are described. The authors of this system accept the polyclimax view of succession, and recognize climatic, edaphic, topographic, topo-edaphic, and zootic climaxes. The overstory union at climax is said to reflect regional climate rather than soil variations, whereas the understory union is said to be more responsive to local variations in soil moisture, chemistry, and microclimate.

The climax associations are used to define *habitat types:* physical environments or parts of the landscape that will support particular climax plant associations in the absence of disturbance. Habitat types are felt to be a more practical classification tool than associations because once the habitat type is defined, so is the seral sequence of plant communities, and the suitability and productivity of the site for different tree species. As a result, habitat types can be recognized whether or not the community has been disturbed.

The habitat type system of classification does not incorporate soils data in the development of the classification, and a given habitat type can include a variety of soil types. A description of soils is included in a description of the habitat types, and soils information may be used to help characterize lower levels in the classification such as

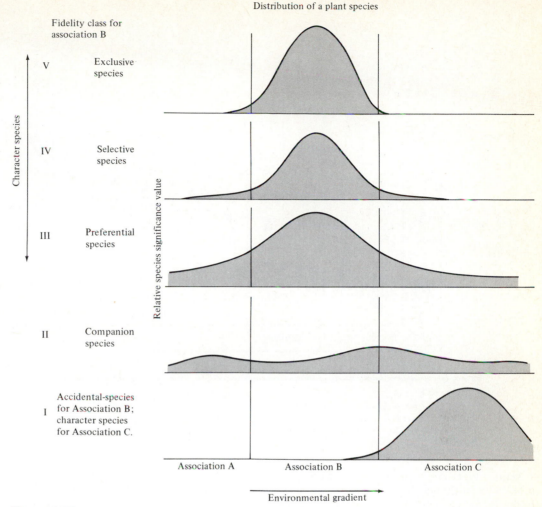

Distribution of a plant species

Fidelity class for
association B

Character species

V   Exclusive
     species

IV   Selective
     species

III Preferential
     species

II   Companion
     species

     Accidental-species
I   for Association B;
     character species
     for Association C.

Relative species significance value

Association A   Association B   Association C

Environmental gradient

Figure 16.7
Diagrammatic illustration of fidelity classes. Relative species significance values are given because fidelity does not imply high absolute significance value.

phases. However, the system is most commonly used at or above the habitat type level, and consequently it has traditionally been a vegetation rather than an ecosystem type of classification.

The explanation for the relative exclusion of soils data from the classification is that an adequate soils classification had not yet been developed for the northwestern U.S. at the time the system was first developed. Although he noted that soil is a critically important ecological factor, Daubenmire felt that vegetation responds to differences in moisture, fertility, temperature, and aeration rather than to parameters such as color, texture, structure, depth, sequence of hori-

zons, and other soil features that are easily observed by the human eye. The latter were the basis for soils classifications available to him at the time he was developing his classification scheme, which led Daubenmire to develop a vegetation-only classification: a classification of the biotic potential of the land as expressed through the vegetation. Daubenmire felt that soils data should be included as ecologically useful soils information became available, and although the system remained largely a vegetation system, recent applications of the method have involved an increasing component of soils data, and it is likely that this trend will continue.

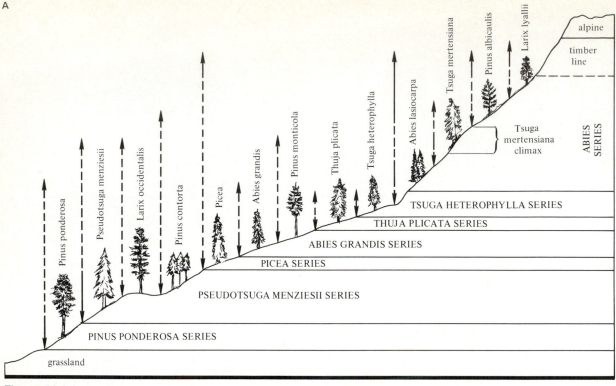

Figure 16.8

Daubenmire's forest habitat type classification. (A) Altitudinal distribution of forest habitat series in northwestern Montana. The vertical lines show the elevational range of the tree species. Dotted line = seral status; the solid line = climax status. (B) Estimated production potential (ft^3 acre^{-1} year^{-1}) of habitat types in western Montana. (After Pfister et al., 1977. Courtesy of the USDA Forest Service and the authors.)

Habitat types are the basis for two different classification hierarchies: a floristic hierarchy and a landscape hierarchy. In the former, habitat types are grouped into *series:* groups of habitat types having the same dominant climax species. Series are successively grouped into subformations and formations on the basis of physiognomic similarities of the dominant vegetation at climax. Figure 16.8 shows a topographic sequence of series in northwestern Montana, and the relationship between habitat types and potential timber yield.

In the landscape hierarchy, habitat types are used to define *vegetation zones:* geographical areas with a uniform climate which supports the same climatic climax association (i.e., has the same habitat type) in zonal ecosystems. Vegetation zones are grouped into *vegetation provinces* based on floristic similarities, and these are grouped into *vegetation regions:* geographic areas having characteristic climate and dominant vegetation of a particular physiognomy. The

highest category in this hierarchy is the *ecoregion,* defined on the basis of major differences in understory and overstory, which are thought to reflect major climatic variations (Pfister, 1976; Pfister and Arno, 1980). Each region is characterized by a typical altitudinal sequence of 5–15 habitat types.

The habitat-type approach is being used through much of northwestern U.S. where it is gaining acceptance as the ecological basis for forest management. A map and description of the ecoregions of the U.S. is available (Bailey, 1976, 1978).

16.5   Ecosystem Classification

In cases where there is a diverse biota that is in equilibrium with its physical environment, where there is detailed knowledge of the relationships between the components of this biota and between the physical environment and the

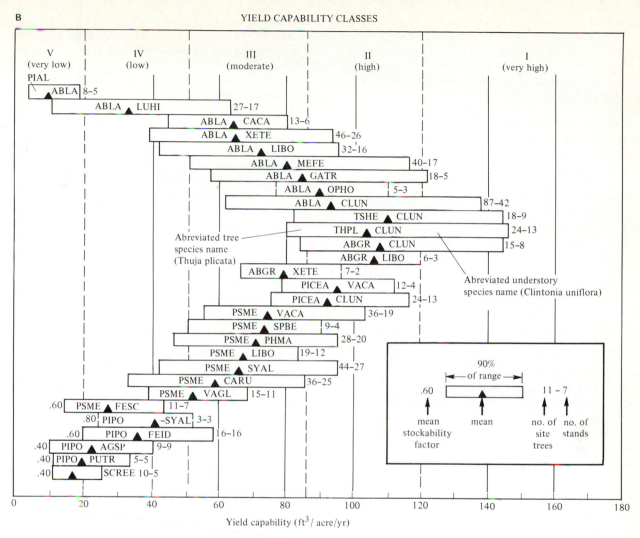

B

YIELD CAPABILITY CLASSES

biota, and where the seral characteristics of particular ecosystems are known, classification based on the biotic community alone has proven to be a very satisfactory approach. Conversely, where the biota is less diverse, where individual species tend to have broader ranges and to be less specific in their environmental tolerances (lower fidelity values), where much of the vegetation has been recently disturbed, and when this situation is coupled with an incomplete knowledge of biotic–environment relationships, a purely vegetation classification may prove to be unsatisfactory for many aspects of forest management. An alternative approach that has become increasingly popular for such situations over the past two decades is ecosystem classifica-

tion, in which the classes are explicitly defined in terms of climate, soils, landforms, and vegetation. Faunal and microbiological parameters belong equally in such classifications but have received less attention than they deserve, for reasons such as lack of knowledge, lack of interest, and/or lack of funds and manpower.

Ecosystem approaches to classification can be divided into two main types: (1) those that focus on vegetation–soil units (ecosystem types or biogeocoenoses), using climatic and/or climatic–vegetation relationships as a broad framework for the classification (e.g., the *biogeoclimatic classification* of British Columbia; also called an *ecosystematic classification*), and (2) those that either focus on the physical environment, incorporating vegetation only in the final stages of the classification, or which classify and map different parameters of the environment separately and subsequently integrate them by overlaying the final maps (e.g., the *biophysical classification* approach developed in Australia and Canada).

A. Biogeoclimatic Classification[2]

1. Introduction to the System.

Biogeoclimatic classification is a hierarchical system of ecosystem classification developed by Krajina (1965, 1969, 1972) in British Columbia. It divides the province initially into major climatic regions using Köppen's classification of climate (Table 16.1). Four *climatic formations* (E, D, BSK, and C) and seven *biogeoclimatic regions* (subdivisions of formations) are identified, primarily on the basis of broad climatic features but also on the basis of broad vegetational and soils characteristics that are induced by climate. These regions are in turn subdivided into *biogeoclimatic zones,* which are defined as: geographical areas characterized by a mosaic of vegetation types and soils, the character of which broadly reflects the regional climate; the spatial boundaries of a zone are defined by the dominant climatic climax vegetation on *mesic* sites that have *zonal* soils. The term ''mesic'' refers to the site *hygrotope* (soil moisture status). Zonal soils are those that have developed primarily under the control of regional climate and the climatically determined vegetation. To understand the biogeoclimatic classification method requires an understanding of the classification of hygrotopes.

2. Classification of Hygrotopes.

The term *mesic* in the biogeoclimatic classification system refers to sites on which the moisture conditions experienced by plants are primarily under the control of the local climate. *Xeric* sites are those sites which are drier than would be expected from local precipitation data. This can be because of rapid drainage of water (steep slopes; thin, coarse soils lacking incorporated organic matter; or very deep coarse soils), low soil moisture storage capacity, and no upslope drainage area (no slope seepage water to augment precipitation inputs). In contrast, *hygric* sites receive an abundant input of water in the form of soil seepage from upslope, and often have good soil moisture storage capacity. Plants on such sites have access

to far more moisture than would be suggested by local precipitation data, but the soils are still well aerated and are rarely saturated in the upper 0.5–1.0 m. *Hydric* sites are those which, because of soil texture, soil organic matter, poor drainage, and/or abundant inputs of slope seepage or spring water have soils that are saturated almost to the surface for much of the year; often, they are semiaquatic.

On xeric, hygric, and hydric sites there is strong edaphic and/or topographic modification of the climatically-determined availability of moisture plants. On *mesic* sites, there is relatively little such modification. Mesic sites can occur on broad flat ridges with fairly deep (1–2 m), medium-textured soil or on midslopes where downslope drainage is balanced by small seepage inputs from above (but insufficient to make the site hygric). Mesic sites can occur on rocky ridges or on coarse soils if the forest floor has accumulated to sufficient depth to be able to hold much of the precipitation input for long enough for the plants to have the opportunity to use it. Thus, mesic sites can occur almost anywhere in the landscape where the moisture conditions experienced by the plants are primarily determined by the local climate. They certainly are not restricted to midslope positions, although mesic conditions are often best developed on midslopes.

Xeric sites can also be found in various topographic positions. Normally an upper slope or ridge-top type, xeric conditions can occur on lower slopes or valley bottoms, where deep, coarse-textured geological deposits elevate the rooting zone well above the slope seepage zone or the phreatic zone (above the groundwater table). Hygric conditions are nearly always found on lower concave seepage slopes with medium soil depth (the seepage zone is within reach of the roots). Hydric conditions are also a lower-slope, valley-bottom condition, but can also be found in poorly drained concave depressions on ridge tops. In exceptionally cool and humid climates, sub-hydric conditions (bogs) may develop almost anywhere on the landscape.

Use of the hygrotope classification is central to the biogeoclimatic classification. Each biogeoclimatic zone and subzone is a mosaic of different climax associations (or their seral equivalents) located at various positions on the landscape. The structure and composition of these associations reflects both the regional climate and the local soil conditions, but the relative importance of climate and soil as controlling factors varies. On xeric, hygric, and hydric sites, soil conditions dominate, and the vegetation does not accurately reflect the regional climate. Only on the mesic site does the vegetation and soil truly indicate the climate of the area. Consequently, the geographical extent of a zone or

---

[2]This method of classification is given more detailed treatment than the others because it is currently in operational use in B.C. as the ecological basis for intensive forest management by government and industry foresters. The method is being applied on an experimental basis in Alberta and Ontario. Biogeoclimatic classifications have been proposed for the Hawaiian Islands (Krajina, 1966) and for Japan (Kojima, 1979).

subzone is defined by the composition and structure of the vegetation and the nature of the soil on the mesic site.

The terms xeric, mesic, hygric, and hydric are measures of relative moisture availability to plants (relative to local precipitation). This means that the absolute moisture tensions experienced by plants on the xeric site, for example, will vary greatly from one subzone to another and from one zone to the next. The absolute moisture status of each hygrotope in each subzone is currently being quantified.

3. Biogeoclimatic Zones and Subzones.

Biogeoclimatic zones are identified and named after the climatic climax vegetation on the mesic site type with zonal soils. The climax vegetation on hygric and xeric sites within a zone reflects these soil moisture conditions and will be similar to the climax vegetation on the mesic sites of the next wetter and drier zones, respectively. For example, ponderosa pine is climax on mesic sites in the Ponderosa pine–Bunchgrass (PPBG) zone in the southern interior valleys of B.C., but is found only on xeric sites in the Interior Douglas-fir (IDF) zone which is elevationally above the PPBG zone and is therefore wetter and cooler. Douglas-fir is restricted to hygric sites in the PPBG zone, is the climatic climax dominant on mesic sites in the IDF zone, and is restricted at climax to the xeric sites in the next wetter zone: the Interior Cedar Hemlock (ICH) (Figure 16.9A). Similarly, a single plant species or plant association may be found in more than one subzone of a zone, and may even occur in more than one zone, but its position on the topographic sequence will vary according to the zone and subzone (Figure 16.9B). The position of an association on the topographic sequence will also be influenced by the soil parent material. On nutrient-rich materials, an association will frequently occur farther upslope (drier) than on nutrient-poor materials. Thus, each zone and subzone is a mosaic of vegetation types, characterized by particular vegetation types on particular sections of the topographic sequence. The province of British Columbia is a mosaic of zones, a predictable sequence of which will be encountered while traveling west to east or south to north through the province, or while ascending a mountain anywhere in the province.

Most of the biogeoclimatic zones are subdivided into two or more subzones according to variations in overstory, understory, and soils that reflect variations in climate. These variations are not sufficient to alter the climax dominant plant species on the mesic site, but they do result in significant variations in soil and vegetation that are of both ecological and management significance. The biogeoclimatic subzone is the level of the classification that dictates overall resource-use strategies. It is significantly more homogeneous than the zone, but the subzone is still not detailed enough for site-specific decisions.

4. Topographic Sequences of Ecosystem Types within a Subzone.

Within each subzone, variable topography results in gradients of soil moisture and fertility (classes of soil fertility are called *trophotopes*). These environmental gradients are associated with characteristic patterns of vegetation and soils that are repeated throughout the subzone. The variation in vegetation along the physical gradients is typically discontinuous, which permits the identification of individual plant communities and biogeocoenoses that have characteristic floristic composition and structure. Figure 16.10 shows a characteristic topographic sequence within one of the subzones of coastal British Columbia. The broad structural features of this sequence can be observed in other subzones in many parts of the province, but of course the floristic details vary from subzone to subzone. Several features of the vegetation structure shown in Figure 16.10 are different in zones with extremes of temperature or low rainfall.

The magnitude of the vegetation discontinuities that occur along a topographically induced gradient of moisture and fertility varies from subzone to subzone. This causes a variation between zones in the ease with which the vegetation can be subdivided into recognizable, discrete classes. Subdivision tends to be easy in zones with steep topographic, soils and climatic gradients, and in which climatic climax vegetation is common. In these areas, the zones of transition between adjacent classes are narrow. Subdivision into discrete classes is more difficult in areas lacking steep environmental gradients, or in which fire or animals (including humans) have created widespread seral conditions. In such areas the transition zones may be as broad as the areas of individual vegetation classes.

5. Methods Used in Biogeoclimatic Classification.

In order to describe and identify zones and subzones and to subdivide the subzones, the vegetation is analyzed using a slightly modified Braun–Blanquet method (described below) and the soils and landforms are analyzed for a variety of parameters using standard soil and landform description and classification methods. Particular attention is paid to the nature and condition of the forest floor (Klinka et al., 1981). The combination of the resulting environmental (soils and landform) and vegetation data form the basis for the definition of *ecosystem types* or biogeocoenoses, while all ecosystem types that have the same plant association are grouped as an *ecosystem association*. Ecosystem types are generally defined and named in terms of the climax condition (which may be determined by either climatic, topo-

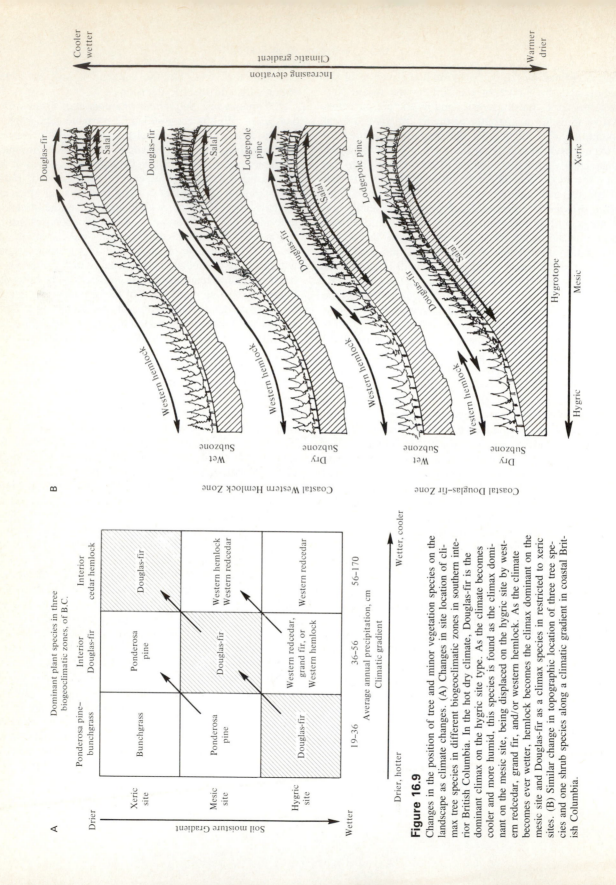

Figure 16.9

Changes in the position of tree and minor vegetation species on the landscape as climate changes. (A) Changes in site location of climax tree species in different biogeoclimatic zones in southern interior British Columbia. In the hot dry climate, Douglas-fir is the dominant climax on the hygric site type. As the climate becomes cooler and more humid, this species is found as the climax dominant on the mesic site, being displaced on the hygric site by western redcedar, grand fir, and/or western hemlock. As the climate becomes ever wetter, hemlock becomes the climax dominant on the mesic site and Douglas-fir as a climax species in restricted to xeric sites. (B) Similar change in topographic location of three tree species and one shrub species along a climatic gradient in coastal British Columbia.

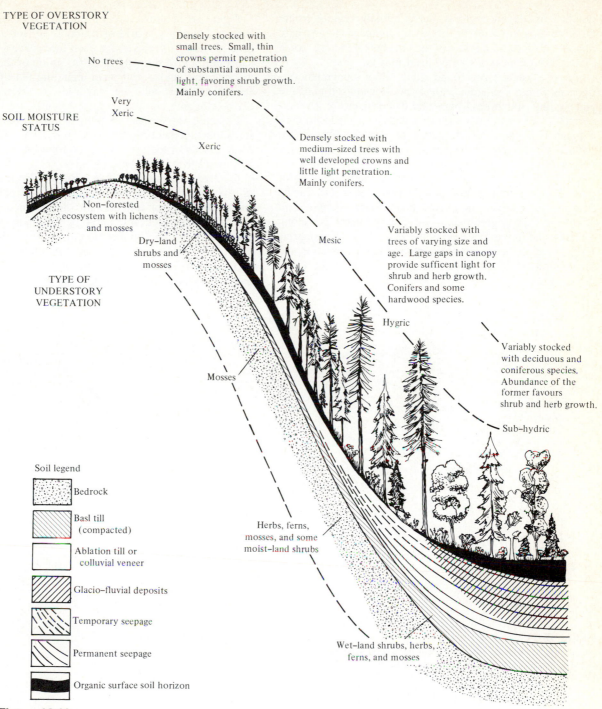

TYPE OF OVERSTORY
VEGETATION

No trees

Densely stocked with
small trees. Small, thin
crowns permit penetration
of substantial amounts of
light, favoring shrub growth.
Mainly conifers.

SOIL MOISTURE
STATUS

Very
Xeric

Xeric

Densely stocked with
medium-sized trees with
well developed crowns and
little light penetration.
Mainly conifers.

Non-forested
ecosystem with lichens
and mosses

Dry-land
shrubs and
mosses

Mesic

Variably stocked with
trees of varying size and
age. Large gaps in canopy
provide sufficent light for
shrub and herb growth.
Conifers and some
hardwood species.

TYPE OF
UNDERSTORY
VEGETATION

Hygric

Variably stocked
with deciduous and
coniferous species.
Abundance of the
former favours
shrub and herb growth.

Mosses

Sub-hydric

Soil legend

Bedrock

Basl till
(compacted)

Ablation till or
colluvial veneer

Glacio-fluvial deposits

Temporary seepage

Permanent seepage

Organic surface soil horizon

Herbs, ferns,
mosses, and some
moist-land shrubs

Wet-land shrubs, herbs,
ferns, and mosses

Figure 16.10
Variation in vegetation structure, soils, and soil moisture along a minor topographic sequence in British Columbia.

graphic, or edaphic factors), but in climatic regions where the disturbance of wind or fire is very frequent and/or where the rate of succession is slow (e.g., the boreal region), some of the ecosystem types recognized may be seral.

The ecosystem types found along minor topographic sequences within a subzone reflect variations in soil moisture and fertility. Other environmental determinants (e.g., temperature, soil aeration) also help to determine the location of a plant association on the sequence, but the former two factors are thought to be particularly important and they play a major role in determining the productivity of trees. The relationship of these two factors to the distribution of plant associations and the productivity of tree species can be broadly summarized in a two-dimensional *edaphic grid* (Remezov and Pogrebnyak, 1969), with hygrotopes along one axis and trophotopes along the second axis. These grids have proven to be a very useful aid in the interpretation and application of the biogeoclimatic classification for forest management.

Figure 16.11 shows a set of three grids for one subzone in British Columbia: a grid of productivity for a tree species (one of these is prepared for each tree species found in the subzone), a grid showing the distribution of the major plant associations, and a grid recommending (1) the major tree species that should be favored in regeneration and (2) postlogging slashburning treatment.

Examples of the use of biogeoclimatic classification in forest management can be found in Klinka et al. (1980a,b). More details of the system can be found in Krajina (1969), Kojima (1981), and Pojar (1983).

6. *Overall Structure of the Biogeoclimatic Classification System.* The biogeoclimatic classification approach subdivides a region into climatic classes according to Köppen, and subdivides these into biogeoclimatic zones according to the climatic climax dominant vegetation on mesic sites with zonal soils. Zones are subdivided into subzones according to floristic and structural differences in the plant community and differences in soils. Within subzones, pat-

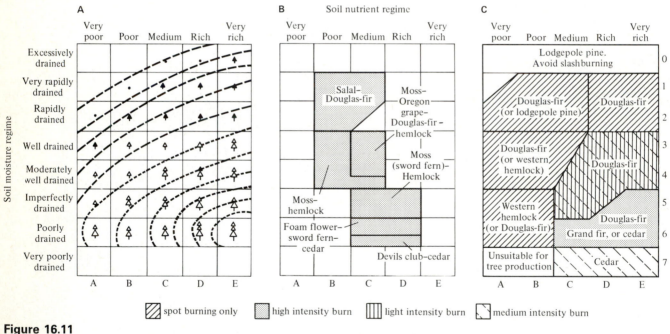

Figure 16.11
Edaphic grids, using the dry subzone of the coastal Western hemlock Biogeoclimatic Zone in British Columbia as an example. (A) Productivity and shade tolerance of Douglas-fir for various combinations of soil moisture and fertility. The size of the diagrammatic trees is proportional to productivity. Open trees indicate that regeneration is light-demanding. Black trees indicate that regeneration is shade-tolerant. Dotted lines are isoclines of tree productivity. (B) Distribution of major plant associations in the subzone with respect to soil moisture and fertility. (C) Major species recommended for regeneration, and recommended slashburning policy. (After Krajina, 1969, and Klinka, 1977. Used with permission of Department of Botany. The University of British Columbia, Ministry of Forests, and authors.)

terns of ecosystem types are identified along topographic sequences. These topographic sequences of ecosystem types, which are associated with gradients of soil moisture and fertility, are summarized in the form of edaphic grids, which then form the ecological basis for the development of guidelines for a variety of silvicultural decisions. The vegetation component of the ecosystem is analyzed according to the Braun–Blanquet system, and standard descriptions of soil and landform are prepared. Because the system is hierarchical and follows the basic principles of systematic taxonomy, this system is said to be an ecosystematic classification: it is a natural, taxonomic classification of ecosystems.

The biogeoclimatic classification consists of five distinct levels (Figure 16.12):

a. *The biogeoclimatic level,* which consists of a hierarchy of categories from formation to region to zone to subzone to variant (biogeoclimatic). Variants represent slight variations in the subzone according to where the subzone is found. This level deals with the mosaic of ecosystem types from a broad regional category down to a local category. Only the lowest two categories are really of practical interest to forest resource managers.

b. *The biogeocoenotic level* is the local site level of the classification. The basic taxonomic unit (taxon) of the entire biogeoclimatic classification system is the biogeocoenose or ecosystem type. This forms the center of a local site hierarchy from ecosystem association to ecosystem type to variant (biogeocoenotic). The biogeocoenotic hierarchy is continuous with the biogeoclimatic hierarchy (ecosystem associations are subdivisions of subzones or biogeoclimatic variants) but is based on vegetation and soils whereas the biogeoclimatic hierarchy is also based on climate and landform. All the categories in the biogeocoenotic hierarchy are of value to foresters.

c. *The phytocoenotic (plant) level.* All the categories in the two levels above can be arranged on the basis of vegetation parameters into a second major hierarchy, which intersects with the biogeocoenotic–biogeoclimatic hierarchy at the ecosystem association. The phytocoenotic hierarchy descends from order to alliance to association to subassociation to variant (phytocoenotic). This level is mainly of interest to plant ecologists.

d. *The functional level.* The various taxa of the above hierarchies can also be classified according to function (cf.

Figure 16.12

Diagrammatic summary of the various "integrative levels" of the biogeoclimatic classification of British Columbia (based on Krajina, 1972). The Biogeoclimatic and Biogeocoenotic hierarchies subdivide the province regionally and locally, respectively, to the level of individual ecosystem types and their variants. The plant community of the ecosystem association is a part of a separate vegetation hierarchy. The nonhierarchical Functional level analyzes the distribution of plant species, their productivity, and various other aspects of ecosystem function along environmental gradients. The Interpretative level applies knowledge from the Functional level to interpret various levels in the Biogeocoenotic and Biogeoclimatic hierarchies in terms of forest management.

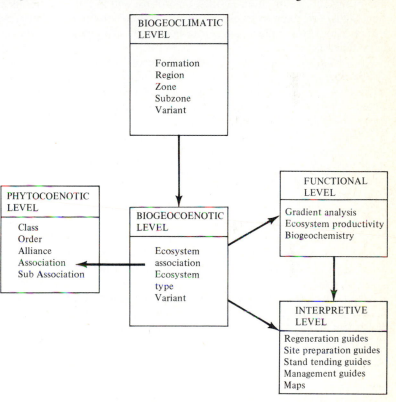

Rodin and Bazilevich, 1967): biomass, productivity, energy transfers, nutrient content, and nutrient cycling. The edaphic grid represents one aspect of the functional level: the variation of tree productivity or the distribution of plant associations along gradients of soil moisture and fertility. This level cannot be developed until the above descriptive levels have been established.

e. *The interpretive level.* This level of the classification is concerned with the application of knowledge developed at the functional level in the form of management guides that can be applied to various categories in the above hierarchies. The tree species selection and slashburning guide based on the edaphic grid (Figure 16.10) is an example of this level.

B. Biophysical Classification

Biophysical classification is an approach that has been developed and used quite widely in Canada for broad classification of large areas. As a logical development from the earlier physiographic approach, it has itself evolved and is now generally referred to as *ecological classification* (Thie and Ironside, 1976). However, the approach is really a series of inventories of climate, soils, landforms, and vegetation, which are then synthesized into a series of environmental categories, rather than a true taxonomic ecological classification.

The biophysical approach generally involves a team of specialists (a geologist, a pedologist, and a plant ecologist). When this team works together with close cooperation and integration, the results should be broadly comparable with the biogeoclimatic approach. However, in practice, the geology, soil, and vegetation inventories are often undertaken independently, and this can result in a number of problems during the final synthesis because of variations in scale of mapping and size of mapping unit. The method has been developed and applied particularly in large-scale reconnaissance inventories of the environment for such purposes as hydroelectric schemes and pipeline projects in Canada and the United States. Mapping has largely been done from aerial photographs with limited ground checking because of access problems and the vast extent of the area being mapped.

The biophysical approach has proved to be enormously successful for many of the purposes for which it has been used, but it has not proven to be the best classification method for forest management. It has tended to be more of a regional than a site-specific system, although there are many examples of its use for specific local resource-development and land-management purposes.

16.6   Mapping of Vegetation

Mapping is the graphic representation, in two dimensions, of patterns of plant communities, physical environments, ecosystems, or some parameter thereof.

Vegetation may be directly mapped as *existing vegetation,* or interpretations may be made about present successional status and future trends to yield a map of *potential vegetation.* The latter requires a detailed knowledge of the ecology of an area if reliable potential vegetation maps are to be derived from studies of existing vegetation, especially where all vestiges of the original (pre-human) vegetation have long since been removed by urbanization, agriculture, forestry, industry, or "natural" disaster. Vegetation mapping may also be conducted as a means of mapping habitats or physical environments. Habitats (geographical locations capable of supporting specific biotic communities) and physical environments can be identified by indicator species that reflect physical, chemical, and/or hydrological conditions of the soil, and meso- or microclimatic conditions.

As already mentioned, most of the earlier climatic classifications utilized vegetation to assist in the definition of major climatic regions. Similarly, interpretation of vegetation is an indispensable part of soil mapping. Soil scientists often use empirically-derived correlations between indicator plant species or associations of plants and certain characteristics of soils to map the soils of a region far more rapidly and accurately than would be possible otherwise. Such indirect mapping of soils and climates requires initial studies to establish the necessary plant–environment correlations.

A. Reasons for Mapping

Vegetation mapping may be undertaken for a variety of purposes (Mueller-Dombois and Ellenberg, 1974):

1. *To provide a framework for research.* Field research results should always be related to a specific set of ecological conditions in order to permit extrapolation of research results to other locations. Sampling represents the measurement of certain parameters of interest on a few representative samples of a homogeneous group or population in order to make predictions or estimates about those parameters for the whole group or population. The accuracy of these predictions is improved if samples are located in homogeneous ecological types and if the extent of these types is known accurately. Ecological maps help in the location of samples and extrapolation of the resulting data.

2. *As an aid in classifying vegetation.* Mapping gives an opportunity to test the adequacy of a classification scheme. It helps to reveal errors and omissions, and tests the ability of the scheme to handle transition or ecotone situations.

3. *As a tool in studies of vegetation structure,* pattern, distribution, succession, and the relationship between vegetation and the physical environment. Comparison of maps of vegetation and various aspects of the physical environment help in understanding the reasons for observed vegetation patterns.

4. *As a basis for resource management.* Ecological site maps, maps of existing and potential vegetation, and maps of potential site productivity are indispensable components of successful resource management. Although maps are not an alternative to adequate ecological knowledge (which all resource managers should have), they provide a permanent record of ecological conditions that facilitates planning in the office, facilitates the transfer of knowledge and experience to new or junior employees, and portrays the variety of ecological conditions to be faced in resource development. When coupled with interpretations of the map units for management, ecological site maps become a powerful factor in improving the quality of management. Maps in general are the main method of summarizing inventory information in resource management.

Maps provide a visual characterization of the earth's features over large areas at a reduced scale, comprehensible to the human mind. They provide for the summarization, storage, and dissemination of geographic, ecological, and management information and facilitate comparisons between remote locations.

Before mapping vegetation, habitats, or ecosystems, a number of questions must be answered: (1) What information is to be included in the map? (2) What scale is to be used in the mapping? (3) What accuracy is required? (4) What form is the information to be presented in? (5) What are the personnel, financial, time, and access constraints? (6) What methods of mapping are to be used? These questions are not all independent. Questions 1 to 4 depend largely on the objectives of the mapping and the ultimate use and application of the maps. They also depend upon the answer to question 5. Question 6 will be answered largely by the answers to the other questions. A full treatment of mapping is beyond the scope of this book, and the interested reader is directed to Kuchler (1967) and Mueller-Dombois and Ellenberg (1974). However, two topics will be treated briefly before proceeding: the question of scale and the implications of succession for mapping.

B. Map Scale

The question of scale is one of the more important decisions that must be made at the outset. The following guide is given by Mueller-Dombois and Ellenberg (1974).

1. *Small-scale maps for a general overview.* Such maps have a scale of 1:1 million or smaller. One centimeter on a 1:1 million map represents 10 km in the field: one square centimeter represents 100 km^2. Such maps can present vegetation formations or biogeoclimatic zones, as, for example, Kuchler's (1964) 1:7.5 million map, "Potential Natural Vegetation" of the United States; the 1:6.4 million map "Forest Regions of Canada" (Rowe, 1972). The smallest feature on the ground that can usefully be represented has a minimum dimension of 1 km.[3] Such maps are useful for regional summaries and for depicting continental vegetation patterns.

2. *Intermediate-scale maps.* These include maps from 1:1 million to about 1:100,000. One centimeter on the 1:100,000 map represents 1 km on the ground. Actual vegetation cannot be presented at this scale, so these maps generally represent potential vegetation. The smallest unit on the ground that can usefully be represented on the map has a minimum dimension of 100 m and a size of 1 ha. Such maps are useful for regional planning or for detailed presentation of vegetation zones at a provincial, state, or national (smaller countries) level.

3. *Large-scale maps.* These include most maps in the range 1:100,000 to 1:10,000. One centimeter on the 1:10,000 map represents 100 m on the ground; 1 cm^2 represents 1 ha. Maps in the range 1:50,000 to 1:20,000 are generally used for detailed forest management purposes. At this scale, nearly all the vegetation units on the ground can be represented, and the boundaries of existing vegetation can be drawn. The smallest feature on the ground that can be represented on such maps has a minimum dimension of 10 m. These maps require a great deal of intensive field and office work, and generally they are prepared only for specific purposes such as park or urban development, research areas, and so on. Some small countries may consider mapping their entire area at this scale range, but normally this would be impractically expensive and time consuming.

4. *Detailed maps at a very large scale.* This includes maps varying in scale from 1:5,000 to 1:1,000. One centimeter on the 1:1,000 map represents 10 m in the field. Such maps are prepared only for research areas, intensive-recreation areas, and situations requiring very detailed permanent records of the existing vegetation.

It is thought by some forest ecologists that mapping below the scale of about 1:50,000 is not justified. Correct (ecological and economical) site-specific management decisions are thought to be better achieved by having knowledgeable people who inspect the site make the decisions,

---

[3] Damman (1977) feels that the smallest vegetation unit that can be mapped is 2.5 times larger than the limits given here.

rather than people who lack the necessary ecological knowledge, but who have detailed ecological maps. The money and time invested in the preparation of such detailed maps is better spent in providing adequate training in local ecology for local management personnel. The need for site inspection as a basis for management decisions rather than office interpretation of maps cannot be overstressed.

At a scale of 1:50,000 mapping can be achieved largely by air-photo interpretation with limited field checking (''ground truth''). For example, mapping of a 100,000-ha watershed at this scale will often involve a couple of weeks of ground reconnaissance with access by road or helicopter. During this period, descriptions will be prepared of all major ecosystem units. Several days will then be spent in a helicopter with air photos and topographic maps in hand, recognizing landform and vegetation features that correlate strongly with soil–habitat–vegetation features (established during the ground reconnaissance and subsequent data analysis) that are to be mapped. Thereafter, the entire watershed can be mapped in the office from air photographs (black and white, infrared, color, and/or color–infrared).

C. Implications of Succession for Mapping

Vegetation is dynamic, as outlined in Chapter 15. Although there are still a few areas of the world left in which relatively undisturbed vegetation still exists, such areas are rapidly shrinking and for the most part future mapping will be dealing with seral (and therefore changing) vegetation. The mapper must therefore decide whether or not to map existing vegetation (which may change, giving the map a short period of usefulness) or potential (i.e., climax) vegetation (a condition that the vegetation may never attain).

The same question arises during the development of a vegetation classification. Should the ecologist sample and describe seral stages or climax communities? If forced to sample seral stages, does the ecologist interpret the probable climax condition of the sample from the composition and structure of the vegetation and group the sampled ecosystems on this basis, or accept classification units based on the vegetation as it presently exists? In northern boreal forests markedly influenced by fire, the vegetation may be almost entirely composed of various seral communities, most of which will be developing rather slowly toward a single climatic climax. In such a case, the only practical option is to classify the vegetation into the vegetation units that exist. On the other hand, in more temperate climates it may be reasonable to classify on the basis of potential climax vegetation, as is done in the Habitat Type classification of Daubenmire, because succession to the climax condition is much more rapid, especially on mesic to hygric sites.

The answer to the question is also influenced by use of the mapped information. In the north we may wish to map existing vegetation for inventory purposes as a part of resource development planning. In more temperate situations we may wish to map site potential as the basis for making site-specific operational management decisions, developing a taxation system for forestland, or in calculating long-term sustainable yields. Understory vegetation tends to achieve climax condition more rapidly than the overstory. Mapping techniques that utilize only the forest overstory will lend themselves more to the mapping of existing vegetation. Those techniques that are based on understory or on the entire plant association permit the mapping of potential vegetation, as do techniques incorporating data on the entire ecosystem.

Classification of ecosystems almost inevitably involves on-the-ground sampling, whereas mapping can be done to a large extent by remote sensing. The interested reader is referred to Lulla (1981), Lilles and Kiefer (1980) and Sabins (1978).

16.7 Summary

Resource management is being practiced in a climate of public opinion that is increasingly intolerant of ''mistakes.'' The need for resource managers to achieve their public statements of intent to practice ''good'' management has never been greater. Thus *resource managers need to be successful* in achieving the objectives of their management.

Success in almost any endeavor in life involves an ability to make reliable predictions about the object of our intentions. The better our ability to predict something, the greater the probability of success in any endeavor in which it is involved. Thus, *to be successful, resource managers must be able to make accurate predictions*.

Making accurate predictions is difficult, but in general, the more we know about something, the better we can predict it. Whether we are buying a car, planning a vacation, or designing and locating a logging road, the more we know about it, the greater the chance that the outcome of our efforts matches our expectations and hopes. Accurate predictions in a simple system are easy. We can predict with complete certainty that the sun will rise in the east and set in the west, and that an apple will fall to the ground upon being released from the branch on which it is growing. Such high predictive power is possible because the few major determinants of these events are fixed and reasonably well understood and quantified. However, it is a basic characteristic of any system in which there are several or many determinants whose action is unknown or poorly quantified that it is difficult to make accurate predictions about events or conditions in that system. Thus reliable prediction in complex, poorly understood systems is inherently difficult. *The only way to ensure good powers of prediction (and thus to be successful) in forest management is to have a good knowledge of the structure and functional processes of the forest ecosystem.*

Knowledge of a determinant in a complex system essentially eliminates the contribution of that determinant to reducing one's powers of prediction. For each determinant that we understand and quantify, we increase our power of prediction (see Chapter 2), until when we have complete knowledge of the system, we can achieve 100% accuracy in our predictions (an ideal that will probably never be obtained in most types of resource management because of economic limitations). However, knowledge on its own is not sufficient to ensure an improvement in the quality of resource management. Among other things, it is also necessary to have a workable system by which we can apply this knowledge in our day-to-day activities. Such a system is provided by classification and, where appropriate, mapping.

Various approaches to classification have been developed, reflecting varying physical and biological conditions, variable access to and basic knowledge of the environment, and variable applications for which the classifications have been developed. There is no single best approach. Each particular situation defines a best approach for the prevailing set of circumstances. However, there has been a historical trend in the development of classifications from broad schemes utilizing very general parameters of the physical environment, to more detailed schemes that incorporate all the major components of the ecosystem. It has generally been found that prediction of ecosystems is more successful when based on an ecosystem classification than on a classification based on only one or a small number of ecosystem parameters. Within the ecosystem approach, classification may either work with entire ecosystem types (e.g., the biogeoclimatic approach) or may classify different components of the ecosystem independently, combining subgroups of these components to define ecosystem units (e.g., the biophysical approach). The merits of the two approaches must be judged by their utility for resource management. Undoubtedly, both approaches will find favor under appropriate circumstances, but it is possible that the former will find more ready acceptance in the silvicultural aspects of forest management.

17 Models and Their Role in Ecology and Resource Management[1]

17.1 Introduction

The complexity of ecosystems has been mentioned several times, as has an important consequence of this complexity: that events and conditions in ecosystems are difficult to predict. A detailed knowledge of ecosystem structure and function greatly improves our ability to make accurate predictions, but this knowledge on its own is not always sufficient. Many ecological phenomena and resource management problems involve so many interacting factors that predictions are difficult in spite of our knowledge. Classification of ecosystems and of our knowledge about them certainly helps, but a major limitation remains: the limited mental capacity of the human brain, which restricts us to thinking at any one time about only a few of the many interacting components of a complex system.

The complexity of natural phenomena has always been a problem for science. In their attempts to describe, define, and explain the world, scientists have traditionally resorted to *scientific reductionism,* the description of phenomena in terms of simple or causal hypotheses. In many cases, this is the only way to advance our knowledge of the details of

processes in systems about which we already know quite a lot, but it is generally not an appropriate method for investigating the overall functioning of little understood ecosystems and the impact of management thereon. Simple, causal explanations for complex phenomena about which we have limited knowledge rarely contribute much to our understanding of those phenomena. An alternative approach, which is being used with increasing frequency, is to incorporate much of the complexity into a comprehensive *model* of the phenomenon, and to use the model to make predictions about the system and its response to perturbations.

A model can take many different forms, but basically it is either an abstract or a physical entity that represents in some way the form and/or the function of real-world entities and processes. A mathematical equation that summarizes a physiological process is a model of that process. Pictures and statues are models. This book is a model of the form and functioning of a forest ecosystem. Many different types of model have played, and will continue to play, useful roles in ecology and resource management, but it is the relatively recent use of a model in conjunction with a computer that makes modeling such a valuable aid in understanding the properties and behavior of complex systems. It was the advent of computer modeling that gave modeling in general the attention and the reputation that it now has.

This chapter will briefly introduce the reader to the variety and nature of models. It starts with a cautionary note on the limitations of models, and a review of different types of model and their attributes. Then, as an example of the historical trend in modeling, a series of models of harvest-induced site nutrient depletion, from the simple models of 25 years ago to a recent ecosystem-level model, is presented. The chapter concludes with a brief treatment of the relationship between modeling and the traditional scientific method. The chapter is intended as a brief introduction to, and overview of, modeling for beginning students of ecology and renewable resource management. No attempt has been made to review the literature or provide a description of the wide variety of modeling techniques, but readers interested in pursuing the topic further are recommended to Sollins et al. (1981) and other papers in Reichle (1981), Linder (1981), Mitsch et al. (1981), Jeffers (1978), Hall and Day (1977), de Wit and Goudriaan (1974), and Smith (1970).

17.2 Limitations of Models

When a model is first developed, it is generally a very inexact representation of the real object or process that it mimics. However, models can be improved. Some can be

---

[1] Chapter 17 was written jointly with K. A. Scoullar.

improved to the point at which they represent reality so well that they are no longer a model, but the reality that they were intended to represent. In other cases this cannot happen. The former are models of human-made objects; the latter are models of natural, living systems. A model airplane becomes a real airplane when it represents the real airplane so closely that it can do everything that a real airplane can. This is possible because model airplanes can be made of the same materials and with the same construction techniques as real airplanes. A model bird which mimics the flight of a bird cannot, however, become a real bird. It cannot mimic all aspects of a bird's morphology, physiology, and behavior since at present we cannot synthesize living tissues and assemble them into living systems. Similarly, a computer model of a tree or an ecosystem can never represent that tree or ecosystem with complete accuracy because the computer model uses different construction materials and techniques. Because of this ultimate restriction on how well a model can duplicate biological reality, no model of biological systems can ever be completely "correct." All models are thus incorrect to some degree. Whether a model is good or not must be judged on whether it provides an acceptably good representation of the reality it is describing, and not on whether it is "right" or "wrong."

17.3 A Catalog of Types of Model

Many different types of model have been produced and used for a wide variety of purposes. For the present, we have grouped models into several broad classes that will be described in sequence, from the most fundamental to the most technically advanced type, the computer simulation model. This sequence starts with conceptual models that exist only in the mind *(internally represented models)* and progresses through a variety of *externally represented models* (Figure 17.1). When a mathematical model is implemented on a computer, it becomes a computer simulation model. Computer models may also be developed directly from word models by translating them directly into computer language, although this almost inevitably involves the use of some mathematical notation.

A. Internally Represented Models or Conceptual Models

Construction of mental models is something we all do every day as part of our normal thinking process. We perceive the conditions and entities around us with our senses of sight, sound, touch, taste, and smell. Each new percep-

tion is combined with previous perceptions to which it relates, and from the sum of these perceptions we develop an understanding of our environment. This understanding, which may or may not be an accurate description of that environment, can be called a *model* because it provides a representation of the form and/or function of the conditions and entities being perceived. Such mental abstractions are commonly referred to as *conceptual models* because they serve to unify related perceptions and because the mental images that embody the model exist only in the thoughts and memory of an individual mind.

The formulation of conceptual models is extremely important in all branches of science. This is the way in which hypotheses are formulated concerning the structure and processes of ecosystems, and conceptual models are the basis on which all other models are developed. These other models are only as good as the original conceptual model.

B. Externally Represented Models That Are Developed from Conceptual Models

1. General Comments About External Representations of Conceptual Models. The conceptual models of our minds can be stored only in our memories, and the *verbal models* that we use for communication exist only while the words are being spoken. Modern acoustical recording equipment allows the verbal model to act as a permanent, though inaccurate, record of the conceptual model and thus provides a means for storing conceptual models external to the memory. However, long before the invention of voice recordings, humans had found other ways to represent conceptual models in permanent, external forms. We carved *physical models* using available tools and materials. We painted *picture models* with less effort but at the expense of three-dimensional reality. We evolved a written form of language so that we could record our verbal communications as *word models*. Science and technology have since allowed us to develop and apply mathematical techniques in the building of *mathematical models* which can be converted into *computer simulation models* by translating the former into computer language.

The distinctions between the different types of externally represented models just mentioned are not always clear. Pictures may be painted or etched so thickly that the forms begin to take physical shape. A written language may evolve from pictures simplified to the symbols of stick drawings. Mathematical models often use words and letters as variable names, and computer simulation models are mathematical models written in a notation recognized by a computer. The different types of models are frequently used

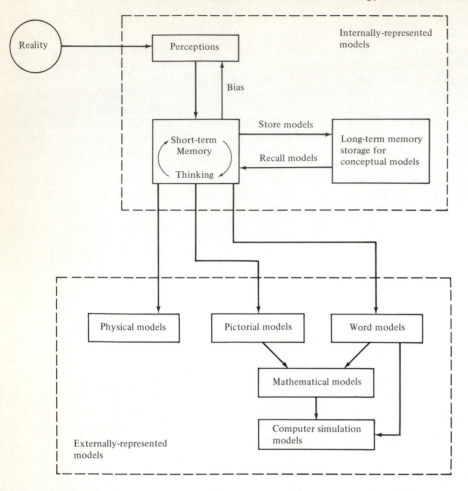

Figure 17.1
Diagram of the relationship between internally and externally represented models, showing various types of the latter. (Kimmins and Scoullar, 1984. Copyright Academic Press, Inc. Used with permission of the publisher and authors.)

in combination, as in the case of a physical model with painted details, a picture model that uses words for labels, and a word model that uses numbers to define quantities.

The conceptual models of our mind may be more *realistic* than externally represented models because they are not subject to constraints imposed by the availability of materials and techniques with which to build or express realistic external models. On the other hand, conceptual models are less *rigorous* than externally represented models because the thoughts that embody our conceptual models are fleeting and tenuous and are not available for scrutiny by other people. For example, we cannot evaluate the conceptual model of a sculptor until he or she converts the vision to a physical model by carving it in solid form. Even though the sculptor may be disappointed in his or her ability to capture the realism that had been envisioned, the finished sculpture is more rigorous than the vision because it is persistent, un-

changing, and available as a perception to other people for evaluation by comparison with their own conceptual model of the object represented in the sculpture. It is this rigorous nature of externally represented models that has resulted in their widespread use.

The procedure that one must follow in order to put a model to use is commonly termed *running* the model. Running a conceptual model involves recalling to mind from long-term memory the thoughts that embody the model. Externally represented models may be run either in the mind or externally to the mind, depending on the kind of model involved. Both picture models and static physical models can be run by perceiving the details of the model and allowing these perceptions to direct the formation of a conceptual model in the mind. In the case of a dynamic physical model (e.g., a model that works like a machine) the model must be turned on and allowed to run on its own.

To run a word model, we must read or hear the words that embody the model. We must recall from memory the thoughts and images that we associate with the words and thus be led to form an appropriate conceptual model. That literate human beings have become adept at running word models is evidenced by the economic success of book publishing companies. The greater pleasure that some people derive from reading a good novel rather than seeing a film based on the novel is often due to the fact that highly personalized and imaginative conceptual models can be developed from the word model (the novel) whereas the film (a picture model) permits little or no conceptual modeling.

Mathematical models are run by completing the series of calculations that constitute the model. The final results of all the calculations are themselves a run of the model. With a mathematical model translated into the form of a computer simulation model, we must run the computer program on a digital computer and allow it to do the calculation for us. The final result or *output* from the computer constitutes a run.

2. A Catalog of Externally Represented Models:

a. WORD MODELS. The word model is the most commonly used method for externally representing our conceptual models. Most scientific articles are word models of the systems under study, often accompanied by picture, graph, and flowchart models (see below).

b. PHYSICAL MODELS. Three-dimensional representations of real objects or systems, which are generally of limited use in forest ecology other than for education and display (e.g., a diorama of the seral stages of post-logging succession on different sites).

c. PICTURE MODELS. Two-dimensional representations of three-dimensional objects are widely used for education and demonstration. A picture may also be used as a static model of the present state of the system. Picture models include maps and histograms.

d. FLOWCHARTS. A flowchart is an externally represented dynamic model, generally with word submodels (labels). It can depict the interactions between the components of a system, the transfer of materials within a system, and/or the sequence of events in a process.

e. GRAPHS. Externally represented dynamic models that generally combine pictures, words, and mathematics, graphs are most commonly used to depict changes in a component or a process over time, or the change in one component or process as another component or process changes.

f. MATHEMATICAL MODELS. A mathematical model, an external representation of a conceptual model or other type of using mathematical notation, may be static (describing *state variables;* analogous to an *inventory*) or dynamic (describing both *state variables* and *system variables,* which define how state variables change over time). Some mathematical models stress the mathematical viewpoint where accuracy of biological description is compromised in favor of using "powerful" and/or convenient types of mathematical techniques. Biologically biased mathematical models compromise the type of mathematics that can be used in favor of accurate description of the biology of the system. Most mathematical models are intermediate between these two extremes.

g. COMPUTER MODELS. Mathematical models can be translated into computer language and implemented on a computer.

3. Stages in the Development of a Computer Simulation Model.

Because of the growing importance of computer simulation models, students of forest ecology and resource management should understand the main stages in the development of this type of model. Construction of such a model is not difficult if the modeling activities are ordered in the right sequence.

1. Establishing the objectives of the model or modeling activity—the goal to be achieved by developing the model.
2. Development of an educated conceptual model. The quality of the predictions of the computer model will depend upon how well the conceptual model describes the real system. There is a tendency to rush this critically important stage and to develop the conceptual model too narrowly. Remember, the success of the modeling activity is largely dependent on how well the conceptual model is developed.
3. Selection of the scope (i.e., the boundaries of the model: how much of the world is described in the model) and resolution of the computer model. The model should only include those processes and components that are necessary to meet the objectives.
4. Representation of the conceptual model in external form. This may involve any combination of word, physical, picture, or other nonmathematical external types of model.
5. Definition of state and system variables. The components of the system must be defined (state variables) as well as the system variables (parameters that define the rates of processes and/or the quantities being transferred between state variables).
6. Selection of the length of the simulation's time steps. How often are the transfers between state variables calculated? Daily, weekly, annually?

7. Formulation of transfer variables—the development of the mathematical equations that are needed to calculate system variables at each time step. This converts the model developed in step 4 into a mathematical model.

8. Construction of a flowchart of model execution. Before the mathematical model can be translated into computer language for implementation on the computer, the order in which the calculations are to be made must be identified. This is often done in the form of a flowchart of model execution.

9. Conversion of the mathematical model into a computer simulation model—translation of the mathematical notation into computer language, and preparation of the necessary input and output files.

10. Running the model on the computer. The computer language must be translated by the computer into machine language, and then run to check for programming errors.

11. Calibration of the model. Parameters in the model are given values that result in realistic predicted values in the output of the model.

12. Validation of the predictions. The reality of the model's predictions must be tested against a data set other than that used for calibration.

13. Gaming with the model: running the model (''gaming'' or ''playing'') to investigate properties of the simulated system, the sensitivity of the model's prediction to the quality of input data and the assumptions that were used in building the model, and/or its response to perturbation.

14. Evolution of the model. Steps 2–13 are repeated in the light of deficiencies revealed during steps 12 and 13 until the model performs acceptably.

15. Using the model for the purpose for which it was intended. Sometimes this is for making predictions. Sometimes it is for generating new hypotheses for experimental testing. Sometimes it is for synthesizing complex sets of data to test our understanding of a system. In some cases the value of building a computer model lies in the learning process involved in building it. When it is finished, it has no further use.

17.4 Application of Different Models to the Study of Site Nutrient Depletion Through Harvesting of Forest Biomass

Most of the types of model described above have been used in both basic and applied forest ecology (i.e., forest resource management). Numerous examples can be found in this book (e.g., the models of ecological succession described in Chapter 15), but to illustrate the diversity of types of model that can be applied to a particular topic, we will consider models that have been used to evaluate the significance for future biomass production of nutrient removals in harvested forest products. Reliable predictions about this effect of harvesting must be based on an understanding of the ecological processes of biomass accumulation, nutrient cycling, and secondary succession, and a recognition of the impact of forest harvesting thereon.

Extensive forest management generally places only moderate to low nutrient demands on a forest site. Harvesting only the largest logs (mainly heartwood, which has low concentrations of nutrients) at infrequent intervals (long rotations) removes only a small proportion of the site nutrient capital; such losses are more than replaced over the next rotation by natural inputs from the geochemical cycle (cf. Chapter 5). This situation changes as one moves from extensive to intensive forest management. Shorter rotations, intermediate harvests (thinning), and intensive utilization of forest biomass [whole-tree (all above-ground biomass) or even complete-tree harvesting (both above and below-ground biomass)] greatly increase nutrient outputs from the ecosystem and may result in a long-term net reduction of the site nutrient capital and productive potential. To reduce the risk of site degradation, the potential for this problem must be evaluated prior to any change from extensive to intensive management.

The forest manager needs to be able to answer this question: Will the increased nutrient withdrawals that accompany the switch from extensive to intensive forest management and biomass utilization result in a decline in the productive capacity of the forest ecosystem? The complex understanding that is required to answer this question has been expressed in a variety of modeling approaches.

A. Conceptual Models

The most fundamental type of modeling that has been used to evaluate this question is the creation of a conceptual model in the mind of the scientist or resource manager who is thinking about it. By considering what one knows of tree nutrition and its relationship to biomass production, by combining this with one's knowledge of the normal geochemical inputs to and outputs from the forest in question, the biogeochemical cycling within the ecosystem, and the internal conservation of nutrients within the trees by internal cycling, one can develop a mental image or conception of the problem from which conclusions can be drawn about whether or not intensive biomass harvesting will affect future productivity in the area.

Such a conceptual model of a forest ecosystem is limited by the mental capacity of the modeler. Just how many of the varied states and processes involved in the problem can be thought of at one time? The mental confusion that attends attempts at conceptual modeling of very complex systems results in a lack of clear definition of the magnitudes of states and of the rates of processes. Consequently, any conclusions are at best broadly qualitative. Because of these deficiencies, attempts at conceptual modeling of harvest-induced site nutrient depletion and yield reduction have frequently led to the next stage—word modeling.

B. Word Models

By carefully describing the conceptual model in words and recording this verbal description in writing or on tape, word models of the risk of nutrient depletion have been produced. These models contain far more detail than can be called to mind at any moment in a conceptual model. Clear definitions of ecosystem components are given, and detailed descriptions of ecosystem processes are provided. Quantitative estimates are placed on the magnitudes of biomass and nutrient compartments and on the rates of processes by including mathematical measurements in the word model. Examples of such word models can be found in the early literature on nutrient removal in harvested products and its effects (observed or predicted) on biomass production. The first of these is probably the writing of a German forest scientist, Ebermeyer (1869). He published a word model (a scientific description) of the effects of litter raking in German pine forests on the nutrient status of the site and the rate of growth of the trees. Decades of litter raking and removal for use in agriculture resulted in a significant reduction in site nutrient status and tree growth. Termination of litter removal resulted in a slow recovery of soil fertility and tree growth rates. Similar word models, complete with tables of numbers defining quantities and amounts (thereby rendering the model a hybrid between word and mathematical models), were presented by the English forest ecologists Rennie (1956, 1957) and Ovington (1957, 1959), who, building on the concerns of Ebermeyer, stimulated the past two decades of interest in this topic. A review-type word model of the problem can be found in Kimmins (1977).

C. Pictorial Models

The word models described above have been summarized into pictorial models with word labels, diagrams or flowcharts that more clearly display the structure of the model. Alternatively, pictorial models of nutrient depletion can be created directly from the original conceptual models. The resulting pictorial models can be qualitative or quantitative,

depending on whether mathematical measurements have been included. Figure 5.1 is an example of a qualitative pictorial model of nutrient cycling. Quantitative pictorial flowcharts of nutrient cycling in forest ecosystems, such as Figure 5.15, can be modified to summarize the problem of nutrient withdrawals at the time of harvest. Alternatively, the word model can be summarized in a diagram that compares the nutrient withdrawals at different intensities of harvest with a static budget of total site nutrient reserves, thereby omitting the information on nutrient dynamics (Figure 17.2).

This type of pictorial-mathematical model shows conditions at one moment in time but fails to describe many of the important ecosystem processes. Small quantities of nutrients being rapidly exchanged and circulated may be more important than large quantities of relatively immobile nutrients, but the rate and magnitude of nutrient turnover are not represented in Figure 17.2. An improvement is obtained by focusing on the rates of nutrient circulation, thereby emphasizing the functional relationships in the system rather than the inventory of nutrient quantities in different components. Figure 17.3 shows an example of this kind of pictorial model for a Corsican pine stand in eastern Scotland. Diagrams of this sort can be prepared for stands of different ages and subject to different conditions, thereby permitting conclusions to be drawn about temporal changes in function and the effects of management thereon. However, this type of model still falls short of a truly dynamic description of ecosystem processes. If enough diagrams of this type were made, each one representing the state of the system each year over a rotation, an animated film could be made and a dynamic pictorial model could be produced.

D. Computer Models

Neither word nor pictorial models have proven to be appropriate tools with which to make quantitative predictions of the risk of management-induced site nutrient depletion. They cannot deal with the complexity and dynamic character of the problem, and most researchers concerned with this topic eventually turn to computer models. Mathematical equations are developed that describe rates of transfer of materials between ecosystem components, and when the system of equations is solved (i.e., the model is run) on a computer, estimates can be obtained of future sizes of various ecosystem components under a variety of circumstances.

Several ecosystem-level models have been developed to examine the problem of site nutrient depletion: FORTNITE (Aber et al., 1978, 1979, 1982; Aber and Mellilo, 1980); STAND (Lindgren and Axelsson, 1980); FORCYTE (Kim-

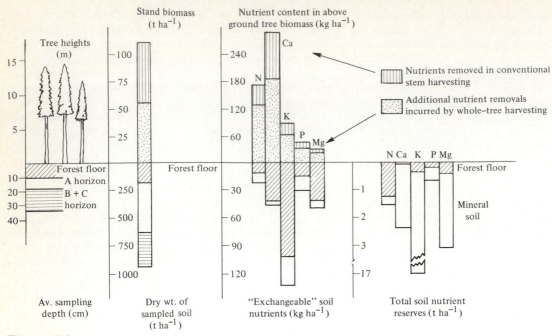

Figure 17.2
Pictorial model of nutrient withdrawals in harvested products at two different levels of utilization. Data for a 65-year-old black spruce stand north of Baie Comeau, Quebec. (After Weetman and Webber, 1972. Copyright National Research Council of Canada. Used with permission of NRC and authors.)

mins, 1981; Kimmins and Scoullar, 1979, 1981, 1983); and an earlier, unnamed model by Mitchell et al. (1975) (see Waide and Swank, 1975, 1977; Swank and Waide, 1980). There are many similarities among FORTNITE, STAND, and FORCYTE, each of which provides a fairly detailed simulation of nutrient cycling and a feedback between nutrient availability and biomass production. FORCYTE will be described as a representative of this generation of models.

The major compartments and transfer processes represented in the tenth version of FORCYTE (*FOR*est nutrient *C*ycling and *Y*ield *T*rend *E*valuator) are shown in Figure 17.4. The model, which simulates the stand cycle (i.e., secondary succession) from the time of a clearcut through herb, shrub, and tree stages to the subsequent clearcut, consists of three compartments: plant biomass, forest floor, and available soil nutrients.

The model is driven by a biomass generator (site-specific increment as a function of age for herbs, shrubs, and a tree crop) which for trees is based ultimately on site-specific stemwood volume yield tables or an empirical stand model. Biomass is added to herb, shrub, and tree populations according to their age and competition for nutrients with the other plant populations, and is lost from these populations through harvest (trees), natural mortality, and annual litterfall. Site and species-specific tissue nutrient concentration data permit the simulation of nutrient accumulation in the biomass, losses with biomass transfers, internal cycling within the plants, and net nutrient uptake demand.

Biomass and nutrients lost from plants are added to the forest floor compartment, the magnitude of which reflects the balance between these inputs and outputs by decomposition. The decomposition process releases carbon to the atmosphere, and either releases nutrients to (mineralization), or takes up nutrients (immobilization) from the available soil nutrient compartment. Immobilized nutrients are returned to the forest floor compartment.

The size of the available soil nutrient pool is determined by inputs from precipitation, mineralization, fertilization, biological fixation (of nitrogen), slope seepage, and mineral weathering, and outputs to immobilization, soil leaching losses and plant uptake. Plant uptake is calculated as the quantity of nutrient required to produce the new biomass, less the amount that can be recirculated within the plants (internal cycling).

The simulated available soil nutrient pool provides the nutritional basis for the simulated plant biomass increment, and forms the basis for two ways in which the model responds to changes in site nutrient status.

1. A direct response of plant growth to the availability of nutrients, and

2. A *site quality* response which regulates decomposition rates, plant tissue chemistry, internal cycling, root/shoot ratio and natural mortality rates.

FORCYTE provides predictions of biomass yields, forest floor biomass changes, and site nutrient status under a variety of management scenarios (rotation length, regeneration

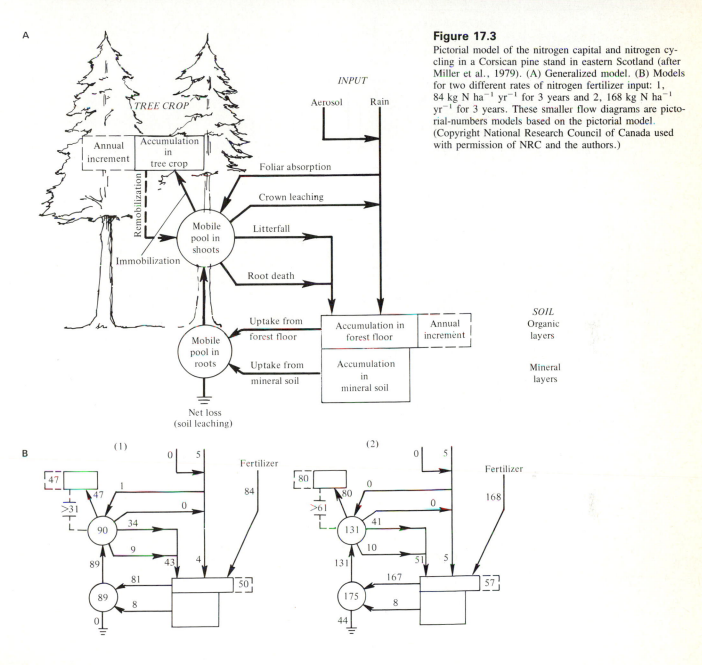

Figure 17.3

Pictorial model of the nitrogen capital and nitrogen cycling in a Corsican pine stand in eastern Scotland (after Miller et al., 1979). (A) Generalized model. (B) Models for two different rates of nitrogen fertilizer input: 1, 84 kg N ha^{-1} yr^{-1} for 3 years and 2, 168 kg N ha^{-1} yr^{-1} for 3 years. These smaller flow diagrams are pictorial-numbers models based on the pictorial model. (Copyright National Research Council of Canada used with permission of NRC and the authors.)

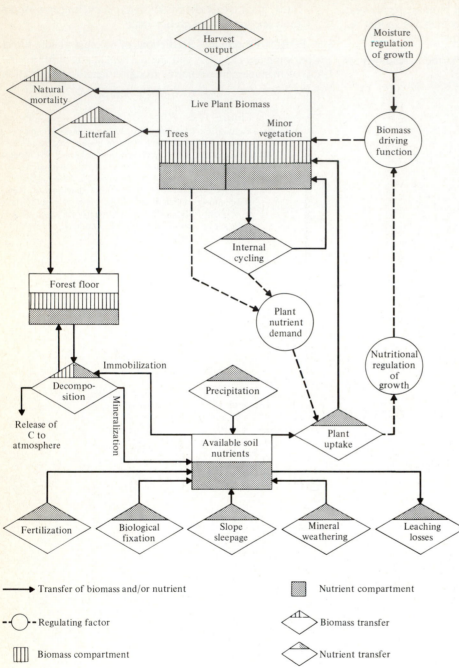

Figure 17.4
FORCYTE-10 flowchart showing the major compartments and transfer processes that are simulated. (After Kimmins and Scoullar, 1984.)

delay, thinning and fertilization regimes, and utilization levels). It also provides an economic and energy-efficiency analysis of the simulated management. The most recent edition of the model (FORCYTE–11) is capable of simulating brush competition and control, slashburning and wildfire, insect defoliation, and coppice regeneration. This version of the model can be used to simulate single, mixed species, or sequential species crops, and it has been modified for use in simulating tropical agro-forestry. FORCYTE–10 simulates the dynamics of a single nutrient. FORCYTE–11 can simulate up to 5 nutrients in a single run.

Some examples of how FORCYTE can be used to ana-

lyze the effects of various different management strategies on yield are shown in Figures 17.5 and 17.6. The former shows the model's predictions of how stem biomass and total biomass yield vary over eight successive 30-year rotations under two different management regimes. The latter summarizes the predictions of tree biomass harvested over 240 years under three different rotations, two different utilization levels and three intensities of stand management. In both figures, the predicted effects of the simulated management on soil nitrogen and soil organic matter (including logging slash, forest floor and mineral soil nitrogen and organic matter) are shown.

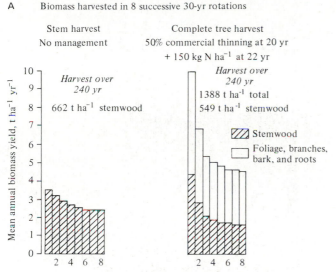

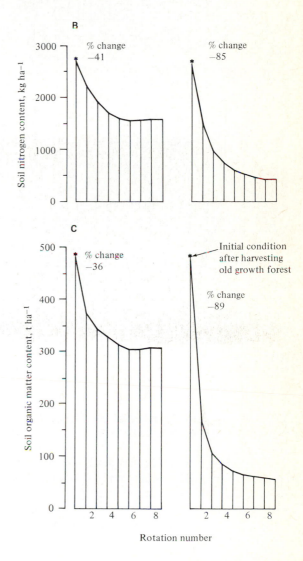

Figure 17.5
Example of the use of FORCYTE-10 to analyze the effects of two intensities of management on biomass yield and soil when the forest is harvested every 30 years. (A) Simulated biomass yield over 8 successive rotations with stem harvesting and no stand management vs. intensive stand management (thinning, fertilization) and complete tree harvesting. (B) Simulated change in soil nitrogen content (N in mineral soil, forest floor, and logging slash) over the 8 rotations. (C) Simulated change in soil organic matter (as for B). (After Kimmins and Scoullar, 1981. Used by permission of Forstliche Bundesversuchsanstalt, Vienna.)

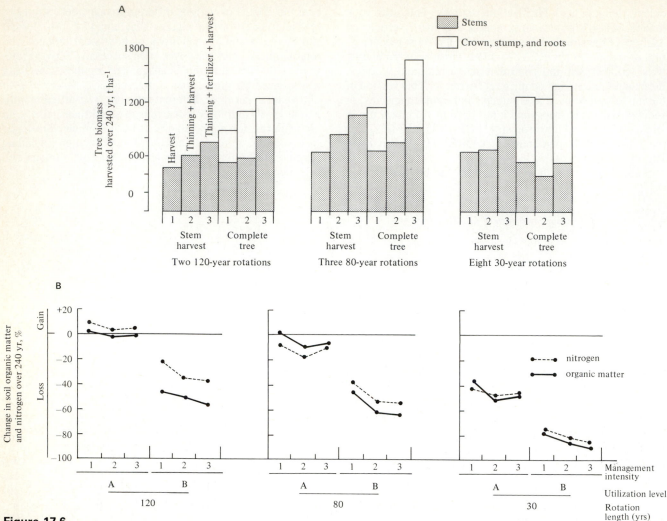

Figure 17.6

FORCYTE-10 predictions of the effects of three rotation lengths, two utilization levels and three intensities of management, on (A) biomass yield over 240 years and (B) change in soil nitrogen and organic matter (defined as in Figure 17.5). (After Kimmins and Scoullar, 1981. Used with permission of Forstliche Bundesversuchsanstalt, Vienna.)

17.5 Why People Model and the Survivorship of Models

If you ask someone who has just completed a modeling project why they did it, what they got out of it, and of what value the completed model is, you are likely to receive a wide variety of replies. This simply reflects the variety of reasons for undertaking modeling (and the success or failure of the modeling activity!).

Models may be built as predictive tools. Relatively little new may be learned in their development. Their value lies in what they can do, not in how they were made. Alternatively, models may be built as a purely heuristic exercise, a way of exploring and synthesizing what we think we know about some system and of identifying what we do not know but would like or need to know. The completed model is of little use, and many models are never used after their development has been completed. Their value is in their development, and not in the completed product.

Many different types of model were produced by ecologists and renewable resource managers during the 1960s and 1970s. These varied greatly in type (e.g., word, picture, physical, mathematical, and computer), in scope and resolution (e.g., models of physiological processes, of individual tree growth, of stand development, of ecosystem processes, or of entire ecosystems), and in purpose (e.g., to describe natural phenomena, to organize existing data, to identify information gaps and research needs, to be a teaching/learning process, or to predict future conditions and response of systems to natural perturbations and/or management).

The diverse types of mathematical and computer models that have been produced have varied notably in lifespan. Some models of restricted application have had a brief though useful existence and have not evolved. Other models or model types have been more persistent. It is of some interest to consider what characteristics have made these models persistent.

The International Biological Program (IBP) of the late 1960s and 1970s provided a major impetus to modeling of ecosystems and ecosystem processes. Large numbers of biologists spent an enormous amount of time producing very detailed conceptual models of the systems they were interested in. The computer models that resulted were highly complex, and many of them produced very acceptable simulations of parts of the real world. The modeling activity proved valuable as a learning experience, for synthesizing complex data sets, and for describing natural systems. It is therefore of interest to learn that most of the models produced have had a short lifespan. Like a shooting star, they were brilliant, but briefly so. Why?

Part of the explanation may be that many of these models had satisfied the modeling objective as soon as they were completed. They were not developed for the purpose of prediction and gaming. Many of the modelers were biologists who were more interested in describing biological systems than in predicting their response to perturbation and management. Their purpose achieved, the models fell into disuse as the modelers turned to other types of research activity. Another component of the explanation may be that adequate data were not available at the time the models were being developed. Many biologists involved in the modeling of that era became disillusioned by having to use so many imaginary parameter values in the models because of lack of empirically derived real numbers and lost faith in the computer modeling method. This problem was exacerbated by the fact that many of the biologists involved in the modeling were process-oriented scientists, who believed that the more detailed the model, the better. As a result,

many of these detailed process models required very large amounts of data for calibration. So great were the information requirements of many of the models that even today the necessary data sets do not exist. This problem has restricted the application of this type of model in resource management.

In contrast to the relatively short-lived, but complex, biological process-oriented ecosystem models, several of the relatively simple tree and stand growth models produced in the 1960s have persisted in either original or modified form. The major reason is that these models were simple, with low data requirements, and served a defined and continuing purpose: the prediction of stemwood volume production. With low-intensity forest management, these models simulated growth acceptably. However, as the need for more accurate predictions of total biomass production under a wider variety of more frequent management disturbances continued to increase, there has been a trend toward developing such models into ecosystem models.

There is now a growing use of computer gaming with models of forest growth and/or succession to examine alternative management strategies, to make predictions about future yields, and to investigate the environmental, economic, and social implications of different methods of forest management. This activity is largely based on models that are basically mensurational descriptions of past and present stemwood biomass accumulation and are short on descriptions of the ecological processes determining that growth. This raises the serious and as yet unanswered question as to how useful such models will prove to be in predicting the consequences of very intensive management for biomass production (see Kimmins, 1985).

Every type of modeling has its own particular set of advantages and limitations; probably no one type of modeling will dominate all others in the future. However, the most dramatic increase is likely to occur in computer modeling, in spite of the early setbacks this method experienced. Greatly increased power of computers, improved ecological knowledge, and the development of management-oriented but ecologically sound ecosystem models will combine to make gaming with computer models a major tool in the conservation and management of ecosystems in the future.

In conclusion, the reader is reminded *to be skeptical of the predictions of models*. External models are only as good as the conceptual models on which they are based and the data used in calibrating the model. These in turn depend on the level of our understanding of the system and the availability of appropriate data. Both of these items are generally in inadequate supply, and all models must fundamentally be considered to be ''wrong.'' Only reality is completely

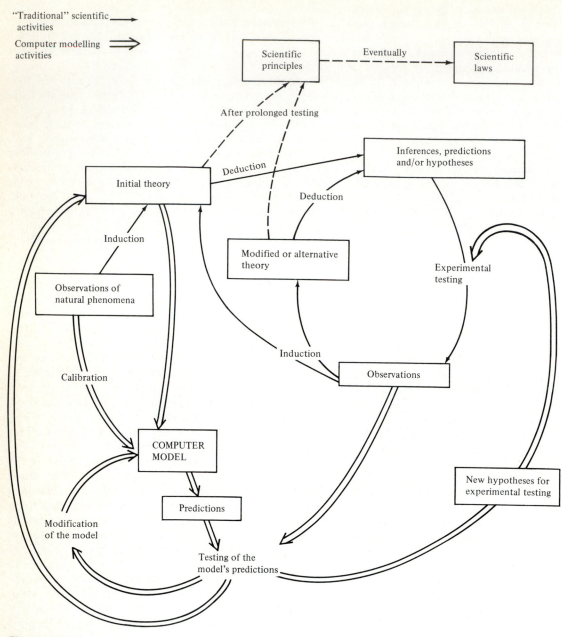

Figure 17.7
Diagram of the traditional scientific method, and the complementary role that computer modelling should play in any program of scientific research.

''right.'' This does not render models and modeling value-less. It merely requires that models be used with discretion and an explicit recognition of their strengths and weaknesses.

17.6 Modeling and the Scientific Method

Before leaving the topic of computer modeling, it is necessary to consider briefly the relationship between this contemporary scientific activity and the more traditional methods of science.

The ''traditional'' scientific method begins with observations/measurements of natural phenomena. From observation of many examples of a phenomenon one develops an initial *theory* about it by the process of induction (specific → general). From this theory one can then deduce (general → specific) certain inferences and make various predictions. From these predictions one can develop *hypotheses* that can be critically tested in an experiment. The results (observations) obtained from experimentation are used inductively to support or reject the initial theory, or to derive an alternative hypothesis for subsequent testing. If after many tests one fails to reject a theory it may be elevated to a *scientific principle*. After many years of evaluation such a principle may be accepted as a *scientific law* (Figure 17.7).

It is a feature of scientific experiments that they often tend to raise more questions than they answer, and as a consequence hypotheses tend to get increasingly narrow as a science advances. Actually, reducing a phenomenon to a series of rather narrow hypotheses is a basic requirement of the traditional scientific method. By convention, hypotheses must be capable of being falsified in a definitive experiment, and this is possible only if the hypothesis is fairly simple. Thus there is a momentum in science that tends to keep a scientist in a reductionist spiral of hypothesis → testing → modified or narrower hypothesis → testing, etc. Ultimately, this is the only way of advancing knowledge of the details of a natural phenomenon. However, the ''traditional'' scientific method has a problem. It may tend to encourage analytical reductionism to the exclusion of synthesis and integration. Unless there is a mechanism to integrate the results of reductionist science, we may fail to achieve our original objective of explaining natural phenomena. Computer modeling can provide such a mechanism. Figure 17.7 shows the complementary role that computer modeling should play in the scientific method, and how it can prevent a research program from getting trapped in a reductionist spiral by integrating the results from many experiments and relating them back to the initial theory.

17.7 Summary

The goal of science is to describe and understand our environment, and scientific knowledge can be used to predict the future conditions in the world's ecosystems and the impacts of our management on these ecosystems. As knowledge expands and our understanding of the components of the ecosystem improves, it becomes necessary for individual scientists to focus their attention on increasingly narrow subcomponents thereof. This tendency is encouraged by the Scientific Method and is the *modus operandi* of the traditional scientific disciplines. Unfortunately, while this trend does increase our knowledge of the subcomponents and processes of a system, it does not always contribute to our understanding of the system as a whole. There is a need for a branch of science that focuses on the system as a whole and facilitates the integration of the parts. Ecology provides this focus, but there is a need for a mechanism by which to examine complex ecological systems and to integrate our rapidly increasing knowledge thereof. Modeling, especially in conjunction with computers, provides such a mechanism.

Modeling is a very ordinary activity indulged in to some extent by all humans. There are many different types of model, from our private thoughts, through pictures, words, and three-dimensional physical representations, to mathematical expressions. It is the mathematical expression implemented on a computer, that most people think of as modeling: the computer model.

Computer models come in two major varieties: (1) those that take advantage of the power and convenience of certain mathematical techniques, but thereby compromise to some extent the accuracy of the biological description in the model, and (2) those that sacrifice mathematical elegance and computational efficiency in order to obtain the best description of the biological attributes of the system being modeled. The user must judge which is the more useful approach for any particular application, and a combination may prove to be the best. The recent trend in model evolution has been toward accurate biological representation.

Irrespective of the approach taken, models can be used for various purposes in ecology and resource management.

1. They can be used to provide a description of an ecosystem, integrating and synthesizing large data sets in a way that cannot be achieved by any other method.
2. They can be developed as a learning activity, for the purpose of exploring our knowledge of a system, identifying information gaps, and suggesting future lines of research.

3. They can be used to make predictions about future states of a system, with and without management treatments.

In the past decade, many ecosystem models of the detailed biological-process type have been produced, largely serving the first two purposes. Building on earlier work in the 1960s, many simple forest growth (i.e., tree growth) models were developed in the 1970s to serve the third objective. Few of these provided an explicit description of the ecosystem, but in the early 1980s several models appeared that predict tree growth within the context of ecosystem processes and other ecosystem components. These promise to provide a very useful framework for integrating ecological information with management and economic considerations to investigate the ecological and economic implications of alternative management strategies. As the power of computers grows over the next few years, computer modeling probably will and certainly should become a commonplace tool of ecologists and resource managers. The greatest contributions of computer modeling may come from those models that are specifically developed for the purposes of gaming to investigate the response of ecosystems to perturbations in general and the effects of our management in particular.

18.1 Introduction

As the human population continues to grow, material and energy resources that are renewable will become of paramount importance to society. The cost of nonrenewable resources will rise at an increasing rate because of their increasing scarcity, until many of them become uneconomic. The cost of renewable resources, on the other hand, will rise more slowly because of their continuing availability. As a consequence, their relative value will continue to increase, as will society's concern for their renewability. This will require a better definition of just what we mean by *renewable* and *nonrenewable*, and an improved understanding of the determinants of resource *renewability*. This final chapter presents definitions of these terms and, by way of example, applies them to the management of forest resources.

18.2 Renewability of Resources

What is the fundamental difference between renewable and nonrenewable resources? These two terms are used commonly, but rarely is their exact meaning defined.

Implicit in the contemporary use of the term *renewable resource* is the assumption that the resource is inherently renewable: that it will renew itself, come what may. Governments have Ministries of Renewable Resources, and universities have Departments of Renewable Resource Management. These are organizations concerned with activities such as forestry, fisheries, agriculture and wildlife which deal with biological resources that are commonly assumed to be, by their very nature, renewable. In contrast, the term *nonrenewable resource* is, by tradition, used to refer to deposits of fossil fuels and mineral materials such as coal and copper: nonliving materials that are considered to be irreplaceable. Implicit in the classification of resources as renewable or nonrenewable is whether or not the resource is living or nonliving; a direct connection is made between *living* and *renewable*.

In contrast to the foregoing usages of these terms, I would submit that the difference between the two types of resource is *not* a direct function of whether or not the resource is living or nonliving: that in fact *renewable* and *nonrenewable* are socioeconomic terms which do not accurately reflect the biological or nonbiological nature of a resource. A renewable resource is basically one that can be restored to the point of reuse after a period of time that is within our current economic or social planning time scale, or which is renewed at a rate that renders investment in its renewal economically attractive. Resources not meeting these criteria would be classified as nonrenewable.

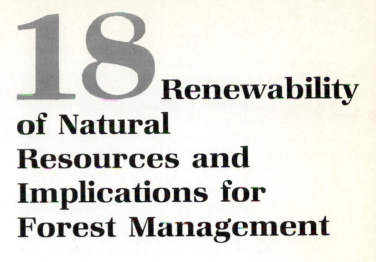

18 Renewability of Natural Resources and Implications for Forest Management

A. Traditionally Renewable Resources

Consider first a classically renewable resource: the forest. Forests are renewed by the biological process of photosynthesis at a rate that generally places the renewal period well within our contemporary time scale. *Eucalyptus* plantations in some tropical countries can reach a height of 25 m in 5 years. They can be managed on rotations as short as 4 years and are therefore not much different from an agricultural crop. Similarly, red alder on the west coast of North America can reach a height of 10 m in about 5 years on some sites. Where there is a market for red alder, it constitutes an eminently renewable resource, attaining exceptionally high rates of biomass accumulation over its first 10–15 years and outgrowing its coniferous competitors for about 35 years. *Tree farming* is indeed an appropriate term for such crops.

Douglas-fir, another western North America tree, can grow as much as 60 m in height in 100 years on very good sites, and this species is capable of producing valuable saw logs in 30–40 years on the best sites. On such land, Douglas-fir also constitutes a very renewable resource, one in which society is very willing to invest capital to assist its renewal. On a dry and infertile site, on the other hand, Douglas-fir might take more than 200 years to reach commercially valuable size. Such a timber resource begins to

475

reach the limits of renewability in the socioeconomic sense, and there is little enthusiasm to invest much in its renewal. Similarly, neither 1000-year-old redwoods in California, valued primarily as a recreational resource, nor 300-year-old oaks in France, planted for the production of very large wine casks, can be considered as renewable resources in the commonly accepted sense of this term. Although these trees are quite capable, under appropriate conditions, of reproducing the above-mentioned values, the time required to do so greatly exceeds society's current economic and/or social time scales.

A value that is not capable of being recreated in less than 1000 years (e.g., large redwoods) or even 300 years (e.g., large-diameter oak trees) is considered by most people to be nonrenewable. Therein lies the general antipathy of the public toward cutting down very large and very old trees which they perceive to be nonrenewable resources. Once cut, the social values that they provided are gone, "never" to be renewed. Certainly, if we are prepared to wait for many centuries, these values may well be recreated. Certainly, in a biological sense the resource value is probably renewable. However, it is renewable on a geological time scale, not a socioeconomic time scale, and therefore we consider it to be nonrenewable.

B. Traditionally Nonrenewable Resources

Consider now a classically nonrenewable resource: mineral deposits. These are generally formed by tectonic or erosion/solution/deposition processes over periods on a geological time scale. However, not all deposits of mineral materials are nonrenewable. Guano phosphate deposits on islands off the west coast of South America at dry, subtropical latitudes have been estimated to have a renewal rate of 190,000 metric tons per year, containing about 8800 metric tons of phosphorus (Hutchinson, 1950). These deposits have been extensively mined as a source of industrial phosphorous, and in this context they can be considered analogous to commercial mineral phosphate deposits elsewhere in the world which have a zero renewal rate. Although the guano deposits have been heavily exploited, they certainly represent a renewable phosphorous deposit, which, if managed properly, could be mined in perpetuity on a sustained yield basis.

Similarly, not all fossil fuels are nonrenewable, even though they have traditionally been considered as such. When we think of fossil fuels, we generally think of oil and coal, which are nonrenewable. But in countries such as Ireland and the U.S.S.R., peat is also very important. As oil becomes increasingly scarce, and/or expensive, peat will probably take its place as an important fossil fuel in several other countries, including Canada. In contrast to coal and oil, peat is being formed continuously and at a rate that makes it a renewable source of energy. If the mining were appropriately regulated, it could become a renewable, locally important, sustained-yield fossil fuel energy supply.

Thus, both living trees and nonliving material deposits may or may not be considered as a renewable resource, depending upon either how long it takes them to generate a particular socioeconomic value or how rapidly the future value of the resource is accumulated. Forests are certainly not an inherently renewable resource, and similarly not all mineral or fossil fuel deposits can be considered intrinsically nonrenewable. The difference between renewable and nonrenewable resources lies more in the rate or time of their renewal than in the physical, chemical, or biological character of the resource per se.

18.3 Nature of a Material Resource

A. Material Resources as Concentration Phenomena

Material resources can be defined as concentrations of energy or materials that are sufficiently greater than the average concentrations of these materials in the earth's crust or at the earth's surface to have value for society. The greater the difference in concentration between the resource and the average concentrations in the environment, the greater the value of that resource to society. This definition will be explained using three examples: precious and semiprecious metals, fossil carbon deposits (fossil fuels), and forests (timber) (Figure 18.1).

Most rocks contain at least a few atoms of most of the precious and semiprecious metals, but whether a particular geological deposit is a copper mine or a gold mine depends on whether or not the concentration is high enough to have economic value. Only rocks containing several percent of copper are currently of value as copper ore; rocks containing 0.005% copper are just rocks. The value of low-grade copper ore is much less than that of high-grade deposits of the same magnitude because of the greater energy (and therefore expense) required for the recovery of the metal. The exact concentration at which the rock becomes a copper resource depends upon the location and extent of the deposit, on the current costs of recovering it, and on the current market value of copper. Thus, as with renewability, the very definition of *resource* is socioeconomic rather than scientific. The dramatic rise in the value of gold in the winter of 1979–1980 resulted in old gold mines being reopened, and old gold mine tailings piles being reworked. The nonresource of yesterday became a valuable gold resource almost overnight.

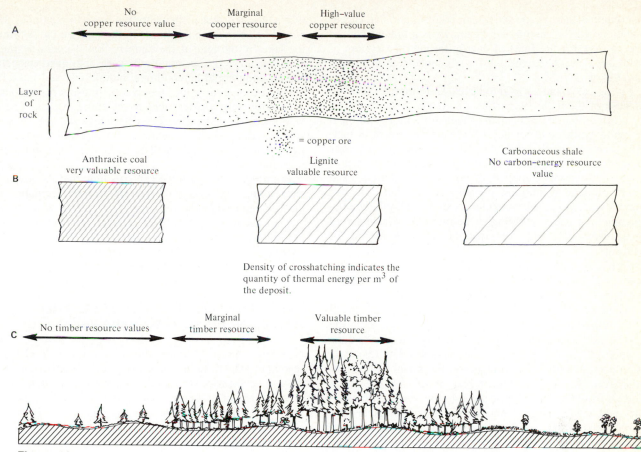

Figure 18.1
Material resources considered as concentration phenomena. (A) Copper deposits in rock. (B) Carbon deposits.
(C) Forests as a timber resource. The concentration of a material that is considered to be a resource depends upon
socioeconomic conditions and will therefore change from time to time.

Among the coals, anthracite coal is more valuable than lignite because of the higher energy content per ton and per cubic meter of anthracite. However, lignite is more valuable than carbonaceous shale, which is not considered to be a fossil fuel resource in spite of the abundant carbonaceous fossils found between the layers of rock. The concentration of carbon in carbonaceous shale is simply too low for the rock to be of value as a fuel, even though the amount of free carbon in such rocks is much greater than the average for rocks in general. Thus the value of carbonaceous deposits as a source of energy is closely related to the concentration of oxidizable carbon per ton or per cubic meter.

Most areas containing trees are capable of yielding some lumber. Even scattered small trees can be cut down and the small pieces of sawn wood that result can be used directly or glued together to yield larger pieces. However, savannah forests or open woodland are not normally considered to be timber resources because the volume of wood per hectare (i.e., the concentration of wood) is too low to make harvesting economical. Only forests with volumes per hectare greater than some threshold value are considered to be timber resources.

B. Rate of Formation of Material Resources as a Function of Energy Flux through the Resource-Forming System

A corollary of the second law of thermodynamics is that the creation and the maintenance of order in a system requires the expenditure of energy (Chapter 4). The creation of a material resource (a concentration of energy or materials) requires energy, and the rate of concentration and accumulation of both energy and chemicals is a function of the rate of flow (or the flux) of energy through the system of processes that are responsible for the concentration and accumulation.

Biological resources tend to have a short time for renewal because of the high energy flux frequently associated with the photosynthetic mechanism of their formation. Although net photosynthetic efficiency is only a few percent of incident solar energy, this still amounts to a large flux of energy in areas where the photosynthetic apparatus of primary producers is adequately supplied by moisture and nutrients, and where climatic conditions are suitable. In those circumstances where the environmental conditions inhibit the photosynthetic process, a biological resource may have a very small energy flux and, consequently, a very long time for renewal.

Similarly, most mineral deposits have a long time for renewal because the energy flux of the geochemical processes involved in their formation tends to be low.

Where both biological and large-scale geochemical mechanisms are involved in resource formation, as in the case of guano phosphate deposits, the renewal time and the resource renewability will be intermediate. The relatively rapid accumulation of phosphate on the guano islands results from the combination of phosphorus-rich water upwelling from the deep Pacific abyss (a low-energy-flux geochemical mechanism), a high-energy-flux biological food web concentration process (beginning with uptake of phosphorus by photosynthetic plankton and ending with predaceous seabirds that nest and defecate on the guano islands), and a relative lack of precipitation, which allows the phosphorus-rich feces and remains of the seabirds to accumulate on the rocky islands.

An analogous, though perhaps tongue-in-cheek, example comes from the suggestion that if the chronic pollution of Lake Erie with phosphorus in the 1960s and early 1970s had continued, the lake would have become a renewable phosphorus resource by the turn of the century. The high-energy-flux processes of mining, refining, manufacturing, and transportation (using fossil fuel energy) have brought large quantities of phosphorus from far-removed locations to the watershed of Lake Erie. There it has been used in the form of detergents, fertilizers, and other chemicals in processes that placed it in urban sewage or agricultural drainage waters, all of which flow to the lake (low-energy-flux process). Once in the lake, food chain concentration processes led to its ultimate deposition in the lake-bottom sediments (medium- to high-energy-flux process). In the early 1970s, when chronic phosphate pollution of lakes was common, it

was suggested that if this situation were to continue, there would be so much phosphorus in the mud on the bottom of the lake by the end of the century that it could be mined economically. If this pollution were continued unabated, such mining could be continued indefinitely and Lake Erie would become a giant, renewable phosphorus resource. Hopefully, this scenario will never come to pass. The development of phosphate-free detergents and the slow but steady reduction in the extent of water pollution should mean that this great lake will never be used as a phosphorus recycling facility.

From this discussion we can conclude that the lower the energy flux, the slower the rate of resource formation and the less renewable the resource.

The fundamental difference between renewable and nonrenewable material resources lies in the magnitude of the energy flux involved in their formation, not in whether the resource is biotic or abiotic per se.

18.4   How Does Our Use of Material Resources Affect Their Renewability?

If this concept of renewability is valid, it is clear that resources which have traditionally been called renewable are not necessarily so, and that resources which are generally thought of as being nonrenewable may be capable of renewal within our socioeconomic time scale. If the efficiency of the energy flux mechanism of a renewable resource is impaired, the time for renewal will be lengthened and its renewability will be diminished, possibly to a point at which it no longer constitutes a socioeconomically renewable resource. If the energy flux mechanism of a nonrenewable resource could be changed from a geochemical to a biogeochemical basis, or if the efficiency of the energy flux mechanism of a marginally renewable biotic resource could be improved, their renewal time would be reduced and they might become renewable.

The distinction between renewable and nonrenewable forests is not an absolute one. In many areas it is largely dependent upon the type of forest management employed. For example, misapplication of the otherwise legitimate practices of clearcutting and slashburning to an area of climax lithosere forest can render a renewable forest condition nonrenewable by retrogressing the area back to the early seral stage of mosses and lichens on exposed rock. On the other hand, careful harvesting of such sites can leave them in a reasonably productive condition. Fertilization of nutrient-poor soils, drainage of excessively wet sites, and careful matching of species to site can greatly improve forest productivity and convert nonrenewable forest resources into renewable ones. The quality and intensity of forest management is therefore the key.

Managers of renewable forest resources must use ecologically sound management techniques if they are to preserve or improve the renewability of the resource. Unfortunately, this has not always occurred. Deforested areas of India, Africa, and China, and recent conversion of tropical rainforest in South America and Asia are classic examples of turning renewable forests into nonrenewable forests, but some contemporary logging in developed countries also falls into this category. If forest management (referring here to the actual way the forest resource is presently being "managed," not to the theoretical definition of the term "forest management") ignores the effects of management on the ecological mechanisms of forest productivity and on the functioning of the resource, it may be no different from the utilization of nonrenewable mineral deposits—an act of exploitation conducted without any thought for the future renewal of the deposit.

18.5 Timber Mining vs. Sustained Yield Management

The profession of forestry has evolved in one form or another at various times and places in our cultural history. In every case, the motivating force behind its development has been to sustain the supply of a variety of desired goods and services from forests. The Ford–Robertson (1971) definition of forestry reflects the same notion of sustained provision of forest products or nonmaterial values: "generally, a profession embracing the science, business and art of creating, conserving and managing forests and forest lands for the continuing use of their resources, material or other." It is not surprising, therefore, to find the classical sustained-yield timber management concept deeply entrenched in the philosophy of forest land management in North America and elsewhere in the world.

The concept of *sustained yield* is the keystone of most modern forest management. Implicit in the term is the assumption that the forest is a renewable resource. However, this assumption should be made *explicit* because many forests constitute a patchwork of renewable and nonrenewable forest conditions. The assumption should be tested for its validity in any particular situation. Under conditions of renewability, the sustained-yield concept may be legitimate because the socioeconomic values are eminently renewable. However, in the nonrenewable condition, "timber management" is tantamount to *timber mining:* that is, the use of

socioeconomic values accumulated in the standing crop over a long period of time, with no prospect of renewal to the point of reuse over the contemporary socioeconomic time scale. To pretend that we are practicing sustained yield in such forests is deluding ourselves.

Ecologically sound management of forestland for timber production, in harmony with wildlife, fish, water, recreation, and other resource values, would seem to be an appropriate land use for the majority of the forests which truly constitute renewable resources. Certainly, there will be frequent conflicts between these alternative resources, but the major question is how to make timber production compatible with the other land uses, not whether timber production should be an objective of land management. On the other hand, the decision to undertake timber production in forests that are not renewable in a socioeconomic sense (i.e., timber mining) requires a much more critical analysis. The determination of whether or not timber mining is desirable must depend upon a comparison of the long-term socioeconomic costs and benefits, and the conclusion may frequently be reached not to harvest the timber.

There can be no a priori conclusion that timber mining is intrinsically a social evil. In some cases, the benefits from timber mining may outweigh the costs, giving a net benefit. For example, extensive high-elevation clearcut logging, which certainly has the potential to be a good example of timber mining in some subalpine forest environments, can result in the expansion of subalpine meadows, with significant long-term benefits for mountain recreation. It is certainly necessary to give serious consideration to the implications of such forest denudation for streams, fisheries, avalanche hazard, wildlife, and the future supply of timber, but in some situations a limited extension of alpine and subalpine plant communities might be both acceptable and desirable. In many other cases, such high-elevation forest removal would undoubtedly be totally unacceptable. Each case would have to be examined on its own merits after an appropriate analysis.

18.6 Sustained Yield and the Concept of Ecological Rotation

As noted above, a fundamental tenet of sustained yield is that the resource is renewable: that we can harvest a forest with justifiable expectations that in the foreseeable future we will once again be able to enjoy the timber, wildlife, watershed protection, recreational, and other values generated by forest cover.

However, there are many forests being harvested today or scheduled for harvesting in the future under the banner of sustained yield which cannot legitimately be considered as a renewable resource. Let me explain by way of a discussion of the concept of *ecological rotation*.

Forest crop rotations (the length of time between successive harvests) can be calculated in a number of ways. A *technical rotation* is that period required to produce a specified type of product: a certain size of log or a log with the outer layers free of branch knots. An *economic rotation* may be the period over which mean annual return on investment is maximized. A *maximum volume rotation* is the period over which mean annual increment is maximized. An *ecological rotation,* on the other hand, would be the period required for a given site managed with a given technology to return to the predisturbance ecological condition (Figure 18.2). We will discuss ecological rotation in terms of ecological succession and site nutrient capital.

A. Succession and Ecological Rotation

Whenever a forest is harvested, the site is reverted to an earlier stage of the successional sequence. This is often both ecologically sound and economically desirable in order to favor a particular species, but if the disturbance is excessive it can be disastrous in terms of future forest productivity.

Figure 18.3 compares the successional consequences of a single high degree of logging disturbance with a moderate degree of logging disturbance, the latter being repeated with a frequency higher than that for an ecological rotation.

The earlier stages of lithic xeroseres are frequently prolonged and unproductive of trees, so it is easy to designate the high degree of disturbance as undesirable. Conversely, the moderate degree of disturbance may be both deliberate and desirable in the first rotation. Unfortunately, if it is repeated at intervals shorter than the time required for complete successional recovery, such a disturbance can result in a gradual retrogression of the area to successively earlier seral conditions, and ultimately this can result in the same nonproductive condition as is produced by the single high degree of disturbance. Thus, a technique which produces moderate disturbance that appears to be quite acceptable over the first one or two rotations may eventually produce undesirable results if not coupled to a rotation of appropriate length (i.e., a successional-recovery ecological rotation).

In terms of the renewability of resources, the single severe disturbance depicted in Figure 18.3 immediately impairs the energy flux through the system, rendering the resources nonrenewable. The moderate disturbance with a short rotation initially sustains the energy flux, changing only the species involved, but as successively earlier seral

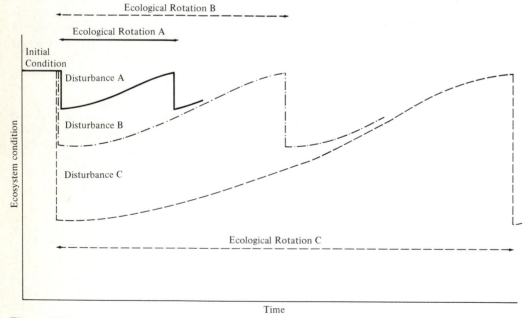

Figure 18.2
Graphical representation of the concept of ecological rotation—period required for ecosystem to recover to original condition. (Based on Kimmins, 1974.)

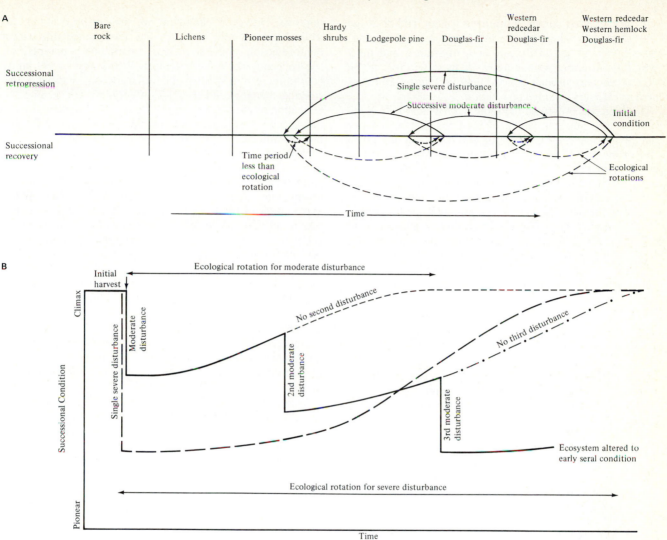

Figure 18.3

The concept of ecological rotation expressed in terms of successional retrogression and recovery. The figure depicts the successional consequences of either a single excessive disturbance or a series of successive, moderate harvesting disturbances in conjunction with rotations equal to or less than the ecological rotation. (A) Successional retrogression and postdisturbance recovery in a hypothetical lithic xerarch succession at low elevation in southern coastal British Columbia. (B) The same events expressed graphically.

stages are created, energy flow is decreased, and this treatment eventually produces the same effect as the severe disturbance.

B. Site Nutrient Capital and Ecological Rotation

As a second example of the concept of ecological rotation, consider the depletion of the site nutrient capital that can accompany harvesting. Among other things, trees need certain nutrients in certain proportions in order to grow. The forest has a certain capital of these nutrients, which exists as a dynamic equilibrium between a variety of inputs and outputs. Harvesting inevitably results in some depletion of the site nutrient capital through losses in harvested materials, as a result of disruption of nutrient retention mechanisms, as a result of increased output in drainage waters, and/or as the result of such postlogging site treatments as slashburning. These losses are gradually replaced, of course, and for a given loss of nutrients on a given site there will be a given nutrient recovery period, which might be referred to as the *nutrient-recovery ecological rotation.*

This idea was presented in Figure 5.17 which showed the effect on site nutrient capital of rotations that are shorter than the nutrient-recovery rotation and the effect of a given level of harvest depletion and rotation length on sites that vary in their rate of recovery. The length of the recovery period is a function of two things: the degree of site nutrient depletion accompanying harvesting and the rate of replacement of the losses. On a site receiving nutrients in seepage water or having large reserves of readily weatherable soil minerals, even substantial losses of these nutrients may be replaced rapidly. On a site with very slow replacement and/or poorly developed nutrient accumulation mechanisms, even a small loss may require a substantial period for replacement.

18.7   Nonrenewable Aspects of the Forest Ecosystem

The discussion so far has focused on the renewability of resources in terms of rates of accumulation of materials. This is not the only aspect of the renewability of forest ecosystems.

A. Genetic Constitution of the Ecosystem

One of the most important nonrenewable aspects of a forest ecosystem is the gene pool. The genotypes of the plants, animals, and microbes that constitute the biocoenose have been fashioned by millions of years of natural selection, which has adapted organisms to the wide variety of physical and biotic environments that exist in any area. As a result, organisms are able to acquire and accumulate biomass in virtually all types of environment present on the earth.

If particular genotypes are lost from the gene pool, they may never be recreated. Although there is a finite possibility that recreation of a particular genotype could occur naturally by means of natural selection operating on a similar genetic population, this possibility is small and the process would probably require a very long time, especially for long-lived organism such as trees. Human beings may be able to speed up the process of recreating particular genotypes or generating new genotypes by artificial selection and breeding, and as the new science of genetic engineering develops, the possibilities of recreating lost genotypes will

improve. However, based on our present knowledge and technologies, it does not seem that it will be feasible within the foreseeable future to recreate a particular genotype if all similar genotypes have been lost. We simply do not know how to recreate a species once it has become extinct. Considering this fact and the lack of certainty concerning the recreation of specific genotypes from similar genetic stocks, the genetic constitution of the biocoenose must, for the present time, be considered to be nonrenewable.

Without appropriately adapted genotypes, ecosystems will not function normally, and possibly not at all. It is of paramount importance that we place top priority on conserving our genetic resources whenever we are planning the exploitation of biological resources. Representative examples of all major types of ecosystem should be set aside in *ecological reserves,* which must be large enough to encompass the local variation of genotypes and to ensure the survival of the genetic diversity (cf Figure 14.24). These reserves will serve as future gene banks for plant, animal, and microbial populations, and will act as long term benchmarks against which we can make future measurements of the long-term impacts of our resource management. Fortunately, programs to establish ecological reserves were set up in many countries in the 1970s, but many more must be created if we are to conserve the world's genetic inheritance.

Timber managers should be particularly concerned with the conservation of tree genotypes. Seed collection and storage, together with gene banks of vegetatively reproduced trees in tree orchards, can make a significant contribution to this genetic conservation, but these mechanisms cannot substitute for having significant areas (perhaps 1% of the forest area) set aside permanently in genetic–ecological reserves. It is the responsibility of professional foresters to ensure that this is done.

B. The Soil Resource

Trees, fish, and terrestrial wildlife are the major biotic crops yielded by forest ecosystems. The basic resource from which these crops develop is the physical environment: the soil and local climate. Except in extreme environments, the latter is neither greatly nor permanently influenced by local forest management, and although there are fears that we may be altering global climatic patterns, from a local perspective one can consider that, like solar energy, local climate is unaffected by resource use (of course, microclimates can be considerably, although temporarily, altered). For soil, the situation is quite different.

Soil is a complex phenomenon that results from the action of physical, chemical, and biological processes acting on soil parent material over a period of time. The time required to produce a given type of soil is highly variable, depending as it does on climate, vegetation, animals, topography, and the nature of the parent material. Some types of soil form relatively rapidly; most do not. Mass wasting of soil that leaves only soil parent material can reduce the productivity of a site for a particular tree species for an extended period (several decades or even several centuries). Where bedrock is exposed, it may be many tens of thousands of years before the original productivity of the site is restored. Thus in many situations soil can be considered as a nonrenewable resource.

The renewability of the soil resource is highly variable. Nitrogen-fixing trees such as red alder can grow very satisfactorily on exposed parent material that is devoid of nitrogen but in which weathering of primary minerals provides an adequate supply of mineral nutrients. In this case the soil could be considered renewable. The same substrate may be totally unsuitable for a later successional species because of the lack of nitrogen and organic matter. The renewability of the soil in terms of the productivity of a particular tree species will thus depend upon the nutritional and moisture adaptations of the species involved. Many tree species grow best in relatively well developed soils, and for these species the soils on most sites can be considered to be nonrenewable. Because of this it seems most appropriate to consider soil in general as a nonrenewable resource which must therefore be conserved in order to maintain the renewability of the plant and animal crops that it produces.

18.8 Concluding Statement

The evolutionary record suggests that only those species that adapt to their changing environment and exist in harmony with that environment survive the test of time. In our recent past, the human species has adopted the alternative strategy of adapting their environment to suit their own changing needs. Rather than balancing our numbers to match the carrying capacity of our niche, we are expanding our niche and increasing the carrying capacity of the environment for our species by the application of technology. We are now discovering, however, that there is an ultimate limit to how far we can go in this direction without very undesirable long-term consequences, and that the time has come to start modifying our behavior to render it more compatible with the environment. This requires a change in attitudes toward our environment and resources, a recognition of the consequences of the current unbridled expropriation of the niches of other organisms, a clear identification of the

maximum level of ecosystem productivity that is compatible with long-term maintenance of ecosystem function, and the acceptance and application of ecologically sound behavior patterns and management practices. Among these changes is the need to learn how to preserve and improve the natural renewability of resources, and how to classify forest resources according to their renewability.

In these days of environmental awareness, the profession of forestry is under increasing scrutiny from a critical public. Areas of nonrenewable forests, which are our heritage from past logging and "site protection treatments" that proved to be inappropriate for the particular site, stand as a mute testimony that in some areas our expectations of sustained yield have been overly optimistic. In some parts of the world, foresters have lost a lot of their public credibility, and if they are to retain their current role as decision makers in the forestry domain, it is important that they do not claim to be practicing sustained yield forestry when they are not. It is important that they be able to demonstrate that sustained-yield management is an environmentally sound way of managing renewable forest resources, and restrict the concept to forests where this is possible. Harvesting of nonrenewable forests almost certainly constitutes timber mining, and this should be made explicit. Timber mining is not necessarily an inappropriate management goal, however. Its danger for the forestry profession is not inherent in the practice itself, but only when it occurs consciously or unconsciously under the guise of sustained yield. To do so only further diminishes the credibility of foresters in the eyes of the public and the scientific community.

Much of traditional economics is concerned with expanding economies, with growth, and with maximizing short-term returns on investment. In this context, economics and ecology are dancing to different tunes. However, economics in its broadest sense is homologous to ecology; it is a branch of human ecology in that it studies the interactions and exchange of energy and materials between individuals in socioeconomic systems. Conversely, ecology might be considered to be the economics of the environment, in that it is concerned with the interactions and exchange of energy and materials between individuals in ecological systems.

The human race is as much involved with ecology in its day-to-day existence as is any other species of animal, and, together with other species, is destined to adjust to the environment or ultimately succumb in the evolutionary struggle. It appears high time that economics and ecology walk the same road, and that an ecological approach be adopted for all aspects of human activity.

Nowhere is this more true than in the management of the world's diminishing forest resources.

Appendix A: Scientific and Common Names of Plant Species

Scientific Name	Common Name	Life Form
Abies alba Mill.	Silver fir	Tree, evergreen conifer
Abies amabilis (Dougl.) Forbes	Pacific silver fir	Tree, evergreen conifer
Abies balsamea (L.) Mill.	Balsam fir	Tree, evergreen conifer
Abies concolor (Gord. & Glend.) Lindl	White fir	Tree, evergreen conifer
Abies fraseri (Pursh.) Poir	Fraser fir	Tree, evergreen conifer
Abies lasiocarpa (Hook.) Nutt.	Subalpine fir	Tree, evergreen conifer
Abies magnifica A. Murr.	California red fir	Tree, evergreen conifer
Acacia cornigera Willd.	Bull's horn acacia	Tree, evergreen broadleaf
Acer circinatum Pursh.	Vine maple	Tree, deciduous broadleaf
Acer glabrum Torr.	Rocky Mountain maple	Tree, deciduous broadleaf
Acer grandidentatum Nutt.	Bigtooth maple, canyon maple	Tree, deciduous broadleaf
Acer japonicum Thunb.	Japanese maple	Tree, deciduous broadleaf
Acer macrophyllum Pursh.	Bigleaf maple	Tree, deciduous broadleaf
Acer pseudoplatanus L.	Sycamore	Tree, deciduous broadleaf
Acer rubrum L.	Red maple	Tree, deciduous broadleaf
Acer saccharum Marsh.	Sugar maple	Tree, deciduous broadleaf
Achillea lanulosa (Nutt.) Piper	Yarrow	Herb, forb
Adenostoma fasciculatum Hook & Arn.	Chamise	Shrub, evergreen
Aesculus mollissima	Chinese chestnut	Tree, deciduous broadleaf
Allium chamaemoly L.	Wild onion	Herb, forb
Alnus rubra Bong.	Red alder	Tree, deciduous broadleaf
Alnus sinuata (Regel) Rydb.	Sitka alder	Tree, deciduous broadleaf
Ammophila arenaria (L.) Link.	Marram grass, beachgrass	Herb, grass
Araucaria spp. Jussieu	Southern pine	Tree, evergreen conifer
Arbutus arizonica (Gray) Sarg.	Arizona madrone	Tree, evergreen broadleaf
Aster canadensis O. Ktze	Horseweed	Herb, forb
Bellis annua L.	Daisy	Herb, forb
Betula nigra L.	River Birch	Tree, deciduous broadleaf
Calamagrostis rubescens Buckl.	Pinegrass	Herb, grass
Callitris spp. Ventenat	Cypress pine	Tree, evergreen conifer
Calluna vulgaris Salisb.	Heather	Shrub, evergreen
Ceanothus spp. L.	Ceanothus	Shrub, deciduous/evergreen
Clematis L.	Clematis	Climbing vine

Scientific Name	Common Name	Life Form
Cornus spp. L.	Dogwood	Tree, deciduous broadleaf
Cryptomeria japonica (L.f) Don	Sugi	Tree, evergreen conifer
Cupressus macrocarpa Hartw.	Monterey cypress	Tree, evergreen conifer
Dicksonia spp.	Tree ferns	Tree, evergreen
Dryas drummondii Richards	Yellow mountain avens	Creeping shrub
Encelia californica Nutt.	Encelia	Shrub
Epilobium angustifolium L.	Fireweed	Herb, forb
Eucalyptus spp. Benth. & Hook.	Mallee, eucalyptus	Tree, evergreen broadleaf
Eucalyptus marginata Sm.	Jarrah	Tree, evergreen broadleaf
Fagus grandifolia Ehrh.	American beech	Tree, deciduous broadleaf
Fagus sylvatica L.	European beech	Tree, deciduous broadleaf
Festuca ovina L.	Sheep fescue	Herb, grass
Fraxinus excellsior Bove ex DC.	European ash	Tree, deciduous broadleaf
Gaultheria shallon Pursh.	Salal	Shrub, evergreen
Hedera helix L.	Ivy	Climbing shrub, evergreen
Hyoseris scabra Pourr.		Herb, forb
Hypericum perforatum L.	Klamath weed, St. John's Wort	Herb, forb
Juglans nigra L.	Black walnut	Tree, deciduous broadleaf
Juniper deppeana Steud.	Alligator juniper	Shrub, evergreen
Kalmia angustifolium L.	Sheep laurel	Shrub, evergreen
Kalmia polifolia Wang	Swamp laurel	Shrub, evergreen
Lantana camara L.	Lantana	Shrub, evergreen
Larix laricina (Du Roi) K. Koch	Tamarack eastern larch	Tree, deciduous conifer
Larix leptolepis Hort. ex Endl.	Japanese larch	Tree, deciduous conifer
Larix occidentalis Nutt.	Western larch	Tree, deciduous conifer
Ledum groenlandicum Oeder	Labrador tea	Shrub, evergreen
Liquidambar styraciflua L.	Sweetgum	Tree, deciduous broadleaf
Liriodendron tulipifera L.	Yellow-poplar	Tree, deciduous broadleaf
Malus diversifolia (Bong.) Roem = *Malus fusca* (Raf.) Schneid	Western crab apple Oregon crab apple	Tree, deciduous broadleaf
Malus pumila (L.) Mill. = *Malus sylvestris* (L.) Mill.	Common crab apple Common apple	Tree, deciduous broadleaf
Metrosideros polymorpha Gaud.	Ohia	Tree, evergreen broadleaf
Myrica gale L.	Sweet gale	Shrub, deciduous
Nothofagus spp. Blume	Southern beech	Tree, deciduous broadleaf
Nothofagus fusca Oerst.	Red beech	Tree, deciduous broadleaf
Opuntia spp. Mill.	Prickly pear cactus	Succulent thorny
Oryza sativa L.	Rice	Herb, grass
Persea americana Mill.	Avocado, alligator-pear	Tree, evergreen broadleaf
Physiocarpus malvaceus (Greene) Kuntze	Mallow ninebark	Shrub, deciduous
Picea abies (L.) Karst.	Norway spruce	Tree, evergreen conifer
Picea engelmannii Parry	Engelmann spruce	Tree, evergreen conifer
Picea glauca (Moench) Voss	White spruce	Tree, evergreen conifer
Picea mariana (Mill.) B.S.P.	Black spruce	Tree, evergreen conifer
Picea sitchensis (Bong.) Carr.	Sitka spruce	Tree, evergreen conifer
Pinus aristata Engelm.	Bristlecone pine, foxtail pine	Tree, evergreen conifer
Pinus ayacahnita Ehreub.	Mexican white pine	Tree, evergreen conifer
Pinus banksiana Lamb.	Jack pine	Tree, evergreen conifer
Pinus cembra L.	Swiss stone pine	Tree, evergreen conifer
Pinus cembroides Zucc.	Mexican pinyon pine	Tree, evergreen conifer
Pinus contorta Dougl.	Lodgepole pine	Tree, evergreen conifer
Pinus densiflora Sieb. & Zucc.	Japanese red pine	Tree, evergreen conifer
Pinus edulis Engelm.	Pinyon pine	Tree, evergreen conifer
Pinus elliottii Engelm.	Slash pine	Tree, evergreen conifer
Pinus lecophylla Schiede & Deppe	Chihuahua pine	Tree, evergreen conifer
Pinus monticola Dougl.	Western white pine	Tree, evergreen conifer

Scientific Name	Common Name	Life Form
Pinus nigra Arnold	Corsican pine	Tree, evergreen conifer
Pinus palustris Mill.	Long leaf pine	Tree, evergreen conifer
Pinus ponderosa Dougl.	Ponderosa pine	Tree, evergreen conifer
Pinus radiata D. Don	Monterey pine	Tree, evergreen conifer
Pinus resinosa Ait.	Red pine	Tree, evergreen conifer
Pinus rigida Mill.	Pitch pine	Tree, evergreen conifer
Pinus strobus L.	Eastern white pine	Tree, evergreen conifer
Pinus sylvestris L.	Scotch (Scots) pine	Tree, evergreen conifer
Pinus taeda L.	Loblolly pine	Tree, evergreen conifer
Plagiomnium insigne Mitt.	Toothed mnium	Moss
Polygonum bistortoides Pursh.	Snakeweed	Herb, forb
Polypodium polypochoides	Polypody fern, licorice fern	Herb, fern
Polytrichum juniperinum Hedw.	Hair-cap moss	Moss
Populus deltoides Bartr.	Eastern cottonwood	Tree, deciduous broadleaf
Populus nigra var *italica* Muench.	Lombardy poplar	Tree, deciduous broadleaf
Populus tremuloides Michx.	Quaking aspen	Tree, deciduous broadleaf
Populus trichocarpa Torr. and Gray	Black cottonwood	Tree, deciduous broadleaf
Prosopis farata L.	Mesquite	Shrub, tree, deciduous broadleaf
Prunus spp. L.	Cherry	Tree, deciduous broadleaf
Prunus serotina Ehrh.	Black cherry	Tree, deciduous broadleaf
Pseudotsuga menziesii (Mirb.) Franco.	Douglas-fir	Tree, evergreen conifer
Pteridium aquilinum (L.) Kuhn	Bracken fern	Herb, fern
Purshia tridentata (Pursh.) DC	Bitter brush, Antelope-brush	Shrub, evergreen
Quercus spp. L.	Oak	Tree, deciduous broadleaf
Quercus arizonica Sarg.	Arizona white oak	Tree, deciduous broadleaf
Quercus borealis (Marsh.) = *Quercus rubra* L.	Northern red oak	Tree, deciduous broadleaf
Quercus emoryi Torr.	Emory oak	Tree, deciduous broadleaf
Quercus gambelii Nutt.	Gambel oak	Tree, deciduous broadleaf
Quercus hypoleucoides A. Camus	Silverleaf oak	Tree, deciduous broadleaf
Quercus lyrata Walt.	Overcup oak	Tree, deciduous broadleaf
Quercus oblongifolia Torr.	Mexican blue oak	Tree, deciduous broadleaf
Quercus petraea	Sessile oak	Tree, deciduous broadleaf
Quercus reticulata Humb & Bonpl = *Quercus rugosa* Nee	Live oak, netleaf oak	Tree, evergreen broadleaf
Quercus rubra L.	Northern red oak	Tree, deciduous broadleaf
Ranunculus testiculatus Crantz	Hornseed buttercup	Herb, forb
Rhus spp. L.	Sumac	Shrub/tree, deciduous broadleaf
Robinia neomexicana Gray	New Mexico locust	Tree, deciduous broadleaf
Robinia pseudoacacia L.	Black locust	Tree, deciduous broadleaf
Rubus spectabilis Pursh.	Salmonberry	Shrub, deciduous
Salix spp. L.	Willow	Tree (or shrub) deciduous broadleaf
Secale cereale L.	Winter rye	Herb, grass
Sequoia sempervirens (D. Don) Endl.	Redwood	Tree, evergreen coniferous
Sheperdia canadensis (L.) Nutt.	Soapberry	Shrub, deciduous
Solidago spp. L.	Goldenrod	Herb, forb
Spirea douglasii Hook.	Hardhack	Shrub, deciduous
Taraxacum officinale Weber	Dandelion	Herb, forb
Taxus brevifolia Nutt.	Pacific yew	Tree, evergreen conifer
Taxus canadensis Marsh.	Canada yew	Tree, evergreen conifer
Thuja occidentalis L.	Northern white cedar	Tree, evergreen conifer
Thuja plicata Donn.	Western redcedar	Tree, evergreen conifer
Thuja standishii (Gord.) Carr.	Japanese arbor-vitae	Tree, evergreen conifer

Scientific Name	Common Name	Life Form
Tsuga canadensis (L.) Carr.	Eastern hemlock	Tree, evergreen conifer
Tsuga heterophylla (Raf.) Sarg.	Western hemlock	Tree, evergreen conifer
Ulmus americana L.	American elm	Tree, deciduous broadleaf
Viburnum edule (Michx.) Raf.	High-bush cranberry	Shrub, deciduous

Appendix B: Common and Scientific Names of Animals

Common Name	Scientific Name	Type of Animal
Alaska black fish	*Dallia pectoralis* (Bean)	fish
Ant	*Pseudomyrex ferruginea* (Smith)	insect
Army worm, nutgrass	*Spodoptera exempta* (Walk.)	insect
Badger (e.g. American badger)	*Taxidea taxus* (Schreber)	mammal
Bears	Ursidae	mammal
Black bear	*Ursus americanus* (Pallas)	mammal
Grizzly bear	*Ursus arctos* (L.)	mammal
Beaver	*Castor canadensis* (Kuhl)	mammal
Budmoth, grey larch	*Zeiraphera griseana* (Hubner)	insect
Budworm, spruce	*Choristoneura fumiferana* (Clemens)	insect
Butterfly, monarch	*Danaus plexippus* (L.)	insect
Caribou, barren-ground	*Rangifer tarandus groenlandicus* (L.)	mammal
Caribou, mountain	*Rangifer tarandus montanus* (Seton)	mammal
Chalcid, golden (parasitic wasp (Aphelinid))	*Aphytis chrysomphali*	insect
Cockroaches	Blattidae	insect
Cougar	*Felis concolor* (L.)	mammal
Cowbird, brown-headed	*Molothrus ater* (Boddaert)	bird
Cowbird, giant	*Scaphidura oryzivora*	bird
Coyotes	*Canis latrans* (Say)	mammal
Cuckoo	*Cuculus canorus*	bird
Deer, black-tailed	*Odocoileus hemionus colombianus* (Richardson)	mammal
Deer, rocky mountain mule	*Odocoileus hemionus hemionus* (Rafinesque)	mammal
Deer, white-tailed	*Odocoileus virginianus* (Zimmermann)	mammal
Dove, rock	*Columba livia* (Gmelin)	bird
Elk	*Cervus elaphus canadensis* (Erxleben)	mammal
Fisher	*Martes pennanti* (Erxleben)	mammal
Fly, fruit	*Drosophila melanogaster* (Meigen.)	insect
Gophers, pocket		mammal
Botta's	*Thomomys bottae* (Eydoux and Gervais)	
Mountain	*Thomomys talpoides* (Richardson)	
Plains	*Geomys bursarius* (Shaw)	
Yellow faced	*Pappogeomys castanops* (Baird)	

Common Name	Scientific Name	Type of Animal
Goshawk	*Accipiter gentilis* (L.)	bird
Grebe, western	*Aechmophorus occidentalis* (Lawrence)	bird
Grouse, red	*Lagopus lagopus scoticus* (L.)	bird
Grouse, ruffed	*Bonasa umbellus* (L.)	bird
Grouse, sharp-tailed	*Tympanuchus phasianellus* (L.)	bird
Grouse, spruce	*Canachites canadensis* (L.)	bird
Grouse, blue	*Dendragopus obscurus* (Say)	bird
Grouse, willow	*Lagopus lagopus* (L.)	bird
Heath hen	*Tympanuchus cupido cupido* (L.)	bird
Hedgehogs	Erinaceidae	mammal
Hummingbirds	Trochilidae	bird
Lemmings (e.g. brown lemming)	*Lemmus sibiricus* (Kerr)	mammal
Little white heron, snowy egret	*Leucophoyx thula*	bird
Looper, pine	*Bupalis piniaria* (L.)	insect
Lynx	*Lynx lynx* (L.)	mammal
Marmot, arctic	*Marmota broweri* (Hall and Gilmore)	mammal
Marten	*Martes americana* (Turton)	mammal
Moose	*Alces alces* (L.)	mammal
Moth, peppered (pepper-and-salt)	*Biston cognataria betularia* (Guenee)	insect
Moth, green oak-roller	*Tortrix viridiana* (L.)	insect
Moth, gypsy	*Porthetria dispar* (L.)	insect
Mouse, field	*Microtus pennsylvanicus* (Ord)	mammal
Mouse, white-footed deer	*Peromyscus maniculatus* (Wagner)	mammal
Musk oxen	*Ovibos moschatus* (Zimmermann)	mammal
Oropendula, chestnut-headed	*Zarynchus wagleri*	bird
Owl, snowy	*Nyctea scandiaca* (L.)	bird
(Parasitic wasp (Aphelinid))	*Aphytis lignanesis*	insect
(Parasitic wasp (Aphelinid))	*Aphytis melinus*	insect
Pheasant, ring-necked	*Phasianus colchicus* (L.)	bird
Pigeon, passenger	*Ectopistes migratorius* (L.)	bird
Pigeons	Columbidae	bird
Pillbug	*Armadillidium vulgare* (Latreille)	isopod
Psyllids	Psyllidae	insect
Ptarmigan, willow arctic	*Lagopus mutus* (Montin)	bird
Quail, bob-white	Colinus virginianus (L.)	bird
Rabbit, snowshoe (varying hare)	*Lepus americanus* (Erxlehen)	mammal
Racoons	*Procyon lotor* (L.)	mammal
Reindeer	*Rangifer tarandus tarandus* (L.)	mammal
Rook	*Corvus frugilegus* (L.)	bird
Salamander	Urodela	amphibian
Salmon, sockeye	*Oncorhynchus nerka* (Walbaum)	fish
Sawfly, European pine	*Diprion pini* (L.)	insect
Scale, California red	*Aonidiella aurantii* (Maskell)	insect
Scale, cottony-cushion	*Icerya purchasi* (Maskell)	insect
Shipworm	*Teredo navalis* (L.)	bivalve
Shrew, masked	*Sorex cinereus* (Kerr)	mammal
Shrew, short-tailed	*Blarina brevicauda* (Say)	mammal
Sowbug	*Porcellio scarber*	isopod
Squirrel, Mohave ground	*Spermophilis mohavensis* (Merriam)	mammal
Squirrel, red	*Tamiasciurus hudsonicus* (Erxlehen)	mammal
Starling (European)	*Sturnus vulgaris* (L.)	bird
Swallow	Hirundinidae	bird
Tern, arctic	*Sterna paradisaea* (Brunnich)	bird
Thar, Himalayan	*Hemitragus jemlahicus* (H. Smith)	mammal
Tit, great	*Parus major* (L.)	bird
Turkey, wild	*Meleagris gallopavo* (Vieillot)	bird

Common Name	Scientific Name	Type of Animal
Tussock moth, Douglas-fir	*Orgyia pseudotsugata* McDunnough	insect
Vedalia (beetle)	*Rodolia cardinalis* (Muls.)	insect
Vole, field	*Microtus pennsylvanicus* (Ord)	mammal
Vole, California	*Microtus californicus* (Peale)	mammal
Weevil, granary	*Sitophilus granarius* (L.)	insect
Wolf	*Canis lupus* (L.)	mammal
Wolverine	*Gulo gulo* (L.)	mammal
Woodland caribou	*Rangifer tarandus caribou* (Gmelin)	mammal

References Cited

Abee, A., and D. P. Lavender. 1972. Nutrient cycling in through-fall and litterfall in a 450-year-old Douglas-fir stand. pp. 133–143. *In* J. F. Franklin et al. (eds.), *Proceedings, Research on Coniferous Forest Ecosystems*. USDA For. Serv. PNW For. Range Exp. Sta., Portland, Ore.

Aber, J. D., and J. M. Melillo. 1982. FORTNITE: An integrated computer model of organic matter and nitrogen dynamics in forest ecosystems. Univ. of Wisconsin Res. Bull. R3130. 49 pp.

———, D. B. Botkin, and J. M. Melillo. 1978. Predicting the effects of different harvesting regimes on forest floor dynamics in northern hardwoods. *Can. J. For. Res.* 8:306–315.

———, D. B. Botkin, and J. M. Melillo. 1979. Predicting the effects of different harvesting regimes on productivity and yield in northern hardwoods. *Can. J. For. Res.* 9:10–14.

———, J. M. Melillo, and C. A. Federer. 1982. Predicting the effects of rotation length, harvest intensity and fertilization on fibre yield from northern hardwood forests in New England. *For. Sci.* 28:31–45.

Agee, J. K. 1974. Environmental impacts from fire management alternatives. Nat. Park Serv., West. Reg. Off. San Francisco, Calif. 92 pp.

Ahlgren, C. E. 1970. Some effects of prescribed burning on jack pine reproduction in northeastern Minnesota. Minn. Agr. Exp. Stat. Misc. Rept. 94. 14 pp.

Ahlgren, I. F. 1974. The effect of fire on soil organisms. pp. 47–72. *In* T. T. Kozlowski and C. E. Ahlgren (eds.), *Fire and Ecosystems*. Academic Press, New York.

———, and C. E. Ahlgren. 1960. Ecological effects of forest fires. *Bot. Rev.* 26:483–533.

———, and C. E. Ahlgren. 1965. Ecology of prescribed burning on soil microorganisms in a Minnesota jack pine forest. *Ecol.* 46:304–310.

Aho, P. E. 1974. Decay. *In* Environmental effects of forest residues management in the Pacific Northwest: a state-of-knowledge compendium. USDA For. Serv. Gen. Tech. Rept. PNW–24.

Ajtay, G. L., P. Ketner, and P. Duvigneaud. 1979. Terrestrial primary production and phytomass. pp. 129–181. *In* B. Bolin, E. T. Degens, S. Kempe, and P. Ketner (eds.), *The Global Carbon Cycle*. Scope Report 13. Wiley, New York.

Albrecht, F. O. 1967. *Polymorphisme phasaire et biologie des acridiènes migrateurs*. Masson, Paris. 192 pp.

Albrecht, W. A. 1958. *Soil Fertility and Animal Health*. Fred Hahne Printing Co., Webster City, Iowa. 232 pp.

Alcock, M. B. 1964. The physiological significance of defoliation on the subsequent regrowth of grass-clover mixtures and cereals. pp. 25–41. *In* A. J. Crisp (ed.), *Grazing in Terrestrial and Marine Environments*. Blackwell Scientific Publications, Oxford.

Alexander, M. E., and F. G. Hawksworth. 1976. Fire and dwarf mistletoes in North American coniferous forests. *J. For.* 74:446–449.

Allee, W. C. 1931. *Animal Aggregations: A Study in General Sociology*. Univ. of Chicago Press. 431 pp.

———. 1951. *Cooperation Amongst Animals, With Human Implications*. Henry Schumann, New York. 233 pp.

———, A. E. Emerson, O. Park, T. Park, and K. P. Schmidt. 1967. *Principles of Animal Ecology*. W. B. Saunders Co., Philadelphia. 837 pp.

Allen, S. E. 1964. Chemical aspects of heather burning. *J. Appl. Ecol.* 1:347–367.

Almer, B. 1974. Effects of acidification on Swedish Lakes. *Ambio* 3(1):30–36.

Amadon, D. 1947. Ecology and evolution of some Hawaiian birds. *Evolution* 1:63–68.

Anderson, J. 1952. Fluctuations in the field hare populations in Denmark compared with certain climatic factors. Papers on Game Research. Finnish Game Foundation. No. 8:41–43.

Andrewartha, H. G., and L. C. Birch. 1954. *The Distribution and Abundance of Animals*. Univ. of Chicago Press. 782 pp.

———, and T. O. Browning. 1961. An analysis of the idea of "resources" in animal ecology. *J. Theoret. Biol.* 1:83–97.

Armson, K. A. 1977. *Forest Soils: Properties and Processes*. Univ. Toronto Press, Toronto. 390 pp.

———, and H. Struik. 1969. The effects of oxygen levels on the growth of black spruce and red pine seedlings. Univ. Toronto Faculty of Forestry, *Glendon Hall Ann. Report* 1967–68.

———, J. McG. Taylor, and E. Astley. 1973. The effect of fire on organic layers of spodosols in the boreal forests of Ontario. *Agron. Abstr.* 1973:137.

Art, H. W., and P. L. Marks. 1971. A summary table of biomass and net annual primary production in forest ecosystems of the world. pp. 3–32. *In Forest Biomass Studies*. IUFRO Univ. Maine, Orono.

——, F. H. Bormann, G. K. Voigt, and G. M. Woodwell. 1974. Barrier Island forest ecosystem: role of meteorologic nutrient inputs. *Sci.* 184:60–62.

Ash, M. J., P. C. Knoblock, and N. Peters. 1980. Energy analysis of energy from forest options. ENFOR Project P-59. Canadian Forest Service, Ottawa. 79 pp.

Attiwill, P. M. 1966. The chemical composition of rainwater in relation to cycling of nutrients in mature *Eucalyptus* forests. *Plant and Science* 24:390–406.

——. 1980. Nutrient cycling in a *Eucalyptus obliqua* (L'Herit) forest. IV. Nutrient uptake and nutrient return. *Aust. J. Bot.* 28:199–222.

Aulitzky, H. 1961. Standortsuntersuchungen in der subalpinen Stufe. 4. Die Bodentemperaturen in der Kampfzone oberhalb der Waldgrenze und im subalpinen Zirben-Larchenwald. *Mitt. Der forst. Bundes-Versuch. Mariabrunn* 59:153–208.

Bailey, R. G. 1976. Ecoregions of the United States. USDA For. Serv. Intermountain Reg., Ogden, Utah. Map, scale 1:7,500,000.

——. 1978. Description of the ecoregions of the United States. USDA For. Serv. Intermountain Reg., Ogden, Utah. 77 pp.

Bajikov, A. D. 1949. Do fish fall from the sky? *Sci.* 109:402.

Baker, F. S. 1950. *The Principles of Silviculture*. McGraw-Hill, New York. 414 pp.

Baker, J. B., and B. G. Blackmon. 1977. Biomass and nutrient accumulation in a cottonwood plantation—the first growing season. *Soil Sci. Soc. Amer. Proc.* 41:632–636.

——, and W. M. Broadfoot. 1979. Site evaluation for commercially important southern hardwoods. USDA For. Serv. Gen. Tech. Rept. SO–26. 51 pp.

Baldwin, I. T., and J. C. Schultz. 1983. Rapid changes in tree leaf chemistry induced by damage: evidence for communication between plants. *Sci.* 221:277–279.

Baldwin, J. P. 1975. A quantitative analysis of the factors affecting plant nutrient uptake from some soils. *J. Soil Sci.* 26:195–206.

Ballard, T. M. 1972. Subalpine soil temperature regimes in southwest British Columbia. *Arctic and Alpine Res.* 4:139–146.

——, and D. W. Cole. 1974. Transport of nutrients to tree root systems. *Can. J. For. Res.* 4:563–564.

——, T. A. Black, and K. G. McNaughton. 1977. Summer energy balance and temperatures in a forest clearcut in southwestern British Columbia. pp. 74–86. *In Energy, Water and the Physical Environment of the Soil*. 6th British Columbia Soil Sci. Workshop Report, Min. Agri., Victoria, B.C.

Bangay, G. E., and C. Riordan. 1983. U.S.—Canada memorandum of intent on transboundary air pollution. Impact Assessment Work Group 1, Final Report. Jan. 1983.

Bange, G. G. J. 1953. On the quantitative explanation of stomatal transpiration. *Acta Bot. Neerl.* 2:255–297.

Banner, A., J. Pojar, and G. E. Rouse. 1983. Postglacial paleoecology and successional relationships of a bog woodland near Prince Rupert, British Columbia. *Can. J. For. Res.* 13:938–947.

Bannikov, A. G. 1967. Some remarks concerning determination of biomass of wild ungulates in natural geographical zones of the USSR. pp. 255–260. *In* K. Petrusewicz (ed.), *Secondary Productivity of Terrestrial Ecosystems (Principles and Methods)*. IBP and Polish Academy of Science. Panstwowe Wydawnictwo Naukowe, Warsaw, Poland.

Barclay-Estrup, P., and C. H. Gimingham. 1969. The description and interpretation of cyclical processes in a heath community. 1. Vegetational change in relation to the *Calluna* cycle. *J. Ecol.* 57:737–758.

Barry, R. G., and R. J. Chorley. 1968. *Atmosphere, Weather and Climate*. Methuen, London. 319 pp.

Bates, C. G., and J. Roeser Jr. 1928. Light intensities required for growth of coniferous seedlings. *Amer. J. Bot.* 15:185–244.

Batra, S. W. T., and L. R. Batra. 1967. The fungus gardens of insects. *Scientific American* 217:112–120.

Bazzaz, F. A. 1979. The physiological ecology of plant succession. *Ann. Rev. Ecol. Syst.* 10:351–371.

——, and S. T. A. Pickett. 1980. Physiological ecology of tropical succession: a comparative review. *Ann. Rev. Ecol. Syst.* 11:287–310.

Beadle, N. C. W. 1940. Soil temperatures during forest fires and their effect on the survival of vegetation. *J. Ecol.* 28:180–192.

——. 1966. Soil phosphate and its role in moulding segments of the Australian flora and vegetation, with special reference to xeromorphylly and sclerophylly. *Ecol.* 47:922–1007.

Beamish, R. J. 1974. Loss of fish populations from unexploited remote lakes in Ontario, Canada, as a consequence of atmospheric fallout of acid. *Water Research* 8:85–95.

——. 1975. Long-term acidification of a lake and resulting effects on fishes. *Ambio* 4(2):98–102.

Beard, J. S. 1973. The physiognomic approach. pp. 355–386. *In* R. H. Whittaker (ed.), Ordination and Classification of Communities. Part 5, *Handbook of Vegetation Science*. W. Junk b.v., Publishers, The Hague.

Beaufait, W. R. 1960. Some effects of high temperatures on the cones and seeds of jack pine. *For. Sci.* 6:194–199.

Beck, S. 1956. The European corn borer, *Pyrausta nubilalis* (Hubn.) and its principle host plant. II. The influence of nutritional factors on larval establishment and development of the corn plant. *Annals of the Entomol. Soc. Amer.* 49:582–588.

Beggs, J. P. 1964. Growth inhibitor in soil. *N.Z. J. Agr.* 108:529–535.

Bell, M. A. M., J. M. Beckett, and W. F. Hubbard. 1974a. Impact of harvesting on forest environments and resources. A review of the literature and evaluation of research needs. Canadian For. Serv., Dept. of Environ., Ottawa. 141 pp.

——, J. M. Beckett, and W. F. Hubbard. 1974b. Impact of harvesting on forest environments and resources. Annotated bibliography. Canadian For. Serv., Dept. of Environ., Ottawa. For. Tech. Rept. 3. 237 pp. + Suppl. No. 1., 1976. 16 pp.

Bell, P. R. 1982. Methane hydrate and the carbon dioxide question, pp. 401–406. *In* W. C. Clark (ed.), *Carbon Dioxide Review: 1982*. Clarendon Press, Oxford.

Bendell, J. F. 1974. Effects of fire on birds and mammals. pp. 73–138. *In* T. T. Kozlowski, and C. E. Ahlgren (eds.), *Fire and Ecosystems*. Academic Press, New York.

Benecke, U., and M. R. Davis. 1980. Mountain environments and subalpine tree growth. For. Res. Inst. NZ For. Serv. Tech. Pap. No. 70. 288 pp.

Bennett, J. 1960. A comparison of selective methods and a test of the pre-adaptation hypothesis. *Heredity* 15:65–77.

Bennett, W. D. 1960. Survey of lightning fire occurrences in Canada's forests: 1950–1959. Pulp Pap. Res. Inst. Can. Tech. Rept. 212.

Bernard, S. 1968. Thermoregulatory function of growing antlers (deer, caribou, goat). *Nature* 218:870–872.

Berndt, H. W. 1971. Early effects of forest fire on streamflow characteristics. USDA For. Serv. PNW For. Range Exp. Sta. Res. Note PNW–148. 9 pp.

———, and W. B. Fowler. 1969. Rime and hoarfrost in upperslope forests of eastern Washington. *J. For.* 67:92–95.

Bessey, E. A. 1950. *Morphology and Taxonomy of the Fungi*. Blakiston Co., Philadelphia. 791 pp.

Bilan, M. V. 1971. Some aspects of tree root distribution. pp. 69–80. *In Mycorrhizae. Proc. 1st N. American Conference on Mycorrhizae*. April 1969. USDA For. Serv., Misc. Publ. 1189.

Billings, W. D. 1954. Temperature inversions in the pinyon-juniper zone of a Nevada mountain range. *Butler Univ. Bot. Studies* 11:112–118.

Binkley, D. 1982. Nitrogen fixation and net primary production in a young Sitka alder stand. *Can. J. Bot.* 60:281–284.

———. 1983. Ecosystem production in Douglas-fir plantations: interaction of red alder and site fertility. *For. Ecol. and Mgmt.* 5:215–227.

Bishop, D. M., and M. E. Stevens. 1964. Landslides in logged areas in southeast Alaska. USDA For. Serv. Res. Pap. NOR-1. 18 pp.

Biswell, J. K. 1960. Danger of wildfires reduced by prescribed burning in ponderosa pine. *Calif. Agr.* 14(10):5–6.

Bjorkman, E. 1970. Mycorrhiza and tree nutrition on poor forest soils. Stud. for. suec. Skogs. #83, 24 pp.

Black, T. A. 1977. Micrometeorological studies of Douglas-fir. *In* J. J. Landsberg, and C. V. Cutting (eds.), *Environmental Effects on Crop Physiology*. Academic Press, New York. (Proc. 5th Symposium, Long Ashton Research Sta., Univ. of Bristol, London, 13–16 April 1975).

Blair-West, J. R., J. P. Coghlan, D. A. Denton et al. 1968. Physiological, morphological and behavioral adaptations to a sodium deficient environment by wild native Australian and introduced species of animal. *Nature* 217:922–928.

Blais, J. R. 1958. The vulnerability of balsam fir to spruce budworm attack in northern Ontario with special reference to the physiological age of the tree. *For. Chron.* 34:405–422.

Blinkenberg, G., H. Brix, S. de Muckadell, and H. Vedel. 1958. Controlled pollinations in *Fagus. Silv. Genet.* 7:116–122.

Bliss, L. C. 1962. Adaptations of arctic and alpine plants to environmental conditions. *Arctic* 15:117–144.

———. 1966. Plant productivity in alpine microenvironments on Mount Washington, New Hampshire. *Ecol. Monogr.* 36:125–155.

Bockheim, J. G., T. M. Ballard, and R. P. Willington. 1975. Soil disturbance associated with timber harvesting in southwestern British Columbia. *Can. J. For. Res.* 5:285–290.

Bodenheimer, F. S. 1928. Welche Faktoren regulieren die Individuenzahl einer Insektenart in der Natur? *Biol. Zentralbl.* 48:714–739.

Boelter, D. H. 1964. Water storage characteristics of several peats in situ. *Soil Sci. Soc. Amer. Proc.* 28:433–435.

Bogert, C. M. 1959. Thermoregulation in reptiles, a factor in evolution. *Evolution* 3:195–211.

Bolin, B. 1970. The carbon cycle. *Sci. Amer.* 223:125–132.

———, E. T. Degens, S. Kempe, and P. Ketner (eds.). 1979. *The Global Carbon Cycle*. Scope Report 13. Wiley, New York. 491 pp.

Bollen, W. B. 1974. Soil microbes. pp. B1–B41. *In* Environmental Effects of Forest Residues Management in the Pacific Northwest. USDA For. Serv. Gen. Tech. Rept. PNW–24.

Bond, G. 1977. Some reflections on *Alnus*-type root nodules. pp. 531–537. *In* W. Newton, J. R. Postgate, and C. Rodrigues-Barrneco (eds.), *Recent Developments in Nitrogen Fixation*. Academic Press, New York.

Bormann, F. H., and G. E. Likens. 1979. *Pattern and Process in a Forested Ecosystem*. Springer-Verlag, New York. 253 pp.

Bornemisza, E., and R. Llanos. 1967. Sulphate movement, adsorption, and resorption in three Costa Rican soils. *Soil Sci. Soc. Amer. Proc.* 31:336–360.

Botkin, D. B. 1980. A grandfather clock down the staircase: stability and disturbance in natural ecosystems. pp. 1–10. *In* R. H. Waring (ed.), *Forests: Fresh Perspectives from Ecosystem Analysis*. Proc. 40th Ann. Biol. Colloquium, Oregon State Univ. Oregon State Univ. Press, Corvallis.

———. 1981. Causality and succession. pp. 36–55. *In* R. H. Waring (ed.), *Forests: Fresh Perspectives from Ecosystem Analysis*. Oregon State Univ. Press, Corvallis.

———, J. F. Janak, and J. R. Wallis. 1972. Some ecological consequences of a computer model of forest growth. *J. Ecol.* 60:849–872.

Boyle, J. R. 1975. Nutrients in relation to intensive culture of forest crops. *Iowa State J. Res.* 49:293–303.

———, and A. R. Ek. 1972. An evaluation of some effects of bole and branch pulpwood harvesting on site macronutrients. *Can. J. For. Res.* 2:407–412.

———, and A. R. Ek. 1973. Whole tree harvesting: nutrient budget evaluation. *J. For.* 71:760–762.

———, J. J. Phillips, and A. R. Ek. 1973. Whole tree harvesting: nutrient budget evaluation. *J. For.* 71:760–872.

Boysen-Jensen, P. 1932. *Die Stoffproduktion der Pflanzen*. Gustav Fisher Verlag, Jena.

Bradshaw, A. D. 1952. Populations of *Agrostis tenuis* resistant to lead and zinc poisoning. *Nature* 169:1098.

Brady, N. C. 1984. *The Nature and Properties of Soils,* 9th ed. Macmillan, New York. 750 pp.

Braekke, F. H. (ed.). 1976. Impact of acid precipitation on forest and freshwater ecosystems in Norway. SNSF-Project, Agric. Res. Council of Norway, Oslo. 111 pp.

Braestrup, F. W. 1940. The periodic die-off in certain herbivorous mammals and birds. *Sci.* 92:354–355.

Bramble, W. C., and W. R. Byrnes. 1972. A long-term ecological study of game food and cover on a sprayed utility right-of-way. Purdue University, Agric. Exper. Sta. Res. Bull. #885. 20 pp.

Bray, J. R. 1961. An estimate of a minimum quantum yield of photosynthesis based on ecological data. *Plant Physiol.* 36:371–373.

———. 1962. Estimates of energy budget for a *Typha* (cattail) marsh. *Sci.* 136:1119–1120.

———, and E. Gorham. 1964. Litter production in the forests of the world. *Adv. Ecol. Res.* 2:101–157.

Brayshaw, T. C. 1970. The dry forests of British Columbia. *Syesis* 3:17–43.

Brink, V. C. 1959. A directional change in the subalpine forest-heath ecotone in Garibaldi Park, British Columbia. *Ecol.* 40:10–16.

Brix, H. 1971. Effects of nitrogen fertilization on photosynthesis and respiration in Douglas-fir. *For. Sci.* 17:407–414.

Broecker, W. S. 1973. Factors controlling CO_2 content in the oceans and atmosphere. pp. 32–50. *In* G. M. Woodwell and E. V. Pecan, (eds.), *Carbon and the Biosphere,* AEC Symp. Series 30. Tech. Info. Center. Office of Info. Services, USAEC.

Brooke, R. C., E. B. Peterson, and V. J. Krajina. 1970. The subalpine mountain hemlock zone. *Ecol. Western N. Amer.* 2:148–439.

Brosset, C. 1973. Air-borne acid. *Ambio* 11(1–2):2–9.

Brouzes, R., J. Lasik, and R. Knowles. 1969. The effect of organic amendment, water content and oxygen on the incorporation of $^{15}N_2$ by some agricultural and forest soils. *Can. J. Microbiol.* 15:899–905.

Brown, J. H., Jr. 1960. The role of fire in altering the species composition of forests in Rhode Island. *Ecol.* 41:310–316.

Brown, S., G. Gertner, A. E. Lugo, and J. Novak. 1981. Carbon dioxide dynamics of the biosphere. pp. 19–28. *In* W. J. Mitsch, R. W. Bossermann and J. M. Klopatek (eds.), *Energy and Ecological Modelling.* Elsevier Sci. Publ., New York.

Browning, T. O. 1962. The environments of animals and plants. *J. Theoret. Biol.* 2:63–68.

Brues, C. T. 1946. *Insect Dietary.* Harvard Univ. Press, Cambridge, Mass. 466 pp.

Brunig, E. F. 1977. The tropical forest—a wasted asset or an essential biospheric resource? *Ambio* 6:187–191.

Bryant, J. 1986. Role of vertebrate herbivores in determining community structure and diversity in the taiga. In K. Van Cleve et al. (eds.), Forest Ecosystems in the Alaskan Taiga. Springer-Verlag, NY. In press.

Bryant, J. P., and P. J. Kuropat. 1980. Selection of winter forage by subarctic browsing vertebrates: the role of plant chemistry. *Ann. Rev. Ecol. Syst.* 11:261–285.

———, F. S. Chapin, III, and D. R. Klein. 1983. Carbon/nutrient balance of boreal plants in relation to vertebrate herbivory. *Oikos* 40:357–368.

Bryson, R. A. 1974. A perspective on climatic change. *Sci.* 184:753–760.

Buchanan, B. A., K. T. Harper, and N. C. Frischknecht. 1978. Allelopathic effects of bur buttercup tissue on germination and growth of various grasses and forbs *in vitro* and in soil. *Great Basin Nat.* 38:19–96.

Buck, C. C. (ed.). 1964. *Winds over wildlands—a guide for forest management.* USDA For. Serv. Agric. Hndbk No. 272. 33 pp.

Budyko, M. I. 1955. *Atlas of Heat Balance,* 2nd ed. (1963) Leningrad. Publ. Meteorol. 19. 35 pp.

———. 1974. *Climate and Life.* Academic Press, New York. 508 pp.

Buffington, L. C., and C. H. Herbel. 1965. Vegetational changes on a semidesert grassland range. *Ecol. Monogr.* 35:139–164.

Bunge, M. 1959. *Causality: The Place of the Causal Principle in Modern Science.* Harvard Univ. Press, Cambridge, Mass. 380 pp.

Burger, D. 1972. Forest site classification in Canada. *Mitt. Ver. Forstl. Standortsk. Forstpflanz.* 21:20–36.

Burges, A. 1963. The microbiology of a podzol profile. pp. 151–157. *In* J. Doekson and J. van der Drift (eds.), *Soil Organisms.* Amsterdam.

———, and F. Raw (eds.). 1967. *Soil Biology.* Academic Press. London and New York. 582 pp.

Burgess, R. L., and D. M. Sharpe (eds.). 1981. *Forest Island Dynamics in Man-Dominated Landscapes.* Springer-Verlag, New York. 311 pp.

Burns, G. P. 1923. Measurement of solar radiant energy in plant habitats. *Ecol.* 4:189–195.

Cain, S. A., and R. C. Friesner. 1929. Some ecological factors in secondary succession: upland hardwood. I. Evaporation studies in the sycamore creek region. *Butler Univ. Bot. Studies Pap.* 1:1–15.

Cajander, A. K. 1926. The theory of forest types. *Acta For. Fenn.* 29(3):1–108.

———. 1949. Forest types and their significance. *Acta For. Fenn.* 56(4):1–71.

———, and Y. Ilvessalo. 1921. Über Waldtypen. II. *Acta For. Fenn.* 20(1):1–77.

Caldwell, M. M. 1968. Solar ultra violet radiation as an ecological factor for alpine plants. *Ecol. Monogr.* 38:243–268.

Callaham, R. Z. 1962. Geographic variability in growth of forest trees. pp. 311–325. *In* T. T. Kozlowski (ed.), *Tree Growth.* Ronald Press, New York.

Cannell, M. G. R. 1982. *World Forest Biomass and Primary Production Data.* Academic Press, New York. 391 pp.

———, and F. T. Last. 1976. *Tree Physiology and Yield Improvement.* Academic Press, New York. 506 pp.

Carlisle, A. 1976. The utilization of forest biomass and forest industry wastes for the production and conservation of energy. Dept. Environ. Can. For. Serv., Ottawa. 54 pp.

————, A. H. F. Brown, and E. J. White. 1966. Litterfall, leaf production and the effects of defoliation by *Tortix viridiana* in a sessile oak (*Quercus petraea*) woodland. *J. Ecol.* 54:65–85.

————, A. H. F. Brown, and E. J. White. 1967. The nutrient content of tree stem flow and ground flora litter and leachates in a sessile oak (*Quercus petraea*) woodland. *J. Ecol.* 55:615–627.

Carmean, W. H. 1959. Litter weight not reduced following clear-cutting of poor site oak stands in S.E. Ohio. *J. For.* 57:207–209.

————. 1975. Forest site quality evaluation in the United States. *Adv. Agronomy* 27:207–269.

Carpenter, J. R. 1940. Insect outbreaks in Europe. *J. Anim. Ecol.* 9:108–147.

Cattelino, P. J., I. R. Noble, R. O. Slatyer, and S. R. Kessell. 1979. Predicting the multiple pathways of plant succession. *Environ. Mgmt.* 3:41–50.

Caughley, G. 1970. Eruption of ungulate populations with emphasis on Himalayan thar in New Zealand. *Ecol.* 51:53–72.

Cavers, P. B., and J. L. Harper. 1966. Germination polymorphism in *Rumex crispus* and *R. obtusifolius*. *J. Ecol.* 54:367–382.

Chandler, R. F., Jr. 1942. The time required for podzol profile formation as evidenced by the Mendenhall glacial deposit near Juneau, Alaska. *Soil Sci. Soc. Amer. Proc.* 7:454–459.

Chapin, F. S. III. 1980. The mineral nutrition of wild plants. *Ann. Rev. Ecol. Syst.* 11:233–260.

Chapman, R. W. 1928. The quantitative analysis of environmental factors. *Ecol.* 9:111–122.

Chatarpaul, L., and A. Carlisle. 1983. Nitrogen fixation: A biotechnological opportunity for Canadian forestry. *For. Chron.* 59:249–259.

Cheng, T. C. 1970. *Symbiosis. Organisms Living Together*. Pegasus, New York. 250 pp.

Chew, R. M., and A. E. Chew. 1970. Energy relationships of the mammals of a desert shrub. *Ecol. Monogr.* 40:1–21.

Chippendale, H. G., and W. E. J. Milton. 1934. On the viable seeds present in the soil beneath pastures. *J. Ecol.* 22:508–531.

Chitty, D. 1960. Population processes in the vole and their relevance to general theory. *Can. J. Zool.* 38:99–113.

————. 1967. The natural selection of self-regulatory behaviour in animal populations. *Proc. Ecol. Soc. Australia* 2:51–78.

Christensen, N. L. 1973. Fire and the nitrogen cycle in California chaparral. *Sci.* 181:66–67.

Christersson, L., and R. Sandstedt. 1978. Short-term temperature variation in needles of *Pinus sylvestris*. *L. Can. J. For. Res.* 8:480–482.

Christian, J. J. 1950. The adreno-pituitary system and population cycles in mammals. *J. Mamm.* 31:247–259.

————. 1961. Phenomena associated with population density. *Proc. Nat. Acad. Sci.* 47:428–448.

————. 1971. Population density and reproductive efficiency. *Biol. Reprod.* 4:248–294.

————, and D. E. Davis. 1964. Endocrines, behavior and population. *Sci.* 146:1550–1560.

Clark, F. B. 1976. The central hardwood forest. pp. 1–8. *In* J. S. Fralish et al. (eds.). Central Hardwood Conference. USDA For. Serv. NC For. Exp. Sta. St. Paul. Minn.

Clark, F. E., and T. Rosswall (eds.). 1981. Terrestrial nitrogen cycles. Processes, Ecosystem Strategies and Management Impacts. Ecol. Bull. No. 33. Swedish Nat. Sci. Res. Council. 714 pp.

Clark, W. C. (ed.). 1982. *Carbon Dioxide Review: 1982*. Clarendon Press, Oxford. 469 pp.

————, K. H. Cook, and G. Marland et al. 1982. The carbon dioxide question: perspectives for 1982. pp. 3–53. *In* W. C. Clark (ed.), *Carbon Dioxide Review: 1982*. Clarendon Press, Oxford.

Clarke, C. H. D. 1936. Fluctuations in numbers of ruffed grouse, *Bonsa umbellus* (Linne.) with special reference to Ontario. Univ. Toronto Studies. Biol. Ser. No. 41. 118 pp.

Clarke, G. L. 1967. *Elements of Ecology*. 3rd ed., Wiley, New York. 560 pp.

Clausen, J. 1965. Population studies of alpine and subalpine races of conifers and willows in the California high Sierra Nevada. *Evolution* 19:56–68.

————, D. D. Keck, and W. M. Hiesey. 1948. Experimental studies on the nature of species. III. Environmental responses of climatic races of *Achillea*. Carnegie Inst. Wash. Publ. 581:1–129.

Clayton, J. L. 1976. Nutrient gains to adjacent ecosystems during a forest fire: an evaluation. *For. Sci.* 27:162–166.

Cleaves, E. T., A. E. Godfrey, and O. P. Bricker. 1970. Geochemical balance of a small watershed and its geomorphic implications. *Geol. Soc. Amer. Bull.* 81:3015–3032.

————, D. W. Fisher, and O. P. Bricker. 1974. Chemical weathering of serpentine in the eastern Piedmont of Maryland. *Geol. Soc. Amer. Bull.* 85:437–444.

Clements, F. E. 1916. Plant succession. An analysis of the development of vegetation. Carnegie Inst. Wash. Publ. 242. 512 pp.

Coale, A. J. 1974. The history of the human population. *Sci. Amer.* 231(3):41–51.

Cochran, P. H. 1969a. Lodgepole pine clearcut size affects minimum temperatures near the soil surface. USDA For. Serv. Pac. Northwest For. Range Exp. Sta. Res. Paper PNW–86. 9 pp.

————. 1969b. Thermal properties and surface temperatures of seedbeds. USDA For. Serv. Pac. Northwest For. Range Exp. Sta. Misc. Publ. 12. 19 pp.

Cody, M. L. 1966. A general theory of clutch size. *Evolution* 20:174–184.

Cole, D. W., and S. P. Gessel, 1963. Movement of elements through a forest soil as influenced by tree removal and fertilizer additions. pp. 95–104. *In* C. T. Youngberg (ed.), *Forest Soil Relationships in North America*. Oregon State Univ. Press, Corvallis.

————, S. P. Gessel, and S. F. Dice. 1967. Distribution and cycling of nitrogen, phosphorus, potassium and calcium in a second-growth Douglas-fir ecosystem. pp. 197–232. *In Symposium on Primary Production and Mineral Cycling in Natural Ecosystems*. Univ. of Maine Press.

————, J. Turner, and C. Bledsoe. 1974. Requirement and uptake of mineral nutrients in coniferous ecosystems. pp. 171–176. *In* J. K. Marshall (ed.), *The Below Ground Ecosystem*. Dowden, Hutchinson and Ross, Stroudsberg, Pa.

———, W. J. B. Crane, and C. C. Grier. 1975. The effect of forest management practices on water chemistry in a second-growth Douglas-fir ecosystem. pp. 195–207. *In* B. Bernier and C. H. Winget (eds.), *Forest Soils and Forest Land Management*. Laval Univ. Press, Quebec.

———, and P. Schiess. 1978. Renovation of wastewater and response of forest ecosystems. The Pack Forest Study. pp. 323–332. *In* H. L. McKim (ed.), *State of Knowledge in Land Treatment of Wastewater*. Vol. I. U.S. Army Corps of Engr. Cold Regions Res. and Engr. Lab., Hanover, N.H.

———, and D. W. Johnson. 1980. Mineral cycling in tropical forests. pp. 341–356. *In* C. T. Youngberg (ed.), *Forest Soils and Land Use*. Proc. 5th N. Amer. For. Soils Conf., Dept. For. and Wood Sci., Colorado State Univ., Fort Collins, Colo.

———, and M. Rapp. 1981. Elemental cycling in forest ecosystems. pp. 341–409. *In* D. E. Reichle (ed.), *Dynamic Properties of Forest Ecosystems*. International Biological Programme 23. Cambridge Univ. Press, Cambridge.

———, C. L. Henry, P. Schiess, and R. J. Zasoski. 1983. The role of forests in sludge and wastewater utilization programs. pp. 125–143. *In* A. L. Page et al. (eds.), *Proc. 1983 Workshop on Utilization of Municipal Wastewater and Sludge on Land*. Univ. Calif., Riverside.

Cole, L. C. 1957. Sketches of general and comparative demography. Cold Spring Harbour Symp. *Quant. Biol.* 22:1–15.

Coley, P. D. 1983. Herbivory and defense characteristics of tree species in a lowland tropical forest. *Ecol. Monogr.* 53:209–233.

Collier, B. D., G. W. Cox, A. W. Johnson, and P. C. Miller. 1973. *Dynamic Ecology*. Prentice-Hall, Englewood Cliffs, N.J. 563 pp.

Connell, J. H. 1972. Community interactions on marine rocky intertidal shores. *Ann. Rev. Ecol. Syst.* 3:169–192.

———, and R. O. Slatyer. 1977. Mechanisms of succession in natural communities and their role in community stability and organization. *Amer. Nat.* 111:1119–1144.

Cook, C., R. R. Askew, and J. A. Bishop. 1970. Increasing frequency of the typical form of the Peppered Moth in Manchester. *Nature* 227:1155.

Cooper, C. F. 1961. The ecology of fire. *Sci. Amer.* 204(4):150–160.

Cooper, R. W. 1973. Trade-offs between smoke from wild and prescribed fires. Proc. Int. Symp. Air Qual. and Smoke from Urban and Forest Fires. Ft. Collins, Colo. Oct. 23–26, 1973.

Cordes, L. D. 1972. An ecological study of the Sitka spruce forest on the west coast of Vancouver Island. Ph.D. thesis, Univ. of B. C., Vancouver. 298 pp.

Corke, C. T. 1958. Nitrogen transformations in Ontario forest podsols. pp. 116–121. *In Proc. 1st N. American For. Soils Conf.*, Mich. State Univ. Agric. Exp. Stat., East Lansing.

Cornforth, I. S. 1970. Reafforestation and nutrient reserves in the humid tropics. *J. Appl. Ecol.* 7:609–615.

Council on Environmental Quality. 1980. *The Global 2000 Report to the President: Entering the Twenty-first Century*. Govt. Printing Office, Wash., D.C. 766 pp.

Cousens, J. 1974. *An Introduction to Woodland Ecology*. Oliver and Boyd, Edinburgh. 151 pp.

Covington, W. W. 1976. Forest floor organic matter and nutrient content and leaf fall during secondary succession in northern hardwoods. Ph.D. thesis, Yale Univ., New Haven. 98 pp.

Cowan, R. L. 1962. Physiology of nutrition as related to deer. pp. 1–8. Proc. 1st National White-tailed Deer Disease Symposium.

Cowles, H. C. 1899. The ecological relations of the vegetation of the sand dunes of Lake Michigan. *Bot. Gaz.* 27:95–117;167–202;281–308;361–391.

Cramer, O. P. 1974a. Air quality influences. *In* O. P. Cramer (ed.) Environmental effects of forest residues management in the Pacific Northwest: A state-of-knowledge compendium. USDA For. Serv. Gen. Tech. Rept. PNW-24.

———. 1974b. Environmental effects of forest residues management in the Pacific Northwest. A state-of-knowledge compendium. USDA For. Serv. Gen. Tech. Rept. PNW-24.

Crawford, H. S. 1975. Soil-site and forest land management in relation to wildlife. pp. 571–581. *In* B. Bernier and C. H. Winget (eds.), *Forest Soils and Forest Land Management*. Laval Univ. Press, Quebec.

Crisp, D. T. 1966. Input and output of minerals for an area of Pennine moorland: the importance of precipitation, drainage, peat erosion and animals. *J. Appl. Ecol.* 3:327–348.

Crocker, R. L., and J. Major. 1955. Soil development in relation to vegetation and surface age of Glacier Bay, Alaska. *J. Ecol.* 43:427–448.

Cummins, K. W. 1980. The multiple linkages of forests to streams. pp. 191–198. *In* R. H. Waring (ed.), *Forests: Fresh Perspectives from Ecosystem Analysis*. Oregon State Univ. Press, Corvallis.

Cunningham, P. M. 1963. The effect of clearing a tropical soil. *J. Soil Sci.* 14:334–345.

Curry, R. R. 1972. Geological and hydrological effects of even-age management on productivity of forest soils, particularly in the Douglas-fir region. pp. 137–178. *In* R. K. Hermann and D. P. Lavender (eds.), *Even-Age Management,* Paper 848. Oregon State Univ., Corvallis.

Curtis, J. P. 1959. *The Vegetation of Wisconsin*. Univ. of Wisconsin Press, Madison. 657 pp.

———, and R. P. McIntosh. 1951. An upland forest continuum in the prairie-forest border region of Wisconsin. *Ecol.* 32:476–496.

Dalton, D. C. 1963. Effect of dilution of the diet with an indigestible filler on feed intake in the mouse. *Nature* 197:909–910.

Damman, A. W. H. 1971. Effect of vegetation changes on the fertility of a Newfoundland forest site. *Ecol. Monogr.* 41:253–270.

———. 1977. The role of vegetation analysis in land classification. pp. 169–193. *In* Ecological Classification of Forest Land in Canada and Northwestern USA. Proc. Center for Cont. Ed., Univ. of B. C., Vancouver.

Daniel, T. W., J. A. Helms, and F. S. Baker. 1979. *Principles of Silviculture*. 2nd ed., McGraw-Hill, New York. 500 pp.

Dansereau, P. 1951. Description and recording of vegetation upon a structural basis. *Ecol.* 32:172–229.

———. 1957. *Biogeography, an Ecological Perspective*. Ronald, New York. 394 pp.

Darling, F. F. 1938. *Bird Flocks and the Breeding Cycle. A Contribution to the Study of Avian Sociality*. Cambridge Univ. Press. 124 pp.

Darlington, P. J. Jr., 1938. The origin of the fauna of the Greater Antilles, with discussion of dispersal of animals over water and through the air. *Quart. Rev. Biol.* 13:274–300.

Darwin, C. R. 1859. *On the Origin of Species by Means of Natural Selection, or the Preservation of Favoured Races in the Struggle for Life*. J. Murray, London. 502 pp.

Daubenmire, R. F. 1952. Forest vegetation of northern Idaho and adjacent Washington, and its bearing on concepts of vegetation classification. *Ecol. Monogr.* 22:301–330.

———. 1954. Alpine timberlines in the Americas and their interpretation. *Butler Univ. Bot. Stud.* 11:119–136.

———. 1968. *Plant Communities: A Textbook of Plant Synecology*. Harper & Row, New York. 300 pp.

———. 1974. *Plants and Environment: A Textbook of Plant Autecology*. Wiley, New York. 422 pp.

———. 1976. The use of vegetation in assessing the productivity of forest lands. *Bot. Rev.* 42:115–143.

———, and J. B. Daubenmire. 1968. Forest vegetation of eastern Washington and northern Idaho. Wash. Agric. Exp. Sta. Tech. Bull. 60. 104 pp.

Davis, G. K. 1968. Mineral elements in the nutrition of larger mammals. *Amer. Zool.* 8:169–174.

Davis, R. B. 1966. Spruce-fir forests of the coast of Maine. *Ecol. Monogr.* 36:79–94.

Davis, T. W. A., and P. W. Richards. 1933 and 1934. The vegetation of Moraballi Creek, British Guiana: an ecological study of a limited area of tropical rain forest. *J. Ecol.* 21:350–384; 22:106–155.

DeAngelis, D. L., R. H. Gardner, and H. H. Shugart Jr. 1981. Productivity of forest ecosystems studied during IBP: the woodlands data set. pp. 567–672. *In* D. E. Reichle (ed.), *Dynamic Properties of Forest Ecosystems*. Cambridge Univ. Press, Cambridge.

DeBach, P., and R. A. Sundby, 1963. Competitive displacement between ecological homologues. *Hilgardia* 34:105–166.

DeBano, L. F., and R. M. Rice. 1973. Water-repellent soils: their implications in forestry. *J. For.* 71:220–223.

———, J. F. Osborn, J. S. Krammes, and J. Letey Jr. 1967. Soil wettability and wetting agents: our current knowledge of the problem. USDA For. Serv. Res. Pap. PSW–43. 13 pp.

Debell, D. S., and C. W. Ralston. 1970. Release of nitrogen by burning light forest fuels. *Soil Sci. Soc. Amer. Proc.* 34:936–938.

DeByle, N. V. 1973. Broadcast burning of logging residues and the water repellency of soils. *Northwest Sci.* 47:77–87.

de Candolle, A. P. A. 1874. Constitution dans le Règne Végétal des Groupes Physiologiques Applicables à la Géographie Ancienne et Modern. Archives des Sciences Physiques et Naturelles, Geneva.

Deevey, E. S., Jr. 1947. Life tables for natural populations of animals. Quart. Rev. Biol. 22:283–314.

———. 1960. The human population. *Sci. Amer.* 203:195–204.

———. 1970. Mineral cycles. *Sci. Amer.* 223:149–158.

———. 1973. Sulphur, nitrogen and carbon in the biosphere. pp. 182–190. *In* G. M. Woodwell and E. V. Pecan (eds.), *Carbon in the Biosphere*. AEC. Symp. Series 30. Tech. Info. Centre, Office of Info. Services, USAEC.

Dell, J. D., and F. R. Ward. 1971. Logging residues on Douglas-fir region clearcuts—weights and volumes. USDA For. Serv. Res. Pap. PNW–115.

DeLury, R. 1932. Astronomical periods in climate and life. pp. 213–221. *In* E. Huntington (ed.), *Matamek Conference on Biological Cycles*. Matamek Factory. Canadian Labrador.

Delwiche, C. C. (ed.). 1981. *Denitrification, Nitrification and Atmospheric Nitrous Oxide*. Wiley, New York. 286 pp.

Development Forum. 1982. U.N. University and Div. Econ. and Social Info. 5(10), p. 8.

de Wit, C. T., and J. Goudriaan. 1974. Simulation of ecological processes. Centre for Agricultural Publishing and Documentation. Wageningen, Netherlands.

DeYoe, D. R., and K. Cromack. 1983. Mycorrhizae—A hidden benefactor to forest trees. Oregon State University Extension Service, EM 8247. June 1983. 10 pp.

Dickerson, R. E. 1978. Chemical evolution and the origin of life. *Sci. Amer.* 239(3):70–86.

Dickinson, R. E. 1982. Modeling climatic changes due to carbon dioxide increases. pp. 103–142. *In* W. C. Clark (ed.), *Carbon Dioxide Review: 1982*. Clarendon Press, Oxford.

Dickson, W. 1975. The acidification of Swedish Lakes. Institute of Freshwater Res. Rept. No. 54. 20 pp.

Diebold, C. H. 1942. Effect of fire and logging upon the depth of the forest floor in the Adirondack region. *Soil Sci. Soc. Amer. Proc.* 6:409–413.

Dittmer, H. J. 1937. A quantitative study of the roots and root hairs of a winter rye plant (*Secale cereale*). *Amer. J. Bot.* 24:417–420.

Dix, R. L. 1960. The effects of burning on the mulch structure and species composition of grasslands in western North Dakota. *Ecol.* 41:438–445.

Dobzansky, T. 1950. Evolution in the tropics. *Amer. Sci.* 38:209–221.

Dochinger, L. S., and T. A. Seliga (eds.). 1976. Proceedings of the first international symposium on acid precipitation and the forest ecosystem. USDA For. Serv. NE. For. Exp. Sta. Gen. Tech. Rept. NE-23. 1072 pp.

Dodge, M. 1972. Forest fuel accumulation—a growing problem. *Sci.* 177:139–142.

Dodson, C. H., R. L. Dressler, H. G. Hills, R. M. Adams, and N. H. Williams. 1969. Biologically active compounds in orchid fragrances. *Sci.* 164:1243–1249.

Dominski, A. 1971. Accelerated nitrate production and loss in the northern hardwood forest ecosystem underlain by podzol soils following clearcutting and addition of herbicides. Ph.D. thesis, Yale Univ., New Haven. 157 pp.

Dorn, H. F. 1962. World population growth: an international dilemma. *Sci.* 135:283–290.

Douglas, A. E. 1919. Climatic cycles and tree growth. Vol. 1. A study of the annual rings of trees in relation to climate and solar activity. Carnegie Inst. Wash. Publ. 289. 127 pp.

Downs, R. J. 1962. Photocontrol of growth and dormancy in woody plants. pp. 133–148. *In* T. T. Kozlowski (ed.), *Tree Growth*. Ronald Press, New York.

Doyle, T. W. 1982. The role of disturbance in the gap dynamics of a montane rain forest: an application of a tropical forest succession model. pp. 56–73. *In* R. H. Waring (ed.), *Forests: Fresh Perspectives from Ecosystem Analysis*. Oregon State Univ. Press, Corvallis.

Drablos, D., and A. Tollan (eds.). 1980. Ecological impact of acid precipitation. Proc. Internat. Conf. Sandfjord, Norway. SWSF Project Oslo, Norway.

Dressler, R. L. 1968. Pollination by euglossine bees. *Evolution* 22:202–210.

Drobikov, A. A. 1969. [Changes in the water regime of brown soils under the influence of fellings]. *Pocvoved* 6:54–62.

Drury, W. H. and I. C. T. Nisbet. 1973. Succession. *J. Arnold Arboretum,* Harv. Univ. 54:331–368.

Duddridge, J. A., A. Malibari, and D. J. Read. 1980. Structure and function of mycorrhizal rhizomorphs with special reference to their role in water transport. *Nature* 287:834–836.

Durzan, D. J., and F. C. Steward. 1967. The nitrogen metabolism of *Picea glauca* (Moench) Voss and *Pinus banksiana* Lamb as influenced by mineral nutrition. *Can. J. Bot.* 45:695–710.

Duvall, V. L., and L. B. Whittaker. 1964. Rotation burning: a forage management system for longleaf pine-bluestem ranges. *J. Range Mgmt.* 17:322–326.

Duvigneaud, P. 1971. Concepts sur la productivité primaire des écosystèmes forestières. pp. 111–140. *In* P. Duvigneaud (ed.), *Productivity of Forest Ecosystems*. UNESCO, Paris.

———, and S. Denaeyer-De Smet. 1970. Biological cycling of minerals in temperate deciduous forests. pp. 199–225. *In* D. E. Reichle (ed.), *Analysis of Temperate Forest Ecosystems,* Springer-Verlag, New York.

Dyrness, C. T. 1965. Soil surface condition following tractor and high-lead logging in the Oregon Cascade. *J. For.* 63:272–275.

———. 1967. Mass soil movements in the H. J. Andrews Experimental Forest. USDA For. Serv. Res. Pap. PNW–42. 12 pp.

Eaton, J. S., G. E. Likens, and F. H. Bormann. 1973. Throughfall and stemflow chemistry in a northern hardwood forest. *J. Ecol.* 61:495–508.

Ebell, L. F. 1972. Cone-induction response of Douglas-fir to form of nitrogen fertilizer and time of treatment. *Can. J. For. Res.* 2:317–326.

———, and E. E. McMullen. 1970. Nitrogenous substances associated with differential cone production responses of Douglas-fir to ammonium and nitrate fertilization. *Can. J. Bot.* 48:2169–2177.

Ebermeyer, E. 1826. *Die gesammte Lehre der Waldstreu mit Rücksicht auf die chemische Statik des Waldbaues*. J. Springer-Verlag, Berlin.

Edwards, C. A., and G. W. Heath. 1963. The role of soil animals in breakdown of leaf material. pp. 76–84. *In* J. Doeksen and J. van der Drift (eds.), *Soil Organisms*. North-Holland Publ., Amsterdam.

———, D. E. Reichle, and D. A. Crossley Jr. 1970. The role of soil invertebrates in turnover of organic matter and nutrients. pp. 145–172. *In* D. E. Reichle (ed.), *Analysis of Temperate Forest Ecosystems*. Springer-Verlag, New York.

Edwards, M. V., J. Atterson, and R. S. Howell. 1963. Wind-loosening of young trees on upland heaths. Forestry Commission: Forest Record #50. London. 16 pp.

Edwards, N. T., H. H. Shugart Jr., S. B. McLauglin, W. F. Harris, and D. E. Reichle. 1981. Carbon metabolism in terrestrial ecosystems. pp. 499–536. *In* D. E. Reichle (ed.), *Dynamic Properties of Forest Ecosystems*. Cambridge Univ. Press, Cambridge.

Egerton, F. N. 1968. Studies of animal populations from Lamarck to Darwin. *J. Hist. Biol.* 1:225–259.

Egler, F. E. 1953. Vegetation management for rights-of-way and roadsides. Smithsonian Inst. Ann. Rept. 1953, pp. 299–320.

———. 1954. Vegetation science concepts. I. Initial floristic composition—a factor in old-field vegetation development. *Vegetatio* 4:412–418.

Ehhalt, D. H. 1973. Methane in the atmosphere. pp. 144–158. *In* G. M. Woodwell and E. V. Pecan (eds.), *Carbon and the Biosphere*. AEC Symp. Series 30. Tech. Info. Centre, Office of Info. Serv. USAEC.

Ehrlich, P. R., and P. H. Raven. 1967. Butterflies and plants. *Sci. Amer.* 216:104–113.

Eis, S. 1962. Statistical analysis of several methods for estimation of forest habitats and tree growth near Vancouver, B.C. For. Bull. No. 4, Fac. For., Univ. of B.C., Vancouver.

Ek, A. R., and R. A. Monserud. 1974. FOREST: A computer model for simulating the growth and reproduction of mixed forest stands. Res. Rept. A2635. Coll. Agric. and Life Sciences. Univ. of Wisconsin, Madison. 14 pp.

Ekern, P. C. 1964. Direct interception of cloud water at Lanaihole, Hawaii. *Soil Sci. Soc. Amer., Proc.* 28:419–421.

Elton, C. 1924. Periodic fluctuations in the numbers of animals: their causes and effects. *Br. J. Exp. Biol.* 2:119–163.

———. 1927. *Animal Ecology*. Sedgwick and Jackson, London. 207 pp.

Epstein, E. 1972. *Mineral Nutrition of Plants: Principles and Perspectives*. Wiley, New York. 412 pp.

Errington, P. L. 1963. *Muskrat Populations*. Chap. 17: The muskrat and population cycles. Iowa State Univ. Press. Ames, Iowa. 665 pp.

Esau, K. 1963. *Plant Anatomy*. Wiley, New York. 5th ed. 735 pp.

Evans, F. C. 1956. Ecosystem as the basic unit in ecology. *Sci.* 123:1127–1128.

Evans, G. C. 1956. An area survey method of investigating the distribution of light intensity in woodlands with particular reference to sunflecks, including an analysis of data from rain forest in Southern Nigeria. *J. Ecol.* 44:391–428.

Ewel, J., C. Berish, B. Brown, N. Price, and J. Raich. 1981. Slash and burn impacts on a Costa Rican wet forest site. *Ecol.* 62:816–829.

Eyre, F. H. (ed.). 1980. *Forest Cover Types of the United States and Canada*. Soc. Amer. For., Wash. D.C. 168 pp.

Eyre, S. R. 1968. *Vegetation and Soils: A World Picture*, 2nd ed. Edward Arnold, London. 328 pp.

Farnworth, E. G., and F. B. Golley (eds.). 1973. *Fragile Ecosystems. Evaluation of research and applications in the neotropics*. Springer-Verlag, New York. 258 pp.

Feeny, P. P. 1968. Effect of oak leaf tannins on larval growth of the winter moth *Operophtera brumata*. *J. Insect. Physiol.* 14:805–817.

———. 1970. Seasonal changes in oak leaf tannins and nutrients as a cause of spring feeding by winter moth caterpillars. *Ecol.* 51:565–581.

———, and H. Bostock. 1968. Seasonal changes in the tannin content of oak leaves. *Phytochem.* 7:871–880.

Feller, M. C. 1974. Initial effects of clearcutting on the flow of chemicals through a forest-watershed ecosystem in southwestern British Columbia. Ph.D. thesis, Univ. of B.C., Vancouver.

———. 1982. The ecological effects of slashburning with particular reference to British Columbia: a literature review. Land Management Report No. 23. ISSN 0702–9861. Ministry of Forests. Province of B.C., Victoria.

———, and J. P. Kimmins. 1984. Effects of clearcutting and slashburning on streamwater chemistry and watershed nutrient budgets in southwestern British Columbia. *Water Resour. Res.* 20:29–40.

———, J. P. Kimmins, and K. M. Tsze. 1983. Nutrient losses to the atmosphere during slashburns in southwestern British Columbia. pp. 128–132. *In Proc. 7th Conf. Fire and Meteorology*. Amer. Met. Soc. Boston, Mass.

Ferreira, M. G. M., J. P. Kimmins, and N. F. Barros. 1984. Impact of intensive management on phosphorus cycling in *Eucalyptus grandis* plantations in the savannah region, Minas Gerais, Brazil. pp. 847–856. *In* Proc. Symp. on *Site Productivity of Fast Grown Plantations*. IUFRO, Pretoria and Pieter Maritzburg, South Africa, Vol. 1.

Fischer, A. G. 1960. Latitudinal variations in organic diversity. *Evolution* 14:64–8.

Fisher, R. T. 1928. Soil changes and silviculture on the Harvard forest. *Ecol.* 9:6–11.

Fitton, E. M., and C. F. Brooks. 1931. Soil temperatures in the United States. *Mo. Weather Rev*. 59:6–16.

Flinn, M. A., and R. W. Wein. 1977. Depth of underground plant organs and theoretical survival during fire. *Can. J. Bot.* 55:2550–2554.

Florence, R. G., and J. R. McWilliam. 1956. The influence of spacing on seed production: its application to forest tree improvement. *Silv. Genet.* 5:97–102.

———, and P. H. Chuong. 1974. The influence of soil type on foliar nutrients in plantations. *Australian J. For. Res.* 6:1–8.

Foil, R. R. 1965. The effects of compaction on soil characteristics and seedling growth. *Dissert. Abstr.* 26(6):2955.

Folk, G. E. Jr. 1974. *Textbook of Environmental Physiology*. 2nd ed., Lea and Febiger, Philadelphia, 465 pp.

Fonda, R. W. 1974. Forest succession in relation to river terrace development in Olympic National Park, Washington. *Ecol.* 55:927–942.

Ford, E. B. 1931. *Mendelism and Evolution*. Methuen, London. 116 pp.

———. 1975. *Ecological Genetics*. 4th ed., Chapman & Hall, London. 442 pp.

Ford-Robertson, F. C. (ed.). 1971. *Terminology of Forest Science, Technology, Practice, and Products*. The Multi-Lingual Forest Terminology Series (English Language Version) No. 1. Soc. Amer. For., Wash. D.C. 349 pp.

Forman, T. T. (ed.). 1979. *Pine Barrens. Ecosystem and Landscape*. Academic Press. New York. 601 pp.

Fortin, J. A., R. Lavallée, and Y. Piche. 1979. Forest utilization for energy and the role of nitrogen fixation. A literature review. Contractors Report. DSS Contract 04SU.KL011–8–0008. ENFOR Project P-9, Can. For. Serv., Chalk River, Ontario. 166 pp.

Foster, N. W., and S. P. Gessel. 1972. The natural addition of nitrogen, potassium and calcium to a *Pinus banksiana* Lamb. forest floor. *Can. J. For. Res.* 2:448–455.

———, and I. K. Morrison. 1976. Distribution and cycling of nutrients in a natural *Pinus banksiana* ecosystem. *Ecol.* 57:110–120.

Fowells, H. A. 1965. *Silvics of Forest Trees of the United States*. USDA For. Serv. Agric. Handbook #271. 762 pp.

Francke-Grosmann, H. 1967. Ecosymbiosis in wood-inhibiting insects. pp. 141–204. *In* S. M. Henry (ed.), *Symbiosis*, Vol. II. Academic Press, New York.

Frank, F. 1957. The causality of microtine cycles in Germany. *J. Wildl. Mgmt.* 21:113–121.

Franklin, J. F., W. H. Moir, G. W. Douglas, and C. Wieberg. 1971. Invasion of subalpine meadows by trees in the Cascade range, Washington and Oregon. *Arctic and Alpine Res.* 3:215–224.

Frediksen, R. L. 1972. Nutrient budget of a Douglas-fir forest on an experimental watershed in western Oregon. pp. 115–131. *In* J. F. Franklin et al. (eds.), *Proceedings, Research on Coniferous Forest Ecosystems*. USDA For. Serv., For. Range Exp. Sta., Portland, Ore.

———, D. G. Moore, and L. A. Norris. 1975. The impact of timber harvest, fertilization and herbicide treatment on streamwater quality in western Oregon and Washington. pp. 283–313. *In* B. Bernier and C. H. Winget (eds.), *Forest Soils and Forest Land Management*. Laval Univ. Press, Quebec.

Freedman, B. 1981. Intensive forest harvest: a review of nutrient budget considerations. Info. Rept. M-X-121. Maritimes For. Res. Centre, Can. For. Serv., Dept. Environ., Fredericton, N.B. 78 pp.

Frejka, T. 1974. World population projections: Alternative paths to zero growth. *Population Bulletin* 29(5).

Frey, T. E. A. 1973. The Finnish school and forest site-types. pp. 405–433. *In* R. H. Whittaker (ed.), Ordination and Classification of Communities, Part 5, *Handbook of Vegetation Science*. W. Junk b.v., Publishers, The Hague.

Fryer, J. H., and F. T. Ledig. 1972. Microevolution of the photosynthetic temperature optimum in relation to the elevational complex gradient. *Can. J. Bot.* 50:1231–1235.

Fujimori, T., S. Kawanabe, H. Saito, C. C. Grier, and T. Shidei. 1976. Biomass and primary production in forests of three major vegetation zones of the northwestern United States. *J. Jap. For. Soc.* 58:360–373.

Fujiwara, K. 1970. [A study on the landslides by aerial photographs.] *Res. Bull. Exp. For., Hokkaido Univ.*, Japan 27:297–345.

Fuller, W. H., S. Shannon, and P. S. Burgess. 1955. Effect of burning on certain forest soils of northern Arizona. *For. Sci.* 1:44–50.

Futuyma, D. J., and M. Slatkin (eds.). 1983. *Coevolution*. Sinaner Associates, Sunderland, Mass. 555 pp.

Gadgil, R. L., and P. D. Gadgil. 1971. Mycorrhiza and litter decomposition. *Nature* 233:133.

———, and P. D. Gadgil. 1975. Suppression of litter decomposition by mycorrhizal roots of *Pinus radiata*. *N.Z. J. For. Sci.* 5:33–41.

Gagnon, J. D. 1966. Free amino acids in needles in *Abies balsamea* and *Picea mariana* growing on different sites. *Nature* 212:884.

Galloway, G., and J. Worrall. 1979. Cladoptosis: a reproductive strategy in black cottonwood? *Can. J. For. Res.* 9:122–125.

Gardner, C. A. 1957. The fire factor in relation to the vegetation of Western Australia. *West. Austr. Nat.* 5:166–173.

Gardner, R. H., and J. B. Mankin. 1981. Analysis of biomass allocation in forest ecosystems of IBP. pp. 451–497. *In* D. E. Reichle (ed.), *Dynamic Properties of Forest Ecosystems*. Cambridge Univ. Press, Cambridge.

Garner, W. W., and H. A. Allard. 1920. Effect of the relative length of the day and night and other factors of the environment on growth and reproduction in plants. *J. Agr. Res.* 18:553–606.

Garrison, G. A., and R. S. Rummel. 1951. First-year effects of logging on ponderosa pine forest range lands of Oregon and Washington. *J. For.* 49:708–713.

Gates, D. M. 1962. *Energy Exchange in the Biosphere*. Harper & Row, New York. 151 pp.

———. 1965. Energy, plants and ecology. *Ecol.* 46:1–24.

———. 1971. The flow of energy in the biosphere. *Sci. Amer.* 225:89–100.

———, and R. Janke. 1966. The energy environment of the alpine tundra. *Oecol. Plant.* 1:39–62.

Gause, G. F. 1934. *The Struggle for Existence*. Williams and Wilkins Co., Baltimore. 163 pp.

———. 1935. Experimental demonstration of Volterra's periodic oscillations in the numbers of animals. *J. Exper. Biol.* 12:44–48.

Geiger, R. 1965. *The Climate near the Ground*. Harvard Univ. Press, Cambridge, Mass. 611 pp.

Geist, V. 1971. *Mountain Sheep: A Study in Behavior and Evolution*. Univ. of Chicago Press, Chicago.

Gerloff, G. C., D. G. Moore, and J. T. Curtin. 1966. Selective absorption of mineral elements by mature plants of Wisconsin. *Plant and Soil* 25:393–405.

Gersper, P. L., and N. Holowaychuck. 1970. Effects of stemflow water on a Miami soil under a beech tree. I. Morphological and physical properties. II. Chemical properties. *Soil Sci. Soc. Amer. Proc.* 34:779–786; 786–794.

Gessell, S. P. 1962. Progress and problems in mineral nutrition of forest trees. pp. 221–235. *In* T. T. Kozlowski (ed.), *Tree Growth*. Ronald, New York.

———, and A. N. Balci. 1965. Amount and composition of forest floors under Washington coniferous forests. pp. 11–23. *In* C. T. Youngberg (ed.), *Forest Soil Relationships in N. America*. Oregon State Univ. Press, Corvallis.

Gholz, H. L. 1982. Environmental limits on aboveground net primary production, leaf area, and biomass in vegetation zones of the Pacific Northwest. *Ecol.* 63:469–481.

Gholz, H. L., F. K. Fitz, and R. H. Waring. 1976. Leaf area differences associated with old-growth forest communities in the western Oregon Cascades. *Can. J. For. Res.* 6:49–57.

Gilbert, J. M. 1959. Forest succession in the Florentine Valley, Tasmania. *Pap. Proc. Royal Soc. Tasmania* 93:129–151.

Gill, A. M. 1975. Fire and the Australian flora: A review. *Aust. For.* 38:1–25.

———, R. H. Groves, and I. R. Noble (eds.). 1981. *Fire and the Australian Biota*. Aust. Acad. Sci., Canberra. 582 pp.

Gilpin, M. E. 1973. Do hares eat lynx? *Amer. Nat.* 107:727–730.

Gimingham, C. H. 1972. *Ecology of Heathlands*. Chapman and Hall, London. 266 pp.

Glass, A. D. M. 1976. The allelopathic potential of phenolic acids associated with the rhizosphere of *Pteridium aquilinum*. Can. J. Bot. 54:2440–2444.

Gleason, H. A. 1926. The individualistic concept of the plant association. *Bull. Torrey Bot. Club* 53:7–26.

———. 1939. The individualistic concept of the plant association. *Amer. Midl. Nat.* 21:92–110.

Godwin, G. E. 1968. The influence of wind on forest management and planning. pp. 60–66. *In* R. W. V. Palmer (ed.), *Wind Effects on the Forest*. Suppl. to *For.* 1968. Oxford Univ. Press, London.

Golding, D. L. 1970. The effects of forests on precipitation. *For. Chron.* 46(5):1–6.

———. 1978. Calculated snowpack evaporation during chinooks along the eastern slope of the Rocky Mountains in Alberta. *J. Appl. Meteorol.* 17:1647–1651.

———, and R. H. Swanson. 1978. Snow accumulation and melt in small forest openings in Alberta. *Can. J. For. Res.* 8:380–388.

Golley, F. B. 1960. Energy dynamics of a food chain in an old-field community. *Ecol. Monogr.* 30:187–206.

———. 1961. Energy values of ecological materials. *Ecol.* 42:581–584.

———. 1977. Insects as regulators of forest nutrient cycling. *Trop. Ecol.* 18:116–123.

———, and E. Medina. 1975. *Tropical ecological systems. Trends in terrestrial and aquatic research*. Ecological Studies. Vol. II. Springer-Verlag, New York. 398 pp.

———, J. T. McGinnis, R. G. Clements, G. I. Child, and M. J. Duever. 1975. *Mineral Cycling in a Tropical Moist Forest Ecosystem*. Univ. Georgia Press, Athens. 248 pp.

Gordon, D. T. 1973. Damage from wind and other causes in mixed white fir-red fir stands adjacent to clearcuttings. USDA For. Serv. Res. Pap. PSW–90, 22 pp.

Gordon, M. S., G. A. Bartholemew, and A. D. Grivell, et al. 1968. *Animal Function: Principles and Adaptations*. MacMillan, New York. 560 pp.

Gore, A. J. P. 1968. The supply of six elements by rain to an upland peat area. *J. Ecol.* 56:483–495.

Gorham, E., P. Vitousek, and W. A. Reiners. 1979. The regulation of chemical budgets over the course of terrestrial ecosystem succession. *Ann. Rev. Ecol. Syst.* 10:53–84.

Gosz, J. R., G. E. Likens, and F. H. Bormann. 1972. Nutrient content of litter fall on the Hubbard Brook experimental forest, New Hampshire. *Ecol.* 53:769–784.

———, G. E. Likens, and F. H. Bormann. 1976. Organic matter and nutrient dynamics of the forest and forest floor in the Hubbard Brook forest. *Oecologia* 22:305–320.

Granat, L., R. O. Hallberg, and H. Rodhe. 1976. The global sulphur cycle. pp. 89–134. *In* B. H. Svensson and R. Söderlund (eds.), Nitrogen, Phosphorus and Sulphur—Global Cycles. Scope Report 7. *Ecol. Bull.* (Stockholm) 22.

Grange, W. B. 1949. *The Way to Game Abundance*. Scribner's, New York. 365 pp.

Granhall, U., and H. Selander. 1973. Nitrogen fixation in a subarctic mire. *Oikos* 24:8–15.

———, and T. Lindberg. 1977. Nitrogen fixation of coniferous forest sites within the SWECON project. Swed. Conif. For. Project. Tech. Rept. 11. 39 pp. Uppsala, Sweden.

Green, G. R., and C. A. Evans. 1940. Studies on a population cycle of snowshoe hares on the Lake Alexander area. *J. Wildl. Mgmt.* 4:220–238, 267–278, 347–358.

Green, G. R., and C. L. Larson. 1938. Shock disease and the snowshoe hare cycle. *Sci.* 87:298–299.

Greenland, D. J., and M. Kowal. 1960. Nutrient content of the moist tropical forest of Ghana. *Plant and Soil* 12:154–174.

Gregory, R. A. 1960. The development of forest soil organic layers in relation to time in south-eastern Alaska. USDA For. Serv. Alaska For. Res. Center Tech. Note No. 47. 3 pp.

Grier, C. C. 1972. Effects of fire on the movement and distribution of elements within a forest ecosystem. Ph.D. thesis, Univ. of Washington, Seattle. 167 pp.

———. 1975. Wildfire effects on nutrient distribution and leaching in a coniferous ecosystem. *Can. J. For. Res.* 5:599–607.

———, and R. H. Waring. 1974. Conifer foliage mass related to sapwood area. *For. Sci.* 20:205–206.

———, and R. S. Logan. 1977. Old growth *Pseudotsuga menziesii* communities of a western Oregon watershed: biomass distribution and production budgets. *Ecol. Monogr.* 47:373–400.

———, and S. W. Running. 1977. Leaf area of mature northwestern coniferous forests; relation to site water balance. *Ecol.* 58:893–899.

———, D. W. Cole, C. T. Dyrness, and R. L. Fredriksen. 1974. Nutrient cycling in 37- and 450-year-old Douglas-fir ecosystems. pp. 21–34. *In* R. H. Waring and R. L. Edwards (eds.), *Integrated Research in the Coniferous Forest Biome*. Conif. For. Biome Bull. No. 5., Ecosystem Analysis Studies, US/IBP. Univ. Washington, Seattle.

———, K. A. Vogt, M. R. Keyes, and R. L. Edmonds. 1981. Biomass distribution and above- and below-ground production in young and mature *Abies amabilis* zone ecosystems of the Washington Cascades. *Can. J. For. Res.* 11:155–167.

Griffith, B. G., E. W. Hartwell, and T. E. Shaw. 1930. The evolution of soils as affected by the old field white pine-mixed hardwood succession in central New England. Harv. For. Bull. 15. 82 pp.

Griggs, R. F. 1946. The timberlines of North America and their interpretation. *Ecol.* 15:80–96.

Grime, J. P. 1966. Shade avoidance and shade tolerance in flowering plants. pp. 187–207. *In* R. Bainbridge et al. (eds.), *Light as an Ecological Factor*. Blackwell Sci. Publ., Oxford.

———, and A. W. Jeffrey. 1965. Seedling establishment in vertical gradients of sunlight. *J. Ecol.* 53:621–642.

Grinnell, J. 1917. The niche-relationship of the California Thrasher. *Auk.* 34:427–433.

Gross, A. O. 1928. The heath hen. Mem. Boston. *Society of Natural History* 6:491–588.

Gullion, G. W. 1984. Managing northern forests for wildlife. Minn. Agr. Exp. Sta. Misc. J. Ser. Publ. 13,442. 72 pp.

Gunn, D. L. 1960. The biological background of locust control. *Ann. Rev. Entomol.* 5:279–300.

Habeck, J. R., and R. W. Mutch. 1973. Fire-dependent forests in the northern Rocky Mountains. *J. Quaternary Res.* 3:408–424.

Hacskaylo, E. 1972. Mycorrhiza: the ultimate in reciprocal parasitism. *BioSci.* 22:577–583.

Hacskaylo, E. (ed.). 1971. Mycorrhizae. *Proc. 1st N. Amer. Conf. on Mycorrhizae*. April 1969. USDA For. Serv. Misc. Publ. 1189.

Haines, E. H. 1922. Influence of varying soil conditions on night air temperatures. *Monthly Weather Rev.* 50:363–366.

Hairston, N. G., F. E. Smith, and L. B. Slobodkin. 1960. Community structure, population control and competition. *Amer. Nat.* 64:421–425.

Hall, C. A. S., and J. W. Day Jr. 1977. *Ecosystem Modelling in Theory and Practice: An Introduction with Case Histories*. Wiley, New York. 684 pp.

Hall, R. B. 1974. Variations in DNA content per cell, and repetitions in DNA of selected populations of *Pinus banksiana* Lamb. Ph.D. thesis, University of Wisconsin, Madison. 209 pp.

Handley, W. R. C. 1963. Mycorrhizae associations and *Calluna* heathland afforestation. Bull. British For. Comm. No. 36.

Hansen, H. P. (ed.). 1966. *Arctic Biology*. 2nd ed., Oregon State Univ. Press, Corvallis.

Hansen, J., A. Johnson, A. Lacas, S. Lebedeff, P. Lee, D. Rind, and G. Russel. 1981. Climatic impact of increasing atmospheric carbon dioxide. *Sci.* 213:957–966.

Harcomb, P. A. 1977a. The influence of fertilization on some aspects of succession in a humid tropical forest. *Ecol.* 58:1375–1383.

———. 1977b. Nutrient accumulation by vegetation during the first year of recovery of a tropical forest ecosystem. pp. 347–378. *In* J. Cairns, K. Dickson, and E. Herricks (eds.), *Recovery and Restoration of Damaged Ecosystems.* Univ. of Virginia Press, Charlottesville.

Hardin, G. 1960. The competitive exclusion principle. *Sci.* 131:1292–1297.

Hardy, C. E., and J. W. Franks. 1963. Forest fires in Alaska. USDA For. Serv. Res. Pap. INT-5. 163 pp.

Harley, J. L. 1952. Associations between micro-organisms in higher plants (mycorrhizae). *Ann. Rev. Micro-Biology* 6:367–386.

———. 1969. *The Biology of Mycorrhiza.* 2nd ed. Leonard Hill, London. 334 pp.

Harper, J. L. 1961. Approaches to the study of plant competition. pp. 1–39. *In* F. L. Milthorpe (ed.), Mechanisms in Biological Competition. *Symp. Soc. Exper. Biol.* 15:1–39.

———. 1969. The role of predation in vegetational diversity. *Brookhaven Symp. in Biology* 22:48–62.

———. 1977. *Population Biology of Plants.* Academic Press, New York. 892 pp.

Harris, A. S., and W. A. Farr. 1974. The forest ecosystem of southeast Alaska. 7. Forest ecology and timber management. USDA For. Serv. Gen. Tech. Rept. PNW–25. 109 pp.

Harris, W. F., D. Santantonio, and D. McGinty. 1980. The dynamic below-ground ecosystems. pp. 119–129. *In* R. H. Waring (ed.), *Forests: Fresh Perspectives from Ecosystem Analysis.* Oregon State Univ. Press, Corvallis, Ore.

Hartog, G. den, and H. L. Ferguson. 1978. Water Balance. Hydrological Atlas of Canada. Fisheries and Environment Canada. Ottawa.

Hartzell, A. 1967. Insect ectosymbiosis. Chap. 2. pp. 107–140. *In* S. M. Henry (ed.), *Symbiosis.* Vol. II. Academic Press, New York.

Harwood, C. E., and W. D. Jackson. 1975. Atmospheric losses of four plant nutrients during a forest fire. *Aust. For.* 38:92–99.

Hase, H., and H. Foelster. 1983. Impact of plantation forestry with teak (*Tectona grandis*) on the nutrient status of young alluvial soils in west Venezuela. *For. Ecol. and Mgmt.* 6:33–57.

Haukioja, E. 1980. On the role of plant defences in the fluctuation of herbivore populations. *Oikos* 35:202–213.

Hauser, P. M. 1971. World Population: retrospect and prospect. pp. 103–122. *In Rapid Population Growth.* N.A.S. Johns Hopkins, Baltimore. 696 pp.

Havranek, W. M., and U. Benecke. 1978. The influence of soil moisture on water potential, transpiration and photosynthesis of conifer seedlings. *Plant and Soil* 49:91–103.

Haydu, E. P., and R. N. Thut. 1971. Effects of forest chemicals on aquatic life in surface waters. pp. 159–171. *In* J. T. Krygier

and J. D. Hall (eds.), *Proc. Symp. Forest Land Uses and the Stream Environment.* Oregon State Univ., Corvallis.

Heal, O. W., M. J. Swift, and J. M. Anderson. 1982. Nitrogen cycling in United Kingdom forests: the relevance of basic ecological research. *Phil. Trans. R. Soc. Lond.* B 296, 427–444.

Heginbottom, J. A. 1971. Some effects of a forest fire on the permafrost active layer at Inuvik, N.W.T. pp. 31–36. *In* R. J. E. Brown (ed.), *Proc. Permafrost Active Layer Conf.* C.N.R.C. Tech. Memo. No. 103.

Heilman, P. E. 1966. Change in distribution and availability of nitrogen with forest succession on north slopes in interior Alaska. *Ecol.* 47:825–831.

———. 1968. Relationship of availability of phosphorus and cations to forest succession and bog formation in interior Alaska. *Ecol.* 49:331–336.

Heinselman, M. L., and H. E. Wright (eds.). 1973. The ecological role of fire in natural conifer forests of western and northern America. *Quaternary Research* 3:317–513.

Hellmers, H. 1962. Temperature effect on optimum tree growth. pp. 275–287. *In* T. T. Kozlowski (ed.), *Tree Growth.* Ronald, New York.

———. 1964. An evaluation of the photosynthetic efficiency of forests. *Quart. Rev. Biol.* 39:249–257.

———. 1966a. Temperature action and interaction of temperature regimes in the growth of red fir seedlings. *For. Sci.* 12:90–96.

———. 1966b. Growth response of redwood seedlings to thermoperiodism. *For. Sci.* 12:276–283.

———, and W. P. Sundahl. 1959. Response of *Sequoia sempervirens* (D.Don) Endl. and *Pseudotsuga menziesii* (Mirb.) Franco seedlings to thermoperiodism. *For. Sci.* 12:276–283.

———, M. K. Genthe, and F. Ronco. 1970. Temperature affects growth and development of Engelman spruce. *For. Sci.* 16:447–452.

Helvey, J. D. 1972. First-year effects of wildfire on water yield and stream temperature in north-central Washington. pp. 308–312. *In* C. S. Csallany et al. (eds.), *Watersheds in Transition.* Amer. Water Resources Assn. & Col. State Univ.

———, and J. H. Patric. 1965. Canopy and litter interception of rainfall by hardwoods of eastern United States. *Water Resources Res.* 1:193–206.

Henderson, G. S., and W. F. Harris. 1975. An ecosystem approach to characterization of the nitrogen cycle in a deciduous forest watershed. pp. 179–193. *In* B. Bernier and C. H. Winget (eds.), *Forest Soils and Forest Land Management.* Laval Univ. Press, Quebec.

Henry, S. M. (ed.). 1967. *Symbiosis.* Vol. I. *Associations of Microorganisms, Plants and Marine Organisms.* Vol. II. *Associations of Invertebrates, Birds, Ruminants and Other Biota.* Academic Press, New York.

Henson, W. R. 1962. Convective transportation of *Choristoneura fumiferana* (Clem.). *XI Internat. Kongr. Für Entomol.,* Vienna 1960. III:44–46.

Hermann, R. K. 1977. Growth and production of tree roots: A review. pp. 7–28. *In* J. K. Marshall (ed.), *The Belowground*

Ecosystem: A Synthesis of Plant-associated Processes. Colorado State Univ., Fort Collins.

———, and W. W. Chilcote. 1965. Effect of seedbeds on germination and survival of Douglas-fir. Res. Pap. Ore. For. Res. Lab. 4:1–28.

Herrera, R., C. F. Jordan, H. Klinge, and E. Medina. 1978. Amazon ecosystems. Their structure and functioning with particular emphasis on nutrients. *Interciencia* 3:223–232.

Heslop-Harrison, J. 1964. Forty years of genecology. *Adv. Ecol. Res.* 2:159–247.

Hewlett, J. D., and W. L. Nutter. 1969. *An Outline of Forest Hydrology*. Univ. of Georgia Press, Athens. 137 pp.

Heyward, F. 1938. Soil temperatures during forest fires in the longleaf pine region. *J. For.* 36:478–491.

Hibbs, D. E. 1979. The age structure of a striped maple population. *Can. J. For. Res.* 9:504–508.

Hiesey, W. M., and H. W. Milner. 1965. Physiology of ecological races and species. *Ann. Rev. Plant Phys.* 16:203–216.

Hill, F. B. 1973. Atmospheric sulphur and its links to the biota. pp. 159–181. *In* G. M. Woodwell and E. V. Pecan (eds.), *Carbon and the Biosphere*. AEC Symposium Series 30. Tech. Info. Center, Office of Info. Services. USAEC.

Hillman, W. S. 1969. Photoperiodism and vernalization. Chap. 16. *In* M. B. Wilkins (ed.), *The Physiology of Growth and Development*. McGraw-Hill, New York.

Hills, G. A. 1976. An integrated, iterative holistic approach to ecosystem classification. pp. 73–97. *In* J. Thie and G. Ironside (eds.), *Ecological (Biophysical) Land Classification in Canada*. Ecological Land Classification Series, No. 1. Lands Directorate, Env. Canada, Ottawa.

Hodges, J. D. 1967. Patterns of photosynthesis under natural conditions. *Ecol.* 48:234–242.

Holden, A. D. 1966. A chemical study of rain and stream waters in the Scottish Highlands. Dept. Agric. Fish., Scotland.

Holdridge, L. R. 1947. Determination of world plant formations from simple climatic data. *Sci.* 105:367–368.

Holling, C. S. 1959. The components of predation as revealed by a study of small mammal predation of the European spruce sawfly. *Can. Entomol.* 9:293–320.

———. 1965. The functional response of predators to prey and its role in mimicry and population regulation. *Mem. Entomol. Soc. Can.* No. 45. 60 pp.

———. 1973. Resilience and stability of ecological systems. *Ann. Rev. Ecol. Syst.* 4:1–23.

Holstener-Jorgensen, H. 1960. [Drift of soil into the western edge of a plantation.] Forstt. Forsogsv. Danm. 26:389–397.

Hoover, W. H., E. S. Johnston, and F. S. Brackett. 1933. Carbon dioxide assimilation in a higher plant. *Smithsonian Inst. Misc. Coll.* 87:1–19.

Hopkins, A. D. 1920. The bioclimatic law. *J. Wash. Acad. Sci.* 10:34–40.

Hopkins, H., and J. Eisen. 1959. Mineral elements in fresh vegetables from different geographic areas. *Agric. Food. Chem.* 7:633–638.

Hori, T. (ed.). 1953. *Studies on Fogs in Relation to Fog-Preventing Forest*. Foreign Books Dept. Tanne Trading Co., Sapporo, Hokkaido, 399 pp.

Horn, H. S. 1971. *The Adaptive Geometry of Trees*. Princeton Univ. Press, Princeton. 144 pp.

———. 1974. The ecology of secondary succession. *Ann. Rev. Ecol. Syst.* 5:25–37.

———. 1976. Succession. pp. 187–204. *In* R. M. May (ed.) *Theoretical Ecology: Principles and Applications*. Blackwell Sci. Publ., Oxford.

Hornbeck, J. W., G. E. Likens, R. S. Pierce, and F. H. Bormann. 1975. Strip cutting as a means of protecting site and streamflow quality when clearcutting northern hardwoods. pp. 209–225. *In* B. Bernier and C. H. Winget (eds.), *Forest Soils and Forest Land Management*. Laval Univ. Press, Quebec.

Horton, K. W. 1956. The ecology of lodgepole pine in Alberta and its role in forest succession. Can. Dept. N. Affairs and Nat. Resources, For. Br., For. Res. Div. Tech. Note 45. 29 pp.

Houghton, R. A., J. E. Hobbie, J. M. Melillo, B. Moore, et al. 1983. Changes in the carbon content of terrestrial biota and soils between 1860 and 1980: a net release of CO_2 to the atmosphere. *Ecol. Monogr.* 53:236–262.

House, H. L. 1965. Effects of low levels of the nutrient content of a food and of nutrient imbalance on the feeding and nutrition of a phytophagous larva, *Celerio euphorbiae* (L.) (Lepidoptera: Sphingidae). *Can. Entomol.* 97:62–68.

———. 1967. The role of nutritional factors in food selection and preference as related to larval nutrition of an insect, *Pseudosarcophaga affinis* (Diptera: Sarcophagidae) on synthetic diets. *Can. Entomol.* 99:1310–1321.

Howard, B. H. 1967. Intestinal micro-organisms of ruminants and other vertebrates. pp. 317–385. *In* S. M. Henry (ed.), *Symbiosis*. Vol. II. Academic Press, New York.

Howard, L. O., and W. F. Fiske. 1911. The importation into the United States of the parasites of the gypsy moth and the brown-tail moth: a report of progress with some consideration of previous and concurrent efforts of this kind. *U.S. Dept. Agr., Bur. Ent. Bull.* 91:105–109.

Hoyle, M. C. 1973. Nature and properties of some forest soils in the White Mountains of New Hampshire. USDA For. Serv. Res. Pap. NE-260. 18 pp.

Huffaker, C. B. 1958. Experimental studies on predation: dispersion factors and predator-prey oscillations. *Hilgardia* 27:343–383.

———, and P. S. Messenger. 1964. The concept and significance of natural control. pp. 74–117. *In* P. DeBach (ed.), *Biological Control of Insect Pests and Weeds*. Chapman and Hall, London.

Humphreys, F. R., and M. Lambert. 1965. Soil temperature profiles under slash and log fires of various intensities. *Aust. J. For. Res.* 1(4):23–29.

Hunt, C. B. 1972. *Geology of Soils. Their Evolution, Classification and Uses*. W. H. Freeman and Co., San Francisco. 344 pp.

Huntington, E. 1945. *Mainsprings of Civilization*. Wiley, New York. 660 pp.

Hurd, R. M. 1971. Annual tree-litter production by successional forest stands, Juneau, Alaska. *Ecol.* 52:881–884.

Hussain, S. B., C. M. Skan, S. M. Bashir, and R. O. Meeuwig. 1969. Infiltrometer studies of water-repellent soils on the east slope of the Sierra Nevada. pp. 127–131. *In Symp. On Water-Repellent Soils,* Univ. of Calif., Riverside.

Hustich, I. 1953. The boreal limits of conifers. *Arctic* 6:149–162.

Hutchinson, G. E. 1950. Survey of contemporary knowledge of biogeochemistry. 3. The biogeochemistry of vertebrate excretion. *Bull. Amer. Mus. Nat. Hist.* 96:1–554.

————. 1957. Concluding remarks. *Cold Spring Harbor Symp. Quant. Biol.* 22:415–427.

————. 1959. Homage to Santa Rosalia, or why are there so many kinds of animals? *Amer. Nat.* 93:145–159.

————, and E. S. Deevey Jr. 1949. Ecological studies on populations. pp. 345–359. *In* G. S. Avery Jr. (ed.), *Survey of Biological Progress,* Vol. 1. Academic Press. New York.

Hutchinson, G. L., R. I. Millington, and D. B. Peters. 1972. Atmospheric ammonia: adsorption by plant leaves. *Sci.* 175:771–772.

Hutt, F. B. 1949. *Genetics of the Fowl.* McGraw-Hill, New York. 590 pp.

Ingestad, T. 1967a. Nutrient needs of seedlings and young trees. pp. 139–141. *In* Proc. Colloq. For. Fertil., Vth Colloq. Internat., Potash Inst. Jyvaskyla, Finland.

————. 1967b. Methods for uniform optimum fertilization of forest tree plants. *Proc. 14th IUFRO Congr.* 3:265–269.

————. 1971. A definition of optimum nutrient requirements in birch seedlings. II. *Physiol. Plant.* 24:118–125.

————. 1979. Mineral nutrient requirements of *Pinus sylvestris* and *Picea abies* seedlings. *Physiol. Plant.* 45:373–380.

————. 1981. Nutrition and growth of birch and grey alder seedlings in low conductivity solutions and at varied relative rates of nutrient addition. *Physiol. Plant.* 52:454–466.

Ingrens-Moller, H. 1957. Ecotypic response to temperature and photoperiod in Douglas-fir. *For. Sci.* 3:78–83.

Irving, L. 1964. Terrestrial animals in cold: birds and mammals. pp. 361–377. *In* D. B. Dill et al. (eds.), *Handbook of Physiology* Section 4. Adaptation to the Environment. Amer. Physiol. Soc., Wash. D.C. Waverly Press, Baltimore.

Isaac, L. A. 1930. Seed flight in the Douglas-fir region. *J. For.* 28:492–499.

————. 1938. Factors affecting Douglas-fir seedlings. USDA Agric. Circ. 486. 45 pp.

————. 1946. Fog drip and rain interception in coastal forests. USDA For. Serv. PNW For. Range Exp. Stat. Paper 34. 16 pp.

Ivanov, M. V. 1981. The global biogeochemical sulphur cycle. pp. 61–78. *In* G. E. Likens (ed.), *Some Perspectives of the Major Biogeochemical Cycles.* SCOPE-17. Wiley, New York.

Ives, J. D. 1974. Permafrost. pp. 159–194. *In* J. D. Ives and R. G. Barry (eds.), *Arctic and Alpine Environments.* Methuen, London.

————, and R. G. Barry (eds.). 1974. *Arctic and Alpine Environments.* Methuen, London. 999 pp.

Iwatsubo, G., and T. Tsutsumi. 1968. On the amount of plant nutrients supplied to the ground by rain water in adjacent open plot and forests. III. On the amount of plant nutrients contained in run-off water. *Bull. Kyoto Univ. For.* No. 40:140–156.

Jackson, R. M., and F. Rowe. 1966. *Life in the Soil. Studies in Biology.* No. 2, Edward Arnold, London. 60 pp.

Jacob, F. H. 1958. Some modern problems in pest control. *Sci. Prog.* 46(181):30–45.

Janzen, D. H. 1966. Coevolution of mutualism between ants and acacias in central America. *Evolution* 20:249–275.

————. 1967. Why mountain passes are higher in the tropics. *Amer. Nat.* 101:233–249.

————. 1970. Herbivores and the number of tree species in tropical forests. *Amer. Nat.* 104:501–528.

————. 1973. Tropical agroecosystems. *Sci.* 182:1212–1219.

————. 1974. Tropical blackwater rivers, animals, and mast fruiting by the Dipterocarpaceae. *Biotropica* 6:69–103.

————. 1979. How to be a fig. *Ann. Rev. Ecol. Syst.* 10:13–51.

Jarvis, P. G., and M. S. Jarvis. 1963. The water relations of tree seedlings. I. Growth and water use in relation to soil water potential. II. Some aspects of the tissue water relations and drought resistance. *Physiol. Plant.* 16:215–235, 501–516.

Jeffers, J. N. R. 1978. *An Introduction to Systems Analysis, with Ecological Applications.* Edward Arnold, London. 198 pp.

Jenkins, D., A. Watson, and G. R. Miller. 1963. Population studies on red grouse, *Lagopus lagopus scoticus* (Lath.) in North-East Scotland. *J. Anim. Ecol.* 32:317–376.

————, A. Watson, G. R. Miller, and N. Picozzi. 1964. Unit of grouse and moorland ecology. Rept. Nat. Conservancy 1964:95–98.

Jennings, D. H., and D. L. Lee (eds.). 1975. *Symbiosis.* Symposia of the Society for Experimental Biology No. XXIV. Cambridge Univ. Press, Cambridge. 633 pp.

Jenny, H. 1941. *Factors of Soil Formation.* McGraw-Hill, New York. 281 pp.

————. 1980. *The Soil Resource. Origin and Behavior.* Ecol. Stud. 37. Springer-Verlag, New York. 377 pp.

Jensen, J. 1962. [Investigations of the plant nutrient content in rain]. *Tidsskr. Planteavl.* 65:894–906.

Johnson, C. G. 1963. The aerial migration of insects. *Sci. Amer.* 209:132–138.

Johnson, D. W., D. W. Cole, and S. P. Gessel. 1979. Acid precipitation and soil sulphate properties in a tropical and in a temperate forest soil. *Biotropica* 11:38–42.

————, D. W. Cole, S. P. Gessel et al. 1977. Carbonic acid leaching in a tropical, temperate, subalpine, and northern forest soil. *Arctic and Alpine Res.* 9:329–343.

————, J. Turner and J. M. Kelley. 1982. The effects of acid rain on forest nutrient status. *Water Resour. Res.* 18:449–461.

Johnson, E. A., and J. S. Rowe. 1975. Fire in the sub-arctic wintering ground of the Beverly Caribou Herd. *Amer. Midl. Nat.* 94:1–14.

Johnson, N. M. 1971. Mineral equilibria in ecosystem geochemistry. *Ecol.* 52:529–531.

Johnson, P. L., and W. T. Swank. 1973. Studies of cation budgets in the southern Appalachians on four experimental watersheds with contrasting vegetation. *Ecol.* 54:70–80.

Jones, J. B., and A. E. Luchsinger. 1979. *Plant Systematics*. McGraw-Hill, NewYork. 388 pp.

Jones, J. R. 1969. Review and comparison of site evaluation methods. USDA For. Serv. Res. Paper RM-51. 27 pp.

Jones, K. 1976. Nitrogen fixing bacteria in the canopy of conifers in a temperate forest. pp. 451–463. *In* C. H. Dickinson and T. F. Preece (eds.), *Microbiology of Aerial Plant Surfaces*. Academic Press, London.

———. 1970. Nitrogen fixation in the phyllosphere of the Douglas-fir, *Pseudotsuga douglasii*. *Annals Bot.*, N.S. 34:239–244.

———. 1982. Nitrogen fixation in the canopy of temperate forest trees: a re-examination. *Annals Bot.* 50:329–334.

———, E. King, and M. Eastlick. 1974. Nitrogen fixation by free-living bacteria in the soil and in the canopy of Douglas-fir. *Annals Bot.* 38:765–772.

Jonsson, B., and R. Sundberg. 1972. Has the acidification by atmospheric pollution caused a growth reduction in Swedish forests? Inst. For Skogproduktion. Rapport 20. 48 pp.

Jordan, C. F. 1971. A world pattern in plant energetics. *Amer. Sci.* 59:425–433.

Jordan, C. F. 1985. *Nutrient Cycling in Tropical Forest Ecosystems*. Wiley, New York. 190 pp.

Juday, C. 1940. The annual energy budget of an inland lake. *Ecol.* 21:438–450.

Kahn, H., and W. Brown. 1975. A world turning point. *The Futurist*. December. 284 pp.

Kale, H. W. II. 1965. Ecology and bioenergetics of the Long-billed Marsh Wren in Georgia salt marshes. Publ. Nuttal Ornith. Club, No. 5.

Kalela, O. 1962. On the fluctuations in the numbers of arctic and boreal small rodents as a problem of production biology. *Ann. Acad. Sci. Fenn.* A IV 66:1–38.

Katagiri, S., and T. Tsutsumi. 1973. The relation between site condition and circulation of nutrients in forest ecosystems. I. Litterfall and nutrient contents. *J. Jap. For. Soc.* 55:83–90.

Katznelson, H. 1965. Nature and importance of the rhizosphere. pp. 187–209. *In* K. F. Baker and W. C. Snyder (eds.), *Ecology of Soil-Borne Plant Pathogens,* Univ. of Calif. Press, Berkeley.

Kayll, A. J. 1968. The role of fire in boreal forest of Canada. Petawawa For. Exp. Stat., Chalk River, Ontario. Info. Rept. PS-X-7.

Keever, C. 1950. Causes of succession on old fields of the Piedmont, North Carolina. *Ecol. Monogr.* 20:229–250.

Keith, L. B. 1963. *Wildlife's Ten-Year Cycle*. Univ. Wisconsin Press, Madison. 201 pp.

———, and L. A. Windberg. 1978. A demographic analysis of the snowshoe hare cycle. Wildl. Monogr. No. 58, 50 pp. Suppl. to *J. Wldl. Mgmt.* 42(2).

Keller, T. 1971. The effect of N nutrition on gas exchange in Norway spruce. *Allgem. Forst. U. Jagdztg.* 142:89–93.

Kellman, M. C. 1970. The viable seed content of some forest soil in coastal British Columbia. *Can. J. Bot.* 48:1383–1385.

Kellogg, W. W., R. D. Cadle, E. R. Allen et al. 1972. The sulphur cycle. *Sci.* 175:587–596.

Kelsall, J. P. 1968. *The Migratory Barren-ground Cariboo in Canada*. Can. Wildl. Serv., Ottawa. Queen's Printer. 340 pp.

Kendeigh, S. C. 1961. *Animal Ecology*. Prentice-Hall, Englewood Cliffs, N.J. 468 pp.

Kerfoot, O. 1968. Mist precipitation on vegetation. *For. Abstr.* 29(1):8–20.

Kershaw, K. A. 1973. *Quantitative and Dynamic Ecology*. Edward Arnold, London. 183 pp.

Kessell, S. R., and M. W. Potter. 1980. A quantitative succession model for nine Montana forest communities. *Environ. Mgmt.* 4:227–240.

Kettlewell, H. B. D. 1956. Further selection experiments on industrial melanism in the *Lepidoptera*. *Heredity* 10:287–301.

———. 1958. A survey of the frequencies of *Biston betulavia* (L.) (Lep.) and its melanic forms in Great Britain. *Heredity* 12:51–72.

Key, K. H. L. 1950. A critique of the phase theory of locusts. *Quart. Rev. Biol.* 25:363–407.

Keyes, M. R., and C. C. Grier. 1981. Above- and below-ground net reproduction in 40-year-old Douglas-fir stands on low and high productivity sites. *Can. J. For. Res.* 11:599–605.

Kilgore, B. M., and G. S. Briggs. 1972. Restoring fire to high elevation forests in California. *J. For.* 70:266–271.

Kilian, C., and G. Lemée. 1956. Les xerophytes: Leur économie d'êau. Handb. *Pflanzen-physiol* 3:787–824.

Kimber, P. C. 1974. The root system of Jarrah (*Eucalyptus marginata*). For. Dept. W. A. Res. Pap. No. 10, 5 pp.

Kimmins, J. P. 1970. Cyclic fluctuations in herbivore populations in northern ecosystems. A general hypothesis. Ph.D. thesis, Yale Univ., New Haven.

———. 1971. Variations in the foliar amino acid composition of flowering and non-flowering balsam fir (*Abies balsamea* (L.) Mill.) and white spruce (*Picea glauca* (Moench) Voss) in relation to outbreaks of the spruce budworm (*Choristoneura fumiferana* (Clem.)). *Can. J. Zool.* 49:1005–1011.

———. 1972. The ecology of forestry: the ecological role of man, the forester, in forest ecosystems. *For. Chron.* 48:301–307.

———. 1973. The renewability of natural resources: implications for forest management. *J. For.* 71:290–292.

———. 1974. Sustained yield, timber mining, and the concept of ecological rotation; a British Columbian view. *For. Chron.* 50:27–31.

———. 1977. Evaluation of the consequences for future tree productivity of the loss of nutrients in whole-tree harvesting. *For. Ecol. Mgmt.* 1(1977):169–183.

———. 1985. Future shock in forest yield forecasting: the need for a new approach. *For. Chron.* 61:503–512

———, and M. C. Feller. 1976. Effect of clearcutting and broadcast slashburning on nutrient budgets, streamwater chemistry and productivity in western Canada. pp. 186–197. Proc. XVI IUFRO World Congress, Div. I.

———, and B. Hawkes. 1978. Distribution and chemical content of fine roots in an old growth white-subalpine fir stand in central B.C. *Can. J. For. Res.* 8:265–279.

————, and K. A. Scoullar. 1979. FORCYTE: A computer simulation approach to evaluating the effect of whole tree harvesting on the nutrient budgets of northwest forests. pp. 266–273. *In* S. P. Gessel et al. (eds.), *Forest Fertilization Conference,* Proc. Inst. For. Resources, Univ. of Wash., Seattle, Contrib. No. 40.

————, and K. A. Scoullar. 1981. FORCYTE—a computer simulation approach to evaluating the effect of whole tree harvesting on nutrient budgets and future forest productivity. *Mitt. D. Forstl. Bundes-versuchsanstalt, Wien* 140:189–205.

————, and K. A. Scoullar. 1983. FORCYTE-10: A User's Manual. Faculty of Forestry, Univ. of B.C. Vancouver. 112 pp. + appen.

————, D. Binkley, L. Chatarpaul, and J. de Catanzaro. 1985. Biogeochemistry of temperate forest ecosystems: Literature on inventories and dynamics of biomass and nutrients. Can. For. Serv., Nat. For. Inst., Petawawa, Ont. Information Rept. PI-X-47 E/F 227 pp.

Kimura, M. 1960. Primary production of the warm-temperate laurel forest in the southern part of Osumi Peninsula, Kyushu, Japan. Misc. Rpt. Res. Inst. Nat. Resources, Tokyo. 52/53:36–47.

King, H. G. C., and C. W. Heath. 1967. The chemical analysis of small samples of leaf material and the relationship between disappearance and composition of leaves. *Pedobiologia* 7:192–197.

Kira, T., and T. Shidae. 1967. Primary production and turnover of organic matter in different forest ecosystems of the western Pacific. *J. Jap. Ecol.* 17:70–87.

————, K. Shinozaki, and K. Hozumi. 1969. Structure of forest canopies as related to their primary productivity. *Plant Cell Physiol.* 10:129–142.

Kitchell, J. F., R. V. O'Neill, and D. Webb et al. 1979. Consumer regulation of nutrient cycling. *BioSci.* 29:28–34.

Kittredge, J. 1940. A comparison of forest floors from plantations of the same age and environment. *J. For.* 38:729–732.

————. 1948. *Forest Influences. The Effects of Woody Vegetation on Climate, Water and Soil.* McGraw-Hill, New York. 394 pp.

Kleiber, M. 1961. *The Fire of Life: An Introduction to Animal Energetics.* Wiley, New York. 454 pp.

Klein, D. R. 1968. The introduction, increase, and crash of reindeer on St. Matthew Island. *J. Wldl. Mgmt.* 32:350–367.

Klemmedson, J. O. 1975. Nitrogen and carbon regimes in an ecosystem of young dense Ponderosa pine in Arizona. *For. Sci.* 21:163–168.

Klinka, K. 1976. Ecosystem units, classification, interpretation and mapping in the UBC Research Forest. Ph.D. thesis, Univ. of British Columbia, Vancouver.

————, W. D. van der Horst, F. C. Nuszdorfer, and R. G. Harding. 1980a. An ecosystematic approach to a subunit plan. Koprino River watershed study. BCFS Land Mgmt. Rept. No. 5. Ministry of Forests, B.C. 118 pp.

————, W. D. van der Horst, F. C. Nuszdorfer, and R. G. Harding. 1980b. An ecosystematic approach to forest planning. *For. Chron.* 56:97–103.

————, R. N. Green, R. L. Trowbridge, and L. E. Lowe. 1981. Taxonomic classification of humus forms in ecosystems of British Columbia. First approximation. Land Management Report Number 8. Ministry of Forests, Victoria, B.C. 54 pp.

Klock, G. O. 1982. Some soil erosion effects on forest soil productivity. pp. 53–66. *In* Determinants of Soil Loss Tolerance. Proc. Symp., Ft. Collins, Colorado. ASA Special Publ. No. 45, *Amer. Soc. Agron.; Soil Sci. Soc. Amer.* Madison, Wisc.

Klomp, H. 1970. The determination of clutch-size in birds. A review. *Ardea* 58:1:124.

Kluijver, H. N. 1951. The population ecology of the Great Tit, *Parus m.major. Ardea* 39:1–135.

Knabe, W. 1976. Effects of sulfur dioxide on terrestrial vegetation. *Ambio* 5:213–218.

Knapp, R. 1974. Cyclic successions and ecosystem approaches in vegetation dynamics. pp. 91–100. *In* R. Knapp (ed.), *Vegetation Dynamics,* Part 8, *Handbook of Vegetation Science.* W. Junk b.v., Publishers, The Hague.

Knight, H. 1966. Loss of nitrogen from the forest floor by burning. *For. Chron.* 42:149–152.

Knowles, P., and M. C. Grant. 1983. Age and size structure analyses of Engelmann spruce, ponderosa pine, lodgepole pine and limber pine in Colorado. *Ecol.* 64:1–9.

Knowles, R. 1965. The significance of non-symbiotic nitrogen fixation. *Soil Sci. Soc. Amer. Proc.* 29:223.

————. 1975. Interpretation of recent ^{15}N studies of nitrogen in forest ecosystems. pp. 53–65. *In* B. Bernier and C. H. Winget (eds.), *Forest Soils and Forest Land Management.* Laval Univ. Press, Quebec.

Koch, P. 1978. Five new machines and six products can triple commodity recovery from southern forests. *J. For.* 76:767–772.

————. 1980. Concept for southern pine plantation operation in the year 2020. *J. For.* 78:78–82.

Kojima, S. 1979. Biogeoclimatic zones of Hokkaido Island, Japan. *J. Coll. Liberal Arts,* Toyama Univ. 12:97–141.

————. 1981. Biogeoclimatic ecosystem classification and its practical use in forestry. *J. Coll. Liberal Arts,* Toyama Univ. 14:41–75.

Komarek, E. V. 1971. Principles of fire ecology and fire management in relation to the Alaskan environment. pp. 1–22. *In* C. W. Slaughter et al. (eds.), *Fire in the Northern Environment—A Symposium.* USDA For. Serv., PNW For. Range Exp. Sta., Portland, Ore.

Koppen, W. 1923. *Die Klimate der Erde: Grundriss der Klimakunde.* DeGruyter, Berlin and Leipzig. 369 pp.

Kormanik, P. P., W. C. Bryan, and R. C. Schultz. 1977. The role of mycorrhizae in plant growth and development. pp. 1–10. *In* H. M. Vines (ed.), Physiol. of Root-Microorganisms Associations. Proc. Symp., S. Sect. Amer. Soc. Plant Physiol., Atlanta.

Kormondy, E. J. (ed.). 1965. *Readings in Ecology.* Prentice-Hall, Englewood Cliffs, N.J. 219 pp.

————. 1969. *Concepts of Ecology.* Prentice-Hall, Englewood Cliffs, N.J. 209 pp.

Korstian, C. F., and N. J. Fetherolf. 1921. Control of stem girdle of spruce transplants caused by excessive heat. *Phytopathology* 11:485–490.

———, and T. S. Coile. 1938. Plant competition in forest stands. Duke Univ. Sch. For. Bull. 3. Durham, N.C. 125 pp.

Koskimmes, J. 1955. Ultimate causes of cyclic fluctuations in numbers in animal populations. Papers on Game Research. Finnish Game Foundation. No. 15. 29 pp.

Kowal, N. E. 1969. Effect of leaching on pine litter decomposition rate. *Ecol.* 50:739–740.

Kozlovsky, D. G. 1968. A critical evaluation of the trophic level concept. 1. Ecological efficiencies. *Ecol.* 49:48–60.

Kozlowski, T. T. 1962. Photosynthesis, climate and tree growth. pp. 149–164. *In* T. T. Kozlowski (ed.), *Tree Growth*. Ronald, New York.

——— (ed.). 1968–1978. *Water deficits and plant growth*. I. 1968. *Development, control and measurement*. II. 1968. *Plant water consumption and response*. III. 1972. *Plant responses and responses and control of water balance*. IV. 1977. *Soil water measurement, plant responses and breeding for drought resistance*. V. 1978. *Water and plant disease*. Academic Press, New York.

———, and C. E. Ahlgren (eds.). 1974. *Fire and Ecosystems*. Academic Press, New York. 542 pp.

Krajina, V. J. 1965. Biogeoclimatic zones in British Columbia. Ecol. West. N. Amer. (Univ. of British Columbia, Vancouver.) 1:1–17.

———. 1966. Biogeoclimatic zones of the Hawaiian Islands and their variation by volcanic activities. Pap. Presented to 11th Pac. Sci. Congr., Tokyo.

———. 1969. Ecology of forest trees in British Columbia. Ecol. West. N. Amer. (Univ. of British Columbia, Vancouver.) 2(1):1–147.

———. 1972. Ecosystem perspectives in forestry. H. R. MacMillan Lectureship in Forestry. Univ. of British Columbia, Vancouver. 31 pp.

Kramer, P. J. 1957. Some effects of various combinations of day and night temperatures and photoperiod on the growth of loblolly pine seedlings. *For. Sci.* 3:45–55.

———, and J. P. Decker. 1944. Relation between light intensity and rate of photosynthesis of loblolly pine and certain hardwoods. *Plant Physiol.* 19:350–358.

———, and T. T. Kozlowski. 1979. *Physiology of Woody Plants*. Academic Press, New York. 811 pp.

Krammes, J. S. 1965. Seasonal debris movement from steep mountainside slopes in southern California. pp. 85–89. *In* U.S. Dept. Agric. Misc. Publ. No. 970.

Kraus, J. F., and A. E. Squillace. 1964. Inheritance of yellow oleoresin and virescent foliage in slash pine. *Silvae Genet.* 13:114–116.

Krebs, C. J. 1964. The lemming cycle at Baker Lake, Northwest Territories, during 1959–62. Arctic Inst. N. Amer. Tech. Pap. No. 15.

———. 1978. *Ecology: The Experimental Analysis of Distribution and Abundance*. 2nd ed. Harper & Row, New York. 678 pp.

———, M. S. Gaines, B. L. Keller, J. H. Myers, and R. H. Tamarin. 1973. Population cycles in small rodents. *Sci.* 179:35–41.

———, and J. Myers. 1974. Population cycles in small mammals. *Adv. Ecol. Res.* 8:267–399.

Krefting, L. W., and H. L. Hansen. 1969. Increasing browse for deer by aerial applications of 2,4–D. *J. Wildl. Mgmt.* 33:784–790.

Kruckeberg, A. R. 1954. The ecology of serpentine soils. III. Plant species in relation to serpentine soils. *Ecol.* 35:267–274.

Krug, E. C., and C. R. Frink. 1983. Acid rain on acid soil. A new perspective. *Sci.* 221:520–525.

Krumlik, G. J. 1979. Comparative study of nutrient cycling in the subalpine Mountain Hemlock Zone of British Columbia. Ph.D. thesis, Univ. of B. C., Vancouver. 195 pp.

Kucera, C. L., and J. H. Ehrenreich. 1962. Some effects of annual burning on central Missouri prairie. *Ecol.* 43:334–336.

Küchler, A. W. 1947. A geographical system of vegetation. *Geogr. Rev.* (N.Y.) 37:233–240.

———. 1964. Potential natural vegetation of the conterminous United States. Manual to accompany map. *Amer. Geogr. Soc. Spec. Publ.* No. 36. 116 pp. + Rev. Map, 1965.

———. 1967. *Vegetation Mapping*. Ronald, New York. 472 pp.

Lack, D. 1947. *Darwin's Finches*. Cambridge Univ. Press, Cambridge. 208 pp.

———. 1954. *The Natural Regulation of Animal Numbers*. Oxford Univ. Press, New York. 343 pp.

Lamprecht, H. 1966. The two exmutants *laciniata* and *asplenifolia* of *Fagus sylvatica* and their genetical basis. *Phyton,* Horn. 11:188–198.

Landsburg, H. E. 1958. Trends in climatology. *Sci.* 128:749–758.

Langmaid, K. K. 1964. Some effects of earthworm invasion in virgin podzols. *Can. J. Soil Sci.* 44:34–37.

Langner, W. 1954. Beitrag zur Lösung des Problems der Befruchtungsoverhältnisse im Wald mittels einer Mendelspaltung. Compte rendus, 11e Congrès, Union internationale des instituts de recherches forestières, 1953:459–467.

Larsen, J. A. 1974. Ecology of the northern forest border. pp. 341–369. *In* J. D. Ives and R. G. Barry (eds.), *Arctic and Alpine Environments*. Methuen, London.

Larsen, P. R. 1963. Stem form development of forest trees. *For. Sci. Monogr.* 5. 42 pp.

Laukhart, J. B. 1957. Animal cycles and food. *J. Wildl. Mgmt.* 21:230–234.

———. 1962. Wildlife population fundamentals. 27th N. Amer. Wildl. Conf. 27:233–242.

Lawrence, D. B. 1939. Some features of the vegetation of the Columbia River gorge with special reference to asymmetry of forest trees. *Ecol. Monogr.* 19:217–257.

———. 1950. Glacier fluctuation for six centuries in southeastern Alaska and its relation to solar activity. *Geogr. Rev.* 40:191–223.

———. 1958. Glaciers and vegetation in southeastern Alaska. *Amer. Sci.* 46:89–122.

———, R. E. Sehonihi, A. Quispel, and G. Bond. 1967. Role of *Dryas drummondi* in vegetation development. *J. Ecol.* 55:793–813.

Leaf, A. L. (ed.). 1979. *Impact of Intensive Harvesting on Forest Nutrient Cycling*. Proc. Symp., Coll. Environ. Sci. and For. State Univ. Syracuse, N.Y. 421 pp.

Ledig, F. T., and J. H. Fryer. 1971. The serotinous cone habit in *Pinus rigida* as related to selection in introgression. Contrib. Pap. Work. Group on Quant. Genetics. IUFRO Congr. Gainesville, Fla. 1971.

———, and D. R. Korbobo. 1983. Adaptation of sugar maple populations along altitudinal gradients: photosynthesis, respiration, and specific leaf weight. *Amer. J. Bot.* 70:256–265.

Lee, J. J., and D. L. Inman. 1975. The ecological role of consumers—an integrated ecosystem view. *Ecol.* 56:1455–1458.

Leonard, R. E. 1961. Interception of precipitation by northern hardwoods. USDA For. Serv., NE For. Exp. Sta., Upper Darby. Station Paper No. 159. 16 pp.

Levitt, J. 1958. Frost, drought and heat resistance. *Protoplasmatologia* 6, 87 pp.

———. 1972. *Responses of Plants to Environmental Stress*. Academic Press, New York. 697 pp.

Lewis, W. M., Jr. 1974. Effects of fire on nutrient movement in a South Carolina pine forest. *Ecol.* 55:1120–1127.

Leyton, L., and L. Z. Rousseau. 1958. Root growth of seedlings in relation to aeration. pp. 467–475. *In* K. V. Thimann (ed.), *Physiology of Forest Trees*. Ronald Press, New York.

Likens, G. E. 1981. *Some Perspectives of the Major Biogeochemical Cycles. Scope 17*. Wiley, New York. 175 pp.

———, F. H. Bormann, and N. M. Johnson. 1969. Nitrification: importance to nutrient losses from a cutover forested ecosystem. *Sci.* 163:1205–1206.

———, F. H. Bormann, N. M. Johnson, D. W. Fisher, and R. S. Pierce. 1970. Effects of forest cutting and herbicide treatment on nutrient budgets in the Hubbard Brook watershed-ecosystem. *Ecol. Monogr.* 40:23–47.

———, F. H. Bormann, R. S. Pierce, J. S. Eaton, and N. M. Johnson. 1977. *Biogeochemistry of a Forested Ecosystem*. Springer-Verlag, New York. 146 pp.

Lillesand, T. M., and R. W. Kiefer. 1980. *Remote Sensing and Image Interpretation*. Wiley, New York. 612 pp.

Lindeman, R. L. 1942. The trophic-dynamic aspect of ecology. *Ecol.* 23:399–418.

Linder, S. (ed.). 1981. Understanding and predicting tree growth. *Studia Forestalia Suecica* No. 160. 87 pp.

Lines, R., and R. S. Howell. 1963. The use of flags to estimate the relative exposure of trial plantations. Forestry Commission: Forestry Record #51. London. 31 pp.

Livingston, B. E., and F. Shreve. 1921. The distribution of vegetation in the United States as related to climatic conditions. Carnegie Inst. Wash. Publ. 284. 590 pp.

Lloyd, P. S. 1971. Effect of fire on the chemical status of herbaceous communities of the Derbyshire Dales. *J. Ecol.* 59:261–273.

Logan, K. T. 1966. Growth of tree seedlings as affected by light intensity: II. Red pine, white pine, jack pine and eastern larch. Dept. For. Can., Publ. 1160. 19 pp.

Longman, K. A., and J. Jenik. 1974. *Tropical Forest and its Environment*. Longman, London. 196 pp.

Lorenz, R. W. 1939. High temperature tolerance of forest trees. Univ. Minn. Agr. Exp. Stat. Tech. Bull. 141. 25 pp.

Lotka, A. J. 1925. *Elements of Physical Biology*. Williams and Wilkins, Baltimore.

Loucks, O. L., A. R. Ek, W. C. Johnson, and R. A. Monserud. 1981. Growth, aging and succession. pp. 37–85. *In* D. E. Reichle (ed.), *Dynamics Properties of Forest Ecosystems*. International Biological Programme 23. Cambridge Univ. Press, Cambridge.

Lovat, Lord. 1911. Moor management. pp. 372–391. *In* Lord Lovat (ed.), *The Grouse in Health and Disease*. London.

Love, D. 1970. Subarctic and subalpine: where and what? *Arctic and Alpine Res.* 2:63–71.

Lovejoy, T. E., and D. C. Oren. 1981. The minimal critical size of ecosystems. pp. 7–12. *In* R. L. Burgess and D. M. Sharpe (eds.), *Forest Island Dynamics in Man-Dominated Landscapes*. Springer-Verlag, New York. 311 pp.

Loveless, A. R. 1961. A nutritional interpretation of sclerophylly based on differences in the chemical composition of sclerophyllous and mesophytic leaves. *Annals Bot.* 25:168–184.

———. 1962. Further evidence to support a nutritional interpretation of sclerophylly. *Annals Bot.* 26:551–561.

Lowe, V. P. W. 1969. Population dynamics of the red deer (*Cervus elaphus* L.) on Rhum. *J. Anim. Ecol.* 38:425–457.

Lull, H. W. 1951. Forest fire smoke of September 1950. *J. For.* 49:286.

Lulla, K. 1981. Remote sensing in ecological studies. *Can. J. Remote Sensing* 7:97–107.

Lutz, H. J. 1956. Ecological effects of forest fires in the interior of Alaska. USDA Tech. Bull. No. 1133. 121 pp.

———, and R. F. Chandler Jr. 1946. *Forest Soils*. Wiley, New York. 514 pp.

MacArthur, R. H., and E. O. Wilson. 1967. *The Theory of Island Biogeography*. Princeton Univ. Press, Princeton.

MacArthur, R. H. 1958. Population ecology of some warblers of north eastern coniferous forests. *Ecol.* 39:599–619.

———, and J. W. MacArthur. 1961. On bird species diversity. *Ecol.* 42:594–598.

MacDougal, D. T., and E. B. Working. 1921. Another high temperature record for growth and endurance. *Sci.* 54:152–153.

MacHattie, L. B. 1963. Winter injury of lodgepole pine foliage. *Weather* (London) 18:301–307.

MacLean, D. A. 1978. Fire and the nutrient cycle of New Brunswick pine and hardwood stands: field studies and computer simulation studies. Ph.D. thesis, Univ. of New Brunswick, Fredericton. 324 pp.

———, and R. W. Wein. 1980. Simulation of wildfire effects on the nitrogen cycle of a *Pinus banksiana* ecosystem in New Brunswick, Canada. *Ecological Modelling* 10:167–192.

———, S. J. Woodley, M. G. Weber, and R. W. Wein. 1981.

Fire and nutrient cycling. Chap. 7. *In* R. W. Wein and D. A. MacLean (eds.). *The Role of Fire in Northern Circumpolar Ecosystems*. Scope 18; Wiley, New York.

MacLulich, D. A. 1937. Fluctuations in the numbers of British tetraonids. *J. Anim. Ecol.* 21:128–153.

MacMahon, J. A. 1980. Ecosystems over time succession and other types of change. pp. 27–58. *In* R. H. Waring (ed.), *Forests: Fresh Perspectives from Ecosystem Analysis*. Oregon State Univ. Press, Corvallis.

Mace, A. C., Jr. 1970. Soil compaction due to tree length and full tree skidding with rubber tired skidders. Minn. For. Res. Note. No. 214. 4 pp.

Machta, L. 1973. Prediction of CO_2 in the atmosphere. pp. 21–31. *In* G. M. Woodwell and E. V. Pecan (eds.), Carbon in the Biosphere. AEC Symp. Series 30, Tech. Info. Center, Off. Of Info. Services. USAEC.

Mackay, J. R. 1970. Disturbances to the tundra and forest tundra environment of the western Arctic. *Can. Geotech. J.* 7:420–432.

Mackenzie, J. M. D. 1952. Fluctuations in the numbers of British tetraonids. *J. Anim. Ecol.* 21:128–153.

Mader, D. L., and H. W. Lull. 1968. Depth, weight and water storage of the forest floor in white pine stands in Massachusetts. USDA For. Serv., NE For. Exp. Sta. Res. Pap. No. NE–109. 35 pp.

Madge, D. S. 1965. Leaf fall and disappearance in a tropical forest. *Pedobiologia* 5:273–288.

Madgewick, H. A. I., and J. D. Ovington. 1959. The chemical composition of precipitation in adjacent forest and open plots. *For.* 32:14–22.

Mahendrappa, M. K. 1974. Chemical composition of stemflow from some eastern Canadian tree species. *Can. J. For. Res.* 4:1–7.

Majawa, A. O. 1977. Phytoecological impacts and management implications of the Douglas-fir tussock moth near Kamloops, British Columbia. M.Sc. thesis, Univ. of B.C., Vancouver.

Major, J. 1951. A functional, factorial approach to plant ecology. *Ecol.* 32:392–412.

————. 1974. Accumulation of ash elements and pH changes. pp. 215–218. *In* R. Knapp (ed.), *Vegetation Dynamics*, Vol. 8, *Handbook of Vegetation Science*. Junk b.v., Publishers, The Hague.

Malcolm, D. C. 1975. The influence of heather on silviculture practice—an appraisal. *Scottish For.* 29(1):14–24.

Malkonen, E. 1974. Annual primary production and nutrient cycle in some scots pine stands. Comm., Inst. For. Fenn. 84.5 87 pp.

Malthus, T. R. 1978. *An Essay on the Principle of Population as it Affects the Future Improvement of Society*. Johnson, London.

Marchand, D. E. 1971. Rates and modes of denudation, White Mountains, eastern California. *Amer. J. Sci.* 270:109–135.

Margalef, R. 1975. Diversity, stability and maturity in natural ecosystems. pp. 151–160. *In* W. H. van Dobben and R. H. Lowe-McConnell (eds.), *Unifying Concepts in Ecology*. W. Junk, b.v., Publishers, The Hague.

Marion, G. M. 1979. Biomass and nutrient removal in long-rotation stands. pp. 98–110. *In Proc. Impact of Intensive Harvesting on Forest Nutrient Cycling*. Coll. Environ. Sci. & For., SUNY, Syracuse, N.Y.

Marks, G. C., and T. T. Kozlowski. 1973. *Ectomycorrhizae: Their Ecology and Physiology*. Academic Press, New York. 444 pp.

Marks, P. 1974. The role of pin cherry (*Prunus pensylvanica* L.) in the maintenance of stability in northern hardwood ecosystems. *Ecol. Monogr.* 44:73–88.

Marriage, P. B., and S. I. Warwick. 1980. The selection of herbicide resistant biotypes of *Chenopodium album* L. *Weed Res.* 20:9–15.

Marshall, A. J., and H. S. deS. Disney. 1957. Experimental induction of the breeding seasons in a xerophilous bird. *Nature* 180:647.

Marshall, W. H. 1954. Ruffed grouse and snowshore hare populations on the Cloquet Experimental Forest, Minnesota. *J. Wildl. Mgmt.* 18:109–112.

Martin, C. W., and R. S. Pierce. 1979. Clearcutting patterns affect nitrate and calcium in streams in New Hampshire. *J. For.* 78:268–272.

Martin, P. S. 1966. Africa and Pleistocene overkill. *Nature* 212:339–342.

————. 1967. Africa and Pleistocene overkill. pp. 75–120. *In* P. S. Martin and H. E. Wright (eds.), *Pleistocene Extinctions*, Yale Univ. Press, New Haven.

Marx, D. H., and W. C. Brian. 1976. The significance of mycorrhizae to forest trees. pp. 107–117. *In* B. Bernier and C. H. Winget (eds.), *Forest Soils and Forest Land Management*. Laval Univ. Press, Quebec.

Mason, B. 1966. *Principles of Geochemistry*. 3rd ed. Wiley, New York. 329 pp.

Mason, D. I. 1915. The life history of lodgepole pine in the Rocky mountains. USDA, For. Serv., Bull. 154. 33 pp.

Materna, J. 1979. The influence of air pollution on the stability of spruce ecosystems. pp. 343–354. *In* E. Klimo (ed.), *Stability of Spruce Forest Ecosystems*. Proc. Symp. MAB/IUFRO, Univ. of Agri., Brno, Czechoslovakia.

Matthews, J. D. 1963. Factors affecting the production of seed by forest trees. *For. Abs.* 24:i–xiii.

Mattson, W. J. Jr. 1980. Herbivory in relation to plant nitrogen content. *Ann. Rev. Ecol. Syst.* 11:119–161.

————, and N. D. Addy. 1975. Phytophagous insects as regulators of forest primary production. *Sci.* 190:515–522.

May, R. H. 1975. Stability in ecosystems: some comments. pp. 161–168. *In* W. H. van Dobben and R. H. Lowe-McConnell (eds.), *Unifying Concepts in Ecology*. W. Junk, b.v., Publishers, The Hague.

————. 1978. The evolution of ecological systems. *Sci. Amer.* 239(3):160–175.

McBeath, J. H., G. P. Juday, G. Weller, and M. Murray (eds.). 1984. The potential effects of carbon dioxide-induced climatic change in Alaska. Conf. Proc. Sch. Agr. and Land Res. Mgmt., Univ. of Alaska, Fairbanks. Misc. Publ. 83–1. 208 pp.

McDermott, R. E. 1954. Seedling tolerance as a factor in bottom-land timber succession. Mo. Agr. Exp. Stat. Res. Bull. 557. 11 pp.

McFee, W. W., and E. L. Stone. 1965. Quantity, distribution and variability of organic matter and nutrients in a forest podzol in New York. *Soil Sci. Soc. Amer. Proc.* 29:432–436.

McLachlin, R. 1983. Winter wren dispersion in coastal western hemlock forest (dry subzone) in southwestern British Columbia. Ph.D. thesis, Univ. of B.C., Vancouver.

McLean, D. L., and M. R. Lockman. 1967. Forest fire losses in Canada, 1966. Can. Dept. Forest and Rural Devel., For. Fire Res. Inst. Rept.

McNaughton, F. G., and T. A. Black. 1973. A study of evapotranspiration from a Douglas-fir forest using the energy balance approach. *Water Resources Res.* 9:1579–1590.

McNaughton, S. J., and L. L. Wolf. 1973. *General Ecology*. Holt, Rinehart and Winston, Inc., New York. 710 pp.

McPhee, W. W., and E. L. Stone. 1965. Quantity, distribution and variability of organic matter and nutrients in a forest podzol in New York. *Soil Sci. Soc. Amer. Proc.* 29:432–436.

McPherson, J. K., and C. H. Muller. 1969. Allelopathic effects of *Adenostoma fasciculatum*, "Chamise" in the California chaparral. *Ecol. Monogr.* 39:177–198.

McWhirter, N., and R. McWhirter. 1975. *Guiness Book of Records*. Guiness Superlatives, Enfield, UK.

Meadows, D. H., D. L. Meadows, J. Randers, and W. W. Behrens III. 1972. *The Limits to Growth. A report for the Club of Rome's Project on the Predicament of Mankind*. Pan Books, London. 205 pp.

Means, J. E. (ed.). 1982. *Forest Successional Stand Development Research in the Northwest*. Forest Res. Lab., Oregon State Univ., Corvallis. 170 pp.

Means, T. H. 1927. Fog precipitated by trees. *J. For.* 25:1015–1016.

Meentmeyer, V. 1978. Macroclimate and lignin control of litter decomposition rates. *Ecol.* 59:465–472.

Meiklejohn, J. 1953. The effect of bush burning on the microflora of some Kenya soils. *Proc. 6th Int. Conf. Microbiol.* 1953 10:317–319.

Mekaru, T., and G. Uehara. 1972. Anion absorption in furruginous tropical soils. *Soil Sci. Soc. Amer. Proc.,* 36:296–300.

Metz, L. J., and M. H. Farrier. 1971. Prescribed burning and soil mesofauna on the Santee Experimental Forest. pp. 100–106. *In* Prescribed Burning Symposium. USDA For. Serv. SE For. Exp. Sta., Ashville, S.C.

Mikola, P. 1962. Temperature and tree growth near the northern timber line. pp. 265–274. *In* T. T. Kozlowski (ed.), *Tree Growth*. Ronald, New York.

———. 1970. Mycorrhizal innoculation in afforestation. *Internat. Rev. For. Res.* 3:123–197.

Miller, G. R., D. Jenkins, and A. Watson. 1966. Heather performance and red grouse populations. 1. Visual estimates of heather performance. *J. Appl. Ecol.* 3:313–326.

Miller, H. G. 1979. The nutrient budgets of even-aged forests. pp. 221–256. *In* E. D. Ford et al. (eds.), *The Ecology of Even-aged Forest Plantations*. Inst. Terrestrial Ecol., Cambridge.

———, and B. L. Williams. 1968. Research on forest soils and tree nutrition. pp. 143–147. *In* Rep. For. Res. London.

———, and J. D. Miller. 1976. Effects of nitrogen supply on net primary production in Corsican pine. *J. Appl. Ecol.* 13:249–256.

———, J. M. Cooper, and J. D. Miller. 1976. Effect of nitrogen supply on nutrients in litter fall and crown leaching in a stand of Corsican pine. *J. Appl. Ecol.* 13:233–248.

———, J. M. Cooper, J. D. Miller, and O. J. Pauline. 1979. Nutrient cycles in pine and their adaptation to poor soils. *Can. J. For. Res.* 9:19–26.

Miller, R. S. 1964. Ecology and distribution of pocket gophers (Geomyidae) in Colorado. *Ecol.* 45:256–272.

Miller, W. F. 1966. Annual changes in foliar nitrogen, phosphorus and potassium levels of loblolly pine (*Pinus taeda* L.) with site and weather factors. *Plant and Soil* 24:369–378.

Milne, A. 1957. The natural control of insect populations. *Can. Entomol.* 89:193–213.

———. 1962. On a theory of natural control of insect population. *J. Theoret. Biol.* 3:19–26, 32–42, 48–50.

Mitchell, J. E., J. B. Waide, and R. L. Todd. 1975. A preliminary compartment model of the nitrogen cycle in a deciduous forest ecosystem. pp. 41–57. *In* F. G. Howell et al. (eds.), *Mineral Cycling in Southeastern Ecosystems*. Tech. Info. Centre, Oak Ridge, TN. 898 pp. CONF-740513.

Mitsch, W. J., R. W. Bosserman, and J. M. Klopatek. 1981. *Energy and Ecological Modelling*. Elsevier Sci. Publ. New York. 839 pp.

Möller, C. M., D. Muller, and J. Nielson. 1954. Graphic presentation of dry matter production of European beech. *Forst. Fors. Danm* 21:327–335.

Moncrief, L. W. 1970. The cultural basis for our environmental crisis. *Sci.* 170:508–512.

Money, D. C. 1972. *Climate, Soils and Vegetation*. 2nd ed., Univ. Tutorial Press, London. 272 pp.

Monk, C. D. 1966. An ecological significance of evergreenness. *Ecol.* 47:504–505.

Montes, R., and E. Medina. 1977. Seasonal changes in nutrient content of leaves of savanna trees with different ecological behaviour. *Geo. Eco. Trop.* 1:295–307.

Mooney, H. A., and F. Shropshire. 1967. Population variability in temperature related to photosynthetic acclimation. *Oecol. Plant.* 2:1–13.

———, and M. Godvan (eds.). 1983. *Disturbance and Ecosystems*. Ecological Studies 44. Springer-Verlag, New York. 297 pp.

Moore, J. M., and R. W. Wein. 1977. Viable seed populations by soil depth and potential site recolonization after disturbance. *Can. J. Bot.* 55:2408–2412.

Moreau, R. E. 1966. *The Bird Faunas of Africa and its Islands*. Academic Press, New York. 424 pp.

Morgenstern, E. K. 1969. Genetic variation in seedlings of *Picea mariana* (Mill.) B.S.P. I. Correlation with ecological factors. II. Variation patterns. *Silv. Genet*. 18:151–160; 161–167.

Morris, R. F. 1963. The dynamics of epidemic spruce budworm populations. *Mem. Entomol. Soc. Can*. 31:1–332.

Morrison, I. K. 1974. Mineral nutrition of conifers with special reference to nutrient status interpretation: A review of literature. Can. For. Serv. No. 1343. 74 pp.

———. 1984. Acid rain. A review of literature on acid deposition effects in forest ecosystems. *For. Abstr*. 45:483–506.

Moser, M. 1959. Die künstliche Mykorrhizaimpfung an Forstpflanzen. III. Die Impfmethodic im Forstgarten. Forstwiss. Cbl. 78:193–202.

Moss, R. 1967a. Food selection and nutrition in ptarmigan (*Lagopus mutus*). Symp. Zool. Soc. Lond. No. 21:207–216.

———. 1967b. Probable limiting nutrients in the main food of red grouse (*Lagopus lagopus scoticus*). pp. 369–379. *In* K. Petrusewicz (ed.), *Secondary Productivity of Terrestrial Ecosystems*. IBP, Krakow, Warsaw.

———. 1972. Food selection by red grouse (*Lagopus l. scoticus*) in relation to chemical composition. *J. Anim. Ecol*. 44:233–244.

Mount, A. B. 1969. Eucalypt ecology as related to fire. *Proc. Tall Timbers Fire Ecol. Conf*. 9:75–108.

Mueller-Dombois, D., and H. Ellenberg. 1974. *Aims and Methods of Vegetation Ecology*. Wiley, New York. 547 pp.

Mukammal, E. I. 1965. Ozone as a cause of tobacco injury. *Agric. Meteorol*. 2:145–165.

Muller-Stoll, W. R. 1947. Der Einfluss der Ernährung auf die xeromorphie der Hochmoor pflanzen. *Planta* 35:225–251.

Muller, C. H. 1969. Allelopathy as a factor in ecological processes. *Vegetatio* 18:348–357.

———. 1970. Phototoxins as plant habitat variables. *Recent Adv. Phytochem* 3:105–121.

———, R. B. Hanawalt, and J. K. McPherson. 1968. Allelopathic control of herb growth in the fire cycle of California chaparral. *Bull. Torrey Bot. Club* 95:225–231.

Murray, K. F. 1965. Population changes during the 1957–58 vole (*Microtus*) outbreak in California. *Ecol*. 46:163–171.

Mustanoja, K. J., and A. L. Leaf. 1965. Forest fertilization research, 1957–1964. *Bot. Rev*. 31:151–246.

Mutch, R. W. 1970. Wildland fires and ecosystems—a hypothesis. *Ecol*. 51:1046–1051.

Myers, K. 1967. Morphological changes in the adrenal glands of wild rabbits. *Nature* 213:147–150.

Myers, N. 1980. *Conversion of Tropical Moist Forest*. Nat. Acad. Sci., Wash. D.C. 205 pp.

Nägeli, W. 1946. Weitere Untersuchungen über die Windverhältnisse im Bereich von Windschutzstreifen. *Mitteil. schweiz. Anstalt forstl. Versuch*., Zürich 24:659–737.

National Academy of Sciences. 1975. *Productivity of World Ecosystems*. Proc. Symp. Nat. Acad. Sci., Washington, D.C. 166 pp.

Neiland, B. J. 1971. The forest-bog complex of southeast Alaska. *Vegetatio* 22:1–64.

Newman, K. 1979. Sapwood basal area as an estimator of individual tree growth. M.Sc. thesis, Sch. For., Ore. State Univ., Corvallis. 65 pp.

Newton, M., B. A. El Hassan, and J. Zavitovski. 1968. Role of red alder in western Oregon forest succession. pp. 73–84. *In* J. M. Trappe et al. (eds.), *Biology of Alder*. USDA For. Serv., PNW For. and Range Exp. Sta., Portland, Ore.

Nicholson, A. J. 1933. The balance of populations. *J. Anim. Ecol*. 2:132–148, 178.

Niciporovic, A. A. 1968. Evaluation of productivity by study of photosynthesis as a function of illumination. pp. 261–270. *In Functioning of Terrestrial Ecosystems at the Primary Production Level*. UNESCO, Paris.

Niering, W. A., and F. E. Egler. 1955. A shrub community of *Viburnum lentago* stable for twenty-five years. *Ecol*. 36:356–360.

Nihlgard, B. 1972. Plant biomass, primary production and distribution of chemical elements in a beech and a planted spruce forest in South Sweden. *Oikos* 23:69–81.

Noble, I. R., and R. O. Slatyer. 1977. Post-fire succession of plants in mediterranean ecosystems. pp. 27–63. *In* Mooney, H. A. and C. E. Conrad (eds.), *Proc.—Symp. on the Environmental Consequences of Fire and Fuel Management in Mediterranean Ecosystem*. USDA For. Serv. Gen. Tech. Rept. WO-3.

———, and R. O. Slatyer. 1980. The effect of disturbance on plant succession. *Proc. Ecol. Soc. Aust*. 10:135–145.

Nortcliff, S., and J. B. Thornes. 1977. Water and cation movement in a tropical rain forest environment. 1. Objectives, experimental design and preliminary results. Discussion Paper No. 62. London School of Economics.

Nuszdorfer, F. C. 1982. Vertical distribution and biomass of fine roots in three subalpine forest plant associations in southwestern British Columbia. M.Sc. thesis, University of B.C., Vancouver. 172 pp.

Nye, P. H. 1954. Some soil forming processes in the humid tropics. I. A field study of a catena in a West African Forest. *J. Soil Sci*. 5:7–21.

———. 1961. Organic matter and nutrient cycles under moist tropical forest. *Plant and Soil* 13:333–346.

———, and D. J. Greenland. 1960. The soil under shifting cultivation. Commonw. Bur. Soil Sci., Harpenden, Tech. Commun. No. 51. 156 pp.

———, and D. J. Greenland. 1964. Changes in the soil after clearcutting tropical forest. *Plant and Soil* 21:101–112.

Oberlander, G. T. 1956. Summer fog precipitation of the San Francisco peninsula. *Ecol*. 37:851–852.

Oberle, M. 1969. Forest fires: suppression policy has its ecological drawbacks. *Sci*. 165:568–571.

O'Connor, F. B. 1957. An ecological study of the enchytraeid worm population of a coniferous forest soil. *Oikos* 8:161–199.

Odum, E. P. 1962. Relationships between structure and function in the ecosystem. *Jap. J. of Ecol.* 12:108–118.

———. 1969. The strategy of ecosystem development. *Sci.* 164:262–270.

———. 1971. *Fundamentals of Ecology.* 3rd ed. W. B. Saunders Co., Toronto, 574 pp.

Odum, H. T. 1956. Efficiencies, size of organisms, and community structure. *Ecol.* 37:592–597.

———. 1957. Trophic structure and productivity of Silver Springs, Florida. *Ecol. Monogr.* 27:55–112.

———, and R. F. Pigeon (eds.). 1970. A tropical rain forest. A study of irradiation and ecology at El Verde, Puerto Rico. Nat. Tech. Info. Serv., Springfield, Vt. 1678 pp.

Oke, T. R. 1978. *Boundary Layer Climates.* Methuen, London. 372 pp.

Old, S. M. 1969. Microclimate, fire and plant production in an Illinois prairie. *Ecol. Monogr.* 39:355–384.

Olmsted, N. W., and J. D. Curtis. 1947. Seeds of the forest floor. *Ecol.* 28:49–52.

O'Loughlin, C. L. 1974. A study of tree root strength deterioration following clearcutting. *Can. J. For. Res.* 4:107–113.

Olson, J. S. 1963. Energy storage and the balance of producers and decomposers in ecological systems. *Ecol.* 44:322–331.

———. 1982. Earth's vegetation and atmospheric carbon dioxide. pp. 388–398. *In* W. C. Clark (ed.), *Carbon Dioxide Review: 1982.* Clarendon Press, Oxford.

O'Neill, R. V. 1976. Ecosystem persistence and heterotrophic regulation. *Ecol.* 57:1244–1253.

———, and D. E. Reichle. 1980. Dimensions of ecosystem theory. pp. 11–26. *In* R. H. Waring (ed.), *Forests: Fresh Perspectives from Ecosystem Analysis.* Oregon State Univ. Press, Corvallis.

———, and D. L. DeAngelis. 1981. Comparative productivity and biomass relations of forest ecosystems. pp. 411–449. *In* D. E. Reichle (ed.), *Dynamic Properties of Forest Ecosystems.* International Biological Programme 23. Cambridge Univ. Press, Cambridge.

———, W. F. Harris, B. S. Ausmus, and D. E. Reichle. 1975. A theoretical basis for ecosystem analysis with particular reference to element cycling. pp. 28–40. *In* F. W. Howell, J. B. Gentry, and M. H. Smith (eds.), *Mineral Cycling in Southeastern Ecosystems.* ERDA Symp. Ser., U.S. Energy Res. and Devel. Admin. CONF-740513.

Oosting, H. J. 1956. *The Study of Plant Communities: An Introduction to Plant Ecology.* 2nd ed. W. H. Freeman and Co., San Francisco. 440 pp.

Oppenheimer, H. R. 1951. Summer drought and water balance of plants growing in the near east. *J. Ecol.* 39:357–362.

Orians, G. H. 1975. Diversity, stability and maturity in natural ecosystems. pp. 139–150. *In* W. H. van Dobben and R. H. Lowe-McConnell (eds.), *Unifying Concepts in Ecology.* W. Junk, b.v., Publishers, The Hague.

———, and F. A. Pitelka. 1960. Range management for the animal ecologist. *Ecol.* 41:406.

Ostman, N. L., and G. T. Weaver. 1982. Autumnal nutrient transfers by retranslocation, leaching and litter fall in a chestnut oak forest in southern Illinois. *Can. J. For. Res.* 12:49–51.

Ovington, J. D. 1957. Dry matter production by *Pinus sylvestris* L. *Ann. Bot.* 21:287–314.

———. 1959. Mineral content of plantations of *Pinus sylvestris* L. *Ann. Bot.* 23:75–88.

———. 1961. Some aspects of energy flow in populations of *Pinus sylvestris. Annals of Botany* N.S. 25:12–20.

———. 1962. Quantitative ecology and the woodland ecosystem concept. *Adv. Ecol. Res.* 1:103–192.

Paine, R. T. 1966. Food web complexity and species diversity. *Amer. Nat.* 100:65–75.

Palmer, R. W. V. (ed.). 1968. *Wind Effects on the Forest.* Suppl. to *For.* Oxford Univ. Press, London. 93 pp.

Park, T. 1962. Beetles; competition and populations. *Sci.* 138:1369–1375.

———, P. H. Leslie, and D. B. Mertz. 1961. Genetic strains of *Tribolium:* Their primary characteristics. *Physiol. Zool.* 34:62–80.

Parker, J. 1953. Photosynthesis of *Picea excelsa* (*P. abies*) in winter. *Ecol.* 34:605–609.

———. 1963. Cold resistance in woody plants. *Bot. Rev.* 29:123–201.

Parkinson, J. A. 1984. Nitrogen and phosphorus retranslocation from needles of Douglas-fir growing on three site-types. M.Sc. thesis, Univ. of B.C., Vancouver. 116 pp.

Pauley, S. S. 1958. Photoperiodism in relation to tree improvement. pp. 557–571. *In* K. V. Thimann (ed.), *The Physiology of Forest Trees.* Ronald, New York.

———, and T. O. Perry. 1954. Ecotypic variation of the photoperiodic response in *Populus. J. Arnold Arbor.* 35:167–188.

Pearman, G. I. (ed.). 1980. *Carbon dioxide and climate: Australian Research.* Aust. Acad. Sci., Canberra. 217 pp.

Pears, N. V. 1968. The natural altitudinal limit of forest in the Scottish Grampians. *Oikos* 19:71–80.

———. 1972. Interpretation problems in the study of tree-line fluctuations. Chap. 3. *In* J. A. Taylor (ed.), *Forest Meteorology: an Aberystinyth Symposium.* Univ. College of Wales, Aberystwyth.

Perrin, C. J. 1981. On the summer regulation of nitrogen and phosphorus transport in a small stream of southwestern British Columbia. M.Sc. thesis, Univ. of B.C., Vancouver. 144 pp.

Perry, T. O. 1962. Racial variation in the day and night temperature requirements of red maple and loblolly pine. *Forest Science* 8:336–344.

———. 1971. Dormancy of trees in winter. *Sci.* 171:29–36.

Pfister, R. D. 1976. Forest habitat type classification, mapping, and ecoregions in the northern Rocky Mountains. Discussion paper, XVI IUFRO Congress, Oslo, 1976.

———, and S. F. Arno. 1980. Classifying forest habitat types based on potential climax vegetation. *For. Sci.* 26:52–70.

———, B. L. Kovalchik, S. F. Arno, and R. C. Presby. 1977. Forest habitat types of Montana. USDA For. Serv. Gen.

Tech. Rept. INT-34. Intermountain For. and Range Exp. Sta. 174 pp.

Phillips, J. 1931. The biotic community. *J. Ecol.* 19:1–24.

———. 1934, 1935a, 1935b. Succession, development, the climax and the complex organism: an analysis of concepts. Parts I, II and III. *J. Ecol.* 22:554–571; 23:210–246, 488–508.

Phillipson, J. 1966. *Ecological Energetics*. Edward Arnold, London. 57 pp.

Pianka, E. R. 1970. On r- and K-selection. *Amer. Nat.* 104:592–597.

Pierce, R. S., C. W. Martin, C. C. Reeves, G. E. Likens, and F. H. Bormann. 1972. Nutrient loss from clearcutting in New Hampshire. pp. 285–295. *In* S.C. Csallany et al. (eds). *Watersheds in Transition,* Proc. Symposium, Ft. Collins, Colo.

Pimentel, D., W. D. Nagel, and J. L. Madden. 1963. Space-time structure of the environment and the survival of parasite-host systems. *Amer. Nat.* 97:141–167.

———, L. E. Hurd, A. C. Bellotti et al. 1973. Food production and the energy crisis. *Sci.* 182:443–449.

———, W. Dritschilo, J. Krummel, and J. Kutzman. 1975. Energy and land constraints in food protein production. *Sci.* 190:754–761.

———, E. C. Terhune, R. Dyson-Hudson et al. 1976. Land degradation: effects on food and energy resources. *Sci.* 194:149–155.

Pisek, A., W. Larcher, W. Moser, and I. Pack. 1969. Kardinale Temperaturbereiche der Photosynthese und Grenztemperaturen des Lebens der Blätter verschiedener Spermatophyten. III Temperaturabhängigkeit und optimaler Temperaturbereich der Netto-Photosynthese. *Flora* (Abt. B) 158:608–630.

Pitelka, F. A. 1957. Some aspects of population structure in the short-term cycle of the brown lemming in northern Alaska. Cold Spr. Hbr. Symp. Quart. *Biol.* 22:237–251.

———. 1964. The nutrient recovery hypothesis for arctic microtive cycles. I. Introduction. pp. 55–56. *In* A. J. Crisp (ed.), *Grazing in Terrestrial and Marine Environments.* Blackwell Sci. Publ., Oxford.

Pogrebniak, P. S. 1930. Über die Methodik von Standortsuntersuchungen in Verbindung mit Waldtypen. Verh.II. Int. Congr. Forstl. Versuchsanstalten, 1929. Stockholm.

Pollard, W. G. 1979. The prevalence of earthlike planets. *Amer. Sci.* 67:653–659.

Polster, H. 1950. *Die physiologischen Grundlagen der Stofferzeugung im Walde*. Bayerischer Landwirtschaftsverlag, München.

Poole, T. B. 1961. An ecological study of the Collembola in a coniferous forest soil. *Pedobiologia* 1:113–137.

Population Reference Bureau. 1983. World Population Data Sheet. Pop. Ref. Bureau, Inc., Washington, D.C.

Precht, H. et al. 1973. *Temperature and Life*. Springer-Verlag, New York. 779 pp.

Preston, F. W. 1962. The canonical distribution of commonness and rarity. *Ecol.* 43:185–215, 410–432.

Price, P. W., C. E. Bouton, and P. Gross et al. 1980. Interactions among three trophic levels: influence of plants on interactions between insect herbivores and natural enemies. *Ann. Rev. Ecol. Syst.* 11:41–65.

Pritchett, W. L. 1979. *Properties and Management of Forest Soils*. Wiley, New York. 500 pp.

Puritch, G. S. 1973. Effects of water stress on photosynthesis, respiration and transpiration of four *Abies* species. *Can. J. For. Res.* 3:293–298.

———. 1981. Nonvisual remote sensing of trees affected by stress. A Review. Can. For. Serv., Pac. For. Res. Cent. For. Tech. Rept. 30. 38 pp.

P'Yavchenko, N. I. 1960. The biological cycle of nitrogen and mineral substances in bog forests. *Soviet Soil Sci*. No. 6. 1960:593–602.

Rafes, P. M. 1970. Estimation of the effects of phytophagous insects on forest production. pp. 100–106. *In* D. E. Reichle (ed.), *Analysis of Temperate Forest Ecosystems.* Springer-Verlag, New York.

———. 1971. Pests and the damage they cause to forests. pp. 357–367. *In* P. Duvigneaud (ed.), *Productivity of Forest Ecosystems.* UNESCO, Paris.

Rainey, R. C. 1973. Airborne pests in the atmospheric environment. *Weather* 28:224–239.

Ralston, C. W., and G. E. Hatchell. 1971. Effects of prescribed burning on physical properties of soil. pp. 68–85. *In* Prescribed Burning Symposium Proceedings. USDA For. Serv., SE For. Exp. Stat., Ashville, S.C.

Ramensky, L. G. 1924. [The main regularities of the vegetation cover] (In Russian). Věstnik opýtnogo děla Sredne-Chernoz. Obl., Voronezh. pp. 37–73.

Ranjitsinh, M. K. 1979. Forest destruction in Asia and the South Pacific. *Ambio* 8:192–201.

Rapp, M., M. C. LeClerc, and P. Loissant. 1979. The nitrogen economy in a *Pinus pinea* L. stand. *For. Ecol. & Mgmt.* 22:221–231.

Raunkiaer, C. 1934. *The Life Forms of Plants and Statistical Plant Geography*. Clarendon Press, Oxford. 632 pp.

Read, R. A. 1964. Tree windbreaks for the central great plains. USDA For. Serv., Rky. Mt. For. Range Exp. Sta. Agr. Hdbk. No. 250. 68 pp.

Redmond, D. R. 1959. Mortality of rootlets of balsam fir defoliated by the spruce budworm. *For. Sci.* 5:64–69.

Reed, K. L., and S. G. Clark. 1976. Succession simulator: a coniferous forest simulator. Coniferous Forest Biome Bull. 11. Univ. of Washington, Seattle.

Reichle, D. E. (ed.). 1981. *Dynamic Properties of Forest Ecosystems*. International Biological Programme 23. Cambridge Univ. Press, Cambridge. 683 pp.

———, R. V. O'Neill, and W. F. Harris. 1975. Principles of energy and materials exchange in ecosystems. pp. 27–43. *In* W. H. van Dobben and R. H. Lowe-Connell (eds.), *Unifying Concepts in Ecology*. W. Junk b.v. Publishers, The Hague.

Reifsnyder, W. E., and H. W. Lull. 1965. Radiant energy in relation to forests. USDA For. Serv. Tech. Bull. No. 1344. 111 pp.

Remezov, N. P., and P. S. Pogrebnyak. 1969. *Forest Soil Science*. Israel Program of Scientific Translations, Jerusalem. 261 pp.

Remmert, H., and K. Wunderling. 1970. Temperature differences between arctic and alpine meadows and their ecological significance. *Oecologia* 4:208–210.

Rennie, P. J. 1955. Uptake of nutrients by mature forest growth. *Plant and Soil* 7:49–95.

———. 1957. The uptake of nutrients by timber forest and its importance to timber production in Britain. *Quart. J. For.* 51:101–115.

Revelle, R. 1974. Food and population. *Sci. Amer.* 231:161–170.

Rice, E. L. 1964. Inhibition of nitrogen-fixing and nitrifying bacteria by seed plants. *Ecol.* 45:824–837.

———. 1965. Inhibition of nitrogen-fixing and nitrifying bacteria by seed plants. II. Characterization and identification of inhibitors. *Physiol. Plant.* 18:255–268.

———. 1967. Chemical warfare between plants. *Bios* (Mt. Vernon, Iowa) 38:67–74.

———. 1968. Inhibition of nodulation of innoculated legumes by pioneer plant species from abandoned fields. *Bull. Torrey Bot. Club* 95:346–358.

———. 1984. *Allelopathy*. 2nd ed. Academic Press, New York. 422 pp.

———, and S. K. Pancholy. 1972. Inhibition of nitrification by climax ecosystems. *Amer. J. Bot.* 59:1033–1040.

Rice, R. M., and G. T. Foggin. 1971. Effects of high intensity storms on soil slippage on mountainous watersheds in Southern California. *Wat. Resour. Res.* 7:1485–1496.

Richards, B. N. 1968. Effect of soil fertility on the distribution of plant communities as shown by pot culture and field trials. *Comm. For. Rev.* 47:200–210.

Richards, P. W. 1952. *The Tropical Rain Forest: An Ecological Study*. Cambridge Univ. Press, London. 450 pp.

———. 1969. Speciation in the tropical rain forest and the concept of the niche. *J. Linn. Soc.* (Biol.) 1:149–153.

———. 1973. The tropical rain forest. *Sci. Amer.* 229:58–67.

———. 1977. Tropical forest and woodlands: an overview. *Agro-ecosystems* 3:225–238.

Ricklefs, R. E. 1973. *Ecology*. Chiron. Press., Portland, Ore. 861 pp.

Robertson, R. A., and G. E. Davis. 1965. Quantities of plant nutrients in heather ecosystems. *J. Appl. Ecol.* 2:211–219.

Rodhe, W. 1955. Can plankton production proceed during winter darkness in subarctic lakes? *Proc. Internat. Assoc. Theor. Appl. Limnol.* 12:117–122.

Rodin, L. E., and N. I. Bazilevich. 1967. *Production and Mineral Cycling in Terrestrial Vegetation*. Oliver & Boyd, London. 288 pp.

Roe, A. L. 1967. Seed dispersal in a bumper spruce seed year. USDA For. Serv. Res. Pap. INT-39, 10 pp.

Rollo, D. 1978. The behavioral ecology of terrestrial slugs. Ph.D. thesis, Univ. of B.C., Vancouver. 444 pp.

Rosen, K., and T. Lindberg. 1980. Biological nitrogen fixation in coniferous forest watershed areas in central Sweden. *Holarct. Ecol.* 3:137–140.

Ross, H. H. 1957. Principles of natural coexistence indicated by leafhopper populations. *Evolution* 11:113–129.

Roussel, L. 1948. Convert et photometrie. *Bull. Soc. For. Franche-Comte* 125:313–326.

Rowe, J. S. 1956. Uses of undergrowth plant species in forestry. *Ecol.* 37:461–473.

———. 1961. The level-of-integration concept and ecology. *Ecol.* 42:420–427.

———. 1972. Forest Regions of Canada. Dept. of Environment, Can. For. Serv., Publ. No. 1300. 172 pp. + maps.

Russell, C. E. 1983. Nutrient cycling and productivity of native and plantation forests at Jari Forestal, Para, Brazil. Ph.D. thesis, Univ. of Georgia, Athens. 133 pp.

Russell, W. M. S. 1969. *Man, Nature and History; Controlling the Environment*. Natural History Press, Garden City, N.Y. 252 pp.

Ruth, R. H. 1967. Silvicultural effects of skyline crane and high-lead yarding. *J. For.* 65:251–255.

Rutter, A. J. 1963. Studies in the water relations of *Pinus sylvestris* in plantation conditions. I. Measurement of rainfall and interception. *J. Ecol.* 51:191–203.

———. 1968. Water consumption by forests. pp. 23–84. *In* T. T. Kozlowski (ed.), *Water Deficits and Plant Growth*. Vol. II. Academic Press, New York.

Ryan, D. F., and F. H. Bormann. 1982. Nutrient resorption in a northern hardwood forest. *BioSci.* 32:29–32.

Sabins, F. F. 1978. *Remote Sensing Principles and Interpretation*. W. H. Freeman and Co., San Francisco. 426 pp.

Salisbury, E. J. 1970. The pioneer vegetation of exposed muds and its biological features. *Phil. Trans. Roy. Soc. B. Biol. Sci.*, London. 259:207–255.

Salisbury, F. B., and C. Ross. 1969. *Plant Physiology*. Wadsworth, Belmont, Calif. 747 pp.

Satchell, J. E. 1967. Lumbricidae. pp. 259–322. *In* A. Burgess and F. Raw (eds.), *Soil Biology*. Academic Press, London and New York.

Satoo, T. 1956. Drought resistance of some conifers at the first summer after their emergence. *Bull. Tokyo Univ. For.* 51:1–108.

———, and H. A. I. Madgwick. 1982. *Forest Biomass*. W. Junk. The Hague. 152 pp.

Satterlund, D. R. 1972. *Wildland Watershed Management*. Wiley, New York. 370 pp.

Sauer, C. O. 1969. *Agricultural Origins and Dispersals*. 2nd ed. M. I. T. Press, Cambridge, Mass. 110 pp.

Savage, S. M. 1974. Mechanism of fire-induced water repellency in soil. *Soil Sci. Soc. Amer. Proc.* 38:652–657.

Sawyer, C. N. 1966. Basic concepts of eutrophication. *J. Water Pollution Con. Fed.* 38:737–744.

Scheffer, V. B. 1951. The rise and fall of a reindeer herd. *Sci. Monthly* 73:356–362.

Schlesinger, W. H. 1977. Carbon balance in terrestrial detritus. *Ann. Rev. Ecol. Syst.* 8:51–81.

———, and W. A. Reiners. 1974. Deposition of water and cations on artificial foliar collectors in fir krummholz of New England mountains. *Ecol.* 55:378–386.

Schneider, S. H. 1974. The population explosion: can it shake the climate. *Ambio* 3(3–4):150–155.

———. 1975. On the carbon dioxide-climate confusion. *J. Atmos. Sci.* 32:2060–2066.

Schneider, S. H., and R. D. Dennett. 1975. Climatic barriers to long-term energy growth. *Ambio* 4:66–74.

Schonland, B. F. J. 1950. *The Flight of the Thunderbolt*. Oxford Univ. Press, Oxford. 152 pp.

Schroter, C. 1926. *Das Pflanzenleben der Alpen*. Raustein, Zurich. 1288 pp.

Schultz, A. M. 1964. The nutrient recovery hypothesis for arctic microtine cycles. II. Ecosystem variables in relation to arctic microtine cycles. pp. 57–68. *In* A. J. Crisp (ed.), *Grazing in Terrestrial and Marine Environments*. Blackwell Sci. Publ., Oxford.

———. 1969. A study of an ecosystem: the arctic tundra. pp. 77–93. *In* G. van Dyne (ed.), *The Ecosystem Concept in Natural Resource Management*. Academic Press, New York.

Schurhoff, P. N. 1924. Die Plastiden. *In* K. Linshaner. *Handbuch der Pflanzen-anatomie*. Vol. I. p. 10.

Schweers, W., and F. H. Meyer. 1970. Einfluss der Mykorrhiza auf den Transport von Assimilaten in die Wurzel. *Der dtsch. Bot. Gesell.* 83:109–119.

Scott, D. R. M. 1955. Amount and chemical composition of the organic matter contributed by overstorey and understorey vegetation to forest soil. Yale Univ. School For. Bull. 62. 73 pp.

Segaard, B. 1969. Resistance studies in *Thuja*. *Forstl. Forso/gsv. Damm*. 31:279–398.

Seidel, S., and D. Keyes. 1983. Can we delay a greenhouse warming? USEPA. Washington, D.C.

Selye, H. 1946. The general adaptation syndrome and the disease of adaptation. *J. Clinical Endocrinology* 6:117–230.

Shea, S. R. 1979. An ecological approach to the control of jarrah dieback. Forest Focus No. 21, April 1979:7–19.

Shelford, V. E. 1951a. Fluctuations of non-forest animal populations in the upper Mississippi Basin. *Ecol. Monogr.* 21:149–181.

———. 1951b. Fluctuations of forest animal populations in east central Illinois. *Ecol. Monogr.* 21:183–214.

Shibata, N., T. Ibaragi, and M. Ishii. 1951. [Studies on the influence of variation of forest conditions on the soil. II. Effects of clear felling on soil in Hinoki forest]. pp. 133–135. Trans. 59th Meeting Jap. For. Soc.

Shimwell, D. W. 1971. *The Description and Classification of Vegetation*. Univ. Washington Press, Seattle. 322 pp.

Shugart, H. H. and D. C. West. 1980. Forest succession models. *BioSci.* 30:308–313.

———, D. C. West, and W. R. Emanuel. 1981. Patterns and dynamics of forests: an application of simulation models. pp. 74–94. D. C. West et al. (eds.), *Forest Succession: Concepts and Application*. Springer-Verlag, New York.

Siivonen, L., and J. Koskimmes. 1955. Population fluctuations and the lunar cycle. Papers on Game Research. Finnish Game Foundation, No. 14. 22 pp.

Silverman, M. P., and E. F. Munoz. 1970. Fungal attack on rock: solubilization and altered infrared spectra. *Sci.* 169:985–987.

Simons, E. L. 1972. *Primate Evolution: An Introduction to Man's Place in Nature*. Macmillan, New York. 322 pp.

Simpson, G. G. 1964. Species density of North American recent mammals. *Syst. Zool.* 13:57–73.

Skutch, A. F. 1967. Adaptive limitation of the reproductive rate of birds. *Ibis* 109:579–599.

Slankis, V. 1958. The role of auxin and other exudates in mycorrhizal symbionts of forest trees. pp. 427–443. *In* K. V. Thimann (ed.), *Physiology of Forest Trees*. Ronald, New York.

———. 1971. Formation of ectomycorrhizae of forest trees in relation to light, carbohydrates and auxins. pp. 151–167. *In* Mycorrhizae. Proc. First N. Amer. Conf. on Mycorrhizae. Misc. Publ. 1189. USDA For. Serv.

Slatyer, R. O. 1967. *Plant-Water Relationships*. Academic Press, London and New York. 366 pp.

———. (ed.). 1977. Dynamic changes in terrestrial ecosystems: patterns of change and techniques for study and applications to management. MAB Technical Notes No. 4. 30 pp. UNESCO.

Slaughter, C. W., R. J. Barney, and G. M. Hansen (eds.). 1971. *Fire in the Northern Environment—A Symposium*. USDA For. Serv. PNW For. Range Exp. Sta., Portland, 275 pp.

Slobodkin, L. B. 1961. *Growth and Regulation of Animal Populations*. Holt, New York.

Small, E. 1972. Photosynthetic rates in relation to nitrogen recycling as an adaptation to nutrient deficiency in peat bog plants. *Can. J. Bot.* 50:2227–2233.

Smith, D. W., and G. C. Bowes. 1974. Loss of some elements in flyash during old-field burns in southern Ontario. *Can. J. Soil Sci.* 54:215–224.

Smith, F. E. 1970. Analysis of ecosystems. pp. 2–18. *In* D. E. Reichle (ed.), *Analysis of Temperate Forest Ecosystems*. Springer-Verlag, Berlin.

Smith, H. S. 1935. The role of biotic factors in the determination of population densities. *J. Econ. Entomol.* 28:873–898.

Smith, N. G. 1968. The advantage of being parasitized. *Nature* 219:690–694.

Smith, R. B., and E. F. Wass. 1976. Soil disturbance, vegetative cover and regeneration on clearcuts in the Nelson forest district, British Columbia. Pacific For. Res. Centre, Victoria, Canada. Report No. BC-X-151. 37 pp.

Smith, R. L. 1966. *Ecology and Field Biology*. Harper & Row, New York. 686 pp.

Smith, W. H. 1985. Forest quality and air quality. *J. For.* 83:82–92.

———, D. M. Post, and F. W. Adrian. 1979. Waste management to maintain or enhance productivity. pp. 304–320. *In Impact of Intensive Harvesting on Forest Nutrient Cycling*. Proc. Symp., Coll. Environ. Sci. and For., SUNY, Syracuse.

Smithers, L. A. 1957. Thinning in lodgepole pine stands in Alberta. Can. Dept. N. Affairs and Nat. Resources, Forest Br., For. Res. Div. Tech. Note 52. 26 pp.

Snell, G. L., S. C. Sterns-Smith, and E. W. Mogren. 1979. Macronutrient transport in relation to harvesting in Colorado spruce-fir forests. Paper distrib. at *Impact of Intensive Harvesting on Forest Nutrient Cycling*. SUNY, Syracuse, N.Y.

Söderlund, R., and B. H. Svensson. 1976. The global nitrogen cycle. pp. 23–73. *In* B. H. Svensson and R. Söderlund (eds.), Nitrogen, Phosphorus and Sulphur—Global Cycles. Scope Report 7. *Ecol. Bull.* (Stockholm) 22.

Soil Science Society of America. 1973. Glossary of Soil Science Terms. Soil Sci. Soc. Amer., Madison, Wisc. 34 pp.

Soil Survey Staff. 1975. *Soil Taxonomy. A basic system of soil classification for making and interpreting soil surveys*. USDA Agric. Handbook 436. Washington, D.C. 754 pp.

Sollins, P., R. A. Goldstein, J. B. Mankin, C. E. Murphy, and G. L. Swartzman. 1981. Analysis of forest growth and water balance using complex ecosystem models. pp. 537–565. *In* D. E. Reichle (ed.), *Dynamic Properties of Forest Ecosystems*. International Biological Programme 23. Cambridge Univ. Press, Cambridge.

Sopper, W. E. 1975. Wastewater recycling on forest lands. pp. 227–243. *In* B. Bernier and C. H. Winget (eds.), *Forest Soils and Forest Land Management*, Laval Univ. Press, Quebec.

——— ; and S. N. Kerr (eds.). 1979. *Utilization of Municipal Sewage Effluent and Sludge on Forest and Disturbed Land*. Pennsylvania State Univ. Press, University Park, Pa. 547 pp.

Southwood, T. R. E. 1961. The number of species of insect associated with various trees. *J. Anim. Ecol.* 30:1–8.

Spears, J. S. 1979. Can the wet tropical forest survive? *Comm. For. Rev.* 58:165–180.

Specht, R. L., P. Rayson, and M. E. Jackman. 1958. Dark Island Heath (Ninety-Mile Plain, South Australia). VI. Pyric succession; changes in composition, coverage, dry weight and mineral status. *Austr. J. Bot.* 6:59–88.

Spilsbury, R. H., and D. S. Smith. 1947. Forest site types of the Pacific Northwest. Dept. Lands and Forests, B.C. For. Serv., Victoria, B.C. 46 pp.

Sprugel, D. G. 1975. Dynamic structure of wave-regenerated *Abies balsamea* forests in the northeastern United States. *J. Ecol.* 64:889–911.

Spurr, S. H. 1957. Local climate in the Harvard Forest. *Ecol.* 38:37–46.

——— , and B. V. Barnes. 1973. *Forest Ecology*. 2nd ed. Ronald, New York. 571 pp.

Staaf, H. 1982. Plant nutrient changes in beech leaves during senescence as influenced by site characteristics. *Oecol. Plant.* 3:161–170.

Stachurska-Hagen, T. 1980. Acidification experiments in conifer forest. 8. Effects of acidification and liming on some soil animals: Protozoa, Rotifera and Nematoda. Internal Report 74/80. SNSF-project, Aas—NLH, Norway.

Stachurski, A., and J. R. Zimka. 1975. Methods of studying forest ecosystems: leaf area, leaf production and withdrawal of nutrients from leaves of trees. *Ekol. Pol.* 23:637–648.

Stark, N. 1972. Nutrient cycling pathways and litter fungi. *BioSci.* 22:355–360.

——— , and C. F. Jordan. 1978. Nutrient retention by the root mat of an Amazonian rain forest. *Ecol.* 59:434–437.

Stark, R. W. 1959. Climate in relation to winter mortality of the lodgepole needle miner, *Recurvaria starki* Free., in Canadian Rocky Mountain Parks. *Can. J. Zool.* 37:753–761.

Statistics Canada. 1976. Profile Studies. The age-sex structure of the Canadian population. 1971 Census of Canada. Catalogue 99–703 Vol:V–Part:1 (Bull. 5.1–3). Ottawa.

Steinberg, R. A. 1951. Correlations between protein-carbohydrate metabolism and mineral deficiencies in plants. pp. 359–386. *In* E. Truog (ed.), *Mineral Nutrition of Plants*. Univ. of Wisc. Press, Madison.

Steinbrenner, E. C. 1955. The effects of repeated tractor trips on the physical properties of forest soils. *Northwest Sci.* 29:155–159.

——— . 1976. Factors that influence the productivity of western hemlock. XVI IUFRO World Congress, Oslo. *Proc. Div.* 1:167–185.

Steinhart, J. S., and C. E. Steinhart. 1974. Energy use in the U.S. food system. *Science.* 184:307–316.

Steinlin, H. J. 1982. Monitoring the world's tropical forests. *Unasylva* 34:2–8.

Stenlid, G. 1958. Salt losses and redistribution of salts in higher plants. *Encyclopedia of Plant Physiol.* 4:615–637.

Stern, K., and L. Roche. 1974. *Genetics of Forest Ecosystems*. Springer-Verlag, New York. 330 pp.

Stewart, O. C. 1956. Fire as the first great force employed by man. pp. 115–133. *In* W. L. Thomas Jr. (ed.), *Man's Role in Changing the Face of the Earth*. Univ. of Chicago Press.

Stewart, W. D. P. 1966. *Nitrogen Fixation in Plants*. Athlone Press, London. 168 pp.

Stoessl, A. 1970. Antifungal compounds produced by higher plants. *Rec. Adv. Phytochem.* (3):143–180.

Stone, E. C. 1957. Dew as an ecological factor. *Ecol.* 38:407–422.

——— . 1958. Dew absorption by conifers. pp. 125–153. *In* K. V. Thimann (ed.), *The Physiology of Forest Trees*. Ronald, New York.

——— , and H. A. Fowells. 1955. Survival value of dew under laboratory conditions with *Pinus ponderosa*. *For. Sci.* 1:183–188.

Strand, L. 1980. Acid precipitation and regional tree ring analyses. Internal Report 73/80. SNSF-project, Aas—NLH, Norway.

Strang, R. M. 1972. Ecology and land use of the barrens of western Nova Scotia. *Can. J. For. Res.* 2:276–290.

——— . 1973. The rate of silt accumulation in the Lower Peel River, Northwest Territories. *Can. J. For. Res.* 3:457–458.

Stuart, T. S. 1968. Revival of respiration and photosynthesis in dried leaves of *Polypodium polypodioides*. *Planta* 83:185–206.

Sturges, F. W., R. T. Holmes, and G. E. Likens. 1974. The role of birds in nutrient cycling in a northern hardwood ecosystem. *Ecol.* 55:149–155.

Stutzbach, S. J., A. L. Leaf, and R. E. Leonard. 1972. Variation in forest floor under a red pine plantation. *Soil Sci.* 114:24–28.

Suchting, H., and Christmann. 1935. [On humus layer destruction in the forest floor. III. Humus destruction during clearcutting.] *Mitteil. Fortswirt. u. Forstwiss.* 6:425–446.

Sukachev, V., and N. Dylis. 1964. *Fundamentals of Forest Biogeocoenology*. Oliver and Boyd, Edinburgh. 672 pp.

Sullivan, T. P. 1978. Conifer seed predation by the deer mouse: a problem in reforestation. Ph.D. thesis, Univ. of B.C., Vancouver. 181 pp.

——— . 1979. The use of alternative foods to reduce conifer seed predation by the deer mouse (*Peromyscus maniculatus*). *J. Appl. Ecol.* 16:475–495.

Sutton, R. F. 1969. Form and development of conifer root systems. Comm. For. Bureau. Comm. Agric. Bureau, Oxford Tech. Communication No. 7. 131 pp.

Swank, W. T., and J. W. Elwood. 1971. The seasonal and annual flux of cations for forested ecosystems in the Appalachian Highlands. Paper. 2nd Nat. Biol. Congr., Miami Beach, Fla. October 23–26, 1971. 34 pp.

Swanson, F. J., and C. T. Dyrness. 1975. Impact of clearcutting and road construction on soil erosion by landslides in the western Cascade Range, Oregon. *Geology* 3:393–396.

Swanston, D. N. 1969. Mass wasting in coastal Alaska. USDA For. Serv., Res. Paper PNW–83, 15 pp.

——— . 1974. Slope stability problems associated with timber harvesting in mountainous regions of the western United States. USDA For. Serv., Gen. Tech. Rept. PNW–21. 14 pp.

Switzer, G. L., and L. E. Nelson. 1972. Nutrient accumulation and cycling in loblolly pine (*Pinus taeda* L.) plantation ecosystems: the first 20 years. *Soil Sci. Soc. Amer. Proc.* 36:143–147.

——— , L. E. Nelson, and W. H. Smith. 1968. The mineral cycle in forest stands. pp. 1–9. *In Forest Fertilization. Theory and Practice*. TVA, Muscle Shoals, Tenn.

Syers, J. K., J. A. Adams, and T. W. Walker. 1970. Accumulation of organic matter in a chronosequence of soils developed on wind-blown sand in New Zealand. *J. Soil Sci.* 21:146–153.

Tamarin, R. H. 1978. *Population Regulation*. Benchmark Papers in Ecology. 7. Dowden, Hutchinson and Ross, Stroudsburg, Pa.

Tamm, C. O. 1976. Acid precipitation and forest soils. pp. 681–684. *In* L. S. Dochinger and T. A. Seliga (eds.). Proc. 1st Int. Symp. Acid Precip. USDA For. Serv., Gen. Tech. Rept. NE–23.

——— , and E. B. Cowling. 1976. Acidic precipitation and forest vegetation. pp. 848–855. *In* L. S. Dochinger and T. A. Seliga (eds.), Proc. 1st Int. Symp. Acid Precip. USDA For. Serv., Gen. Tech. Rept. NE–23.

Tanner, J. T. 1966. Effects of population density on growth rates of animal populations. *Ecol.* 47:733–745.

Tansley, A. G. 1920. The classification of vegetation and the concept of development. *J. Ecol.* 8:118–149.

——— . 1935. The use and abuse of vegetational concepts and terms. *Ecol.* 16:284–307.

——— . 1939. *The British Islands and Their Vegetation*. Cambridge Univ. Press, Cambridge. 930 pp.

——— . 1941. Note on the status of salt-marsh vegetation and the concept of "formation". *J. Ecol.* 29:212–214.

Tarrant, R. F., and J. M. Trappe. 1971. The role of *Alnus* in improving the forest environment. *Plant and Soil*, Spec. vol.: 335–348.

Theodorou, C., and G. D. Bowen. 1970. Mycorrhizal responses of radiata pine in experiments with different fungi. *Aust. For.* 34:183–191.

Thie, J., and G. Ironside (eds.). 1976. *Ecological (Biophysical) Land Classification in Canada*. Ecol. Land. Classif. Ser. No. 1. Lands Directorate, Environ. Canada.

Thielges, B. A. 1968. Altered polyphenol metabolism in the foliage of *Pinus sylvestris* associated with European pine sawfly attack. *Can. J. Bot.* 46:724–725.

Thirgood, J. V. 1981. *Man and the Mediterranean Forest*. Academic Press, New York. 180 pp.

Thomas, B. R., and E. R. Burroughs Jr. 1975. Significance of soil classification in forest land management. pp. 599–616. *In* B. Bernier and C. H. Winget (eds.), *Forest Soils and Forest Land Management*. Laval Univ. Press, Quebec.

Thomas, W. A. 1969. Accumulation and cycling of calcium by dogwood trees. *Ecol. Monogr.* 39:101–120.

Thompson, J. N. 1982. *Interaction and Coevolution*. Wiley Interscience, New York. 180 pp.

Thornthwaite, C. W. 1948. An approach towards a rational classification of climate. *Geogr. Rev.* 38:55–94.

——— , and F. K. Hare. 1955. Climatic classification in forestry. UNASYLVA 9:50–59.

Timmer, V. R., and E. L. Stone. 1978. Comparative foliar analysis of young balsam fir fertilized with NPK. and lime. *Soil Sci. Soc. Amer. J.* 42:125–130.

Tinbergen, L. 1960. The natural control of insects in pinewoods. 1. Factors influencing the intensity of predation by songbirds. *Arch. Neerl. Zool.* 13:265–343.

Ting, I. P., and W. M. Duggar Jr. 1968. Non-autotrophic carbon dioxide metabolism in cacti. *Bot. Gazette* 129:9–15.

Tisdale, S. L., and W. L. Nelson. 1966. *Soil Fertility and Fertilizers*. Macmillan, New York. 694 pp.

Tollan, A. (ed.). 1978. Annotated bibliography 1974–1977. SNSF project. Acid precipitation—effects on forest and fish. Aas—NLH, Norway. 39 pp.

Tomlinson, G. H. 1981. Tree die-back in Quebec and the N.E. United States—a hypothesis suggesting the cause and a proposed experimental investigation. Res. Memo., Rept. #3. Proj. #74-7124-13. Res. Centre, Senneville, Quebec.

Torrenueva, A. L. 1975. Variation in mineral flux to the forest floors of a pine and a hardwood stand in the Georgia piedmont. Ph.D. thesis, Univ. Georgia, Athens. 110 pp.

Toumey, J. W., and R. Kienholz. 1931. Trenched plots under forest canopies. Yale Univ. School For. Bull. No. 30. 31 pp.

Tranquillini, W. 1954. Über den Einfluss von Übertemperaturen der Blätter bei Dauereinschluss in Küvetten auf die ökologische CO_2–Assimilationsmessung. *Ber. Deut. Bot. Ges.* 67:191–204.

——— . 1959. Die Stoffproduktion der Zirbe (*Pinus cembra* L.) an der Waldgrenze während eines Jahres: I Standertsklima und CO_2–Assimilation. II. Zuwachs und CO_2–Bilanz. *Planta* 54:107–151.

——— , and W. Schutz. 1971. Über den Einfluss von Warme auf das Photosynthesevermogen der Zirbe (*Pinus cembra* L.) und der Alpen rose (*Rhododendron ferrugineum* L.) in winter. Rep. Kevo. Subarctic Res. Stat. 8:158–166.

Transeau, E. N. 1926. The accumulation of energy by plants. *Ohio J. Sci.* 26:1–10.

Treshow, M. 1970. *Environment and Plant Response*. McGraw-Hill, New York. 422 pp.

Trewartha, G. T. 1954. *An Introduction to Climate*. McGraw-Hill, New York. 402 pp.

Triska, F. J., and K. Cromack Jr. 1980. The role of wood debris in forests and streams. pp. 171–190. *In* R. H. Waring (ed.), *Forests: Fresh Perspectives from Ecosystem Analysis*. Oregon State Univ. Press, Corvallis.

Truog, E. 1947. Soil reaction influence on availability of plant nutrients. *Soil Sci. Soc. Amer. Proc.* 11:305–308.

Trust, T. J., and R. W. Coombs. 1973. Antibacterial activity of β-thujaplicin. *Can. J. Microbiol.* 19:1341–1346.

Tsutsumi, T. 1971. Accumulation and circulation of material elements in forest ecosystems. pp. 543–552. *In* P. Duvigneaud (ed.), *Productivity of Forest Ecosystems*. UNESCO, Paris.

Tubbs, C. H. 1973. Allelopathic relationships between yellow birch and sugar maple seedlings. *For. Sci.* 19:139–145.

Tucker, G. F., and W. H. Emmingham. 1977. Morphological changes in leaves of residual western hemlock after clear and shelterwood cutting. *For. Sci.* 23:195–203.

Tukey, H. B., Jr. 1969. Implications of allelopathy in agricultural plant science. *Bot. Rev.* 35:1–16.

———. 1970. The leaching of substances from plants. *Ann. Rev. Plant Physiol.* 21:305–324.

———, and J. V. Morgan. 1963. Injury to foliage and its effects upon the leaching of nutrients from aboveground plant parts. *Physiol. Plant.* 16:557–564.

Turmanina, V. I. 1965. The strength of tree roots. *Bjull. Mosk. Obsc. Ispty. Prir. (Otd. Biol.)* 70:36–45.

Turner, J. 1975. Nutrient cycling in a Douglas-fir ecosystem with respect to age and nutrient status. Ph.D. thesis, Univ. of Wash., Seattle.

———. 1977. Effect of nitrogen availability on nitrogen cycling in a Douglas-fir stand. *For. Sci.* 23:307–316.

———, and M. J. Singer. 1976. Nutrient distribution and cycling in a subalpine coniferous forest ecosystem. *J. Appl. Ecol.* 13:295–301.

Turner, N. 1963. The gypsy moth problem. Conn. Agric. Exp. Sta. Bull. 655.

Turrell, F. M. 1934. Leaf surface of a twenty-one-year-old catalpa tree. *Iowa Acad. Sci. Proc.* 41:79–84.

———. 1936. The area of the internal exposed surface of dicotyledon leaves. *Amer. J. Bot.* 23:255–264.

Ugolini, F. C. 1966. Soils. pp. 29–72. *In* Soil Development and Ecological Succession in a Deglaciated Area of Muir Inlet, southeastern Alaska. Institute for Polar Studies, Report 20, Part 3. Ohio State Univ., Columbus.

———, and D. H. Mann. 1979. Biopedological origin of peatlands in south east Alaska. *Nature* 281:366–368.

Ulrich, B., R. Mayer, and P. K. Khanna. 1980. Chemical changes due to acid precipitation in a loess-derived soil in central Europe. *Soil Sci.* 130:193–199.

———, P. Benecke, and W. F. Harris et al. 1981. Soil processes. pp. 265–338. *In* D. E. Reichle (ed.), *Dynamic Properties of Forest Ecosystems*. International Biological Programme 23. Cambridge Univ. Press, Cambridge.

UN Univ. & Div. Economic and Social Info./DPI. 1982. Development Forum 10(5):8.

UNESCO. 1978. *Tropical Forest Ecosystems. A state-of-knowledge report*. UNESCO/UNEP/FAO. Nat. Resour. Res. UNESCO.

U.S. Corps of Engineers. 1956. *Snow hydrology*. Summary Report of the Snow Investigations. North Pac. Dw. USCE. Portland, Oregon. 437 pp.

U.S. Department of Agriculture. 1958. Alpine snowfields gain moisture from air. USDA For. Serv., Rocky Mt. For. Range Exp. Sta. Ann. Rept. 1957:3–4.

———. 1964. *Winds over Wild Lands—A Guide for Forest Management*. USDA For. Serv. Agric. Handbook No. 272. Washington, D.C. 33 pp.

———. 1971. Prescribed Burning Symposium. USDA For. Serv., SE For. Exp. Sta., Ashville, S.C. 160 pp.

———. 1979. Effects of Fire on Soil. USDA For. Serv., Gen. Tech. Rept. WO-7, 34 pp.

———. 1980. Environmental consequences of timber harvesting. Symp. Proc. USDA For. Serv., Gen. Tech. Rept. INT-90, Ogden, Utah. 526 pp.

Uvarov, B. P. 1931. Insects and climate. *Trans. Entomol. Soc. London* 79:1–247.

———. 1961. Quantity and quality in insect populations. *Proc. Royal Entomol. Soc. London*(C). 25:52–59.

Vaartaja, O. 1952. Forest humus quality and light conditions as factors influencing damping-off. *Phytopathol.* 42:501–506.

———. 1959. Evidence of photoperiodic ecotypes in trees. *Ecol. Monogr.* 29:91–111.

———, and P. J. Salisbury. 1965. Mutual effects *in vitro* of micro-organisms isolated from tree seedlings, nursery soil and forests. *For. Sci.* 11:160–168.

Van Arsdel, E. P. 1965. Micrometeorology and plant disease epidemiology. *Phytopathol.* 55:945–950.

Van Cleve, K., and L. L. Noonan. 1971. Physical and chemical properties of the forest floor in birch and aspen stands in interior Alaska. *Proc. Soil Sci. Soc. Amer.* 35:356–360.

———, and L. A. Viereck. 1981. Forest succession in relation to nutrient cycling in the boreal forest of Alaska. pp. 185–211. *In* D. C. West, H. H. Shugart and D. B. Botkin (eds.), *Forest Succession. Concepts and Application*. Springer-Verlag, New York.

Van den Burg, J. 1976. Problems related to analysis of soil fertility. XVI IUFRO World Congress, Oslo. Proc. Div. 1:148–163.

Van den Driessche, R. 1974. Prediction of mineral nutrient status of trees by foliar analyses. *Bot. Rev.* 40:347–394.

Van der Maarel, E. (ed.). 1980. *Succession*. W. Junk b.v., The Hague. 151 pp.

Van der Tak, J., C. Haub, and E. Murphy. 1979. Our population predicament: a new look. *Population Bulletin* 34(5). 48 pp.

Vandermeer, J. H. 1969. The competitive structure of communities: an experimental approach with protozoa. *Ecol.* 50:362–371.

Van Dyne, G. M. 1969. *The Ecosystem Concept in Natural Resource Management.* Academic Press, New York. 383 pp.

Van Eimern, J., R. Karschon, L. A. Razumova, and G. W. Robertson. 1964. Windbreaks and shelterbelts. Tech. Note No. 59. World Meteorological Organization. WMO. No. 147. TP. 70. Geneva.

Van Vechten, G. W. 1960. The ecology of the timberline and alpine vegetation of the Three Sisters, Oregon. Ph.D. thesis, Oregon State Univ., Corvallis. 111 pp.

Van Wagner, C. E. 1972. Duff consumption by fire in eastern pine stands. *Can. J. For. Res.* 2:34–39.

Varley, G. C. 1970. The concept of energy flow applied to a woodland community. pp. 389–405. *In* A. Watson (ed.), *Animal Populations in Relation to Their Food Resources.* Blackwell, Oxford.

———, G. R. Gradwell, and M. P. Hassel. 1973. *Insect Population Ecology: An Analytical Approach.* Blackwell Sci. Publ. 212 pp.

Vasil'eva, I. N. 1968. Physical properties and water requirements of soils in the Sereboyanyi Bor experimental forest. pp. 10–50. *In* L. P. Rysin and M. V. Nadezhdina (eds.), *Long-Term Biogeocoenotic Investigations in the Southern Taiga Zone.* Transl. 1964 Symposium, USDA and Natural Science Foundation, Washington, D.C.

Veihmeyer, F. J. 1956. Soil Moisture. *Handb. Pflanzen physiol.* 3:64–123.

Vézina, P. E., and D. W. K. Boulter. 1966. The spectral composition of near ultraviolet and visible radiation beneath forest canopies. *Can. J. Bot.* 44:1267–1284.

Viereck, L. A. 1965. Relationship of white spruce to lenses of perennially frozen ground, Mount McKinley National Park, Alaska, *Arctic* 18:262–267.

———. 1970. Forest succession and soil development adjacent to the Chena River in interior Alaska. *Arctic and Alpine Res.* 2(1):1–26.

———. 1973. Ecological effects of river flooding and forest fires on permafrost in the taiga of Alaska. pp. 60–67. *In* Permafrost. The N. Amer. Contrib. To the Second Internat. Conf. Nat. Acad. Sci. Washington, D.C.

Vince-Prue, D. 1975. *Photoperiodism in Plants.* McGraw-Hill, New York. 444 pp.

Viro, P. J. 1953. Loss of nutrients and the natural nutrient balance of the soil in Finland. *Com. Inst. For. Fenn.* 42:1–50.

———. 1974. Effects of forest fire on soil. pp. 7–45. *In* T. T. Kozlowski and C. E. Ahlgren (eds.), *Fire and Ecosystems.* Academic Press, New York.

Vitousek, P. M. 1977. The regulation of element concentrations in mountain streams in the northeastern United States. *Ecol. Monogr.* 47:65–87.

———. 1981. Clearcutting and the nitrogen cycle. pp. 631–642. *In* F. E. Clark and T. H. Rosswall (eds.), Nitrogen Cycling in Terrestrial Ecosystems: Processes, Ecosystem Strategies, and Management Implications. *Ecol. Bull.* 33, Swedish Nat. Sci. Research Council, Stockholm.

———, and W. A. Reiners. 1975. Ecosystem succession and nutrient retention: a hypothesis. *BioSci.* 25:376–381.

———, J. R. Gosz, C. C. Grier, J. M. Melillo, W. A. Reiners, and R. L. Todd. 1979. Nitrate losses from disturbed ecosystems. *Sci.* 204:469–473.

———, J. R. Gosz, C. C. Grier, J. M. Melillo, and W. A. Reiners. 1982. A comparative analysis of potential nitrification and nitrate mobility in forest ecosystems. *Ecol. Monogr.* 52:155–177.

Vogt, K. A., R. L. Edmonds, C. C. Grier, and S. R. Piper. 1980. Seasonal changes in mycorrhizal and fibrous-textured root biomass in 23- and 180-year-old Pacific silver fir stands in western Washington. *Can. J. For. Res.* 10:523–529.

———, R. L. Edwards, C. C. Grier, and S. R. Piper. 1981. Seasonal changes in biomass and vertical distribution of mycorrhizal and fibrous-textured conifer fine roots in 23- and 180-year-old subalpine *Abies amabilis* stands. *Can. J. For. Res.* 11:223–229.

———, C. C. Grier, C. E. Meier, and R. L. Edmonds. 1982. Mycorrhizal role in net primary production and nutrient cycling in *Abies amabilis* ecosystems in western Washington. *Ecol.* 63:370–380.

———, C. C. Grier, C. E. Meier, M. R. Keyes. 1983. Organic matter and nutrient dynamics in forest floors of young and mature *Abies amabilis* stands in western Washington, as affected by fine-root input. *Ecol. Monogr.* 53:139–157.

Voigt, G. K. 1960. Distribution of rainfall under forest stands. *For. Sci.* 6:2–9.

———. 1968. Variation in nutrient uptake by trees. pp. 20–27. *In Forest Fertilization, Theory and Practice.* Proc. Symp., Gainesville, Fla. TVA, Muscle Shoals, Ala.

———. 1971. Mycorrhizae and nutrient immobilization. pp. 122–131. *In* Mycorrhizae. Proc. 1st N. Amer. Conf. on Mycorrhizae. USDA For. Serv., Misc. Publ. 1189.

———, B. N. Richards, and E. C. Mannion. 1964. Nitrogen utilization by young pitch pine. *Soil Sci. Soc. Amer. Proc.* 28:707–709.

Volterra, V. 1926. Variazioni e gluttnazioni del numero d'individui in specie animali conviventi. Mem. Acad. Lincei Roma. 2:31–113.

Von Frisch, K. 1967. *The Dance Language and Orientation of Bees.* Harvard Univ. Press, Cambridge. 566 pp.

Wagener, W. W. 1961. Past fire incidence in Sierra Nevada forest. *J. For.* 59:739–748.

Wahl, E. W. 1968. A comparison of the climate of the eastern United States during the 1830's with the current normals. *Monthly Weather Rev.* 96:73–82.

———, and T. L. Lawson. 1970. The climate of the mid nineteenth century United States compared to current normals. *Monthly Weather Rev.* 98:259–265.

Waide, J. B., and W. T. Swank. 1975. Nutrient recycling and the stability of ecosystems: implications for forest management in the southeastern U.S. pp. 404–424. *In Proc. 1975 SAF Annual Meeting.* S.A.F., Wash., D.C.

———, and W. T. Swank. 1977. Simulation of potential effects of forest utilization on the nitrogen cycle in different southeastern ecosystems. pp. 767–789. *In* D. L. Correll (ed.). Watershed Research in Eastern North America. A workshop to compare results. Vol. II. Chesapeake Bay Cntr. Environ. Studies. Smithsonian Inst., Edgewater, Md.

Waksman, S. A. 1932. *Principles of Soil Microbiology*. 2nd ed. Wilkins and Wilkins Co., Baltimore. 894 pp.

Wali, M. K., and V. J. Krajina. 1973. Vegetation environment relationships of some sub-boreal spruce zone ecosystems in British Columbia. *Vegetatio* 26:237–381.

Wallwork, J. A. 1970. *Ecology of Soil Animals*. McGraw-Hill, New York.

Waloff, Z. 1966. The upsurges and recessions of the desert locust plague: A historical survey. *Anti-locust Memoirs* 8:1–111.

Walter, H., E. Harnickell, and D. Mueller-Dombois. 1975. *Climate-diagram maps of the individual continents and the ecological climatic regions of the earth*. Suppl. to *Veg. Monogr.* 36 pp. and 9 maps. Springer-Verlag, Berlin.

Wang, J. Y. 1960. A critique of the heat unit approach to plant response studies. *Ecol.* 41:785–790.

Wardle, P. 1968. Engelmann spruce (*Picea engelmannii* Engel.) at its upper limits on the Front Range, Colorado. *Ecol.* 49:483–495.

———. 1974. Alpine timberlines. Chap. 7. *In* J. D. Ives and R. G. Barry (eds.), *Arctic and Alpine Environments*. Methuen, London.

Wareing, P. F. 1969. Germination and dormancy. Chap. 17. *In* M. B. Wilkins (ed.), *The Physiology of Plant Growth and Development*. McGraw-Hill, New York.

Waring, R. H. 1980. Vital signs of forest ecosystems. pp. 131–136. *In* R. H. Waring (ed.), *Forests: Fresh Perspectives from Ecosystem Analysis*. Oregon State Univ. Press, Corvallis.

———, W. H. Emmingham, H. L. Gholz, and C. C. Grier. 1978. Variation in maximum leaf area of coniferous forests in Oregon and its ecological significance. *For. Sci.* 24:131–140.

———, and J. F. Franklin. 1979. Evergreen coniferous forests of the Pacific Northwest. *Sci.* 204:1380–1386.

———, R. H., K. Newman, and J. Bell. 1981. Efficiency of tree crowns and stemwood production at different canopy densities. *For.* 54:129–137.

———, J. J. Rogers, and W. T. Swank. 1981. Water relations and hydrologic cycles. pp. 205–264. *In* D. E. Reichle (ed.) *Dynamic Properties of Forest Ecosystems*. Internat. Biol. Programme 23. Cambridge Univ. Press, Cambridge.

———, W. G. Thies, and D. Muscato. 1980. Stem growth per unit of leaf area: a measure of tree vigour. *For. Sci.* 26:112–117.

Warming, E. 1909. *Oecology of Plants: An Introduction to the Study of Plant Communities*. Oxford Press. 422 pp.

Wassink, E. C. 1959. Efficiency of light energy conversion in plant growth. *Plant Physiol.* 34:356–361.

Watt, A. S. 1947. Pattern and process in the plant community. *J. Ecol.* 35:1–22.

———. 1955. Bracken versus heather, a study in plant sociology. *J. Ecol.* 43:490–506.

Watt, K. E. 1968. Large-scale biological wave phenomena: fur bearer predator-prey cycles in the boreal forest and outbreaks of insect pests. pp. 143–156. *In Ecology and Resource Management*. McGraw-Hill, New York.

Watts, J. A. 1982. The carbon dioxide question: data sampler. pp. 431–469. *In* W. C. Clark (ed.), *Carbon Dioxide Review: 1982*. Clarendon Press, Oxford.

Weaver, H. 1951. Fire as an ecological factor in the southwestern ponderosa pine forests. *J. For.* 49:93–98.

Weaver, J. E. 1968. *Prairie Plants and Their Environment*. University of Nebraska Press, Lincoln. 276 pp.

———, and F. E. Clements, 1938. *Plant Ecology*. 2nd ed. McGraw-Hill, New York. 601 pp.

———, and N. W. Roland. 1952. Effects of excessive natural mulch on development, yield and structure of native grassland. *Bot. Gazette* 114:1–19.

Webber, B. D. 1977. Biomass and nutrient distribution patterns in a young *Pseudotsuga menziesii* ecosystem. *Can. J. For. Res.* 7:326–334.

Webster, J. R., J. B. Waide, and B. C. Patten. 1975. Nutrient recycling and the stability of ecosystems. pp. 1–27. *In* Howell, F. G. et al. (eds.), Mineral Cycling in Southeastern Ecosystems. Tech. Info. Centre, U.S. Energy Res. & Devel. Admin. CONF-740513.

Weetman, G. F. 1967. Nitrogen deficient black spruce on raw humus soils in northern Quebec—response to thinning and urea treatments. Proc. XIVth IUFRO Congress, München. IV:608–611.

———, and R. Fournier. 1983. Graphical diagnoses of lodgepole pine responses to fertilization. *Soil Sci. Soc. Amer. J.* 46:1280–1289.

———, and V. Timmer. 1967. Feather moss growth and nutrient content under upland black spruce. Woodland Res. Index No. 183. Pulp Pap. Res. Instit. Can. 38 pp.

———, and B. Webber. 1972. The influence of wood harvesting on the nutrient status of two spruce stands. *Can. J. For. Res.* 2:351–369.

Wein, R. W. 1978. The role of fire in the degradation of ecosystems. pp. 193–209. *In* M. W. Holdgate and M. J. Woodman (eds.), *The Breakdown and Restoration of Ecosystems*. Plenum, New York. 322 pp.

———, and J. M. Moore. 1977. Fire history and rotations in the New Brunswick Acadian forest. *Can. J. For. Res.* 7:285–294.

———, and D. A. MacLean (eds.). 1981. *The Role of Fire in Northern Circumpolar Ecosystems*. Scope; Wiley and Co., Toronto. 322 pp.

Weir, J. 1969. Importation of nutrients into woodlands by rooks. *Nature* 221:487–488.

Weiser, C. J. 1970. Cold resistance and injury in woody plants. *Sci.* 169:1269–1278.

Wellington, W. G. 1952. Air mass climatology of Ontario north of Lake Huron and Lake Superior before outbreaks of the spruce budworm and the forest tent caterpillar. *Can. J. Zool.* 30:114–127.

———. 1954. Weather and climate in forest entomology. *Meteorol. Monogr.* 2:11–18.

———. 1957. Individual differences as a factor in population dynamics: the development of a problem. *Can. J. Zool.* 35:293–323.

————. 1960. Qualitative changes in animal populations during changes in abundance. *Can. J. Zool.* 38:289–314.

————. 1964. Qualitative changes in populations in unstable environments. *Can. Entomol.* 96:436–451.

————. 1965. Some maternal influences on progeny quality in the western tent caterpillar *Malacosoma pluviale* (Dyar.). *Can. Entomol.* 97:1–14.

Wells, C. G., and L. J. Metz. 1963. Variation in nutrient content of loblolly pine needles with season, age, soil and position on the crown. *Soil Sci. Soc. Amer. Proc.* 27:90–93.

————, and J. R. Jorgensen. 1975. Nutrient cycling in loblolly pine plantations. pp. 137–158. *In* B. Bernier and C. H. Winget (eds.), *Forest Soils and Forest Land Management.* Laval Univ. Press, Quebec.

————, R. E. Campbell, and L. F. Debano et al. 1979. Effects of fire on soil. A state-of-knowledge review. USDA For. Serv., Gen. Tech. Rept. WO-7. 34 pp.

Wells, P. V. 1965. Scarp woodlands, transported soils, and concept of grassland climate in the Great Plains region. *Sci.* 148:246–249.

Welty, J. C. 1962. *The Life of Birds.* Saunders, Philadelphia. 546 pp.

Went, F. W., and N. Stark. 1968. Mycorrhiza. *BioSci.* 18:1035–1039.

Wertz, W. A., and J. F. Arnold. 1975. Land stratification for land-use planning. pp. 617–629. *In* B. Bernier and C. H. Winget (eds.), *Forest Soils and Forest Land Management.* Laval Univ. Press, Quebec.

West, D. C., H. H. Shugart, and D. B. Botkin. 1981. *Forest Succession: Concepts and Application.* Springer-Verlag, New York. 517 pp.

Westhoff, C. F. 1974. The populations of the developed countries. *Sci. Amer.* 230:108–120.

Westhoff, V., and E. van der Maarel. 1973. The Braun-Blanquet approach. pp. 617–726. *In* R. H. Whittaker (ed.), *Ordination and Classification of Communities,* Part 5. Handbook of Vegetation Science. W. Junk, b.v., Publishers, The Hague.

Wetselaar, R., J. R. Simpson, and T. Rosswall (eds.). 1981. *Nitrogen cycling in South East Asian wet monsoonal ecosystems.* Proc. Scope/UNEP Workshop. Aust. Acad. Sci., Canberra. 215 pp.

White, L. 1967. The historical roots of our ecological crisis. *Sci.* 155:1203–1207.

White, T. R. C. 1969. An index to measure weather-induced stress of trees associated with outbreaks of Psyllids in Australia. *Ecol.* 50:905–909.

————. 1974. A hypothesis to explain outbreaks of looper caterpillars, with special reference to populations of *Selidosema suavis* in a plantation of *Pinus radiata* in New Zealand. *Oecologia* 16:279–301.

————. 1976. Weather, food and plagues of locusts. *Oecologia* 22:119–134.

Whitehead, F. H. 1968. Physiological effects of wind exposure in plants. pp. 38–44. *In* Wind Effects on the Forest. *Suppl. to For.* 1968.

Whittaker, R. H. 1953. A consideration of climax theory: the climax as a population and pattern. *Ecol. Monogr.* 23:41–78.

————. 1956. Vegetation of the Great Smoky Mountains. *Ecol. Monogr.* 26:1–80.

————. 1960. Vegetation of the Siskiyou mountains, Oregon and California. *Ecol. Monogr.* 30:279–338.

————. 1970. The biochemical ecology of higher plants. pp. 43–70. *In* E. Sondheimer and J. B. Simeone (eds.), *Chemical Ecology.* Academic Press, New York.

————. (ed.). 1973a. Ordination and Classification of Communities. Part 5, *Handbook of Vegetation Science.* R. Tuxen (ed.), W. Junk, b.v., Publishers, The Hague.

————. 1973b. Dominance types. pp. 387–402. *In* R. H. Whittaker (ed.), Ordination and Classification of Communities. Part 5, *Handbook of Vegetation Science.* W. Junk, b.v., Publishers, The Hague.

————. 1974. Climax concepts and recognition. pp. 139–154. *In* R. Knapp (ed.), Vegetation Dynamics. Part 8, *Handbook of Vegetation Science.* W. Junk, b.v., Publishers, The Hague.

————. 1975. *Communities and Ecosystems.* 2nd ed., Macmillan, New York. 385 pp.

————, and G. M. Woodwell. 1968. Dimension and production relations of trees and shrubs in the Brookhaven Forest, New York. *J. Ecol.* 56:1–25.

————, and G. M. Woodwell. 1969. Structure, production and diversity of the oak-pine forest at Brookhaven, New York. *J. Ecol.* 57:155–175.

————, and G. M. Woodwell. 1971. Measurement of net primary production of forests. pp. 159–175. *In* P. Duvigneaud (ed.), *Productivity of Forest Ecosystems.* UNESCO, Paris.

————, and G. E. Likens. 1973. Carbon in the biota. pp. 281–302. *In* G. M. Woodwell and E. V. Pecan (eds.). *Carbon and the Biosphere.* AEC Symposium Series 30. Technical Information Center, USAEC.

Wiebes, J. T. 1979. Co-evolution of figs and their insect pollinators. *Ann. Rev. Ecol. Syst.* 10:1–12.

Wiegert, R. G., and F. C. Evans. 1967. Investigations of secondary productivity in grasslands. pp. 499–518. *In* K. Petrusewicz (ed.), *Secondary Productivity of Terrestrial Ecosystems.* Polish Acad. Sci., Warsaw.

————, and D. F. Owen. 1971. Trophic structure, available resources and population density in terrestrial vs. aquatic ecosystems. *J. Theoret. Biol.* 30:69–81.

Williams, G. R. 1954. Population fluctuations in some northern hemisphere game birds (*Tetraonidae*). *J. Anim. Ecol.* 23:1–34.

Wilson, B. F. 1970. *The Growing Tree.* Univ. Massachusetts Press, Amherst, Mass. 152 pp.

Wilson, J. W. 1959. Notes on wind and its effects in arctic-alpine vegetation. *J. Ecol.* 47:415–427.

Winters, R. K. 1974. *The Forest and Man.* Vantage Press, New York. 393 pp.

Witkamp, M. 1966. Decomposition of leaf litter in relation to environment, microflora, and microbial respiration. *Ecol.* 47:194–200.

Wittich, W. H. L. 1962. Classification, mapping and interpretation of soils for forestry purposes. *Proc. 5th World For. Congr.,* Seattle, Washington 1960. 5:502–507.

Wollum, A. G. II, and G. B. Davey. 1975. Nitrogen accumulation, transformation and transport in forest soils. pp. 67–106. *In* B. Bernier and C. H. Winget (eds.), *Forest Soils and Forest Land Management.* Laval Univ. Press, Quebec.

Wong, S. C. 1980. Effects of elevated partial pressure of CO_2 on rate of CO_2 assimilation and water use efficiency. pp. 159–166. *In* G. I. Pearman (ed.), *Carbon Dioxide and Climate.* Australian Research. Aust. Acad. Sci., Canberra.

Woodwell, G. M. 1970. The energy cycle of the biosphere. *Sci. Amer.* 223:64–74.

———. 1982. Earth's vegetation and the carbon dioxide question. pp. 399–400. *In* W. C. Clark (ed.), *Carbon Dioxide Review: 1982.* Clarendon Press, Oxford.

———, and R. H. Whittaker. 1967. Primary production and the cation budget of the Brookhaven forest. pp. 151–166. *In Proc. Symp. Primary Production and Mineral Cycling in Natural Ecosystems.* Univ. of Maine Press.

———, and D. B. Botkin. 1970. Metabolism of terrestrial ecosystems by gas exchange techniques: The Brookhaven approach. pp. 73–85. *In* D. E. Reichle (ed.), *Analysis of Temperate Forest Ecosystems.* Springer-Verlag, New York.

———, R. H. Whittaker, W. A. Reiners, G. E. Likens, C. C. Delwiche, and D. B. Botkin. 1978. The biota and the world carbon budget. *Sci.* 199:141–146.

Wooldridge, D. D. 1960. Watershed disturbance from tractor and skyline crane logging. *J. For.* 58:369–372.

Wright, H. E., Jr. 1974. Landscape development, forest fires, and wilderness management. *Sci.* 186:487–495.

Wyne-Edwards, V. C. 1962. *Animal Dispersion in Relation to Social Behavior.* Oliver and Boyd, Edinburgh. 653 pp.

———. 1964. Population control in animals. *Sci. Amer.,* 211(2): 68–74.

———. 1965. Self-regulating systems in populations of animals. *Sci.* 147:1543–1548.

Yarie, J. 1980. The role of understory vegetation in the nutrient cycle of forested ecosystems in the Mountain Hemlock Biogeoclimatic Zone. *Ecol.* 61:1498–1514.

———. 1981. Forest fire cycles and life tables: a case study from interior Alaska. *Can. J. For. Res.* 11:554–564.

Young, H. E. 1968. Challenge of complete tree utilization. *Forest Prod. J.* 18:83–86.

———. 1972. Woody fibre farming: an ecologically sound and productive use of right-of-ways. Univ. Maine Sch. For. Res. Pap. 19 pp.

Youngberg, C. T. 1966. Forest floors in Douglas-fir forests: dry weight and chemical properties. *Soil Sci. Soc. Amer. Proc.* 30:406–409.

Zavitovski, J., and M. Newton. 1968a. Ecological importance of snowbrush *Ceanothus velutinus* in the Oregon Cascades. *Ecol.* 49:1134–1145.

———, and M. Newton. 1968b. Effect of organic matter and combined nitrogen on nodulation and nitrogen fixation in red alder. pp. 209–223. *In* J. M. Trappe et al. (eds.), *Biology of Alder.* USDA For. Serv., PNW For. Range Exp. Sta., Portland, Ore.

Zeman, L. J. 1973. Chemistry of trophospheric fallout and streamflow in a small mountainous watershed near Vancouver, British Columbia. Ph.D. thesis, Univ. of B.C., Vancouver.

———. 1975. Hydrochemical balance of a British Columbian mountainous watershed. *Catena* 2:81–94.

Zimmerman, R. R., J. P. Greenberg, S. O. Wandiga, and P. J. Crutzen. 1982. Termites: a potentially large source of atmospheric methane, carbon dioxide and molecular hydrogen. *Sci.* 218:563–565.

Zlotin, R. I., and K. S. Khodashova. 1980. *The Role of Animals in Biological Cycling of Forest-Steppe Ecosystems.* Dowden, Hutchinson and Ross, Stroudsburg, Pa. 221 pp.

Zobel, D. B., W. A. McKee, G. M. Hawk, and C. T. Dyrness. 1974. Correlation of forest communities with environment and phenology on the H. J. Andrews Experimental Forest, Oregon. pp. 48–56. *In* R. H. Waring and R. L. Edmonds (eds.), *Integrated Research in the Coniferous Forest Biome* Bull. No. 5. Conif. For. Biome, US/IBP, Univ. Washington, Seattle.

———, A. McKee, G. M. Hawk, and C. T. Dyrness. 1976. Relationship of environment to composition, structure and diversity of forest communities of the central western Cascades of Oregon. *Ecol. Monogr.* 46:135–156.

Zwolinski, M. J. 1971. Effects of fire on water infiltration rate in a ponderosa pine stand. *Hydrol. Water Resour. Ariz. and Southwest* 1:107–112.

Index